2012
Photograph[ ]
MARKL[ ]

D1403787

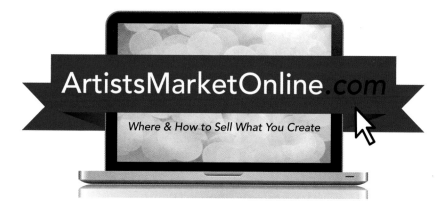

ArtistsMarketOnline.com

Where & How to Sell What You Create

THE ULTIMATE MARKET RESEARCH TOOL FOR PHOTOGRAPHERS

To register your *2012 Photographer's Market* book and **start your FREE 1-year online subscription**, scratch off the block below to reveal your activation code*, then go to www.ArtistsMarketOnline.com. Click on "Sign Up Now" and enter your contact information and activation code. It's that easy!

Carefully scratch off the block with a coin. **Do not use a key.**

DISCARD

UPDATED MARKET LISTINGS

EASY-TO-USE SEARCHABLE DATABASE • RECORD-KEEPING TOOLS

INDUSTRY NEWS • PROFESSIONAL TIPS & ADVICE

*Valid through 12/31/12

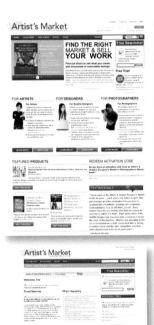

35TH ANNUAL EDITION

2012

Photographer's

MARKET

Mary Burzlaff Bostic, Editor

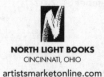

NORTH LIGHT BOOKS
CINCINNATI, OHIO
artistsmarketonline.com

Publisher and Community Leader, Fine Art Community: Jamie Markle
Editorial Director, North Light Books: Pam Wissman
Managing Editor, North Light Books: Mona Michael
Market Books Assistant, North Light Books: Stacy Heyderhoff

Artist's Market Online website: www.artistsmarketonline.com
Artist's Network website: www.artistsnetwork.com
North Light Shop website: www.northlightshop.com

Distributed in Canada by Fraser Direct
100 Armstrong Avenue
Georgetown, ON, Canada L7G 5S4
Tel: (905) 877-4411

Distributed in the U.K. and Europe by F&W Media International, LTD
Brunel House, Forde Close, Newton Abbot, Devon, TQ12 4PU, UK
Tel: (+44) 1626 323200, Fax: (+44) 1626 323319
E-mail: enquiries@fwmedia.com

Distributed in Australia by Capricorn Link
Loder House, 126 George Street
Windsor, NSW 2756 Australia
Tel: (02) 4577-3555

ISSN: 0147-247X
ISBN-13: 978-1-4403-1419-3
ISBN-10: 1-4403-1419-5

Cover design by Laura Spencer
Interior design by Claudean Wheeler
Interior layout by Jessica Schultz and Kelly Volz
Production coordinated by Greg Nock

Attention Booksellers: This is an annual directory of F+W Media, Inc.
Return deadline for this edition is December 31, 2012.

fw
media

CONTENTS

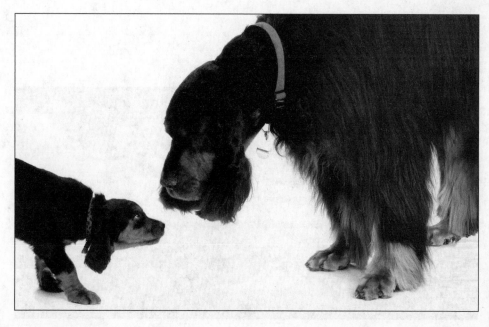

© Vik Orenstein

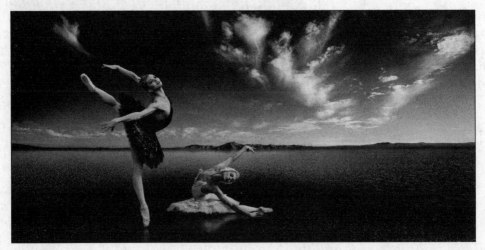

© David Allan Brandt

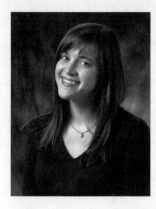

FROM
THE
EDITOR

Each year we look for new and better ways to give you the tools you need to make the most of your photography career with *Photographer's Market*. And, I have to say, I am really excited to share this year's edition with you. We've increased the number of up-to-date market listings to more than 1500 contacts, and we've doubled the number of business features and interviews. We added so much new material, we had to increase the page count!

On some of those new pages you'll find lots of advice for improving your photography business and selling your work. Check out the special features on selling more photography in 2012, secrets to social media success, exploring new niches, bringing new life to an old business, generating referrals and managing your clients. Then read on for tips and advice from the pros, including Q&As with photo rep Norman Maslov and American Photographic Artists CEO Stephen Best.

You'll also find inspiring and informative interviews with successful professionals, including sports photographer Rick Wilson, fine art photographer Kathleen McFadden, wedding photographer Marissa Bowers and Harley-Davidson's chief photographer Brad Chaney.

These freelancers turned their passions into their day jobs, and you can too. Read on, keep creating and good luck!

Mary Burzlaff Bostic

Mary Burzlaff Bostic
photomarket@fwmedia.com
www.artistsmarketonline.com

P.S. Don't forget to register at **Artist's Market Online, which you get FREE for a year with the purchase of this book**. Your free 1-year subscription will provide you with everything *Photographer's Market* has to offer and then some. You'll be able to search listings, track your submissions, read up on the latest market news, and much more. Use the activation code from the front insert to access your free subscription today.

HOW TO USE THIS BOOK

//

The first thing you'll notice about most of the listings in this book is the group of symbols that appears before the name of each company. Scanning the listings for symbols can help you quickly locate markets that meet certain criteria. (You'll find a quick-reference key to the symbols as well as a sample listing on the back inside cover of the book.) Here's what each symbol stands for:

    ⊕ This photo buyer is new to this edition of the book.

    ↻ This photo buyer is located in Canada.

    ↪ This photo buyer is located outside the U.S. and Canada.

    ◎ This photo buyer uses only images created on assignment.

    ⊕ This photo buyer uses only stock images.

COMPLAINT PROCEDURE ///

If you feel you have not been treated fairly by a company listed in *Photographer's Market*, we advise you to take the following steps:

- First, try to contact the listing. Sometimes one phone call, e-mail, or letter can quickly clear up the matter.
- Document all your correspondence with the listing. If you write to us with a complaint, provide the details of your submission, the date of your first contact with the listing, and the nature of your subsequent correspondence.
- We will enter your letter into our files.
- The number and severity of complaints will be considered in our decision whether to delete the listing from the next edition.

🖱 This photo buyer accepts submissions in digital format.

🎞 This photo buyer uses film or other audiovisual media.

⚖ This art fair is a juried event; a juror or committee of jurors views applicants' work and selects those whose work fits within the guidelines of the event.

PAY SCALE

We asked photo buyers to indicate their general pay scale based on what they typically pay for a single image. Their answers are signified by a series of dollar signs before each listing. Scanning for dollar signs can help you quickly identify which markets pay at the top of the scale. However, not every photo buyer answered this question, so don't mistake a missing dollar sign as an indication of low pay rates. Also keep in mind that many photo buyers are willing to negotiate.

$ Pays $1–150

$$ Pays $151–750

$$$ Pays $751–1,500

$$$$ Pays more than $1,500

OPENNESS

We also asked photo buyers to indicate their level of openness to freelance photography. Looking for these symbols can help you identify buyers who are willing to work with newcomers, as well as prestigious buyers who only publish top-notch photography.

○ Encourages beginning or unpublished photographers to submit work for consideration; publishes new photographers. May pay only in copies or have a low pay rate.

◐ Accepts outstanding work from beginning and established photographers; expects a high level of professionalism from all photographers who make contact.

● Hard to break into; publishes mostly previously published photographers.

⊘ May pay at the top of the scale. Closed to unsolicited submissions.

SUBHEADS

Each listing is broken down into sections to make it easier to locate specific information (see sample listing on the back inside cover of this book). In the first section of each listing you'll find mailing addresses, phone numbers, e-mail and website addresses, and the name of the person you should contact. You'll also find general information about photo buyers, including when their business was established and their publishing philosophy. Each listing will include one or more of the following subheads:

FREQUENTLY ASKED QUESTIONS

1 How do companies get listed in the book?

No company pays to be included—all listings are free. Every company has to fill out a detailed questionnaire about their photo needs. All questionnaires are screened to make sure the companies meet our requirements. Each year we contact every company in the book and ask them to update their information.

2 Why aren't other companies I know about listed in this book?

We may have sent these companies a questionnaire, but they never returned it. Or if they did return a questionnaire, we may have decided not to include them based on our requirements.

3 Some publishers say they accept photos with or without a manuscript. What does that mean?

Essentially, the word manuscript means a written article that will be published by a magazine. Some magazines will only consider publishing your photos if they accompany a written article. Other publishers will consider publishing your photos alone, without a manuscript.

4 I sent a CD with large digital files to a photo buyer who said she wanted to see my work. I have not heard from her, and I am afraid that my photos will be used without my permission and without payment. What should I do?

Do not send large, printable files (300 dpi or larger) unless you are sure the photo buyer is going to use them, and you know what you will be paid for their usage and what rights the photo buyer is requesting. If a photo buyer shows interest in seeing your work in digital format, send small JPEGs at first so they can "review" them—i.e., determine if the subject matter and technical quality of your photos meet their requirements. Until you know for sure that the photo buyer is going to license your photos and you have some kind of agreement, do not send high-resolution files. The exception to this rule would be if you have dealt with the photo buyer before or perhaps know someone who has. Some companies receive a large volume of submissions, so sometimes you must be patient. It's a good idea to give any company listed in this book a call before you submit anything and be sure nothing has changed since we contacted them to gather or update information. This is true whether you submit slides, prints, or digital images.

5 A company says they want to publish my photographs, but first they will need a fee from me. Is this a standard business practice?

No, it is not a standard business practice. You should never have to pay to have your photos reviewed or to have your photos accepted for publication. If you suspect that a company may not be reputable, do some research before you submit anything or pay their fees. The exception to this rule is contests. It is not unusual for some contests listed in this book to have entry fees (usually minimal—between five and twenty dollars).

Needs. Here you'll find specific subjects each photo buyer is seeking. (Use the subject index at the end of the book to help you narrow your search.) You'll also find the average number of freelance photos a buyer uses each year, which will help you gauge your chances of publication.

Audiovisual Needs. If you create images for media such as filmstrips or overhead transparencies, or you shoot videotape or motion picture film, look here for photo buyers' specific needs in these areas.

Specs. Look here to see in what format the photo buyer prefers to receive accepted images. Many photo buyers will accept both digital and film (slides, transparencies, prints) formats. However, many photo buyers are reporting that they accept digital images only, so make sure you can provide the format the photo buyer requires before you send samples.

Exhibits. This subhead appears only in the Galleries section of the book. Like the Needs subhead, you'll find information here about the specific subjects and types of photography a gallery shows.

Making Contact & Terms. When you're ready to make contact with a photo buyer, look here to find out exactly what they want to see in your submission. You'll also find what the buyer usually pays and what rights they expect in exchange. In the Stock section, this subhead is divided into two parts, Payment & Terms and Making Contact, because this information is often lengthy and complicated.

Handles. This subhead appears only in the Photo Representatives section. Some reps also represent illustrators, fine artists, stylists, make-up artists, etc., in addition to photographers. The term "handles" refers to the various types of "talent" they represent.

Tips. Look here for advice and information directly from photo buyers in their own words.

HOW TO START SELLING YOUR WORK

If this is your first edition of *Photographer's Market*, you're probably feeling a little overwhelmed by all the information in this book. Before you start flipping through the listings, read the eleven steps below to learn how to get the most out of this book and your selling efforts.

1. Be honest with yourself. Are the photographs you make of the same quality as those you see published in magazines and newspapers? If the answer is yes, you may be able to sell your photos.

2. Get someone else to be honest with you. Do you know a professional photographer who would critique your work for you? Other ways to get opinions about your work: join a local camera club or other photo organization; attend a stock seminar led by a professional photographer; attend a regional or national photo conference or a workshop where they offer daily critiques.

- You'll find workshop and seminar listings in the Markets section.
- You'll find a list of photographic organizations in the Resource section.
- Check your local camera store for information about camera clubs in your area.

3. Get organized. Create a list of subjects you have photographed and organize your images into subject groups. Make sure you can quickly find specific images and keep track of any sample images you send out. You can use database software on your home computer to help you keep track of your images.

Other resources:

- *Photo Portfolio Success* by John Kaplan (Writer's Digest Books).
- *Sell and Re-Sell Your Photos* by Rohn Engh (Writer's Digest Books).

- *The Photographer's Market Guide to Building Your Photography Business* by Vik Orenstein (Writer's Digest Books)

4. Consider the format. Are your pictures color snapshots, black-and-white prints, color slides, or digital captures? The format of your work will determine, in part, which markets you can approach. Below are some general guidelines for where you can market various photo formats. Always check the listings in this book for specific format information.

- **digital**—nearly all newspapers, magazines, stock agencies, ad agencies, book and greeting card publishers
- **black-and-white prints**—some galleries, art fairs, private collectors, literary/art magazines, trade magazines, newspapers, book publishers
- **color prints**—some newsletters, very small trade or club magazines
- **large color prints**—some galleries, art fairs, private collectors
- **color slides (35mm)**—a few magazines, newspapers, some greeting card and calendar publishers, a very few book publishers, textbook publishers, stock agencies
- **color transparencies (2¼×2¼ and 4×5)**—a few magazines, book publishers, calendar publishers, ad agencies, stock agencies. Many of these photo buyers have begun to accept only digital photos, especially stock agencies.

5. Do you want to sell stock images or accept assignments? A stock image is a photograph you create on your own and then sell to a publisher. An assignment is a photograph created at the request of a specific buyer. Many of the listings in *Photographer's Market* are interested in both stock and assignment work.

⊕ Listings that are only interested in stock photography are marked with this symbol.

◎ Listings that are only interested in assignment photography are marked with this symbol.

6. Start researching. Generate a list of the publishers that might buy your images—check the newsstand, go to the library, search the Web, read the listings in this book. Don't forget to look at greeting cards, stationery, calendars, and CD covers. Anything you see with a photograph on it, from a billboard advertisement to a cereal box, is a potential market.

7. Check the publisher's guidelines. Do you know exactly how the publisher you choose wants to be approached? Check the listings in this book first. If you don't know the format, subject, and number of images a publisher wants in a submission, you should check their website first. Often, guidelines are posted there. Or you can send a short letter with a self-addressed, stamped envelope (SASE) or e-mail asking those questions. A quick call to the receptionist might also yield the answers.

8. Check out the market. Get in the habit of reading industry magazines.

9. Prepare yourself. Before you send your first submission, make sure you know how to respond when a publisher agrees to buy your work.

Pay rates

Most magazines and newspapers will tell you what they pay, and you can accept or decline. However, you should become familiar with typical pay rates. Ask other photographers what they charge—preferably ones you know well or who are not in direct competition with you. Many will be willing to tell you to prevent you from devaluing the market by undercharging.

Other resources:

- *Pricing Photography: The Complete Guide to Assignment & Stock Prices*, by Michal Heron and David MacTavish (Allworth Press).
- *fotoQuote*, a software package that is updated each year to list typical stock photo and assignment prices, (800)679-0202, www.cradocfotosoftware.com.
- *Negotiating Stock Photo Prices*, by Jim Pickerell (www.jimpickerell.com).

Copyright

You should always include a copyright notice on any slide, print, or digital image you send out. While you automatically own the copyright to your work the instant it is created, the notice affords extra protection. The proper format for a copyright notice includes the word or symbol for copyright, the date and your name: © 2012 Jane Photographer. To fully protect your copyright and recover damages from infringers, you must register your copyright with the Copyright Office in Washington D.C.

Rights

In most cases, you will not actually be selling your photographs, but rather, the rights to publish them. If a publisher wants to buy your images outright, you will lose the right to resell those images in any form or even display them in your portfolio. Most publishers will buy one-time rights and/or first rights.

Other resources:

- *Legal Guide for the Visual Artist*, by Tad Crawford (Allworth Press).

Contracts

Formal contract or not, you should always agree to any terms of sale in writing. This could be as simple as sending a follow-up letter restating the agreement and asking for confirmation, once you agree to terms over the phone. You should always keep copies of any correspondence in case of a future dispute or misunderstanding.

Other resources

- *Business and Legal Forms for Photographers*, by Tad Crawford (Allworth Press).

10. Prepare your submission. The number one rule when mailing submissions is: "Follow the directions." Always address letters to specific photo buyers. Always include a SASE of sufficient size and with sufficient postage for your work to be safely returned to you. Never send originals when you are first approaching a potential buyer. Try to include something in your submission that the potential buyer can keep on file, such as a tearsheet and your résumé. In fact, photo buyers prefer that you send something they don't have to return to you. Plus, it saves you the time and expense of preparing a SASE.

Other Resources

- *Photo Portfolio Success*, by John Kaplan (Writer's Digest Books).

11. Continue to promote yourself and your work. After you've made that first sale (and even before), it is important to promote yourself. Success in selling your work depends in part on how well and how often you let photo buyers know what you have to offer. This is known as self-promotion. There are several ways to promote yourself and your work. You can send postcards or other printed material through the mail; send an e-mail with an image and a link to your website; and upload your images to a website that is dedicated to showcasing your work and your photographic services.

RUNNING YOUR BUSINESS

Photography is an art that requires a host of skills, some which can be learned and some which are innate. To make money from your photography, the one skill you can't do without is business savvy. Thankfully, this skill can be learned. We'll cover:

- Submitting Your Work
- Digital Submission Guidelines
- Using Essential Business Forms
- Stock List
- Charging for Your Work
- Figuring Small Business Taxes
- Self-Promotion
- Organizing & Labeling Your Images
- Protecting Your Copyright

SUBMITTING YOUR WORK

Editors, art directors, and other photo buyers are busy people. Many spend only 10 percent of their work time actually choosing photographs for publication. The rest of their time is spent making and returning phone calls, arranging shoots, coordinating production, and doing a host of other unglamorous tasks that make publication possible. They want to discover new talent, and you may even have the exact image they're looking for, but if you don't follow a market's submission instructions to the letter, you have little chance of acceptance.

To learn the dos and don'ts of photography submissions, read each market's listing carefully and make sure to send only what they ask for. Don't send prints if they only want slides. Don't send color if they only want black and white. Check their website or send for guidelines whenever they are available to get the most complete and up-to-date submission advice. When in doubt, follow these ten rules when sending your work to a potential buyer:

1. Don't forget your SASE—Always include a self-addressed, stamped envelope whether you want your submission back or not. Make sure your SASE is big enough, has enough packaging, and has enough postage to ensure the safe return of your work.

2. Don't over-package—Never make a submission difficult to open and file. Don't tape down all the loose corners. Don't send anything too large to fit in a standard file.

3. Don't send originals—Try not to send things you must have back. Never, ever send originals unsolicited.

4. Label everything—Put a label directly on the slide mount or print you are submitting. Include your name, address, and phone number, as well as the name or number of the image. Your slides and prints will almost certainly get separated from your letter.

5. Do your research—Always research the places to which you want to sell your work. Request sample issues of magazines, visit galleries, examine ads, look at websites, etc. Make sure your work is appropriate before you send it out. A blind mailing is a waste of postage and a waste of time for both you and the art buyer.

6. Follow directions—Always request submission guidelines. Include an SASE for reply. Follow *all* the directions exactly, even if you think they're silly.

7. Include a business letter—Always include a cover letter, no more than one page, that lets the potential buyer know you are familiar with their company, what your photography background is (briefly), and where you've sold work before (if it pertains to what you're trying to do now). If you send an e-mail, follow the same protocol as you would for a business cover letter and include the same information.

8. Send to a person, not a title—Send submissions to a specific person at a company. When you address a cover letter to Dear Sir or Madam, it shows you know nothing about the company you want to buy your work.

9. Don't forget to follow through—Follow up major submissions with postcard samples several times a year.

10. Have something to leave behind—If you're lucky enough to score a portfolio review, always have a sample of your work to leave with the art director. Make it small enough to fit in a file but big enough not to get lost. Always include your contact information directly on the leave-behind.

DIGITAL SUBMISSION GUIDELINES

Today, almost every publisher of photographs prefers digital images. Some still accept "analog" images (slides and prints) as well as digital images, but most accept only digital images. There are a few who still do not accept digital images at all, but their number is rapidly decreasing. Follow each buyer's size and format guidelines carefully.

STARTING A BUSINESS

To learn more about starting a business:

- Take a course at a local college. Many community colleges offer short-term evening and weekend courses on topics like creating a business plan or finding financial assistance to start a small business.
- Contact the Small Business Administration at (800)827-5722 or check out their website at www.sba.gov. The U.S. Small Business Administration was created by Congress in 1953 to help America's entrepreneurs form successful small enterprises. Today, SBA's program offices in every state offer financing, training, and advocacy for small firms.
- Contact the Small Business Development Center at (202)205-6766. The SBDC offers free or low-cost advice, seminars, and workshops for small business owners.
- Read a book. Try *Commercial Photography Handbook: Business Techniques for Professional Digital Photographers*, by Kirk Tuck (Amhearst Media) or *The Business of Studio Photography*, by Edward R. Lilley (Allworth Press). The business section of your local library will also have many general books about starting a small business.

Previews

Photo buyers need to see a preview of an image before they can decide if it will fit their needs. In the past, photographers mailed slides or prints to prospective photo buyers so they could review them, determine their quality, and decide whether or not the subject matter was something they could use. Or photographers sent a self-promotion mailer, often a postcard with one or more representative images of their work. Today, preview images can be e-mailed to prospective photo buyers, or they can be viewed on a photographer's website. This eliminates the hassle and expense of sending slides through the mail and wondering if you'll ever get them back.

The important thing about digital preview images is size. They should be no larger than 3×5 inches at 72 dpi. E-mailing larger files to someone who just wants a peek at your work could greatly inconvenience them if they have to wait a long time for the files to open or if their e-mail system cannot handle larger files. If photo buyers are interested in using your photographs, they will definitely want a larger, high-resolution file later, but don't overload their systems and their patience in the beginning with large files. Another option is sending a CD with preview images. This is not as efficient as e-mail or a website since the photo buyer has to put the CD in the computer and view the images one by one. If you send a CD, be sure to include a printout of thumbnail images: If the photo buyer does not have time to put the CD in the computer and view the images, she can at least glance at the printed thumbnails. CDs and DVDs are probably best reserved for high-resolution photos you know the photo buyer wants and has requested from you.

Size & quality

Size and quality might be the two most important aspects of your digital submission. If the quality is not there, photo buyers will not be interested in buying your image regardless of its subject matter. Find out what the photo buyer needs. If you scan your slides or prints, make sure your scanning quality is excellent: no dirt, dust, or scratches. If the file size is too small, they will not be able to do much with it either. A resolution of 72 dpi is fine for previews, but if a photo buyer wants to publish your images, they will want larger, high-resolution files. While each photo buyer may have different needs, there are some general guidelines to follow. Often digital images that are destined for print media need to be 300 dpi and the same size as the final, printed image will be (or preferably a little larger). For example, for a full-page photo in a magazine, the digital file might be 8×10 inches at 300 dpi. However, always check with the photo buyer who will ultimately be publishing the photo. Many magazines, book publishers, and stock photo agencies post digital submission guidelines on their websites or will provide copies to photographers if they ask. Photo buyers are usually happy to inform photographers of their digital guidelines since they don't want to receive images they won't be able to use due to poor quality.

Note: Many of the listings in this book that accept digital images state the dpi they require for final submissions. They may also state the size they need in terms of megabytes (MB). See subhead "Specs" in each listing.

Formats

When you know that a photo buyer is definitely going to use your photos, you will then need to submit a high-resolution digital file (as opposed to the low-resolution 72 dpi JPEGs used for previews). Photo buyers often ask for digital images to be saved as JPEGs or TIFFs. Again, make sure you know what format they prefer. Some photo buyers will want you to send them a CD or DVD with the high-resolution images saved on it. Most photo buyers appreciate having a printout of thumbnail images to review in addition to the CD. Some may allow you to e-mail images directly to them, but keep in mind that anything larger than 9 megabytes is usually too large to e-mail. Get the permission of the photo buyer before you attempt to send anything that large via e-mail.

Another option is FTP (file transfer protocol). It allows files to be transferred over the Internet from one computer to another. This option is becoming more prevalent.

Note: Most of the listings in this book that accept digital images state the format they require for final digital submissions. See subhead "Specs" in each listing.

Color space

Another thing you'll need to find out from the photo buyer is what color space they want photos to be saved in. RGB (red, green, blue) is a very common one. You might also encounter

CMYK (cyan, magenta, yellow, black). Grayscale is for photos that will be printed without any color (black and white). Again, check with the photo buyer to find out what color space they require.

USING ESSENTIAL BUSINESS FORMS

Using carefully crafted business forms will not only make you look more professional in the eyes of your clients, it will make bills easier to collect while protecting your copyright. Forms from delivery memos to invoices can be created on a home computer with minimal design skills and printed in duplicate at most quick-print centers. When producing detailed contracts, remember that proper wording is imperative. You want to protect your copyright and, at the same time, be fair to clients. Therefore, it's a good idea to have a lawyer examine your forms before using them.

The following forms are useful when selling stock photography, as well as when shooting on assignment:

Delivery memo

This document should be mailed to potential clients along with a cover letter when any submission is made. A delivery memo provides an accurate count of the images that are enclosed, and it provides rules for usage. The front of the form should include a description of the images or assignment, the kind of media in which the images can be used, the price for such usage, and the terms and conditions of paying for that usage. Ask clients to sign and return a copy of this form if they agree to the terms you've spelled out.

FORMS FOR PHOTOGRAPHERS

Where to learn more about forms for photographers:
- Editorial Photographers (EP), www.editorialphoto.com.
- *Business and Legal Forms for Photographers*, by Tad Crawford (Allworth Press).
- *Legal Guide for the Visual Artist*, by Tad Crawford (Allworth Press).
- *ASMP Professional Business Practices in Photography*, (Allworth Press).
- The American Society of Media Photographers offers traveling business seminars that cover issues from forms to pricing to collecting unpaid bills. Write to them at 14 Washington Rd., Suite 502, Princeton Junction NJ 08550, for a schedule of upcoming business seminars, or visit www.asmp.org.
- The Volunteer Lawyers for the Arts, 1 E. 53rd St., 6th Floor, New York NY 10022, (212)319-2910. The VLA is a nonprofit organization, based in New York City, dedicated to providing all artists, including photographers, with sound legal advice.

PROPERTY RELEASE

In consideration of $_____ and/or _____, receipt of which is acknowledged, I being the legal owner of or having the right to permit the taking and use of photographs of certain property designated as _____, do hereby give _____, his/her assigns, licensees, and legal representatives the irrevocable right to use this image in all forms and media and in all manners, including composite or distorted representations, for advertising, trade, or any other lawful purposes, and I waive any rights to inspect or approve the finished product, including written copy that may be created in connection therewith.

Short description of photographs: _____

Additional information: _____

I am of full age. I have read this release and fully understand its contents.

Please Print:

Name _____

Address _____

City _____ State _____ Zip Code _____

Sample property release

Terms & conditions

This form often appears on the back of the delivery memo, but be aware that conditions on the front of a form have more legal weight than those on the back. Your terms and conditions should outline in detail all aspects of usage for an assignment or stock image. Include copyright information, client liability, and a sales agreement. Also, be sure to include conditions covering the alteration of your images, the transfer of rights, and digital storage. The more specific your terms and conditions are to the individual client, the more legally binding they will be. If you create your forms on your computer, seriously consider altering your standard contract to suit each assignment or other photography sale.

Invoice

This is the form you want to send more than any of the others, because mailing it means you have made a sale. The invoice should provide clients with your mailing address, an explanation of usage, and the amount due. Be sure to include a reasonable due date for payment, usually thirty days. You should also include your business tax identification number or Social Security number.

Model/property releases

Get into the habit of obtaining releases from anyone you photograph. They increase the sales potential for images and can protect you from liability. A model release is a short form, signed by the person(s) in a photo, that allows you to sell the image for commercial purposes. The property release does the same thing for photos of personal property. When photographing children, remember that a parent or guardian must sign before the release is legally binding. In exchange for signed releases, some photographers give their subjects copies of the photos; others pay the models. You may choose the system that works best for you, but keep in mind that a legally binding contract must involve consideration, the exchange of something of value. Once you obtain a release, keep it in a permanent file.

You do not need a release if the image is being sold editorially. However, magazines now require such forms in order to protect themselves, especially when an image is used as a photo illustration instead of as a straight documentary shot. You always need a release for advertising purposes or for purposes of trade and promotion. In works of art, you only need a release if the subject is recognizable. When traveling in a foreign country, it is a good idea to carry releases written in that country's language. To translate releases into a foreign language, check with an embassy or a college language professor.

STOCK LIST

Some market listings in this book ask for a stock list, so it is a good idea to have one on hand. Your stock list should be as detailed and specific as possible. Include all the subjects you have in your photo files, breaking them into logical categories and subcategories.

CHARGING FOR YOUR WORK

No matter how many books you read about what photos are worth and how much you should charge, no one can set your fees for you. If you let someone try, you'll be setting yourself up for financial ruin. Figuring out what to charge for your work is a complex task that will require a lot of time and effort. But the more time you spend finding out how much you need to charge, the more successful you'll be at targeting your work to the right markets and getting the money you need to keep your business, and your life, going.

MODEL RELEASE

In consideration of $ _____ and/or _____,
receipt of which is acknowledged, I, _____, do
hereby give _____, his/her assigns, licensees, and
legal representatives the irrevocable right to use my image in all forms and
media and in all manners, including composite or distorted representations, for
advertising, trade, or any other lawful purposes, and I waive any rights to in-
spect or approve the finished product, including written copy that may be created in connection therewith. The following name may be used in reference to
these photographs:

My real name, or _____

Short description of photographs: _____
_____

Additional information: _____

Please print:

Name _____

Address _____

City _____ State _____ Zip code _____

Country _____

CONSENT

(If model is under the age of 18) I am the parent or guardian of the minor named
above and have the legal authority to execute the above release. I approve the
foregoing and waive any rights in the premises.

Please print:

Name _____

Address _____

City _____ State _____ Zip code _____

Country _____

Signature _____

Witness _____ Date _____

Sample model release

STOCK LIST

INSECTS
Ants
Aphids
Bees
Beetles
Butterflies
Grasshoppers
Moths
Termites
Wasps

PROFESSIONS
Bee Keeper
Biologist
Firefighter
Nurse
Police Officer
Truck Driver
Waitress
Welder

LANDMARKS
Asia
 Angkor Wat
 Great Wall of China

Europe
 Big Ben
 Eiffel Tower
 Louvre
 Stonehenge

United States
 Empire State Building
 Grand Canyon
 Liberty Bell
 Mt. Rushmore
 Statue of Liberty

TRANSPORTATION
Airplanes and helicopters
Roads
 Country roads
 Dirt roads
 Interstate highways
 Two-lane highways

WEATHER
Clouds
 Cumulus
 Cirrus
 Nimbus
 Stratus
Flooding
Lightning
Snow and Blizzards
Storm Chasers
Rainbows
Tornadoes
Tornado Damage

Sample stock list

Keep in mind that what you charge for an image may be completely different from what a photographer down the street charges. There is nothing wrong with this if you've calculated your prices carefully. Perhaps the photographer works in a basement on old equipment and you have a brand new, state-of-the-art studio. You'd better be charging more. Why the disparity? For one thing, you've got a much higher overhead, the continuing costs of running your business. You're also probably delivering a higher-quality product and are more able to meet client requests quickly. So how do you determine just how much you need to charge in order to make ends meet?

Setting your break-even rate

All photographers, before negotiating assignments, should consider their break-even rate—the amount of money they need to make in order to keep their studios open. To arrive at the actual price you'll quote to a client, you should add onto your base rate things like usage, your experience, how quickly you can deliver the image, and what kind of prices the market will bear.

Start by estimating your business expenses. These expenses may include rent (office, studio), gas and electric, insurance (equipment), phone, fax, Internet service, office supplies, postage, stationery, self-promotions/portfolio, photo equipment, computer, staff salaries and taxes. Expenses like film and processing will be charged to your clients.

Next, figure your personal expenses, which will include food, clothing, medical, car and home insurance, gas, repairs and other car expenses, entertainment, and retirement savings and investments, etc.

PRICING INFORMATION

Where to find more information about pricing:

- *Pricing Photography: The Complete Guide to Assignment and Stock Prices*, by Michal Heron and David MacTavish (Allworth Press).
- *ASMP Professional Business Practices in Photography*, (Allworth Press).
- fotoQuote, a software package produced by the Cradoc Corporation, is a customizable, annually updated database of stock photo prices for markets from ad agencies to calendar companies. The software also includes negotiating advice and scripted telephone conversations. Call (800)679-0202, or visit www.cradocfotosoftware.com for ordering information.
- Stock Photo Price Calculator, a website that suggests fees for advertising, corporate and editorial stock, photographersindex.com/stockprice.htm.
- Editorial Photographers (EP), www.editorialphoto.com.

Before you divide your annual expenses by the 365 days in the year, remember you won't be shooting billable assignments every day. A better way to calculate your base fee is by billable weeks. Assume that at least one day a week is going to be spent conducting office business and marketing your work. This amounts to approximately ten weeks. Add in days for vacation and sick time, perhaps three weeks, and add another week for workshops and seminars. This totals fourteen weeks of non-billable time and thirty-eight billable weeks throughout the year.

Now estimate the number of assignments/sales you expect to complete each week and multiply that number by 38. This will give you a total for your yearly assignments/sales. Finally, divide the total overhead and administrative expenses by the total number of assignments. This will give you an average price per assignment, your break-even or base rate.

As an example, let's say your expenses come to $65,000 per year (this includes $35,000 of personal expenses). If you complete two assignments each week for thirty-eight weeks, your average price per assignment must be about $855. This is what you should charge to break even on each job. But, don't forget, you want to make money.

Establishing usage fees

Too often, photographers shortchange themselves in negotiations because they do not understand how the images in question will be used. Instead, they allow clients to set prices and prefer to accept lower fees rather than lose sales. Unfortunately, those photographers who shortchange themselves are actually bringing down prices throughout the industry. Clients realize if they shop around they can find photographers willing to shoot assignments at very low rates.

There are ways to combat low prices, however. First, educate yourself about a client's line of work. This type of professionalism helps during negotiations because it shows buyers that you are serious about your work. The added knowledge also gives you an advantage when negotiating fees because photographers are not expected to understand a client's profession.

For example, if most of your clients are in the advertising field, acquire advertising rate cards for magazines so you know what a client pays for ad space. You can also find print ad rates in the *Standard Rate and Data Service* directory at the library. Knowing what a client is willing to pay for ad space and considering the importance of your image to the ad will give you a better idea of what the image is really worth to the client.

For editorial assignments, fees may be more difficult to negotiate because most magazines have set page rates. They may make exceptions, however, if you have experience or if the assignment is particularly difficult or time-consuming. If a magazine's page rate is still too low to meet your break-even price, consider asking for extra tearsheets and copies of the issue in which your work appears. These pieces can be used in your portfolio and as mailers, and the savings they represent in printing costs may make up for the discrepancy between the page rate and your break-even price.

There are still more ways to negotiate sales. Some clients, such as gift and paper product manufacturers, prefer to pay royalties each time a product is sold. Special markets, such as galleries and stock agencies, typically charge photographers a commission of 20 to 50 percent for displaying or representing their images. In these markets, payment on sales comes from the purchase of prints by gallery patrons, or from fees on the "rental" of photos by clients of stock agencies. Pricing formulas should be developed by looking at your costs and the current price levels in those markets, as well as on the basis of submission fees, commissions, and other administrative costs charged to you.

Bidding for jobs

As you build your business, you will likely encounter another aspect of pricing and negotiating that can be very difficult. Like it or not, clients often ask photographers to supply bids for jobs. In some cases, the bidding process is merely procedural and the assignment will go to the photographer who can best complete it. In other instances, the photographer who submits the lowest bid will earn the job. When asked to submit a bid, it is imperative that you find out which bidding process is being used. Putting together an accurate estimate takes time, and you do not want to waste your efforts if your bid is being sought merely to meet some budget quota.

If you decide to bid on a job, it's important to consider your costs carefully. You do not want to bid too much on projects and repeatedly get turned down, but you also don't want to bid too low and forfeit income. When a potential client calls to ask for a bid, consider these dos and don'ts:

1. Always keep a list of questions by the telephone so you can refer to it when bids are requested. The answers to the questions should give you a solid understanding of the project and help you reach a price estimate.
2. Never quote a price during the initial conversation, even if the caller pushes for a "ballpark figure." An on-the-spot estimate can only hurt you in the negotiating process.
3. Immediately find out what the client intends to do with the photos, and ask who will own copyrights to the images after they are produced. It is important to note that many clients believe if they hire you for a job they'll own all the rights to the images you create. If they insist on buying all rights, make sure the price they pay is worth the complete loss of the images.
4. If it is an annual project, ask who completed the job last time, then contact that photographer to see what he charged.

5. Find out who you are bidding against and contact those people to make sure you received the same information about the job. While agreeing to charge the same price is illegal, sharing information about reaching a price is not.

6. Talk to photographers not bidding on the project and ask them what they would charge.

7. Finally, consider all aspects of the shoot, including preparation time, fees for assistants and stylists, rental equipment, and other materials costs. Don't leave anything out.

FIGURING SMALL BUSINESS TAXES

Whether you make occasional sales from your work or you derive your entire income from your photography skills, it's a good idea to consult with a tax professional. If you are just starting out, an accountant can give you solid advice about organizing your financial records. If you are an established professional, an accountant can double-check your system and maybe find a few extra deductions. When consulting with a tax professional, it is best to see someone who is familiar with the needs and concerns of small business people, particularly photographers. You can also conduct your own tax research by contacting the Internal Revenue Service.

Self-employment tax

As a freelancer it's important to be aware of tax rates on self-employment income. All income you receive over $400 without taxes being taken out by an employer qualifies as self-

---

TAX INFORMATION

To learn more about taxes, contact the IRS. There are free booklets available that provide specific information, such as allowable deductions and tax rate structure:

- Tax Guide for Small Business, 334
- Travel, Entertainment, Gift, and Car Expenses, 463
- Tax Withholding and Estimated Tax, 505
- Business Expenses, 535
- Accounting Periods and Methods, 538
- Business Use of Your Home, 587

To order any of these booklets, phone the IRS at (800)829-3676. IRS forms and publications, as well as answers to questions and links to help, are available on the Internet at www.irs.gov.

employment income. Normally, when you are employed by someone else, the employer shares responsibility for the taxes due. However, when you are self-employed, you must pay the entire amount yourself.

Freelancers frequently overlook self-employment taxes and fail to set aside a sufficient amount of money. They also tend to forget state and local taxes. If the volume of your photo sales reaches a point where it becomes a substantial percentage of your income, then you are required to pay estimated tax on a quarterly basis. This requires you to project the amount of money you expect to generate in a three-month period. However burdensome this may be in the short run, it works to your advantage in that you plan for and stay current with the various taxes you are required to pay. Read IRS Publication 505 (Tax Withholding and Estimated Tax).

Deductions

Many deductions can be claimed by self-employed photographers. It's in your best interest to be aware of them. Examples of 100-percent-deductible claims include production costs of résumé, business cards and brochures; photographer's rep commissions; membership dues; costs of purchasing portfolio materials; education/business-related magazines and books; insurance; and legal and professional services.

Additional deductions can be taken if your office or studio is home-based. The catch here is that your work area must be used only on a professional basis; your office can't double as a family room after hours. The IRS also wants to see evidence that you use the work space on a regular basis via established business hours and proof that you've actively marketed your work. If you can satisfy these criteria, then a percentage of mortgage interests, real estate taxes, rent, maintenance costs, utilities, and homeowner's insurance, plus office furniture and equipment, can be claimed on your tax form at year's end.

In the past, to qualify for a home-office deduction, the space you worked in had to be "the most important, consequential, or influential location" you used to conduct your business. This meant that if you had a separate studio location for shooting but did scheduling, billing and record keeping in your home office, you could not claim a deduction. However, as of 1999, your home office will qualify for a deduction if you "use it exclusively and regularly for administrative or management activities of your trade or business and you have no other fixed location where you conduct substantial administrative or management activities of your trade or business." Read IRS Publication 587 (Business Use of Your Home) for more details.

If you are working out of your home, keep separate records and bank accounts for personal and business finances, as well as a separate business phone. Since the IRS can audit tax records as far back as seven years, it's vital to keep all paperwork related to your business. This includes invoices, vouchers, expenditures and sales receipts, canceled checks, deposit slips, register tapes, and business ledger entries for this period. The burden of proof will be on you if the IRS questions any deductions claimed. To maintain professional status in the eyes of the IRS, you will need to show a profit for three years out of a five-year period.

Sales tax

Sales taxes are complicated and need special consideration. For instance, if you work in more than one state, use models or work with reps in one or more states, or work in one state and store equipment in another, you may be required to pay sales tax in each of the states that apply. In particular, if you work with an out-of-state stock photo agency that has clients over a wide geographic area, you should explore your tax liability with a tax professional.

As with all taxes, sales taxes must be reported and paid on a timely basis to avoid audits and/or penalties. In regard to sales tax, you should:

- Always register your business at the tax offices with jurisdiction in your city and state.
- Always charge and collect sales tax on the full amount of the invoice, unless an exemption applies.
- If an exemption applies because of resale, you must provide a copy of the customer's resale certificate. If an exemption applies because of other conditions, such as selling one-time reproduction rights or working for a tax-exempt, nonprofit organization, you must also provide documentation.

SELF-PROMOTION

There are basically three ways to acquaint photo buyers with your work: through the mail, over the Internet, or in person. No one way is better or more effective than another. They each serve an individual function and should be used in concert to increase your visibility and, with a little luck, your sales.

IDEAS FOR GREAT SELF-PROMOTION

Where to find ideas for great self-promotion:
- *HOW* magazine's self-promotion annual (October issue).
- *Photo District News*, magazine's self-promotion issue (October issue).
- *The Photographer's Guide to Marketing & Self-Promotion*, by Maria Piscopo (Allworth Press).
- *The Business of Photography: Principles and Practices*, by Mary Virginia Swanson, available at www.mvswanson.com.

Self-promotion mailers

When you are just starting to get your name out there and want to begin generating assignments and stock sales, it's time to design a self-promotion campaign. This is your chance to do your best, most creative work and package it in an unforgettable way to get the attention of busy photo buyers. Self-promotions traditionally are sample images printed on card stock and sent through the mail to potential clients. If the image you choose is strong and you carefully target your mailing, a traditional self-promotion can work.

But don't be afraid to go out on a limb here. You want to show just how amazing and creative you are, and you want the photo buyer to hang onto your sample for as long as possible. Why not make it impossible to throw away? Instead of a simple postcard, maybe you could send a small, usable notepad with one of your images at the top, or a calendar the photo buyer can hang up and use all year. If you target your mailing carefully, this kind of special promotion needn't be expensive.

If you're worried that a single image can't do justice to your unique style, you have two options. One way to get multiple images in front of photo buyers without sending an overwhelming package is to design a campaign of promotions that builds from a single image to a small group of related photos. Make the images tell a story and indicate that there are more to follow. If you are computer savvy, the other way to showcase a sampling of your work is to point photo buyers to an online portfolio of your best work. Send a single sample that includes your Internet address, and ask buyers to take a look.

Websites

Websites are steadily becoming more important in the photographer's self-promotion repertory. If you have a good collection of digital photographs—whether they have been scanned from film or are from a digital camera—you should consider creating a website to showcase samples of your work, provide information about the type of work you do, and display your contact information. The website does not have to be elaborate or contain every photograph you've ever taken. In fact, it is best if you edit your work very carefully and choose only the best images to display on your website. The benefit of having a website is that it makes it so easy for photo buyers to see your work. You can send e-mails to targeted photo buyers and include a link to your website. Many photo buyers report that this is how they prefer to be contacted. Of course, your URL should also be included on any print materials, such as postcards, brochures, business cards, and stationery. Some photographers even include their URL in their credit line.

Portfolio presentations

Once you've actually made contact with potential buyers and piqued their interest, they'll want to see a larger selection of your work—your portfolio. Once again, there's more than one way to get this sampling of images in front of buyers. Portfolios can be digital—stored on a disk or CD-ROM, or posted on the Internet. They can take the form of a large box or binder and require a special visit and presentation by you. Or they can come in a small binder and be sent through the mail. Whichever ways you choose to showcase your best work, you should always have more than one portfolio, and each should be customized for potential clients.

Keep in mind that your portfolios should contain your best work (dupes only). Never put originals in anything that will be out of your hands for more than a few minutes. Also, don't include more than twenty images. If you try to show too many pieces you'll overwhelm the buyer, and any image that is less than your best will detract from the impact of your strongest work. Finally, be sure to show only work a buyer is likely to use. It won't do any good to show a shoe manufacturer your shots of farm animals or a clothing company your food pictures. For more detailed information on the various types of portfolios and how to select which photos to include and which ones to leave out, see *Photo Portfolio Success*, by John Kaplan (Writer's Digest Books).

Do you need a résumé?

Some of the listings in this book say to submit a résumé with samples. If you are a freelancer, a résumé may not always be necessary. Sometimes a stock list or a list of your clients may suffice, and may be all the photo buyer is really looking for. If you do include a résumé, limit the details to your photographic experience and credits. If you are applying for a position teaching photography or for a full-time photography position at a studio, corporation, newspaper, etc., you will need the résumé. Galleries that want to show your work may also want to see a résumé, but, again, confine the details of your life to significant photographic achievements.

ORGANIZING & LABELING YOUR IMAGES

It will be very difficult for you to make sales of your work if you aren't able to locate a particular image in your files when a buyer needs it. It is imperative that you find a way to organize your images—a way that can adapt to a growing file of images. There are probably as many ways to catalog photographs as there are photographers. However, most photogra-

---

IMAGE ORGANIZATION & STORAGE

To learn more about selecting, organizing, labeling and storing images, see:
- *Photo Portfolio Success*, by John Kaplan (Writer's Digest Books).
- *Sell & Re-Sell Your Photos*, by Rohn Engh, 5th edition (Writer's Digest Books).

phers begin by placing their photographs into large, general categories such as landscapes, wildlife, countries, cities, etc. They then break these down further into subcategories. If you specialize in a particular subject—birds, for instance—you may want to break the bird category down further into cardinal, eagle, robin, osprey, etc. Find a coding system that works for your particular set of photographs. For example, nature and travel photographer William Manning says, "I might have slide pages for Washington, DC (WDC), Kentucky (KY), or Italy (ITY). I divide my mammal subcategory into African wildlife (AWL), North American wildlife (NAW), zoo animals (ZOO)."

After you figure out a coding system that works for you, find a method for naming your digital files or captioning your slides. Images with complete information often prompt sales: Photo editors appreciate having as much information as possible. Always remember to include your name and the copyright symbol © on each image. If you're working with slides, computer software can make this job a lot easier. Programs such as Caption Writer (www. hindsightltd.com), allow photographers to easily create and print labels for their slides.

The computer also makes managing your photo files much easier. Programs such as fotoBiz (www.cradocfotosoftware.com) and StockView (www.hindsightltd.com) are popular with freelance assignment and stock photographers. FotoBiz has an image log and is capable of creating labels. It can also track your images and allows you to create documents such as delivery memos and invoices. StockView also tracks your images, has labeling options, and can create business documents.

PROTECTING YOUR COPYRIGHT

There is one major misconception about copyright: Many photographers don't realize that once you create a photo it becomes yours. You (or your heirs) own the copyright, regardless of whether you register it for the duration of your lifetime plus seventy years.

The fact that an image is automatically copyrighted does not mean that it shouldn't be registered. Quite the contrary. You cannot even file a copyright infringement suit until you've registered your work. Also, without timely registration of your images, you can only recover actual damages—money lost as a result of sales by the infringer plus any profits the infringer earned. For example, recovering $2,000 for an ad sale can be minimal when weighed against the expense of hiring a copyright attorney. Often this deters photographers from filing lawsuits if they haven't registered their work. They know that the attorney's fees will be more than the actual damages recovered, and, therefore, infringers go unpunished.

Registration allows you to recover certain damages to which you otherwise would not be legally entitled. For instance, attorney fees and court costs can be recovered. So too can statutory damages—awards based on how deliberate and harmful the infringement was.

PROTECTING YOUR COPYRIGHT

How to learn more about protecting your copyright:

- Call the United States Copyright Office at (202)707-3000 or check out their website, www.copyright.gov, for answers to frequently asked questions.
- American Society of Media Photographers (ASMP), www.asmp.org/ tutorials/copy-right-overview.html.
- Editorial Photographers (EP), www.editorialphoto.com.
- *Legal Guide for the Visual Artist*, by Tad Crawford, Allworth Press.
- Society of Photographers and Artists Representatives (SPAR), www.spar.org.

Statutory damages can run as high as $100,000. These are the fees that make registration so important.

In order to recover these fees, there are rules regarding registration that you must follow. The rules have to do with the timeliness of your registration in relation to the infringement:

- **Unpublished images** must be registered before the infringement takes place.
- **Published images** must be registered within three months of the first date of publication or before the infringement began.

The process of registering your work is simple. Visit the United States Copyright Office's website at www.copyright.gov to file electronically. Registration costs $35, but you can register photographs in large quantities for that fee. For bulk registration, your images must be organized under one title, for example, "The works of John Photographer, 2009–2011." It's still possible to register with paper forms, but this method requires a higher filing fee ($65). To request paper forms, contact the Library of Congress, Copyright Office-COPUBS, 101 Independence Avenue, SE, Washington, DC 20559-6304, (202) 707-9100, and ask for Form VA (works of visual art).

The copyright notice

Another way to protect your copyright is to mark each image with a copyright notice. This informs everyone reviewing your work that you own the copyright. It may seem basic, but in court this can be very important. In a lawsuit, one avenue of defense for an infringer is "innocent infringement"—basically the "I didn't know" argument. By placing a copyright notice on your images, you negate this defense for an infringer.

The copyright notice basically consists of three elements: the symbol, the year of first publication, and the copyright holder's name. Here's an example of a copyright notice for an image published in 2012: © 2012 John Q. Photographer. Instead of the symbol ©, you can use the word "Copyright" or simply "Copr." However, most foreign countries prefer © as a common designation.

Also consider adding the notation "All rights reserved" after your copyright notice. This phrase is not necessary in the U.S. since all rights are automatically reserved, but it is recommended in other parts of the world.

Know your rights

The digital era is making copyright protection more difficult. As this technology grows, more and more clients will want digital versions of your photos. Don't be alarmed, just be careful. Your clients don't want to steal your work. When you negotiate the usage of your work, consider adding a phrase to your contract that limits the rights of buyers who want digital versions of your photos. You might want them to guarantee that images will be removed from their computer files once the work appears in print. You might say it's okay to perform limited digital manipulation, and then specify what can be done. The important thing is to discuss what the client intends to do and spell it out in writing.

It's essential not only to know your rights under the Copyright Law, but also to make sure that every photo buyer you deal with understands them. The following list of typical image rights should help you in your dealings with clients:

- **One-time rights.** These photos are "leased" or "licensed" on a one-time basis; one fee is paid for one use.
- **First rights.** This is generally the same as purchase of one-time rights, though the photo buyer is paying a bit more for the privilege of being the first to use the image. He may use it only once unless other rights are negotiated.
- **Serial rights.** The photographer has sold the right to use the photo in a periodical. This shouldn't be confused with using the photo in "installments." Most magazines will want to be sure the photo won't be running in a competing publication.
- **Exclusive rights.** Exclusive rights guarantee the buyer's exclusive right to use the photo in his particular market or for a particular product. A greeting card company, for example, may purchase these rights to an image with the stipulation that it not be sold to a competing company for a certain time period. The photographer, however, may retain rights to sell the image to other markets. Conditions should always be put in writing to avoid any misunderstandings.
- **Electronic rights.** These rights allow a buyer to place your work on electronic media such as CD-ROMs or websites. Often these rights are requested with print rights.
- **Promotion rights.** Such rights allow a publisher to use a photo for promotion of a publication in which the photo appears. The photographer should be paid for promotional use in addition to the rights first sold to reproduce the image. Another form of this—agency promotion rights—is common among stock photo agencies. Likewise, the terms of this need to be negotiated separately.

- **Work for hire.** Under the Copyright Act of 1976, section 101, a "work for hire" is defined as: "(1) a work prepared by an employee within the scope of his or her employment; or (2) a work … specially ordered or commissioned for use as a contribution to a collective, as part of a motion picture or audiovisual work or as a supplementary work . . . if the parties expressly agree in a written instrument signed by them that the work shall be considered a work made for hire."
- **All rights.** This involves selling or assigning all rights to a photo for a specified period of time. This differs from work for hire, which always means the photographer permanently surrenders all rights to a photo and any claims to royalties or other future compensation. Terms for all rights—including time period of usage and compensation—should only be negotiated and confirmed in a written agreement with the client.

It is understandable for a client not to want a photo to appear in a competitor's ad. Skillful negotiation usually can result in an agreement between the photographer and the client that says the images will not be sold to a competitor, but could be sold to other industries, possibly offering regional exclusivity for a stated time period.

ADAPT AND SELL MORE PHOTOGRAPHY IN 2012

Lori McNee

> "Enjoying success requires the ability to adapt. Only by being open to change will you have a true opportunity to get the most from your talent."
>
> —*Nolan Ryan*

Most likely if you are reading this article right now, you are interested in selling more art in 2012. There is no magic bullet or quick way to success; however, photographers who are open to new ideas and have a willingness to adapt to the ever-changing marketplace will have a head start over their peers and competitors. It is time for you to take charge of your art career.

In this challenging economy, being a successful artist not only consists of creating great art, but is also about building a strong business. The small businesses that have succeeded over the past few years have been based on *adaptability*, *trust*, *longevity* and *personal branding*.

As an artist myself, I understand that artisans tend to be frugal. Nevertheless, it does take some money to make money. The good news is, many of the ideas listed below can be accomplished with little or no monetary investment other than good ole' sweat equity.

Lori McNee is an internationally recognized professional artist and art-marketing expert, who writes about art and marketing tips on her blog FineArtTips.com. Lori is an exhibiting member of Oil Painters of America and ranks as one of the most influential artists and powerful women on Twitter. She was named a Twitter Powerhouse by *The Huffington Post*.

Implementing the following marketing tips into your photography business plan will lead you toward more art sales.

DETERMINE YOUR GOALS

Goal setting is important, because once you have your goals in place it is easier to achieve them. Goals are much like a road map with mile-markers along the way. They give you a clear plan that details where you are going and how you are going to get there.

To begin, you need to determine what you want. Identify your *short-term* and *long-term* goals. Goals do not have to be overwhelming. For instance, let's say you are an amateur photographer, but you dream of having your work represented by a top gallery in New York City. Most likely that goal would be unrealistic and difficult to achieve in one step. It is easier and more realistic to set your goal within workable units, like mile-markers.

1. A short-term and reachable goal would be to first start perfecting your craft.
2. The next goal would be to develop a cohesive and consistent body of work.
3. Then, progress into building your collector base by selling your photographs in a co-op gallery or coffee shop, or from your studio.
4. The next goal would be to enter a juried exhibition, arts and crafts show, or local gallery for representation.
5. Next, the fifth goal might be attained once you have consistently sold your photography, gained the respect of your fellow art peers, have been solicited by galleries, and have had your art published in national magazines.
6. The long-term goal would be to approach that top New York gallery for representation.

Visualize where you would like to see yourself and your photography career in one year, then in five years. Do you understand your potential market? Where does your work belong? Your potential market might include commercial galleries, university galleries, art fairs, art salons, juried exhibitions, public art projects, co-op galleries, museums, and more. Write them down and tack a list of goals next to your computer or bathroom mirror. Think big, but start small. Small decisions are important for your long-term success. Be patient and reward yourself when you meet each goal or mile-marker along the way.

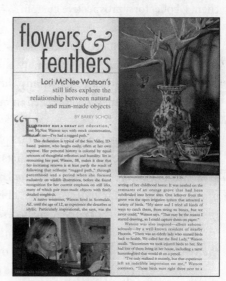

Garnering a feature in a national magazine helps build exposure, credibility and respect amongst your peers.

SELL YOURSELF

Years ago, while working in retail, I learned this valuable lesson: The number one ingredient to successful sales in any business is to know how to sell yourself. If you can sell yourself, you can sell anything.

BUILD YOUR BRAND

A great way to begin "selling yourself" is to build your brand identity. A strong brand is invaluable and serves to communicate credibility to your prospective customers and colleagues.

This is equally important for all fine artists, designers, crafters, photographers, illustrators and freelance artists and more. You want your brand to reside in the hearts and minds of your clients, collectors, prospective customers and competitors.

For example, famous photographers such as Ansel Adams, Mathew Brady, Walker Evans, Dorothea Lange, Cindy Sherman, Alfred Stieglitz and James Van Der Zee's distinctive brands are forever etched in our minds. Your brand identity will help set you apart from the pack.

Think of your profile picture as your personal logo. A great profile picture immediately states who and what you are. Your picture should be friendly and it is best to make eye contact with the camera. I chose to wear red because it is a "power color" and grabs attention, but the blue apron helps to calm it down. Blue builds trust and confidence. This attention to detail will enhance your brand.

Start a Facebook fan page for your photography business. With a fan page you can promote your photography and products, and share your portfolio and videos. This is a great way to build your fan and collector base. Use the other social media sites to build your brand, like Twitter, LinkedIn and YouTube to promote yourself and your art business. (See the article "Secrets to Social Media Success.")

Be sure to personalize your online image and brand with your picture or avatar. Using the same recognizable image on all your online sites will further promote your brand.

Deliver what you promise. One of the primary motivators of brand loyalty is trust and a consistent experience. If you say you're going to have the proofs ready by Friday, make sure they are ready. A reputation takes a lifetime to build and an instant to destroy. Protect your brand.

UPDATE YOUR WEBSITE AND START A BLOG

Most likely you have a website with information about your photography and pricing, your bio and résumé, and maybe a cool video or two. You might be wondering why no one is visiting your website.

The easiest way for people to discover your website is to start a blog.

On your blog, write about things your fans, photographers, and collectors care about. Encourage feedback on your blog and be sure to personally answer all incoming comments and questions. Customers will enjoy the extra information and personal touch. Potential collectors will have reasons to choose you.

Technology is becoming more and more important in your client's life, so you must stay current. There are many free business-

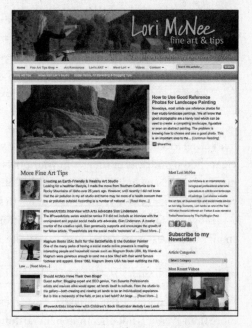

A good blog is easy to navigate and has a variety of content and interesting illustrations to grab the attention of the reader. You can see that I have made my social media buttons and newsletter subscription link easily accessible.

EXTRA BLOGGING TIPS

There are many simple and free blog templates. It has become very easy to create your own blog these days through WordPress, Blogger, LiveJournal, and TypePad, just to name a few. Follow the instructions to set up your own blog through any of these blog template providers.

- Don't rush writing your posts. It is better to wait an extra day or two than to post a half-hearted article. Posting once a week or even a few times a month is plenty enough to get you started. Link to other articles within your site to help keep your readers' attention and make your blog "sticky."

- Keep your titles interesting. Make sure the content reflects the title. Add variety to your posts by using bullet points, diagrams and images. Break up long paragraphs.

- Content is king. Use content to engage your audience, both customers and prospects. Some estimate 90 percent of purchase decisions start with online search. Readers will skim an article in under 30 seconds to determine whether or not they want to read it. Make it easy to read. Find your own voice and write about things that nobody else writes about. Offer services, and sell your own product.

> • Although the industry standard is somewhere between 250–600 words, there is no set rule for the perfect post length. However, a mix of short and long posts keeps your blog from getting too predictable. Use Google Analytics to measure and monitor your website and blog traffic and watch it grow! Your main goal for the blog is to convert your readers into business prospects.

marketing tools that can be used to promote your site. For example, you can easily embed video, audio podcasts or images in your posts. Be sure to integrate widgets and your social media channels including, Facebook "like" buttons, Tweet This and Share to drive traffic to your site and make it easy for your readers to share your interesting content.

Blogs are far more versatile than traditional websites and are one of the best ways for small businesses to gain exposure, especially if you are an artist, photographer or crafter.

FOCUS ON CUSTOMER COMMITMENT AND RELATIONSHIPS

With the onslaught of social media, customer intimacy is easy to provide and is expected more than ever. It is not uncommon for customers, collectors and potential clients to engage with each other on sites such as Facebook and Twitter *before* they engage with you.

The Internet has changed the way we do business. Everything happens so quickly and the competition is increasing. A client's continuing patronage is no longer guaranteed. Photographers must encourage their customer's loyalty and advocacy through word of mouth. As a result, photographers have to find a way to quickly respond to their customer's wants and needs because consumer loyalty is a thing of the past.

If you do not react quickly, your client will find another artist who will. Stop thinking of your potential clients as dollar bills and understand them as real people whose lives are positively affected by what you can do and provide for them.

Provide top-drawer service, and do not neglect repeat customers. It takes five times the effort to acquire new clients than to repeat a sale to an existing customer. Keep the Pareto principle or 80/20 rule in mind: 20 percent of your collectors will produce 80 percent of your sales.

DIRECT MARKETING

Direct marketing is being revolutionized by commingling old-world direct marketing techniques and mediums with current methods of the new digital marketing tools. This new "hybrid-marketing" is a blend of online and offline methods. Direct marketing now consists of the Internet, mobile and direct mail.

The experts say you will find your marketing power double by simply diverting your traditional advertising dollars into direct marketing, and that will drive better return on investment for your photography brand and business. This is good news considering many photographers have drastically reduced their marketing budgets. Nevertheless, competition increases during a recession, which generates new talent and innovation. It is not a time for you to lay low.

Return to the marketplace

Marketing began hundreds of years ago by literally going to a marketplace to sell a good or service. Artisans and craftsmen would engage buyers face to face. Today, people still want to buy from those they *know*, like and trust—gallery receptions, arts and crafts shows, social media and blogging helps make this possible. It is important to think of your product as an extension of yourself.

Get online

Consider art registries and websites like deviantART, Flickr, Etsy and eBay. Many of these sites allow individuals to sell arts and crafts without having to operate a storefront business of their own. Market your art business and product via social media such as Twitter, Facebook and YouTube, and remember to start a blog.

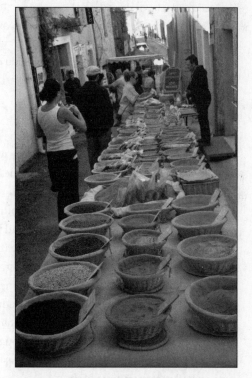

Business cards

Be prepared. It's a good idea to have a professional stack of business cards on hand. In this day and age be sure to include your name, e-mail address, website/blog URL address as well as any social media handles, and your cell phone number. Add a logo or an image of your art to further your brand identity. Tip: Print up bookmarks with the same information and leave a stack at your local bookstore and coffee shop!

Business relationships

Don't forget to nurture your existing relationships with your galleries and their employees. Reach out to interior decorators, real estate agents, house stagers, restaurant own-

Similar to social media, the French marketplace is a vibrant community. Without the middleman, vendors and buyers communicate directly on a one-on-one basis in order to buy or sell goods.

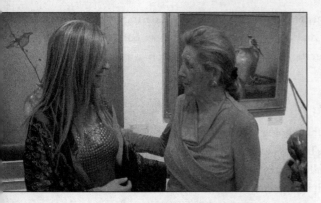

With the increased use of social media by artists and photographers, trust and open communication is needed more than ever between the gallery owner and the creative. In this photo, Kneeland Gallery owner Diane Kneeland and I share a laugh at my recent exhibition.

ers, corporate art buyers and private art dealers and let them bring the clients.

Photographers have a tendency to concentrate on personal excellence, career achievement and individual sales. However, there are wonderful rewards to be made from building alliances amongst your peers. These mutually beneficial friendships help to facilitate an environment filled with inspiration and abundance, rather than an environment of isolation and competition.

Create a simple system to manage your new friends and contacts. There is software available to help you with these tasks; record new contacts in a database, phone book, or whatever works best for you. After you exchange cards with a new friend or prospective client, jot down where you met, what you discussed and how and when you should follow up as a reminder.

Send out a newsletter

Once you have your blog up and running, be sure to send out a newsletter. Dollar for dollar, newsletters are one of the most effective ways to reach your targeted market. Creating newsletters can be hard work, though. Decide on the number of newsletters you will be able to produce each year and stick to it.

Use your newsletter to further build your credibility, brand and professionalism. The newsletter will inform your subscribers and prospective collectors of special announcements, offers and coming events. Make sure it is unique and reflects your brand.

Of course you want to sell your product, but you can't ask subscribers to "buy" all at once. If you spam your readers, they will unsubscribe to your newsletter. Instead, try including just one *call to action* in each individual newsletter. Focus on just one promotion and your customers will likely pay better attention.

Note: E-mail is *not* for everyone. Although most people prefer e-mail, there are those who still prefer getting their mail the old-fashioned way. Consider sending a postcard or paper newsletter from time to time.

HELPFUL LINKS

en.wikipedia.org/wiki/Relationship_
marketing

twitter.com

facebook.com

youtube.com

gettag.mobi.com

en.wikipedia.org/wiki/Pareto_
principle

FineArtTips.com

Customer relationship management
software:

act.com

artworkspro.com

salesforce.com

Newsletter services:

icontact.com

constantcontact.com

mailchimp.com

Wordpress newsletter plugin:

www.satollo.net/plugins/
newsletter-pro

MOBILE MARKETING

Mobile marketing describes marketing with a mobile device, such as a cell phone. This has exploded with Apple's iPhone, Google's Android operating system, the iPad and smart phones. In fact, as of 2011, over 50 percent of all U.S. homes owned at least one smart phone.

Mobile devices are redefining the shopping habits of customers. Smart phones and other mobile devices act as research and shopping tools.

Today, more and more artists, galleries and museums are using smart phones for marketing. For instance, imagine a slide show of your photographs, a video demo, or your website being instantly delivered to a potential collector's smart phone. By using a tag you can make that vision a reality.

A tag is a barcode that can be placed in magazines, business cards, brochures, and postcards, or even hanging next to your photographs in a gallery. After the tag reader application is downloaded onto a smart phone, the phone's camera becomes a "scanner." The lens will detect the code that will trigger the information to be displayed on your client's phone. Keep in mind, to be successful, the mobile activity must be engaging and relevant, and there must be a call to action. Tag readers have helped to revive the print marketing industry!

SOCIAL MEDIA

Over the years, "social media" has become a buzzword. Wikipedia's definition of social media is "a blending of technology and social interaction for the co-creation of value driven content." The "co-creation of content" means that social media is about *we*, not about *me*.

Social media is a fundamental shift in the way we communicate. Artists should embrace the free marketing power of social media. Millions of people could possibly become customers. This is not possible in the off-line world.

Build your brand

Social media is the quickest way to build brand recognition for you and your art business. A strong brand is invaluable and serves to communicate credibility to your prospective customers and business associates.

Marketing

Social media is already changing the rules of the marketplace across the globe. We now have access to literally millions of potential customers. These prospective buyers feel more comfortable about a brand if they can interact with it via social media. Use social media channels to send out videos, images of your photographs, and links to your latest blog post, and to share interesting content. You can easily drive huge amounts of traffic to your website or blog using social media. Utilize social media to get the word out about your photography business in a way that promotes conversation and leads to sales.

Networking

Being a photographer can be a solitary occupation, but with social networking, you're not alone! Use social media to get instant feedback on your latest photograph or blog post, or ask for a critique on your work. You will learn from other photographers and business leaders, gain inspiration from others and build lasting relationships.

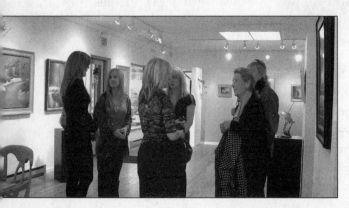

Networking with other photographers and building a good working relationship between you and your gallery is key to your success and will eventually lead to more sales. This synergy also builds a sense of community, trust and propriety.

Keep your finger on the pulse

Remember, creatives are the movers and shakers of the world. We need to *stay informed* and on the cutting edge. Photographers should be aware of new trends in design, decorating, fashion and technology and how it influences photography and sales.

TAKE CALCULATED RISKS

People like to stay with what is familiar and safe. But, if we eliminate calculated risks, we remove the opportunity for growth in business and in our craft. As a small business entrepreneur, if you try something new and it doesn't work, you can easily change your strategy. But, you need to be accountable for the inherent risks and the outcome.

Go where the action is. Visit gallery receptions and rub elbows with successful photographers and gallery owners. Attend lectures, symposiums and events held in museums and art centers. Enter juried exhibitions, art fairs, local photography contests and competitions.

Send press releases to local newspapers. Call the editor of the photography magazines within your niche and request an interview. Contact a popular photography blog and submit a guest article. Network outside your circle. Think creatively. Talk to your banker, accountant, dentist, florist and doorman. Ask them for business referrals and do a favor for them in return.

During these uncertain times of economic challenges it is tempting to escape into a creative safe haven in your studio and withdraw from extra challenges. But remember Neil Simon's words of wisdom, "If no one ever took risks, Michelangelo would have painted the Sistine floor."

DON'T BE AFRAID TO FAIL

There is no real secret to success. In order to succeed, you must challenge yourself, be passionate about your craft, perfect your skill as a photographer, and learn from your mistakes along the way.

The greatest barrier to success is the fear of failure and an inability to adapt to change. Some of the ideas listed in this article might seem unconventional and intimidating. But, if you adapt just a few of these new ideas into your photography marketing strategy, you will begin to see favorable results, which will lead to more sales in 2012. Good luck and I hope to see you on Twitter!

SECRETS TO SOCIAL MEDIA SUCCESS

Twitter, Facebook and YouTube

....

by Lori McNee

By now, most photographers probably use social media in one form or another. On a daily basis I meet creatives with a natural liking for social media and its networking capabilities. However, many of these talented individuals still do not understand how to harness the power of social media to their advantage.

Social media offers large-scale reach for little cost other than your time. The successes you reap from social media will directly depend upon the amount of time you are willing to devote to this free marketing medium. There has never been another era in business when an individual could reach out to hundreds or even thousands of customers in one day. Social marketing eliminates the middleman and provides photographers with the unique opportunity to have a direct relationship with their customers.

For me, the main purpose of social media is to drive traffic back to my blogs, LoriMc-Nee.com and FineArtTips.com. Social media has put my name on the map, given me international recognition, and been the lifeblood to my blogs and art business. Twitter, Facebook and YouTube are the fastest ways to build brand recognition for you and your photography business. I use all three of these social media channels quite differently.

Twitter is possibly the most intimidating social platform because everything happens so quickly. Once you jump in and start engaging, you will see that Twitter also has the broadest reach. Twitter updates reach like-minded people quickly and can effectively market a

---

Lori McNee is an internationally recognized professional artist and art-marketing expert, who writes about art and marketing tips on her blog FineArtTips.com. Lori is an exhibiting member of Oil Painters of America and ranks as one of the most influential artists and powerful women on Twitter. She was named a Twitter Powerhouse by *The Huffington Post*.

person or a service. Twitter offers an immediate response and is very addictive once you get the hang of it.

Twitter is much like a cocktail party where you can quickly meet and exchange information. But, the social etiquette rules still apply. Would you just walk up to someone and say, "Hey, please buy my photographs." No, that is just rude. You need to connect and build a relationship first.

Facebook on the other hand, is more like a dinner party, where you build upon conversations and further develop your relationships. Facebook is about connecting with people and prospective customers you have already met. Facebook is a bit easier to market tangible products, such as photographs.

Facebook's platform appeals to the social butterfly and can also be very addictive because it allows people to connect with old and new friends. In fact, Facebook has replaced e-mail, chat and photo sharing for many users.

YouTube is like inviting the person into your home movie theater to learn more about you, your product or service, and what you do. Currently, YouTube is the favorite site when searching for online video.

Remember this: Nearly every single person who uses social media wants to sell you something, whether it is art, real estate, travel, information or a service. This is the trick— how do you learn to market and brand yourself correctly on social media?

Brand identity differentiates you from the rest of the pack. We have all heard the old saying, "Don't judge a book by its cover." But, on social media sites, your cover or *profile* is judged and very quickly.

Read on for my secrets to your social media success:

TWITTER TIPS

Name

Your name is the first thing that people will see on Twitter. Use the name you want to represent your photography brand. For example, when I first started on Twitter I used @lorimcnee, but quickly changed my Twitter handle to @lorimcneeartist and rapidly gained loyal followers. Why? Because it is easier for people to instantly associate me as an artist this way. Also, when people do a Twitter search for "artist," my name appears.

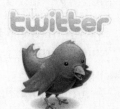

At first glance, the famous Twitter logo might look like child's play. But, don't let this little bluebird fool you; there is a lot of power in a tweet!

Avatar

On Twitter it is important to make your profile picture friendly. Recent studies have found that your profile picture or *avatar* is more than just a pretty face. In fact, one's avatar affects how a message is received, and also how individuals interpret it. The higher the friendliness of the avatar, the more intimate people are willing to be with strangers. It is not a rule, but I suggest using an image of yourself rather than a business logo or a photograph as your avatar.

To further your brand identity, it is a good idea to use the same avatar on all your social media sites. You can change your photo, but, be forewarned, this will confuse some of your followers. It is best to wait until you have a loyal following before you make any major changes.

Profile/bio

On any social media channel, the profile or bio is your big branding opportunity to make your unique mark. This is your virtual personality. Sound interesting, witty, or clever, but, whatever you do, choose your profile words wisely. These few words will say a lot to the world about who and what you are. Make sure to include the link to your blog or website. If you don't have a website, link to your Facebook page.

Custom landing page

Consider creating a custom Twitter landing page by using a site such as Twitbacks or Free Twitter Designer. A custom page is another branding opportunity. Potential followers and customers will immediately understand who and what you are just by your custom page. I made a collage of my artwork, together with some images of me painting in the field—at once, this states, "artist."

Get followers

Once you have an informative and engaging profile page, you will automatically start attracting new followers. You have already begun to build your brand.

Interestingly, I have found that most creatives use Twitter as a way to connect with other creatives. True, this is a great networking opportunity, but they are missing an important marketing opportunity to reach out to prospective customers.

Be a good follower

Decide if you want to actively engage with your followers, and also if you want to follow everyone back. Do what works best for you. It is nice to reach out to your friends and followers. Do not forget the little guys as your following grows. They helped you get to where you are now, and they are loyal. I do my best to thank my followers because I truly appreciate them.

Twitter is all about making friendly connections in order to build a strong social networking community through your following.

It is good to reach out to some of the bigger Twitter names. These tweeters have a lot of experience and if they retweet (RT) you, it helps with your own Twitter influence.

What to tweet

To gain new followers, be sure to pass along good content. Your followers are looking for tweets with value. If they do not find it, they will either delete you or forget you.

Engage with your followers and don't focus on selling. Focus on giving. Learn to speak *with* your audience, not *at* them. You are here to build valuable, real relationships. By engaging your market, you are creating a community around your brand. This will lead to trust and eventually sales. About 80 percent of my tweets and retweets share useful information and resources, including links to my blog. The remaining 20 percent of the tweets are reaching out to my following, small talk, inquiries and relationship building.

Share photos of your latest painting using Twitpic or yfrog, ask for feedback from your followers and get instant replies, or share inspiring quotes. Link to your YouTube or Vimeo videos as a great way to engage your following in conversation and strengthen your brand. Learn how to abbreviate your tweets. You can use URL shorteners such as bit.ly or TinyURL. Manage your Twitter following with helpful applications such as TweetDeck or HootSuite. To be effective, plan to tweet at least once a day. Ten to fifteen minutes of tweeting is enough to keep a consistent presence on Twitter.

Share links to your latest blog posts, and recycle your blog's old content. Make sure your *Twitter stream* is interesting and vary the content and cadence of your tweets. Be consistent with quality. You can tweet a lot or just a few times a day—this is a personal and business choice.

Make sure your last tweet counts. At the end of each Twitter session, leave a valuable tweet. Your potential followers will judge whether or not to follow you by your last Twitter update.

Reach beyond your niche on Twitter

When I first started tweeting back in 2009, my target niche was artists and art collectors. To my surprise, my tweets and blog posts began to capture the attention of a much broader audience.

Why? My Twitter updates have an appeal that reaches beyond my own art niche. How? I am able to reach beyond my art readers by understanding that

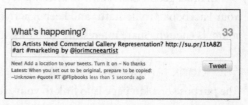

Twitter asks, "What's happening?" above the update box. This is where you share your "tweet." Here, I typed the title and then the link to one of my blog posts. I added the hashtags #art and #marketing to get more views. After I click the "Tweet" button, this update will be seen by thousands, if not millions of Twitter friends—amazing!

most people have broad interests. I tweet about art, and share my other interests that include blogging, social media, nature, quotes, photography, outdoors and more. Not only can I attract my own niche readers, but also I can appeal to multiple profiles while staying true to my target audience.

FACEBOOK TIPS

Facebook is the largest online social networking site. It allows people to interact and to share photos, videos, links, and more. Facebook is an invaluable tool for small businesses for its networking and marketing capabilities.

Facebook offers three ways to build your brand, and there are a few major differences between each: *profiles* are for people, *fan pages* are for businesses and *groups* are for special discussions and events. Each of these entities provide for different networking and marketing opportunities. However, you must have a personal profile before you can add or create a page or a group. Many photographers incorrectly use their personal profiles instead of fan pages for their photography businesses. For branding, both the profile and the fan page are necessary. As a photographer you need a profile to network and promote your personal brand while using a fan page to promote your photography business.

Facebook profile page

Your profile gives you visibility as a real person. Be sure to set up your profile with your real name. It is against the Facebook terms to use a profile for your business. Profiles limit Facebook users to 5,000 friends. I like to use my profile to connect with my family and art friends. However, I can still connect with friends on a business level via my profile. Nowadays, people want to connect with the person behind the brand; this is a good way to interact with them.

In order get the best *return on investment (*ROI) out of your Facebook experience, update your Facebook profile status and keep it active. Once a day, or a few times a week at minimum, is enough. Share interesting thoughts, links, and videos or informative content.

Facebook fan page

The purpose of a fan page is to link to your website or blog. Fan pages are set up to target your customers with bigger viral marketing potential. Pages are public and can be linked to externally. Fan pages are an important part of your *search engine optimization* (SEO), while profiles are not. Fan pages allow you an unlimited number of "fans." Facebook has been touting the pages as the strongest marketing vehicle.

The pages allow you to customize a welcome page, add your company's newsletter sign-up box, embed widgets and other social media buttons, and add on applications.

The fan page of Facebook marketing expert Mari Smith is a great example of a welcome page that invites more followers and provides a sneak preview of her service.

Facebook also allows you to have multiple fan pages. This is important for people who want to promote more than one business. Using a fan page allows you and your photography business to connect with current or prospective customers. Your followers and customers can easily receive any offers, special announcements and promotions. The pages allow for extra applications to be added. Pages are generally better for long-term relationships with your fans, readers and customers. In order to simplify my life, I manage just one fan page. My fan page, Fine Art Tips, is named after my art blog.

Mari Smith is one of the world's foremost experts on using Facebook as a marketing channel. Her friendly welcome page immediately explains what you can expect to receive when you "like" her fan page.

Facebook group

The main advantage of a group is that it offers the ability to message all the members via Facebook e-mail, and these messages will show up in their personal e-mail inboxes. A Facebook group is set up around a special group of people rather than your photography business or brand. Unlike fan pages, groups allow

---

EXTRA FAN PAGE TIPS

- Choose a page name that reflects your brand. Once you have one hundred connections, you will not be able to edit or change your fan page name.
- To gain more fans and followers, add a Facebook widget on your blog. By adding a fan box or "like" button to your blog, you will encourage visitors to join your page.
- You should always post your blog links to your fan page wall. You can choose to use a blogging network such as NetworkedBlogs or Blogged to automatically integrate a feed of your latest posts.
- A good rule of thumb for the frequency of Facebook updates is at least four times a week, but no more than five times a day with these postings preferably spaced apart. You might start to get complaints if you flood your followers' feed with too many updates.

you to send out bulk invites that easily invite all your friends to join. These people become members and can also send out invites. Groups are generally better for hosting quick, active discussions that attract attention for a specific purpose. For instance, I set up the PowerArtists Club group. This group consists of the artists who I have interviewed on my blog for their excellence in the arts and social media.

YOUTUBE TIPS

Photographers should discover the value of video marketing. The basic marketing idea behind video is to drive traffic back to your website or blog. Video marketing will help your website ranking and page results on Google, Yahoo and all the other search engines.

Since 2008, YouTube has been recognized as the number two search engine, behind Google. YouTube has continued to dominate as a specialist social network for video content. This means millions of people choose to use YouTube as a general search engine for researching and gathering information. Approximately 65 percent of all people are visual learners. Once your video is uploaded it is immediately available to the rest of the world. YouTube's compelling statistics cannot be ignored.

YouTube stats

Here are YouTube's impressive statistics at the time of printing:

- YouTube exceeds 2 billion views per day.
- The average person spends 15 minutes each day on YouTube.
- More video is uploaded to YouTube in 60 days than the major U.S. networks created in 60 years.
- 24 hours of video is uploaded every minute.
- 70 percent of YouTube's traffic comes from outside the U.S.

You don't have to be the next James Cameron to create an entertaining video that generates views and increases traffic to your site. Keep reading for tips on making video marketing work for you.

Make videos geared toward your audience

There are many topics you may want to cover in your videos:

- Demonstrations
- How to
- Product reviews
- Interviews
- Portfolio presentations
- Gallery tours
- Upload relevant and entertaining video

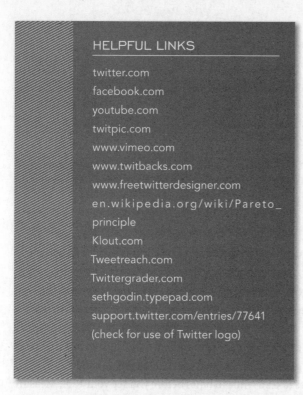

HELPFUL LINKS

twitter.com

facebook.com

youtube.com

twitpic.com

www.vimeo.com

www.twitbacks.com

www.freetwitterdesigner.com

en.wikipedia.org/wiki/Pareto_principle

Klout.com

Tweetreach.com

Twittergrader.com

sethgodin.typepad.com

support.twitter.com/entries/77641

(check for use of Twitter logo)

Create a video title that stands out

Use keywords within the title of your video. For SEO purposes, use keywords that are applicable to your product, service or brand.

Video length

The most popular videos on YouTube average about 3 minutes in length. People's attention span begins to wander after only 8 seconds—keep the video short so you do not lose them. The optimum video length is 2 to 4 minutes long.

Copyright laws

Intellectual property law protects digital music and other recorded music, just like it protects the rights of visual artists. Just because you have bought a CD or can download music for free does not mean you can use the music without paying a royalty for it. The use of copyrighted works for nonprofit documentaries or educational purposes may be considered, but ask permission of the artist. Consider purchasing a legal music license from royalty-free music websites such as Premiumbeat.com. You can choose from thousands of soundtracks by paying a one-time affordable fee. YouTube will take down your video if it violates copyright law.

Tag and categorize for video SEO

Use description words or tags that users most likely will be searching for on the Web. Add as many keywords as you can, and try and match to the existing content—this will help your video become "recommended" in the sidebar. Video optimization is becoming more important as a mainstream aspect of SEO.

Include your URL

When you post a video, make sure to add the URL to your website or blog at the top of the descriptive text. This way, when the "more info" is collapsed, the user will still see your link and can click it.

Create a channel

Creating a YouTube channel is your first step towards becoming a video creator. A channel gives you the opportunity to create a profile for yourself and your content with links back to your website and blog. To be successful on YouTube, you should consider adding video consistently. This will help build your brand and help people find you, and, as a result, will drive more traffic to your site.

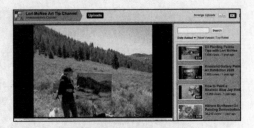

A custom YouTube channel is a great way to brand yourself as a professional in your niche. Create a variety of short, interesting, entertaining and informative videos to keep your viewers happy.

Promote your video

Use your social media networks such as Twitter and Facebook to virally market your - video.

See, there really is a method to this social media madness: When used properly, the various platforms work together to give value to your audience, and then social media drives the traffic back to you! This in turn grows your brand and your business and is the purpose of a successful social media strategy. Be sure to *pull* in your audience through engagement and relationship building, rather than *pushing* and forcing your message upon them.

Any new small business venture takes a while to build before you see your ROI. Measure your ROI and influence with social media measuring tools such as Klout, TweetReach, and Twitter Grader. Be patient and do not expect it all at once. Just like with your art or craft, it takes time to develop your skill.

Remember, compensation comes in many forms. Yes, I have sold artwork via Twitter and Facebook, but, more importantly, social media has provided me with unique business opportunities and relationships that would never have happened without this new marketing medium. In fact, I wrote this article because of my social media relationships.

. . . .

"Marketing is no longer about the stuff that you make, but about the stories you tell."

—*Seth Godin*

. . . .

BREAKING AWAY

Exploring New Niches

....

by Vik Orenstein

//

There are any number of reasons photographers leave one area of specialty for another, or add a new specialty to their existing one. The realities of their market may cause them to steer their careers away from the type of images they feel passionate about, and so they come back to their desired subjects and styles later in their lives. They may love the subject matter/images they get to create but dislike the particular industry or marketplace in which they are forced to compete. Their market, interests or the economy might change and force them into new areas. They may lose the physical stamina required for location work and turn to studio photography. They may crave a new creative outlet and new challenges.

AND NOW FOR SOMETHING COMPLETELY DIFFERENT—OR SOMEWHAT SIMILAR

Entering a new niche doesn't have to mean switching from underwater fish photography to weddings or from architecture to head shots. Often the change is much less extreme. A wedding photographer, finding his market suddenly crowded with upstarts willing to give away copyrights, might make a shift into lifestyle shooting—an area that requires a similar style and the same equipment but sells to a different market with a different fee structure.

Vik Orenstein is a photographer, writer and teacher. She founded KidCapers Portraits in 1988, followed by Tiny Acorn Studio in 1994. In addition to her work creating portraits of children, she has photographed children for such commercial clients as Nikon, Pentax, Microsoft and 3M. Vik teaches several photography courses at BetterPhoto.com.

For a period of about five years I added child commercial shooting on top of my child portrait work—same subject but different market, fee structure and style. An architectural photographer may keep shooting editorial work for design magazines but also market to commercial architectural suppliers—same work, different market. Often finding a new niche involves some tweaking, not wholesale changes.

WHEN TO MAKE THE MOVE

It doesn't matter whether you're in the beginning, middle or later stages of your career—if your existing market falters, if a golden opportunity presents itself or if your heart wanders in a new direction—you should follow your gut. Of course, changing or adding new niches will create different pros and cons depending on what career stage you're in. A change at the beginning of your career, while it may prove necessary, will probably be extra difficult, given that you'll still be in the learning stages regarding both your art and your business. But on the pro side, you're young, you're supple, you're energetic and you're willing to do anything to succeed. You don't yet have a huge ego involvement or an emotional tie to your original area of specialty, so you're freer to try new markets.

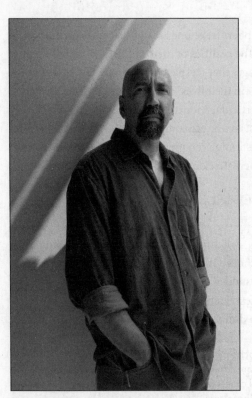

Ibarionex Perello fuses his talents for portraiture, storytelling, and street photography to create portraits of California Poets. This is Gar Anthony Haywood.

Making the change in your business' midlife can come with a bigger emotional price tag—you're committed to your specialty and your business is probably still appreciating significant growth, even if your market or the economy is failing. So making a change at this stage of life is cause for pause. Is this really necessary? You'll have your doubts. On the other hand, you're well into your career, and while the learning never really stops, you've got enough experience and resources behind you to make this kind of a transition easier.

Changing niches late in life can be a godsend or a heartbreak, depending on the motivation for the change. If you're making the change to pursue your dreams and make the images you've always imagined you'd one day make, then it will be easy.

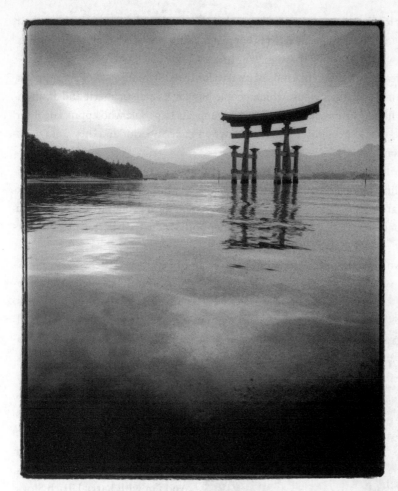

Doug Beasley's fine art images are well received by his corporate and commercial clients, like this one of Torji Gate, Miya Jima.

But if you're a well-established shooter with a glorious career whose market suddenly dries up and forces you to start over in some new niche, well, that's heartbreak. You're used to being a big dog; now you're practically starting over with the little dogs again. But there's a hidden plus here: Once you get over the angst, you might actually like starting over. Some of that good wholesome fear, that thrill of the unknown that you had at the very beginning, might come back. It could provide a new lease on your creative life.

CRAIG BLACKLOCK: A NATURE PHOTOGRAPHER MAKES A NATURAL TRANSITION

Craig Blacklock's late father and partner, Les, was one of the pioneers in the field of nature photography. When Craig joined his father in 1974, they were like kids in a candy store, shooting anything and any place they desired. There was always someone out there willing to pay top dollar for their images. While they didn't take assignments, they did keep their audience always in mind. "To be an artist is not just making yourself happy, it also means communicating with your public through your images," says Blacklock.

Blacklock creates two different kinds of images for two different kinds of art appreciators: "I have my more abstract work, which people buy for its artistic merit and as an investment. And I have my more literal work, which appeals to people who appreciate it for its regional value—they spent part of their summer on Lake Superior and they want to extend their vacation."

As the nature field became crowded and its practitioners increasingly disregarded standard industry billing and copyright protocol, it became very difficult to earn a living. Blacklock loved and cared deeply about his subject matter, so he wasn't about to give up nature photography. But he responded to the grim realities of the industry by creating new markets for his work.

"I opened two art galleries: Waters of Superior and Blacklock Gallery," says Blacklock. Thus he created his own retail market for his fine art photos. And as the calendar market faltered, with fees for images dropping up to 65 percent, Blacklock began to publish his own calendars and books. "I still sell images for editorial use and to designers and corporate art consultants, the people who do interior design for places like hospitals and banks. And I'm with Larry Ulrich Stock Photography, Inc. But to continue to thrive in this field, I've had to add to the ways I sell my images."

By applying his creativity to his business as well as his art, Blacklock has managed to thrive and to maintain his integrity in an increasingly difficult market. He has found a large high-paying niche in artwork sales to institutions, with the surprising addition of nature video sales.

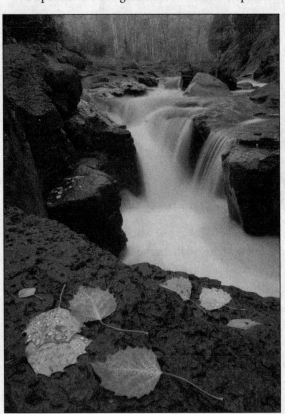

Craig Blacklock's fine art nature images sell well as decorative art for hospitals and hotels.

"The biggest upside for me has been hospitals and hotels buying large numbers of prints. I am now complementing that work by doing nature videos that are played in hospitals. This is a niche I've worked in for many years, and now that many hospitals are remodeling or expanding, they're using more video—it is really paying off. Some sales have come in directly, but most sales come from art consultants that take 40 percent of the sale—and they are worth it! I've worked with some of these consultants for around thirty years. I always try to deliver ahead of schedule, and they know they can trust that when they place an order, their client's expectations will be exceeded."

Blacklock's large increase in sales to institutions has helped offset a drop in his sales to individual photography collectors, though there are still a few serious collectors buying large numbers of prints. And this has also served to offset the dwindling market for fine art books and stock images.

"Over the past decade or so I've put more and more emphasis on my print and self-published book sales. Stock continues to sell but is a very small part of my overall income. The biggest change recently has been the drop in high-end book sales. Last year I came out with a sixty-dollar book that included a three-hour DVD. It was a good value, reproduced very well, won awards and got many good reviews, and the movie played on public television. But the economy tanked, and with it, high-end book sales."

VIK ORENSTEIN: SAME BAT TIME, DIFFERENT BAT CHANNEL

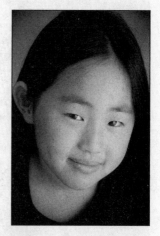

I opened up my first studio, KidCapers (then called KidShooters) in 1988. My portrait prices were by necessity higher than those of studios that specialized in direct color or even standard black-and-white work because of the labor intensity of creating hand-processed, hand-painted fine art prints. My average client spent over $2,000 at that time on a photo session, portraits and frames, and I developed a reputation for being expensive.

The reality, though, was that I offered my hand-painted portraits at a price substantially lower—per portrait—than my closest competitors. The myth that my studio was expensive arose from that high average purchase; it wasn't that my portraits were more expensive, it was that my clients made bigger purchases. For clients who both desired and could afford the best, this was no problem. But my friend and, at that time, employee Pat Lelich noticed that quite often we were losing clients because of this perceived expensiveness. Since it

Even such a seemingly straightforward specialty such as portraiture can be established in a variety of niches, from point of purchase to retail; from wall art to photobooks; from fine art prints to machine prints. Here's one of my portraits.

wasn't possible to offer our current product at a lower price and remain profitable, we became partners in Tiny Acorn Portraits, Inc., and opened our first retail studio in 1994. Tiny Acorn portraits were still custom hand printed and hand colored, but we eliminated much of the labor by simplifying the product. The prints were not sepia-toned and were not otherwise stabilized, so were not strictly archival. The coloring was done with transparent watercolor pencils rather than artist's oils (oils are more difficult to manipulate and take much longer to dry), and we offered pre-made frames rather than the extensive custom design and framing services offered at KidCapers. The result was a product that we could sell for nearly 50 percent less than the product at our original point of destination studio.

At first there were a lot of doomsayers: "You're competing against yourself!" "Everyone will go to the cheaper, more visible and convenient retail studio and no one will come to KidCapers anymore!" "Are you crazy?"

I didn't feel I was competing against myself at all. Though the portraits offered at both studios were hand painted, the similarities stopped there. Each business had a different niche,

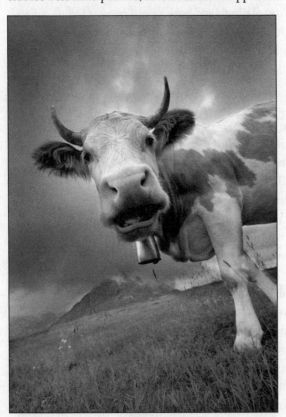

A popular category for stock is "funny animals." This one is by Jim Zuckerman.

a different price point and therefore a different client base. (Although it's true, there was some client overlap.) Only time would tell. At the end of the first year, the Tiny Acorn Studio had paid back its initial start-up costs and was even nominally profitable—a really successful start, in my book. And during that year KidCapers enjoyed the same growth rate of 20 percent that it had for the previous four years. So the doomsayers were wrong. Tiny Acorn Portraits was a legitimate new niche. Sure, it looked similar, but ultimately it proved to be different.

Tiny Acorn Portraits became such a successful business that in August 2008, I was able to sell it to a current and a former employee who now own and operate it. I continue to own and operate KidCapers Portraits. Both businesses are successful.

KAREN MELVIN: ARCHITECTURAL INTERIOR PHOTOGRAPHER CREATES A MARRIAGE OF CONVENIENCE

When Karen Melvin started her career in architectural photography, she marketed herself primarily to local architecture firms and magazines. She also marketed to local hospitals, banks and any institution that might need architectural images. For the most part, she focused on generating editorial work. While the editorial field in general offers better than average creative freedom and prestige, editorial rates are typically far lower than commercial rates.

So eventually Karen started to market her work nationally to product manufacturers such as window and tile companies who supply architects and builders. The results thrilled her. "This niche pays more, and there's a bigger client base to draw from," she says. "There's more production value, more legwork—and I love that part!"

Melvin still shoots editorial work that winds up in such acclaimed publications as *Architectural Record*. She has successfully wedded her editorial and commercial specialties. But more and more, her work is in advertising.

Any regrets?

"Only that I didn't plumb this niche earlier," Melvin says.

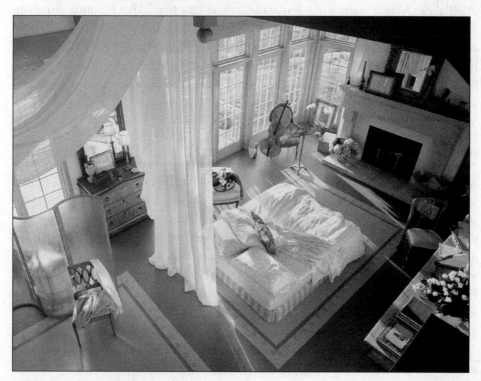

An interior photograph by Karen Melvin.

ROY BLAKEY: COMMERCIAL PORTRAIT AND FINE ART PHOTOGRAPHER SHOWS NAKED AMBITION

After teaching himself photography in the army (he bought his first camera in the PX [post exchange store] in Germany) and traveling the world as a professional ice skater in the touring show "Holiday on Ice," Roy Blakey came to live in New York in 1967. He began his photography career shooting head shots for actors, dancers and models. "It was wonderful. I was the very person for it because I cared so much about these people and about making them look their most beautiful," he says. Blakey shot his share of celebrities, including Chita Rivera, Tommy Tune, Felicia Rashad, and Debbie Allen. Eventually his work wound its way into such magazines as *Time* and *Gentleman's Quarterly*. He loved his work and yet there was a new fine art niche he wanted to try: the male nude. "There was no market for it, obviously. When I had a body of work I started calling editors to see about getting it published. They told me I was crazy," recalls Blakey. So he self-published *70s Nudes* in 1972. He presold all five-thousand-plus copies he had printed. Exactly thirty years later—to the day— the book was reissued to critical acclaim. Referring to the fact that his subjects were dancers and models at the peak of physical condition, Blakey says, "We used to joke that the book should be called, *Blakey's Bird's Eye Boys—Frozen at the Peak of Perfection!*"

Blakey's foray into this niche was made early in his career. After his initial print run sold out, he stored his nude photographs in boxes, forgotten until another fine art photographer found them and encouraged Blakey to find a publisher to reissue them. While the huge majority of Blakey's career was—and still is—spent making commercial head shots, his brief detour into the world of the fine art male nude gave him a new creative outlet and a place in the history of fine art photography.

ROB LEVINE: PHOTOJOURNALIST AND COMMERCIAL PHOTOGRAPHER—FROM STAFF EMPLOYED TO SELF-EMPLOYED

Rob Levine began his career in 1983 as a photojournalist, working on staff for the Minneapolis *StarTribune*. Now he is self-employed, sharing a warehouse studio with another photographer, and shooting publicity and commercial images. He also hosts websites where photographers can display and sell their images, including stock, and he sells studio management software through GripSoftware.com. While it was Levine's dream to be a photojournalist, the realities of working in the industry left him cold. "I just didn't feel they were treating me very well," he says. When asked why he didn't try to work for a different newspaper to see if working conditions were better elsewhere, he says, "Because the *StarTribune* was one of the best in that regard."

Far from the gritty, grainy, black-and-white images of his earlier specialty, Levine now shoots incredibly colorful high-resolution publicity stills for the Children's Theatre Company of Minneapolis, Minnesota. He gives this client maximum bang for its buck by

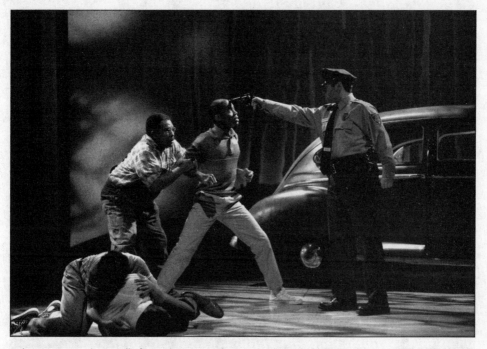

Rob Levine eased naturally from photojournalism into editorial photography, creating images like this one for the Minneapolis Children's Theater Company.

hosting their website. "The site contains literally hundreds of media contacts. People can sign in to browse or use the images, and when there are new pictures, we send out e-mail notifications to the whole list. It's a very efficient and cost-effective way of publicizing the theater."

While Levine is passionate about his career as it is today, he says his heart is still in photojournalism. "It's all about going out alone, and I love going out alone," Levine says. "But I'm very happy with my career now. I have no regrets."

RANDY LYNCH: A PORTRAIT PHOTOGRAPHER GOES FORENSIC

When Randy Lynch constructed his home in 1990, he built in a home studio. His intention was to shoot portraits there—and for a while, he did. He also took a job as a forensic photographer with a county sheriff's department. The home studio became a playroom for his kids, never to be used again.

Lynch is a genuine, extroverted people person. You can see how he'd be successful at portraiture and every aspect of that business. But when he talks about his experiences as a forensic photographer, he gets fire in his eyes. Words like *nanometer, omni chrome* and *luminal* sprinkle his speech, and he's too engrossed with his topic to notice that those who are listening might get lost in his dust.

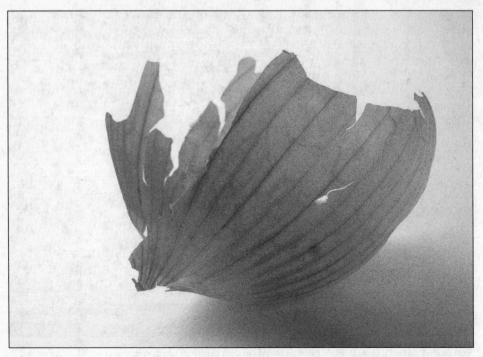

Leo Kim had worked for years in macro and landscape photography. When an illness forced him to stay in his home more than he liked, he found compelling subjects to photograph right in his own kitchen, and now he creates decorative wall art.

I asked him if it didn't get boring, taking hundreds of pictures of one pair of jeans, each with a different filter, trying to illuminate blood or semen stains.

"It's never boring," he states emphatically. "When you find blood or semen, you've helped to stop a murderer or a rapist. How can that be boring?" Lynch worked for the sheriff's department for ten years and ultimately left because of political and personality issues within the department. "If it weren't for those issues, I'd still be working there today. I loved it."

But just as his issues with his forensic job were coming to a boil, he was offered an opportunity to buy into a photo lab in the busy Minneapolis skyway system.

"It was perfect," he says, "because there's one big crunch time when everybody drops off or picks up their film in the skyway, and that's lunchtime, so that's when I'm at the lab. The rest of the time I spend visiting commercial clients and taking care of business."

Lynch also has established himself in a third photographic niche—he shoots weddings.

"Nobody ever asks me for the negs," he says, "because I'm their lab! A lot of my wedding clients are my regular lab clients, so I've printed their work for them for years."

These are some great success stories. But trying a new niche is no guarantee of a happy ending. I once tried to offer a less expensive direct color product at KidCapers Studio.

Not only did no one buy it—not one family—but the very existence of this new product confused some of our clients and spurred rumors that the studio had gone out of business.

And you'd think that going from a huge, glamorous market like New York to a medium-sized market would be a breeze—that your little niche would be right there waiting for you. But when Roy Blakey brought his head shot business from New York to the Midwest, "It took forever for people to catch on to me. They all knew Ann Marsden (the reigning head shot queen of the time) and no one knew me. But I stuck to it, and now it's back to business."

GUARANTEE? WHAT GUARANTEE?

While adding or changing to a new niche is no guarantee of a heftier income, there are precautions you can take that will increase your chances of success.

- **Keep your finger in the pie.** This is the photographer's mid-career equivalent of the warning, "Keep your day job!" Don't drop your original specialty until your new one has proven lucrative enough to warrant it.

- **Don't rob Peter to pay Paul.** Do not, I repeat, *do not* enter into a new niche if doing so requires that you take needed resources away from your original one. If becoming a dirt bike–racing photographer requires you to buy equipment with money you would have otherwise used to send out your spring portrait mailing, don't do it. Or if going out and becoming a field photographer leaves no one at your studio to answer the phone, forget it. The risk won't be worth it.

- **Categorize your new niche.** Is it simply a new product you can offer at your old studio or a whole new business that requires a new venue and identity? Is it an entirely new specialty area or just a different market for your current work? Is it a different product for your existing client base or a similar product for an altogether different client base? Once the answers to these questions have solidified in your mind, you'll be better able to create a business plan, just as if you were starting out from scratch.

- **Question the mass migration.** When your market becomes saturated and other photographers head for greener pastures, you might want to stay put and bide your time. You may find yourself (happily) alone in a suddenly less crowded specialty.

You can see the logic in the progression of the niche-jumping photographers whose stories I've shared with you. That's because their stories have already happened and we know how they come out—that's called 20/20 hindsight. If you're contemplating a similar leap, you don't have the luxury of knowing whether you'll have a happy ending. But then again, neither did they.

BREAKING OUT

Bringing New Life to an Old Business

....

by Vik Orenstein

Congratulations! Your photography business has survived the treacherous start-up stage. You've learned how to weather the cash flow roller coaster, you know how to win and keep clients and you've been profitable for several years—more so than you had dared to hope! You're out of the woods, right? Or is there a little voice in the back of your head whispering, "Famous last words"?

DROPPING THE BALL

Oh boy, you've been in business for a while and people seem to know who you are. You call prospects and say, "Hi, I'm Stanley Kowalski," and they say, "Oh, yes, Stanley, I've seen your work." You have a solid client base and it's been a long time since you've gotten that fluttering, sick feeling in the pit of your stomach when things are a little slow. Maybe your business has even shown good growth every year since you started. Maybe you're even turning away work. You're enjoying the prime of your business life. So what do you do? You relax a little. You don't send out that spring postcard. And it doesn't matter; spring is just as busy as you expect it to be. Then you skip the newsletter, and you stop sending those thank-you letters to clients who send you referrals. Still no adverse effects. You don't leap at the phone

Vik Orenstein is a photographer, writer and teacher. She founded KidCapers Portraits in 1988, followed by Tiny Acorn Studio in 1994. In addition to her work creating portraits of children, she has photographed children for such commercial clients as Nikon, Pentax, Microsoft and 3M. Vik teaches several photography courses at BetterPhoto.com.

anymore when it rings, and you get a little lax in your costumer service. You stop putting new work in your book. A year of this and still no ill effects. Two years, and your gross isn't up anymore, but it's stable. Three years: You're not turning away jobs anymore, but you're not worried. But the four-year mark comes, and suddenly you're wondering where everybody went. Where are your loyal clients?

When you're not on top of your game, you won't see an immediate drop in business. It's gradual erosion that often is not apparent until it's too late. You'll be like Wile E. Coyote when he chases the roadrunner off the edge of a cliff, but he doesn't realize he's already doomed to plummet to the earth until he looks down.

By the time you look down, you'll be scrambling to get a marketing plan back in place, freshen up your portfolio, renew acquaintances with old clients and glad hand a few new ones, and brush up those customer service skills, all just in the name of damage control.

If only you hadn't dropped the ball, you'd still be growing your business right now instead of trying to build it back up again.

Avoid the mistakes complacency breeds.

- **Keep marketing**—Even McDonald's still advertises. As successful stock photographer Jim Zuckerman says, "You have to market constantly. Perpetually. You never stop moving."

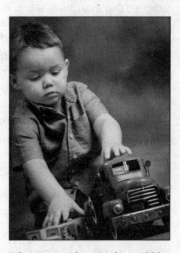

- **Keep your website up-to-date**—You still need to show the world the best face you possibly can. And if you're a commercial or fashion shooter, your portfolio needs to be up to date as well, even if you don't show it much anymore. You never know when someone is going to ask for it.

- **Answer your phone and reply to e-mail promptly**—They are still your most powerful sales and marketing tools.

When I started my studio in 1988, I shot only small children with their pets and families. I offered only black-and-white, sepia-toned, and hand-colored images to my portraits clients. Not being a big fan of direct color film, I shot color transparencies for commercial clients only (and only shot for commercial clients when the project included kids).

- **Keep up the customer relations**—They're still the reason you're in business.

- **Remember, you're one of the lucky ones**—You're living your dream.

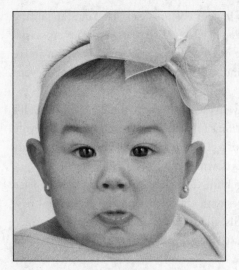

When I embraced digital capture and learned image editing, I was finally able to offer color prints that I felt looked beautiful enough to hang on a wall. This was stimulating for me creatively, and it gave me a new product to introduce to my clients, helping me maintain an edge in my marketplace.

DISILLUSIONMENT

Another pitfall the owner of a newer studio can encounter is disillusionment, and even bitterness. The honeymoon is over; you're living with the day-to-day reality of a photography business. The work isn't always as creative has you'd hoped it would be. You're working in the studio and in the office more than you'd anticipated. Some of your clients have proven to be less loyal than you thought they were. The paperwork is a pain in the backside. It's sometimes hard to collect payment. You're still shooting solid, technically excellent pictures, but some of the market has moved onto the next new thing. The new thing isn't as good as your thing, and it'll only be a flash in the pan. You know this, you've seen it before, but it still insults your integrity. Other shooters are leapfrogging past you and snapping up some of "your" market. You aren't in touch with the beautiful parts of the business anymore. You can't remember what made you want to get into this. You are disillusioned.

Disillusionment is a very dangerous place. If you don't change your attitude, your business will fizzle away.

• **Take a break.** If you're like most entrepreneurs I know, the word vacation isn't in your vocabulary. Your work is your life. You find relaxing more tiring than working. You worry that if you leave town one big client is going to up and leave you. Or that you'll miss out on the mother of all jobs because you weren't there to answer the phone. Or some competitor is going to spring up across the street while you're gone. Probably you believe your studio will burn down if you're not there to protect it by sheer force of will. Get over it. The burnout you'll suffer from working without a break will be worse than anything that could happen to your business in your absence.

I speak from experience. I worked five to seven days a week with almost no reprieve for the first five years after I opened my studio. I loved my job. I had boundless energy. But then, during Christmas season number five, I suddenly hated everybody. My clients, myself, my neighbors, the person in line ahead of me at the supermarket, the other drivers on the road, my friends and family—everybody! I hated going to work. I started to fantasize about going back to waiting tables, marrying rich and winning the lottery. I'd had it with photography.

I really thought that my work was my problem. But a conversation with a friend who was a pediatric ICU nurse—a woman who, needless to say, knew a lot about stress and job burnout—told me what was really going on.

"You need a vacation," she said. "You've got job burnout. You go away, you come back, you like your work again."

I thought she was nuts—and right at that moment I didn't like her too much, either. I didn't take her advice until six months later. By then I didn't care if the studio burned down while I was away.

She was right! I went to central Mexico for two weeks to visit friends who lived there. I saw original works by Freda Kahlo and Diego Rivera; I visited pyramids and artists' colonies and ate fruit my friends called "snot grenades." It was a very exciting and intriguing trip, but in reality it probably wouldn't have mattered if I'd been holed up in a Motel 6 with nothing else to do. The point was taking a break from work. When I came back, I loved my clients, I loved myself, I loved my work—although I still didn't love the other drivers on the road.

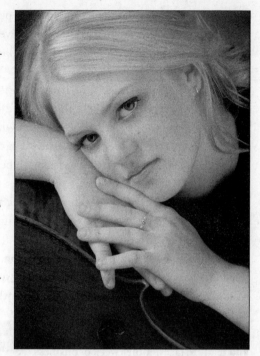

As my client base aged and their kids grew up, I wound up shooting senior pictures for the kids that I had worked with since they were babies. I found that direct color images really appeal to teenagers.

• **Volunteer.** We experience disillusionment when we reach a point in our careers in which we feel our business isn't giving us enough. Ironically, one surefire way to overcome this feeling is to give more to the community and the world. Volunteer to teach photography to low-income kids or physically challenged people and see how fast you're reminded of the magic and the beauty of the darkroom, of the view through your lens. You needn't limit your volunteer efforts to photography-oriented work. If you need a total break from your regular grind, do something totally unrelated. Join an adult literacy program; become a Guardian Ad Litem; read to the blind. Are you missing the chaos and action you experienced when your business was new?

• **Test shoot.** Part of your disillusionment may stem from one of the paradoxes with which the photo business is fraught; you open your studio because you want to do creative work but as you become more successful you do less and less of what you really love.

So take some time for yourself and do some personal work. It may be hard to motivate yourself at first, since you're used to being driven by the client and by the almighty buck. Shooting something for pleasure will seem alien at first. But do it. It'll breathe life back into your drudgery.

• **Count your blessings.** Sure, it sounds trite, simplistic and vaguely religious. But it works. Make a written list of all the things you're thankful for that your business has brought you: a good income, the freedom to be your own boss, job stability (you're not likely to lay yourself off, are you?), some creative expression, the satisfaction of knowing that people are willing to pay you for your creative vision … I bet you can think of a few more. Save the list and consult it from time to time.

• **Explore alternatives.** Go career shopping and see what's out there. You may find a totally different field that you'll be even happier in. Or, more likely, you'll come back to your list of blessings with a few more to add.

• **Have a good old-fashioned gripe session.** For years, I used to meet with a group of photographers for happy hour on Fridays after work. Inevitably the conversation would turn to all the aggravations we'd encountered at work that week. It always started out negative, but by the time we'd complained a little bit, we'd all wind up laughing and jocular, and ready to face another week of business. It's not a matter of dwelling on the negative; it's a matter of letting the negative pass through you so you don't wind up carrying it around.

EXPANSION /CONTRACTION

Sooner or later your growing business will come to the point where it's almost unmanageable. You're at a crossroads. Do you take on more employees and a larger studio to accommodate additional business? You're doing well, so you can, but should you? Before you make the commitment, ask yourself the following questions.

What do I want my role to be?

Until now you've been a photographer: you shoot, you sell, you do the books, you empty the wastebasket, you do what you must

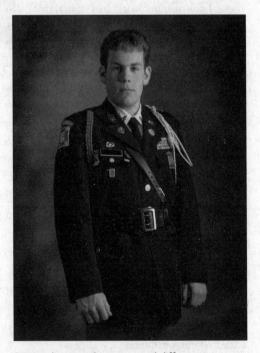

Seniors love anything new and different, so working with them allowed me to exploit new artistic treatments in Photoshop that weren't possible before.

to keep your batteries charged. But the bigger you get, the more removed you will become from these day-to-day, hands-on realities of operation. You will become a manager. You will oversee people who will do your shooting, do your books and empty your wastebasket. You will have to help them keep their batteries charged. You will become one step removed from your product and your clients. If this doesn't sound good to you, think twice before expanding.

Not sure if you view a role change from photographer to photographer/manager as a positive or a negative? Answer the following statements true or false.

1. It's easier to do something myself than to try to explain to someone else how to do it.
2. No one else will be able to do my work as well as I do.
3. There's only one way to do things: the right way.

If you answered "true" to any of these statements, you might not be manager material. It's true that in the short term, it's easier to do things yourself than to shift down a gear and teach someone else how to do it, but ultimately it will save you time to delegate many of your responsibilities.

And while it's true that no one else will do your work exactly the same way you would do it, they may still arrive at an equally good or valid outcome.

There's always more than one way to do anything. If you think there's only one way, you probably shouldn't be a manager; you should keep flying solo. Remember, though, even Batman had Robin.

Can I make do with contractors?

Is it possible for me to take on temporary help in the form of contractors to get through this busy time? Or do I need permanent employees? If your surge in business is thanks to just one or two huge clients, you may be wise to tough it out by hiring temporary help and renting extra temporary space as needed. I've seen many small businesses make the mistake of thinking all they need to justify expansion is that one big client because that client will be theirs forever. *Nothing* is forever. On the other hand, expansion may be warranted if your business has been growing steadily over time and if your client base is diverse.

Am I making enough money now?

How much money is enough money? Is there ever enough? Human nature dictates that there is not. And yet—are you happy with your lifestyle? Because expansion is a risk. You may or may not increase your income by expanding. It's no sure thing. But what is a sure thing is that you'll be increasing your fixed overhead—the kiss of death for many businesses. If you're happy with your livelihood now, you may want to leave well enough alone, as difficult as that may be to do.

Is there some other way I can increase my profitability without taking on additional fixed overhead?

If you're so busy you're turning away business (you poor thing!) maybe the answer to your problem is not to expand but to raise your prices. That way, the clients who can't or don't want to afford your services will naturally fall away and you'll be doing the same amount of work (possibly even less) and making more money. Or perhaps instead of taking on more staff or a bigger studio you could generate more business by going on location or selling your existing images for stock, greeting cards, fine art or other applications.

WHY BIGGER ISN'T ALWAYS BETTER

"You can be a big small business, cruise along and do fine for years," says wedding/portrait shooter Bob Dale. "But then say a large corporation comes into your market and they have a billion-dollar marketing budget, they can suck up all your business and they don't even have to be profitable to survive."

Obviously if you have a bigger business and it's operating profitably, you'll realize more income than a smaller one. But when bad times hit—and there will be bad times—the operations with larger fixed overhead can be more vulnerable to failure than the smaller ones.

Reduced margins are the blessing of small businesses. I enjoy being a manager—I love to motivate, teach and coach. I like interacting with my employees as much as my clients. So it was no hardship for me to evolve in my role as my studios grew. But I discovered a disturbing trend after several years: The bigger my business got, the smaller my profit was. In my first year in business I had one studio and I only grossed $8,000, but I was almost 90 percent profitable. In my twelfth year, I had three studios and grossed $2 million, but my profitability dropped precipitously. It is possible to have a huge business, work really hard and still have a smaller net profit than the other guy who stays small and works half as hard. In my experience, the larger the operation, the higher your fixed overhead (rent for three retail locations instead of one, for instance), and the layers of employees and managers required increases.

Here's an example: Mom and Pop open a portrait studio in a trendy retail district. They own and operate it, and after two years they are making a net profit of $150,000 each year. It's a huge success! So much so that they decide to open another portrait studio across town. To do this, they need to hire employees to run the old studio and do all the things they used to do themselves. They need a manager, a photographer, an assistant and possibly even more employees. So they wind up with $90,000 worth of extra payroll, and they still have to spend time not only opening up the new studio but overseeing the operations of the old studio. Now they're working more hours than they did before. As it turns out, the new location isn't quite as profitable as the old one. It earns a net profit of only $40,000 each year. Now Mom and Pop are working more hours for $50,000 less a year. If the economy goes

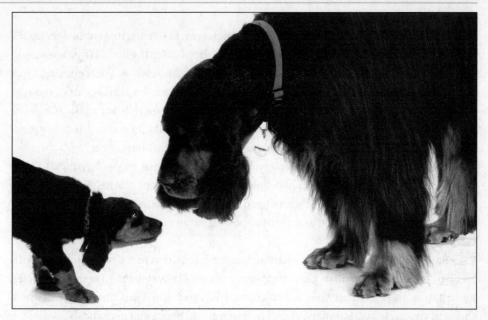

I noticed that many of my clients bought pets when their kids were about to go off to college. So when they brought their seniors in for portraits, I recommended that they bring their new family members, as well.

through a tough period or a big construction project blocks traffic for a few months at one of their locations—or any number of other unforeseen difficulties arise—their profit margin may go down even further, but they'll still be working just as hard.

Sometimes small businesses wind up contracting rather than expanding. There's no shame in this—and it could make you more profitable. The trick here is to close one of the studios before the situation is desperate. Don't wait until you have to file chapter eleven and crawl away wounded. Make the move before your profitability drops to dangerous levels.

"At one time I had four studios," says commercial/fine art shooter Doug Beasley. "And I'm a location shooter! Imagine. Now I only shoot on location, I have no studios and I'm much happier."

LEARNING BY REPETITION

When I became an employer, I had the naïve notion that I would have to train each employee only once, tell them their job description once and send them off to work. Then they'd know what to do and they'd do it. Imagine my surprise when I realized I actually had to train them repeatedly for the same tasks and remind them what their jobs were over and over again.

Then I realized I operate the same way my employees do: I need to retrain myself, re-learn lessons I already know and tell myself my job description ad nauseum. We're all human. We need to brush up occasionally. We need continuing education.

It's easy for me to continually educate my employees. I hold meetings or in-service sessions during the slow times of the year. These workshops cover the brass tacks, answering the phone, closing a sale, selling up, customer service—all the basics. At the beginning, I was afraid the employees would rebel. "Why are you telling me all this stuff again?" I thought they'd do what my five-year-old does when I repeat myself. She rolls her eyes, crosses her arms, tips her head, and says, "Mommy, I already know that." But to my surprise, they seem to enjoy the meetings. I suppose the coffee and doughnuts don't hurt either.

It's harder to reteach yourself. First, you need to realize that you've forgotten to practice some key policy, procedure or philosophy—ideally before your business begins to suffer for it. Then you have to figure out where to go for a refresher course. Can you do it yourself or do you need the inspiration and motivation that a more formal setting, like a seminar, can provide?

• **Surf the Net.** This is one time when surfing the Internet isn't a waste of time. Start with an open mind and enter a few pertinent words: photography+business+marketing+sales, for instance. Then go where your search engine leads you. You'll probably find many sites that lead you to classes, seminars, clubs and groups, and books and periodicals.

• **Write out your job description.** Sounds silly, doesn't it? Why on earth would you need a job description? You're probably thinking, "I know what I do, and the only person I have to report to is myself." But do you really know what you do? And since it is yourself to whom you're reporting, how do you hold yourself to a high level of accountability?

I didn't always know exactly what it was that I did. I found out when I went to apply for disability insurance. The insurance company needed to know, not just what my title was, but what my functions were, in order to determine what it would cost to replace me.

"I'm a photographer—I take pictures," I told them.

"What else do you do?"

"Well, nothing, really."

"Who does your marketing?"

"I do."

"Who does your product development?"

"I do."

"Who does your sales?"

"I do." And so on. It suddenly occurred to me that I was doing more than I thought I was. I rushed back to my office and wrote myself a job description. By writing down and categorizing what I did, I was able to figure out what things I could or should be doing more, and what things I needed to start doing that I wasn't currently doing at all.

So take a minute to sit down and list all the functions you perform in your business. Then decide what areas you may be lagging in, and punch 'em hard. I look at my old job description and create a new one once a year.

• **Take a seminar.** Chances are if you've been in business for a number of years, you're not going to learn much that you don't already know by attending a seminar—possibly a few tidbits or possibly nothing. But what a seminar will do for you is reinforce those things you already know, and remind you to practice them. I regularly attend marketing seminars, for instance. I have attended the John Hartman Marketing Boot Camp twice. I usually don't leave these meetings saying to myself, "Oh boy, that's news to me!" But I do say to myself, "Oh, yeah! I forgot all about doing that. I should start doing that again." And I do.

• **Revisit your past work.** Sometimes you can be your own best mentor. Dig out your old promotional material, your old schedule books, your old lighting notes—anything that documents how you've done things over the years. You may be surprised to find that some of the things you used to do were pretty darn good. Maybe even better than the things you're doing now. Reincorporate them into your repertoire.

• **Teach someone else.** Nothing reinforces what you already know better than teaching someone else. I always wind up energized, recharged and on my game after teaching classes on business and creative techniques. I learn—and relearn—as much or more than I impart to my students. If you're not into standing in front of a class full of people, you can take it one student at a time by becoming a mentor, or taking on an apprentice or intern.

• **Join business and professional groups.** Becoming involved in business networking and professional groups, you'll find opportunities to both speak and be spoken to on a variety of germane topics, and you may expand your client base in the bargain. I've given talks to groups that focus on women in business, church groups, the Junior League, the Woman's Club of Minneapolis, Kiwanis Club, small business owners and many others.

• **Read (or reread) a book or periodical.** Pick a book or magazine. It could be on sales, marketing, public speaking, motivation, management, general business practices, relationships—anything that you can apply to your business. You can skim, speed read, open up the book and start reading on the page that falls open, or do the whole in-depth, cover to cover thing. All that matters is that you tickle those memory cells enough to refresh your perspective on your day-to-day business.

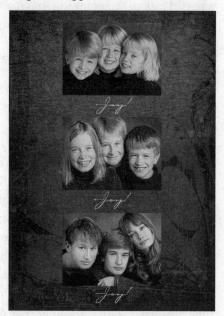

Another new product I've been able to offer due to digital technology is press-printed holiday cards and birth announcements. New services give clients yet another reason to come back.

TRACKING PERSONAL ECONOMY, INDUSTRY ECONOMY AND NATIONAL ECONOMY

In order to really see how your business is doing, you need to separate out the layers of different economic states that are affecting its development. In this way you'll be able to get a clearer picture of where you've been, where you are now and where you're likely to go. Let's say you've been in business five years now. Make yourself a graph. From left to right, start with the year you opened your doors and progress to the present year. From bottom to top, indicate units of measure. Now use a red line to chart your personal economic progression. Use a different color line to indicate what the national economy was doing that year. You can use different factors in determining this: consumer index, unemployment rate, the stock market, etc. Or you can factor them all together and create your own subjective impression of the economy over your years in business. Use a third color to create a line indicating your local industry economy. Did your market lose any major clients in a given year? Did any agencies start shooting out of town? Did a big corporate competitor come to town, or did a big crop of small studios open up near you? When you've finished all three lines, take a good look at them and see how you did. Did your personal economy grow even in years when the national economy was flagging? Did your personal economy flag when your local market was growing? Spot the trends. Adapt accordingly.

PROS AND CONS OF MIDDLE AGE

Just as with anything in life, there's always a trade-off. You give up one thing to get another. The thrill and anxiety of youth gives way to the confidence and boredom of middle age.

Topping out

Eventually your business growth will level out. It will have reached maturity, much like a child who enters her young adult years and stops getting taller. I didn't believe this until it happened to me. I had at least 20 percent growth every year for twelve years. No matter what the economy did, no matter what my competition did, no matter what my local market did. I thought that "topping out" was just a nasty little rumor—an urban myth. (But then, there was also a time I believed I was never going to die, either.) Then, in year thirteen, the growth started slowing down. In year fourteen, it stopped altogether. My business had reached maturity. This is good, because I'm stable, I'm secure, I can anticipate what my income will be from month to month and year to year. But it's also bad, because the excitement of watching the growth is over. Gone are the days of looking at quarterly comparisons and saying, "Oh my gosh, look how much we're up over last year!" Ironically, this mature, stable stage was what I eagerly looked forward to when I was a start-up. Now I look back fondly at the start-up stage. There's just no pleasing some people.

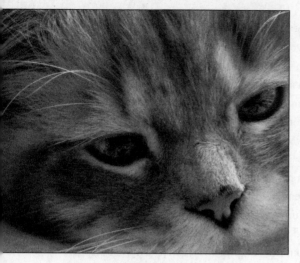

A pet portrait by Vik Orenstein.

Fear and the lack of it

When you're new in business, everything is scary. There are monsters under your bed. Are you good enough? Is someone else better? Will there be images on the film when it comes back from the lab? How do I file those government forms again? What if the client doesn't like my work? What if the client doesn't pay? What if I can't take the pressure and I wind up at a nature retreat weaving baskets with my toes? What if I fail and I have to go back to my day job? What if I fail and I can't get another day job? What if I lose my life savings?

The fear is with you all the time. You have to face it down every morning when you get out of bed. You wear it all day and you go to sleep with it at night. And that's the good news!

The fear certainly is a powerful motivator. It's hard to live with but it makes it easy to keep on keeping on. Sometimes I think fear is just another word for enthusiasm. When you've been in business long enough to be really confident in your abilities you need to replace the fear with satisfaction as a motivating factor.

"I was outside a church prior to a wedding, and I watched the photographers shoot it," says sixteen-year wedding photography veteran Hilary Bullock. "There were two young girls, all dressed very hip and edgy, and they descended in a frenzy on one big floral arrangement and shot it crazily from every possible angle. I would have taken just one shot, because I'd know the shot I got would be 'the one.' Enthusiasm or experience, either one will get the job done. But, boy, they sure look different from the outside."

DEALING WITH LOOK-ALIKES

If you stay in business long enough, eventually someone is going to imitate one of your innovations—whether it be your visual style, how you sell, your fee structure or how you position yourself in the market. Take heart! When this happens to you, you'll know you've arrived. It means someone is impressed enough with your work to want to go out and do it themselves. Imitation is the sincerest form of flattery, and all that. But it can be aggravating, too. Especially if someone swipes your idea, and a little piece of your market goes with it. What can you do to stay ahead of the folks who want to jump on your bandwagon?

- **Raise the bar.** Refine your art and hone your market to pull yourself above the crowd. Make yourself the best darn photographer in your market.

- **Keep innovating.** By the time you've been doing something long enough for a competitor to take notice and knock off your concept, it's probably time to do something else anyway. That way, when you see someone imitating your old visual style or your old marketing methods, you can honestly say, "Oh, that. I was doing that three years ago."
- **Stay the course.** Almost always, the original of anything is the best. Those who come after can try to re-create your work—and your success—but it will often result in a pale imitation.
- **Put it in perspective.** As we've often heard it said, "There's nothing new under the sun." Ideas and inspiration go around and come around. I once thought I was doing something really original and unique by grouping portraits into diptychs, triptychs and other arrangements and framing them together. One day I went to a friend's home and saw a similar grouping hanging on her wall. "Aha! Someone is copying me!" I thought. But upon closer examination I realized I was wrong. It would have been tricky for this photographer to have copied my idea. As it turned out, this was a popular look from the 1930s into the 1960s. Oh well. At least I was in good company.

FINDING SATISFACTION AND EXCITEMENT OUTSIDE OF WORK

In the early years of my business, my work was my life and my studios were my babies. It was easy to throw myself into every aspect of photography, because I was hungry, I was passionate, I was energetic—and I was scared. I never really believed I had any images on my film until I got it back from the lab—and then I breathed a huge sigh of relief. At the time I didn't realize it, but I was having the most fun of my life. I never appreciated that early stage when I was in it; all I wanted was to be around long enough to stop being scared, stop feeling like an impostor, stop scrambling and basically be able to say, "Hah! I've arrived. I'm the old kid on the block." I was like a little kid wanting to grow up too fast.

And let's face it: You can't go home again. You simply can't re-create the excitement and the rewards you derived from your business when you were an upstart and it was a start-up. But you still crave that excitement—I'll even venture to say you need it. So, after you've been around for a while, you need to get it elsewhere—outside of the studio, outside of the office and even outside of the field of photography. It's imperative that you fight boredom at all costs. A bored photographer is a bad photographer; a bored entrepreneur is a bad entrepreneur.

This is a great time to develop a Plan B—a side business or investment that can help build your nest egg or float you through the tough economic times. If you already have a Plan B, now is the time to take it out of the closet, shake it off and fluff it up.

Wedding/portrait photographer Bob Dale knew he wanted to be a photographer since he was in the eighth grade, but he has never limited his entrepreneurial focus to the photography business.

"All along I've been into other things," he says, "like the stock market and real estate. I'm probably not going to have a salable commodity when I retire. I hope to, but I can't count on it. And I'm not counting on Social Security for a comfortable lifestyle. So I've always looked at my studio as a way to generate cash to make investments."

Or perhaps this is the time for you to finally write that novel that's been simmering on your back burner. Or make a sculpture, or dust off that cello—dabble in a complementary creative field and you'll probably feel refreshed.

END GAMES

Typically, middle age is when you start to think seriously about your retirement. Many entrepreneurs in other fields open their businesses with the intent of one day selling them. In fact that's often when they make the big bucks—not when they're actually growing the business. But if you're a photographer, what exactly will you have to sell?

You have a client list. You have goodwill, as its called by those in the legal profession. You either own a building or you hold a lease on a commercial space. You have equipment, props, backdrops, etc. You have an image (also referred to as "corporate identity"), a proven system of operation, a product, and you have your expertise. You also have some big problems.

- How do you arrive at a price for your business?
- How do you find someone who can afford to buy your business? "Who has fifty, sixty, one hundred K or more lying around?" asks Bob Dale.
- How can you convince your potential buyers that your client base will stick around even after you're gone?

There are many different formulas for determining the value of a business. My personal favorite is to figure out your average net for the last four years and multiply that by three to five.

Your accountant, lawyer or a business broker can give you an opinion on how to value your business. Be forewarned: A business appraisal can cost up to several thousand dollars.

Finding a buyer can be another sticky wicket. CPA Jim Orenstein has some suggestions on how a photographer might target a qualified buyer and make the transition between owners successful and beneficial for everyone involved.

He recommends dealing with someone you know. It could be a person you already employ or even one of your clients who may have expressed an interest in learning to do what you do. Chances are you'll need to finance them partially, but don't loan them the entire purchase price. If they have some capital invested up front they'll work harder to make a go of it.

Jim's method of passing on the business takes roughly two years from start to finish. The original owner/photographer brings in the new owner as a sort of partner, maintaining a presence while teaching the newbie the trade and helping him build credibility in the minds of his clients. The new owner earns a livable salary while paying the balance of the profit to the original owner toward the purchase price of the studio. Of course, until it is paid off, the loan from the original owner to the new owner is accruing interest. Commercial/fine art photographer Leo Kim calls this the "someday this will all be yours" approach to selling your business. He has very gradually begun to do this with a protégé who is not yet a photographer but who has business experience and has shown a talent for visual art. "He really wants to be a photographer," says Kim, "and he already has the business experience. In six or seven years, when I turn it over to him, I think he will do very well."

Just as the start-up has its hazards, so does the middle age of a small business. But if you apply the same energy and ingenuity to your studio when it's in its prime that you did when it was new, you might just find that this stage has its rewards, too.

SOMETHING TO TALK ABOUT

4 Strategies for Generating Referrals

....

by Peleg Top

Your marketing toolbox probably includes your blog, e-newsletters, social media, face-to-face networking—all the usual suspects. But to really grow your business, developing a steady stream of qualified, intentional referrals should be the tool at the top of the box. Of all your marketing initiatives, generating referrals takes the least amount of time, costs almost nothing and yields the greatest results.

When a close friend tells you about a new restaurant, there's a pretty good chance that you'll take the recommendation seriously and give the place a try, right? Now turn that power of referrals from "trusted others" into a marketing force that works for your design business. Your most satisfied, enthusiastic clients are your biggest fans, and each of them also is a trusted other for an untapped network of potential clients who are just waiting to hear about you from their friends.

If you don't pay attention to who's talking about you and what they're saying, you may attract the wrong prospects—or none at all.

Peleg Top is a business development coach and professional mentor to creative entrepreneurs. He specializes in helping creative agency owners improve their business and marketing skills and become better leaders. www.pelegtop.com
Excerpted from the September 2010 issue of *HOW* magazine. Used with the kind permission of *HOW* magazine, a publication of F+W Media, Inc. Visit www.howdesign.com to subscribe.

Good word of mouth can transform a business. But, if you don't pay attention to who's talking about you and what they're saying, you may attract the wrong prospects—or none at all. Your goal in generating referrals is to control the process. And for that to happen, you need a system—one that produces qualified referrals from your best clients on an ongoing basis.

People are willing to make referrals not because they want *you* to make more money or grow your business, but because they want to help their friends. Your clients will think about recommending you when they encounter someone else who needs design services. Harness this natural human drive by making it easier for your best clients to be your representatives in the world because they believe that what you do serves others and they want to be part of that helping cause.

A referral system will be most effective if it supplements an existing marketing machine for your business. So for the sake of this article, I'm going to assume that you have a marketing infrastructure in place that supports your expertise and showcases your talent. What you say about your business will support what other people say about you. Furthermore, your own marketing will encourage referrals through the effect of what I like to call "The Three Rs"—when people see your marketing they *react*, *remember* and *recommend*.

Step 1: Serve

When you truly serve your clients and help them transform their businesses and experience success, they will naturally want to tell others. Serving your clients well and doing exceptional work is the foundation to cultivating good referrals. As simple as it sounds, holding yourself to the highest standards and providing the best work possible to every one of your clients is step 1 in the process. Clients won't refer you based on a merely good experience; they refer based on an exceptional experience. Ask yourself: "Are my clients astonished by my work?" If you strive to wow people with the work you create, you'll naturally put the wheels of referrals in motion.

Step 2: Ask

Many creative professionals are either afraid to ask their clients to refer them or don't ask properly. They worry that they might come across as desperate, so they don't ask at all. Or they ask in such a general way ("Would you mind handing my business card out to people you know?") that the client doesn't know what to do with the request.

You can get over these feelings if you re-frame the intent of your request. Feelings of desperation come from thinking that you're asking the client to help you. Instead, frame the "ask" as an offer to be a resource for helping your client help somebody else. Then, further help your client by being specific about exactly the kinds of services that you can provide to the people they might refer you to.

Come from a place of true service to others. Share with your clients the joy and satisfaction you get when you see their business thrive through the work you do for them. Then ask them if they can think of anyone else that could benefit from a similar experience. That's a powerful question. It's not about you. You're asking them if *they* want to help someone else.

In your request, help the other person understand what kind of people and companies you serve best. Be specific. Instead of saying, "Do you know anyone in the nonprofit industry that could use our help?" try: "Our best work happens when we work directly with marketing managers in small to mid-size nonprofits who are looking to grow their donor base and promote fund-raising events. Is there anyone you know that could use help with this type of challenge?"

Finally, ask your client to make the introduction for you. You want them to call their contact and share their experience of working with you. A personal phone call is far more powerful than an e-mail.

Step 3: Thank

When you finish a major project, promptly and effusively thank your client for their business, and use that as an opportunity to open the door to referrals. With the thank you, ask them if they'd be open to passing along some information about your agency (most would be delighted) and give them the tools to do so. Send them brochures, business cards or any other promotional items that would help them make a connection on your behalf. Remember, your raving fans become your marketing agents. Help them help you.

The thanks don't stop with you. When you land that new client based on a referral, ask them to call the person who recommended them to you to say thanks, as well. That contact shows the person who referred you the great impact they had on someone's life. And the double thanks feels double great.

TIME IT RIGHT //

Knowing when to ask for a referral is a big part of the challenge. There are three ideal times to be in asking mode:

1. At the get-go. When you bring a new client onboard, ask them about making referrals later on. It'll be easier for you to make a formal request. Plus, it plants a seed that may sprout at any moment: They may have a friend who needs a logo right now.

2. While the iron is hot. During the course of your project, when your client is wowed by your design solution and loves the experience of working with you, remind them that you'd appreciate a referral.

3. At the close of a job. Your client is thrilled. Ride that momentum and ask them to connect you with people they know.

Step 4: Inform

This part of the referral process is the one most creative professionals overlook, and yet they still somehow hope that others will think about them. How would anyone who refers you know the truly great impact of your work if you don't tell them about it?

Make it a point to contact the people who recommend you on an ongoing basis and inform them of the progress of your work with their friend. That relationship building and goodwill leads to more referrals.

The easiest, cheapest, most effective tool in your marketing toolbox is waiting to be used. You're likely sitting on a database of raving fans who would be happy to refer you to others if you reminded them that you're interested and available. You're already providing great service, right? Ask your best clients to connect you with someone else who needs your help, and thank them when they do. Finally, when you've started work with that new customer, get back to the old client with regular information on how it's going. You'll be keeping the wheels of referrals in motion.

MANAGING YOUR CLIENTS

Two Skills That Will Put You Back in the Driver's Seat in Your Client Relationships

by Ilise Benun

You run your own freelance business so you can make a living doing something you love with people who won't make your life miserable. Right?

Even if that's not your current reality, it could be—if you decide to be the boss. That means taking charge of the way you run your business, rather than letting your clients boss you around. Isn't the customer always right? To an extent.

If you want more control over your time, you must train your clients to work on your schedule.

Two skills can help you retain control of your work, your schedule and your sanity: No. 1, choosing the right clients, and No. 2, managing their expectations. You need both of those capabilities, because if you choose the wrong clients, all your excellent client-management skills will have little effect. And if you manage the right clients poorly, you'll create avoidable problems for yourself and for them.

Ilise Benun is an author, consultant and national speaker, the founder of Marketing-Mentor.com and the co-producer of the Creative Freelancer Conference. Her books include *The Designer's Guide to Marketing and Pricing* (HOW Books), *Stop Pushing Me Around!: A Workplace Guide for the Timid, Shy and Less Assertive* (Career Press) and *The Creative Professional's Guide to Money* (HOW Books). Sign up for her tips here: www.marketing-mentortips.com.

Excerpted from the November 2010 issue of *HOW* magazine. Used with the kind permission of *HOW* magazine, a publication of F+W Media, Inc. Visit www.howdesign.com to subscribe.

SKILL NO. 1: CHOOSING THE RIGHT CLIENTS

Start by accepting the fact that not every client who comes your way is a good fit.

Who is a good fit? That's up to you to decide, and the definition changes over time. But we can say that clients who respect and value your work and are willing—and able—to pay for it in a timely manner are most likely to be your ideal customers.

Often, it's easier to spot those prospects who aren't right for you than it is to identify those who are. These red flags seem obvious, but if you're feeling desperate or unsure about where the next job is coming from, you'll probably ignore them.

Watch for these warning signs:

- Their first question is, "How much does it cost?"
- They want it yesterday.
- They don't answer your questions completely—or at all.
- They don't know what they want or keep changing their mind.
- They don't want to pay your rates, or they keep trying to renegotiate the project fee.

Being the boss of your business means you stop ignoring those ominous signals and politely decline the clients who don't fit, so you can find clients who do and then get busy managing them.

SKILL NO. 2: MANAGING EXPECTATIONS

Although you can't control your clients, you can manage their expectations. But you have to train them first—which you're actually already doing, whether you're aware of it or not. With every action, you set precedents, which are very hard to change once they're in place. Respond to their first e-mail right away, and your client will think that's normal for you and come to expect it. Turn a project around in a day because you happen to have the time, and from now on they'll assume that's your style.

If you want more control over your time, you must train your clients to work on *your* schedule. Veteran Los Angeles-area solopreneur Luke Mysse suggests dedicating one day per week to focus on your business, with no client work or contact. "This may seem impossible at first," he acknowledges. "How will they wait a whole day when they can barely stand to wait an hour for you to return their call?

"They will," Mysse affirms. "If you set aside one day a week, or even one morning a week to start, they will eventually get used to your new schedule, especially if you give them some warning so they can prepare."

What else can you do to manage your clients' expectations? Here are several strategies:

Put absolutely everything in writing, in detail. That's what Kristin Maija Peterson of Grand Ciel Design in St. Paul, Minnesota, does. "In our first meeting, I outline the process so they know what to expect," she says. "Once they sign off on a proposal, I back up my verbal process with written phases of the project and time line. I include what needs to happen at the end of each phase. I adjust my level of communication to accommodate their style and schedule—they know I'm there for them. In return, they're equally respectful of my time and schedule."

Recap key information verbally. Sometimes, putting it in writing isn't enough, because clients often don't read a detailed agreement. So Heather Parlato, of Parlato Design Studio in Los Angeles, has learned to preempt potential problems by verbally highlighting certain details. "I've learned to tell clients everything up front," Parlato says. "I tell them what my process involves, what a typical time line will look like for the project in question and the limitations. I'll say, 'We do two rounds of revisions to refine the content, and that is included in the price. But if there are additional revisions that cannot be avoided, those will be extra, so anything we can do to revise as completely as possible in those two rounds is best.'"

Most important, address the questions your clients may not know to ask. Parlato outlines the points in her contract that are most often misunderstood, especially regarding payments, usage rights and ownership. "Clients don't read the fine print, and they react much better to what's in the contract when it's explained verbally," she says.

Make sure their expectations are realistic. Parlato also asks up front about the client's expected results for the project. "Often, my clients don't have a firm success metric they're looking for, so I define what I think we can achieve," she says. "I make sure clients know that the final piece alone won't double their sales. Discussing this also helps me know if a client's expectations are putting too much pressure on the outcome of this one project."

Copywriter Deidre Rienzo, of Connect with Copy in Tappan, New York, also makes a point of determining the client's goals at the outset. "If they start out with expectations that aren't realistic, or that I'm not capable of meeting, then these expectations will be nearly impossible to manage," she says. "So I start by talking frankly about their goals. I want to make sure I'm equipped to give them what they want. If clients expect magic, I don't work with them (unless I can make magic for them)."

Keep them in the loop. Constant communication is a key to managing expectations. You can't read your clients' minds and they can't read yours. That's why keeping clients in the loop is worth the extra effort and attention. Sometimes all it takes is a quick phone call or an e-mail update. Rienzo sends a lot of messages saying, "Your bio is 75 percent ready. I'm putting on the finishing touches and will send it over for your review on Friday. "

Parlato also sends little reminders or check-ins about a project's progress, especially if a problem crops up, as often happens. "I contact them as soon as I know I might have to reschedule something," she says. "That way, even if a milestone isn't on the exact date we'd planned, they know I care about their work and won't leave them with any surprises."

Being the boss with your clients isn't about being a bully or getting your own way. "To me, it boils down to being a professional," Mysse says. "Take control and lead others to greater prosperity and understanding. A bully sticks around and tries to force his way, no matter how bad the fit. Be a professional and know when things don't fit. A pro knows when he's a bad match and when to bow out."

NORMAN MASLOV

AGENT INTERNATIONALE

....

by Ric Deliantoni

Norman Maslov, a native San Franciscan, is an artist's agent, representing commercial photographers nationally from his hometown by the Bay. His photography agency, Maslov: Agent Internationale opened in 1986. I first met Norman while working with the extremely successful commercial photographer Michele Clement. At that time he was working as her business manager, running the operation from his perch in the studio's loft. His boom voice at times seemed like the Great Oz coming from the heavens and certainly got our attention. Several years later,

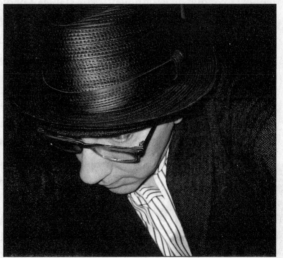

© Norman Maslov

Here Norman shows his own photography skills and his passion for hats.

when I started my studio, his advice and help was invaluable. He always took the time to review my new work and consulted with the development of my book. Although we never

Ric Deliantoni is professional photographer and director with thirty years of experience, with a focus on still-life and lifestyle imagery for advertising, design and publishing. He has developed a unique style that has been described as impressionistic and bold. Ric has also spent much of his career teaching and mentoring students of all levels to better themselves as artists.

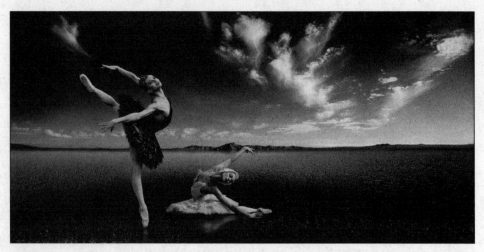

worked together as rep and photographer, he did funnel work my way whenever he could through tips and advice on how I could land assignments. His stable of photographers includes some of the best and most sought after shooters in the country. He has a keen eye for recognizing talent. The success of his company and his photographers is a true testament to this ability.

Many of David Allan Brandt's photographs include romantic worldscapes combining people with urban structures and whimsical dreamlike environments.

Talk a bit about the services you offer to your artists.

I work with them in editing and organizing their portfolios and websites. I consult with them about the direction they want to go style-wise and in terms of testing for themselves.

I collaborate with them to create a marketing plan and promotional campaigns. I market them to potential clients in adverting, design and corporations and negotiate assignments and licensing agreements.

Talk a bit about the services you offer to the clients.

I offer them a variety of photographers with artistic and production experience. I suggest specific photographers depending on their

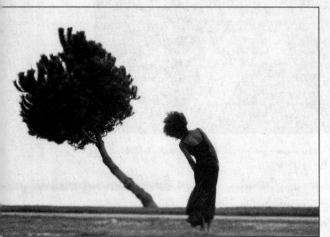

Diptychs of human images partnered with natural forms comprise Cristiana Ceppas's latest series of photographs.
© Cristiana Ceppas

needs. I work to try to match them with my artists and attempt to create a budget that fits within theirs.

How do you go about finding photographers to rep?

I keep an eye on work I see in publications like *Photo District News* (*PDN*), *Communication Arts*, *Graphis* and so on. I also see work from direct mail and e-mail promotions and social sites such as Facebook. Also, clients and buyers occasionally refer new photographers to me. I also do portfolio reviews at some of the art schools and at events sponsored by American Photographic Artists (APA) and American Society of Media Photographers (ASMP) and other photo organizations.

Do you rep other art professionals?

No, except for one digital post artisan retoucher.

How many artists do you rep?

Presently I have twelve photographers in my stable.

What are your thoughts on specialization?

It's good to specialize at first to get noticed and then expand out over time. However, some specializations are very specific like food and product or sports photography. You can't be all of over the map when you start out. You have to focus and stay consistent with your work. Create several series that work together thematically or stylistically, once you are known for those styles, you then can afford to grow into other areas.

How do you market your artists?

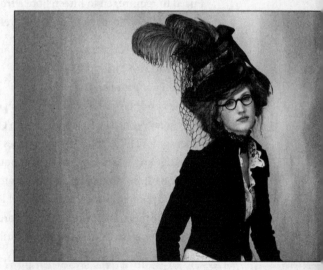

Calling and visiting clients I have relationships with. Promoting to new clients when I see or hear that they represent certain products. Direct and e-mail promotions. In person Portfolio Donut Road shows. Directory and website advertising. Social network and business sites and so on. You have to be everywhere!

How do you break down or share marketing expenses with your artists?

They pay their way and I pay mine. They all get major group discounts in some of the printed and online directories by being included in my group, in my stable.

Michele Clement's dramatic black-and-white portraits and lifestyle images evoke a timeless style.
© Michele Clement

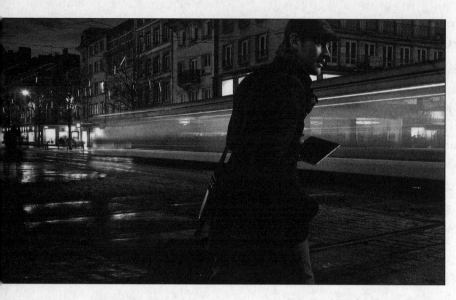

Harold Lee Miller has worked as a magazine managing editor in New York, a newspaper reporter and editor in the Midwest and Northeast, and for the last twenty years, as an advertising photographer.
© Harold Lee Miller

What is your cut of a job, and is this a set percentage or does it fluctuate?

I receive 25–30 percent of fees. This includes assignment shoot fees and relicensing fees.

Give us your thoughts on the portfolio and what you require from your artists?

I used to require ten to fifteen books from each photographer. I now only need one or two, mostly for in-person shows, as everything else is presented online.

What are your thoughts on the digital age, and how has it affected you, your business and the industry in whole?

It's been good and bad.

The good: It's quicker to see if you got the shot immediately. You can shoot many more images and the cost really doesn't add up as it did when you needed to shoot and process more film. You can send images to clients faster and promote the work quicker. It's easier and faster to get new work out. It's easier to promote yourself.

The bad: Everyone has a digital camera, and everyone seems to think they are professional photographers. Many are not learning to use lighting as they feel they can fix it in Photoshop. There are so many more "photographers" now. Clients shoot more for themselves or have "friends" who will shoot cheap for them.

Do any of your artists shoot on film? If so, is this driven by the client or the artists?

Hardly at all. Only in a rare instance when a photographer uses a certain style or look. For instance, Polaroid (if even possible) or Holga cameras. Very special and specific processes.

Do any of your artists shoot video? If so, how does this affect the way you represent them?

Yes, this is growing fast, especially since the Canon cameras can shoot both stills and HD video. I've had clients (usually food and pharmaceutical) want video pieces, mostly for the Web. They seem to think you can simply add it on during a shoot, but you have to be careful and explain that the lighting needs to be different and separate. We charge a separate fee for video and bring in a gaffer to light. It's good for photographers who want to, to practice with motion. But don't give it away. Educate the client on the process. Clients seem to think it is easy to add it to a print shoot. But it is not.

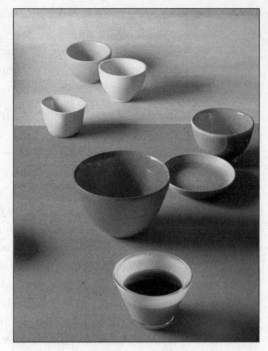

Deborah Jones's wonderful still-life and food photography can be seen in over two dozen books.

Do you belong to a professional association? If so, which one?

Both the APA and ASMP.

What are the reasons for this decision?

These associations support the industry in whole. They support the business of photography in terms of copyright and so on. They are also offer great opportunities for networking both locally and nationally.

In recent years there has been some talk about developing a set of professional standards to govern the business photography, what are your thoughts on this subject?

There is always talk of this. There are so-called standards already in place. Some choose to follow them and others don't. You can't force it on anyone but simply try to educate. It's human nature.

What are your thoughts on licensing photographers, akin to other professionals such as contractors, CPAs, and the like?

Not needed in the world I work in. It's like Rock & Roll!

Do you encourage or work with your artists in entering competitions or organizing public showings of their work?

Yes. Any way to get their work shown. And they need to shoot all of the time. When they are not on an assignment, they should work on new series of personal images. Shoot for yourself. Always keep fresh. Don't stop, or you'll get stale and die.

Do you have any parting words of wisdom you would like to share about the future of the profession of photography?

I am just starting my twenty-fifth year as an agent. Twenty-five years in business for myself. It's been a wonderful journey with a few bumps along the way. A few recent tempestuous years of "end of the world" talk … are coming to an end. I'm actually feeling more optimistic right now. Yes, there have been major changes, and the axis of the planet has tilted in a different direction, but new possibilities are also opening up to those who have the courage and stamina to continue.

There are countless articles about how assignments have been chipped away: the recession, stock imagery, reductions in magazine advertising, digital photography where every person has a camera and sees themselves as a pro … And of course there is the reduction of licensing images for a limited time and the expansion of image libraries for use in perpetuity. Some assignments have looked like those all-you-can-eat Vegas buffets for $2.99. And then there are the shooters who just give it all away in exchange for the fame of seeing their name in print or images published. We can freeze up, get pissed about it, or we can jump in and look towards the wonderful new possibilities.

Socializing is back big time. The obvious is connecting through networks such as Facebook and writing personal blogs. Our markets and potential connections have actually expanded, but it is still necessary to keep those personal connections intact. Pressing the flesh, no matter how upset or discouraged you may get about the present and future of our industry, it is so important to be respected and trusted. This is how I have always tried to run my business. Treat everyone with honesty and respect, and he or she will come back again and again. Take interest! Be personal!

I am so proud of the artists I represent, and I know that it is difficult for them when assignments don't come through, but we will continue to persevere and move forward. They will continue to shoot work for themselves, and I will do my best to showcase their talent and keep my personal connections alive. I will continue to get them their auditions whenever possible.

I think Arthur Miller said it wonderfully through his character Willie Loman in *Death of a Salesman*, "The man who makes an appearance in the business world, the man who creates a personal interest, is the man who gets ahead. Be liked and you will never want."

STEPHEN BEST

American Photographic Artists CEO

....

by Ric Deliantoni

Several years ago I had the opportunity to work with Stephen Best, who at that time was the studio manager for Ambrosi San Francisco. This was one of the best experiences I have had in my thirty years as a photographer. The team he put together for Ambrosi was top-notch and produced great work, exceeding all of the clients' expectations. Thus I was not surprised to hear that he was chosen to head up the American Photographic Artists (APA). Under his watch I am sure that great things will happen for this organization. The following is a bit on Best's history and his thoughts on working in photography today.

Tell us a bit about your photography career.

When I entered college I was thinking of being a lawyer, so I went through college with that plan. My last quarter before graduation I needed one more elective. Someone suggested a photo class, which exposed me to a new passion. Having no photo knowledge, I enrolled in a technical school to study and received an A.S. in photography.

During those two years I did an internship at a studio that hired me as soon as I graduated, so I was lucky to start off immediately as a photographer and soon had management responsibilities for the in-house lab. After four years at that studio I then moved to Atlanta, Georgia, managing an in-house studio for an advertising agency specializing in retail advertising.

Ric Deliantoni is professional photographer and director with thirty years of experience, with a focus on still-life and lifestyle imagery for advertising, design and publishing. He has developed a unique style that has been described as impressionistic and bold. Ric has also spent much of his career teaching and mentoring students of all levels to better themselves as artists.

During those years I maintained a daily photo schedule, shooting anything that came through the door: room sets, tabletop, fragrance, jewelry and food. The last few years in Atlanta I was photographing a lot of fashion.

In 1997 I was recruited to manage the Robinsons-May department store advertising studios in Los Angeles. When Macy's and May merged, it was time to move again. Ambrosi, an agency in Chicago, recruited me to open a studio in San Francisco. Later, when the San Francisco office closed, Ambrosi transferred me to their studio in Atlanta. Going back to Atlanta was like going back home, but soon that studio also closed and I was on my own as a photographer for the first time. It was a bad time in the economy to experience that.

Currently, I'm the CEO for American Photographic Artists (APA), a nonprofit professional photographer's association. During the 1990s and early 2000s I was on the board of directors of Professional Photographers of America. All during that time I really enjoyed the association business. When the CEO position for APA was advertised, I applied and after several interview steps, was hired. It has been a great two years, and I look forward to the years ahead.

Even though I haven't been behind a camera for over ten years, I've always been involved with photography. It's still a passion but from another side.

Talk a bit about your education?

My B.A. from Emory and Henry College in Emory, Virginia, is an interdisciplinary degree in history, sociology and economics. My photography training was technical rather than art-oriented. I received an A.S. in photography from Randolph Technical Institute (now Randolph Community College) in Asheboro, North Carolina. I also went back to school in 1997 and earned an M.B.A. from Georgia State University in Atlanta.

How would you rate an education vs. a mentor program?

Education is very important, not necessarily to photography, but some college experience is valuable to life experience. Photography education gives a great basis for understanding the medium. It gives someone a head start in my opinion and combined with an internship or mentor program would greatly increase one's desirability.

Do you have a mentor or someone you look up to?

I've had two people I call mentors. The man that first hired me out of school gave me so many experiences and opportunities. The second is the person was who hired me for my first job in Atlanta. Again, he had a lot of experience, and he placed me in positions that allowed me to grow.

How does the APA go about marketing?

We use websites, e-mail marketing and social media extensively. Sponsorship and partner programs are also important to us for cross-promotion to the photo industry. We also have partnerships with private photo social networks.

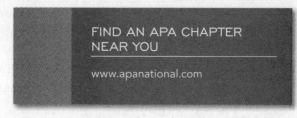

How do you use e-mail as a tool?

We use e-mail a lot. Our two e-mail marketing vendors are My Emma and ADBASE Emailer.

What social media sites do you use?

Facebook, Twitter and LinkedIn.

Do you send out printed marketing promos?

Not often. We do have a printed membership brochure that we use at events and conventions.

What are your thoughts on artists' reps?

Can be great, but they're not always necessary. Know where your strengths are, and use one if you need it.

Talk about the APA—costs, benefits, community development, etc.

APA's mission is Successful Professional Photographers. We offer discounts from major photo vendors; benefits such as business insurance and financial services; a find-a-photographer site with portfolios for members; and partnerships with some photo social communities like Photocrew and One Eyeland. We also offer a downloadable business manual online. (Some sections are public and some are member-only.)

Fees range from $55 per year for students to $350 per year for professional photographers. We believe in advocacy for photographers focused on copyright laws, protections and enforcement. We make several trips to Capitol Hill each year and belong to the Copyright Alliance as well as Authors Coalition of America. We are also a member and supporter of Picture Licensing Universal System (PLUS), an organization establishing standards for licensing images around the world. APA has also been a founder and contributor to UPDIG, a coalition of organizations drafting standards for workflow issues in digital image management.

In recent years there has been some talk about developing a set of professional standards to govern the business photography. What are your thoughts on this subject?

> Business standards or best practices are very much needed. Learning from the experience of others is great. There may not be set standards that are usable for everyone, but guidelines are good to have.

What are your thoughts on licensing photographers, akin to other professionals such as contractors, CPAs and the like?

> I'm mixed on that. I do think the public can see a credential or certificate as a positive. Wedding and portrait photographers may gain from that. In commercial and advertising work, I don't think it would mean that much. Art buyers look at portfolios and want to personally connect with someone working for them.

What are your thoughts on style development and specialization as a photographer?

> Style is a personal matter. I think style can be something that crosses over between specialties. My photo experience was great from small product illustration to large room scenes, jewelry to pots and pans, fashion to cars, location to studio. Through all that I think I had a style that can be identifiable as my work.
>
> Specialization can be successful but I've heard from several photographers that they have to be more varied in their work in today's economy. I think you can be diverse in your work and still maintain a style that is unique to you.

RICK WILSON

A Career in Sports Photography

....

by Crystal Pirri

Rick Wilson was "discovered" in his hometown of Troy, Ohio, at a young age. He joined the high school newspaper as a junior, after taking his first photography class the year before. As luck would have it, working at the high school paper meant he worked in the same offices as the town's professional paper, the *Troy Daily News*.

Rick was developing his photos in the newsroom for all to see, and soon the photo editors took notice. They gave him photo assignments within months. Rick remembers, "By the time I was a senior in high school I

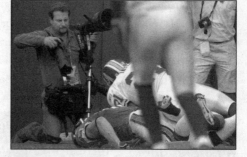

Rick Wilson almost becomes part of the action while covering the Washington Redskins game against the Jacksonville Jaguars at FedEx Field in Landover, Maryland.

Emily Barnes/The Florida Times-Union

was doing assignments on a daily basis, covering Cincinnati Reds games, Cincinnati Bengals games, Ohio State football games, and high school sports almost every night. At a younger age I had an opportunity to do more prestigious sporting events than a normal person." His early sports background would stay with him his entire career.

Rick left Troy and went to college at the Ohio University, studying for a digital communications degree. Bit by the photo bug, he didn't just stick to the books. Rick flew coast-to-coast, interning as a photographer at the *Corvallis Daily Times* in Oregon and later the *Providence Journal* in Rhode Island. After he graduated, he immediately landed the chief

Crystal Pirri is based in Akron, Ohio. You can find her on the Web at www.crystalpirri.com.

photography position at his hometown paper, but he didn't stay long. He then went to Flagstaff, Arizona, and Lewiston, Maine. He explains, "I just wanted to try something different. I was young, I didn't have kids, I wanted to live in different parts of the country, to experience different things, and all the while expanding my photographic horizons."

Still heavily involved in sports, he covered local high school, college and professional events wherever he went. He was at the Lewiston paper less than a year, he says, when he received an unexpected phone call: "The director of photography at the *Florida Times-Union* called me and said that the city of Jacksonville had been awarded the Jacksonville Jaguar NFL franchise and [offered me] a staff photography position covering the Jaguars. They gave me an offer I couldn't refuse. I've been in Jacksonville for the past sixteen years."

SPORTS PHOTOGRAPHER

Rick's official job title at the *Florida Times-Union* was Lead Jaguars/Sports Photographer. He was to follow the Jaguars extensively, including practice sessions, training camps, and every pre-season and regular season game, home and away.

Aside from his job photographing the Jaguars, Rick has an impressive résumé from the off-season. He routinely covered the PGA Tour Players Championship, Daytona Speed Week leading up to the Daytona 500, the Sony Ericsson Women's Professional Tennis Tour, the Gator Bowl, national championship football and basketball games, the 2005 Super Bowl, and a host of University of Florida football, basketball and baseball events.

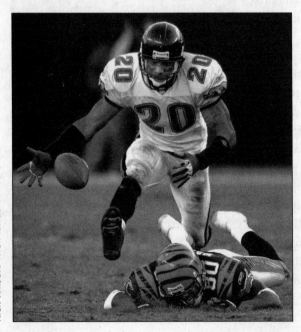

Rick Wilson/The Florida Times-Union

If that sounds too glamorous, his job had its downsides, too. While Floridians were scrambling for safety in the wake of natural disasters like floods, wildfires and hurricanes, Rick was tirelessly taking pictures and sometimes having to drive hours to get out of the affected area in order to find a wireless signal that would allow him to send his photos back to the newsroom.

Jacksonville Jaguars safety #20 Donovin Darius (top) flattens Cincinnati Bengals receiver #80 Peter Warrick while breaking up and almost intercepting a pass during an NFL game in Cincinnati, Ohio.

Rick explains, "In the newspaper industry, getting photographs back to the office is crucial, in fact it's the most important part of the job. Regardless if you're at a sporting event or a spot news event, it doesn't matter how fantastic the images are, if you can't get them to the office to be published, it doesn't matter."

Rick tells of a game around ten years ago, in which Florida State played in Louisville, Kentucky: "It was a blinding rainstorm. The game was on a Thursday night at eight o'clock and the newspaper was on deadline. [The game] was like a trade-off, big play after big play, and it seemed like I was shooting a couple photos and then running up to the press box to transmit those photos and then running down to the field and shooting some more photos and running back up to the press box and transmitting those photos. It was a very interesting night."

Rick has also witnessed his share of memorable events: "Crashes at Daytona, covering the Jags

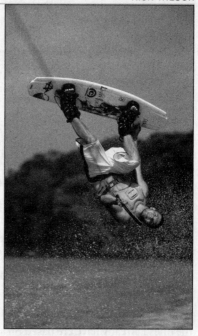

An instructor from Epic Sessions wake boarding school performs an aerial trick on the waters of Black Creek in Clay County, Florida.

Rick Wilson/Rick Wilson Photography

… I've had people come up and say, 'Hey, I remember that picture you took.' There was a woman I was talking to the other day about a picture I had taken of Tiger Woods over ten years ago, and she remembered that picture. The thing with covering sporting events is you never know when you'll be a part of history."

NO LONGER A TEAM

It was during Rick's time at the paper that other publications and companies began approaching him to do freelance work. Working at the *Times-Union* kept him busy, though, and he really didn't have time to pursue it. He explains, "Other newspapers were actually my freelance clients, like *USA Today* and the *Washington Post*, the *New York Post*, the *New York Times*. Any time they had a writer working on a story in the Jacksonville or the north Florida area, they would need a photographer to go shoot pictures for the story, so I was able to get some freelance work that way."

After shooting the Jaguars for fifteen years (1995–2010) Rick decided he'd been "long enough at one entity doing one thing" and started his own freelance business. While he says he's not quite making what he used to, he's off to a great start: "This past week I made more money as a freelancer working less time than I did in a normal week at the newspaper."

DON'T SHOOT

Rick is no doubt a sports photographer, and he's branding his business as such. But what about the other opportunities that come his way? "When you're a photographer, you're approached to do weddings," he says.

Rick does not accept these job opportunities: "I have friends and pals who run wedding photography businesses. Once I left the *Times-Union*, it was very important to me to not directly compete with people who were established photographers. The few weddings I've shot, people say, 'You'd be an amazing wedding photographer.' Well, I know there are several other photographers in Jacksonville that make a living doing weddings, and I don't want to take away from that, to be competing with them."

He continues, "I'm taking a different approach with my business. First and foremost I'm concentrating on sports and lifestyle photography for editorial and corporate clients. The easy answer when you're running your own business is, yeah, you'll take work from anybody that pays you, regardless of whether it's weddings or architecture or medical photography or whatever. But my marketing aspects reaching out to potential clients on top of the ones I already have are based on sports and lifestyle."

HOME-FIELD ADVANTAGE

I asked Rick if he thought being in Florida gave him an advantage as a sports photographer, since the warm weather draws sporting events year-round.

He responded, "It does on one hand. There are a lot of events happening in Florida and being based in Jacksonville certainly helps. But I believe if you're a talented photographer who takes unique and creative images, if you develop a client list who appreciate the work that you do, you can find work anywhere."

Rick further explains that, no matter where photographers are based, a publication or client will often pay to send them across the globe for a photo shoot.

He notes, "It's just like *Sports Illustrated*'s staff photographers. [*Sports Illustrated* will] send them to the Olympics, even though, say, the next summer games are in London, and there might be some great photographers based in London. Certain publications are going to send their own photographers who they've worked with for years and years. They trust their work."

He continues, "In some aspects it doesn't matter where you're based at, especially in the sports world. If you're a wedding photographer, unless you do travel or destination weddings, then all [your] clients are in that area where [you] live. The same with family portraits, the same if you're shooting senior pictures, the same if you're working for a real estate company. But sports photography—on one hand, yes, you can do the little league thing and high school thing, selling images to parents, but, on a bigger scale, covering major sporting events affords you the opportunity to travel, especially if you're good enough."

PHOTOGRAPHERS VS. PEOPLE WITH CAMERAS

Many professional photographers face the market flood of non-professionals with expensive equipment. Arguably more than in any other profession, an untrained, unexperienced camera owner can bill themselves as a professional photographer. While Rick acknowledged the challenges that professional photographers face in today's culture, he wasn't too concerned.

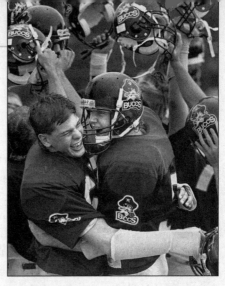

Members of the Covington (Ohio) Buccaneers high school football celebrate their first win of the season against rival Bradford.

He explains, "There is competition from everybody with a camera, but I think you can rise above that. There's plenty of work for established professional photographers. I believe that there are photo directors and photo buyers and companies out there that respect professional photography, they respect creativity, and they respect a unique vision. If there's a company that's willing to accept free photography and marketing managers and so forth that establish friendships with, what I call 'prosumer'-type photographers, then those aren't companies or entities that I want to work with anyway. They don't value quality necessarily."

He continues, "I'm going to rely on the philosophy that if I work hard and take outstanding photographs, present them to my clients and potential future clients, then that's going to help me get work. I've never made any income in my entire life other than from photography, from the time I was sixteen years old. I've never had any other job, I've never had a part-time job when I was in college. From the time I was sixteen I started working at my hometown newspaper, until now. I've never earned a cent from anything else."

Rick notes, "There are lots of photographers [on the field] that have fancy equipment and you find out that they're not even full-time photographers. They're lawyers that can afford fancy equipment, and somebody got them a pass. Lots of [those types of] photographers basically shoot for free, for the passes and provide the images for free, in exchange for the pass. [But] there's a difference between shooting a professional football game and getting some good stop-action photographs because of the gear that you're using."

Rick goes on to explain what separates the professionals from the "every guy with a camera"-type:

"There might be three plays that lead up to the last-second touchdown pass that tell a story. A lot of people that are just there for the fun of it aren't even aware of the essence of the sport and what makes it remarkable." Telling that story with your photos, he says, is

the difference between being a photojournalist and being a fan with a camera.

HOW TO SHOOT LIKE A PRO

Throughout the interview, Rick shared his tips
for newcomers to photography. His advice is
for anyone starting out in the business, but
also covers best-practices for photographers
who may not have had formal training.

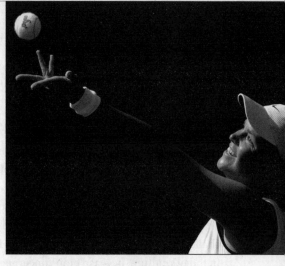

Lindsay Davenport tosses a tennis ball to
serve on stadium court at Amelia Island Plantation during her semi-final victory over
Nadia Petrova in the Bausch & Lomb Champ-
ionships in Fernandina Beach, Florida.
Rick Wilson/The Florida Times-Union

1. Be a creative photographer. Rick tells
   the story of a high school photographer he'd met recently in Jacksonville.
   The student had named his business
   something that meant "innovative."
   Rick asked him, "What's so special
   about your work? How are you being innovative? What are you doing
   differently than everybody else?" The
   student said, "Nothing, I just want to
   do what everybody else is doing—portraits, weddings, all that stuff." Rick's advice:
   be innovative with your photography, not with your business name. Finding out
   what makes you different from everyone else will give you a place to start from with
   your marketing, as well as a way to stand out from the crowd.

   He explains, "I think your name is your reputation. Everybody tries to come
   up with a catchy name for their business. If you have to have 'Exotic Photography'
   [as a business name] … if you have to rely on some crazy name to attract business,
   then you may not be a very good, creative photographer."

2. Get credentials. Rick notes, "I may like to draw pictures of houses, but I'm not a professional architect. I shouldn't promote myself as one just because I have some cool
   houses I designed. I don't think any architectural firm is going to hire me without
   a college degree and without training." At the very least, a few photography classes
   in the basics of using your camera will take you further in your goals than merely
   turning your wheel to "auto."

3. Conduct yourself professionally. Rick explains, "Photography isn't about pressing the button, it's also about how you conduct yourself in a certain situation.
   There have been many guys with cameras at football games that are seeking out
   autographs and stopping the players after the game and asking them to pose for
   pictures, and people that spend more time shooting the cheerleaders than the ac-

tual game. That's not a way to conduct yourself if you're a professional at a sporting event." Even though you're at a major football game and the adrenaline is high, you're still working. Treating your photography assignments like work instead of parties will help ensure you get more assignments.

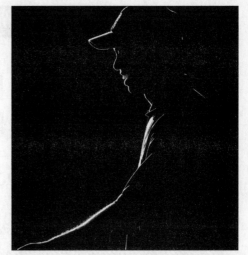

PGA Tour golfer Tiger Woods is illuminated by the setting sun behind him as he walks along the second fairway during first round play of The Players Championship on the Stadium Course at TPC Sawgrass in Ponte Vedra Beach, Florida.

4. Be a businessperson. Rick encourages photographers to "learn the ins and outs of the business. Do it the right way." Get your Tax ID Number and business insurance. Find out what you need to operate professionally in your state.

5. Market yourself specifically. Rick notes, "Many editorial photographers can shoot fantastic images of anything, any genre, so that makes it hard...to decide what genre are you going to focus on, to brand your business." He says many freelancers "go the wedding route, the family portrait route. That's the easiest to market in a way. It's easy to put galleries up on Facebook. Doing weddings can't be extremely lucrative, and you're still competing with the guy with a camera who shoots weddings for $200." Rick talked extensively about sticking to one field. If you're a flower photographer, do that. If you shoot weddings, excel there. You'll want to be known for your brand, and you'll get more calls for further assignments in the area you pursue the heaviest.

6. Pay your dues. He explains, "I went to college, I paid my dues by working at small town newspapers before I got a break and was hired by a big newspaper." Rick shot for at least six years before he was recognized by a large paper. If you don't spend your free time interning at newspapers all over America, it can take even longer.

7. Take excellent photos. "The cream rises to the top," Rick says. He explains, "It's subtle changes in what you do and how you use your camera that makes a picture go from ordinary to extraordinary. Sometimes it doesn't take much, but it takes the thought and vision and creativity to accomplish that. And I think that's what separates a lot of OK photographers from really exceptional photographers. It takes great skill to envision something that other people don't see standing right next to you."

KATHLEEN MCFADDEN

Fine Art Photographer

....

by Crystal Pirri

According to Kathleen Mc-Fadden, "You can learn German by taking German classes, or you learn German by going to Germany and immersing yourself in the culture. That's how I learned photography, I immersed myself in the culture of photography and the industry."

Kathleen has not only immersed herself in photography, she's become an expert in all aspects of her craft. She's been shooting for over thirty years and has her own successful gallery in Colorado Springs.

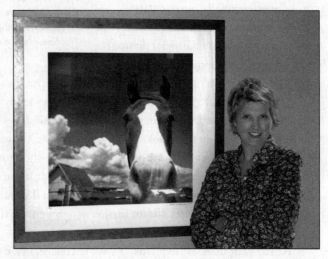

Kathleen's successful Colorado Springs gallery shows her work exclusively.

What you might not expect, however, is this: Kathleen doesn't shoot digitally. She shoots entirely with film cameras, using a collection you'll see in museums in a few years. Some of her iconic pieces include a 1927 Kodak Brownie, a 1937 Zeiss Ikon, an 1960s original Diana camera, and an 8×10 Deardorff with accordion-style leather bellows.

Crystal Pirri is based in Akron, Ohio. You can find her on the Web at www.crystalpirri.com.

"Capturing [photos] in a modern way but with old instruments, that's something I really dig about using the old cameras," Kathleen explains. She says she's "really marrying the old technology and the new technology, the old world and the new world, the past and the present."

Her gallery is a diverse mix of image styles and sizes. Kathleen observes, "Because of the different formats that I use, some of the toy cameras, or the old Brownies, you can't print very large. I use a lot of medium and large formats, so I have some very big images as well … People come in and think it's several photographers because I don't have just one set style. I call it Americana."

ALL-AMERICAN HISTORY

Kathleen's Americana roots begin in Texas. Having been born and raised in Amarillo, she says, made her a better photographer: "My grandparents had a farm and it was a very slow pace of life, not a whole lot going on, so it really made me observant. It influenced my Americana style … Amarillo is not the most beautiful place, outwardly, when you just glance at it. Having grown up there and having liked photography and liking the instruments, I got to looking, and I would look carefully. I would look at things and look at the way the light hit the lamppost or look at the radiator … Growing up in a place that wasn't just outwardly gorgeous really influenced my style, so far as looking at common things that were familiar to me and waiting until the light hit them just right in order to capture them in a way that would show people how I felt about them."

Kathleen continues, "My photography is all American photography, mostly western America. That's where I was born and raised and that's where my heart is. I know the soul of western America and I think that's what draws people to my images and why I've done so well … because I shoot what I know."

Kathleen first received a Kodak Instamatic 110 at eight years old, when her immersion began. She calls it "a great little camera with a flip flash," which soon led to buying her "first real camera," a Canon AE-1 when she was thirteen. She proudly tells, "I bought it with my own money from a camera store that I later went to work in when I was sixteen. I lied about my age to be able to work [there] selling cameras."

At the same time, she also worked on the yearbook staff in junior high and high school. Despite starting with this early experience and working in commercial labs while she went to college, Kathleen didn't study photography professionally. Instead, she earned a journalism/environmental studies degree that she never used. She explains, "I didn't have the self-confidence in my artistic creative ability to [study photography in school]. I wish I'd had the confidence then that I have now at forty-three."

Even what she considers low confidence certainly didn't set her back. After college, Kathleen and a partner, a camera store manager she worked under previously, opened their

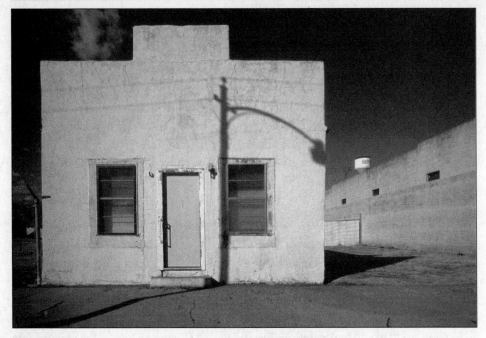

Kathleen tries to show the beauty of places and things that most people wouldn't ordinarily find appealing.

own camera store together in downtown San Luis Obispo, California, which remained open for twelve years. Eventually she opened a gallery next door to the camera store, which was another experiment in immersion: "I used to hang my images in the camera store and nobody ever bought one. When we opened the gallery next door, all of a sudden people were buying my work—some of the same work that I had in the camera store!" She explains, "The difference [was] the environment, the presentation. When people go in [a gallery] they're expecting to look at art that's for sale. Hanging your artwork in a store or restaurant or a café just doesn't work because people don't go there expecting to buy art. You've got to show this level of respect for your work if you expect people to respect it enough to [buy it]."

That respect for her work led her to dive into developing, framing and displaying her work. Kathleen explains, "[I frame my own work] not just because I do panoramics. It's also so I have complete control from start to finish, from pushing the shutter button to developing the film, [from] printing my own images and framing them and presenting them and lighting them. I have total control over every aspect of that image and so, from an artistic standpoint, it is technically perfect and presented as well as it possibly can be presented."

BEHIND THE GALLERY

While the gallery is popular and has its own following, Kathleen doesn't rely on gallery sales exclusively. Diversifying her income streams, she says, takes the pressure off her creative side. She explains, "The framing end of things and the printing … supplements the gallery, complements the gallery, [but it] also takes the pressure off the gallery, that way I can put anything I want in [there]. I don't have to think, 'Is it a money shot?'" She says, "If I tried to rely exclusively on gallery sales … I think that would take the fun out of it."

Obviously, Kathleen's technical precision in her own work keeps her in high demand with her customers, and she teaches her craft to budding photographers as well. Her four workshops are designed to carry the amateur photographer through the process of learning the craft and finally, presenting it well in a portfolio.

In her first workshop, "Point and Shoot Like a Pro," Kathleen teaches photography using only point-and-shoot cameras. She explains, "It's not all about the equipment. You're not going to get great images if you have an expensive camera. Likewise, you're not a professional photographer if you have an expensive camera. You can take great images with a point-and-shoot … but you need to know how it works. You need to know the basics."

Practicing what she preaches, Kathleen carries an Olympus Epic 35mm point-and-shoot with her everywhere she goes. "There are some images in [the gallery] that I wouldn't have gotten if I didn't have it."

Her second workshop "F-What and Shutter Who?" is for taking photography a step further. After you master the basics of using your instrument, Kathleen explains, you can be more comfortable getting creative with it.

"Composition: Why Other People's Vacation Photos Are Boring" is Kathleen's third workshop and is her take on "shoot what you know." When someone's on vacation, she says, they don't know the heart and soul of the place, and they can't capture what they don't know. She emphasizes that photographers should think about what they're looking at and determine how to capture "the soul of it" without taking another touristy sunset, or typical beach background.

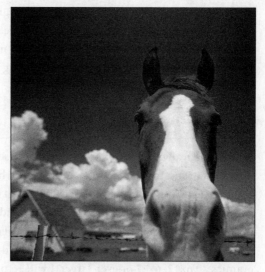

After her students have learned to take an interesting photograph on any continent, she offers a fourth workshop, a portfolio review and presentation class that teaches people how to present their work in a professional manner. Kathleen explains, "A portfolio review is not just me reviewing, looking over their portfolio and telling them if they have good

Kathleen encourages photographers to pay attention to detail from step one rather than relying on Photoshop to fix faulty shots.

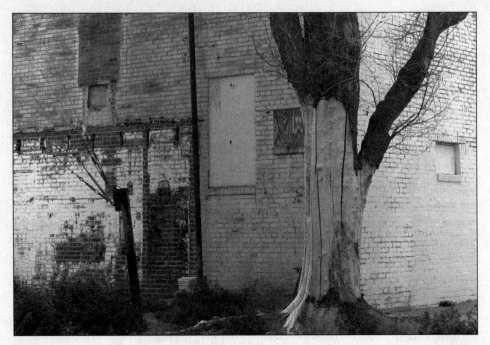

Kathleen explains that when you "shoot what you know," you're able to capture the heart and soul of a place.

shots or not. I want them to understand how to look at their own work critically and know if they have a good shot. A lot of times a photographer will gloss right over a really great shot and they'll lean towards one that's not so great. Maybe they like the not-so-great photo because the subject matter, or … they had this fond memory [of taking it]." Drawing on her own experience of learning the business by being in business, she also teaches how to avoid the pitfalls of trying to sell your work.

HOW SHE DOES IT

With so many digital options on the market these days, I asked Kathleen what she uses behind the curtain to scan, develop and produce her images. She describes her process for scanning negatives: "I use a Coolscan 9000. That is the best scanner that Nikon ever made, and when I had the camera store I played around with all different kinds of scanners, and this scanner gave me the best results. It has a very high dynamic range, extremely sharp optic, decent resolution, especially when you're doing larger negatives. When I do my panoramics … 6×12, 6×17 or even larger, I will actually physically sacrifice the negative and scan it in pieces and then use a stitching software that will handle very large files. That way I'm able to get that great incredibly sharp scan."

For enlarging, Kathleen explains, "I have my 4×5 color head enlarger so I can do anything 35mm to 4×5, including panoramics. I exclusively do black-and-white with that [because] color printing isn't that much fun."

When she talks about silver gelatin prints, you can hear the smile in her voice: "I enjoy the craft of black-and-white. There is a big difference in looking at a silver gelatin print versus an inkjet black-and-white when you're dealing with a contrasty image. A lot of times here in Colorado [we have] high contrast because we have bright sun."

She continues, "Even though I may scan the negatives so I'm digitizing them and I'm losing some of that tonal range that I gained by shooting film (because film does have the greatest tonal range), I'm not so far behind the eight ball because I started with a different kind of capture. I started with extremely high resolutions and a great tonal range. Though I'm losing tonal range by digitizing, it's still going to have a great look to me ... a filmlike look and there's a difference, there's a romance to it that digital doesn't have."

ON HER LOVE OF FILM

Kathleen in staunch in her defense of working with film: "People think I'm backwards, and they think I don't know the benefits of digital or I don't understand it and that's why I don't shoot digital, but I sold digital cameras for eleven of the twelve years I was in the business. I know them backwards and forwards, I know what they can do, I can train people on how to use them, I know Photoshop, all of that."

She goes on to say, "I know [my] cameras so well that I know exactly how [a photo is] going to look with each different camera, and so certain scenes require certain cameras to get this look that I want. When I'm holding a camera from 1937, a folding Zeiss 645, and I cock that shutter and I trip it, the feel of it, the smell of the leather bellows, that's part of the whole sensual experience of photography for me. I love the feel of the camera, the act the whole process of taking the photo is as important to me as what comes out of it. That's the thing with old cameras, each camera has its own character and style and so each camera will represent a subject differently."

Even with her extensive knowledge of the digital camera industry, she's unimpressed. She explains, "I think [the availability of digital cameras has] made it harder for somebody who is serious about [photography], who has taken the time to learn it, who really wants to get into it. It's made it harder, but on the other hand I think when some things are more difficult it weeds out people who aren't serious. If you're serious about it, you're going to keep going, and in the long run it's like a bad economy—it shakes out the people who aren't really great at what they do, and so the ones that are left are the really strong ones, the ones that were able to buckle down or ... be persistent."

ADVICE FOR BEGINNING PHOTOGRAPHERS

Kathleen's recommendations for newcomers to the industry:

1. "Learn [the craft] backwards and forwards, like you would a language. You want to be completely fluent in it." It's the foundation, she says, "if you don't know your craft, you can't consistently produce fine images. You have to be consistent if you want to make it in the business. If you know you have a good image and if you've done your homework and you have taken a great shot and it's exposed properly and it looks great, it deserves to be printed and framed properly and presented well."

2. Pay attention to detail from step one. Kathleen observes, "That's the thing with Photoshop—a lot of people think 'I'll fix it later.' Don't do that. Get everything right when you're out in the field, because you can't make a silk purse of a sow's ear. If you take care and you take pride, it will show."

3. Establish a style. She explains, "That's what's going to set you apart."

4. Try as many types of photography as you can. Kathleen notes, "I've tried everything … anytime anybody came up with a project for me to shoot I would try it. I've shot pregnancy photos, baby shots, portraits, weddings, kids in parties, product shots … I've done it all. You've got to do it all in order to find out what you like, but also what you're good at."

THE GIFT OF PHOTOGRAPHY

For Kathleen, the rewards of photography are great. She explains, "The greatest thing [about photography] is that it makes you appreciate looking around. You're observant, you see more things than other people see, you're always looking. I'm not always looking for a shot—I'm just always looking and observing. What a fabulous gift that is, to be observant of your surroundings because so many people just rush past and they don't notice what's happening … they're just intent on their struggles and their day-to-day activities. You just miss what's around you. What a great gift photography is to notice the light and notice subjects."

She concludes, "Photography can be a huge tool in teaching you to be present in the here and now. That is the best thing we can take out of the whole idea of going into photography for fun or for a living … that's what life is all about, really."

MARISSA BOWERS

A Designer Starting Out on a New Path

by Ric Deliantoni

When I started as managing photographer at F+W Media, Marissa was my counterpart as the managing designer for the craft community. We collaborated on many book projects as a creative team, and we worked together to schedule both of our teams, matching talents and personalities to get the best results for our projects. About a year ago, Marissa made the decision to follow her passion for photography. She left her position to start on a new career path. Since then, we have talked on many occasions and have shared information. I thought that with one year under her belt, this would be a good time to get her thoughts on this decision and where she is now.

Marissa made a leap of faith, leaving behind a promising graphic design career to pursue a new career in wedding and family-portrait photography.

Marissa, talk a bit about you education and what prompted your decision to follow your passion for photography.

In college I had a secondary interest in photography, and, had I not wanted to complete school as quickly as I could, I would have double majored or at least minored in photography. Unfortunately, the "quick path" won out, and I finished a degree in visual communications (focusing on graphic design) in 1997 from the Illinois Institute of Art in Chicago. I went on to work in design for ten years. When I began my de-

Ric Deliantoni is professional photographer and director with thirty years of experience, with a focus on still-life and lifestyle imagery for advertising, design and publishing. He has developed a unique style that has been described as impressionistic and bold. Ric has also spent much of his career teaching and mentoring students of all levels to better themselves as artists.

sign path as a book designer for a publishing company and began art directing photo shoots, my love for photography resurfaced. Encouraged by the professional photographers I worked with, I began shooting family and engagement sessions in 2007. This naturally evolved into full-time work in wedding photography.

How would you rate an education vs. a mentor program working as an assistant?

While I think my career path has evolved a little from both, I think it is important for those aspiring to work in photography to have some schooling in the arts. Mentoring and peer learning, hands down, is the best way to learn real-world experience. I would not be where I am today had I not stood back, learned quickly, and observed what works from those in the field who are already doing it. Peer professionals told me that I had an eye and encouraged me to branch out. I think my background as an art director let me "virtually" assist for a number of years without knowing it.

Since breaking out on my own this year, I have especially benefitted from taking a back seat some, assisting another professional wedding photographer at several weddings. Assisting takes away some of the stress you'd have if it were a wedding you had personally booked. It allows you to step back, observe and, most importantly, learn. And, in the meantime, you get some great shots that you wouldn't have otherwise had the opportunity to take!

Do you have a mentor or someone you look up to?

I try to be inspired by all types of photographers, not just those that work in the genre of clientele that I work with. When I first became interested in pursuing photography as a creative outlet with just photographing my children, I was inspired by the work of California-based family photographer Tara Whitney (www.tarawhitney.com). On the flip side, I am also inspired by the creative and over-the-top brilliant photography of Jeremy Cowart (www.jeremycowart.com). He is a graphic-designer-turned-photographer just like myself, and it is inspiring to set my goals as high as the level of work he is producing for the music and entertainment industries.

I think it is important to follow photography "celebrity" blogs, such as the ones I mentioned, but it is also important to have someone in your local circle or on a similar level to you who can also inspire you a bit more personally. For me, I've been incredibly blessed to meet a fellow wedding photographer this year, Nathan Peel (www.fyrefly.com) and to be able to just talk "business" and gain perspective from having similar interests and goals. Nathan is the head of a local photography meet-up group that I started attending at the beginning of 2010. I would highly recommend finding something like this in whatever city you are in and finding a mentor of your own. It is a very good thing!

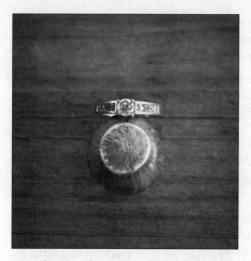

Natural surroundings inspired Marissa's shot of the bride's engagement ring.

What inspires you to create?

At first it was my children, then I opened up to the wedding world. Looking at wedding blogs helps, but I also just try to walk around and find surroundings that inspire me. It usually happens by chance on an actual shoot, but I use the moment and find what I need. For instance, I took this ring shot at a wedding in late 2009. It was a warm early fall day, and I was walking the grounds of the ceremony site, looking for a good spot for the groom and groomsmen group photos. I kept stepping on these buckeyes that were falling from trees as I checked out a perfect tree-lined area. The idea popped into my head to use the buckeyes as a "resting place" for the ring in the ring shot. I stuffed a few in my pocket and walked back to a picnic table, set it up quickly, and instantly had the elements for creating an awesome ring shot. This is a case of letting my surroundings inspire me, which is what I often do to kick-start my creative process.

Talk a bit about your creative process, and how you approach your commercial work. Does this differ when you shoot for your portfolio?

I always shoot with the goal of being creatively different from the rest of the pack. I approach my photographic process the same way I would a design process, asking what I need to do to make my work a notch above the rest. I have always been a bit of a perfectionist when it comes to my work (design and now photography). I want the work I am producing to be the most creative piece of work it can be.

My creative process doesn't usually differ when I'm thinking of things to use for my portfolio. If something is going to stand out, it does immediately, and then I know that I need to share it on my blog or website for past, current and future clientele to see.

What are your thoughts on specializing?

I think people will fit with the specific field they choose to do. I am a firm believer in this. I have seen it during my design career and think it is even more evident as a factor of determining if a person is outstanding or not in their photography field. You can tell when they are really into what they are shooting.

Your personality needs to fit with the job. A wedding photographer needs to create on the fly, to not be creatively stifled by changing schedules (which always happens on wedding days!). The wedding photographer has to always be on the lookout for the "perfect spot," even if you just saw that perfect spot in brief passing during the first ten minutes you were at the venue the day of the wedding. A successful wedding photographer also has to have a calming effect to the bride and her family and to be able to make anyone instantly at ease in front of the camera. The wedding photographer cannot let on that she is stressed, even if she is. It is all about being calm, cool and collected.

What are your thoughts on the development of a personal style?

Personal style certainly plays a role in how I approach my work and the images I choose to show on my blog. If you don't take the time to really figure out what your own personal style is, it is easy to blend in with all of the other photographers out there doing the same thing. Without a personal style of your own, you are just imitating what you see your peers doing. Being creative (and bold!) in photography takes risk, but the risk is well worth the reward. With wedding photography being so oversaturated with professionals, I can see how it would be easy to just settle and do what everyone else is doing. I personally make the choice not to fall into that trap. I approach each job with the clear picture that I do not want to copy, but would rather be copied.

What are your specialties?

I focus on wedding and family portraits in a non-traditional style. I am not your typical wedding photographer. I have a photojournalistic style and approach to the wedding day, but, even more than that, I try to just "tell the story" of a couple's big day. I do this by being creative with environment and positioning, as well as capturing detail images that will transport the bride and groom back to the day they always want to remember months, even years, later. Being creative with the bride's shoes, for instance, or thinking of a special meaning for the ring shot is how I tell the story. I also like to think that one of my specialties is how I choose to process an image after the wedding day when I am editing their final set for their collection. Not every image calls for a vintage post-process, but maybe one image clearly sticks out to be finished in a way that makes the viewer recall the memory in a special way.

How do you present your work?

On my combined blog/website: issadesign.squarespace.com.

Talk about your thoughts on marketing. How do you go about it?

There's a lot to think about in marketing yourself these days, and I attempt to do a combination of it all, eventually. I start by blogging my favorites from a session on my blog/website. This serves as a sneak peek for the actual client and allows current or potential clients to see my capabilities at a quick glance. It serves as an interest sparker, which will then hopefully lead potential clients to my portfolio where they can see what my other capabilities and style of imagery are. I am pretty careful about showing my absolute favorites from a session or a wedding, rather than throwing everything up that is just "good."

I then put the same link up on Twitter and Facebook. My tweets instantly feed into my personal Facebook page as well, so even if someone isn't a fan of my business page on Facebook, they'll see my link and might just venture on over to the blog and check things out. Who knows, maybe an old friend from high school has a sister who just got engaged. This is how you market to and maximize each page in different ways.

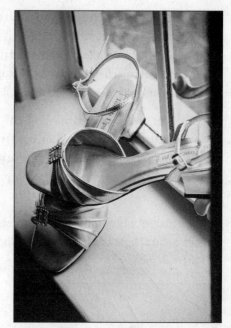

Do you use e-mail as a tool?

I do try to do an e-mail promotion every couple of months, and I try to be specific with who I send it and market it to. For example, last year I had a marketable e-mail list of brides from a local bridal show that I attended as a vendor, and I focused the e-mail promotion to pertain to the season (or month) a bride was getting married in.

Do you send out printed marketing promos?

Not yet, but I may in the upcoming year.

Creative shots transport the bride and groom back to their special day.

Do you have a rep?

Not yet!

Do you belong to a professional association? What are the reasons for this decision?

No, I just haven't figured out quite yet what association I should belong to and why. There are tons out there to choose from, and I am still early in the process of deciding which one would benefit me the most.

In recent years there has been some talk about developing a set of professional standards to govern the business photography. What are your thoughts on this subject?

I think there might be some value in this and would consider it a positive step in an ever-changing industry that does need some clarification on who is considered a professional and who is not.

What are your thoughts on licensing photographers, akin to other professionals such as contractors and CPAs?

I think licensing might take it a little too far, but I think there may be a specific association or rule standard that makes it easier for people to verify that they are getting a top-notch, respected professional.

What are your thoughts on the digital age, and how has it affected you, your business and the industry in whole?

I began as a digital photographer and think that my ability to do things digitally makes me an asset to a client. If new technology isn't embraced, you will get left behind. Photographers must keep up with technology and learn the new ways of doing things.

Do you ever shoot your work on film?

I don't currently shoot on film, but I would like to add it to my services if a particular shoot or wedding called for it to have a certain aesthetic that only film could capture.

Where do you shoot the majority of your work, location (indoors/outdoors) or in the studio?

The majority is outdoors and with natural light as often as possible. I do like using the natural light of a home in an indoor situation when shooting families at home, in their element.

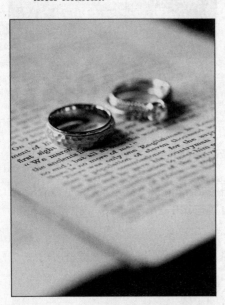

Marissa tries to think of a special meaning for the ring shot to help tell the couple's story.

Recent innovations in DSLR cameras have included HD video capabilities. What are your thoughts on developing skills to shoot moving images, and do you shoot any video yourself?

I don't currently shoot video, but I don't shy away from thinking about it for the future. Last year, Tara Whitney (the photographer I mentioned earlier) began showing her collaborative efforts with a videographer on her blog. She did the stills, he did the video, and they combined the two into an awesome package for a family. With DSLRs starting to have both, it opens up a new scope of possibility for the photographer.

Talk a bit about what's in your camera bag and lighting kit.

I use a Canon 50D, Canon 50mm f1.8 lens, Canon 100mm macro lens f2.8, Canon kit lens

18-55mm (currently shopping around for the best wide angle lens to buy to replace this). I rent what I think I may need additionally for a wedding after studying the venue (usually an L-series wide angle). I currently also rent a Canon Speedlite when I have a wedding coming up, but plan to purchase one in 2011. I also hope to upgrade to the Canon 5D Mark II in 2011.

Do you have any parting words of wisdom to share?

Photography is a rewarding occupation and can take you on an even more rewarding path. In the time I've been photographing professionally, I have come to realize what an awesome creative outlet it is. The "side benefit" of getting to capture memories for people and their families is that those images will stay with a family for long after I'm gone. Knowing this couldn't be a more humbling and rewarding feeling. I strive to get even more creative and better with each shoot, each month, and now each year. It is my goal that a couple who hires me for their wedding will come back to me when they are pregnant, when the new baby arrives, and when that baby (or babies!) grows up. I want their lives to be a documentary, and I want to be the one given the opportunity to document it, just as I document my own family.

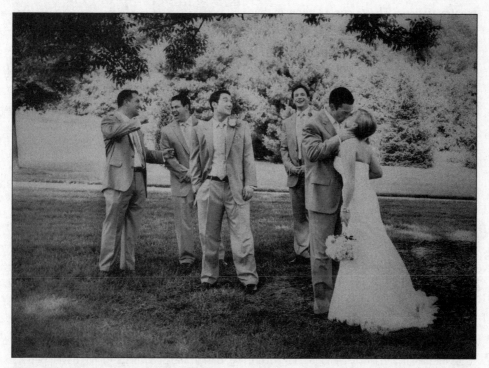

Marissa explains that this image just works in a sepia-toned, vintage style and doesn't have the same emotion when viewed as the true-to-color image.

BRAD CHANEY

Harley-Davidson's Chief Photographer

....

by Ric Deliantoni

Brad Chaney is the chief photographer for Harley-Davidson in Milwaukee. He's my mentor and one of best people I know in the business. He gave me my first job after graduation and has become a great friend and the guy I go to when I need advice, both in life and in photography. This interview is a rare opportunity as he is a very private person who has never loved the limelight. His guidance was invaluable when I opened my first studio, helping me through the maze of stuff I had no clue how to deal with, and he

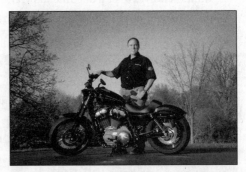

Brad is just as happy coaching his son's sports teams as he is in the studio.

has always been there to answer questions and share his sense of humor and sage insights. If we should seek to emulate someone, Brad would be at the top of my list.

Tell us about yourself and your career in photography. Have you always been a photographer or involved in photography?

I attended UC Santa Barbara and earned a B.A. in physical geography. After college I worked several part-time and summer jobs, and soon realized that a geography degree

Ric Deliantoni is professional photographer and director with thirty years of experience, with a focus on still-life and lifestyle imagery for advertising, design and publishing. He has developed a unique style that has been described as impressionistic and bold. Ric has also spent much of his career teaching and mentoring students of all levels to better themselves as artists.

wasn't in big demand in the job market. I evaluated my interests and returned to Santa Barbara, attending Brooks Institute of Photographic Arts and Science. I majored in illustration, focusing on advertising photography.

After photo school I was offered an internship at Walter Swarthout Studios in San Francisco. At the time this was one of the bigger advertising photography studios on the West Coast, and it was my intention to treat the eight-week "no pay" position as one last class before I set out to job hunt for real. However, I stayed at Swarthout Studios for thirteen years. I was hired as a photo assistant, which evolved into a staff photographer position. I eventually bought into the business, and we became Swarthout and Chaney Photography for several years. We shot still life and people, and worked both in the studio and on location. After that, I broke out on my own and opened a studio in San Francisco and kept that business for

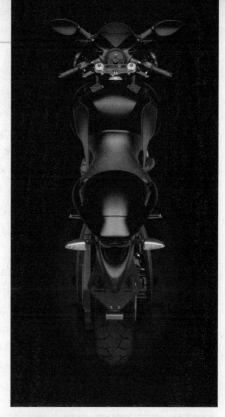

Brad describes his photography as "honest, clean and crisp with a bit of humor tossed in at times."

nine years until my wife and I moved our family to Wisconsin. Once we were settled in Milwaukee, I set up my studio. Then, three years later, I was offered and took the position of staff photographer at Harley-Davidson. I'm now in my tenth year at Harley.

How do you view the mentor vs. education question?

My training at Brooks is the only way I would have gotten the opportunity to work in Walter Swarthout's studio. He became my mentor and taught me the business. It was key that I went to school to learn the basics of my trade, and it was even more important that I worked for such a prolific and talented professional. As a young man, Walter assisted for Irving Penn in New York, and his whole approach was based on his experience working for one of the icons of advertising photography. I'm quite fortunate to have that heritage in my background.

What or who inspires you to create?

Early in my career I was primarily influenced by the big names in advertising photography, the New York guys like Avedon, Turner and Penn. I tried to impress myself by emulating their simplicity and graphic styles. I wanted to create clean, memorable images. My art director wife also inspired me, as I tried to impress her as well. We would talk for hours about style and trends and work on portfolio shots together. All the work was aimed at commercial advertising buyers, and I ended up trying to do too many styles for too many markets. I wanted to be good at everything, but I only got better when I settled down and worked in the area I was trained for, large format still life. Once I came to this realization, I built a food and product portfolio and have made a living for thirty years following this path.

Talk a bit about your creative process and how you approach your commercial work.

I still to this day use the studio lighting skills I learned from Walter Swarthout back in the '70s and '80s. I'm not sure how to describe my personal style other than possibly honest, clean and crisp with a bit of humor tossed in at times. I have never depended on postproduction effects or heavy image manipulation. It's always been clean, simple subjects and soft box lighting, with "in camera effects," using a mastery of craft, based on a lifetime of 8×10 studio still-life work.

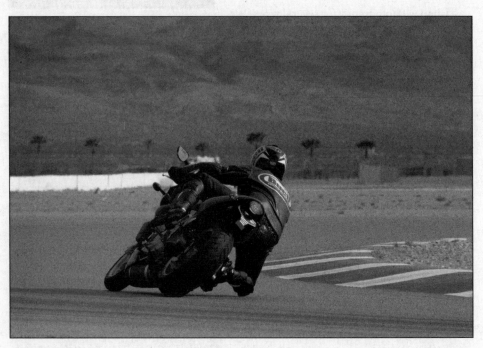

Brad describes himself as an "old film guy," but he now works in digital capture only and has come to respect it.

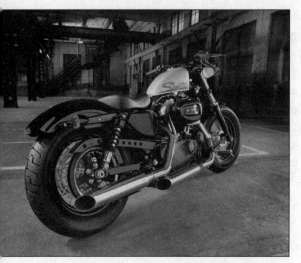

When shooting motorcycles for Harley-Davidson, Brad falls back on the studio lighting skills he developed in the 1970s and `80s.

I was hired at Harley-Davidson because they needed an experienced studio shooter who could handle the specific problems of their chrome, glass and metal subject matter. When I shoot the motorcycles I'm tested, and thankfully my years of lighting so many different jobs for such a wide variety of clients is always there to fall back on.

How did you present your work when you had the studios? Did you use an artist rep?

When I had my own business and photo studios for all those years, it was always color transparency originals mounted in handmade black mats. In my portfolio I showed the medium I delivered to clients: 8×10 and 4×5 chromes. I've never had a website.

When I took the job at Harley, I transitioned to digital within two years. If I were a freelance shooter today, of course I would have a website.

When I had my own studio I advertised in the big national promotional books like *American Showcase* and the *BlackBook*. I sent out endless printed promotional pieces. I had reps that carried the portfolio to client appointments.

Have you belonged to a professional association?

I attended my first American Photographic Artists (APA) meeting in San Francisco in 1980. Prior to that, the American Society of Media Photographers (ASMP) was the most popular source for business practice standards. Professional business practice standards for advertising photographers have been encouraged for over thirty years now, and there have been standardized estimate forms, model and property release forms, and change of work orders for that entire time. Usage rate guidelines for assignment photography have also been available for decades. The APA was huge in setting up these standards and helping to explain copyright laws. I've served on APA boards and have always believed in raising the quality of business awareness in our industry.

What are your thoughts on the digital age, and how has it affected you, your business, and the industry in whole?

I'm an old "film guy," and there will always be a part of me that dearly misses the craft and discipline of those days. I went into the digital age kicking and screaming. But, I've thrown my fit, and now I only work with digital capture and have grown to respect it. I also do not miss the uncertainty of waiting for my film to come out of the lab.

I do not by any means consider myself a strong technical shooter. I'm self-taught with regard to digital capture and know just enough to get the job done. Digital photography is complex, and it's my most pressing professional challenge. Fortunately, Harley-Davidson has provided training and equipment. For studio still shots of motorcycles and motorcycle related products, I use a digital Hasselblad with a Phase One capture back. For small camera event coverage or action shots of motorcycles, I use a Nikon D700. Studio strobes are Speedotrons and location strobes are Alien Bees. Practically everything else is Mathews, Gitzo, Pocket Wizard, and Calumet, and Apple computers, of course.

Do you have any parting words of wisdom you would like to share?

For several years I taught a photo class at the Academy of Art in San Francisco. Those students always asked about how to break into the advertising photography business. I told them there was no formula. For every successful studio there is an individual story. It's like all freelance careers in that there is always room for good talent. It's up to each person to recognize and take advantage of contacts, opportunities and responsibilities. Hard work means everything. Longevity and patience is essential.

I would point out that you need to get to a place where taking the picture is the easiest part of your day. That's the part a pro is trained and ready for. Taking the picture is the bonus we all work so hard to attain. The difficult part is getting the job to come in the door in the first place. That's where a freelancer earns his money … promoting, networking, hosting clients, estimating well, making sound business decisions, and staying fresh.

Now that I'm in a corporate environment, some of those tasks aren't so vital, but the images are still the fun part, and staying fresh is key because every day brings new people and projects.

CONSUMER PUBLICATIONS

//

Research is the key to selling any kind of photography. If you want your work to appear in a consumer publication, you're in luck. Magazines are the easiest market to research because they're available on newsstands and at the library and at your doctor's office and . . . you get the picture. So, do your homework. Before you send your query or cover letter and samples, and before you drop off your portfolio on the prescribed day, look at a copy of the magazine. The library is a good place to see sample copies because they're free, and there will be at least a year's worth of back issues right on the shelf.

Once you've read a few issues and feel confident your work is appropriate for a particular magazine, it's time to hit the keyboard. Most first submissions take the form of a query or cover letter and samples. So, what kind of letter do you send? That depends on what kind of work you're selling. If you simply want to let an editor know you're available for assignments or have a list of stock images appropriate for the publication, send a cover letter, a short business letter that introduces you and your work and tells the editor why your photos are right for the magazine. If you have an idea for a photo essay or plan to provide the text and photos for an article, you should send a query letter, a one- to one-and-a-half-page letter explaining your story or essay idea and why you're qualified to shoot it. You can send your query letter through the U.S. postal system, or you can e-mail it along with a few JPEG samples of your work. Check the listing for the magazine to see how they prefer to be contacted initially.

Both kinds of letters can include a brief list of publication credits and any other relevant information about yourself. Both also should include a sample of your work—a tearsheet, a slide or a printed piece, but never an original negative. Be sure your sample photo is of something the magazine might publish. It will be difficult for the editor of a biking magazine to appreciate your skills if you send a sample of your fashion work.

If your letter piques the interest of an editor, she may want to see more. If you live near the editorial office, you might be able to schedule an appointment to show your portfolio in person. Or you can inquire about the drop-off policy—many magazines have a day or two each week when artists can leave their portfolios for art directors to review. If you're in Wichita and the magazine is in New York, you'll have to send your portfolio through the mail. Consider using FedEx or UPS; both have tracking services that can locate your book if it gets waylaid on its journey. If the publication accepts images in a digital format (most do these days), you can send more samples of your work via e-mail or on a CD—whatever the publication prefers. Make sure you ask first. Better yet, if you have a website, you can provide the photo buyer with the link.

To make your search for markets easier, consult the Subject Index. The index is divided into topics, and markets are listed according to the types of photographs they want to see.

4-WHEEL ATV ACTION

25233 Anza Dr., Valencia CA 91355. (661)295-1910. Fax: (661)295-1278. E-mail: atv@hi-torque.com. Website: www.4wheelatv.com. Joe Kosch, editor-at-large (joeatvaction@yahoo.com); Tim Tolleson, editor (timt@hi-torque.com); Cody Hooper, associate editor. Estab. 1986. Circ. 65,000. Monthly. Emphasizes all-terrain vehicles and anything closely related to them.

NEEDS Buys 4 photos from freelancers/issue; 50 photos/year. Needs photos of adventure, events, hobbies, sports. "We are interested only in ATVs and UTVs and very closely related ride-on machines with more than two wheels—no cars, trucks, buggies or motorcycles. We're looking for scenic riding areas with ATVs or UTVs in every shot, plus unusual or great looking ATVs." Reviews photos with or without a manuscript. Model/property release preferred. Photo captions preferred; include location, names.

SPECS Uses 8×10 glossy color prints; 35mm transparencies. Accepts images in digital format. Send via ZIP, e-mail as JPEG files at 300 dpi.

MAKING CONTACT & TERMS Send query letter with photocopies or e-mail JPEGs. Does not keep samples on file; cannot return material. Responds only if interested; send nonreturnable samples. Simultaneous submissions and previously published work OK. Pays $50-100 for color cover; $15-25 for color inside. Credit line given. Buys one-time rights, first rights; negotiable.

TIPS "*4-Wheel ATV Action* offers a good opportunity for amateur but serious photographers to get a credit line in a national publication."

540 RIDER

TMB Publications, P.O. Box 1156, Lake Oswego OR 97035. (503)236-2524. Fax: (503)620-3800. E-mail: dano@gosportz.com. Website: www.540rider.com. **Contact:** Dan Kesterson, publisher. Estab. 2002. Circ. 100,000. Quarterly. Emphasizes action sports for youth: snowboarding, skateboarding and other board sports. Features high school teams, results, events, training, "and kids that just like to ride." Sample copy available with 8×10 SASE and 75¢ first-class postage. Photo guidelines available by e-mail request or online.

NEEDS Buys 10-20 photos from freelancers/issue; 40-80 photos/year. Needs photos of sports. Reviews photos with or without a manuscript. Model/property release preferred. Photo captions preferred.

SPECS Accepts images in digital format only. Send via CD as TIFF files at 300 dpi.

MAKING CONTACT & TERMS Send query via e-mail. Provide self-promotion piece to be kept on file for possible future assignments. Responds only if interested; send nonreturnable samples. Simultaneous submissions OK. Pays $25 minimum for b&w and color covers and inside photos. Pays on publication. Credit line given. Buys all rights.

TIPS "Send an e-mail ahead of time to discuss. Send us stuff that even you don't like, because we just might like it."

AAA MIDWEST TRAVELER

AAA Auto Club of Missouri, 12901 N. 40 Dr., St. Louis MO 63141. (314)523-7350 ext. 6301. Fax: (314)523-6982. E-mail: dreinhardt@aaamissouri.com. Website: www.aaa.com/traveler. **Contact:** Deborah Reinhardt, managing editor. Estab. 1901. Circ. 500,000. Bimonthly. Emphasizes travel and driving safety. Readers are members of the Auto Club of Missouri. Sample copy and photo guidelines free with SASE (use large manila envelope) or online.

NEEDS Buys 3-5 photos/issue. "We use four-color photos inside to accompany specific articles. Our magazine covers topics of general interest, historical (of Midwest regional interest), profile, travel, car care and driving tips. Our covers are full-color photos mainly corresponding to an article inside. Except for cover shots, we use freelance photos only to accompany specific articles." Model release preferred. Photo captions required.

SPECS Accepts images in digital format. Send via ZIP as TIFF files at minimum of 300 dpi.

MAKING CONTACT & TERMS Send query letter with résumé of credits and list of stock photo subjects. Does not keep samples on file; include SASE for return of material. Responds in 1 month. Simultaneous submissions and previously published work OK. Pays $400 for color cover; $75-200 for color inside. **Pays on acceptance.** Credit line given. Buys first, second and electronic rights.

TIPS "Send an 8½×11 SASE for sample copies and study the type of covers and inside work we use. Photo needs driven by an editorial calendar/schedule. Write to request a copy and include SASE."

$ ◐ ADIRONDACK LIFE

P.O. Box 410, Jay NY 12941-0410. (518)946-2191. Fax: (518)946-7461. E-mail: astoltie@adirondacklife.com. Website: www.adirondacklife.com. Kelly Hofschneider, photo editor. **Contact:** Annie Stoltie, editor. Estab. 1970. Circ. 50,000.

NEEDS Photos of environmental, landscapes/scenics, wildlife. Reviews photos with or without a manuscript.

SPECS Accepts color transparencies of any size; b&w prints no larger than 8×10. Digital images output to paper may be submitted.

MAKING CONTACT & TERMS Pays $400 maximum for color cover. Pays $150 maximum for b&w or color inside. Credit line given.

ADVENTURE CYCLIST

Adventure Cycling Assn., Box 8308, Missoula MT 59807. (406)721-1776, ext. 222. Fax: (406)721-8754. E-mail: magazine@adventurecycling.org. Website: www.adventurecycling.org. Greg Siple, art director. Estab. 1975. Circ. 43,000. Published 9 times/year. Emphasizes bicycle touring and travel.

NEEDS People riding bicycles, cultural, detail, architectural, people historic, vertical, horizontal. Identification of subjects, model releases required.

SPECS Reviews color transparencies and digital files.

TIPS Sample copy and photo guidelines free with 9×12 SAE and 4 first-class stamps. Guidelines also available on website at www.adventurecycling.org/mag/submissions.cfm.

ADVOCATE, PKA'S PUBLICATION

1881 Little Westkill Rd., Prattsville NY 12468. (518)299-3103. E-mail: advoad@localnet.com. Website: Advocatepka.weebly.com or www.facebook.com/pages/Advocate-PKAs-Publication/111826035499969. **Contact:** Patricia Keller, publisher. Estab. 1987. Circ. 12,000. Bimonthly. "PKA's *Advocate* is an advertiser-supported tabloid, publishing original, previously unpublished poetry, short stories, art and photos on many subjects. The publication has a strong horse orientation."

NEEDS Equine of strong interest but look at many different types and styles.

SPECS Accepts print photos in b&w and color, no larger than 8½×14.

○ AFRICAN AMERICAN GOLFER'S DIGEST

139 Fulton St., Suite 209, New York NY 10038. (212)571-6559. E-mail: debertcook@aol.com. Website: www.africanamericangolfersdigest.com. **Contact:** Debert Cook, managing editor. Estab. 2003. Circ. 20,000. Quarterly. Emphasizes golf lifestyle, health, travel destinations, golfer profiles, golf equipment reviews. Editorial content focuses on the "interests of our market demographic of African Americans and categories of high interest to them—historical, artistic, musical, educational (higher learning), automotive, sports, fashion, entertainment." Sample copy available for $4.50.

NEEDS Photos of golf, golfers, automobiles, entertainment, health/fitness/beauty, sports. Interested in lifestyle.

SPECS Accepts images in digital format. Send JPEG or GIF files, 4×6 at 300 dpi.

TIPS Reviews photos with or without a manuscript.

🌐 ◎ ◐ AFRICAN PILOT

Wavelengths 10 (Pty) Ltd., P.O. Box 30620, Kyalami 1684 South Africa. +27 11 466-8524. Fax: +27 11 466 8496. E-mail: Editor@Africanpilot.co.za. Website: www.Africanpilot.co.za. **Contact:** Athol Franz, editor. Estab. 2001. Circ. 7,000+ online; 6,000+ print. "*African Pilot* is southern Africa's premier monthly aviation magazine. It publishes a high-quality magazine that is well-known and respected within the aviation community of southern Africa. The magazine offers a number of benefits to readers and advertisers, including a weekly e-mail newsletter, annual service guide, pilot training supplement, executive wall calendar and an extensive website that mirrors the paper edition. The magazine offers clean layouts with outstanding photography and reflects editorial professionalism as well as a responsible approach to journalism. The magazine offers a complete and tailored promotional solution for all aviation businesses operating in the African region."

MAKING CONTACT & TERMS Send e-mail with samples. Samples are kept on file. Portfolio not required. Credit line given.

TIPS "*African Pilot* is an African aviation specific publication and therefore preference is given to articles, illustrations and photographs that have an African theme. The entire magazine is online in exactly the same format as the printed copy for the viewing of our style and quality. Contact me for specific details on our publishing requirements for work to be submitted. Articles together with a selection of about ten thumbnail pictures to be submitted so that a decision can be made on the relevance of the article and what pictures are available to be used to illustrate the article. If we decide to go ahead with the article, we will request high-resolution images from the portfolio already submitted as thumbnails."

⑨ ○ AFTER FIVE

P.O. Box 492905, Redding CA 96049. (530)275-1716. E-mail: editorial@after5online.com. Website: www. after5online.com. **Contact:** Craig Harrington, publisher. Estab. 1986. Circ. 32,000. Monthly tabloid. Emphasizes news, arts and entertainment.

NEEDS Buys 1-2 photos from freelancers/issue; 2-24 photos/year. Needs scenic photos of northern California. Also wants regional images of wildlife, rural, adventure, automobiles, entertainment, events, health/fitness, hobbies, humor, performing arts, sports, travel. Model release preferred. Photo captions preferred.

SPECS Accepts images in digital format. Send via e-mail, as TIFF, JPEG, EPS files at 150 dpi.

MAKING CONTACT & TERMS Provide résumé, business card, brochure, flier or tearsheets to be kept on file for possible future assignments. Responds in 2 weeks. Previously published work OK. Pays $60 for b&w or color cover; $20 for b&w or color inside. Pays on publication. Credit line given. Buys one-time rights.

TIPS "Need photographs of subjects north of Sacramento to Oregon-California border, plus southern Oregon. Query first."

AKRON LIFE

Baker Media Group, 90 S. Maple St., Akron OH 44302. (330)253-0056. Fax: (330)253-5868. E-mail: kmoorhouse@bakermediagroup.com; editor@bakermediagroup.com. Website: www.akronlife.com. Georgina Carson, editor. **Contact:** Kathy Moorhouse, art director. Estab. 2002. Circ. 15,000. "*Akron Life & Leisure* is a monthly lifestyles publication committed to providing information that enhances and enriches the experience of living in or visiting Akron and the surrounding region of Summit, Portage, Medina and Stark Counties. Each colorful, thoughtfully designed issue profiles interesting places, personalities

and events in the arts, sports, entertainment, business, politics and social scene. We cover issues important to the Greater Akron area and significant trends affecting the lives of those who live here."

NEEDS Essays, general interest, historical, how-to, humor, interview, photo feature, travel. Query with published clips.

⑨ ⓓ ALABAMA LIVING

Alabama Rural Electric Assn., P.O. Box 244014, Montgomery AL 36124. (334)215-2732. Fax: (334)215-2733. E-mail: dgates@areapower.com. Website: www. alabamaliving.com. Michael Cornelison, art director. **Contact:** Darryl Gates, editor. Estab. 1948. Circ. 400,000. Monthly. Covers topics of interest to rural and suburban Alabamians.

NEEDS Photos of Alabama specific scenes, particularly seasonal. Special photo needs include vertical scenic cover shots. Photo captions preferred; include place and date.

SPECS Accepts images in digital format. Send via CD, Zip as EPS, JPEG files at 400 dpi.

MAKING CONTACT & TERMS Send query letter with stock list or transparencies ("dupes are fine") in negative sleeves. Keeps samples on file; include SASE for return of material. Responds in 1 month. Simultaneous submissions and previously published work OK "if previously published out-of-state."

ALARM

Alarm Press, 53 W. Jackson Blvd., Suite 315, Chicago IL 60604. (312)341-1290. E-mail: info@alarmpress. com. Website: www.alarmpress.com. **Contact:** Art Director. Published 6 times/year. "It does one thing, and it does it very well: it publishes the best new music and art. From our headquarters in a small Chicago office, along with a cast of contributing writers spread across the country, we listen to thousands of CDs, view hundreds of gallery openings, and attend lectures and live concerts in order to present inspirational artists who are fueled by an honest and contagious obsession with their art."

MAKING CONTACT & TERMS Submit by e-mail with the subject line "ALARM Magazine Submissions." "Please send your work as part of the body of an e-mail; we cannot accept attachments." Alternatively, submissions may be sent by regular mail to Submissions Dept. "*ALARM* is not responsible for the return, loss of, or damage to unsolicited manuscripts, unsolicited art work, or any other unsolicited materials. Those submitting manuscripts, art work, or any other materials should not send originals." Art event listings should be e-mailed to artlistings@alarmpress.com.

🄢🄢🄢 ALASKA

301 Arctic Slope Ave., Suite 300, Anchorage AK 99518-3035. (907)272-6070. Fax: (907)258-5360. E-mail: tim.woody@alaskamagazine.com; andy.hall@alaska magazine.com. Website: www.alaskamagazine. com. **Contact:** Tim Woody, editor. Estab. 1935. Circ. 180,000. *Alaska Magazine* actively solicits photo-feature ideas having in-depth treatments of single subjects. The ideal photo essay would tell a story of a subject while having compelling content with vibrant color and contrast, and would include both the macro and the micro. Buys 500 photos/year, supplied mainly by freelancers. Photo captions required.

NEEDS Photographic submissions must be high-res digital images that are sharp and properly exposed. Please note: slides, transparencies and prints will not be accepted. Also, no digital composites, please. Historical b&w prints for which negatives are not available can be submitted in any size. All photo submissions will be carefully packaged before being returned. *Alaska* assumes no responsibility for unsolicited photographs.

SPECS Images made with a digital camera of 5 megapixels or better are acceptable. Images may be submitted on CD, DVD or flash drive. Photo manipulations of any kind must be clearly noted and defined. Digital composites will not be accepted.

MAKING CONTACT & TERMS Send carefully edited, captioned submission of 35mm, 2¼×2¼ or 4×5 transparencies. Include SASE for return of material. Also accepts images in digital format; check guidelines before submitting. Responds in 1 month. Send submissions to Alaska Magazine Photo Submissions.

♻ ALTERNATIVES JOURNAL

University of Waterloo, Faculty of Environmental Studies, Waterloo ON N2L 3G1, Canada. (519)888-4442. Fax: (519)746-0292. E-mail: editor@alternatives journal.ca. Website: www.alternativesjournal.ca. **Contact:** Nicola Ross, editor-in-chief; Marcia Ruby, production coordinator. Estab. 1971. Circ. 5,000. Bimonthly. Emphasizes environmental issues. Readers are activists, academics, professionals, policy makers.

Sample copy free with 9×12 SASE and 2 first-class stamps.

○ "*Alternatives* is a nonprofit organization whose contributors are all volunteer. We are able to give a small honorarium to artists and photographers. This in no way should reflect the value of the work. It symbolizes our thanks for their contribution to *Alternatives*."

NEEDS Buys 4-8 photos from freelancers/issue; 48-96 photos/year. Subjects vary widely depending on theme of each issue. "Strong action photos or topical environmental issues are needed—preferably with people. We also print animal shots. We look for positive solutions to problems and prefer to illustrate the solutions rather than the problems. Freelancers need a good background understanding of environmental issues." Check website for upcoming themes. Reviews photos with or without a manuscript. Photo captions preferred; include who, when, where, environmental significance of shot.

SPECS Accepts images in digital format. Send via CD, e-mail as JPEG files at 300 dpi. "E-mail your web address/electronic portfolio." Simultaneous submissions and previously published work OK. Pays on publication. Buys one-time rights; negotiable.

TIPS "You need to know the significance of your subject before you can powerfully present its visual perspective."

🄢 ○ AMC OUTDOORS

Appalachian Mountain Club, 5 Joy St., Boston MA 02108. (617)523-0655. Fax: (617)523-0722. E-mail: amcpublications@outdoors.org. Website: www.out doors.org. Estab. 1908. Circ. 70,000. Published 6 times/year. "Our 94,000 members do more than just read about the outdoors; they get out and play. More than just another regional magazine, *AMC Outdoors* provides information on hundreds of AMC-sponsored adventure and education programs. With award-winning editorial, advice on Northeast destinations and trip planning, recommendations and reviews of the latest gear, AMC chapter news and more, *AMC Outdoors* is the primary source of information about the Northeast outdoors for most of our members." Photo guidelines available at www.outdoors.org/publications/outdoors/contributor-guidelines.cfm.

NEEDS Buys 6-12 photos from freelancers/issue; 75 photos/year. Needs photos of adventure, environmental, landscapes/scenics, wildlife, health/fitness/beauty, sports, travel. Other specific photo needs: people, including older adults (50+ years), being active outdoors. "We seek powerful outdoor images from the Northeast U.S., or non-location-specific action shots (hiking, skiing, snowshoeing, paddling, cycling, etc.). Our needs vary from issue to issue, based on content, but are often tied to the season."

SPECS Uses color prints or 35mm slides. Prefers images in digital format. Send via CD or e-mail as TIFF, JPEG files at 300 dpi. Low-res OK for review of digital photos.

MAKING CONTACT & TERMS Previously published work OK. Pays $300 (negotiable) for color cover; $50-100 (negotiable) for color inside. Pays on publication. Credit line given.

TIPS "We do not run images from other parts of the U.S. or from outside the U.S. unless the landscape background is 'generic.' Most of our readers live and play in the Northeast, are intimately familiar with the region in which they live, and enjoy seeing the area and activities reflected in living color in the pages of their magazines."

⊕⊕ AMERICAN ANGLER

P.O. Box 810, Arlington VA 05250. (706)823-3538. E-mail: steve.walburn@morris.com. Website: www.americanangler.com. Wayne Knight, art director (wayne.knight@morris.com). **Contact:** Steve Walburn, editor. Estab. 1976. Circ. 60,000. Bimonthly. Covers fly fishing. "More how-to than where-to, but we need shots from all over. More domestic than foreign. More trout, salmon and steelhead than bass or saltwater." Sample copy available for $6 and 9×12 SASE with Priority Mail Flat Rate Envelope with $4.05. Photo guidelines available on website. Buys 10 photos from freelancers/issue; 60 photos/year. "Most of our photos come from writers of articles."

NEEDS Photos that convey "the spirit, essence and exhilaration of fly fishing. Always need good fish-behavioral stuff—spawning, rising, riseforms, etc."

SPECS Prefers slides or digital images via CD or e-mail at 300 dpi; must be very sharp with good contrast.

MAKING CONTACT & TERMS "We prefer to work from e-mailed queries whenever possible, and you should send an e-mail outlining your article before submitting a manuscript. A query can save you the frustration and disappointment of making a futile submission, and it allows us to fine-tune an idea to suit our editorial needs. We read and respond to all queries, but expect at least a six-week wait for that response. Be patient, please. But squeak gently if you don't hear from us within 6-8 weeks. Send query letter with samples, brochure, stock photo list, tearsheets. Provide résumé, business card, self-promotion piece or tearsheets to be kept on file for possible future assignments. Portfolio review by prior arrangement. Query deadline: 6-10 months prior to cover date. Submission deadline: 5 months prior to cover date. Responds in 6 weeks to queries; 1 month to samples. Simultaneous submissions and previously published work OK—"but only for inside 'editorial' use—not for covers, prominent feature openers, etc."

TIPS "We don't want the same old shots: grip and grin, angler casting, angler with bent rod, fish being released. Sure, we need them, but there's a lot more to fly fishing. Don't send us photos that look exactly like the ones you see in most fishing magazines. Think like a storyteller. Let me know where the photos were taken, at what time of year, and anything else that's pertinent to a fly fisher."

AMERICAN ARCHAEOLOGY

The Archaeological Conservancy, 5301 Central Ave. NE, #902, Albuquerque NM 87108-1517. (505)266-9668. Fax: (505)266-0311. E-mail: tacmag@nm.net. Website: www.americanarchaeology.org. **Contact:** Michael Bawaya, editor; Vicki Singer, art director. Estab. 1997. Circ. 35,000. Quarterly. "We're a popular archaeology magazine. Our readers are very interested in this science. Our features cover important digs, prominent archaeologists, and most any aspect of the science. We only cover North America." Sample copies available.

SPECS Uses 35mm, 2¼×2¼, 4×5 transparencies. Accepts images in digital format.

MAKING CONTACT & TERMS Send via CD at 300 dpi or higher. Send query letter with résumé, photocopies and tearsheets. Provide résumé, business card, self-promotion piece to be kept on file for possible future assignments. Responds in 2 months to queries. Previously published work OK.

TIPS "Read our magazine. Include accurate and detailed captions."

⊕ AMERICAN FITNESS

15250 Ventura Blvd., Suite 200, Sherman Oaks CA 91403. (800)446-2322, ext. 200. E-mail: american fitness@afaa.com. Website: www.afaa.com. **Contact:** Meg Jordan, editor. Estab. 1983. Circ. 42,900. Buys 20-40 photos from freelancers/issue; 120-240 photos/year. Assigns 90% of work. Payment is issued post-publication. Send query letter with samples, list of stock photo subjects; include SASE for return of material. Responds in 2 weeks. Simultaneous submissions and previously published work OK. Pays $10-35 for b&w or color photo; $50 for text/photo package. Pays 4-6 weeks after publication. Credit line given. Buys first North American serial rights.

NEEDS Action photography of runners, aerobic classes, swimmers, bicyclists, speedwalkers, in-liners, volleyball players, etc. Also needs food choices, babies/children/teens, celebrities, couples, multicultural, families, parents, senior fitness, people enjoying recreation, cities/urban, rural, adventure, entertainment, events, hobbies, humor, performing arts, sports, travel, medicine, product shots/still life, science. Interested in alternative process, fashion/glamour, seasonal. Model release required.

SPECS Uses b&w prints; 35mm, 2¼×2¼ transparencies. Cover: Color slides, transparencies (2" preferred size) or high-res 300 dpi, TIFF, or PDF files of at least 8¾×11¼. Interior/Editorial: Color slides, transparencies or high-res 300 dpi, TIFF, PDF, or JPEG files; glossy print.

TIPS "Over-40 sports leagues, youth fitness, family fitness and senior fitness are hot trends. Wants high-quality, professional photos of people participating in high-energy activities—anything that conveys the essence of a fabulous fitness lifestyle. Also accepts highly stylized studio shots to run as lead artwork for feature stories. Since we don't have a big art budget, freelancers usually submit spin-off projects from their larger photo assignments."

🟢🟢 🔵 AMERICAN FORESTS

734 15th St. NW, 8th Floor, Washington D.C. 20005. (202)737-1944, ext. 203. Fax: (202)737-2457. E-mail: info@amfor.org. Website: www.americanforests. org/productsandpubs/magazine. Estab. 1895. Circ. 25,000. Quarterly publication of American Forests. Emphasizes use, enjoyment and management of forests and other natural resources. Readers are "people from all walks of life, from rural to urban settings, whose main common denominator is an abiding love for trees, forests or forestry." Sample copy and photo

guidelines free with magazine-sized envelope and 7 first-class stamps.

NEEDS Buys 32 photos from freelancers/issue; 128 photos/year. Needs woods scenics, wildlife, woods use/management, and urban forestry shots. "Also shots of national champion trees; contact editor for details." Photo captions required; include who, what, where, when and why.

SPECS Uses 35mm or larger. Prefers images in digital format. Send link to viewing platform, or send via CD or FTP as TIFF files at 300 dpi.

MAKING CONTACT & TERMS "We regularly review portfolios from photographers to look for potential images for upcoming issues or to find new photographers to work with." Send query letter with résumé of credits. Include SASE for return of material. Responds in 4 months. Pays $500 for color cover; $90-200 for color inside; $75-100 for b&w inside; $250-2,000 for text/photo package. **Pays on acceptance.** Credit line given. Buys one-time rights and rights for use in online version of magazine.

TIPS "Please identify species in tree shots if possible."

🟢 🟠 THE AMERICAN GARDENER

7931 E. Boulevard Dr., Alexandria VA 22308-1300. (703)768-5700. Fax: (703)768-7533. E-mail: editor@ ahs.org; myee@ahs.org. Website: www.ahs.org. **Contact:** Mary Yee, art director. Estab. 1922. Circ. 20,000. Bimonthly. "This is the official publication of the American Horticultural Society (AHS), a national, nonprofit, membership organization for gardeners, founded in 1922." Sample copy available for $5. Photo guidelines free with SASE or via e-mail request. Uses 35-50 photos/issue. Reviews photos with or without a manuscript. "Lists of plant species for which photographs are needed are sent out to a selected list of photographers approximately 10 weeks before publication. We currently have about 20 photographers on that list. Most of them have photo libraries representing thousands of species. Before adding photographers to our list, we need to determine both the quality and quantity of their collections. Therefore, we ask all photographers to submit both some samples of their work, either as digital files or slides (these will be returned immediately if sent with a SASE) and a list indicating the types and number of plants in their collection. After reviewing both, we may decide to add the photographer to our photo call for a trial period of 6 issues (1 year)."

NEEDS Photos of plants, gardens, landscapes.

SPECS Prefers color, 35mm slides and larger transparencies or high-res JPEG or TIFF files with a minimum size of 5×7 at 300 dpi. Digital images should be submitted on a CD or posted to an online photo gallery.

MAKING CONTACT & TERMS Send query letter with samples, stock list via mail or e-mail. Will contact for portfolio review if interested. Does not keep samples on file; include SASE for return of material.

⑤⑤ AMERICAN HUNTER

NRA, 11250 Waples Mill Rd., Fairfax VA 22030-9400. (703)267-1336. Fax: (703)267-3971. E-mail: publications@nrahq.org; americanhunter@nrahq.org, lcromwell@nrahq.org. Website: www.americanhunter.org. **Contact:** J. Scott Olmsted, editor-in-chief. Circ. 1,000,000. Monthly magazine of the National Rifle Association. "*American Hunter* contains articles dealing with various sport hunting and related activities both at home and abroad. With the encouragement of the sport as a prime game management tool, emphasis is on technique, sportsmanship and safety. In each issue hunting equipment and firearms are evaluated, legislative happenings affecting the sport are reported, lore and legend are retold and the business of the Association is recorded in the Official Journal section." Uses wildlife shots and hunting action scenes. Seeks general hunting stories on North American and African game.

SPECS Send via CD as TIFF, GIF, or RAW files at 300 dpi. Vertical format required for cover.

MAKING CONTACT & TERMS Sample copy and photo guidelines free with 9×12 SASE. Send material by mail for consideration; include SASE for return of material.

TIPS "Most successful photographers maintain a file in our offices so editors can select photos to fill holes when needed. We keep files on most North American big game, small game, waterfowl, upland birds, and some exotics. We need live hunting shots as well as profiles and portraits in all settings. Many times there is not enough time to call photographers for special needs. This practice puts your name in front of the editors more often and increases the chances of sales."

⑤ AMERICAN MOTORCYCLIST

13515 Yarmouth Dr., Pickerington OH 43147. (614)856-1900. E-mail: grassroots@ama-cycle.org. Website: www.american-motorcyclist.com. **Contact:** Bill Wood, director of communications; Grant Parsons, managing editor. Estab. 1947. Circ. 260,000. Monthly magazine of the American Motorcyclist Association. Emphasizes people involved in, and events dealing with, all aspects of motorcycling. Readers are "enthusiastic motorcyclists, investing considerable time in road riding or all aspects of the sport."

NEEDS "The cover shot is tied in with the main story or theme of that issue and generally needs to be submitted with accompanying manuscript. Show us experience in motorcycling photography, and suggest your ability to meet our editorial needs and complement our philosophy."

SPECS Prefers images in digital format. Send via CD as TIFF, GIF, JPEG files at 300 dpi.

MAKING CONTACT & TERMS Send query letter with samples to be kept on file for possible future assignments. Responds in 3 weeks.

⑤ ⑨ ◐ AMERICAN TURF MONTHLY

747 Middle Neck Rd., Great Neck NY 11024. (516)773-4075. Fax: (516)773-2944. E-mail: jcorbett@americanturf.com; editor@americanturf.com. Website: www.americanturf.com. **Contact:** Joe Girardi, editor; James Corbett, editor-in-chief. Estab. 1946. Circ. 30,000. Monthly. Covers Thoroughbred horse racing, especially aimed at horseplayers and handicappers.

NEEDS Buys 10 photos from freelancers/issue; 120 photos/year. Needs photos of celebrities, racing action, horses, owners, trainers, jockeys. Reviews photos with or without a manuscript. Photo captions preferred; include who, what, where.

SPECS Uses glossy color prints. Accepts images in digital format. Send via CD, floppy disk, ZIP as TIFF, JPEG files at 300 dpi.

MAKING CONTACT & TERMS Send query letter with CD, prints. Provide business card to be kept on file for possible future assignments. Responds only if interested; send nonreturnable samples.

TIPS "Like horses and horse racing."

ANCHOR NEWS

75 Maritime Dr., Manitowoc WI 54220. (920)684-0218; (866)724-2356. Fax: (920)684-0219. E-mail:

museum@wisconsinmaritime.org. Website: www. wisconsinmaritime.org. Norma Bishop, exec. director. **Contact:** curator. Circ. 1,100. Quarterly publication of the Wisconsin Maritime Museum. Emphasizes Great Lakes maritime history. Readers include learned and lay readers interested in Great Lakes history. Sample copy available with 9×12 SASE and $3 postage. Photo guidelines free with SASE.

NEEDS Uses 8-10 photos/issue; infrequently supplied by freelance photographers. Needs historic/nostalgic; personal experience; Great Lakes environmental issues, including aquatic invasive species and other topics of interest to environmental educators; and general interest articles on Great Lakes maritime topics. How-to and technical pieces and model ships and ship-building are OK. Special needs include historic photography or photos that show current historic trends of the Great Lakes; photos of waterfront development, bulk carriers, sailors, recreational boating, etc. Model release required. Photo captions required.

SPECS Accepts images in digital format. Send via CD, e-mail as JPEG files at 300 dpi minimum.

MAKING CONTACT & TERMS Send 4×5 or 8×10 glossy b&w prints by mail for consideration; include SASE for return of material. Simultaneous submissions and previously published work OK. Pays in copies on publication. Credit line given. Buys first North American serial rights.

TIPS "Besides historic photographs, I see a growing interest in underwater archaeology, especially on the Great Lakes, and underwater exploration—also on the Great Lakes. Sharp, clear photographs are a must. Our publication deals with a wide variety of subjects; however, we take a historical slant with our publication. Therefore, photos should be related to a historical topic in some respect. Also, there are current trends in Great Lakes shipping. A query is most helpful. This will let the photographer know exactly what we are looking for and will help save a lot of time and wasted effort."

ANIMAL TRAILS MAGAZINE

2660 Petersborough St., Herndon VA 20171. E-mail: animaltrails@yahoo.com. Website: animaltrails magazine.doodlekit.com. **Contact:** Shannon Bridget Murphy. Quarterly. "*Animal Trails* is an anchor for memories that are made as a result of experiences with animals. Through writing, photography and illustrations animals are given a voice."

NEEDS Photos of environmental, landscapes/scenics, wildlife, architecture, cities/urban, gardening, interiors/decorating, pets, religious, rural, performing arts, agriculture, product shots/still life—as related to animals. Interested in alternative process, avant garde, documentary, fashion/glamour, fine art, historical/vintage, seasonal. Reviews photos with or without a manuscript. Model/property release preferred.

SPECS Uses glossy or matte color and b&w prints.

MAKING CONTACT & TERMS Send query letter via e-mail or online form at website. Provide résumé, business card, self-promotion piece to be kept on file for possible future assignments. "A photograph or two is requested but not required. Illustrations and artwork are also accepted." Responds within 1 month to queries; 1 week to portfolios. Simultaneous submissions and previously published work OK. **Pays on acceptance.** Credit line given. Buys one-time rights, first rights; negotiable.

APERTURE

547 W. 27th St., 4th Floor, New York NY 10001. (212)505-5555. E-mail: editorial@aperture.org. Website: www.aperture.org. **Contact:** Michael Famigehtti, managing editor. Circ. 30,000. Quarterly. Emphasizes fine-art and contemporary photography, as well as social reportage. Readers include photographers, artists, collectors, writers.

NEEDS Uses about 60 photos/issue; biannual portfolio review. Model release required. Photo captions required.

MAKING CONTACT & TERMS Submit portfolio for review in January and July; include SASE for return of material. Responds in 2 months. No payment. Credit line given.

TIPS "We are a nonprofit foundation. Do not send portfolios outside of January and July."

APOGEE PHOTO

11121 Wolf Way, Westminster CO 80031. (904)619-2010 (Florida contact). E-mail: meier@qadas.com. Website: apogeephoto.com. **Contact:** Marla Meier, editorial director. A free online monthly magazine designed to inform, educate and entertain photographers of all ages and levels.

NEEDS Digital photography, photo technique articles, product reviews, business and marketing, nature and wildlife photography, photographer profiles/interviews and all other photography-related articles.

TIPS "Please do a search by subject before submitting your article to see if your article covers a new subject or brings a new perspective on a particular subject or theme."

🔵 ⏺ APPALACHIAN TRAIL JOURNEYS

P.O. Box 807, Harpers Ferry WV 25425. (304)535-6331. Fax: (304)535-2667. E-mail: jfolgar@appalachiantrail. org. Website: www.appalachiantrail.org. Estab. 2005. Circ. 38,000. Bimonthly publication of the Appalachian Trail Conservancy. Uses only photos related to the Appalachian Trail. Readers are conservationists, hikers. Photo guidelines available on website.

NEEDS Buys 4-5 photos from freelancers/issue in addition to 2- to 4-page "Vistas" spread each issue; 50-60 photos/year. Most frequent need is for candids of hikers enjoying the trail. Photo captions and release required.

SPECS Accepts high-res digital images (300 dpi). Uses 35mm transparencies.

MAKING CONTACT & TERMS Send query letter with ideas by mail, e-mail. Duplicate slides preferred over originals for query. Responds in 3 weeks. Simultaneous submissions and previously published work OK. Pays on publication. Pays $300 for cover; variable for inside. Credit line given. Rights negotiable.

APPALOOSA JOURNAL

2720 West Pullman Rd., Moscow ID 83843. (208)882-5578. Fax: (208)882-8150. E-mail: editor@ appaloosajournal.com; drice@appaloosajournal.com; artdirector@appaloosajournal.com;. Website: www. appaloosajournal.com. Laura Vander Hoek, art director (artdirector@appaloosajournal.com). **Contact:** Diane Rice; Dana Russell, editor. Estab. 1946. Circ. 25,000. Monthly association magazine. "*Appaloosa Journal* is the official publication of the Appaloosa Horse Club. We are dedicated to educating and entertaining Appaloosa enthusiasts from around the world." Readers are Appaloosa owners, breeders and trainers, child through adult. Complimentary sample copies available. Photo guidelines free with SASE or online. Buys 3 photos from freelancers/issue; 36 photos/year. "The Appaloosa Horse Club is a not-for-profit organization. Serious inquiries within specified budget only." In photographer's samples, wants to see "high-quality color photos of world-class, characteristic (coat patterned) Appaloosa horses in appealing, picturesque outdoor environments."

NEEDS Photos for cover, and to accompany features and articles. Specifically wants photographs of high-quality Appaloosa horses, especially in winter scenes. Model release required. Photo captions required.

SPECS Uses glossy color prints; 35mm transparencies; digital images 300 dpi at 5×7 or larger, depending on use. Send query letter with résumé, slides, prints, or e-mail as PDF or GIF. Keeps samples on file. Responds only if interested; send nonreturnable samples. Simultaneous submissions OK.

MAKING CONTACT & TERMS Send a letter introducing yourself and briefly explaining your work. If you have inflexible preset fees, be upfront and include that information.

TIPS "Be patient. We are located at the headquarters; although an image might not work for the magazine, it might work for other printed materials. Work has a better chance of being used if allowed to keep on file. If work must be returned promptly, please specify. Otherwise, we will keep it for other departments' consideration."

🔵 ⏺ AQUARIUM FISH INTERNATIONAL

Bowtie, Inc., P.O. Box 6050, Mission Viejo CA 92690-6050. (949)855-8822. Fax: (949)855-3045. E-mail: aquariumfish@bowtieinc.com. Website: www.fishchannel.com. Clay Jackson, editor. **Contact:** Patricia Knight, managing editor. Estab. 1988. Monthly. Covers fish and other aquatic pets. 90% freelance written. "Our focus is on beginning and intermediate fish keeping; we also run one advanced saltwater article per issue. Most of our articles concentrate on general fish and aquarium care, but we will also consider other types of articles that may be helpful to those in the fishkeeping hobby. Freshwater and saltwater tanks, and ponds are covered."

　🔵 "For beginning to advanced fish hobbyists: freshwater and saltwater. We also have an annual pond magazine."

NEEDS Freshwater and saltwater species and aquariums. Also needs ponds.

SPECS See photo guidelines before submitting digital images. Accepts TIFF/JPEG formats at 300 dpi. Also accepts 35mm transparencies. Responds within 6 months. Portfolio not required. Credit line given.

MAKING CONTACT & TERMS Send query letter or e-mail with SASE.

ARCHAEOLOGY

Archaeological Institute of America, 36-36 33rd St., Long Island NY 11106. (718)472-3050. Fax: (718)472-3051. E-mail: cvalentino@archaeology.org. E-mail: editorial@archaeology.org. Website: www.archaeology.org. **Contact:** Editor-in-chief. Estab. 1948. Circ. 750,000. *ARCHAEOLOGY* combines worldwide archaeological findings with photography, specially rendered maps, drawings, and charts. Covers current excavations and recent discoveries, and includes personality profiles, technology updates, adventure, travel and studies of ancient cultures

● ARIZONA WILDLIFE VIEWS

2221 W. Greenway Rd., Phoenix AZ 85053. (800)777-0015. E-mail: awv@azgfd.gov. Website: www.azgfd.gov/magazine. **Contact:** Julie Hammonds, assoc. editor. Circ. 22,000. Bimonthly official magazine of the Arizona Game & Fish Department. "*Arizona Wildlife Views* is a general interest magazine about Arizona wildlife, wildlife management and outdoor recreation (specifically hunting, fishing, wildlife watching, boating and off-highway vehicle recreation). We publish material that conforms to the mission and policies of the Arizona Game and Fish Department. Topics include habitat issues and historical articles about wildlife and wildlife management."

NEEDS Photos of sports, environmental, landscapes/scenics, wildlife in Arizona. Reviews photos with or without a manuscript. Model release required only if the subject matter is of a delicate or sensitive nature. Captions required.

SPECS "We prefer and primarily use professional-quality 35mm and larger color transparencies. Submitted transparencies must be numbered, identified by artist, and an inventory list must accompany each shipment. The highest resolution digital images are occasionally used." Send JPEG or GIF files. See new information for photographers online at website.

MAKING CONTACT & TERMS Before contacting, please read the appropriate submission guidelines: www.azgfd.gov/i_e/pubs/contributorguidelines.shtml. "Half of the written content of *Arizona Wildlife Views* magazine is generated by freelance writers and photographers. Payment is made upon publication. We prefer queries by e-mail. Sample copies are available on request. The magazine does not accept responsibility for any submissions. It is the artist's responsibility to insure his work." Pays $400 for front cover; $350 for back cover; $250 for inside half-page or larger; $150 for inside smaller than half-page. Pays following publication. Credit line given. Buys one-time rights.

TIPS "Unsolicited material without proper identification will be returned immediately."

$ ASTRONOMY

Kalmbach Publishing, 21027 Crossroads Circle, P.O. Box 1612, Waukesha WI 53187-1612. (800)533-6644. Fax: (262)796-1615. Website: www.astronomy.com. Carole Ross, art director. Estab. 1973. Circ. 122,000. Monthly. Emphasizes astronomy, science and hobby. Median reader: 52 years old, 86% male. Submission guidelines free with SASE or via website. Buys 70 photos from freelancers/issue; 840 photos/year.

NEEDS Photos of astronomical images.

SPECS "If you are submitting digital images, please send TIFF or JPEG files to us via our FTP site. Send duplicate images by mail for consideration." Keeps samples on file. Responds in 1 month. Pays on publication. Credit line given.

$$ ◎ ◐ ATLANTA HOMES & LIFESTYLES

1100 Johnson Ferry Rd., NE, Suite 595, Atlanta GA 30342. (404)252-6670. Fax: (404)252-6673. E-mail: gchristman@nci.com. Website: www.atlantahomesmag.com. Clinton Ross Smith, editor. **Contact:** Susan Uedelhofen, art director. Estab. 1983. Circ. 30,000. Monthly. Covers residential design (home and garden); food, wine and entertaining; people, lifestyle subjects in the metro Atlanta area. Sample copy available for $4.95.

NEEDS Photos of homes (interior/exterior), people, decorating ideas, products, gardens. Model/property release required. Photo captions preferred.

SPECS Accepts images in digital format only.

MAKING CONTACT & TERMS Contact creative director to review portfolio. Provide résumé, business card, brochure, flyer or tearsheets to be kept on file for possible future assignments. Responds in 2 months. Simultaneous submissions and previously published work OK. Pays $150-750/job. **Pays on acceptance**. Credit line given. Buys one-time rights.

○ AUTO RESTORER

Bowtie, Inc., 3 Burroughs, Irvine CA 92618. (949)855-8822, ext. 412. Fax: (949)855-3045. E-mail: tkade@fancypubs.com; editors@mmminc.org. Website:

www.autorestorermagazine.com. **Contact:** Ted Kade, editor. Estab. 1989. Circ. 60,000. Offers no additional payment for photos accepted with ms. Interview the owner of a restored car. Present advice to others on how to do a similar restoration. Seek advice from experts. Go light on history and nonspecific details. Make it something that the magazine regularly uses. Do automotive how-tos.

NEEDS Photos of auto restoration projects and restored cars.

SPECS Prefers images in high-res digital format. Send via CD at 240 dpi with minimum width of 5 inches. Uses transparencies, mostly 35mm, 2¼×2¼.

MAKING CONTACT & TERMS Submit inquiry and portfolio for review. Provide résumé, business card, brochure, flier or tearsheets to be kept on file for possible future assignments. Responds in 1 month. Simultaneous submissions OK.

AVIATION HISTORY

Weider History Group, 19300 Promenade Dr., Leesburg VA 20176. E-mail: aviationhistory@weiderhistory group.com. Website: www.thehistorynet.com. Estab. 1990. Circ. 45,000. "It aims to make aeronautical history not only factually accurate and complete, but also enjoyable to a varied subscriber and newsstand audience."

MAKING CONTACT & TERMS Reviews contact sheets, negatives, transparencies. Identification of subjects required. Buys one time rights.

● BABYTALK

Bonnier Corporation, 460 N. Orlando Ave., Suite 200, Winter Park FL 32789. (407)628-4802. Website: www. babytalk.com. **Contact:** Nancy Smith, art director. Estab. 1937. Monthly. Non-newstand circulation of 2 million; distributed via subscription and through physicians' offices and retail outlets. Readers are new mothers and pregnant women. Sample copies available upon request.

MAKING CONTACT & TERMS Send query letter and printed samples; include URL for your website. After introductory mailing, send follow-up postcard every 3 months. Samples are kept on file. Responds only if interested. Portfolios not required. **Pays on acceptance.** Buys one-time rights, reprint rights, all rights, electronic rights. Finds freelancers through agents, artists' submissions, word of mouth and sourcebooks.

TIPS "Please, no calls or e-mails. Postcards or mailers are best. We don't look at portfolios unless we request them. Websites listed on mailers are great."

BACKHOME

Wordsworth Communications, Inc., P.O. Box 70, Hendersonville NC 28793. (828)696-3838. Fax: (828)696-0700. E-mail: backhome@ioa.com. Website: www.backhomemagazine.com. Estab. 1990. Circ. 42,000. Bimonthly. "*BackHome* encourages readers to take more control over their lives by doing more for themselves: productive organic gardening; building and repairing their homes; utilizing renewable energy systems; raising crops and livestock; building furniture; toys and games and other projects; creative cooking. *BackHome* promotes respect for family activities, community programs, and the environment."

SPECS Reviews color prints, 35mm slides, JPEG photo attachments at 300 dpi

MAKING CONTACT & TERMS Reviews color prints, 35mm slides, JPEG photo attachments at 300 dpi. Identification of subjects required. Buys one-time rights.

⊜⊜ ❶ BACKPACKER MAGAZINE

2520 55th St., Suite 210, Boulder CO 80301. E-mail: jvandenoever@backpacker.com. Website: www.back packer.com. **Contact:** Julia Vandenoever, photo editor. Published 9 times/year. Readers are male and female, ages 35-45. Photo guidelines available on website (www.backpacker.com/guidelines) or free with SASE marked Attn: Guidelines.

NEEDS Buys 80 photos from freelancers/issue; 720 photos/year. Needs transparencies of people backpacking, camping, landscapes/scenics. Reviews photos with or without a manuscript. Model/property release required.

SPECS Accepts images in digital format. Send via CD, ZIP, e-mail as JPEG files at 72 dpi for review (300 dpi needed to print).

MAKING CONTACT & TERMS Send query letter with résumé of credits, photo list and example of work to be kept on file. Sometimes considers simultaneous submissions and previously published work. Pays $500-1,000 for color cover; $100-600 for color inside. Pays on publication. Credit line given. Rights negotiable.

BASEBALL

2660 Petersborough St., Herndon VA 20171. E-mail: shannonaswriter@yahoo.com. **Contact:** Shannon Bridget Murphy. Quarterly. Covers baseball. Photo guidelines available by e-mail request.

NEEDS Photos of baseball scenes featuring children and teens; photos of celebrities, couples, multicultural, families, parents, environmental, landscapes/scenics, wildlife, agriculture—as related to the sport of baseball. Interested in alternative process, avant garde, documentary, fine art, historical/vintage, seasonal. Reviews photos with or without a manuscript.

SPECS Uses glossy or matte color and b&w prints.

MAKING CONTACT & TERMS Send query letter via e-mail. "If possible, please do not include photographs in files if they are sent through e-mail. A disc with your photographs is acceptable. If you plan to send a disc, photographs or portfolio, please send an e-mail stating this." Provide résumé, business card, self-promotion piece to be kept on file for possible future assignments. "Photographs sent with CDs are requested but not required. Write to request guidelines for artwork and illustrations." Responds within 1 month to queries; 1 week to portfolios. Simultaneous submissions and previously published work OK. **Pays on acceptance.** Credit line given. Buys one-time, first rights; negotiable.

BC OUTDOORS HUNTING AND SHOOTING

OP Publishing Ltd, 200 West Esplanade, Suite 500, Vancouver BC V7M 1A4, Canada. (604)998-3310. Fax: (604)998-3320. E-mail: info@oppublishing.com. E-mail: mmitchell@outdoorgroupmedia.com; production@outdoorgroupmedia.com. Website: www.bcoutdoorsmagazine.com. Paul Bielicki, art director/production; Shannon Swanson, art director (sswanson@oppublishing.com). **Contact:** Mike Mitchell, editor. Estab. 1945. Circ. 30,000.

NEEDS Buys 30-35 photos from freelancers/issue; 60-70 photos/year. Prefers images in digital format. Send via e-mail at 300 dpi. Send by mail for consideration actual 5×7 or 8×10 color prints; 35mm, 2¼×2¼, 4×5 or 8×10 color transparencies; color contact sheet. If color negative, send jumbo prints, then negatives only on request. E-mail high-res electronic images. Send query letter with list of stock photo subjects. Include SASE or IRC. Pays in Canadian currency. Simultaneous submissions not acceptable if competitor. Edi-

tor determines payments. Pays on publication. Credit line given. Buys one-time rights for inside shots; for covers, "we retain the right for subsequent promotional use."

BC OUTDOORS SPORT FISHING

1080 Howe St., Suite 900, Vancouver BC V6Z 2T1, Canada. (604)606-4644. E-mail: production@outdoor groupmedia.com. Website: www.bcosportfishing. com. **Contact:** Paul Bielicky; Chelsea Whitteker, managing editor. Estab. 1945. Circ. 35,000. Published 7 times/year. Emphasizes fishing, both fresh and salt water. Sample copy available for $4.95 Canadian.

NEEDS Buys 30-35 photos from freelancers/issue; 180-210 photos/year. "Fishing (in our territory) is a big need—people in the act of catching or releasing fish. Family oriented. By far, most photos accompany manuscripts. We are always on the lookout for good covers—fishing, wildlife, recreational activities, people in the outdoors—of British Columbia, vertical and square format. Photos with manuscripts must, of course, illustrate the story. There should, as far as possible, be something happening. Photos generally dominate lead spread of each story. They are used in everything from double-page bleeds to thumbnails. Column needs basically supplied in-house." Model/property release preferred. Photo captions or at least full identification required.

SPECS Prefers images in digital format. Send via e-mail at 300 dpi.

MAKING CONTACT & TERMS *No unsolicited submissions.* Send by mail for consideration actual 5×7 or 8×10 color prints; 35mm, 2¼×2¼, 4×5 or 8×10 color transparencies; color contact sheet. If color negative, send jumbo prints, then negatives only on request. E-mail high-resolution electronic images. Send query letter with list of stock photo subjects. Include SASE or IRC. Pays in Canadian currency. Simultaneous submissions not acceptable if competitor. Editor determines payments. Pays on publication. Credit line given. Buys one-time rights for inside shots; for covers, "we retain the right for subsequent promotional use."

THE BEAR DELUXE MAGAZINE

Orlo, 810 SE Belmont #5, Portland OR 97214. (503)242-1047. E-mail: bear@orlo.org. Website: www.orlo.org. Kristin Rogers Brown, art director. **Contact:** Tom Webb, editor-in-chief. Estab. 1993. Circ. 19,000. "*The Bear Deluxe Magazine* is a national independent environmental arts magazine publishing significant works of reporting, creative nonfiction, literature, visual art and design. Based in the Pacific Northwest, it reaches across cultural and political divides to engage readers on vital issues effecting the environment. Published twice per year, *The Bear Deluxe* includes a wider array and a higher-percentage of visual art work and design than many other publications. Artwork is included both as editorial support and as stand alone or independent art. It has included nationally recognized artists as well as emerging artists. As with any publication, artists are encouraged to review a sample copy for a clearer understanding of the magazine's approach. Unsolicited submissions and samples are accepted and encouraged. *The Bear Deluxe* has been recognized for both its editorial and design excellence."

MAKING CONTACT & TERMS "Send us your current work samples and a brief cover letter outlining your availability and turn-around time estimates. Let us know if you'd like to be considered for editorial illustration/photography, or only independent art. Send slides (not more than one sheet), prints, high-quality photocopies, or high-resolution scans (TIFF files please) on a ZIP drive or CD. If you submit via e-mail, send PDF format files only, or a url address for us to visit. (Note on e-mail submissions and url suggestions, we prefer hard-copy work samples but will consider electronic submissions and links. We cannot, however, guarantee a response to electronic submissions.) Send SASE for the return of materials. No faxes. Assumes no liability for submitted work samples."

○ BELLINGHAM REVIEW

Mail Stop 9053, Western Washington University, Bellingham WA 98225. (360)650-4863. E-mail: bhreview@wwu.edu. Website: www.wwu.edu/bhreview. Brenda Miller, editor-in-chief. **Contact:** Christopher Carlson, managing editor. Estab. 1977. Circ. 1,500. Annual nonprofit magazine. "Literature of palpable quality: poems stories and essays so beguiling they invite us to touch their essence. The *Bellingham Review* hungers for a kind of writing that nudges the limits of form, or executes traditional forms exquisitely.

NEEDS Babies/children/teens, couples, multicultural, families, parents, senior citizens, architecture, cities/urban, gardening, pets, rural, disasters, environment, landscapes, wildlife, adventure, event.

MAKING CONTACT & TERMS Send an e-mail with sample photographs. Accepts JPEG samples at 72 dpi. Samples not kept on file. Portfolio not required. Pays on publication.

THE BINNACLE

University of Maine at Machias, 116 O'Brien Ave., Machias ME 04654. E-mail: ummbinnacle@maine.edu. Website: www.umm.maine.edu/binnacle. Estab. 1957. Circ. 300. Semiannual alternative paper format covering general arts. "We publish an alternative format journal of literary and visual art. The Binnacle accepts submissions from the students, faculty, and staff of the University of Maine at Machias and from writers and artists anywhere in the world. Please submit photography and other works of visual art, both color and black and white."

SPECS Files in JPEG, GIF, or PSD are preferable; BMP or TIFF are normally fine.

MAKING CONTACT & TERMS "We prefer submissions of all types in electronic form. Digital images should be submitted via postal mail on a CD or posted on a website for our viewing. Please do not send these in attachments. Please include SASE if you would like the media returned." Buys one-time rights.

⊕ $ ◐ BIRD WATCHER'S DIGEST

P.O. Box 110, Marietta OH 45750. (740)373-5285; (800)879-2473. Fax: (740)373-8443. E-mail: editor@birdwatchersdigest.com. E-mail: submissions@birdwatchersdigest.com. Website: www.birdwatchersdigest.com. **Contact:** Bill Thompson III, editor. Estab. 1978. Circ. 125,000. Bimonthly; digest size. Emphasizes birds and bird watchers. "We use images to augment our magazine's content, so we often look for non-traditional shots of birds, including images capturing unusual behavior or settings. For our species profiles of birds we look for more traditional images: sharp, well-composed portraits of wild birds in their natural habitat." Readers are bird watchers/birders (backyard and field, veterans and novices). Sample copy available for $3.99. Photo guidelines available online.

NEEDS Buys 25-35 photos from freelancers/issue; 150-210 photos/year. "If you are just starting out, we suggest an initial submission of 20 or fewer images so that we can judge the quality of your work." Needs photos of North American species.

SPECS Accepts high-res (300 dpi) digital images via CD or DVD. "We appreciate quality thumbnails to accompany digital images. Our preferred formats for digital images are JPEG or TIFF. Images taken with digital cameras should be created using the highest-quality JPEG setting (usually marked 'fine' or 'high') on your camera. TIFF images should be saved with LZW compression. Please make all images Mac compatible."

MAKING CONTACT & TERMS Send query letter with list of stock photo subjects, samples, SASE to Editorial Dept. Responds in 2 months. *Work previously published in other bird publications should not be submitted.* Pays $75 for color inside. Credit line given. Buys one-time rights.

TIPS "Query with slides or digital images on a CD to be considered for photograph want-list. Send a sample of no more than 20 images for consideration. Sample will be reviewed and responded to in 8 weeks."

BIRD WATCHING

Bauer Active, Media House, Lynch Wood, Peterborough PE2 6EA, Wales. 01733 468 201. Fax: (44)(733)465-376. E-mail: trevor.ward@bauermedia.co.uk. Website: www.birdwatching.co.uk. **Contact:** Dominic Mitchell, editor. Estab. 1986. Circ. 22,000. Monthly hobby magazine for bird watchers. Sample copy free with SASE (first-class postage/IRC).

NEEDS Photos of "wild birds photographed in the wild, mainly in action or showing interesting aspects of behavior. Also stunning landscape pictures in birding areas and images of people with binoculars, telescopes, etc." Also considers travel, hobby and gardening shots related to bird watching. Reviews photos with or without a manuscript. Photo captions preferred.

SPECS Uses 35mm, 2¼×2¼ transparencies. Accepts images in digital format. Send via CD, e-mail as TIFF, EPS, JPEG files at 200 dpi.

MAKING CONTACT & TERMS Provide résumé, business card, self-promotion piece or tearsheets to be kept on file for possible future assignments. Returns unsolicited material if SASE enclosed. Responds in 1 month. Simultaneous submissions OK. Pays £70-100 for color cover; £15-120 for color inside. Pays on publication. Buys one-time rights.

TIPS "All photos are held on file here in the office once they have been selected. They are returned when used or a request for their return is made. Make sure all slides are well labeled: bird, name, date, place taken, photographer's name and address. Send sample of images to show full range of subject and photographic techniques."

BLACKFLASH

P.O. Box 7381, Station Main, Saskatoon SK S7K 4J3, Canada. (306)374-5115. E-mail: editor@blackflash.ca. Website: www.blackflash.ca. **Contact:** John Shelling, managing editor. Estab. 1983. Circ. 1,700. Canadian journal of photo-based and electronic arts published 3 times/year.

NEEDS Lens-based and new media contemporary fine art and electronic arts practitioners. Reviews photos with or without a manuscript.

SPECS Accepts images in digital format. Send via CD, Zip, e-mail as TIFF, EPS, BMP, JPEG files at 300 dpi.

MAKING CONTACT & TERMS Send query letter with résumé, digital images. Does not keep samples on file; will return material with SASE only. Simultaneous submissions OK. Pays when copy has been proofed and edited. Credit line given. Buys one-time rights.

TIPS "We need alternative and interesting contemporary photography. Understand our mandate and read our magazine prior to submitting."

BLUE RIDGE COUNTRY

Leisure Publishing, 3424 Brambleton Ave., Roanoke VA 24018. (540)989-6138. Fax: (540)989-7603. E-mail: krheinheimer@leisurepublishing.com. Website: www.blueridgecountry.com. **Contact:** Kurt Rheinheimer, editor. Estab. 1988. Circ. 425,000. Bimonthly. Emphasizes outdoor scenics, recreation, travel destinations in 9-state Blue Ridge Mountain region. Photo guidelines available for SASE or on website.

"We're looking for feature photography and cover images, and we're connecting covers to the stories inside the magazine, so we're not just looking for general mountain scenics. We're looking for scenes with and without people, for outdoor recreation from soft to extreme. We can especially use more images from Kentucky, South Carolina and Alabama as well as our other coverage states: Virginia, West Virginia, Maryland, Georgia, Tennessee and North Carolina. For each issue's travel destinations and weekend getaways, we are looking for scenics, town shots, people, outdoor recreation, historical attractions, etc. All should be shot within the season they are to appear (green, autumn, winter)."

NEEDS Photos of travel, scenics and wildlife. Seeking more scenics with people in them. Buys 20-40 photos from freelancers/issue; 100-300 photos/year. Model release preferred. Photo captions required.

SPECS Uses 35mm, 2¼×2¼, 4×5 transparencies. Accepts images in digital format. Send via CD, e-mail, or FTP (contact editor for information) at 300 dpi; low-res images OK for initial review, but accepted images must be high-res.

MAKING CONTACT & TERMS Send query letter with list of stock photo subjects, samples with caption info and SASE. Responds in 2 months.

🌀 BOAT INTERNATIONAL USA

Boat International Media, 41-47 Hartfield Rd., London SW19 3RQ, United Kingdom. (954)522-2628. Fax: (954)522-2240. E-mail: marilyn.mower@boat internationalmedia.com. Website: www.boat international.com. **Contact:** Marilyn Mower, US editor-in-chief; Richard Taranto, art director. Estab. 1995. Circ. 55,000. "Luxury yachting publication aimed at the world's discerning yachting audience. We provide the most exclusive access to superyachts over 100 feet worldwide."

💲 🕊 ○ BOROUGH NEWS

2941 N. Front St., Harrisburg PA 17110. (717)236-9526. Fax: (717)236-8164. E-mail: caccurti@boroughs.org. Website: www.boroughs.org. **Contact:** Courtney Accurti, editor. Estab. 2001. Circ. 6,000. Monthly magazine of Pennsylvania State Association of Boroughs. Emphasizes borough government in Pennsylvania. Readers are officials in municipalities in Pennsylvania. Sample copy free with 9×12 SASE and 5 first-class stamps.

NEEDS Number of photos/issue varies with inside copy. Needs "color photos of scenics (Pennsylvania), local government activities, Pennsylvania landmarks, ecology—for cover photos only; authors of articles supply their own photos." Special photo needs include street and road maintenance work; wetlands scenic. Model release preferred. Photo captions preferred; include identification of place and subject.

SPECS Uses color prints and 35mm transparencies. Accepts images in digital format. Send via CD, ZIP, e-mail as TIFF, EPS, JPEG, PSD files at 300 dpi.

MAKING CONTACT & TERMS Send query letter with résumé of credits and list of stock photo subjects. Send unsolicited photos by mail for consideration; include SASE for return of material. Provide résumé, business card, brochure, flier or tearsheets to be kept on file for possible future assignments. Responds in 1 month. Pays $30 for color. Pays on publication. Buys one-time rights.

TIPS "We're looking for a variety of scenic shots of Pennsylvania for front covers of the magazine, especially special issues such as engineering, street/road maintenance, downtown revitalization, technology, tourism and historic preservation, public safety and economic development, and recreation."

BOWHUNTER

InterMedia Outdoors, 6385 Flank Dr., Suite 800, Harrisburg PA 17112. (717)695-8085. Fax: (717)545-2527. E-mail: dwight.schuh@imoutdoors.com; curt. wells@imoutdoors.com. Website: www.bowhunter. com. Mark Olszewski, art director; Dwight Schuh, editor-at-large; Jeff Waring, publisher. **Contact:** Curt Wells, editor. Estab. 1971. Circ. 126,480. Published 9 times/year. Emphasizes bow and arrow hunting. Sample copy available for $2. Submission guidelines free with SASE.

NEEDS Buys 40-50 photos/year. Wants scenic (showing bowhunting) and wildlife (big and small game of North America) photos. "No cute animal shots or poses. We publish informative, entertaining bowhunting adventure, how-to and where-to-go articles."

SPECS Digital submissions should be 300 dpi in RAW, JPEG, or TIFF format; CMYK preferred, provided on CD or DVD named in a simple and logical system with accompanying contact sheet.

MAKING CONTACT & TERMS Send query letter with samples, SASE. Responds in 2 weeks to queries; 6 weeks to samples. Reviews high-res digital images. Reviews photos with or without a manuscript. Offers $50-300/photo. Pays $50-125 for b&w inside; $75-300 for color inside; $600 for cover, "occasionally more if photo warrants it." **Pays on acceptance.** Captions required. Credit line given. Buys one-time publication rights.

TIPS "Know bowhunting and/or wildlife and study several copies of our magazine before submitting any material. We're looking for better quality, and we're using more color on inside pages. Most purchased photos are of big game animals. Hunting scenes are second. In b&w we look for sharp, realistic light, good contrast. Color must be sharp; early or late light is best. We avoid anything that looks staged; we want natural settings, quality animals. Send only your best, and, if at all possible, let us hold those we indicate interest in. Very little is taken on assignment; most comes from our files or is part of the manuscript package. If your work is in our files, it will probably be used."

BOYS' LIFE

(972)580-2366. Fax: (972)580-2079. Website: www.boyslife.org. J.D. Owen, editor-in-chief, Michael Goldman, managing editor; Aaron Derr, senior writer. Estab. 1911. Circ. 1.1 million. Photo guidelines free with SASE. Boy Scouts of America Magazine Division also publishes *Scouting* magazine. "Most photographs are from specific assignments that freelance photojournalists shoot for *Boys' Life*. Interested in all photographers, but do not send unsolicited images."

MAKING CONTACT & TERMS Send query letter with list of credits. Pays $500 base editorial day rate against placement fees, plus expenses. **Pays on acceptance.** Buys one-time rights.

TIPS "Learn and read our publications before submitting anything."

🍁 ◯ BRIARPATCH

2138 McIntyre St., Regina SK S4P 2R7, Canada. (306)525-2949. E-mail: editor@briarpatchmagazine.com. Website: www.briarpatchmagazine.com. **Contact:** Dave Mitchell, editor. Estab. 1973. Circ. 3,000. Published 6 times/year. Emphasizes Canadian and international politics, labor, environment, women, peace. Readers are socially progressive and politically engaged. Sample copy available for $6 plus shipping.

NEEDS Buys 5-20 photos from freelancers/issue; 30-120 photos/year. Photos of Canadian and international politics, labor, environment, women, peace and personalities. Model/property release preferred. Photo captions preferred; include names in photo.

SPECS Minimum 300 dpi color or b&w prints.

MAKING CONTACT & TERMS Send query letter with samples or link to online portfolio. Do not send slides. Provide résumé, business card, brochure, flyer, or tearsheets to be kept on file for possible future assignments. Include SASE for return of material. Responds in 1 month. Simultaneous submissions and previously published work OK. Pays $20 per published photo and $100 for cover. Credit line given. Buys one-time rights. Submission guidelines available online.

$ ◐ BRIDAL GUIDES MAGAZINE

2660 Petersborough St., Herndon VA 20171. E-mail: BridalGuides@yahoo.com. **Contact:** Shannon Bridget Murphy. Estab. 1998. Quarterly. Photo guidelines available by e-mail request.

NEEDS Buys 12 photos from freelancers/issue; 48-72 photos/year. Photos of babies/children/teens, celebrities, couples, multicultural, families, parents, cities/urban, environmental, landscapes/scenics, wildlife, architecture, gardening, interiors/decorating, pets, religious, rural, adventure, entertainment, events, food/drink, health/fitness, performing arts, travel, agriculture—as related to weddings. Interested in alternative process, avant garde, documentary, fashion/glamour, fine art, historical/vintage, seasonal. Also wants photos of weddings "and those who make it all happen, both behind and in front of the scene." Reviews photos with or without a manuscript. Model/property release preferred.

SPECS Uses glossy or matte color and b&w prints.

MAKING CONTACT & TERMS Send query letter via e-mail. "If possible, please do not include photographs in files if they are sent through e-mail. A disc with your photographs is acceptable. If you plan to send a disc, photographs or portfolio, please send an e-mail stating this." Provide résumé, business card or self-promotion piece to be kept on file for possible future assignments. A photograph or 2 sent with CD is requested but not required. Illustrations and artwork are also accepted. Write to request guidelines for artwork and illustrations. Responds within 1 month to queries; 1 week to portfolios. Simultaneous submissions and previously published work OK. **Pays on acceptance.** Credit line given. Buys one-time rights, first rights; negotiable.

THE BRIDGE BULLETIN

American Contract Bridge League, 6575 Windchase Dr., Horn Lake MS 38637-1523. (662)253-3156. Fax: (662)253-3187. E-mail: editor@acbl.org. E-mail: brent.manley@acbl.org. Website: www.acbl.org. Paul Linxwiler, managing editor. **Contact:** Brent Manley, editor. Estab. 1938. Circ. 155,000. Monthly association magazine for tournament/duplicate bridge players. Sample copies available. Buys 6-10 photos/year.

SPECS Prefers high-res digital images, color only.

MAKING CONTACT & TERMS Query by phone. Responds only if interested; send nonreturnable samples. Previously published work OK. Credit line given. Photos must relate to bridge. Call first.

🌀 BURKE'S BACKYARD

Locked Bag 1000, Artarmon NSW 1570, Australia. (61)(2)9414-4800. Fax: (61)(2)9414-4850. E-mail: magazine@burkesbackyard.com.au; photos@burkes backyard.com.au. Website: www.burkesbackyard.com.au. Circ. 60,000. Monthly. Provides trusted, informative ideas and information for Australian homes and gardens.

SPECS The ideal format is 300 dpi (high-res) or a JPEG saved to "best quality."

🟢🟢 BUSINESS NH MAGAZINE

55 S. Commercial St., Manchester NH 03101. (603)626-6354. Fax: (603)626-6359. E-mail: hcopeland@ BusinessNHmagazine.com. Website: www.millyard communications.com. **Contact:** Heidi Copeland, publisher. Estab. 1983. Circ. 15,000. Monthly. Covers business, politics, and people of New Hampshire. Readers are male and female top management, average age 45. Sample copy free with 9×12 SASE and 5 first-class stamps. Offers internships for photographers. Looks for "people in environment shots, interesting lighting, lots of creative interpretations, a definite personal style."

NEEDS Photos of couples, families, rural, entertainment, food/drink, health/fitness, performing arts, travel, business concepts, industry, science, technology/computers.

SPECS Uses 3-6 photos/issue. Accepts images in digital format.

MAKING CONTACT & TERMS Send via CD, ZIP as TIFF, JPEG files at 300 dpi. Arrange personal interview to show portfolio. Provide résumé, business card, brochure, flyer or tearsheets to be kept on file for possible future assignments. Responds in 3 weeks.

TIPS "If you're just starting out and want excellent statewide exposure to the leading executives in New Hampshire, you should talk to us. Send letter and samples, then arrange for a portfolio showing."

🟢🟢 CALLIOPE

Cobblestone Publishing Co., 30 Grove St., Suite C, Peterborough NH 03458-1454. (603)924-7209. Fax: (603)924-7380. E-mail: cfbakeriii@meganet.net. Website: www.cobblestonepub.com. Lou Waryncia, editorial director; Ann Dillon, art director. **Contact:** Rosalie Baker and Charles Baker, co-editors. Estab. 1990. Circ. 13,000. Published 9 times/year (May/June, July/August, November/December). Emphasis on non-United States history. Readers are children ages 8-14. "To be considered for publication, photographs must relate to a specific theme. Writers are encouraged to submit available photos with their query or article." Sample copies available for $5.95 with 9×12 or larger SASE and 5 first-class stamps. Photo guidelines available on website or free with SASE.

NEEDS Contemporary shots of historical locations, buildings, artifacts, historical reenactments and costumes.

SPECS Uses b&w and color prints; 35mm transparencies.

MAKING CONTACT & TERMS If you have photographs pertaining to any upcoming theme, please contact the editor by mail or fax, or send them with your query. You may also send images on speculation. Send query letter with stock photo list. Provide résumé, business card, brochure, flyer or tearsheets to be kept on file for possible future assignments. Responds within 5 months. Simultaneous submissions and previously published work OK.

TIPS "Given our young audience, we like to have pictures that include people, both young and old. Pictures must be dynamic to make history appealing. Submissions must relate to themes in each issue."

🔵🟢🔵 CANADA LUTHERAN

302-393 Portage Ave., Winnipeg MB R3B 3H6, Canada. (204)984-9172. Fax: (204)984-9185. E-mail: tgallop@elcic.ca. Website: www.elcic.ca/clweb. **Contact:** Trina Gallop, editorial director. Estab. 1986. Circ. 8,000. Monthly publication of Evangelical Lutheran Church in Canada. Emphasizes faith/religious content, Lutheran denomination. Readers are members of the Evangelical Lutheran Church in Canada. Sample copy available for $5 Canadian (includes postage).

NEEDS Buys 1-2 photos from freelancers/issue; 12-24 photos/year. Photos of people in worship, at work/play, diversity, advocacy, youth/young people, etc. Canadian sources preferred.

SPECS Accepts images in digital format. Send via CD, e-mail as JPEG at 300 dpi minimum.

MAKING CONTACT & TERMS Send sample prints and photo CDs by mail (include SASE for return of material) or send low-re images by e-mail. Pays $20-

75 for a photo, depending on how it is used. Covers claim the greatest return: $40-75. Feature photos next: $25-50. News photos: $20-30. Prices are in Canadian dollars. Pays on publication. Credit line given. Buys one-time rights.

TIPS "Give us many photos that show your range. We prefer to keep them on file for at least a year. We have a short-term turnaround and turn to our file on a monthly basis to illustrate articles or cover concepts. Changing technology speeds up the turnaround time considerably when assessing images, yet forces publishers to think farther in advance to be able to achieve promised cost savings. U.S. photographers—send via U.S. mail. We sometimes get wrongly charged duty at the border when shipping via couriers."

CANADIAN HOMES & COTTAGES

The In-Home Show, Ltd., 2650 Meadowvale Blvd., Unit 4, Mississauga ON L5N 6M5, Canada. (905)567-1440. Fax: (905)567-1442. E-mail: jnaisby@ homesandcottages.com. E-mail: oliver@homesand cottages.com. Website: www.homesandcottages.com. **Contact:** Oliver Johnson, managing editor. Estab. 1987. Circ. 92,340.

NEEDS Photos of landscapes/scenics, architecture, interiors/decorating. Does not keep samples on file; cannot return material.

MAKING CONTACT & TERMS Photo guidelines free with SASE. Responds only if interested; send nonreturnable samples.

THE CANADIAN ORGANIC GROWER

1205 Route 915, New Horton NB E4H 1W1, Canada. E-mail: janet@cog.ca; office@cog.ca; publications@ cog.ca. Website: www.cog.ca/magazine.htm. **Contact:** Janet Wallace, managing editor. Estab. 1975. Circ. 4,000. Quarterly. For organic gardeners, farmers and consumers in Canada. Depends entirely on freelancers. Deadlines: October 15 for winter issue, January 15 for spring, April 15 for summer, and July 15 for fall. Please see website for more guidelines: www. cog.ca/our-services/magazine/guide-for-magazine-contributors/

NEEDS Photos of gardening, rural, agriculture, organic gardening and farming in Canada.

SPECS Accepts images in digital format. Send JPEG or GIF files. With digital photos, we need high-res shots. A good rule of thumb is to ensure that the file

size of the photo is at least 800KB (preferably 1-3 MB) in size.

TIPS "Try to get pictures of people actively working in their gardens or field. Please indicate who or what is in each photo. List groups of people from left to right and from back row to front row. Try to capture the same person, place or thing from more than one angle as you take pictures. Tell us who the photographer is for the list of credits."

CANADIAN RODEO NEWS

2116 27th Ave., NE, #223, Calgary AB T2E 7A6, Canada. (403)250-7292. Fax: (403)250-6926. E-mail: editor@rodeocanada.com. Website: www.rodeo canada.com. **Contact:** Darell Hartlen, editor. Estab. 1964. Circ. 4,000. Monthly tabloid. Promotes professional rodeo in Canada. Readers are male and female rodeo contestants and fans of all ages.

NEEDS Photos of professional rodeo action or profiles.

SPECS Uses color and b&w prints. Accepts images in digital format. Send via CD or e-mail as JPEG or TIFF files at 300 dpi.

MAKING CONTACT & TERMS Send low-res unsolicited photos by e-mail for consideration. Call to confirm if photos are usable. Keeps samples on file. Simultaneous submissions and previously published work OK. Pays $25 for color cover; $15 for b&w or color inside. Pays on publication. Credit line given. Rights negotiable.

TIPS "Photos must be from or pertain to professional rodeo in Canada. Phone to confirm if subject/material is suitable before submitting. *CRN* is very specific in subject."

CANADIAN YACHTING

800-2 St. Clair Ave., E., Toronto ON M4T 2T5, Canada. (416)258-9948. Fax: (416)513-0348. E-mail: eakerr@ kerrwil.com. Website: www.canadianyachting.ca. **Contact:** Elizabeth A. Kerr. Estab. 1976. Circ. 31,000. Bimonthly. Emphasizes sailing (and powerboats). Readers are mostly male, highly educated, high income, well read. Sample copy free upon request.

NEEDS Buys 28 photos from freelancers/issue; 168 photos/year. Needs photos of all sailing/boating-related (keelboats, dinghies, racing, cruising, etc.). Model/property release preferred. Photo captions preferred.

MAKING CONTACT & TERMS Submit portfolio for review or query with SASE, stock photo list and transparencies. Responds in 1 month. Simultaneous submissions and previously published work OK. Pays $150-350 for color cover; $30-70 for b&w or color inside. Pays on publication. Buys one-time rights.

☺ ⑨⑨ ◑ CANOE & KAYAK

Source Interlink Media, 236 Avenida Fabricante, Suite 201, San Clemente CA 92672. (425)827-6363. E-mail: jeff@canoekayak.com; joe@canoekayak.com; dave@canoekayak.com. Website: www.canoekayak.com. Joe Carberry, managing editor; Dave Shively, associate editor. **Contact:** Jeff Moag, editor-in-chief. Estab. 1972. Circ. 70,000. Bimonthly, published 6 times a year in March, May, June, July, August, December. Packed with destination reviews and features a different region of North America, paddling techniques, photography from seasoned canoeists and expert reviews of paddle and camping gear. It is the world's largest paddle sports publication. Emphasizes a variety of paddle sports, as well as how-to material and articles about equipment. For upscale canoe and kayak enthusiasts at all levels of ability. Also publishes special projects. Sample copy free with 9×12 SASE.

NEEDS Buys 25 photos from freelancers/issue; 150 photos/year. Photos of canoeing, kayaking, ocean touring, canoe sailing, fishing when compatible to the main activity, canoe camping but not rafting. No photos showing disregard for the environment, be it river or land; no photos showing gasoline-powered, multi-hp engines; no photos showing unskilled persons taking extraordinary risks to life, etc. Accompanying manuscripts for "editorial coverage striving for balanced representation of all interests in today's paddling activity. Those interests include paddling adventures (both close to home and far away), camping, fishing, flatwater, whitewater, ocean kayaking, poling, sailing, outdoor photography, how-to projects, instruction and historical perspective. Regular columns feature paddling techniques, conservation topics, safety, interviews, equipment reviews, book/movie reviews, new products and letters from readers." Photos only occasionally purchased without accompanying manuscript. Model release preferred "when potential for litigation." Property release required. Photo captions preferred.

SPECS Uses 5×7, 8×10 glossy b&w prints; 35mm, 2¼×2¼, 4×5 transparencies; color transparencies for cover; vertical format preferred. Accepts images in digital format. Send via CD, ZIP as TIFF, EPS, JPEG files at 300 dpi.

MAKING CONTACT & TERMS Include SASE for return of material. Responds in 1 month. Simultaneous submissions and previously published work OK, in noncompeting publications. Pays $500-700 for color cover; $75-200 for b&w inside; $75-350 for color inside. Captions, identification of subjects, model releases required. Pays on publication. Credit line given. Buys one-time rights, first serial rights and exclusive rights.

TIPS "We have a highly specialized subject, and readers don't want just any photo of the activity. We're particularly interested in photos showing paddlers' *faces*; the faces of people having a good time. We're after anything that highlights the paddling activity as a lifestyle and the urge to be outdoors." All photos should be "as natural as possible with authentic subjects. We receive a lot of submissions from photographers to whom canoeing and kayaking are quite novel activities. These photos are often clichéd and uninteresting. So consider the quality of your work carefully before submission if you are not familiar with the sport. We are always in search of fresh ways of looking at our sport. All paddlers must be wearing life vests/PFDs."

⑨ ◑ CAPE COD LIFE

13 Steeple St., Suite 204, P.O. Box 1439, Mashpee MA 02649. (508)419-7381. E-mail: sdewey@capecodlife.com. Website: www.capecodlife.com. **Contact:** Susan Dewey, managing editor. Estab. 1979. Circ. 45,000. Bimonthly. Emphasizes Cape Cod lifestyle. Also publishes *Cape Cod & Islands Home*. Readers are 55% female, 45% male, upper income, second home, vacation homeowners. Sample copy available for $4.95. Photo guidelines free with SASE.

NEEDS Buys 30 photos from freelancers/issue; 180 photos/year. Needs "photos of Cape and Island scenes, southshore and south coast of Massachusetts, people, places; general interest of this area." Subjects include boating and beaches, celebrities, families, environmental, landscapes/scenics, wildlife, architecture, gardening, interiors/decorating, rural, adventure, events, travel. Interested in fine art, historical/vintage, seasonal. Reviews photos with or without a manuscript. Model release required; property release preferred. Photo captions required; include location.

SPECS Uses 35mm, 2¼×2¼, 4×5 transparencies. Accepts images in digital format. Send via e-mail or FTP as TIFF files at 300 dpi.

MAKING CONTACT & TERMS Submit portfolio for review. "Photographers should not drop by unannounced. We prefer photographers to mail portfolio, then follow up with a phone call 1 to 2 weeks later." Send unsolicited photos by mail for consideration. Keeps samples on file. Simultaneous submissions and previously published work OK. Pays $225 for color cover; $25-175 for b&w or color inside, depending on size. Pays 30 days after publication. Credit line given. Buys one-time rights; reprint rights for *Cape Cod Life* reprints; negotiable.

TIPS "Write for photo guidelines. Mail photos to the attention of our art director. Photographers who do not have images of Cape Cod, Martha's Vineyard, Nantucket or the Elizabeth Islands should not submit." Looks for "clear, somewhat graphic slides. Show us scenes we've seen hundreds of times with a different twist and elements of surprise. Photographers should have a familiarity with the magazine and the region first. Prior to submitting, photographers should send a SASE to receive our guidelines. They can then submit works (via mail) and follow up with a brief phone call. We love to see images by professional-calibre photographers who are new to us, and prefer it if the photographer can leave images with us at least 2 months, if possible."

☼ ❸❸ THE CAPILANO REVIEW

2055 Purcell Way, North Vancouver BC V7J 3H5, Canada. (604)984-1712. E-mail: contact@the capilanoreview.ca; tcr@capilanou.ca. E-mail: tcr@ capilanou.ca. Website: www.thecapilanoreview.ca. **Contact:** Tamara Lee, managing editor. Estab. 1972. Circ. 800. Publishes an 8- to 16-page visual section by 1 or 2 artists/issue. "Read the magazine before submitting. *TCR* is an avant garde literary and visual arts publication that wants innovative work. We've previously published photography by Barrie Jones, Roy Kiyooka, Robert Keziere, Laiwan, and Colin Browne."

NEEDS Work that is new in concept and in execution.

MAKING CONTACT & TERMS Send an artist statement and list of exhibitions. Submit a group of photos with SASE (with Canadian postage or IRCs). "We do *not* accept submissions via e-mail or on disc."

❸ ❹ CAPPER'S

1503 SW 42nd St., Topeka KS 66609-1265. (800)678-4883. Fax: (800)274-4305. E-mail: editor@cappers. com. Website: www.cappers.com. **Contact:** Hank Will, editor-in-chief. Estab. 1879. Circ. 100,000. Bimonthly. Emphasizes small town life, country lifestyle, or "hobby" farm-oriented material. Readership is national. Sample copy available for $6.

NEEDS Buys 24+ photos/year with accompanying stories and articles; 90% from freelancers. Needs, on a regular basis, photos of small-farm livestock, animals, farm labor, gardening, produce and related images. "Be certain pictures are well composed, properly exposed and pin sharp. Must be *shot* at high-res (no less than 300 dpi). No cheesecake. No pictures that cannot be shown to any member of the family. No pictures that are out of focus or over- or under-exposed. No ribbon-cutting, check-passing or hand-shaking pictures. Story subjects include all aspects of the hobby or country lifestyle farm, such as livestock, farm dogs, barn cats, sowing and hoeing, small tractors, fences, etc." Photo captions required. "Any image that stands alone must be accompanied by 50-100 words of meaningful caption information."

SPECS Uses 35mm, high-res digital images. Send digital images via e-mail, one at a time, as JPEG files at 300 dpi resolution.

MAKING CONTACT & TERMS Study the magazine. "We use a beautiful country scene for 'Reverie,' the last page in each issue. Take a look at previous issues to get a sense of the sort of shot we're looking for." Send material by mail with SASE for consideration. Responds ASAP. Pay is negotiable. Rarely uses b&w, and only if "irresistibly atmospheric." Pays on publication. Buys shared rights; negotiable.

❸ CAREERFOCUS

7300 W. 110th St., 7th Floor, Overland Park KS 66210. (913)317-2888. Fax: (913)317-1505. E-mail: nmpaige@ careerfocusmagazine.com; editorial@careerfocus magazine.com. Website: www.careerfocusmagazine. com. **Contact:** N. Michelle Paige, executive editor. Estab. 1988. Circ. 250,000. Bimonthly. Emphasizes career development. Readers are male and female African-American and Hispanic professionals, ages 21-45. Sample copy free with 9×12 SASE and 4 first-class stamps. Photo guidelines available online.

NEEDS Uses approximately 40 photos/issue. Needs technology photos and shots of personalities; career people in computer, science, teaching, finance, engineering, law, law enforcement, government, high-tech, leisure. Model release preferred. Photo captions required; include name, date, place, why.

MAKING CONTACT & TERMS Send query letter via e-mail with résumé of credits and list of stock photo subjects. Keeps samples on file. Simultaneous submissions and previously published work OK. Responds in 1 month. Pays $10-50 for color photos; $5-25 for b&w photos. Pays on publication. Credit line given. Buys one-time rights.

TIPS "Freelancer must be familiar with our magazine to be able to submit appropriate manuscripts and photos."

💲💲 CARIBBEAN TRAVEL & LIFE

460 N. Orlando Ave., Suite 200, Winter Park FL 32789. (407)571-4704. E-mail: editor@caribbeantravelmag. com. Website: www.caribbeantravelmag.com. Estab. 1985. Circ. 150,000. Published 9 times/year. Emphasizes travel, culture and recreation in islands of Caribbean, Bahamas and Bermuda. Readers are male and female, frequent Caribbean travelers, ages 32-52. Sample copy available for $4.95. Photo guidelines free with SASE.

NEEDS Uses about 100 photos/issue; 90% supplied by freelance photographers: 10% assignment and 90% freelance stock. "We combine scenics with people shots. Where applicable, we show interiors, food shots, resorts, water sports, cultural events, shopping and wildlife/underwater shots. We want images that show intimacy between people and place. Provide thorough caption information. Don't submit stock that is mediocre."

SPECS Uses 4-color photography.

MAKING CONTACT & TERMS Query by mail or e-mail with list of stock photo subjects and tearsheets. Responds in 3 weeks. Pays $1,000 for color cover; $450/spread; $325/full+ page; $275/full page; $200/½+ page; $150/½ page; $120/⅓ page; $90/¼ page or less. Pays after publication. Buys one-time rights. Does not pay shipping, research or holding fees.

TIPS Seeing trend toward "fewer but larger photos with more impact and drama. We are looking for particularly strong images of color and style, beautiful island scenics and people shots—images that are powerful enough to make the reader want to travel to the region; photos that show people doing things in the destinations we cover; originality in approach, com-

position, subject matter. Good composition, lighting and creative flair. Images that are evocative of a place, creating story mood. Good use of people. Submit stock photography for specific story needs; if good enough can lead to possible assignments. Let us know exactly what coverage you have on a stock list so we can contact you when certain photo needs arise."

CARLSBAD MAGAZINE

P.O. Box 2089, Carlsbad CA 92018. (760)729-9099. Fax: (760)729-9011. E-mail: tim@wheelhousemedia. com. Website: www.clickoncarlsbad.com. **Contact:** Tim Wrisley, editorial department. Estab. 2004. Circ. 37,000. Bimonthly. Covers the people, places, events and arts in Carlsbad, California. "We are a regional magazine highlighting all things pertaining specifically to Carlsbad. We focus on history, events, people and places that make Carlsbad interesting and unique. Our audience is both Carlsbad residents and visitors or anyone interested in learning more about Carlsbad." Sample copy available for $2.31.

NEEDS Photos of gardening, entertainment, events, performing arts. Interested in historical/vintage, lifestyle. "People, places, events, arts in Carlsbad, California."

SPECS Accepts images in digital format. Send as GIF or JPEG files.

MAKING CONTACT & TERMS Pays $15-400/photo. Pays on publication. Credit line given. Buys one-time rights.

TIPS "E-mail is the preferred method for queries."

◎ 💲 ◐ CAT FANCY

Fancy Publications, BowTie Inc., P.O. Box 6050, Mission Viejo CA 92690. (949)855-8822. Fax: (949)855-3045. E-mail: query@catfancy.com; catsupport@catchannel.com. E-mail: slogan@bowtieinc.com. Website: www.catfancy.com; www.catchannel.com. **Contact:** Susan Logan, editor. Estab. 1965. Circ. 290,000. "*Cat Fancy* is the undisputed premier feline magazine that is dedicated to better lives for pet cats. Always a presence within the cat world, *Cat Fancy* and its sister website CatChannel.com are where cat owners, lovers and rescue organizations go for education and entertainment." Monthly magazine. Readers are men and women of all ages interested in all aspects of cat ownership.

NEEDS Editorial "lifestyle" shots of cats in beautiful, modern homes; cats with attractive people (infant to middle-age, variety of ethnicities); cat behavior (good and bad, single and in groups); cat and kitten care (grooming, vet visits, feeding, etc.); household shots of CFA- or TICA-registered cats and kittens. Buys 20-30 photos from freelancers/issue; 240-360 photos/year.

SPECS "Sharp, focused images only (no prints). Accepts images in digital format. Send via CD as TIFF or JPEG files at 300 dpi minimum; include contact sheet (thumbnails with image names). Also accepts 35mm slides and 2¼ color transparencies; include SASE. Lifestyle focus. Indoor cats preferred. Send SASE for list of specific photo needs."

MAKING CONTACT & TERMS Photo guidelines and needs free with SASE or on website.

CHA

E-mail: editors@asiancha.com; j@asiancha.com. E-mail: submissions@asiancha.com. Website: www.asiancha.com. Tammy Ho Lai-Ming, co-editor. **Contact:** Eddie Tay, reviews editor. Estab. 2007. "*Cha* is the first Hong Kong-based English online literary journal; it is dedicated to publishing quality poetry, fiction, creative non-fiction, reviews, photography and art. *Cha* has a strong focus on Asian-themed creative work and work done by Asian writers and artists. It also publishes established and emerging writers/artists from around the world. *Cha* is an affiliated organization of the Asia-Pacific Writing Partnership and is catalogued in the School of Oriental and African Studies (SOAS) Library, among other universities."

SPECS Submit all visual work in JPEG format.

MAKING CONTACT & TERMS Submit 1-5 pieces. Include a brief biography (no more than 100 words). "Simultaneous submissions are accepted, but notify us as soon as possible if your work is accepted for publication elsewhere."

CHARISMA

600 Rinehart Rd., Lake Mary FL 32746. (407)333-0600. Fax: (407)333-7100. E-mail: magcustsvc@charismamedia.com. Website: www.charismamedia.com. **Contact:** Bill Johnson, marketing design director. Estab. 1975. Formerly Strang Communications. Publishes religious magazines and books for Sunday school and general readership as well as gift books and children's books. Photos used for text illustrations, promotional materials, book covers, dust jackets. Examples of recently published titles: *Cha-*

risma; New Man Magazine; Ministry Today; Christian Retailing; Vida Cristiana (all editorial, cover).

NEEDS Buys 75-100 photos/year; offers 75-100 freelance assignments/year. Needs photos of people, environmental portraits, situations. Reviews stock photos. Model/property release preferred for all subjects. Photo captions preferred; include who, what, when, where.

SPECS Uses 8×10 prints; 35mm, 2¼×2¼, 4×5 transparencies. Accepts images in digital format for Mac (Photoshop). Send via CD, e-mail.

MAKING CONTACT & TERMS Arrange a personal interview to show portfolio or call and arrange to send portfolio. Send query letter with samples. Provide résumé, business card, brochure, flyer or tearsheets to be kept on file for possible future assignments. Works with freelancers on assignment only. Keeps samples on file. Simultaneous submissions and previously published work OK. Pays $5-75 for b&w photos; $50-550 for color photos; negotiable with each photographer. Pays on publication and receipt of invoice. Credit line given. Buys one-time, first-time, book, electronic and all rights; negotiable.

CHESAPEAKE BAY MAGAZINE

1819 Bay Ridge Ave., Annapolis MD 21403. (410)263-2662, ext. 32. Fax: (410)267-6924. E-mail: chesapeakeboating@gmail.com. Website: www.chesapeakeboating.net. Karen Ashley, art director; T.F. Sayles, editor. **Contact:** Ann Levelle, managing editor. Estab. 1972. Circ. 46,000. Monthly. Emphasizes boating—Chesapeake Bay only. Readers are "people who use Chesapeake Bay for recreation." Sample copy available with SASE.

Chesapeake Bay is CD-equipped and does corrections and manipulates photos in-house.

NEEDS Photos that are Chesapeake Bay related (must); "vertical powerboat shots are badly needed (color)." Special needs include "vertical 4-color slides showing boats and people on Bay." Buys 27 photos from freelancers/issue; 324 photos/year.

SPECS Uses 35mm, 2¼×2¼, 4×5, 8×10 transparencies. Accepts images in digital format. Send via CD as TIFF files at 300 dpi, at least 8×10 (16×10 for spreads). "A proof sheet would be helpful.

MAKING CONTACT & TERMS Interested in reviewing work from newer, lesser-known photographers. Send query letter with samples or list of stock photo subjects. Responds only if interested. Simultaneous submissions OK. Pays $400 for color cover; $75-250 for color *stock* inside, depending on size; $200-1,200 for *assigned* photo package. Pays on publication. Credit line given. Buys one-time rights.

TIPS "We prefer Kodachrome over Ektachrome. Looking for boating, bay and water-oriented subject matter. Qualities and abilities include fresh ideas, clarity, exciting angles and true color. We're using larger photos—more double-page spreads. Photos should be able to hold up to that degree of enlargement. When photographing boats on the Bay, keep safety in mind. People hanging off the boat, drinking, women 'perched' on the bow are a no-no! Children must be wearing life jackets on moving boats. We must have IDs for *all* people in close-up to medium-view images."

CHESS LIFE

P.O. Box 3967, Crossville TN 38557-3967. (931)787-1234. Fax: (931)787-1200. E-mail: dlucas@uschess.org; fbutler@uschess.org. Website: www.uschess.org. Francesca "Frankie" Butler, art director. **Contact:** Daniel Lucas, editor. Estab. 1939. Circ. 85,000. Monthly publication of the U.S. Chess Federation. Emphasizes news of all major national and international tournaments; includes historical articles, personality profiles, columns of instruction, occasional fiction, humor for the devoted fan of chess. Sample copy and photo guidelines free with SASE or on website.

NEEDS News photos from events around the country; shots for personality profiles.

SPECS Accepts prints or high-res digital images. Send digital images as JPEG or TIFF files at 300 dpi—via CD for multiple-image submissions; e-mail for single-shot submission. Contact art director for further details on submission options and specifications.

MAKING CONTACT & TERMS Query with samples via e-mail (preferred). Responds in 1 month, "depending on when the deadline crunch occurs." Simultaneous submissions and previously published work OK.

TIPS Using "more color, and more illustrative photography. The photographer's name, address and date of the shoot should appear on the back of all photos. Also, name of persons in photograph and event should be identified." Looks for "clear images, good composition and contrast with a fresh approach to interest the viewer. Typical 'player sitting at chessboard' photos are not what we want. Increasing emphasis on strong portraits of chess personalities, especially Americans. Tournament photographs of winning players and key games are in high demand."

$ CHESS LIFE FOR KIDS

P.O. Box 3967, Crossville TN 38557. (732)252-8388. E-mail: gpetersen@uschess.org. Website: www.uschess.org. **Contact:** Glenn Petersen, editor. Estab. 2006. Circ. 28,000. Bimonthly association magazine geared for the young reader, age 12 and under, interested in chess; fellow chess players; tournament results; and instruction. Sample copy available with SASE and first-class postage. Photo guidelines available via e-mail.

NEEDS Photos of babies/children/teens, celebrities, multicultural, families, senior citizens, events, humor. Some aspect of chess must be present: playing, watching, young/old contrast. Reviews photos with or without a manuscript. Property release is required. Captions required.

SPECS Accepts images in digital format. Send via ZIP or e-mail. Contact Frankie Butler at fbutler@uschess.org for more information on digital specs. Uses glossy color prints.

MAKING CONTACT & TERMS E-mail query letter with link to photographer's website. Provide self-promotion piece to be kept on file. Responds in 1 week to queries and portfolios. Simultaneous submissions and previously published work OK. Pays $150 minimum/$300 maximum for color cover. Pays $35 for color inside. Pays on publication. Credit line given. Rights are negotiable. Will negotiate with a photographer unwilling to sell all rights.

TIPS "Read the magazine. What would appeal to *your* 10-year-old? Be original. We have plenty of people to shoot headshots and award ceremonies. And remember, you're competing against proud parents as well."

🍁 ◐ CHICKADEE

10 Lower Spadina Ave., Suite 400, Toronto ON M5V 2Z2, Canada. (416)340-2700, ext. 318. Fax: (416)340-9769. E-mail: deb@owlkids.com. Website: www.owlkids.com. **Contact:** Deb Yea, photo researcher. Estab. 1979. Circ. 92,000. Published 10 times/year. A discovery magazine for children ages 6-9. Sample copy available for $4.95 with 9×12 SASE and $1.50 money order to cover postage. Photo guidelines available with SASE or via e-mail.

○ *chickaDEE* has received Magazine of the Year, Parents' Choice, Silver Honor, Canadian Children's Book Centre Choice and several Distinguished Achievement awards from the Association of Educational Publishers.

NEEDS Photo stories, photo puzzles, children ages 6-10, multicultural, environmental, wildlife, pets, adventure, events, hobbies, humor, performing arts, sports, travel, science, technology, animals in their natural habitats. Interested in documentary, seasonal. Model/property release required. Photo captions required.

SPECS Prefers images in digital format. E-mail as JPEG files at 72 dpi; 300 dpi required for publication.

MAKING CONTACT & TERMS Previously published work OK. Credit line given. Buys one-time rights.

○ ◑ CHIRP

10 Lower Spadina Ave., Suite 400, Toronto ON M5V 2Z2, Canada. (416)340-2700, ext. 318. Fax: (416)340-9769. E-mail: owl@owlkids.com. Website: www.owlkids.com. Estab. 1997. Circ. 85,000. Published 10 times/year. A discovery magazine for children ages 3-6. Sample copy available for $4.95 with 9×12 SASE and $1.50 money order to cover postage. Photo guidelines available with SASE or via e-mail.

○ *Chirp* has received Best New Magazine of the Year, Parents' Choice, Canadian Children's Book Centre Choice and Distinguished Achievement awards from the Association of Educational Publishers.

NEEDS Photo stories, photo puzzles, children ages 5-7, multicultural, environmental, wildlife, adventure, events, hobbies, humor, animals in their natural habitats. Interested in documentary, seasonal. Model/property release required. Photo captions required.

SPECS Prefers images in digital format. E-mail as TIFF, JPEG files at 72 dpi; 300 dpi required for publication.

MAKING CONTACT & TERMS Request photo packages before sending photos for review. Responds in 3 months. Previously published work okay. Credit line given. Buys one-time rights.

○ ◎ ◑ THE CHRONICLE OF THE HORSE

P.O. Box 46, Middleburg VA 20118-0046. (540)687-6341. Fax: (540)687-3937. E-mail: slieser@chronofhorse.com. Website: www.chronofhorse.com. Contact: Sara Lieser, managing editor. Estab. 1937. Circ. 18,000. Weekly. Emphasizes English horse sports. Readers range from young to old. "Average reader is a college-educated female, middle-aged, well-off financially." Sample copy available for $2. Photo guidelines free with SASE or on website. Buys 10-20 photos from freelancers/issue.

NEEDS Photos from competitive events (horse shows, dressage, steeplechase, etc.) to go with news story or to accompany personality profile. "A few stand alone. Must be cute, beautiful or newsworthy. Reproduced in b&w." Prefers purchasing photos with accompanying manuscript.

SPECS Uses b&w and color prints, slides (reproduced b&w). Accepts images in digital format at 300 dpi.

MAKING CONTACT & TERMS "We do not want to see portfolio or samples. Contact us first, preferably by letter; include SASE for reply. Responds in 6 weeks.

TIPS "Know horse sports."

○ ◑ CHRONOGRAM

314 Wall St., Kingston NY 12401. (845)334-8600. Fax: (845)334-8610. E-mail: dperry@chronogram.com. Website: www.chronogram.com. **Contact:** David Perry, art director. Estab. 1993. Circ. 50,000. Monthly arts and culture magazine with a focus on green living and progressive community building in the Hudson Valley. Tends to hire regional photographers, or photographers who are showing work regionally. Sample copy available for $5. Photo guidelines available on website.

NEEDS Buys 16 photos from regional freelancers/issue; 192 photos/year. Interested in alternative process, avant garde, fashion/glamour, fine art, historical/vintage, artistic representations of anything. "Striking, minimalistic and good! Great covers!" Reviews photos with or without a manuscript. Model/property release preferred. Photo captions required; include title, date, artist, medium.

SPECS Prefers images in digital format. Send via CD as TIFF files at 300 dpi or larger at printed size.

MAKING CONTACT & TERMS Send query letter with résumé and digital images or prints. Provide self-promotion piece to be kept on file for possible future assignments. Responds only if interested; send non-returnable samples. Pays $200 maximum for color inside. Pays 1 month after publication. Credit line given. Buys one-time rights; negotiable.

TIPS "Colorful, edgy, great art! See our website—look at the back issues and our covers, and check out back issues and our covers before submitting."

● CITY LIMITS

Community Service Society of New York, 105 E. 22nd St., Suite 901, New York NY 10010. (212)479-3344. Fax: (212)344-6457. E-mail: citylimits@citylimits.org; magazine@citylimits.org. E-mail: editor@citylimits. org. Website: www.citylimits.org. Jarrett Murphy, editor-in-chief; Tracie McMillan, art director. **Contact:** Mark Anthony Thomas, director. Estab. 1976. Circ. 5,000. "*City Limits* is an urban policy monthly offering intense journalistic coverage of New York City's low-income and working-class neighborhoods." Sample copy available for 8×11 SAE with $1.50 first-class postage. Photo guidelines available for SASE.

NEEDS Assigned portraits, photojournalism, action, ambush regarding stories about people in low-income neighborhoods, government or social service sector, babies/children/teens, families, parents, senior citizens, cities/urban. Interested in documentary. Reviews photos with or without a manuscript. Special photo needs: b&w photo essays about urban issues.

SPECS Uses 5×7 and larger b&w prints. Accepts images in digital format. Send via CD, ZIP, e-mail as TIFF, EPS, JPEG files at 600 dpi. Inside photos are b&w; cover is 4-color.

MAKING CONTACT & TERMS "Send query letter with samples, tearsheets, self-promotion cards. Provide résumé, business card, self-promotion piece or tearsheets to be kept on file for possible future assignments. Art director will contact photographer for portfolio review if interested. Portfolio should include b&w prints and tearsheets. Keeps samples on file; cannot return material. Responds only if interested; send nonreturnable samples. Simultaneous submissions and previously published work OK."

TIPS "We need good photojournalists who can capture the emotion of a scene. We offer huge pay for great photos."

CLEVELAND MAGAZINE

City Magazines, Inc., 1422 Euclid Ave., Suite 730, Cleveland OH 44115. (216)771-2833. Fax: (216)781-6318. E-mail: gleydura@clevelandmagazine.com; miller@clevelandmagazine.com; kessen@cleveland magazine.com. Website: www.clevelandmagazine. com. **Contact:** Kristen Miller, art director. Estab.

1972. Circ. 50,000. Monthly. Emphasizes Cleveland, Ohio. General interest to upscale audience.

NEEDS Photos of architecture, business concepts, education, entertainment, environmental, events, food/drink, gardening, health/fitness, industry, interiors/decorating, landscapes/scenics, medicine, people (couples, families, local celebrities, multicultural, parents, senior citizens), performing arts, political, product shots/still life, sports, technology, travel, interested in documentary and fashion/glamour.

SPECS Prefers images in digital format.

MAKING CONTACT & TERMS Please provide self-promotions, JPEG samples or tearsheets via e-mail or mail to be kept on file for possible future assignments. We will respond if interested. Send via CD, e-mail as TIFF, JPEG files at 300 dpi. Also uses color and b&w prints.

●●● ● COBBLESTONE

30 Grove St., Suite C, Peterborough NH 03458. (800)821-0115. Fax: (603)924-7380. E-mail: customer service@caruspub.com. Website: www.cobblestone pub.com. Circ. 15,000. Published 9 times/year, September-May. Emphasizes American history; each issue covers a specific theme. Writers are encouraged to submit available photos with their query or article. We buy one-time use. Readers are children ages 9-14, parents, teachers. Sample copy available for $4.95 and 9×12 SASE with 5 first-class stamps. Photo guidelines free with SASE. Mail queries to Editorial Dept. "Reporting dates depend on how far ahead of the issue the photographer submits photos. We work on issues 6 months ahead of publication." Simultaneous submissions and previously published work OK. See guidelines on website at: www.cobblestonepub.com/guides_cob.html.

NEEDS Buys 10-20 photos from freelancers/issue; 90-180 photos/year. Photos of children, multicultural, landscapes/scenics, architecture, cities/urban, agriculture, industry, military. Interested in fine art, historical/vintage, reenacters. "We need photographs related to our specific themes (each issue is theme-related) and urge photographers to request our themes list."

SPECS Uses 8×10 glossy prints; 35mm, 2¼×2¼ transparencies. Accepts images in digital format.

MAKING CONTACT & TERMS Send via CD, Sy-Quest, ZIP as TIFF files at 300 dpi, saved at 8×10 size.

Send query letter with samples or list of stock photo subjects; include SASE for return of material.

TIPS "Most photos are of historical subjects, but contemporary color images of, for example, a Civil War battlefield, are great to balance with historical images. However, the amount varies with each monthly theme. Please review our theme list and submit related images."

⑤ ⓘ COLLECTIBLE AUTOMOBILE

7373 N. Cicero Ave., Lincolnwood IL 60712. (847)676-3470. Fax: (847)676-3671. E-mail: jbiel@pubint.com. Estab. 1984. Bimonthly. "*CA* features profiles of collectible automobiles and their designers as well as articles on literature, scale models, and other topics of interest to automotive enthusiasts." Sample copy available for $8 and 10½×14 SASE with $3.50 first-class postage. Photo guidelines available with #10 SASE.

NEEDS "For digital photography, we require our files to have a minimum resolution of A) no less than 25 MB in their uncompressed state or B) approximately 3500-4000 pixels on the largest side or C) 12-14 inches on the largest side at 300 dpi. Raw TIFF is best, but lightly compressed JPEGs are acceptable as well. For film shoots, 2-3 rolls of 35mm, 2-3 rolls of 2¼×2¼, and 4-8 4×5 exposures. Complete exterior views, interior and engine views, and close-up detail shots of the subject vehicle are required."

SPECS Uses 35mm, 2¼×2¼, 4×5 transparencies.

MAKING CONTACT & TERMS Send query letter with transparencies and stock list. Provide business card to be kept on file for possible future assignments. Responds only if interested; send nonreturnable samples. Previously published work OK. Pays bonus if image is used as cover photo; $300-350 plus costs for standard auto shoot. **Pays on acceptance**. Photography is credited on an article-by-article basis in an "Acknowledgments" section at the front of the magazine. Buys all intellectual and digital property rights.

TIPS "Read our magazine for good examples of the types of backgrounds, shot angles and overall quality that we are looking for."

⑤ COLLEGE PREVIEW

7300 W. 110th St., 7th Floor, Overland Park KS 66210. (913)317-2888. Fax: (913)317-1505. E-mail: nmpaige@collegepreviewmagazine.com; editorial@collegepreviewmagazine.com. Website: www.collegepreviewmagazine.com. **Contact:** Michelle

Paige, executive editor. Circ. 600,000. Quarterly. Emphasizes college and college-bound African-American and Hispanic students. Readers are African American, Hispanic, ages 16-24. Sample copy free with 9×12 SASE and 4 first-class stamps.

NEEDS Uses 30 photos/issue. Needs photos of students in class, at work, in interesting careers, on campus. Special photo needs include computers, military, law and law enforcement, business, aerospace and aviation, health care. Model/property release required. Photo captions required; include name, age, location, subject.

MAKING CONTACT & TERMS Send query letter with résumé of credits. Simultaneous submissions and previously published work OK. Pays $10-50 for color photos; $5-25 for b&w inside. Pays on publication. Buys first North American serial rights.

COMMUNITY OBSERVER

Ann Arbor Observer Co., 201 Catherine St., Ann Arbor MI 48104. (734)769-3175. Fax: (734)769-3375. E-mail: editor@arborweb.com. Website: www.washtenawguide.com. John Hilton, editor. Circ. 20,000. Quarterly. "The *Community Observer* serves three historic communities facing rapid change. We provide an intelligent, informed perspective on the most important news and events in the communities we cover." Sample copy available for $2.

SPECS Uses contact sheets, negatives, transparencies, prints. Accepts images in digital format; GIF or JPEG files.

MAKING CONTACT & TERMS Negotiates payment individually. Pays on publication. Buys one-time rights.

⑤ ⓒ COMPANY

Company Magazine, c/o The Jesuit Conference of the United States, 1016 16th St. NW, Suite 400, Washington D.C. 20036. (800)955-5538. Fax: (773)761-9443. E-mail: editor@companymagazine.org. Website: www.companysj.com. Estab. 1983. Circ. 114,000. Quarterly magazine published by the Jesuits (Society of Jesus). Emphasizes Jesuit works/ministries and the people involved in them. Sample copy available with 9×12 SASE.

NEEDS Photos and photo-stories of Jesuit and allied ministries and projects. Reviews photos with or without manuscript. Photo captions required.

SPECS Accepts images in digital format. Send via CD, ZIP, e-mail "at screen resolution as long as higher-res is available."

MAKING CONTACT & TERMS Query with samples; include SASE for return of material. Provide résumé, business card, brochure, flier or tearsheets to be kept on file for possible future assignments. Pays on publication. Credit line given. Buys one-time rights; negotiable.

TIPS "Avoid large-group, 'smile at camera' photos. We are interested in people/activity photographs that tell a story about Jesuit ministries."

COMPETITOR

9477 Waples St., Suite 150, San Diego CA 92121. (858)768-6776. E-mail: rheaton@competitorgroup. com. Website: www.competitor.com. **Contact:** Rebecca Heaton. Circ. 95,000. Monthly. Covers running, mountain biking, road racing, snowboarding, both alpine and Nordic skiing, kayaking, hiking, climbing, mountaineering, and other individual sports.

NEEDS Photos of adventure, running, mountain biking, road racing, snowboarding, both alpine and Nordic skiing, kayaking, hiking, climbing, mountaineering, and other individual sports. Interested in lifestyle. Editorial calendar: March: running; April: adventure; May: triathlon; June: climbing/paddling/mountain biking; July: summer travel; August: organic; September: women; October: gym/fitness; November: snow sports; December: snow sports. Reviews photos with or without a manuscript. Model release required. Captions required; include identification of subjects.

SPECS Accepts images in digital format. Send JPEG or TIFF files at 300 dpi minimum.

MAKING CONTACT & TERMS Payment negotiated. Pays on publication. Credit line given. Buys one-time rights.

TIPS "Think fun. Don't be afraid to try something new. We like new."

COMPLETE WOMAN

Associated Publications, Inc., 875 N. Michigan Ave., Suite 3434, Chicago IL 60611. (312)266-8680. Fax: (312)573-3020. Website: www.thecompletewoman magazine.com. Kourtney McKay, art director. Estab. 1980. Circ. 300,000. Bimonthly general interest magazine for women. Readers are "females, ages 21-40, from all walks of life."

NEEDS Uses 50-60 photos/issue; 300 photos/year. High-contrast shots of attractive women, how-to beauty shots, celebrities, couples, health/fitness/beauty, business concepts. Interested in fashion/glamour. Model release required.

SPECS Uses color transparencies (slide and large-format). Accepts images in digital format. Send via CD as TIFF, JPEG files at 300 dpi.

MAKING CONTACT & TERMS Portfolio may be dropped off and picked up by appointment only. Provide résumé, business card, brochure, flyer or tearsheets to be kept on file for possible future assignments. Send color prints and transparencies. "Each print/transparency should have its own protective sleeve. Do not write or make heavy pen impressions on back of prints; identification marks will show through, affecting reproduction." Responds in 1 month. Simultaneous submissions and previously published work OK. Pays $75-150 for color inside. Pays on publication. Credit line given. Buys one-time rights.

TIPS "We use photography that is beautiful and flattering, with good contrast and professional lighting. Models should be attractive, ages 18-28, and sexy. We're always looking for nice couple shots."

CONDE NAST TRAVELLER

4 Times Square, 14th Floor, New York NY 10036. (212)286-2860. Fax: (212)286-5931. E-mail: cn traveller@condenast.co.uk; hazel.lubbock@condenast.co.uk. Website: www.cntraveller.com. Sarah Miller, editor. **Contact:** Alice Walker and Hazel Lubbock, editorial assistants. Provides the experienced traveler with an array of diverse travel experiences encompassing art, architecture, fashion, culture, cuisine and shopping. This magazine has very specific needs and contacts a stock agency when seeking photos.

CONFRONTATION

Confrontation Press, English Dept., C.W. Post Campus Long Island University, 720 Northern Blvd., Brookville NY 11548-1300. (516)299-2720. Fax: (516)299-2735. E-mail: confrontation@liu.edu; martin.tucker@liu.edu. Website: www.liu.edu/ confrontation. **Contact:** Jonna Semeiks, editor. Estab. 1968. Circ. 2,000. Semiannual. Covers all forms and genres of stories, poems, essays, memoirs, and plays. A special section contains book reviews and cultural commentary.

MAKING CONTACT & TERMS Send query letter with résumé of credits, stock list. Responds in 1 month. Simultaneous submissions OK.

⊗ ⊕ ○ CONSCIENCE

Catholics for Choice, 1436 U St. NW, Suite 301, Washington D.C. 20009-3997. (202)986-6093. E-mail: conscience@catholicsforchoice.org. Website: www.catholicsforchoice.org. **Contact:** Kim Puchir; David Nolan. Estab. 1980. Circ. 12,000. Quarterly news journal of Catholic opinion. "Conscience offers in-depth coverage of a range of topics, including contemporary politics, Catholicism, women's rights in society and in religions, U.S. politics, reproductive rights, sexuality and gender, ethics and bioethics, feminist theology, social justice, church and state issues, and the role of religion in formulating public policy."

NEEDS Photos of multicultural, religious, Catholic-related news.

SPECS Uses glossy color and b&w prints. Accepts high-res digital images. Send as TIFF, JPEG files.

MAKING CONTACT & TERMS Send query letter with tearsheets. Responds only if interested; send nonreturnable samples. Simultaneous submissions and previously published work OK. Model/property release preferred. Photo captions preferred; include title, subject, photographer's name. Pays $300 maximum for color cover; $50 maximum for b&w inside. Pays on publication. Credit line given.

CONTEMPORARY BRIDE

North East Publishing, Inc., 216 Stelton Rd., Unit D-1, Piscataway NJ 08854. (908)561-6010. E-mail: gary@contemporarybride.com. Website: www.contemporarybride.com. Linda Paris, executive editor. **Contact:** Gary Paris, publisher. Estab. 1994. Circ. 120,000. Biannual bridal magazine with wedding planner; 4-color publication with editorial, calendars, check-off lists and advertisers. Sample copy available for first-class postage.

NEEDS Photos of travel destinations, fashion, bridal events. Reviews photos with accompanying manuscript only. Model/property release preferred. Photo captions preferred; include photo credits.

SPECS Accepts images in digital format. Send as high-res files at 300 dpi.

MAKING CONTACT & TERMS Send query letter with samples. Art director will contact photographer for portfolio review if interested. Provide b&w and color prints, disc. Keeps samples on file; cannot return material. Responds only if interested; send nonreturnable samples. Simultaneous submissions and previously published work OK. Payment negotiable. Buys all rights, electronic rights.

TIPS "Digital images preferred with a creative eye for all wedding-related photos. Give us the *best* presentation."

⊗ ⊕ ○ CONTINENTAL NEWSTIME

Continental News Service, Inc., 501 W. Broadway, Plaza A, PMB #265, San Diego CA 92101-3802. (858)492-8696. E-mail: Continentalnewsservice@yahoo.com. Website: www.continentalnewsservice.com. **Contact:** Gary P. Salamone, editor-in-chief. Estab. 1987. Twice-monthly general interest magazine of news and commentary on U.S. national and world news, with travel columns, entertainment features, humor pieces, comic strips, general humor panels, and editorial cartoons. Covers the unreported and under-reported national (U.S.) and international news. Sample copy available for $4.50 in US and $6.50 CAN/foreign.

NEEDS Buys variable number of photos from freelancers. Photos of public figures, U.S. and foreign government officials/cabinet ministers, breaking/unreported/under-reported news. Reviews photos with or without a manuscript. Model/property release required. Photo captions required.

SPECS Uses 8×10 color and b&w prints.

MAKING CONTACT & TERMS Send query letter with résumé, photocopies, tearsheets, stock list. Provide résumé to be kept on file for possible future assignments. Responds only if interested in absence of SASE being received; send nonreturnable samples. Simultaneous submissions OK. Pays $10 minimum for b&w cover. Pays on publication. Credit line given. Buys one-time rights.

TIPS "Read our magazine to develop a better feel for our photo applications/uses and to satisfy our stated photo needs."

⊘ COSMOPOLITAN

224 W. 57th St., 8th Floor, New York NY 10019. (212)649-2000. E-mail: cosmo@hearst.com. Website: www.cosmopolitan.com. *Cosmopolitan* targets young women for whom beauty, fashion, fitness, career, relationships and personal growth are top priorities. It includes articles and columns on nutrition and food,

travel, personal finance, home/lifestyle and celebrities. *Query before submitting.*

COUNTRY WOMAN

Reiman Publications, 5400 South 60th St., Greendale WI 53129. (414)423-0100. E-mail: editors@country womanmagazine.com. Website: www.country womanmagazine.com. Estab. 1970. Bimonthly. Supported entirely by subscriptions and accepts no outside advertising. Emphasizes rural life and a special quality of living to which country women can relate; at work or play, in sharing problems, etc. Sample copy available for $2. Photo guidelines free with SASE.

NEEDS Uses 75-100 photos/issue; most supplied by readers, rather than freelance photographers. "Covers are usually supplied by professional photographers; they are often seasonal in nature and generally feature a good-looking country woman (mid-range to close up, shown within her business setting or with a hobby, craft or others; static pose or active)." Photos purchased with or without accompanying manuscript. Also interested in unique or well-designed country homes and interiors. Some work assigned for interiors. Works 6 months in advance. "No poor-quality color prints, posed photos, etc." Photo captions required.

SPECS Prefers color transparencies, all sizes. Accepts images in digital format. Send via lightboxes, CD/DVD with printed thumbnails and caption sheet, or e-mail if first review selection is small (12 or less).

MAKING CONTACT & TERMS Send material by mail for consideration; include SASE. Provide brochure, calling card, letter of inquiry, price list, résumé and samples to be kept on file for possible future assignments. Responds in 3 months. Previously published work OK. "If the material you are submitting has been published previously, we ask that you please let us know. We accept color prints, slides or high-res digital photos. Digital images should be about 4×6 at a minimum resolution of 300 dpi and sent as JPEGs on a CD or via e-mail. We cannot use photos that are printed on an ink-jet printer. After you share a story and photos, please be patient. We receive a lot of mail, and it takes our small staff a while to catch up. We may hold your material for consideration in a future issue without informing you first, but we will let you know if we publish it. If we publish your material, we will send you a complimentary copy of the issue and any payment mentioned in the original solicitation upon publication, or at our normal contributor's rates."

Pays $300-800 for text/photo package depending on quality of photos and number used; $300 minimum for front cover; $200 minimum for back cover; $100-300 for partial page inside, depending on size. No b&w photos used. **Pays on acceptance.** Buys one-time rights.

TIPS Prefers to see "rural scenics, in various seasons; include a variety of country women—from traditional farm and ranch women to the new baby-boomer, rural retiree; slides appropriately simple for use with poems or as accents to inspirational, reflective essays, etc."

CRUISING WORLD

The Sailing Co., 55 Hammarlund Way, Middletown RI 02842. (401)845-5100. Fax: (401)845-5180. E-mail: elaine.lembo@cruisingworld.com; bill.roche@bonniercorp.com. Website: www.cruisingworld.com. **Contact:** Elaine Lembo; Bill Roche, art director. Estab. 1974. Circ. 155,000. Emphasizes sailboat maintenance, sailing instruction and personal experience. For people interested in cruising under sail. Sample copy free with 9×12 SASE.

NEEDS Buys 25 photos/year. Needs "shots of cruising sailboats and their crews anywhere in the world. Shots of ideal cruising scenes. No identifiable racing shots, please." Also wants exotic images of cruising sailboats, people enjoying sailing, tropical images, different perspectives of sailing, good composition, bright colors. For covers, photos "must be of a cruising sailboat with strong human interest, and can be located anywhere in the world." Prefers vertical format. Allow space at top of photo for insertion of logo. Model release preferred; property release required. Photo captions required; include location, body of water, make and model of boat. See guidelines at www.cruisingworld.com/writer_and_photographer_guidelines.jsp.

SPECS Prefers images in digital format via CD. Accepts 35mm color slides.

MAKING CONTACT & TERMS "Submit original 35mm slides—*no* duplicates—or digital images. We look for good color balance, very sharp focus, the ability to capture sailing, good composition and action. Always looking for *cover shots*." Responds in 2 months. Pays $600 for color cover; $50-300 for color inside. Pays on publication. Credit line given. Buys all rights, but may reassign to photographer after publication; first North American serial rights; or one-time rights.

CYCLE CALIFORNIA! MAGAZINE

1702-L Meridian Ave., #289, San Jose CA 95125. (408)924-0270. Fax: (408)292-3005. E-mail: tcorral@cyclecalifornia.com; BMack@cyclecalifornia.com. Website: www.cyclecalifornia.com. **Contact:** Tracy L. Corral; Bob Mack, publisher. Estab. 1995. Circ. 26,000 print; 4,700 digital. Monthly. Provides readers with a comprehensive source of bicycling information, emphasizing the bicycling life in northern California and northern Nevada; promotes bicycling in all its facets. Sample copy available with 9×12 SASE and $1.39 first-class postage. Photo guidelines available with SASE.

NEEDS Buys 3-5 photos from freelancers/issue; 45 photos/year. Needs photos of recreational bicycling, bicycle racing, triathlons, bicycle touring and adventure racing. Cover photos must be vertical format, color. All cyclists must be wearing a helmet if riding. Reviews photos with or without manuscript. Model release required; property release preferred. Photo captions preferred; include when and where photo is taken; if an event, include name, date and location of event; for nonevent photos, location is important.

SPECS High-res TIFF images preferred (2000×3000 pixel minimum). Cover photos are 7×9.

MAKING CONTACT & TERMS Send query letter with CD/disc or e-mail. Keeps usable images on file; include SASE for return of material. Responds in 3 weeks. Simultaneous submissions OK. Pays $125 for color cover; $50 for inside. Pays on publication.

TIPS "We are looking for photographic images that depict the fun of bicycle riding. Your submissions should show people enjoying the sport. Read the magazine to get a feel for what we do. Label images so we can tell what description goes with which image."

⑤ CYCLE WORLD

1499 Monrovia Ave., Newport Beach CA 92663. (949)720-5300. E-mail: dedwards@hfmus.com; cycleworld@neodata.com. Website: www.cycleworld.com. **Contact:** David Edwards, editor-in-chief. Circ. 300,000. Monthly. Readers are active motorcyclists who are "affluent, educated and very perceptive."

NEEDS Buys 10 photos/issue. Wants "outstanding" photos relating to motorcycling. Prefers to buy photos with manuscripts. For "Slipstream" column, see instructions in a recent issue.

SPECS Prefers high-res digital images at 300 dpi or quality 35mm color transparencies.

MAKING CONTACT & TERMS Send photos for consideration; include SASE for return of material. Responds in 6 weeks. "Cover shots are generally done by the staff or on assignment." Pays $50-200/photo. Pays on publication. Buys first publication rights.

TIPS "Editorial contributions are welcomed, but must be guaranteed exclusive to *Cycle World*. We are not responsible for the return of unsolicited material unless accompanied by an SASE."

⑤ ⑪ ○ DAKOTA OUTDOORS

P.O. Box 669, Pierre SD 57501. (605)224-7301. E-mail: publisher@capjournal.com. Website: www.sdoinsider.com. Lee Harstad, editor; Rachel Engbrecht, managing editor. **Contact:** Steve Baker, publisher. Estab. 1978. Circ. 8,000. Monthly. Emphasizes hunting and fishing in the Dakotas. Readers are sportsmen interested in hunting and fishing, ages 35-45. Sample copy available with 9×12 SASE and 3 first-class stamps. Photo guidelines free with SASE.

NEEDS Uses 15-20 photos/issue; 8-10 supplied by freelancers. Needs photos of hunting and fishing. Reviews photos with or without a manuscript. Special photo needs include: scenic shots of sportsmen, wildlife, fish. Model/property release required. Photo captions preferred.

SPECS Uses 3×5 b&w and color prints; 35mm b&w and color transparencies. Accepts images in digital format. Send via ZIP, e-mail as EPS, JPEG files.

MAKING CONTACT & TERMS Send query letter with samples. Keeps samples on file; include SASE for return of material. Responds in 3 weeks. Pays $20-75 for b&w cover; $10-50 for b&w inside; payment negotiable. Pays on publication. Credit line given. Usually buys one-time rights; negotiable.

TIPS "We want good-quality outdoor shots, good lighting, identifiable faces, etc.—photos shot in the Dakotas. Use some imagination and make your photo help tell a story. Photos with accompanying story are accepted."

◑ DANCE

2660 Petersborough St., Herndon VA 20171. E-mail: shannonaswriter@yahoo.com. **Contact:** Shannon Bridget Murphy. Quarterly. Features international dancers.

NEEDS Performing arts, product shots/still life as related to international dance for children and teens. Interested in alternative process, avant garde, documentary, fashion/glamour, fine art, historical/vintage, seasonal. Reviews photos with or without a manuscript. Model/property release preferred.

SPECS Uses glossy or matte color and b&w prints.

MAKING CONTACT & TERMS Send query letter via e-mail. Provide résumé, business card, self-promotion piece to be kept on file for possible future assignments. "Photographs sent along with CDs are requested but not required. Write to request guidelines for artwork and illustrations." Responds within 1 month to queries; 1 week to portfolios. Simultaneous submissions and previously published work OK. **Pays on acceptance.** Credit line given. Buys one-time rights, first rights; negotiable.

DEER & DEER HUNTING

F+W Media, Inc., 700 E. State St., Iola WI 54990-0001. (715)445-2214. E-mail: dan.schmidt@fwmedia.com. Website: www.deeranddeerhunting.com. **Contact:** Dan Schmidt, editor-in-chief. Estab. 1977. Circ. 200,000. Published 9 times/year. Emphasizes whitetailed deer and deer hunting. Readers are "a cross-section of American deer hunters—bow, gun, camera." Sample copy and photo guidelines free with 9×12 SASE with 7 first-class stamps. Photo guidelines also available on website.

NEEDS Buys 20 photos from freelancers/issue; 180 photos/year. Photos of deer in natural settings. Model release preferred. Photo captions preferred.

SPECS Accepts images in digital format. Send contact sheet.

MAKING CONTACT & TERMS Send query letter with résumé of credits and samples. "If we judge your photos as being usable, we like to hold them in our file. Send originals—include SASE if you want them returned." Responds in 2-4 weeks. Pays $800 for color cover; $75-250 for color inside; $50 for b&w inside. Pays net 30 days of publication. Credit line given. Buys one-time rights.

TIPS Prefers to see "adequate selection of 35mm color transparencies; action shots of whitetail deer only, as opposed to portraits. We also need photos of deer hunters in action. We are currently using almost all color—very little b&w. Submit a limited number of quality photos rather than a multitude of marginal photos. Include your name on all entries. Cover shots must have room for masthead."

● ⑤ ① DIGITAL PHOTO

Bauer Consumer Media, Media House, Lynch Wood, Peterborough PE2 6EA, United Kingdom. 44 1733 468 546. Fax: 44 1733 468 387. E-mail: dp@bauerconsumer.co.uk. Website: www.photoanswers.co.uk. Estab. 1997. Circ. 60,792. Monthly. "UK's best-selling photography and imaging magazine."

NEEDS Stunning, digitally manipulated images of any subject and Photoshop or Elements step-by-step tutorials of any subject. Reviews photos with or without a manuscript. Model/property release preferred. Photo captions preferred.

SPECS Accepts images in digital format. Send via CD as PSD, TIFF or JPEG files at 300 dpi, or via e-mail as JPEG.

MAKING CONTACT & TERMS Send e-mail with résumé, low-res tearsheets, low-res JPEGs. Responds in 1 month to queries. Rates negotiable, but typically 60 GBP per page. Pays on publication. Credit line given. Buys first rights.

TIPS "Study the magazine to check the type of images we use, and send a sample of images you think would be suitable. The broader your style, the better for general acceptance, while individual styles appeal to our Gallery section. Step-by-step technique pieces must be formatted to house style, so check magazine before submitting. Supply a contact sheet or thumbnail of all the images supplied in electronic form to make it easier for us to make a quick decision on the work."

DOG FANCY

P.O. Box 6050, Mission Viejo CA 92690-6050. (949)855-8822. Fax: (949)855-3045. E-mail: barkback@dogfancy.com. Website: www.dogfancy.com. Estab. 1970. Circ. 268,000. Monthly. Readers are "men and women of all ages interested in all aspects of dog ownership." Photo guidelines free with SASE or on website.

NEEDS Three specific breeds featured in each issue. Prefers "photographs that show the various physical and mental attributes of the breed. Include both environmental and action photographs. Dogs must be well groomed and, if purebred, good examples of their breed. By good example, we mean clean, healthy-looking dogs who conform to their breed standard (found at www.akc.org or www.ukcdogs.com). We also need for high-quality, interesting photographs of pure or mixed-breed dogs in canine situations (dogs with veterinarians; dogs eating, drinking, playing, swimming, etc.) for use with feature articles. Shots should have natural, modern background, style and setting, avoiding studio backgrounds. Photographer is responsible for model releases.

SPECS Prefers high-res digital images either TIFF or JPEG at least 5 inches at 300 dpi. Can be sent on disc or via FTP site. Instructions for FTP submittal provided upon request. Send CD or DVD.

MAKING CONTACT & TERMS Address submission to "Photo Editor." Present a professional package, disc with photographer's name on it separated by subject with contact sheets. Pays $300 for color cover; $25-100 for color inside; $200 for 4-color centerspreads. Credit line given. Buys first North American print rights and non-exclusive rights to use in electronic media.

TIPS "Send a variety of shots. We mainly want to see candid outdoor and action photos of dogs alone and dogs with people. Once we review your images, we will notify you whether we will be adding you to our list of freelance photographers. Poor lighting, focus, and composition in photographs are what make a particular photographer a likely candidate for rejection."

◯ DOGS IN CANADA

Apex Publishing, Ltd., 200 Ronson Dr., Suite 401, Etobicoke ON M9W 5Z9, Canada. (416)798-9778. Fax: (416)798-9671. E-mail: editor@dogsincanada.com. Website: www.dogsincanada.com. Kelly Caldwell, art director. Estab. 1889. Circ. 41,769. Monthly. "*Dogs in Canada* is a reliable and authoritative source of information about dogs. Our mix of editorial content and photography must satisfy a diverse readership, including breed fanciers and serious pet fanciers. Photography is of central importance." Sample copy available for $4.95 and 8×10 SASE with postage. Request photo guidelines via e-mail.

NEEDS Buys 10-30 photos/year. Photos from any category as long as there is a purebred dog in the shot. Reviews photos with or without a manuscript. Model/property release preferred. Photo captions preferred; include breed of dog.

SPECS Only accepts images in digital format. Send via CD as TIFF or EPS files at 300 dpi.

MAKING CONTACT & TERMS E-mail query letter with link to photographer's website and JPEG samples at 72 dpi. Send query letter with slides, prints. Provide résumé, business card, self-promotion piece to be kept on file for possible future assignments. Responds only

if interested; send nonreturnable samples. Considers previously published work. Pays $80-600 for b&w or color cover; $50-300 for b&w or color inside. Pays on publication. Credit line given. Buys first rights, electronic rights.

TIPS "Well-composed, high-quality photographs are expected. A creative approach catches our eye. Photos that capture a moment in time and the essence of a dog are preferred to a staged portrait."

DOWNBEAT

102 N. Haven Rd., Elmhurst IL 60126. (630)941-2030. E-mail: editor@downbeat.com. Website: www.downbeat.com. Estab. 1934. Circ. 90,000. Monthly. Emphasizes jazz musicians. Sample copy available with SASE.

NEEDS Buys 20 photos from freelancers/issue; 240 photos/year. Needs photos of live music performers/posed musicians/equipment, primarily jazz and blues. Photo captions preferred.

SPECS Accepts images in digital format. "Do not send unsoliciated high-res images via e-mail!" Send 8×10 b&w prints; 35mm, 2¼×2¼, 4×5, 8×10 transparencies; b&w or color contact sheets by mail.

MAKING CONTACT & TERMS Unsolicited samples will not be returned unless accompanied by SASE. Provide résumé, business card, brochure, flyer or tearsheets to be kept on file for possible future assignments. Responds only when needed. Simultaneous submissions and previously published work OK. Pay rates vary by size. Credit line given. Buys one-time rights.

TIPS "We prefer live shots and interesting candids to studio work."

THE DRAKE MAGAZINE

1600 Maple St., Fort Collins CO 80521. (949)218-8642. E-mail: info@drakemag.com. Website: www.drakemag.com. Estab. 1998. Quarterly. For fly-fishing enthusiasts.

NEEDS Buys 50 photos from freelancers/issue. Needs creative flyfishing shots. Reviews photos with or without a manuscript.

SPECS Uses digital photos; 35mm transparencies.

MAKING CONTACT & TERMS Send query letter with slides. Provide business card to be kept on file for possible future assignments. Responds in 6 months to queries. Pays $200 minimum for color cover; $40 minimum for b&w inside. Pays on publication. Credit line given. Buys one-time rights.

TIPS "No 'grip and grins' for fishing photos. Think creative. Show me something new."

$$ DUCKS UNLIMITED MAGAZINE

One Waterfowl Way, Memphis TN 38120. (901)758-3864. E-mail: jhoffman@ducks.org. Website: www.ducks.org. **Contact:** John Hoffman, photo editor. Estab. 1937. Circ. 700,000. Bimonthly association magazine of Ducks Unlimited Inc., a nonprofit organization. Emphasizes waterfowl hunting and conservation. Readers are professional males, ages 40-50. Sample copy available for $3. Photo guidelines available on website, via e-mail or with SASE.

NEEDS Images of wild ducks and geese, waterfowling and scenic wetlands. Special photo needs include waterfowl hunters, dynamic shots of waterfowl interacting in natural habitat. Buys 84 photos from freelancers/issue; 504 photos/year

SPECS Accepts images in digital format. Send via CD as TIFF, JPEG, EPS files at 300 dpi; include thumbnails.

MAKING CONTACT & TERMS Responds in 1 month. Previously published work *will not be considered.* Pays on publication. Credit line given. Buys one-time rights "plus permission to reprint in our Mexican and Canadian publications."

$ EASYRIDERS

Paisano Publications, 28210 Dorothy Dr., Agoura Hills CA 91301. (818)889-8740. E-mail: davenichols@easyriders.net. Website: www.easyriders.com. **Contact:** Dave Nichols, editorial director. Estab. 1971. Monthly. Emphasizes "motorcycles (Harley-Davidsons in particular), motorcycle women, bikers having fun." Readers are "adult men who own, or desire to own, custom motorcycles; the individualist—a rugged guy who enjoys riding a custom motorcycle and all the good times derived from it." Sample copy free. Photo guidelines free with SASE.

NEEDS Uses about 60 photos/issue; majority supplied by freelancers; 70% assigned. Photos of "motorcycle riding (rugged chopper riders), motorcycle women, good times had by bikers, etc." Model release required. Also interested in technical articles relating to Harley-Davidsons.

SPECS Prefers images in digital format. Send via CD at 300 dpi ("raw from camera, no effects added"). Call for digital guidelines.

MAKING CONTACT & TERMS Send b&w prints, color prints, 35mm transparencies by mail for consideration. Include SASE. Call for appointment for portfolio review. Responds in 3 months. Pays $30-100 for b&w photos; $40-250 for color photos; $30-1,700 for complete package. Other terms for bike features with models to satisfaction of editors. Pays 30 days after publication. Credit line given. Buys all rights. All material must be exclusive.

TIPS Trend is toward "more action photos, bikes being photographed by photographers on bikes to create a feeling of motion." In samples, wants photos "clear, in-focus, eye-catching and showing some emotion. Read magazine before making submissions. Be critical of your own work. Check for sharpness. Also, label photos/slides clearly with name and address."

THE ELKS MAGAZINE

425 W. Diversey Pkwy., Chicago IL 60614-6196. (773)755-4740. E-mail: elksmag@elks.org. Website: www.elks.org/elksmag. **Contact:** Cheryl T. Stachura, editor/publisher. Estab. 1922. Circ. 1,037,000.

NEEDS Buys 10 cover photos/year; mostly from stock photo houses; approximately 20 photos/month for interior use. "Photographs of elks in action are particularly welcome." Reviews photos with or without a manuscript. Photo captions required; include location.

SPECS Accepts high-res digital images.

MAKING CONTACT & TERMS Send query letter with samples. Does not keep samples on file; include SASE for return of material. Responds in 2 months to queries. Simultaneous submissions OK. Pays $475 for color cover. Pays on publication. Credit line given. Buys one-time rights.

TIPS "Artistry and technical excellence are as important as subject matter. We are now purchasing 90% of our photographs from photographic stock houses."

$$ ◐ ENTREPRENEUR

2445 McCabe Way, Suite 400, Irvine CA 92614. (949)261-2325. E-mail: queries@entrepreneur.com. Website: www.entrepreneur.com. Megan Roy, creative director. Estab. 1977. Circ. 650,000. Monthly. Emphasizes business. Readers are existing and aspiring small business owners.

NEEDS Uses 40 photos/issue; 10% supplied by freelance photographers; 80% on assignment; 10% from stock. Needs people at work, home office, business situations. "I want to see colorful shots in all formats and styles." Model/property release preferred. Photo captions required; include names of subjects.

SPECS Accepts images in digital format and film. Send via ZIP, CD, e-mail as TIFF, EPS, JPEG files at 300 dpi.

MAKING CONTACT & TERMS All magazine queries should be e-mailed to: queries@entrepreneur.com. Responds in 6 weeks. No phone calls, please. Entrepreneur Media Inc. assumes no responsibility for unsolicited manuscripts or photos. Provide résumé, business card, brochure, flyer or tearsheets to be kept on file for possible future assignments. Pays $2,000 for color cover; $700 for color inside. **Pays on acceptance.** Credit line given. Buys one-time North American rights; negotiable.

TIPS "I am looking for photographers who use the environment creatively; I do not like blank walls for backgrounds. Lighting is also important. I prefer medium-format for most shoots. I think photographers are going back to the basics—a good, clean shot, different angles and bright colors. I also like gelled lighting. I prefer examples of your work—promo cards and tearsheets—along with business cards and résumés."

[●] $ [O] EOS MAGAZINE

Robert Scott Publishing, The Old Barn, Ball Lane, Tackley, Kidlington, Oxfordshire 0X5 3AG, United Kingdom. (44)(186)933-1741. Fax: (44)(186)933-1641. E-mail: editorial@eos-magazine.com. Website: www.eos-magazine.com. **Contact:** Angela August, editor. Estab. 1993. Circ. 20,000. Quarterly. For all users of Canon EOS cameras. Photo guidelines free.

NEEDS Looking for quality stand-alone images as well as photos showing specific photographic techniques and comparison pictures. All images must be taken with EOS cameras but not necessarily with Canon lenses. Model release preferred. Photo captions required; include technical details of photo equipment and techniques used.

SPECS Accepts images in digital format exclusively.

MAKING CONTACT & TERMS E-mail to request 'Notes for Contributors' (put this in the subject line). You will be e-mailed with further information about how to submit images, current requirements, and rates of payment. Pays on publication. Credit line given. Buys one-time rights.

TIPS "We are more likely to use images from photographers who submit a wide selection of top-quality images (40-60 images)."

[O] EVENT

Douglas College, P.O. Box 2503, New Westminster BC V3L 5B2, Canada. (604)527-5293. Fax: (604)527-5095. E-mail: event@douglas.bc.ca. Website: www.douglas.bc.ca/visitors/event-magazine.html. Estab. 1971. Circ. 1,250. Published every 4 months. Emphasizes literature (short stories, reviews, poetry, creative nonfiction). Sample back issue available for $9. Current issue is $12.

NEEDS Buys approximately 3 photographs/year. Has featured photographs by Mark Mushet, Lee Hutzulak and Anne de Haas. Assigns 50% of photographs to new and emerging photographers. Uses freelancers mainly for covers. "We look for art that is adaptable to a cover, particularly images that are self-sufficient and don't lead the reader to expect further artwork within the journal."

MAKING CONTACT & TERMS "Please send photography/artwork (no more than 10 images) to *Event*, along with SASE (Canadian postage or IRCs only) for return of your work. We also accept e-mail submissions of cover art. We recommend that you send low-res versions of your photography/art as small JPEG or PDF attachments. If we are interested, we will request high-res files. We do not buy the actual piece of art; we only pay for the use of the image." Simultaneous submissions OK. Pays $150 on publication. Credit line given. Buys one-time rights.

FACES

Cobblestone Publishing, 30 Grove St., Suite C, Peterborough NH 03458. (603)924-7209; (800)821-0115. Fax: (603)924-7380. E-mail: customerservice@caruspub.com. Website: www.cobblestonepub.com. Estab. 1984. Circ. 15,000. Published 9 times/year, September-May. Emphasizes cultural anthropology for young people ages 8-14. Sample copies available; see website. Photo guidelines and themes available online or free with SASE.

NEEDS Uses about 30-35 photos/issue; 75% supplied by freelancers. "Photos (color) for text must relate to themes; cover photos (color) should also relate to themes." Send SASE for themes. Photos purchased with or without accompanying manuscript. Model release preferred. Photo captions preferred.

MAKING CONTACT & TERMS Query with stock photo list and/or samples. Responds in 1 month. Simultaneous submissions and previously published work OK. Pays $200-350 for color cover; $25-100 color inside. Pays on publication. Buys one-time rights. Credit line given.

TIPS "Photographers should request our theme list. Most of the photographs we use are of people from other cultures. We look for an ability to capture people in action—at work or play. We primarily need photos showing people, young and old, taking part in ceremonies, rituals, customs and with artifacts and architecture particular to a given culture. Appropriate scenics and animal pictures are also needed. All submissions must relate to a specific future theme."

FAITH & FRIENDS

The Salvation Army, 2 Overlea Blvd., Toronto ON M4H 1P4, Canada. (416)422-6226. Fax: (416)422-6120. E-mail: faithandfriends@can.salvationarmy.org. Website: www.faithandfriends.ca. **Contact:** Geoff Moulton, senior editor. Circ. 43,000. Monthly. "Our mission: To show Jesus Christ at work in the lives of real people, and to provide spiritual resources for those who are new to the Christian faith."

NEEDS Photos of religion.

SPECS Accepts images in digital format. Send JPEG or GIF files. Uses prints.

MAKING CONTACT & TERMS Payment negotiated. Captions required. Buys one-time rights.

FAMILY MOTOR COACHING

8291 Clough Pike, Cincinnati OH 45244. (513)474-3622. Fax: (513)388-5286. E-mail: rgould@fmca.com. Website: www.fmca.com. **Contact:** Robbin Gould, editor. Estab. 1963. Circ. 140,000. Monthly publication of the Family Motor Coach Association. Emphasizes motor homes. Readers are members of national association of motor home owners. Sample copy available for $3.99 ($5 if paying by credit card). Writer's/photographer's guidelines free with SASE or via e-mail.

NEEDS Buys 55-60 photos from freelancers/issue; 660-720 photos/year. Each issue includes varied subject matter—primarily needs photos depicting motor home travel, travel with scenic shots, couples, families, senior citizens, hobbies and how-to material. Photos purchased with accompanying manuscript only. Model release preferred. Photo captions required.

SPECS Accepts images in digital format. Send via CD as EPS, TIFF files at 300 dpi.

MAKING CONTACT & TERMS Send query letter with résumé of credits, samples, contact sheets; include SASE for return of material. Responds in 3 months. Pays $100 for color cover; $25-100 for b&w and color inside. $125-500 for text/photo package. **Pays on acceptance.** Credit line given if requested. Prefers first North American rights, but will consider one-time rights on photos *only*.

TIPS Photographers are "welcome to submit brochures or copies of their work. We'll keep them in mind should a freelance photography need arise."

$ FELLOWSHIP

P.O. Box 271, Nyack NY 10960. (845)358-4601 ext. 42. E-mail: editor@forusa.org. Website: www.forusa.org. **Contact:** Ethan Vesely-Flad, editor. Estab. 1935. Circ. 5,000. Publication of the Fellowship of Reconciliation published 4 times/year. Emphasizes peace-making, social justice, nonviolent social change. Readers are interested in peace, justice, nonviolence and spirituality. Sample copy available for $7.50.

NEEDS Buys 0-2 photos from freelancers/issue; 4-10 photos/year. Needs stock photos of people, civil disobedience, demonstrations—Middle East, Latin America, Caribbean, prisons, anti-nuclear, children, gay/lesbian, human rights issues, Asia/Pacific. Captions required.

MAKING CONTACT & TERMS Provide résumé, business card, brochure, flyer or tearsheets to be kept on file for possible future assignments. "Call for specs." Responds in 4-6 weeks. Simultaneous submissions and previously published work OK. Pays $100 for color cover; $35 for b&w inside. Pays on publication. Credit line given. Buys one-time rights.

TIPS "You must want to make a contribution to peace movements. Money is simply token."

$ FIELD & STREAM

2 Park Ave., New York NY 10016. (212)779-5238. E-mail: amy.berkley@bonniercorp.com; Anna.Armienti@bonniercorp.com. Website: www.fieldandstream.com. **Contact:** Amy Berkley, photo editor. Circ. 1.5 million. Broad-based service magazine published 11 times/year. Editorial content ranges from very basic "how it's done" filler stories that tell in pictures and words how an outdoor technique is accomplished or device is made, to feature articles of penetrating depth

about national conservation, game management and resource management issues; also recreational hunting, fishing, travel, nature and outdoor equipment. Photo guidelines available.

NEEDS Photos using action and a variety of subjects and angles in color and occasionally b&w. "We are always looking for cover photographs, in color, vertical or horizontal. Remember: a cover picture must have room for cover lines." Also looking for interesting photo essay ideas related to hunting and fishing. Query photo editor by mail. Needs photo information regarding subjects, the area, the nature of the activity and the point the picture makes. First Shots: these photos appear every month (2/issue). Prime space, 2-page spread. One of a kind, dramatic, impactful images, capturing the action and excitement of hunting and fishing. Great beauty shots. Unique wildlife images. See recent issues. "Please do not submit images without reviewing past issues and having a strong understanding of our audience."

SPECS Uses 35mm slides. Will also consider large-format photography. Accepts images in digital format. Send via CD, e-mail as JPEG files at 300 dpi.

MAKING CONTACT & TERMS Submit photos by registered mail. Send slides in 8½×11 plastic sheets, and pack slides and prints between cardboard. Include SASE for return of material. Drop portfolios at receptionist's desk, ninth floor. Buys first North American serial rights.

FINESCALE MODELER

Kalmbach Publishing Co., P.O. Box 1612, Waukesha WI 53187. (414)796-8776. Website: www.finescale. com. Circ. 60,000. Published 10 times/year. Emphasizes "how-to information for hobbyists who build non-operating scale models." Readers are "adult and juvenile hobbyists who build non-operating model aircraft, ships, tanks and military vehicles, cars and figures." Photo and submission guidelines free with SASE or online.

NEEDS Buys 10 photos from freelancers/issue; 100 photos/year. Needs "in-progress how-to photos illustrating a specific modeling technique; photos of full-size aircraft, cars, trucks, tanks and ships." Model release required. Photo captions required.

SPECS Prefers prints and transparencies; will accept digital images if submission guidelines are followed.

MAKING CONTACT & TERMS Provide résumé, business card, brochure, flyer or tearsheets to be kept on file for possible future assignments. "Will sometimes accept previously published work if copyright is clear. Pays for photos on publication, for text/photo package on acceptance. Credit line given. Buys all rights.

TIPS Looks for "sharp color prints or slides of model aircraft, ships, cars, trucks, tanks, figures and science-fiction subjects. In addition to photographic talent, must have comprehensive knowledge of objects photographed and provide complete caption material. Freelance photographers should provide a catalog stating subject, date, place, format, conditions of sale and desired credit line before attempting to sell us photos. We're most likely to purchase color photos of outstanding models of all types for our regular feature, 'Showcase.'"

FLAUNT

1422 N. Highland Ave., Los Angeles CA 90028. (323)836-1000. E-mail: info@flauntmagazine.com. Website: www.flaunt.com. **Contact:** Lee Corbin, art director; Andrew Pogany, senior editor. Estab. 1998. Circ. 100,000. Monthly. Covers culture, arts, entertainment, literature. "*Flaunt* features the bold work of emerging photographers, writers, artists and musicians. The quality of the content is mirrored in the sophisticated, interactive format of the magazine, using advanced printing techniques, fold-out articles, beautiful papers, and inserts to create a visually stimulating, surprisingly readable and intelligent book that pushes the magazine format into the realm of art object."

NEEDS Photos of celebrities, architecture, cities/urban, entertainment, performing arts, avant garde, lifestyle. Reviews photos with or without a manuscript. Model release required. Captions required; include identification of subjects.

SPECS Accepts images in digital format. Send JPEG or GIF files. Reviews contact sheets, any size transparencies and prints.

MAKING CONTACT & TERMS E-mail query letter with link to photographer's website. Credit line given. Buys one-time rights.

FLORIDA SPORTSMAN

Wickstrom Communications, Intermedia Outdoors, 2700 S. Kanner Hwy., Stuart FL 34994. (772)219-7400. Fax: (772)219-6900. E-mail: editor@florida sportsman.com. Website: www.floridasportsman. com. Circ. 115,000. Edited for the boatowner and offshore, coastal, and fresh water fisherman. It provides a how, when, and where approach in its articles, which also includes occasional camping, diving, and hunting stories—plus ecology; in-depth articles and editorials attempting to protect Florida's wilderness, wetlands, and natural beauty.

SPECS High-res digital images on CD preferred. Reviews 35mm transparencies, 4×5 and larger prints.

MAKING CONTACT & TERMS Pays up to $750 for cover photos. Buys all rights.

$ ⚑ ◐ FLY ROD & REEL

P.O. Box 370, Camden ME 04843. (207)594-9544. Fax: (207)594-5144. E-mail: editor@flyrodreel.com. Website: www.flyrodreel.com. **Contact:** Paul Guernsey, editor-in-chief. Estab. 1979. Circ. 61,941. Quarterly. Emphasizes fly-fishing. Readers are primarily fly-fishers ages 30-60. Sample copy and photo guidelines free with SASE; photo guidelines also available via e-mail.

NEEDS Buys 15-20 photos from freelancers/issue; 90-120 photos/year. Needs "photos of fish, scenics (preferably with anglers in shot), equipment." Photo captions preferred; include location, name of model (if applicable).

SPECS Uses 35mm slides; 2¼×2¼, 4×5 transparencies.

MAKING CONTACT & TERMS Send query letter with list of stock photo subjects. Send unsolicited photos by mail for consideration; include SASE for return of material. Provide résumé, business card, brochure, flier or tearsheets to be kept on file for possible future assignments. Responds in 1 month. Pays $600-800 for color cover photo; $75 for b&w inside (seldom needed); $75-200 for color inside. Pays on publication. Credit line given. Buys one-time rights.

TIPS "Photos should avoid appearance of being too 'staged.' We look for bright color (especially on covers), and unusual, visually appealing settings. Trout and salmon are preferred for covers. Also looking for saltwater fly-fishing subjects. Ask for guidelines, then send 20 to 40 shots showing breadth of work."

◯ FOLIATE OAK LITERARY MAGAZINE

University of Arkansas-Monticello, P.O. Box 3460, Monticello AR 71656. (870)460-1247. E-mail: foliateoak@uamont.edu. Website: www.foliateoak. Uamont.edu. **Contact:** Online submission manager. Estab. 1973. Circ. 500. "We are a university general literary magazine publishing new and established artists." Has featured Terry Wright, Brett Svelik, Lucita Peek, David Swartz and Fariel Shafee. No samples kept on file.

NEEDS People, architecture, cities, gardening, landscapes, wildlife, environmental, natural disasters, adventure, humor, alternative, avant garde, documentary, erotic, fashion/glamour, fine art, historical, and lifestyle photographs. Photo captions are preferred.

MAKING CONTACT & TERMS Online submission manager must be used to submit all artwork.

TIPS "We are unable to pay our contributors but we love to support freelancers. We solicit work for our online magazine and our annual print anthology. Read submission guidelines online."

$ $ FOOD & WINE

1120 Avenue of the Americas, New York NY 10036. (212)382-5600. Website: www.foodandwine.com. **Contact:** Fredrika Stjarne, director of photography. Estab. 1978. Circ. 950,000. Monthly. Emphasizes food and wine. Readers are "upscale people who cook, entertain, dine out and travel stylishly."

NEEDS Uses 25-30 photos/issue; 85% freelance photography on assignment basis; 15% freelance stock. "We look for editorial reportage specialists who do restaurants, food on location, and travel photography." Model release required. Photo captions required.

MAKING CONTACT & TERMS Drop off portfolio on Wednesday (attn: Rebecca Jacobs). Call for pickup. Submit flyers, tearsheets, etc., to be kept on file for possible future assignments and stock usage. Pays $450/color page; $100-450 for color photos. **Pays on acceptance.** Credit line given. Buys one-time world rights.

FORTUNE

Time, Inc., 1271 Avenue of the Americas, New York NY 10020. (212)522-1212. Fax: (212)522-0810. E-mail: fortunemail_letters@fortunemail.com. Website: www.fortune.com. Scott Thode, deputy picture editor. Circ. 1,066,000. Emphasizes analysis of news in the business world for management personnel.

MAKING CONTACT & TERMS Picture editor reviews photographers' portfolios on an overnight drop-off basis. Photos purchased on assignment only. Day rate on assignment (against space rate): $500; page rate for space: $400; minimum for b&w or color usage: $200.

FORWARD IN CHRIST

WELS Communication Services, 2929 N. Mayfair Rd., Milwaukee WI 53222-4398. (414)256-3210. Fax: (414)256-3210. E-mail: fic@wels.net. Website: www.wels.net. John A. Braun, executive editor. **Contact:** Julie K. Wietzke, managing editor. Estab. 1913. Circ. 42,000. Official monthly magazine covering Wisconsin Evangelical Lutheran Synod (WELS) news, topics, issues. The material usually must be written by or about WELS members.

MAKING CONTACT & TERMS Reviews contact sheets. Captions, identification of subjects, model releases required. Negotiates payment individually. Buys one-time rights, plus 1 month on Web and in archive.

FRANCE MAGAZINE

Archant House, Oriel Rd., Cheltenham, Gloucestershire GL50 1BB, United Kingdom. +44 1242 216001. E-mail: miller.hogg@archant.co.uk; editorial@francemag.com. Website: www.francemag.com; www.archant.co.uk. **Contact:** Adam Vines, art editor. Estab. 1990. Circ. 40,000. Monthly, about France. Readers are male and female, ages 45 and over; people who holiday in France.

NEEDS Photos of France and French subjects: people, places, customs, curiosities, produce, towns, cities, countryside. Photo captions required; include location and as much information as is practical.

SPECS Uses 35mm, medium-format transparencies; high-quality digital.

MAKING CONTACT & TERMS "E-mail in the first instance with list of subjects. Please do not send digital images. We will add you to our photographer list and contact you on an ad-hoc basis for photographic requirements."

THE FREEFALL REVIEW

Undead Poets Press, 15735 Kerstyn St., Taylor MI 48180-4891. E-mail: shootanyangle@yahoo.com. Website: www.freefallreview.t35.com. **Contact:** James Hannibal. Estab. 1997. Circ. 250. "*The Freefall Review* is a literary magazine showcasing b&w photography inside and color photography on the cover. The cover is a horizontal color photo that wraps around to the back cover (please make sure your cover submissions are horizontal and that the right and left half of the photo can stand on their own as well as together, bear-

ing in mind that just the right half of the photo will be on the front)."

TIPS "Please carefully review our submission guidelines at our website before submitting."

FRESHLY BAKED FICTION

Isis International, P.O. Box 510232, Saint Louis MO 63151. (314)315-5200. E-mail: editor@freshlybakedfiction.com. Website: www.freshlybakedfiction.com. **Contact:** John Ferguson, editor. Estab. 2009. Circ. 8,000+ monthly. "*Freshly Baked Fiction* is a non-genre specific publication. We publish short stories, novellas, poetry, art, and more. Our audience is everyone that loves to read. Our website is free to all and updated daily with new fiction and classic works. *Freshly Baked Fiction* is a place where new and published authors can get opinions and insight from readers and other authors relating to their own work. Taking advantage of technology, we have set out goals on being the new way people read. We will be offering readers a chance to get daily fiction on eBook readers, via RSS, e-mail, iPhone, and other electronic devices that have yet to hit the market."

NEEDS Style photography: alternative process, avant garde, documentary, erotic, fine art, historical/vintage, lifestyle and seasonal. Samples not kept on file. Portfolio not required. Credit line given.

MAKING CONTACT & TERMS Send an e-mail with samples in zipped TIFF, GIF or JPEG format.

TIPS "We like to use technology. We look for creative artists and photographers willing to use multiple medias to create work. Also, make sure you send work as attachments. Zipped or unzipped is good. Technology is here to stay, so I recommend you learn to use it."

FT. MYERS MAGAZINE

And Pat, LLC, 15880 Summerlin Rd., Suite 189, Fort Myers FL 33908. (941)433-3884. E-mail: ftmyers@optonline.net. Website: www.ftmyersmagazine.com. Estab. 2001. Circ. 20,000. Bimonthly. Covers regional arts and living for educated, active, successful and creative residents of Lee and Collier counties (FL) and guests at resorts and hotels in Lee County.

NEEDS Buys 3-6 photos from freelancers/year. Photos of celebrities, architecture, gardening, interiors/decorating, medicine, product shots/still life, environmental, landscapes/scenics, wildlife, entertainment, events, food/drink, health/fitness/beauty, performing arts, sports, travel. Interested in alternative process, avant garde, documentary, fashion/glamour, fine art, historical/vintage. Also needs beaches, beach scenes/sunsets over beaches, boating/fishing, palm trees. Reviews photos with or without a manuscript. Model release required. Photo captions preferred; include description of image and photo credit.

SPECS Uses 4×5, 8×10 glossy or matte color and b&w prints; 35mm, 2×2, 4×5, 8×10 transparencies ("all are acceptable, but we prefer prints or digital"). Accepts images in digital format. Send via CD or e-mail (preferred) as TIFF, EPS, PICT, JPEG, PDF files (prefers TIFF or JPEG) at 300-600 dpi.

MAKING CONTACT & TERMS Send query letter via e-mail with digital images and stock list. Responds only if interested; send nonreturnable samples. Simultaneous submissions and previously published work OK. Pays $100 for b&w or color cover; $25-100 for b&w or color inside. Pays on publication. Credit line given. Buys one-time rights.

FUR-FISH-GAME

2878 E. Main St., Columbus OH 43209-9947. E-mail: ffgcox@ameritech.net. Website: www.furfishgame.com. **Contact:** Mitch Cox, editor. Estab. 1900. Circ. 111,000. Monthly. For outdoorsmen of all ages who are interested in hunting, fishing, trapping, dogs, camping, conservation, and related topics.

NEEDS Buys 4 photos from freelancers/issue; 50 photos/year. Photos of freshwater fish, wildlife, wilderness and rural scenes. Reviews photos with or without a manuscript. Photo captions required; include subject.

SPECS Reviews transparencies, color 5×7 or 8×10 prints, digital photos on CD only with thumbnail sheet of small images and a numbered caption sheet.

MAKING CONTACT & TERMS Send query letter "and nothing more." Does not keep samples on file; include SASE for return of material. Responds in 1 month to queries. Simultaneous submissions and previously published work OK. Pays $35 minimum for b&w and color inside. Pays on publication. Credit line given. Buys one-time rights.

GAME & FISH

(770)953-9222. Fax: (770)933-9510. E-mail: ken.dunwoody@inoutdoors.com. Website: www.gameandfishmag.com. Ron Sinfelt, photo editor. Estab. 1975. Circ. 570,000. Publishes 31 different monthly outdoors magazines: *Alabama Game & Fish, Arkansas Sportsman, California Game & Fish, Flor-*

ida Game & Fish, Georgia Sportsman, Great Plains Game & Fish, Illinois Game & Fish, Indiana Game & Fish, Iowa Game & Fish, Kentucky Game & Fish, Louisiana Game & Fish, Michigan Sportsman, Mid-Atlantic Game & Fish, Minnesota Sportsman, Mississippi/Louisana Game & Fish, Missouri Game & Fish, New England Game & Fish, New York Game & Fish, North Carolina Game & Fish, Ohio Game & Fish, Oklahoma Game & Fish, Pennsylvania Game & Fish, Rocky Mountain Game & Fish, South Carolina Game & Fish, Tennessee Sportsman, Texas Sportsman, Virginia Game & Fish, Washington-Oregon Game & Fish, West Virginia Game & Fish, Wisconsin Sportsman, and North American Whitetail. All magazines (except *Whitetail*) are for experienced hunters and fishermen and provide information about where, when and how to enjoy the best hunting and fishing in their particular state or region, as well as articles about game and fish management, conservation and environmental issues. Photo guidelines and current needs list free with SASE.

NEEDS 50% of photos supplied by freelance photographers; 5% assigned. Photos of live game animals/birds in natural environments and hunting scenes; game fish photos and fishing scenes. Photo captions required; include species identification and location. Number slides/prints.

SPECS Accepts images in digital format. Send via CD at 300 dpi with output of 8×12.

MAKING CONTACT & TERMS Send 5×7, 8×10 glossy b&w prints or 35mm transparencies (preferably Fujichrome, Kodachrome) with SASE for consideration. Responds in 1 month. Simultaneous submissions not accepted. Pays 60 days prior to publication. Tearsheet provided. Credit line given. Buys one-time rights.

TIPS "Send separate CD and proof sheet for each species, with digital submissions. We'll return photos we don't expect to use and hold remainder in-house so they're available for monthly photo selections. Please do not send dupes. Photos will be returned upon publication or at photographer's request."

GARDENING HOW-TO

12301 Whitewater Dr., Minnetonka MN 55317. (952)936-9333. E-mail: editors@gardeningclub.com. Website: www.gardeningclub.com. **Contact:** Lisa Samoilenko, art director. Estab. 1996. Circ. 708,000. Association magazine published 6 times/year. Emphasizes gardening subjects for the avid home gardener, from beginner to expert. Readers are 78% female, average age of 51. Sample copies available.

NEEDS Buys 50 photos from freelancers/issue; 300 photos/year. Needs photos of gardening. Offers assignment work shooting specific gardens around the country. Reviews photos with or without a manuscript. Model/property release preferred. Photo captions preferred.

SPECS Prefers images in digital format. Send via CD as TIFF, EPS, JPEG files at 300 dpi. "FTP site available for digital images." Also uses 35mm, 2¼×2¼, 4×5, 8×10 transparencies.

MAKING CONTACT & TERMS Query art director. Provide self-promotion piece to be kept on file for possible future assignments. Responds only if interested; send nonreturnable samples. Previously published work OK. Pays $750 for cover; payment for inside depends on size. **Pays on acceptance.** Credit line given. Buys one-time rights, first rights, electronic rights; negotiable.

TIPS "Looking for tack-sharp, colorful general gardening photos and will send specific wants if interested in your work. Send a complete list of photos along with slides or CD in package."

GEORGIA STRAIGHT

1701 W. Broadway, Vancouver BC V6J 1Y3, Canada. (604)730-7000. Fax: (604)730-7010. E-mail: contact@straight.com; photos@straight.com. Website: www.straight.com. **Contact:** Charlie Smith, editor. Estab. 1967. Circ. 117,000. Weekly tabloid. Emphasizes entertainment. Readers are generally well-educated people, ages 20-45. Sample copy free with 10×12 SASE.

NEEDS Buys 3 photos from freelancers/issue; 364 photos/year. Needs photos of entertainment events and personalities. Photo captions essential.

MAKING CONTACT & TERMS Send query letter with list of stock photo subjects. Provide résumé, business card, brochure, flier or tearsheets to be kept on file for possible future assignments. Responds in 1 month. Simultaneous submissions and previously published work OK. Include SASE for return of material. Pays $250-300 for cover; $100-200 for inside. Pays on publication. Credit line given. Buys one-time rights.

TIPS "Almost all needs are for in-Vancouver assigned photos, except for high-quality portraits of film stars. We rarely use unsolicited photos, except for Vancouver photos for our content page."

GERMAN LIFE

Zeitgeist Publishing, Inc., 1068 National Hwy., LaVale MD 21502. (301)729-6190. Fax: (301)729-1720. E-mail: mslider@germanlife.com. Website: www.germanlife.com. **Contact:** Mark Slider. Estab. 1994. Circ. 40,000. Bimonthly. Focuses on history, culture, and travel relating to German-speaking Europe and German-American heritage. Sample copy available for $5.95.

MAKING CONTACT & TERMS Reviews color transparencies, 5×7 color or b&w prints. Buys one-time rights.

GHOST TOWN

2660 Petersborough St., Herndon VA 20171. E-mail: shannonsdustytrails@yahoo.com. **Contact:** Shannon Bridget Murphy. Estab. 1998. Quarterly. Photo guidelines available by e-mail request.

NEEDS Buys 12 photos from freelancers/issue; 48-72 photos/year. Photos of babies/children/teens, celebrities, couples, multicultural, families, parents, disasters, environmental, landscapes/scenics, wildlife, architecture, cities/urban, education, gardening, interiors/decorating, pets, religious, rural, adventure, events, food/drink, sports, travel, agriculture, medicine, military, political, product shots/still life, science, technology—as they are related to archaeology and ghost towns. Interested in alternative process, avant garde, documentary, fashion/glamour, fine art, historical/vintage, seasonal. Wants photos of archaeology sites and excavations in progress of American ghost towns. "Would like photographs from ghost towns and western archaeological sites." Reviews photos with or without a manuscript. Model/property release preferred.

SPECS Uses glossy or matte color and b&w prints.

MAKING CONTACT & TERMS Send query letter via e-mail. "If possible, please do not include photographs in files if they are sent through e-mail. A CD sent with your photographs is acceptable." Provide résumé, business card or self-promotion piece to be kept on file for possible future assignments. "Photographs sent with CDs are requested but not required. Illustrations and artwork are also accepted." Responds within 1 month to queries; 1 week to portfolios. Simultaneous submissions and previously published work OK. **Pays on acceptance.** Credit line given. Buys one-time rights, first rights; negotiable.

$ ◎ GIRLS LIFE

4529 Harford Rd., Baltimore MD 21214. (410)426-9600. Fax: (410)254-0991. E-mail: katiea@girlslife.com. Website: www.girlslife.com. **Contact:** Katie Abbondanza, senior editor. Estab. 1994. Bimonthly. Emphasizes advice, relationships, school, current news issues, entertainment, quizzes, fashion and beauty pertaining to preteen girls. Readers are preteen girls (ages 10-15). *Girls' Life* accepts unsolicited manuscripts on a speculative basis only. First, send an e-mail or letter query with detailed story ideas. No telephone solicitations, please. Guidelines available online.

NEEDS Buys 65 photos from freelancers/issue. Submit seasonal material 3 months in advance.

SPECS Uses 5×8, 8½×11 color and b&w prints; 35mm, 4×5 transparencies.

MAKING CONTACT & TERMS Send query letter with stock list. E-mail queries are responded to within 90 days. Works on assignment only. Keeps samples on file. Responds in 3 weeks. Simultaneous submissions and previously published work OK. Pays on usage. Credit line given.

TIPS Please familiarize yourself with the voice and content of *Girls' Life* before submitting.

🍁 ● GOLF CANADA

Chill Media Inc., 77 John St., Suite 4, Oakville ON L6K 3W3, Canada. (905)337-1886. Fax: (905)337-1887. E-mail: scotty@chillmag.ca; stacy@chillonline.ca. Website: www.golfcanada.ca. Stacy Bradshaw, associate editor. **Contact:** Scott Stevenson, publisher. Estab. 1994. Circ. 159,000. Published 4 times/year. Covers Canadian golf. The official magazine of the Royal Canadian Golf Association, published to entertain and enlighten members about RCGA-related activities and to generally support and promote amateur golf in Canada.

GOLF TIPS

Werner Publishing Corp., 12121 Wilshire Blvd., 12th Floor, Los Angeles CA 90025-1176. (310)820-1500. Fax: (310)826-5008. E-mail: editors@golftipsmag.com. Website: www.golftipsmag.com. Warren Keating, art director. Estab. 1986. Circ. 300,000. Published 9 times/year. Readers are "hardcore golf enthusiasts." Sample copy free with SASE. Submission guidelines at www.golftipsmag.com/submissions.html.

NEEDS Buys 40 photos from freelancers/issue; 360 photos/year. Photos of golf instruction (usually prearranged, on-course), equipment; health/fitness, travel. Interested in alternative process, documentary, fashion/glamour. Reviews photos with accompanying manuscript only. Model/property release preferred. Photo captions required.

SPECS Uses prints; 35mm, 2¼×2¼, 4×5, 8×10 transparencies. Accepts images in digital format. Send via ZIP as TIFF files at 300 dpi.

MAKING CONTACT & TERMS Send query letter with résumé of credits. Submit portfolio for review. Cannot return material. Responds in 1 month. Pays $500-1,000 for b&w or color cover; $100-300 for b&w inside; $150-450 for color inside. Pays on publication. Buys one-time rights; negotiable.

GO

INK Publishing, 68 Jay St., Suite 315, Brooklyn NY 11201. (347)294-1220. Fax: (917)591-6247. E-mail: editorial@airtranmagazine.com. E-mail: trcrosby@mailaaa. Website: www.airtranmagazine.com. **Contact:** Shane Luitjens, art director. Estab. 2003. Circ. 100,000. "*Go Magazine* is an inflight magazine covering travel, general interest and light business."

MAKING CONTACT & TERMS Reviews GIF/JPEG files. Buys one-time rights.

GOOD HOUSEKEEPING

Hearst Corp., 300 W. 57th St., 28th Floor, New York NY 10019. (212)649-2200. Website: www.goodhousekeeping.com. **Contact:** Melissa Paterno, art director; Toni Paciello, photo editor; Laura Mathews, fiction editor. Circ. 5,000,000. Articles focus on food, fitness, beauty and childcare, drawing upon the resources of the Good Housekeeping Institute. Editorial includes human interest stories and articles that focus on social issues, money management, health news and travel. Photos purchased mainly on assignment. *Query before submitting.*

🍁 O GOSPEL HERALD

5 Lankin Blvd., Toronto ON M4J 4W7, Canada. (416)461-7406. Fax: (416)424-1850. E-mail: editorial@gospelherald.org. Website: www.gospelherald.org. **Contact:** Max Craddock, managing editor. Estab. 1936. Circ. 1,300. Monthly. Emphasizes Christianity. Readers are primarily members of the Churches of Christ. Sample copy free with SASE.

NEEDS Uses 2-3 photos/issue. Photos of babies/children/teens, families, parents, landscapes/scenics, wildlife, seasonal, especially those relating to readership—moral, religious and nature themes.

SPECS Uses b&w, any size and any format. Accepts images in digital format. Send via CD, ZIP, e-mail as JPEG files.

MAKING CONTACT & TERMS Send unsolicited photos by mail for consideration. Payment not given, but photographer receives credit line.

TIPS "We have never paid for photos. Because of the purpose of our magazine, both photos and stories are accepted on a volunteer basis."

GRACE ORMONDE WEDDING STYLE

Elegant Publishing, Inc., P.O. Box 89, Barrington RI 02806. (401)245-9726. Fax: (401)245-5371. E-mail: jessica@weddingstylemagazine.com. Website: www. weddingstylemagazine.com. **Contact:** Jessica Latimer. Estab. 1997. Circ. 500,000. Semiannual. Covers weddings catering to the affluent bride.

MAKING CONTACT & TERMS Reviews transparencies. Negotiates payment individually.

GRAND RAPIDS FAMILY MAGAZINE

Gemini Publications, 549 Ottawa Ave., NW, Suite 201, Grand Rapids MI 49503-1444. (616)459-4545. Fax: (616)459-4800. E-mail: cvalade@geminipub.com. Website: www.grfamily.com. **Contact:** Carole Valade. Circ. 30,000. Monthly. Covers local parenting issues. *Grand Rapids Family* seeks to inform, instruct, amuse, and entertain its readers and their families.

NEEDS Buys 20-50 photos from freelancers/issue; 240-600 photos/year. Needs photos of families, children, education, infants, play, etc. Model/property release required. Photo captions preferred; include who, what, where, when.

MAKING CONTACT & TERMS Send query letter with résumé of credits, stock list. Sometimes keeps samples on file; include SASE for return of material. Responds in 1 month, only if interested. Simultaneous submissions and previously published work OK. Pays $200 minimum for color cover; $35-75 for inside. Pays on publication. Credit line given. Buys one-time rights, all rights; negotiable.

TIPS "We are not interested in clip art variety photos. We want the honesty of photojournalism; photos that speak to the heart, that tell a story, that add to the story told."

GRAND RAPIDS MAGAZINE

Gemini Publications, 549 Ottawa Ave., NW, Suite 201, Grand Rapids MI 49503-1444. (616)459-4545. Fax: (616)459-4800. E-mail: cvalade@geminipub.com. Website: www.grmag.com. **Contact:** Carole Valade, editor. Estab. 1964. Circ. 20,000. Monthly. Emphasizes community-related material of metro Grand Rapids area and West Michigan; local action and local people.

NEEDS Photos of animals, nature, scenic, travel, sport, fashion/beauty, photo essay/photo feature, fine art, documentary, human interest, celebrity/personality, humorous, wildlife, vibrant people shots and special effects/experimental. Wants, on a regular basis, West Michigan photo essays and travel-photo essays of any area in Michigan. Model release required. Photo captions required.

SPECS Prefers images in digital format. Send via CD at 300 dpi minimum. Also uses 2¼×2¼, 4×5 color transparencies for cover, vertical format required. "High-quality digital also acceptable."

MAKING CONTACT & TERMS Send material by mail for consideration; include SASE for return. Provide business card to be kept on file for possible future assignments; "only people on file with us are those we have met and personally reviewed." Arrange a personal interview to show portfolio. Responds in 3 weeks. Pays $35-100 for color photos; $100 minimum for cover. Buys one-time rights, exclusive product rights, all rights; negotiable.

TIPS "Most photography is by our local freelance photographers, so you should sell us on the unique nature of what you have to offer."

THE GREYHOUND REVIEW

P.O. Box 543, Abilene KS 67410. (785)263-4660. E-mail: nga@ngagreyhounds.com. Website: www. ngagreyhounds.com. Estab. 1911. Circ. 3,500. Monthly publication of The National Greyhound Association. Emphasizes Greyhound racing and breeding. Readers are Greyhound owners and breeders. Sample copy free with SASE and 11 first-class stamps.

NEEDS Buys 1 photo from freelancers/issue; 12 photos/year. Needs "anything pertinent to the Greyhound that would be of interest to Greyhound owners." Photo captions required.

MAKING CONTACT & TERMS Query via e-mail first. After response, send b&w or color prints and contact sheets by mail for consideration. Provide résumé, business card, brochure, flier or tearsheets to be kept on file for possible future assignments. Can return unsolicited material if requested; include SASE for return of material. Responds in 1 month. Simultaneous submissions and previously published work OK. Pays $85 for color cover; $25-100 for color inside. **Pays on acceptance**. Credit line given. Buys one-time and North American rights.

TIPS "We look for human-interest or action photos involving Greyhounds. No muzzles, please, unless the Greyhound is actually racing. When submitting photos for our cover, make sure there's plenty of cropping space on all margins around your photo's subject; full breeds on our cover are preferred."

◎ ❶ ○ GRIT MAGAZINE

1503 SW 42nd St., Topeka KS 66609. (785)274-4300. Fax: (785)274-4305. E-mail: Grit@Grit.com. Website: www.grit.com. **Contact:** Jean Teller, senior associate editor; Caleb Regan, associate editor. Estab. 1882. Circ. 230,000. "*Grit* focuses on rural lifestyles, country living and small farming. We are looking for useful, practical information on livestock, gardening, farm equipment, home and yard improvement and related topics."

NEEDS Buys 24+ photos/year with accompanying stories or articles; 90% from freelancers. Needs, on a regular basis, photos of small-farm livestock, animals, farm labor, gardening, produce and related images. "Be certain pictures are well composed, properly exposed and pin sharp. Must be *shot* at high resolution (no less than 300 dpi). No cheesecake. No pictures that cannot be shown to any member of the family. No pictures that are out of focus or over- or underexposed. No ribbon-cutting, check-passing or handshaking pictures. Story subjects include all aspects of the hobby or country lifestyle farm, such as livestock, farm dogs, barn cats, sowing and hoeing, small tractors, fences, etc. Photo captions required. Any image that stands alone must be accompanied by 50-100 words of meaningful caption information."

SPECS 35mm, slides and high-res digital images. Send digital images via CD or e-mail; ZIP as JPEG files at 300 dpi. Model and property releases are preferred. Photo captions are required (who, what, when, where, why, how).

MAKING CONTACT & TERMS "Study the magazine. We use a beautiful country scene for 'Reverie,' the last page in each issue. Take a look at previous issues to get a sense of the sort of shot we're looking for." Send material by mail with SASE for consideration. Responds ASAP. Pay is negotiable up to $1,000 for color cover; $35-200 for color inside; $25-100 for b&w inside. Rarely uses b&w, and only if "irresistibly atmospheric." Pays on publication. Buys shared rights; negotiable.

GUERNICA

165 Bennett Ave., 4C, New York NY 10040. E-mail: editors@guernicamag.com; art@guernicamag.com; publisher@guernicamag.com. Website: www.guernica mag.com. **Contact:** Dan Eckstein, art/photography. Estab. 2005. Biweekly. "*Guernica* is one of the Web's most acclaimed new magazines. *Guernica* is called a "great online literary magazine" by *Esquire*. Contributors come from dozens of countries and write in nearly as many languages."

❸❸ ○ GUIDEPOSTS

P.O. Box 5814, Harlan IA 51593. (800)431-2344. E-mail: submissions@guidepostsmag.com. Website: www.guideposts.org. **Contact:** Candice Smilow, photo editor. Estab. 1945. Circ. 2.6 million. Monthly. Emphasizes tested methods for developing courage, strength and positive attitudes through faith in God. Free sample copy and photo guidelines with 6×9 SASE.

NEEDS Uses 90% assignment, 10% stock on a story-by-story basis. Photos are mostly environmental portraiture, editorial reportage. Stock can be scenic, sports, fine art, mixed variety. Model release required.

SPECS Uses 35mm, 2¼×2¼ transparencies; vertical for cover, horizontal or vertical for inside. Accepts images in digital format. Send via CD at 300 dpi.

MAKING CONTACT & TERMS Send photos or arrange a personal interview. Responds in 1 month. Simultaneous submissions OK. Pays by job or on a per-photo basis; $800 minimum for color cover; $150-400 for color inside; negotiable. **Pays on acceptance.** Credit line given. Buys one-time rights.

TIPS "I'm looking for photographs that show people in their environment; straight portraiture and people interacting. We're trying to appear more contemporary. We want to attract a younger audience and yet maintain a homey feel. For stock—scenics; graphic images in color. *Guideposts* is an 'inspirational' magazine. No violence, nudity, sex. No more than 20 images at a time. Write first and ask for a sample issue; this will give you a better idea of what we're looking for."

GUITAR WORLD

149 5th Ave., 9th Floor, New York NY 10010. (650)872-1642. E-mail: gwedit@aol.com; soundingboard@guitarworld.com. Website: www.guitarworld.com. Circ. 150,000. Written for guitar players categorized as either professionals, semi-professionals or amateur players. Every issue offers broad-ranging interviews that cover technique, instruments, and lifestyles. "To submit a GuitarWorldBlips story, you must be logged in. If you already have an account on GuitarWorldBlips, please log in. Or join GuitarWorldBlips—it's free and fast. Just fill out the form and enter the URL, title, and description. Your story will appear once we've validated your e-mail address."

NEEDS Buys 20 photos from freelancers/issue; 240 photos/year. Photos of guitarists. Reviews photos with or without a manuscript. Property release preferred. Photo captions preferred.

SPECS Uses glossy or matte color and b&w prints; 35mm, 2¼×2¼ transparencies. Accepts images in digital format. Send via e-mail as TIFF, EPS, JPEG files at 300 dpi.

MAKING CONTACT & TERMS Send query letter with slides, prints, photocopies, tearsheets. Keeps samples on file. Responds in 2 weeks to queries. Previously published work OK. Pay rates vary by size. **Pays on acceptance.** Credit line given. Buys one-time rights.

HADASSAH MAGAZINE

50 W. 58th St., New York NY 10019. (212)688-0227. Fax: (212)446-9521. E-mail: magazine@hadassah.org. Website: www.hadassah.org. **Contact:** Rachel Fyman Schwartzberg. Circ. 300,000. Monthly publication of the Hadassah Women's Zionist Organization of America. Emphasizes Jewish life, Israel. Readers are 85% females who travel and are interested in Jewish affairs, average age 59. Photo guidelines free with SASE.

NEEDS Uses 10 photos/issue; most supplied by freelancers. Photos of travel, Israel and general Jewish life. Photo captions preferred; include where, when, who and credit line.

SPECS Accepts images in digital format. Send via CD as JPEG files at 300 dpi. High-res, digital photos preferred. Pays $80-$100/image.

MAKING CONTACT & TERMS Submit portfolio for review. Send unsolicited photos by mail for consideration. Keeps samples on file; include SASE for return of material. Responds in 3 months. Pays $450 for color cover; $125-175 for quarter page color inside. Pays on publication. Credit line given. Buys one-time rights.

TIPS "We frequently need travel photos, especially of places of Jewish interest."

HAMILTON MAGAZINE

Town Media, 1074 Cooke Blvd., Burlington ON L7T 4A8, Canada. (905)522-6117 or (905)634-8003. Fax: (905)634-7661 or (905)634-8804. E-mail: david@townmedia.ca; info@townmedia.ca. Website: www.hamiltonmagazine.com. Kate Sharrow, art director. Estab. 1978. "Our mandate: to entertain and inform by spotlighting the best of what our city and region have to offer. We invite readers to take part in a vibrant community by supplying them with authoritative and dynamic coverage of local culture, food, fashion and design."

NEEDS Photos of cities/urban, entertainment, food/drink, health/fitness/beauty, fashion/glamour, lifestyle. Reviews photos with or without a manuscript. Captions required; include identification of subjects.

SPECS Accepts images in digital format. Send JPEG files at 8×10 at 300 dpi. Uses 8×10 prints.

MAKING CONTACT & TERMS Pays on publication. Credit line given.

HARPER'S MAGAZINE

666 Broadway, 11th Floor, New York NY 10012. (212)420-5720. Fax: (212)228-5889. E-mail: readings@harpers.org. Website: www.harpers.org. **Contact:** Stacey Clarkson, art director. Estab. 1850. Circ. 230,000. Monthly literary magazine. "The nation's oldest continually published magazine providing fiction, satire, political criticism, social criticism, essays." *Harper's Magazine* encourages national discussion on current and significant issues in a format that offers arresting facts and intelligent opinions.

NEEDS Buys 8-10 photos from freelancers/issue; 120 photos/year. Needs photos of human rights issues, environmental, political. Interested in alternative process, avant garde, documentary, fine art, historical/vintage. Model/property release preferred.

SPECS Uses any format. Accepts images in digital format. Send preferably via e-mail to alyssa@harpers.org or on CD; TIFF, EPS, JPEG files at 72 dpi.

MAKING CONTACT & TERMS Send query letter with résumé, slides, prints, photocopies, tearsheets, transparencies. Portfolio may be dropped off last Wednesday of the month. Provide self-promotion piece to be kept on file for possible future assignments. Responds in 1 week. Pays $200-800 for b&w/color cover; $250-400 for b&w/color inside. Pays on publication. Credit line given. Buys one-time rights; negotiable.

TIPS "*Harper's* is geared more toward fine art photos or artist's portfolios than to 'traditional' photo usages. For instance, we never do fashion, food, travel (unless it's for political commentary), lifestyles or celebrity profiles. A good understanding of the magazine is crucial for photo submissions. We consider all styles and like experimental or nontraditional work. Please don't confuse us with *Harper's Bazaar!*"

◐ HEALING LIFESTYLES & SPAS MAGAZINE

JLD Publications, P.O. Box 271207, Louisville CO 80027. (303)917-7124. Fax: (303)926-4099. E-mail: melissa@healinglifestyles.com. Website: www.healinglifestyles.com. Laura Kayata, art director. **Contact:** Melissa B. Williams, editorial director. Estab. 1997. *HL&S* is an online-only publication—a trusted leading social media platform for the spa/wellness industry, focusing on spas, retreats, therapies, food and beauty geared toward a mostly female audience, offering a more holistic and alternative approach to healthy living. Photo guidelines available with SASE.

NEEDS Buys 3 photos from freelancers/issue; 6-12 photos/year. Photos of multicultural, environmental, landscapes/scenics, adventure, health/fitness/beauty, food, yoga, travel. Reviews photos with or without a manuscript. Model/property release preferred. Photo captions required; include subject, location, etc.

SPECS Prefers images in digital format. Send via CD, ZIP, e-mail as TIFF, EPS, JPEG files at 300 dpi. Also uses 35mm or large-format transparencies.

MAKING CONTACT & TERMS Send query letter with résumé, prints, tearsheets. Provide résumé, business card, self-promotion piece to be kept on file for possible future assignments. Responds in 1 month. Responds only if interested; send nonreturnable samples. Simultaneous submissions OK. Pays on assignment. Credit line given. Buys one-time rights.

TIPS "We strongly prefer digital submissions, but will accept all formats. We're looking for something other than the typical resort/spa shots—everything from at-home spa treatments to far-off, exotic locations. We're also looking for reliable lifestyle photographers who can shoot yoga-inspired shots, healthy cuisine, ingredients, and spa modalities in an interesting and enlightening way."

◎ ○ HEARTLAND BOATING

The Waterways Journal, Inc., 319 N. Fourth St., Suite 650, St. Louis MO 63102. (314)241-4310. Fax: (314)241-4207. E-mail: Lbraff@Heartlandboating.com. Website: www.Heartlandboating.com. **Contact:** John R. Cassady, art director. Estab. 1989. Circ. 12,000. "*Heartland Boating*'s content is both informative and humorous—describing boating life as the heartland boater knows it. The content reflects the challenge, joy, and excitement of our way of life afloat. We are devoted to both power and sailboating enthusiasts throughout middle America; houseboats are included. The focus is on the freshwater inland rivers and lakes of the heartland, primarily the waters of the Arkansas, Tennessee, Cumberland, Ohio, Missouri, Illinois, and Mississippi rivers, the Tennessee-Tombigbee Waterway, the Gulf Intracoastal Waterway, and the lakes along these waterways."

NEEDS Hobby or sports photos, primarily boating.

MAKING CONTACT & TERMS Send query letter with samples or postcard sample. No follow-ups. Samples kept on file. Portfolio not required. Credit line given.

TIPS "Please read the magazine first. Go to the website to obtain three free copies. Our rates are low, but we do our best to take care of and promote our contributors. *Note: any e-mail submission will be deleted unread.* Submissions must come during our window, May 1-July 1, and be hard-copy form only. Remember to include all of your contact info!"

◑ HERITAGE RAILWAY MAGAZINE

P.O. Box 43, Horncastle, Lincolnshire LN9 6JR, United Kingdom. (44)(507)529300. Fax: (44)(507)529301. E-mail: robinjones@mortons.co.uk. Website: www.heritagerailway.co.uk. **Contact:** Mr. Robin Jones, editor. Circ. 15,000. Monthly leisure magazine emphasizing preserved railways; covering heritage steam, diesel and electric trains with over 30 pages of news in each issue.

NEEDS Interested in railway preservation. Reviews photos with or without a manuscript. Photo captions required.

SPECS Uses glossy or matte color and b&w prints; 35mm, 2¼×2¼, 4×5, 8×10 transparencies. No digital images accepted.

MAKING CONTACT & TERMS Send query letter with slides, prints, transparencies. Query with online contact form. Does not keep samples on file; include SASE for return of material. Responds in 1 month to queries. Simultaneous submissions OK. Buys one-time rights.

HIGHLIGHTS FOR CHILDREN

803 Church St., Honesdale PA 18431-1824. (570)253-1080. Fax: (570)251-7847. Website: www.Highlights. com. Christine French Clark, editor-in-chief; Cindy Faber Smith, art director. **Contact:** Manuscript Coordinator. Estab. 1946. Circ. approx. 2.5 million. Monthly. For children ages 2-12. Sample copy free.

○ *Highlights* is currently expanding photographic needs.

NEEDS Buys 100 or more photos/year. "We will consider outstanding photo essays on subjects of high interest to children." Reviews photos with accompanying manuscript only. Wants no single photos without captions or accompanying manuscript.

SPECS Accepts images in digital format. Send via CD at 300 dpi. Also accepts transparencies of all sizes.

MAKING CONTACT & TERMS Send photo essays with SASE for consideration. Responds in 7 weeks. Pays $30 minimum for b&w photos; $50 minimum for color photos; $100 minimum for manuscript. Buys all rights.

TIPS "Tell a story that is exciting to children. We also need mystery photos, puzzles that use photography/collage, special effects, anything unusual that will visually and mentally challenge children."

HIGHWAYS

Affinity Group, Inc., 2575 Vista Del Mar Dr., Ventura CA 93001. (805)667-4100. E-mail: highways@goodsamclub.com. Website: www.goodsamclub.com/highways. Estab. 1966. Circ. 975,000. Monthly. Covers recreational vehicle lifestyle. Sample copy free with 8½×11 SASE.

SPECS Accepts images in digital format. Send via CD or e-mail at 300 dpi.

MAKING CONTACT & TERMS Editorial director will contact photographer for portfolio review if in-terested. Pays $500 for cover; $75-350 for inside. Buys one-time rights.

HOME EDUCATION MAGAZINE

P.O. Box 1083, Tonasket WA 98855. (800)236-3278; (509)486-1351. Fax: (509)486-2753. E-mail: articles@homeedmag.com. Website: www.homeedmag.com. **Contact:** Jeanne Faulconer, articles editor. Estab. 1983. Circ. 120,000. Bimonthly. Emphasizes homeschooling. Readership includes parents, educators, researchers, media.—anyone interested in homeschooling. Sample copy available for $6.50. Photo guidelines free with SASE or via e-mail.

NEEDS Number of photos used/issue varies based on availability; 50% supplied by freelance photographers. Photos of babies/children/teens, multicultural, families, parents, senior citizens, education. Special photo needs include homeschool personalities and leaders. Model/property release preferred. Photo captions preferred.

SPECS Uses color prints in normal print size. "Enlargements not necessary." Accepts images in digital format. Send via CD, ZIP, e-mail as TIFF files at 300 dpi.

MAKING CONTACT & TERMS Send unsolicited color prints by mail with SASE for consideration. Responds in 1 month. Pays $100 for color cover; $12.50 for color inside; $50-150 for photo/text package. Pays on publication. Credit line given. Buys first North American serial rights.

TIPS In photographer's samples, wants to see "sharp, clear photos of children doing things alone, in groups, or with parents. Know what we're about! We get too many submissions that are simply irrelevant to our publication."

HOOF BEATS

750 Michigan Ave., Columbus OH 43215. E-mail: hoofbeats@ustrotting.com. Website: www.hoofbeatsmagazine.com. Estab. 1933. Circ. 13,500. Monthly publication of the U.S. Trotting Association. Emphasizes harness racing. Readers are participants in the sport of harness racing. Sample copy free.

NEEDS Buys 6 photos from freelancers/issue; 72 photos/year. Needs "artistic or striking photos that feature harness horses for covers; other photos on specific horses and drivers by assignment only."

MAKING CONTACT & TERMS Send query letter with samples; include SASE for return of material. Responds in 3 weeks. Simultaneous submissions OK.

Pays $150 minimum for color cover; $25-150 for b&w inside; $50-200 for color inside; freelance assignments negotiable. Pays on publication. Credit line given if requested. Buys one-time rights.

TIPS "We look for photos with unique perspective and that display unusual techniques or use of light. Send query letter first. Know the publication and its needs before submitting. Be sure to shoot pictures of harness horses only, not thoroughbred or riding horses. We always need good night racing action or creative photography."

THE HORSE

P.O. Box 919003, Lexington KY 40591-9003. (859)278-2361. Fax: (859)276-4450. E-mail: schurch@thehorse.com. Website: www.thehorse.com. **Contact:** Stephanie Church; Megan Arszman, photo/newsletter editor. Estab. 1983. Circ. 55,000. Monthly. Emphasizes equine health. Readers are equine veterinarians, hands-on horse owners, trainers and barn managers. Sample copy free with large SASE. Photo guidelines free with SASE and on website.

NEEDS Buys 20-30 photos from freelancers/issue; 240-360 photos/year. Needs generic horse shots, horse health such as farrier and veterinarian shots. "We use all breeds and all disciplines." Model/property release preferred. Photo captions preferred.

SPECS Uses color transparencies. Accepts images in digital format. Send via CD, floppy disk, ZIP, e-mail as TIFF, EPS, JPEG files at 300 dpi (4×6). "All photos must have metadata included in them before sending to photo editor."

MAKING CONTACT & TERMS Send unsolicited photos by mail for consideration. Keeps samples on file. Previously published work OK. Pays $350 for color cover; $40-120 for color inside. Pays on publication. Buys one-time rights.

TIPS "Please include name, address, and phone number of photographer; date images were sent; whether images may be kept on file or should be returned; date by which images should be returned; number of images sent. Usually 10-20 samples is adequate. Do not submit originals. E-mail photo editor before you send photos."

HORSE ILLUSTRATED

BowTie, Inc., P.O. Box 8237, Lexington KY 40533. (859)260-9800. Fax: (859)260-1154. E-mail: horse illustrated@bowtieinc.com. Website: www.horse illustrated.com. **Contact:** Elizabeth Moyer, editor. Es-tab. 1976. Circ. 160,660. Readers are "primarily adult horsewomen, ages 18-40, who ride and show mostly for pleasure, and who are very concerned about the well being of their horses. Editorial focus covers all breeds and all riding disciplines." Sample copy available for $4.99. Photo guidelines free with SASE.

NEEDS Buys 30-50 photos from freelancers/issue. Needs stock photos of riding and horse care. "Photos must reflect safe, responsible horsekeeping practices. We prefer all riders to wear protective helmets; prefer people to be shown only in action shots (riding, grooming, treating, etc.). We like all riders—especially those jumping—to be wearing protective headgear."

SPECS Prefer digital images—high-res JPEGs on a CD with printout of thumbnails.

MAKING CONTACT & TERMS Send by mail for consideration. Responds in 2 months. Pays $250 for color cover; $65-250 for color inside. Credit line given. Buys one-time rights.

TIPS "Looks for clear, sharp color shots of horse care and training. Healthy horses, safe riding and care atmosphere is standard in our publication. Send SASE for a list of photography needs, photo guidelines, and to submit work. Photo guidelines are also available on our website."

🐾 💲 🄴 HUNGER MOUNTAIN

Vermont College of Fine Arts, 36 College St., Montpelier VT 05602. (802)828-8517. E-mail: hungermtn@vermontcollege.edu. Website: www.hungermtn.org. Estab. 2002.

NEEDS Buys no more than 10 photos/year. Interested in avant garde, documentary, fine art, seasonal. Reviews photos with or without a manuscript.

MAKING CONTACT & TERMS Send query letter with résumé, slides, prints, tearsheets. Does not keep samples on file; include SASE for return of material. Responds in 3 months to queries and portfolios. Simultaneous submissions OK. Pays $30-45 for inside photos; cover negotiable. Pays on publication. Credit line given. Buys first rights.

TIPS Fine art photography—no journalistic/media work. Particularly interested in b&w. "Keep in mind that we only publish twice per year with a minimal amount of artwork. Considering publication of a special edition of all b&w photos. Interested in photography with a literary link."

IDEALS MAGAZINE

2630 Elm Hill Pike., Suite 100, Nashville TN 37214. (615)333-0478. Fax: (888)815-2759. Website: www.idealsbooks.com. **Contact:** Melinda Rathjen Rumbaugh, editor. Estab. 1944. Circ. 25,000. Published 2 times/year. Emphasizes an idealized, nostalgic look at America through poetry and short prose, using seasonal themes. Average reader has a college degree. Sample copy available for $4. Photo guidelines free with SASE or available on website.

NEEDS Buys 30 photos from freelancers/issue; 120 photos/year. Photos of "bright, colorful flowers, scenics, still life, children, pets, home interiors; subject-related shots depending on issue." Model/property release required. No research fees.

SPECS Prefers medium- to large-format transparencies; no 35mm.

MAKING CONTACT & TERMS Submit tearsheets to be kept on file. No color copies. Will send photo needs list if interested. Do not submit unsolicited photos or transparencies. Keeps samples on file. Simultaneous submissions and previously published work OK. Payment negotiable. Pays on publication. Credit line given. Buys one-time rights.

TIPS "We want to see *sharp* shots. No mood shots, please. No filters. We suggest the photographer study several recent issues of *Ideals* for a better understanding of our requirements."

IMAGE BY DESIGN LICENSING

7 Hunting Gate, Hitchen, Herts SG4 OTJ, UK. 44 0 7462 4244. E-mail: lucy@ibd-licensing.co.uk. Website: www.Ibd-licensing.co.uk. **Contact:** Lucy Brenham. Agency specializing in art licensing. Serves fine artists, illustrators, and photographers. Interested in reviewing fine art, design, and photography.

MAKING CONTACT & TERMS Send a link to a website with résumé, bio, brochure of work, photocopies or digital images in low-res JPEG format.

TIPS Be aware of current trends.

INDIANAPOLIS MONTHLY

Emmis Publishing Corp., 1 Emmis Plaza, 40 Monument Cir., Suite 100, Indianapolis IN 46204. (317)237-9288. E-mail: dzivan@indymonthly.emmis.com. Website: www.indianapolismonthly.com. **Contact:** David Zivan, editor. Estab. 1977. Circ. 50,000. "*Indianapolis Monthly* attracts and enlightens its upscale, well-educated readership with bright, lively editorial on subjects ranging from personalities to social issues, fashion to food. Its diverse content and attention to service make it the ultimate source by which the Indianapolis area lives." Sample copy available for $4.95 and 9×12 SASE.

NEEDS Buys 10-12 photos from freelancers/issue; 120-144 photos/year. Needs seasonal, human interest, humorous, regional; subjects must be Indiana- or Indianapolis-related. Model release preferred. Photo caption information required.

SPECS Glossy prints; transparencies, digital. Send via CD, e-mail as TIFF, EPS, JPEG files at 300 dpi at actual size.

MAKING CONTACT & TERMS Send query letter with samples, SASE. Responds in 1 month. Previously published work on occasion OK, if different market. Pays $300-1,200 for color cover; $75-350 for b&w inside; $75-350 for color inside. Pays on publication. Credit line given. Buys first North American serial rights.

TIPS "Read publication. Send photos similar to those you see published. If you see nothing like what you are considering submitting, it's unlikely we will be interested. We are always interested in photo essay queries if they are Indiana-specific."

INSIDE TRIATHLON

9477 Waples St., Suite 150, San Diego CA 92121. (858)768-6776. Website: www.insidetriathlon.com. Circ. 40,000 (paid). Monthly journal of triathlons; includes news, features, profiles.

NEEDS Looking for "action and feature shots that show the emotion of triathlons, not just finish-line photos with the winner's arms in the air. Need shots of triathletes during training sessions (non-racing) for our 'Training' section." Reviews photos with or without a manuscript. Photo captions required; include identification of subjects.

SPECS Uses digital files, negatives and transparencies.

MAKING CONTACT & TERMS Send samples of work or tearsheets with assignment proposal. Query before sending manuscript. Responds in 3 weeks. Pays $325 for color cover; $24-72 for b&w inside; $48-300 for color inside. Pays on publication. Credit line given. Buys one-time rights.

TIPS "Photos must be timely."

⊛⊛ ◐ INSIGHT MAGAZINE

Review and Herald Publishing, 55 W. Oak Ridge Dr., Hagerstown MD 21740. (301)393-4038. Fax: (301)393-4055. E-mail: insight@rhpa.org. Website: www.insightmagazine.org. Estab. 1970. Circ. 20,000. Weekly Seventh-Day Adventist teen magazine. "We print teens' true stories about God's involvement in their lives. All stories, if illustrated by a photo, must uphold moral and church organization standards while capturing a hip, teen style." Sample copy free.

NEEDS Model/property release required. Photo captions preferred; include who, what, where, when.

MAKING CONTACT & TERMS "Send query letter with photo samples so we can evaluate style." Provide résumé, business card, self-promotion piece or tearsheets to be kept on file for possible future assignments. Responds only if interested; send nonreturnable samples. Simultaneous submissions and previously published work OK. Pays $200-300 for color cover; $200-400 for color inside. Pays 30-45 days after receiving invoice and contract. Credit line given. Buys first rights. Submission guidelines available online.

◐ INSTINCT MAGAZINE

303 N. Glenoaks Blvd., Suite L-120, Burbank CA 91502. (818)286-0071; (818)843-1536 x102. E-mail: editor@instinctmag.com. Website: instinctmag.com. **Contact:** Mike Wood, editor-in-chief. Estab. 1997. Circ. 115,000. Monthly gay men's magazine. "*Instinct* is geared towards a gay male audience. The slant of the magazine is humor mingled with entertainment, travel, and health and fitness." Sample copies available. Photo guidelines available via website.

NEEDS Buys 50-75 photos from freelancers/issue; 500-750 photos/year. Needs photos of celebrities, couples, cities/urban, entertainment, health/fitness, humor, travel. Interested in lifestyle, fashion/glamour. High emphasis on humorous and fashion photography. Reviews photos with or without a manuscript. Model release required; property release preferred. Photo captions preferred.

SPECS Uses 8×10 glossy color prints; 2¼×2¼ transparencies. Accepts images in digital format. Send via CD, Jaz, ZIP as TIFF files at least 300 dpi.

MAKING CONTACT & TERMS Portfolio may be dropped off every weekday. Provide résumé, business card, self-promotion piece to be kept on file for possible future assignments. Responds in 2 weeks.

Simultaneous submissions OK. Payment negotiable. Pays on publication. Credit line given.

TIPS "Definitely read the magazine. Keep our editor updated about the progress or any problems with the shoot."

INTERVAL WORLD

P.O. Box 431920, Miami FL 33243-1920. (305)666-1861. E-mail: kimberly.dewees@intervalintl.com. Website: www.intervalworld.com. **Contact:** Kimberly Dewees, photo editor. Estab. 1982. Circ. 1,080,000. Quarterly publication of Interval International. Emphasizes vacation exchange and travel. Readers are members of the Interval International vacation exchange network.

NEEDS Uses 100 or more photos/issue. Needs photos of travel destinations, vacation activities. Model/property release required. Photo captions required; all relevant to full identification.

MAKING CONTACT & TERMS Send query letter with stock list. Provide business card, brochure, flyer or tearsheets to be kept on file for possible future assignments. Cannot return materials. Simultaneous submissions and previously published work OK. Payment negotiable. Pays on publication. Credit line given for editorial use. Buys one-time rights; negotiable.

TIPS Looking for beautiful scenics; family-oriented, fun travel shots; superior technical quality.

⊛⊛ ◐ IN THE WIND

Paisano Publications, P.O. Box 3000, Agoura Hills CA 91376-3000. (818)889-8740; (800)879-4247. Fax: (818)889-1252. E-mail: k.peterson@paisanopub.com; photos@easyriders.net. Website: www.easyriders.com. **Contact:** Kim Peterson, editor. Estab. 1978. Circ. 65,000. Quarterly. Displays the exhilaration of riding American-made V-twin (primarily Harley-Davidson) street motorcycles, the people who enjoy them, and the fun involved. Motto: "If It's Out There, It's In Here." Photo guidelines free with SASE.

NEEDS Photos of celebrities, couples, landscapes/scenics, adventure, events, travel. Interested in erotic, historical/vintage. Other specific photo needs: action photos of people—men or women—riding Harley-Davidson motorcycles. "Ideally, with no helmets; full-frame without wheels cropped off on the bikes. No children." Reviews photos with or without a manuscript. Model release required on posed and nude photos.

SPECS Uses 4×6, 5×7, 8×10 glossy color and b&w prints; 35mm transparencies. Accepts images in digital format. Send via CD, e-mail as TIFF, JPEG files at 300 dpi, 5×7 size. 3 megapixel minimum (2048 x 1536) Resolution: 5×7, 300 dpi minimum - RGB Color Mode. Acceptable Formats: TIFF, Photoshop (PSD), Kodak Photo CDs, JPEG. GIF format is NOT acceptable.

MAKING CONTACT & TERMS There is an online submission form. Send query letter with slides, prints, transparencies. Does not keep samples on file; include SASE for return of material. Responds in 6 weeks to queries; 3 months to portfolios. Responds only if interested; send nonreturnable samples. Pays $30-200 for b&w cover; $30-200 for color cover; $30-500 for b&w inside; $30-500 for color inside; inset photos usually not paid extra. Assignment photography for features pays up to $1,500 for bike and model. Pays on publication. Credit line given. Buys all rights; negotiable.

TIPS "Get familiar with the magazine. Shoot sharp, in-focus pictures; fresh views and angles of bikes and the biker lifestyle. Send SASE for return of material. Label each photo with name, address and caption information, i.e., where and when picture was taken."

THE IOWAN MAGAZINE

300 Walnut, Suite 6, Des Moines IA 50309. (515)246-0402. Fax: (515)282-0125. E-mail: editor@iowan.com; artdirector@iowan.com. Website: www.iowan.com. **Contact:** Bobbie Russie, art director. Estab. 1952. Circ. 22,000. Bimonthly. Emphasizes "Iowa's people, places, events, nature and history." Readers are over age 40, college-educated, middle-to-upper income. Sample copy available for $4.50 plus shipping/handling; call the distribution center toll-free at (877)899-9977. Photo guidelines available on website or via e-mail.

NEEDS "We print only Iowa-related images from Iowa photographers, illustrators, and artists. Show us Iowa's residents, towns, environmental, landscape/scenics, wildlife, architecture, rural, entertainment, events, performing arts, travel." Interested in Iowa heritage, historical/vintage, seasonal. Accepts unsolicited stock photos related to above. Editorial stock photo needs available on website or via e-mail. Model/property release preferred. Photo captions required.

SPECS Digital format preferred on clearly labeled CD/DVD with submission form, printed contact sheet, and image reference. See website for details. Press resolution is 300 dpi at 9×12. Digital materials will not be returned. Uses 35mm, color transparencies, which will be returned following press deadline.

MAKING CONTACT & TERMS Pays $50-250 for stock photo one-time use, depending on size printed; pays on publication. Contract rates run $200-500/day for assigned editorials; pays within 60 days of receipt of invoice.

ISLANDS

Bonnier Corporation, 460 N. Orlando Ave., Suite 200, Winter Park FL 32789. (407)571-4930; (407)628-4802. Fax: (407)628-7061. E-mail: editor@islands.com. Website: www.islands.com. **Contact:** Lori Barbely, photo editor. Circ. 200,000. Published 8 times/year. "From Bora Bora to the Caribbean, Tahiti to Bali and beyond, *Islands* is your passport to the world's most extraordinary destinations. Each issue is filled with breathtaking photography and detailed first-hand accounts of the fascinating cultural experiences and tranquil, relaxing escapes unique to each vibrant locale."

NEEDS Buys 50 photos from freelancers/issue; 400 photos/year. Needs photos of island travel. Reviews photos with or without a manuscript. Model/property release preferred. Detailed captions required (please use metadata); include name, phone, address, subject information.

SPECS Prefers images in digital format. Send via CD, e-mail, web gallery, FTP site as JPEG files at 72 dpi (must have 300 dpi file available if image is selected for use). Film is not desired.

MAKING CONTACT & TERMS Send query letter with tearsheets. Provide business card and self-promotion piece or tearsheets to be kept on file for possible future assignments. You will be contacted if additional information or a portfolio is desired. Keeps samples on file. Simultaneous submissions OK. Pays $600-1,000 for color cover; $100-500 for inside. Pays 45 days after publication. Credit line given. Buys one-time rights. No phone calls.

ITALIAN AMERICA

219 E St., NE, Washington D.C. 20002. (202)547-2900. Website: www.osia.org. Estab. 1996. Circ. 65,000. Quarterly. "*Italian America* is the official publication of the Order Sons of Italy in America, the nation's oldest and largest organization of American men and women of Italian heritage. *Italian America* strives to provide timely information about OSIA, while report-

ing on individuals, institutions, issues and events of current or historical significance in the *Italian American* community." Sample copy and photo guidelines free and available online.

NEEDS Buys 5-10 photos from freelancers/issue; 25 photos/year. Needs photos of travel, history, personalities; anything Italian or Italian-American. Reviews photos with or without a manuscript. Special photo needs include travel in Italy. Model release preferred. Photo captions required.

SPECS Accepts images in digital format. Send via CD, e-mail as TIFF, EPS, PICT, BMP, GIF, JPEG files at 400 dpi.

MAKING CONTACT & TERMS Send query letter with tearsheets. Provide résumé, business card, self-promotion piece or tearsheets to be kept on file for possible future assignments. Art director will contact photographer for portfolio review if interested. Portfolio should include color tearsheets. Responds only if interested; send nonreturnable samples. Simultaneous submissions OK. Pays $250 for b&w or color cover; $50-250 for b&w or color inside. Pays on publication. Credit line given. Buys one-time rights.

$$ JEWISH ACTION

Orthodox Union, 11 Broadway, New York NY 10004. (212)613-8146. Fax: (212)613-0646. E-mail: ja@ou.org; carmeln@ou.org. Website: www.ou.org/jewish_action. Ed Hamway, art director. **Contact:** Nechama Carmel, editor; Anna Socher, assistant editor. Estab. 1986. Circ. 40,000. Quarterly. Covers a vibrant approach to Jewish issues, Orthodox lifestyle, and values. Sample copy available for $5 or on website.

NEEDS Buys 30 photos/year. Photos of Jewish lifestyle, landscapes and travel photos of Israel, and occasional photo essays of Jewish life. Reviews photos with or without a manuscript. Model/property release preferred. Photo captions required; include description of activity, where taken, when.

SPECS Uses color and b&w prints. Accepts images in digital format. Send CD, Jaz, ZIP as TIFF, GIF, JPEG files.

MAKING CONTACT & TERMS Send query letter with samples, brochure or stock photo list. Keeps samples on file. Responds in 2 months. Simultaneous submissions OK. Pays $250 maximum for b&w cover; $400 maximum for color cover; $100 maximum for b&w inside; $150 maximum for color inside. Pays within 6 weeks of publication. Credit line given. Buys one-time rights.

TIPS "Be aware that models must be clothed in keeping with Orthodox laws of modesty. Make sure to include identifying details. Don't send work depicting religion in general. We are specifically Orthodox Jewish."

$$ JOURNAL OF ASIAN MARTIAL ARTS

Via Media Publishing Co., 941 Calle Mejia, #822, Santa Fe NM 87501. (505)983-1919. E-mail: info@goviamedia.com. Website: www.goviamedia.com. Estab. 1991. Circ. 10,000. "An indexed, notch-bound quarterly magazine exemplifying the highest standards in writing and graphics available on the subject. Comprehensive, mature and eye-catching. Covers all historical and cultural aspects of Asian martial arts." Sample copy available for $10. Photo guidelines free with SASE.

NEEDS Buys 120 photos from freelancers/issue; 480 photos/year. Photos of health/fitness, sports, action shots; technical sequences of martial arts; photos that capture the philosophy and aesthetics of Asian martial traditions. Interested in alternative process, avant garde, digital, documentary, fine art, historical/vintage. Model release preferred for photos taken of subjects not in public demonstration; property release preferred. Photo captions preferred; include short description, photographer's name, year taken.

SPECS Uses color and b&w prints; 35mm, 2¼×2¼, 4×5, 8×10 transparencies. Accepts images in digital format. Send via CD, ZIP as TIFF files at 300 dpi.

MAKING CONTACT & TERMS Send query letter with samples, stock list. Provide résumé, business card, self-promotion piece or tearsheets to be kept on file for possible future assignments. Art director will contact photographer for portfolio review if interested. Keeps samples on file. Responds in 2 months. Previously published work OK. Pays $100-500 for color cover; $10-100 for b&w inside. Credit line given. Buys first rights and reprint rights.

TIPS "Read the journal. We are unlike any other martial arts magazine and would like photography to complement the text portion, which is sophisticated with the flavor of traditional Asian aesthetics. When submitting work, be well organized and include a SASE."

◎ JOURNEY MAGAZINE

AAA, 1745 114th Ave., S.E., Bellevue WA 98004. E-mail: nicolemeoli@aaawin.com. **Contact:** Nicole Meoli, editor. Circ. 550,000. Bimonthly. For members of AAA Washington reaches readers in Washington, and northern Idaho.

○ "Photographers interested in submitting work to *Journey* magazine are encouraged to send a link to their website, along with a stock listing of regions and subjects of specialty for us to review. You are encouraged to familiarize yourself with *Journey* before sending in submissions. We review photographers' stock lists and samples and keep the names of potential contributors on file to contact as needed. We do not post our photo needs online or elsewhere. To be considered for an assignment, send links to journey@aaawin.com."

MAKING CONTACT & TERMS "We run all articles with high-quality photographs and illustrations. If you are a published photographer, let us know but please do not submit any photos unless requested. To be considered for an assignment, mail a query along with three samples of published work or send links to journey@aaawin.com."

❸❺ ◐ JUDICATURE

2700 University Ave., Des Moines IA 50311. (773)973-0145. Fax: (773)338-9687. E-mail: drichert@ajs.org. Website: www.ajs.org. **Contact:** David Richert, editor. Estab. 1917. Circ. 5,000. Bimonthly publication of the American Judicature Society. Emphasizes courts, administration of justice. Readers are judges, lawyers, professors, citizens interested in improving the administration of justice. Sample copy free with 9×12 SASE and 6 first-class stamps.

NEEDS Buys 1-2 photos from freelancers/issue; 6-12 photos/year. Needs photos relating to courts, the law. "Actual or posed courtroom shots are always needed." Interested in fine art, historical/vintage. Model/property release preferred. Photo captions preferred.

SPECS Uses b&w and color prints. Accepts images in digital format. Send via CD, ZIP, e-mail as JPEG files at 600 dpi.

MAKING CONTACT & TERMS Submit samples via e-mail. Simultaneous submissions and previously published work OK. Pays $250 for b&w cover; $350 for color cover; $125-250 for b&w inside; $125-300 for color inside. Pays on publication. Credit line given. Buys one-time rights.

❸❺ JUVENILE DIABETES RESEARCH FOUNDATION INTERNATIONAL

26 Broadway, 14th Floor, New York NY 10004. (800)533-2873. Fax: (212)785-9595. E-mail: info@jdrf.org. Website: www.jdrf.org. Estab. 1970. Produces 4-color, 48-page quarterly magazine to deliver research information to a lay audience.

NEEDS Buys 60 photos/year; offers 20 freelance assignments/year. Photos of babies/children/teens, families, events, food/drink, health/fitness, medicine, product shots/still life, science. Needs "mostly portraits of people, but always with some environmental aspect." Reviews stock photos. Model release preferred. Photo captions preferred.

SPECS Uses 2¼×2¼ transparencies. Accepts images in digital format. Send via CD, ZIP as TIFF, EPS, JPEG files at 300 dpi.

MAKING CONTACT & TERMS Send query letter with samples. Provide résumé, business card, brochure, flyer or tearsheets to be kept on file for possible future assignments. Cannot return material. Responds as needed. Pays $500 for color photos; $500-700 per day. Also pays by the job—payment depends on how many days, shots, cities, etc. Credit line given. Buys nonexclusive perpetual rights.

TIPS Looks for "a style consistent with commercial magazine photography—upbeat, warm, personal, but with a sophisticated edge. Call and ask for samples of our publications before submitting any of your own samples so you will have an idea of what we are looking for in photography. Nonprofit groups have seemingly come to depend more and more on photography to get their messages across. The business seems to be using a variety of freelancers, as opposed to a single in-house photographer."

❸❺ ◐ KANSAS!

Kansas Department of Commerce, 1000 SW Jackson St., Suite 100, Topeka KS 66612-1354. (785)296-3479. Fax: (785)296-6988. E-mail: ksmagazine@kansas commerce.com. Website: www.kansmag.com. Estab. 1945. Circ. 45,000. Quarterly magazine published by the Travel & Tourism Development Division of the Kansas Department of Commerce. Emphasizes Kansas travel, scenery, arts, recreation and people. Photo guidelines available on website.

NEEDS Buys 60-80 photos from freelancers/year. Subjects include animal, human interest, nature, seasonal, rural, scenic, sport, travel, wildlife, photo essay/photo feature, all from Kansas. No nudes, still life or fashion photos. Will review photographs with or without a manuscript. Model/property release mandatory.

SPECS Images must be digital at 300 dpi for 8×10.

MAKING CONTACT & TERMS Send material by mail for consideration. Previously published work is accepted if no longer under contract. Pays on acceptance. Credit line given. Buys one-time FNAR for 90 days or perpetual rights depending on assignment/gallery/cover/calendar.

TIPS Kansas-oriented material only. Prefers Kansas photographers. "Follow guidelines, submission dates specifically. Shoot a lot of seasonal scenics."

$ ◐ KASHRUS MAGAZINE

The Kashrus Institute, P.O. Box 204, Brooklyn NY 11204. (718)336-8544. E-mail: editorial@kashrusmagazine.com. Website: www.kashrusmagazine.com. **Contact:** Rabbi Wikler, editor. Estab. 1981. Circ. 10,000. "The periodical for the kosher consumer. We feature updates including mislabeled kosher products and recalls. Important for vegetarians, lactose intolerant and others with allergies."

NEEDS 25% freelance written. Prefers to work with published/established writers, but will work with new/unpublished writers.

SPECS Uses 2¼×2¼, 3½×3½ or 7½×7½ matte b&w and color prints.

MAKING CONTACT & TERMS Send unsolicited photos by mail with SASE for consideration. Provide business card, brochure, flier or tearsheets to be kept on file for possible future assignments. Responds in 1 week. Simultaneous submissions and previously published work OK. Pays $40-75 for b&w cover; $50-100 for color cover; $25-50 for b&w inside; $75-200/job; $50-200 for text for photo package. Pays part on acceptance, part on publication. Buys one-time rights, first North American serial rights, all rights; negotiable. Byline given. Submit seasonal materials 2 months in advance. Responds in 2 weeks.

TIPS "Seriously in need of new photo sources, but *call first* to see if your work is appropriate before submitting samples."

$ ○ KENTUCKY MONTHLY

P.O. Box 559, Frankfort KY 40602-0559. (502)227-0053; (888)329-0053. Fax: (502)227-5009. E-mail: kymonthly@kentuckymonthly.com; steve@kentuckymonthly.com. Website: www.kentuckymonthly.com. **Contact:** Stephen Vest, editor. Estab. 1998. Circ. 40,000. Monthly. Focuses on Kentucky and Kentucky-related stories. Sample copy available for $4.

NEEDS Buys 10 photos from freelancers/issue; 120 photos/year. Photos of celebrities, wildlife, entertainment, landscapes. Reviews photos with or without a manuscript. Model release required. Photo captions required.

SPECS Uses glossy prints; 35mm transparencies. Accepts images in digital format. Send via CD, e-mail at 300 dpi.

MAKING CONTACT & TERMS Send query letter. Provide self-promotion piece to be kept on file for possible future assignments. Responds in 1 month. Simultaneous submissions OK. Pays $25 minimum for inside photos. Pays the 15th of the following month. Credit line given. Buys one-time rights.

KIWANIS

(317)875-8755; (800)549-2647 [dial 411] (US and Canada only). Fax: (317)879-0204. E-mail: magazine@kiwanis.org; shareyourstory@kiwanis.org. Website: www.kiwanis.org. **Contact:** Jack Brockley, editor. Estab. 1917. Circ. 240,000. Published 6 times/year. Emphasizes organizational news, plus major features of interest to business and professional men and women involved in community service. Sample copy available with SASE and 5 first-class stamps. Photo guidelines available via website at www.kiwanismagazine.org. Look for "magazine submission guidelines" link.

NEEDS Photos of babies/children/teens, multicultural, families, parents, senior citizens, landscapes/scenics, education, business concepts, medicine, science, technology/computers. Interested in fine art. Reviews photos with or without ms.

SPECS Uses 5×7 or 8×10 glossy b&w prints; accepts 35mm but prefers 2¾×2¾ and 4×5 transparencies. Accepts images in digital format. Send via CD, e-mail as TIFF, BMP files.

MAKING CONTACT & TERMS Send résumé stock photos. Provide brochure, business card or flier to be kept on file for future assignments. Assigns 95% of work. Pays $100-1,000 for color photos. Buys primarily one-time rights.

TIPS "We can offer the photographer a lot of freedom to work *and* worldwide exposure. And perhaps an award or two if the work is good. We are now using more conceptual photos. We also use studio set-up shots for most assignments. When we assign work, we want to know if a photographer can follow a concept into finished photo without on-site direction." In portfolio or samples, wants to see "studio work with flash and natural light."

$$ ● KNOWATLANTA

450 Northridge Parkway, Suite 202, Atlanta GA 30350. (770)650-1102. Fax: (770)650-2848. E-mail: chris@knowatlanta.com. Website: www.knowatlanta.com. **Contact:** Chris Colwell, publisher. Estab. 1986. Circ. 48,000. Quarterly. Serves as a relocation guide to the Atlanta metro area with a corporate audience. Photography reflects regional and local material as well as corporate-style imagery.

NEEDS Buys more than 10 photos from freelancers/issue; more than 40 photos/year. Photos of cities/urban, events, performing arts, business concepts, medicine, technology/computers. Reviews photos with or without a manuscript. Model release required; property release preferred. Photo captions preferred.

SPECS Uses 8×10 glossy color prints; 35mm, transparencies. Accepts images in digital format. Send via CD, ZIP, e-mail as TIFF, EPS, JPEG files at 300 dpi.

MAKING CONTACT & TERMS Send query letter with photocopies. Provide résumé, business card, self-promotion piece to be kept on file for possible future assignments. Responds only if interested; send non-returnable samples. Pays $600 maximum for color cover; $300 maximum for color inside. Pays on publication. Credit line given. Buys first rights.

TIPS "Think like our readers. What would they want to know about or see in this magazine? Try to represent the relocated person if using subjects in photography."

◎ $ ○ LACROSSE MAGAZINE

113 W. University Pkwy., Baltimore MD 21210. (410)235-6882. Fax: (410)366-6735. E-mail: gferraro@uslacrosse.org; blogue@uslacrosse.org. Website: www.uslacrosse.org. **Contact:** Gabriella O'Brien, art director; Brian Logue, director of communications. Estab. 1978. Circ. 235,000. Publication of U.S. Lacrosse. Monthly. Emphasizes sport of lacrosse. Readers are male and female lacrosse enthusiasts of all ages. Sample copy free with general information pack.

NEEDS Buys 15-30 photos from freelancers/issue; 120-240 photos/year. Needs lacrosse action shots. Photo captions required; include rosters with numbers for identification.

SPECS Accepts images in digital format. Digital photographs should be submitted in the form of original, unedited JPEGs. Suggested captions are welcome. Photographs may be submitted via CD or e-mail. Prints also are accepted and are returned upon request. Photographer credit is published when supplied. Original RAW/NEF files or 300 dpi TIFFs.

MAKING CONTACT & TERMS Send unsolicited photos by mail with SASE for consideration. Provide résumé, business card, brochure, flier or tearsheets to be kept on file for possible future assignments. Responds in 3 weeks. Simultaneous submissions and previously published work OK. Pays $250 for color cover; $75-150 inside. Pays on publication. Credit line given. Buys one-time rights.

$$ LADIES HOME JOURNAL

125 Park Ave., 20th Floor, New York NY 10017. (212)455-1033. Website: www.lhj.com. Circ. 6 million. Monthly. Features women's issues. Readership consists of women with children and working women in 30s age group.

NEEDS Uses 90 photos/issue; 100% supplied by freelancers. Needs photos of children, celebrities and women's lifestyles/situations. Reviews photos only without manuscript. Model release preferred. Photo captions preferred.

MAKING CONTACT & TERMS Provide résumé, business card, brochure, flier or tearsheet to be kept on file for possible assignment. "Do not send slides or original work; send only promo cards or disks." Responds in 3 weeks. Pays $500/page. **Pays on acceptance.** Credit line given. Buys one-time rights.

$ LAKELAND BOATING MAGAZINE

727 South Dearborn St., Suite 812, Chicago IL 60605. (312)276-0610. Fax: (312)276-0619. E-mail: ljohnson@lakelandboating.com. Website: www.lakelandboating.com. **Contact:** Lindsay Johnson, editor; Brook Poplawski, art/production manager. Estab. 1945. Circ. 60,000. Monthly. Emphasizes powerboating in

the Great Lakes. Readers are affluent professionals, predominantly men over age 35.

NEEDS Shots of particular Great Lakes ports and waterfront communities. Model release preferred. Photo captions preferred.

MAKING CONTACT & TERMS Send query letter with list of stock photo subjects. Provide résumé, business card, brochure, flyer or tearsheets to be kept on file for possible future assignments. Pays $25-100 for photos. Pays on publication. Credit line given.

LAKE SUPERIOR MAGAZINE

Lake Superior Port Cities, Inc., P.O. Box 16417, Duluth MN 55816-0417. (218)722-5002. Fax: (218)722-4096. E-mail: edit@lakesuperior.com. Website: www.lakesuperior.com. Estab. 1979. Circ. 20,000. Bimonthly. "Beautiful picture magazine about Lake Superior." Readers are male and female, ages 35-55, highly educated, upper-middle and upper-management level through working. Sample copy available for $4.95 plus $5.95 S&H. Photo guidelines free with SASE or via website.

NEEDS Buys 21 photos from freelancers/issue; 126 photos/year. Also buys photos for calendars and books. Needs photos of landscapes/scenics, travel, wildlife, personalities, boats, underwater—all Lake Superior-related. Photo captions preferred.

SPECS Uses mainly images in digital format. Send via CD with at least thumbnails on a printout.

MAKING CONTACT & TERMS Send unsolicited photos by mail with SASE for consideration. Provide résumé, business card, brochure, flier or tearsheets to be kept on file for possible future assignments. Responds in 2 months. Simultaneous submissions OK. Pays $150 for color cover; $50 for b&w or color inside. Pays on publication. Credit line given. Buys first North American serial rights; reserves second rights for future use.

TIPS "Be aware of the focus of our publication—Lake Superior. Photo features concern only that. Features with text can be related. We are known for our fine color photography and reproduction. It has to be tops. We try to use images large; therefore, detail quality and resolution must be good. We look for unique outlook on subject, not just snapshots. Must communicate emotionally. Some photographers send material we can keep in-house and refer to, and these will often get used."

LINCOLNSHIRE LIFE

P.O. Box 81, Lincoln LN1 1HD, United Kingdom. (44)(152)252-7127. Fax: (44)(152)256-0035. E-mail: editorial@lincolnshirelife.co.uk. Website: www.lincolnshirelife.co.uk. Estab. 1961. Circ. 10,000. Monthly county magazine featuring the culture and history of Lincolnshire. Sample copy available for £2. Photo guidelines free.

NEEDS Buys 10 photos from freelancers/issue; 120 photos/year. Needs photos of Lincolnshire scenes, animals, people. Photo captions required.

SPECS Color transparencies with vertical orientation for cover. Accepts color prints for inside.

MAKING CONTACT & TERMS Send query letter with samples. Art director will contact photographer for portfolio review if interested. Portfolio should include slides or transparencies. Keeps samples on file. Responds in 1 month. Previously published work OK. Payment negotiable. Pays on publication. Credit line given. Buys first rights.

THE LION

300 W. 22nd St., Oak Brook IL 60523-8842. (630)571-5466. E-mail: jay.copp@lionsclubs.org. Website: www.lionsclubs.org. **Contact:** Jay Copp, senior editor. Estab. 1918. Circ. 490,000. Monthly magazine for members of the Lions Club and their families. Emphasizes Lions Club activities and membership. Sample copy and photo guidelines free.

NEEDS Uses 50-60 photos/issue. Needs photos of Lions Club service or fundraising projects. "All photos must be as candid as possible, showing an activity in progress. Please, no award presentations, meetings, speeches, etc. Generally, photos are purchased with manuscript (300-1,500 words) and used as a photo story. We seldom purchase photos separately." Model release preferred for young or disabled children. Photo captions required.

SPECS Uses 5×7, 8×10 glossy color prints; 35mm transparencies; also accepts digital images via e-mail at 300 dpi or larger.

MAKING CONTACT & TERMS Works with freelancers on assignment only. Provide résumé to be kept on file for possible future assignments. Query first with résumé of credits or story idea. Pays $150-600 for text/photo package. "Must accompany story on the service or fundraising project of the The Lions Club." **Pays on acceptance.** Buys all rights; negotiable.

TIPS "Query on specific project and photos to accompany manuscript."

⑤ ○ LIVING FREE

P.O. Box 969, Winnisquam NH 03289. (603)455-7368. E-mail: free@natnh.com. Website: www.natnh.com/LF/index.html. **Contact:** Tom Caldwell, editor-in-chief. Estab. 1987. Quarterly electronic magazine succeeding Naturist Life International's online e-zine. Emphasizes nudism. Readers are male and female nudists. Sample copy available on CD for $10. Photo guidelines free with SASE. We periodically organize naturist photo safaris to shoot nudes in nature.

NEEDS Buys 36 photos from freelancers/issue; 144 photos/year. Photos depicting family-oriented nudist/naturist work, recreational activity and travel. Reviews photos with or without a manuscript. Model release required (including Internet use) for recognizable nude subjects. Photo captions preferred.

SPECS Prefers digital images submitted on CD or via e-mail; 8×10 glossy color and b&w prints.

MAKING CONTACT & TERMS Send query letter with résumé of credits. Send unsolicited photos by mail or e-mail for consideration; include SASE for return of material. Provide résumé, business card, brochure, flier or tearsheets to be kept on file for possible future assignments. Responds in 2 weeks. Pays $50 for color cover; $10-25 for others. Pays on publication. Credit line given. "Prefer to own all rights but sometimes agree to one-time publication rights."

TIPS "The ideal photo shows ordinary-looking people of all ages doing everyday activities, in the joy of nudism. We do not want 'cheesecake' glamour images or anything that emphasizes the erotic."

⑤⑤ ⓘ LOG HOME LIVING

Home Buyer Publications, Inc., 4125 Lafayette Center Dr., Suite 100, Chantilly VA 20151. (703)222-9411; (800)826-3893. Fax: (703)222-3209. E-mail: editor@loghomeliving.com; ksmith@homebuyerpubs.com. Website: www.loghomeliving.com. Estab. 1989. Circ. 132,000. Monthly. Emphasizes planning, building and buying a log home. Sample copy available for $4. Photo guidelines available online.

NEEDS Buys 90 photos from freelancers/issue; 120 photos/year. Needs photos of homes—living room, dining room, kitchen, bedroom, bathroom, exterior, portrait of owners, design/decor—tile sunrooms, furniture, fireplaces, lighting, porch and deck, doors. Close-up shots of details (roof trusses, log stairs, railings, dormers, porches, window/door treatments) are appreciated. Model release required.

SPECS Prefers to use digital images or 4×5 color transparencies/Kodachrome or Ektachrome color slides; smaller color transparencies and 35mm color prints also acceptable.

MAKING CONTACT & TERMS Send unsolicited photos by mail for consideration. Keeps samples on file. Responds only if interested. Previously published work OK. Pays $2,000 maximum for color feature. Cover shot submissions also accepted; fee varies, negotiable. **Pays on acceptance.** Credit line given. Buys first World-one-time stock serial rights; negotiable.

TIPS "Send photos of log homes, both interiors and exteriors."

⑤ LOYOLA MAGAZINE

820 N. Michigan Ave., Chicago IL 60611. (312)915-6930. E-mail: abusiek@luc.edu. Website: www.luc.edu/loyolamagazine. **Contact:** Anastasia Busiek, editor. Estab. 1971. Circ. 120,000. Loyola University alumni magazine. Quarterly. Emphasizes issues related to Loyola University Chicago. Readers are Loyola University Chicago alumni—professionals, ages 22 and up.

NEEDS Buys 20 photos from freelancers/issue; 60 photos/year. Needs Loyola-related or Loyola alumni-related photos only. Model release preferred. Photo captions preferred.

SPECS Uses 8×10 b&w and color prints; 35mm, 2¼×2¼ transparencies. Accepts high-res digital images. Query before submitting.

MAKING CONTACT & TERMS Best to query by mail before making any submissions. If interested, will ask for résumé, business card, brochure, flier or tearsheets to be kept on file for possible future assignments. Simultaneous submissions and previously published work OK. **Pays on acceptance.** Credit line given.

TIPS "Send us information, but don't call."

ⓓ ○ LULLWATER REVIEW

Emory University, P.O. Box 122036, Atlanta GA 30322. Fax: (404)727-7367. E-mail: lullwater@lullwaterreview.com. **Contact:** Arina Korneva, editor-in-chief. Estab. 1990. Circ. 2,000. "We're a small, student-run literary magazine published out of Emory University in Atlanta, GA with two issues yearly—one in the fall and one in the spring. You can find us in the *Index* of *American Periodical Verse*, the *American Humanities Index* and as a member of the Council of Literary Magazines and Presses. We welcome work that brings a fresh perspective, whether through language or the visual arts."

NEEDS Architecture, cities/urban, rural, landscapes, wildlife, alternative process, avant garde, fine art and historical/vintage photos.

MAKING CONTACT & TERMS Send an e-mail with photographs. Samples kept on file. Portfolio should include b&w, color, photographs and finished, original art. Credit line given when appropriate.

TIPS "Read our magazine. We welcome work of all different types, and we encourage submissions that bring a fresh or alternative perspective. Submit at least 5 works. We frequently accept 3-5 pieces from a single artist and like to see a selection."

⊗⊗ ◐ THE LUTHERAN

8765 W. Higgins Rd., 5th Floor, Chicago IL 60631-4183. (800)638-3522, ext. 2540. Fax: (773)380-2409. E-mail: michael.watson@thelutheran.org; lutheran@thelutheran.org. Website: www.thelutheran.org. **Contact:** Michael Watson, art director. Estab. 1988. Circ. 300,000. Monthly publication of Evangelical Lutheran Church in America. "Please send samples of your work that we can keep in our files. Though we prefer to review online portfolios, a small number of slides, prints or tearsheets, a brochure, or even a few photocopies are acceptable as long as you feel they represent you."

NEEDS Buys 10-15 photos from freelancers/issue; 120-180 photos/year. Current news, mood shots. Subjects include babies/children/teens, couples, multicultural, families, parents, senior citizens, disasters, landscapes/scenics, cities/urban, education, religious. Interested in fine art, seasonal. "We usually assign work with exception of 'Reflections' section." Model release required. Photo captions preferred.

SPECS Accepts images in digital format. Send via CD or e-mail as TIFF or JPEG files at 300 dpi.

MAKING CONTACT & TERMS Send query letter with list of stock photo subjects. Provide résumé, brochure, flier or tearsheets to be kept on file for possible future assignments. Pays $300-500 for color cover; $175-300 for color inside; $300 for half day; $600 for full day. Pays on publication. Credit line given. Buys one-time rights; credits the photographer.

TIPS Trend toward "more dramatic lighting; careful composition." In portfolio or samples, wants to see "candid shots of people active in church life, preferably Lutheran. Church-only photos have little chance of publication. Submit sharp, well-composed photos with borders for cropping. Send printed or duplicate samples to be kept on file; no originals. If we like your style, we will call you when we have a job in your area."

THE MAGAZINE ANTIQUES

Brant Publications, 575 Broadway, New York NY 10012. (212)941-2800. Fax: (212)941-2819. E-mail: tmaedit@brantpub.com (JavaScript required to view). Website: www.themagazineantiques.com. **Contact:** Editorial. Estab. 1922. Circ. 61,754. Bimonthly. Emphasizes art, antiques, architecture. Readers are male and female collectors, curators, academics, interior designers, ages 40-70. Sample copy available for $10.50. Buys 24-48 photos from freelancers/issue; 288-576 photos/year.

NEEDS Photos of interiors, architectural exteriors, objects. Reviews photos with or without a manuscript.

SPECS Uses 8×10 glossy prints; 4×5 transparencies; JPEGs at 300 dpi.

MAKING CONTACT & TERMS Submit portfolio for review; phone ahead to arrange drop-off. Does not keep samples on file; include SASE for return of material. Responds in 6 weeks. Previously published work OK. Payment negotiable. Pays on publication. Credit line given.

⊗⊗ MARLIN

P.O. Box 8500, Winter Park FL 32790. (407)628-4802. Fax: (407)628-7061. E-mail: dave.ferrell@bonniercorp.com. Website: www.marlinmag.com. Estab. 1982. Circ. 50,000. Published 8 times/year. Emphasizes offshore big game fishing for billfish, tuna and other large pelagics. Readers are 94% male, 75% married, average age 43, very affluent businessmen. Sample copy free with 8×10 SASE. Photo guidelines free with SASE or online.

NEEDS Buys 45 photos from freelancers/issue; 270 photos/year. Photos of fish/action shots, scenics and how-to. Special photo needs include big game fishing action and scenics (marinas, landmarks, etc.). Model release preferred. Photo captions preferred.

SPECS Uses 35mm transparencies. Also accepts high-res images on CD or via FTP.

MAKING CONTACT & TERMS Contract required. Send unsolicited photos by mail with SASE for consideration. Responds in 1 month. Simultaneous submissions OK with notification. Pays $1,200 for color cover; $100-300 for color inside. Pays on publication. Buys first North American rights.

TIPS "Send sample material with SASE. No phone call necessary. Don't hesitate to call Editor Dave Ferrel or Managing Editor Charlie Levine at (407)628-4802 anytime you have any general or specific questions about photo needs, submissions or payment."

ⓢⓢ ○ METROSOURCE MAGAZINE

137 W. 19th St., 2nd Floor, New York NY 10011. (212)691-5127. E-mail: letters@metrosource.com. Website: www.metrosource.com. **Contact:** Editor. Estab. 1990. Circ. 145,000. Upscale, gay men's luxury lifestyle magazine published 6 times/year. Emphasizes fashion, travel, profiles, interiors, film, art. Sample copies free.

NEEDS Buys 10-15 photos from freelancers/issue; 50 photos/year. Photos of celebrities, architecture, interiors/decorating, adventure, food/drink, health/fitness, travel, product shots/still life. Interested in erotic, fashion/glamour, seasonal. Also needs still-life drink shots for spirits section. Reviews photos with or without a manuscript. Model/property release preferred. Photo captions preferred.

SPECS Uses 8×10 glossy or matte color and b&w prints; 2¼×2¼, 4×5 transparencies. Prefers images in digital format. Send via CD, Zip, e-mail as TIFF, EPS, JPEG files at 300 dpi.

MAKING CONTACT & TERMS Send query letter with self-promo cards. "Please call first for portfolio drop-off." Provide self-promotion piece to be kept on file for possible future assignments. Responds only if interested; send nonreturnable samples. Simultaneous submissions and previously published work OK. Pays $500-800 for cover; up to $300 for inside. Pays on publication. Credit line given. Buys one-time rights.

TIPS "We work with creative established and newly-established photographers. Our budgets vary depending on the importance of story. Have an e-mail address on card so we can see more photos or whole portfolio online."

○ MGW NEWSMAGAZINE

Guess What Media, LLC, 1123 21st St., Suite 201, Sacramento CA 95811. (916)441-6397. Fax: (206)339-5864. E-mail: editor@momguesswhat.com. Website: www.mgwnews.com. **Contact:** Matthew Burlingame, editorial director. Estab. 1978. Circ. 21,000.

NEEDS Photo subjects include events, personalities, culture, entertainment, fashion, food, travel. Model release required. Photo captions required.

SPECS Accepts images in digital format. Send via CD, e-mail preferred as TIFF, EPS, JPEG, PDF files at 300 dpi.

MAKING CONTACT & TERMS Arrange a personal interview to show portfolio. Send 8×10 glossy color or b&w prints by mail for consideration; include SASE for return of material. Previously published work OK. "Currently only using volunteer/pro bono freelance photographers but will consider all serious inquiries from local professionals." Credit line given.

TIPS "In portfolios, prefers to see gay/lesbian-related stories, human/civil rights, some 'artsy' photos; *no* nudes or sexually explicit photos. E-mail is always the best way to contact us. Uses photographers as interns (contact editor for details)."

MICHIGAN OUT-OF-DOORS

P.O. Box 30235, Lansing MI 48909. (517)371-1041. Fax: (517)371-1505. E-mail: magazine@mucc.org. Website: www.mucc.org. Estab. 1947. Circ. 40,000. Monthly. For people interested in "outdoor recreation, especially hunting and fishing; conservation; environmental affairs." Sample copy available for $3.50; editorial guidelines free.

NEEDS Buys 6-12 photos from freelancers/issue; 72-144 photos/year. Photos of animals/wildlife, nature, scenics, sports (hunting, fishing, backpacking, camping, cross-country skiing, other forms of noncompetitive outdoor recreation). Materials must have a Michigan slant. Photo captions preferred.

MAKING CONTACT & TERMS Digital photos only. Include SASE for return of material. Responds in 1 month. Pays $275 for cover; $20 minimum for b&w inside; $40 for color inside. Credit line given. Buys first North American serial rights.

ⓢ ⓞ ⓞ MINNESOTA GOLFER

Minnesota Golf Association, 6550 York Ave. S., Suite 211, Edina MN 55435. (952)927-4643; (800)642-4405. Fax: (952)927-9642. E-mail: editor@mngolf.org; wp@

mngolf.org. Website: www.mngolf.org. **Contact:** W.P. Ryan, editor. Estab. 1970. Circ. 60,000. Bimonthly association magazine covering Minnesota golf scene. Sample copies available.

NEEDS Works on assignment only. Buys 25 photos from freelancers/issue; 150 photos/year. Photos of golf, golfers, and golf courses only. Will accept exceptional photography that tells a story or takes specific point of view. Reviews photos with or without manuscript. Model/property release required. Photo captions required; include date, location, names and hometowns of all subjects.

SPECS Accepts images in digital format. Send via DVD or CD, e-mail as TIFF files.

MAKING CONTACT & TERMS Send query letter with digital medium. Portfolios may be dropped off every Monday. Provide business card or self-promotion piece to be kept on file for possible future assignments. Responds only if interested; send nonreturnable samples. Pays on publication. Credit line given. Buys one-time rights. Will negotiate one-time or all rights, depending on needs of the magazine and the MGA.

TIPS "We use beautiful golf course photography to promote the game and Minnesota courses to our readers. We expect all submissions to be technically correct in terms of lighting, exposure, and color. We are interested in photos that portray the game and golf courses in new, unexpected ways. For assignments, submit work with invoice and all expenses. For unsolicited work, please include contact, fee, and rights terms submitted with photos; include captions where necessary. Artist agreement available upon request."

$ ○ MISSOURI LIFE

515 E. Morgan St., Boonville MO 65233. (660)882-9898. Fax: (660)828-9899. E-mail: sarah@missourilife.com. Website: www.missourilife.com. **Contact:** Sarah Herrera, graphic designer/assistant editor. Estab. 1973. Circ. 22,000. Bimonthly. "*Missouri Life* celebrates Missouri people and places, past and present, and the unique qualities of our great state with interesting stories and bold, colorful photography." Sample copy available for $4.95 and SASE with $2.44 first-class postage. Photo guidelines available on website.

NEEDS Buys 80 photos from freelancers/issue; more than 500 photos/year. Needs photos of environmental, seasonal, landscapes/scenics, wildlife, architecture, cities/urban, rural, adventure, historical sites, entertainment, events, hobbies, performing arts, travel. Reviews photos with or without manuscript. Model/property release required. Photo captions required; include location, names and detailed identification (including any title and hometown) of subjects.

SPECS Prefers images in high-res digital format (minimum 300 ppi at 8×10). Send via e-mail, CD, ZIP as EPS, JPEG, TIFF files.

MAKING CONTACT & TERMS Send query letter with résumé, stock list. Provide self-promotion piece to be kept on file for possible future assignments. Responds in 1 month. Pays $100-150 for color cover; $50 for color inside. Pays on publication. Credit line given. Buys first rights, nonexclusive rights, limited rights.

TIPS "Be familiar with our magazine and the state of Missouri. Provide well-labeled images with detailed caption and credit information."

$ ◎ ⓗ ◐ MORPHEUS TALES

Morpheus Tales, 116 Muriel St., London N1 9QU, UK. E-mail: morpheustales@blueyonder.co.uk. Website: www.morpheustales.com. **Contact:** Adam Bradley, publisher. Estab. 2008. Circ. 1,000. Publishes experimental fiction, fantasy, horror and science fiction. Publishes 4-6 titles/year.

NEEDS "Look at magazine and website for style."

MAKING CONTACT & TERMS Portfolio should include b&w, color, finished and original art. Responds within 30 days. Model and property release are required.

MOTHER JONES

Foundation for National Progress, 222 Sutter St., Suite 600, San Francisco CA 94108. (415)321-1700. E-mail: query@motherjones.com. Website: www.motherjones.com. Mark Murrmann, assoc. photo editor. Estab. 1976. Circ. 240,000. "Recognized worldwide for publishing groundbreaking work by some of the most talented photographers, *Mother Jones* is proud to include the likes of Antonin Kratochvil, Eugene Richards, Sebastião Salgado, Lana Šlezić, and Larry Sultan as past contributors. We remain committed to championing the best in photography and are always looking for exceptional photographers with a unique visual style. It's best to give us a URL for a portfolio website. For photo essays, describe the work that you've done or propose to do; and if possible, provide a link to view the project online. We will contact you if we are interested in seeing more work. Or you can mail nonreturnable samples or discs to: Mark Murrmann."

TIPS "Please do not submit original artwork or any samples that will need to be returned. *Mother Jones* cannot be responsible for the return or loss of unsolicited artwork."

MOTOR BOATING MAGAZINE

Bonnier Corporation, 460 N. Orlando Ave., Suite 200, Winter Park FL 32789. (407)628-4802. Fax: (407)628-7061. E-mail: editor@yachtingmagazine.com or via online contact form. Website: www.motorboating.com; www.bonniercorp.com/brands/Motor-Boating.html. Lianna Sisinni, managing editor. **Contact:** Emilie Whitcomb, art director. Estab. 1907. Circ. 132,000. Monthly. Addresses the interests of both sail and powerboat owners, with the emphasis on high-end vessels. Includes boating events, boating-related products, gear and how-to.

MAKING CONTACT & TERMS Send query letter with tearsheets. Provide self-promotion piece to be kept on file for possible future assignments. Responds only if interested; send nonreturnable samples. Pays on publication. Buys first rights.

TIPS "Read the magazine, and have a presentable portfolio."

MOTORING & LEISURE

Britannia House, 21 Station St., Brighton BN1 4DE, United Kingdom. E-mail: magazine@csmaclub.co.uk. Website: www.csma.uk.com. Circ. 300,000. In-house magazine of CSMA (Civil Service Motoring Association); 144 pages printed 10 times/year (double issue July/August and November/December). Covers car reviews, worldwide travel features, lifestyle and leisure, gardening. Sample copy available.

NEEDS Innovative photos of cars and motorbikes, old and new, to give greater choice than usual stock shots; motoring components (tires, steering wheels, windscreens); car manufacturer logos; UK traffic signs, road markings, general traffic, minor roads and motorways; worldwide travel images; UK villages, towns and cities; families on UK outdoor holidays; caravans, motor homes, camping, picnics sites. Reviews photos with or without manuscript. Photo captions preferred; include location.

SPECS Prefers images in digital format. Send JPEG files via e-mail, 300 dpi where possible, or 72 dpi at the largest possible image size. Maximum limit per e-mail is 8MB so may need to send images in separate e-mails or compress byte size. Most file formats (EPS, TIFF, PDF, PSD) accepted for PC use. Unable to open Mac files. TIFFs and very large files should be sent on a CD.

MAKING CONTACT & TERMS Prefers to be contacted via e-mail. Simultaneous submissions and previously published work OK. Payment negotiated with individual photographers and image libraries. Credit line sometimes given if asked. Buys one-time rights.

MOUNTAIN LIVING

Network Communications, Inc., 1777 S. Harrison St., Suite 903, Denver CO 80210. (303)248-2062; (303)248-2063. Fax: (303)248-2064. E-mail: hscott@mountainliving.com; cdeorio@mountainliving.com. Website: www.mountainliving.com. **Contact:** Holly Scott, publisher; Christine DeOrio, editor-in-chief. Estab. 1994. Circ. 48,000. Published 10 times/year covering architecture, interior design and lifestyle issues for people who live in, visit, or hope to live in the mountains.

NEEDS Buys 10 photos from freelancers/issue; 120 photos/year. Photos of home interiors, architecture. Reviews photos with accompanying manuscript only. Model/property release required. Photo captions preferred.

SPECS Prefers images in digital format. Send via CD as TIFF files at 300 dpi. Also uses 35mm, 2¼×2¼, 4×5 transparencies.

MAKING CONTACT & TERMS Submit portfolio for review. Send query letter with stock list. Provide résumé, business card, brochure, flyer or tearsheets to be kept on file for possible future assignments. Responds in 6 weeks. Pays $500-600/day; up to $600 for color inside. **Pays on acceptance.** Credit line given. Buys one-time and first North American serial rights as well as rights to use photos on the *Mountain Living* website and in promotional materials; negotiable.

MUSCLEMAG INTERNATIONAL

Robert Kennedy Publishing, 400 Matheson Blvd. W., Mississauga ON L5R 3M1, Canada. (888)254-0767; (905)507-3545. Fax: (905)507-2372. Website: www.emusclemag.com. **Contact:** Art director. Estab. 1974. Circ. 300,000. Monthly. Emphasizes hardcore bodybuilding for men and women. Sample copy available for $6.

NEEDS Buys 3,000 photos/year; 50% assigned; 50% stock. Needs bodybuilding, celebrity/personality, swimsuit, how-to, special effects/experimental and spot news. "We require action exercise photos of bodybuilders and fitness enthusiasts training with sweat and strain." Wants on a regular basis "different" pics of top names, bodybuilders or film stars famous for their physiques (i.e., Schwarzenegger, The Hulk, etc.). No photos of mediocre bodybuilders. "They have to be among the top 100 in the world or top film stars exercising." Photos may be purchased with accompanying manuscript. Photo captions preferred.

SPECS Uses 8×10 glossy b&w prints; 35mm, 2¼×2¼ or 4×5 transparencies; high-resolution digital thumbnails; vertical format preferred for cover.

MAKING CONTACT & TERMS Send material by mail for consideration; send $3 for return postage. Send query letter with contact sheet. Responds in 1 month. Pays $20-50/b&w photo; $40-100/color photo; $500-1,000/cover photo. Pays on publication. Credit line given. Buys all rights.

TIPS "We would like to see photographers take up the challenge of making exercise photos look like exercise motion. In samples we want to see sharp, color-balanced, attractive subjects, no grain, artistic eye. Someone who can glamorize bodybuilding on film. To break in get serious: read, ask questions, learn, experiment and try, try again. Keep trying for improvement—don't kid yourself that you are a good photographer when you don't even understand half the attachments on your camera. Immerse yourself in photography. Study the best; study how they use light, props, backgrounds, angles. Current biggest demand is for swimsuit-type photos of fitness men and women (splashing in waves, playing/posing in sand, etc.). Shots must be sexually attractive."

MUSHING.COM MAGAZINE

P.O. Box 1195, Willow AK 99688. (907)495-2468. E-mail: editor@mushing.com. Website: www.mushing.com. **Contact:** Greg Sellentin, managing editor. Estab. 1987. Circ. 10,000.

NEEDS Uses 50 photos/issue; most supplied by freelancers. Needs action photos: all-season and wilderness; still and close-up photos: specific focus (sledding, carting, dog care, equipment, etc.). Special photo needs include skijoring, feeding, caring for dogs, summer carting or packing, 1- to 3-dog-sledding, and kids mushing. Model release preferred. Photo captions preferred.

SPECS Accepts images in digital format. Send via CD, ZIP, e-mail as JPEG files at 300 dpi.

MAKING CONTACT & TERMS Send unsolicited photos by mail for consideration. Responds in 6 months. Pays $175 maximum for color cover; $15-40 for b&w inside; $40-50 for color inside. Pays $10 extra for 1 year of electronic use rights on the Web. Pays within 60 days after publication. Credit line given. Buys first serial rights and second reprint rights.

TIPS Wants to see work that shows "the total mushing adventure/lifestyle from environment to dog house." To break in, one's work must show "simplicity, balance and harmony. Strive for unique, provocative shots that lure readers and publishers. Send 10-40 images for review. Allow for 2-6 months' review time for at least a screened selection of these."

MUZZLE BLASTS

P.O. Box 67, Friendship IN 47021. (812)667-5131. Fax: (812)667-5136. E-mail: mblastdop@seidata.com. Website: www.nmlra.org. Estab. 1939. Circ. 18,500. Publication of the National Muzzle Loading Rifle Association. Monthly. Emphasizes muzzleloading. Sample copy free. Photo guidelines free with SASE.

NEEDS Interested in muzzleloading, muzzleloading hunting, primitive camping. "Ours is a specialized association magazine. We buy some big-game wildlife photos but are more interested in photos featuring muzzleloaders, hunting, powder horns and accoutrements." Model/property release required. Photo captions preferred.

SPECS Accepts images in digital format. Send via e-mail or on a CD in JPEG or TIFF format. Also accepts 3×5 color transparencies, quality color and b&w prints; sharply contrasting 35mm color slides are acceptable.

MAKING CONTACT & TERMS Send query letter with stock list. Keeps samples on file; include SASE for return of material. Responds in 2 weeks. Simultaneous submissions OK. Pays $300 for color cover; $25-50 for b&w inside. Pays on publication. Credit line given. Buys one-time rights.

NA'AMAT WOMAN

350 Fifth Ave., Suite 4700, New York NY 10118. (212)563-5222. Fax: (212)563-5710. E-mail: naamat@naamat.org; judith@naamat.org. Website: www.

naamat.org. **Contact:** Judith Sokoloff, editor. Estab. 1926. Circ. 15,000. Quarterly organization magazine focusing on issues of concern to contemporary Jewish families and women.

NEEDS Buys 5-10 photos from freelancers/issue; 50 photos/year. Photos of Jewish themes, Israel, women, babies/children/teens, families, parents, senior citizens, landscapes/scenics, architecture, religious, travel. Interested in documentary, fine art, historical/vintage, seasonal. Reviews photos with or without manuscript. Photo captions preferred.

SPECS Uses color and b&w prints. Accepts images in digital format. Contact editor before sending.

MAKING CONTACT & TERMS Provide résumé, business card, self-promotion piece or tearsheets to be kept on file for possible future assignments. Art director will contact photographer for portfolio review if interested. Keeps samples on file; include SASE for return of material. Responds in 6 weeks. Pays $250 maximum for cover; $35-75 for inside. Pays on publication. Credit line given. Buys one-time, first rights.

⊘ NATIONAL GEOGRAPHIC

1145 17th St., NW, Washington D.C. 20036. E-mail: ngsforum@nationalgeographic.com. Website: www. nationalgeographic.com. David Griffin, director of photography. Estab. 1919. Circ. 7 million. Monthly publication of the National Geographic Society.

○ This is a premiere market that demands photographic excellence. *National Geographic* does not accept unsolicited work from freelance photographers. Photography internships and faculty fellowships are available. Contact Susan Smith, deputy director of photography, for application information.

◑ ◎◎ ⊘ NATIONAL PARKS MAGAZINE

National Parks Conservation Association, 777 6th St., NW, Suite 700, Washington D.C. 20001-3723. (202)223-6722; (800)628-7275. Fax: (202)454-3333. E-mail: npmag@npca.org. Website: www.npca.org/magazine. **Contact:** Scott Kirkwood, editor-in-chief. Estab. 1919. Circ. 340,000. Quarterly. Emphasizes the preservation of national parks and wildlife. Sample copy available for $3 and 8½×11 or larger SASE. Photo guidelines available online.

SPECS "Photographers who are new to *National Parks* may ONLY submit digitally for an initial re-view—we prefer links to clean, easily-navigable and searchable websites, or lightboxes with well-captioned images. We DO NOT accept and are not responsible for unsolicited slides, prints, or CDs."

MAKING CONTACT & TERMS "The best way to break in is to send a brief, concise e-mail message to Sarah Rutherford. See guidelines online. Less than 1 percent of our image needs are generated from unsolicited photographs, yet we receive dozens of submissions every week. Photographers are welcome to send postcards or other simple promotional materials that we do not have to return or respond to." Photographers who are regular contributors may submit images in the following forms: digitally, via CD, DVD, or e-mail (as in attachments or a link to a lightbox or FTP site) physically, as slides or prints, via courier mail. Pays within 30 days after publication. Buys one-time rights.

TIPS "When searching for photos, we frequently use www.agpix.com to find photographers who fit our needs. If you're interested in breaking into the magazine, we suggest setting up a profile and posting your absolute best parks images there."

◎ ◑ NATIVE PEOPLES MAGAZINE

5333 N. 7th St., Suite C-224, Phoenix AZ 85014. (602)265-4855. Fax: (602)265-3113. E-mail: dgibson@nativepeoples.com; kcoochwytewa@native peoples.com. Website: www.nativepeoples.com. **Contact:** Daniel Gibson, editor; Kevin Coochwytewa, art director. Estab. 1987. Circ. 40,000. Bimonthly. "Dedicated to the sensitive portrayal of the arts and lifeways of the native peoples of the Americas." Photo guidelines free with SASE or on website.

NEEDS Buys 20-50 photos from freelancers/issue; 120-300 photos/year. Needs Native American lifeways photos (babies/children/teens, celebrities, couples, multicultural, families, parents, senior citizens, events). Also uses photos of entertainment, performing arts, travel. Interested in fine art. Model/property release preferred. Photo captions preferred; include names, location and circumstances.

SPECS Uses transparencies, all formats. Accepts images in digital format. Send via CD, ZIP, e-mail as TIFF, JPEG, EPS files at 300 dpi.

MAKING CONTACT & TERMS Submit portfolio for review. Send unsolicited photos by mail for consideration; include SASE for return of material. Responds in 1 month. Pays $250 for color cover; $45-150 for color or b&w inside. Pays on publication. Buys one-time rights.

TIPS "Send samples, or, if in the area, arrange a visit with the editors."

⊗⊗ NATURAL HISTORY

105 W. Highway 54, Suite 265, Durham NC 27713-6650. (646)356-6500. Fax: (919)933-1867. E-mail: sblack@nhmag.com; nhmag@naturalhistorymag.com. Website: www.nhmag.com. **Contact:** Steve Black, art director. Circ. 200,000. Printed 10 times/year. Readers are primarily well-educated people with interests in the sciences. Free photo guidelines available by request.

NEEDS Buys 400-450 photos/year. Subjects include animal behavior, photo essay, documentary, plant and landscape. "We are interested in photo essays that give an in-depth look at plants, animals, or people and that are visually superior. We are also looking for photos for our photographic feature, 'The Natural Moment.' This feature focuses on images that are both visually arresting and behaviorally interesting." Photos used must relate to the social or natural sciences with an ecological framework. Accurate, detailed captions required.

SPECS Uses 35mm, 2¼×2¼, 4×5, 6×7, 8×10 color transparencies; high-res digital images. Covers are always related to an article in the issue.

MAKING CONTACT & TERMS Send query letter with résumé of credits. "We prefer that you come in and show us your portfolio, if and when you are in New York. Please don't send us any photographs without a query first, describing the work you would like to send. No submission should exceed 30 original transparencies or negatives. However, please let us know if you have additional images that we might consider. Potential liability for submissions that exceed 30 originals shall be no more than $100 per slide." Responds in 2 weeks. Previously published work OK but must be indicated on delivery memo. Pays (for color and b&w) $400-600 for cover; $350-500 for spread; $300-400 for oversize; $250-350 for full-page; $200-300 for ¼ page; $175-250 for less than ¼ page. Pays $50 for usage on contents page. Pays on publication. Credit line given. Buys one-time rights.

◐ ⊗ ◑ NATURE FRIEND MAGAZINE

4253 Woodcock Lane, Dayton VA 22821. (540)867-0764. E-mail: photos@naturefriendmagazine.com.

Website: www.dogwoodridgeoutdoors.com; www.naturefriendmagazine.com. **Contact:** Kevin Shank, editor. Estab. 1982. Circ. 13,000. Monthly. Children's magazine covering nature. Sample copy available for $5 plus $2 first-class postage.

NEEDS Buys 5-10 photos from freelancers/issue; 100 photos/year. Photos of wildlife, wildlife interacting with each other, humorous wildlife, all natural habitat appearance. Reviews photos with or without manuscript. Model/property release preferred. Photo captions preferred.

SPECS Prefers images in digital format. Send via CD or DVD as TIFF files at 300 dpi at 8×10 size; provide color thumbnails when submitting photos. "Transparencies are handled and stored carefully; however, we do not accept liability for them so discourage submissions of them."

MAKING CONTACT & TERMS Responds in 1 month to queries; 2 weeks to portfolios. "Label contact prints and digital media with your name, address, and phone number so we can easily know how to contact you if we select your photo for use." Please send articles rather than queries. We try to respond within 4-6 months. Simultaneous submissions and previously published work OK. Pays $75 for front cover; $50 for back cover; $15-25 for inside photos. Pays on publication. Credit line given. Buys one-time rights.

TIPS "We're always looking for photos of wild animals doing something unusual or humorous. Please label every sheet of paper or digital media with name, address and phone number. We may need to contact you on short notice, and you do not want to miss a sale. Also, photos are selected on a monthly basis, after the articles. What this means to a photographer is that photos are secondary to writings and cannot be selected far in advance. High-res photos in our files the day we are making selections will stand the greatest chance of being published. "

⊗ NATURE PHOTOGRAPHER

P.O. Box 220, Lubec ME 04652. (207)733-4201. E-mail: nature_photographer@yahoo.com. Website: www.naturephotographermag.com. Estab. 1990. Circ. 41,000. Quarterly 4-color, high-quality magazine. Emphasizes "conservation-oriented, low-impact nature photography" with strong how-to focus. Readers are male and female nature photographers of all ages. Sample copy available with 10×13 SASE with 6 first-class stamps.

○ *Nature Photographer* charges $80/year to be a "field contributor."

NEEDS Buys 90-120 photos from freelancers/issue; 400 photos/year. Needs nature shots of "all types—abstracts, animals/wildlife, flowers, plants, scenics, environmental images, etc. Shots must be in natural settings; no set-ups, zoo or captive animal shots accepted." Reviews photos (slides or digital images on CD) with or without ms 4 times/year: May (for fall issue); August (for winter issue); November (for spring issue); and January (for summer issue). Photo captions required; include description of subject, location, type of equipment, how photographed.

MAKING CONTACT & TERMS Contact by e-mail or with SASE for guidelines before submitting images. Prefers to see 35mm transparencies or CD of digital images. Send digital images via CD.

TIPS Recommends working with "the best lens you can afford and slow-speed slide film; or, if shooting digital, using the RAW mode." Suggests editing with a 4× or 8× loupe (magnifier) on a light board to check for sharpness, color saturation, etc. "Color prints are not normally used for publication in our magazine. When editing digital captured images, please enlarge to the point that you are certain that the focal point is tack sharp. Also avoid having grain in the final image."

◎ ○ NECROLOGY SHORTS: TALES OF MACABRE AND HORROR

Isis International, P.O. Box 510232, Saint Louis MO 63151. E-mail: editor@necrologyshorts.com; submit@necrologyshorts.com. Website: www.necrologyshorts.com. **Contact:** John Ferguson, editor. Estab. 2009. Circ. 20,000. Consumer publication published online daily and through Amazon Kindle. Also offers an annual collection. "*Necrology Shorts* is an online publication that publishes fiction, articles, cartoons, artwork, and poetry daily. Embracing the Internet, e-book readers, and new technology, we aim to go beyond the long-time standard of a regular publication to bring our readers a daily flow of entertainment. We will also be publishing an annual collection for each year in print, e-book reader, and Adobe PDF format. Our main genre is suspense horror, similar to H.P. Lovecraft and Robert E. Howard. We also publish science fiction and fantasy. We would love to see work continuing the Cthulhu Mythos, but we accept all horror. We also hold contests, judged by our readers, to select the top stories and artwork. Winners of contests receive various prizes, including cash."

NEEDS Alternative process, avant garde, documentary, erotic, fine art, historical/vintage, lifestyle, seasonal.

MAKING CONTACT & TERMS Submit transparencies, prints, or GIF/JPEG files by e-mail at submit@necrologyshorts.com. Requires model releases and identification of subjects.

TIPS "*Necrology Shorts* is looking to break out of the traditional publication types to use the Internet, e-book readers, and other technology. We not only publish works of artists, we let them use their published works to brand themselves and further their profits of their hard work. We love to see traditional artwork, but we also look forward to those that go beyond that to create multimedia works. The best way to get to us is to let your creative side run wild and not send us the typical fare. Don't forget that we publish horror, sci-fi, and fantasy. We expect deranged, warped, twisted, strange, sadistic, and things that question sanity and reality."

$ $ NEW MEXICO MAGAZINE

Lew Wallace Bldg., 495 Old Santa Fe Trail, Santa Fe NM 87501. (505)827-7447. E-mail: queries@nmmagazine.com. Website: www.nmmagazine.com. Estab. 1923. Circ. 100,000. Monthly. For affluent people ages 35-65 interested in the Southwest or who have lived in or visited New Mexico. Sample copy available for $4.95 with 9×12 SASE and 3 first-class stamps. Photo guidelines available online.

NEEDS Buys 10 photos from freelancers/issue; 120 photos/year. Needs New Mexico photos only—landscapes, people, events, architecture, etc. Model release preferred.

SPECS Uses 300 dpi digital files with contact sheets (8-12 per page). Photographers must be in photodata. Photo captions required; include who, what, where.

MAKING CONTACT & TERMS Submit portfolio; include SASE for return of material, or e-mail with web gallery link. Pays $450/day; $300 for color or b&w cover; $60-100 for color or b&w stock. Pays on publication. Credit line given. Buys one-time rights.

TIPS "*New Mexico Magazine* is the official magazine for the state of New Mexico. Photographers should know New Mexico. We are interested in the less common stock of the state. The magazine is editorial driven, and all photos directly relate to a story in the magazine." Cover photos usually relate to the main feature in the magazine.

NEWSWEEK

251 W. 57th St., New York NY 10019. (212)445-4000. E-mail: editors@newsweek.com. Website: www.news week.com. Circ. 3,180,000. *Newsweek* reports the week's developments on the newsfront of the world and the nation through news, commentary and analysis. News is divided into National Affairs; International; Business; Society; Science & Technology; and Arts & Entertainment. Relevant visuals, including photos, accompany most of the articles. Query before submitting.

$ ○ NEW YORK STATE CONSERVATIONIST MAGAZINE

NYSDEC, 625 Broadway, Albany NY 12233-4502. (518)402-8047. E-mail: magazine@gw.dec.state.ny.us. Website: www.dec.ny.gov. Estab. 1946. Circ. 100,000. Bimonthly nonprofit, New York State government publication. Emphasizes natural history, environmental and outdoor interests pertinent to New York State. Sample copy available for $3.50. Photo guidelines free with SASE or online.

NEEDS Uses 40 photos/issue; 80% supplied by freelancers. Needs wildlife shots, people in the environment, outdoor recreation, forest and land management, fisheries and fisheries management, environmental subjects. Also needs landscapes/scenics, cities, travel, historical/vintage, seasonal. Model release preferred. Photo captions required.

SPECS Accepts images in digital format. Send via CD as TIFF files at 300 dpi. Also uses 35mm, 2¼×2¼, 4×5, 8×10 transparencies.

MAKING CONTACT & TERMS Send material by mail for consideration, or submit portfolio for review. Provide résumé, bio, business card, brochure, flyer or tearsheets to be kept on file for possible future assignments. Responds in 3 weeks. Simultaneous submissions and previously published work OK. Pays $50 for cover photos; $15 for b&w or color inside. Pays on publication. Buys one-time rights.

TIPS Looks for "artistic interpretation of nature and the environment; unusual ways of picturing environmental subjects (even pollution, oil spills, trash, air pollution, etc.); wildlife and fishing subjects at all seasons. Try for unique composition, lighting. Technical excellence a must."

THE NEW YORK TIMES MAGAZINE

620 8th Ave., New York NY 10018. (212)556-1234. Fax: (212)556-3830. E-mail: magazine@nytimes.com; thearts@nytimes.com. Website: www.nytimes.com/pages/magazine. **Contact:** Gerald Marzorati, editor. Circ. 1.8 million. *The New York Times Magazine* appears in *The New York Times* on Sunday. The *Arts and Leisure* section appears during the week. The *Op Ed* page appears daily.

NEEDS Number of freelance photos purchased varies. Model release required. Photo captions required.

MAKING CONTACT & TERMS "Please FedEx all submissions." Include SASE for return of material. Responds in 1 week. Pays $345 for full page; $260 for half page; $230 for quarter page; $400/job (day rates); $750 for color cover. **Pays on acceptance.** Credit line given. Buys one-time rights.

$ ◑ NORTH AMERICAN WHITETAIL

2250 Newmarket Pkwy., Suite 110, Marietta GA 30067. (678)589-2000. Fax: (678)279-7512. E-mail: ron.sinfelt@imoutdoors.com. Website: www.north americanwhitetail.com. Estab. 1982. Circ. 125,000. Published 7 times/year (July-February) by InterMedia Outdoors. Emphasizes trophy whitetail deer hunting. Sample copy available for $4. Photo guidelines free with SASE.

NEEDS Buys 5 photos from freelancers/issue; 35 photos/year. Needs photos of large, live whitetail deer, hunter posing with or approaching downed trophy deer, or hunter posing with mounted head. Also uses photos of deer habitats and signs. Model release preferred. Photo captions preferred; include when and where scene was photographed.

SPECS Accepts images in digital format. Send via CD at 300 dpi with output of 8×12 inches. Also uses 35mm transparencies.

MAKING CONTACT & TERMS Send query letter with résumé of credits and list of stock photo subjects. Will return unsolicited material in 1 month if accompanied by SASE. Simultaneous submissions not accepted. Pays $400 for color cover; $75 for color inside. Tearsheets provided. Pays 60 days prior to publication. Credit line given. Buys one-time rights.

TIPS "In samples we look for extremely sharp, well-composed photos of whitetailed deer in natural settings. We also use photos depicting deer hunting scenes. Please study the photos we are using before making submission. We'll return photos we don't expect to use and hold the remainder for potential use. Please do not send dupes. Use an 8×10 envelope to ensure sharpness of images, and put name and identifying number on all slides and prints. Photos returned at time of publication or at photographer's request."

$ NORTH CAROLINA LITERARY REVIEW

East Carolina University, ECU Mailstop 555 English, Greenville NC 27858-4353. (252)328-1537. Fax: (252)328-4889. E-mail: nclrsubmissions@ecu.edu; bauerm@ecu.edu. Website: www.nclr.ecu.edu. Estab. 1992. Circ. 750. Annual literary magazine with North Carolina focus. *NCLR* publishes poetry, fiction and nonfiction by and interviews with NC writers, and articles and essays about NC literature, literary history and culture. Photographs must be NC-related. Sample copy available for $15. Photo guidelines available on website.

NEEDS Buys 3-6 photos from freelancers/issue. Model/property release preferred. Photo captions preferred.

SPECS Accepts images in digital format, 5×7 at 300 dpi. Inquire first; request, submit TIFF, GIF files at 300 dpi to nclrsubmissions@ecu.edu.

MAKING CONTACT & TERMS Send query letter with website address to show sample of work. If selected, art acquisitions editor will be in touch. Pays $50-250 for cover; $5-100 for b&w inside. Pays on publication. Credit line given. Buys first rights.

TIPS "*Only NC photographers.* Look at our publication—1998-present back issues. See our website."

$$ ◐ NORTH DAKOTA HORIZONS

P.O. Box 1091, Bismarck ND 58502. (866)462-0744. Fax: (701)223-4645. E-mail: ndhorizons@btinet.net. Website: www.ndhorizons.com. **Contact:** Andrea W. Collin, editor. Estab. 1971. Quality regional magazine. Photos used in magazines, audiovisual, calendars.

NEEDS Buys 50 photos/year; offers 25 assignments/year. Scenics of North Dakota events, places and people. Also wildlife, cities/urban, rural, adventure, entertainment, events, hobbies, performing arts, travel, agriculture, industry. Interested in historical/vintage, seasonal. Model/property release preferred. Photo captions preferred.

SPECS Prefers images in digital format. Send via CD, as TIFF, EPS files at 600 dpi.

MAKING CONTACT & TERMS Prefers e-mail query letter. Pays by the project, varies ($300-500); negotiable. Pays on usage. Credit line given. Buys one-time rights; negotiable.

TIPS "Know North Dakota events and places. Have a strong quality of composition and light."

NORTHERN WOODLANDS MAGAZINE

(802)439-6292. Fax: (802)439-6296. E-mail: dave@northernwoodlands.org. Website: www.northernwoodlands.org. Anne Margolis, managing editor. Estab. 1994. Circ. 15,000. Quarterly. "Created to inspire landowners' sense of stewardship by increasing their awareness of the natural history and the principles of conservation and forestry that are directly related to their land; to encourage loggers, foresters, and purchasers of raw materials to continually raise the standards by which they utilize the forest's resources; to increase the public's awareness and appreciation of the social, economic, and environmental benefits of a working forest; to raise the level of discussion about environmental and natural resource issues; and to educate a new generation of forest stewards." Sample copies available for $6. Photo guidelines available on website.

NEEDS Buys 10-50 photos from freelancers/year. Photos of forestry, environmental, landscapes/scenics, wildlife, rural, adventure, travel, agriculture, science. Interested in historical/vintage, seasonal. Other specific photo needs: vertical format, photos specific to assignments in northern New England and upstate New York. Reviews photos with or without a manuscript. Model release preferred. Photo captions required.

SPECS Uses glossy or matte color and b&w prints; 35mm, 2¼×2¼ transparencies. Prefers images in digital format. Send via CD, ZIP, e-mail as TIFF, EPS files at 300 dpi minimum. No e-mails larger than 10MB.

MAKING CONTACT & TERMS Send cover photo submissions as either slides or digital photos. Digital photos, less than 1MB each, can be e-mailed in JPEG, PDF, or TIFF format. If yours is chosen, we will request a higher-resolution image. You may also mail us a CD of your images to Attn: Cover Photos. Send query letter with slides. We have an online e-mail form available. Provide self-promotion piece to be kept on file for possible future assignments. Responds only if interested; send nonreturnable samples. Previously published work OK. Pays $150 for color cover; $25-75 for b&w inside. "We might pay upon receipt or as late as publication." Credit line given. Buys one-time rights. "We will hold your photos until publication of the magazine for which they are being considered, unless you ask otherwise. All materials will be returned by certified mail."

NORTHWEST TRAVEL MAGAZINE

4969 Hwy. 101 N., Suite 2, Florence OR 97439. (800)348-8401. E-mail: barb@ohwy.com; rosemary@nwmags.com. Website: www.northwestmagazines.com. **Contact:** Rosemary Camozzi, editor. Estab. 1991. Circ. 50,000. Bimonthly. Emphasizes travel in Oregon, Washington, Idaho, western Montana, and British Columbia, Canada. Sample copy available for $6. Photo guidelines free with SASE or online.

NEEDS Buys 3-5 photos from freelancers/issue; 18-30 photos/year. Wants seasonal scenics. Model release required. Photo captions required; include specific location and description. "Now only accepting digital images. Please include metadata."

SPECS Uses 35mm, 2¼×2¼, 4×5 positive transparencies. Do not e-mail images. We recommend acquiring model releases for any photos that include people, but we don't require releases except for photos used on covers or in advertising. Photos must be current, shot within the last five years. Digital photos must be sent on CDs as high-res (300 dpi) TIFF, JPEG, or EPS files without compression. Images should be 8½×11½. Include clear, color contact sheets of all images (no more than 8 per page). CDs are not returned. To be considered for calendars, photos must have horizontal formats.

MAKING CONTACT & TERMS Annual deadline for calendars is August 15. Responds in 1 month. Pays $425 for color cover; $100 for calendar usage; $25-50 for b&w inside; $25-100 for color inside; $100-250 for photo/text package. Credit line given. Buys one-time rights. We do not sign for personal delivery. SASE or return postage required.

TIPS "Send slide film that can be enlarged without graininess (50-100 ASA). We don't use color filters. Send 20-40 slides. Protect slides with sleeves put in plastic holders. Don't send in little boxes. We work about 3 months ahead, so send spring images in winter, summer images in spring, etc."

NOTRE DAME MAGAZINE

University of Notre Dame, 538 Grace Hall, Notre Dame IN 46556-5612. (574)631-5335. E-mail: Ndmag@Nd.edu. Website: Magazine.Nd.edu. Kerry Prugh, art

director. Estab. 1972. Circ. 150,000. "We are a university magazine with a scope as broad as that found at a university, but we place our discussion in a moral, ethical, and spiritual context reflecting our Catholic heritage."

NEEDS People, cities, education, architecture, business, science, environmental and landscapes. Model and property releases are required. Photo captions are required.

MAKING CONTACT & TERMS E-mail (JPEG samples at 72 dpi) or send a postcard sample.

NOW & THEN

Box 70556 ETSU, 807 University Pkwy., Johnson City TN 37614-1707. (423)439-5348. Fax: (423)439-6340. E-mail: wardenc@etsu.edu. Website: www.etsu.edu/cass. **Contact:** Charlie Warden, photo editor. Estab. 1984. Circ. 1,000. Literary magazine published twice/year. *Now & Then* tells the story of Appalachia, the mountain region that extends from northern Mississippi to southern New York state. The magazine presents a fresh, revealing picture of life in Appalachia, past and present, with engaging articles, personal essays, fiction, poetry and photography. Sample copy available for $8 plus $2 shipping. Photo guidelines free with SASE or online.

NEEDS Photos of environmental, landscapes/scenics, architecture, cities/urban, rural, adventure, performing arts, travel, agriculture, political, disasters. Interested in documentary, fine art, historical/vintage. Photographs must relate to theme of issue. Themes are posted on the website or available with guidelines. "We publish photo essays based on the magazine's theme." Reviews photos with or without a manuscript. Model/property release preferred. Photo captions preferred; include where the photo was taken, identify places/people.

SPECS Require images in digital format sent as e-mail attachments as JPEG or TIFF files at 300 dpi minimum.

MAKING CONTACT & TERMS Send query letter with résumé, photocopies. Provide self-promotion piece to be kept on file for possible future assignments. Responds only if interested; send nonreturnable samples. Simultaneous submissions OK. Credit line given along with a free issue of the magazine in which the photography is featured.

TIPS "Know what our upcoming themes are. Keep in mind we cover only the Appalachian region. (See the website for a definition of the region)."

OCEAN MAGAZINE

P.O. Box 84, Rodanthe NC 27968-0084. (252)256-2296. E-mail: Diane@oceanmagazine.org. Website: www.Oceanmagazine.org. **Contact:** Diane Buccheri, publisher. Estab. 2004. Circ. 40,000. *"OCEAN Magazine* serves to celebrate and protect the greatest, most comprehensive resource for life on earth, our world's ocean. *OCEAN* publishes articles, stories, poems, essays, and photography about the ocean—observations, experiences, scientific and environmental discussions—written with fact and feeling, illustrated with images from nature."

NEEDS People, disasters, environmental, adventure, landscape, wildlife, pets, documentary, sports, travel, fine art, lifestyle and seasonal photographs. Identification of subjects, model releases required. Reviews 3×5, 4×6, 5×7, 8×10, 10×12 prints, JPEG files. Negotiates payment individually. Buys one-time rights.

MAKING CONTACT & TERMS E-mail with photographs and samples. Samples kept on file. Portfolio not required.

TIPS "Purchase an issue to learn what *OCEAN* publishes."

OFF THE COAST

Resolute Bear Press, P.O. Box 14, Robbinston ME 04671. (207)454-8026. E-mail: poetrylane2@gmail.com. E-mail: poetrylane2@gmail.com. Website: www.off-the-coast.com. Michael Brown, Editor & Publisher. **Contact:** Valerie Lawson, editor and publisher. Estab. 1994. "The Mission of *Off the Coast* is to become recognized around the world as Maine's international poetry journal, a publication that prizes quality, diversity and honesty in its publications and in its dealings with poets. *Off the Coast*, a quarterly journal, publishes poetry, artwork and reviews. Arranged much like an anthology, each issue bears a title drawn from a line or phrase from one of its poems."

MAKING CONTACT & TERMS "We accept b&w graphics and photos to grace the pages of *Off the Coast*, and color or b&w for the cover. Send 3-6 images in JPEG format. We prefer you select and send images rather than send a link to your website."

OKLAHOMA TODAY

P.O. Box 1468, Oklahoma City OK 73101-1468. (405)230-8450; (800)777-1793. Fax: (405)230-8650. E-mail: megan@oklahomatoday.com. Website: www.oklahomatoday.com. **Contact:** Megan Rossman, associate editor. Estab. 1956. Circ. 45,000. Bimonthly. "We cover all aspects of Oklahoma, from history to people profiles, but we emphasize travel." Readers are "Oklahomans, whether they live in-state or are exiles; studies show them to be above average in education and income." Sample copy available for $4.95. Photo guidelines free with SASE or online.

NEEDS Buys 45 photos from freelancers/issue; 270 photos/year. Needs photos of "Oklahoma subjects only; the greatest number are used to illustrate a specific story on a person, place or thing in the state. We are also interested in stock scenics of the state." Other areas of focus are adventure—sport/travel, reenactment, historical and cultural activities. Model release required. Photo captions required.

SPECS Uses 8×10 glossy b&w prints; 35mm, 2¼×2¼, 4×5, 8×10 transparencies. Accepts images in digital format. Send via CD or e-mail.

MAKING CONTACT & TERMS Send query letter with samples; include SASE for return of material. Responds in 2 months. Simultaneous submissions and previously published work OK (on occasion). Pays $50-150 for b&w photos; $50-250 for color photos; $125-1,000/job. Pays on publication. Buys one-time rights with a 4-month from publication exclusive, plus right to reproduce photo in promotions for magazine without additional payment with credit line.

TIPS To break in, "read the magazine. Subjects are normally activities or scenics (mostly the latter). I would like good composition and very good lighting. I look for photographs that evoke a sense of place, look extraordinary and say something only a good photographer could say about the image. Look at what Ansel Adams and Eliot Porter did and what Muench and others are producing, and send me that kind of quality. We want the best photographs available, and we give them the space and play such quality warrants."

ONBOARD MEDIA

1691 Michigan Ave., Suite 600, Miami Beach FL 33139. (305)673-0400. Fax: (305)673-3575. E-mail: beth@onboard.com; sirena@onboard.com; info@onboard.com. Website: www.onboard.com. **Contact:** Beth Wood and Sirena Andras, co-art directors. Estab.

1990. Circ. 792,184. 90 annual and quarterly publications. Emphasize travel in the Caribbean, Europe, Mexican Riviera, Bahamas, Alaska, Bermuda, Las Vegas. Custom publications reach cruise vacationers and vacation/resort audience. Photo guidelines free with SASE.

NEEDS Photos of scenics, nature, prominent landmarks based in Caribbean, Mexican Riviera, Bahamas, Alaska, Europe and Las Vegas. Model/property release required. Photo captions required; include where the photo was taken and explain the subject matter. Credit line information requested.

SPECS Uses 35mm, 2¼×2¼, 4×5, 8×10 transparencies. Prefers images in digital format RAW data. Send via CD at 300 dpi.

MAKING CONTACT & TERMS Send query letter with stock list. Provide résumé, business card, brochure, flyer or tearsheets to be kept on file for possible future assignments. Keeps samples on file. Responds in 3 weeks. Previously published work OK. Rates negotiable per project. Pays on publication. Credit line given.

⊗ ⓞ ONE

1011 First Ave., New York NY 10022. (212)826-1480. Fax: (212)826-8979. E-mail: cnewa@cnewa.org. Website: www.cnewa.org. Estab. 1974. Circ. 90,000. Bimonthly. Official publication of Catholic Near East Welfare Association, "a papal agency for humanitarian and pastoral support." *ONE* informs Americans about the traditions, faiths, cultures and religious communities of the Middle East, Northeast Africa, India and Eastern Europe. Sample copy and photo guidelines available for 8½×11 SASE.

NEEDS Freelancers supply 80% of photos. Prefers to work with writer/photographer team. Looking for evocative photos of people—not posed—involved in activities: work, play, worship. Liturgical shots also welcome. Extensive captions required if text is not available.

MAKING CONTACT & TERMS Send query letter first. "Please do not send an inventory; rather, send a letter explaining your ideas." Include 8½ ×11 SASE. Responds in 3 weeks; acknowledges receipt of material immediately. Simultaneous submissions and previously published work OK, "but neither is preferred. If previously published, please tell us when and where." Pays $75-100 for b&w cover; $150-200 for color cover; $50-100 for b&w inside; $75-175 for color inside. Pays

on publication. Credit line given. "Credits appear on page 3 with masthead and table of contents." Buys first North American serial rights.

TIPS "Stories should weave current lifestyles with issues and needs. Avoid political subjects; stick with ordinary people. Photo essays are welcome. Write requesting sample issue and guidelines, then send query. We rarely use stock photos but have used articles and photos submitted by single photojournalist or writer/photographer team."

OREGON COAST

4969 Highway 101 N. #2, Florence OR 97439. E-mail: Rosemary@nwmags.com. Website: www.northwest magazines.com. **Contact:** Rosemary Camozzi. Estab. 1982. Circ. 50,000. Bimonthly. Emphasizes Oregon coast life. Sample copy available for $6, including postage. Photo guidelines available with SASE or on website.

NEEDS Buys 3-5 photos from freelancers/issue; 18-30 photos/year. Needs scenics. Especially needs photos of typical subjects—waves, beaches, lighthouses—with a fresh perspective. Needs mostly vertical format. Model description in megadata and on caption sheet. "Now only accepting digital images. We recommend acquiring model releases for any photos that include people, but we don't require releases except for photos used on covers or in advertising. Photos must be current, shot within the last five years."

MAKING CONTACT & TERMS Digital photos must be sent on CDs as high-res (300 dpi) TIFF, JPEG, or EPS files without compression. Images should be 8½×11. Include clear, color contact sheets of all images (no more than 8 per page). CDs are not returned. To be considered for calendars, photos must have horizontal formats. The annual deadline for calendars is August 15. Responds in 3 months. Pays $425 for color cover; $100 for calendar usage; $25-50 for b&w inside; $25-100 for color inside; $100-250 for photo/text package. Credit line given. Buys one-time rights. We do not sign for personal delivery. SASE or return postage required.

⊗⊗ ⓞ OUTDOOR AMERICA

Izaak Walton League of America, 707 Conservation Ln., Gaithersburg MD 20878. (301)548-0150. Fax: (301)548-9409. E-mail: oa@iwla.org. Website: www. iwla.org. **Contact:** Dawn Merritt, communications director. Estab. 1922. Circ. 36,500. Quarterly. Covers conservation topics, from clean air and water to public lands, fisheries and wildlife. Also focuses on outdoor recreation issues and covers conservation-related accomplishments of the League's membership.

NEEDS Vertical wildlife photos or shots of campers, boaters, anglers, hunters and other traditional outdoor recreationists for cover. Reviews photos with or without a manuscript. Model release required. Photo captions preferred; include date taken, model info, location and species.

SPECS Uses 35mm, 6×9 transparencies or negatives. Accepts images in digital format. Send via CD, ZIP, e-mail as TIFF, EPS, JPEG files at 300 dpi.

MAKING CONTACT & TERMS "Tearsheets and non-returnable samples only. Not responsible for return of unsolicited material." Simultaneous submissions and previously published work OK. **Pays on acceptance.** Credit line given. Buys one-time rights and occasionally web rights.

TIPS "We prefer the unusual shot—new perspectives on familiar objects or subjects. We occasionally assign work. Approximately one half of the magazine's photos are from freelance sources."

OUTDOOR CANADA MAGAZINE

25 Sheppard Ave. W., Suite 100, Toronto ON M2N 6S7, Canada. (416)733-7600. Fax: (416)227-8296. E-mail: editorial@outdoorcanada.ca. Website: www.outdoorcanada.ca. Estab. 1972. Circ. 90,000. 4-color magazine for Canadian anglers and hunters. Stories on fishing, hunting and conservation. Readers are 81% male. Publishes 8 regular issues/year. "We are looking for strong, attention-grabbing images that capture the love our readers have for hunting and fishing. We're interested in finding and cultivating new Canadian talent and appreciate submissions from new photographers and illustrators to add to our list."

NEEDS Buys 200-300 photos/year. Needs photos of wildlife; fishing, hunting, ice-fishing; action shots. *Canadian content only.* Photo captions required; include identification of fish, bird or animal.

SPECS Accepts images in digital format. Photographers interested in sending originals should send a small portfolio of 100 (or less) well-edited images. Naturally, we would expect photographers to send images that are in line with the magazine's content (i.e., fishing, hunting, conservation). Label each frame with your name, and provide details such as species of fish or shot location. We usually do not purchase

images in advance, but will solicit images from your library when packaging stories or features. We'll return them by Express Post as soon as we can after viewing. We also are happy to accept electronic submissions via e-mail.

MAKING CONTACT & TERMS "Send a well-edited selection of transparencies with return postage for consideration. E-mail/CD portfolios also accepted." Responds in 1 month. Pays on invoice. Buys one-time rights.

TIPS "When sending unsolicited submissions, please send dupes, color copies or tear sheets of your work that we can keep on file. We get hundreds of promotional pieces each year, so we can't possibly respond to them all, but we'll do our best. If we'd like to see more of your portfolio or assign work to you, we'll contact you. Art guidelines are available."

OUTDOOR LIFE MAGAZINE

2 Park Ave., New York NY 10016-5604. (212)779-5000. Fax: (212)779-5366. E-mail: OLphotos@bonniercorp.com. Website: www.outdoorlife.com. **Contact:** Margaret McKenna and Jason Beckstead, assistant art directors. Estab. 1897. Circ. 900,000. Emphasizes hunting, fishing and shooting. Readers are "outdoor enthusiasts of all ages." Sample copy "not for individual requests." Photo guidelines available with SASE.

NEEDS Buys 100 photos from freelancers/issue; 1,000-2,000 photos/year. Needs photos of "all species of wildlife and game fish, especially in action and in natural habitat; how-to and where-to." Interested in historical/vintage hunting and fishing photos. Photo captions preferred.

SPECS Prefers 35mm slides. Accepts images in digital format. Send via CD, e-mail as JPEG files at 100 dpi, 3×5 size.

MAKING CONTACT & TERMS Send 35mm or 2¾×2¾ transparencies by certified mail with SASE for consideration. Prefers dupes. Responds in 1 month. Pays $1,000 minimum for color cover; $100-850 for color inside. Rates are negotiable. Pays on publication. Credit line given. Buys one-time rights.

TIPS "Print name and address clearly on each photo to ensure return; send in 8×10 plastic sleeves. Multiple subjects encouraged. E-mail examples and list of specific animal species and habitats. All of our images are hunting and fishing related. We are about adventure (hunting & fishing!) and 'how-to!' Query first with SASE; will not accept, view or hold artist's work without first receiving a signed copy of our waiver of liability."

☺ ◑ OWL MAGAZINE

10 Lower Spadina Ave., Suite 400, Toronto ON M5V 2Z2, Canada. (416)340-2700. Fax: (416)340-9769. E-mail: melissa.kilpatrick@owlkids.com;owl@owlkids.com. Website: www.owlkids.com. **Contact:** Debbie Yea, photo editor. Estab. 1976. Circ. 80,000. Published 10 times/year. A discovery magazine for children ages 9-13. Sample copy available for $4.95 and 9×12 SAE with $1.50 money order for postage. Photo guidelines free with SAE or via e-mail.

NEEDS Photo stories, photo puzzles, photos of children ages 12-14, extreme weather, wildlife, science, technology, environmental, pop culture, multicultural, events, adventure, hobbies, humor, sports, extreme sports. Interested in documentary, seasonal. Model/property release required. Photo captions required. Will buy story packages.

SPECS Accepts images in digital format. E-mail as JPEG files at 72 dpi. Requires 300 dpi for publication.

MAKING CONTACT & TERMS Accepts no responsibility for unsolicited material. Previously published work OK. Credit line given. Buys one-time rights.

TIPS "Photos should be sharply focused with good lighting, and engaging for kids. We are always on the lookout for humorous, action-packed shots; eye-catching, sports, animals, bloopers, etc. Photos with a 'wow' impact."

☺ OXYGEN

Canusa Products/St. Ives, Inc., 5775 McLaughlin Rd., Mississauga ON L5R 3P7, Canada. (905)507-3545; (888)254-0767. Fax: (905)507-2372. E-mail: editorial@oxygenmag.com. Website: www.oxygenmag.com. Estab. 1997. Circ. 340,000. Monthly. Emphasizes exercise and nutrition for women. Readers are women ages 20-39. Sample copy available for $5.

NEEDS Buys 720 photos from freelancers/issue. Needs photos of women weight training and exercising aerobically. Model release required. Photo captions preferred; include names of subjects.

SPECS Accepts high-res digital images. Uses 35mm, 2¼×2¼ transparencies. Prints occasionally acceptable.

MAKING CONTACT & TERMS Send unsolicited photos by mail for consideration. Does not keep samples on file; include SASE for return of material. Responds in 3 weeks. Pays $200-400/hour; $800-1,500/day; $500-1,500/job; $500-2,000 for color cover; $50-100 for color or b&w inside. **Pays on acceptance.** Credit line given. Buys all rights.

TIPS "We are looking for attractive, fit women working out on step machines, joggers, rowers, treadmills, ellipticals; with free weights; running for fitness; jumping, climbing. Professional pictures only, please. We particularly welcome photos of female celebrities who are into fitness; higher payments are made for these."

OYEZ REVIEW

Roosevelt University, Dept. of Literature & Languages, 430 S. Michigan Ave., Chicago IL 60605-1394. (312)341-3500. E-mail: oyezreview@roosevelt.edu. Website: legacy.roosevelt.edu/roosevelt.edu/oyez review. Estab. 1965. Circ. 600. Annual magazine of the Creative Writing Program at Roosevelt University, publishing fiction, creative nonfiction, poetry, and art. There are no restrictions on style, theme, or subject matter. Each issue has 100 pages: 92 pages of text and an 8-page b&w spread of one artist's work (usually drawing, painting or photography), with the front and back covers as well, totaling 10 pieces. Accepts outstanding work from beginning and established photographers. Expects a high level of professionalism from all photographers who make contact. Reviews photos with or without a manuscript.

NEEDS Accepts 10 photos from freelancers/issue; 10 photos/year. Needs babies/children/teens, senior citizens, cities/urban, pets, religious, rural, military, political, product shots/still life, disasters, environmental, landscapes/scenics, wildlife, adventure, automobiles, events, hobbies, humor, performing arts, sports, travel, avant garde, documentary, fine art, seasonal

SPECS Submit in b&w only. Send via CD, e-mail as JPEG files.

MAKING CONTACT & TERMS Send query letter, e-mail with b&w photocopies, SASE, photographs, JPEG samples at 72 dpi. Model and property release is preferred. Photo captions are preferred.

☺ PACIFIC YACHTING

OP Publishing, Ltd., 200 West Esplanade, Suite 500, North Vancouver BC V7M 1A4, Canada. (604)998-3310. Fax: (604)998-3320. E-mail: editor@pacific yachting.com. Website: www.pacificyachting.com.

Contact: Dale Miller, editor. Estab. 1968. Circ. 19,000. Monthly. Emphasizes boating on West Coast. Readers are ages 35-60; boaters, power and sail. Sample copy available for $6.95 Canadian plus postage.

NEEDS Buys 75 photos from freelancers/issue; 900 photos/year. Photos of landscapes/scenics, adventure, sports. Interested in historical/vintage, seasonal. "All should be boating related. Reviews photos with accompanying manuscript only. Always looking for covers; must be shot in British Columbia."

MAKING CONTACT & TERMS Keeps samples on file. Simultaneous submissions and previously published work OK. Pays $400 Canadian for color cover. Payment negotiable. Credit line given. Buys one-time rights.

PAKN TREGER

National Yiddish Book Center, 1021 West St., Amherst MA 01002. (413)256-4900. E-mail: aatherley@bikher.org; pt@bikher.org; bwolfson@bikher.org. Website: www.yiddishbookcenter.org. Betsey Wolfson, photography. **Contact:** Anne Atherley, editor's assistant. Estab. 1980. Circ. 20,000. Literary magazine published 3 times/year; focuses on modern and contemporary Jewish and Yiddish culture.

NEEDS Photos of families, parents, senior citizens, education, religious, humor, historical/vintage, Jewish and Yiddish culture. Reviews photos with or without a manuscript. Captions required; include identification of subjects.

SPECS Accepts images in digital format. Send JPEG or GIF files.

MAKING CONTACT & TERMS Negotiates payment. Pays on publication. Credit line given. Buys one-time rights.

🟢🟢 PENNSYLVANIA ANGLER & BOATER

P.O. Box 67000, Harrisburg PA 17106-7000. (717)705-7844. E-mail: sgearhart@state.pa.us. Website: www.fish.state.pa.us. **Contact:** Spring Gearhart, editor. Bimonthly. "*Pennsylvania Angler & Boater* is the Keystone State's official fishing and boating magazine, published by the Pennsylvania Fish & Boat Commission." Readers are anglers and boaters in Pennsylvania. Sample copy and photo guidelines free with 9×12 SASE and 9 oz. postage, or online.

NEEDS Buys 8 photos from freelancers/issue; 48 photos/year. Needs "action fishing and boating shots." Model release required. Photo captions required.

MAKING CONTACT & TERMS "Don't submit without first considering contributor guidelines, available online. Then send query letter with résumé of credits. Send 35mm or larger transparencies by mail for consideration; include SASE for return of material. Send low-res images on CD; we'll later request high-res images of those shots that interest us." Responds in several weeks. Pays $400 maximum for color cover; $30 minimum for color inside; $50-300 for text/photo package. Pays between acceptance and publication. Credit line given.

🟢 PENNSYLVANIA GAME NEWS

2001 Elmerton Ave., Harrisburg PA 17110-9797. (717)787-3745. E-mail: robmitchel@state.pa.us. Website: www.pgc.state.pa.us. **Contact:** Robert Mitchell. Circ. 75,000. Monthly. Published by the Pennsylvania Game Commission. Readers are people interested in hunting, wildlife management and conservation in Pennsylvania. Sample copy available with 9×12 SASE. Editorial guidelines free.

NEEDS Considers photos of "any outdoor subject (Pennsylvania locale), except fishing and boating." Reviews photos with accompanying manuscript. Manuscript not required.

MAKING CONTACT & TERMS The agency expects all photos to be accompanied with a photo credit (e.g., Jake Dingel/PGC Photo). E-mail Robert Mitchell at robmitchel@state.pa.us with questions about images and policy. Send prints or slides. "No negatives, please." Include SASE for return of material. Will accept electronic images via CD only (no e-mail). Will also view photographer's website if available. Responds in 2 months. Pays $40-300. **Pays on acceptance.**

🟢 PENNSYLVANIA MAGAZINE

P.O. Box 755, Camp Hill PA 17011. (717)697-4660. E-mail: pamag@aol.com. Website: www.pa-mag.com. **Contact:** Matthew K. Holliday, editor. Circ. 30,000. Bimonthly. Emphasizes history, travel and contemporary topics. Readers are 40-70 years old, professional and retired. Samples available upon request. Photo guidelines free with SASE or via e-mail.

NEEDS Uses about 40 photos/issue; most supplied by freelancers. Needs include travel, wildlife and scenic. All photos must be taken in Pennsylvania. Reviews photos with or without accompanying manuscript. Photo captions required.

MAKING CONTACT & TERMS Send query letter with samples. Send digital submissions for consideration. Sharpness is more important than pixel size. If your submitted images are of interest, the editor will communicate as to sizes needed. Responds in 1 month. Simultaneous submissions and previously published work OK with notification. Pays $100-150 for color cover; $35 for color inside; $50-500 for text/photo package. Credit line given. Buys one-time, first rights or other rights as arranged.

TIPS Look at several past issues and review guidelines before submitting.

Ⓞ PENTHOUSE

2 Penn Plaza, Suite 1125, New York NY 10121. (212)702-6000. Fax: (212)702-6262. Website: www.penthouse.com. Monthly. For the sophisticated male. Editorial scope ranges from outspoken contemporary comment to photography essays of beautiful women. Features interviews with personalities, sociological studies, humor, travel, food and wines, and fashion and grooming for men. Query before submitting.

◗ Ⓢ PERIOD IDEAS

21-23 Phoenix Court, Hawkins Rd., Colchester, Essex CO2 8JY, United Kingdom. (44)(1206)505976. E-mail: jeannine@aceville.co.uk. Website: www.periodideas.com. **Contact:** Jeannine McAndrew; Rebecca Winward, editor. Circ. 38,000. Monthly home interest magazine for readers with period properties which they wish to renovate sympathetically.

NEEDS Photos of architecture, interiors/decorating, gardens, events. Reviews photos with or without ms.

SPECS Uses glossy color prints; 35mm transparencies. Accepts images in digital format. Send via CD as TIFF, JPEG files at 300 dpi.

MAKING CONTACT & TERMS Send query letter with prints, transparencies. Does not keep samples on file; include SASE for return of material. Responds only if interested; send nonreturnable samples. Previously published work OK. Prices for covers/packages/single shots negotiated one-on-one (please indicate expectations). Pays at the end of the cover-dated publication date. Credit line sometimes given. Buys one-time rights.

TIPS "Label each image with what it is, name and contact address/telephone number of photographer."

❷❸ ◗ PERSIMMON HILL

1700 NE 63rd St., Oklahoma City OK 73111. (405)478-6404. Fax: (405)478-4714. E-mail: editor@national cowboymuseum.org. Website: www.nationalcowboy museum.org. **Contact:** Judy Hilovsky. Estab. 1970. Circ. 7,500. Quarterly publication of the National Cowboy and Western Heritage Museum. Emphasizes the West, both historical and contemporary views. Has diverse international audience with an interest in preservation of the West. Sample copy available for $10.50 and 9×12 SAE with 10 first-class stamps. Photo guidelines free with SASE or on website.

◯ This magazine has received Outstanding Publication honors from the Oklahoma Museums Association, the International Association of Business Communicators, Ad Club and Public Relations Society of America.

NEEDS Buys 65 photos from freelancers/issue; 260 photos/year. "Photos must pertain to specific articles unless it is a photo essay on the West." Western subjects include celebrities, couples, families, landscapes, wildlife, architecture, interiors/decorating, rural, adventure, entertainment, events, hobbies, travel. Interested in documentary, fine art, historical/vintage, seasonal. Model release required for children's photos. Photo captions required; include location, names of people, action. Proper credit is required if photos are historic.

SPECS Accepts images in digital format. Send via CD.

MAKING CONTACT & TERMS Submit portfolio for review by mail, directly to the editor, or with a personal visit to the editor. Responds in 6 weeks. Pays $150-500 for color cover; $100-150 for b&w cover; $50-150 for color inside; $25-100 for b&w inside. Credit line given. Buys first North American serial rights.

TIPS "Make certain your photographs are high quality and have a story to tell. We are using more contemporary portraits of things that are currently happening in the West and using fewer historical photographs. Work must be high quality, original, innovative. Photographers can best present their work in a portfolio format and should keep in mind that we like to feature photo essays on the West in each issue. Study the magazine to understand its purpose. Show only the work that would be beneficial to us or pertain to the traditional Western subjects we cover."

PHI DELTA KAPPAN

408 N. Union St., Bloomington IN 47402. 800-766-1156. Fax: 812-339-0018. E-mail: cbucheri@pdkintl.org; akincaid@pdkintl.org. Website: www.pdkintl.org/kappan/kappan.htm. Ashley McDonald Kincaid, director of marketing & communications. **Contact:** Carol Bucheri, design director. Estab. 1915. Circ. 30,000. Produces *Kappan* magazine and supporting materials. Photos used in magazine, flyers and subscription cards. Photo guidelines available online at: www.pdkintl.org/kappan/write.htm.

NEEDS Uses high-quality royalty-free, model-released stock photos and stock illustrations on education topics. Especially interested in photos of educators and students at all levels, pre-K through university depicting a variety of people in different educational settings; teacher-to-teacher interactions with or without students (e.g., teachers' meetings, in-service, professional development settings). Photo caption preferred; include who, what, when, where.

SPECS All visual materials should be submitted in high-resolution digital format, preferably JPEG (300 dpi at a minimum of 2100×3000 pixels). When taking photos, use the largest or finest format available. Images should be at least a few MB in size. Secure signed releases from parents before submitting any images of students/minors. In cases where an author is submitting work (photos or artwork) done by another person, obtain that person's written permission and include information crediting that person. Releases should be transmitted to *Kappan* along with the images. Submit images in digital format only.

MAKING CONTACT & TERMS Credit line and tearsheets given. Buys one-time rights. Payment is for print and electronic use in one issue, which may include distribution of, through third party vendors such as EBSCO, JSTOR, and HighWire, PDFs of articles that include illustrations, photographs, and cartoons. Provides a copy of the issue in which the photographs or illustrations appear.

TIPS "We will definitely consider purchasing collections of royalty-free, copyright-free, model-released stock work if the majority of the images are relevant."

PHOTOGRAPHER'S FORUM MAGAZINE

813 Reddick St., Santa Barbara CA 93103. (805)963-6425. Fax: (805)965-0496. E-mail: julie@serbin.com. Website: www.pfmagazine.com. **Contact:** Julie Simp-

son, managing editor. Quarterly magazine for the serious student and emerging professional photographer. Includes feature articles on historic and contemporary photographers, interviews, book reviews, workshop listings, new products.

PHOTO LIFE

Apex Publications, 185 St. Paul St., Quebec City QC G1K 3W2, Canada. (800)905-7468. Fax: (800)664-2739. E-mail: editor@photolife.com. Website: www.photolife.com. **Contact:** Editor. Circ. 60,000. Published 6 times/year. Readers are amateur, advanced amateur and professional photographers. Sample copy free with SASE. Photo guidelines available on website. Priority is given to Canadian photographers.

NEEDS Buys 70 photos from freelancers/issue; 420 photos/year. Needs landscape/wildlife shots, fashion, scenics, b&w images and so on.

SPECS Accepts images in digital format. Send via CD at 300 dpi.

MAKING CONTACT & TERMS Send query letter with résumé of credits, SASE. Pays on publication. Buys first North American serial rights and one-time rights.

TIPS "Looking for good writers to cover any subject of interest to the amateur and advanced photographer. Fine art photos should be striking, innovative. General stock and outdoor photos should be presented with a strong technical theme."

PHOTO TECHNIQUES

Editorial Offices, 1755 Avenida de Mercado, P.O. Box 1022, Mesilla MN 88046. (575)523-0208. E-mail: pschranz@phototechmag.com. Website: www.phototechmag.com. **Contact:** Paul Schranz, editor. Estab. 1979. Circ. 20,000. Bimonthly. For advanced traditional and digital photographers. Sample copy available for $6. Photo guidelines free with SASE or available online.

NEEDS Publishes expert technical articles about photography. Needs photos of rural, landscapes/scenics, "but if extensively photographed by others, ask yourself if your photo is sufficiently different." Also "some urban or portrait if it fits theme of article." Especially needs digital ink system testing and coloring and alternative processes articles. Reviews photos with or without a manuscript. Photo captions required; include technical data.

SPECS Uses any and all formats.

MAKING CONTACT & TERMS "E-mail queries work best." Send article or portfolio for review. Portfolio should include b&w and color prints, slides or transparencies. Keeps samples on file; include SASE for return of material. "Prefer that work not have been previously published in any competing photography magazine; small, scholarly, or local publication OK." Pays $300 for color cover; $100-150/page. Pays on publication. Credit line given. Buys one-time rights.

TIPS "We need people to be familiar with our magazine before submitting/querying. Include return postage/packaging. Also, we much prefer complete, finished submissions. When people ask, 'Would you be interested in...?' often the answer is simply, 'We don't know! Let us see it.' Most of our articles are written by practicing photographers and use their work as illustrations."

PILOT GETAWAYS MAGAZINE

Airventure Publishing LLC, P.O. Box 550, Glendale CA 91209-0550. (818)241-1890. Fax: (818)241-1895. E-mail: info@pilotgetaways.com. Website: www.pilotgetaways.com. Estab. 1999. Circ. 25,000. Bimonthly. Focuses on travel by private aircraft. Includes sections on back country, bush and mountain flying. Emphasizes private pilot travel—weekend getaways, fly-in dining, bush flying, and complete flying vacations. Readers are mid-life males, affluent.

NEEDS Uses assignment photos. Needs photos of adventure, travel, product shots/still life. Model release required. Photo captions required.

SPECS Accepts medium-format and 35mm slides. Accepts images in digital format. Send via CD as TIFF files at 300 dpi.

MAKING CONTACT & TERMS Provide résumé, business card or tearsheets to be kept on file for possible future assignments; contact by e-mail. Simultaneous submissions OK. Prefers previously unpublished work. Pays 30 days after publication. Credit line given. Buys all rights; negotiable.

TIPS "Exciting, fresh and unusual photos of airplanes used for recreation. Aerial landscapes, fly-in destinations. Outdoor recreation: skiing, hiking, fishing and motor sports. Affluent back-country lifestyles: homes, hangars and private airstrips. Query first. Don't send originals—color copies or low-res digital OK for evaluation."

PILOT MAGAZINE

3 The Courtyard, Denmark Street, Wokingham, Berkshire RG40 2AZ, United Kingdom. +44(0)118 989 7246. Fax: +44(0)7834 104843. Website: www.pilotweb.aero. Estab. 1968. Circ. 15,754. "The UK's best-selling aviation monthly magazine." Photo guidelines available.

NEEDS Photos of aviation. Reviews photos with or without a manuscript. Photo captions required.

SPECS Uses glossy, color prints; 35mm, 2¼×2¼, 4×5, 8×10 transparencies. Accepts images in digital format. Send via CD, ZIP as JPEG files at 300 dpi.

MAKING CONTACT & TERMS Does not keep samples on file; include SASE for return of material. Previously published work OK. Pays £30 for color inside. Pays on publication. Credit line given. Buys one-time rights.

TIPS "Read our magazine. Label all photos with name and address. Supply generous captions."

PLANET

P.O. Box 44, Aberystwyth SY23 3ZZ, Wales. (44)(1970)611255. Fax: (44)(1970)611197. E-mail: planet.enquiries@planetmagazine.org.uk. Website: www.planetmagazine.org.uk. Estab. 1970. Circ. 1,400. Bimonthly cultural magazine devoted to Welsh culture, current affairs, the arts, the environment, but set in broader international context. Audience based mostly in Wales.

NEEDS Photos of environmental, performing arts, sports, agriculture, industry, political, science. Interested in fine art, historical/vintage. Reviews photos with or without manuscript. Model/property release preferred. Photo captions required; include subject, copyright holder.

SPECS Uses glossy color and b&w prints; 4×5 transparencies. Accepts images in digital format. Send as JPEG files at 300 dpi.

MAKING CONTACT & TERMS Send query letter with résumé, slides, prints, photocopies. Does not keep samples on file; include SASE for return of material. Simultaneous submissions and previously published work OK. Pays on publication. Credit line given. Buys first rights.

TIPS "Read the magazine first to get an idea of the kind of areas we cover so incompatible/unsuitable material is not submitted. Submission guidelines available online."

⊘⊘ ● PLAYBOY MAGAZINE

680 N. Lake Shore Drive, Chicago IL 60611. (312)373-2700. Fax: (312)587-9046. E-mail: gcole@playboy.com. Website: www.playboy.com. Gary Cole, contributing editor. Estab. 1953. Monthly magazine and website with daily updates. Pay site: Playboy Cyber Club. This is a premier market that demands photographic excellence. *Playboy* frequently uses freelancers but only those with superior quality work. *Playboy* accepts model submissions from all photographers but copies of model photo ID showing they are at least 18 years of age must be included with submission. Playmate finder's fees are paid. Readers are 75% male, 25% female, ages 18-70; come from all economic, ethnic and regional backgrounds.

NEEDS Photographic needs focus primarily on glamour/pretty girls with nudity. Also includes still life, fashion, food, personalities, travel.

SPECS Raw digital file preferred with a minimum of 40-50MB.

MAKING CONTACT & TERMS Pay is negotiable depending on job. Finder's fee for a published Playmate is $500. The modeling fee for a published Playmate is $25,000. **Pays on acceptance.** Buys all rights.

TIPS "Lighting and attention to detail is most important when photographing women, especially the ability to use strobes indoors. Refer to magazine for style and quality guidelines."

PLAYBOY'S SPECIAL EDITIONS

680 N. Lake Shore Dr., Chicago IL 60611. (312)373-2273. Fax: (312)751-2818. E-mail: specialeditions@playboy.com. Website: www.playboyse.com. Estab. 1984. Bimonthly magazine and 18 newsstand specials for male sophisticates (25 issues/year). Photo guidelines available on website.

NEEDS Photos of beautiful women. Model/property release required. Models must be 18 years or older with two forms of valid ID. Photo captions required.

SPECS Uses 35mm color transparencies or high-res digital. Accepts images in digital format. Send via e-mail to sesubmissions@playboy.com.

MAKING CONTACT & TERMS Send query letter with samples. Does not keep samples on file; include SASE for return of material. Responds in 4-6 weeks. **Pays on acceptance.** Credit line given. Buys all rights.

ⓓ POPULAR PHOTOGRAPHY & IMAGING

Bonnier Corporation, 460 N. Orlando Ave., Suite 200, Winter Park FL 32789. (407)628-4802. Fax: (407)628-7061. E-mail: mleuchter@hfmus.com; popeditor@hfmus.com. Website: www.popularphotography.com; online at PopPhoto.com. **Contact:** Miriam Leuchter, managing editor. Estab. 1937. Circ. 450,000. Monthly. Readers are male and female photographers, amateurs to professionals of all ages. Photo guidelines free with SASE.

NEEDS "We are primarily interested in articles on new or unusual phases of photography which we have not covered recently or in recent years. We do not want general articles on photography which could just as easily be written by our staff. We reserve the right to rewrite, edit, or revise any material we are interested in publishing."

MAKING CONTACT & TERMS "Queries should be accompanied by a sampling of how-to pictures (particularly when equipment is to be constructed or a process is involved), or by photographs which support the text. Please send duplicates only; do not send negatives or original slides. We are not responsible for the loss of original work. The sender's name and address should be clearly written on the back of each print, on the mount of each slide, watermarked on digitally sent sample images, and on the first and last pages of all written material, including the accompanying letter. Technical data should accompany all pictures, including the camera used, lens, film (or image format if digital), shutter speed, aperture, lighting, and any other points of special interest on how the picture was made. Material mailed to us should be carefully wrapped or packaged to avoid damage. All submissions must be accompanied by a SASE. The rate of payment depends upon the importance of the feature, quality of the photographs, and our presentation of it. Upon acceptance, fees will be negotiated by the author/photographer and the editors of the magazine. We are unable to accept individual portfolios for review. However, we do welcome samples of your work in the form of promotional mailers, press kits, or tear sheets for our files. These shoud be sent to the attention of Miriam Leuchter, managing editor, at the above address or via e-mail at mleuchter@hfmus.com"

TIPS The Annual Reader's Picture Contest gives photographers the opportunity to have their work recognized in the largest photo magazine in the world, as well as on PopPhoto.com. See website for submission guidelines, or e-mail acooper@hfmus.com.

POWER & MOTORYACHT

Source Interlink Media, 261 Madison Ave., 6th Floor, New York NY 10016. (212)915-4313; (212)915-4000. Fax: (212)915-4328. E-mail: richard.thiel@powerand motoryacht.com. Website: www.powerandmotor yacht.com. Aimee Colon, art director. **Contact:** Richard Thiel, editor-in-chief. Estab. 1985. Circ. 157,000. Monthly. Covers powerboats 24 feet and larger with special emphasis on the 35-foot-plus market. "Readers have an average of 33 years experience boating, and we give them accurate advice on how to choose, operate, and maintain their boats as well as what electronics and gear will help them pursue their favorite pastime. In addition, since powerboating is truly a lifestyle and not just a hobby for them, *Power & Motoryacht* reports on a host of other topics that affect their enjoyment of the water: chartering, sportfishing, and the environment, among others."

😊😊 🌑 POZ MAGAZINE

462 Seventh Ave., 19th Floor, New York NY 10018-7424. (212)242-2163. Fax: (212)675-8505. E-mail: editor-in-chief@poz.com; webmaster@poz.com. Website: www.poz.com. **Contact:** Michael Halliday, art production manager. Circ. 100,000. Monthly. Focuses exclusively on HIV/AIDS news, research and treatment.

NEEDS Buys 10-25 photos from freelancers/issue; 120-300 photos/year. Reviews photos with or without a manuscript. Model release preferred. Photo captions required.

SPECS Prefers online portfolios.

MAKING CONTACT & TERMS Send query letter with nonreturnable samples. Provide self-promotion piece to be kept on file for possible future assignments. Responds only if interested; send nonreturnable samples. Simultaneous submissions and previously published work OK. Pays $400-1,000 for color cover; $100-500 for color inside. Pays on publication. Credit line given.

☺ 😊 😊 🌑 THE PRAIRIE JOURNAL

P.O. Box 68073, 28 Crowfoot Terrace NW, Calgary AB Y3G 3N8, Canada. E-mail: editor@prairiejournal. org (queries only); prairiejournal@yahoo.com. Website: prairiejournal.org. **Contact:** A.E. Burke, literary editor. Estab. 1983. Circ. 600. Literary magazine published twice/year. Features mainly poetry and artwork. Sample copy available for $6 and 7×8½ SAE. Photo guidelines available for SAE and IRC.

NEEDS Buys 4 photos/year. Needs literary only, artistic.

SPECS Uses b&w prints. Accepts images in digital format. Send via e-mail "if your query is successful."

MAKING CONTACT & TERMS Send query letter with photocopies only (no originals) by mail. Provide self-promotion piece to be kept on file. Responds in 6 months, only if interested; send nonreturnable samples. Pays $10-50 for b&w cover or inside. Pays on publication. Credit line given. Buys first rights.

TIPS "Black & white literary, artistic work preferred; not commercial. We especially like newcomers. Read our publication or check out our website. You need to own copyright for your work and have permission to reproduce it. We are open to subjects that would be suitable for a literary arts magazine containing poetry, fiction, reviews, interviews. We do not commission but choose from your samples."

☺ 😊 🌑 PRAIRIE MESSENGER

Benedictine Monks of St. Peter's Abbey, P.O. Box 190, Muenster SK S0K 2Y0, Canada. (1)(306)682-1772. Fax: (1)(306)682-5285. E-mail: Pm.canadian@ Stpeterspress.ca. Website: www.prairiemessenger. ca. **Contact:** Maureen Weber, associate editor. Estab. 1904. Circ. 5,000. Weekly Catholic publication published by the Benedictine Monks of St. Peter's Abbey in Muenster, SK. Canada. Has a strong focus on ecumenism, social justice, interfaith relations, aboriginal issues, arts and culture.

NEEDS People, religious, agriculture, industry, military, environmental, entertainment, performing arts, lifestyle, seasonal photographs. Buys 50 photos/year. "I usually need photos to illustrate columns and occasionally use 'filler' feature photos with captions I either make up or seek quotations for. This means a range of themes is possible, including seasonal, environmental, religious, etc. Also, we carry a weekly poem submitted by freelancers, but I use stock photos to illustrate the poems."

MAKING CONTACT & TERMS Accepts photos as TIFF or JPEG format. E-mail with JPEG samples at 72 dpi. Credit line given.

PRINCETON ALUMNI WEEKLY

194 Nassau St., Suite 38, Princeton NJ 08542. (609)258-4722. Fax: (609)258-2247. E-mail: mnelson@princeton.edu. Website: www.princeton.edu/paw. **Contact:** Marianne Nelson, art director. Circ. 60,000. Published 15 times/year. Emphasizes Princeton University and higher education. Readers are alumni, faculty, students, staff and friends of Princeton University. Sample copy available for $2 with 9×12 SASE and 2 first-class stamps.

NEEDS Assigns local and out-of-state photographers and purchases stock. Needs photos of people, campus scenes; subjects vary greatly with content of each issue.

MAKING CONTACT & TERMS Arrange a personal interview to show portfolio. Provide sample card to be kept on file for possible future assignments. Payment varies according to usage, size, etc. Pays on publication. Buys one-time rights.

[A] $ ○ PROCEEDINGS

U.S. Naval Institute, 291 Wood Rd., Annapolis MD 21402-5034. (410)268-6110. Fax: (410)295-7940. E-mail: articlesubmissions@usni.org. Website: www.usni.org; www.navalinstitute.org. **Contact:** Paul Merzlak, editor-in-chief; Amy Voight, photo editor. Estab. 1873. Circ. 60,000. Monthly trade magazine dedicated to providing an open forum for national defense. Sample copy available for $3.95. Photo guidelines free with SASE.

NEEDS Buys 10 photos from freelancers/issue; 120 photos/year. Needs photos of industry, military, political. Model release preferred. Photo captions required; include time, location, subject matter, service represented—if necessary.

SPECS Uses glossy color prints. Accepts images in digital format. Send via CD, ZIP as TIFF, JPEG files at 300 dpi.

MAKING CONTACT & TERMS Send query letter with résumé, prints. Does not keep samples on file; include SASE for return of material. Responds only if interested; send nonreturnable samples. Simultaneous submissions and previously published work OK. Pays $200 for color cover; $25-75 for color inside. Pays on publication. Credit line given. Buys one-time and sometimes electronic rights.

TIPS "We look for original work. The best place to get a feel for our imagery is to see our magazine or look at our website."

◎ $ ○ THE PROGRESSIVE

409 E. Main St., Madison WI 53703. (608)257-4626. Fax: (608)257-3373. E-mail: editorial@progressive.org; mattr@progressive.org. Website: www.progressive.org. Estab. 1909. Monthly political magazine. "Grassroots publication from a left perspective, interested in foreign and domestic issues of peace and social justice." Photo guidelines free and online.

NEEDS Buys 5-10 photos from freelancers/issue; 50-100 photos/year. Looking for images documenting the human condition and the social/political environments of contemporary society. Special photo needs include "labor activities, environmental issues and political movements." Photo captions required; include name, place, date, credit information.

SPECS Accepts low-res JPEGs via e-mail.

MAKING CONTACT & TERMS Send query letter with photocopies; include SASE. Provide stock list to be kept on file for possible future assignments. Art director will contact photographer for portfolio review if interested. Responds once every month. Simultaneous submissions and previously published work OK. Pays $50-150 for b&w inside. Pays on publication. Credit line given. Buys one-time rights. All material returned with SASE.

TIPS "Most of the photos we publish are of political actions. Interesting and well-composed photos of creative actions are the most likely to be published. We also use 2-3 short photo essays on political or social subjects per year." For detailed photo information, see the website.

$ ◎ ◐ RACQUETBALL MAGAZINE

1685 W. Uintah, Colorado Springs CO 80904-2906. (719)635-5396. Fax: (719)635-0685. E-mail: jhiser@usra.org. Website: www.usaracquetball.com. Estab. 1990. Circ. 30,000. Bimonthly magazine of USA Racquetball. Emphasizes racquetball. Sample copy available for $4.50. Photo guidelines available.

NEEDS Buys 6-12 photos from freelancers/issue; 36-72 photos/year. Needs photos of action racquetball. Model/property release preferred. Photo captions required.

SPECS Accepts images in digital format. Send via CD as EPS files at 900 dpi.

MAKING CONTACT & TERMS Provide résumé, business card, brochure, flier or tearsheets to be kept on file for possible future assignments. Responds in 1 month. Previously published work OK. Pays $200 for color cover; $3-5 for b&w inside; $25-75 for color inside. Pays on publication. Credit line given. Buys all rights; negotiable.

REFORM JUDAISM

633 Third Ave., 7th Floor, New York NY 10017-6778. (212)650-4240. Fax: (212)650-4249. E-mail: rjmagazine@urj.org. Website: www.reformjudaismmag.org. Estab. 1972. Circ. 310,000. Quarterly publication of the Union for Reform Judaism. Offers insightful, incisive coverage of the challenges faced by contemporary Jews. Readers are members of Reform congregations in U.S. Sample copy available for $3.50. Photo guidelines available via e-mail or on website.

NEEDS Buys 3 photos from freelancers/issue; 12 photos/year. Needs photos relating to Jewish life or Jewish issues, Israel, politics. Model release required for children. Photo captions required.

MAKING CONTACT & TERMS Provide website. Responds in 1 month. Simultaneous submissions and previously published website work OK. Include self-addressed, stamped postcard for response. Pays on publication. Credit line given. Buys one-time rights, first North American serial rights.

TIPS Wants to see "excellent photography: artistic, creative, evocative pictures that involve the reader."

RELOCATING TO THE LAKE OF THE OZARKS

Cliffside Corporate Center, 2140 Bagnell Dam Blvd., Suite 303E, Lake Ozark MO 65049. (573)365-2323. Fax: (573)365-2351. E-mail: spublishingco@msn.com. Website: www.relocatingtothelakeoftheozarks.com. **Contact:** Dave Leathers. Annual relocation guides, free for people moving to the area.

Guidelines available online.

SPECS "Only digital images are accepted. Digital images must be submitted with resolutions of 300 dpi and can be submitted as JPEG, EPS, TIFF and/or PSD files. They must be submitted with physical width of 6 inches wide at the very least and should preferably be submitted as being set to CMYK mode."

REVOLUTIONARY WAR TRACKS

2660 Petersborough St., Herndon VA 20171. E-mail: revolutionarywartracks@yahoo.com. **Contact:** Shannon Bridget Murphy. Estab. 2005. Quarterly. "Bringing Revolutionary War history alive for children and teens." Photo guidelines available by e-mail request.

NEEDS Buys 12-24 photos/year. Photos of babies/children/teens, multicultural, families, parents, disasters, environmental, landscapes/scenics, wildlife, cities/urban, education, religious, rural, adventure, events, food/drink, sports, travel, agriculture, medicine, military, political, product shots/still life, science, technology—as related to Revolutionary War history. Interested in alternative process, avant garde, documentary, fashion/glamour, fine art, historical/vintage, seasonal. Reviews photos with or without a manuscript. Model/property release preferred.

SPECS Uses glossy or matte color and b&w prints.

MAKING CONTACT & TERMS Send query letter via e-mail. "If possible, please do not include photographs in files if they are sent through e-mail. A disc with your photographs is acceptable." Provide résumé, business card or self-promotion piece to be kept on file for possible future assignments. "Photographs sent with CDs are requested but not required." Responds within 1 month to queries; 1 week to portfolios. Simultaneous submissions and previously published work OK. **Pays on acceptance.** Credit line given. Buys one-time rights, first rights; negotiable.

RHODE ISLAND MONTHLY

The Providence Journal Co., 717 Allens Ave., Suite 105, Providence RI 02905. (401)649-4800. E-mail: dwelshman@rimonthly.com. Website: www.rimonthly.com. **Contact:** Dean Welshman, art director. Estab. 1988. Circ. 41,000. Monthly regional publication for and about Rhode Island. *Rhode Island Monthly* is a general interest consumer magazine with a strict Rhode Island focus.

NEEDS Buys 15 photos from freelancers/issue; 200 photos/year. "Almost all photos have a local slant: portraits, photo essays, food, lifestyle, home, issues."

SPECS Accepts images in digital format.

MAKING CONTACT & TERMS Portfolio may be dropped off. Provide self-promotion piece to be kept on file for possible future assignments. Will return anything with SASE. Responds in 2 weeks. Pays "a month after invoice is submitted." Credit line given. Buys one-time rights.

TIPS "Freelancers should be familiar with *Rhode Island Monthly* and should be able to demonstrate their proficiency in the medium before any work is assigned."

THE ROANOKER

Leisure Publishing Co., Leisure Publishing Co., 3424 Brambleton Ave., Roanoke VA 24018. (540)989-6138. Fax: (540)989-7603. E-mail: jwood@leisurepublishing. com. Website: www.theroanoker.com. **Contact:** Jeff Wood. Estab. 1974. Circ. 14,000. Bimonthly. Emphasizes Roanoke region and western Virginia. Readers are upper-income, educated people interested in their community. Sample copy available for $3.

NEEDS Buys 30 photos from freelancers/issue; 180 photos/year. Needs photos of couples, multicultural, families, parents, senior citizens, architecture, cities/urban, education, interiors/decorating, entertainment, events, food/drink, health/fitness/beauty, performing arts, sports, travel, business concepts, medicine, technology/computers, seasonal. Needs "travel and scenic photos in western Virginia; color photo essays on life in western Virginia." Model/property release preferred. Photo captions required.

MAKING CONTACT & TERMS Accepts digital format. Send via CD, e-mail as TIFF, EPS, JPEG files at 300 dpi, minimum print size 8×10 with cutlines and thumbnails. Responds in 1 month. Simultaneous submissions and previously published work OK. Pays $100-150 for color cover; $15-25 for b&w inside, $25-100 for color inside; $100/day. Pays on publication. Credit line given. Rights purchased vary; negotiable.

ROLLING STONE

Wenner Media, 1290 Avenue of the Americas, New York NY 10104. (212)484-1616. Fax: (212)484-1664. E-mail: letters@rollingstone.com. Website: www. rollingstone.com. **Contact:** Jann S. Wenner. Circ. 1,254,200. Monthly. Emphasizes film, CD reviews, music groups, celebrities, fashion. Readers are young adults interested in news of popular music, politics and culture.

NEEDS Photos of celebrities, political, entertainment, events. Interested in alternative process, avant garde, documentary, fashion/glamour.

SPECS Accepts images in digital format. Send as TIFF, JPEG files at 300 dpi.

MAKING CONTACT & TERMS Portfolio may be dropped off every Wednesday and picked up on Friday afternoon. Provide business card, self-promotion piece to be kept on file for possible future assignments. Responds only if interested; send nonreturnable samples.

TIPS "It's not about a photographer's experience, it's about a photographer's talent and eye. Lots of photographers have years of professional experience but their work isn't for us. Others might not have years of experience, but they have this amazing eye."

Ⓢ ROMANTIC HOMES

2400 E. Katella Ave., Suite 300, Anaheim CA 92806. (714)939-9991, ext. 2700. Fax: (714)939-9909. E-mail: jdemontravel@beckett.com. Website: www.romantic homes.com. **Contact:** Jacqueline Demontravel, editor. Estab. 1983. Circ. 140,000. Monthly. For women who want to create a warm, intimate and casually elegant home. Provides how-to advice, along with information on furniture, home decorating ideas, floor and window coverings, artwork, travel, etc. Sample copy available with SASE.

NEEDS Buys 20-30 photos from freelancers/issue; 240-360 photos/year. Needs photos of gardening, interiors/decorating, travel. Reviews photos with accompanying manuscripts only. Model/property release required. Photo captions preferred.

SPECS Uses 2¼×2¼ transparencies.

MAKING CONTACT & TERMS Send query letter with transparencies, stock list. Provide self-promotion piece to be kept on file for possible future assignments. Responds in 3 weeks. Simultaneous submissions OK. Pays net 30 days for images and on publication for articles. Credit line/byline given. Buys all rights; negotiable.

THE ROTARIAN

Rotary International, One Rotary Center, 1560 Sherman Ave., Evanston IL 60201. (847)866-3000. Fax: (847)328-8554. E-mail: rotarian@rotary.org. Website: www.rotary.org. Estab. 1911. Circ. 510,000. Monthly organization magazine for Rotarian business and professional men and women and their families. "Dedicated to business and professional ethics, community life, and international understanding and goodwill." Sample copy and photo guidelines free with SASE.

NEEDS Assigns photography to freelancers and staff photographers; Subject varies from studio to location, from environmental portraiture to photojournalism, but there is always a Rotary connection.

SPECS Digital images only. Prefers RAW files, but will accept high-res JPEG.

MAKING CONTACT & TERMS Send query e-mail, fee schedule and link to online portfolio. Clearly identify your location in the subject of your e-mail. Creative director will contact photographer. No calls please. Keeps e-mail, promotion samples on file. Do not send unsolicited originals. Responds in 3 weeks. Payment negotiable. **Pays on acceptance**. Credit line given. Buys one-time rights; occasionally all rights; negotiable.

TIPS "We prefer high-res digital images in most cases. The key words for the freelance photographer to keep in mind are *internationality* and *variety*. Study the magazine. Read the kinds of articles we publish. Think how your photographs could illustrate such articles in a dramatic, storytelling way."

RUNNING TIMES

P.O. Box 20627, Boulder CO 80308. (203)761-1113. Fax: (203)761-9933. E-mail: editor@runningtimes. com. Website: www.runningtimes.com. Estab. 1977. Circ. 102,000. Published 10 times/year. Covers distance running and racing. "*Running Times* is the national magazine for the experienced running participant and fan. Our audience is knowledgeable about the sport and active in running and racing. All editorial relates specifically to running: improving performance, enhancing enjoyment, or exploring events, places, and people in the sport."

MAKING CONTACT & TERMS Identification of subjects required. Negotiates payment individually. Buys one time rights.

RURAL HERITAGE

P.O. Box 2067, Cedar Rapids IA 52406. (319)362-3027. E-mail: editor@ruralheritage.com. Website: www. ruralheritage.com. **Contact:** Gail Damerow, editor. Estab. 1976. Circ. 9,500. Bimonthly journal in support of modern-day farming and logging with draft animals (horses, mules, oxen). Sample copy available for $8 ($10 outside the U.S.). Photo guidelines available online or via e-mail.

NEEDS "Quality photographs of draft animals working in harness."

SPECS "For interior pages we use glossy color prints, high-quality slides, or high-res images (300 dpi or greater) shot with a quality digital camera. For covers we use 5×7 glossy color prints, large-format transparencies, or high-res images shot with a quality digital camera. Digital images must be original (not resized, cropped, etc.) files from a digital camera; scans unacceptable."

MAKING CONTACT & TERMS Send query letter with samples. "Please include SASE for the return of your material, and put your name and address on the back of each piece." Pays $100 for color cover; $10-25 for b&w inside. Also provides 2 copies of issue in which work appears. Pays on publication.

TIPS "Animals usually look better from the side than from the front. We like to see all the animal's body parts, including hooves, ears and tail. For animals in harness, we want to see the entire implement or vehicle. We prefer action shots (plowing, harvesting hay, etc.). Watch out for shadows across animals and people. Please include the name of any human handlers involved, the farm, the town (or county), state, and the animals' names (if possible) and breeds. You'll find current guidelines in the 'Business Office' of our website."

RUSSIAN LIFE

RIS Publications, P.O. Box 567, Montpelier VT 05601. Website: www.russianlife.net. Estab. 1956. Circ. 15,000. Bimonthly. Uses 25-35 photos/issue. Offers 10-15 freelance assignments/year.

NEEDS Photojournalism related to Russian culture, art and history.

SPECS Send 35mm, 2¼×2¼, 4×5, 8×10 transparencies; digital format.

MAKING CONTACT & TERMS Send query letter. After inquiry and response, be prepared to send digital thumbnails or links to same online. We no longer accept submissions by mail. Responds in 1 month. Pays $20-50 (color photo with accompanying story), depending on placement in magazine. Pays on publication. Credit line given. Buys one-time and nonexclusive electronic rights.

TIPS "Our readers are informed Russophiles with an avid interest in all things Russian. But we do not publish personal travel journals or the like."

⊛⊛ ❶ SAIL

98 N. Washington St., Suite 107, Boston MA 02114. (617)720-8600. Fax: (617)723-0912. E-mail: rjolley@ sailmagazine.com. Website: www.sailmagazine.com. **Contact:** Ryan Jolley, art director. Estab. 1970. Circ. 200,000. Monthly. Emphasizes all aspects of sailing. Readers are managers and professionals, average age 44. Photo guidelines free with SASE and on website.

NEEDS Buys 50-100 images/issue. "Particularly interested in photos for cover and 'pure sail' sections.

Ideally, these photos would be digital files @300 dpi with a run size of approximately 9×12 for cover, 9×16 for 'pure sail.'" Also accepts 35mm transparencies. Vertical cover shots also needed. Photo captions required.

SPECS Accepts images in digital format. Send high-res JPEG, TIFF and RAW files via CD, DVD or FTP (contact for FTP log-in info). Also accepts all forms of transparencies and prints with negatives.

MAKING CONTACT & TERMS Send unsolicited 35mm and 2¼×2¼ transparencies by mail with SASE for consideration. Pays $1,000 for color cover; $50-800 for color inside; also negotiates prices on a per day, per hour and per job basis. Pays on publication. Credit line given. Buys one-time North American rights. Photo shoots commissioned using half- or full-day rates.

⊖⊖ ◐ SAILING

P.O. Box 249, Port Washington WI 53074. (262)284-3494. Fax: (262)284-7764. E-mail: editorial@sailingmagazine.net. Website: www.sailingmagazine.net. **Contact:** Greta Schanen, managing editor. Circ. 50,000. Monthly. Emphasizes sailing. Readers are experienced sailors who race, cruise and daysail on all types of boats: dinghies, large and small mono and multihulls. Sample copy available with 11×15 SASE and 9 first-class stamps. Photo guidelines free with SASE.

NEEDS "We are a large-format journal, with a strong emphasis on top-notch photography backed by creative, insightful writing. Need photos of sailing, both long shots and on-deck. We encourage creativity; send me a sailing photograph I have not seen before." Photo captions required; include boat and people IDs, location, conditions, etc.

SPECS Uses 35mm and larger transparencies. Accepts images in digital format. Send via CD as TIFF, JPEG files at 300 dpi. Include printed thumbnails with CD. If photos are also being submitted by e-mail, they should be sent as low-res attachments, and under no circumstances, be embedded in a Word document. Only submit photos via e-mail or ftp upon request.

MAKING CONTACT & TERMS Send query letter with samples; include SASE for return of material. Portfolios may be dropped off by appointment. Send submissions by mail; e-mail samples or portfolios will not be considered. Responds in 3 months. "Tell us of simultaneous submissions; previously published work OK if not with other sailing publications who compete with us." Pays $250-500 for color cover; $50-500 for color inside. Pays 30 days after publication.

SAILING WORLD

World Publications, 55 Hammarlund Way, Middletown RI 02842. (401)845-5100. Fax: (401)848-5180. E-mail: editorial@sailingworld.com. Website: www.sailingworld.com. **Contact:** Dave Reed, editor; Shannon Cain, associate art director. Estab. 1962. Circ. 65,000. Monthly. Emphasizes performance sailing and racing for upper-income sailors. Readers are males ages 35-45, females ages 25-35 who are interested in sailing. Sample copy available for $7. Photo guidelines available online.

NEEDS Freelance photography in a given issue: 20% assignment and 80% freelance stock. Covers most sailing races. Needs photos of adventure, health/fitness, humor, sports. "We will send an updated e-mail listing our photo needs on request."

SPECS Uses 35mm for covers; vertical and square (slightly horizontal) formats; digital 300-dpi 5×7 JPEGs.

MAKING CONTACT & TERMS Responds in 1 month. Pays $650 for cover; $75-400 for inside. Pays on publication. Credit line given. Buys first North American serial rights.

TIPS "We look for photos that are unusual in composition, lighting and/or color that feature performance sailing at its most exciting. We would like to emphasize speed, skill, fun and action. Photos must be of high quality. We prefer Fuji Velvia film. We have a format that allows us to feature work of exceptional quality. A knowledge of sailing and experience with on-the-water photography is a requirement. Please call with specific questions or interests. We cover current events and generally only use photos taken in the past 30-60 days."

◐ SALT HILL LITERARY JOURNAL

Syracuse University, 401 Hall of Languages, Syracuse NY 133244. Website: www.salthilljournal.net. **Contact:** Art editor. Circ. 1,000. *Salt Hill* seeks unpublished 2D art-drawings, paintings, photography, mixed media, documentation of 3D art, typographic art diagrams, maps, etc., for its semiannual publication. We offer all colors, shapes, and stripes.

NEEDS Seeking graphic novels, literary and experimental art. Sample copy available for $6. Responds in 3 months.

MAKING CONTACT & TERMS See website for specifications.

$$ ◐ SALT WATER SPORTSMAN

460 N. Orlando Ave., Suite 200, Winter Park FL 32789. (407)628-4802. Fax: (407)628-7601. E-mail: editor@saltwatersportsman.com. Website: www.saltwatersportsman.com. Estab. 1939. Circ. 175,000. Monthly. Emphasizes all phases of saltwater sport fishing for the avid beginner-to-professional saltwater angler. "Number-one monthly marine sport fishing magazine in the U.S." Sample copy free with 9×12 SASE and 7 first-class stamps. Photo guidelines free.

NEEDS Buys photos (including covers) without manuscript; 20-30 photos/issue with manuscript. Needs saltwater fishing photos. "Think fishing action, scenery, mood, storytelling close-ups of anglers in action. Make it come alive—and don't bother us with the obviously posed 'dead fish and stupid fisherman' back at the dock." Wants, on a regular basis, cover shots (clean verticals depicting saltwater fishing action). For accompanying manuscript, needs fact/feature articles dealing with marine sport fishing in the U.S., Canada, Caribbean, Central and South America. Emphasis on how-to.

SPECS Uses 35mm or 2¼×2¼ transparencies; vertical format preferred for covers. Accepts images in digital format. Send via CD, ZIP; format as 8-bit, unconverted, 300 dpi, RGB TIFF. A confirming laser or proof of each image must accompany the media. A printed disk directory with each new name written next to each original name must be provided.

MAKING CONTACT & TERMS Send material by mail for consideration, or query with samples. Provide résumé or tearsheets to be kept on file for possible future assignments. Holds slides for 1 year and will pay as used; include SASE for return of material. Responds in 1 month. Pays $2,500 maximum for cover; $100-500 for color inside; $500 minimum for text-photo package. **Pays on acceptance.**

TIPS "Prefer to see a selection of fishing action and mood; must be sport fishing-oriented. Read the magazine! No horizontal cover slides with suggestions it can be cropped, etc. Don't send Ektachrome. We're using more 'outside' photography—that is, photos not submitted with manuscript package. Take lots of verticals and experiment with lighting."

$ ◐ SANDLAPPER MAGAZINE

Sandlapper Society, Inc., 3007 Millwood Ave., Columbia SC 29205. (803)779-8763. Fax: (803)254-4833. E-mail: elaine@sandlapper.org. Website: www.sandlapper.org. **Contact:** Elaine Gillespie, executive director. Estab. 1969. Circ. 8,000. Quarterly. Emphasizes South Carolina topics only.

NEEDS Uses about 10 photographers/issue. Photos of anything related to South Carolina in any style, "as long as they're not in bad taste." Model release preferred. Photo captions required; include places and people.

SPECS Uses 8×10 color and b&w prints; 35mm, 2¼×2¼, 4×5, 8×10 transparencies. Accepts images in digital format. Send via CD, ZIP as TIFF, JPEG files at 300 dpi. "Do not format exclusively for PC. RGB preferred. Submit low- and high-res files, and label them as such."

MAKING CONTACT & TERMS Send query letter with samples. Keeps samples on file; include SASE for return of material. Responds in 1 month. Pays $100 for color cover; $50-100 for color inside. Pays 1 month *after* publication. Credit line given. Buys first rights plus right to reprint.

TIPS "We see plenty of beach sunsets, mountain waterfalls, and shore birds. Would like fresh images of people working and playing in the Palmetto state."

SANTA BARBARA MAGAZINE

25 E. De La Guerra St., Santa Barbara CA 93101-2217. (805)965-5999. Fax: (805)965-7627. E-mail: alisa@sbmag.com. Website: www.sbmag.com. **Contact:** Jennifer Smith Hale, publisher; Alisa Baur, art director; Gina Tolleson, editor. Estab. 1975. Circ. 40,000. Bimonthly. Emphasizes Santa Barbara community and culture. Sample copy available for $4.95 with 9×12 SASE.

NEEDS Buys 64-80 photos from freelancers/issue; 384-480 photos/year. Needs portrait, environmental, architectural, travel, celebrity, etc. Reviews photos with accompanying manuscript only. Model release required. Photo captions preferred.

MAKING CONTACT & TERMS Provide résumé, business card, brochure, flier or tearsheets to be kept on file for possible future assignments; "portfolio drop-off 24 hours." Cannot return unsolicited material. Pays $75-250 for b&w or color. Pays on publication. Credit line given. Buys first North American serial rights.

$ SCHOLASTIC MAGAZINES

557 Broadway, New York NY 10012. (212)343-7147. Fax: (212)389-3913. E-mail: sdiamond@scholastic.com. Website: www.scholastic.com. **Contact:** Steven Diamond, executive director of photography. Estab. 1920. Publication of magazines varies from weekly to monthly. "We publish 27 titles on topics from current events, science, math, fine art, literature and social studies. Interested in featuring high-quality, well-composed images of students of all ages and all ethnic backgrounds. We publish hundreds of books on all topics, educational programs, Internet products and new media."

NEEDS Photos of various subjects depending upon educational topics planned for academic year. Model release required. Photo captions required. "Images must be interesting, bright and lively!"

SPECS Accepts images in digital format. Send via CD, e-mail.

MAKING CONTACT & TERMS Send query letter with résumé, business card, brochure, flyer or tearsheets to be kept on file for possible future assignments. Material cannot be returned. Previously published work OK. Pays on publication.

TIPS Especially interested in good photography of all ages of student population. All images must have model/property releases.

THE SCHOOL ADMINISTRATOR

801 N. Quincy St., Suite 700, Arlington VA 22203-1730. (703)528-0753. Fax: (703)841-1543. E-mail: lgriffin@aasa.org. E-mail: info@aasa.org. Website: www.aasa.org. **Contact:** Liz Griffin, managing editor. Circ. 20,000. Monthly magazine of the American Association of School Administrators. Emphasizes K-12 education. Readers are school district administrators including superintendents, ages 50-60. Sample copy available for $10.

NEEDS Uses 8-10 photos/issue. Needs classroom photos (K-12), photos of school principals, superintendents and school board members interacting with parents and students. Model/property release preferred for physically handicapped students. Photo captions required; include name of school, city, state, grade level of students, and general description of classroom activity.

SPECS Accepts images in digital format: TIFF, JPEG files at 300 dpi. Send via link to FTP site.

MAKING CONTACT & TERMS "Send a link to your FTP site with photos of children in public school settings, grades K-12. Do not send originals or e-mails of your work or website. Check our website for our editorial calendar. Familiarize yourself with topical nature and format of magazine before submitting work." Work assigned is 3-4 months prior to publication date. Keeps samples on file; include SASE for return of material. Simultaneous submissions and previously published work OK. Pays $50-75 for inside photos. Credit line given. Buys one-time rights.

TIPS "Prefer photos with interesting, animated faces and hand gestures. Always looking for the unusual human connection where the photographer's presence has not made subjects stilted."

SCIENTIFIC AMERICAN

415 Madison Ave., New York NY 10017. (212)754-0550. Fax: (212)755-1976. E-mail: editors@sciam.com. Website: www.sciam.com. Edward Bell, art director. **Contact:** Emily Harrison, photography editor. Estab. 1845. Circ. 710,000. Emphasizes science, policy, technology and people involved in science. Seeking to broaden our 20-40 year-old readership.

NEEDS Buys 100 photos from freelancers/issue. Needs all kinds of photos. Model release required; property release preferred. Photo captions required.

MAKING CONTACT & TERMS Arrange a personal interview to show portfolio. "Do not send unsolicited photos." Provide résumé, business card, brochure, flier or tearsheets to be kept on file for possible future assignments and note photo website. Cannot return material. Responds in 1 month. Pays $600/day; $1,000 for color cover. Pays on publication. Credit line given. Buys one-time rights and world rights. Frequently leads to re-use buying and develops relationships with scientists and writers needing photo work.

TIPS Wants to see strong natural and artificial lighting, location portraits and location shooting. Intelligent artistic photography and photo-illustration welcomed. Send business cards and promotional pieces frequently when dealing with magazine editors. Find a niche.

SCRAP

1615 L St., NW, Suite 600, Washington D.C. 20036-5664. (202)662-8547. Fax: (202)626-0947. E-mail: kentkiser@scrap.org. Website: www.scrap.org. **Contact:** Kent Kiser, publisher/editor-in-chief. Estab. 1987. Circ. 8,278. Bimonthly magazine of the Institute of Scrap Recycling Industries. Emphasizes scrap recycling for owners and managers of recycling operations worldwide. Sample copy available for $8.

NEEDS Buys 0-15 photos from freelancers/issue; 15-70 photos/year. Needs operation shots of companies being profiled and studio concept shots. Model release required. Photo captions required.

SPECS Accepts images in digital format. Send via CD, Zip, e-mail as JPEG or TIFF file at 300 dpi.

MAKING CONTACT & TERMS Provide résumé, business card, brochure, flyer or tearsheets to be kept on file for possible future assignments. Previously published work OK. Pays $800-1,500/day; $100-400 for b&w inside; $200-600 for color inside. Pays on delivery of images. Credit line given. Rights negotiable.

TIPS Photographers must possess "ability to photograph people in corporate atmosphere, as well as industrial operations; ability to work well with executives, as well as laborers. We are always looking for good color photographers to accompany our staff writers on visits to companies being profiled. We try to keep travel costs to a minimum by hiring photographers located in the general vicinity of the profiled company. Other photography (primarily studio work) is usually assigned through freelance art director."

🅢 ⭕ SEA

Duncan McIntosh Co., 17782 Cowan, Suite A, Irvine CA 92614. (949)660-6150. Fax: (949)660-6172. E-mail: editorial@seamag.com. Website: seamag. com. Jeff Fleming, associate editor/publisher. **Contact:** Mike Werling, managing editor. Circ. 50,000. Monthly magazine. Emphasizes "recreational boating in 13 Western states (including some coverage of Mexico and British Columbia) for owners of recreational power boats." Sample copy and photo guidelines free with 10×13 SASE.

NEEDS Uses about 50-75 photos/issue; most supplied by freelancers; 10% assignment; 75% requested from freelancers, existing photo files, or submitted unsolicited. Needs "people enjoying boating activity (families, parents, senior citizens) and scenic shots (travel, regional); shots that include parts or all of a boat are preferred." Photos should have West Coast angle. Model release required. Photo captions required.

SPECS Accepts images in digital format. Send via CD, FTP, e-mail as TIFF, EPS, JPEG files at least 300 dpi. E-mail editorial assistant, lisa@seamag.com for FTP instructions.

MAKING CONTACT & TERMS Send query letter with samples; include SASE for return of material. Responds in 1 month. Pay rate varies according to size published (range is $50-200 for color). Pays on publication. Credit line given. Buys one-time North American rights and retains reprint rights via print and electronic media.

TIPS "We are looking for sharp images with good composition showing pleasure boats in action, and people having fun aboard boats in a West Coast location. Digital shots are preferred; they must be at least 5 inches wide and a minimum of 300 dpi. We also use studio shots of marine products and do personality profiles. Send samples of work with a query letter and a résumé or clips of previously published photos. *Sea* does not pay for shipping; will hold photos up to 6 weeks."

SHARING THE VICTORY

Fellowship of Christian Athletes, 8701 Leeds Rd., Kansas City MO 64129. (816)921-0909. Fax: (816)921-8755. E-mail: stv@fca.org. Website: www.fca.org. **Contact:** Jill Ewert, managing editor. Estab. 1959. Circ. 80,000. Monthly association magazine featuring stories and testimonials of prominent athletes and coaches in sports who proclaim a relationship with Jesus Christ. Sample copy available for $1 and 9×12 SASE. No photo guidelines available.

NEEDS Photos of sports. "We buy photos of persons being featured in our magazine. We don't buy photos without story being suggested first." Reviews photos with accompanying manuscript only. "All submitted stories must be connected to the FCA Ministry." Model release preferred; property release required. Photo captions preferred.

SPECS Uses glossy or matte color prints; 35mm, 2¼×2¼ transparencies. Accepts images in digital format. Send via CD, ZIP, e-mail as TIFF, JPEG files at 300 dpi.

MAKING CONTACT & TERMS Contact through e-mail with a list of types of sports photographs in stock. Do not send samples. Simultaneous submissions OK. Pays $150 maximum for color cover; $100 maximum for color inside. Pays on publication. Credit line given. Buys one-time rights.

TIPS "We would like to increase our supply of photographers who can do contract work."

SHINE BRIGHTLY

GEMS Girls' Clubs, P.O. Box 7259, Grand Rapids MI 49510. (616)241-5616. Fax: (616)241-5558. E-mail: shinebrightly@gemsgc.org. Website: www.gemsgc.org. **Contact:** Jan Boone, editor; Kelli Ponstein, managing editor. Estab. 1970. Circ. 17,000. Monthly publication of GEMS Girls' Club. Emphasizes "girls ages 9-14 in action. The magazine is a Christian girls' publication that inspires, motivates, and equips girls to become world changers." Sample copy and photo guidelines available for $1 with 9×12 SASE.

NEEDS Uses about 5-6 photos/issue. Photos suitable for illustrating stories and articles: photos of babies/children/teens, multicultural, religious, girls aged 9-14 from multicultural backgrounds, close-up shots with eye contact." Model/property release preferred.

SPECS Uses 5×7 glossy color prints. Accepts images in digital format. Send via ZIP, CD as TIFF, BMP files at 300 dpi.

MAKING CONTACT & TERMS Send 5×7 glossy color prints by mail (include SASE), electronic images by CD only (no e-mail) for consideration. Will view photographer's website if available. Responds in 2 months. Simultaneous submissions OK. Pays $50-75 for cover; $35 for color inside. Pays on publication. Credit line given. Buys one-time rights.

TIPS "Make the photos simple. We prefer to get a spec sheet or CDs rather than photos, and we'd really like to hold photos for our annual theme update and try to get photos to fit the theme of each issue." Recommends that photographers "be concerned about current trends in fashions, hair styles, and realize that all girls don't belong to 'families.' Please, no slides, no negatives and no e-mail submissions."

$ $ ◐ SHOOTING SPORTS USA

11250 Waples Mill Rd., Fairfax VA 22030. (703)267-1310. E-mail: shootingsportsusa@nrahq.org. Website: www.nrapublications.org. **Contact:** Chip Lohman, editor. Monthly publication of the National Rifle Association of America. Emphasizes competitive shooting sports (rifle, pistol and shotgun). Readers range from beginner to high master. Past issues available online. Editorial guidelines free via e-mail.

NEEDS 15-25 photos from freelancers/issue; 180-300 photos/year. Needs photos of how-to, shooting positions, specific shooters. Quality photos preferred with accompanying manuscript. Model release required. Photo captions preferred.

SPECS Accepts images in digital format. Send via CD or e-mail as TIFF files at 300 dpi.

MAKING CONTACT & TERMS Send query letter with photo and editorial ideas by e-mail. Include SASE. Responds in 1 week. Previously published work OK when cleared with editor. Pays $150-400 for color cover; $50-150 for color inside; $250-500 for photo/text package; amount varies for photos alone. Pays on publication. Credit line given. Buys first North American serial rights.

TIPS Looks for "generic photos of shooters shooting, obeying all safety rules and using proper eye protection and hearing protection. If text concerns certain how-to advice, photos are needed to illuminate this. Always query first. We are in search of quality photos to interest both beginning and experienced shooters."

SHOTGUN SPORTS MAGAZINE

P.O. Box 6810, Auburn CA 95604. (530)889-2220. Fax: (530)889-9106. E-mail: shotgun@shotgunsportsmagazine.com. Website: www.shotgunsportsmagazine.com. **Contact:** Linda Martin, production coordinator.

SPECS On disk or e-mailed at least 5-inches and 300 dpi (contact graphics artist for details).

◐ SHOTS

P.O. Box 27755, Minneapolis MN 55427-0755. E-mail: shots@shotsmag.com. Website: www.shotsmag.com. **Contact:** Russell Joslin, editor/publisher. Circ. 2,000. Quarterly fine art photography magazine. "We publish b&w fine art photography by photographers with an innate passion for personal, creative work." Sample copy available for $6.50. Photo guidelines free with SASE or on website.

NEEDS Fine art photography of all types accepted for consideration (but not bought). Reviews photos with or without a manuscript. Model/property release preferred. Photo captions preferred.

SPECS Uses 8×10 b&w prints. Accepts images in digital format. Send via CD as TIFF files at 300 dpi. "See website for further specifications."

MAKING CONTACT & TERMS Send query letter with prints. There is a $16 submission fee for nonsubscribers (free for subscribers). Include SASE for return of material. Responds in 3 months. Credit line given. Does not buy photographs/rights.

SIERRA

85 Second St., 2nd Floor, San Francisco CA 94105. (415)977-5656. Fax: (415)977-5799. E-mail: sierra.magazine@sierraclub.org. Website: www.sierraclub.org. Estab. 1893. Circ. 695,000. Bimonthly. Emphasizes conservation and environmental politics for people who are well educated, activist, outdoor-oriented, and politically well informed with a dedication to conservation.

🍁 $ $ SKI CANADA

117 Indian Rd., Toronto ON M6R 2V5, Canada. (416)538-2293. Fax: 416-538-2475. E-mail: design@skicanadamag.com. Website: www.skicanadamag.com. **Contact:** Iain MacMillan, editor. Circ. 50,000. Published monthly, September-February. Readership is 65% male, ages 25-44, with high income. Sample copy free with SASE.

NEEDS Buys 80 photos from freelancers/issue; 480 photos/year. Needs photos of skiing—travel (within Canada and abroad), new school, competition, equipment, instruction, news and trends. Photo captions preferred.

SPECS Uses 35mm color transparencies. Accepts images in digital format. Send via e-mail.

MAKING CONTACT & TERMS Send unsolicited photos by mail for consideration; include SASE for return of material. Provide résumé, business card, brochure, flier or tearsheets to be kept on file for possible future assignments. Responds in 1 month. Simultaneous submissions OK. Pays $400 for cover; $50-200 for inside. Pays within 30 days of publication. Credit line given.

TIPS "Please see travel.canoe.ca/SkiCanada/mediakit.html#editorial for the annual editorial lineup."

SKIING MAGAZINE

Bonnier Corp., 5720 Flatiron Parkway, Boulder CO 80301. (303)448-7600. Fax: (303)448-7638. E-mail: editor@skiingmag.com. Website: www.skinet.com/skiing. Estab. 1936. Circ. 430,000. *Skiing Magazine* is an online ski-lifestyle publication written and edited for recreational skiers. Its content is intended to help them ski better (technique), buy better (equipment and skiwear), and introduce them to new experiences, people, and adventures.

SKIPPING STONES: A MULTICULTURAL LITERARY MAGAZINE

P.O. Box 3939, Eugene OR 97403-0939. (541)342-4956. Fax: Call for number. E-mail: Editor@Skippingstones.org. Website: www.skippingstones.org. **Contact:** Arun Toke, editor. Estab. 1988. Circ. 2,200 print, plus web. "We promote multicultural awareness, international understanding, nature appreciation, and social responsibility. We suggest authors not make stereotypical generalizations in their articles. We like when authors include their own experiences, or base their articles on their personal immersion experiences in a culture or country." Has featured Xuan Thu Pham, Soma Han, Jon Bush, Zarouhie Abdalian, Elizabeth Zunon and Najah Clemmons.

NEEDS Buys babies/teens/children, celebrities, multicultural, families, disasters, environmental, landscapes, wildlife, cities, education, gardening, rural, events, health/fitness/beauty, travel, documentary and seasonal. Reviews 4×6 prints, low-res JPEG files. Captions required.

MAKING CONTACT & TERMS Send query letter or e-mail with photographs (digital JPEGs at 72 dpi).

TIPS "We are a multicultural magazine for youth and teens. We consider your work as a labor of love that contributes to the education of youth. We publish photoessays on various cultures and countries/regions of the world in each issue of the magazine to promote international and intercultural (and nature) understanding. Tell us a little bit about yourself, your motivation, goals, and mission."

SKYDIVING

1725 N. Lexington Ave., DeLand FL 32724. (386)736-9779. Fax: (386)736-9786. E-mail: sue@skydivingmagazine.com. Website: www.skydivingmagazine.com. **Contact:** Sue Clifton, editor. Estab. 1979. Circ. 14,200. "*Skydiving* is a news magazine. Its purpose is to deliver timely, useful and interesting information about the equipment, techniques, events, people and places of parachuting. Our scope is national. *Skydiving*'s audience spans the entire spectrum of jumpers, from first-jump students to veterans with thousands of skydives. Some readers are riggers with a keen interest in the technical aspects of parachutes, while others are weekend 'fun' jumpers who want information to help them make travel plans and equipment purchases." Readers are "sport parachutists worldwide, dealers and equipment manufacturers." Sample copy available for $3. Photo guidelines free with SASE or online.

NEEDS Buys 5 photos from freelancers/issue; 60 photos/year. Selects photos from wire service, photographers who are skydivers and freelancers. Interested in anything related to skydiving—news or any dramatic illustration of an aspect of parachuting. Model release preferred. Photo captions preferred; include who, what, why, when, how.

SPECS Digital files are preferred. Send via CD, DVD, FTP, e-mail as JPEG, TIFF files at 300 dpi (minimum). Also accepts prints and transparencies.

MAKING CONTACT & TERMS Send digital files after reviewing guidelines, or send 5×7 or larger b&w or color prints or 35mm or 2¼×2¼ transparencies by mail for consideration. Keeps samples on file; include SASE for return of material. Responds in 1 month. Pays $50 for color cover; $5-25 for b&w inside; $25-50 for color inside. Pays on publication. Credit line given. Buys all rights.

⊘ SMITHSONIAN MAGAZINE

MRC 513, P.O. Box 37012, Washington D.C. 20012-7012. (202)633-6090. Fax: (202)633-6095. E-mail: smithsonianmagazine@si.edu. Website: www.smithsonianmagazine.com. **Contact:** Molly Roberts, photo editor. Monthly. *Smithsonian* chronicles the arts, environment, sciences and popular culture of the times for today's well-rounded individuals with diverse, general interests, providing its readers with information and knowledge in an entertaining way. Visit website for photo submission guidelines. *Does not accept unsolicited photos or portfolios.* Use online submission form. Query before submitting.

SOLDIER OF FORTUNE

2135 11th St., Boulder CO 80302-4045. (303)449-3750. E-mail: editorsof@aol.com. Website: www.sofmag.com. **Contact:** Lt. Col. Robert A. Brown, editor/publisher. Estab. 1975. Circ. 60,000. Monthly. Covers military, paramilitary, police, combat subjects, and action/adventure.

MAKING CONTACT & TERMS Reviews contact sheets, transparencies. Captions, identification of subjects required. Pays $500 for cover photo. Buys one-time rights.

SOUTHCOMM PUBLISHING COMPANY, INC.

541 Buttermilk Pike, Suite 100, Crescent Springs KY 41017. (678)624-1075. Fax: (678)623-9979. E-mail: cwwalker@southcomm.com. Website: www.southcomm.com. **Contact:** Carolyn Williams-Walker. Estab. 1985. "We publish approximately 35 publications throughout the year. They are primarily for chambers of commerce throughout the Southeast (Georgia, Tennessee, South Carolina, North Carolina, Alabama, Virginia, Florida). We are expanding to the Northeast (Pennsylvania) and Texas. Our publications are used for tourism, economic development and marketing purposes. We also are a custom publishing company, offering brochures and other types of printed material."

NEEDS "We are only looking for photographers who can travel to the communities with which we're working as we need shots that are specific to those locations. We will not consider generic stock-type photos. Images are generally for editorial purposes; however, advertising shots sometimes are required." Model/property release preferred. Photo captions required. "Identify people, buildings and as many specifics as possible."

SPECS Prefers images in digital format. Send via CD, saved as TIFF, GIF or JPEG files for Mac at no less than 300 dpi. "We prefer digital photography for all our publications."

MAKING CONTACT & TERMS Send query letter with résumé and photocopies. Keeps samples on file; provide business card. Responds only if interested; send nonreturnable samples. Pays $40 minimum; $60 maximum for color inside. Pays a flat rate that ranges between $400 and $1,200 for projects. Each has its own specific budget, so rates fluctuate. We pay the same rates for cover images as for interior shots because, at times, images identified for the cover cannot be used as such. They are then used in the interior instead." **Pays on acceptance.** Credit line given. "Photos that are shot on assignment become the property of SouthComm Publishing Company, Inc. They cannot be released to our clients or another third party. We will purchase one-time rights to use images from photographers should the need arise." Will negotiate with a photographer unwilling to sell all rights.

TIPS "We are looking for photographers who enjoy traveling and are highly organized and can communicate well with our clients as well as with us. Digital photographers *must* turn in contact sheets of all images shot in the community, clearly identifying the subjects."

$$ ◐ SOUTHERN BOATING

330 N. Andrews Ave., Ft. Lauderdale FL 33301. (954)522-5515. Fax: (954)522-2260. E-mail: info@southernboating.com. Website: www.southernboating.com. Louisa Beckett. **Contact:** Jon Hernandez, art director. Estab. 1972. Circ. 40,000. Monthly. Emphasizes "powerboating, sailing, and cruising in the southeastern and Gulf Coast U.S., Bahamas and the Caribbean." Readers are "concentrated in 30-60 age group, mostly male, affluent, very experienced boat owners." Sample copy available for $7.

NEEDS Number of photos/issue varies; many supplied by freelancers. Seeks "boating lifestyle" cover shots. Buys stock only. No "assigned covers." Model release required. Photo captions required.

SPECS Accepts images in digital format. Send via CD or e-mail as JPEG, TIFF files, minimum 4×6 at 300 dpi.

MAKING CONTACT & TERMS Send query letter with list of stock photo subjects, SASE. Response time varies. Simultaneous submissions and previously published work OK. Pays $300 minimum for color cover; $70 minimum for color inside; photo/text package negotiable. Pays within 30 days of publication. Credit line given. Buys one-time print and electronic/website rights.

TIPS "We want lifestyle shots of saltwater cruising, fishing or just relaxing on the water. Lifestyle or family boating shots are actively sought."

SPECIALIVING

P.O. Box 1000, Bloomington IL 61702. (309)962-2003. E-mail: gareeb@aol.com. Website: www.specialiving.com. Estab. 2001. Circ. 12,000. Quarterly. For physically disabled people. Emphasizes travel, home modifications, products, info, inspiration. Sample copy available for $5.

NEEDS Any events/settings that involve physically disabled people (who use wheelchairs), not developmentally disabled. Reviews photos with or without a manuscript. Model release preferred. Photo captions required.

SPECS Uses glossy or matte color and b&w prints. Accepts images in digital format. Send via CD, ZIP, e-mail as TIFF, JPEG files at 300 dpi.

MAKING CONTACT & TERMS Send query letter with prints. Online e-mail form available on website. Does not keep samples on file; include SASE for return of material. Responds in 3 weeks. Simultaneous submissions and previously published work OK. Pays $50 minimum for b&w cover; $100 maximum for color cover; $10 minimum for b&w or color inside. Pays on publication. Credit line given. Buys one-time rights.

TIPS "Need good-quality photos of someone in a wheelchair involved in an activity. Need caption and where I can contact subject to get story if wanted."

$ O SPFX: SPECIAL EFFECTS MAGAZINE

95 N. Route 17, Paramus NJ 07652. (201)391-8788. E-mail: thedeadlyspawn@aol.com. Website: www.deadlyspawn.com. **Contact:** Ted A. Bohus, editor. Estab. 1978. Circ. 6,000-10,000. Biannual film magazine emphasizing science fiction, fantasy and horror films of the past, present and future. Includes feature articles, interviews and rare photos. Sample copy available for $5. Photo guidelines free.

NEEDS Film stills and film personalities. Reviews photos with or without a manuscript. Special photo needs include rare film photos. Model/property release preferred. Photo captions preferred.

SPECS Uses any size prints. Accepts images in digital format. Send via CD, ZIP, e-mail as TIFF, EPS files at 300 dpi.

MAKING CONTACT & TERMS Send query letter with samples. Provide résumé, business card, self-promotion piece or tearsheets to be kept on file for possible future assignments. To show portfolio, photographer should follow up with letter after initial query. Art director will contact photographer for portfolio review if interested. Portfolio should include b&w and color, prints, tearsheets, slides, transparencies or thumbnails. Responds only if interested; send nonreturnable samples. Previously published work OK. Pays $150-200 for color cover; $10-50 for b&w and color inside. Pays on publication. Credit line given.

SPORT FISHING

Bonnier Corporation, 460 N. Orlando Ave., Suite 200, Winter Park FL 32789. (407)628-4802. Fax: (407)628-7061. E-mail: missie.prichard@bonniercorp.com. Website: www.sportfishingmag.com. **Contact:** Missie Prichard. Estab. 1985. Circ. 250,000. "*Sport Fishing*'s readers are middle-aged, affluent, mostly male, who are generally proficient in and very educated to their sport. We are about fishing from boats, not from surf or jetties." Emphasizes saltwater sport fishing. Sample copy available for $2.50, 9×12 SASE and 6 first-class stamps. Photo guidelines available on website, via e-mail or with SASE.

NEEDS Buys 50% or more photos from freelancers/issue. Needs photos of saltwater fish and fishing—especially good action shots. "Are working more from stock—good opportunities for extra sales on any given assignment." Model release not generally required.

SPECS Prefers images in RAW, unaltered/undoctored digital format, especially for the option to run images very large, with accompanying low-res JPEGs for quick review. Original 35mm (or larger) transparencies are accepted for smaller images, but no longer for the cover or two-page spreads. All guidelines, rates, suggestions available online; click on "Editorial Guidelines" at bottom of home page.

MAKING CONTACT & TERMS Send query letter with samples. Send unsolicited photos by mail or low-res digitals by e-mail for consideration. Provide business card, brochure, flyer or tearsheets to be kept on file for possible future assignments. Responds in 3 weeks. Pays $1,000 for cover; $75–400 for inside. Buys one-time rights unless otherwise agreed upon.

TIPS "Sharp focus critical; avoid 'kill' shots of big game fish, sharks; avoid bloody fish in/at the boat. The best guideline is the magazine itself. Know your market. Get used to shooting on, in or under water using the RAW setting of your camera. Most of our needs are found in the magazine. If you have first-rate photos and questions, e-mail us."

SPORTS AFIELD

Field Sports Publishing, 15621 Chemical Ln., Suite B, Huntington Beach CA 92649. (714)373-4910. E-mail: letters@sportsafield.com. Website: www.sportsafield.com. **Contact:** Jerry Gutierrez, art director. Estab. 1887. Circ. 50,000.

NEEDS Hunting/wildlife themes only. Considers all media.

SPECS Reviews 35mm slides transparencies, TIFF/JPEG files.

MAKING CONTACT & TERMS Captions, model releases required. Buys first time rights.

🜚 SPORTSCAR

Haymarket Worldwide LLC., 16842 Von Karman Ave., Suite 125, Irvine CA 92606. (949)417-6700. Fax: (949)417-6116. E-mail: sportscar@haymarketworldwide.com. Website: www.sportscarmag.com. **Contact:** Philip Royle, editor. Estab. 1944. Circ. 50,000. Monthly magazine of the Sports Car Club of America. Emphasizes sports car racing and competition activities. Sample copy available for $4.99.

NEEDS Uses 75-100 photos/issue; 75% from assignment and 25% from freelance stock. Needs action photos from competitive events, personality portraits and technical photos.

MAKING CONTACT & TERMS Prefers electronic submissions on CD with query letter. Provide résumé, business card, brochure or flier to be kept on file for possible future assignments. Responds in 1 month. Simultaneous submissions OK. Pays $250-400 for color cover; $25-100 for color inside; negotiates all other rates. Pays on publication. Credit line given.

SPORTS ILLUSTRATED

Time, Inc., Sports Illustrated Bldg., 135 W. 50th St., New York NY 10020. (212)522-1212. E-mail: story_queries@simail.com. Website: sportsillustrated.cnn.com. Estab. 1954. Circ. 3,339,000. *Sports Illustrated* reports and interprets the world of sports, recreation and active leisure. It previews, analyzes and comments on major games and events, as well as those noteworthy for character and spirit alone. In addition, the magazine has articles on such subjects as fashion, physical fitness and conservation. Query before submitting.

🜚 ○ STICKMAN REVIEW

721 Oakwater Ln., Port Orange FL 32128. (386)756-1795. E-mail: art@stickmanreview.com. Website: www.stickmanreview.com. **Contact:** Anthony Brown, editor. Estab. 2001. Biannual literary magazine publishing fiction, poetry, essays and art for a literary audience. Sample copies available on website.

NEEDS Accepts 1-2 photos from freelancers/issue; 4 photos/year. Interested in alternative process, avant garde, documentary, erotic, fine art. Reviews photos with or without a manuscript.

SPECS Accepts images in digital format. Send via e-mail as JPEG, GIF, TIFF, PSD files at 72 dpi (500K maximum).

MAKING CONTACT & TERMS Contact through e-mail only. Does not keep samples on file; cannot return material. Do not query, just submit the work you would like considered. Responds 2 months to portfolios. Simultaneous submissions OK. Pays $25-50. Credit line given.

TIPS "Please check out the magazine on our website. We are open to anything, so long as its intent is artistic expression."

STRANGE, WEIRD, AND WONDERFUL MAGAZINE

313 N. Washington, Smith Center KS 66967-1930. (785)686-4155. E-mail: Sblack@strangeweirdand wonderful.com. Website: www.strangeweirdand wonderful.com. **Contact:** Sharon Black, editor. Estab. 2007. Circ. 26,530. Covering horror, fantasy and sci-fi, paranormal fiction and related nonfiction articles and artwork. "Online magazine with 7 stories each quarter and artwork for each story. We also have a rotating editorial and *Hey!* article by the editors, Sharon Black and DL Russell; Green Watch article; advertisements; and awards chosen by the readers. Article each issue by John Minser. The feature story has two artworks, one for the cover and one to introduce the story, illustrated by the same artist."

NEEDS Based on the story assigned. Reviews JPEG files. Pays $20 per photo. Purchases all rights on photos.

MAKING CONTACT & TERMS Send e-mail with résumé and samples. Samples not kept on file. Portfolio not required.

TIPS "The artwork should entice the reader to want to read the story and our magazine. Our stories are strange, weird and/or wonderful, and we want the artwork to be the same. Always include the story title and author name in the artwork, except on the cover artwork. Submit the artwork by the deadline."

THE SUN

107 N. Roberson St., Chapel Hill NC 27516. (919)942-5282. Fax: (919)932-3101. Website: www.thesun magazine.org. Sy Safransky, editor. **Contact:** Luc Sanders, editorial associate. Estab. 1974. Circ. 69,500. Monthly literary magazine featuring personal essays, interviews, poems, b&w photos and photo essays. Sample copy available for $5. Photo guidelines free with SASE or on website.

NEEDS Buys 10-30 photos/issue; 200-300 photos/year. Needs "slice of life" photographs of people and environments. Photographs that relate to political, spiritual, and social themes. Documentary-style images considered. "Most of our photos of people feature unrecognizable individuals, although we do run por-

traits in specific places, including the cover." Model/property release strongly preferred.

SPECS Uses 5×7 to 11×17 glossy or matte b&w prints. Slides are not accepted, and color photos are discouraged. "We cannot review images via e-mail or website. If you are submitting digital images, please send high-quality digital prints first. If we accept your images for publication, we will request the image files on CD or DVD media (Mac or PC) in uncompressed TIFF grayscale format at 300 dpi or greater."

MAKING CONTACT & TERMS Include SASE for return of material. Responds in 3 months. Simultaneous submissions and previously published work OK. "Submit no more than 30 of your best b&w prints. Please do not e-mail images." Pays $500 for b&w cover; $100 for b&w inside. Pays on publication. Credit line given. Buys one-time rights.

◎ ◑ SURFACE MAGAZINE

12 W. 27th St., 10th Floor, New York NY 10001. (212)343-0210. E-mail: advertising@quadramediallc. com. Website: www.surfacemag.com. Estab. 1994. Circ. 112,000. Published 6 times/year. "*Surface* is the definitive American source for engaging, curated content covering all that is inventive and compelling in the design world. Contains profiles of emerging designers and provocative projects that are reshaping the creative landscape."

NEEDS Buys 200 photos from freelancers/issue; 1,600 photos/year. Needs photos of environmental, landscapes/scenics, architecture, cities/urban, interiors/decorating, performing arts, travel, product shots/still life, technology. Interested in avant garde, fashion, portraits, fine art, seasonal.

SPECS Uses 11×17 glossy matte prints; 35mm, 2¼×2¼, 4×5, 8×10 transparencies. Accepts images in digital format. Send via CD, ZIP as TIFF, JPEG files at 300 dpi.

MAKING CONTACT & TERMS Contact through rep or send query letter with prints, photocopies, tearsheets. Provide self-promotion piece to be kept on file for possible future assignments. "Portfolios are reviewed on Friday each week. Submitted portfolios must be clearly labelled and include a shipping account number or postage for return. Please call for more details." Responds only if interested; send nonreturnable samples. Simultaneous submissions OK. Credit line given.

⊛⊛ ◐ SURFING MAGAZINE

P.O. Box 73250, San Clemente CA 92673. (949)492-7873. E-mail: tony.perez@sorc.com; peter@surfing magazine.com. Website: www.surfingthemag.com. **Contact:** Tony Perez, publisher; Peter Taras, photo editor. Circ. 180,000. Monthly. "Emphasizes surfing action and related aspects of beach lifestyle. Travel to new surfing areas covered as well. Average age of readers is 17 with 95% being male. Nearly all drawn to publication due to high-quality, action-packed photographs." Sample copy available with legal-size SASE and 9 first-class stamps. Photo guidelines free with SASE or via e-mail.

NEEDS Buys an average of 10 photos from freelancers/issue. Needs "in-tight, front-lit surfing action photos, as well as travel-related scenics. Beach lifestyle photos always in demand."

SPECS Uses 35mm transparencies. Accepts digital images via CD; contact for digital requirements before submitting digital images.

MAKING CONTACT & TERMS Send samples by mail for consideration; include SASE for return of material. Responds in 1 month. Pays $750-1,000 for color cover; $25-330 for color inside; $600 for color poster photo. Pays on publication. Credit line given. Buys one-time rights.

TIPS Prefers to see "well-exposed, sharp images showing both the ability to capture peak action, as well as beach scenes depicting the surfing lifestyle. Color, lighting, composition and proper film usage are important. Ask for our photo guidelines prior to making any film/camera/lens choices."

TECHNICAL ANALYSIS OF STOCKS & COMMODITIES

4757 California Ave. SW, Seattle WA 98116. (206)938-0570. E-mail: editor@traders.com. Website: www.traders.com. Christine M. Morrison, art director. Estab. 1982. Circ. 65,000. "Magazine covers methods of investing and trading stocks, bonds and commodities (futures), options, mutual funds, and precious metals using technical analysis."

MAKING CONTACT & TERMS Captions, identification of subjects, model releases required. Pays $60-350 for b&w or color negatives with prints or positive slides. Buys one-time and reprint rights.

TEXAS GARDENER

Suntex Communications, Inc., P.O. Box 9005, Waco TX 76714-9005. (254)848-9393. Fax: (254)848-9779. E-mail: info@texasgardener.com. Website: www.texas gardener.com. Estab. 1981. Circ. 20,000. Bimonthly. Emphasizes gardening. Readers are "51% male, 49% female, home gardeners, 98% Texas residents." Sample copy available for $4.

NEEDS Buys 18-27 photos from freelancers/issue; 108-162 photos/year. Needs color photos of gardening activities in Texas. Special needs include cover photos shot in vertical format. Must be taken in Texas. Photo captions required.

SPECS Prefers high-res digital images. Send via e-mail as JPEG files at 300 dpi.

MAKING CONTACT & TERMS Send query letter with samples, SASE. Responds in 3 weeks. Pays $100-200 for color cover; $25-100 for color inside. Pays on publication. Credit line given. Buys one-time rights.

TIPS "Provide complete information on photos. For example, if you submit a photo of watermelons growing in a garden, we need to know what variety they are and when and where the picture was taken."

TEXAS HIGHWAYS

Box 141009, Austin TX 78714-1009. (800)839-4997. Website: www.texashighways.com. Estab. 1974. Circ. 250,000. Monthly. "Texas Highways interprets scenic, recreational, historical, cultural and ethnic treasures of the state and preserves the best of Texas heritage. Its purpose is to educate and entertain, to encourage recreational travel to and within the state, and to tell the Texas story to readers around the world." Readers are ages 45 and over (majority), $24,000 to $60,000/year salary bracket with a college education. Photo guidelines and online submission form available on website.

NEEDS Buys 30-60 photos from freelancers/issue; 360-420 photos/year. Needs "travel and scenic photos in Texas only." Special needs include "fall, winter, spring and summer scenic shots and wildflower shots (Texas only)." Photo captions required; include location, names, addresses and other useful information.

SPECS "We take only color originals, 35mm or larger transparencies. No negatives or prints." Accepts images in digital format. Prefers camera RAW files with tweaks and captions in sidecar files. Consult guidelines before submitting.

MAKING CONTACT & TERMS Send query letter with samples, SASE. Provide business card and tearsheets to be kept on file for possible future assignments. Responds in 1 month. Simultaneous submissions OK. Pays $400 for color cover; $60-170 for color inside. Pays $15 extra for electronic usage. Pays on publication. Credit line given. Buys one-time rights. Online feedback form is used for correspondence with all magazine staff.

TIPS "Look at our magazine and format. We accept only high-quality, professional-level work—no snapshots. Interested in a photographer's ability to edit own material and the breadth of a photographer's work. Look at 3-4 months of the magazine. Query not just for photos but with ideas for new/unusual topics."

TEXAS MONTHLY

Emmis Publishing LP, P.O. Box 1569, Austin TX 78767-1569. (512)320-6900. Fax: (512)476-9007. E-mail: lbaldwin@texasmonthly.com. Website: www.texasmonthly.com. Scott Dadich, art director. **Contact:** Jake Silverstein, editor; Leslie Baldwin, photo editor. Estab. 1973. Circ. 300,000. *Texas Monthly* is edited for the urban Texas audience and covers the state's politics, sports, business, culture and changing lifestyles. It contains lengthy feature articles, reviews and interviews, and presents critical analysis of popular books, movies and plays.

NEEDS Uses about 50 photos/issue. Photos of celebrities, sports, travel.

MAKING CONTACT & TERMS "Please feel free to submit your photography or illustration portfolio to us. The best way to do this is by e-mailing us a link to your work. If you do not have a website, simply attaching a few images of your work in an e-mail is fine. Send samples or tearsheets. No preference on printed material—b&w or color. Responds only if interested. Keeps samples on file."

TIPS "Visit www.texasmonthly.com/artguide for information on sending portfolios."

THIN AIR MAGAZINE

English Department, Northern Arizona University, Bldg. 18, Room 133, Flagstaff AZ 86011. (928)523-6743. E-mail: editors@thinairmagazine.com. Website: thinairmagazine.com. Estab. 1995. Circ. 400. Annual literary magazine. Emphasizes arts and literature—poetry, fiction and essays. Readers are collegiate, academic, writerly adult males and females interested in arts and literature. Sample copy available for $6.

NEEDS Buys 2-4 photos from freelancers/issue; 4-8 photos/year. Needs scenic/wildlife shots and b&w photos that portray a statement or tell a story. Looking for b&w or color cover shots. Model/property release preferred. Photo captions preferred; include name of photographer, date of photo.

SPECS Uses 8×10 b&w prints.

MAKING CONTACT & TERMS Send unsolicited photos by mail with SASE for consideration. Photos accepted August through May only. Keeps samples on file. Responds in 3 months. Simultaneous submissions and previously published work OK. Pays 2 contributor's copies. Credit line given. Buys one-time rights.

TIDE MAGAZINE

6919 Portwest Dr., Suite 100, Houston TX 77024. (713)626-4234; (800)201-FISH. Fax: (713)626-5852. E-mail: ccantl@joincca.org. Website: www.joincca.org. Estab. 1979. Circ. 80,000. Bimonthly magazine of the Coastal Conservation Association. Emphasizes coastal fishing, conservation issues—exclusively along the Gulf and Atlantic Coasts. Readers are mostly male, ages 25-50, coastal anglers and professionals.

NEEDS Buys 12-16 photos from freelancers/issue; 72-96 photos/year. Needs photos of *only* Gulf and Atlantic coastal activity, recreational fishing and coastal scenics/habitat, tight shots of fish (saltwater only). Model/property release preferred. Photo captions not required, but include names, dates, places and specific equipment or other key information.

MAKING CONTACT & TERMS Send query letter with stock list. Responds in 1 month. Simultaneous submissions and previously published work OK. Pays $250 for color cover; $50-200 for color inside; $300-400 for photo/text package. Pays on publication. Credit line given. Buys one-time rights; negotiable.

TIPS Wants to see "fresh twists on old themes—unique lighting, subjects of interest to my readers. Take time to discover new angles for fishing shots. Avoid the usual poses, i.e., 'grip-and-grin.' We see too much of that already."

TIKKUN

2342 Shattack Ave., #1200, Berkeley CA 94704. (510)644-1200. Fax: (510)644-1255. E-mail: magazine@tikkun.org; or via online contact form. Website: www.

tikkun.org. **Contact:** Managing editor. Estab. 1986. Circ. 25,000. Bimonthly. Jewish and interfaith critique of politics, culture and society. Readers are 60% Jewish, professional, middle-class, literary people, ages 30-60.

NEEDS Uses 15 photos/issue; 30% supplied by freelancers. Needs political, social commentary; Middle East and U.S. photos. Reviews photos with or without a manuscript.

SPECS Uses b&w and color prints. Accepts images in digital format for Mac.

MAKING CONTACT & TERMS Response time varies. "Turnaround is 4 months, unless artist specifies other." Previously published work OK. Pays $50 for b&w inside. Pays on publication. Credit line given. Buys all rights; negotiable.

TIPS "Look at our magazine and suggest how your photos can enhance our articles and subject material. Send samples."

⊘ TIME

Time/Life Building, 1271 Avenue of the Americas, New York NY 10020. E-mail: letters@time.com. Website: www.time.com. **Contact:** Art director. Estab. 1923. Circ. 4,034,000. *TIME* is edited to report and analyze a complete and compelling picture of the world, including national and world affairs, news of business, science, society and the arts, and the people who make the news. Query before submitting.

● TIMES OF THE ISLANDS

Times Publications, Ltd., P.O. Box 234, Lucille Lightbourne Bldg., #7, Providenciales Turks & Caicos Islands, British West Indies. (649)946-4788. Fax: (649)946-4788. E-mail: timespub@tciway.tc. Website: www.timespub.tc. Estab. 1988. Circ. 10,000. Quarterly. Focuses on in-depth topics specifically related to Turks & Caicos Islands. Targeted beyond mass tourists to homeowners, investors, developers and others with strong interest in learning about these islands. Sample copy available for $6. Photo guidelines available on website.

NEEDS Buys 5 photos from freelancers/issue; 20 photos/year. Needs photos of environmental, landscapes/scenics, wildlife, architecture, adventure, travel. Interested in historical/vintage. Also scuba diving, islands in TCI beyond main island of Providenciales. Reviews photos with or without a manuscript. Photo captions required; include specific location, names of any people.

SPECS Prefers high resolution digital images. Send via CD or e-mail as JPEG files.

MAKING CONTACT & TERMS Send query e-mail with photo samples. Provide business card, self-promotion piece to be kept on file for possible future assignments. Responds in 6 weeks to queries. Simultaneous submissions and previously published work OK. Pays $100-300 for color cover; $50-100 for inside. Pays on publication. Credit line given. Buys one-time rights; negotiable.

TIPS "Make sure photo is specific to Turks & Caicos and location/subject accurately identified."

❸ ◑ TRACK & FIELD NEWS

2570 El Camino Real, Suite 480, Mountain View CA 94040. (650)948-8188. Fax: (650)948-9445. E-mail: editorial@trackandfieldnews.com. Website: www.trackandfieldnews.com. **Contact:** Jon Hendershott, associate editor (features/photography). Estab. 1948. Circ. 25,000. Monthly. Emphasizes national and world-class track and field competition and participants at those levels for athletes, coaches, administrators and fans. Sample copy free with 9×12 SASE. Photo guidelines free.

NEEDS Buys 10-15 photos from freelancers/issue; 120-180 photos/year. Wants, on a regular basis, photos of national-class athletes, men and women, preferably in action. "We are always looking for quality pictures of track and field action, as well as offbeat and different feature photos. We also welcome shots from road and cross-country races for both men and women. Any photos may eventually be used to illustrate news stories in *T&FN*, feature stories in *T&FN*, or may be used in our other publications (books, technical journals, etc.). Any such editorial use will be paid for, regardless of whether material is used directly in *T&FN*. About all we don't want to see are pictures taken with someone's Instamatic. No shots of someone's child or grandparent running. Professional work only." Photo captions required; include subject name (last name first), meet date/name.

SPECS Images must be in digital format. Send via CD, e-mail; all files at 300 dpi.

MAKING CONTACT & TERMS Send query letter with samples, SASE. Responds in 10–14 days. Pays $225 for color cover; $25 for b&w inside (rarely used); $50 for color inside ($100 for full-page interior color;

$175 for interior 4-color poster). Payment is made monthly. Credit line given. Buys one-time rights.

TIPS "No photographer is going to get rich via *T&FN*. We can offer a credit line, nominal payment and, in some cases, credentials to major track and field meets. Also, we can offer the chance for competent photographers to shoot major competitions and competitors up close, as well as being the most highly regarded publication in the track world as a forum to display a photographer's talents."

TRAILER BOATS MAGAZINE

Ehlert Publishing Group, Inc., 20700 Belshaw Ave., Carson CA 90746-3510. Website: www.trailerboats. com. **Contact:** Jim Hendricks, publisher/editorial director. Estab. 1971. Circ. 100,000. Distributed 9 times/year. "We are the only magazine devoted exclusively to trailerable boats and related activities" for owners and prospective owners.

NEEDS Uses 15 photos/issue; 95-100% of freelance photography comes from assignment, 0-5% from stock. Needs how-to trailerable boat, travel (with manuscript). For accompanying manuscripts, needs articles related to trailer boat activities. Photos purchased with or without accompanying manuscript. "Photos must relate to trailer boat activities. No long list of stock photos or subject matter not related to editorial content." Photo captions preferred; include location of travel pictures.

SPECS Accepts images in digital format. Send as JPEG files at 300 dpi.

MAKING CONTACT & TERMS Query or send photos or contact sheet by mail with SASE for consideration. Pays per text/photo package or on a per-photo basis. **Pays on acceptance.** Credit line given.

TIPS "Shoot with imagination and a variety of angles. Don't be afraid to 'set up' a photo that looks natural. Think in terms of complete feature stories: photos and manuscripts."

TRAIL RUNNER

Big Stone Publishing, 417 Main St., Unit N, Carbondale CO 81623. (970)704-1442. Fax: (970)963-4965. E-mail: aarnold@bigstonepub.com. Website: www. trailrunnermag.com. **Contact:** Michael Benge, editor; Ashley Arnold, associate editor. Estab. 1999. Circ. 29,000. Bimonthly. The nation's only magazine covering all aspects of trail running. *Trail Runner* regularly features stunning photography of trail running destinations, races, adventures and faces of the sport.

Sample copy available for 9×12 SAE with $1.65 postage. Photo guidelines available on website.

NEEDS Buys 5-10 photos from freelancers/issue; 50-100 photos/year. Needs photos of landscapes/scenics, adventure, health/fitness, sports, travel. Interested in anything related to running on trails and the outdoors. Reviews photos with or without a manuscript. Model/property release preferred. Photo captions required.

SPECS Uses glossy color prints; 35mm transparencies. Accepts images in digital format. Send via CD, e-mail as TIFF files at 600 dpi.

MAKING CONTACT & TERMS Send query letter via e-mail to photo editor. Contact photo editor for appointment to drop off portfolio. Provide résumé, business card or self-promotion piece to be kept on file for possible future assignments. Responds in 3 weeks. Simultaneous submissions OK. Pays $500 for color cover; $50-200 for b&w inside; $50-250 for color inside; $350 for spread (color). Pays 30 days from date of publication. Credit line given. Buys one-time rights, first rights; negotiable.

TIPS "Read our magazine. Stay away from model shots, or at least those with make-up and spandex clothing. No waving at the camera."

💮 💲 TRAVELLER MAGAZINE & PUBLISHING

45-49 Brompton Road, London SW3 1DE, United Kingdom. (44)(207)581-6156; (44)(207)589-0500. Fax: (44)(207)581-8476. E-mail: traveller@and-publishing.co.uk. Website: www.traveller.org.uk; www.traveller@and-publishing.co.uk. **Contact:** Amy Sohanpaul, editor. Circ. 25,000. Quarterly. Readers are predominantly male, professional, ages 35 and older. Sample copy available for £4.95.

NEEDS Uses 75-100 photos/issue; all supplied by freelancers. Needs photos of travel, wildlife, tribes. Reviews photos with or without a manuscript. Photo captions preferred.

MAKING CONTACT & TERMS Send at least 20 original color slides or b&w prints. Or send at least 20 low-res scans by e-mail or CD (include printout of thumbnails); high-res (300 dpi) scans will be required for final publication. Does not keep samples on file; include SASE for return of material. Responds in 3 months. Pays £150 for color cover; £80 for full page; £50 for other sizes. Pays on publication. Buys one-time rights.

TIPS Look at guidelines for contributors on website.

⑤ ◐ TRAVELWORLD INTERNATIONAL MAGAZINE

531 Main St., #902, El Segundo CA 90245. (310)836-8712. Fax: (310)836-8769. E-mail: helen@natja.org. Website: www.natja.org, www.travelworldmagazine. com. **Contact:** Helen Hernandez, CEO. Estab. 1992. Circ. 75,000. Quarterly online magazine of the North American Travel Journalists Association (NATJA). Emphasizes travel, food, wine, and hospitality industries.

NEEDS Photos of food/drink, travel.

SPECS Uses color and b&w. Prefers digital images.

MAKING CONTACT & TERMS Send query via e-mail.

TIPS Only accepts submissions from members.

TRICYCLE

92 Vandam St., New York NY 10013. (212)645-1143. Fax: (212)645-1493. E-mail: editorial@tricycle.com. Website: www.tricycle.com. Estab. 1991. Circ. 60,000. Quarterly nonprofit magazine devoted to the exploration of Buddhism, literature and the arts.

NEEDS Buys 10 photos from freelancers/issue; 40 photos/year. Reviews photos with or without a manuscript. Model/property release preferred. Photo captions preferred.

SPECS Uses glossy b&w and color prints; 35mm transparencies. Accepts images in digital format. Send via CD, ZIP, e-mail as TIFF, EPS, BMP, GIF, JPEG files at 300 dpi.

MAKING CONTACT & TERMS "We prefer to receive copies or CDs of photographs or art, rather than originals, in both color and b&w. For the safety of your own work, please do not send anything which you would fear losing, as we cannot assume responsibility for the loss of unsolicited artwork. If you would like to receive a reply from us and wish your work returned, you must include a SASE with sufficient postage."

TIPS "Read the magazine to get a sense of the kind of work we publish. We don't only use Buddhist art; we select artwork depending on the content of the piece."

⑤ ⑤ ◐ TRIUMPH WORLD

P.O. Box 978, Peterborough PE1 9FL, United Kingdom. +44 (0)1959 541444. Fax: +44 (0)1959 541400. E-mail: tw.ed@kelseypb.co.uk. Website: www.triumph-world.co.uk. Estab. 1995. Bimonthly. For enthusiasts and owners of Triumph cars.

NEEDS Buys 60 photos from freelancers/issue; 360 photos/year. Needs photos of Triumph cars. Reviews photos with or without a manuscript. Photo captions preferred.

SPECS Uses color and b&w prints; 35mm, 2¼×2¼, 4×5 transparencies. Accepts images in digital format. Send as JPEG files.

MAKING CONTACT & TERMS Send query letter with samples, tearsheets. Pays 6 weeks after publication. Credit line given. Buys first rights.

TURKEY & TURKEY HUNTING

F+W Media, Inc., 700 E. State St., Iola WI 54990-0001. (715)445-4612. E-mail: brian.lovett@fwmedia.com. Website: www.turkeyandturkeyhunting.com. Jim Schlender, editor. **Contact:** Brian Lovett. Estab. 1982. Circ. 40,000. Published 6 times/year. Provides features and news about wild turkeys and turkey hunting. Photo guidelines available on website.

TURKEY COUNTRY

(803)637-3106. Fax: (803)637-0034. E-mail: info@nwtf. net; turkeycountry@nwtf.net. E-mail: klee@nwtf.net. Website: www.turkeycountrymagazine.com. Gregg Powers, managing editor; P.J. Perea, senior editor; Matt Lindler, photo editor. **Contact:** Karen Lee, editor. Estab. 1973. Circ. 180,000. Bimonthly. For members of the National Wild Turkey Federation—people interested in conserving the American wild turkey. Sample copy available for $5 with 9×12 SASE. Images may be submitted to accompany specific assignments or on speculation. See photograph submission information and send speculative images to the photo editor at the NWTF shipping address. Photo guidelines free with SASE or on website at www.turkeycountrymagazine. com/contributor_guidelines.html.

NEEDS Buys at least 100 photos/year. Needs photos of "wildlife, including wild turkeys, upland birds, North American Big Game; wild turkey hunting; wild turkey management techniques (planting food, trapping for relocation, releasing); wild turkey habitat; families, women, children and people with disabilities hunting or enjoying the outdoors." Photo captions required.

SPECS Prefers images in digital format from 6mp or higher resolution cameras. Send via CD/DVD at 300 ppi with thumbnail page (see guidelines for more details).

MAKING CONTACT & TERMS Send copyrighted photos to editor for consideration; include SASE. Responds in 6 weeks. Pays $800 for cover; $400 maximum for color inside. We purchase both print rights and for electronic usage on turkeycountrymagazine.com, which includes a digital version of the magazine. Additional usage on the website, other than in the digital magazine, will be negotiated. Pays on publication. Credit line given. Buys one-time rights.
TIPS "No poorly posed or restaged shots, no mounted turkeys representing live birds, no domestic animals representing wild animals. Photos of dead animals in a tasteful hunt setting are considered. Contributors must agree to the guidelines before submitting."

TV GUIDE

Gemstar-TV Guide International, Inc., 1211 Avenue of the Americas, 4th Floor, New York NY 10036. (212)852-7500. Fax: (212)852-7470. Website: www.tvguide.com. Catherine Suhocki, associate art director. Estab. 1953. Circ. 9,097,762. *TV Guide* watches television with an eye for how TV programming affects and reflects society. It looks at the shows and the stars, and covers the medium's impact on news, sports, politics, literature, the arts, science and social issues through reports, profiles, features and commentaries.
MAKING CONTACT & TERMS Works only with celebrity freelance photographers. "Photos are for one-time publication use. Mail self-promo cards to photo editor at above address. No calls, please."

☻ UP HERE

P.O. Box 1350, Yellowknife NT X1A 3T1, Canada. (867)766-6710. Fax: (867)873-9876. E-mail: katharine@uphere.ca; patrick@uphere.ca (for photography). Website: www.uphere.ca. **Contact:** Katharine Sandiford, editor. Estab. 1984. Circ. 22,000. Published 8 times/year. Emphasizes Canada's North. Readers are educated, affluent men and women ages 30 to 60.
NEEDS Buys 18-27 photos from freelancers/issue; 144-216 photos/year. Needs photos of Northern Canada environmental, landscapes/scenics, wildlife, adventure, performing arts. Interested in documentary, seasonal. Purchases photos with or without accompanying manuscript. Photo captions required.
SPECS Accepts images in digital format. Send via CD, e-mail. Also uses color transparencies, not prints, labeled with the photographer's name, address, phone number, and caption.

MAKING CONTACT & TERMS Provide résumé, business card, brochure, flyer or tearsheets to be kept on file for possible future assignments. Pays $350-400 for color cover, up to $300 for color inside. Pays on publication. Credit line given. Buys one-time rights.
TIPS "We are a *people* magazine. We need stories that are uniquely Northern (people, places, etc.). Few scenics as such. We approach local freelancers for given subjects, but routinely complete commissioned photography with images from stock sources. Please let us know about Northern images you have." Wants to see "sharp, clear photos, good color and composition. We always need verticals to consider for the cover, but they usually tie in with an article inside."

VELONEWS

Inside Communications, Inc., 3002 Sterling Circle, Suite 100, Boulder CO 80301. (303)440-0601. Fax: (303)444-6788. E-mail: velonews@pcspublink.com. Website: www.velonews.com. Estab. 1972. Circ. 48,000.

⊙ Covers road racing, mountain biking and recreational riding. Sample copy free with 9×12 SASE.

NEEDS Uses photos of bicycle racing (road, mountain and track). "Looking for action and feature shots that show the emotion of cycling, not just finish-line photos with the winner's arms in the air." No bicycle touring. Photos purchased with or without accompanying manuscript. Uses news, features, profiles. Photo captions required.
SPECS Uses negatives and transparencies.
MAKING CONTACT & TERMS Send samples of work or tearsheets with assignment proposal. Query first. Pays on publication. Credit line given. Buys one-time rights.
TIPS "Photos must be timely."

⑨ ◑ VERMONT MAGAZINE

P.O. Box 900, Arlington VT 05250. (802)375-1366. E-mail: prj@vermontmagazine.com. Website: www.vermontmagazine.com. **Contact:** Philip Jordan, editor. Estab. 1989. Circ. 50,000. Bimonthly. Emphasizes all facets of Vermont culture, business, sports, restaurants, real estate, people, crafts, art, architecture, etc. Readers are people interested in Vermont, including residents, tourists and second home owners. Sample copy available for $4.95 with 9×12 SASE and 5 first-class stamps. Photo guidelines free with SASE.

NEEDS Buys 10 photos from freelancers/issue; 60 photos/year. Needs animal/wildlife shots, travel, Vermont scenics, how-to, products and architecture. Special photo needs include Vermont activities such as skiing, ice skating, biking, hiking, etc. Model release preferred. Photo captions required.

MAKING CONTACT & TERMS Send query letter with résumé of credits, samples, SASE. Send 8×10 b&w prints or 35mm or larger transparencies by mail for consideration. Submit portfolio for review. Provide tearsheets to be kept on file for possible future assignments. Responds in 2 months. Previously published work OK, depending on "how it was previously published." Pays $300 for color cover; $150 color page rate; $50-150 for color and b&w inside; $250/day. Pays on publication. Credit line given. Buys one-time rights and first North American serial rights; negotiable.

TIPS In portfolio or samples, wants to see tearsheets of published work and at least 40 35mm transparencies. Explain your areas of expertise. Looking for creative solutions to illustrate regional activities, profiles and lifestyles. "We would like to see more illustrative photography/fine art photography where it applies to the articles and departments we produce."

● VERSAL

Postbus 3865, Amsterdam 1054 EJ , The Netherlands. +31 (0)63 433 8875. E-mail: Info@wordsinhere.com. Website: www.wordsinhere.com. Shayna Schapp, assistant art editor (artists); Megan Garr, editor (designers). **Contact:** Megan M. Garr, editor. Estab. 2002. Circ. 650. "*Versal*, published each May by *wordsinhere*, is the only literary magazine of its kind in the Netherlands and publishes new poetry, prose and art from around the world. *Versal* and the writers behind it are also at the forefront of a growing translocal European literary scene, which includes exciting communities in Amsterdam, Paris and Berlin. *Versal* seeks work that is urgent, involved and unexpected."

MAKING CONTACT & TERMS Submission guidelines online. Samples not kept on file. Portfolio not required. Credit line is given. Work accepted by submission period (September–January).

TIPS "After reviewing the journal, if you are interested in what we're doing and would like to get involved, please send a query and CV to editor Megan Garr at Megan@wordsinhere.com. Artists submitting to *Versal* must follow our submission guidelines online

and submit during our review period, September to January. Others interested in helping should always send an inquiry with a cover letter and CV. Please do not submit images of artwork via e-mail."

◎ ○ THE VIEW FROM HERE

E-mail: Editor@Viewfromheremagazine.com. Website: www.viewfromheremagazine.com. **Contact:** Mike French, senior editor. Estab. 2008. Circ. 8,000. "We are a print and online literary magazine with author interview, book reviews, original fiction and poetry and articles. Designed and edited by an international team we bring an entertaining mix of wit, insight and intelligence all packaged in beautifully designed pages that mix the new with the famous. We publish our fiction at *The Front View* and our poetry at *The Rear View*, where we showcase the weird, unusual, thought provoking and occasionally bizarre. We classify ourselves as 'Bohemian Eclectic'—yes, we coined the term. Our stories and poems will make you wonder, laugh, cry and generally *feel* something."

NEEDS Avant garde, entertainment and fine art photographs.

MAKING CONTACT & TERMS Send an e-mail with résumé and JPEG samples. Portfolio not required. Credit line given.

⊛⊛ ○ VILLAGE PROFILE

33 N. Geneva St., Elgin IL 60120. (847)468-6800. Fax: (847)468-9751. E-mail: smikutis@villageprofilemail. com. Website: www.villageprofile.com. **Contact:** Juli Schatz, vice president/production. Estab. 1988. Circ. 5-15,000 per publication; average 240 projects/year. Publication offering community profiles, chamber membership directories, maps. "Village Profile has published community guides, chamber membership directories, maps, atlases and builder brochures in 45 states. Community guides depict the towns served by the chamber with 'quality of life' text and photos, using a brochure style rather than a news or documentary look." Sample copy available with 10×13 SASE. Photo guidelines free with SASE.

NEEDS Buys 50 photos from freelancers/issue; 5,000 photos/year. Needs photos of babies/children/teens, multicultural, families, parents, senior citizens, cities/urban, food/drink, health/fitness/beauty, business concepts, industry, medicine, technology/computers. Interested in historical/vintage, seasonal. Points of interest specific to the communities being profiled.

Reviews photos with or without a manuscript. Model/property release preferred. Photo captions required. **SPECS** Uses up to 8×10 glossy prints; 35mm, 2¼×2¼ transparencies. Accepts images in digital format. Send via ZIP as TIFF files at 300 dpi.

MAKING CONTACT & TERMS Send query letter with photocopies, tearsheets, stock list, locale/travel ability. Provide résumé, business card, self-promotion piece to be kept on file for possible future assignments. Responds in 1 week to queries. Previously published work OK. Pays $500 minimum/project; negotiates higher rates for multiple-community projects. **Pays on acceptance.** Credit line given. Buys all rights.

TIPS "We want photographs of, and specific to, the community/region covered by the *Profile*, but we always need fresh stock photos of people involved in healthcare, shopping/dining, recreation, education and business to use as fillers. E-mail anytime to find out if we're doing a project in your neighborhood. Do NOT query with or send samples or tearsheets of scenics, landscapes, wildlife, nature—see stock needs list above. We only purchase stock images in batches if the price is comparable to stock photo CDs available on the market—don't expect $100 per image."

THE WASHINGTON BLADE

529 14th St., NW, Washington D.C. 20045. (202)747-2077. Fax: (202)747-2070. E-mail: knaff@washblade.com. Website: www.washblade.com. Estab. 1969. Circ. 30,000. Weekly tabloid for and about the gay community. Readers are gay men and lesbians; moderate-to upper-level income; primarily Washington, D.C., metropolitan area. Sample copy free with 9×12 SASE plus 11 first-class stamps.

⊙ *The Washington Blade* stores images on CD; manipulates size, contrast, etc.—but not content.

NEEDS Uses about 6–7 photos/issue. Needs "gay-related news, sports, entertainment, events; profiles of gay people in news, sports, entertainment, other fields." Photos purchased with or without accompanying manuscript. Model release preferred. Photo captions preferred.

SPECS Accepts images in digital format. Send via e-mail.

MAKING CONTACT & TERMS Send query letter with résumé of credits. Provide résumé, business card and tearsheets to be kept on file for possible future assignments. Responds in 1 month. Simultaneous sub-

missions and previously published work OK. Pays $10 fee to go to location, $15/photo, $5/reprint of photo; negotiable. Pays within 30 days of publication. Credit line given. Buys all rights when on assignment, otherwise one-time rights.

TIPS "Be timely! Stay up-to-date on what we're covering in the news, and call if you know of a story about to happen in your city that you can cover. Also, be able to provide some basic details for a caption (*tell us what's happening, too*). It's especially important to avoid stereotypes."

WASHINGTON TRAILS

705 2nd Ave., Suite 300, Seattle WA 98104. (206)625-1367. E-mail: lace@wta.org. Website: www.wta.org/trail-news/magazine. **Contact:** Lace Thornberg, editor. Estab. 1966. Circ. 9,000. Magazine of the Washington Trails Association, published 6 times/year. Emphasizes "backpacking, hiking, cross-country skiing, all nonmotorized trail use, outdoor equipment and minimum-impact camping techniques." Readers are "people active in outdoor activities, primarily backpacking; residents of the Pacific Northwest, mostly Washington; age group: 9-90; family-oriented; interested in wilderness preservation, trail maintenance." Photo guidelines free with SASE or online.

NEEDS Uses 10–15 photos from volunteers/issue; 100–150 photos/year. Needs "wilderness/scenic; people involved in hiking, backpacking, skiing, snowshoeing, wildlife; outdoor equipment photos, all with Pacific Northwest emphasis." Photo captions required.

MAKING CONTACT & TERMS Send JPEGs by e-mail for consideration. Responds in 1–2 months. Simultaneous submissions and previously published work OK. No payment for photos. A 1-year subscription offered for use of color cover shot. Credit line given.

TIPS "Photos must have a Pacific Northwest slant. Photos that meet our cover specifications are always of interest to us. Familiarity with our magazine will greatly aid the photographer in submitting material to us. Contributing to *Washington Trails* won't help pay your bills, but sharing your photos with other backpackers and skiers has its own rewards."

⊙⊙ ○ WATERCRAFT WORLD

2575 Vista Del Mar, Ventura CA 93001. (805)667-4100. Fax: (805)667-4336. E-mail: gmansfield@affinitygroup.com. Website: www.watercraftworld.com. **Contact:** Gregg Mansfield, editorial director. Estab. 1987. Circ.

75,000. Published 6 times/year. Emphasizes personal watercraft (Jet Skis, Wave Runners, Sea-Doo). Readers are 95% male, average age 37, boaters, outdoor enthusiasts. Sample copy available for $4.

NEEDS Buys 7-12 photos from freelancers/issue; 42-72 photos/year. Needs photos of personal watercraft travel, race coverage. Model/property release required. Photo captions preferred.

SPECS Accepts images in digital format. Send via CD, ZIP, e-mail as TIFF, EPS, GIF, JPEG files at 300 dpi.

MAKING CONTACT & TERMS Send query letter with résumé of credits. Provide résumé, business card, brochure, flyer or tearsheets to be kept on file for possible future assignments. "Call with ideas." Responds in 1 month. Pays $25-200 for b&w inside; $50-250 for color inside; cover rate negotiable. Pays on publication. Credit line given. Rights negotiable.

TIPS "Call to discuss project. We take and use many travel photos from all over the United States (very little foreign). We also cover many regional events (e.g., charity rides, races)."

✆✆ WATERSKI

460 N. Orlando Ave., Suite 200, Winter Park FL 32789. (407)628-4802. Fax: (407)628-7061. E-mail: bill.doster@bonniercorp.com; todd.ristorcelli@bonniercorp.com. Website: www.waterskimag.com. Russ Moore, art director. **Contact:** Bill Doster, photo editor; Todd Ristorcelli, editor. Estab. 1978. Circ. 105,000. Published 8 times/year. Emphasizes water skiing instruction, lifestyle, competition, travel. Readers are 36-year-old males, average household income $65,000. Sample copy available for $2.95. Photo guidelines free with SASE.

NEEDS Buys 20 photos from freelancers/issue; 160 photos/year. Needs photos of instruction, travel, personality. Model/property release preferred. Photo captions preferred; include person, trick described.

MAKING CONTACT & TERMS Query with good samples, SASE. Keeps samples on file. Responds within 2 months. Pays $200–500/day; $500 for color cover; $50–75 for b&w inside; $75–300 for color inside; $150/color page rate; $50–75/b&w page rate. Pays on publication. Credit line given. Buys first North American serial rights.

TIPS "Clean, clear, tight images. Plenty of vibrant action, colorful travel scenics and personality. Must be able to shoot action photography. Looking for photographers in other geographic regions for diverse coverage."

THE WATER SKIER

1251 Holy Cow Rd., Polk City FL 33868. (863)324-4341. Fax: (863)325-8259. E-mail: satkinson@usawaterski.org. Website: www.usawaterski.org. **Contact:** Scott Atkinson, editor. Estab. 1951. Circ. 30,000. Magazine of USA Water Ski, published 7 times/year. Emphasizes water skiing. Readers are male and female professionals, ages 20-45. Sample copy available for $3.50. Photo guidelines available.

NEEDS Buys 1-5 photos from freelancers/issue; 9-45 photos/year. Needs photos of sports action. Model/property release required. Photo captions required.

MAKING CONTACT & TERMS Call first. Pays $50-150 for color photos. Pays on publication. Credit line given. Buys all rights.

WATERWAY GUIDE

P.O. Box 1125, 16273 General Puller Hwy., Deltaville VA 23043. (804)776-8999. Fax: (804)776-6111. E-mail: slandry@waterwayguide.com. Website: www.waterwayguide.com. **Contact:** Susan Landry, editor. Estab. 1947. Circ. 30,000. Cruising guide with 4 annual regional editions. Emphasizes recreational boating. Readers are men and women ages 25-65, management or professional, with average income $138,000. Sample copy available for $39.95 and $3 shipping. Photo guidelines free with SASE.

NEEDS Buys 10-15 photos from freelancers/issue. Needs aerial photos of waterways. Expects to use more coastal shots from Maine to the Bahamas; also Hudson River, Great Lakes, Lake Champlain and Gulf of Mexico. Model release required. Photo captions required.

SPECS Accepts images in digital format. Send as EPS, TIFF files at 300 dpi.

MAKING CONTACT & TERMS Send unsolicited photos by mail with SASE for consideration. Responds in 4 months. Pay varies; negotiable. Pays on publication. Credit line given. Must sign contract for copyright purposes.

☺ WAVELENGTH MAGAZINE

Wild Coast Publishing, #6-10 Commercial St., Nanaimo BC V9R 5G2, Canada. (250)244-6437; (866)984-6437. Fax: (250)244-1937; (866)654-1937. E-mail: editor@wavelengthmagazine.com. Website: www.wavelengthmagazine.com. **Contact:** John Kimantas, editor. Estab. 1991. Circ. 65,000 print and electronic readers. Quarterly. Emphasizes safe, ecologically sensitive paddling. For sample copy, see downloadable PDF version online.

NEEDS Buys 10 photos from freelancers/issue ("usually only from authors"); 60 photos/year. Needs kayaking shots. Photos should have sea kayak in them. Reviews photos with or without a manuscript. Model/property release preferred. Photo captions preferred.

SPECS Prefers digital submissions, but only after query. Send as low-res for assessment.

MAKING CONTACT & TERMS Send query letter first. Provide business card or self-promotion piece to be kept on file for possible future assignments. Responds in 2 months to queries. Absolutely no simultaneous submissions or previously published work accepted. Pays $100-200 for color cover; $25-50 for inside. Pays on publication. Credit line given. Buys one-time print rights including electronic archive rights.

TIPS "Look at free downloadable version online and include kayak in picture wherever possible. Always need vertical shots for cover!"

$$ ◐ WESTERN OUTDOORS

185 Avenida La Pata, San Clemente CA 92673. (949)366-0030. E-mail: rich@wonews.com. Website: www.wonews.com. **Contact:** Rich Holland, editor. Estab. 1961. Circ. 100,000. Published 9 times/year. Emphasizes fishing and boating "for Far West states." Sample copy free. Editorial and photo guidelines free with SASE.

NEEDS Uses 80-85 photos/issue; 70% supplied by freelancers; 80% comes from assignments, 25% from stock. Needs photos of fishing in California, Oregon, Washington, Baja. Most photos purchased with accompanying manuscript. Model/property release preferred for women and men in brief attire. Photo captions required.

SPECS Prefers images in digital format.

MAKING CONTACT & TERMS Query or send photos with SASE for consideration. Responds in 3 weeks. Pays $50-150 for color inside; $300-400 for color cover; $400-600 for text/photo package. **Pays on acceptance.** Buys one-time rights for photos only; first North American serial rights for articles; electronic rights are negotiable.

TIPS "Submissions should be of interest to Western fishermen, and should include a 1,120- to 1,500-word manuscript; a Trip Facts Box (where to stay, costs, special information); photos; captions; and a map of the area. Emphasis is on fishing how-to, somewhere-to-go. Submit seasonal material 6 months in advance. Query only; no unsolicited manuscripts. Make your photos tell the story, and don't depend on captions to explain what is pictured. Get action shots, live fish. In fishing, we seek individual action or underwater shots. For cover photos, use vertical format composed with action entering picture from right; leave enough left-hand margin for cover blurbs, space at top of frame for magazine logo. Add human element to scenics to lend scale. Get to know the magazine and its editors. Ask for the year's editorial schedule (available through advertising department), and offer cover photos to match the theme of an issue. In samples, looks for color saturation, pleasing use of color components; originality, creativity; attractiveness of human subjects, as well as fish; above all—sharp, sharp, sharp focus! "

$ ◐ WEST SUBURBAN LIVING MAGAZINE

C2 Publishing, Inc., P.O. Box 111, Elmhurst IL 60126. (630)834-4994. Fax: (630)834-4996. E-mail: wsl@westsuburbanliving.net. Website: www.westsuburbanliving.net. Estab. 1995. Circ. 25,000. Bimonthly regional magazine serving the western suburbs of Chicago. Sample copies available.

NEEDS Photos of babies/children/teens, couples, families, senior citizens, landscapes/scenics, architecture, gardening, interiors/decorating, entertainment, events, food/drink, health/fitness/beauty, performing arts, travel. Interested in seasonal. Model release required. Photo captions required.

MAKING CONTACT & TERMS Responds only if interested; send nonreturnable samples. Simultaneous submissions and previously published work OK. Credit line given. Buys one-time rights, first rights, all rights; negotiable.

$$ WOODMEN LIVING

Woodmen Tower, 1700 Farnam St., Omaha NE 68102. (402)342-1890. Fax: (402)271-7269. E-mail: service@woodmen.com. Website: www.woodmen.org. **Contact:** Billie Jo Foust, editor. Estab. 1890. Circ. 480,000. Quarterly magazine published by Woodmen of the World/Omaha Woodmen Life Insurance Society. Emphasizes American family life. Sample copy and photo guidelines free.

NEEDS Buys 10-12 photos/year. Needs photos of the following themes: historic, family, insurance, humorous, photo essay/photo feature, human interest and health. Model release required. Photo captions preferred.

SPECS Uses 8×10 glossy b&w prints on occasion; 35mm, 2¼×2¼, 4×5 transparencies; for cover: 4×5 transparencies, vertical format preferred. Accepts images in digital format. Send high-res scans via CD.

MAKING CONTACT & TERMS Send material by mail with SASE for consideration. Responds in 1 month. Previously published work OK. Pays $500-600 for cover; $250 minimum for color inside. **Pays on acceptance.** Credit line given on request. Buys one-time rights.

TIPS "Submit good, sharp pictures that will reproduce well."

WHISKEY ISLAND MAGAZINE

Cleveland State University, English Dept., 2121 Euclid Ave., Cleveland OH 44115-2214. (216)687-2000. E-mail: whiskeyisland@csuohio.edu. Website: www.csuohio.edu/class/english/whiskeyisland. "This is a nonprofit literary magazine that has been published (in one form or another) by students of Cleveland State University for over 30 years. Also features the Annual Student Creative Writing Contest." Biannual literary magazine publishing extremely contemporary writing. Sample copy available for $6. Photo guidelines available with SASE.

NEEDS Uses 10 photos/issue; 20 photos/year. Interested in mixed media, alternative process, avant garde, fine art. Surreal and abstract are welcome. Do not send sentimental images, "rust-belt" scenes, photos of Cleveland, straight landscapes, or anything that can be viewed as "romantic." Model/property release preferred. Photo captions required; include title of work, photographer's name, address, phone number, e-mail, etc.

SPECS Accepts images in digital format. Send via e-mail attachment as individual, high-res JPEG files. No TIFFs. No disks.

MAKING CONTACT & TERMS E-mail with sample images. Do not just send your website link. Does not keep samples on file; responds in 3 months. Pays 2 contributor's copies and a 1-year subscription. Credit line given. Include as much contact information as possible.

$ $ WINE & SPIRITS

2 W. 32nd St., Suite 601, New York NY 10001. (212)695-4660, ext. 15. E-mail: elenab@wineandspiritsmagazine.com; info@wineandspiritsmagazine.com. Website: www.wineandspiritsmagazine.com. **Contact:** Elena Bessarabova, art director. Estab. 1985. Circ. 70,000. Bimonthly. Emphasizes wine. Readers are male, ages 39-60, married, parents, $70,000-plus income, wine consumers. Sample copy available for $4.95; Special issues are $4.95-6.50 each.

NEEDS Buys 0-30 photos from freelancers/issue; 0-180 photos/year. Needs photos of food, wine, travel, people. Photo captions preferred; include date, location.

SPECS Accepts images in digital format. Send via SyQuest, ZIP at 300 dpi.

MAKING CONTACT & TERMS Submit portfolio for review. Provide résumé, business card, brochure, flier or tearsheets to be kept on file for possible future assignments. Responds in 2 weeks, if interested. Simultaneous submissions OK. Pays $200-1,000/job. Pays on publication. Credit line given. Buys one-time rights.

$ WISCONSIN SNOWMOBILE NEWS

P.O. Box 182, Rio WI 53960-0182. (920)992-6370. Website: www.sledder.net. **Contact:** Cathy Hanson, editor. Estab. 1969. Circ. 30,000. Published 7 times/year. Official publication of the Association of Wisconsin Snowmobile Clubs. Emphasizes snowmobiling. Sample copy free with 9×12 SASE and 5 first-class stamps.

NEEDS Buys very few stand-alone photos from freelancers. "Most photos are purchased in conjunction with a story (photo/text) package. Photos need to be Midwest region only!" Needs photos of family-oriented snowmobile action, posed snowmobiles, travel. Model/property release preferred. Photo captions preferred; include where, what, when.

SPECS Uses 8×10 glossy color and b&w prints; 35mm, 2¼×2¼, 4×5, 8×10 transparencies. Digital files accepted at 300 dpi.

MAKING CONTACT & TERMS Submit portfolio for review. Send unsolicited photos by mail for consideration; include SASE for return of material. Provide résumé, business card, brochure, flier or tearsheets to be kept on file for possible future assignments. Responds in 2 weeks. Simultaneous submissions and previously published work OK. Pays $10-50 for color photos. Pays on publication. Credit line given. Buys one-time rights, all rights; negotiable.

WOODSHOP NEWS

Soundings Publications, Inc., 10 Bokum Rd., Essex CT 06426. (860)767-8227. Fax: (860)767-1048. E-mail: editorial@woodshopnews.com. Website: www.woodshopnews.com. **Contact:** Tod Riggio, editor. Estab. 1986. Circ. 60,000. Monthly trade magazine (tabloid format) covering all areas of professional woodworking. Sample copies available.

NEEDS Buys 12 sets of cover photos from freelancers/year. Photos of celebrities, architecture, interiors/decorating, industry, product shots/still life. Interested in documentary. "We assign our cover story, which is always a profile of a professional woodworker. These photo shoots are done in the subject's shop and feature working shots, portraits and photos of subject's finished work." Photo captions required; include description of activity contained in shots. "Photo captions will be written in-house based on this information."

SPECS Prefers digital photos.

MAKING CONTACT & TERMS Send query letter with résumé, photocopies, tearsheets. Provide self-promotion piece to be kept on file for possible future assignments. Responds only if interested; send nonreturnable samples. Previously published work OK occasionally. Pays $600-800 for color cover. Note: "We want a cover photo 'package'—one shot for the cover, others for use inside with the cover story." **Pays on acceptance.** Credit line given. Buys "perpetual" rights, but will pay a lower fee for one-time rights.

TIPS "I need a list of photographers in every geographical region of the country—I never know where our next cover profile will be done, so I need to have options everywhere. Familiarity with woodworking is a definite plus. Listen to our instructions! We have very specific lighting and composition needs, but some photographers ignore instructions in favor of creating 'artsy' photos, which we do not use, or poorly lighted photos, which we cannot use."

$$ ◎ ● YANKEE MAGAZINE

1121 Main St., P.O. Box 520, Dublin NH 03444. (603)563-8111. E-mail: heatherm@yankeepub.com. Website: www.yankeemagazine.com. **Contact:** Heather Marcus, photo editor; Lori Pedrick, art director. Estab. 1935. Circ. 350,000. Monthly. Emphasizes general interest within New England, with national distribution. Readers are of all ages and backgrounds; majority are actually outside of New England. Sample copy available for $1.95. Photo guidelines free with SASE or on website. "We give assignments to experienced professionals. If you want to work with us, show us a portfolio of your best work. Contact our photo editor before sending any photography to our art department. Please do not send any unsolicited original photography or artwork."

NEEDS Buys 56–80 photos from freelancers/issue; 672–960 photos/year. Needs photos of landscapes/scenics, wildlife, gardening, interiors/decorating. "Always looking for outstanding photo essays or portfolios shot in New England." Model/property release preferred. Photo captions required; include name, locale, pertinent details.

MAKING CONTACT & TERMS Submit portfolio for review. Keeps samples on file; include SASE for return of material. Responds in 1 month. Simultaneous submissions and previously published work OK. Pays $800–1,000 for color cover; $150–700 for color inside. Credit line given. Buys one-time rights; negotiable.

TIPS "Submit only top-notch work. Submit the work you love. Prefer to see focused portfolio, even of personal work, over general 'I can do everything' type of books."

$ YOUTH RUNNER MAGAZINE

P.O. Box 1156, Lake Oswego OR 97035. (503)236-2524. Fax: (503)620-3800. E-mail: dank@youthrunner.com. Website: www.youthrunner.com. **Contact:** Dan Kesterson, editor. Estab. 1996. Circ. 100,000. Publishes 10 issues per year. Features track, cross country and road racing for young athletes, ages 8-18. Photo guidelines available on website.

NEEDS Uses 30–50 photos/issue. Also uses photos on website daily. Needs action shots from track, cross country and indoor meets. Model release preferred; property release required. Photo captions preferred.

SPECS Accepts images in digital format only. Send via e-mail or CD.

MAKING CONTACT & TERMS Send low-res photos via e-mail first or link to gallery for consideration. Responds to e-mail submissions immediately. Simultaneous submissions OK. Pays $25 minimum. Credit line given. Buys electronic rights, all rights.

NEWSPAPERS

When working with newspapers, always remember that time is of the essence. Newspapers have various deadlines for each of their sections. An interesting feature or news photo has a better chance of getting in the next edition if the subject is timely and has local appeal. Most of the markets in this section are interested in regional coverage. Find publications near you and contact editors to get an understanding of their deadline schedules.

More and more newspapers are accepting submissions in digital format. In fact, most newspapers prefer digital images. However, if you submit to a newspaper that still uses film, ask the editors if they prefer certain types of film or if they want color slides or black-and-white prints. Many smaller newspapers do not have the capability to run color images, so black-and-white prints are preferred. However, color slides and prints can be converted to black and white. Editors who have the option of running color or black-and-white photos often prefer color film because of its versatility.

Although most newspapers rely on staff photographers, some hire freelancers as stringers for certain stories. Act professionally and build an editor's confidence in you by supplying innovative images. For example, don't get caught in the trap of shooting "grip-and-grin"' photos when a corporation executive is handing over a check to a nonprofit organization. Turn the scene into an interesting portrait. Capture some spontaneous interaction between the recipient and the donor. By planning ahead you can be creative.

When you receive assignments, think about the image before you snap your first photo. If you are scheduled to meet someone at a specific location, arrive early and scout around. Find a proper setting or locate some props to use in the shoot. Do whatever you can to show the editor you are willing to make that extra effort.

Always try to retain resale rights to shots of major news events. High news value means high resale value, and strong news photos can be resold repeatedly. If you have an image with national appeal, search for larger markets, possibly through the wire services. You also may find buyers among national news magazines such as *Time* or *Newsweek*.

While most newspapers offer low payment for images, they are willing to negotiate if the image will have a major impact. Front-page artwork often sells newspapers, so don't underestimate the worth of your images.

🄯🅢 ✇ AMERICAN SPORTS NETWORK

Box 6100, Rosemead CA 91770. (626)280-0000. Fax: (626)280-0001. E-mail: info@asntv.com. Website: www.fitnessamerica.com. Circ. 873,007. Publishes 4 newspapers covering "general collegiate, amateur and professional sports, e.g., football, baseball, basketball, wrestling, boxing, powerlifting and bodybuilding, fitness, health contests, etc." Also publishes special bodybuilder annual calendar, collegiate and professional football pre-season and post-season editions.

NEEDS Buys 10–80 photos from freelancers/issue for various publications. Needs "sport action, hard-hitting contact, emotion-filled photos." Model release preferred. Photo captions preferred.

MAKING CONTACT & TERMS Send 8×10 glossy b&w prints, 4×5 transparencies, video demo reel, or film work by mail for consideration. Include SASE for return of material. Provide résumé, business card, brochure, flyer or tearsheets to be kept on file for possible future assignments. Simultaneous submissions and previously published work OK. Negotiates rates by the job and hour. Pays on publication. Buys first North American serial rights.

🄯 THE ANGLICAN JOURNAL

(416)924-9192. Fax: (416)921-4452. E-mail: editor@anglicanjournal.com. Website: www.anglicanjournal.com. Estab. 1875. Circ. 175,000. Covers news of interest to Anglicans in Canada and abroad.

SPECS Reviews GIF/JPEG files (high resolution at 300 ppi).

MAKING CONTACT & TERMS Identification of subjects required. Negotiates payment individually. Buys all rights.

🄯 O AQUARIUS

1035 Green St., Roswell GA 30075. (770)641-9055. Fax: (770)641-8502. E-mail: felica@aquarius-atlanta.com; gloria@aquarius-atlanta.com. Website: www.aquarius-atlanta.com/. **Contact:** Felica Hicks, creative director; Gloria Parker, publisher/editor. Estab. 1991. Circ. 50,000; readership online: 110,000. Monthly. "Emphasizes New Age, metaphysical, holistic health, alternative religion; environmental audience primarily middle-aged, college-educated, computer-literate, open to exploring new ideas. Our mission is to publish a newspaper for the purpose of expanding awareness and supporting all those seeking spiritual growth. We are committed to excellence and integrity in an atmo-sphere of harmony and love." Sample copy available with SASE.

NEEDS "We use photos of authors, musicians, and photos that relate to our articles, but we have no budget to pay photographers at this time. We offer byline in paper, website, and copies." Needs photos of New Age and holistic health, celebrities, multicultural, environmental, religious, adventure, entertainment, events, health/fitness, performing arts, travel, medicine, technology, alternative healing processes. Interested in coverage on environmental issues, genetically altered foods, photos of "anything from Sufi Dancers to Zen Masters." Model/property release required. Photo captions required; include photographer's name, subject's name, and description of content.

SPECS Uses color and b&w photos. Accepts images in digital format. Send via ZIP, e-mail as JPEG files at 300 dpi.

MAKING CONTACT & TERMS Send query letter with photocopies and/or tearsheets, or e-mail samples with cover letter. Provide résumé, business card or self-promotion piece to be kept on file for possible future assignments. Pays in copies, byline with contact info (phone number, e-mail address published if photographer agrees).

🄯 🅢 O CATHOLIC SENTINEL

P.O. Box 18030, Portland OR 97218. (503)281-1191 or (800)548-8749. E-mail: sentinel@catholicsentinel.org. Website: www.sentinel.org. **Contact:** Robert Pfohman, editor. Estab. 1870. Circ. 8,000. Weekly. "We are the newspaper for the Catholic community in Oregon." Sample copies available with SASE. Photo guidelines available via e-mail.

NEEDS Buys 15 photos from freelancers/issue; 800 photos/year. Needs photos of religious and political subjects. Interested in seasonal. Model/property release preferred. Photo captions required; include names of people shown in photos, spelled correctly.

SPECS Prefers images in digital format. Send via e-mail or FTP as TIFF or JPEG files at 300 dpi. Also uses 5×7 glossy or matte color and b&w prints; 35mm 2×2, 4×5, 8×10 transparencies.

MAKING CONTACT & TERMS Send query letter with résumé and tearsheets. Portfolio may be dropped off every Thursday. Keeps samples on file. Responds only if interested; send nonreturnable samples. Simultaneous submissions and previously published work OK. Pays on publication or on receipt of photographer's invoice. Credit line given. Buys first rights and electronic rights.

TIPS "We use photos to illustrate editorial material, so all photography is on assignment. Basic knowledge of Catholic Church (e.g., don't climb on the altar) is a big plus. Send accurately spelled cutlines. Prefer images in digital format."

$ CHILDREN'S DEFENSE FUND

25 E St., NW, Washington D.C. 20001. (800)233-1200. E-mail: cdfinfo@childrensdefense.org. Website: www.childrensdefense.org. Children's advocacy organization.

NEEDS Buys 20 photos/year. Buys stock and assigns work. Wants to see photos of children of all ages and ethnicity—serious, playful, poor, middle class, school setting, home setting and health setting. Subjects include babies/children/teens, families, education, health/fitness/beauty. Some location work. Domestic photos only. Model/property release required.

SPECS Uses b&w and some color prints. Accepts images in digital format. Send via e-mail as TIFF, EPS, JPEG files at 300 dpi or better.

MAKING CONTACT & TERMS Provide résumé, business card, self-promotion piece or tearsheets to be kept on file for possible future assignments. Keeps photocopy samples on file. Previously published work OK. Pays on usage. Credit line given. Buys one-time rights; occasionally buys all rights.

TIPS Looks for "good, clear focus, nice composition, variety of settings and good expressions on faces."

🌐 $ THE CHURCH OF ENGLAND NEWSPAPER

14 Great College St., London SW1P 3RX, United Kingdom. +44(020)7878 1002. E-mail: cen@churchnewspaper.com; colin.blakely@churchnewspaper.com. Website: www.churchnewspaper.com. **Contact:** Colin Blakely, editor; Peter May, graphic designer. Estab. 1828. Circ. 12,000. Weekly religious newspaper. Sample copies available.

NEEDS Buys 2-3 photos from freelancers/issue; 100 photos/year. Needs political photos. Reviews photos with or without a manuscript. Photo captions required.

SPECS Uses glossy color prints; 35mm transparencies.

MAKING CONTACT & TERMS Does not keep samples on file; include SASE for return of material. Responds only if interested; send nonreturnable samples. Pays on publication. Credit line given. Buys one-right rights.

$ THE CLARION-LEDGER

201 S. Congress St., Jackson MS 39201. (601)961-7073; (877)850-5343. E-mail: dhampton@clarionledger.com. Website: www.clarionledger.com. **Contact:** David Hampton, editorial director. Circ. 95,000. Daily. Emphasizes photojournalism: news, sports, features, fashion, food and portraits. Readers are in a very broad age range of 18-70 years, male and female. Sample copies available.

NEEDS Buys 1-5 photos from freelancers/issue; 365-1,825 photos/year. Needs news, sports, features, portraits, fashion and food photos. Special photo needs include food and fashion. Model release required. Photo captions required.

SPECS Uses 8×10 matte b&w and color prints; 35mm slides/color negatives. Accepts images in digital format. Send via CD, e-mail as JPEG files at 200 dpi.

MAKING CONTACT & TERMS Provide résumé, business card, brochure, flyer or tearsheets to be kept on file for possible future assignments. Pays on publication. Credit line given. Buys one-time or all rights; negotiable.

$ [◎] [O] FULTON COUNTY DAILY REPORT

190 Pryor St. SW, Atlanta GA 30303. (404)521-1227. Fax: (404)659-4739. E-mail: jbennitt@alm.com. Website: www.dailyreportonline.com. **Contact:** Jason R. Bennitt, art director. Daily (5 times/week). Emphasizes legal news and business. Readers are male and female professionals, age 25+, involved in legal field, court system, legislature, etc. Sample copy available for $2 with 9¾×12¾ SASE and 6 first-class stamps.

NEEDS Buys 1–2 photos from freelancers/issue; 260-520 photos/year. Needs informal environmental photographs of lawyers, judges and others involved in legal news and business. Some real estate, etc. Photo captions preferred; include complete name of subject and date shot, along with other pertinent information. Two or more people should be identified from left to right.

SPECS Accepts images in digital format. Send via CD or e-mail as JPEG files at 200–600 dpi.

MAKING CONTACT & TERMS Submit portfolio for review. Mail or e-mail samples. Keeps samples on file.

Simultaneous submissions and previously published work OK. "Freelance work generally done on an assignment-only basis." Pays $75–100 for color cover; $50–75 for color inside. Credit line given.

TIPS Wants to see ability with "casual, environmental portraiture, people—especially in office settings, urban environment, courtrooms, etc.—and photojournalistic coverage of people in law or courtroom settings." In general, needs "competent, fast freelancers from time to time around the state of Georgia who can be called in at the last minute. We keep a list of them for reference. Good work keeps you on the list." Recommends that "when shooting for *FCDR*, it's best to avoid law-book-type photos if possible, along with other overused legal clichés."

◎ $ ◐ GRAND RAPIDS BUSINESS JOURNAL

549 Ottawa Ave., NW, Suite 201, Grand Rapids MI 49503-1444. (616)459-4545. Fax: (616)459-4800. E-mail: cvalade@geminipub.com. Website: www.grbj.com. Estab. 1983. Circ. 6,000. Weekly tabloid. Emphasizes West Michigan business community. Sample copy available for $1.

NEEDS Buys 5–10 photos from freelancers/issue; 520 photos/year. Needs photos of local community, manufacturing, world trade, stock market, etc. Model/property release required. Photo captions required.

MAKING CONTACT & TERMS Send query letter with résumé of credits, stock list. Responds in 1 month. Simultaneous submissions and previously published work OK. Pays on publication. Credit line given. Buys one-time rights and first North American serial rights; negotiable.

🍁 $ ◐ THE LAWYERS WEEKLY

123 Commerce Valley Dr., E., Suite 700, Markham ON L3T 7W8, Canada. (905)479-2665; (800)668-6481. Fax: (905)479-3758. E-mail: tim.wilbur@lexisnexis.ca. Website: www.thelawyersweekly.ca. **Contact:** Tammy Leung, art director; Tim Wilbur, managing editor. Estab. 1983. Circ. 20,300.

NEEDS Uses 12-20 photos/issue; 5 supplied by freelancers. Needs head shots of lawyers and judges mentioned in stories, as well as photos of legal events.

SPECS Accepts images in digital format. Send as JPEG, TIFF files.

MAKING CONTACT & TERMS Provide résumé, business card, brochure, flyer or tearsheets to be kept on file for possible future assignments. Deadlines: 1- to 2-day turnaround time. Does not keep samples on file; include SASE for return of material. Responds only when interested. **Pays on acceptance.** Credit line not given.

TIPS "We need photographers across Canada to shoot lawyers and judges on an as-needed basis. Send a résumé, and we will keep your name on file. Mostly b&w work."

$ ◎ ◐ THE LOG NEWSPAPER

17782 Cowan, Suite A, Irvine CA 92614. (949)660-6150. Fax: (949)660-6172. E-mail: eston@goboating.com. Website: www.thelog.com. **Contact:** Eston Ellis, editor. Estab. 1971. Circ. 41,018.

NEEDS Buys 5-10 photos from freelancers/issue; 130-260 photos/year. Needs photos of marine-related, recreational sailing/powerboating in Southern California. Photo captions required; include location, name and type of boat, owner's name, race description if applicable.

SPECS Accepts images in digital format. Send via e-mail as TIFF, EPS, JPEG files at 300 dpi or greater.

MAKING CONTACT & TERMS Simultaneous submissions and previously published work OK. Pays on publication. Credit line given. Buys all rights; negotiable.

TIPS "We want timely and newsworthy photographs! We always need photographs of people enjoying boating, especially power boating. 95% of our images are of California subjects."

$ NATIONAL MASTERS NEWS

P.O. Box 1117, Orangevale CA 95662. (916)989-6667. E-mail: nminfo@nationalmastersnews.com. Website: www.nationalmastersnews.com. Estab. 1977. Circ. 8,000. Monthly tabloid. Official world and U.S. publication for Masters (ages 30 and over)—track and field, long distance running, and race walking. Sample copy free with 9×12 SASE.

NEEDS Uses 25 photos/issue; 30% assigned and 70% from freelance stock. Needs photos of Masters athletes (men and women over age 30) competing in track and field events, long distance running races or racewalking competitions. Photo captions required.

MAKING CONTACT & TERMS Send any size matte or glossy b&w prints by mail for consideration; include SASE for return of material. Responds in 1 month. Simultaneous submissions and previously published work OK. Pays on publication. Credit line given. Buys one-time rights.

THE NEW YORK TIMES ON THE WEB

500 7th Ave., New York NY 10018. E-mail: web editor@nytimes.com. Website: www.nytimes.com. Circ. 1.3 million. Daily newspaper. "Covers breaking news and general interest." Sample copy available with SASE or online.

NEEDS Photos of celebrities, architecture, cities/urban, gardening, interiors/decorating, industry, medicine, military, political, product shots/still life, science, technology/computers, disasters, environmental, landscapes/scenics, wildlife, automobiles, entertainment, events, food/drink, health/fitness/beauty, hobbies, performing arts, sports, travel, alternative process, avant garde, documentary, fashion/glamour, fine art, breaking news. Model release required. Photo captions required.

SPECS Accepts images in digital format. Send via CD, e-mail as TIFF, JPEG files.

MAKING CONTACT & TERMS E-mail query letter with link to photographer's website. Provide business card, self-promotion piece to be kept on file for possible future assignments. Simultaneous submissions OK. Pays on publication. Credit line given. Buys one-time rights and electronic rights.

STREETPEOPLE'S WEEKLY NEWS

P.O. Box 270942, Dallas TX 75227-0942. E-mail: sw_n@yahoo.com. **Contact:** Lon G. Dorsey, Jr., publisher. Estab. 1977. Sample copy no longer available temporarily. "Seeking help to launch homeless television show and photo gallery."

Photographers needed in every metropolitan city in the U.S.

NEEDS Photos of babies/children/teens, celebrities, couples, multicultural, families, parents, senior citizens, cities/urban, education, pets, religious, rural, events, food/drink, health/fitness, hobbies, humor, political, technology/computers. Interested in alternative process, documentary, fine art, historical/vintage, seasonal. Subjects include: photojournalism on homeless or street people. Model/property release required. "All photos *must* be accompanied by *signed* model releases." Photo captions required.

SPECS Accepts images in digital format. Send via CD, e-mail as GIF, JPEG files. "Items to be considered for publishing must be in PDF from a *SWNews*-certified

photographer. Write first to gain certification with publisher."

MAKING CONTACT & TERMS "Hundreds of photographers are needed to show national state of America's homeless." Do not send unsolicited materials. Responds promptly. Pay scale information provided to *SWNews*-certified photographers. Pays extra for electronic usage (negotiable). Pays on acceptance or publication. Credit line sometimes given. Buys all rights; negotiable.

SUN

1000 American Media Way, Boca Raton FL 33464-1000. (561)989-1154. E-mail: acharles@amisunmag.com. **Contact:** Ann Charles, photo editor. Weekly tabloid. Readers are housewives, college students, middle Americans. Sample copy free with extra-large SASE.

NEEDS Buys 30 photos from freelancers/issue; 1,560 photos/year. Wants varied subjects: prophesies and predictions, amazing sightings (e.g., Jesus, Elvis, angels), stunts, unusual pets, health remedies, offbeat medical, human interest, inventions, spectacular sports action; offbeat pix and stories; and celebrity photos. "We are always in need of interesting, offbeat, humorous stand-alone pics." Model release preferred. Photo captions preferred.

SPECS Uses 8×10 b&w prints; 35mm transparencies. Accepts images in digital format.

MAKING CONTACT & TERMS Send query letter with stock list and samples. Responds in 2 weeks. Simultaneous submissions and previously published work OK. Pays on publication. Buys one-time rights.

TIPS "We are specifically looking for the unusual, offbeat, freakish true stories and photos. *Nothing* is too far out for consideration. We suggest you send for a sample copy and take it from there."

THE SUNDAY POST

2 Albert Square, Dundee DD1 9QJ, Scotland. (44)(1382)223131. Fax: (44)(1382)201064. E-mail: mail@sundaypost.com. Website: www.sundaypost.com. **Contact:** Alan Morrison, picture editor. Estab. 1919. Circ. 328,129. Readership 901,000. Weekly family newspaper.

NEEDS Photos of "UK news and news involving Scots," sports. Other specific needs: exclusive news pictures from the UK, especially Scotland. Reviews photos with accompanying manuscript only. Model/property release preferred. Photo captions required;

include contact details, subjects, date. "Save in the caption field of the file info METEADATA, so they can be viewed on our picture desk system. Mac users should ensure attachments are PC-compatible as we use PCs."

SPECS Prefers images in digital format. Send via e-mail as JPEG files. "We need a minimum 11MB file saved at quality level 9/70% or above, ideally at 200 ppi/dpi."

MAKING CONTACT & TERMS Send query letter with tearsheets, stock list. Does not keep samples on file; include SASE for return of material. Responds in 2 weeks to queries. Simultaneous submissions OK. Pays $150 (USD) for b&w or color cover; $100 (USD) for b&w or color inside. Pays on publication. Credit line not given. Buys single use, all editions, one date, worldwide rights; negotiable.

TIPS "Offer pictures by e-mail before sending: lo-res only, please—72 ppi, 800 pixels on the widest side; no more than 10 at a time. Make sure the daily papers aren't running the story first and that it's not being covered by the Press Association (PA). We get their pictures on our contracted feed."

SYRACUSE NEW TIMES

Alltimes Publishing, LLC, 1415 W. Genesee St., Syracuse NY 13204. E-mail: menglish@syracusenewtimes.com. E-mail: editorial@syracusenewtimes.com. Website: newtimes.rway.com. **Contact:** Molly English. Estab. 1969. Circ. 40,000. "*Syracuse New Times* is an alternative weekly that is topical, provocative, irreverent, and intensely local." 50% freelance written. Publishes ms an average of 1 month after acceptance. Submit seasonal material 3 months in advance. Sample copy available with 8×10 SASE.

NEEDS Photos of performing arts. Interested in alternative process, fine art, seasonal. Reviews photos with or without a manuscript. Model/property release required. Photo captions required; include names of subjects.

SPECS Uses 5×7 b&w prints; 35mm transparencies.

MAKING CONTACT & TERMS Send query letter with résumé, stock list. Does not keep samples on file; include SASE for return of material. Responds in 6 weeks. Responds only if interested; send nonreturnable samples. Previously published work OK. Pays on publication. Credit line given. Buys one-time rights.

TIPS "Realize the editor is busy and responds as promptly as possible."

🍁 $$ TORONTO SUN PUBLISHING

333 King St. E., Toronto ON M5A 3X5, Canada. (416)947-2399. Fax: (416)947-1664. E-mail: jim.thomson@sunmedia.ca. Website: www.torontosun.com. **Contact:** Jim Thomson, photo editor. Estab. 1971. Circ. 180,000. Daily. Emphasizes sports, news and entertainment. Sample copy free with SASE.

NEEDS Uses 30–50 photos/issue; occasionally uses freelancers (spot news pics only). Needs photos of Toronto personalities making news out of town. Also disasters, beauty, sports, fashion/glamour. Reviews photos with or without a manuscript. Photo captions preferred.

SPECS Accepts images in digital format. Send via CD or e-mail.

MAKING CONTACT & TERMS Arrange a personal interview to show portfolio. Send any size color prints; 35mm transparencies; press link digital format. Deadline: 11 p.m. daily. Does not keep samples on file. Responds in 1–2 weeks. Simultaneous submissions and previously published work OK. Pays on publication. Credit line given. Buys one-time and other negotiated rights.

TIPS "The squeaky wheel gets the grease when it delivers the goods. Don't try to oversell a questionable photo. Return calls promptly."

VENTURA COUNTY REPORTER

700 E. Main St., Ventura CA 93001. (805)648-2244. Fax: (805)648-2245. E-mail: editor@vcreporter.com. Website: www.vcreporter.com. Enrique Candioti, art director (artdirector@vcreporter.com). **Contact:** Michael Sullivan, editor. Circ. 35,000. Weekly tabloid covering local news (entertainment and environment).

NEEDS Uses 12-14 photos/issue; 40-45% supplied by freelancers. "We require locally slanted photos (Ventura County, CA)." Model release required.

SPECS Accepts images in digital format. Send via e-mail or CD.

MAKING CONTACT & TERMS Send sample b&w or color original photos; include SASE for return of material. Simultaneous submissions OK. Pays on publication. Credit line given. Buys one-time rights.

$ WATERTOWN PUBLIC OPINION

120 3rd Ave., NW, P.O. Box 10, Watertown SD 57201. (605)886-6901. Fax: (605)886-4280. E-mail: dougm@thepublicopinion.com. Website: www.thepublic

opinion.com. **Contact:** Doug Mack, creative coordinator. Estab. 1887. Circ. 15,000. Daily. Emphasizes general news of the region; state, national and international news.

NEEDS Uses up to 8 photos/issue. Reviews photos with or without a manuscript. Model release required. Photo captions required.

SPECS Uses b&w or color prints. Accepts images in digital format. Send via CD.

MAKING CONTACT & TERMS Send unsolicited photos by mail for consideration. Does not keep samples on file; include SASE for return of material. Responds in 1-2 weeks. Simultaneous submissions OK. Pays on publication. Credit line given. Buys one-time rights; negotiable.

🍁 $ ◐ THE WESTERN PRODUCER

P.O. Box 2500, 2310 Millar Ave., Saskatoon SK S7K 2C4, Canada. (306)665-9629. Fax: (306)933-9536. E-mail: robert.magnell@producer.com. Website: www.producer.com. **Contact:** Robert Magnell, creative director. Estab. 1923. Circ. 70,000. Weekly. Emphasizes agriculture and rural living in western Canada. Photo guidelines free with SASE.

NEEDS Buys 5–8 photos from freelancers/issue; 260–416 photos/year. Needs photos of farm families, environmental, gardening, science, livestock, nature, human interest, scenic, rural, agriculture, day-to-day rural life and small communities. Interested in documentary. Model/property release preferred. Photo captions required; include person's name, location, and description of activity.

SPECS Accepts images in digital format. Send via CD, ZIP, e-mail as TIFF, EPS, PICT files at 300 dpi.

MAKING CONTACT & TERMS Send material for consideration by mail or e-mail to the attention of the news editor; include SASE for return of material if sending by mail. Previously published work OK, "but let us know." Pays on publication. Credit line given. Buys one-time rights.

TIPS Needs current photos of farm and agricultural news. "Don't waste postage on abandoned, derelict farm buildings or sunset photos. We want modern scenes with life in them—people or animals, preferably both." Also seeks items on agriculture, rural western Canada, history and contemporary life in rural western Canada.

TRADE PUBLICATIONS

Most trade publications are directed toward the business community in an effort to keep readers abreast of the ever-changing trends and events in their specific professions. For photographers, shooting for these publications can be financially rewarding and can serve as a stepping stone toward acquiring future assignments.

As often happens with this category, the number of trade publications produced increases or decreases as professions develop or deteriorate. In recent years, for example, magazines involving new technology have flourished as the technology continues to grow and change.

Trade publication readers are usually very knowledgeable about their businesses or professions. The editors and photo editors, too, are often experts in their particular fields. So, with both the readers and the publications' staffs, you are dealing with a much more discriminating audience. To be taken seriously, your photos must not be merely technically good pictures, but also should communicate a solid understanding of the subject and reveal greater insights.

In particular, photographers who can communicate their knowledge in both verbal and visual form will often find their work more in demand. If you have such expertise, you may wish to query about submitting a photo/text package that highlights a unique aspect of working in a particular profession or that deals with a current issue of interest to that field.

Many photos purchased by these publications come from stock—both freelance inventories and stock photo agencies. Generally, these publications are more conservative with their freelance budgets and use stock as an economical alternative. For this reason, some listings in this section will advise sending a stock list as an initial method of contact. (See sample stock list in "Running Your Business.") Some of the more established publications with larger circulations and advertising bases will sometimes offer assignments as they become familiar with a particular photographer's work. For the most part, though, stock remains the primary means of breaking in and doing business with this market.

⑤ ➊ ⓞ AAP NEWS

141 Northwest Point Blvd., Elk Grove Village IL 60007. (847)434-4755. Fax: (847)434-8000. E-mail: mhayes@aap.org. Website: www.aapnews.org. **Contact:** Michael Hayes, art director/production coordinator. Estab. 1985. Monthly tabloid newspaper. Publication of American Academy of Pediatrics.

NEEDS Uses 60 photos/year. Needs photos of babies/children/teens, families, health/fitness, sports, travel, medicine, pediatricians, health care providers—news magazine style. Interested in documentary. Model/property release required as needed. Photo captions required; include names, dates, locations and explanations of situations.

SPECS Accepts images in digital format. Send via CD, floppy disk, Jaz, ZIP, e-mail as TIFF, EPS, JPEG files at 300 dpi.

MAKING CONTACT & TERMS Provide résumé, business card or tearsheets to be kept on file (for 1 year) for possible future assignments. Cannot return material. Simultaneous submissions and previously published work OK. Pays $50–150 for one-time use of photo. Pays on publication. Buys one-time or all rights; negotiable.

TIPS "We want great photos of real children in real-life situations—the more diverse the better."

⑤⑤⑤ ● ABA BANKING JOURNAL

Simmons-Boardman Publishing Corp., 345 Hudson St., 12th Floor, New York NY 10014. (212)620-7200. E-mail: scocheo@sbpub.com; wwilliams@sbpub.com. Website: www.ababj.com. **Contact:** Steve Cocheo, executive editor; Wendy Williams, art director. Estab. 1909. Circ. 30,000. Monthly magazine. Emphasizes "how to manage a bank better. Bankers read it to find out how to keep up with changes in regulations, lending practices, investments, technology, marketing and what other bankers are doing to increase community standing."

NEEDS Buys 6 photos/year; freelance photography is 20% assigned, 80% from stock. Personality, and occasionally photos of unusual bank displays or equipment. "We need candid photos of various bankers who are subjects of articles." Photos purchased with accompanying ms or on assignment.

SPECS Uses 35mm transparencies. Accepts images in digital format. Send via CD, e-mail as CMYK JPEG files at 300 dpi.

MAKING CONTACT & TERMS Send query letter with samples, postcards; include SASE for return of material. Responds in 1 month. Pays $400-1,500/photo. **Pays on acceptance.** Credit line given. Buys one-time rights.

TIPS "Send postcard. We hire by location, city."

ACRES U.S.A.

P.O. Box 91299, Austin TX 78709-1299. (512)892-4400. Fax: (512)892-4448. E-mail: editor@acresusa.com. Website: www.acresusa.com. Estab. 1970. Circ. 18,000. "Monthly trade journal written by people who have a sincere interest in the principles of organic and sustainable agriculture."

SPECS Reviews GIF/JPEG/TIFF files.

MAKING CONTACT & TERMS Captions, identification of subjects required. Negotiates payment individually. Buys one time rights.

➊ ⑤ ⓞ AFTERMARKET BUSINESS WORLD

Advanstar Communications, 24950 Country Club Blvd., Suite 200, North Olmsted OH 44070. (440)891-2746. Fax: (440)891-2675. E-mail: kmcnamara@advanstar.com. Website: www.aftermarketbusiness.com. **Contact:** Krista McNamara, content manager. Estab. 1936. Circ. 41,821. The mission of *Aftermarket Business World* (formerly *Aftermarket Business*) involves satisfying the needs of U.S. readers who want to do business here and elsewhere and helping readers in other countries who want to do business with U.S. companies. "Being an electronic publication assures us that we can reach just about anybody, anywhere." New editorial material for *Aftermarket Business World* will focus on news, trends and analysis about the international automotive aftermarket. The publication features a new column, "Beyond Borders," by Karen Fierst, a well-known and well-traveled global consultant. Fierst's monthly column provides in-depth understanding of countries around the world including the cultural, political, marketing and logistical information that make each country unique. Written for corporate executives and key decision-makers responsible for buying automotive products (parts, accessories, chemicals) and other services sold at retail to consumers and professional installers. It's the oldest continuously published business magazine covering the retail automotive aftermarket and is the only publication dedicated to the specialized needs of this industry." Sample copies available; call (888)527-7008 for rates.

NEEDS Buys 0-1 photo from freelancers/issue; 12-15 photos/year. Needs photos of automobiles, product shots/still life. "Review our editorial calendar to see what articles are being written. We use lots of conceptual material." Model/property release preferred.

SPECS Prefers images in digital format. Send via CD, Zip, e-mail as TIFF, JPEG files at 300 dpi. Also uses 35mm, 2¼×2¼ transparencies.

MAKING CONTACT & TERMS Send query letter with slides, transparencies, stock list. Provide business card or self-promotion piece to be kept on file for possible future assignments. Responds only if interested; send nonreturnable samples. Pay negotiable. Pays on publication. Credit line given. "Corporate policy requires all freelancers to sign a print and online usage contract for stories and photos." Usually buys one-time rights.

TIPS "We can't stress enough the importance of knowing our audience. We are not a magazine aimed at car dealers. Our readers are auto parts distributors. Looking through sample copies will show you a lot about what we need. Show us a variety of stock and lots of it. Send only dupes."

AG WEEKLY

Lee Agri-Media, P.O. Box 507, Twin Falls ID 83303. (208)735-3221. Fax: (208)734-9667. E-mail: mark.conlon@lee.net. Website: www.agweekly.com. **Contact:** Mark Conlon, editor. Circ. 12,402. *Ag Weekly* is an agricultural publication covering production, markets, regulation, politics.

SPECS Reviews GIF/JPEG files.

MAKING CONTACT & TERMS Captions required. Offers $10/photo. Buys one time rights.

🔊 💲 🅾 AIR LINE PILOT

1625 Massachusetts Ave., NW, Washington D.C. 20036. (703)698-2270. E-mail: magazine@alpa.org. Website: www.alpa.org. **Contact:** Pete Janhunen, publications manager. Estab. 1931. Circ. 90,000. Publication of Air Line Pilots Association. Publishes 10 issues/year. Emphasizes news and feature stories for airline pilots. Photo guidelines available online.

NEEDS Buys 3–4 photos from freelancers/issue; 18–24 photos/year. Needs dramatic 35mm transparencies, prints or high-res images on disk or CD of commercial aircraft, pilots and co-pilots performing work-related activities in or near their aircraft. "Pilots must be ALPA members in good standing. Our editorial staff can verify status." Special needs include dramatic images technically and aesthetically suitable for full-page magazine covers. Especially needs vertical composition scenes. Model release required. Photo captions required; include aircraft type, airline, location of photo/scene, description of action, date, identification of people and which airline they work for. "Our greatest need is for strikingly original cover photographs featuring ALPA flight deck crew members and their airlines in their operating environment. See list of airlines with ALPA Pilots online."

SPECS Accepts images in digital format. Uses original 35mm or larger slides; Fuji Velvia 50 film preferred.

MAKING CONTACT & TERMS Send query letter with samples. Send unsolicited photos by mail with SASE for consideration. "Currently use 2 local outside vendors for assignment photography. Occasionally need professional news photographer for location work. Most freelance work is on speculative basis only." No simultaneous submissions. Pays $350 for cover (buys all rights); Fees for inside are negotiable (buys one-time rights). **Pays on acceptance.**

TIPS In photographer's samples, wants to see "strong composition, poster-like quality and high technical quality. Photos compete with text for space, so they need to be very interesting to be published. Be sure to provide brief but accurate caption information and send only professional-quality work. Cover images should show airline pilots at work or in the airport going to work. For covers, please shoot vertical images. Check website for criteria and requirements. Send samples of slides to be returned upon review. Make appointment to show portfolio."

● AMERICAN BAR ASSOCIATION JOURNAL

321 N. Clark St., 20th Floor, Chicago IL 60654. (312)988-6018; (800)285-2221. E-mail: robert.fernandez@americanbar.org; debora.clark@americanbar.org. Website: www.abajournal.com. **Contact:** Robert Fernandez, design director; Debora Clark, deputy design director. Estab. 1915. Circ. 500,000. Monthly magazine of the American Bar Association. Emphasizes law and the legal profession. Readers are lawyers. Photo guidelines available.

NEEDS Buys 45-90 photos from freelancers/issue; 540-1,080 photos/year. Needs vary; mainly shots of lawyers and clients by assignment only.
SPECS Prefers digital images sent via CD as TIFF files at 300 dpi.
MAKING CONTACT & TERMS "Send us your website address to view samples. If samples are good, portfolio will be requested." Cannot return unsolicited material. Payment negotiable. Credit line given. Buys one-time rights.
TIPS "No phone calls! The *ABA Journal* does not hire beginners."

$ AMERICAN BEE JOURNAL

51 S. Second St., Hamilton IL 62341. (217)847-3324. Fax: (217)847-3660. E-mail: editor@americanbeejournal.com. Website: www.americanbeejournal.com. **Contact:** Joe B. Graham, editor. Estab. 1861. Circ. 13,500. Monthly trade magazine. Emphasizes beekeeping for hobby and professional beekeepers. Sample copy free with SASE.
NEEDS Buys 1–2 photos from freelancers/issue; 12–24 photos/year. Needs photos of beekeeping and related topics, beehive products, honey and cooking with honey. Special needs include color photos of seasonal beekeeping scenes. Model release preferred. Photo captions preferred.
MAKING CONTACT & TERMS Send query e-mail with samples. Send thumbnail samples to e-mail. Send 5×7 or 8½×11 color prints by mail for consideration; include SASE for return of material. Responds in 2 weeks. Pays $75 for color cover; $25 for color inside. Pays on publication. Credit line given. Buys all rights. Submission guidelines available online.

$ ◎ ◐ AMERICAN POWER BOAT ASSOCIATION

17640 E. Nine Mile Rd., Box 377, Eastpointe MI 48021-0377. (586)773-9700. Fax: (586)773-6490. E-mail: propeller@apba-racing.com. Website: www.apba-racing.com. **Contact:** Tana Moore, publications editor. Estab. 1903. Sanctioning body for U.S. power boat racing; monthly magazine. Majority of assignments made on annual basis. Photos used in monthly magazine, brochures, audiovisual presentations, press releases, programs and website.
NEEDS Photos of APBA boat racing—action and candid. Interested in documentary, historical/vintage. Photo captions or class/driver ID required.
SPECS Accepts images in digital format. Send via CD, e-mail as TIFF, EPS, JPEG files at 300 dpi.
MAKING CONTACT & TERMS Initial personal contact preferred. Suggests initial contact by e-mail; JPEG samples or link to website welcome. Provide business card to be kept on file for possible future assignments. Responds in 2 weeks when needed. Payment varies. Standard is $25 for color cover; $15 for interior pages. Credit line given. Buys one-time rights; negotiable. Photo usage must be invoiced by photographer within the month incurred.
TIPS Prefers to see selection of shots of power boats in action or pit shots, candids, etc., (all identified). Must show ability to produce clear color action shots of racing events. "Send a few samples with e-mail, especially if related to boat racing."

ANGUS BEEF BULLETIN

Angus Productions, Inc., 3201 Frederick Ave., St. Joseph MO 64506-2997. (816)383-5270. Fax: (816)233-6575. E-mail: shermel@angusjournal.com. Website: www.angusbeefbulletin.com. **Contact:** Shauna Rose Hermel, editor. Estab. 1985. Circ. 97,000. Mailed free to commercial cattlemen who have purchased an Angus bull and had the registration transferred to them and to others who sign a request card.
SPECS Reviews 5×7 transparencies, 5×7 glossy prints.
MAKING CONTACT & TERMS Identification of subjects required. Offers $25/photo. Buys all rights.

ANGUS JOURNAL

Angus Productions Inc., 3201 Frederick Ave., St. Joseph MO 64506-2997. (816)383-5270. Fax: (816)233-6575. E-mail: shermel@angusjournal.com. Website: www.angusjournal.com. Estab. 1919. Circ. 13,500. The *Angus Journal* is the official magazine of the American Angus Association. Its primary function as such is to report to the membership association activities and information pertinent to raising Angus cattle.
SPECS Reviews 5×7 glossy prints.
MAKING CONTACT & TERMS Identification of subjects required. Offers $25-400/photo. Buys all rights.

$ ◐ ANIMAL SHELTERING

2100 L St., Washington D.C. 20037. (301)258-3008. Fax: (301)721-6468. E-mail: asm@hsus.org. Website: www.animalsheltering.org. Carrie Allan, editor. **Contact:** Shevaun Brannigan, production/marketing manager. Estab. 1978. Circ. 6,000. Published 6 times a year; magazine of The Humane Society of the United States. Magazine for animal care professionals and volunteers, dealing with animal welfare issues faced by animal shelters, animal control agencies, and rescue groups. Emphasis on news for the field and professional, hands-on work. Readers are shelter and animal control directors, kennel staff, field officers, humane investigators, animal control officers, animal rescuers, foster care volunteers, general volunteers, shelter veterinarians, and anyone concerned with local animal welfare issues. Sample copy free.

NEEDS Buys about 2–10 photos from freelancers/issue; 30 photos/year. Needs photos of pets interacting with animal control and shelter workers; animals in shelters, including farm animals and wildlife; general public visiting shelters and adopting animals; humane society work, functions, and equipment. Photo captions preferred.

SPECS Accepts color images in digital or print format. Send via CD, ZIP, e-mail as TIFF, JPEG files at 300 dpi.

MAKING CONTACT & TERMS Provide samples of work to be kept on file for possible future use or assignments; include SASE for return of material. Responds in 1 month. Pays $150 for cover; $75 for inside. Pays on publication. Credit line given. Buys one-time and electronic rights.

TIPS "We almost always need good photos of people working with animals in an animal shelter or in the field. We do not use photos of individual dogs, cats and other companion animals as often as we use photos of people working to protect, rescue or care for dogs, cats and other companion animals. Contact us for upcoming needs."

💲💲 ◐ AOPA PILOT

421 Aviation Way, Frederick MD 21701. (301)695-2371. Fax: (301)695-2375. E-mail: pilot@aopa.org; mike. kline@aopa.org. Website: www.aopa.org. **Contact:** Michael Kline, design director. Estab. 1958. Circ. 400,000. Monthly association magazine. "The world's largest aviation magazine. The audience is primarily pilot and aircraft owners of General Aviation airplanes." Sample copies and photo guidelines available online.

NEEDS Buys 5–25 photos from freelancers/issue; 60–300 photos/year. Photos of couples, adventure, travel, industry, technology. Interested in documentary. Reviews photos with or without a manuscript. Model/property release preferred. Photo captions preferred.

SPECS Uses images in digital format. Send via CD, DVD as TIFF, EPS, JPEG files at 300 dpi. *AOPA Pilot* prefers original 35mm color transparencies (or larger), although high-quality color enlargements sometimes can be used if they are clear, sharp, and properly exposed. (If prints are accepted, the original negatives should be made available.) Slides should be sharp and properly exposed; slower-speed films (ISO 25 to ISO 100) generally provide the best results. We are not responsible for unsolicited original photographs; send duplicate slides and keep the original until we request it.

MAKING CONTACT & TERMS Send query letter. Provide self-promotion piece to be kept on file for possible future assignments. Responds only if interested; send nonreturnable samples. Pays $800–2,000 for color cover; $200–720 for color inside. **Pays on acceptance.** Credit line given. Buys one-time, all rights; negotiable.

TIPS "A knowledge of our subject matter, airplanes, is a plus. Show range of work and not just one image."

APA MONITOR

750 First St., NE, Washington D.C. 20002-4242. (202)336-5500; (800)374-2721. Circ. 150,000. Monthly magazine. Emphasizes "news and features of interest to psychologists and other behavioral scientists and professionals, including legislation and agency action affecting science and health, and major issues facing psychology both as a science and a mental health profession." Sample copy available for $3 and 9×12 SASE envelope.

NEEDS Buys 60-90 photos/year. Photos purchased on assignment. Needs portraits, feature illustrations and spot news.

SPECS Prefers images in digital format; send TIFF files at 300 dpi via e-mail. Uses 5×7 and 8×10 glossy prints.

MAKING CONTACT & TERMS Arrange a personal interview to show portfolio or query with samples. Pays by the job; $100/hour; $175 minimum; $200 for stock. Pays on receipt of invoice. Credit line given. Buys first serial rights.

TIPS "Become good at developing ideas for illustrating abstract concepts and innovative approaches to clichés such as meetings and speeches. We look for quality in technical reproduction and innovative approaches to subjects."

$$ AQUA MAGAZINE

Athletic Business Publications, Inc., 4130 Lien Rd., Madison WI 53704-3602. (608)249-0186. Fax: (608)249-1153. E-mail: scott@aquamagazine.com. Website: www.aquamagazine.com. **Contact:** Scott Maurer, art director. Estab. 1976. Circ. 15,000. Business publication for spa and pool professionals. Monthly magazine. "*AQUA* serves spa dealers, swimming pool dealers and/or builders, spa/swimming pool maintenance and service, casual furniture/patio dealers, landscape architects/designers and others allied to the spa/swimming pool market. Readers are qualified owners, GM, sales directors, titled personnel."

NEEDS Photos of residential swimming pools and/or spas (hot tubs) that show all or part of pool/spa. "The images may include grills, furniture, gazebos, ponds, water features." Photo captions including architect/builder/designer preferred.

MAKING CONTACT & TERMS "OK to send promotional literature, and to e-mail contact sheets/web gallery or low-res samples, but do not send anything that has to be returned (e.g., slides, prints) unless asked for." Simultaneous submissions and previously published work OK, "but should be explained." Pays $400 for color cover (negotiable); $200 for color inside. Pays on publication. Credit line given. Buys all rights; negotiable.

TIPS Wants to see "visually arresting images, high quality, multiple angles, day/night lighting situations. Photos including people are rarely published."

$$ [A] [◐] ARCHITECTURAL LIGHTING

One Thomas Circle, NW, Suite 600, Washington D.C. 20005. (202)729-3647. Fax: (202)785-1974. E-mail: edonoff@hanleywood.com. Website: www.archlighting.com. **Contact:** Elizabeth Donoff, editor. Estab. 1981. Circ. 25,000. Published 7 times/year. Emphasizes architecture and architectural lighting. Readers are architects and lighting designers. Sample copy free.

NEEDS Buys 3-5 photos/feature story. Needs photos of architecture and architectural lighting.

SPECS Prefers images in digital format. Send via e-mail as TIFF files at 300 dpi, minimum 4×6 inches.

MAKING CONTACT & TERMS Query *first* by e-mail to obtain permission to e-mail digital samples. Keeps samples on file. Cannot return material. Responds in 1-2 weeks. Simultaneous submissions OK. Pays $300-400 for color cover; $50-125 for color inside. Pays net 40 days point of invoice submission. Credit line given. Buys all rights for all media, including electronic media.

TIPS "Looking for a strong combination of architecture and architectural lighting."

$ [A] [O] ASIAN ENTERPRISE MAGAZINE

Asian Business Ventures, Inc., P.O. Box 1126, Walnut CA 91788. (909)896-2865; (909)319-2306. E-mail: alma.asianent@gmail.com; almag@asianenterprise.com. Website: www.asianenterprise.com. Estab. 1993. Circ. 100,000. Monthly trade magazine. "Largest Asian American small business focus magazine in U.S." Sample copy available with SASE and first-class postage. Editorial calendar available online.

NEEDS Buys 3-5 photos from freelancers/issue; 36-60 photos/year. Needs photos of multicultural, business concepts, senior citizens, environmental, architecture, cities/urban, education, travel, military, political, technology/computers. Reviews photos with or without a manuscript. Model/property release required.

SPECS Uses 4×6 matte b&w prints. Accepts images in digital format. Send via ZIP as TIFF, JPEG files at 300-700 dpi.

MAKING CONTACT & TERMS Send query letter with prints. Provide self-promotion piece to be kept on file for possible future assignments. Responds only if interested; send nonreturnable samples. Simultaneous submissions OK. Pays $50-200 for color cover; $25-100 for b&w inside. Pays on publication. Credit line given. Buys one-time rights.

[🍁] THE ATA MAGAZINE

11010 142nd St., NW, Edmonton AB T5N 2R1, Canada. (780)447-9400. Fax: (780)455-6481. E-mail: government@teachers.ab.ca. Website: www.teachers.ab.ca. **Contact:** Editor. Estab. 1920. Circ. 42,100. Quarterly magazine covering education.

SPECS Reviews 4×6 prints.

MAKING CONTACT & TERMS Captions required. Negotiates payment individually. Negotiates rights.

⊖⊙ ATHLETIC BUSINESS

Athletic Business Publications, Inc., 4130 Lien Rd., Madison WI 53704. (800)722-8764, x119. Fax: (608)249-1153. E-mail: editors@athleticbusiness.com. Website: www.athleticbusiness.com. **Contact:** Cathy Liewen, art director. Estab. 1977. Circ. 44,000. The leading resource for athletic, fitness and recreation professionals. Monthly magazine. Emphasizes athletics, fitness and recreation. Readers are athletic, park and recreational directors and club managers, ages 30-65. Sample copy available for $8. The magazine can also be viewed digitally at www.athleticbusiness.com. Become a fan on Facebook or LinkedIn.
NEEDS Buys 2-3 photos from freelancers per issue; 24-26 photos/year. Needs photos of college and high school team sports, coaches, athletic equipment, recreational parks, and health club/multi-sport interiors." Model/property release preferred. Photo captions preferred.
MAKING CONTACT & TERMS Use online e-mail to contact. "Feel free to send promotional literature, but do not send anything that has to be returned (e.g., slides, prints) unless asked for." Simultaneous submissions and previously published work OK, "but should be explained." Pays $400 for color cover (negotiable); $200 for color inside. Pays on publication. Credit line given. Buys all rights; negotiable.
TIPS Wants to see "visually arresting images, ability with subject and high quality photography." To break in, "shoot a quality and creative shot (that is part of our market) from more than one angle and at different depths."

⊙ ATHLETIC MANAGEMENT

31 Dutch Mill Rd., Ithaca NY 14850-9785. (607)257-6970. Fax: (607)257-7328. E-mail: ef@momentummedia.com. Website: www.athleticmanagement.com. **Contact:** Eleanor Frankel, editor-in-chief. Estab. 1989. Circ. 30,000. Bimonthly magazine. Emphasizes the management of athletics. Readers are managers of high school and college athletic programs.
NEEDS Uses 10–20 photos/issue; 50% supplied by freelancers. Needs photos of athletic events and athletic equipment/facility shots; college and high school sports action photos. Model release preferred.
MAKING CONTACT & TERMS Previously published work OK. Pays $600-800 for color cover; $200-400 for color inside. Pays on publication. Credit line given. Buys first North American serial rights; negotiable.

◑ ⊙ AUTO GLASS

National Glass Association, 1945 Old Gallows Rd., Suite 750, Vienna VA 22182. (866)342-5642. Fax: (703)442-0630. E-mail: mslovic@glass.org; editorial info@glass.org. Website: www.glass.org. **Contact:** Matt Slovick, managing editor. Estab. 1990. Circ. 14,000. Trade magazine emphasizing automotive use of glass. Published 7 times/year. Sample copies available with 9×12 SASE and $1.25 first-class postage.
NEEDS Buys 1-3 photos from freelancers/issue; 7-21 photos/year. Needs photos of cities/urban, automobiles. All photos should feature glass prominently. Reviews photos with or without ms. Photo caption required.
SPECS Uses 4×6 minimum, glossy color prints. Accepts images in digital format. Send via CD, ZIP, e-mail, FTP upload as TIFF, EPS files at 300 dpi.
MAKING CONTACT & TERMS Send query letter with tearsheets, stock list. Provide self-promotion piece to be kept on file for possible future assignments. Responds only if interested, send nonreturnable samples. Payment depends on freelancer and position of photo in the magazine. **Pays on acceptance.** Credit line given. Buys one-time rights.

AUTOINC.

Automotive Service Association, P.O. Box 929, Bedford TX 76095. (800)272-7467. Fax: (817)685-0225. E-mail: leonad@asashop.org. Website: www.autoinc.org. Estab. 1952. Circ. 14,000. The mission of *AutoInc.,* ASA's official publication, is to be the informational authority for ASA and industry members nationwide. Its purpose is to enhance the professionalism of these members through management, technical and legislative articles, researched and written with the highest regard for accuracy, quality, and integrity.
SPECS Reviews 2×3 transparencies, 3×5 prints, high resolution digital images.
MAKING CONTACT & TERMS Captions, identification of subjects, model releases required. Negotiates payment individually. Buys one-time and electronic rights.

◯ AUTOMATED BUILDER

CMN Associates, Inc., 1445 Donlon St., Suite 16, Ventura CA 93003. (805)642-9735; (800)344-2537. Fax: (805)642-8820. E-mail: info@automatedbuilder.com. Website: www.automatedbuilder.com. **Contact:** Don O. Carlson, editor/publisher. Estab. 1964. Circ. 25,000.

Monthly. Emphasizes home and apartment construction. Readers are "factory and site builders and dealers of all types of homes, apartments and commercial buildings." Sample copy free with SASE.

NEEDS Needs in-plant and job site construction photos and photos of completed homes and apartments. Reviews photos purchased with accompanying manuscript only. Photo captions required.

SPECS Wants 4×5, 5×7, or 8×10 glossies or disks.

MAKING CONTACT & TERMS Query editor by phone on story ideas related to industrialized housing industry." Send 3×5 color prints; 35mm or 2¼×2¼ transparencies by mail with SASE for consideration. Will consider dramatic, preferably vertical cover photos. Responds in 2 weeks.

TIPS "Study sample copy."

AUTOMOTIVE NEWS

1155 Gratiot Ave., Detroit MI 48207-2997. (313)446-0371. E-mail: rjohnson@crain.com. Website: www.autonews.com. **Contact:** Richard Johnson, managing editor. Estab. 1926. Circ. 77,000. Weekly tabloid. Emphasizes the global automotive industry. Readers are automotive industry executives, including people in manufacturing and retail. Sample copies available.

NEEDS Buys 5 photos from freelancers/issue; 260 photos/year. Needs photos of automotive executives (environmental portraits), auto plants, new vehicles, auto dealer features. Photo captions required; include identification of individuals and event details.

SPECS Uses 8×10 color prints; 35mm, 2¼×2¼, 4×5 transparencies. Accepts images in digital format. Send as JPEG files at 300 dpi (at least 6" wide).

MAKING CONTACT & TERMS Send unsolicited photos by mail with SASE for consideration. Provide résumé, business card, brochure, flyer or tearsheets to be kept on file for possible future assignments. Keeps samples on file. Responds in 2 weeks. Simultaneous submissions and previously published work OK. Pays on publication. Credit line given. Buys one-time rights, possible secondary rights for other Crain publications.

○ AUTO RESTORER

Bowtie, Inc., 3 Burroughs, Irvine CA 92618. (949)855-8822, ext. 412. Fax: (949)855-3045. E-mail: tkade@fancypubs.com; editors@mmminc.org. Website: www.autorestorermagazine.com. **Contact:** Ted Kade, editor. Estab. 1989. Circ. 60,000. Offers no additional payment for photos accepted with ms. Interview the owner of a restored car. Present advice to others on how to do a similar restoration. Seek advice from experts. Go light on history and nonspecific details. Make it something that the magazine regularly uses. Do automotive how-tos.

NEEDS Photos of auto restoration projects and restored cars.

SPECS Prefers images in high-res digital format. Send via CD at 240 dpi with minimum width of 5 inches. Uses transparencies, mostly 35mm, 2¼×2¼.

MAKING CONTACT & TERMS Submit inquiry and portfolio for review. Provide résumé, business card, brochure, flier or tearsheets to be kept on file for possible future assignments. Responds in 1 month. Simultaneous submissions OK.

$$ ◐ AVIONICS MAGAZINE

(301)354-1818. E-mail: bcarey@accessintel.com. Website: www.avionicsmagazine.com. **Contact:** Bill Carey, editor-in-chief. Estab. 1978. Circ. 20,000. Monthly magazine. Emphasizes aviation electronics. Readers are avionics and air traffic management engineers, technicians, executives. Sample copy free with 9×12 SASE.

NEEDS Buys 1–2 photos from freelancers/issue; 12–24 photos/year. Needs photos of travel, business concepts, industry, technology, aviation. Interested in alternative process, avant garde. Reviews photos with or without a manuscript. Photo captions required.

SPECS Prefers images in digital format. Send as JPEG files at 300 dpi minimum.

MAKING CONTACT & TERMS Query by e-mail. Provide résumé, business card, brochure, flier or tearsheets to be kept on file for possible future assignments. Simultaneous submissions OK. Responds in 2 months. Pay varies; negotiable. **Pays on acceptance.** Credit line given. Rights negotiable.

$ BALLINGER PUBLISHING

41 N. Jefferson St., Suite 402, Pensacola FL 32502. (850)433-1166. E-mail: kelly@ballingerpublishing.com. Website: www.ballingerpublishing.com. **Contact:** Kelly Oden, executive editor. Estab. 1990. Circ. 15,000. Monthly magazines. Emphasize business, lifestyle. Readers are executives, ages 35-54, with average annual income of $80,000. Sample copy available for $1.

NEEDS Photos of Florida topics: technology, government, ecology, global trade, finance, travel, regional and life shots. Model/property release required. Photo captions preferred.

SPECS Uses 5×7 b&w and color prints; 35mm. Prefers images in digital format. Send via CD, Zip as TIFF, EPS files at 300 dpi.

MAKING CONTACT & TERMS Send unsolicited photos by mail or e-mail for consideration; include SASE for return of material sent by mail. Provide résumé, business card, brochure, flyer or tearsheets to be kept on file for possible future assignments. Responds in 3 weeks. Pays $100-300 for color cover; $7 for b&w or color inside. Pays on publication. Buys one-time rights.

BARTENDER MAGAZINE

Foley Publishing, P.O. Box 158, Liberty Corner NJ 07938. (908)766-6006. Fax: (908)766-6607. E-mail: barmag@aol.com. Website: www.bartender.com. Doug Swenson, art director. **Contact:** Jackie Foley, editor. Estab. 1979. Circ. 150,000. Magazine published 4 times/year. *Bartender Magazine serves full-service drinking establishments (full-service means able to serve liquor, beer and wine).* "We serve single locations, including individual restaurants, hotels, motels, bars, taverns, lounges and all other full-service on-premises licensees." Sample copy available for $2.50. Number of photos/issue varies; number supplied by freelancers varies. Reviews photos with or without a manuscript.

NEEDS Photos of liquor-related topics, drinks, bars/bartenders

MAKING CONTACT & TERMS Model/property release required. Photo captions preferred. Provide résumé, business card, brochure, flier or tearsheets to be kept on file for possible future assignments; include SASE for return of material. Previously published work OK. Payment negotiable. Pays on publication. Credit line given. Buys all rights; negotiable.

BEDTIMES

501 Wythe St., Alexandria VA 22314-1917. (571)482-5442. Fax: (703)683-4503. E-mail: jpalm@sleep products.org. Website: www.bedtimesmagazine. com. **Contact:** Julie Palm, editor-in-chief. Estab. 1917. Monthly association magazine; 40% of readership is overseas. Readers are manufacturers and suppliers in bedding industry. Sample copies available.

NEEDS Head shots, events, product shots/still life, conventions, shows, annual meetings. Reviews photos with or without a manuscript. Photo captions required; include correct spelling of name, title, company, return address for photos.

SPECS Prefers digital images sent as JPEGs via e-mail.

MAKING CONTACT & TERMS Send query letter with résumé, photocopies. Responds in 3 weeks to queries. Simultaneous submissions and previously published work may be OK—depends on type of assignment. Pays $1,000 minimum for color cover; $100-750 for b&w or color inside. Pays on publication. Credit line given. Buys one-time rights; negotiable.

BEE CULTURE

P.O. Box 706, Medina OH 44256-0706. Fax: (330)725-5624. E-mail: kim@beeculture.com. Website: www.beeculture.com. **Contact:** Mr. Kim Flottum, editor. Estab. 1873. Monthly trade magazine emphasizing beekeeping industry—how-to, politics, news and events. Sample copies available. Photo guidelines available on website. Buys 1-2 photos from freelancers/issue; 6-8 photos/year.

NEEDS Needs photos of honey bees and beekeeping, honey bees on flowers, etc.

SPECS Send via e-mail as TIFF, EPS, JPEG files at 300 dpi. Low-res for review encouraged.

MAKING CONTACT & TERMS Reviews photos with or without a manuscript. Accepts images in digital format. Does not keep samples on file; include SASE for return of material. E-mail contact preferred. Responds in 2 weeks to queries. Payment negotiable. **Pays on acceptance.** Credit line given.

TIPS "Read 2-3 issues for layout and topics. Think in vertical!"

BEEF TODAY

P.O. Box 958, Mexico MO 65265. (210)957-4474. E-mail: kwatson@farmjournal.com. Website: www.agweb.com. **Contact:** Kim Watson Potts, editor. Circ. 220,000. Monthly magazine. Emphasizes American agriculture. Readers are active farmers, ranchers or agribusiness people. Sample copy and photo guidelines free with SASE.

NEEDS Buys 5–10 photos from freelancers/issue; 180–240 photos/year. "We use studio-type portraiture (environmental portraits), technical, details, scenics." Wants photos of environmental, livestock (feeding transporting, worming cattle), landscapes/scenics (from different regions of the U.S.). Model release preferred. Photo captions required.

SPECS Accepts images in digital format. Send via CD or e-mail as TIFF, EPS, JPEG files, color RGB only.

MAKING CONTACT & TERMS Arrange a personal interview to show portfolio. Send query letter with résumé of credits along with business card, brochure, flyer or tearsheets to be kept on file for possible future assignments. Do not send originals! Responds in 2 weeks. Simultaneous submissions OK. Payment negotiable. "We pay a cover bonus." **Pays on acceptance.** Credit line given. Buys one-time rights.

TIPS In portfolio or samples, likes to see "about 20 slides showing photographer's use of lighting and ability to work with people. Know your intended market. Familiarize yourself with the magazine and keep abreast of how photos are used in the general magazine field."

$$ BEVERAGE DYNAMICS

17 High St., 2nd Floor, Norwalk CT 06851. (203)855-8499. E-mail: rbrandes@m2media360.com. Website: www.adamsbevgroup.com. **Contact:** Richard Brandes, editor. Circ. 67,000. Quarterly. Emphasizes distilled spirits, wine and beer. Readers are retailers (liquor stores, supermarkets, etc.), wholesalers, distillers, vintners, brewers, ad agencies and media.

NEEDS Uses 5-10 photos/issue. Needs photos of retailers, products, concepts and profiles. Special needs include good retail environments, interesting store settings, special effect photos. Model/property release required. Photo captions required.

MAKING CONTACT & TERMS Send query letter with samples and list of stock photo subjects. Provide business card to be kept on file for possible future assignments. Keeps samples on file; send nonreturnable samples, slides, tearsheets, etc. Simultaneous submissions OK. Pays on publication. Credit line given. Buys one-time rights or all rights.

TIPS "We're looking for good location photographers who can style their own photo shoots or have staff stylists. It also helps if they are resourceful with props."

$ ○ BIZTIMES MILWAUKEE

BizTimes Media, 126 N. Jefferson St., Suite 403, Milwaukee WI 53202-6120. (414)277-8181. Fax: (414)277-8191. E-mail: shelly.tabor@biztimes.com. Website: www.biztimes.com. **Contact:** Shelly Tabor, art director. Estab. 1994. Circ. 15,000. Biweekly business-to-business publication.

NEEDS Buys 2-3 photos from freelancers/issue; 200 photos/year. Needs photos of Milwaukee, including cities/urban, business men and women, business concepts. Interested in documentary.

SPECS Uses various sizes of glossy color prints. Accepts images in digital format. Send via CD as TIFF files at 300 dpi.

MAKING CONTACT & TERMS Provide résumé, business card, self-promotion piece to be kept on file for possible future assignments. Responds only if interested; send nonreturnable samples. Simultaneous submissions and previously published work OK. Pays $250 maximum for color cover; $80 maximum for inside. **Pays on acceptance.**

TIPS "Readers are owners/managers/CEOs. Cover stories and special reports often need conceptual images and portraits. Clean, modern and cutting edge with good composition. Covers have lots of possibility! Approximate one-week turnaround. Most assignments are for the Milwaukee area."

$$ ◐ BOXOFFICE MAGAZINE

Boxoffice Media, LLC, 230 Park Ave., Suite 1000, New York NY 10169. (212)922-9800. E-mail: help@boxoffice.com; amy@boxoffice.com; peter@boxoffice.com; ken@boxoffice.com; phil@boxoffice.com. Website: www.BoxOffice.com; www.BoxofficeMagazine.com. **Contact:** Amy Nicholson, editor; Peter Cane, publisher; Kenneth James Bacon, creative director; Phil Contrino, boxoffice.com editor. Estab. 1920. Circ. 6,000. Magazine about the motion picture industry for executives and managers working in the film business, including movie theater owners and operators, Hollywood studio personnel and leaders in allied industries.

NEEDS All photos must be of movie theaters and management. Reviews photos with accompanying manuscript only.

SPECS Send via CD, ZIP as TIFF files at 300 dpi.

MAKING CONTACT & TERMS Send query letter with résumé, tearsheets. Does not keep samples on file; cannot return material. Responds in 1 month to queries. Responds only if interested; send nonreturnable samples. Previously published work OK.

BUILDINGS

Editorial Department, P.O. Box 1888, Cedar Rapids IA 52406-1888. (319)364-6167. E-mail: kylie.wroblaski@buildings.com, janelle.penny@buildings.com. Website: www.buildings.com. **Contact:** Kylie Wroblaski or Janelle Penny, associate editors. Estab. 1906. Circ. 72,000. Monthly magazine. Emphasizes commercial real estate. Readers are building owners and facilities managers. Sample copy available for $8.

NEEDS Buys 5 photos from freelancers/issue; 60 photos/year. Needs photos of concept, building interiors and exteriors, company personnel and products. Model/property release preferred. Photo caption preferred.

SPECS Prefers images in digital format. Send TIFF files at 300 dpi minimum.

MAKING CONTACT & TERMS Provide résumé, business card, brochure, flyer or tearsheets to be kept on file for possible future assignments. Responds as needed. Simultaneous submissions OK. Payment is negotiable. Pays on publication. Credit line given. Rights negotiable.

CANADIAN GUERNSEY JOURNAL

5653 Highway 6 N, RR 5, Guelph ON N1H 6J2, Canada. (519)836-2141. Fax: (519)763-6582. E-mail: info@guernseycanada.ca. Website: www.guernseycanada.ca. **Contact:** Doris Curran, administration. Estab. 1927. Annual journal of the Canadian Guernsey Association. Emphasizes dairy cattle, purebred and grade guernseys. Readers are dairy farmers and agriculture-related companies. Sample copy available for $15.

NEEDS Photos of guernsey cattle: posed, informal, scenes. Photo captions preferred.

MAKING CONTACT & TERMS Contact through administration office. Keeps samples on file.

$ CASINO JOURNAL

505 E. Capovilla Ave., #102, Las Vegas NV 89119. (702)794-0718. Fax: (702)794-0799. E-mail: gizickit@bnpmedia.com. Website: www.casinojournal.com. **Contact:** Tammie Gizicki, art director. Estab. 1985. Circ. 35,000. Monthly journal. Emphasizes casino operations. Readers are casino executives, employees and vendors. Sample copy free with 11×14 SASE. Ascend Media Gaming Group also publishes *IGWB*, *Slot Manager*, and *Indian Gaming Business*. Each magazine has its own photo needs.

NEEDS Buys 0-2 photos from freelancers/issue; 12-24 photos/year. Needs photos of gaming tables and slot machines, casinos and portraits of executives. Model release required for gamblers, employees. Photo captions required.

MAKING CONTACT & TERMS Send query letter with résumé of credits, stock list. Pays on publication. Credit line given. Buys all rights; negotiable.

TIPS "Read and study photos in current issues."

CATHOLIC LIBRARY WORLD

100 North St., Suite 224, Pittsfield MA 01201-5109. (413)443-2CLA. Fax: (413)442-2252. E-mail: cla@cathla.org. Website: www.cathla.org/cathlibworld.html. **Contact:** Jean R. Bostley, SSJ, executive director. Estab. 1929. Circ. 1,100. Quarterly magazine of the Catholic Library Association. Emphasizes libraries and librarians (community/school libraries; academic/research librarians; archivists). Readers are librarians who belong to the Catholic Library Association; other subscribers are generally employed in Catholic institutions or academic settings. Sample copy available for $15.

NEEDS Uses 2-5 photos/issue. Needs photos of authors of children's books, and librarians who have done something to contribute to the community at large. Special needs include photos of annual conferences. Model release preferred for photos of authors. Photo captions preferred.

MAKING CONTACT & TERMS Send electronically in high-res, 450 dpi or greater. Deadlines: January 2, April 1, July 1, October 1. Responds in 2 weeks. Credit line given. Acquires one-time rights.

$ CEA ADVISOR

Connecticut Education Association, Capitol Place, Suite 500, 21 Oak St., Hartford CT 06106. (860)525-5641; (800)842-4316. Fax: (860)725-6356; (860)725-6323. E-mail: kathyf@cea.org. Website: www.cea.org. Michael Lydick, man. editor. **Contact:** Kathy Frega, director of communications. Circ. 42,000. Monthly tabloid. Emphasizes education. Readers are public school teachers. Sample copy free with 6 first-class stamps.

NEEDS Buys 1-2 photos from freelancers/issue; 12-24 photos/year. Needs "classroom scenes, students, school buildings." Model release preferred. Photo captions preferred.

MAKING CONTACT & TERMS Send b&w contact sheet by mail for consideration. Provide résumé, business card, brochure, flyer or tearsheets to be kept on file for possible future assignments. Cannot return material. Responds in 1 month. Simultaneous submissions and previously published work OK. Pays $50 for b&w cover; $25 for b&w inside. Pays on publication. Credit line given. Buys all rights.

◐ CHEF

Talcott Communications, 233 N. Michigan Ave., Suite #1780, Chicago IL 60610. (312)849-2220. Fax: (312)849-2174. E-mail: bsmith@talcott.com. Website: www.chefmagazine.com. **Contact:** Brooke Smith, managing editor. Estab. 1956. Circ. 50,000. Trade magazine. "We are a food magazine for chefs. Our focus is to help chefs enhance the bottom lines of their businesses through food preparation, presentation, and marketing the menu."

NEEDS Buys 1-2 photos from freelancers/issue. Needs photos of food/drink. Other specific photo needs: chefs, establishments. Reviews photos with or without a ms. Model/property release preferred. Photo captions preferred.

SPECS Prefers images in digital format. Send via CD, Jaz, ZIP as TIFF, EPS, JPEG files at 300 dp minimum, 5×7.

MAKING CONTACT & TERMS Send query letter with résumé, photocopies, tearsheets, stock list. Provide résumé, business card or self-promotion piece to be kept on file for possible future assignments. Responds in 1 month to queries; 3 months to portfolios. Previously published work OK. Pays on publication. Credit line given. Buys one-time rights (prefers one-time rights to include electronic).

$ CHILDHOOD EDUCATION

17904 Georgia Ave., Suite 215, Olney MD 20832. (301)570-2111; (800)423-3563. Fax: (301)570-2212. E-mail: abauer@acei.org; bherzig@acei.org; editorial@acei.org. Website: www.acei.org. **Contact:** Anne Watson Bauer, editor/director of publications. Estab. 1924. Circ. 15,000. Bimonthly journal of the Association for Childhood Education International. Emphasizes the education of children from infancy through early adolescence. Readers include teachers, administrators, day-care workers, parents, psychologists, student teachers, etc. Sample copy free with 9×12 SASE and $1.44 postage. Submission guidelines available online.

NEEDS Uses 1 photos/issue; 2-3 supplied by freelance photographers. Uses freelancers mostly for covers. Subject matter includes children, infancy-14 years, in groups or alone, in or out of the classroom, at play, in study groups; boys and girls of all races and in all cities and countries. Wants close-ups of children, unposed. Reviews photos with or without accompanying manuscript. Special needs include photos of minority children; photos of children from different ethnic groups together in one shot; boys and girls together. Model release required.

SPECS Accepts images in digital format, 300 dpi.

MAKING CONTACT & TERMS Send unsolicited photos by e-mail to abauer@acei.org and bherzig@acei.org. Responds in 1 month. Simultaneous submissions and previously published work are discouraged but negotiable. Pays $200 for color cover; $75-100 for b&w inside. Pays on publication. Credit line given. Buys one-time rights.

TIPS "Send pictures of unposed children in educational settings, please."

$ ● THE CHRONICLE OF PHILANTHROPY

1255 23rd St., NW, 7th Floor, Washington D.C. 20037. (202)466-1200. Fax: (202)466-2078. E-mail: creative@chronicle.com; editor@philanthropy.com. Website: philanthropy.com. **Contact:** Sue LaLumia, art director. Estab. 1988. Biweekly tabloid. Readers come from all aspects of the nonprofit world such as charities, foundations and relief agencies such as the Red Cross. Sample copy free.

NEEDS Buys 10-15 photos from freelancers/issue; 260-390 photos/year. Needs photos of people (profiles) making the news in philanthropy and environmental shots related to person(s)/organization. Most shots arranged with freelancers are specific. Model release required. Photo caption required.

SPECS Accepts images in digital format. Send via CD or Zip.

MAKING CONTACT & TERMS Arrange a personal interview to show portfolio. Send 35mm, 2¼×2¼ transparencies and prints by mail for consideration. Provide résumé, business card, brochure, flyer or tearsheets to be kept on file for possible future assignments. Responds in 2 days. Previously published work OK. Pays (color and b&w) $275 plus expenses/half day; $450 plus expenses/full day; $100 for web publication (2-week period). Pays on publication. Buys one-time rights.

💲 🔰 ◑ CIVITAN MAGAZINE

P.O. Box 130744, Birmingham AL 35213-0744. (205)591-8910. E-mail: magazine@civitan.org. Website: www.civitan.org. Estab. 1920. Circ. 24,000. Quarterly publication of Civitan International. Emphasizes work with mental retardation/developmental disabilities. Readers are men and women, college age to retirement, usually managers or owners of businesses. Sample copy free with 9×12 SASE and 2 first-class stamps.

NEEDS Buys 1-2 photos from freelancers/issue; 6-12 photos/year. Always looking for good cover shots (multicultural, travel, scenic and how-to), babies/children/teens, families, religious, disasters, environmental, landscapes/scenics. Model release required. Photo captions preferred.

SPECS Accepts images in digital format. Send via CD or e-mail at 300 dpi only.

MAKING CONTACT & TERMS Send sample of unsolicited 2¼×2¼ or 4×5 transparencies by mail for consideration. Provide résumé, business card, brochure, flier or tearsheets to be kept on file for possible future assignments. Responds in 1 month. Simultaneous submissions and previously published work OK. Pays $50-200 for color cover; $20 for color inside. **Pays on acceptance.** Buys one-time rights.

💲 CLASSICAL SINGER

P.O. Box 1710, Draper UT 84020. (801)254-1025; (877)515-9800. Fax: (801)254-3139. E-mail: info@ classicalsinger.com. Website: www.classicalsinger. com. Estab. 1988. Circ. 9,000. Glossy monthly trade magazine for classical singers. Sample copy free.

NEEDS Looking for photos in opera or classical singing. E-mail for calendar and ideas. Photo captions preferred; include where, when, who.

SPECS Uses b&w and color prints or high-res digital photos.

MAKING CONTACT & TERMS Responds in 1 month to queries. Simultaneous submissions and previously published work OK. Pays honorarium plus 10 copies. Pays on publication. Credit line given. Buys one-time rights. Photo may be used in a reprint of an article on paper or website. "In an effort to reduce spam, we are no longer providing our e-mail addresses from our website. Please use the online form to contact individual staff members.

TIPS "Our publication is expanding rapidly. We want to make insightful photographs a big part of that expansion."

💲 ◑ CLEANING & MAINTENANCE MANAGEMENT

NTP Media, 19 British American Blvd. West, Latham NY 12110. (518)783-1281, ext. 3137. Fax: (518)783-1386. E-mail: rdipaolo@ntpmedia.com. Website: www.cmmonline.com. **Contact:** Rich Dipaolo, senior editor. Estab. 1963. Circ. 38,300. Monthly. Emphasizes management of cleaning/custodial/housekeeping operations for commercial buildings, schools, hospitals, shopping malls, airports, etc. Readers are middle- to upper-level managers of in-house cleaning/custodial departments, and managers/owners of contract cleaning companies. Sample copy free (limited) with SASE.

NEEDS Uses 10-15 photos/issue. Needs photos of cleaning personnel working on carpets, hardwood floors, tile, windows, restrooms, large buildings, etc. Model release preferred. Photo captions required.

MAKING CONTACT & TERMS Provide résumé, business card, brochure, flyer or tearsheets to be kept on file for possible future assignments. "Send query letter with specific ideas for photos related to our field." Responds in 1-2 weeks. Simultaneous submissions and previously published work OK. Pays $25 for b&w inside. Credit line given. Rights negotiable.

TIPS "Query first and shoot what the publication needs."

∅ COMMERCIAL CARRIER JOURNAL

3200 Rice Mine Rd., NE, Tuscaloosa AL 35406. (800)633-5953. Fax: (205)750-8070. E-mail: avise@ ccjdigital.com. Website: www.ccjmagazine.com. **Contact:** Avery Vise, editorial director. Estab. 1911. Circ. 105,000. Monthly magazine. Emphasizes truck and bus fleet maintenance operations and management.

NEEDS Spot news (of truck accidents, Teamster activities and highway scenes involving trucks). Photos purchased with or without accompanying manuscript, or on assignment. Model release required. Detailed captions required.

SPECS Prefers images in digital format. Send via e-mail as JPEG files at 300 dpi. For covers, uses medium-format transparencies (vertical only).

MAKING CONTACT & TERMS Does not accept unsolicited photos. Query first; send material by mail with SASE for consideration. Responds in 3 months. Pays on a per-job or per-photo basis. **Pays on acceptance.** Credit line given. Buys all rights.

TIPS Needs accompanying features on truck fleets and news features involving trucking companies.

CONSTRUCTION EQUIPMENT GUIDE

470 Maryland Dr., Ft. Washington PA 19034. (215)885-2900 or (800)523-2200. E-mail: editorial@cegltd.com. Website: www.cegltd.com. **Contact:** Craig Mongeau, editor-in-chief. Estab. 1957. Circ. 120,000. Biweekly trade newspaper. Emphasizes construction equipment industry, including projects ongoing throughout the country. Readers are males and females of all ages; many are construction executives, contractors, dealers and manufacturers. Free sample copy.

NEEDS Buys 35 photos from freelancers/issue; 910 photos/year. Needs photos of construction job sites and special event coverage illustrating new equipment applications and interesting projects. Call to inquire about special photo needs for coming year. Model/property release preferred. Photo captions required for subject identification.

MAKING CONTACT & TERMS Send any size matte or glossy b&w prints by mail with SASE for consideration. Provide résumé, business card, brochure, flier or tearsheets to be kept on file for possible future assignments. Responds in 3 weeks. Payment negotiable. Pays on publication. Credit line given. Buys all rights; negotiable.

THE COOLING JOURNAL

3000 Village Run Road, Suite 103, #221, Wexford PA 15090. (724)799-8415. Fax: (724)799-8416. E-mail: info@narsa.org. Website: www.narsa.org. Estab. 1956. Magazine (10 issues per annum) of NARSA—The International Heat Exchange Association. Emphasis on thermal management products and services for transportation, energy and industry.

NEEDS Buys photos, images, and stories about people, organizations, processes, technologies, and products in heat exchange industry which includes: automotive, heavy truck and mobile machinery engine and transmission cooling; automotive, heavy truck, and mobile machinery air conditioning and cabin heating; engine and transmission cooling for marine applications; engine and transmission cooling for vehicle high performance and racing; heat exchange for energy exploration and generation; construction, mining, agricultural applications for heat exchange products and services; metals joining including welding and brazing; heat exchange product fabrication, design and engineering.

MAKING CONTACT & TERMS Send inquiry for current story board, rates, and deadlines. Pays on publication.

COTTON GROWER MAGAZINE

Cotton Media Group, 65 Germantown Ct., Suite #202, Cordova TN 38018-4246. (901)756-8822. E-mail: mccue@meistermedia.com. **Contact:** Mike McCue, editor. Circ. 43,000. Monthly trade magazine. Emphasizes "cotton production; for cotton farmers." Sample copies and photo guidelines available.

NEEDS Photos of agriculture. "Our main photo needs are cover shots of growers. We write cover stories on each issue."

SPECS Prefers high-res digital images; send JPEGs at 300 dpi via e-mail or CD. Uses high-quality glossy prints from 35mm.

MAKING CONTACT & TERMS Send query letter with slides, prints, tearsheets. **Pays on acceptance.** Credit line given. Buys all rights.

TIPS Most photography hired is for cover shots of cotton growers.

😊😊 CROPLIFE

37733 Euclid Ave., Willoughby OH 44094. (440)942-2000. E-mail: erics@croplife.com. Website: www.croplife.com. Estab. 1894. Circ. 24,500. Monthly magazine. Serves the agricultural distribution channel delivering fertilizer, chemicals and seed from manufacturer to farmer. Sample copy and photo guidelines free with 9×12 SASE.

NEEDS Buys 6-7 photos/year; 5-30% supplied by freelancers. Needs photos of agricultural chemical and fertilizer application scenes (of commercial—not farmer—applicators), people shots of distribution channel executives and managers. Model release preferred. Photo captions required.

SPECS Uses 8×10 glossy b&w and color prints; 35mm slides, transparencies.

MAKING CONTACT & TERMS Send query letter first with résumé of credits. Simultaneous submissions and previously published work OK. **Pays on acceptance.** Buys one-time rights.

⊙⊙ DAIRY TODAY

P.O. Box 958, Mexico MO 65265. (573)581-6387. E-mail: jdickrell@farmjournal.com. Website: www.agweb.com/livestock/dairy/. **Contact:** Jim Dickrell, editor. Circ. 50,000. Monthly magazine. Emphasizes American agriculture. Readers are active farmers, ranchers or agribusiness people. Sample copy and photo guidelines free with SASE.

NEEDS Buys 5-10 photos from freelancers/issue; 60-120 photos/year. "We use studio-type portraiture (environmental portraits), technical, details, scenics." Wants photos of environmental, landscapes/scenics, agriculture, business concepts. Model release preferred. Photo captions required.

MAKING CONTACT & TERMS Arrange a personal interview to show portfolio. Send query letter with résumé of credits along with business card, brochure, flyer or tearsheets to be kept on file for possible future assignments. "Portfolios may be submitted via CD." *Do not send originals!* Responds in 2 weeks. Simultaneous submissions OK. Pays $75-400 for color photo; $200-400/day. "We pay a cover bonus." **Pays on acceptance.** Credit line given, except in advertorials. Buys one-time rights.

TIPS In portfolio or samples, likes to see "about 40 slides showing photographer's use of lighting and ability to work with people. Know your intended market. Familiarize yourself with the magazine and keep abreast of how photos are used in the general magazine field."

⊙ ❶ DISPLAY DESIGN IDEAS

1145 Sanctuary Pkwy., Suite 355, Alpharetta GA 30004. (770)291-5510. E-mail: jessie.bove@ddionline.com. Website: www.ddimagazine.com. **Contact:** Jessie Bove, managing editor/web editor. Estab. 1988. Circ. 21,500. Monthly magazine. Emphasizes retail design, store planning, visual merchandising. Readers are retail architects, designers and retail executives. Sample copies available.

NEEDS Buys 7 or fewer photos from freelancers/issue; 84 or fewer photos/year. Needs photos of architecture, mostly interior. Property release preferred.

SPECS Prefers digital submissions. Send as TIFF or JPEG files at 300 dpi.

MAKING CONTACT & TERMS Send query letter with résumé of credits. Provide résumé, business card, brochure, flier or tearsheets to be kept on file for pos-sible future assignments. Responds in 3 weeks. Credit line given. Rights negotiable.

TIPS Looks for architectural interiors, ability to work with different lighting. "Send samples (photocopies OK) and résumé."

DM NEWS

Haymarket Media, Inc., 114 W. 26th St., New York NY 10001. (646)638-6000. Fax: (212)925-8754. E-mail: carol.krol@dmnews.com; news@dmnews.com. Website: www.dmnews.com. **Contact:** Carol Krol, editor-in-chief. Estab. 1979. Circ. 50,300. Company publication for Courtenay Communications Corporation. Weekly newspaper. Emphasizes direct, interactive and database marketing. Readers are decision makers and marketing executives, ages 25-55. Sample copy available for $2.

NEEDS Uses 20 photos/issue; 3-5 supplied by freelancers. Needs news head shots, product shots. Reviews photos purchased with accompanying manuscript only. Photo captions required.

MAKING CONTACT & TERMS Provide résumé, business card, brochure, flyer or tearsheets to be kept on file for possible future assignments. Responds in 1-2 weeks. Payment negotiable. **Pays on acceptance.** Buys worldwide rights.

TIPS "News and business background are a prerequisite."

ELECTRICAL APPARATUS

Barks Publications, Inc., 400 N. Michigan Ave., Chicago IL 60611-4104. (312)321-9440. Fax: (312)321-1288. **Contact:** Elsie Dickson, associate publisher; Kevin Jones, senior editor. Estab. 1967. Circ. 16,000. Monthly trade magazine. Emphasizes industrial electrical machinery maintenance and repair for the electrical aftermarket. Readers are "persons engaged in the application, maintenance and servicing of industrial and commercial electrical and electronic equipment." Sample copies available.

NEEDS "Assigned materials only. We welcome innovative industrial photography, but most of our material is staff-prepared." Photos purchased with accompanying manuscript or on assignment. Model release required "when requested." Photo captions preferred.

MAKING CONTACT & TERMS Send query letter with résumé of credits. Contact sheet or contact sheet with negatives OK; include SASE for return of material. Responds in 3 weeks. Pays $200 for color. Pays on publication. Credit line given. Buys all rights, but exceptions are occasionally made.

⊖⊖ ◑ ELECTRIC PERSPECTIVES

701 Pennsylvania Ave. NW, Washington D.C. 20004. (202)508-5584. E-mail: eblume@eei.org; bcannon@eei.org. Website: www.eei.org/ep. **Contact:** Eric Blume, editor; LaVonne Rose, photo coordinator. Estab. 1976. Circ. 11,000. Bimonthly magazine of the Edison Electric Institute. Emphasizes issues and subjects related to shareholder-owned electric utilities. Sample copy available on request.

NEEDS Photos relating to the business and operational life of electric utilities—from customer service to engineering, from executive to blue collar. Model release required. Photo captions preferred. All high-resolution non-postscript formats accepted.

SPECS Uses 8×10 glossy color prints; 35mm, 2¼×2¼, 4×5 transparencies. Accepts images in digital format. All high-resolution non-postscript formats accepted. Send via ZIP, e-mail as TIFF, JPEG files at 300 dpi and scanned at a large size, at least 4×5.

MAKING CONTACT & TERMS Send query letter with stock list or send unsolicited photos by mail for consideration. Provide electronic résumé, business card, or brochure to be kept on file for possible future assignments. Keeps samples on file. Pays $300-500 for color cover; $100-300 for color inside; $200-350 color page rate; $750-1,500 for photo/text package. Pays on publication. Buys one-time rights; negotiable (for reprints).

TIPS "We're interested in annual-report-quality images in particular. Quality and creativity are often more important than subject."

EL RESTAURANTE MEXICANO

P.O. Box 2249, Oak Park IL 60303-2249. (708)488-0100. Fax: (708)488-0101. E-mail: kfurore@restmex.com. Estab. 1997. Circ. 27,000. Bimonthly trade magazine for restaurants that serve Mexican, Tex-Mex, Southwestern and Latin cuisine. Sample copies available.

NEEDS Buys at least 1 photo from freelancers/issue; at least 6 photos/year. Needs photos of food/drink. Reviews photos with or without a manuscript.

SPECS Uses 35mm transparencies. Accepts images in digital format. Send via e-mail as TIFF, JPEG files of at least 300 dpi.

MAKING CONTACT & TERMS Send query letter with slides, prints, photocopies, tearsheets, transparencies or stock list. Provide résumé, business card, self-promotion piece to be kept on file for possible future assignments. Responds in 2 months to queries. Previously published work OK. Pays $450 maximum for color cover; $125 maximum for color inside. Pays on publication. Credit line given. Buys all rights; negotiable.

TIPS "We look for outstanding food photography; the more creatively styled, the better."

ESL TEACHER TODAY

2660 Petersborough St., Herndon VA 20171. E-mail: shannonaswriter@yahoo.com. **Contact:** Shannon Bridget Murphy. Quarterly trade magazine. Photo guidelines available via e-mail.

NEEDS Buys 12-24 photos/year. Needs photos of babies/children/teens, multicultural, families, parents, disasters, environmental, landscapes/scenics, wildlife, cities/urban, education, religious, rural, adventure, events, food/drink, sports, travel, agriculture, medicine, military, political, product shots/still life, science, technology—as related to teaching ESL (English as a Second Language) around the globe. Interested in alternative process, avant garde, documentary, fashion/glamour, fine art, historical/vintage, seasonal. Reviews photos with or without a manuscript. Model/property release preferred.

SPECS Uses glossy or matte color and b&w prints.

MAKING CONTACT & TERMS Send query letter via e-mail. "If possible, please do not include photographs in files if they are sent through e-mail. A disc with your photographs sent to *ESL Teacher Today* is acceptable." Provide résumé, business card or self-promotion piece to be kept on file for possible future assignments. Responds within 1 month to queries; 1 week to portfolios. Simultaneous submissions and previously published work OK. **Pays on acceptance.** Credit line given. Buys one-time rights, first rights; negotiable.

⊖⊖ FARM JOURNAL

P.O. Box 958, Mexico MO 65265. (573)581-6387. E-mail: cfinck@farmjournal.com. Website: www.agweb.com. **Contact:** Anna McBrayer, art director; Charlene Finck, editor. Estab. 1877. Circ. 600,000. Monthly magazine. Emphasizes the business of agriculture: "Good farmers want to know what their peers are doing and how to make money marketing their products." Free sample copy upon request.

○ *Farm Journal* has received the Best Use of Photos/Design from the American Agricultural Editors' Association (AAEA).

NEEDS Freelancers supply 60% of the photos. Photos having to do with the basics of raising, harvesting and marketing of all the farm commodities, farm animals and international farming. People-oriented shots are encouraged. Also uses human interest and interview photos. All photos must relate to agriculture. Photos purchased with or without accompanying manuscript. Model release required. Photo captions required.

SPECS Uses glossy or semigloss color prints; 35mm, 2¼×2¼ transparencies; all sizes for covers. Accepts images in digital format. Send via CD as TIFF, EPS, JPEG files at 300 dpi.

MAKING CONTACT & TERMS Arrange a personal interview or send photos by mail. Provide calling card and samples to be kept on file for possible future assignments. Responds in 1 month. Simultaneous submissions OK. Pays per assignment or photo. Pays $200-400/job; $400-1,200 for color cover (plus cover bonus); $150-500 for color inside. **Pays on acceptance**. Credit line given. Buys one-time rights; negotiable.

TIPS "Be original and take time to see with the camera. Be selective. Look at use of light—available or strobed—and use of color. I look for an easy rapport between photographer and subject. Take as many different angles of subject as possible. Use fill where needed. Send nonreturnable samples of agriculture-related photos only. We are always looking for photographers located in the Midwest and other areas of the country where farming is a way of life. Don't forget to shoot vertical versions of everything to be used as possible cover shots."

FIRE CHIEF

Primedia Business, 330 N. Wabash Ave., Suite 2300, Chicago IL 60611. (312)595-1080. Fax: (312)595-0295. E-mail: glenn.bischoff@penton.com. Website: www.firechief.com. **Contact:** Glenn Bischoff, editor. Estab. 1956. Circ. 53,000. Monthly magazine. Focus on fire department management and operations. Readers are primarily fire officers and predominantly chiefs of departments. Sample copy free. Request photo guidelines via e-mail or view online.

NEEDS Fire and emergency response, especially leadership themes—if you do not have fire or EMS, please do not contact.

SPECS Digital format preferred, file name less than 15 characters. Send via e-mail, CD, ZIP as TIFF, EPS files at highest possible resolution.

MAKING CONTACT & TERMS Send low-res JPEGs for consideration along with caption, date, time, and location. Samples are kept on file. Expect confirmation/response within 1 month. Payment 90 days after publication. Buys first serial rights; negotiable.

TIPS "As the name *Fire Chief* implies, we prefer images showing a leading officer (white, yellow, or red helmet) in action—on scene of a fire, disaster, accident/rescue, hazmat, etc. Other subjects: administration, communications, decontamination, dispatch, EMS, foam, heavy rescue, incident command, live fire training, public education, SCBA, water rescue, wildland fire."

FIRE ENGINEERING

PennWell Corporation, 21-00 Route 208 S., Fair Lawn NJ 07410. (800)962-6484, ext. 5047. E-mail: dianef@pennwell.com. Website: www.fireengineering.com. **Contact:** Diane Feldman, executive editor. Estab. 1877. Training magazine for firefighters. Photo guidelines free.

NEEDS Uses 400 photos/year. Needs action photos of disasters, firefighting, EMS, public safety, fire investigation and prevention, rescue. Photo captions required; include date, what is happening, location and fire department contact.

SPECS Accepts images in digital format. Send via e-mail or mail on CD as JPEG files at 300 dpi minimum.

MAKING CONTACT & TERMS Send unsolicited photos by mail for consideration. Pays on publication. Credit line given. We retain copyright.

TIPS "Firefighters must be doing something. Our focus is on training and learning lessons from photos."

✿✿ ✪ ◑ FIREHOUSE MAGAZINE

3 Huntington Quadrangle, Suite 301N, Melville NY 11747. (631)845-2700. E-mail: harvey.eisner@cygnuspub.com. Website: www.firehouse.com. **Contact:** Harvey Eisner, editor-in-chief. Estab. 1976. Circ. 90,000. Monthly. Emphasizes "firefighting—notable fires, techniques, dramatic fires and rescues, etc." Readers are "paid and volunteer firefighters, EMTs."

Sample copy available for $5 with 9×12 SASE and 7 first-class stamps. Photo guidelines free with SASE or online.

NEEDS Buys 20 photos from freelancers/issue; 240 photos/year. Needs photos of fires, terrorism, firefighter training, natural disasters, highway incidents, hazardous materials, dramatic rescues. Model release preferred.

SPECS Uses 3×5, 5×7, 8×10 matte or glossy b&w or color prints; 35mm transparencies. Accepts images in digital format. Send via CD, e-mail as TIFF, EPS, JPEG files at 300 dpi.

MAKING CONTACT & TERMS "Photos must not be more than 30 days old." Include SASE. "Photos cannot be returned without SASE." Responds ASAP. Pays up to $200 for color cover; $20-100 for b&w inside; $20-200 for color inside. Pays on publication. Credit line given. Buys one-time rights.

TIPS "Mostly we are looking for action-packed photos—the more fire, the better the shot. Show firefighters in full gear; do not show spectators. Fire safety is a big concern. Much of our photo work is freelance. Try to be in the right place at the right time as the fire occurs. Be sure that photos are clear, in focus, and show firefighters/EMTs at work. Firehouse encourages submissions of high-quality action photos that relate to the firefighting/EMS field. Please understand that while we encourage first-time photographers, a minimum waiting period of 3-6 months is not unusual. Although we are capable of receiving photos online, please be advised that there are color variations. Include captions. Photographers must include a SASE, and we cannot guarantee the return of unsolicited photos. Mark name and address on the back of each photo."

$ ◐ FIRE-RESCUE MAGAZINE

525 B St., Suite 1800, San Diego CA 92101. (800)266-5367. Fax: (619)699-6396. E-mail: s.pieper@elsevier.com; jfoskett@elsevier.com. Website: www.firefighternation.com. **Contact:** Shannon Pieper, deputy editor. Estab. 1997. Circ. 50,000. Monthly. Emphasizes techniques, equipment, action stories of fire and rescue incidents. Editorial slant: "Read it today, use it tomorrow."

NEEDS Photos of fires, fire ground scenes, commanders operating at fires, company officers/crews fighting fires, disasters, emergency medical services, rescue scenes, transport, injured victims, equipment and personnel, training, earthquake rescue operations. Special photo needs include strong color shots showing newsworthy rescue operations, including a unique or difficult firefighting, rescue/extrication, treatment, transport, personnel, etc.; b&w showing same. Photo captions required.

SPECS Accepts images in digital format. Prefers digital format submitted via e-mail or FTP (info.jems.com/ftp/). Send via ZIP, e-mail, Jaz, CD as TIFF, EPS, JPEG files at 300 dpi.

MAKING CONTACT & TERMS Pays $300 for cover; $22-137 for color inside. Pays on publication. Credit line given. Buys one-time rights.

$$ ◎ ◐ ⊛ FLORAL MANAGEMENT MAGAZINE

1601 Duke St., Alexandria VA 22314. (703)836-8700. Fax: (703)836-8705. E-mail: kpenn@safnow.org. Website: www.safnow.org. **Contact:** Kate Penn, editor-in-chief. Estab. 1894. National trade association magazine representing growers, wholesalers and retailers of flowers and plants. Photos used in magazine and promotional materials.

NEEDS Offers 15-20 assignments/year. Needs photos of floral business owners, employees on location, and retail environmental portraits. Reviews stock photos. Model release required. Photo captions preferred.

SPECS Prefers images in digital format. Send via CD or e-mail as TIFF files at 300 dpi. Also uses b&w prints; transparencies.

MAKING CONTACT & TERMS Send query letter with samples. Provide résumé, business card, brochure, flyer or tearsheets to be kept on file for possible future assignments. Responds in 1 week. Pays $150-600 for color cover; $75-150/hour; $125-250/job; $75-500 for color inside. Credit line given. Buys one-time rights.

TIPS "We shoot a lot of tightly composed, dramatic shots of people, so we look for these skills. We also welcome input from the photographer on the concept of the shot. Our readers, as business owners, like to see photos of other business owners. Therefore, people photography, on location, is particularly popular." Photographers should approach magazine "via letter of introduction and sample. We'll keep name in file and use if we have a shoot near photographer's location."

⑤ ⓐ ○ FOREST LANDOWNER

900 Circle 75 Parkway, Suite 205, Atlanta GA 30339. (800)325-2954; (404)325-2954. Fax: (404)325-2955. E-mail: info@forestlandowners.com. Website: www. forestlandowners.com. Estab. 1942. Circ. 10,000. Bimonthly magazine of the Forest Landowners Association. Emphasizes forest management and policy issues for private forest landowners. Readers are forest landowners and forest industry consultants; 94% male between the ages of 46 and 55. Sample copy available for $3 (magazine), $30 (manual).

NEEDS Uses 15-25 photos/issue; 3-4 supplied by freelancers. Needs photos of unique or interesting private southern forests. Other subjects: environmental, regional, wildlife, landscapes/scenics. Model/property release preferred. Photo captions preferred.

SPECS Accepts images in digital format. Send via CD, ZIP, e-mail as TIFF, EPS files at 300 dpi.

MAKING CONTACT & TERMS Send ZIP disk, color prints, negatives or transparencies by mail or e-mail for consideration. Send query letter with stock list. Keeps samples on file. SASE. Responds in 3 weeks. Simultaneous submissions and previously published work OK. Pays $100-150 for color cover; $25-50 for b&w inside; $35-75 for color inside. Pays on publication. Credit line given. Buys one-time and all rights; negotiable.

TIPS "We most often use photos of timber management, seedlings, aerial shots of forests, and unique southern forest landscapes. Mail ZIP, CD or slides of sample images. Captions are important."

FRAME BUILDING NEWS

F+W Media, Inc., 700 E. State St., Iola WI 54990-0001. (715)445-4612, ext. 428. Fax: (715)445-4087. E-mail: jim.austin@fw.media.com. Website: www. framebuildingnews.com. Estab. 1990. Circ. 20,000. "*Frame Building News* is the official publication of the National Frame Builders Association, which represents contractors who specialize in post-frame building construction."

SPECS Reviews GIF/JPEG files.

MAKING CONTACT & TERMS Captions, identification of subjects required. Negotiates payment individually. Buys all rights.

FRUIT GROWERS NEWS

Great American Publishing, P.O. Box 128, Sparta MI 49345. (616)887-9008. Fax: (616)887-2666. E-mail: fgnedit@fruitgrowersnews.com. Website: www.fruit growersnews.com. Kimberly Warren, editorial director. **Contact:** Matt Milkovich, managing editor. Estab. 1961. Circ. 16,429. Monthly. Emphasizes all aspects of tree fruit and small fruit growing as well as farm marketing. Readers are growers but include anybody associated with the field. Sample copy available for $6.

NEEDS Buys 3 photos from freelancers/issue; 25 photos/year. Needs portraits of growers, harvesting, manufacturing, field shots for stock photography—anything associated with fruit growing. Photo captions required.

SPECS Accepts images in digital format. Send via CD as JPEG, TIFF or EPS files at 300 dpi, at least 4×6.

MAKING CONTACT & TERMS Query about prospective jobs. Simultaneous submissions and previously published work OK. Payment rates to be negotiated between editorial director and individual photographer. Pays on publication. Credit line given. Buys first North American rights.

TIPS "Learn about the field. Great American Publishing also publishes *The Vegetable Growers News*, *Spudman*, *Fresh Cut*, *Museums & More*, *Party & Paper Retailer and Stationery Trends*. Contact the editorial director for information on these publications."

GEOSYNTHETICS

1801 County Road B W., Roseville MN 55113. (651)222-2508 or (800)225-4324. Fax: (651)225-6966. E-mail: generalinfo@ifai.com; rwbygness@ifai.com. Website: www.geosyntheticsmagazine.com; www.ifai. com. **Contact:** Ron Bygness, editor. Estab. 1983. Circ. 18,000. Association magazine published 6 times/year. Emphasizes geosynthetics in civil engineering applications. Readers are civil engineers, professors and consulting engineers. Sample copies available.

NEEDS Uses 10-15 photos/issue; various number supplied by freelancers. Needs photos of finished applications using geosynthetics; photos of the application process. Reviews photos with accompanying manuscript only. Model release required. Photo captions required; include project, type of geosynthetics used and location.

SPECS Prefers images in high-res digital format.

MAKING CONTACT & TERMS "Please call before submitting samples!" Keeps samples on file. Responds in 1 month. Simultaneous submissions OK. Credit line given. Buys all rights; negotiable.

GLASS MAGAZINE

National Glass Association, 1945 Old Gallows Rd., Suite 750, Vienna VA 22182. (866)342-5642, ext.253. Fax: (703)442-0630. E-mail: editorialinfo@glass.org. Website: www.glass.org. **Contact:** Matt Slovick, editor-in-chief. Estab. 1948. Circ. 23,000. Monthly trade magazine emphasizing architectural, commercial use of glass. Sample copies available with 9×12 SASE and $1.25 first-class postage.

NEEDS Buys 1-3 photos/year. Needs photos of architecture, cities/urban, interiors/decorating (doors and windows only), business concepts, industry. All photos should feature glass prominently. Architectural shots must be accompanied by names of companies that produced and installed the glass. Reviews photos with or without ms. Photo caption required.

SPECS Uses 4×6 or larger glossy color prints. Accepts images in digital format. Send via CD, ZIP, e-mail, FTP upload as TIFF, EPS files at 300 dpi.

MAKING CONTACT & TERMS Send query letter with tearsheets, stock list. Provide self-promotion piece to be kept on file for possible future assignments. Responds only if interested, send nonreturnable samples. Payment depends on freelancer and position of photo in the magazine. **Pays on acceptance.** Credit line given. Buys one-time rights.

GOVERNMENT TECHNOLOGY

100 Blue Ravine Rd., Folsom CA 95630. (916)932-1300. Fax: (916)932-1470. E-mail: kmartinelli@govtech.com. Website: www.govtech.net. **Contact:** Kelly Martinelli, creative director. Estab. 2001. Circ. 60,000. Monthly trade magazine. Emphasizes information technology as it applies to state and local government. Readers are government executives.

NEEDS Buys 2 photos from freelancers/issue; 20 photos/year. Needs photos of government officials, disasters, environmental, political, technology/computers. Reviews photos with accompanying manuscript only. Model release required; property release preferred. Photo captions required.

SPECS Accepts images in digital format only. Send via DVD, CD, ZIP, e-mail as TIFF, JPEG files at 300 dpi.

MAKING CONTACT & TERMS Send query letter with résumé, prints, tearsheets. Provide business card, self-promotion piece to be kept on file for possible future assignments. Responds only if interested; send nonreturnable samples. Simultaneous submissions and previously published work OK. Payment is dependent upon pre-publication agreement between photographer and *Government Technology*. Pays on publication. Credit line given. Buys one-time rights, electronic rights.

TIPS "View samples of magazines for style, available online at www.govtech.com/gt/magazines."

GRAIN JOURNAL

Country Journal Publishing Co., 3065 Pershing Ct., Decatur IL 62526. (800)728-7511. Fax: (217)877-6647. E-mail: ed@grainnet.com. Website: www.grainnet. com. **Contact:** Ed Zdrojewski, editor. Estab. 1972. Circ. 12,000. Bimonthly trade magazine. Emphasizes grain industry. Readers are "elevator and feed mill managers primarily, as well as suppliers and others in the industry." Sample copy free with #10 SASE.

NEEDS Uses about 1-2 photos/issue. "We need photos concerning industry practices and activities. We look for clear, high-quality images without a lot of extraneous material." Photo captions preferred.

SPECS Accepts images in digital format minimum 300 dpi resolution. Send via e-mail, floppy disk, ZIP.

MAKING CONTACT & TERMS Send query letter with samples and list of stock photo subjects. Responds in 1 week. Pays $100 for color cover; $30 for b&w inside. Pays on publication. Credit line given. Buys all rights; negotiable.

HARD HAT NEWS

Lee Publications, Inc., 6113 State Highway 5, Palatine Bridge NY 13428. (518)673-3237. Fax: (518)673-2381. E-mail: joncasey88@gmail.com. Website: www. hardhat.com. **Contact:** Jon Casey, editor. Estab. 1980. Circ. 15,000. Biweekly trade newspaper for heavy construction. "Our readers are contractors and heavy construction workers involved in excavation, highways, bridges, utility construction, and underground construction." Readership includes owners, managers, senior construction trades. Photo guidelines available via e-mail only.

NEEDS Buys 12 photos from freelancers/issue; 280 photos/year. Specific photo needs: heavy construction in progress, construction people. Reviews photos with accompanying manuscripts only. Property release preferred. Photo captions required.

SPECS Only high-res digital photographs. Send via e-mail as JPEG files at 300 dpi.

MAKING CONTACT & TERMS E-mail only. Simultaneous submissions OK. Pays on publication. Credit line given. Buys first rights.

TIPS "Include caption and brief explanation of what picture is about."

⊙ HEARTH AND HOME

P.O. Box 1288, Laconia NH 03246. (603)528-4285. Fax: (603)527-3404. E-mail: production@villagewest.com. Website: hearthandhome.com. Circ. 16,000. Monthly magazine. Emphasizes hearth, barbecue and patio news and industry trends for specialty retailers and manufacturers of solid fuel and gas appliances, barbeque grills, hearth appliances inside and outside and casual furnishings. Sample copy available for $5.

NEEDS Buys 3 photos from freelancers/issue; 36 photos/year. Photos of inside and outside fireplace and patio furnishings, gas grills, outdoor room shots emphasizing BBQs, furniture, and outdoor fireplaces. Assignments available for conferences." Model release required. Photo captions preferred.

SPECS Accepts digital images with color proof; highres, 300 dpi preferred.

MAKING CONTACT & TERMS Contact before submitting material. Responds in 2 weeks. Simultaneous and photocopied submissions OK. Pays $50-200 for color photos; $250-1,200/on location job. Pays within 30 days after publication prints. Credit line given. Buys various rights.

TIPS "Call first and ask what we need. We're *always* on the lookout for gorgeous outdoor room material."

⊙ HEREFORD WORLD

Hereford Cattle Association, P.O. Box 014059, Kansas City MO 64101. (816)842-3757. Fax: (816)842-6931. E-mail: cvaught@hereford.org. Website: www.herefordworld.org. **Contact:** Caryn Vaught, production manager. Estab. 1947. Circ. 5,600. Monthly (11 issues with 7 glossy issues) association magazine. Emphasizes Hereford cattle for registered breeders, commercial cattle breeders and agribusinessmen in related fields. A tabloid-type issue is produced 4 times — January, February, August and October— and mailed to an additional 20,000 commercial cattlemen. "We also publish a commercial edition with a circulation of 20,000."

NEEDS "*Hereford World* includes timely articles and editorial columns that provide readers information to help them make sound management and marketing decisions. From basic how-to articles to in-depth reports on cutting-edge technologies, *Hereford World* offers its readers a solid package of beef industry information."

SPECS Uses b&w and color prints.

MAKING CONTACT & TERMS Query. Responds in 2 weeks. Pays $5 for b&w print; $100 for color print. Pays on publication.

TIPS Wants to see "Hereford cattle in quantities, in seasonal and scenic settings."

☼ ⊙⊙ ◑ HPAC: HEATING PLUMBING AIR CONDITIONING

1 Mount Pleasant Rd., Toronto ON M4Y 2Y5, Canada. (416)764-2000. Fax: (416)764-1746. E-mail: kerry.turner@hpacmag.rogers.com. Website: www.hpacmag.mercuryemail.com. **Contact:** Kerry Turner, editor. Estab. 1927. Circ. 17,000. Bimonthly magazine plus annual buyers guide. Emphasizes heating, plumbing, air conditioning, refrigeration. Readers are predominantly male mechanical contractors, ages 30-60. Sample copy available for $4.

NEEDS Buys 5-10 photos from freelancers/issue; 30-60 photos/year. Needs photos of mechanical contractors at work, site shots, product shots. Model/property release preferred. Photo captions preferred.

SPECS Prefers images in digital format. Send via CD, e-mail as TIFF, JPEG files at 300 dpi minimum. Also uses 4×6 glossy/semi-matte color and b&w prints; 35mm transparencies.

MAKING CONTACT & TERMS Send unsolicited photos by mail for consideration. Cannot return material. Responds in 1 month. Simultaneous submissions and previously published work OK. Pays $400 for b&w or color cover; $50-200 for b&w or color inside (payment in Canadian dollars). Pays on publication. Credit line given. Buys one-time rights; negotiable.

⊙⊙ ◑ IEEE SPECTRUM

3 Park Ave., New York NY 10016. (212)419-7555. Fax: (212)419-7570. E-mail: r.silberman@ieee.org. Website: www.spectrum.ieee.org. **Contact:** Randi Silberman, photo editor. Circ. 375,000. Monthly magazine of the Institute of Electrical and Electronics Engineers, Inc. (IEEE). Emphasizes electrical and electronics field and high technology for technology innovators, business leaders, and the intellectually curious. Spectrum explores future technology trends and the im-

pact of those trends on society and business. Readers are technology professionals and senior executives worldwide in the high technology sectors of industry, government, and academia. Subscribers include engineering managers and corporate and financial executives, deans and provosts at every major engineering university and college throughout the world; males/females, educated, ages 20-70.

NEEDS Uses 20-30 photos/issue. Purchases stock photos in following areas: technology, energy, medicine, military, sciences and business concepts. Hires assignment photographers for location shots and portraiture, as well as product shots. Model/property release required. Photo captions required.

SPECS Accepts images in digital format. Send via CD as TIFF, JPEG files at 300 dpi.

MAKING CONTACT & TERMS Provide promos or tearsheets to be kept on file for possible future assignments. Pays $1,200 for color cover; $200-600 for inside. **Pays on acceptance.** Credit line given. Buys one-time rights.

TIPS Wants photographers who are consistent, have an ability to shoot color and b&w, display a unique vision, and are receptive to their subjects. "As our subject matter is varied, *Spectrum* uses a variety of imagemakers."

IGA GROCERGRAM

8745 W Higgins Rd., Suite 350, Chicago IL 60631. (773)693-5902. E-mail: apage@igainc.com. Website: www.iga.com/igagrocergram.aspx. **Contact:** Ashley Page, communications. Quarterly magazine of the Independent Grocers Alliance. This comprehensive quarterly magazine—which evolved from the monthly that has chronicled the Alliance since its birth in 1926—is published in four seasonal editions each year and distributed to a worldwide audience. The glossy keep-sake issues profile IGA and its members through in-depth stories featuring stimulating interviews and informative analyses. Emphasizes food industry. Readers are IGA retailers. Sample copy available upon request.

NEEDS Needs in-store shots, food (appetite appeal). Prefers shots of IGA stores. Model/property release required. Photo captions required.

SPECS Accepts images in digital format. Send as TIFF files at 300 dpi.

MAKING CONTACT & TERMS Send samples by e-mail or link to website for consideration. Provide

résumé, business card, brochure, flier or tearsheets to be kept on file for possible future assignments. Keeps samples on file. Responds in 3 weeks. Simultaneous submissions and previously published work OK. Pay negotiable. **Pays on acceptance.** Credit line given. Buys one-time rights.

INDEPENDENT RESTAURATEUR

P.O. Box 917, Newark OH 43058. (740)345-5542. Fax: (740)345-5557. E-mail: jim@theindependent restaurateur.com. Website: www.theindependent restaurateur.com. **Contact:** Jim Young, publisher. Estab. 1986. Circ. 32,000. (Formerly My Foodservice News.) Bimonthly magazine. "*Independent Restaurateur* is designed and written exclusively for the independent restaurant owner. Our editorial style is crisp and relevant. Each issue highlights the originality and exceptional qualities of peer restaurants, restaurateurs or chefs worthy of national attention. Plus useful news and ideas on topics like food and beverage, equipment and technology, staff training and service, menus and recipes, industry and consumer trends, food safety, and marketing. In short, every issue is packed with stories that specifically seek to inform, inspire and invigorate independent restaurateurs."

NEEDS Upon request.

SPECS Accepts images in digital format only. Send via CD, e-mail as JPEG files at 300-800 dpi.

MAKING CONTACT & TERMS Send e-mail. Provide self-promotion piece to be kept on file for possible future assignments. Responds only if interested; send nonreturnable samples. Simultaneous submissions OK. Pay is based on experience. Pays on publication. Credit line given. Buys first rights.

ITE JOURNAL

1627 Eye St. NW, Suite 600, Washington D.C. 20006. (202)785-0060. Fax: (202)785-0609. E-mail: ite_staff@ite.org. Website: www.ite.org. **Contact:** Newton D. Holt, managing editor. Estab. 1930. Circ. 17,000. Monthly journal of the Institute of Transportation Engineers. Emphasizes surface transportation, including streets, highways and transit. Readers are transportation engineers and professionals.

NEEDS One photo used for cover illustration per issue. Needs "shots of streets, highways, traffic, transit systems. No airports, airplanes, or bridges." Also considers landscapes, cities, rural, automobiles, travel, industry, technology, historical/vintage. Model release required. Photo captions preferred; include location, name or number of road or highway, and details.

MAKING CONTACT & TERMS Send query letter with list of stock photo subjects. Send 35mm slides or 2¼×2¼ transparencies by mail for consideration. Provide résumé, business card, brochure, flier or tearsheets to be kept on file for possible future assignments. "Send originals; no dupes, please." Simultaneous submissions and previously published work OK. Pays $200 for color cover. Pays on publication. Credit line given. Buys multiple-use rights.

TIPS "Send a package to me in the mail; package should include samples in the form of slides and transparencies."

$ ◐ JOURNAL OF ADVENTIST EDUCATION

12501 Old Columbia Pk., Silver Spring MD 20904-6600. (301)680-5075. Fax: (301)622-9627. E-mail: rumbleb@gc.adventist.org. Website: education.gc.adventist.org/jae. **Contact:** Beverly J. Robinson-Rumble, editor. Estab. 1939. Circ. 11,000 in English; 13,000 in other languages. Published 5 times/year in English, 2 times/year in French, Spanish and Portuguese. Emphasizes procedures, philosophy and subject matter of Christian education. Official professional organ of the Department of Education covering elementary, secondary and higher education for all Seventh-day Adventist educational personnel (worldwide).

NEEDS Buys 5-15 photos from freelancers/issue; up to 75 photos/year. Needs photos of children/teens, multicultural, parents, education, religious, health/fitness, technology/computers with people, committees, offices, school photos of teachers, students, parents, activities at all levels, elementary though graduate school. Reviews photos with or without a manuscript. Model release preferred. Photo captions preferred.

SPECS Uses mostly digital color images but also accepts color prints; 35mm, 2¼×2¼, 4×5 transparencies. Send digital photos via ZIP, CD or DVD (preferred); e-mail as TIFF, GIF, JPEG files at 300 dpi. Do not send large numbers of photos as e-mail attachments.

MAKING CONTACT & TERMS Send query letter with prints, photocopies, transparencies. Provide self-promotion piece to be kept on file for possible future assignments. Responds in 1 month to queries. Simultaneous submissions and previously published work OK. Pays $100-350 for color cover; $50-100 for color inside. Willing to negotiate on electronic usage of photos. Pays on publication. Credit line given. Buys one-time rights for use in magazine and on website.

TIPS "Get good-quality people shots—close-ups, verticals especially; use interesting props in classroom shots; include teacher and students together, teachers in groups, parents and teachers, cooperative learning and multi-age, multicultural children. Pay attention to backgrounds (not too busy) and understand the need for high-res photos!"

$ JOURNAL OF PSYCHOACTIVE DRUGS

856 Stanyan St., San Francisco CA 94117. (415)752-7601. E-mail: hajournal@comcast.net. Website: www.hajpd.com. Estab. 1967. Circ. 1,400. Quarterly. Emphasizes "psychoactive substances (both legal and illegal)." Readers are "professionals (primarily health) in the drug abuse treatment field."

NEEDS Uses 1 photo/issue; supplied by freelancers. Needs "full-color abstract, surreal, avant garde or computer graphics."

MAKING CONTACT & TERMS Send query letter with 4×6 color prints or 35mm slides. Online and e-mail submissions are accepted. Include SASE for return of material. Responds in 2 weeks. Simultaneous submissions and previously published work OK. Pays $50 for color cover. Pays on publication. Credit line given. Buys one-time rights.

$$ ◐ JUDICATURE

2700 University Ave., Des Moines IA 50311. (773)973-0145. Fax: (773)338-9687. E-mail: drichert@ajs.org. Website: www.ajs.org. **Contact:** David Richert, editor. Estab. 1917. Circ. 5,000. Bimonthly publication of the American Judicature Society. Emphasizes courts, administration of justice. Readers are judges, lawyers, professors, citizens interested in improving the administration of justice. Sample copy free with 9×12 SASE and 6 first-class stamps.

NEEDS Buys 1-2 photos from freelancers/issue; 6-12 photos/year. Needs photos relating to courts, the law. "Actual or posed courtroom shots are always needed." Interested in fine art, historical/vintage. Model/property release preferred. Photo captions preferred.

SPECS Uses b&w and color prints. Accepts images in digital format. Send via CD, ZIP, e-mail as JPEG files at 600 dpi.

MAKING CONTACT & TERMS Submit samples via e-mail. Simultaneous submissions and previously published work OK. Pays $250 for b&w cover; $350 for color cover; $125-250 for b&w inside; $125-300 for color inside. Pays on publication. Credit line given. Buys one-time rights.

THE LAND

Free Press Co., P.O. Box 3169, Mankato MN 56002-3169. (507)345-4523. E-mail: editor@thelandonline.com. Website: www.thelandonline.com. Estab. 1976. Circ. 33,000. Weekly tabloid covering farming in Minnesota and Northern Iowa.

SPECS Reviews contact sheets.

MAKING CONTACT & TERMS Negotiates payment individually. Buys one time rights.

$ LANDSCAPE ARCHITECTURE

636 Eye St., NW, Washington D.C. 20001-3736. (202)898-2444. Fax: (202)898-1185. E-mail: cmcgee@asla.org; lspeckhardt@asla.org. Website: www.asla.org. **Contact:** Christopher McGee, art director; Lisa Speckhardt, managing editor. Estab. 1910. Circ. 22,000. Monthly magazine of the American Society of Landscape Architects. Emphasizes "landscape architecture, urban design, parks and recreation, architecture, sculpture" for professional planners and designers.

NEEDS Buys 5-10 photos from freelancers/issue; 50-120 photos/year. Needs photos of landscape- and architecture-related subjects as described above. Special needs include aerial photography and environmental portraits. Model release required. Credit, caption information required.

MAKING CONTACT & TERMS Send query letter with samples or list of stock photo subjects. Provide brochure, flyer or tearsheets to be kept on file for possible future assignments. Response time varies. Previously published work OK. Pays $300-600/day. Pays on publication. Credit line given. Buys one-time rights.

TIPS "We take an editorial approach to photographing our subjects."

🍁 $ © THE MANITOBA TEACHER

191 Harcourt St., Winnipeg MB R3J 3H2, Canada. (204)888-7961; (800)262-8803. Fax: (204)831-0877; (800)665-0584. E-mail: gstephenson@mbteach.org. Website: www.mbteach.org. **Contact:** George Stephenson, editor. Magazine of the Manitoba Teachers' Society published 7 times/year. Emphasizes education in Manitoba—specifically teachers' interests. Readers are teachers and others in education. Sample copy free with 10×12 SASE and Canadian stamps.

NEEDS Buys 3 photos from freelancers/issue; 21 photos/year. Needs action shots of students and teachers in education-related settings. Model release required.

MAKING CONTACT & TERMS Send 8×10 glossy b&w prints by mail for consideration; include SASE for return of material. Submit portfolio for review. Provide résumé, business card, brochure, flier or tearsheets to be kept on file for possible future assignments. Responds in 1 month. Pays $40/photo for single use.

TIPS "Always submit action shots directly related to major subject matter of publication and interests of readership."

🍁 $$$ MANUFACTURING AUTOMATION & ADVANCED MANUFACTURING

Annex Publishing and Printing, 240 Edwards St., Aurora ON L4G 3S9, Canada. (905)727-0077 or (905)713-4378. E-mail: editor@automationmag.com. Website: www.automationmag.com. **Contact:** Mary Del Ciancio, editor. Estab. 1998. Circ. 19,020. Bimonthly trade magazine providing a window on the world of advanced manufacturing. Sample copies available for SASE with first-class postage.

NEEDS Occasionally buys photos from freelancers. Subjects include industry and technology. Reviews photos with or without a manuscript. Model release required. Photo captions preferred.

SPECS Uses 5×7 color prints; 4×5 transparencies. "We prefer images in high-res digital format. Send as FTP files at a minimum of 300 dpi."

MAKING CONTACT & TERMS Send query letter with résumé, stock list. Provide self-promotion piece to be kept on file for possible future assignments. Responds only if interested. Simultaneous submissions and previously published work OK. Pays $400-600 for color cover and inside images. Pays 30-45 days after invoice date. Credit line given. Buys one-time rights, electronic rights; negotiable.

TIPS "Read our magazine. Put yourself in your clients' shoes. Meet their needs and you will excel. Understand your audience and the editors' needs. Meet deadlines, be reasonable and professional."

⊘⊘ ○ MARKETING & TECHNOLOGY GROUP

1415 N. Dayton, Chicago IL 60622. (312)274-2216. E-mail: qburns@meatingplace.com. Website: www. meatingplace.com. **Contact:** Queenie Burns, vice president of design and production. Estab. 1993. Circ. 18,000. Publishes magazines that emphasize meat and poultry processing. Readers are predominantly male, ages 35-65, generally conservative. Sample copy available for $4.

NEEDS Buys 1-6 photos from freelancers/issue. Needs photos of processing plant tours and product shots. Model/property release preferred. Photo captions preferred.

MAKING CONTACT & TERMS Provide résumé, business card, brochure, flier or tearsheets to be kept on file for possible future assignments. Submit portfolio for review. Keeps samples on file. Responds in 1 month. Simultaneous submissions and previously published work OK. Payment negotiable. Pays on publication. Credit line given.

TIPS "Work quickly and meet deadlines. Follow directions when given; and when none are given, be creative while using your best judgment."

○ ○ MEETINGS & INCENTIVE TRAVEL

1 Mount Pleasant Rd., 7th Floor, Toronto ON M4Y 2Y5, Canada. (416)764-1635. E-mail: lindsey.mrav@ mtg.rogers.com. Website: www.meetingscanada.com. **Contact:** Lindsey Mrav, art director. Estab. 1970. Circ. 10,500. Bimonthly trade magazine emphasizing meetings and travel.

NEEDS Buys 1-5 photos from freelancers/issue; 7-30 photos/year. Needs photos of environmental, landscapes/scenics, cities/urban, interiors/decorating, events, food/drink, travel, business concepts, technology/computers. Reviews photos with or without a manuscript. Model/property release required. Photo captions required; include location and date.

SPECS Uses 8×12 prints depending on shoot and size of photo in magazine. Accepts images in digital format. Send via CD as TIFF files at 300 dpi.

MAKING CONTACT & TERMS Contact through rep or send query letter with tearsheets. Portfolio may be dropped off every Tuesday. Provide résumé, business card, self-promotion piece to be kept on file for possible future assignments. Responds only if interested; send nonreturnable samples. Simultaneous submissions and previously published work OK. "Payment

depends on many factors." Credit line given. Buys one-time rights.

TIPS "Send samples to keep on file."

○ MILITARY OFFICER MAGAZINE

201 N. Washington St., Alexandria VA 22314. (800)234-6622. E-mail: editor@moaa.org. Website: www.moaa.org. **Contact:** Jill Akers, photo editor. Estab. 1945. Circ. 400,000. Monthly publication of the Military Officers Association of America. Represents the interests of military officers from the 7 uniformed services: Army, Navy, Air Force, Marine Corps, Coast Guard, Public Health Service and National Oceanic and Atmospheric Administration. Emphasizes military history (particularly Vietnam and Korea), travel, health, second-career job opportunities, military family lifestyle and current military/political affairs. Readers are commissioned officers or warrant officers and their families. Sample copy available on request with 9×12 SASE.

NEEDS Buys 8 photos from freelancers/issue; 96 photos/year. "We're always looking for good color images of active-duty military people and healthy, active mature adults with a young 50s look—our readers are 55-65."

SPECS Uses digital images as well as 2¼×2¼ or 4×5 transparencies. Send digital images via e-mail as JPEG files at 300 dpi.

MAKING CONTACT & TERMS Send query letter with list of stock photo subjects. Provide résumé, brochure, flyer to be kept on file. "Do NOT send original photos unless requested to do so." Payment negotiated. "Photo rates vary with size and position." Pays on publication. Credit line given. Buys one-time rights. Submission guidelines available online.

⊘⊘ ○ NAILPRO

7628 Densmore Ave., Van Nuys CA 91406. (818)782-7328. Fax: (818)782-7450. E-mail: mjames@creative age.com. E-mail: nailpro@creativeage.com. Website: www.nailpro.com. Estab. 1989. Circ. 65,000. Monthly magazine published by Creative Age Publications. Emphasizes topics for professional manicurists and nail salon owners. Readers are females of all ages. Sample copy available for $2 with 9×12 SASE.

NEEDS Buys 10-12 photos from freelancers/issue; 120-144 photos/year. Needs photos of beautiful nails illustrating all kinds of nail extensions and enhancements; photographs showing process of creating and decorating nails, both natural and artificial. Also needs salon interiors, health/fitness, fashion/glamour. Model release required. Photo captions required; identify people and process if applicable.

SPECS Accepts images in digital format. Send via ZIP, e-mail as TIFF, EPS files at 300 dpi or better.

MAKING CONTACT & TERMS Send query letter; responds only if interested. Call for portfolio review. "Art directors are rarely available, but photographers can leave materials and pick up later (or leave nonreturnable samples)." Send color prints; 35mm, 2¼×2¼, 4×5 transparencies. Keeps samples on file. Responds in 1 month. Previously published work OK. Pays $500 for color cover; $50-250 for color inside.

TIPS "Talk to the person in charge of choosing art about photo needs for the next issue and try to satisfy that immediate need; that often leads to assignments. Submit samples and portfolios with letter stating specialties or strong points."

⑨ NAILS MAGAZINE

Bobit Business Media, 3520 Challenger St., Torrance CA 90503. (310)533-2400; (310)533-2537 (art director). Fax: (310)533-2507. E-mail: danielle.parisi@bobit. com. Website: www.nailsmag.com. **Contact:** Danielle Parisi, art director. Estab. 1982. Circ. 60,000. Monthly trade publication for nail technicians and beauty salon owners. Sample copies available.

NEEDS Buys up to 10 photos from freelancers/issue. Needs photos of celebrities, buildings, historical/vintage. Other specific photo needs: salon interiors, product shots, celebrity nail photos. Reviews photos with or without a ms. Model release required. Photo captions preferred.

SPECS Uses 35mm transparencies. Accepts images in digital format. Send via CD, ZIP as TIFF, EPS files at 266 dpi.

MAKING CONTACT & TERMS Send query letter with résumé, slides, prints. Keep samples on file. Responds in 1 month on queries. **Pays on acceptance.** Credit line sometimes given if it's requested. Buys all rights.

⑨⑨ THE NATIONAL NOTARY

9350 De Soto Ave., Chatsworth CA 91311-4926. (800)876-6827. E-mail: publications@national notary.org. Website: www.nationalnotary.org. Circ. 300,000+. Bimonthly association magazine. Emphasizes "Notaries Public and notarization—goal is to impart knowledge, understanding and unity among notaries nationwide and internationally." Readers are employed primarily in the following areas: law, government, finance and real estate.

NEEDS Number of photos purchased varies with each issue. "Photo subject depends on accompanying story/theme; some product shots used." Reviews photos with accompanying manuscript only. Model release required.

MAKING CONTACT & TERMS Send query letter with samples. Provide business card, tearsheets, résumé or samples to be kept on file for possible future assignments. Prefers to see prints as samples. Cannot return material. Previously published work OK. Pays on publication. Credit line given "with editor's approval of quality." Buys all rights.

TIPS "Since photography is often the art of a story, the photographer must understand the story to be able to produce the most useful photographs."

⑨ ⑨ ⓞ NAVAL HISTORY

U.S. Naval Institute, 291 Wood Rd., Annapolis MD 21402. (410)295-1071. Fax: (410)295-1049. E-mail: avoight@usni.org. Website: www.usni.org/magazines/navalhistory. **Contact:** Amy Voight, photo editor. Estab. 1873. Circ. 50,000. Bimonthly association publication. Emphasizes Navy, Marine Corps, Coast Guard. Readers are male and female naval officers (enlisted, retirees), civilians. Photo guidelines free with SASE.

NEEDS 40 photos from freelancers/issue; 240 photos/year. Needs photos of foreign and U.S. Naval, Coast Guard and Marine Corps vessels, industry, military, personnel and aircraft. Interested in historical/vintage. Photo captions required.

SPECS Uses 8×10 glossy or matte b&w and color prints (color preferred); transparencies. Accepts images in digital format. Send via CD, ZIP, e-mail as JPEG files at 300 dpi.

MAKING CONTACT & TERMS "We prefer to receive photo images digitally. We accept cross-platform (must be Mac and PC compatible) CDs with CMYK images at 300 dpi resolution (TIFF or JPEG). If e-mailing an image, send submissions to photo editor. We do not return prints or slides unless specified with a SASE, so please do not send original photographs. Payment for any use of photography is based upon a space rate fee of $25 for inside editorial, $50 for an article opener, and $200 for a cover. We negotiate fees with photographers who provide a volume of images for publication in books or as magazine pictorials. We sponsor three annual photo contests." For additional information please contact the photo editor. Responds in 1 month. Simultaneous submissions and previously published work OK. Pays on publication. Credit line given. Buys one-time and electronic rights.

🚫 NEVADA FARM BUREAU AGRICULTURE AND LIVESTOCK JOURNAL

2165 Green Vista Dr., Suite 205, Sparks NV 89431. (775)674-4000. E-mail: zacha@nvfb.org. Website: www.nvfb.org. **Contact:** Zach Allen, editor. Circ. 1,500. Monthly magazine. Emphasizes Nevada agriculture. Readers are primarily Nevada Farm Bureau members and their families; men, women and youth of various ages. Members are farmers and ranchers. Sample copy free with 10×13 SASE with 3 first-class stamps.

NEEDS Uses 5 photos/issue; 30% occasionally supplied by freelancers. Needs photos of Nevada agriculture people, scenes and events. Model release preferred. Photo captions required.

MAKING CONTACT & TERMS Send 3×5 and larger b&w or color prints, any format and finish, by mail with SASE for consideration. Responds in 1 week. Pays $10 for b&w cover, $50 for color cover; $5 for b&w inside. **Pays on acceptance.** Credit line given. Buys one-time rights.

TIPS In portfolio or samples, wants to see "newsworthiness, 50%; good composition, 20%; interesting action, 20%; photo contrast/resolution, 10%. Try for new angles on stock shots: awards, speakers, etc. We like 'Great Basin' agricultural scenery such as cows on the rangelands and high desert cropping. We pay little, but we offer credits for your résumé."

🌐 💲 🌑 NEWDESIGN

6A New St., Warwick, Warwickshire CV34 4RX, United Kingdom. +44 (0)1926 408207. E-mail: info@newdesignmagazine.co.uk; tanya@newdesign magazine.co.uk. Website: www.newdesignmagazine. co.uk. Estab. 2000. Circ. 5,000. Published 10 times/ year. Emphasizes product design for product designers: informative, inspirational. Sample copies available.

NEEDS Photos of product shots/still life, technology. Reviews photos with or without a manuscript.

SPECS Uses glossy color prints; 35mm transparencies. Accepts images in digital format. Send via CD as TIFF, JPEG files at 300 dpi.

MAKING CONTACT & TERMS Send query letter with résumé. Provide self-promotion piece to be kept on file for possible future assignments. Cannot return material. Responds only if interested; send nonreturnable samples. Pays on publication. Credit line given.

NFPA JOURNAL

1 Batterymarch Park, Quincy MA 02169-7471. (617)984-7568. E-mail: ssutherland@nfpa.org. Website: www.nfpa.org. **Contact:** Scott Sutherland, executive editor. Circ. 85,000. Bimonthly magazine of the National Fire Protection Association. Emphasizes fire and life safety information. Readers are fire professionals, engineers, architects, building code officials, ages 20-65. Sample copy free with 9×12 SASE or via e-mail.

NEEDS Buys 5-7 photos from freelancers/issue; 30-42 photos/year. Needs photos of fires and fire-related incidents. Model release preferred. Photo captions preferred.

MAKING CONTACT & TERMS Send query letter with list of stock photo subjects. Provide résumé, business card, brochure, flyer or tearsheets to be kept on file for possible future assignments. Send color prints and 35mm transparencies in 3-ring slide sleeve with date. Responds in 3 weeks. Payment negotiated. Pays on publication. Credit line given.

TIPS "Send cover letter, 35mm color slides, preferably with manuscripts and photo captions."

🌙 NORTHWEST TERRITORIES EXPLORER'S GUIDE

P.O. Box 610, Yellowknife NT X1A 2N5, Canada. (800)661-0788. Fax: (867)873-4059. E-mail: communications@spectacularnwt.com; info@spectacular nwt.com. Website: www.spectacularnwt.com. Estab. 1996. Circ. 90,000. Annual tourism publication for Northwest Territories. Sample copies available.

NEEDS Photos of babies/children/teens, couples, multicultural, families, senior citizens, landscapes/ scenics, wildlife, adventure, automobiles, events, travel. Interested in historical/vintage, seasonal. Also needs photos of Northwest Territories, winter and road touring.

SPECS Uses 35mm transparencies.

MAKING CONTACT & TERMS Send query letter with résumé, slides, prints, photocopies, tearsheets, transparencies, stock list. Portfolio may be dropped off Monday—Saturday. Provide résumé, business card, self-promotion piece to be kept on file for possible future assignments. Responds in 1 week to queries. Simultaneous submissions OK. **Pays on acceptance.**

🍁 $ THE ONTARIO TECHNOLOGIST

10 Four Seasons Pl., Suite 404, Etobicoke ON M9B 6H7, Canada. (416)621-9621. Fax: (416)621-8694. E-mail: editor@oacett.org. Website: www.oacett.org. **Contact:** Colleen Mellor, editor-in-chief. Circ. 23,000. Bimonthly publication of the Ontario Association of Certified Engineering Technicians and Technologists. Emphasizes engineering and applied science technology. Sample copy free with SASE and IRC.

NEEDS Uses 10-12 photos/issue. Needs how-to photos—"building and installation of equipment; similar technical subjects." Model release preferred. Photo captions preferred.

MAKING CONTACT & TERMS Prefers business card and brochure for files. Send 5×7 glossy color prints or high-res digital images at 300 dpi for consideration. Responds in 1 month. Previously published work OK. Payment varies; negotiable. Pays on publication. Credit line given. Buys one-time rights.

$$ THE PARKING PROFESSIONAL

P.O. Box 7167, Fredericksburg VA 22404. (540)371-7535. Fax: (540)371-8022. E-mail: fernandez@parking.org. Website: www.parking.org. **Contact:** Kim Fernandez, editor. Estab. 1984. Circ. 10,000. Monthly magazine of the International Parking Institute. Emphasizes parking and transportation: public, private, institutional, etc. Readers are male and female public parking and transportation managers, ages 30-60. Sample copy free.

NEEDS Buys 4-5 photos from freelancers/issue; 48-60 photos/year. Model release required. Photo captions preferred; include location, purpose, type of operation.

SPECS Uses 5×7, 8×10 color and b&w prints; 35mm, 2¼×2¼, 4×5, 8×10 transparencies.

MAKING CONTACT & TERMS Contact through rep. Arrange a personal interview to show portfolio for review. Send query letter with résumé of credits. Provide résumé, business card, brochure, flyer or tearsheets to be kept on file for possible future assignments. Responds in 2 weeks. Previously published work OK. Pays $100-300 for color cover; $25-100 for b&w or color inside; $100-500 for photo/text package. Pays on publication. Credit line given. Buys one-time, all rights; negotiable.

$$ PEDIATRIC ANNALS

6900 Grove Rd., Thorofare NJ 08086. (856)848-1000. Fax: (856)848-6091. E-mail: editor@PediatricSuperSite.com. Website: www.pediatricsupersite.com. Monthly journal. Readers are practicing pediatricians. Sample copy free with SASE.

NEEDS Uses 5-7 photos/issue; primarily stock. Occasionally uses original photos of children in medical settings.

SPECS Color photos preferred. Accepts images in digital format. Send as EPS, JPEG files at 300 dpi.

MAKING CONTACT & TERMS Request editorial calendar for topic suggestions. E-mail query with links to samples. Simultaneous submissions and previously published work OK. Pays varies; negotiable. Pays on publication. Credit line given. Buys unlimited North American rights including any and all subsidiary forms of publication, such as electronic media and promotional pieces.

🌐 $ ◐ PEOPLE MANAGEMENT

17 Britton St., London EC1M 5TP, United Kingdom. E-mail: rima@peoplemanagement.co.uk. Website: www.peoplemanagement.co.uk. **Contact:** Rima Evans, editor. Circ. 120,000. Official publication of the Chartered Institute of Personnel and Development. Biweekly trade journal for professionals in personnel, training and development.

NEEDS Photos of industry, medicine. Interested in alternative process, documentary. Reviews photos with or without a manuscript. Model release preferred. Photo captions preferred.

SPECS Accepts images in digital format. Send via CD, Jaz, ZIP, e-mail, ISDN as TIFF, EPS, JPEG files at 300 dpi.

MAKING CONTACT & TERMS Send query letter with samples. To show portfolio, photographer should follow-up with call. Portfolio should include b&w prints, slides, transparencies. Keeps samples on file. Responds only if interested; send nonreturnable samples. Pays £500 for cover; £500 including expenses for inside. Pays on publication. Rights negotiable.

$ ◐ PET PRODUCT NEWS

P.O. Box 6050, Mission Viejo CA 92690-6040. (949)855-8822. Fax: (949)855-3045. E-mail: ppneditor@

bowtieinc.com; scollins@bowtieinc.com. Website: www.petproductnews.com. **Contact:** Sherri Collins, editor. Monthly tabloid. Emphasizes pets and the pet retail business. Readers are pet store owners and managers. Sample copy available for $5. Photo guidelines free with SASE or online.

NEEDS Buys 16-50 photos from freelancers/issue; 192-600 photos/year. Needs photos of people interacting with pets, retailers interacting with customers and pets, pets doing "pet" things, pet stores and vets examining pets. Also needs wildlife, events, industry, product shots/still life. Interested in seasonal. Reviews photos with or without a manuscript. Model/property release preferred. "Enclose a shipment description with each set of photos detailing the type of animal, name of pet store, names of well-known subjects and any procedures being performed on an animal that are not self-explanatory."

SPECS Accepts images in digital format. Send via CD, ZIP, e-mail as TIFF, EPS, JPEG files at 300 dpi.

MAKING CONTACT & TERMS "We cannot assume responsibility for submitted material, but care is taken with all work. Freelancers must include a SASE for returned work." Send sharp 35mm color slides or prints by mail for consideration. Responds in 2 months. Previously published work OK. Pays $75 for color cover; $50 for color inside. Pays on publication. Photographer also receives 2 complimentary copies of issue in which their work appears. Credit line given; name and identification of subject must appear on each slide or photo. Buys one-time rights.

TIPS Looks for "appropriate subjects, clarity and framing, sensitivity to the subject. No avant garde or special effects. We need clear, straight-forward photography. Definitely no 'staged' photos; keep it natural. Read the magazine before submission. We are a trade publication and need business-like, but not boring, photos that will add to our subjects."

💲💲 PLANNING

American Planning Association, 205 N. Michigan Ave., Suite 1200, Chicago IL 60601. (312)431-9100. Fax: (312)786-6700. E-mail: slewis@planning.org. Website: www.planning.org. Richard Sessions, art director. **Contact:** Sylvia Lewis, editor. Estab. 1972. Circ. 44,000. Monthly magazine. "We focus on urban and regional planning, reaching most of the nation's professional planners and others interested in the topic." Sample copy and photo guidelines free with 10×13 SASE and 4 first-class stamps (do not send cash or checks).

NEEDS Buys 4-5 photos from freelancers/issue; 60 photos/year. Photos purchased with accompanying manuscript and on assignment. Photo essay/photo feature (architecture, neighborhoods, historic preservation, agriculture); scenic (mountains, wilderness, rivers, oceans, lakes); housing; transportation (cars, railroads, trolleys, highways). "No cheesecake; no sentimental shots of dogs, children, etc. High artistic quality is very important. We publish high-quality nonfiction stories on city planning and land use. Ours is an association magazine but not a house organ, and we use the standard journalistic techniques: interviews, anecdotes, quotes. Topics include energy, the environment, housing, transportation, land use, agriculture, neighborhoods and urban affairs." Photo captions required.

SPECS Uses 4-color prints; 35mm, 4×5 transparencies. Accepts images in digital format. Send via ZIP, CD as TIFF, EPS, JPEG files at 300 dpi and around 5×7 in physical size.

MAKING CONTACT & TERMS Send query letter with samples; include SASE for return of material. Responds in 1 month. Previously published work OK. Pays $50-100 for b&w photos; $75-200 for color photos; $375 maximum for cover; $200-600 for manuscript. Pays on publication. Credit line given.

TIPS "Subject lists are only minimally useful, as are website addresses. How the work looks is of paramount importance. Please don't send original slides or prints with the expectation of them being returned. Your best chance is to send addresses for your website showing samples of your work. We no longer keep paper on file. If we like your style we will commission work from you."

💲 PLASTICS NEWS

1725 Merriman Rd., Akron OH 44313-5283. (330)836-9180. Fax: (330)836-2322. E-mail: dloepp@crain.com. Website: www.plasticsnews.com. **Contact:** Don Loepp, managing editor. Estab. 1989. Circ. 60,000. Weekly tabloid. Emphasizes plastics industry business news. Readers are male and female executives of companies that manufacture a broad range of plastics products; suppliers and customers of the plastics processing industry. Sample copy available for $1.95.

NEEDS Buys 1-3 photos from freelancers/issue; 52-156 photos/year. Needs photos of technology related to use and manufacturing of plastic products. Model/property release preferred. Photo captions required.

MAKING CONTACT & TERMS Send unsolicited photos by mail for consideration. Provide résumé, business card, brochure, flyer or tearsheets to be kept on file for possible future assignments. Send query letter with stock list. Keeps samples on file; include SASE for return of material. Responds in 2 weeks. Simultaneous submissions and previously published work OK. Pays $125-175 for color cover; $100-150 for b&w inside; $125-175 for color inside. Pays on publication. Credit line given. Buys one-time and all rights.

$$$ ◐ PLASTICS TECHNOLOGY

6915 Valley Ave., Cincinnati OH 45244. (513) 527-8800, (800)950-8020. Fax: (646)827-4859. E-mail: sbriggs@gardnerweb.com. Website: www.ptonline.com. **Contact:** Sheri Briggs, art director. Estab. 1954. Circ. 50,000. Monthly trade magazine. Sample copy available for first-class postage.

NEEDS Buys 1-3 photos from freelancers/issue. Needs photos of agriculture, business concepts, industry, science, technology. Model release required. Photo captions required.

SPECS Accepts images in digital format. Send via CD, ZIP, e-mail as TIFF, EPS, JPEG files at 300 dpi.

MAKING CONTACT & TERMS Send query letter with résumé, photocopies, tearsheets. Provide business card, self-promotion piece to be kept on file for possible future assignments. Responds only if interested; send nonreturnable samples. Simultaneous submissions OK. Pays $1,000-1,300 for color cover; $300 minimum for color inside. Pays on publication. Credit line given. Buys one-time rights, all rights; negotiable.

POETS & WRITERS MAGAZINE

90 Broad St., Suite 2100, New York NY 10004. (212)226-3586. E-mail: editor@pw.org. Website: www.pw.org. **Contact:** Suzanne Pettypiece, managing editor. Estab. 1987. Circ. 60,000. Bimonthly literary trade magazine. "Designed for poets, fiction writers and creative nonfiction writers. We supply our readers with information about the publishing industry, conferences and workshop opportunities, grants and awards available to writers, as well as interviews with contemporary authors."

NEEDS Needs photos of contemporary writers: poets, fiction writers, writers of creative nonfiction. Photo captions required.

SPECS Digital format.

MAKING CONTACT & TERMS Provide URL, self-promotion piece or tearsheets to be kept on file for possible future assignments. Managing editor will contact photographer for portfolio review if interested. Pays on publication. Credit line given.

TIPS "We seek photographs to accompany articles and profiles. We'd be pleased to have photographers' lists of author photos."

POLICE AND SECURITY NEWS

DAYS Communications, Inc., 1208 Juniper St., Quakertown PA 18951-1520. (215)538-1240. Fax: (215)538-1208. E-mail: jdevery@policeandsecuritynews.com; dyaw@policeandsecuritynews.com. Website: www.policeandsecuritynews.com. Al Menear, assoc. publisher. **Contact:** James Devery, editor; David Yaw, publisher. Estab. 1984. Circ. 24,000. Bimonthly trade journal. "*Police and Security News* is edited for middle and upper management and top administration. Editorial content is a combination of articles and columns ranging from the latest in technology, innovative managerial concepts, training and industry news in the areas of both public law enforcement and Homeland security." Sample copy free with 13×10 SASE and $2.24 first-class postage.

NEEDS Buys 2 photos from freelancers/issue; 12 photos/year. Needs photos of law enforcement and security related. Reviews photos with or without a manuscript. Photo captions preferred.

SPECS Uses color and b&w prints.

MAKING CONTACT & TERMS Provide résumé, business card, self-promotion piece or tearsheets to be kept on file for possible future assignments. Art director will contact photographer for portfolio review if interested. Portfolio should include b&w and/or color prints or tearsheets. Keeps samples on file; include SASE for return of material. Simultaneous submissions and previously published work OK. Pays $20-40 for color inside. Pays on publication. Credit line given. Buys one-time rights; negotiable.

◐ POLICE MAGAZINE

3520 Challenger St., Torrance CA 90503. (310)533-2400; (704)527-5182. Fax: (310)533-2507. E-mail: david.griffith@policemag.com; info@policemag.

com. Website: www.policemag.com. **Contact:** David Griffith, editor. Estab. 1976. Monthly. Emphasizes law enforcement. Readers are various members of the law enforcement community, especially police officers. Sample copies available. Photo guidelines free via e-mail.

NEEDS Uses in-house photos and freelance submissions. Needs law enforcement-related photos. Special needs include photos relating to daily police work, crime prevention, international law enforcement, police technology and humor. Model release required; property release preferred. Photo captions preferred.

SPECS Uses color photos only. Accepts images in digital format. Send via e-mail or CD; no ZIP files.

MAKING CONTACT & TERMS Send contact sheet or samples by e-mail or mail for consideration. Simultaneous submissions OK. Payscale available in photographer's guidelines. Pays on publication. Buys all rights.

TIPS "Send for our editorial calendar and submit photos based on our projected needs. If we like your work, we'll consider you for future assignments. A photographer we use must grasp the conceptual and the action shots."

$ O POLICE TIMES/CHIEF OF POLICE

6350 Horizon Dr., Titusville FL 32780. (321)264-0911. E-mail: peterc@aphf.org. Website: www.aphf.org. **Contact:** Peter Connolly, publications editor. Circ. *Police Times*: quarterly trade magazine (circ. 155,000); *Chief of Police*: bimonthly trade magazine (circ. 33,000). Readers are law enforcement officers at all levels. *Police Times* is the official journal of the American Federation of Police and Concerned Citizens. Sample copy available for $2.50. Photo guidelines free with SASE.

NEEDS Buys 60-90 photos/year. Needs photos of police officers in action, civilian volunteers working with the police, and group shots of police department personnel. Wants no photos that promote other associations. Police-oriented cartoons also accepted on spec. Model release preferred. Photo captions preferred.

MAKING CONTACT & TERMS Send glossy b&w and color prints for consideration; include SASE for return of material. Responds in 3 weeks. Simultaneous submissions and previously published work OK. Pays $10-25 for b&w, $25-50 for color. **Pays on acceptance.** Credit line given if requested; editor's option. Buys all rights, but may reassign to photographer after publication; includes online publication rights.

TIPS "We are open to new and unknowns in small communities where police are not given publicity."

$ ◎ PRODUCE RETAILER

Vance Publishing Corp., 400 Knightsbridge Pkwy., Lincolnshire IL 60069. (512)906-0733. Fax: (847)634-4379. E-mail: pamelar@produceretailer.com. Website: produceretailer.com. **Contact:** Pamela Riemenschneider, editor. Estab. 1988. Circ. 12,000. Monthly magazine, e-mail newsletters, and website. Emphasizes the retail end of the fresh produce industry. Readers are male and female executives who oversee produce operations in U.S. and Canadian supermarkets as well as in-store produce department personnel. Sample copies available.

NEEDS Buys 0-2 photos from freelancers/issue; 5-10 photos/year. Needs in-store shots, environmental portraits for cover photos or display pictures. Photo captions required; include subject's name, job title and company title—all verified and correctly spelled.

SPECS Accepts images in digital format. Send via e-mail as TIFF, JPEG files.

MAKING CONTACT & TERMS E-mail only. Response time "depends on when we will be in a specific photographer's area and have a need." Pays $500-750 for color cover; $25-50/color photo. **Pays on acceptance.** Credit line given. Buys all rights.

TIPS "We seek photographers who serve as our on-site art director to ensure capture of creative angles and quality images."

PROFESSIONAL PHOTOGRAPHER

Professional Photographers of America, 229 Peachtree St. NE, Suite 2200, International Tower, Atlanta GA 30303. (404)522-8600, ext. 260. Fax: (404)614-6406. E-mail: cbishopp@ppa.com. Website: www.ppmag.com. Debbie Todd, art director. **Contact:** Cameron Bishopp, director of publications. Estab. 1907. Circ. 26,000. Monthly magazine. Emphasizes professional photography in the fields of portrait, wedding, commercial/advertising, sports, corporate and industrial. Readers include professional photographers and photographic services and educators. Approximately half the circulation is Professional Photographers of America members. Sample copy available for $5 postpaid.

💬 PPA members submit material unpaid to promote their photo businesses and obtain recognition. Images sent to *Professional Photographer* should be technically perfect, and photographers should include information about how the photo was produced.

NEEDS Buys 25-30 photos from freelancers/issue; 300-360 photos/year. "We only accept material as illustration that relates directly to photographic articles showing professional studio, location, commercial and portrait techniques. A majority are supplied by Professional Photographers of America members." Reviews photos with accompanying manuscript only. "We always need commercial/advertising and industrial success stories; how to sell your photography to major accounts, unusual professional photo assignments. Also, photographer and studio application stories about the profitable use of electronic still imaging for customers and clients." Model release preferred. Photo captions required.

SPECS Prefers images in digital format. Send via CD, e-mail as TIFF, EPS, JPEG files at 72 dpi minimum. Also uses 8×10 unmounted glossy b&w and color prints; 35mm, 2¼×2¼, 4×5, 8×10 transparencies.

MAKING CONTACT & TERMS Send query letter with résumé of credits. "We prefer a story query, or complete manuscript if writer feels subject fits our magazine. Photos will be part of manuscript package." Responds in 2 months. Credit line given.

PUBLIC POWER

1875 Connecticut Ave. NW, Suite 1200, Washington D.C. 20009-5715. (202)467-2900. Fax: (202)467-2910. E-mail: DBlaylock@publicpower.org. Website: www.publicpowermedia.org. **Contact:** David L. Blaylock, editor. Estab. 1942. Publication of the American Public Power Association, published eight times a year. Emphasizes electric power provided by cities, towns and utility districts. Sample copy and photo guidelines free.

NEEDS Buys photos on assignment only.

SPECS Prefers digital images; call art director (Robert Thomas) at (202)467-2983 to discuss.

MAKING CONTACT & TERMS Send query letter with samples. Provide résumé, business card, brochure, flyer or tearsheets to be kept on file for possible future assignments. **Pays on acceptance.** Credit line given. Buys one-time rights.

QSR

4905 Pine Cone Dr., Suite 2, Durham NC 27707. (919)489-1916. Fax: (919)489-4767. E-mail: blair@qsrmagazine.com. Website: www.qsrmagazine.com. **Contact:** Blair Chancey, editor. Estab. 1997. Trade magazine directed toward the business aspects of quick-service restaurants (fast food). "Our readership is primarily management level and above, usually franchisors and franchisees. Our goal is to cover the quick-service and fast, casual restaurant industries objectively, offering our readers the latest news and information pertinent to their business." Photo guidelines free.

NEEDS Buys 10-15 photos/year. Needs corporate identity portraits, images associated with fast food, general food images for feature illustration. Reviews photos with or without a manuscript. Model/property release preferred.

SPECS Prefers images in digital format. Send via CD/DVD, ZIP as TIFF, EPS files at 300 dpi.

MAKING CONTACT & TERMS Send query letter with samples, brochure, stock list, tearsheets. Art director will contact photographer for portfolio review if interested. Portfolio should include slides and digital sample files. Keeps samples on file. Responds only if interested; send nonreturnable samples. Simultaneous submissions and previously published work OK. Pays $250-500 for color cover; $250-500 for color inside. Pays on publication. Publisher only interested in acquiring all rights unless otherwise specified.

TIPS "Willingness to work with subject and magazine deadlines essential. Willingness to follow artistic guidelines necessary but should be able to rely on one's own eye. Our covers always feature quick-service restaurant executives with some sort of name recognition (e.g., a location shot with signage in the background, use of product props which display company logo)."

QUICK FROZEN FOODS INTERNATIONAL

2125 Center Ave., Suite 305, Fort Lee NJ 07024-5898. (201)592-7007. Fax: (201)592-7171. E-mail: JohnQFFI@aol.com. Website: www.qffintl.com. **Contact:** John M. Saulnier, chief editor/publisher. Circ. 15,000. Quarterly magazine. Emphasizes retailing, marketing, processing, packaging and distribution of frozen foods around the world. Readers are international executives involved in the frozen food industry: manufacturers, distributors, retailers, brokers, importers/exporters, warehousemen, etc. Sample copy available for $20.

NEEDS Buys 10-25 photos/year. Uses photos of agriculture, plant exterior shots, step-by-step in-plant processing shots, photos of retail store frozen food cases, head shots of industry executives, etc. Photo captions required.

SPECS Accepts digital images via CD at 300 dpi, CMYK. Also accepts 5×7 glossy b&w and/or color prints.

MAKING CONTACT & TERMS Send query letter with résumé of credits. Responds in 1 month. Payment negotiable. Pays on publication. Buys all rights but may reassign to photographer after publication.

TIPS A file of photographers' names is maintained; if an assignment comes up in an area close to a particular photographer, she/he may be contacted. "When submitting your name, inform us if you are capable of writing a story if needed."

RANGEFINDER

11835 W. Olympic Blvd., #500-E, Los Angeles CA 90064. (310)481-8036. Fax: (310)481-8037. E-mail: bhurter@rfpublishing.com. Website: www.rangefindermag.com. **Contact:** Bill Hunter, editor. Estab. 1952. Circ. 61,000. Monthly magazine. Emphasizes topics, developments and products of interest to the professional photographer. Readers are professionals in all phases of photography. Sample copy free with 11×14 SASE and 2 first-class stamps. Photo guidelines free with SASE.

NEEDS Buys very few photos from freelancers/issue. Needs all kinds of photos; almost always run in conjunction with articles. "We prefer photos accompanying 'how-to' or special interest stories from the photographer." No pictorials. Special needs include seasonal cover shots (vertical format only). Model release required; property release preferred. Photo captions preferred.

MAKING CONTACT & TERMS Send query letter with résumé of credits. Keeps samples on file; include SASE for return of material. Responds in 1 month. Previously published work occasionally OK; give details. Payment varies. Covers submitted gratis. Pays on publication. Credit line given. Buys first North American serial rights; negotiable.

⊕ READING TODAY

800 Barksdale Rd., P.O. Box 8139, Newark DE 19714-8139. (800)336-7323. Fax: (302)731-1057. E-mail: jmicklos@reading.org; readingtoday@reading.org. Website: www.reading.org. **Contact:** John Miklos, Jr., editor-in-chief. Estab. 1983. Circ. 70,000. Bimonthly newspaper of the International Reading Association. Emphasizes reading education. Readers are educators who belong to the International Reading Association. Sample copies available. Photo guidelines free with SASE.

NEEDS Buys 1 or 2 photos from freelancers/issue; 6-12 photos/year. Needs classroom shots and photos of people of all ages reading in various settings. Reviews photos with or without a manuscript. Model/property release needed. Photo captions preferred; include names (if appropriate) and context of photo.

SPECS Uses 3½×5 or larger color and b&w prints. Prefers images in digital format. Send via CD, e-mail as JPEG files.

MAKING CONTACT & TERMS Send query letter with résumé of credits and stock list. Send unsolicited photos by mail or e-mail for consideration; include SASE for return of material. Responds in 1 month. Simultaneous submissions and previously published work OK. Pays $100 for editorial use. **Pays on acceptance.** Credit line given. Buys one-time rights for print use and rights to post editorially on the IRA website.

⊕ ◐ RECOMMEND

Worth International Media Group, 5979 NW 151st St., Suite 120, Miami Lakes FL 33014. (305)828-0123; (800)447-0123. Fax: (305)826-6950. E-mail: janet@recommend.com; rick@recommend.com. Website: www.recommend.com; www.worthit.com. Rick Shively, editor-in-chief. Estab. 1985. Circ. 55,000. Monthly. Emphasizes travel. Readers are travel agents, meeting planners, hoteliers, ad agencies.

NEEDS Buys 16 photos from freelancers/issue; 192 photos/year. "Our publication divides the world into 7 regions. Every month we use travel destination-oriented photos of animals, cities, resorts and cruise lines; feature all types of travel photography from all over the world." Model/property release required. Photo captions preferred; identification required on every photo.

SPECS Accepts images in digital format. Send via CD, ZIP as TIFF, EPS files at 300 dpi minimum. "We do not accept 35mm slides or transparencies."

MAKING CONTACT & TERMS "Contact via e-mail to view sample of photography." Simultaneous submissions and previously published work OK. Pays $75-150 for color cover; $50 for front cover less than 80 square inches; $25-50 for color inside. Pays 30 days after publication. Credit line given. Buys one-time rights.

TIPS Prefers to see high-res digital files.

REFEREE

Referee Enterprises, Inc., P.O. Box 161, Franksville WI 53126. Fax: (262)632-5460. E-mail: submissions@referee.com. Website: www.referee.com. **Contact:** Julie Sternberg, managing editor. Estab. 1976. Circ. 40,000. Monthly magazine. Readers are mostly male, ages 30-50. Sample copy free with 9×12 SASE and 5 first-class stamps. Photo guidelines free with SASE.

NEEDS Buys 25-40 photos from freelancers/issue; 300-400 photos/year. Needs action officiating shots—all sports. Photo needs are ongoing. Photo captions required; include officials' names and hometowns.

SPECS Prefers to use digital files (minimum 300 dpi submitted on CD only—no DVDs) and 35mm slides. Also uses color prints.

MAKING CONTACT & TERMS Send unsolicited photos by mail or to submissions@referee.com for consideration. Responds in 2 weeks. Simultaneous submissions and previously published work OK. Pays $100 for color cover; $35 for color inside. Pays on publication. Credit line given. Rights purchased negotiable.

TIPS "Prefer photos that bring out the uniqueness of being a sports official. Need photos primarily of officials at or above the high school level in baseball, football, basketball, softball, volleyball and soccer in action. Other sports acceptable, but used less frequently. When at sporting events, take a few shots with the officials in mind, even though you may be on assignment for another reason. Don't be afraid to give it a try. We're receptive, always looking for new freelance contributors. We are constantly looking for pictures of officials/umpires. Our needs in this area have increased. Names and hometowns of officials are required."

REGISTERED REP

249 W. 17th St., 3rd Floor, New York NY 10011-5300. (212)204-4260. Fax: (212)206-3923. E-mail: sean.barrow@penton.com. Website: www.registeredrep.com; www.rrmag.com. **Contact:** Sean Barrow, art director. Estab. 1976. Circ. 100,000. Monthly magazine. Emphasizes stock brokerage and financial services industries. Magazine is "requested and read by 90% of the nation's top financial advisors."

NEEDS Uses about 8 photos/issue—3 supplied by freelancers. Needs environmental portraits of financial and brokerage personalities, and conceptual shots of financial ideas—all by assignment only. Model/property release is photographer's responsibility. Photo captions required.

SPECS Prefers 100 ISO film or better. Accepts images in digital format. Send electronically, or via CD.

MAKING CONTACT & TERMS Provide brochure, flyer or tearsheets to be kept on file for possible future assignments. Cannot return material. Due to space limitations, please obtain permission *prior* to sending digital samples via e-mail. Simultaneous submissions and previously published work OK. Pays $500-1,500 for cover; $200-800 for inside. Pays 30 days after publication. Credit line given. Buys one-time rights. Publisher requires signed rights agreement.

TIPS "We're always looking for young talent. The focus of our magazine is on design, so talent and professionalism are key."

RELAY MAGAZINE

417 E. College Ave., Tallahassee FL 32301. (850)224-3314, ext. 4. Fax: (850)224-2831. E-mail: gholmes@publicpower.com. Website: www.publicpower.com/relay.shtml. **Contact:** Garnie Holmes, editor. Estab. 1957. Circ. 5,000. Quarterly industry magazine of the Florida Municipal Electric Association. Emphasizes energy, electric, utility and telecom industries in Florida. Readers are utility professionals, local elected officials, state and national legislators, and other state power associations.

NEEDS Number of photos/issue varies; various number supplied by freelancers. Needs photos of electric utilities in Florida (hurricane/storm damage to lines, utility workers, power plants, infrastructure, telecom, etc.); cityscapes of member utility cities. Model/property release preferred. Photo captions required.

SPECS Uses 3×5, 4×6, 5×7, 8×10 b&w and color prints. Accepts images in digital format.

MAKING CONTACT & TERMS Send query letter with description of photo or photocopy. Keeps samples on file. Simultaneous submissions and previously published work OK. Payment negotiable. Rates negotiable. Pays on use. Credit line given. Buys one-time rights, repeated use (stock); negotiable.

TIPS "Must relate to our industry. Clarity and contrast important. Always query first."

$ ◐ REMODELING

HanleyWood, LLC, One Thomas Circle NW, Suite 600, Washington D.C. 20005. (202)452-0800. Fax: (202)785-1974. E-mail: salfano@hanleywood.com; ibush@hanleywood.com. Website: www.remodelingmagazine.com. **Contact:** Sal Alfano, editorial director. Estab. 1985. Circ. 80,000. Published 13 times/year. "Business magazine for remodeling contractors. Readers are small contractors involved in residential and commercial remodeling." Sample copy free with 8×11 SASE.

NEEDS Uses 10-15 photos/issue; number supplied by freelancers varies. Needs photos of remodeled residences, both before and after. Reviews photos with "short description of project, including architect's or contractor's name and phone number. We have one regular photo feature: *Before and After* describes a whole-house remodel. Request editorial calendar to see upcoming design features." Wants "interior and exterior photos of residences that emphasize the architecture over the furnishings."

SPECS Accepts images in digital format. Send via ZIP as TIFF, GIF, JPEG files at 300 dpi.

MAKING CONTACT & TERMS Provide résumé, business card, brochure, flier or tearsheets to be kept on file for possible future assignments. Responds in 1 month. **Pays on acceptance.** Credit line given. Buys one-time rights; web rights.

$$ RENTAL MANAGEMENT

1900 19th St., Moline IL 61265. (309)764-2475. Fax: (309)764-2747. E-mail: wayne.walley@ararental.org. Website: www.rentalmanagementmag.com. **Contact:** Wayne Walley, editor. Estab. 1970. Circ. 18,000. Monthly business management magazine for managers in the equipment rental industry—no appliances, furniture, cars, "rent to own" or real estate (property or apartments). Sample copies available.

NEEDS Buys 0-5 photos from freelancers/issue; 5-10 photos/year. Needs photos of business concepts, technology/computers. Projects: construction, landscaping, remodeling, parties, and events with rental companies involved. Business scenes: rental stores, communication, planning, training, financial management, HR issues, etc. Reviews photos with or without a manuscript. Model/property release preferred. Photo captions preferred; include identification of people.

SPECS Digital format requested. Send via CD, FTP, e-mail, ZIP as TIFF, EPS, JPEG files at 300 dpi/8×10 minimum (CMYK).

MAKING CONTACT & TERMS Send query letter with résumé, samples, stock list. Provide résumé, business card or self-promotion piece to be kept on file for possible future assignments. Responds only if interested; send nonreturnable samples. Previously published work OK "if not in our industry." Usually pays $200-500 for color cover; $100-400 for color inside. Negotiates fee and rights prior to assignment or purchase of existing photos. **Pays on acceptance.** Credit line given. Buys one-time rights, first rights.

TIPS "We occasionally use photographers to shoot pictures to accompany freelance articles. We also sometimes buy stock shots to help illustrate freelance and staff-written articles."

$$ ◐ RESTAURANT HOSPITALITY

Penton Media, 1300 E. Ninth St., Cleveland OH 44114. (216)931-9942. Fax: (216)696-0836. E-mail: chris.roberto@penton.com. Website: www.restaurant-hospitality.com. **Contact:** Chris Roberto, group creative director; Michael Sanson, editor-in-chief. Estab. 1919. Circ. 100,000. Monthly magazine. Emphasizes "ideas for full-service restaurants" including business strategies and industry menu trends. Readers are restaurant owners/operators and chefs for full-service independent and chain concepts.

NEEDS Assignment needs vary; 10-15 photos from freelancers/issue, plus stock; 120 photos/year. Needs "on-location portraits, restaurant interiors and details, and occasional project specific food photos." Special needs include subject-related photos: industry chefs, personalities and food trends. Model release preferred. Photo captions preferred.

SPECS Accepts images in digital format. Send via FTP, download link or e-mail.

MAKING CONTACT & TERMS Send postcard samples and e-mail with link to website. Previously published work OK. Pay varies; negotiable. Cover fees on per project basis. **Pays on acceptance.** Credit line given. Buys one-time rights plus usage in all media.

TIPS "Send a postcard that highlights your work and website. If you mainly shoot in one specific metro area, it's very helpful to know what city you're based in—seems that many photographers tastefully use only a web address on a mailer without including other information."

RETAILERS FORUM

383 E. Main St., Centerport NY 11721. (800)635-7654. E-mail: forumpublishing@aol.com. **Contact:** Martin Stevens, publisher. Estab. 1981. Circ. 70,000. Monthly magazine. Readers are entrepreneurs and retail store owners. Sample copy available for $7.50.

NEEDS Buys 3-6 photos from freelancers/issue; 36-72 photos/year. "We publish trade magazines for retail variety goods stores and flea market vendors. Items include jewelry, cosmetics, novelties, toys, etc. (five-and-dime-type goods). We are interested in creative and abstract impressions—not straight-on product shots. Humor a plus." Model/property release required.

SPECS Uses color prints. Accepts images in digital format. Send via e-mail at 300 dpi.

MAKING CONTACT & TERMS Send unsolicited photos by mail or e-mail for consideration. Does not keep samples on file; include SASE for return of material. Responds in 2 weeks. Simultaneous submissions and previously published work OK. Pays $100 for color cover; $50 for color inside. **Pays on acceptance.** Buys one-time rights.

RTOHQ: THE MAGAZINE

1504 Robin Hood Tr., Austin TX 78703. (800)204-2776. Fax: (512)794-0097. E-mail: nferguson@rtohq.org. Website: www.rtohq.org. **Contact:** Neil Ferguson, editor. Estab. 1980. Circ. 5,500. (Formerly *Progressive Rentals*.) Bimonthly magazine published by the Association of Progressive Rental Organizations. Emphasizes the rental-purchase industry. Readers are owners and managers of rental-purchase stores in North America, Canada, Great Britain and Australia.

NEEDS Buys 1-2 photos from freelancers/issue; 6-12 photos/year. Needs "strongly conceptual, cutting-edge photos that relate to editorial articles on business/management issues. Also looking for photographers to capture unique and creative environmental

portraits of our members." Model/property release preferred.

MAKING CONTACT & TERMS Provide brochure, flyer or tearsheets to be kept on file for possible future assignments. Simultaneous submissions and previously published work OK. Pays $200-450/job; $350-450 for cover; $200-450 for inside. Pays on publication. Credit line given. Buys one-time and electronic rights.

TIPS "Understand the industry and the specific editorial needs of the publication, i.e., don't send beautiful still-life photography to a trade association publication."

SCIENCE SCOPE

National Teachers Association, 1840 Wilson Blvd., Arlington VA 22201. (703)243-7100. Fax: (703)243-7177. E-mail: wthomas@nsta.org; scope@nsta.org. Website: www.nsta.org. **Contact:** Will Thomas. Journal published 9 times/year during the school year. Emphasizes "activity-oriented ideas—ideas that teachers can take directly from articles." Readers are mostly middle school science teachers. Sample copy available for $6.25. Photo guidelines free with SASE.

NEEDS About half our photos are supplied by freelancers. Needs photos of classroom activities with students participating. "In some cases, say for inter-disciplinary studies articles, we'll need a specialized photo." Model release required. Need for photo captions "depends on the type of photo."

SPECS Uses slides, negatives, prints. Accepts images in digital format. Send via CD, e-mail as TIFF, EPS files at 300 dpi minimum.

MAKING CONTACT & TERMS Arrange a personal interview to show portfolio. Send query letter with stock list. Provide résumé, business card, brochure, flyer or tearsheets to be kept on file for possible future assignments. Considers previously published work; "prefer not to, although in some cases there are exceptions." Pays $250 for cover photos and $100 for small b&w photos. Pays on publication. Sometimes pays kill fee. Credit line given. Buys one-time rights; negotiable.

TIPS "We look for clear, crisp photos of middle-level students working in the classroom. Shots should be candid with students genuinely interested in their activity. (The activity is chosen to accompany manuscript.) Please send photocopies of sample shots along with listing of preferred subjects and/or listing of stock photo topics."

$ SECURITY DEALER & INTEGRATOR

3 Huntington Quadrangle, Suite 301N, Melville NY 11747. (631)845-2700. Fax: (631)845-2721. E-mail: deborah.omara@cygnusb2b.com. Website: www.securityinfowatch.com. **Contact:** Deborah L. O'Mara, editor-in-chief. Estab. 1967. Circ. 28,000. Monthly magazine. Emphasizes security subjects. Readers are business owners who install alarm, security, CCTV, home automation and access control systems. Sample copy free with SASE. "*SD&I* seeks credible, reputable thought leaders to provide timely, original editorial content for our readers—security value-added resellers, integrators, systems designers, central station companies, electrical contractors, consultants and others—on rapidly morphing new communications and signaling technologies, networking, standards, business acumen, project information and other topics to hone new skills and build business. Content must add value to our pages and provide thought-provoking insights on the industry and its future. In most cases, content must be vendor-neutral, unless the discussion is on a patented or proprietary technology."

NEEDS Uses 2-5 photos/issue; none at present supplied by freelance photographers. Needs photos of security-application-equipment. Model release preferred. Photo captions required.

SPECS Photos must be JPEG, TIFF or EPS form for any section of the magazine, including product sections (refer to the editorial calendar). We require a 300 dpi image at a minimum 100% size of 2×3 for product submissions. *SD&I* has a File transfer Protocol (FTP) site to send images over 10MB; visit www.cygnusb2b.com and note the Cygnus Web FTP icon on the bottom of the home page. Or, consult the editor for FTP instructions. See more complete guidelines online at: www.securityinfowatch.com/magazine/sdi/editorialguidelines.

MAKING CONTACT & TERMS Send b&w and color prints by mail for consideration; include SASE for return of material. Responds "immediately." Simultaneous submissions and/or previously published work OK.

TIPS "Do not send originals; send dupes only, and only after discussion with editor."

SPECIALTY TRAVEL INDEX

Alpine Hansen, P.O. Box 458, San Anselmo CA 94979. (415)455-1643. E-mail: info@specialtytravel.com. Website: www.specialtytravel.com. Estab. 1980. Circ. 35,000. Biannual trade magazine. Directory of special interest travel. Readers are travel agents. Sample copy available for $6.

NEEDS Contact for want list. Buys photo/manuscript packages. Photo captions preferred.

SPECS Uses digital images. Send via CD or photographer's website. "No e-mails for photo submissions!"

MAKING CONTACT & TERMS Send query letter with résumé, stock list and website link to view samples. Does not keep samples on file; include SASE for return of material. Responds in 2 months to queries. Simultaneous submissions and previously published work OK. Pays $25/photo. **Pays on acceptance.** Credit line given.

$ $ SUCCESSFUL MEETINGS

Northstar Travel Media, Northstar Travel Media, 100 Lighting Way, Secaucus NJ 07094. (646)380-6247. E-mail: valonzo@ntmllc.com; jruf@ntmllc.com. Website: www.successfulmeetings.com. **Contact:** Vincent Alonzo, editor-in-chief; Jennifer Ruf, art director. Estab. 1955. Circ. 70,000. Monthly. Emphasizes business group travel for all sorts of meetings. Readers are business and association executives who plan meetings, exhibits, conventions and incentive travel. Sample copy available for $10.

NEEDS Special needs include high-quality corporate portraits; conceptual, out-of-state shoots.

MAKING CONTACT & TERMS Arrange a personal interview to show portfolio. Send query letter with résumé of credits and list of stock photo subjects. Responds in 2 weeks. Simultaneous submissions and previously published work OK, "only if you let us know." Pays $500-750 for color cover; $50-150 for b&w inside; $75-200 for color inside; $150-250/b&w page; $200-300/color page; $50-100/hour; $175-350/¾ day. **Pays on acceptance**. Credit line given. Buys one-time rights.

THE SURGICAL TECHNOLOGIST

6 W. Dry Creek Circle, Suite 200, Littleton CO 80120-8031. (303)694-9130. Fax: (303)694-9169. E-mail: kludwig@ast.org. Website: www.ast.org. **Contact:** Karen Ludwig, editor/publisher. Circ. 23,000. Monthly journal of the Association of Surgical Technologists.

Emphasizes surgery. Readers are operating room professionals, well educated in surgical procedures, ages 20-60. Sample copy free with 9×12 SASE and 5 first-class stamps. Photo guidelines free with SASE.

NEEDS Needs "surgical, operating room photos that show members of the surgical team in action." Model release required.

MAKING CONTACT & TERMS Send low-res JPEGs with query via e-mail. Responds in 4 weeks after review by editorial board. Simultaneous submissions and previously published work OK. Payment negotiable. **Pays on acceptance.** Credit line given. Buys all rights.

$ ◐ TECHNIQUES

1410 King St., Alexandria VA 22314. (703)683-3111; 800-826-9972. Fax: (703)683-7424. E-mail: techniques@acteonline.org. Website: www.acteonline.org. **Contact:** Susan Emeagwali, managing editor. Estab. 1926. Circ. 42,000. Monthly magazine of the Association for Career and Technical Education. Emphasizes education for work and on-the-job training. Readers are teachers and administrators in high schools and colleges. Sample copy free with 10×13 SASE.

💬 This publication is now outsourced and offers little opportunity for freelance photography.

NEEDS Buys 1-2 photos from freelancers/issue; 12-24 photos/year. Needs "students in classroom and job training settings; teachers; students in work situations." Model release preferred for children. Photo caption preferred; include location, explanation of situation.

SPECS Uses 5×7 color prints; 35mm transparencies.

MAKING CONTACT & TERMS Send query letter with list of stock photo subjects. Send unsolicited photos by mail for consideration. Provide résumé, business card, brochure, flyer or tearsheets to be kept on file for possible future assignments. Responds as needed. Simultaneous submissions and previously published work OK. Pays $400 minimum for color cover; $30 minimum for b&w inside; $50 minimum for color inside; $500-1,000/job. Pays on publication. Credit line given. Buys one-time rights; sometimes buys all rights; negotiable.

$ $ TEXAS REALTOR MAGAZINE

P.O. Box 2246, Austin TX 78768. (800)873-9155; (512)370-2286. Fax: (512)370-2390. E-mail: jmathews@texasrealtors.com. Website: www.texasrealtors.com. **Contact:** Joel Mathews, art director. Estab. 1972. Circ. 50,000. Monthly magazine of the Texas Association of Realtors. Emphasizes real estate sales and related industries. Readers are male and female realtors, ages 20-70. Sample copy free with SASE.

NEEDS Buys 10 photos from freelancers/issue; 120 photos/year. Needs photos of architectural details, business, office management, telesales, real estate sales, commercial real estate, nature. Property release required.

MAKING CONTACT & TERMS Pays $75-300/color photo; $1,500/job. Buys one-time rights; negotiable.

$ ◎ TEXTILE RENTAL MAGAZINE

1800 Diagonal Rd., Suite 200, Alexandria VA 22314. (877)770-9274. Fax: (703)519-0026. E-mail: jmorgan@trsa.org. Website: www.trsa.org. Monthly magazine of the Textile Rental Services Association of America. Emphasizes the linen supply, industrial and commercial textile rental and service industry. Readers are "heads of companies, general managers of facilities, predominantly male; national and international readers."

NEEDS Photos needed on assignment basis only. Model release preferred. Photo captions preferred or required "depending on subject."

MAKING CONTACT & TERMS "We contact photographers on an as-needed basis from a directory. We also welcome inquiries and submissions." Cannot return material. Previously published work OK. Pays $350 for color cover plus processing; "depends on the job." **Pays on acceptance.** Credit line given if requested. Buys all rights.

THOROUGHBRED TIMES

2008 Mercer Rd., P.O. Box 8237, Lexington KY 40533. (859)260-9800. E-mail: tlaw@thoroughbredtimes.com. Estab. 1985. Circ. 20,000. Weekly tabloid news magazine. Emphasizes Thoroughbred breeding and racing. Readers are wide demographic range of industry professionals. Photo guidelines available upon request.

NEEDS Buys 10-15 photos from freelancers/issue; 520-780 photos/year. Looks for photos "only from desired trade (Thoroughbred breeding and racing)." Needs photos of specific subject features (personality, farm or business). Model release preferred. Photo captions preferred. "File info required."

MAKING CONTACT & TERMS Provide business card, brochure, flier or tearsheets to be kept on file for possible future assignments. Responds in 1 month. Previously published work OK. Pays $100 for color or b&w cover; $50 for b&w inside; $50 for color; $250/day. Pays on publication. Credit line given. Buys one-time rights.

$ TOBACCO INTERNATIONAL

Lockwood Publications, Inc., 26 Broadway, Floor 9M, New York NY 10004. (212)391-2060. Fax: (212)827-0945. E-mail: e.leonard@lockwoodpublications.com; editor@tobaccointernational.com. Website: www.tobaccointernational.com. **Contact:** Emerson Leonard, editor. Estab. 1886. Circ. 5,000. Monthly international business magazine. Emphasizes cigarettes, tobacco products, tobacco machinery, supplies and services. Readers are executives, ages 35-60. Sample copy free with SASE.

NEEDS Uses 20 photos/issue. "Prefer photos of people smoking, processing or growing tobacco products from all around the world, but any interesting newsworthy photos relevant to subject matter is considered." Model and/or property release preferred.

MAKING CONTACT & TERMS Send query letter with photocopies, transparencies, slides or prints. Does not keep samples on file; include SASE for return of material. Responds in 3 weeks. Simultaneous submissions OK (not if competing journal). Pays $50/color photo. Pays on publication. Credit line may be given.

[O] TODAY'S PHOTOGRAPHER

American Image Press, P.O. Box 42, Hamptonville NC 27020-0042. (336)468-1138. Fax: (336)468-1899. E-mail: homeoffice@ainewsservice.net. Website: www.aipress.com. **Contact:** Vonda H. Blackburn, editor-in-chief. Estab. 1986. Circ. 78,000. Published once a year in print, twice/year online. Magazine of the International Freelance Photographers Organization. Emphasizes making money with photography. Readers are 90% male photographers. Sample copy available for 9×12 SASE. Photo guidelines free with SASE.

NEEDS Buys 40 photos from freelancers/issue; 240 photos/year. Model release required. Photo captions preferred. Only buys content from members of IFPO ($74 membership fee, plus $7 shipping).

MAKING CONTACT & TERMS Send 35mm, 2¼×2¼, 4×5, 8×10 b&w and color prints or transparencies by mail for consideration; include SASE for return of material. Responds at end of quarter. Simultaneous submissions and previously published work OK. Payment negotiable. Credit line given. Buys one-time rights, per contract.

$$ TOP PRODUCER

383 N. Downey St., Walcott IA 52773. (563)284-5054. E-mail: drafferty@farmjournal.com. Website: www.agweb.com. **Contact:** Dana Rafferty, art director; Jeanne Bernick, editor. Circ. 120,000. Monthly. Emphasizes American agriculture. Readers are active farmers, ranchers or agribusiness people. Sample copy and photo guidelines free with SASE.

NEEDS Buys 5-10 photos from freelancers/issue; 60-100 photos/year. "We use studio-type portraiture (environmental portraits), technical, details and scenics." Model release preferred. Photo captions required.

MAKING CONTACT & TERMS Send query letter with résumé of credits along with business card, brochure, flyer or tearsheets to be kept on file for possible future assignments. "Do not send originals!" Please send information for online portfolios/websites, as we often search for stock images on such sites. Digital files and portfolios may be sent via CD to the address noted above." Simultaneous submissions and previously published work OK. Pays $75-400 for color photos; $200-400/day, with additional bonus for cover usage. **Pays on acceptance.** Credit line given. Buys one-time rights.

TIPS In portfolio or samples, likes to see "about 40 samples showing photographer's use of lighting and ability to work with people. Know your intended market. Familiarize yourself with the magazine and keep abreast of how photos are used in the general magazine field."

$ TRANSPORTATION MANAGEMENT & ENGINEERING

Scranton Gillette Communications, Inc., 3030 W. Salt Creek Lane, Suite 201, Arlington Heights IL 60016. (847)391-1000. Fax: (847)390-0408. E-mail: bwilson@sgcmail.com. Website: www.roadsbridges.com. **Contact:** Bill Wilson, editor. Estab. 1994. Circ. 18,000. Quarterly supplement. "*TM&E* is a controlled publication targeted toward 18,000 traffic/transit system planners, designers, engineers and managers in North America." Sample copies available.

NEEDS Buys 1-2 photos from freelancers/issue; 5-10 photos/year. Needs photos of landscapes/scenics, transportation-related, traffic, transit. Reviews photos with or without ms. Property release preferred. Photo captions preferred.

SPECS Uses 5×7 glossy prints; 35mm transparencies. Accepts images in digital format. Send via CD as TIFF, EPS files at 300 dpi.

MAKING CONTACT & TERMS Send query letter with prints. Portfolio may be dropped off every Monday. Responds in 3 weeks to queries. Responds only if interested; send nonreturnable samples. Pays $100-1,000 for color cover; $50-500 for color inside. Pays on publication. Credit line sometimes given. Buys all rights; negotiable.

TIPS "Read our magazine."

⊕ TRANSPORT TOPICS

950 N. Glebe Rd., Suite 210, Arlington VA 22203. (703)838-1770. Fax: (703)838-7916. E-mail: nabt@trucking.org. Website: www.ttnews.com. **Contact:** Neil Abt, news editor. Estab. 1935. Circ. 31,000. Weekly tabloid. Publication of American Trucking Associations. Emphasizes the trucking industry and freight transportation. Readers are executives, ages 35-65.

NEEDS Uses approximately 12 photos/issue; amount supplied by freelancers "depends on need." Needs photos of truck transportation in all modes. Model/property release preferred. Photo captions preferred.

MAKING CONTACT & TERMS Send unsolicited JPEGs by e-mail for consideration. Provide résumé, business card, brochure, flyer or tearsheets to be kept on file for possible future assignments. Does not keep samples on file; include SASE for return of material. Responds in 1 month. Simultaneous submissions and previously published work OK. Payment negotiable. Pays standard "market rate" for color cover photo. **Pays on acceptance**. Credit line given. Buys one-time or permanent rights; negotiable.

TIPS "Trucks/trucking must be dominant element in the photograph—not an incidental part of an environmental scene."

TREE CARE INDUSTRY MAGAZINE

Tree Care Industry Association, 136 Harvey Rd., Suite 101, Londonderry NH 03053. (800)733-2622 or (603)314-5380. Fax: (603)314-5386. E-mail: staruk@tcia.org. Website: www.treecareindustry.org. **Contact:** Don Staruk, editor. Estab. 1990. Circ. 27,500. Monthly trade magazine for arborists, landscapers and golf course superintendents interested in professional tree care practices. Sample copy available for $5.

NEEDS Buys 3-6 photos/year. Needs photos of environment, landscapes/scenics, gardening. Reviews photos with or without a manuscript.

SPECS Uses color prints. Accepts images in digital format. Send via e-mail as TIFF files at 300 dpi.

MAKING CONTACT & TERMS Send query letter with stock list. Does not keep samples on file; include SASE for return of material. Pays $100 maximum for color cover; $25 minimum for color inside. Pays on publication. Credit line given. Buys one-time rights and online rights.

$ UNITED AUTO WORKERS (UAW)

UAW Solidarity House, 8000 E. Jefferson Ave., Detroit MI 48214. (313)926-5291. E-mail: uawsolidarity@uaw.net. Website: www.uaw.org. **Contact:** Jennifer John, editor. Trade union representing 650,000 workers in auto, aerospace, agricultural-implement industries, government and other areas. Publishes *Solidarity* magazine. Photos used for magazine, brochures, newsletters, posters and calendars.

NEEDS Buys 85 freelance photos/year; offers 12-18 freelance assignments/year. Needs photos of workers at their place of employment, and social issues for magazine story illustrations. Reviews stock photos. Model release preferred. Photo captions preferred.

SPECS Uses 8×10 prints.

MAKING CONTACT & TERMS Arrange a personal interview to show portfolio. In portfolio, prefers to see b&w and color workplace shots. Send query letter with samples and SASE by mail for consideration. Prefers to see published photos as samples. Provide résumé or tearsheets to be kept on file for possible future assignments. Notifies photographer if future assignments can be expected. Responds in 2 weeks. Pays $75-175 for b&w or color; $300/half-day; $600/day. Credit line given. Buys one-time rights and all rights; negotiable.

VETERINARY ECONOMICS

Advanstar Veterinary Healthcare Communications, 8033 Flint, Lenexa KS 66214. (800)255-6864. Fax: (913)871-3808. E-mail: ve@advanstar.com. Website: www.vetecon.com. Estab. 1960. Circ. 54,000. Monthly trade magazine emphasizing practice management for veterinarians.

NEEDS Photographers on an "as needed" basis for editorial portraits; must be willing to sign license agreement; 2-3 photo portraits/year. License agreement required. Photo captions preferred.

SPECS Prefers images in digital format. Send via FTP, e-mail as JPEG files at 300 dpi.

MAKING CONTACT & TERMS Send 1 e-mail with sample image less than 1 MB; repeat e-mails are deleted. Does not keep samples on file. **Pays on acceptance**. Credit line given.

WATER WELL JOURNAL

National Ground Water Association, 601 Dempsey Rd., Westerville OH 43081. Fax: (614)898-7786. Website: www.ngwa.org. **Contact:** Thad Plumley, director of publications; Mike Price, associate editor. Circ. 24,000. Monthly association publication. Emphasizes construction of water wells, development of ground water resources and ground water cleanup. Readers are water well drilling contractors, manufacturers, suppliers, and ground water scientists. Sample copy available for $15 U.S., $36 foreign.

NEEDS Buys 1-3 freelance photos/issue plus cover photos; 12-36 photos/year. Needs photos of installations and how-to illustrations. Model release preferred. Photo captions required.

SPECS Accepts images in digital format. Send via CD, ZIP as TIFF files at 300 dpi.

MAKING CONTACT & TERMS Send query letter with samples. "We'll contact you." Pays $250 for color cover; $50 for b&w or color inside; "flat rate for assignment." Pays on publication. Credit line given. Buys all rights.

TIPS "E-mail or send written inquiries; we'll reply if interested. Unsolicited materials will not be returned."

THE WHOLESALER

1838 Techny Court, Northbrook IL 60062. (847)564-1127. E-mail: editor@thewholesaler.com. Website: www.thewholesaler.com. Estab. 1946. Circ. 35,000. Monthly news tabloid. Emphasizes wholesaling/distribution in the plumbing, heating, air conditioning, piping (including valves), fire protection industry. Readers are owners and managers of wholesale distribution businesses; manufacturer representatives. Sample copy free with 11×15¾ SASE and 5 first-class stamps.

NEEDS Buys 3 photos from freelancers/issue; 36 photos/year. Interested in field and action shots in the warehouse, on the loading dock, at the job site. Property release preferred. Photo captions preferred—"just give us the facts."

MAKING CONTACT & TERMS Send query letter with stock list. Send any size glossy color and b&w prints by mail with SASE for consideration. Responds in 2 weeks. Simultaneous submissions and previously published work OK. Pays on publication. Buys one-time rights.

$$ WINES & VINES

1800 Lincoln Ave., San Rafael CA 94901. (415)453-9700. Fax: (415)453-2517. E-mail: edit@winesandvines.com. Website: www.winesandvines.com. **Contact:** Kerry Kirkham, technical editor. Estab. 1919. Circ. 5,000. Monthly magazine. Emphasizes winemaking, grape growing, and marketing in North America and internationally for wine industry professionals, including winemakers, grape growers, wine merchants and suppliers.

NEEDS Color cover subjects—on a regular basis.

SPECS Accepts images in digital format. Send via CD, ZIP, e-mail as TIFF, or JPEG files at 400 dpi.

MAKING CONTACT & TERMS Prefers e-mail query with link to portfolio; or send material by mail for consideration. Will e-mail if interested in reviewing photographer's portfolio. Provide business card to be kept on file for possible future assignments. Responds in 3 months. Previously published work considered. Pays $100-350 for color cover, or negotiable ad trade out. Pays on publication. Credit line given. Buys one-time rights.

$ WISCONSIN ARCHITECT

321 S. Hamilton St., Madison WI 53703-4000. (608)257-8477. E-mail: editor@aiaw.org. Website: www.aiaw.org. Estab. 1931. Circ. 3,700. Annual magazine of the American Institute of Architects Wisconsin. Emphasizes architecture. Readers are design/construction professionals.

NEEDS Uses approximately 100 photos/issue. "Photos are almost exclusively supplied by architects who are submitting projects for publication. Of these, approximately 65% are professional photographers hired by the architect."

MAKING CONTACT & TERMS "Contact us using online submission/contact form." Keeps samples on file. Responds when interested. Simultaneous submissions and previously published work OK. Pays on publication. Credit line given. Rights negotiable.

🟦 💲💲 🌑 WORLD TOBACCO

Quartz Business Media, Westgate House, 120/130 Station Road, Redhill, Surrey RH1 1ET, United Kingdom. +44(1737)855000. Fax: +44(1737)855327. E-mail: anja.helk@konradin.de; stefanie.rossel@konradin.de; william.mcewen@konradin.de. Website: www.world tobacco.co.uk. William McEwen, editor. **Contact:** Anja Helk, editor. Circ. 4,300. Trade magazine. "Focuses on all aspects of the tobacco industry from international trends to national markets, offering news and views on the entire industry from leaf farming to primary and secondary manufacturing, to packaging, distribution and marketing." Sample copies available. Request photo guidelines via e-mail.

NEEDS Buys 5-10 photos from freelancers/issue; agriculture, product shots/still life. "Anything related to tobacco and smoking. Abstract smoking images considered, as well as international images."

SPECS Accepts almost all formats. Minimum resolution of 300 dpi at the size to be printed. Prefers TIFFs to JPEGs, but can accept either.

MAKING CONTACT & TERMS E-mail query letter with link to photographer's website, JPEG samples at 72 dpi. Provide self-promotion piece to be kept on file for possible future assignments. Pays £200 maximum for cover photo. **Pays on acceptance.** Credit line given.

TIPS "Check the features list on our website."

WRITER'S DIGEST

F+W Media, Inc., 4700 E. Galbraith Rd., Cincinnati OH 45236. (513)531-2690, ext. 11483. E-mail: wd submissions@fwmedia.com. Website: www.writers digest.com. Estab. 1920. Monthly consumer magazine. "Our readers write fiction, nonfiction, plays and scripts. They're interested in improving their writing skills and the ability to sell their work, and finding new outlets for their talents." Photo guidelines free with SASE or via e-mail.

NEEDS Occasionally buys photos from freelancers. Needs photos of education, hobbies, writing life, business concepts, product shots/still life. Other specific photo needs: photographers to shoot authors on location for magazine cover. Model/property release required. Photo captions required; include your copyright notice.

SPECS Uses 8×10 color and/or digital (resizable) images. Accepts images in digital format if hired. Send via CD as TIFF, EPS, JPEG files at 300 dpi (at hire).

MAKING CONTACT & TERMS Prefers postal mail submissions to keep on file. Final art may be sent via e-mail. Buys one-time rights. **Pays on acceptance:** $500-1,000 for color cover; $100-800 for color inside. Responds only if interested; send nonreturnable samples. Credit line given. Buys one-time rights.

TIPS "I like having several samples to look at. Online portfolios are great. Submissions are considered for other *Writer's Digest* publications as well. For stock photography, please include pricing/sizes of b&w usage if available."

WRITERS' JOURNAL

Val-Tech Media, P.O. Box 394, Perham MN 56573-0394. (218)346-7921. Fax: (218)346-7924. E-mail: writersjournal@writersjournal.com. Website: www.writersjournal.com. **Contact:** Leon Ogroske, editor. Estab. 1980. Circ. 15,000. Bimonthly trade magazine. "*Writers' Journal* is read by thousands of aspiring writers whose love of writing has taken them to the next step: writing for money. We are an instructional manual giving writers the tools and information necessary to get their work published. We also print works by authors who have won our writing contests." Sample copy available for $6.

NEEDS Buys 1 photo from freelancers/issue; 6 photos/year. Needs photos of landscapes/scenics or wildlife; more recently, uses photos about reading or writing.

SPECS Uses 8×10 color prints. "Digital images must be accompanied by a hardcopy printout."

MAKING CONTACT & TERMS Does not keep samples on file; include SASE for return of material. Responds in 2 months. Pays $50 for color cover. Pays on publication. Credit line given. Buys one time North American rights.

BOOK PUBLISHERS

There are diverse needs for photography in the book publishing industry. Publishers need photos for the obvious (covers, jackets, text illustrations, and promotional materials), but they may also need them for use on CD-ROMs and websites. Generally, though, publishers either buy individual or groups of photos for text illustration, or they publish entire books of photography.

Those in need of text illustration use photos for cover art and interiors of textbooks, travel books, and nonfiction books. For illustration, photographs may be purchased from a stock agency or from a photographer's stock, or the publisher may make assignments. Publishers usually pay for photography used in book illustration or on covers on a per-image or per-project basis. Some pay photographers hourly or day rates, if on an assignment basis. No matter how payment is made, however, the competitive publishing market requires free-lancers to remain flexible.

To approach book publishers for illustration jobs, send a cover letter with photographs or slides and a stock photo list with prices, if available. (See sample stock list in "Running Your Business.") If you have a website, provide a link to it. If you have published work, tearsheets are very helpful in showing publishers how your work translates to the printed page.

PHOTO BOOKS

Publishers who produce photography books usually publish books with a theme, featuring the work of one or several photographers. It is not always necessary to be well-known to publish your photographs as a book. What you do need, however, is a unique perspective, a salable idea, and quality work.

For entire books, publishers may pay in one lump sum or with an advance plus royalties (a percentage of the book sales). When approaching a publisher for your own book of photographs, query first with a brief letter describing the project, and include sample photographs. If the publisher is interested in seeing the complete proposal, you can send additional information in one of two ways depending on the complexity of the project.

Prints placed in sequence in a protective box, along with an outline, will do for easy-to-describe, straightforward book projects. For more complex projects, you may want to create a book dummy. A dummy is basically a book model with photographs and text arranged as they will appear in finished book form. Book dummies show exactly how a book will look, including the sequence, size, format and layout of photographs and accompanying text. The quality of the dummy is important, but keep in mind that the expense can be prohibitive.

To find the right publisher for your work, first check the Subject Index in the back of the book to help narrow your search, then read the appropriate listings carefully. Send for catalogs and guidelines for those publishers that interest you. You may find guidelines on publishers' websites as well. Also, become familiar with your local bookstore or visit the site of an online bookstore such as Amazon.com. By examining the books already published, you can find those publishers who produce your type of work. Check for both large and small publishers. While smaller firms may not have as much money to spend, they are often more willing to take risks, especially on the work of new photographers. Keep in mind that photo books are expensive to produce and may have a limited market.

ACTION PUBLISHING

P.O. Box 391, Glendale CA 91209. (323)478-1667. Fax: (323)478-1767. Website: www.actionpublishing.com. Estab. 1996.

SPECS Uses all formats.

MAKING CONTACT & TERMS Art, illustration and photography samples should be c/o the art director. Samples are reviewed and filed for future reference. In general, don't expect a response unless there is a specific interest. Samples returned with SASE.

TIPS "We use a small number of photos. Promo is kept on file for reference if potential interest. If book proposal, send query letter first with web link to sample photos if available."

AERIAL PHOTOGRAPHY SERVICES

2511 S. Tryon St., Charlotte NC 28203. (704)333-5144. Fax: (704)333-4911. Website: www.aps-1.com. Estab. 1960. Publishes pictorial books, calendars, postcards, etc. Photos used for text illustrations, book covers, souvenirs. Examples of recently published titles: *Blue Ridge Parkway Calendar*; *Great Smoky Mountain Calendar*; *North Carolina Calendar*; *North Carolina Outer Banks Calendar*—all depicting the seasons of the year. Photo guidelines free with SASE.

NEEDS Buys 100 photos/year. Wants landscapes/scenics, mostly seasons. Reviews stock photos. Model/property release preferred. Photo captions required; include location.

SPECS Uses 5×7, 8×10 matte color prints; 35mm, 2¼×2¼, 4×5 transparencies; C41 120mm film mostly. Accepts images in digital format on CD.

MAKING CONTACT & TERMS Send unsolicited photos by mail with SASE for consideration. Works with local freelancers on assignment only. Responds in 3 weeks. Simultaneous submissions OK. Payment negotiable. **Pays on acceptance.** Credit line given. Buys all rights; negotiable.

TIPS "Looking for fresh looks; creative, dynamic, crisp images. We use a lot of nature photography, scenics of the Carolinas area including Tennessee and the mountains. We like to have a nice variety of the 4 seasons. We also look for quality chromes good enough for big reproduction. Only submit images that are very sharp and well exposed. For the fastest response time, please limit your submission to only the highest-quality transparencies. Seeing large-format photography (the most 120mm–4×5). If you would like to submit images on a CD, that is also acceptable."

ALLYN & BACON PUBLISHERS

75 Arlington St., Suite 300, Boston MA 02116. Website: www.ablongman.com. Find local rep to submit materials via online rep locator. Publishes college textbooks. Photos used for text illustrations, book covers. Examples of recently published titles: *Criminal Justice*; *Including Students With Special Needs*; *Social Psychology* (text illustrations and promotional materials). Offers one assignment plus 80 stock projects/year.

NEEDS Photos of babies/children/teens, celebrities, couples, multicultural, families, parents, senior citizens, disasters, education, special education, science, technology/computers. Interested in fine art, historical/vintage. Also uses multi-ethnic photos in education, health and fitness, people with disabilities, business, social sciences, and good abstracts. Reviews stock photos. Model/property release required.

SPECS Uses b&w prints, any format; all transparencies. Accepts images in digital format.

MAKING CONTACT & TERMS Send via CD, ZIP, e-mail as TIFF, EPS, PICT, GIF, JPEG files at 72 dpi for review, 300 dpi for use. See photo and art specifications online.

TIPS "Send tearsheets and promotion pieces. Need bright, strong, clean abstracts and unstaged, nicely lit people photos."

APPALACHIAN MOUNTAIN CLUB BOOKS

5 Joy St., Boston MA 02108. (617)523-0636. Fax: (617)523-0722. E-mail: amcpublications@outdoors. org. Website: www.outdoors.org. **Contact:** Editor-in-chief. Estab. 1876. Publishes hardcovers and trade paperbacks. Photos used for text illustrations, book covers. Examples of recently published titles: *Discover* series, *Best Day Hikes* series, *Trail Guide* series. Model release required. Photo captions preferred; include location, description of subject, photographer's name and phone number. Uses print-quality color and grayscale images.

NEEDS Looking for photos of nature, hiking, backpacking, biking, paddling, skiing in the Northeast.

SPECS AD, LS, LI, SP

MAKING CONTACT & TERMS E-mail light boxes. Art director will contact photographer if interested. Keeps samples on file. Responds only if interested.

🔲 ⬤ BARBOUR PUBLISHING, INC.

1800 Barbour Dr., P.O. Box 719, Urichsville OH 44683. (740)922-6045. E-mail: editors@barbourbooks.com; aschrock@barbourbooks.com. E-mail: fiction submit@barbourbooks.com. Website: www.barbourbooks.com. Paul Muckley, senior editor (nonfiction). **Contact:** Ashley Schrock, creative director. Estab. 1981. Publishes adventure, humor, juvenile, romance, religious, young adult, coffee table, cooking and reference books. Specializes in inspirational fiction. "We're an inspirational company—no graphic or provocative images are used. Mostly scenic, non-people imagery/illustration."

NEEDS Inspirational/traditional. Publishes over 150 titles/year.

MAKING CONTACT & TERMS Send e-mail including digital images, samples and a URL. Follow up every 3-4 months. Responds only if interested. $400-1600 for covers, $200-600 for inside shots.

TIPS "Faithfulness to the Bible and Jesus Christ are the bedrock values behind every book Barbour's staff produces."

BEARMANOR MEDIA

P.O. Box 1129, Duncan OK 73534. (580)252-3547. Fax: (814)690-1559. E-mail: Books@Benohmart.com. Website: www.bearmanormedia.com. **Contact:** Ben Ohmart, publisher. Estab. 2000. Publishes 70 titles/year. Payment negotiable. Responds only if interested. Catalog available online or free with a 9×12 SASE submission.

TIPS "Potential freelancers should be familiar with our catalog, be able to work comfortably and timely with project managers across 12 time zones, and be computer savvy. Like many modern publishing companies, different facets of our company are located in different regions from Japan to both U.S. coasts. Potential freelancers *must* be knowledgeable in the requirements of commercial printing in regards to resolution, colorspace, process printing and contrast levels. Please provide some listing of experience and payment requirements."

🔲🔲 🔲 ⬤ BEDFORD/ST. MARTIN'S

75 Arlington St., Boston MA 02116. (617)399-4000. E-mail: ddennison@bedfordstmartins.com. Website: www.bedfordstmartins.com. Estab. 1981. Publishes college textbooks. Subjects include English composition, literature, history, communications, philosophy, music. Photos used for text illustrations, promotional materials, book covers. Examples of recently published titles: Bartholomae/Petrosky, *Ways of Reading*, 9th edition (text illustration, book cover); McCornack, *Reflect and Relate*, 2nd edition (text illustration, book cover).

NEEDS "We use photographs editorially, tied to the subject matter of the book." Needs mostly historical photos. Also wants artistic, abstract, conceptual photos; people—predominantly American; multicultural, cities/urban, education, performing arts, political, product shots/still life, business concepts, technology/computers. Interested in documentary, fine art, historical/vintage. Not interested in photos of children or religious subjects. Also uses product shots for promotional material. Reviews stock photos. Model/property release required.

SPECS Prefers images in digital format. Send via CD, ZIP as TIFF, EPS, JPEG files at 300 dpi.

MAKING CONTACT & TERMS Send query letter with nonreturnable samples. Provide résumé, business card, brochure, flyer or tearsheets to be kept on file for possible future assignments. Previously published work OK. Pays $50-1,000 for cover. Credit line always included for covers, never on promo. Buys one-time rights and all rights in every media; depends on project; negotiable.

TIPS "We like web portfolios."

◎ 🔲 BENTLEY PUBLISHERS

1734 Massachusetts Ave., Cambridge MA 02138. (617)547-4170. Fax: (617)876-9235. E-mail: michael.bentley@bentleypublishers.com. Website: www.bentleypublishers.com. **Contact:** Michael Bentley, president. Estab. 1950. Publishes professional, technical, consumer how-to books. Photos used for text illustrations, promotional materials, book covers, dust jackets. Examples of published titles: *Porsche: Genesis of Genius; Toyota Prius Repair and Maintenance Manual.*

NEEDS Buys 70-100 photos/year; offers 5-10 freelance assignments/year. Looking for motorsport, automotive technical and engineering photos. Reviews stock photos. Model/property release required. Photo captions required; include date and subject matter.

SPECS Uses 8×10 transparencies. Accepts images in digital format.

MAKING CONTACT & TERMS Send query letter with samples. Provide résumé, business card, brochure, flyer or tearsheets to be kept on file for possible future assignments. Keeps samples on file; cannot return material. Works on assignment only. Responds in 6 weeks. Simultaneous submissions and previously published work OK. Payment negotiable. Credit line given. Buys electronic and one-time rights.

TIPS "Bentley Publishers publishes books for automotive enthusiasts. We are interested in books that showcase good research, strong illustrations, and valuable technical information."

$$ ◐ BREWERS ASSOCIATION

736 Pearl St., Boulder CO 80302. (888)822-6273; (303)447-0816. E-mail: allison@brewersassociation.org. Website: www.beertown.org. **Contact:** Allison Esser, art director. Estab. 1978. Publishes beer how-to, cooking with beer, trade, hobby, brewing, beer-related books. Photos used for text illustrations, promotional materials, books, magazines. Examples of published magazines: *Zymurgy* (front cover and inside); *The New Brewer* (front cover and inside). Examples of published book titles: *Sacred & Herbal Healing Beers* (front/back covers and inside); *Standards of Brewing* (front/back covers).

NEEDS Buys 15-30 photos/year; offers freelance assignments. Needs photos of food/drink, beer, hobbies, humor, agriculture, business, industry, product shots/still life, science. Interested in alternative process, fine art, historical/vintage.

SPECS Uses b&w prints; 35mm, 2¼×2¼, 4×5 transparencies. Accepts images in digital format. Send via CD, e-mail as TIFF, EPS, JPEG files at 300 dpi.

MAKING CONTACT & TERMS Send query letter with nonreturnable samples. Provide résumé, business card, brochure, flyer or tearsheets to be kept on file for possible future assignments. Simultaneous submissions and previously published work OK. Payment negotiable; all jobs done on a quote basis. Pays by the project: $700-800 for cover shots; $300-600 for inside shots. Pays 60 days after receipt of invoice. Preferably buys one-time usage rights; negotiable.

TIPS "Send nonreturnable samples for us to keep in our files that depict whatever your specialty is, plus some samples of beer-related objects, equipment, events, people, etc."

$ ◐ CAPSTONE PRESS

151 Good Counsel Dr., P.O. Box 669, Mankato MN 56002. (800)747-4992. Fax: (888)262-0705. E-mail: d.barton@capstonepress.com. Website: www.capstonepress.com. **Contact:** Dede Barton. Estab. 1991. Publishes juvenile nonfiction and educational books. Subjects include animals, ethnic groups, vehicles, sports, history, scenics. Photos used for text illustrations, promotional materials, book covers. "To see examples of our products, please visit our website." Submission guidelines available online.

NEEDS Buys about 3,000 photos/year. "Our subject matter varies (usually 100 or more different subjects/year); editorial-type imagery preferable although always looking for new ways to show an overused subject or title (fresh)." Model/property release preferred. Photo captions preferred; include "basic description; if people of color, state ethnic group; if scenic, state location and date of image."

SPECS Uses various sizes of color and b&w prints (if historical); 35mm, 2¼×2¼, 4×5 transparencies. Accepts images in digital format for submissions as well as for use. Digital images must be at least 8×10 at 300 dpi for publishing quality (TIFF, EPS or original camera file format preferred).

MAKING CONTACT & TERMS Send query letter with stock list. Provide résumé, business card, brochure, flyer or tearsheets to be kept on file for possible future assignments. Keeps samples on file. Responds in 6 months. Simultaneous submissions and previously published work OK. Pays $200 for cover; $75 for inside. Pays after publication. Credit line given. Looking to buy worldwide all language rights for print and digital rights. Producing online projects (interactive websites and books); printed books may be bound up into binders and etc.

TIPS "Be flexible. Book publishing usually takes at least 6 months. Capstone does not pay holding fees. Be prompt. The first photos in are considered for covers first."

◎ ◐ CENTERSTREAM PUBLICATION LLC

P.O. Box 17878, Anaheim CA 92807. (714)779-9390. E-mail: centerstrm@aol.com. Website: www.centerstream-usa.com. **Contact:** Ron Middlebrook, owner. Estab. 1982. "*Centerstream* is known for its unique publications for a variety of instruments. From instructional and reference books and biographies, to fun song collections and DVDs, our products are created by experts who offer insight and invaluable information to players and collectors." Publishes music history, biographies, DVDs, music instruction (all instruments). Photos used for text illustrations, book covers. Examples of published titles: *Dobro Techniques*; *History of Leedy Drums*; *History of National Guitars*; *Blues Dobro*; *Jazz Guitar Christmas* (book covers).

NEEDS Reviews stock photos of music. Model release preferred. Photo captions preferred.

SPECS Uses color and b&w prints; 35mm, 2¼×2¼, 4×5 transparencies. Accepts images in digital format. Send via ZIP as TIFF files.

MAKING CONTACT & TERMS Send query letter with samples and stock list. Send unsolicited photos by mail for consideration. Provide résumé, business card, brochure, flyer or tearsheets to be kept on file for possible future assignments. Works on assignment only. Responds in 1 month. Simultaneous submissions and previously published work OK. Payment negotiable. Pays on receipt of invoice. Credit line given. Buys all rights.

$ ○ CHIVALRY BOOKSHELF

3305 Mayfair Lane, Highland Village TX 75077. (888)275-5769. E-mail: brian@chivalrybookshelf.com. Website: www.chivalrybookshelf.com. **Contact:** Editorial staff. Estab. 1996. Publishes hardcover and trade paperback originals and reprints. Subjects include art/architecture, history, government/politics, military, sports. Photos used for text illustrations, promotional materials, book covers, dust jackets. Examples of recently published titles: *Deeds of Arms*; *The Medieval Art of Swordsmanship*; *Arte of Defense*. Catalog free with #10 SASE. Photo guidelines available on website.

NEEDS Buys 50-100 freelance photos/year. Needs photos of military, product shots/still life, events, hobbies, sports. Interested in documentary, fine art, historical/vintage. Model/property release required. Photo captions preferred; include subject, context, photographer's name.

SPECS Uses glossy b&w and color prints. Accepts images in digital format. Send via CD, e-mail as TIFF files at 600 dpi.

MAKING CONTACT & TERMS Send query letter with tearsheets. Provide résumé, business card, self-promotion piece to be kept on file for possible future assignments. Responds in 2-4 weeks. Pays on publication. Credit line given. Buys all rights; negotiable. Complete submission guidelines available online.

◎ $$ CLEIS PRESS

(510)845-8000 or (800)780-2279. Fax: (510)845-8001. E-mail: cleis@cleispress.com. E-mail: bknight@cleispress.com. Website: www.cleispress.com and www.vivaeditions.com. Kara Wuest, publishing coordinator; Frédérique Delacoste, art director. **Contact:** Brenda Knight, associate publisher. Estab. 1980. Cleis Press publishes provocative, intelligent books in the areas of sexuality, gay and lesbian studies, erotica, fiction, gender studies, and human rights. Publishes fiction, nonfiction, trade and gay/lesbian erotica. Photos used for book covers. Buys 20 photos/year. Reviews stock photos. Works with freelancers on assignment only. Keeps samples on file. Pays on publication.

NEEDS Fiction, nonfiction, trade and gay/lesbian erotica; photos used for book covers.

SPECS Uses color and/or b&w prints.

MAKING CONTACT & TERMS Query via e-mail only. Provide résumé, business card, brochure, flier or tearsheets to be kept on file for possible future assignments.

$$ CONARI PRESS

665 Third St., Suite 400, San Francisco CA 94107. E-mail: info@redwheelweiser.com. Website: www.redwheelweiser.com. Estab. 1987. Publishes hardcover and trade paperback originals and reprints. Subjects include women's studies, psychology, parenting, inspiration, home and relationships (all nonfiction titles). Photos used for text illustrations, book covers, dust jackets.

NEEDS Buys 5-10 freelance photos /year. Looking for artful photos; subject matter varies. Interested in reviewing stock photos of most anything except high-tech, corporate or industrial images. Model release required. Photo caption s preferred; include photography copyright.

SPECS Prefers images in digital format.

MAKING CONTACT & TERMS Provide résumé, business card, self-promotion piece or tearsheets to be kept on file for possible future assignments. Art director will contact photographer for portfolio review if interested. Portfolio should include prints, tearsheets, slides, transparencies or thumbnails. Keeps samples on file. Simultaneous submissions and previously published work OK. Pays by the project: $400-1,000 for color cover; rates vary for color inside. Pays on publication. Credit line given on copyright page or back cover.

TIPS "Review our website to make sure your work is appropriate."

THE COUNTRYMAN PRESS

(802)457-4826. Fax: (802)457-1678. E-mail: countrymanpress@wwnorton.com;khummel@wwnorton.com. Website: www.countrymanpress.com. Estab. 1973. "Countryman Press publishes books that encourage physical fitness and appreciation for and understanding of the natural world, self-sufficiency, and adventure." Publishes hardcover originals, trade paperback originals and reprints. Subjects include travel, nature, hiking, biking, paddling, cooking, Northeast history, gardening and fishing. Examples of recently published titles: *The King Arthur Flour Baker's Companion* (book cover); *Vermont: An Explorer's Guide* (text illustrations, book cover). Catalog available for 6¾×10½ envelope.

NEEDS Needs photos of environmental, landscapes/scenics, wildlife, architecture, gardening, rural, sports, travel. Interested in historical/vintage, seasonal. Model/property release preferred. Photo captions preferred; include location, state, season.

SPECS Accepts high-res images in digital format. Send via CD, ZIP as TIFF files at 350 dpi.

MAKING CONTACT & TERMS Send query letter to the attention of "Submissions," with résumé, slides, tearsheets, stock list. Provide résumé, business card, self-promotion piece to be kept on file for possible future assignments. Responds in 2 months, only if interested. Simultaneous submissions and previously published work OK. Pays $100-600 for color cover. Pays on publication. Credit line given. Buys all rights for life of edition (normally 2-7 years); negotiable.

TIPS "Our catalog demonstrates the range of our titles and shows our emphasis on travel and the outdoors. Crisp focus, good lighting, and strong contrast are goals worth striving for in each shot. We prefer images that invite rather than challenge the viewer, yet also look for eye-catching content and composition."

$ CRABTREE PUBLISHING COMPANY

PMB 59051, 350 Fifth Ave., 59th Floor, New York NY 10118. (212)496-5040; (800)387-7650. Fax: (800)355-7166. Website: www.crabtreebooks.com. Estab. 1978. Publishes juvenile nonfiction, library and trade. Subjects include science, cultural events, history, geography (including cultural geography), sports. Photos used for text illustrations, book covers. Examples of recently published titles: *The Mystery of the Bermuda Triangle, Environmental Activist, Paralympic Sports Events, Presidents' Day, Plant Cells, Bomb and Mine Disposal Officers.*

🗨 This publisher also has offices in Canada, United Kingdom and Australia.

NEEDS Buys 20-50 photos/year. Wants photos of cultural events around the world, animals (exotic and domestic). Model/property release required for children, photos of artwork, etc. Photo captions preferred; include place, name of subject, date photographed, animal behavior.

SPECS Uses high-res digital files (no compressed JPEG files).

MAKING CONTACT & TERMS *Does not accept unsolicited photos.* Provide résumé, business card, brochure, flyer or tearsheets to be kept on file for possible future assignments. Simultaneous submissions and previously published work OK. Pays $100 for color photos. Pays on publication. Credit line given. Buys non-exclusive, worldwide and electronic rights.

TIPS "Since our books are for younger readers, lively photos of children and animals are always excellent." Portfolio should be diverse and encompass several subjects, rather than just 1 or 2; depth of coverage of subject should be intense so that any publishing company could, conceivably, use all or many of a photographer's photos in a book on a particular subject."

$ ○ CREATIVE EDITIONS

P.O. Box 227, Mankato MN 56002. (800)445-6209. E-mail: info@thecreativecompany.us. E-mail: artdirector@thecreativecompany.us. Website: www.thecreativecompany.us. Estab. 1989. Publishes hardcover originals. Subjects include photo essays, biography, poetry, stories designed for children. Photos used for text illustrations, book covers, dust jackets. Examples of recently published titles: *Spartacus the Spider* (text illustrations, book cover, dust jacket); *Skywriting: Poems to Fly* (text illustrations, book cover, dust jacket). Catalog available.

NEEDS Looking for photo-illustrated documentaries or gift books. Must include some text. Publishes 5 books/year.

SPECS Uses any size glossy or matte color and/or b&w prints. Accepts images in digital format for Mac only. Send via CD as JPEG files at 72 dpi minimum (high-res upon request only).

MAKING CONTACT & TERMS Send query letter with publication credits and project proposal, prints, photocopies, tearsheets of previous publications, stock list for proposed project. Responds in 1 month to queries. Simultaneous submissions and previously published work OK. Advance to be negotiated. Credit line given. Buys world rights for the book; photos remain property of photographer.

TIPS "Creative Editions publishes unique books for the book-lover. Emphasis is on aesthetics and quality. Completed manuscripts are more likely to be accepted than preliminary proposals. Please do not send slides or other valuable materials."

CREATIVE HOMEOWNER

24 Park Way, Upper Saddle River NJ 07458. (201)934-7100, ext. 375. Fax: (201)934-8971 or (201)934-7541. E-mail: info@creativehomeowner.com; rweisman@creativehomeowner.com; mdolan@creativehome owner.com. Website: www.creativehomeowner.com. **Contact:** Rich Weisman, president; Mary Dolan, photo researcher. Estab. 1978. Publishes soft cover originals, mass market paperback originals. Photos used for text illustrations, promotional materials, book covers. Creative Homeowner's books and online information are known by consumers for their complete and easy-to-follow instructions, up-to-date information, and extensive use of color photography. Among its best-selling titles are *Char-broil's Everybody Grills!, Ultimate Guide: Wiring, and Landscaping with Stone.* Catalog available. Photo guidelines available via fax.

NEEDS Buys 1,000 freelance photos/year. Needs photos of architecture, interiors/decorating, some gardening. Other needs include interior and exterior design photography; garden beauty shots. Photo captions required; include photographer credit, designer credit, location, small description, if possible.

SPECS Accepts images in digital format. Send via CD as TIFF files at 300 dpi.

MAKING CONTACT & TERMS Send query letter with résumé, photocopies, tearsheets, transparencies, stock list. Provide résumé, business card, self-promotion piece to be kept on file for possible future assignments. Responds in 2 weeks to queries. Simultaneous submissions and previously published work OK. Pays $800 for color cover; $100-150 for color inside; $200 for back cover. Pays on publication. Credit line given. Buys one-time rights.

TIPS "Be able to pull submissions for fast delivery. Label and document all transparencies for easy in-office tracking and return."

⊕ $ ◐ DOWN THE SHORE PUBLISHING CORP.

P.O. Box 100, West Creek NJ 08092. (609)978-1233. Fax: (609)597-0422. E-mail: info@down-the-shore.com. Website: www.down-the-shore.com. **Contact:** Raymond G. Fisk, publisher. Estab. 1984. Publishes regional calendars; seashore, coastal, and regional books (specific to the mid-Atlantic shore and New Jersey). Photos used for text illustrations, scenic calendars (New Jersey and mid-Atlantic only). Examples of recently published titles: *Great Storms of the Jersey Shore* (text illustrations); *NJ Lighthouse Calendar* (illustrations, cover); *Shore Stories* (text illustrations, dust jacket). Photo guidelines free with SASE or on website.

NEEDS Buys 30-50 photos/year. For calendars, needs scenic coastal shots, photos of beaches and New Jersey lighthouses (New Jersey and mid-Atlantic region). Interested in seasonal. Reviews stock photos. Model release required; property release preferred. Photo captions preferred; *specific location* identification essential.

SPECS Digital submissions via high-res files on DVD/CD. Provide reference prints. Accepts 35mm, 2¼×2¼, 4×5 transparencies. Refer to guidelines before submitting.

MAKING CONTACT & TERMS Send query letter with stock list. Provide résumé, business card, brochure, flier or tearsheets to be kept on file for possible future requests. Responds in 6 weeks. Previously published work OK. Pays $100-200 for b&w or color cover; $10-100 for b&w or color inside. Pays 90 days from publication. Credit line given. Buys one-time or book rights; negotiable.

TIPS "We are looking for an honest depiction of familiar scenes from an unfamiliar and imaginative perspective. Images must be specific to our very regional needs. Limit your submissions to your best work. Edit your work very carefully."

⊙ $$ ⊕ ◐ ECW PRESS

2120 Queen St. E., Suite 200, Toronto ON M4E 1E2, Canada. (416)694-3348. Fax: (416)698-9906. E-mail: info@ecwpress.com. Website: www.ecwpress.com. **Contact:** Jack David, publisher. Estab. 1974. Publishes hardcover and trade paperback originals. Subjects include entertainment, biography, sports, travel, fiction, poetry. Photos used for text illustrations, book covers, dust jackets.

NEEDS Buys hundreds of freelance photos/year. Looking for color, b&w, fan/backstage, paparazzi, action, original, rarely used. Reviews stock photos. Property release required for entertainment or star shots. Photo captions required; include identification of all people.

SPECS Accepts images in digital format. Send via CD as TIFF files at 300 dpi.

MAKING CONTACT & TERMS "For photo and art submissions, it is best to contact us by e-mail and direct us to your work online. Please also describe what area(s) you specialize in. If you do send us artwork by mail that you wish returned, make sure to include a SASE with sufficient postage (for those outside Canada, include an International Reply Coupon). Since our projects vary in topic, we will keep you on file in case we publish something along the lines of your subject(s)." Pays by the project: $250-600 for color cover; $50-125 for color inside. Pays on publication. Credit line given. Buys one-time book rights (all markets).

TIPS "We have many projects on the go. Query for projects needing illustrations. Please check our website before querying."

FARCOUNTRY PRESS

P.O. Box 5630, Helena MT 59604. (800)821-3874. Fax: (406)443-5480. E-mail: shirley.machonis@farcountrypress.com. Website: www.farcountrypress. com. **Contact:** Shirley Machonis. Estab. 1980. Award-winning publisher Farcountry Press specializes in softcover and hardcover color photography books showcasing the nation's cities, states, national parks, and wildlife. Farcountry also publishes several children's series, as well as guidebooks, cookbooks, and regional history titles nationwide. The staff produces about 25 books annually; the backlist has grown to more than 300 titles. Photographer guidelines are available on our website.

NEEDS Seeking color photography of landscapes (including recreation), cityscapes, and wildlife in the United States.

SPECS For digital photo submissions, please send 8- or 16-bit TIFF files (higher preferred), at least 350 dpi or higher, formatted for Macs, RGB profile. All images should be flattened—no channels or layers. Information, including watermarks, should not appear directly on the images. Include either a contact sheet or a folder with low-resolution files for quick editing. Include copyright and caption data. Model releases are required for all images featuring recognizable individuals. Note on the mount or in the metadata that a model release is available. Do not submit images that do not have model releases.

MAKING CONTACT & TERMS Send query letter with stock list. Unsolicited submissions of photography WILL NOT be accepted and WILL NOT be returned. Simultaneous submissions and previously published work OK.

FIFTH HOUSE PUBLISHERS

Fitzhenry & Whiteside, 195 Allstate Parkway, Markham ON L3R 4&8, Canada. (403)571-5230; (800)387-9776. E-mail: stewart@fifthhousepublishers.ca. Website: www.fifthhousepublishers.ca; www.fitzhenry.ca/about_fifthhouse.aspx. **Contact:** Stephanie Stewart, publisher. Estab. 1982. "Fifth House Publishers is committed to 'bringing the West to the rest' by publishing approximately 15 books a year about the land and people who make this region unique. We publish the acclaimed *Going Wild* series, Pierre Berton's *History for Young Canadians*, *Keepers of Life*, the *Western Canadian Classics* series, the *Prairie Gardening* series, and more. Our books are selected for their quality and contribution to the understanding of western-Canadian (and Canadian) history, culture and environment."

NEEDS Buys 15-20 photos/year. Looking for photos of Canadian weather. Model/property release preferred. Photo captions required; include location and identification.

MAKING CONTACT & TERMS Send query letter with samples and stock list. Keeps samples on file. Pays $400 Canadian/calendar image. Pays on publication. Credit line given. Buys one-time rights.

FIREFLY BOOKS

66 Leek Crescent, Richmond Hill ON L4B 1H1, Canada. E-mail: publicity@fireflybooks.com. Website: www.fireflybooks.com. Estab. 1974. Publishes high quality non-fiction. Photos used for text illustrations, book covers and dust jackets.

NEEDS "We're looking for book-length ideas, *not* stock. We pay a royalty on books sold, plus advance."

SPECS Prefers images in digital format, but will accept 35mm transparencies.

MAKING CONTACT & TERMS Send query letter with résumé of credits. Does not keep samples on file; include SAE/IRC for return of material. Simultaneous submissions OK. Payment negotiated with contract. Credit line given.

FLASHLIGHT PRESS

527 Empire Blvd., Brooklyn NY 11225. (718)288-8300. Fax: (718)972-6307. E-mail: editor@flashlightpress. com. Website: www.flashlightpress.com. **Contact:** Shari Dash Greenspan, editor. Estab. 2004. Publishes 2-3 picture books/year. 50% of books by first-time authors. Fiction: Picture books: contemporary, humor, multicultural. Average word length: 1,000. Recently published: *Pobble's Way*, by Simon Van Booy, illustrated by Wendy Edelson (ages 4-8, picture book); *That Cat Can't Stay*, by Thad Krasnesky, illustrated by David Parkins (ages 4-8, picture book); *I Always, ALWAYS Get My Way*, by Thad Krasnesky, illustrated by David Parkins (ages 4-8, picture book); *I Need My Monster*, by Amanda Noll, illustrated by Howard McWilliam (ages 4-8, picture book); *I'm Really Not Tired*, by Lori Sunshine, illustrated by Jeffrey Ebbeler (ages 4-8, picture book).

TIPS "Since I accept only e-mail submissions, I'd love for the sample images to be pasted into the e-mail so I don't have to open multiple files. Include URLs if you have online portfolios."

● FOCAL PRESS

225 Wyman St., Waltham MA 02451. (781)663-5284. Fax: (781)313-4880. E-mail: d.oconnell@elsevier. com. Website: www.focalpress.com. **Contact:** Dan O'Connell, publicity manager. Estab. 1938.

NEEDS "We publish professional reference titles, practical guides and student textbooks in all areas of media and communications technology, including photography and digital imaging. We are always looking for new proposals for book ideas. Send e-mail for proposal guidelines."

MAKING CONTACT & TERMS Simultaneous submissions and previously published work OK. Buys all rights; negotiable.

FORT ROSS INC. INTERNATIONAL RIGHTS

26 Arthur Pl., Yonkers NY 10701. (914)375-6448. E-mail: fortross@optonline.net. Website: www.fort rossinc.com. **Contact:** Dr. Kartsev, executive direc-

tor. Estab. 1992. "Generally, we publish Russia-related books in English or Russian. Sometimes we publish various fiction and nonfiction books in collaboration with the east European publishers in translation. We are looking mainly for well-established authors." Publishes paperback originals. Receives 100 queries received/year; 100 mss received/year. Pays 6-8% royalty on wholesale price or makes outright purchase of $500-1,500; negotiable advance. Buys and sells rights for more than 500 titles per year, mostly in Russian and in Russia. Genres include children adapted classics, adventure, fantasy, horror, romance, science fiction, biography, history and self-help.

NEEDS Photos of couples and pets.

TIPS "We will gladly take a look at your portfolio and buy the secondary rights for works. Looking for images already used on American book covers or images from an original portfolio."

GRYPHON HOUSE, INC.

(800)638-0928. Fax: (301)595-0051. E-mail: kathy@ ghbooks.com. Website: www.gryphonhouse.com. **Contact:** Kathy Charner, editor-in-chief. Estab. 1981. Publishes educational resource materials for teachers and parents of young children. Examples of recently published titles: *Great Games for Young Children* (text illustrations); *Starting With Stories* (book cover). Looking for b&w and color photos of young children (from birth to 6 years.) Reviews stock photos.

NEEDS Model release required.

SPECS Uses 5×7 glossy color (cover only) and b&w prints. Accepts images in digital format. Send via CD, ZIP, e-mail as TIFF files at 300 dpi.

MAKING CONTACT & TERMS Send query letter with samples and stock list. Keeps samples on file. Simultaneous submissions OK. Payment negotiable. Pays on receipt of invoice. Credit line given. Buys book rights.

◐ ❸ GUERNICA EDITIONS, INC.

489 Strathmore Blvd, Toronto ON M4C 1N8, Canada. Website: www.guernicaeditions.com. Estab. 1978. Publishes adult trade (literary). Photos used for book covers. Examples of recently published titles: *Barry Callagan: Essays on His Work*, edited by Priscila Uppal; *Mary Di Michele: Essays on Her Works*, edited by Joseph Pivato; *Maria Mazziotti: Essays on Her Works*, edited by Sean Thomas Doughtery; *Mary Melfi: Essays on Her Works*, edited by William Anselmi.

NEEDS Buys varying number of photos/year; "often" assigns work. Needs life events, including characters; houses. Photo captions required.

SPECS Uses color and/or b&w prints. Accepts images in digital format. Send via CD, ZIP as TIFF, GIF files at 300 dpi minimum.

MAKING CONTACT & TERMS Prefers to receive manuscript queries by e-mail (via online contact form). "Before inquiring, please check our website to determine the type of material that best fits our publishing house." Sometimes keeps samples on file. Cannot return material. Responds in 2 weeks. Pays $150 for cover. Pays on publication. Credit line given. Buys book rights. "Photo rights go to photographers. All we need is the right to reproduce the work."

TIPS "Look at what we do. Send some samples. If we like them, we'll write back."

HANCOCK HOUSE PUBLISHERS

(604)538-1114. Fax: (604)538-2262. E-mail: karen@ hancockwildlife.org. Website: www.hancockwild life.org. **Contact:** David Hancock. Estab. 1971. Publishes trade books. Photos used for text illustrations, promotions, book covers. Examples of recently published titles: *Meet the Sasquatch* by Chris Murhydd (over 500 color images); *Alaska in the Wake of the North Star* by Loel Schuler; *Pheasants of the World* (350 color photos).

NEEDS Photos of birds/nature. Reviews stock photos. Model release preferred. Photo captions preferred.

MAKING CONTACT & TERMS Send query letter with samples, SASE. Responds in 1 month. Simultaneous submissions and previously published work OK. Payment negotiable. Credit line given. Buys non-exclusive rights.

▌● HARPERCOLLINS CHILDREN'S BOOKS / HARPERCOLLINS PUBLISHERS

10 East 53rd, New York NY 10022. (212)207-6901. E-mail: Dana.fritts@Harpercollins.com. E-mail: Mischa.Rosenberg@Harpercollins.com. Website: www.Harpercollins.com. **Contact:** Mischa Rosenberg, assistant designer; Dana Fritts, designer. Publishes hardcover originals and reprints, trade paperback originals and reprints, mass market paperback originals and reprints, and audiobooks. 500 titles/year.

NEEDS Babies/children/teens, couples, multicultural, pets, food/drink, fashion, lifestyle. "We would be interested in seeing samples of map illustrations, chapter spots, full page pieces, etc. We are open to half-tone and line art illustrations for our interiors." Negotiates a flat payment fee upon acceptance. Will contact if interested. Catalog available online.

TIPS "Be flexible and responsive to comments and corrections. Hold to scheduled due dates for work. Show work that reflects the kinds of projects you *want* to get, be focused on your best technique and showcase the strongest, most successful examples."

○ HERALD PRESS

616 Walnut Ave., Scottdale PA 15683. (724)887-8500. Fax: (724)887-3111. E-mail: design@mpn.net. Website: www.mpn.net. **Contact:** Design director. Estab. 1908. Photos used for book covers, dust jackets. Examples of published titles: *Saving the Seasons, Mennonite Girls Can Cook*.

NEEDS Buys 5 photos/year; offers occasional freelance assignments. Subject matter varies. Reviews stock photos of people and other subjects including religious, environmental. Model/property release required. Photo captions preferred; include identification information.

SPECS Prefers images in digital format. Submit URL or link to web pages or light box.

MAKING CONTACT & TERMS Send query letter or e-mail with samples. Provide résumé, business card, brochure, flyer or tearsheets to be kept on file for possible future assignments. Keeps samples on file. Works on assignment only or selects from file of samples. Simultaneous submissions and previously published work OK. Payment negotiable. **Pays on acceptance.** Credit line given. Buys book rights; negotiable.

TIPS "We put your résumé and samples on file. It is best to direct us to your website."

⊕⊕ ○ HOLT MCDOUGAL

1900 S. Batavia Ave., Geneva IL 60134. 800-462-6595. Fax: (888)872-8380. Website: www.hrw.com. Estab. 1866. Publishes textbooks in multiple formats. Photos are used for text illustrations, promotional materials and book covers.

NEEDS Uses 6,500+ photos/year. Wants photos that illustrate content for mathematics, sciences, social studies, world languages and language arts. Model/property release preferred. Photo captions required; include scientific explanation, location and/or other detailed information.

SPECS Prefers images in digital format. Send via CD or broadband transmission.

MAKING CONTACT & TERMS Send a query letter with a sample of work (nonreturnable photocopies, tearsheets, printed promos) and a list of subjects in stock. Self-promotion pieces kept on file for future reference. Include promotional website link if available. "Do not call!" Will respond only if interested. Payment negotiable depending on format and number of uses. Credit line given.

TIPS "Our book image programs yield an emphasis on rights-managed stock imagery, with a focus on teens and a balanced ethnic mix. Though we commission assignment photography, we maintain an in-house studio with 2 full-time photographers. We are interested in natural-looking, uncluttered photographs labeled with exact descriptions, that are technically correct and include no evidence of liquor, drugs, cigarettes or brand names."

◉◉ HUMAN KINETICS PUBLISHERS

P.O. Box 5076, Champaign IL 61825-5076. (800)747-4457. Fax: (217)351-1549. E-mail: acquisitions@hkusa.com. Website: www.hkusa.com. Estab. 1979. Publishes hardcover originals, trade paperback originals, textbooks, online courses and CDs. Subjects include sports, fitness, physical therapy, sports medicine, nutrition, physical activity. Photos used for text illustrations, promotional materials, catalogs, magazines, web content, book covers. Examples of recently published titles: *Serious Tennis* (text illustrations, book cover); *Beach Volleyball* (text illustrations, book cover). Photo guidelines available via e-mail only.

NEEDS Buys 2,000 freelance photos/year. Photos of babies/children/teens, multicultural, families, education, events, food/drink, health/fitness, performing arts, sports, medicine, military, product shots/still life. All photos purchased must show some sort of sport, physical activity, health and fitness. "Expect ethnic diversity in all content photos." Model release preferred.

SPECS Prefers images in digital format. Send via CD, ZIP as TIFF, JPEG files at 300 dpi at 9×12 inches; will accept 5×7 color prints, 35mm transparencies.

MAKING CONTACT & TERMS Send query letter and URL via e-mail to view samples. Responds only if interested. Simultaneous submissions and previously published work OK. Pays $250-500 for b&w or color cover; $75-125 for b&w or color inside. Pays extra for electronic usage of photos. Pays on publication. Credit line given. Buys one-time rights. Prefers world rights, all languages, for one edition; negotiable.

TIPS "Go to Borders or Barnes & Noble and look at our books in the sport and fitness section. We want and need peak action, emotion and razor-sharp images for future projects. The pay is below average, but there is opportunity for exposure and steady income to those with patience and access to a variety of sports and physical education settings. We have a high demand for quality shots of youths engaged in physical education classes at all age groups. We place great emphasis on images that display diversity and technical quality. Do not contact us if you charge research or holding fees. Do not contact us for progress reports. Will call if selection is made, or return images. Typically, we hold images 4 to 6 months. If you can't live without the images that long, don't contact us. Don't be discouraged if you don't make a sale in the first 6 months. We work with over 200 agencies and photographers. Photographers should check to see if techniques demonstrated in photos are correct with a local authority. Most technical photos and submitted work are rejected on content, not quality."

◎ ● HYPERION BOOKS FOR CHILDREN

114 Fifth Ave., New York NY 10011. (914)288-4100. Website: www.hyperionbooks.com. Publishes children's books, including picture books and books for young readers. Subjects include adventure, animals, history, multicultural, sports. Catalog available with 9×12 SASE and 3 first-class stamps.

NEEDS Photos of multicultural subjects.

MAKING CONTACT & TERMS Provide résumé, business card, self-promotion piece to be kept on file for possible future assignments. Pays royalties based on retail price of book, or a flat fee.

◑ ◉ ◐ IMMEDIUM

P.O. Box 31846, San Francisco CA 94131. (415)452-8546. Fax: (360)937-6272. E-mail: submissions@immedium.com. Website: www.immedium.com. **Contact:** Amy Ma, acquisitions editor. Estab. 2005. "*Immedium* focuses on publishing eye-catching children's picture books, Asian American topics, and contemporary arts, popular culture, and multicultural issues."

NEEDS Babies/children/teens, multicultural, families, parents, entertainment, lifestyle. Photos for dust jackets, promotional materials and book covers.

MAKING CONTACT & TERMS Send query letter with résumé, samples and/or SASE. Photo captions and property releases are required. Rights are negotiated and will vary with project.

TIPS "Look at our catalog, it's colorful and a little edgy. Tailor your submission to our catalog. We need responsive workers."

⊖⊖ ☺ ◐ INNER TRADITIONS/BEAR & COMPANY

1 Park St., Rochester VT 05767. (802)767-3174. Fax: (802)767-3726. E-mail: peris@innertraditions.com. Website: www.innertraditions.com. **Contact:** Peri Ann Swan, art director. Estab. 1975. Publishes adult trade and teen self-help. Subjects include new age, health, self-help, esoteric philosophy. Photos used for text illustrations, book covers. Examples of recently published titles: *Tibetan Sacred Dance* (cover, interior); *Tutankhamun Prophecies* (cover); *Animal Voices* (cover, interior).

NEEDS Buys 10-50 photos/year; offers 5-10 freelance assignments/year. Photos of babies/children/teens, multicultural, families, parents, religious, alternative medicine, environmental, landscapes/scenics. Interested in fine art, historical/vintage. Reviews stock photos. Model/property release required. Photo captions preferred.

SPECS Prefers images in digital format. Send via CD, ZIP as TIFF, EPS, JPEG files at 300 dpi or provide comps via e-mail.

MAKING CONTACT & TERMS Provide résumé, business card, brochure, flyer or tearsheets to be kept on file for possible future assignments. Works with freelancers on assignment only. Simultaneous submissions OK. Pays $150-600 for color cover; $50-200 for b&w and color inside. Pays on publication. Credit line given. Buys book rights; negotiable.

⊖ ◐ KEY CURRICULUM PRESS

1150 65th St., Emeryville CA 94608. (800)995-6284. Fax: (800)541-2442. Website: www.keypress.com. Estab. 1971. Publishes textbooks, CDs, software. Subjects include mathematics. Photos used for text illustrations, promotional materials, book covers. Examples of recently published titles: *Discovering Algebra* (text illustrations, promotional materials, book cover); *The Heart of Mathematics* (text illustrations, promotional materials, book cover). Catalog available for first-class postage.

NEEDS Photos of babies/children/teens, couples, multicultural, families, environmental, landscapes/scenics, wildlife, architecture, cities/urban, education, rural, health/fitness/beauty, performing arts, sports, science, technology/computers. Interested in documentary, fine art. Also needs technology with female adults performing professional tasks. Female professionals, not just in office occupations. Model/property release required. Photo captions preferred; include type of technology pictured.

SPECS Accepts images in digital format. Send via CD as TIFF, EPS files at 300 dpi (72 dpi for FPOs).

MAKING CONTACT & TERMS Send query letter with résumé, photocopies, tearsheets, stock list. Provide business card, self-promotion piece to be kept on file for possible future assignments. Responds only if interested, send nonreturnable samples. Simultaneous submissions and previously published work OK. Pays $250-500 for b&w cover; $250-1,000 for color cover; by the project, $250-1,000 for cover shots; $150-200 for b&w inside; $150-300 for color inside; by the project, $100-900 for inside shots. **Pays on acceptance.** Credit line given. Buys all rights to assignment photography.

TIPS "Provide website gallery. Call prior to dropping off portfolio."

⊖⊖ ◐ LERNER PUBLISHING GROUP, INC.

1251 Washington Ave., N, Minneapolis MN 55401. (612)332-3344; (800)328-4929. Fax: (800)332-1132. E-mail: dwallek@igigraphics.com. Website: www.lernerbooks.com. **Contact:** Dan Wallek, director of electronic content and photo research. Estab. 1959. Publishes educational books for grades K-12. Subjects include animals, biography, history, geography, science, vehicles, and sports. Photos used for editorial purposes for text illustrations, promotional materials, book covers. Examples of recently published titles: *A Temperate Forest Food Chain—Follow That Food* (text illustrations, book cover); *Protecting Earth's Water Supply—Saving Our Living Earth* (text illustrations, book cover).

NEEDS Buys more than 6,000 photos/year; occasionally offers assignments. Photos of children/teens, celebrities, multicultural, families, disasters, environmental, landscapes/scenics, wildlife, cities/urban, education, pets, rural, hobbies, sports, agriculture, industry, political, science, vehicles, technology/computers. Model/property release preferred when photos are of social issues (e.g., the homeless). Photo captions required; include who, where, what and when.

SPECS Prefers images in digital format. Send via FTP, CD, or e-mail as TIFF or JPEG files at 300 dpi.

MAKING CONTACT & TERMS Send query letter with detailed stock list by mail, fax or e-mail. Provide current editorial use pricing. "No calls, please." Cannot return material. Responds only if interested. Previously published work OK. Pays by the project: $150-400 for cover; $50-150 for inside. Pays on receipt of invoice. Credit line given. Licenses images for book based on print-run rights, electronic rights, all language rights, worldwide territory rights. Submission guidelines available online.

TIPS Prefers crisp, clear images that can be used editorially. "Send in as detailed a stock list as you can (including fees for clearing additional rights), and be willing to negotiate price."

💲 🌓 LITURGY TRAINING PUBLICATIONS

3949 S. Racine Ave., Chicago IL 60609-2523. (773)579-4900; (800)933-1800. Fax: (773)579-4929; (800)933-7094. E-mail: mfox@ltp.org. Website: www.LTP.org. **Contact:** John Thomas, director; Mary Fox, editor. Estab. 1964. Publishes materials that assist parishes, institutions and households in the preparation, celebration and expression of liturgy in Christian life. Photos used for text illustrations, book covers. Examples of recently published titles: *Infant Baptism: A Parish Celebration* (text illustrations); *The Postures of the Assembly During the Eucharistic Prayer* (cover); *Teaching Christian Children About Judaism* (text illustrations).

NEEDS Buys 50-60 photos/year; offers 1 freelance assignment/year. Needs photos of processions, assemblies with candles in church, African-American Catholic worship, sacramental/ritual moments. Interested in fine art. Model/property release required. Photo captions preferred.

SPECS Uses 5×7 glossy b&w prints; 35mm transparencies; digital scans.

MAKING CONTACT & TERMS Arrange personal interview to show portfolio or submit portfolio for review. Send query letter with résumé of credits, samples and stock list. Provide résumé, business card, brochure, flyer or tearsheets to be kept on file for possible future assignments. Responds only if interested; send nonreturnable samples. Simultaneous submissions

and previously published work OK. Pays $25-200 for b&w; $50-225 for color. Pays on publication. Credit line given. Buys one-time rights; negotiable.

TIPS "Please realize that we are looking for very specific things—Catholic liturgy-related photos including people of mixed ages, races, socio-economic backgrounds; post-Vatican II liturgical style; candid photos; photos that are not dated. We are *not* looking for generic religious photography. We're trying to use more photos, and will if we can get good ones at reasonable rates."

☾ MAGENTA PUBLISHING FOR THE ARTS

151 Winchester St., Toronto ON M4X 1B5, Canada. E-mail: info@magentafoundation.org. Website: www.magentafoundation.org. **Contact:** Submissions. Estab. 2004. "The Magenta Foundation is a charitable arts publishing house, the first of its kind in Canada. It fills the very specific niche of establishing a place for Canadian artists in the international arts community, and it provides a vehicle for galleries to join forces and promote the work of Canadian artists internationally through the publication of books and exhibitions. Magenta will bring the photographic community together and work in tandem with key players to help bring increased recognition to Canadians through U.S. and international representation. Magenta intends to set the standard for community collaboration and partner with other organizations to create the domestic and international presence Canadians need to succeed. Sign up for our e-newsletter to stay in touch and find out what we are doing."

NEEDS "We are looking for complete bodies of work *only* (80% finished). Please do not send works in progress. We are looking for work in all related arenas of photography."

MAKING CONTACT & TERMS See website for open submissions and sign up for e-newsletter for alerts.

TIPS "Please do not contact the office to inquire about the state of your proposal."

☺ MBI INC.

47 Richards Ave., Norwalk CT 06857. (203)853-2000. E-mail: webmail@mbi-inc.com. Website: www.mbi-inc.com/publishing.asp. Estab. 1965.

○ Our book division is Easton Press. Maintains one of America's largest private archives of specially commissioned illustrations, book introductions, and literary criticism.

⊛⊛⊛ ○ MCGRAW-HILL

1333 Burr Ridge Pkwy., Floors 2-5, Burr Ridge IL 60527. (630)789-4000. Fax: (630)789-6594. Website: www.mhhe.com. Publishes hardcover originals, textbooks, CDs. Photos used for book covers.

NEEDS Buys 20 freelance photos/year. Needs photos of business concepts, industry, technology/computers.

SPECS Uses 8×10 glossy prints; 35mm, 2¼×2¼, 4×5 transparencies. Accepts images in digital format. Send via CD.

MAKING CONTACT & TERMS Contact through local sales rep (see submission guidelines online) or via online form. Provide business card, self-promotion piece to be kept on file for possible future assignments. Responds only if interested. Previously published work OK. Pays $650-1,000 for b&w cover; $650-1,500 for color cover. Pays extra for electronic usage of photos. Pays on publication. Credit line given. Buys one-time rights.

MEADOWBROOK PRESS

5451 Smetana Dr., Minnetonka MN 55343. Fax: (952)930-1940. E-mail: info@meadowbrookpress. com. Website: www.meadowbrookpress.com. **Contact:** Art director. Estab. 1974. "Meadowbrook is a family-oriented press. We specialize in pregnancy, baby care, child care, humorous poetry for children, party planning, and children's activities. We are also the number one publisher of baby name books in the country, with eight baby-naming books in print." Publishes trade paperback originals and reprints. 12 titles/year.

NEEDS Babies/children/teens. Receives 1,500 queries/year. No SASE returns. Responds only if interested. Guidelines available online. Book catalog for #10 SASE.

TIPS "Send me a new postcard at least every 3 months. I may not be looking for your style this month, but I may be in six months. I receive a pile of them every day, I will not reply until I need your style, but I enjoy looking at every single one, and I will keep them on file for 6 months. Don't worry about showing me everything, just show me what you do best."

⊕ ○ MITCHELL LANE PUBLISHERS, INC.

P.O. Box 196, Hockessin DE 19707. (302)234-9426. Fax: (866)834-4164. E-mail: barbaramitchell@mitchell lane.com. Website: www.mitchelllane.com. **Contact:**
Barbara Mitchell, publisher. Estab. 1993. Publishes hardcover originals for library market. Subjects include biography and other nonfiction for children and young adults. Photos used for text illustrations, book covers. Examples of recently published titles: *Meet Our New Student From Nigeria* (text illustrations and book cover); *A Backyard Flower Garden for Kids* (text illustrations, book cover).

NEEDS Photo captions required.

SPECS Accepts images in digital format. Send via CD as TIFF, JPEG files at 300 dpi.

MAKING CONTACT & TERMS Send query letter with stock list (stock photo agencies only). Does not keep samples on file; cannot return material. Responds only if interested. Pays on publication. Credit line given. Buys one-time rights.

○ MONDIAL

(212)851-3252. Fax: (208)361-2863. E-mail: contact@ mondialbooks.com. Website: www.mondialbooks. com; www.librejo.com. **Contact:** Andrew Moore, editor. Estab. 1996. Publishes mainstream fiction, romance, history and reference books. Specializes in linguistics.

NEEDS Landscapes, travel and erotic. Printing rights are negotiated according to project. Illustrations are used for text illustration, promotional materials and book covers. Publishes 20 titles/year. Responds only if interested.

MAKING CONTACT & TERMS Payment on acceptance.

○ MUSEUM OF NORTHERN ARIZONA

3101 N. Fort Valley Rd., Flagstaff AZ 86001. (928)774-5213. E-mail: info@mna.mus.az.us; publications@ mna.mus.az.us. Website: www.musnaz.org. **Contact:** Publications Department. Estab. 1928. Subjects include biology, geology, archaeology, anthropology and history. Photos used for *Plateau: Land and People of the Colorado Plateau* magazine, published twice/ year (May, October).

NEEDS Buys approximately 80 photos/year. Biology, geology, history, archaeology and anthropology—subjects on the Colorado Plateau. Reviews stock photos. Photo captions preferred; include location, description and context.

SPECS Uses 8×10 glossy b&w prints; 35mm, 2¼×2¼, 4×5 and 8×10 transparencies. Prefers 2¼×2¼ transparencies or larger. Possibly accepts images in digital format. Submit via ZIP.

MAKING CONTACT & TERMS Send query letter with samples, SASE. Responds in 1 month. Simultaneous submissions and previously published work OK. Pays $55-250/color photo; $55-250/b&w photo. Credit line given. Buys one-time and all rights; negotiable. Offers internships for photographers.

TIPS Wants to see top-quality, natural history work. To break in, send only pre-edited photos.

➕ ➋ ➌➍ MUSIC SALES GROUP

14-15 Berners St., London W1T 3LJ, UK. +44 (020) 7612 7400. Fax: +44 (020) 7612 7547. E-mail: music@musicsales.co.uk. Website: www.musicsales.com. Publishes instructional music books, song collections and books on music. Photos used for covers and interiors. Examples of recently published titles: *Bob Dylan: 100 Songs and Photos*; *Paul Simon: Surprise*; *AC/DC: Backtracks*.

NEEDS Buys 200 photos/year. Model release required on acceptance of photo. Photo captions required.

SPECS Uses 8×10 glossy prints; 35mm, 2×2, 5×7 transparencies. High-res digital 3000 x 4000 pixels.

MAKING CONTACT & TERMS Send query letter first with résumé of credits. Provide business card, brochure, flyer or tearsheets to be kept on file for possible future assignments. Responds in 2 months. Simultaneous submissions and previously published work OK. Pays $75-100 for b&w, $250-750 for color.

TIPS In samples, wants to see "the ability to capture the artist in motion with a sharp eye for framing the shot well. Portraits must reveal what makes the artist unique. We need rock, jazz, classical—onstage and impromptu shots. Please send us an inventory list of available stock photos of musicians. We rarely send photographers on assignment and buy mostly from material on hand." Send business card and tearsheets or prints stamped 'proof' across them. Due to the nature of record releases and concert events, we never know exactly when we may need a photo. We keep photos on permanent file for possible future use."

➒ ➓ ◑ NEW LEAF PRESS, INC.

P.O. Box 726, Green Forest AR 72638. (800)999-3777. Website: www.nlpg.com. Publishes Christian adult trade, gifts, devotions and homeschool. Photos used for book covers, book interiors and catalogs. Example of recently published title: *The Hand That Paints the Sky*.

NEEDS Buys 5 freelance photos/year. Needs photos of landscapes, dramatic outdoor scenes, "anything that could have an inspirational theme." Reviews stock photos. Model release required. Photo captions preferred.

SPECS Uses 35mm slides and transparencies. Accepts images in digital format. Send via CD, Jaz, ZIP, e-mail as TIFF, EPS files at 300 dpi.

MAKING CONTACT & TERMS Send query letter with copies of samples and list of stock photo subjects. "Not responsible for submitted slides and photos from queries. Please send copies, no originals unless requested." Does not assign work. Responds in 2-3 months. Simultaneous submissions and previously published work OK. Pays $50-100 for b&w photos; $100-175 for color photos. Credit line given. Buys one-time and book rights.

TIPS "In order to contribute to the company, send color copies of quality, crisp photos. Trend in book publishing is toward much greater use of photography."

➒ ➓ ◑ NICOLAS-HAYS, INC.

P.O. Box 540206, Lake Worth FL 33454-0206. E-mail: info@nicolashays.com; info@ibispress.net. Website: www.nicolashays.com. Estab. 1976. Publishes trade paperback originals and reprints. Subjects include Eastern philosophy, Jungian psychology, New Age how-to. Photos used for book covers. Example of recently published title: *Dervish Yoga for Health and Longevity: Samadeva Gestual Euphony—The Seven Major Arkanas* (book cover). Catalog available upon request.

NEEDS Buys 1 freelance photo/year. Needs photos of landscapes/scenics.

SPECS Uses color prints; 35mm, 2¼×2¼, 4×5 transparencies. Accepts images in digital format.

MAKING CONTACT & TERMS Send query letter with photocopies, tearsheets. Provide self-promotion piece to be kept on file for possible future assignments. Responds only if interested; send nonreturnable samples. Simultaneous submissions and previously published work OK. Pays $100-200 for color cover. **Pays on acceptance**. Credit line given. Buys one-time rights.

TIPS "We are a small company and do not use many photos. We keep landscapes/seascapes/skyscapes on hand—images need to be inspirational."

W.W. NORTON AND COMPANY

500 Fifth Ave., New York NY 10110. (212)354-5500. Fax: (212)869-0856. Website: www.wwnorton.com. **Contact:** Trish Marks. Estab. 1923. Photos used for text illustrations, book covers, dust jackets.

NEEDS Variable. Photo captions preferred.

SPECS Accepts images in all formats; digital images at a minimum of 300 dpi for reproduction and archival work.

MAKING CONTACT & TERMS "Due to the workload of our editorial staff and the large volume of materials we receive, we are no longer able to accept unsolicited submissions. If you are seeking publication, we suggest working with a literary agent who will represent you to the house."

RICHARD C. OWEN PUBLISHERS, INC.

P.O. Box 585, Katonah NY 10536. (914)232-3903; (800)262-0787. E-mail: richardowen@rcowen.com. Website: www.rcowen.com. **Contact:** Richard Owen, publisher. Estab. 1982. Publishes picture/storybook fiction and nonfiction for 5- to 7-year-olds; author autobiographies for 7- to 10-year-olds; professional books for educators. Photos used for text illustrations, promotional materials, book covers. Examples of recently published titles: *Maker of Things* (text illustrations, book cover); *Springs* (text illustrations, book cover).

NEEDS Number of photos bought annually varies; offers 3-10 freelance assignments/year. Needs unposed people shots and nature photos that suggest storyline. "For children's books, must be child-appealing with rich, bright colors and scenes, no distortions or special effects. For professional books, similar, but often of classroom scenes, including teachers. Nothing posed; should look natural and realistic." Reviews stock photos of children involved with books and classroom activities, ranging from kindergarten to 6th grade. Also wants photos of babies/children/teens, multicultural, families, environmental, landscapes/scenics, wildlife, architecture, cities/urban, pets, adventure, automobiles, sports, travel, science. Interested in documentary. (All must be of interest to children ages 5-9.) Model release required for children and adults. Children (under the age of 21) must have signature of legal guardian. Property release preferred. Photo captions required; include "any information we would need for acknowledgments, including if special permission was needed to use a location."

SPECS "For materials that are to be used, we need 35mm mounted transparencies or high-definition color prints. We usually use full-color photos."

MAKING CONTACT & TERMS Submit copies of samples by mail for review. Provide brochure, flyer or tearsheets to be kept on file for possible future assignments; no slides or disks. Include a brief cover letter with name, address, and daytime phone number, and indicate *Photographer's Market* as a source for correspondence. Works with freelancers on assignment only. "For samples, we like to see any size color prints (or color copies)." Keeps samples on file "if appropriate to our needs." Responds in 1 month. Simultaneous submissions OK. Pays $10-100 for color cover; $10-100 for color inside; $250-800 for multiple photo projects. "Each job has its own payment rate and arrangements." **Pays on acceptance.** Credit line sometimes given, depending on the project. "Photographers' credits appear in children's books and in professional books, but not in promotional materials for books or company." For children's books, publisher retains ownership, possession and world rights, which apply to first and all subsequent editions of a particular title and to all promotional materials. "After a project, (children's books) photos can be used by photographer for portfolio."

TIPS Wants to see "real people in natural, real life situations. No distortion or special effects. Bright, clear images with jewel tones and rich colors. Keep in mind what would appeal to children. Be familiar with what the publishing company has already done. Listen to the needs of the company. Send tearsheets, color photocopies with a mailer. No slides, please."

PAULIST PRESS

997 MacArthur Blvd., Mahwah NJ 07430-9990. (201)825-7300. Fax: (201)825-8345. E-mail: info@paulistpress.com; dcrilly@paulistpress.com. Website: www.paulistpress.com. **Contact:** Donna Crilly, editorial. Estab. 1865. Publishes hardcover and trade paperback originals, textbooks. Types of books include religion, theology and spirituality including biography. Specializes in academic and pastoral theology. Recent titles include *He Said Yes, Finding Purpose in Narnia* and *Our Daily Bread*. Publishes 80 titles/year; 5% requires freelance illustration; 5% require freelance design.

NEEDS Works with 5 illustrators and 10 designers/year. Prefers local freelancers. Works on assignment only. Book design assigns 8 freelance design jobs/year. Jackets/covers assigns 15 freelance design jobs/year. Pays by the project, $400-800.

MAKING CONTACT & TERMS Send query letter with brochure, résumé and tearsheets. Samples are filed. Portfolio review not required. Negotiates rights purchased. Originals are returned at job's completion if requested.

● PELICAN PUBLISHING COMPANY

1000 Burmaster St., Gretna LA 70053. (504)368-1175. Fax: (504)368-1195. E-mail: editorial@pelicanpub.com. Website: www.pelicanpub.com. **Contact:** Nina Kooij, editor-in-chief. Estab. 1926. Publishes adult trade, how-to, cooking, and art books; also religious inspirational and business motivational. Photos used for book covers. Books have a "high-quality, conservative and detail-oriented" look. Examples of published titles: *Brownies to Die For*; *Abraham Lincoln's Execution*.

NEEDS Needs Buys 8 photos/year; offers 3 freelance assignments/year. Needs photos of cooking/food, business concepts, nature/inspirational. Reviews royalty-free stock photos of people, nature, etc. Model/property release required. Photo captions required.

SPECS Uses 8×10 glossy color prints; 35mm, 4×5 transparencies. Accepts images in digital format. Send via CD as TIFF files at 300 dpi or higher.

● PRAKKEN PUBLICATIONS, INC.

(734)975-2800. Fax: (734)975-2787. E-mail: pam@eddigest.com. E-mail: susanne@eddigest.com. Sharon K. Miller, art/design/production manager. **Contact:** Susanne Peckham, book editor. Estab. 1934. "We publish books for educators in career/vocational and technology education, as well as books for the machine trades and machinists' education. Currently emphasizing machine trades." Publishes *The Education Digest* (magazine for teachers and administrators), *Tech Directions* (magazine for technology and career/technical educators), text and reference books for technology and career/technical education, and posters. Photos used for text illustrations, promotional materials, book covers, magazine covers and posters. Photo guidelines available at website.

NEEDS Wants photos of education "in action," especially technology, career/technical education and general education; prominent historical figures, technology/computers, industry. Photo captions required; include scene location, activity.

SPECS Uses all media; any size. Accepts images in digital format. Send via CD, or e-mail, TIFF, EPS, JPEG files at 300 dpi.

MAKING CONTACT & TERMS Send query letter with samples. Send unsolicited photos by mail for consideration. Keeps samples on file. Payment negotiable. Methods of payment to be arranged. Credit line given. Rights negotiable.

TIPS Wants to see "high-quality action shots in tech/career tech-ed and general education classrooms" when reviewing portfolios. Send inquiry with relevant samples to be kept on file. "We buy very few freelance photographs but would be delighted to see something relevant."

❸ ❹ ❶ PROSTAR PUBLICATIONS INC.

3 Church Cir., Suite 109, Annapolis MD 21401. (800)481-6277. Fax: (800)487-6277. E-mail: editor@prostarpublications.com. Website: www.prostarpublications.com. Estab. 1991. Publishes trade paperback originals (how-to, nonfiction). Subjects include history, nature, travel, nautical. Photos used for book covers. Examples of recently published titles: *The Age of Cunard*; *California's Channel Islands*; *Pacific Seaweeds*. Photo guidelines free with SASE.

NEEDS Buys less than 100 photos/year; offers very few freelance assignments/year. Reviews stock photos of nautical (sport). Prefers to review photos as part of a manuscript package. Model/property release required. Photo captions required.

SPECS Uses color and b&w prints.

MAKING CONTACT & TERMS Send query letter with stock list or contact to see if accepting submissions. Does not keep samples on file; include SASE for return of material. Responds in 1 month. Simultaneous submissions and previously published work OK. Pays $10-50 for color or b&w photos. Pays on publication. Credit line given. Buys book rights; negotiable.

● ❸ ❶ QUARTO PUBLISHING PLC.

226 City Rd., London EC1V 2TT, United Kingdom. +44 020 7700 9000. Fax: +44 020 7253 4437. E-mail: info@quarto.com. Website: www.quarto.com. Publishes nonfiction books on a wide variety of topics including arts, crafts, natural history, home and garden, reference. Photos used for text illustrations, book cov-

ers, dust jackets. Examples of recently published titles: *The Color Mixing Bible*; *Garden Birds*; *The Practical Geologist*. Contact for photo guidelines.

NEEDS Buys 1,000 photos/year. Subjects vary with current projects. Needs photos of multicultural, environmental, wildlife, architecture, gardening, interiors/decorating, pets, religious, adventure, food/drink, health/fitness, hobbies, performing arts, sports, travel, product shots/still life, science, technology/computers. Interested in fashion/glamour, fine art, historical/vintage. Special photo needs include arts, crafts, alternative therapies, New Age, natural history. Model/property release required. Photo captions required; include full details of subject and name of photographer.

SPECS Uses all types of prints. Accepts images in digital format. Send via CD, floppy disk, ZIP, e-mail as TIFF, EPS, JPEG files at 72 dpi for viewing, 300 dpi for reproduction.

MAKING CONTACT & TERMS Provide résumé, business card, samples, brochure, flyer or tearsheets to be kept on file for future reference. Arrange a personal interview to show portfolio. Simultaneous submissions and previously published work OK. Pays $30-60 for b&w photos; $60-100 for color photos. Pays on publication. Credit line given. Buys one-time rights; negotiable.

TIPS "Be prepared to negotiate!"

⊕⊖ ◑ RUNNING PRESS BOOK PUBLISHERS

2300 Chestnut St., Suite 200, Philadelphia PA 19103. (215)567-5080. Fax: (215)567-4636. E-mail: bill.jones@perseusbooks.com; perseus.promos@perseusbooks.com. Website: www.runningpress.com. **Contact:** Bill Jones, art director. Estab. 1972. Publishes hardcover originals, trade paperback originals. Subjects include adult and children's fiction and nonfiction; cooking; crafts, lifestyle, kits; miniature editions used for text illustrations, promotional materials, book covers, dust jackets. Examples of recently published titles: *Skinny Bitch, Eat What You Love, The Ultimate Book of Sports Movies, The Baseball Hall of Fame, Wine Drinking For Inspired Thinking, The South Park Guide to Life, The Big Lebowski Kit*.

NEEDS Buys a few hundred freelance photos/year and lots of stock images. Photos for gift books; photos of wine, food, lifestyle, landscapes/scenics, wildlife, architecture, gardening, rural, hobbies, sports.

Model/property release preferred. Photo captions preferred; include exact locations, names of pertinent items or buildings, names and dates for antiques or special items of interest.

SPECS Prefers images in digital format. Send via CD/DVD, via ftp/e-mail as TIFF, EPS files at 300 dpi.

MAKING CONTACT & TERMS Send URL and provide contact info. Do not send original art or anything that needs to be returned. Responds only if interested. Simultaneous submissions and previously published work OK. Pays $500-1000 for color cover; $100-250 for inside. Pays 45 days after receipt of invoice. Credits listed on separate copyright or credit pages. Buys one-time rights.

TIPS Submission guidelines available online.

SCHOLASTIC LIBRARY PUBLISHING

90 Old Sherman Turnpike, Danbury CT 06816. (203)797-3500. Fax: (203)797-3197. Website: www.scholastic.com/librarypublishing. Estab. 1895. "Scholastic Library is a leading publisher of reference, educational, and children's books. We provide parents, teachers, and librarians with the tools they need to enlighten children to the pleasure of learning and prepare them for the road ahead." Publishes 7 encyclopedias plus specialty reference sets in print and online versions. Photos used for text illustrations. Examples of published titles: *The New Book of Knowledge*; *Encyclopedia Americana*.

NEEDS Buys 5,000 images/year. Needs excellent-quality editorial photographs of all subjects A-Z and current events worldwide. All images must have clear captions and specific dates and locations, and natural history subjects should carry Latin identification.

SPECS Uses 8×10 glossy b&w and/or color prints; 35mm, 4×5, 8×10 (reproduction-quality dupes preferred) transparencies. Accepts images in digital format. Send via photo CD, floppy disk, Zip as JPEG files at requested resolution.

MAKING CONTACT & TERMS Send query letter, stock lists and printed examples of work. Cannot return unsolicited material and does not send guidelines. Include SASE only if you want material returned. Pricing to be discussed if/when you are contacted to submit images for specific project. Please note, encyclopedias are printed every year, but rights are requested for continuous usage until a major revision of the article in which an image is used (including online images).

TIPS "Send subject lists and small selection of samples. Printed samples *only*, please. In reviewing samples, we consider the quality of the photographs, range of subjects, and editorial approach. Keep in touch, but don't overdo it—quarterly e-mails are more than enough for updates on subject matter."

SCHOOL GUIDE PUBLICATIONS

210 North Ave., New Rochelle NY 10801. (800)433-7771. E-mail: mridder@schoolguides.com. Website: www.schoolguides.com. **Contact:** Miles Ridder, publisher. Estab. 1935. Publishes mass market paperback originals. Photos used for promotional materials, book covers.

NEEDS Needs photos of college students.

SPECS Accepts images in digital format; send via CD, ZIP, e-mail as TIFF or JPEG files.

MAKING CONTACT & TERMS E-mail query letter. **Pays on acceptance.**

SILVER MOON PRESS

400 E. 85th St., New York NY 10028. (800)874-3320. Fax: (212)988-8112. E-mail: mail@silvermoonpress.com. Website: silvermoonpress.com. **Contact:** Hope Killcoyne, managing editor. Publishes juvenile fiction and general nonfiction. Photos used for text illustrations, book covers, dust jackets. Examples of recently published titles: *Leo Politi: Artist of the Angels* by Ann Stalcup; *The War Between the States* by David Rubel.

NEEDS Buys 5-10 photos/year; offers 1 freelance assignment/year. Looking for general-children, subject-specific photos and American historical fiction photos. Reviews general stock photos. Photo captions preferred.

MAKING CONTACT & TERMS Provide résumé, business card, brochure, flyer or tearsheets to be kept on file for possible future assignments. Keeps samples on file. Responds in 1 month. Simultaneous submissions and previously published work OK. Pays $25-100 for b&w photos. Pays on publication. Credit line given. Buys all rights; negotiable.

🍁 TIGHTROPE BOOKS

602 Markham St., Toronto ON M6G 2L8, Canada. (647)348-4460. E-mail: shirarose@tightropebooks.com. Website: www.tightropebooks.com. **Contact:** Shirarose Wilensky, editor. Estab. 2005. Publishes hardcover and trade paperback originals.

NEEDS Publishes 12 titles/year. SASE returned. Responds only if interested. Catalog and guidelines free upon request and online.

MAKING CONTACT & TERMS Send an e-mail with résumé, digital images and artist's website, if available.

TILBURY HOUSE, PUBLISHERS

103 Brunswick Ave., Gardiner ME 04345. (800)582-1899. Fax: (207)582-8227. E-mail: tilbury@tilburyhouse.com. Website: www.tilburyhouse.com. **Contact:** Karen Fisk, associate children's book editor. Estab. 1990.

MAKING CONTACT & TERMS Send photocopies of photos/artwork.

⊕ $$$ ◐ TYNDALE HOUSE PUBLISHERS

351 Executive Dr., Carol Stream IL 60188. (800)323-9400. Fax: (800)684-0247. Website: www.tyndale.com. Estab. 1962. Publishes hardcover and trade paperback originals. Subjects include Christian content. Photos used for promotional materials, book covers, dust jackets. Examples of recently published titles: *Inside the Revolution, First Things First.* Photo guidelines free with #10 SASE.

NEEDS Buys 5-20 freelance photos/year. Needs photos of babies/children/teens, couples, multicultural, families, parents, senior citizens, landscapes/scenics, cities/urban, gardening, religious, rural, adventure, entertainment. Model/property release required.

SPECS Accepts hard copy samples only.

MAKING CONTACT & TERMS Send query letter with prints, tearsheets. Provide self-promotion piece to be kept on file for possible future assignments. Responds only if interested; send nonreturnable samples. Simultaneous submissions OK. Pays by the project; $200-1,750 for cover; $100-500 for inside. **Pays on acceptance**. Credit line given.

TIPS "We don't have portfolio viewings. Negotiations are different for every project. Have every piece submitted with legible contact information."

VINTAGE BOOKS

1745 Broadway, 15-3, New York NY 10019. (212)572-2444. E-mail: vintageanchorpublicity@randomhouse.com. Website: www.randomhouse.com. Publishes trade paperback reprints; fiction. Photos used for book covers. Examples of recently published titles: *Selected*

Stories by Alice Munro (cover); *The Fight* by Norman Mailer (cover); *Bad Boy* by Thompson (cover).

NEEDS Buys 100 freelance photos/year. Model/property release required. Photo captions preferred.

MAKING CONTACT & TERMS Send query letter with samples, stock list. Portfolios may be dropped off every Wednesday. Keeps samples on file. Responds only if interested; send nonreturnable samples. Pays by the project, per use negotiation. Pays on publication. Credit line given. Buys one-time and first North American serial rights.

TIPS "Show what you love. Include samples with name, address and phone number."

◎ VISITOR'S CHOICE MAGAZINE

102 E. 4th Ave., Vancouver BC V5T 1G2, Canada. (604)608-5180. E-mail: art@visitorschoice.com. Website: www.visitorschoice.com. Estab. 1977. Publishes full-color visitor guides for 16 communities and areas of British Columbia. Photos used for text illustrations, book covers, web sites. Photo guidelines available via e-mail upon request.

NEEDS Looking for photos of attractions, mountains, lakes, views, lifestyle, architecture, festivals, people, sports and recreation—specific to British Columbia region. Specifically looking for people/activity shots. Model release required; property release preferred. Photo captions required—make them detailed but brief.

SPECS Uses color prints; 35mm transparencies. Prefers images in digital format.

MAKING CONTACT & TERMS Send query letter or e-mail with samples; include SASE for return of material. Works with Canadian photographers. Keeps digital images on file. Responds in 3 weeks. Previously published work OK. Payment varies with size of photo published. Pays in 30-60 days. Credit line given.

TIPS "Please submit photos that are relevant to our needs only. Photos should be specific, clear, artistic, colorful, with good lighting."

VOYAGEUR PRESS

Quayside Publishing Group, 400 First Avenue North, Suite 300, Minneapolis MN 55401. (800)458-0454. Fax: (612)344-8691. E-mail: mdregni@voyageurpress.com. Website: voyageurpress.com. **Contact:** Michael Dregni, publisher. Estab. 1972. Publishes adult trade books, hardcover originals and reprints. Subjects include regional history, nature, popular culture, travel, wildlife, Americana, collectibles, lighthouses, quilts, tractors, barns and farms. Photos used for text illustrations, book covers, dust jackets, calendars. Examples of recently published titles: *Legendary Route 66: A Journey Through Time Along America's Mother Road; Illinois Central Railroad; Birds in Love: The Secret Courting & Mating Rituals of Extraordinary Birds; Backroads of New York; How to Raise Cattle; Knitknacks; Much Ado About Knitting; Farmall: The Red Tractor that Revolutionized Farming; Backroads of Ohio; Farmer's Wife Baking Cookbook; John Deere Two-Cylinder Tractor Encyclopedia* (text illustrations, book covers, dust jackets). Photo guidelines free with SASE.

◔ Voyageur Press is an imprint of MBI Publishing Company (see separate listing in this section).

NEEDS Buys 500 photos/year. Wants photos of wildlife, Americana, environmental, landscapes/scenics, cities/urban, gardening, rural, hobbies, humor, travel, farm equipment, agricultural. Interested in fine art, historical/vintage, seasonal. "Artistic angle is crucial—books often emphasize high-quality photos." Model release required. Photo captions preferred; include location, species, "interesting nuggets," depending on situation.

MAKING CONTACT & TERMS "Photographic dupes must be of good quality for us to fairly evaluate your photography. We prefer 35mm and large format transparencies; will accept images in digital format for review only; prefers transparencies for production. Send via CD, ZIP, e-mail as TIFF, BMP, GIF, JPEG files at 300 dpi." Simultaneous submissions OK. Pays $300 for cover; $75-175 for inside. Pays on publication. Credit line given, "but photographer's website will not be listed." Buys all rights; negotiable.

TIPS "We are often looking for specific material (crocodiles in the Florida Keys; farm scenics in the Midwest; wolf research in Yellowstone), so subject matter is important. However, outstanding color and angles and interesting patterns and perspectives are strongly preferred whenever possible. If you have the capability and stock to put together an entire book, your chances with us are much better. Though we use some freelance material, we publish many more single-photographer works. Include detailed captioning info on the mounts."

$ ◐ WAVELAND PRESS, INC.

4180 Illinois Route 83, Suite 101, Long Grove IL 60047-9580. (847)634-0081. Fax: (847)634-9501. E-mail: info@waveland.com. Website: www.waveland.com. **Contact:** Jan Weissman, photo editor. Estab. 1975. Publishes college-level textbooks and supplements. Photos used for text illustrations, book covers. Examples of recently published titles: *Our Global Environment: A Health Perspective, 7th Edition*; *Juvenile Justice, 2nd Edition.*

NEEDS Number of photos purchased varies depending on type of project and subject matter. Subject matter should relate to college disciplines: criminal justice, anthropology, speech/communication, sociology, archaeology, etc. Photos of multicultural, disasters, environmental, cities/urban, education, religious, rural, health/fitness, agriculture, political, technology. Interested in fine art, historical/vintage. Model/property release required. Photo captions preferred.

SPECS Accepts images in digital format. Send via CD, ZIP, e-mail as TIFF, EPS, JPEG files at 300 dpi.

MAKING CONTACT & TERMS Send query letter with stock list. Provide résumé, business card, brochure, flier or tearsheets to be kept on file for possible future assignments. Simultaneous submissions and previously published work OK. Pays $100-200 for cover; $50-100 for inside. Pays on publication. Credit line given. Buys one-time and book rights.

TIPS "Mail stock list and price list." See guidelines at www.waveland.com/manusc.htm.

🍁 WEIGL EDUCATIONAL PUBLISHERS LIMITED

6325 10th St., SE, Calgary AB T2H 2Z9, Canada. (403)233-7747. Fax: (403)233-7769. E-mail: linda@weigl.com. Website: www.weigl.com. Estab. 1979. Publishes textbooks, library and multimedia resources. Subjects include social studies, biography, life skills, environment/science studies, multicultural, language arts, geography. Photos used for text illustrations, book covers. Examples of recently published titles: *Land Mammals* (text illustrations, book cover); *Fossils* (text illustrations, book cover), *Opossums* (text illustrations, book cover); *Eiffel Tower* (text illustrations, book cover).

NEEDS Buys 2,000 photos/year. Needs photos of social issues and events, politics, celebrities, technology, people gatherings, multicultural, architecture, cities/urban, religious, rural, agriculture, disasters, environment, science, performing arts, life skills, landscape, wildlife, industry, medicine, biography and people doing daily activities, Canadiana, famous landmarks, aboriginal people. Interested in historical/vintage, seasonal. Model/property release required. Photo captions required.

SPECS Prefers images in digital format. Send via CD, e-mail, FTP as TIFF files at 300 dpi. Uses 5×7, 8×10 color prints (b&w for historical only); 35mm, 2¼×2¼ transparencies.

MAKING CONTACT & TERMS Send query letter with stock list. Provide tearsheets to be kept on file for possible future assignments. "Tearsheets or samples that don't have to be returned are best. We get in touch when we actually need photos." Simultaneous submissions and previously published work OK. Pays $0-250 for color cover; $0-100 for color inside. Credit line given upon request (photo credits are listed in appendix). Buys one-time, book and all rights; negotiable.

TIPS Needs "clear, well-framed shots that don't look posed. Action, expression, multicultural representation are important, but above all, educational value is sought. People must know what they are looking at. Please keep notes on what is taking place, where and when. As an educational publisher, our books use specific examples as well as general illustrations."

WILLOW CREEK PRESS

(715)358-7010. Fax: (715)358-2807. E-mail: jpetrie@willowcreekpress.com. Website: www.willowcreekpress.com. **Contact:** Jeremy Petrie, vice president of sales. Estab. 1986. Publishes hardcover, paperback and trade paperback originals; hardcover and paperback reprints and calendars. Subjects include pets, outdoor sports, gardening, cooking, birding, wildlife. Photos used for text illustrations, promotional materials, book covers, dust jackets, and calendars. Examples of recently published titles: *Pug Principles, Just Sons, It's a Dad Thing, Spirit of the Wolf.* Catalog free with #10 SASE. Photo guidelines free with #10 SASE or on website.

NEEDS Buys 2,000 freelance photos/year. Needs photos of gardening, pets, outdoors, recreation, landscapes/scenics, wildlife. Model/property release required. Photo captions required.

MAKING CONTACT & TERMS Send query letter with sample of work. Provide self-promotion piece to be kept on file. Responds only if interested. Simultaneous submissions and previously published work

OK. Pays by the project. Pays on publication. Credit line given. Buys one-time rights.

TIPS "We specialize in nature, outdoor, and sporting topics, including gardening, wildlife, and animal books. Pets, cookbooks, and a few humor books and essays round out our titles. Currently emphasizing pets (mainly dogs and cats), wildlife, outdoor sports (hunting, fishing). De-emphasizing essays, fiction."

⊕ $ ◐ WILSHIRE BOOK COMPANY

(818)700-1522. Fax: (818)700-1527. E-mail: mpowers@mpowers.com. Website: www.mpowers.com. **Contact:** Rights Department. Estab. 1947. Publishes trade paperback originals and reprints. Photos used for book covers. Model release required. Responds in 6 weeks. Simultaneous submissions and previously published work OK. Pays $250 for color cover. **Pays on acceptance**. Credit line given.

NEEDS photos of horses

SPECS Uses 35mm, 2¼×2¼, 4×5 transparencies. Accepts images in digital format.

MAKING CONTACT & TERMS Send via disk, e-mail. Send query letter with slides, prints, transparencies. Portfolio may be dropped off Monday through Friday. Does not keep samples on file; include SASE for return of material.

$ WOMEN'S HEALTH GROUP

Rodale, 33 E. Minor St., Emmaus PA 18098. (212)573-0296. Website: www.rodale.com. **Contact:** Yelena Nesbit, communications director. Publishes hardcover originals and reprints, trade paperback originals and reprints, one-shots. Subjects include healthy, active living for women, including diet, cooking, health, beauty, fitness and lifestyle.

NEEDS Photos of babies/children/teens, couples, multicultural, families, parents, senior citizens, food/drink, health/fitness/beauty, sports, travel, women, Spanish women, intimacy/sexuality, alternative medicine, herbs, home remedies. Model/property release preferred.

SPECS Uses color and b&w prints; 35mm, 2¼×2¼, 4×5 transparencies. Accepts images in digital format. Send via CD, ZIP, e-mail as TIFF, EPS, JPEG files at 300 dpi.

MAKING CONTACT & TERMS Send query letter with résumé, prints, photocopies, tearsheets, stock list. Provide résumé, business card, self-promotion piece to be kept on file for possible future assignments. Responds only if interested; send nonreturnable samples. Simultaneous submissions and previously published work OK. Pays $600 maximum for b&w cover; $900 maximum for color cover; $400 maximum for b&w inside; $500 maximum for color inside. Pays additional 20% for electronic promotion of book cover and designs for retail of book. **Pays on acceptance**. Credit line given. Buys one-time rights, electronic rights; negotiable.

TIPS "Include your contact information on each item that is submitted."

GREETING CARDS, POSTERS & RELATED PRODUCTS

The greeting card industry takes in more than $7.5 billion per year—the lion's share through the giants American Greetings and Hallmark Cards. Naturally, these big companies are difficult to break into, but there is plenty of opportunity to license your images to smaller companies.

There are more than 3,000 greeting card companies in the United States, many of which produce low-priced cards that fill a niche in the market, focusing on anything from the cute to the risqué to seasonal topics. A number of listings in this section produce items like calendars, mugs, and posters, as well as greeting cards.

Before approaching greeting card, poster, or calendar companies, it's important to research the industry to see what's being bought and sold. Start by checking out card, gift, and specialty stores that carry greeting cards and posters. Pay attention to the selections of calendars, especially the large seasonal displays during December. Studying what you see on store shelves will give you an idea of what types of photos are marketable.

Greetings etc., published by Edgell Publications, is a trade publication for marketers, publishers, designers, and retailers of greeting cards. The magazine offers industry news and information on trends, new products, and trade shows. Look for the magazine at your library or visit their website: www.greetingsmagazine.com. Also the National Stationery Show (www.nationalstationeryshow.com) is a large trade show held every year in New York City. It is the main event of the greeting card industry.

APPROACHING THE MARKET

After your initial research, query companies you are interested in working with and send a stock photo list. (See sample stock list in "Running Your Business.") You can help narrow your search by consulting the Subject Index in the back of this book. Check the index for companies interested in the subjects you shoot.

Since these companies receive large volumes of submissions, they often appreciate knowing what is available rather than actually receiving samples. This kind of query can lead to future sales even if your stock inventory doesn't meet their immediate needs. Buyers know they can request additional submissions as their needs change. Some listings in this section advise sending quality samples along with your query while others specifically request only a list. As you plan your queries, follow the instructions to establish a good rapport with companies from the start.

Some larger companies have staff photographers for routine assignments but also look for freelance images. Usually, this is in the form of stock, and images are especially desirable if they are of unusual subject matter or remote scenic areas for which assignments—even to staff shooters—would be too costly. Freelancers are usually offered assignments once they have established track records and demonstrated a flair for certain techniques, subject matter, or locations. Smaller companies are more receptive to working with freelancers, though they are less likely to assign work because of smaller budgets for photography.

The pay in this market can be quite lucrative if you provide the right image at the right time for a client in need of it, or if you develop a working relationship with one or a few of the better-paying markets. You should be aware, though, that one reason for higher rates of payment in this market is that these companies may want to buy all rights to images. But with changes in the copyright law, many companies are more willing to negotiate sales that specify all rights for limited time periods or exclusive product rights rather than complete surrender of copyright. Some companies pay royalties, which means you will earn the money over a period of time based on the sales of the product.

⑨⑨ ⑩ ADVANCED GRAPHICS

466 N. Marshall Way, Layton UT 84041. (801)499-5000 or (800)488-4144. Fax: (801) 499-5001. E-mail: info@ advancedgraphics.com. Website: www.advanced graphics.com. Estab. 1984. Specializes in life-size standups and cardboard displays, decorations and party supplies.

NEEDS Photos of celebrities (movie and TV stars, entertainers), babies/children/teens, couples, multicultural, families, parents, senior citizens, wildlife. Interested in seasonal. Reviews stock photos.

SPECS Uses 4×5, 8×10 transparencies. Accepts images in digital format. Send via CD, ZIP, e-mail.

MAKING CONTACT & TERMS Send query letter with stock list. Keeps samples on file. Responds in 1 month. Pays $400 maximum/image; royalties of 7-10%. Simultaneous submissions and previously published work OK. **Pays on acceptance.** Credit line given. Buys exclusive product rights; negotiable.

TIPS "We specialize in publishing life-size, standup cardboard displays of celebrities. Any pictures we use must show the entire person, head to toe. We must also obtain a license for each image that we use from the celebrity pictured or from that celebrity's estate. The image should be vertical and not too wide."

☺ ART IN MOTION

425-625 Agnes St., New Westminster BC V3M 5Y4, Canada. (604)525-3900 or (800)663-1308. Fax: (604)525-6166 or (877)525-6166. E-mail: contactus@ artinmotion.com. Website: www.artinmotion.com. **Contact:** Art relations. Specializes in open edition reproductions, framing prints, wall decor and licensing.

NEEDS "We are publishers of fine art reproductions, specializing in the decorative and gallery market. In photography, we often look for alternative techniques such as hand coloring, polaroid transfer, or any process that gives the photograph a unique look."

SPECS Accepts unzipped digital images sent via e-mail as JPEG files at 72 dpi.

MAKING CONTACT & TERMS Submit portfolio for review. Pays royalties of 10%. Royalties paid monthly. "Art In Motion covers all associated costs to reproduce and promote your artwork."

TIPS "Contact us via e-mail, or direct us to your website; also send slides or color copies of your work (all submissions will be returned)."

◎ ⑩ ART RESOURCES INTERNATIONAL, LTD.

66 Fort Point St., Norwalk CT 06855. (203)845-8888. E-mail: info@bonartique.com. Website: www. bonartique.com. **Contact:** Brett Bennist, art coordinator. Estab. 1980. Art publisher, poster company, licensing and design studio. Publishes/distributes fine art prints, canvas transfers, unlimited editions, offset reproductions and posters. Clients: Internet purveyors of art, picture frame manufacturers, catalog companies, distributors.

NEEDS Buys 50 images/year. Artistic/decorative photos (not stock photos) of landscapes/scenics, wildlife, architecture, cities/urban, gardening, interiors/ decorating, rural, adventure, health/fitness, extreme sports. Interested in fine art, cutting edge b&w, sepia photography. Model release required. Photo captions preferred.

SPECS Uses high-res digital files.

MAKING CONTACT & TERMS Send unsolicited photos by mail with SASE for consideration. Works on assignment only. Responds in 3 months. Simultaneous submissions and previously published work OK. Pays advance against royalties—specific dollar amount is subjective to project. Pays on publication. Credit line given if required. Buys all rights; exclusive reproduction rights.

TIPS "Send us new and exciting material; subject matter with universal appeal. Submit color copies, slides, transparencies, actual photos of your work; if we feel the subject matter is relevant to the projects we are currently working on, we'll contact you."

⊘ ARTVISIONS™: FINE ART LICENSING

12117 SE 26th St., Bellevue WA 98005-4118. E-mail: See website for contact form. Website: www.art visions.com. **Contact:** Neil Miller, president. Estab. 1993. Licenses "fashionable, decorative fine art photography and high-quality art to the commercial print, décor and puzzle/game markets."

NEEDS Handles fine art and photography licensing only.

MAKING CONTACT & TERMS "See website. Not currently seeking new talent. However, we are always willing to view the work of top-notch established artists and photographers. If you fit this category, please contact ArtVisions via e-mail and include a link to a website where your art can be seen." Exclusive worldwide representation for licensing is required. Written contract provided.

TIPS "To gain an idea of the type of art we license, please view our website. Animals, children, people and pretty places should be generic, rather than readily identifiable (this also prevents potential copyright issues and problems caused by not having personal releases for use of a 'likeness'). We prefer that your original work be in the form of high-resolution TIFF files from a 'pro-quality' digital camera. Note: scans/digital files are not to be interpolated or compressed in any way. We are firmly entrenched in the digital world; if you are not, then we cannot represent you. If you need advice about marketing your art, please visit: www.artistsconsult.com."

⊛⊛ ⦾ AVANTI PRESS INC.

6 W. 18 St., 6th Floor, New York NY 10011. (212)414-1025. E-mail: artsubmissions@avantipress.com. Website: www.avantipress.com. Estab. 1980. Specializes in photographic greeting cards. Photo guidelines free with SASE or on website.

NEEDS Buys approximately 200 images/year; all are supplied by freelancers. Interested in humorous, narrative, colorful, simple, to-the-point photos of babies, children (4 years old and younger), mature adults, human characters (not models), animals (in humorous situations) and exceptional florals. Has specific deadlines for seasonal material. Does not want travel, sunsets, landscapes, nudes, high-tech. Reviews stock photos. Model/property release required.

SPECS Accepts all mediums and formats. Accepts images in digital format. Send via CD as TIFF, JPEG files.

MAKING CONTACT & TERMS Do not submit original material. Pays on license. Credit line given. Buys 5-year worldwide, exclusive card rights.

⦾ BENTLEY PUBLISHING GROUP

1410 Lesnick Ln., Walnut Creek CA 94597. (925)935-3186 or (800)227-1666. Fax: (925)935-0213. E-mail: info@bentleypublishinggroup.com. Website: www. bentleypublishinggroup.com. Estab. 1986. Publishes posters.

NEEDS Interested in figurative, architecture, cities, urban, gardening, interiors/decorating, rural, food/drink, travel—b&w, color or hand-tinted photography. Interested in alternative process, avant garde, fine art, historical/vintage. Reviews stock photos and slides. Model/property release required. Include location, date, subject matter or special information.

SPECS Mainly uses 16×20, 22×28, 18×24, 24×30, 24×36 color and b&w prints; 4×5 transparencies from high-quality photos. Accepts images in digital format. Send via CD as TIFF or JPEG files.

MAKING CONTACT & TERMS Mail in the online artist submission form, include photos, printouts, transparencies, disks or other marketing materials. If you send a disk, please include a printout showing thumbnail images of the contents. Please include SASE. You can also e-mail JPEGs, along with contact information, to artist@bentleypublishinggroup.com. All submissions will be considered. Due to the large volume of submissions received, we can only respond if interested.

⊛ ⦿ ⦾ BLUE SKY PUBLISHING

P.O. Box 19974, Boulder CO 80308. (303)530-4654 or (800)875-9493. Fax: (800)432-6168. E-mail: bspinfo @blueskypublishing.net. Website: www.bluesky publishing.net. Estab. 1989. Specializes in fine art and photographic greeting cards.

NEEDS Buys 12-24 images/year; all are supplied by freelancers. Interested in Rocky Mountain winter landscapes, dramatic winter scenes featuring wildlife in mountain settings, winter scenes from the Southwest, unique and creative Christmas still life images, and scenes that express the warmth and romance of the holidays. Submit seasonal material December-April. Reviews stock photos. Model/property release preferred.

SPECS Uses 35mm, 4×5 (preferred) transparencies. Accepts images in digital format.

MAKING CONTACT & TERMS Submit 24-48 of your best images for review. Provide résumé, business card, self-promotion piece or tearsheets to be kept on file for possible future assignments. "We try to respond within 1 month, but it could take 2 months." Simultaneous submissions and previously published work OK. **Pays on acceptance.**

TIPS "Due to the volume of calls we receive from photographers, we ask that you refrain from calling regarding the status of your submission. We will contact you within 2 months to request more samples of your work if we are interested. We do not return unsolicited samples."

THE BOREALIS PRESS

35 Tenney Hill, Blue Hill ME 04614. (207)370-6020 or (800)669-6845. E-mail: info@borealispress.net. Website: www.borealispress.net. **Contact:** Mark Baldwin. Estab. 1989. Specializes in greeting cards, magnets and "other products for thoughtful people." Photo guidelines available for SASE.

NEEDS Buys more than 100 images/year; 90% are supplied by freelancers. Needs photos of humor, babies/children/teens, couples, families, parents, senior citizens, adventure, events, hobbies, pets/animals. Interested in documentary, historical/vintage, seasonal. Photos must tell a story. Model/property release preferred.

SPECS Low-res files are fine for review. Any media OK for finals. Uses 5×7 to 8×10 prints; 35mm, 2¼×2¼, 4×5, 8×10 transparencies. Accepts images in digital format. Send via CD. Send low-resolution files if e-mailing. Send images to art@borealispress.net.

MAKING CONTACT & TERMS Send query letter with slides (if necessary), prints, photocopies, SASE. Send no originals on initial submissions. "Artist's name must be on every image submitted." Responds in 2 weeks to queries; 3 weeks to portfolios. Previously published work OK. Pays by the project, royalties. **Pays on acceptance**, receipt of contract.

TIPS "Photos should have some sort of story, in the loosest sense. They can be in any form. We do not want multiple submissions to other card companies. Include SASE, and put your name on every image you submit."

CENTRIC CORP.

6712 Melrose Ave., Los Angeles CA 90038. (323)936-2100. Fax: (323)936-2101. E-mail: centric@juno.com. Website: www.centriccorp.com. Estab. 1986. Specializes in products that have nostalgic, humorous, thought-provoking images or sayings on them and in the following product categories: T-shirts, watches, pens, clocks, pillows, and drinkware.

NEEDS Photos of cities' major landmarks, attractions and things for which areas are well-known, and humorous or thought-provoking images. Submit seasonal material 5 months in advance. Reviews stock photos.

SPECS Uses 8×12 color and/or b&w prints; 35mm transparencies. Accepts images in digital format. Send via CD as PDF or JPEG files.

MAKING CONTACT & TERMS Submit portfolio online for review or query with résumé of credits. Provide résumé, business card, self-promotion piece or tearsheets to be kept on file for possible future assignments. Responds in 2 weeks. Works mainly with local freelancers. Pays by the job; negotiable. **Pays on acceptance.** Rights negotiable.

TIPS "Research the demographics of buyers who purchase Elvis, Lucy, Marilyn Monroe, James Dean, Betty Boop and Bettie Page products to know how to 'communicate a message' to the buyer."

COMSTOCK CARDS

600 S. Rock Blvd., Suite 15, Reno NV 89502. (775)856-9400 or (800)326-7825. Fax: (775)856-9406 or (888)266-2610. E-mail: production@comstockcards.com. Website: www.comstockcards.com. Estab. 1986. Specializes in greeting cards, invitations, notepads, games, gift wrap. Photo guidelines free with SASE.

NEEDS Buys/assigns 30-40 images/year; all are supplied by freelancers. Wants wild, outrageous and shocking adult humor; seductive images of men or women. Definitely does not want to see traditional, sweet, cute, animals or scenics. "If it's appropriate to show your mother, we don't want it!" Frontal nudity in both men and women is OK and now being accepted as long as it is professionally done—no snapshots from home. Submit seasonal material 10 months in advance. Model/property release required. Photo captions preferred.

SPECS Uses 5×7 color prints; 35mm, 2¼×2¼ color transparencies. Accepts images in digital format.

MAKING CONTACT & TERMS Send query letter with samples, tearsheets, SASE. Responds in 2 months. Pays on publication. Buys all rights; negotiable.

TIPS "Submit with SASE if you want material returned."

DELJOU ART GROUP

1616 Huber St., Atlanta GA 30318. (404)350-7190 or (800)237-4638. Fax: (404)350-7195. E-mail: info@deljouartgroup.com. Website: www.deljouartgroup.com. Estab. 1980. Specializes in wall decor, fine art.

NEEDS All images supplied by freelancers. Specializes in artistic images for reproduction for high-end art market. Work sold through art galleries as photos or prints. Needs nature photos. Reviews stock photos of graphics, b&w photos. No tourist photos: only high-quality, artistic photos.

SPECS Uses color and/or b&w prints; 35mm, 2¼×2¼, 4×5, 8×10 transparencies. Accepts images in digital format. Prefers initial digital submissions via e-mail, but will accept CDs. Final, accepted images must be high-res, of at least 300 dpi.

MAKING CONTACT & TERMS Submit portfolio for review; include SASE for return of material. Also send portfolio via e-mail. Simultaneous submissions and previously published work OK. Pays royalties on sales. Credit line sometimes given depending upon the product. Rights negotiable.

TIPS "Abstract-looking photographs OK. Hand-colored b&w photographs needed."

DESIGN DESIGN, INC.

P.O. Box 2266, Grand Rapids MI 49501. (616)771-8359. Fax: (616)774-4020. E-mail: susan.birnbaum@designdesign.us. Website: www.designdesign.us. Estab. 1986. Specializes in greeting cards and paper-related product development.

NEEDS Licenses stock images from freelancers and assigns work. Specializes in humorous topics. Submit seasonal material 1 year in advance. Model/property release required.

SPECS Uses 35mm transparencies. Accepts images in digital format. Send via ZIP.

MAKING CONTACT & TERMS Submit portfolio for review. Provide résumé, business card, self-promotion piece or tearsheets to be kept on file for possible future assignments. Do not send original work. Pays royalties. Pays upon sales. Credit line given.

☺ DODO GRAPHICS INC.

P.O. Box 585, Plattsburgh NY 12901. (518)561-7294. Fax: (518)561-6720. E-mail: dodographics@aol.com. Website: www.dodographicsinc.com. **Contact:** Frank How, president. Estab. 1979. Specializes in posters and framing prints.

NEEDS Buys 50-100 images/year; 100% are supplied by freelancers. Offers 25-50 assignments/year. Needs all subjects. Submit seasonal material 3 months in advance. Reviews stock photos. Model/property release preferred. Photo captions preferred.

SPECS Uses color and/or b&w prints; 35mm, 4×5 transparencies; CDs.

MAKING CONTACT & TERMS Submit portfolio for review. Send query letter with samples and stock list or CDs. Works on assignment only. Keeps samples on file. Responds in 1 month. Simultaneous submissions

OK. Payment negotiable. **Pays on acceptance.** Credit line given. Buys all rights; negotiable.

☺ ⊘ IMPACT PHOTOGRAPHICS

4961 Windplay Dr., El Dorado Hills CA 95762. (916)939-9333. Website: www.impactphotographics.com. Estab. 1975. Specializes in calendars, postcards, magnets, bookmarks, mugs, CDs, posters, books for the tourist industry. Photo guidelines and fee schedule free with SASE.

> ◯ This company sells to specific tourist destinations; their products are not sold nationally. They need material that will be sold for at least a 5-year period.

NEEDS Photos of wildlife, scenics, U.S. travel destinations, national parks, theme parks and animals. Buys stock. Buys 3,000 photos/year. Submit seasonal material 4-5 months in advance. Model/property release required. Photo captions preferred.

SPECS Uses 35mm, 2¼×2¼, 4×5, 8×10 transparencies. Accepts images in digital format. Send via CD, Zip as TIFF, JPEG files at 300 dpi.

MAKING CONTACT & TERMS "Must have submissions request before submitting samples. No unsolicited submissions." Send query letter with stock list. Provide business card, self-promotion piece or tearsheets to be kept on file for possible future assignments. Simultaneous submissions and previously published work OK. Request fee schedule; rates vary by size. Pays on usage. Credit line and printed samples of work given. Buys one-time and nonexclusive product rights.

⊖ ⊖ INTERCONTINENTAL GREETINGS LTD.

38 W. 32nd St., Suite 910, New York NY 10001. (212)683-5830. Fax: (212)779-8564. E-mail: art@intercontinental-ltd.com. Website: www.intercontinental-ltd.com. **Contact:** Jerra Parfitt, creative director. Estab. 1967. Sells reproduction rights of designs to manufacturers of multiple products around the world. Represents artists in 50 different countries. "Our clients specialize in greeting cards, giftware, giftwrap, calendars, postcards, prints, posters, stationery, paper goods, food tins, playing cards, tabletop, bath and service ware and much more."

NEEDS Approached by several hundred artists/year. Seeking creative decorative art in traditional and computer media (Photoshop and Illustrator work accepted). Prefers artwork previously made with few or no rights pending. Graphics, sports, occasions (e.g., Christmas, baby, birthday, wedding), humorous, "soft touch," romantic themes, animals. Accepts seasonal/holiday material any time. Prefers artists/designers experienced in greeting cards, paper products, tabletop and giftware.

MAKING CONTACT & TERMS Send unsolicited CDs or DVDs by mail or low-res JPEGs by e-mail. "Please do not send original artwork." Upon request, submit portfolio for review. Provide résumé, business card, brochure, flyer, or tear sheets to be kept on file for possible future assignments. "Once your art is accepted, we require original color art—Photoshop files on disc (TIFF, 300 dpi). We will respond only if interested (will send back non-accepted artwork in SASE if provided)." Pays on publication. No credit line given. Offers advance when appropriate. Sells one-time rights and exclusive product rights. Simultaneous submissions and previously published work OK. "Please state reserved rights, if any."

TIPS Recommends the annual New York SURTEX and Licensing shows. In photographer's portfolio samples, wants to see "a neat presentation, perhaps thematic in arrangement."

JILLSON & ROBERTS

3300 W. Castor St., Santa Ana CA 92704-3908. (714)424-0111. Fax: (714)424-0054. E-mail: janel.kaden@jillsonroberts.com. Website: www.jillsonroberts.com. **Contact:** Janel Kaden, art director. Estab. 1974. Specializes in gift wrap, totes, printed tissues, accessories. Photo guidelines free with SASE. Eco-friendly products.

NEEDS Specializes in everyday and holiday products. Themes include babies, sports, pets, seasonal, weddings. Submit seasonal material 3-6 months in advance.

MAKING CONTACT & TERMS Submit portfolio for review or query with samples. Provide résumé, business card, self-promotion piece or tearsheets to be kept on file for possible future assignments. The review process can take up to 4 months. Pays average flat fee of $250.

TIPS "Please follow our guidelines!"

🪙🪙 ⚫ MCGAW GRAPHICS, INC.

100 Dutch Hill Rd., Suite 230, Orangeburg NY 10962. (845)353-8600. Fax: (845)353-8907 or (800)446-8230. Website: www.mcgawgraphics.com. **Contact:** Katy Murphy, product development manager. Estab. 1979. Specializes in posters, framing prints, wall decor.

NEEDS Licenses 250-300 images/year in a variety of media; 10-15% in photography. Interested in b&w: still life, floral, figurative, landscape; color: landscape, still life, floral. Also considers celebrities, environmental, wildlife, architecture, rural, fine art, historical/vintage. Does not want images that are too esoteric or too commercial. Model/property release required for figures, personalities, images including logos or copyrighted symbols. Photo captions required; include artist's name, title of image, year taken. Not interested in stock photos.

SPECS Uses color and b&w prints; 35mm, 2¼×2¼, 4×5, 8×10 transparencies. Accepts images in digital format at 300 dpi.

MAKING CONTACT & TERMS Submit portfolio for review. "Review is typically 2 weeks on portfolio drop-offs. Be certain to leave phone number for pick up." Provide résumé, business card, self-promotion piece or tearsheets to be kept on file for possible future assignments. "Do not send originals!" Responds in 1 month. Simultaneous submissions and previously published work OK. Pays royalties on sales. Pays quarterly following first sale and production expenses. Credit line given. Buys exclusive product rights for all wall decor.

TIPS "Work must be accessible without being too commercial. Our posters/prints are sold to a mass audience worldwide who are buying art prints. Images that relate a story typically do well for us. The photographer should have some sort of unique style or look that separates him from the commercial market. It is important to take a look at our catalog or website before submitting work to get a sense of our aesthetic. You can view the catalog in any poster shop. We do not typically license traditional stock-type images—we are a decorative house appealing to a higher-end market. Send your best work (20-60 examples)."

🪙🪙 🅾 MODERNART EDITIONS

165 Chubb Ave., Lyndhurst NJ 07071. (201)842-8500 or (800)760-3058. Fax: (201)842-8546. E-mail: modernarteditions@theartpublishinggroup.com. Website: www.modernarteditions.com. Specializes in posters, wall decor, open edition fine art prints.

NEEDS Interested in b&w or sepia tone, seasonal, landscapes, seascapes, European scenes, floral still lifes, abstracts, cities, gardening, sports, fine art. Model/property release required.

SPECS Uses 8×10 color and b&w prints; 2¼×2¼, 4×5 transparencies. Accepts images in digital format. Send JPEG files for review via e-mail.

MAKING CONTACT & TERMS Submit portfolio for review. Keeps samples on file. Include SASE for return of material. Simultaneous submissions OK. Responds within 2 months. Pays on usage. Credit line given. Buys one-time, all, and exclusive product rights.

🅞 NEW YORK GRAPHIC SOCIETY PUBLISHING GROUP

130 Scott Rd., Waterbury CT 06705. (203)847-2000 or (800)677-6947. Fax: (203)757-5526. Website: www. nygs.com. Estab. 1925. Specializes in fine art reproductions, prints, posters, canvases.

NEEDS Buys 150 images/year; 125 are supplied by freelancers. "Looking for variety of images."

SPECS Prefers digital format. Send low-res JPEGs via e-mail; no ZIP files.

MAKING CONTACT & TERMS Send query letter with samples to Attn: Artist Submissions. Does not keep samples on file; include SASE for return of material. Responds in 3 months. Payment negotiable. Pays on usage. Credit line given. Buys exclusive product rights. No phone calls.

TIPS "Visit website to review artist submission guidelines and to see appropriate types of imagery for publication."

🅢 🅞 NOVA MEDIA INC.

1724 N. State St., Big Rapids MI 49307-9073. (231)796-4637. E-mail: trund@netonecom.net. Website: www. novamediainc.com. **Contact:** Thomas J. Rundquist, chairman. Estab. 1981. Specializes in CDs, CDs/tapes, games, limited edition plates, posters, school supplies, T-shirts. Photo guidelines free with SASE.

NEEDS Buys 100 images/year; most are supplied by freelancers. Offers 20 assignments/year. Seeking art fantasy photos. Photos of children/teens, celebrities, multicultural, families, landscapes/scenics, education, religious, rural, entertainment, health/fitness/beauty, military, political, technology/computers. Interested in documentary, erotic, fashion/glamour, fine art, historical/vintage. Submit seasonal material 2 months in advance. Reviews stock photos. Model release required. Photo captions preferred.

SPECS Uses color and b&w prints. Accepts images in digital format. Send via CD.

MAKING CONTACT & TERMS Send query letter with samples. Accepts e-mail submissions. Responds in 1 month. Keeps samples on file; does not return material. Simultaneous submissions and previously published work OK. Payment negotiable. Pays extra for electronic usage of photos. Pays on usage. Credit line given. Buys electronic rights; negotiable.

TIPS "The most effective way to contact us is by e-mail or regular mail. Visit our website."

OHIO WHOLESALE, INC.

5180 Greenwich Rd., Seville OH 44273. (330)769-1059. Fax: (330)769-1961. E-mail: annev@ohiowholesale. com. Website: www.ohiowholesale.com. **Contact:** Anne Secoy, vice president of product development. Estab. 1978. Home decor, giftware, seasonal. Produces collectible figurines, decorative housewares, decorations, gifts, mugs, ornaments and textiles.

MAKING CONTACT & TERMS Send an e-mail query with brochure, photographs and SASE. Samples not kept on file. Company will contact artist for portfolio if interested. Pays by the project. Rights negotiated.

TIPS "Be able to work independently with your own ideas—use your 'gift' and think outside the box. *Wow me!*"

OUT OF THE BLUE

1022 Hancock Ave., Sarasota FL 34232. (941)966-4042. Fax: (941)966-8914. E-mail: outoftheblue.us@mac. com; artlicensing@comcast.net. Website: www.out-of-the-blue.us. **Contact:** Michael Woodward, president; Jane Mason, licensing manager. Estab. 2003. "We represent artists, photographers and designers who wish to establish a licensing program for their work. We are particularly interested in photographic images that we can license internationally particularly for fine art prints and posters and giclees for interior design projects and home and office decor. "We require substantial portfolios of work that can generate good incomes, or concepts that have wide commercial appeal."

NEEDS "We prefer concepts that have a unique look or theme and that are distinctive: florals, landscapes, inspirational, bathroom art, European street scenes, lake scenes, forest scenes, nature and spectacular landscapes and exotic beach scenes for murals (large format). Images for prints and posters must be in pairs or series paying attention to future trends and color palettes related to the home décor market."

SPECS "Our standard commission rate is 50% with no expenses to the photographer as long as the photographer provides high-resolution digital files at 300 dpi to print 30-36 inches." Send SASE if you want material returned.

MAKING CONTACT & TERMS "E-mail JPEGs or details of your website for an honest evaluation. No postal submissions, please."

TIPS "Pay attention to trends and color palettes. Artists need to consider actual products when creating new art. Look at products in retail outlets and get a feel for what is selling well. Get to know the markets you want to sell your work to."

○ PAPER PRODUCTS DESIGN

60 Galli Dr., Novato CA 94949. (415)883-1888. Fax: (415)883-1999. E-mail: carol@ppd.co. Website: www. paperproductsdesign.com. **Contact:** Carol Florsheim. Estab. 1992. Specializes in napkins, plates, candles, porcelain.

NEEDS Buys 500 images/year; all are supplied by freelancers. Needs photos of babies/children/teens, architecture, gardening, pets, food/drink, humor, travel. Interested in avant garde, fashion/glamour, fine art, historical/vintage, seasonal. Submit seasonal material 6 months in advance. Model release required. Photo captions preferred.

SPECS Uses glossy color and b&w prints; 35mm, 2¼×2¼, 4×5, 8×10 transparencies. Accepts images in digital format. Send via ZIP, e-mail at 350 dpi.

MAKING CONTACT & TERMS Send query letter with photocopies, tearsheets. Responds in 1 month to queries, only if interested. Simultaneous submissions and previously published work OK.

○ ○○ ○ PI CREATIVE ART

1180 Caledonia Rd., Toronto ON M6A 2W5, Canada. (416)789-7156. Fax: (416)789-7159. E-mail: dow@ pifineart.com. Website: www.picreativeart.com. **Contact:** Darounny (Dow) Marcus, creative director. Estab. 1976. Specializes in posters/prints. Photo guidelines available.

NEEDS Photos of landscapes/scenics, floral, architecture, cities/urban, European, hobbies. Interested in alternative process, avant garde, fine art, historical/vintage. Interesting effects, Polaroids, painterly or hand-tinted submissions welcome. Submit seasonal material 2 months in advance. Model/property

release preferred. Photo captions preferred; include date, title, artist, location.

SPECS Accepts images in digital format. Send via CD, ZIP, e-mail as low-res JPEG files for review. Images of interest will be requested in minimum 300 dpi TIFF files.

MAKING CONTACT & TERMS Send query letter with résumé, slides, prints, photocopies, tearsheets, transparencies, stock list. Provide business card, self-promotion piece to be kept on file for possible future assignments. Responds in 2 weeks to queries; 5 weeks to portfolios. Simultaneous submissions OK. Pays royalties of 10% minimum. Buys worldwide rights for approximately 4-5 years to publish in poster form.

TIPS "Keep all materials in contained unit. Provide easy access to contact information. Provide any information on previously published images. Submit a number of pieces. Develop a theme (we publish in series of 2, 4, 6, etc.). B&w performs very well. Vintage is also a key genre; sepia great, too. Catalog is published with supplement 2 times/year. We show our images in our ads, supporting materials and website."

○ ○ PORTFOLIO GRAPHICS, INC.

4680 Kelly Cir., Salt Lake City UT 84117. (801)424-2574. E-mail: info@portfoliographics.com. Website: www.nygs.com. **Contact:** Kent Barton, creative director. Estab. 1986. Publishes and distributes open edition fine art prints, posters, and canvases as well as images and designs on alternative substrates such as metal, wooden plaques and wall decals.

NEEDS Buys 100 images/year; nearly all are supplied by freelancers. Seeking creative, fashionable, and decorative art for commercial and designer markets. Clients include galleries, designers, poster distributors (worldwide), framers and retailers. For posters, "keep in mind that we need decorative art that can be framed and hung in home or office." Submit seasonal material on an ongoing basis. Reviews stock photos. Photo captions preferred.

SPECS Uses prints, transparencies, high res digital files recommended.

MAKING CONTACT & TERMS E-mail JPEGs, PDF, or website links. Send photos, transparencies, tearsheets or gallery booklets with SASE. Does not keep samples on file; must include SASE for return of material. Art director will contact photographer for portfolio review if interested. Responds in 3 months. Pays royalties of 10% on sales. Quarterly royalties paid per pieces sold. Credit line given. Buys exclusive product rights license per piece.

TIPS "We find artists through galleries, magazines, art exhibits and submissions. We are looking for a variety of artists, styles and subjects that are fresh and unique."

⊗⊗ ◑ RECYCLED PAPER GREETINGS, INC.

111 N. Canal St., Suite 700, Chicago IL 60606-7206. (800)777-9494. Website: www.recycled.com. **Contact:** Art director. Estab. 1971. Specializes in greeting cards. Photo guidelines available on website.

NEEDS All RPG cards are created by freelancers. Wants "primarily humorous photos for greeting cards. Unlikely subjects and offbeat themes have the best chance, but we'll consider all types. Text ideas required with all photo submissions." Photos of babies/children/teens, landscapes/scenics, wildlife, pets, humor. Interested in alternative process, fine art, historical/vintage, seasonal. Model release required.

MAKING CONTACT & TERMS "We currently don't accept submissions electronically. One reason is that with the number of people involved in the review process at RPG, we have found that everything moves along a lot quicker if we already have a hard copy version of the submission. More importantly, we want to get the best representation of what the finished product will look like, which is why we request that submissions look as much like greeting cards as possible. The standard format for a greeting card is 5×7. Artwork and any corresponding words should be on the front of the card with the message appearing on the inside. *It is also important to note that because we believe strongly that the artwork and the message go hand in hand, we also do not accept submissions that include a message without any accompanying artwork.*" See www.recycled.com/artists for complete submission guidelines.

TIPS "We believe the strongest cards come from individuals expressing their feelings in their own style, which is why we strongly recommend you send messages with your artwork. Experience has shown us that the art makes the customer pick up a card, but it is the message that makes them buy it."

◐ ⊗⊗ RIG

500 Paterson Plank Rd., Union City NJ 07087. (201)863-4500. Website: www.rightsinternational.

com. Estab. 1996. Licensing agency specializing in the representation of photographers and artists to manufacturers for licensing purposes. Manufacturers include greeting card, calendar, poster and home furnishing companies.

NEEDS Photos of architecture, entertainment, humor, travel, floral, coastal. "Globally influenced—not specific to one culture. Moody feel." See website for up-to-date needs. Reviews stock photos. Model/property release required.

SPECS Uses prints, slides, transparencies. Accepts images in digital format. Send via CD, e-mail as JPEG files.

MAKING CONTACT & TERMS Submit portfolio for review. Keeps samples on file. Simultaneous submissions and previously published work OK. Payment negotiable. Pays on license deal. Credit line given. Buys exclusive product rights.

◑ SANTORO GRAPHICS, LTD.

Rotunda Point, 11 Hartfield Crescent, Wimbledon London SW19 3RL, United Kingdom. +44 20878 11100. Fax: +44 20878 11101. E-mail: Submissions@ santorographics.com. Website: www.santoro.co.uk. Estab. 1983.

NEEDS Features landscapes/scenics, wildlife, humor and historical/vintage photography.

SPECS Model/property release required.

MAKING CONTACT & TERMS E-mail query letter. Accepts EPS files at 300 dpi.

SPENCER'S

6826 Black Horse Pk., Egg Harbor Twp. NJ 08234-4197. Website: www.spencersonline.com. Estab. 1947. Specializes in packaging design, full-color art, novelty gifts, brochure design, poster design, logo design, promotional P.O.P.

○ Products offered by store chain include posters, T-shirts, games, mugs, novelty items, cards, 14K jewelry, neon art, novelty stationery. Spencer's is moving into a lot of different product lines, such as custom lava lights and Halloween costumes and products. Visit a store if you can to get a sense of what they offer.

NEEDS Photos of babies/children/teens, couples, party scenes (must have releases), jewelry (gold, sterling silver, body jewelry—earrings, chains, etc.). Interested in fashion/glamour. Model/property release required. Photo captions preferred.

SPECS Uses transparencies. Accepts images in digital format. Send via CD, DVD at 300 dpi. Contracts some illustrative artwork. All styles considered.

MAKING CONTACT & TERMS Send query letter with photocopies. Portfolio may be dropped off any weekday, 9-5. Provide self-promotion piece to be kept on file for possible future assignments. Responds only if interested; send *only* nonreturnable samples. Pays by the project, $250-850/image. Pays on receipt of invoice. Buys all rights; negotiable. Will respond upon need of services.

🍁 $ [A] ◐ TELDON

Unit 100 - 12751 Vulcan Way, Richmond BC V6V 1N6, Canada. E-mail: photo@teldon.com. Website: www.teldonmarketing.com. **Contact:** Photo editor. Estab. 1969. Publishes high-quality dated and nondated promotional products, including wall calendars, desk calendars, magnets, newsletters, postcards, etc. E-mail for photo guidelines—waiting list applies.

NEEDS Buys over 1,000 images/year; 70% are supplied by freelancers. Photos of lifestyles (babies/children/teens, couples, multicultural, families, parents, senior citizens, wildlife (North American), architecture (exterior residential homes–property released only), gardening, interiors/decorating (property released only), adventure, sports, travel (world), motivational, inspirational, landscape/scenic. Reviews stock photos. Model/property release required for trademarked buildings, residential houses, people. Photo captions required; include complete detailed description of destination (e.g., Robson Square, Vancouver, British Columbia, Canada); month picture taken also helpful.

SPECS Accepts mostly digital submissions now. Contact photo editor for details.

MAKING CONTACT & TERMS Send query letter or e-mail. "No submissions accepted unless photo guidelines have been received and reviewed." Responds in 1 month, depending on workload. Simultaneous submissions and previously published work OK. Works with freelancers and stock agencies. Pays $150 for one-time use, non-negotiable. Pays in September of publication year. Credit line and complementary calendar copies given. Photos used for one-time use in dated products, North American rights, unlimited print runs.

TIPS City shots should be no older than 1 year. "Examine our catalog on our website carefully, and you will see what we are looking for."

$$ [A] ◐ TIDE-MARK PRESS

P.O. Box 20, Windsor CT 06095. (860)683-4499, ext. 107. Fax: (860)683-4055. E-mail: scott@tide-mark.com. Website: www.tidemarkpress.com. **Contact:** Mara Braverman, acquisitions editor. Estab. 1979. Specializes in calendars. Photo guidelines available on website.

NEEDS Buys 1,000 images/year; 800 are supplied by freelancers. Categories: landscapes/scenics, wildlife, architecture, gardening, interiors/decorating, pets, religious, adventure, automobiles, entertainment, events, food/drink, health/fitness, hobbies, humor, performing arts, sports, travel. Interested in fine art, historical/vintage; Native American; African American. Needs "complete calendar concepts that are unique but also have identifiable markets; groups of photos that could work as an entire calendar; ideas and approach must be visually appealing and innovative but also have a definable audience. No general nature or varied subjects without a single theme." Submit seasonal material 18 months in advance. Reviews stock photos. Model release preferred. Photo captions required.

SPECS Uses film and digital images. Accepts low-res images in PDF or JPEG format for initial review; send high-res only on selection.

MAKING CONTACT & TERMS "Offer specific topic suggestions that reflect specific strengths of your stock." Send e-mail with sample images. Editor will contact photographer for portfolio review if interested. Responds in 3 weeks. Pays $150-350/color image for single photos; royalties on net sales if entire calendar supplied. Pays on publication or per agreement. Credit line given. Buys one-time rights.

TIPS "We tend to be a niche publisher and rely on photographers with strong stock to supply our needs. Check the website, then call or send a query suggesting a specific calendar concept."

$ ◐ TRAILS MEDIA GROUP

333 W. State St., Milwaukee WI 53201. Fax: (414)647-4723. E-mail: mchristiansen@wistrails.com. Website: www.wistrails.com. Estab. 1960. Specializes in calendars (horizontal and vertical) portraying seasonal

scenics. Also publishes regional books and magazines, including *Wisconsin Trails*.

NEEDS Buys 300 photos/year. Needs photos of nature, landscapes, wildlife and regional (Wisconsin, Michigan, Iowa, Minnesota, Indiana, Illinois) activities. Makes selections in January for calendars, 6 months ahead for magazine issues. Photo captions required.

SPECS Uses 35mm, 2¼×2¼, 4×5 transparencies. Accepts images in digital format. Send via CD, ZIP, Jaz as TIFF, EPS files at 300-1,250 dpi.

MAKING CONTACT & TERMS Submit material by mail with SASE for consideration. Responds in 1 month. Simultaneous submissions OK "if we are informed, and if there's not a competitive market among them." Previously published work OK. Buys one-time rights.

TIPS "Be sure to inform us how you want materials returned and include proper postage. Calendar scenes must be horizontal to fit 8¾×11 format, but we also want vertical formats for engagement calendars. See our magazine and books and be aware of our type of photography. E-mail for an appointment."

☉ ❹ ◐ ZITI CARDS

601 S. Sixth St., St. Charles MO 63301. (800)497-5908. Fax: (636)352-2146. E-mail: Mail@Ziticards.com. Website: www.ziticards.com. **Contact:** Salvatore Ventura, owner. Estab. 2006. Produces greeting cards. Specializes in holiday cards for architects and construction businesses. Art guidelines available via e-mail.

NEEDS Buys 20+ freelance photographs per year. Produces material for greeting cards, mainly Christmas. Submit seasonal material at any time. Final art size should be proportional to and at least 5×7. "We purchase exclusive rights for the use of photographs on greeting cards and do not prevent photographers from using images on other non-greeting card items. Photographers retain all copyrights and can end the agreement for any reason." Pays $50 advance and 5% royalties at the end of the season. Finds freelancers through submissions. Accepts prints, transparencies, and digital formats.

MAKING CONTACT & TERMS E-mail query letter with résumé, link and samples or send a query letter with résumé slides, prints, tearsheets and/or transparencies. Samples not kept on file, include SASE for return of material.

TIPS "Pay attention to details, look at other work that publishers use, follow up on submissions, have good presentations. We need unusual and imaginative photographs for general greeting cards and especially the Christmas holiday season. Architecture plus snow, holiday decorations/colors/symbols, etc. Present your ideas for cards if your portfolio does not include such work."

⑤⑤ ◐ THE ZOLAN COMPANY, LLC

9947 E. Desert Jewel Dr., Scottsdale AZ 85255. (480)306-5680. E-mail: donaldz798@aol.com. Website: www.zolan.com. **Contact:** Jennifer Zolan, president/art director. Commercial and fine art business. Photos used for artist reference in oil paintings.

NEEDS Buys 8-10 images/year; works on assignment; looking for photographs of Farmall tractors, especially model M, C, H, 1066, Farmall Cub, Farmall 1206, f20. John Deere tractors are also needed. Looking for photos of puppies and dogs for paintings. Reviews stock photos.

SPECS Uses any size color and b&w prints. Prefers images in digital format. Send via e-mail, PDF, GIF, JPEG files at 72 dpi for preview.

MAKING CONTACT & TERMS Request photo guidelines by e-mail. Does not keep samples on file; include SASE for return of material. Responds in 2 months to queries. Pays $100-300 per photo. **Pays on acceptance**.

TIPS "Call or e-mail before submitting work. We are happy to work with amateur and professional photographers. Will work on assignment shoots with photographers who have access to Farmall tractors. Will also purchase what is in stock if it fits the needs."

STOCK PHOTO AGENCIES

If you are unfamiliar with how stock agencies work, the concept is easy to understand. Stock agencies house large files of images from contracted photographers and market the photos to potential clients. In exchange for licensing the images, agencies typically extract a 50-percent commission from each use. The photographer receives the other 50 percent.

In recent years, the stock industry has witnessed enormous growth, with agencies popping up worldwide. Many of these agencies, large and small, are listed in this section. However, as more and more agencies compete for sales, there has been a trend toward partnerships among some small to mid-size agencies. Other agencies have been acquired by larger agencies and essentially turned into subsidiaries. Often these subsidiaries are strategically located to cover different portions of the world. Typically, smaller agencies are bought if they have images that fill a need for the parent company. For example, a small agency might specialize in animal photographs and be purchased by a larger agency that needs those images but doesn't want to search for individual wildlife photographers.

The stock industry is extremely competitive, and if you intend to sell stock through an agency, you must know how they work. Below is a checklist that can help you land a contract with an agency.

- Build a solid base of quality images before contacting any agency. If you send an agency 50–100 images, they are going to want more if they're interested. You must have enough quality images in your files to withstand the initial review and get a contract.
- Be prepared to supply new images on a regular basis. Most contracts stipulate that photographers must send additional submissions periodically—perhaps quarterly, monthly, or annually. Unless you are committed to shooting regularly, or unless you have amassed a gigantic collection of images, don't pursue a stock agency.

- Make sure all of your work is properly cataloged and identified with a file number. Start this process early so that you're prepared when agencies ask for this information. They'll need to know what is contained in each photograph so that the images can be properly keyworded on websites.
- Research those agencies that might be interested in your work. Smaller agencies tend to be more receptive to newcomers because they need to build their image files. When larger agencies seek new photographers, they usually want to see specific subjects in which photographers specialize. If you specialize in a certain subject area, be sure to check out our Subject Index in the back of the book, which lists companies according to the types of images they need.
- Conduct reference checks on any agencies you plan to approach to make sure they conduct business in a professional manner. Talk to current clients and other contracted photographers to see if they are happy with the agency. Also, some stock agencies are run by photographers who market their own work through their own agencies. If you are interested in working with such an agency, be certain that your work will be given fair marketing treatment.
- Once you've selected a stock agency, contact them via e-mail or whatever means they have stipulated in their listing or on their website. Today, almost all stock agencies have websites and want images submitted in digital format. If the agency accepts slides, write a brief cover letter explaining that you are searching for an agency and that you would like to send some images for review. Wait to hear back from the agency before you send samples. Then send only duplicates for review so that important work won't get lost or damaged. Always include a SASE when sending samples by regular mail. It is best to send images in digital format; some agencies will only accept digital submissions.
- Finally, don't expect sales to roll in the minute a contract is signed. It usually takes a few years before initial sales are made.

SIGNING AN AGREEMENT

There are several points to consider when reviewing stock agency contracts. First, it's common practice among many agencies to charge photographers fees, such as catalog insertion rates or image duping fees. Don't be alarmed and think the agency is trying to cheat you when you see these clauses. Besides, it might be possible to reduce or eliminate these fees through negotiation.

Another important item in most contracts deals with exclusive rights to market your images. Some agencies require exclusivity to sales of images they are marketing for you. In other words, you can't market the same images they have on file. This prevents photographers from undercutting agencies on sales. Such clauses are fair to both sides as long as you can continue marketing images that are not in the agency's files.

An agency also may restrict your rights to sign with another stock agency. Usually such clauses are designed merely to keep you from signing with a competitor. Be certain your contract allows you to work with other agencies. This may mean limiting the area of distribution for each agency. For example, one agency may get to sell your work in the United States, while the other gets Europe. Or it could mean that one agency sells only to commercial clients, while the other handles editorial work. Before you sign any agency contract, make sure you can live with the conditions, including 40/60 fee splits favoring the agency.

Finally, be certain you understand the term limitations of your contract. Some agreements renew automatically with each submission of images. Others renew automatically after a period of time unless you terminate your contract in writing. This might be a problem if you and your agency are at odds for any reason. Make sure you understand the contractual language before signing anything.

REACHING CLIENTS

One thing to keep in mind when looking for a stock agent is how they plan to market your work. A combination of marketing methods seems the best way to attract buyers, and most large stock agencies are moving in that direction by offering catalogs, CDs, and websites.

But don't discount small, specialized agencies. Even if they don't have the marketing muscle of big companies, they do know their clients well and often offer personalized service and deep image files that can't be matched by more general agencies. If you specialize in regional or scientific imagery, you may want to consider a specialized agency.

MICROSTOCK

A relatively new force in the stock photography business is microstock. The term microstock comes from the "micro payments" that these agencies charge their clients—often as little as one dollar (the photographer gets only half of that), depending on the size of the image. Compare that to a traditional stock photo agency, where a rights-managed image could be licensed for hundreds of dollars, depending on the image and its use. Unlike the traditional stock agencies, microstock agencies are more willing to look at work from amateur photographers, and they consider their content "member generated." However, they do not accept all photos or all photographers; images must still be vetted by the microstock site before the photographer can upload his collection and begin selling. Microstock sites are looking for the lifestyle, people, and business images that their traditional counterparts often seek. Unlike most traditional stock agencies, microstock sites offer no rights-managed images; all images are royalty free.

So if photographers stand to make only fifty cents from licensing an image, how are they supposed to make money from this arrangement? The idea is to sell a huge quantity of photos at these low prices. Microstock agencies have tapped into a budget-minded client that the traditional agencies have not normally attracted—the small business, nonprofit organization, and even the individual who could not afford to spend $300 for a photo for their newsletter or brochure. There is currently a debate in the photography community about the viability of microstock as a business model for stock photographers. Some say it is driving down the value of *all* photography and making it harder for all photographers to make a living selling their stock photos. While others might agree that it is driving down the value of photography, they say that microstock is here to stay and photographers should find a way to make it work for them or find other revenue streams to counteract any loss of income due to the effects of microstock. Still others feel no pinch from microstock: They feel their clients would never purchase from a microstock site and that they are secure in knowing they can offer their clients something unique.

If you want to see how a microstock site works, see the following websites, which are some of the more prominent microstock sites. You'll find directions on how to open an account and start uploading photos.

- www.shutterstock.com
- www.istockphoto.com
- www.bigstockphoto.com
- www.fotolia.com
- www.dreamstime.com

DIGITAL IMAGING GUIDELINES AND SYSTEMS

The photography industry is in a state of flux as it grapples with the ongoing changes that digital imaging has brought. In an effort to identify and promote digital imaging standards, the Universal Photographic Digital Imaging Guidelines (UPDIG, www.updig.org) were established. The objectives of UPDIG are to:

- Make digital imaging practices more clear and reliable
- Develop an Internet resource for imaging professionals (including photo buyers, photographers, and nonprofit organizations related to the photography industry)
- Demonstrate the creative and economic benefits of the guidelines to clients
- Develop industry guidelines and workflows for various types of image reproduction, including RAW file delivery, batch-converted files, color-managed master files, and CMYK with proofs.

PLUS (Picture Licensing Universal System) is a cooperative, multi-industry initiative designed to define and categorize image usage around the world. It does not address pricing or negotiations, but deals solely with defining licensing language and managing license data so that photographers and those who license photography can work with the same systems and use the same language when licensing images. To learn more about PLUS, visit www.useplus.com.

MARKETING YOUR OWN STOCK

If you find the terms of traditional agencies unacceptable, there are alternatives available. Many photographers are turning to the Internet as a way to sell their stock images without an agent and are doing very well. Your other option is to join with other photographers sharing space on the Internet. Check out PhotoSource International at www.photosource .com and www.agpix.com.

If you want to market your own stock, it is not absolutely necessary that you have your own website, but it will help tremendously. Photo buyers often "google" the keyword they're searching for—that is, they use an Internet search engine, keying in the keyword plus "photo." Many photo buyers, from advertising firms to magazines, at one time or another, either have found the big stock agencies too unwieldy to deal with, or they simply did not have exactly what the photo buyer was looking for. Googling can lead a photo buyer straight to your site; be sure you have adequate contact information on your website so the photo buyer can contact you and possibly negotiate the use of your photos.

One of the best ways to get into stock is to sell outtakes from assignments. The use of stock images in advertising, design, and editorial work has risen in the last five years. As the quality of stock images continues to improve, even more creatives will embrace stock as an inexpensive and effective means of incorporating art into their designs. Retaining the rights to your assignment work will provide income even when you are no longer able to work as a photographer.

LEARN MORE ABOUT THE STOCK INDUSTRY

There are numerous resources available for photographers who want to learn about the stock industry. Here are a few of the best.

- **PhotoSource International**, (715)248-3800, website: www.photosource.com, e-mail: info@photosource.com. Owned by author/photographer Rohn Engh, this company produces several newsletters that can be extremely useful for stock photographers. A few of these include *PhotoStockNotes*, *PhotoDaily*, *PhotoLetter*, and *PhotoBulletin*. Engh's *Sell & Re-Sell Your Photos* (Writer's Digest Books) tells how to sell stock to book and magazine publishers.
- **Selling Stock**, (301)251-0720, website: www.pickphoto.com, e-mail: Jim@scphoto. com. This newsletter is published by one of the photo industry's leading insiders, Jim Pickerell. He gives plenty of behind-the-scenes information about agencies and is a huge advocate for stock photographers.
- **Negotiating Stock Photo Prices** 5th edition, by Jim Pickerell and Cheryl Pickerell DiFrank, 110 Frederick Ave., Suite A, Rockville MD 20850, (301)251-0720. This is the most comprehensive and authoritative book on selling stock photography.

- **The Picture Archive Council of America**, (800)457-7222, website: www.pacaoffice. org. Anyone researching an American agency should check to see if the agency is a member of this organization. PACA members are required to practice certain standards of professionalism in order to maintain membership.
- **British Association of Picture Libraries and Agencies**, (44)(020)7713-1780, website: www.bapla.org.uk. This is PACA's counterpart in the United Kingdom and is a quick way to examine the track record of many foreign agencies.
- Photo District News, website: www.pdn-pix.com. This monthly trade magazine for the photography industry frequently features articles on the latest trends in stock photography, and publishes an annual stock photography issue.
- Stock Artists Alliance, website: www.stockartistsalliance.org. This trade organization focuses on protecting the rights of independent stock photographers.

✛ THE 3D STUDIO

P.O. Box 30623, Mesa AZ 85205. (602)388-8536. E-mail: Tracy@The3dStudio.com. Website: www.the3dstudio.com. **Contact:** Tracy Eau Claire, director of business development. Estab. 1996. Stock agency. Has 300,000 photos in files. Clients include: advertising agencies, businesses, newspapers, postcard publishers, public relations firms, book publishers, calendar companies, audiovisual firms, magazine publishers, greeting card companies and web usage.

NEEDS Special subject needs include 3D models, renders and vector images.

SPECS Accepts digital images in digital format. Send via CD or ZIP as TIFF, EPS or JPEG. "We accept uploads via our website and CDs for large submitters."

PAYMENT & TERMS Buys photos, film and video outright on a case-by-case basis. E-mail for more information. Member royalties start at 60% paid to photographers and can increase depending on affiliate program, Member Loyalty Program, etc. Enforces strict minimum prices. No volume discounts offered to customers. Discount sales terms not negotiable. Photographer contract negotiable. Agency contracts do not renew automatically with additional submissions. Photographers have access to their accounts 24/7 and sales are reported in real time. Model and property release are preferred.

HOW TO CONTACT Photographers are welcome to create a member account and begin uploading at any time. Samples not kept on file; cannot return material. Photo guidelines, catalog copy, and market tips sheet available on website.

TIPS "Submit your best work and have a basic understanding of the commercial use of stock photography."

⊛ 911 PICTURES

63 Gardiners Ln., East Hampton NY 11937. (631)324-2061. Fax: (631)329-9264. E-mail: 911pix@optonline.net. Website: www.911pictures.com. **Contact:** Michael Heller, president. Estab. 1996. Stock agency. Has 3,500 photos in files. Clients include: advertising agencies, public relations firms, audiovisual firms, businesses, book publishers, magazine publishers, calendar companies, insurance companies, public safety training facilities.

NEEDS Photos of disaster services, public safety/emergency services, fire, police, EMS, rescue, hazmat. Interested in documentary.

SPECS Accepts images in digital format on CD at minimum 300 dpi, 8 inches minimum short dimension. Images for review may be sent via e-mail, CD as BMP, GIF, JPEG files at 72 dpi.

PAYMENT & TERMS Pays 50% commission for b&w and color photos; 75% for film and videotape. Enforces minimum prices. Offers volume discounts to customers. Works with photographers on contract basis only. Offers nonexclusive contract. Charges any print fee (from negative or slide) or dupe fee (from slide). Statements issued/sale. Payment made/sale. Photographers allowed to review account records in cases of discrepancies only. Offers one-time rights. Informs photographers and allows them to negotiate when client requests all rights. Model release preferred. Photo captions preferred; include photographer's name and a short caption as to what is occurring in photo.

HOW TO CONTACT Send query letter with résumé, slides, prints, photocopies, tearsheets. "Photographers can also send e-mail with thumbnail (low-res) attachments." Does not keep samples on file; include SASE for return of material. Responds only if interested; send nonreturnable samples. Photo guidelines sheet free with SASE.

TIPS "Keep in mind that there are hundreds of photographers shooting hundreds of fires, car accidents, rescues, etc., every day. Take the time to edit your own material, so that you are only sending in your best work. We are especially in need of hazmat, police and natural disaster images. At this time, 911 Pictures is only soliciting work from those photographers who shoot professionally or who shoot public safety on a regular basis. We are not interested in occasional submissions of 1 or 2 images."

ACCENT ALASKA/KEN GRAHAM AGENCY

P.O. Box 272, Girdwood AK 99587. (907)783-2796. Fax: (907)783-3247. E-mail: info@accentalaska.com. Website: www.accentalaska.com. **Contact:** Ken Graham, owner. Estab. 1979. Stock agency. Has 18,000 photos online. Clients include: advertising agencies, public relations firms, audiovisual firms, businesses, book publishers, magazine publishers, newspapers, calendar companies, greeting card companies, postcard publishers, CD encyclopedias.

NEEDS Modern stock images of Alaska, Antarctica. "Please do not submit material we already have in our files."

SPECS Uses images from digital cameras 10 mega-pixels or greater; no longer accepting film but will review and select then you return us scanned images with metadata embedded. Send via CD, ZIP, e-mail lightbox URL.

PAYMENT & TERMS Pays 50% commission. Negotiates fees at industry-standard prices. Works with photographers on contract basis only. Offers nonexclusive contract. Payment made quarterly. "We are a rights managed agency."

HOW TO CONTACT "See our website contact page. Any material must include SASE for returns." Expects minimum initial submission of 60 images. Prefers online web gallery for initial review.

TIPS "Realize we specialize in Alaska although we do accept images from Antarctica. The bulk of our sales are Alaska-related. We are always interested in seeing submissions of sharp, colorful and professional-quality images with model-released people when applicable. Do not want to see same material repeated in our library."

ACE STOCK LIMITED

10 Clove Lea, Godalming Surrey GU7 3QQ, United Kingdom. (44)(208)944 9944. Fax: (44)(208)944-9940. E-mail: library@acestock.com; web@acestock.com. Website: www.acestock.com. **Contact:** John Panton, director. Estab. 1980. Stock photo agency. Has approximately 500,000 photos on file; over 65,000 online. Clients include: ad agencies, audiovisual firms, businesses, book/encyclopedia publishers, magazine publishers, postcard companies, calendar companies, greeting card companies, design companies, direct mail companies.

NEEDS Photos of babies/children/teens, couples, multicultural, families, parents, senior citizens, environmental, landscapes/scenics, wildlife, pets, adventure, automobiles, food/drink, health/fitness, hobbies, humor, sports, travel, business concepts, industry, medicine, product shots/still life, science, technology/computers. Interested in alternative process, avant garde, documentary, fashion/glamour, seasonal.

SPECS High-quality digital submissions only. Scanning resolutions for low-res at 72 dpi and high-res at 300 dpi with 30MB minimum size. Send via CD, or e-mail low-res samples.

PAYMENT & TERMS Pays 50% commission on net receipts. Average price per image (to clients): $400. Works with photographers on contract basis only.

Offers limited regional exclusivity. Contracts renew automatically for 2 years with each submission. No charges for scanning. Charges $200/image for catalog insertion. Statements issued quarterly. Payment made quarterly. Photographers permitted to review sales records with 1-month written notice. Offers one-time rights, first rights or mostly nonexclusive rights. Informs photographers when client requests to buy all rights, but agency negotiates for photographer. Model/property release required for people and buildings. Photo captions required; include place, date and function. "Prefer data as IPTC-embedded within Photoshop File Info 'caption' for each scanned image."

HOW TO CONTACT Send e-mail with low-res attachments or website link or FTP. Alternatively, arrange a personal interview to show portfolio or post 50 sample transparencies. Responds within 1 month. Photo guidelines sheet free with SASE. Online tips sheet for contracted photographers.

TIPS Prefers to see "definitive cross-section of your collection that typifies your style and prowess. Must show originality, command of color, composition and general rules of stock photography. All people must be mid-Atlantic to sell in UK. No dupes. Scanning and image manipulation is all done in-house. We market primarily via online search engines and e-mail promos. In addition, we distribute printed catalogs and CDs."

A+E

9 Hochgernstr, Stein D-83371, Germany. (49)8621-61833. Fax: (49)8621-63875. E-mail: apluse@aol.com. Website: www.apluse.de. **Contact:** Elisabeth Pauli, director. Estab. 1987. Picture library. Has over 30,000 photos in files. Clients include newspapers, postcard publishers, book publishers, calendar companies, magazine publishers.

NEEDS Photos of nature/landscapes/scenics, pets, "only your best material."

SPECS Uses 35mm, 6×6 transparencies, digital. Accepts images in digital format. Send via CD as JPEG files at 100 dpi for referencing purposes only.

PAYMENT & TERMS Pays 50% commission. Average price per image (to clients): $15-100 for b&w photos; $75-1,000 for color photos. Offers volume discounts to customers. Works with photographers on contract basis only. Offers nonexclusive contract. Subject exclusivity may be negotiated. Statements issued annually. Payment made annually. Photographers allowed to review account records in cases of discrepancies only. Offers one-time rights. Model/property release required. Photo captions must include country, date, name of object (person, town, landmark, etc.)

HOW TO CONTACT Send query letter with your qualification, description of your equipment, transparencies or CD, stock list. Include SASE for return of material in Europe. Cannot return material outside Europe. Expects minimum initial submission of 100 images with annual submissions of at least 100 images. Responds in 1 month.

TIPS "Judge your work critically. Only technically perfect photos will attract a photo editor's attention—sharp focus, high colors, creative views."

✵ AERIAL ARCHIVES

Petaluma Airport, 561 Sky Ranch Dr., Petaluma CA 94954. (415)771-2555. Fax: (707)769-7277. E-mail: www.aerialarchives.com/contact.htm; herb@aerial archives.com. Website: www.aerialarchives.com. **Contact:** Herb Lingl. Estab. 1989. Has 100,000 photos in files. Has 2,000 hours of film, video footage. Clients include: advertising agencies, public relations firms, audiovisual firms, businesses, book publishers, magazine publishers, newspapers, calendar companies.

NEEDS Aerial photography only.

SPECS Accepts images in digital format only, unless they are historical. Uses 2¼×2¼, 4×5, 9×9 transparencies; 70mm, 5 in. and 9×9 (aerial film). Other media also accepted.

PAYMENT & TERMS Buys photos, film, videotape outright only in special situations where requested by submitting party. Pays on commission basis. Average price per image (to clients): $325. Enforces minimum prices. Offers volume discounts to customers. Photographers can choose not to sell images on discount terms. Works with photographers on contract basis only. Statements issued quarterly. Payment made monthly. Photographers allowed to review account records in cases of discrepancies only. Offers one-time rights, electronic media rights, agency promotion rights. Informs photographers and allows them to negotiate when client requests all rights. Property release preferred. Photo captions required; include date, location, and altitude if available.

HOW TO CONTACT Send query letter with stock list. Provide résumé, business card, self-promotion piece to be kept on file. Expects minimum initial submission of 100 images with quarterly submissions of at least 50 images. Responds only if interested; send nonreturnable samples. Photo guidelines sheet available via e-mail.

TIPS "Supply complete captions with date and location; aerial photography only."

☉ AFLO FOTO AGENCY

7F Builnet 1, 6-16-9, Ginza, Chuo-ku Tokyo 104-0061, Japan. +81 3-5550-2120. E-mail: support@aflo.com. Website: www.aflo.com (Japanese); www.afloimages. com (English). Estab. 1980. Stock agency, picture library and news/feature syndicate. Japan's largest photo agency, employing over 120 staff based in Tokyo and Osaka. Clients include: advertising agencies, designers, public relations firms, new media, book publishers, magazine publishers, educational users and television. Member of the Picture Archive Council of America (PACA). Has 1 million photos in files. "We have other offices in Tokyo and Osaka."

NEEDS Photos of babies/children/teens, celebrities, couples, multicultural, families, parents, senior citizens, disasters, environmental, landscapes/scenics, wildlife, architecture, cities/urban, education, gardening, interiors/decorating, pets, religious, rural, adventure, automobiles, entertainment, events, food/drink, health/fitness, hobbies, humor, performing arts, sports, travel, agriculture, business concepts, industry, medicine, military, political, product shots/still life, science, technology/computers. Interested in alternative process, avant garde, documentary, erotic, fashion/glamour, fine art, historical/vintage, lifestyle, seasonal.

SPECS Uses 35mm, 2¼×2¼, 4×5, 8×10 transparencies. Accepts images in digital format. Send via CD, e-mail as TIFF, JPEG files. When making initial submission via e-mail, files should total less than 3MB.

PAYMENT & TERMS Pays commission. Average price per image (to clients): $195 minimum for b&w photos; $250 minimum for color photos, film, videotape. Offers volume discounts to customers; terms specified in photographers' contracts. Photographers can choose not to sell images on discount terms. Works with photographers with or without a contract; negotiable. Contract type varies. Statements issued quarterly. Payment made quarterly. Photographers allowed to review account records. Model/property release preferred. Photo captions required.

HOW TO CONTACT Send all inquiries regarding images or submissions to support@aflo.com. Any submission inquiries should be accompanied by gallery links or image sets.

AGE FOTOSTOCK

Bretón de los Herreros, 59 bajos B E-28003 Madrid , Spain. (34)91 451 86 00. Fax: (34)91 451 86 01. E-mail: agemadrid@agefotostock.com. Website: www.age fotostock.com. Estab. 1973. Stock agency. Photographers may submit their images to Barcelona directly. Clients include: advertising agencies, businesses, newspapers, postcard publishers, public relations firms, book publishers, calendar companies, audiovisual firms, magazine publishers, greeting card companies. See website for other locations.

NEEDS "We are a general stock agency and are constantly uploading images onto our website. Therefore, we constantly require creative new photos from all categories."

SPECS Accepts all formats. Details available upon request, or see website ("Photographers/submitting images").

PAYMENT & TERMS Pays 50% commission for all formats. Terms specified in photographer's contract. Works with photographers on contract basis only. Offers image exclusivity worldwide. Statements issued monthly. Payment made monthly. Photographers allowed to review account records. Model/property release required. Photo captions required.

HOW TO CONTACT "Send query letter with résumé and 100 images for selection. Download the photographer's info pack from our website."

AGSTOCKUSA INC.

25315 Arriba del Mundo Dr., Carmel CA 93923. (831)624-8600. Fax: (831)626-3260. E-mail: edyoung@agstockusa.com. Website: www.agstockusa.com. Estab. 1996. Stock photo agency. Has 100,000 photos. Clients include: advertising agencies, graphic design firms, businesses, public relations firms, book/encyclopedia publishers, calendar companies, magazine publishers, greeting card companies.

NEEDS Photos should cover all aspects of agriculture worldwide: fruits, vegetables and grains in various growth stages; studio work, aerials; harvesting, processing, irrigation, insects, weeds, farm life, agricultural equipment, livestock, plant damage and plant disease.

SPECS Uses 35mm, 2¼×2¼, 4×5, 6×7, 6×17 transparencies. Accepts images in digital format. Send as high-res TIFF files.

PAYMENT & TERMS Pays 50% commission for color photos. Average price per image (to clients): $100-25,000 for color photos. Works with photographers on contract basis only. Offers nonexclusive contract. Contracts renew automatically with additional submissions for 2 years. Charges 50% website insertion fee. Statements issued monthly. Payment made monthly. Photographers allowed to review account records. Offers unlimited use and buyouts if photographer agrees to sale. Informs photographer when client requests all rights; final decision made by agency. Model/property release preferred. Photo captions required; include location of photo and all technical information (what, why, how, etc.).

HOW TO CONTACT "Review our website to determine if work meets our standards and requirements." Submit low-res JPEGs on CD for review. Call first. Keeps samples on file; include SASE for return of material. Expects minimum initial submission of 250 images. Responds in 3 weeks. Photo guidelines available on website. Agency newsletter distributed yearly to contributors under contract.

TIPS "Build up a good file (quantity and quality) of photos before approaching any agency. A portfolio of 16,000 images is currently displayed on our website. CD catalog with 7,600 images available to qualified photo buyers."

AKM IMAGES, INC.

109 Bushnell Pl., Mooresville NC 28115. E-mail: um83@yahoo.com. Website: www.akmimages. com. **Contact:** Annie-Ying Molander, president. Estab. 2002. Stock agency. Has over 100,000 photos in files (and still increasing). Clients include: advertising agencies, book publishers, magazine publishers, newspapers, calendar and greeting card companies, and postcard publishers.

NEEDS Photos of agriculture, city/urban, food/wine, gardening, multicultural, religious, rural, landscape/scenic, bird, wildlife, wildflower, butterfly, insect, cat, dog, farm animals, fishing, outdoor activity, travel and underwater images. "We also need landscape and culture from Asian countries, Nordic countries (Sweden, Norway, Finland), Alaska, Greenland and Iceland." Also need culture about Sami and Lapplander from Nordic countries and Native American.

SPECS Uses 35mm transparencies, Accepts images in digital format. Send via CD/DVD at JPEG or TIFF files at low and high-res files (300 dpi) for Windows.

PAYMENT & TERMS Pays 48% commission for color photos. Terms specified in photographers' submission guidelines. Works with photographers with a contract. Offers nonexclusive contract. Contracts renew automatically with additional submissions. Offers one-time rights. Model/property release required. Photo captions required.

HOW TO CONTACT Send query letter by e-mail with image samples and stock list. Does not keep samples on file. Include SASE for return of material. Expects minimum initial submission of 100 images. Responds in 1 month to samples. Photo submission guidelines available free with SASE or via e-mail.

ALASKA STOCK IMAGES

2505 Fairbanks St., Anchorage AK 99503. (907)276-1343. Fax: (907)258-7848. E-mail: info@alaskastock.com. Website: www.alaskastock.com. **Contact:** Jeff Schultz, owner. Stock photo agency. Member of the Picture Archive Council of America (PACA) and ASMP. Has 200,000 photos in files. Clients include: international and national advertising agencies; businesses; magazines and newspapers; book/encyclopedia publishers; calendar, postcard and greeting card publishers.

NEEDS Photos of everything related to Alaska, including babies/children/teens, couples, multicultural, families, parents, senior citizens involved in winter activities and outdoor recreation, wildlife, environmental, landscapes/scenics, cities/urban, pets, adventure, travel, industry. Interested in alternative process, avant garde, documentary (images which were or could have been shot in Alaska), historical/vintage, seasonal, Christmas.

SPECS Accepts images in digital format only. Send via CD as JPEG files at 72 dpi for review purposes. "Put together a gallery of low-res images on your website and send us the URL, or send via PC-formatted CD as JPEG files no larger than 9×12 at 72 dpi for review purposes." Accepted images must be 50MB minimum shot as raw originals.

PAYMENT & TERMS Pays 40% commission for color and b&w photos; minimum use fee $125. No charges for catalog, dupes, etc. Offers volume discounts to customers; inquire about specific terms. Photographers can choose not to sell images on discount terms.

Works with photographers on contract basis only. Offers nonexclusive contract; exclusive contract for images in promotions. Contracts renew automatically with additional submissions; nonexclusive for 3 years. Statements issued monthly. Payment made monthly. Photographers allowed to review account records. Offers negotiable rights. Informs photographer and negotiates rights for photographer when client requests all rights. Model/property release preferred for any people and recognizable personal objects (boats, homes, etc.). Photo captions required; include who, what, when, where.

HOW TO CONTACT Send query letter with samples. Keeps samples on file; include SASE for return of material. Expects minimum initial submission of 200 images with periodic submissions of 100-200 images 1-4 times/year. Responds in 3 weeks. Photo guidelines free on request. Market tips sheet distributed 2 times/year to those with contracts. "View our guidelines online at www.alaskastock.com/prospectivephotographers.asp."

TIPS "E-mailed sample images should be sent in one file, not separate images. For photographers shooting digital images, Alaska Stock assumes that you are shooting RAW format and are able to properly process the RAW image to meet our 50MB minimum standards with acceptable color, contrast and density range."

🌀 🌐 AMANAIMAGES INC.

2-2-43 Higashi-Shinagawa, Shinagawa-ku, Tokyo 140-0002, Japan. +81-3-3740-1018. Fax: +81-3-3740-4036. E-mail: planet_info@amanaimages.com; a.ito@amanaimages.com. Website: amanaimages.com. **Contact:** Mr. Akihiko Ito, partner relations. Estab. 1979. Stock photo agency. Member of the Picture Archive Council of America (PACA). Has 2,500,000 digital files and continuously growing. Clients include: advertising agencies, public relations firms, businesses, book/encyclopedia publishers, magazine publishers, newspapers, postcard publishers, calendar companies, greeting card companies, and TV stations.

NEEDS Photos of babies/children/teens, celebrities, couples, multicultural, families, parents, senior citizens, disasters, environmental, landscapes/scenics, wildlife, architecture, cities/urban, education, gardening, interiors/decorating, pets, religious, rural, adventure, automobiles, entertainment, events, food/drink, health/fitness, hobbies, humor, performing arts, sports, travel, agriculture, business concepts, medicine, military, political, industry, product shots/still life, science, technology/computers. Interested in documentary, erotic, fashion/glamour, fine art, historical/vintage, seasonal.

SPECS Digital format by single-lens reflex camera, data size should be larger than 30MB with 8-bit, AdobeRGB, JPEG format. Digital high-res image size: larger than 48MB for CG, 3D, etc. using editing software, e.g. Photoshop or Shade, digital change made by scanning, composed images, collage images.

PAYMENT & TERMS Based on agreement.

HOW TO CONTACT Send 30-50 sample images (shorter side has to be 600 pixel as JPEG file) and your profile by e-mail. "After inspection of your images we may offer you an agreement. Submissions are accepted only after signing the agreement."

AMERICAN MUSEUM OF NATURAL HISTORY LIBRARY, PHOTOGRAPHIC COLLECTION

Library Services, Central Park West, 79th St., New York NY 10024. (212)769-5419. Fax: (212)769-5009. E-mail: speccol@amnh.org. Website: www.amnh.org; library.amnh.org/index.php. **Contact:** Barbara Mathe, museum archivist. Estab. 1869. Provides services for authors, film and TV producers, general public, government agencies, picture researchers, scholars, students, teachers and publishers.

NEEDS "We accept only donations with full rights (nonexclusive) to use; we offer visibility through credits." Model release required. Photo captions required.

PAYMENT & TERMS Credit line given. Buys all rights.

THE ANCIENT ART & ARCHITECTURE COLLECTION, LTD.

15 Heathfield Court, Heathfield Terrace, Chiswick, London W4 4LP, England. +44 (0)20 8995 0895. Fax: +44 (0)20 8429 4646. E-mail: library@aaacollection.co.uk. Website: www.aaacollection.com. Picture library. Has 150,000 photos in files. Represents C.M. Dixon Collection. Clients include: advertising agencies, book/encyclopedia publishers, magazine publishers, newspapers.

NEEDS Photos of ancient/archaeological site, sculptures, objects, artifacts of historical nature. Interested in fine art, historical/vintage.

SPECS Digital images only. JPEG format; minimum 34MB file size.

PAYMENT & TERMS Pays commission on quarterly basis. Works with photographers on contract basis only. Non-exclusive contract. Contracts renew automatically with additional submissions. Statements issued quarterly. Payment made quarterly. Photographers allowed to review account records. Offers one-time rights. Detailed photo captions required.

HOW TO CONTACT Send query letter with samples, stock list, SASE.

TIPS "Material must be suitable for our specialist requirements. We cover historical and archeological periods from 25,000 B.C. to the 19th century A.D., worldwide. All civilizations, cultures, religions, objects and artifacts as well as art may be included. Pictures with tourists, cars, TV aerials, and other modern intrusions not accepted. Send us a submission of CD by mail with a list of other material that may be suitable for us."

ANDES PRESS AGENCY

26 Padbury Ct., Shoreditch, London E2 7EH, United Kingdom. +44 (0)20 7613 5417. Fax: +44 (0)20 7739 3159. E-mail: apa@andespressagency.com. Website: andespressagency.com. Picture library and news/feature syndicate. Has 300,000 photos in files. Clients include: magazine publishers, businesses, book publishers, non-governmental charities, newspapers.

NEEDS Photos of multicultural, senior citizens, disasters, environmental, landscapes/scenics, architecture, cities/urban, education, religious, rural, travel, agriculture, business, industry, political. "We have color and b&w photographs on social, political and economic aspects of Latin America, Africa, Asia and Britain, specializing in contemporary world religions."

SPECS Uses 35mm and digital files.

PAYMENT & TERMS Works with photographers on contract basis only. Offers nonexclusive contract. Contracts renew with additional submissions. Statements issued bi-monthly. Payment made bi-monthly. Offers one-time rights. "We never sell all rights; photographer has to negotiate if interested." Model/property release preferred. Photo captions required.

HOW TO CONTACT Send query via e-mail. Do not send unsolicited images.

TIPS "We want to see that the photographer has mastered one subject in depth. Also, we have a market for photo features as well as stock photos. Please write to us first via e-mail."

ANIMALS ANIMALS/EARTH SCENES

17 Railroad Ave., Chatham NY 12037. (518)392-5500. Fax: (518)392-5550. E-mail: info@animalsanimals. com. Website: www.animalsanimals.com. **Contact:** Nancy Carrizales. Member of Picture Archive Council of America (PACA). Has 1.5 million photos in files. Clients include: ad agencies, public relations firms, businesses, audiovisual firms, book publishers, magazine publishers, encyclopedia publishers, newspapers, postcard companies, calendar companies, greeting card companies.

NEEDS *"We are currently not reviewing any new portfolios."*

SPECS Accepts images in digital and transparency formats.

PAYMENT & TERMS Pays 50% commission. Works with photographers on contract basis only. Offers exclusive contract. Photographers allowed to review account records to verify sales figures "if requested and with proper notice and cause." Statements issued quarterly. Payment made quarterly. Offers one-time rights; other uses negotiable. Informs photographers and allows them to negotiate when client requests all rights. Model release required if used for advertising. Photo captions required; include Latin names ("they must be correct!").

TIPS "First, pre-edit your material. Second, know your subject."

ANTHRO-PHOTO FILE

33 Hurlbut St., Cambridge MA 02138. (617)868-4784. Fax: (617)484-6428. E-mail: cdevore@anthrophoto. com. Website: www.anthrophoto.com. **Contact:** Nancy DeVore. Estab. 1969. Stock photo agency specializing in anthropology and behavioral biology. Has 10,000 photos in files (including tribal peoples, peasant societies, hunter-gatherers, human evolution, animal behavior, natural history). Clients include: book publishers, magazine publishers.

NEEDS Photos of anthropologists at work.

SPECS Uses b&w prints; 35mm transparencies. Accepts images in digital format.

PAYMENT & TERMS Pays 50% commission. Average price per image (to clients): $170 minimum for b&w photos; $200 minimum for color photos. Offers volume discounts to customers; discount terms negotiable. Works with photographers with contract.

Contracts renew automatically. Statements issued annually. Payment made annually. Photographers allowed to review account records. Offers one-time rights. Photo captions required.

HOW TO CONTACT Send query letter with stock list. Keeps samples on file; include SASE for return of material. See website for image delivery options.

TIPS Photographers should e-mail first.

ANT PHOTO LIBRARY

P.O. Box 576, Mornington Victoria, VIC 3931, Australia. 03 5978 8877. Fax: 03 5978 8411. E-mail: images@ antphoto.com.au. Website: www.antphoto.com.au. Estab. 1982. Has 170,000 photos in files, with 30,000 high-res files online. Clients include: advertising agencies, public relations firms, businesses, book publishers, magazine publishers, newspapers, calendar companies, greeting card companies, postcard publishers.

NEEDS Photos of "flora and fauna of Australia, Asia and Antarctica, and the environments in which they live."

SPECS "Use digital camera files supplied as a minimum of 16-bit TIFF files from a minimum of 8-megapixel SLR digital camera. Full specs on our website."

PAYMENT & TERMS Offers volume discounts to customers. Discount sales terms not negotiable. Discount sales terms negotiable. Works with photographers on contract basis only. Offers limited regional exclusivity. Statements issued quarterly. Payment made quarterly. Model release required. Photo captions required; include species, common name and scientific name on supplied Excel spreadsheet.

HOW TO CONTACT Send e-mail with 10 of your best images attached (images must be relevant to our needs). Expects minimum initial submission of 200 images with regular submissions of at least 100 images. Photo guidelines available on website. Market tips sheet "available to all photographers we represent."

TIPS "Our clients come to us for images of all common and not-so-common wildlife species from around the world particularly. Good clean shots. Good lighting and very sharp."

APPALIGHT

230 Griffith Run Rd., Spencer WV 25276. (304)927-2978. E-mail: wyro@appalight.com. Website: www. appalight.com. **Contact:** Chuck Wyrostok, director. Estab. 1988. Stock photo agency. Has over 30,000

photos in files. Clients include advertising agencies, public relations firms, businesses, book/encyclopedia publishers, magazine publishers, calendar companies, greeting card companies, graphic designers.

○ Currently not accepting submissions. This agency also markets images through the Photo Source Bank.

NEEDS General subject matter with emphasis on the people, natural history, culture, commerce, flora, fauna, and travel destinations of the Appalachian Mountain region.

SPECS Uses 8×10 glossy b&w prints; 35mm, 2¼×2¼, 4×5 transparencies and digital images.

PAYMENT & TERMS Pays 50% commission. Works with photographers on nonexclusive contract basis only. Contracts renew automatically for 2-year period with additional submissions. Payment made quarterly. Photographers allowed to review account records during regular business hours or by appointment. Offers one-time rights, electronic media rights. Model release preferred. Photo captions required.

HOW TO CONTACT AppaLight is not currently accepting submissions.

TIPS "We look for a solid blend of topnotch technical quality, style, content and impact. Images that portray metaphors applying to ideas, moods, business endeavors, risk-taking, teamwork and winning are especially desirable."

ARCHIVO CRIOLLO

Ignacio San María, e3-30 y nuñez de vela edificio, Metropoli 6to piso oficina 603 , Ecuador. (593 2) 60 38 748. Fax: (593 9) 52 50 615. E-mail: info@archivocriollo. com. Website: www.archivocriollo.com. **Contact:** Diana Santander, administrator. Estab. 1998. Picture library. Has 20,000 photos in files. Clients include: advertising agencies, businesses, newspapers, postcard publishers, calendar companies, magazine publishers, greeting card companies, travel agencies.

NEEDS Photos of multicultural, environmental, landscapes/scenics, wildlife, architecture, cities/urban, religious, rural, adventure, travel, art and culture, photo production, photo design, press photos. Interested in alternative process, documentary, fine art, historical/vintage.

SPECS Uses 35mm transparencies. Accepts images in digital format. Send via CD, ZIP, e-mail or FTP as JPEG files at 300 dpi, 11 inches.

PAYMENT & TERMS Average price per image (to clients): $50-150 for color photos; $450-750 for videotape. Enforces minimum prices. Offers volume discounts to customers; terms specified in photographers' contracts. Photographers can choose not to sell images on discount terms. Works with photographers with or without a contract; negotiable. Offers nonexclusive contract. Charges 50% sales fee. Payment made quarterly. Photographers allowed to review account records. Informs photographers and allows them to negotiate when client requests all rights. Photo captions preferred.

HOW TO CONTACT Send query letter with stock list. Responds only if interested. Catalog available.

ARGUS PHOTO, LTD. (APL)

Room 2001-4 Progress Commercial Bldg., 9 Irving St., Causeway Bay, Hong Kong. (852)2890-6970. Fax: (852)2881-6979. E-mail: argus@argusphoto. com. Website: www.argusphoto.com. **Contact:** Lydia Li, photo editor. Estab. 1992. Stock photo agency with branches in Beijing and Guangzhou. Has over 1 million searchable photos online. Clients include: advertising agencies, graphic houses, corporations, real estate developers, book and magazine publishers, postcard, greeting card, calendar and paper product manufacturers.

NEEDS "We are a quality image provider specializing in high-end lifestyle, luxurious interiors/home decor, club scene, food and travel, model in fashion or jewelry to promote an upscale lifestyle, well-being, gardenscape and asian/oriental images. High-quality features on home and garden, travel and leisure, fashion and accessories, and celebrities stories are welcome."

SPECS Accepts high-quality digital images only. Send 50MB JPEG files at 300 dpi via DVD or website link for review. English captions and keywords are required.

PAYMENT & TERMS Pays 50% commission. Average price per image (to U.S. clients): $100-6,000. Offers volume discounts to customers. Works with photographers on contract basis only. Statements/payment made quarterly. Informs photographers and allows them to negotiate when client requests all rights. Model/property release may be required. Expects minimum initial submission of 200 images.

ARKRELIGION.COM

Art Directors & Trip Photo Library, 57 Burdon Lane, Cheam Surrey SM2 7BY, England. E-mail: images@artdirectors.co.uk. Website: www.arkreligion.com. Estab. 2004. Stock agency. Has 100,000 photos on file. Clients include: advertising agencies, businesses, newspapers, postcard publishers, calendar companies, magazine publishers, greeting card companies.

NEEDS Photos of major, minor and alternative religions. This covers all aspects of religion from birth to death.

SPECS Prefers digital submissions. Initial submission: 1MB JPEG. High-res requirement: 50MB TIFF. See contributors' page on website for full details. "We require an extremely broad cross-section of images from all religions, from mainstream to alternate, to include ceremonies from birth to death, festivals and important events, peoples—priests, pilgrims, worshipers, artifacts, churches/temples—interior and exterior, holy books, worship—including inside the home, meals and food and daily rituals. If you are actively involved with your religion, we would be very interested in hearing from you and would particularly like to hear from any Muslim photographers who have undertaken or are intending to undertake the pilgrimage to Makkah."

PAYMENT & TERMS Average price per image (to clients): $65-1,000 for b&w or color photos. Enforces strict minimum prices. Offers volume discounts to customers. Discount sales terms not negotiable. Works with photographers on contract basis only. Offers nonexclusive contract. Statements issued quarterly. Payment made quarterly. Photographers allowed to review account records in cases of discrepancies only. Offers one-time rights, electronic media rights. Model/property release preferred. Photo captions required; include as much relevant information as possible.

HOW TO CONTACT Please use the contact page, if you have any questions, before making a submission. Contact by e-mail. Does not keep samples on file. Expects minimum initial submission of 50 images with periodic submissions of at least 50 images. Photo guidelines available on website.

TIPS "Fully caption material and follow the full requirements for digital submissions as detailed on the website. Will only accept slides/transparencies where these represent exceptional and/or difficult-to-obtain images."

ART DIRECTORS & TRIP PHOTO LIBRARY

57 Burdon Ln., Cheam, Surrey SM2 7BY, United Kingdom. (44)(20)8642 3593. Fax: (44)(20)8395 7230. E-mail: images@artdirectors.co.uk. Website: www.artdirectors.co.uk. Estab. 1992. Stock agency. Has 1 million photos in files. Clients include: advertising agencies, businesses, newspapers, postcard publishers, public relations firms, book publishers, calendar companies, magazine publishers, greeting card companies.

NEEDS Photos of babies/children/teens, couples, multicultural, families, parents, senior citizens, disasters, environmental, landscapes/scenics, wildlife, architecture, cities/urban, education, gardening, interiors/decorating, pets, religious, rural, adventure, automobiles, entertainment, events, food/drink, health/fitness, hobbies, humor, performing arts, sports, travel, agriculture, business concepts, industry, medicine, military, political, product shots/still life, science, technology/computers. Interested in alternative process, avant garde, documentary, historical/vintage, seasonal.

SPECS Prefers digital submissions. Initial submission: 1MB JPEG. High-res requirement: 50MB TIFF. See contributors' page on website for full details. Uses 35mm, 2¼×2¼, 4×5, 8×10 transparencies.

PAYMENT & TERMS Pays 50% commission for b&w or color photos when submitted digitally; pays 40% commission when film is submitted. Average price per image (to clients): $65-1,000 for b&w or color photos. Enforces strict minimum prices. Offers volume discounts to customers. Discount sales terms not negotiable. Works with photographers on contract basis only. Offers nonexclusive contract. Statements issued quarterly. Payment made quarterly. Photographers allowed to review account records in cases of discrepancies only. Offers one-time rights, electronic media rights. Model/property release preferred. Photo captions required; include as much relevant information as possible.

HOW TO CONTACT Contact by e-mail. Does not keep samples on file. Expects minimum initial submission of 50 images with periodic submissions of at least 50 images. Responds in 6 weeks to queries. Photo guidelines available on website.

TIPS "Fully caption material and follow the full requirements for digital submissions as detailed on the website. Will only accept slides/transparencies where these represent exceptional and/or difficult-to-obtain images."

ART LICENSING INTERNATIONAL INC.

1022 Hancock Ave., Sarasota FL 34232. (941)966-8912. E-mail: artlicensinginc@gmail.com. Website: www.out-of-the-blue.com. **Contact:** Michael Woodward, president; Jane Mason, licensing manager. Estab. 1986. "We represent artists, photographers and designers who wish to establish a licensing program for their work. We are particularly interested in photographic images that we can license internationally, particularly for fine art posters, canvas giclees for mass market retailers and interior design projects and home and office decor."

NEEDS "We prefer concepts that have a unique look or theme and that are distinctive from the generic designs produced in-house by publishers and manufacturers. Images for prints and posters must be in pairs or sets of 4 or more with a regard for trends and color palettes related to the home décor and interior design trends. Nature themes and landscapes are of particular interest. We need landscapes, trees, poppies, roosters, Tuscany scenes, cafe scenes, as well as florals."

PAYMENT & TERMS "Our general commission rate is 50% with no expenses to the photographer as long as the photographer provides high-resolution digital files at 300 dpi to print 30-36 inches."

HOW TO CONTACT E-mail JPEGs or details of your website. Send SASE if you want material returned.

TIPS "We require substantial portfolios of work that can generate good incomes, or concepts that have wide commercial appeal."

ART RESOURCE

536 Broadway, 5th Floor, New York NY 10012. (212)505-8700. Fax: (212)505-2053. E-mail: requests@artres.com; dreeve@artres.com. Website: www.artres.com. **Contact:** Ryan Jensen. Estab. 1970. Stock photo agency specializing in fine arts. Member of the Picture Archive Council of America (PACA). Has access to 3 million photos. Clients include: advertising agencies, public relations firms, audiovisual firms, businesses, book/encyclopedia publishers, magazine publishers, newspapers, postcard publishers, calendar companies, greeting card companies, all other publishing.

NEEDS Photos of painting, sculpture, architecture *only*.

SPECS Digital photos at 300 dpi.

PAYMENT & TERMS Pays 50% commission. Average price per image (to client): $185-10,000 for color photos. Negotiates fees below standard minimum prices. Offers volume discounts to customers; terms specified in photographer's contract. Discount sales terms not negotiable. Offers one-time rights, electronic media rights, agency promotion and other negotiated rights. Photo captions required.

HOW TO CONTACT Send query letter with stock list.

TIPS "We represent European fine art archives and museums in the U.S. and Europe but occasionally represent a photographer with a specialty in photographing fine art."

ARTWERKS STOCK PHOTOGRAPHY

5045 Brennan Bend, Idaho Falls ID 83406. (208)523-1545. E-mail: photojournalistjerry@msn.com. **Contact:** Jerry Sinkovec, owner. Estab. 1984. News/feature syndicate. Has 100,000 photos in files. Clients include: advertising agencies, public relations firms, businesses, book publishers, magazine publishers, calendar companies, postcard publishers.

NEEDS Photos of American Indians, ski action, ballooning, British Isles, Europe, Southwest scenery, disasters, environmental, landscapes/scenics, wildlife, adventure, events, food/drink, hobbies, performing arts, sports, travel, business concepts, industry, product shots/still life, science, technology/computers. Interested in documentary, fine art, historical/vintage, lifestyle.

SPECS Uses 8×10 glossy color and/or b&w prints; 35mm, 2¼×2¼, 4×5 transparencies. Accepts images in digital format. Send via CD, Zip as JPEG files.

PAYMENT & TERMS Pays 50% commission. Average price per image (to clients): $125-800 for b&w photos; $150-2,000 for color photos; $250-5,000 for film and videotape. Negotiates fees below stated minimums depending on number of photos being used. Offers volume discounts to customers; terms not specified in photographers' contracts. Discount sales terms not negotiable. Works with photographers with or without a contract, negotiable. Offers nonexclusive contract. Charges 100% duping fee. Statements issued quarterly. Payment made quarterly. Offers one-time rights. Does not inform photographers or allow them to negotiate when a client requests all rights. Model/property release preferred. Photo captions preferred.

HOW TO CONTACT Send query letter with brochure, stock list, tearsheets. Provide résumé, business card. Portfolios may be dropped off every Monday. Agency will contact photographer for portfolio review if interested. Portfolio should include slides, tearsheets, transparencies. Works with freelancers on assignment only. Does not keep samples on file; include SASE for return of material. Expects minimum initial submission of 20 images. Responds in 2 weeks.

ASIA IMAGES GROUP

15 Shaw Rd., #08-02, Teo Bldg., 367953, Singapore. (65)6288-2119. Fax: (65)6288-2117. E-mail: info@asiaimagesgroup.com. Website: www.asiapix.com. **Contact:** Alexander Mares-Manton, founder and creative director. Estab. 2001. Stock agency. We specialize in creating, distributing and licensing locally relevant Asian model-released lifestyle and business images. Our image collections reflect the visual trends, styles and issues that are current in Asia. We have three major collections: Asia Images (rights managed); AsiaPix (royalty free); and Picture India (royalty free). Clients include: advertising agencies, corporations, public relations firms, book publishers, calendar companies, magazine publishers.
NEEDS Photos of babies/children/teens, couples, families, parents, senior citizens, health/fitness/beauty, science, technology. "We are only interested in seeing images about or from Asia."
SPECS Accepts images in digital format. "We want to see 72 dpi JPEGs for editing and 300 dpi TIFF files for archiving and selling."
PAYMENT & TERMS "We have minimum prices that we stick to unless many sales are given to one photographer at the same time. Works with photographers on image-exclusive contract basis only. We need worldwide exclusivity for the images we represent, but photographers are encouraged to work with other agencies with other images. Statements issued monthly. Payment made monthly. Photographers allowed to review account records. Offers one-time rights, electronic media rights. Model and property releases are required for all images."

AURORA PHOTOS

20 W. 22nd St., Suite 603, New York NY 10010. (212)995-1900, ext. 113; Cell: (646)250-5404. Fax: (212)995-1901. Website: www.auroraphotos.com. **Contact:** José Azel, owner. Estab. 1993. Stock agency,

news/feature syndicate. Member of the Picture Archive Council of America (PACA). Has 500,000 photos in files. Clients include: advertising agencies, businesses, book publishers, magazine publishers, newspapers, calendar companies, postcard publishers.
NEEDS Photos of babies/children/teens, celebrities, couples, multicultural, families, parents, senior citizens, disasters, environmental, landscapes/scenics, wildlife, architecture, cities/urban, education, rural, adventure, events, sports, travel, agriculture, industry, military, political, science, technology/computers.
SPECS Accepts digital submissions only; contact for specs.
PAYMENT & TERMS Pays 50% commission for film. Average price per image (to clients): $225 minimum-$30,000 maximum. Offers volume discounts to customers. Works with photographers on image-exclusive contract basis only. Statements issued monthly. Payment made monthly. Photographers allowed to review account records once/year. Offers one-time rights, electronic media rights. Model/property release required. Photo captions required.
HOW TO CONTACT "We are not accepting new contributors to our rights managed collections at this time. We are accepting inquiries from photographers interested in contributing to our outstanding outdoor adventure and lifestyle royalty free collection, open. Aurora's Open Collection combines the user-friendliness of royalty free licensing with a picture archive that captures the breadth of sports, recreation and outdoor lifestyles. View Aurora's Open collection on IPNstock.com We are exclusively seeking photographers with outstanding, model released outdoor sports and lifestyle imagery. If you are interested in having your images reviewed, please send a link to your website portfolio for review to Open at open@auroraphotos.com." Does not keep samples on file; does not return material. Responds in 1 month. Photo guidelines available after initial contact.
TIPS "Review our website closely. List area of photo expertise/interest and forward a personal website address where your photos can be found."

AUSCAPE INTERNATIONAL

P.O. Box 1024, Bowral NSW 2576, Australia. (61)(024)885-2245. E-mail: auscape@auscape.com.au. Website: www.auscape.com.au. **Contact:** Sarah Tahourdin, director. Has 250,000 photos in files. Clients include: advertising agencies, book publishers, magazine publishers, newspapers, calendar companies, greeting card companies.

NEEDS Photos of environmental, landscapes/scenics, wildlife, pets, health/fitness, medicine, model-released Australian lifestyle.

SPECS Uses 35mm, 2¼×2¼, 4×5, 8×10 transparencies. Accepts images in digital format. Send via CD or DVD as TIFF files at 300 dpi.

PAYMENT & TERMS Pays 40% commission for color photos. Enforces minimum prices. Offers volume discounts to customers. Works with photographers on contract basis only. Requires exclusive contract. Statements issued quarterly. Payment made quarterly. Photographers allowed to review account records. Charges scan fees for all transparencies scanned in-house; all scans placed on website. Offers one-time rights. Photo captions required; include scientific names, common names, locations.

HOW TO CONTACT Does not keep samples on file. Expects minimum initial submission of 200 images with monthly submissions of at least 50 images. Responds in 3 weeks to samples. Photo guidelines sheet free.

TIPS "Send only informative, sharp, well-composed pictures. We are a specialist natural history agency and our clients mostly ask for pictures with content rather than empty-but-striking visual impact. There must be passion behind the images and a thorough knowledge of the subject."

AUTHOR PICTURES AT LEBRECHT

3 Bolton Rd., London NW8 0RJ, United Kingdom. E-mail: pictures@lebrecht.co.uk. Website: www.authorpictures.co.uk. **Contact:** Ms. E. Lebrecht. Estab. 1992. Picture library has 120,000 high-res images online; thousands more not yet scanned. Clients include: advertising agencies, newspapers, public relations firms, book publishers, calendar companies, magazine publishers, greeting card companies.

NEEDS Photos of authors, writers, historians, plays, playwrights, philosophers, etc.

SPECS Accepts images in digital format only.

PAYMENT & TERMS Pays 50% commission for b&w and color photos. Offers volume discounts to customers. Works with photographers on contract basis only. Offers limited regional exclusivity. Statements issued quarterly. Offers one-time rights. Informs photographers and allows them to negotiate when a client requests all rights. Photo captions required; include who is in photo, location, date.

HOW TO CONTACT Send e-mail.

BANNER IMAGE PHOTOGRAPHY

Alamu Photo, 12415 Archwood St., Suite 10, North Hollywood CA 91606-1350. (310)809-5929. E-mail: info@alamuphoto.com or Bannerimage@yahoo.com. Website: alamuphoto.com/. **Contact:** Eric Jackson, art editor. Estab. 1989.

Photo categories include: People: babies/children/teens, couples, multicultural, families, parents, senior citizens; Home & Garden: cities/urban, education, religious, rural; Business & Technology: agriculture, industry, medicine, military, political, technology/computers; Recreation: adventure, humor, performing arts, sports, travel; Business & Technology: agriculture, industry, medicine, military, political, technology/computers; Style: documentary, lifestyle.

NEEDS Images with focus on people of African descent that suggest a storyline. Quality prints of individuals and/or groups involved in business, leisure, travel, etc. A few examples are people involved with rural and urban communities—farms, courts, law enforcement, transit, construction, aviation, military, formal balls, musicians, temples, churches, mosques, and synagogues. Sport images involving fencing, deep sea and/or sky diving, motorcycle clubs, marathons, chess clubs, etc. Bottom line: give us something we have not seen within the communities of African-Americans, African-Europeans, African-South Americans. Buys 150 images annually; 100% are supplied by freelancers. Buys stock photos only. Specializes in calendars, posters, t-shirts, documentary books. Accepts outstanding work from beginning and established photographers; expects a high level of professionalism from all photographers who make contact. Guidelines free with #10 SASE, or request guidelines via e-mail.

SPECS People of African descent involved in work, play, and family events. Looking for interracial couples interacting. Format: 8×10 matte, color prints. Accepts images in digital format. Send CD as TIFF files at 300 dpi.

PAYMENT & TERMS Pays by the project, $1/min-$50/max per image. Does not pay extra for electronic usage of photos. Pays on publication. Buys one-time rights with credit line given. Model release and property release are preferred. Photo captions required.

HOW TO CONTACT E-mail query letter with link to photographer's website; JPEG samples at 72 dpi. Does not keep samples on file; cannot return material. Responds only if interested, send nonreturnable samples. Considers simultaneous submissions or previously published work.

THE BERGMAN COLLECTION

P.O. Box AG, Princeton NJ 08542-0872. (609)921-0749. E-mail: information@pmiprinceton.com. Website: pmiprinceton.com. **Contact:** Victoria B. Bergman, vice president. Estab. 1980. Collection established in the 1930s. Stock agency. Has 20,000 photos in files. Clients include: advertising agencies, book publishers, audiovisual firms, magazine publishers.

NEEDS "Specializes in medical, technical and scientific stock images of high quality and accuracy."

SPECS Uses color and/or b&w prints; 35mm, 2¼×2¼ transparencies. Accepts images in digital format. Send via CD, ZIP, e-mail as TIFF, BMP, JPEG files.

PAYMENT & TERMS Pays on commission basis. Works with photographers on contract basis only. Offers one-time rights. Model/property release required. Photo captions required; must be medically, technically, scientifically accurate.

HOW TO CONTACT "Do not send unsolicited images. Call, write, fax or e-mail to be added to our database of photographers able to supply, on an as-needed basis, specialized images not already in the collection. Include a description of the field of medicine, technology or science in which you have images. We contact photographers when a specific need arises."

TIPS "Our needs are for very specific images that usually will have been taken by specialists in the field as part of their own research or professional practice. A good number of the images placed by The Bergman Collection have come from photographers in our database."

BIOLOGICAL PHOTO SERVICE AND TERRAPHOTOGRAPHICS

P.O. Box 490, Moss Beach CA 94038. (650)359-6219. E-mail: bpsterra@pacbell.net. Website: www.agpix. com/biologicalphoto. **Contact:** Carl W. May, photo agent. Estab. 1980. Stock photo agency. Has 80,000 photos in files. Clients include: ad agencies, businesses, book/encyclopedia publishers, magazine publishers.

NEEDS All subjects in the pure and applied life and earth sciences. Stock photographers must be scientists. Subject needs include: electron micrographs of all sorts; biotechnology; modern medical imaging; marine and freshwater biology; diverse invertebrates; organisms used in research; tropical biology; and land and water conservation. All aspects of general and pathogenic microbiology, normal human biology, petrology, volcanology, seismology, paleontology, mining, petroleum industry, alternative energy sources, meteorology and the basic medical sciences, including anatomy, histology, medical microbiology, human embryology and human genetics.

SPECS Uses 4×5 through 11×14 glossy, high-contrast b&w prints for EM's; 35mm, 2¼×2¼, 4×5, 8×10 transparencies. "Dupes acceptable for rare and unusual subjects, but we prefer originals." Welcomes images in digital format as 50-100MB TIFF files.

PAYMENT & TERMS Pays 50% commission for b&w and color photos. General price range (for clients): $75-500, sometimes higher for advertising uses. Works with photographers with or without a contract, but only as an exclusive agency. Photographers may market directly on their own, but not through other agencies or portals. Statements issued quarterly. Payment made quarterly; "one month after end of quarter." Photographers allowed to review account records to verify sales figures "by appointment at any time." Offers only rights-managed uses of all kinds; negotiable. Informs photographers and allows them veto authority when client requests a buyout. Model/property release required for photos used in advertising and other commercial areas. Thorough scientific photo captions required; include complete identification of subject and location.

HOW TO CONTACT Interested in receiving work from scientific and medical photographers if they have the proper background. Send query letter or e-mail with stock list, résumé of scientific and photographic background; include SASE for return of material. Responds in 2 weeks. Photo guidelines free with query, résumé and SASE. Tips sheet distributed intermittently to stock photographers only. "Nonscientists should not apply."

TIPS "When samples are requested, we look for proper exposure, maximum depth of field, adequate visual information and composition, and adequate technical and general information in captions. Digital files should have image information in IPTC and EXIF fields. We avoid excessive overlap among our photographer/scientists. Our three greatest problems with potential photographers are: 1) inadequate captions/metadata; 2) inadequate quantities of *fresh* and *diverse* photos; 3) poor sharpness/depth of field/grain/composition in photos."

BLEND IMAGES

501 E. Pine St., Suite 200, Seattle WA 98122. (888)721-8810, ext. 5. Fax: (206)749-9391. E-mail: rebecca@blendimages.com. Website: www.blendimages.com. **Contact:** Rebecca LaGuire, submission and content manager. Estab. 2005. Stock agency. Clients include: advertising agencies, businesses, public relations firms, magazine publishers. Blend Images represents a "robust, high-quality collection of ethnically diverse lifestyle and business imagery.

NEEDS Photos of babies/children/teens, couples, multicultural, families, parents, senior citizens, business concepts; interested in lifestyle. Photos must be ethnically diverse.

SPECS Accepts images in digital format only. Images should be captured using professional-level SLRs of 11+ megapixels, pro digital backs, or high-end scanners that can deliver the required quality. Final media should be 48-52MB, 24-bit RGB (8 bits per channel), uncompressed TIFF files at 300 dpi. Images should be fully retouched, color-corrected, and free from dust, dirt, posterization, artifacing or other flaws. Files should be produced in a color-managed environment with Adobe RGB 1998 as the desired color space.

HOW TO CONTACT E-mail your photographic background and professional experience, along with 30-50 tightly edited, low-resolution JPEGs in one of the following ways: 1. URL with your personal website. 2. Web photo gallery. (Web galleries can be created using your imaging software. Reference your owner's manual for instructions.) 3. Spring-loaded hot link—a clickable link that provides downloadable JPEGs.

THE BRIDGEMAN ART LIBRARY

65 E. 93rd St., New York NY 10128. (212)828-1238. Fax: (212)828-1255. E-mail: newyork@bridgemanart.com. Website: www.bridgemanart.com. Estab. 1972. Member of the Picture Archive Council of America (PACA). Has 400,000 photos online, over 1 million offline. Has branch offices in London, Paris and Berlin. Clients include: advertising agencies, public relations firms, audiovisual firms, businesses, book publishers, magazine publishers, newspapers, calendar companies, greeting card companies, postcard publishers.

NEEDS Interested in fine art, historical photography.

SPECS Uses 4×5, 8×10 transparencies and 50MB+ digital files.

PAYMENT & TERMS Pays 50% commission for color photos. Enforces minimum prices. Offers volume discounts to customers; terms specified in photographers' contracts. Discount sales terms not negotiable. Works with photographers on contract basis only. Charges 100% duping fee. Statements issued quarterly. Photographers allowed to review account records. Offers one-time rights, electronic media rights, agency promotion rights.

HOW TO CONTACT Send query letter with photocopies, stock list. Does not keep samples on file; include SASE for return of material. Expects minimum initial submission of 20 images. Responds only if interested; send nonreturnable samples. Catalog available.

BSIP

34 rue Villiers-de-l'Isle-Adam, 75020 Paris , France. +33(0)1 43 58 69 87. Fax: +33(0)1 43 58 62 14. E-mail: international@bsip.com. Website: www.bsip.com. Estab. 1990. Member of Coordination of European Picture Agencies Press Stock Heritage (CEPIC). Has 200,000 downloadable high-res images online. Clients include: advertising agencies, book publishers, magazine publishers, newspapers.

NEEDS Photos of environmental, food/drink, health/fitness, medicine, science, nature and animals.

SPECS Accepts images in digital format only. Send via CD, DVD, FTP as TIFF or JPEG files at 330 dpi, 3630×2420 pixels.

PAYMENT & TERMS Offers volume discounts to customers; terms specified in photographers' contracts. Discount sales terms not negotiable. Works with photographers with or without a contract; negotiable. Offers guaranteed subject exclusivity. Contracts renew automatically with additional submissions for 5 years. Statements issued monthly. Payment made monthly. Photographers allowed to review account records. Offers one-time rights, electronic media rights, agency promotion rights. Model release required. Photo captions required.

HOW TO CONTACT Send query letter. Portfolio may be dropped off Monday–Friday. Keeps samples on file. Expects minimum initial submission of 50 images with monthly submissions of at least 20 images. Photo guidelines sheet available on website. Catalog free with SASE. Market tips sheet available.

CALIFORNIA VIEWS/MR. PAT HATHAWAY HISTORICAL PHOTO COLLECTION

469 Pacific St., Monterey CA 93940-2702. (831)373-3811. E-mail: hathaway@caviews.com. Website: www.caviews.com. **Contact:** Mr. Pat Hathaway, photo archivist. Estab. 1970. Picture library; historical collection. Has 80,000 b&w images; 10,000 35mm color images in files. Clients include: advertising agencies, public relations firms, audiovisual firms, book/encyclopedia publishers, magazine publishers, museums, postcard companies, calendar companies, television companies, interior decorators, film companies.

NEEDS Historical photos of California from 1855 to today, including disasters, landscapes/scenics, rural, agricultural, automobiles, travel, military, portraits, John Steinbeck and Edward F. Rickets.

PAYMENT & TERMS Payment negotiable. Offers volume discounts to customers.

HOW TO CONTACT "We accept donations of California photographic material in order to maintain our position as one of California's largest archives. Please do not send unsolicited images." Does not keep samples on file; cannot return material.

CAMERA PRESS LTD.

21 Queen Elizabeth St., London SE1 2PD, United Kingdom. +44 (0)20 7378 1300. Fax: +44 (0)20 7278 5126. E-mail: info@camerapress.com. Website: www.camerapress.com. Quality syndication service and picture library. Clients include: advertising agencies, public relations firms, audiovisual firms, book/encyclopedia publishers, magazine publishers, newspapers, postcard companies, calendar companies, greeting card companies and TV stations. Clients principally press but also advertising, publishers, etc.

Camera Press sends and receives images via ISDN, FTP, and e-mail. Has a fully operational electronic picture desk to receive/send digital images via modem/ISDN lines, FTP.

NEEDS Celebrities, world personalities (e.g., politics, sports, entertainment, arts), news/documentary, scientific, human interest, humor, women's features, stock.

SPECS Accepts images in digital format as TIFF, JPEG files, as long as they are a minimum of 300 dpi or 16MB.

PAYMENT & TERMS Standard payment term: 50% net commission. Statements issued every 2 months along with payments.

TIPS "Camera Press, one of the oldest and most celebrated family-owned picture agencies, represents some of the top names in the photographic world but also welcome emerging talents and gifted newcomers. We seek quality celebrity images; lively, colorful features which tell a story; and individual portraits of world personalities, both established and up-and-coming. Accurate captions are essential. Remember there is a big worldwide demand for celebrity premieres and openings. Other needs include: scientific development and novelties; beauty, fashion, interiors, food and women's interests; humorous pictures featuring the weird, the wacky and the wonderful."

CAMERIQUE INC. INTERNATIONAL

P.O. Box 175, Blue Bell PA 19422. (610)272-4000. Fax: (610)539-9558. E-mail: info@camerique.com. Website: www.camerique.com. **Contact:** Christopher C. Johnson, photo director. Estab. 1973. Representatives in Los Angeles, New York City, Montreal, Tokyo, Calgary, Buenos Aires, Rio de Janerio, Amsterdam, Hamburg, Barcelona, Athens, Rome, Lisbon and Hong Kong. Has 1 million photos in files. Clients include: advertising agencies, public relations firms, audiovisual firms, businesses, book/encyclopedia publishers, magazine publishers, newspapers, postcard companies, calendar companies, greeting card companies.

NEEDS General stock photos, all categories. Emphasizes people, activities, all seasons. Always needs large-format color scenics from all over the world. No fashion shots.

SPECS Accepts digital files only.

PAYMENT & TERMS Sometimes buys photos outright; pays $10-25/photo. Also pays 50-60% commission for b&w or color after sub-agent commissions. General price range (for clients): $300-500. Works with photographers on contract basis only. Offers non-exclusive contract. Contracts are valid "indefinitely until canceled in writing." Charges 50% catalog insertion fee for advertising, CD and online services. Statements issued monthly. Payment made monthly; within 10 days of end of month. Photographers allowed to review account records. Offers one-time rights, electronic media and multi-rights. Informs photographers and allows them to negotiate when client requests all rights. Model/property release required for people, houses, pets. Photo captions required; include "date, place, technical detail and any descriptive information that would help to market photos."

HOW TO CONTACT Send query letter with stock list. Send unsolicited photos by mail with SASE for consideration. "Send letter first; we'll send our questionnaire and spec sheet. You must include correct return postage for your material to be returned." Tips sheet distributed periodically to established contributors.

TIPS Prefers to see "well-selected, edited color on a variety of subjects. Well-composed, well lit shots, featuring contemporary styles and clothes. Be creative, selective, professional and loyal. Communicate openly and often." Review guidelines on website before submitting.

🌐 ⊛ CAPITAL PICTURES

85 Randolph Ave., London W9 1DL, United Kingdom. (44)(207)286-2212. E-mail: sales@capitalpictures. com, phil@capitalpictures.com. Website: www.capital pictures.com. Estab. 1980. Picture library. Has 500,000 photos on file. Clients include: advertising agencies, book publishers, magazine publishers, newspapers. Specializes in high-quality photographs of famous people (politics, royalty, music, fashion, film and television).

NEEDS "We have a lot of clients looking for 'pictures of the capital.' We need very high-quality images of London, postcard-type images for international sales. Not just large files, but great content; famous landmarks photographed at the best time, from the best angle, creating interesting and evocative images. Try looking online for pictures of London for some inspiration."

SPECS High-quality digital format only. Send via CD or e-mail as JPEG files.

PAYMENT & TERMS Pays 50% commission of money received. "We have our own price guide but will negotiate competitive fees for large quantity usage or supply agreements." Offers volume discounts to customers. Discount sales terms negotiable. Works with photographers with or without a contract; negotiable, whatever is most appropriate. No charges. 50% commission for sales. Statements issued monthly.

Payment made monthly. Photographers allowed to review account records. Offers any rights they wish to purchase. Informs photographers and allows them to negotiate when client requests all rights." Photo captions preferred; include date, place, event, name of subjects.

HOW TO CONTACT Send query letter with samples. Agency will contact photographer for portfolio review if interested. Keeps samples on file. Expects minimum initial submission of 24 images with monthly submissions of at least 24 images. Responds in 1 month to queries.

CATHOLIC NEWS SERVICE

3211 4th St., NE, Washington D.C. 20017. (202)541-3250. Fax: (202)541-3255. E-mail: photos@catholic news.com. Website: www.catholicnews.com. News service transmitting news, features, photos and graphics to Catholic newspapers and religious publishers.

NEEDS Timely news and feature photos related to the Catholic Church or Catholics, head shots of Catholic newsmakers or politicians, and other religions or religious activities, including those that illustrate spirituality. Also interested in photos of family life, modern lifestyles, teenagers, poverty and active seniors.

SPECS Prefers high-res JPEG files, 8×10 at 200 dpi. If sample images are available online, send URL via e-mail, or send samples via CD.

PAYMENT & TERMS Pays for unsolicited news or feature photos accepted for one-time editorial use in the CNS photo service. Include full-caption information. Unsolicited photos can be submitted via e-mail for consideration. Some assignments made, mostly in large U.S. cities and abroad, to experienced photojournalists; inquire about assignment terms and rates.

HOW TO CONTACT Query by mail or e-mail; include samples of work. Calls are fine, but be prepared to follow up with letter and samples.

TIPS "See our website for an idea of the type and scope of news covered. No scenic, still life, or composite images."

⊛ CHARLTON PHOTOS, INC.

3605 Mountain Dr., Brookfield WI 53045. (262)781-9328. E-mail: jim@charltonphotos.com. Website: www.charltonphotos.com. **Contact:** James Charlton, director of research. Estab. 1981. Stock photo agency. Has 475,000 photos. Clients include: ad agencies, public relations firms, audiovisual firms, businesses, book/encyclopedia publishers, magazine publishers, newspapers, calendar companies.

NEEDS "We handle photos of agriculture, rural lifestyles and pets."

SPECS Uses color photos; digital only. Also uses video.

PAYMENT & TERMS Pays 60/40% commission. Average price per image (to clients): $500-650 for color photos. Offers volume discounts to customers; terms specified in photographers' contracts. Works with photographers on contract basis only. Prefers exclusive contract, but negotiable based on subject matter submitted. Contracts renew automatically with additional submissions for 3 years minimum. Charges duping fee, 50% catalog insertion fee and materials fee. Statements issued monthly. Payment made monthly. Photographers allowed to review account records that relate to their work. Model/property release required for identifiable people and places. Photo captions required; include who, what, when, where.

HOW TO CONTACT Query by phone before sending any material. Expects initial submission of 1,000 images. Responds in 2 weeks. Photo guidelines free with SASE. Market tips sheet distributed quarterly to contract freelance photographers; free with SASE.

TIPS "Provide our agency with images we request by shooting a self-directed assignment each month. Visit our website."

CODY IMAGES

2 Reform St., Beith KA15 2AE, Scotland. (08)(45) 223-5451. E-mail: sam@codyimages.com. Website: www.codyimages.com. **Contact:** Ted Nevill. Estab. 1989. Picture library. Has 100,000 photos in files. Clients include: advertising agencies, newspapers, book publishers, calendar companies, audiovisual firms, magazine publishers.

NEEDS Photos of historical and modern aviation and warfare.

SPECS Accepts images in digital format.

PAYMENT & TERMS Pays commission. Average price per image (to clients): $80 minimum. Offers volume discounts to customers. Discount sales terms not negotiable. Works with photographers with or without a contract; negotiable. Offers nonexclusive contract. Contracts renew automatically with additional submissions. Statements issued quarterly. Payment

made quarterly. Photographers allowed to review account records. Offers one-time rights, electronic media rights. Informs photographers and allows them to negotiate when a client requests all rights. Model/property release preferred. Photo captions preferred.

HOW TO CONTACT Send e-mail with examples and stock list. Provide résumé, business card, self-promotion piece to be kept on file. Expects minimum initial submission of 1,000 images. Responds in 1 month.

EDUARDO COMESAÑA AGENCIA DE PRENSA/BANCO FOTOGRÁFICO

Av. Olleros 1850 4 to. "F", Buenos Aires C1426CRH, Argentina. (54)(11)4771-9418. E-mail: info@comesana.com. Website: www.comesana.com. **Contact:** Eduardo Comesaña, managing director. Estab. 1977. Stock agency, news/feature syndicate. Has 500,000 photos in files. Clients include: advertising agencies, businesses, newspapers, postcard publishers, book publishers, calendar companies, magazine publishers.

NEEDS Photos of babies/children/teens, celebrities, couples, families, parents, disasters, environmental, landscapes/scenics, wildlife, education, adventure, entertainment, events, health/fitness, humor, performing arts, travel, agriculture, business concepts, industry, medicine, political, science, technology/computers. Interested in documentary, fine art, historical/vintage.

SPECS Accepts images in JPEG format only, minimum 300 dpi.

PAYMENT & TERMS Offers volume discounts to customers; terms specified in photographer's contracts. Photographers can choose not to sell images on discount terms. Works with photographers with or without a contract; negotiable. Offers limited regional exclusivity. Contracts renew automatically with additional submissions. Statements issued quarterly. Payment made quarterly. Photographers allowed to review account records in cases of discrepancies only. Offers one-time rights. Model release preferred; property release required.

HOW TO CONTACT Send query letter with tearsheets, stock list. Provide self-promotion piece to be kept on file. Expects minimum initial submission of 200 images in low-res files with monthly submissions of at least 200 images. Responds only if interested; send nonreturnable samples.

CORBIS

250 Hudson St., 4th Floor, New York NY 10013. (212)777-6200; (800)260-0444. Fax: (212)375-7700. Website: www.corbis.com. Estab. 1991. Stock agency, picture library, news/feature syndicate. Member of the Picture Archive Council of America (PACA). Corbis also has offices in London, Paris, Dusseldorf, Tokyo, Seattle, Chicago and Los Angeles. Clients include: advertising agencies, businesses, newspapers, public relations firms, book publishers, calendar companies, audiovisual firms, magazine publishers, greeting card companies, businesses/corporations, media companies.

HOW TO CONTACT "Please check 'About Corbis' on our website for current submission information."

☺ CRESTOCK CORPORATION

3 Concorde Gate, 4th Floor, Toronto ON M3C 3N7, Canada. E-mail: help@crestock.com. Website: www. crestock.com. "Crestock is a growing player in micropayment royalty-free stock photography, helping clients with small budgets find creative images for their projects. With a fast and reliable image upload system, Crestock gives photographers and illustrators a great platform for licensing their creative work. Over 1,000,000 photographs, illustrations and vectors are available for purchase and download online. Masterfile Corporation acquired the agency in 2010. Crestock has a general collection of photographs, illustrations and vectors available in a wide-range of sizes. Crestock sells single images, as well offers a selection of subscription and credit packages.Clients include designers, advertising agencies, small business owners, corporations, newspapers, public relations firms, publishers as well as greeting card and calendar companies."

NEEDS Looking for model-released photographs, as well as illustrations and vectors on a wide-range of subjects, including business, finance, holidays, sports and leisure, travel, nature, animals, technology, education, health and beauty, shopping, green living, architecture, still-life as well as conceptual and general lifestyle themes. For an up-to-date list of specific ideas and themes, see www.crestock.com/forum/microstock-101.

SPECS Accepts images in digital format. Submissions must be uploaded for review via website or FTP as JPEG, EPS or AI. For full technical requirements, see www.crestock.com/technical-requirements.aspx.

PAYMENT & TERMS Pays contributors based on request, once a minimum amount is reached. Requires Model and/or Property releases on particular images. For more information, see: www.crestock.com/modelrelease.aspx Artists are required to caption and keyword their own material in English before submission. In order to join Crestock, register at www.crestock.com and submit photos for approval. To see general information for artists, see www.crestock.com/information-for-contributors.aspx.

TIPS "Crestock is among the most selective microstock agencies, so be prepared for strict quality standards."

DDB STOCK PHOTOGRAPHY, LLC

P.O. Box 80155, Baton Rouge LA 70898. (225)763-6235. Fax: (225)763-6894. E-mail: info@ddbstock.com. Website: www.ddbstock.com. **Contact:** Douglas D. Bryant, president. Estab. 1970. Stock photo agency. Member of American Society of Picture Professionals. Rights managed stock only, no RF. Currently represents 105 professional photographers. Has 500,000 original color transparencies and 25,000 b&w prints in archive, and 125,000 high-res digital images with 45,000 available for download on website. Clients include: text-trade book/encyclopedia publishers, travel industry, museums, ad agencies, audiovisual firms, magazine publishers, CD publishers and many foreign publishers.

NEEDS Specializes in picture coverage of Latin America with emphasis on Mexico, Central America, South America, and the Caribbean. Needs photos of anthropology/archeology, art, commerce, crafts, secondary and university education, festivals and ritual, geography, history, indigenous people and culture, museums, parks, political figures, religion. Also uses teens 6th-12th grade/young adults college age, couples, multicultural, families, parents, senior citizens, architecture, rural, adventure, entertainment, events, food/drink, restaurants, health/fitness, performing arts, business concepts, industry, science, technology/computers.

SPECS Prefers images in TIFF digital format on DVD at 10 megapixels or higher. Prepare digital submissions filling IPTC values. Caption, copyright, and keywords per instructions at: www.ddbstock.com/submissionguidelines.html. Accepts uncompressed JPEGs, TIFFs, and original 35mm transparencies.

PAYMENT & TERMS Pays 40% commission for color photos; 25% on foreign sales through foreign agents. Payment rates: $50-$20,000. Average price per image (to clients): $225. Offers volume discount to customers; terms specified in photographers' contracts. 4-year initial minimum holding period for original transparencies. Payment made quarterly. Does not allow independent audits. "We are a small agency and do not have staff to oversee audits." Offers one-time, print/electronic media, world and all language rights. Model/property release preferred for ad set-up shots. Photo captions required; include location and detailed description. "We have a geographic focus and need specific location info on captions (Geocode latitude/longitude if you carry a GPS unit, and include latitude/longitude in captions)."

HOW TO CONTACT Interested in receiving work from professional photographers who regularly visit Latin America. Send query letter with brochure, tearsheets, stock list. Expects minimum initial submission of 300 digital images/original transparencies and yearly submissions of at least 500 images. Responds in 6 weeks. Photo guidelines available on website.

TIPS "Speak Spanish and spend 1-6 months shooting in Latin America and the Caribbean every year. Follow our needs list closely. Call before leaving on assignment. Shoot digital TIFFs at 12 megapixels or larger. Shoot RAW/NEF/DNG adjust and convert to TIFF or Fuji professional transparency film if you have not converted to digital. Edit carefully. Eliminate images with focus, framing, excessive grain/noise, or exposure problems. The market is far too competitive for average pictures and amateur photographers. Review guidelines for photographers on our website. Include coverage from at least 3 Latin American countries or 5 Caribbean Islands. No one-time vacation shots! Shoot subjects in demand listed on website."

DINODIA PHOTO LIBRARY

13-15 Vithoba Ln., Vithalwadi, Kalbadevi, Bombay 400 002, India. (91)(22)2240-4026. Fax: (91)(22)2240-1675. E-mail: jagdish@dinodia.com. Website: www.dinodia.com. **Contact:** Jagdish Agarwal, founder. Estab. 1987. Stock photo agency celebrating 25 years in business. Has 500,000 photos on website. Clients include: advertising agencies, public relations firms, audiovisual firms, businesses, book/encyclopedia publishers, magazine publishers, newspapers, post-card companies, calendar companies, greeting card companies.

NEEDS Photos of babies/children/teens, celebrities, couples, multicultural, families, parents, senior citizens, disasters, environment, landscapes/scenics, wildlife, architecture, cities/urban, education, gardening, interiors/decorating, pets, religious, rural, adventure, automobiles, entertainment, events, food/drink, health/fitness/beauty, hobbies, humor, performing arts, sports, travel, agriculture, business concepts, industry, medicine, military, political, product shots/still life, science, technology/computers. Interested in alternative process, avant garde, documentary, erotic, fashion/glamour, fine art, historical/vintage, seasonal.

SPECS "At the moment we are only accepting digital. Initially it is better to send a link to your website for our review."

PAYMENT & TERMS Pays 50% commission for b&w and color photos. General price range (to clients): US $50-600. Negotiates fees below stated minimum prices. Offers volume discounts to customers; inquire about specific terms. Discount sales terms not negotiable. Works with photographers on contract basis only. Offers limited regional exclusivity; "prefer exclusive for India." Contracts renew automatically with additional submissions for 5 years. Statement issued monthly. Payment made monthly. Photographers permitted to review sales figures. Informs photographers and allows them to negotiate when client requests all rights. Offers one-time rights. Model release preferred. Photo captions required.

HOW TO CONTACT Send query e-mail with résumé of credits, link to your website. Responds in 1 week. Photo guidelines free with SASE. Dinodia news distributed monthly to contracted photographers.

TIPS "We look for style—maybe in color, composition, mood, subject matter, whatever—but the photos should have above-average appeal." Sees trend that "market is saturated with standard documentary-type photos. Buyers are looking more often for stock that appears to have been shot on assignment."

DK STOCK, INC.

3524 78th St., Suite 29A, Jackson Heights NY 11372. (866)362-4705. Fax: (678)384-1883. E-mail: david@dkstock.com. Website: www.dkstock.com. **Contact:** David Deas, photo editor. Estab. 2000. "A multicultural stock photo company based in New York City.

Prior to launching DK Stock, its founders worked for years in the advertising industry as a creative team specializing in connecting clients to the $1.6 trillion multicultural market. This market is growing, and DK Stock's goal is to service it with model-released, well composed, professional imagery." Member of the Picture Archive Council of America (PACA). Has 15,000 photos on file. Clients include: advertising agencies, public relations firms, graphic design businesses, book publishers, magazine publishers, newspapers, calendar companies, greeting card companies.

NEEDS "Looking for contemporary lifestyle images that reflect the black and Hispanic Diaspora." Wants photos of babies/children/teens, celebrities, couples, multicultural, families, parents, senior citizens, education, adventure, entertainment, health/fitness/beauty, hobbies, humor, performing arts, sports, travel, agriculture, business concepts, industry, medicine, military, political, science, technology/computers. Interested in historical/vintage, lifestyle. "Images should include models of Hispanics and/or people of African descent. Images of Caucasian models interacting with black people or hispanic people can also be submitted. Be creative, selective and current. Visit website to get an idea of the style and range of representative work. E-mail for a current copy of 'needs list.'"

SPECS Accepts images in digital format. 50MB, 300 dpi.

PAYMENT & TERMS Pays 50% commission for b&w or color photos. Average price per image (to clients): $485. Enforces minimum prices. Offers volume discounts to customers; terms specified in photographers' contracts. Photographers can choose not to sell images on discount terms. Works with photographers on contract basis only. Offers non-exclusive contract. Contracts renew automatically with additional submissions for 5 years. Statements issued monthly. Payment made monthly. Photographers allowed to review account records. Model/property release required. Photo captions not necessary.

HOW TO CONTACT Send query letter with disc or DVD. Portfolio may be dropped off every Monday-Friday. Does not keep samples on file; include SASE for return of material. Expects minimum initial submission of 50 images with 5 times/year submissions of at least 200 images. Responds in 2 weeks to samples, portfolios. Photo guidelines free with SASE. Catalog free with SASE.

TIPS "We love working with talented people. If you have 10 incredible images, let's begin a relationship. Also, we're always looking for new and upcoming talent as well as photographers who can contribute often. There is an increasing demand for lifestyle photos of multicultural people. Our clients are based in the Americas, Europe, Asia and Africa. Be creative, original and technically proficient."

● DRK PHOTO

100 Starlight Way, Sedona AZ 86351. (928)284-9808. E-mail: info@drkphoto.com. Website: www.drkphoto. com. "We handle only the personal best of a select few photographers—not hundreds. This allows us to do a better job aggressively marketing the work of these photographers." Member of Picture Archive Council of America (PACA) and American Society of Picture Professionals (ASPP). Clients include: ad agencies; PR and AV firms; businesses; book, magazine, textbook and encyclopedia publishers; newspapers; postcard, calendar and greeting card companies; branches of the government; and nearly every facet of the publishing industry, both domestic and foreign.

NEEDS "Especially need marine and underwater coverage." Also interested in S.E.Ms, African, European and Far East wildlife, and good rainforest coverage.

SPECS Digital capture, digital scans.

PAYMENT & TERMS General price range (to clients): $100-" into thousands." Works with photographers on contract basis only. Contracts renew automatically. Statements issued quarterly. Payment made quarterly. Offers one-time rights; "other rights negotiable between agency/photographer and client." Model release preferred. Photo captions required.

HOW TO CONTACT "With the exception of established professional photographers shooting enough volume to support an agency relationship, we are not soliciting open submissions at this time. Those professionals wishing to contact us in regards to representation should query with a brief letter of introduction."

● DW STOCK PICTURE LIBRARY

108 Beecroft Rd., Beecroft New South Wales 2119, Australia. (61)2 9869 0717. E-mail: info@dwpicture. com.au. Website: www.dwpicture.com.au. Estab. 1997. Has more than 200,000 photos on file and 30,000 online. "Strengths include historical images, marine life, African wildlife, Australia, travel, horticulture, agriculture, people and lifestyles." Clients include: adver-

tising agencies, designers, printers, book publishers, magazine publishers, calendar companies.

NEEDS Photos of babies/children/teens, families, parents, senior citizens, disasters, gardening, pets, rural, health/fitness, travel, industry. Interested in lifestyle.

SPECS Accepts images in digital format. Send as low-res JPEG files via CD.

PAYMENT & TERMS Average price per image (to clients): $200 for color photos. Enforces minimum prices. Offers volume discounts to customers. Works with photographers on contract basis only. Statements issued quarterly. Photographers allowed to review account records in cases of discrepancies only. Offers one-time rights. Model release preferred. Photo captions required.

HOW TO CONTACT Send query letter with images; include SASE if sending by mail. Expects minimum initial submission of 200 images.

E&E PICTURE LIBRARY

Clerks Court, 18-20 Farringdon Lane, London EC1R 3AU, United Kingdom. +44(0)20 7251 7100. Fax: +44 (0)20 7434 0673. E-mail: angela.davies@heritage-images.com. Website: www.heritage-images.com. Estab. 1998. Member of BAPLA (British Association of Picture Libraries and Agencies). Has 250,000+ images on file. Clients include: advertisers/designers, businesses, book publishers, magazine publishers, newspapers, calendar/card companies, merchandising, TV.

NEEDS Worldwide religion, faith, spiritual images, buildings, clergy, festivals, ceremony, objects, places, food, ritual, monks, nuns, stained glass, carvings, the unusual. Mormons, Shakers, all groups/sects, large or small. Death: burial, funerals, graves, gravediggers, green burial, commemorative. Ancient/heritage/Biblelands/saints/eccentricities/festivals: curiosities, unusual oddities like follies, signs, symbols. Architecture, religious or secular. Manuscripts and illustrations, old and new, linked with any of the subjects above.

SPECS Accepts images in digital format. Send via CD, JPEG files in medium to high-res. Uses 35mm, 2¼×2¼, 4×5 transparencies.

PAYMENT & TERMS Average price per image (to clients): $140-200 for color photos. Offers volume discounts to customers. Works with photographers on contract basis for 5 years, offering exclusive/nonexclu-

sive contract renewable automatically with additional submissions. Offers one-time rights. Model release where necessary. Photo captions very important and must be accurate; include what, where, any special features or connections, name, date (if possible), and religion.

HOW TO CONTACT Send query letter with slides, tearsheets, transparencies/CD. Expects minimum initial submission of 40 images. Photo guidelines sheet and "wants list" available via e-mail.

TIPS "Decide on exact subject of image. *Get in close and then closer.* Exclude all extraneous matter. Fill the frame. Dynamic shots. Interesting angles, light. No shadows or miniscule subject matter far away. Tell us what is important about the picture. No people in shot unless they have a role in the proceedings as in a festival or service, etc."

ECOSCENE

Empire Farm, Throop Rd., Templecombe, Somerset BA8 0HR, United Kingdom. (44)(196)337-1700. E-mail: sally@ecoscene.com, pix@ecoscene.com. Website: www.ecoscene.com. **Contact:** Sally Morgan, director. Estab. 1988. Picture library. Has 80,000 photos in files. Clients include: advertising agencies, businesses, book/encyclopedia publishers, magazine publishers, newspapers, online, multimedia.

NEEDS Photos of disasters, environmental, energy issues, sustainable development, wildlife, gardening, rural, agriculture, medicine, science, pollution, industry, energy, indigenous peoples.

SPECS Accepts digital submissions only. High-quality JPEG at 300 dpi, minimum file size when opened of 50MB.

PAYMENT & TERMS Pays 55% commission for color photos. Average price per image (to clients): $70 minimum for color photos. Negotiates fees below stated minimum prices, depending on quantity reproduced by a single client. Offers volume discounts to customers. Discount sales terms not negotiable. Works with photographers on contract basis only. Offers nonexclusive contract. Contracts renew automatically with additional submissions, 4 years minimum. Statements issued quarterly. Payment made quarterly. Offers one-time and electronic media rights. Informs photographers and allows them to negotiate when client requests all rights. Model/property release required. Photo captions required; include location, subject matter, keywords and common and Latin names of wildlife and any behavior shown in pictures.

HOW TO CONTACT Send e-mail with résumé of credits. Digital submissions only. Keeps samples on file; include SASE for return of material. Expects minimum initial submission of 100 images with annual submissions of at least 100 images. Responds in 2 months. Photo guidelines free with SASE. Market tips sheets distributed quarterly to anybody who requests, and to all contributors.

TIPS "Photographers should carry out a tight EDT, no fillers, and be critical of their own work."

⊙ EMPICS

Pavilion House, 16 Castle Blvd., Nottingham NG7 1FL, United Kingdom. +44(0)1158 447 447. Fax: +44(0)1158 447 448. E-mail: info@empics.com. Website: www.empics.com; www.pressassociation. com. Formerly Empics Sports Photo Agency. Picture library. Has over 3 million news, sports and entertainment photos (from around the world, past and present) online. Clients include: advertising agencies, newspapers, public relations firms, book publishers, magazine publishers, web publishers, television broadcasters, sporting bodies, rights holders.

NEEDS Photos of news, sports and entertainment.

SPECS Uses glossy or matte color and b&w prints; 35mm transparencies. Accepts the majority of images in digital format.

PAYMENT & TERMS Negotiates fees below stated minimums. Offers volume discounts to customers. Works with photographers on contract basis only. Rights offered varies.

HOW TO CONTACT Send query letter or e-mail. Does not keep samples on file; cannot return material.

⊛ ESTOCK PHOTO, LLC

27-28 Thomson Ave., Suite 628, Long Island City NY 11101. (800)284-3399. Fax: (212)545-1185. E-mail: submissions@estockphoto.com. Website: www. estockphoto.com. **Contact:** Laura Diez, president. Member of Picture Archive Council of America (PACA). Has over 1 million photos in files. Clients include: ad agencies, public relations and AV firms; businesses; book, magazine and encyclopedia publishers; newspapers, calendar and greeting card companies; textile firms; travel agencies and poster companies.

NEEDS Photos of travel, destination, people, lifestyles, business.

SPECS Accepts images in digital format. Requires images to be taken with a minimum 12 megapixel camera. In order to view new work as efficiently as possible, we can only handle images submitted digitally, as follows: 1. If you have a website, or have your images displayed in another forum on the web, please send us your URL. 2. You may e-mail us 50-75 of your best images following these guidelines: Images must be in RGB or JPEG format and the overall file size of your e-mail cannot exceed 4MB. (Messages exceeding this size will be rejected by our mail server). You may use our form on our website to send us an e-mail.

PAYMENT & TERMS Price depends on quality and quantity. Usually pays 50% commission. General price range (to clients): $125-6,500. Works with photographers on contract basis only. Offers exclusive and limited regional exclusive contracts. Contracts renew automatically for 3 years. Offers to clients "any rights they want to have; payment is calculated accordingly." Statements issued, and payment made, bi-monthly and quarterly. Photographers allowed to review account records to verify their sales figures. Offers one-time and electronic media rights. Informs photographers and allows them to negotiate when client requests all rights; some conditions. Model release required; "depends on subject matter." Photo captions preferred.

HOW TO CONTACT Send query letter with samples, a list of stock photo subjects or submit portfolio for review. Response time depends; often the same day. Photo guidelines free with SASE.

TIPS "Photos should show what the photographer is all about. They should show technical competence—photos that are sharp, well-composed, have impact; if color, they should show color."

EWING GALLOWAY INC.

100 Merrick Rd., Rockville Centre NY 11570. (516)764-8620. Fax: (516)764-1196. Estab. 1920. Stock photo agency. Member of Picture Archive Council of America (PACA), American Society of Media Photographers (ASMP). Has 3 million+ photos in files. Clients include: advertising agencies, public relations firms, audiovisual firms, businesses, book/encyclopedia publishers, magazine publishers, newspapers, postcard companies, calendar companies, greeting card companies, religious organizations.

NEEDS General subject library. Does not carry personalities or news items. Lifestyle shots (model released) are most in demand.

PAYMENT & TERMS Price: $400-450. Charges catalog insertion fee. Statements issued monthly. Payment made monthly. Offers one-time rights; also unlimited rights for specific media. Model/property release required. Photo captions required; include location, specific industry, etc.

HOW TO CONTACT Send query letter with samples. Send unsolicited photos by mail for consideration; must include SASE. Photo guidelines available with SASE. Market tips sheet distributed monthly, with SASE.

TIPS Wants to see "high quality—sharpness, subjects released, shot only on best days—bright sky and clouds. Medical and educational material is currently in demand. We see a trend toward photography related to health and fitness, high-tech industry and mixed race in business and leisure."

☻ EYE UBIQUITOUS

65 Brighton Rd., Shoreham West Sussex N43 6RE, United Kingdom. +44(0)1273 440113. Fax: +44(0)1273 440116. Website: www.eyeubiquitous.com. Estab. 1988. Picture library. Has 300,000+ photos in files. Clients include: ad agencies, public relations firms, businesses, book/encyclopedia publishers, magazine publishers, newspapers, television companies.

NEEDS Photos of worldwide social documentary and general stock.

SPECS Transparencies and 50MB files at 300 dpi.

PAYMENT & TERMS Offers volume discounts to customers; inquire about specific terms. Discount sales terms not negotiable. Works with photographers on contract basis only. Offers exclusive, limited regional exclusivity and nonexclusive contracts. Contracts renew automatically with additional submissions. Charges to photographers "discussed on an individual basis." Payment made quarterly. Photographers allowed to review account records. Buys one-time, electronic media and agency promotion rights; negotiable. Does not inform photographers or allow them to negotiate when client requests all rights. Model/property release preferred for people, "particularly Americans." Photo captions required; include where, what, why, who.

HOW TO CONTACT Submit portfolio for review. Works with freelancers only. Keeps samples on file.

Include SASE for return. No minimum number of images expected in initial submission, but "the more the better." Responds as time allows. Photo guidelines free with SASE. Catalog free with SASE. Market tips sheet distributed to contributors "when we can" free with SASE.

TIPS "Find out how picture libraries operate. This is the same for all libraries worldwide. Amateurs can be very good photographers, but very bad at understanding the industry after reading some irresponsible and misleading articles. Research the library requirements."

☻ FAMOUS PICTURES & FEATURES AGENCY

13 Harwood Rd., London SW6 4QP, United Kingdom. +44(0)20 7731 9333. Fax: +44(0)20 7731 9330. E-mail: info@famous.uk.com. Website: www.famous.uk.com. Estab. 1985. Picture library, news/feature syndicate. Has more than 500,000 photos on database. Clients include: advertising agencies, book publishers, magazine publishers, newspapers, calendar companies, postcard publishers and poster publishers.

NEEDS Photos of music, film, TV personalities; international celebrities; live, studio, party shots (paparazzi) with stars of all types.

SPECS Prefers images in digital format. Send via FTP or e-mail as JPEG files at 300 dpi or higher.

PAYMENT & TERMS Offers volume discounts to customers. Photographers can choose not to sell images on discount terms. Works with photographers with or without a contract; contracts available for all photographers. Offers limited regional exclusivity. Statements issued monthly. Payment made monthly. Photographers allowed to review account records. Offers one-time rights. Photo captions preferred.

HOW TO CONTACT E-mail, phone or write, provide samples. Provide résumé, business card, self-promotion piece or tearsheets to be kept on file. Agency will contact photographer for portfolio review if interested. Keeps samples in online database. Will return material with SAE/IRC.

TIPS "We are solely marketing images via computer networks. Our fully searchable archive of new and old pictures is online. Send details via e-mail for more information. When submitting work, please caption pictures correctly."

⊛ ⊛ FIRST LIGHT ASSOCIATED PHOTOGRAPHERS

9 Davies Ave., Suite 410, Toronto ON M4M 2A6, Canada. (416)597-8625. Fax: (416)597-2035. E-mail: info@firstlight.com. Website: www.firstlight.com. **Contact:** Anne Bastarache, director, photography. Estab. 1984. Stock agency and image partner of Getty Images, represents over 150 photographers and 40 rights-managed and royalty-free collections. Over one million images available online. Clients include: advertising agencies, public relations firms, audiovisual firms, businesses, book/encyclopedia publishers, magazine publishers, newspapers, calendar companies.

NEEDS Commercial imagery in all categories. Special emphasis on model-released people, lifestyle, conceptual, business and Canadian images. "Our broad files require a variety of subjects." Sister company WAVE royalty-free also requires environmentally relevant imagery; contact First Light for more information.

SPECS "For initial review submission we prefer low-res JPEG files via e-mail; for final submissions we require clean 50MB (minimum) high-res TIFF files."

PAYMENT & TERMS Photographer's imagery is represented as rights-managed. 45% commission rate. Works on contract basis only, nonexclusive. Statements issued monthly. Payment made monthly. Offers one-time rights. Informs photographers and allows them to negotiate when client requests buy-out. Model releases required. IPTC embedding required for all final files. Photo captions required.

HOW TO CONTACT Send query letter via e-mail.

TIPS "Wants to see tightly edited submissions. Well-produced, non-candid imagery."

⊛ THE FLIGHT COLLECTION

4 Craster Court, Oxford Road, Banbury OX16 9AG, United Kingdom. +44(0)1295 278146. E-mail: flight@uniquedimension.com. Website: www.theflightcollection.com. Estab. 1983. Has 1 million+ photos in files. Clients include: advertising agencies, public relations firms, audiovisual firms, businesses, book publishers, magazine publishers, newspapers, calendar companies, greeting card companies, postcard publishers.

NEEDS Photos of aviation.

SPECS Accepts all transparency film sizes: Send a sample of 50 for viewing. Accepts images in digital format. Send via CD as TIFF files at 300 dpi.

PAYMENT & TERMS Enforces minimum prices. Offers volume discounts to customers. Discount sales terms not negotiable. Works with photographers on contract basis only. Offers nonexclusive contract. Contracts renew automatically with additional submissions, no specific time. Statements issued monthly. Payment made monthly. Offers one-time rights. Model/property release required. Photo captions required; include name, subject, location, date.

HOW TO CONTACT Send query letter with transparencies or CD. Does not keep samples on file; include SASE for return of material. Expects minimum initial submission of 50 images. Photo guidelines sheet free via e-mail.

TIPS "Caption slides/images properly. Provide a list of what's submitted."

FOODPIX

601 N. 34th St., Seattle WA 98103. (206)925-5000. E-mail: sales@gettyimages.com. Website: www.gettyimages.com. Estab. 1994. Stock agency. Member of the Picture Archive Council of America (PACA). Has 40,000 photos in files. Clients include: advertising agencies, businesses, newspapers, book publishers, calendar companies, design firms, magazine publishers.

NEEDS Food, beverage and food/lifestyle images.

SPECS Accepts analog and digital images. Review and complete the online submission questionnaire on the website before submitting work.

PAYMENT & TERMS Enforces minimum prices. Offers volume discounts to customers; terms specified in photographers' contracts. Works with photographers on contract basis only. Offers exclusive contract only. Statements issued monthly. Payment made quarterly. Offers one-time rights. Model/property release required. Photo captions required.

HOW TO CONTACT Send query e-mail with samples. Expects maximum initial submission of 50 images. Catalog available.

FOTOAGENT.COM/FOTOCONCEPT, INC.

E-mail: werner@fotoagent.com. Website: www.fotoagent.com. **Contact:** Werner J. Bertsch, president. Estab. 1985. Stock photo agency. Has 1.5 million photos in files. Clients include: magazines, advertising agencies, newspapers, publishers.

NEEDS General worldwide travel, medical and industrial.

SPECS Uses digital files only. Upload your files on website.

PAYMENT & TERMS Pays 50% commission for b&w or color photos. Average price per image (to clients): $175 minimum for b&w or color photos. Works with photographers on contract basis only. Offers non-exclusive contract. Contracts renew automatically with each submission for 1 year. Statements issued monthly. Payment made monthly. Photographers allowed to review account records to verify sales figures. Offers one-time rights. Model release required. Photo captions required.

HOW TO CONTACT Use the "Contact Us" feature on website.

TIPS Wants to see "clear, bright colors and graphic style. Looking for photographs with people of all ages with good composition, lighting and color in any material for stock use."

FOTO-PRESS TIMMERMANN

Speckweg 34A, Moehrendorf D-91096, Germany. (49)(9131)42801. Fax: (49)(9131)450528. E-mail: info@f-pt.com. Website: www.f-pt.com. **Contact:** Wolfgange Timmermann. Stock photo agency. Has 750,000 photos in files. Clients include: advertising agencies, audiovisual firms, businesses, book/encyclopedia publishers, magazine publishers, newspapers, calendar companies.

NEEDS Landscapes, countries, travel, tourism, towns, people, business, nature, babies/children/teens, couples, families, parents, senior citizens, adventure, entertainment, health/fitness/beauty, hobbies, industry, medicine, technology/computers. Interested in erotic, fine art, seasonal, lifestyle.

SPECS Uses 2¼×2¼, 4×5, 8×10 transparencies (no prints). Accepts images in digital format. Send via CD, ZIP as TIFF files.

PAYMENT & TERMS Pays 50% commission for color photos. Works on nonexclusive contract basis (limited regional exclusivity). First period: 3 years; contract automatically renewed for 1 year. Photographers allowed to review account records. Statements issued quarterly. Payment made quarterly. Offers one-time rights. Informs photographers and allows them to negotiate when a client requests to buy all rights. Model/property release preferred. Photo captions required; include state, country, city, subject, etc.

HOW TO CONTACT Send query letter with stock list. Send unsolicited photos by mail for consideration; include SAE/IRC for return of material. Responds in 1 month.

FOTOSCOPIO

Jaramillo 3894, 8vo. Piso, Depto. 18, C1430AGJ, Capital Federal, Buenos Aires 1203AAQ, Argentina. (54)(114)542-3512. Fax: (54)(114)542-3512. E-mail: info@fotoscopio.com. Website: www.fotoscopio.com. **Contact:** Gustavo Di Pace, director. Estab. 1999. Latin American stock photo agency. Has 50,000 photos in files. Clients include: advertising agencies, businesses, postcard publishers, book publishers, calendar companies, magazine publishers, greeting card companies.

NEEDS Photos of Hispanic people, Latin American countries, babies/children/teens, celebrities, couples, multicultural, families, senior citizens, disasters, environmental, landscapes/scenics, wildlife, architecture, cities/urban, interiors/decorating, pets, religious, adventure, automobiles, entertainment, health/fitness/beauty, hobbies, sports, travel, agriculture, business concepts, industry, product shots/still life, technology/computers. Interested in documentary, fine art, historical/vintage.

SPECS Uses 35mm, 2¼×2¼, 4×5, 8×10 transparencies. Accepts images in digital format. Send via CD, ZIP.

PAYMENT & TERMS Average price per image (to clients): $50-300 for b&w photos; $50-800 for color photos. Negotiates fees below stated minimums. Offers volume discounts to customers; terms specified in photographer's contracts. Discount sales terms not negotiable. Works with photographers on contract basis only. Offers nonexclusive contract. Contracts renew automatically with additional submissions for 1 year. Statements issued and payment made whenever one yields rights of reproduction of his photography. Photographers allowed to review account records in cases of discrepancies only. Offers one-time and electronic media rights. Model release required; property release preferred. Photo captions preferred.

HOW TO CONTACT Send query letter with résumé, slides, prints, photocopies, tearsheets, transparencies, stock list. Provide résumé, business card, self-promotion piece to be kept on file. Expects minimum initial submission of 100 images. Responds in 1 month to samples. Photo guidelines sheet free with SASE.

FUNDAMENTAL PHOTOGRAPHS

210 Forsyth St., Suite 2, New York NY 10002. (212)473-5770. Fax: (212)228-5059. E-mail: mail@fphoto.com. Website: www.fphoto.com. **Contact:** Kip Peticolas, partner. Estab. 1979. Stock photo agency. Applied for membership into the Picture Archive Council of America (PACA). Has 100,000 photos in files. Searchable online database. Clients include: textbook/encyclopedia publishers, advertising agencies, science magazine publishers, travel guide book publishers, corporate industrial.

NEEDS Photos of medicine, biology, microbiology, environmental, industry, weather, disasters, science-related business concepts, agriculture, technology/computers, optics, advances in science and industry, green technologies, pollution, physics and chemistry concepts.

SPECS Accepts 35mm and all large-format transparencies but digital is strongly preferred. Send digital as RAW or TIFF unedited original files at 300 dpi, 11×14 or larger size. Please e-mail for current submission guidelines.

PAYMENT & TERMS Pays 50% commission for color photos. General price range (to clients): $100-500 for b&w photos; $150-1,200 for color photos; depends on rights needed. Enforces strict minimum prices. Offers volume discount to customers. Works with photographers on contract basis only. Offers guaranteed subject exclusivity. Contracts renew automatically with additional submissions for 2 or 3 years. Charges $5/image scanning fee; can increase to $15 if corrective Photoshop work required. Charges copyright registration fee (optional). Statements issued and payment made quarterly for any sales during previous quarter. Photographers allowed to review account records with written request submitted 2 months in advance. Offers one-time and electronic media rights. Gets photographer's approval when client requests all rights; negotiation conducted by the agency. Model release required. Photo captions required; include date and location.

HOW TO CONTACT E-mail request for current photo guidelines. Contact via e-mail to arrange digital submission. Submit link to web portfolio for review. Send query e-mail with résumé of credits, samples or list of stock photo subjects. Keeps samples on file; include SASE for return of material if sending by post. Expects minimum initial submission of 100 images. E-mail crucial for communicating current photo needs.

TIPS "Our primary market is science textbooks. Photographers should research the type of illustration used and tailor submissions to show awareness of saleable material. We are looking for science subjects ranging from nature and rocks to industrials, medicine, chemistry and physics; macro photography, photomicrography, stroboscopic; well-lit still-life shots are desirable. The biggest trend that affects us is the need for images that document new discoveries in sciences and ecology. Please avoid images that appear dated, images with heavy branding, soft focus or poorly lit subjects."

GEOSLIDES & GEO AERIAL PHOTOGRAPHY

4 Christian Fields, London SW16 3JZ, United Kingdom. +44(115)981-9418. E-mail: geoslides@geo-group.co.uk. Website: www.geo-group.co.uk. **Contact:** John Douglas, marketing director. Estab. 1968. Picture library. Has approximately 100,000 photos in files. Clients include: advertising agencies, public relations firms, audiovisual firms, businesses, book/encyclopedia publishers, magazine publishers, newspapers, calendar companies, television.

NEEDS Accent on travel/geography and aerial (oblique) shots. Wants photos of disasters, environmental, landscapes/scenics, wildlife, architecture, rural, adventure, travel, agriculture, industry, medicine, military, political, product shots/still life, science, technology/computers. Interested in documentary, historical/vintage.

SPECS High-res digital.

PAYMENT & TERMS Pays 50% commission for b&w or color photos. General price range (to clients) $75-750. Works with photographers with or without a contract; negotiable. Offers nonexclusive contract. Charges mailing costs. Statements issued monthly. Payment made upon receipt of client's fees. Offers one-time rights and first rights. Does not inform photographers or allow them to negotiate when clients request all rights. Model release required. Photo captions required; include description of location, subject matter and sometimes the date.

HOW TO CONTACT Send query letter or e-mail with résumé of credits, stock list; include SAE/IRC for return of material. Photo guidelines available for SAE/IRC. No samples until called for.

TIPS Looks for "technical perfection, detailed captions, must fit our needs, especially location needs. Increasingly competitive on an international scale. Quality is important. Needs large stocks with frequent renewals." To break in, "build up a comprehensive (i.e., in subject or geographical area) collection of photographs that are well documented."

GETTY IMAGES

601 N. 34th St., Seattle WA 98103. (206)925-5000. Website: www.gettyimages.com. "Getty Images is the world's leading imagery company, creating and distributing the largest and most relevant collection of still and moving images to communication professionals around the globe and supporting their work with asset management services. From news and sports photography to contemporary and archival imagery, Getty Images' products are found each day in newspapers, magazines, advertising, films, television, books and websites. Gettyimages.com is the first place customers turn to search, purchase, download and manage powerful imagery. Seattle-headquartered Getty Images is a global company with customers in more than 100 countries."

HOW TO CONTACT Visit www.gettyimages.com/contributors.

🌑 ✸ GRANATAIMAGES.COM

Milestone Media SRL, 95 Via Vallazze, Milan 20131, Italy. (39)(02)26680702. Fax: (39)(02)26681126. E-mail: paolo.granata@granataimages.com. Website: www.milestonemedia.it. Estab. 1985. Stock and press agency. Member of CEPIC. Has 2 million photos in files and 800,000 images online. Clients include: advertising agencies, newspapers, book publishers, calendar companies, audiovisual firms, magazine publishers, production houses.

NEEDS Photos of celebrities, people.

SPECS Uses high-res digital files. Send via ZIP, FTP, e-mail as TIFF, JPEG files.

PAYMENT & TERMS Pays 60% commission for color photos. Negotiates fees below stated minimums in cases of volume deals. Offers volume discounts to customers. Photographers can choose not to sell images on discount terms. Works with photographers on contract basis only. Offers exclusive contract only. Contracts renew automatically with additional submissions for 1 year. Statements issued monthly. Photographers allowed to review account records in cases of discrepancies only. Offers one-time rights. Model/property release preferred. Photo captions required; include location, country and any other relevant information.

HOW TO CONTACT Send query letter with digital files.

GRANT HEILMAN PHOTOGRAPHY, INC.

506 West Lincoln Ave., Lititz PA 17543. (717)626-0296 or (800)622-2046. Fax: (717)626-0971. E-mail: info@heilmanphoto.com. Website: www.heilmanphoto.com. Estab. 1948. Member of the Picture Archive Council of America (PACA). Has one million photos in files. Now representing Photo Network Stock. Sub agents in Canada, Europe, England, Japan. Clients include: advertising agencies, public relations firms, businesses, book/textbook publishers, magazine publishers, calendar companies, greeting card companies, postcard publishers.

NEEDS Photos of environmental, landscapes/scenics, wildlife, gardening, pets, rural, agriculture, science, renewable energies and resources, technology/computers. Interested in seasonal.

SPECS Uses 35mm, 2¼×2¼, 4×5 transparencies. Accepts images in digital format. Send via CD, floppy disk, Jaz, ZIP, as TIFF, EPS, PICT, JPEG files.

PAYMENT & TERMS Pays on commission basis. Enforces minimum prices. Offers volume discounts to customers. Works with photographers on contract basis only. Offers guaranteed subject exclusivity (within files). Contracts renew automatically with additional submissions per contract definition. Charges determined by contract. Statements issued quarterly. Payment made quarterly. Photographers allowed to review account records. Offers one-time rights, electronic media rights, agency promotion rights. Model/property release required. Photo captions required; include all known information.

HOW TO CONTACT Send query letter with résumé, slides, prints, photocopies, tearsheets, transparencies, stock list. Provide résumé, business card, self-promotion piece to be kept on file. Expects minimum initial submission of 200 images.

TIPS "Make a professional presentation."

🌑 HUTCHISON PICTURE LIBRARY

65 Brighton Rd., Shoreham-by-Sea, West Sussex BN43 6RE, United Kingdom. E-mail: library@hutchison pictures.co.uk. Website: www.hutchisonpictures.

co.uk. **Contact:** Stephen Rafferty, manager. Stock photo agency, picture library. Has around 500,000 photos in files. Clients include: ad agencies, public relations firms, audiovisual firms, businesses, book/encyclopedia publishers, magazine publishers, newspapers, postcard companies, calendar companies, television and film companies.

NEEDS "We are a general, documentary library (no news or personalities). We file mainly by country and aim to have coverage of every country in the world. Within each country we cover such subjects as industry, agriculture, people, customs, urban, landscapes, etc. We have special files on many subjects such as medical (traditional, alternative, hospital, etc.), energy, environmental issues, human relations (relationships, childbirth, young children, etc., but all real people, not models). We constantly require images of Spain and Spanish-speaking countries. Also interested in babies/children/teens, couples, multicultural, families, parents, senior citizens, disasters, architecture, education, gardening, interiors/decorating, religious, rural, health/fitness, travel, military, political, science, technology/computers. Interested in documentary, seasonal. We are a color library."

SPECS Uses 35mm transparencies. Accepts images in digital format: 50MB at 300 dpi, cleaned of dust and scratches at 100%, color corrected.

PAYMENT & TERMS Pays 40% commission for exclusive; 35% for nonexclusive. Statements issued semiannually. Payment made semiannually. Sends statement with check in June and January. Offers one-time rights. Model release preferred. Photo captions required.

HOW TO CONTACT Always willing to look at new material or collections. Arrange a personal interview to show portfolio. Send letter with brief description of collection and photographic intentions. Responds in about 2 weeks, depends on backlog of material to be reviewed. "We have letters outlining working practices and lists of particular needs (they change)." Distributes tips sheets to photographers who already have a relationship with the library.

TIPS Looks for "collections of reasonable size (rarely less than 1,000 transparencies) and variety; well captioned (or at least well indicated picture subjects; captions can be added to mounts later); sharp pictures, good color, composition; and informative pictures. Prettiness is rarely enough. Our clients want information, whether it is about what a landscape looks like or how people live, etc. The general rule of thumb is that we would consider a collection which has a subject we do not already have coverage of or a detailed and thorough specialist collection. Please do not send *any* photographs without prior agreement."

ICP DI ALESSANDRO MAROSA

Via Bressanone 8/2, Milano 20151, Italy. Milan: +390289954751; Rome: +3906452217748; Torino: +3901123413919; UK: +44 2078553279. Fax: +390248195625; UK: +3902700567952. E-mail: icp@icponline.it. Website: www.icponline.it. **Contact:** Mr. Alessandro Marosa, CEO. Estab. 1970. Stock photo agency. Clients include: advertising agencies, public relations firms, audiovisual firms, businesses, book/encyclopedia publishers, magazine publishers, postcard publishers, calendar companies and greeting card companies.

SPECS High-res digital (A3-A4, 300 dpi), keyworded (English and, if possible, Italian).

PAYMENT & TERMS Pays 50% commission for color photos. Offers volume discounts to customers; terms specified in photographer's contract. Discount sales terms not negotiable. Contracts renew automatically with additional submissions, for 3 years. Statements issued monthly. Payment made monthly. Photographers permitted to review account records to verify sales figures or deductions. Offers one-time, first and sectorial exclusive rights. Model/property release required. Photo captions required.

HOW TO CONTACT Arrange a personal interview to show portfolio. Send query letter with samples and stock list. Works on assignment only. No fixed minimum for initial submission. Responds in 3 weeks, if interested.

THE IMAGE FINDERS

2570 Superior Ave., Suite 200, Cleveland OH 44114. (216)781-7729 or (440)413-6104. E-mail: imagefinders@sbcglobal.net. Website: agpix.com/theimagefinders. **Contact:** Jim Baron, owner. Estab. 1988. Stock photo agency. Has 500,000+ photos in files. Clients include: advertising agencies, public relations firms, businesses, book/encyclopedia publishers, magazine publishers, calendar companies, greeting card companies.

NEEDS General stock agency. Always interested in good Ohio images. Also needs babies/children/teens, couples, multicultural, families, senior citizens, landscapes/scenics, wildlife, architecture, gardening, pets, automobiles, food/drink, sports, travel, agriculture, business concepts, industry, medicine, political, technology/computers. Interested in fashion/glamour, fine art, seasonal.

SPECS Accepts only digital images; see guidelines before submitting. Send via CD.

PAYMENT & TERMS "This is a small agency and we will, on occasion, go below stated minimum prices." Offers volume discounts to customers; terms specified in photographers' contracts. Works with photographers on contract basis only. Contracts renew automatically with additional submissions for 2 years. Statements issued monthly if requested. Payment made monthly. Photographers allowed to review account records. Offers one-time rights; negotiable depending on what the client needs and will pay for. Informs photographers and allows them to negotiate when client requests all rights. "This is rare for us. I would inform photographer of what the client wants and work with photographer to strike the best deal." Model/property release preferred. Photo captions required; include location, city, state, country, type of plant or animal, etc.

HOW TO CONTACT Send query letter with stock list or send e-mail with link to your website. Call before you send anything that you want returned. Expects minimum initial submission of 100 images with periodic submission of at least 100-500 images. Photo guidelines free with SASE. Market tips sheet distributed 2-4 times/year to photographers under contract.

TIPS Photographers must be willing to build their file of images. "We need more people images, industry, lifestyles, wildlife, travel, etc. Scenics and landscapes must be outstanding to be considered. Please call or e-mail before submitting anything. We are taking on very few new photographers and only after we have reviewed their work."

IMAGES.DE FULFILLMENT

Potsdamer Str. 96D, Berlin 10785, Germany. +49(0)30-2579 28980. Fax: +49(0)30-2579 28999. E-mail: info@images.de. Website: www.images.de. Estab. 1997. News/feature syndicate. Has 50,000 photos in files. Clients include: advertising agencies, newspapers, public relations firms, book publishers, magazine publishers. "We are a service company with 10 years experience on the picture market. We offer fulfillment services to picture agencies, including translation, distribution into Fotofiner and APIS picturemaxx, customer communication, invoicing, media control, cash delivery, and usage control."

NEEDS Photos of babies/children/teens, couples, multicultural, families, parents, senior citizens, environment, entertainment, events, food/drink, health/fitness, hobbies, travel, agriculture, business concepts, industry, medicine, political, science, technology/computers.

SPECS Accepts images in digital format. Send via FTP, CD.

PAYMENT & TERMS Pays 50% commission for b&w photos; 50% for color photos. Average price per image (to clients): $50-1,000 for b&w photos or color photos. Offers volume discounts to customers. Discount sales terms not negotiable. Works with photographers with or without a contract; negotiable. Offers limited regional exclusivity. Statements issued monthly. Payment made monthly. Photographers allowed to review account records in cases of discrepancies only. Offers one-time rights, electronic media rights. Informs photographers and allows them to negotiate when client requests all rights. Model release preferred; property release required. Photo captions required.

HOW TO CONTACT Send query letter with CD or link to website. Expects minimum initial submission of 100 images.

THE IMAGE WORKS

P.O. Box 443, Woodstock NY 12498. (845)679-8500 or (800)475-8801. Fax: (845)679-0606. E-mail: info@theimageworks.com. Website: www.theimageworks.com. **Contact:** Mark Antman, president. Estab. 1983. Stock photo agency. Member of Picture Archive Council of America (PACA). Has over 1 million photos in files. Clients include: ad agencies, book/encyclopedia publishers, magazine publishers, newspapers, postcard publishers, greeting card companies, documentary video.

NEEDS "We are always looking for excellent documentary photography. Our prime subjects are people-related subjects like family, education, health care, workplace issues, worldwide historical, technology, fine arts."

SPECS All images must be in digital format; contact for digital guidelines. Rarely accepts 35mm, 2¼×2¼ transparencies and prints.

PAYMENT & TERMS Works with photographers on contract basis only. Offers nonexclusive contract. Statements issued monthly. Payments made monthly. Photographers allowed to review account records to verify sales figures by appointment. Offers one-time, agency promotion and electronic media rights. Informs photographers and allows them to negotiate when clients request all rights. Model release preferred. Photo captions required.

HOW TO CONTACT Send e-mail with description of stock photo archives. Expects minimum initial submission of 500 images.

TIPS "The Image Works was one of the first agencies to market images digitally. All digital images from photographers must be of reproduction quality. When making a new submission to us, be sure to include a variety of images that show your range as a photographer. We also want to see some depth in specialized subject areas. Thorough captions are a must. We will not look at uncaptioned images. Write or call first."

INMAGINE

2650 Fountain View Dr; Suite 332, Houston TX 77057. (800)810-3888. Fax: (866)234-5310. E-mail: photo@inmagine.com. Website: www.inmagine.com. **Contact:** Esther Tea, head of business development, international. Estab. 2000. Stock agency, picture library. Member of the Picture Archive Council of America (PACA). Has 6,000,000 photos in files. Branch offices in USA, Hong Kong, Australia, Malaysia, Thailand, United Arab Emirates, Singapore, Indonesia, and China. Clients include: advertising agencies, businesses, newspapers, public relations firms, magazine publishers.

NEEDS Photos of babies, children, teens, couples, multicultural, families, parents, education, business concepts, industry, medicine, environmental and landscapes, adventure, entertainment, events, food and drink, health, fitness, beauty, hobbies, sports, travel, fashion/glamour, and lifestyle.

SPECS Accepts images in digital format. Submit online via submission.inmagine.com or send JPEG files at 300 dpi.

PAYMENT & TERMS Pays 50% commission for color photos. Average price per image (to clients): $100 minimum, maximum negotiable. Negotiates fees below stated minimums. Offers volume discounts to customers, terms specified in photographers' contracts. Works with photographers on a contract basis only. Offers nonexclusive contract. Payments made monthly. Photographers are allowed to view account records in cases of discrepancies only. Offers one-time rights. Model and property release required. Photo caption required.

HOW TO CONTACT Contact through website. Expects minimum initial submission of 5 images. Responds in 1 week to samples. Photo guidelines available online.

TIPS "Complete the steps as outlined in the IRIS submission pages. E-mail us if there are queries. Send only the best of your portfolio for submission, stock-oriented materials only. EXIF should reside in file with keywords and captions."

INTERNATIONAL PHOTO NEWS

2902 29th Way, West Palm Beach FL 33407. (561)683-9090. E-mail: jkravetz1@earthlink.net. **Contact:** Jay Kravetz, photo editor. News/feature syndicate. Has 50,000 photos in files. Clients include: newspapers, magazines, book publishers. Previous/current clients include: newspapers that need celebrity photos with story.

NEEDS Photos of celebrities, entertainment, events, health/fitness/beauty, performing arts, travel, politics, movies, music and television, at work or play. Interested in avant garde, fashion/glamour.

SPECS Accepts images in digital format. Send via CD, ZIP, e-mail as TIFF, JPEG files at 300 dpi. Uses 5×7, 8×10 glossy b&w prints.

PAYMENT & TERMS Pays $10 for b&w photos; $25 for color photos; 5-10% commission. Average price per image (to clients): $25-100 for b&w photos; $50-500 for color photos. Works with photographers on contract basis only. Offers nonexclusive contract. Contracts renew automatically with additional submissions; 1-year renewal. Photographers allowed to review account records. Statements issued monthly. Payment made monthly. Offers one-time rights. Model/property release preferred. Photo captions required.

HOW TO CONTACT Send query letter with résumé of credits. Solicits photos by assignment only. Responds in 1 week.

TIPS "We use celebrity photographs to coincide with our syndicated columns. Must be approved by the celebrity."

THE IRISH IMAGE COLLECTION

#101, 10464 - 176 St., Edmonton AB , Canada. 780-447-5433. E-mail: kristi@theirishimagecollection.com. Website: www.theirishimagecollection.ie. **Contact:** Kristi Bennell, office manager. Stock photo agency and picture library. Has 50,000+ photos in files. Clients include: advertising agencies, public relations firms, businesses, book/encyclopedia publishers, magazine publishers, newspapers and designers.

NEEDS Consideration is given only to Irish or Irish-connected subjects.

SPECS Uses 35mm and all medium-format transparencies.

PAYMENT & TERMS Pays 40% commission for color photos. Average price per image (to client): $85-2,000. Works on contract basis only. Offers exclusive contracts and limited regional exclusivity. Contracts renew automatically with additional submissions. Statements issued quarterly. Payment made quarterly. Photographers allowed to review account records. Offers one-time and electronic media rights. Informs photographer when client requests all rights, but "we take care of negotiations." Model release required. Photo captions required.

HOW TO CONTACT Send query letter with list of stock photo subjects. Does not return unsolicited material. Expects minimum initial submission of 250 transparencies; 1,000 images annually. "A return shipping fee is required: important that all similars are submitted together. We keep our contributor numbers down and the quantity and quality of submissions high. Send for information first by e-mail."

TIPS "Our market is Ireland and the rest of the world. However, our continued sales of Irish-oriented pictures need to be kept supplied. Pictures of Irish-Americans in Irish bars, folk singing, Irish dancing, in Ireland or anywhere else would prove to be useful. They would be required to be beautifully lit, carefully composed with attractive, model-released people."

THE IRISH PICTURE LIBRARY

69b Heather Rd., Sandyford Industrial Estate, Dublin 18, Ireland. (353)1 295 0799. Fax: (353)1295 0705. E-mail: ipl@fatherbrowne.com. Website: www.fatherbrowne.com/ipl. Estab. 1990. Picture library. Has 60,000+ photos in files. Clients include: advertising agencies, businesses, book publishers, magazine publishers, newspapers, calendar companies.

NEEDS Photos of historic Irish material. Interested in alternative process, fine art, historical/vintage.

SPECS Uses any prints. Accepts images in digital format. Send via CD as TIFF, JPEG files at 400 dpi.

PAYMENT & TERMS Enforces minimum prices. Offers volume discounts to customers. Photographers can choose not to sell images on discount terms. Works with photographers on contract basis only. Statements issued quarterly. Payment made quarterly. Photographers allowed to review account records. Offers one-time rights, electronic media rights. Property release required. Photo captions required.

HOW TO CONTACT Send query letter with photocopies. Does not keep samples on file; include SAE/IRC for return of material.

ISOPIX

Werkhuizenstraat 7-9 Rue des Ateliers, Brussel-Bruxelles 1080, Belgium. +32 2 420 30 50. Fax: 32 2 420 41 22. E-mail: isopix@isopix.be. Website: www.isopix.be. Estab. 1984. News/feature syndicate. Has 2.5 million photos on website, including press (celebrities, royalty, portraits, news sports, archival), stock (contemporary and creative photography) and royalty-free. Clients include: advertising agencies, public relations firms, businesses, book publishers, magazine publishers, newspapers, calendar companies, postcard publishers.

NEEDS Photos of teens, celebrities, couples, families, parents, senior citizens, disasters, environmental, landscapes/scenics, wildlife, education, religious, events, food/drink, health/fitness, hobbies, humor, agriculture, business concepts, industry, medicine, science, technology/computers. Interested in alternative process, avant garde, documentary, fashion/glamour, fine art, historical/vintage, seasonal.

SPECS Accepts images in digital format; JPEG files only.

PAYMENT & TERMS Enforces strict minimum prices. Works with photographers with or without a contract; negotiable. Offers limited regional exclusivity. Contracts renew automatically with additional submissions. Statements issued monthly. Payment made monthly. Photographers allowed to review account records in cases of discrepancies only. Model/property release preferred. Photo captions required.

HOW TO CONTACT Contact through rep. Does not keep samples on file; include SAE/IRC for return of material. Expects minimum initial submission of 1,000 images with quarterly submissions of at least 500 images.

ISRAELIMAGES.COM

POB 60, Kammon 20112, Israel. (972)(4)908-2023. Fax: (972)(4)990-5783. E-mail: israel@israelimages.com. Website: www.israelimages.com. **Contact:** Israel Talby, managing director. Estab. 1991. Has 650,000 photos in files. Clients include: advertising agencies, web designers, businesses, book publishers, magazine publishers, newspapers, calendar companies, greeting card and postcard publishers, multimedia producers, schools and universities, etc.

NEEDS "We are interested in everything about Israel, Judaism (worldwide) and The Holy Land."

SPECS Uses digital material only, minimum accepted size 2000×3000 pixels. Simply upload your pictures directly to the site. "When accepted, we need TIFF or JPEG files at 300 dpi, RGB, saved at quality '11' in Photoshop."

PAYMENT & TERMS Average price per image (to clients): $50-3,000/picture. Negotiates fees below standard minimum against considerable volume that justifies it. Offers volume discounts to customers. Works with photographers on contract basis only. Offers limited regional exclusivity, nonexclusive contract. Contracts renew automatically with additional submissions. Sales reports are displayed on the site at the Contributor's personal account. Payments are constantly made. Photographers allowed to review account records. Offers one-time rights, electronic media rights, agency promotion rights. Informs photographers and allows them to negotiate when a client requests all rights. Model/property release preferred. Photo captions required (what, who, when, where).

HOW TO CONTACT E-mail any query to: Israel@israelimages.com. No minimum submission. Responds within 1-2 days.

TIPS "We strongly encourage everyone to send us images to review. When sending material, a strong edit is a must. We don't like to get 100 pictures with 50 similars. Last, don't overload our e-mail with submissions. Make an e-mail query, or better yet, view our submission guidelines on the website. Good luck and welcome!"

JAYAWARDENE TRAVEL PHOTO LIBRARY

7A Napier Rd., Wembley, Middlesex HA0 4UA, United Kingdom. (44)(208)795-3581. Fax: (44)(202)975-4083. E-mail: jaytravelphotos@aol.com. Website: www.jaytravelphotos.com. **Contact:** Rohith or Franco, partners. Estab. 1992. Stock photo agency and picture library. Has 250,000 photos in files. Clients include: advertising agencies, businesses, book/encyclopedia publishers, magazine publishers, newspapers, postcard publishers, tour operators/travel companies.

NEEDS Travel and tourism-related images worldwide.

SPECS Accepts digital, minimum 12 megapixel SLR (see website for guidelines). Uses 35mm up to 6×7cm original transparencies.

PAYMENT & TERMS Pays 60% commission for digital images and 50% for transparencies. Average price per image (to clients): $125-1,000. Enforces minimum prices of $125, "but negotiable on quantity purchases." Offers volume discounts to customers; inquire about specific terms. Discount sales terms not negotiable. Works with photographers on contract basis only. Offers limited regional exclusivity contract. Statements issued quarterly. Payment made quarterly, within 30 days of payment received from client. Offers one-time and exclusive rights for fixed periods. Does not inform photographers or allow them to negotiate when client requests all rights. Model/property release preferred. Photo captions required; include country, city/location, subject description.

HOW TO CONTACT Send e-mail with stock list, or call. Expects a minimum initial submission of 300 images with quarterly submissions of at least 100 images. Responds in 3 weeks.

TIPS "Study our guidelines on our website on what to submit. If you're planning a photo shoot anywhere, you need to give us an itinerary, with as much detail as possible, so we can brief you on what kind of pictures the library may need."

JEROBOAM

120 27th St., San Francisco CA 94110. (415)312-0198. E-mail: jeroboamster@gmail.com. **Contact:** Ellen Bunning, owner. Estab. 1972. Has 200,000 b&w photos, 200,000 color slides in files. Clients include: text and trade book, magazine and encyclopedia publishers, editorial (mostly textbooks), greeting cards, and calendars.

NEEDS "We want people interacting, relating photos, comic, artistic/documentary/photojournalistic images, especially ethnic and handicapped. Images must have excellent print quality—contextually interesting and exciting and artistically stimulating." Photos of babies/children/teens, couples, multicultural, families, parents, senior citizens, disasters, environmental, cities/urban, education, gardening, pets, religious, rural, adventure, health/fitness, humor, performing arts, sports, travel, agriculture, industry, medicine, military, political, science, technology/computers. Interested in documentary, historical/vintage, seasonal. Needs shots of school, family, career and other living situations. Child development, growth and therapy, medical situations. No nature or studio shots.
SPECS Uses 35mm transparencies.
PAYMENT & TERMS Works on consignment only; pays 50% commission. Average price per image (to clients): $150 minimum for b&w and color photos. Works with photographers without a signed contract. Statements issued monthly. Payment made monthly. Photographers allowed to review account records to verify sales figures. Offers one-time and electronic media rights. Informs photographers and allows them to negotiate when client requests all rights. Model/property release preferred for people in contexts of special education, sexuality, etc. Photo captions preferred; include "age of subject, location, etc."
HOW TO CONTACT "Call if in the Bay Area; if not, query with samples and list of stock photo subjects; send material by mail for consideration or submit portfolio for review. Let us know how long you've been shooting." Responds in 2 weeks.
TIPS "The Jeroboam photographers have shot professionally a minimum of 5 years, have experienced some success in marketing their talent, and care about their craft excellence and their own creative vision. New trends are toward more intimate, action shots; more ethnic images needed."

✳ JOAN KRAMER AND ASSOCIATES, INC.
10490 Wilshire Blvd., Suite 1701, Los Angeles CA 90024. (310)446-1866. Fax: (310)446-1856. E-mail: ekeeeek@earthlink.net. Website: www.erwinkramer.com. Joan Kramer, president. **Contact:** Erwin Kramer. Member of Picture Archive Council of America (PACA). Has 1 million photos in files. Clients include: ad agencies, magazines, recording companies, photo researchers, book publishers, greeting card companies, promotional companies, AV producers.
NEEDS "We use any and all subjects! Stock slides must be of professional quality." Subjects on file include travel, cities, personalities, animals, flowers, lifestyles, underwater, scenics, sports and couples.
SPECS Uses 8×10 glossy b&w prints; any size transparencies.
PAYMENT & TERMS Pays 50% commission. Offers all rights. Model release required.
HOW TO CONTACT Send query letter or call to arrange an appointment. Do not send photos before calling.

KIMBALL STOCK
1960 Colony St., Mountain View CA 94043. (650)969-0682. Fax: (650)969-0485; (888)562-5522. E-mail: submissions@kimballstock.com. Website: www.kimballstock.com. Estab. 1970. Has 1 million photos in files. Clients include: advertising agencies, businesses, newspapers, postcard publishers, public relations firms, book publishers, calendar companies, magazine publishers, greeting card companies. "Kimball Stock strives to provide automotive and animal photographers with the best medium possible to sell their images. In addition, we work to give every photographer a safe, reliable, and pleasant experience."
NEEDS Photos of dogs, cats, lifestyle with cars and domestic animals, landscapes/scenics, wildlife (outside of North America). Interested in seasonal.
SPECS Prefers images in digital format, minimum of 12-megapixel digital camera, although 16-megapixel is preferred. Send via e-mail as JPEG files or send CD to mailing address. Uses 35mm, 120mm, 4×5 transparencies.
PAYMENT & TERMS Pays 50% commission for color photos. Works with photographers with a contract; negotiable. Offers nonexclusive contract. Statements issued quarterly. Payments made quarterly. Photographers allowed to review account records. Offers one-time rights, electronic media rights. Model/property release required. Photo captions required.
HOW TO CONTACT Send query letter with transparencies, digital files, stock list. Provide self-promotion piece to be kept on file. Expects minimum initial submission of 250 images with quarterly submissions of at least 200 images. Responds only if interested; send nonreturnable samples. Photo guidelines available online at www.kimballstock.com/submissions.asp.

LAND OF THE BIBLE PHOTO ARCHIVE

P.O. Box 8441, Jerusalem 91084, Israel. (972)(2)566-2167. Fax: (972)(2)566-3451. E-mail: radovan@net vision.net.il. Website: www.biblelandpictures.com. **Contact:** Zev Radovan. Estab. 1975. Picture library. Has 50,000 photos in files. Clients include: book publishers, magazine publishers, newspapers, calendar companies, postcard publishers.

NEEDS Photos of museum objects, archaeological sites. Also multicultural, landscapes/scenics, architecture, religious, travel. Interested in documentary, fine art, historical/vintage.

SPECS Uses high-res digital system.

PAYMENT & TERMS Average price per image (to clients): $80-700 for b&w, color photos. Offers volume discounts to customers; terms specified in photographers' contracts.

TIPS "Our archives contain tens of thousands of color slides covering a wide range of subjects: historical and archaeological sites, aerial and close-up views, museum objects, mosaics, coins, inscriptions, the myriad ethnic and religious groups individually portrayed in their daily activities, colorful ceremonies, etc. Upon request, we accept assignments for in-field photography."

LATITUDE STOCK

14 High St., Goring-on-Thames, Reading Berks RG8 9AR, United Kingdom. (44)(1491)873011. Fax: (44)(1491)875558. E-mail: info@latitudestock.com. Website: www.latitudestock.com. Has over 115,000 photos in files. Clients include: advertising agencies, businesses, newspapers, public relations firms, book publishers, calendar companies, audiovisual firms, magazine publishers, greeting card companies.

NEEDS Photos of multicultural, environmental, landscapes/scenics, wildlife, architecture, cities/urban, gardening, religious, rural, adventure, events, food/drink, health/fitness/beauty, hobbies, sports, travel.

SPECS Uses 35mm and medium-format transparencies. Accepts images in digital format. See website for details.

PAYMENT & TERMS Pays on a commission basis. Enforces minimum prices. Offers volume discounts to customers. Works with photographers on contract basis only. Offers exclusive contract only. Statements issued quarterly. Payment made quarterly. Photographers allowed to review account records. Offers one-

time rights. Model/property release required. Photo captions required.

HOW TO CONTACT "Please e-mail first."

LIGHTWAVE PHOTOGRAPHY

170 Lowell St., Arlington MA 02174. (781)354-7747. E-mail: paul@lightwavephoto.com. Website: www.lightwavephoto.com. **Contact:** Paul Light. Has 250,000 photos in files. Clients include: advertising agencies, textbook publishers.

NEEDS Candid photos of people in school, work and leisure activities, lifestyle.

SPECS Uses digital photographs.

PAYMENT & TERMS Pays $210/photo; 50% commission. Works with photographers on contract basis only. Offers nonexclusive contract. Contracts renew automatically each year. Statements issued annually. Payments made "after each usage." Offers one-time rights. Informs photographers and allows them to negotiate when client requests all rights. Model/property release preferred. Photo captions preferred.

HOW TO CONTACT "Create a small website and send us the URL."

TIPS "Photographers should enjoy photographing people in everyday activities. Work should be carefully edited before submission. Shoot constantly and watch what is being published. We are looking for photographers who can photograph daily life with compassion and originality."

LINEAIR FOTOARCHIEF

van der Helllaan 6, Arnhem 6824 HT, Netherlands. (31)(26)4456713. E-mail: info@lineairfoto.nl. Website: www.lineairfoto.nl. **Contact:** Ron Giling, manager. Estab. 1990. Stock photo agency and since 2001 also an image-research department as service to publishers and other customers. Has more than 1.6 million downloadable images available through the website. Clients include advertising agencies, public relations firms, book/encyclopedia publishers, magazine publishers. Library specializes in images from Asia, Africa, Latin America, Eastern Europe and nature in all forms on all continents. Member of WEA, a group of international libraries that use the same server to market each other's images, uploading only once.

NEEDS Photos of disasters, environment, landscapes/scenics, wildlife, cities/urban, education, religious, adventure, travel, agriculture, business concepts, industry, political, science, technology/computers, health, education. Interested in everything that has to do with the development of countries all over the world, especially in Asia, Africa and Latin America.

SPECS Accepts images in digital format only. Send via CD, DVD (or use our FTP) as high-quality JPEG files at 300 dpi. "Photo files need to have IPTC information!"

PAYMENT & TERMS Pays 50% commission. Average price per image (to clients): $100-500. Enforces minimum prices. Offers volume discounts to customers; inquire about specific terms. Photographers can choose not to sell images on discount terms. Works with or without a signed contract; negotiable. Offers limited regional exclusivity. Statements issued quarterly. Payments made quarterly. Photographers allowed to review account records. "They can review bills to clients involved." Offers one-time rights. Informs photographers and allows them to negotiate when client requests all rights. Photo captions required; include country, city or region, description of the image.

HOW TO CONTACT Submit portfolio or e-mail thumbnails (20KB files) for review. There is no minimum for initial submissions. Responds in 3 weeks. Market tips sheet available upon request. View website to seesubject matter and quality.

TIPS "We like to see high-quality pictures in all aspects of photography. So we'd rather see 50 good ones than 500 for us to select the 50 out of. Send contact sheets upon our request. We will mark the selected pictures for you to send as high-res, including the very important IPTC (caption and keywords)."

LONELY PLANET IMAGES

150 Linden St., Oakland CA 94607. (510)893-8555 or (800)275-8555. Fax: (510)625-0306. E-mail: lpi@lonelyplanet.com. Website: www.lonelyplanetimages.com. International stock photo agency with offices in Oakland, London and Footscray (outside Melbourne). Clients include: advertising agencies, public relations firms, book/encyclopedia publishers, magazine publishers, newspapers, calendar companies, greeting card companies, design firms.

NEEDS Photos of international travel destinations.

SPECS Uses original color transparencies in all formats; digital images from 6-megapixel and higher DSLRs.

PAYMENT & TERMS Pays 40-50% commission. Works with photographers on contract basis only. Offers image exclusive contract. Contract renews automatically. Model/property release preferred. Photo captions required.

HOW TO CONTACT Download submission guidelines from website—click on Photographers tab, then click on Prospective Photographers.

TIPS "Photographers must be technically proficient, productive, and show interest and involvement in their work."

LONE PINE PHOTO

22 Robinson Crescent, Saskatoon S7L 6N9, Canada. (306)683-0889. Fax: (306)384-5811. E-mail: lone pinephoto@shaw.ca. Website: www.lonepinephoto.ca. **Contact:** Clarence W. Norris. Estab. 1991. Lone Pine Photo is a photo stock agency specializing in well-edited images of Canada. Our library consists of: 60,000+ 35mm slides, 20,000+ digital images. All images are rights managed. A licensing fee is required for the use of all of our images. All images provided are copyrighted to the photographers that we represent. We have updated our website on which clients may browse through a variety of galleries. Each gallery bears a gallery description summarizing the contents and useful search tips. Full caption information is displayed. Click on a thumbnail for larger image and more image info. Keywords allow clients to refine their searches.

SPECS "We are seeking stock photographers who have the following attributes: Excellent technical and creative skills to produce top-quality images based on our submission guidelines, subject want lists and on their specific photographic interests and travels. The ability to carefully edit their own work and to send us only the very best with detailed captions. An existing image file to provide us with 500+ images to start. The time and resources to photograph regularly and to submit 500+ images annually for our review. The ability to work together as part of a team to develop a top-quality Canadian stock photo agency." All rights managed. Credit line.

LUCKYPIX

1658 N. Milwaukee, #324, Chicago IL 60647. (773)235-2000. Fax: (773)235-2030. E-mail: info@luckypix.com. Website: www.luckypix.com. **Contact:** Director of photography. Estab. 2001. Stock agency. Has 9,000 photos in files (adding constantly). Clients include: advertising agencies, businesses, book publishers, design companies, magazine publishers.

NEEDS Outstanding people/lifestyle images.

SPECS 50+MB TIFFs, 300 dpi, 8-bit files. Photos for review: upload to website or e-mail info@luckypix.com. Final: CD/DVD as TIFF files.

PAYMENT & TERMS 50% commission for net revenues. Enforces minimum prices. Offers exclusivity by image and similars. Contracts renew automatically annually. Statements and payments issued quarterly. Model/property release required.

HOW TO CONTACT Call or upload sample from website (preferred). Responds in 1 week. See website for guidelines.

TIPS "Have fun shooting. Search the archives before deciding what pictures to send."

☉ ⊜ ⊕ MASTERFILE

3 Concorde Gate, 4th Floor, Toronto ON M3C 3N7, Canada. (800)387-9010. E-mail: portfolio@masterfile.com. Website: www.masterfile.com. General stock agency offering rights-managed and royalty-free images. The combined collection exceeds 2.5 million images online. Clients include: major advertising agencies, broadcasters, graphic designers, public relations firms, book and magazine publishers, producers of greeting cards, calendars and packaging.

SPECS Accepts images in digital format only, in accordance with submission guidelines.

PAYMENT & TERMS Pays photographers 40% royalties of amounts received by Masterfile. Contributor terms outlined in photographer's contract, which is image-exclusive. Photographer sales statements and royalty payments issued monthly.

HOW TO CONTACT Refer to www.masterfile.com/info/artists/submissions.html for submission guidelines.

TIPS "Do not send transparencies or prints as a first-time submission. We also prefer not receiving discs. In order to view new work as efficiently as possible, we can only handle images submitted digitally, as follows: Submission methods: You can show us a sample in two ways: If you have a website, or are listed in a web-based visual directory, please send us your URL. You may e-mail us 20-30 of your best images following these guidelines: Images must be in RGB JPEG format. The overall file size of your e-mail cannot exceed 4MB. (Messages exceeding this size will be rejected

by our mail server). If we like what we see, you will be contacted by Artist Recruitment to submit additional work, and high resolution files for a technical review. Please note: we require images to be taken with a minimum 12 megapixel camera. Due to the large volume of submissions, we will contact only those artists we are interested in."

⊛ MICHELE MATTEI PHOTOGRAPHY

1714 Wilton Place, Los Angeles CA 90028. (323)462-6342. Fax: (323)462-7568. E-mail: michele@michelemattei.com. Website: http://michelemattei.net. **Contact:** Michele Mattei, director. Estab. 1974. Stock photo agency. Clients include: book/encyclopedia publishers, magazine publishers, television, film.

TIPS "Shots of celebrities and home/family stories are frequently requested." In samples, looking for "high-quality, recognizable personalities and current newsmaking material. We are interested mostly in celebrity photography. Written material on personality or event helps us to distribute material faster and more efficiently."

☉ ⊛ MAXX IMAGES, INC.

1433 Rupert St., Suite 3A, North Vancouver BC V7J 1G1, Canada. (604)985-2560. Fax: (604)985-2590. E-mail: newsubmissions@maxximages.com; info@maxximages.com. Website: www.maxximages.com. **Contact:** Dave Maquignaz, president. Estab. 1994. Stock agency. Member of the Picture Archive Council of America (PACA). Has 3.2 million images online. Has 350 hours of video footage. Clients include: advertising agencies, public relation firms, audiovisual firms, businesses, book publishers, magazine publishers, newspapers, calendar companies, postcard publishers, video production, graphic design studios.

NEEDS Photos of people, lifestyle, business, recreation, leisure.

SPECS Uses all formats.

HOW TO CONTACT Send e-mail. Review submission guidelines on website prior to contact.

THE MEDICAL FILE INC.

279 E. 44th St., 21st Floor, New York NY 10017. (212)883-0820 or (917)215-6301. E-mail: themedicalfile@gmail.com. Website: www.peterarnold.com. **Contact:** Barbara Gottlieb, president. Estab. 2005. Clients include: advertising agencies, public relations firms, businesses, book/encyclopedia publishers,

magazine publishers, postcard companies, calendar companies, greeting card companies.

NEEDS Photos of any medically related imagery including fitness and food in relation to health care.

SPECS Accepts digital format images only on CD or DVD. Images can be downloaded to FTP site.

PAYMENT & TERMS Average price per image (for clients): $250 and up. Works on exclusive and nonexclusive contract basis. Contracts renew automatically with each submission for length of original contract. Payments made quarterly. Offers one-time rights. Informs photographers when clients request all rights or exclusivity. Model release required. Photo captions required.

HOW TO CONTACT Arrange a personal interview to show portfolio. Submit portfolio for review. Tips sheet distributed as needed to contract photographers only.

TIPS Wants to see a cross-section of images for style and subject. "Photographers should not photograph people *before* getting a model release. The day of the 'grab shot' is over."

MEDISCAN

2nd Floor Patman House, 23-27 Electric Parade, George Lane South Woodford, London E18 2LS, United Kingdom. +44(0)20 8530 7589. Fax: +44(0)20 8989 7795. E-mail: info@mediscan.co.uk. Website: www.mediscan.co.uk. Estab. 2001. Picture library. Has over 1 million photos and over 2,000 hours of film/video footage on file. Subject matter includes medical personnel and environment, diseases and medical conditions, surgical procedures, microscopic, scientific, ultrasound/CT/MRI scans and x-rays. Online catalog on website. Clients include: advertising and design agencies, business-to-business, newspapers, public relations, book and magazine publishers in the health care, medical and science arenas.

NEEDS Photos of babies/children/teens/senior citizens; health/lifestyle/fitness/beauty; medicine, especially plastic surgery, rare medical conditions; model-released images; science, including microscopic imagery, botanical and natural history.

SPECS Accepts negatives; 35mm and medium format transparencies; digital images (make contact before submitting samples).

PAYMENT & TERMS Pays up to 50% commission. Statements issued quarterly. Payment made quarterly. Model/property release required, where necessary.

HOW TO CONTACT E-mail or call.

MEGAPRESS IMAGES

1751 Richardson, Suite 2205, Montreal QC H3K 1G6, Canada. (514)279-9859. Fax: (514)279-9859. E-mail: info@megapress.ca. Website: www.megapress.ca. Estab. 1992. Stock photo agency. Has 500,000 photos in files. Has 2 branch offices. Clients include: book/encyclopedia publishers, magazine publishers, postcard publishers, calendar companies, greeting card companies, advertising agencies.

NEEDS Photos of people (babies/children/teens; couples, people at work, medical); animals including puppies in studio; industries; celebrities and general stock. Also needs families, parents, senior citizens, disasters, environmental, landscapes/scenics, wildlife, gardening, pets, religious, adventure, automobile, food/drink, health/fitness/beauty, sports, travel, business concepts, still life, science. "Looking only for the latest trends in photography and very high-quality images. A part of our market is Quebec's local French market."

SPECS Accepts images in digital format only. Send via CD, floppy disk, ZIP as JPEG files at 300 dpi.

PAYMENT & TERMS Pays 50% commission for color photos. Average price per image (to client): $100. Enforces minimum prices. Will not negotiate below $60. Works with photographers with or without a contract. Statements issued semiannually. Payments made semiannually. Offers one-time rights. Model release required for people and controversial news.

HOW TO CONTACT Submit link first by e-mail. "If interested, we'll get back to you." Does not keep samples on file; include SAE/IRC for return of material. Expects minimum initial submission of 250 images with periodic submission of at least 1,000 digital pictures per year. Make first contact by e-mail. Accepts digital submissions only.

TIPS "Pictures must be very sharp. Work must be consistent. We also like photographers who are specialized in particular subjects. We are always interested in Canadian content. Lots of our clients are based in Canada."

MPTV (MOTION PICTURE AND TELEVISION PHOTO ARCHIVE)

16735 Saticoy St., Suite 109, Van Nuys CA 91406. (818)997-8292. Fax: (818)997-3998. E-mail: sales@mptvimages.com. Website: www.mptvimages.com. Estab. 1988. "Established over 20 years ago, mptv is a unique stock photo agency that is passionate about preserving the memory of some of the greatest legends of our time through the art of still photography. We offer one of the largest and continually expanding collections of entertainment photography in the world—images from Hollywood's Golden Age and all the way up to the present day. Our unbelievable collection includes some 1 million celebrity and entertainment-related images taken by more than 60 photographers from around the world. Many of these photographer's are represented exclusively through mptv and can't be found anywhere else. While mptv is located in Los Angeles, our images are used worldwide and can be seen in galleries, magazines, books, advertising, online and in various products."

HOW TO CONTACT If interested in representation, send an e-mail to photographers@mptvimages.com.

● MUSIC & ARTS PICTURES AT LEBRECHT

3 Bolton Rd., London NW8 0RJ, United Kingdom. E-mail: pictures@lebrecht.co.uk. Website: www.lebrecht.co.uk. **Contact:** Ms. E. Lebrecht. Estab. 1992. Has 120,000 high-res images online; thousands more not yet scanned. Clients include: book publishers, magazine publishers, newspapers, calendar companies, film production companies, greeting card companies, public relations firms, advertising agencies.

NEEDS Photos of arts personalities, performing arts, instruments, musicians, dance (ballet, contemporary and folk), orchestras, opera, concert halls, jazz, blues, rock, authors, artists, theater, comedy, art and artists. Interested in historical/vintage.

SPECS Accepts images in digital format only.

PAYMENT & TERMS Pays 50% commission for b&w or color photos. Offers volume discounts to customers. Works with photographers on contract basis only. Offers limited regional exclusivity. Statements issued quarterly. Offers one-time rights. Informs photographers and allows them to negotiate when a client requests all rights. Model release required. Photo captions required; include subject name, location, date.

HOW TO CONTACT Send e-mail.

NOVASTOCK

1306 Matthews Plantation Dr., Matthews NC 28105-2463. (888)894-8622. Fax: (704)841-8181. E-mail: Novastock@aol.com. Website: www.creativeshake.com/profile.html?MyUrl=Novastock. **Contact:** Anne Clark, submission department. Estab. 1993. Stock agency. Clients include: advertising agencies, businesses, postcard publishers, public relations firms, book publishers, calendar companies, magazine publishers, greeting card companies, and international network of subagents.

NEEDS "We need commercial stock subjects such as lifestyles, fitness, business, science, medical, family, etc. We also are looking for unique and unusual imagery. We have one photographer who burns, scratches and paints on his film." Wants photos of babies/children/teens, couples, multicultural, families, parents, senior citizens, disasters, environmental, wildlife, rural, adventure, health/fitness, travel, business concepts, military, science, technology/computers.

SPECS Prefers images in digital format as follows: (1) Original digital camera files. (2) Scanned images in the 30-50MB range. "When sending files for editing, please send small files only. Once we make our picks, you can supply larger files. Final large files should be a uncompressed TIFF. NEVER sharpen or use contrast and saturation filters. Always flatten layers. Files and disks must be readable on Windows PC."

PAYMENT & TERMS Pays 50% commission for b&w and color photos. "We never charge the photographer for any expenses whatsoever." Works with photographers on contract basis only. "We need exclusivity only for images accepted, and similars." Photographer is allowed to market work not represented by Novastock. Statements and payments are made in the month following receipt of income from sales. Informs photographers and discusses with photographer when client requests all rights. Model/property release required. Photo captions required; include who, what and where. "Science and technology need detailed and accurate captions. Model releases must be cross-referenced with the appropriate images."

HOW TO CONTACT Contact by e-mail or send query letter with digital files, slides, tearsheets, transparencies.

TIPS "Digital files on CD/DVD are preferred. All images must be labeled with caption and marked with model release information and your name and copyright. We market agency material through more than 50 agencies in our international subagency network. The photographer is permitted to freely market non-similar work any way he/she wishes."

● OKAPIA

Website: www.okapia.de. Stock photo agency and picture library. Has 700,000+ photos in files. Clients include: ad agencies, book/encyclopedia publishers, magazine publishers, newspapers, postcard companies, calendar companies, greeting card companies, school book publishers.

NEEDS Photos of natural history, babies/children/teens, couples, families, parents, senior citizens, gardening, pets, adventure, health/fitness, travel, agriculture, industry, medical, science, technology/computers, general interest.

SPECS Uses 35mm, 2¼×2¼, 4×5 transparencies. Accepts digital images. Send via DVD, CD as JPEG files at 355 dpi.

PAYMENT & TERMS Pays 50% commission for color photos. Average price per image (to clients): $60-120 for color photos. Enforces strict minimum prices. Offers volume discounts to customers. Discount sales terms not negotiable. Works with photographers on contract basis only. Offers nonexclusive contract, limited regional exclusivity and guaranteed subject exclusivity (within files). Contracts renew automatically for 1 year with additional submissions. Charges catalog insertion fee. Statements issued quarterly, semiannually or annually, depending on money photographers earn. Payment made quarterly, semiannually or annually with statement. Photographers allowed to review account records in cases of discrepancies only. Offers one-time, electronic media and agency promotion rights. Does not permit photographers to negotiate when client requests all rights. Model/property release preferred. Photo captions required.

TIPS "We need every theme which can be photographed." For best results, "send pictures continuously."

🌀 ONASIA

30 Cecil St., Prudential Tower Level 15, 049712, Singapore. (66)2655-4683. Fax: (66)2655-4682. E-mail: info@onasia.com. Website: www.onasia.com. **Contact:** Peter Charlesworth or Yvan Cohen, directors. An Asia-specialized agency offering rights-managed stock, features and assignment services. Represents over 180 photographers and has over 180,000 high-res images available online and 400,000 photos in files. Offices in Singapore and Bangkok. Clients include: advertising and graphic design agencies, newspapers, magazines, book publishers, calendar and gift card companies.

NEEDS Model-released Asia-related conceptual, lifestyle and business imagery as well as a broad range of nonreleased editorial imagery including current affairs, historical collections, travel and leisure, economics as well as social and political trends. Please note: "We only accept images from or relating to Asia."

SPECS Accepts images in digital format. Send via CD or to our FTP site as 12×18 JPEG files at 300 dpi. All files must be retouched to remove dust and dirt. Photo captions required; include dates, location, country and a detailed description of image, including names where possible.

PAYMENT & TERMS Pays 50% commission to photographers. Terms specified in photographer contracts. Photographers are required to submit on an image-exclusive basis. Statements issued monthly.

HOW TO CONTACT E-mail queries with low-res JPEG samples or a link to photographer's website. Does not keep samples on file; cannot return material. Expects minimum initial submission of 150 images. Photo guidelines available via e-mail.

TIPS "Provide a well-edited low-res portfolio for initial evaluation. Ensure that subsequent submissions are tightly edited, sized to Onasia's specs, retouched and submitted with full captions."

ONREQUEST IMAGES

1415 Western Ave., Suite 300, Seattle WA 98101. (206)774-1555 or (877)202-5025. Fax: (206)774-1291. E-mail: photographer.manager@onrequestimages.com. Website: www.onrequestimages.com. "OnRequest Images is the leading provider of powerful, custom imagery and photo production services for the Global 2000. Having the world's largest photo production services network enables our clients to utilize the best fully vested resources the world has to offer, including photographers, stylists, locations and crews. Combined with OnPro™, our collaborative workflow system which underpins every detail of a production, OnRequest Images delivers brand-aligned, cost effective, fast photography solutions for marketers, brand leaders and creative teams. We have the talent, tenacity and technology to make things happen even on the grandest scale. OnRequest Images is headquartered in Seattle, with offices in New York, Chicago, Denver, Los Angeles, Miami, San Francisco, London, Paris and Barcelona."

NEEDS Photos of babies, multicultural, families, parents, senior citizens, environmental, landscapes/scenics, architecture, education, interiors/decorating, pets, rural, adventure, food/drink, health/fitness/beauty, travel, agriculture, business concepts, science, technology/computers. Interested in lifestyle, seasonal.

SPECS Accepts images in digital format as TIFF files at 300 dpi. Send via e-mail or upload.

PAYMENT & TERMS Offers volume discounts to customers; terms specified in photographers' contracts. Photographers can choose not to sell images on discount terms. Works with photographers on contract basis only. Offers nonexclusive contract; guaranteed subject exclusivity (within files). Statements issued quarterly. Payments made within 45 days. Rights offered depend on contract. Informs photographers and allows them to negotiate when a client requests all rights. Model release/property release required. Captions required.

HOW TO CONTACT E-mail query letter with link to photographer's website. Provide self-promotion piece to be kept on file. Expects minimum initial submission of 15 images. Photo guidelines sheet available.

TIPS "Be honest about what you specialize in."

⬤ OPÇÃO BRASIL IMAGENS

(55)(21)2256-9007. Fax: (55)(21)2256-9007. E-mail: pesquisa@opcaobrasil.com.br. Website: www.opcaobrasil.com.br. Estab. 1993. Has 600,000+ photos in files. Clients include: advertising agencies, book publishers, magazine publishers, calendar companies, postcard publishers, publishing houses.

NEEDS Photos of babies/children/teens, couples, families, parents, wildlife, health/fitness, beauty, education, hobbies, sports, industry, medicine. "We need photos of wild animals, mostly from the Brazilian fauna. We are looking for photographers who have images of people who live in tropical countries and must be brunette."

SPECS Accepts images in digital format.

PAYMENT & TERMS Pays 50% commission for b&w or color photos. Negotiates fees below standard minimum prices only in cases of renting at least 20 images. Offers volume discounts to customers. Works with photographers on contract basis only. Offers limited regional exclusivity. Contracts renew automatically with additional submissions for 3 years. Charges $200/image for catalog insertion. Statements issued quarterly. Payment made quarterly. Photographers allowed to review account records in cases of discrepancies only. Offers one-time rights, electronic media rights, agency promotion rights. Model release required; property release preferred. Photo captions required.

HOW TO CONTACT Initial contact should be by e-mail or fax. Explain what kind of material you have. Provide business card, self-promotion piece to be kept on file. "If not interested, we return the samples." Expects minimum initial submission of 500 images with quarterly submissions of at least 300 images.

TIPS "We need creative photos presenting the unique look of the photographer on active and healthy people in everyday life at home, at work, etc., showing modern and up-to-date individuals. We are looking for photographers who have images of people with the characteristics of Latin American citizens."

OUTSIDE IMAGERY

4548 Beachcomber Ct., Boulder CO 80301. (303)530-3357. E-mail: John@outsideimagery.com. Website: www.outsideimagery.com. **Contact:** John Kieffer, president. Estab. 1986. Stock agency. Has 200,000 images in keyword-searchable, online database. Clients include: advertising agencies, businesses, multimedia, greeting card and postcard publishers, book publishers, graphic design firms, magazine publishers.

NEEDS Photos showing a diversity of people participating in an active and healthy lifestyle in natural and urban settings, plus landscapes and cityscapes. Photos of people enjoying the outdoors. Babies/children/teens, couples, multicultural, families, senior citizens. Activities and subjects include: recreation, cityscapes, skylines, environmental, landscapes/scenics, wildlife, rural, adventure, health/fitness, sports, travel, wildlife, agriculture, business and technology.

SPECS Requires images in high-res digital format. No film. Send low-res files via CD or e-mail in JPEG format at 72 dpi.

PAYMENT & TERMS Pays 50% commission for all imagery. Average price per image (to clients): $150-3,500 for all imagery. Will often work within a buyer's budget. Offers volume discounts to customers. Offers nonexclusive contract. Payments made quarterly. Model release required; property release preferred. Photo captions and keywords required.

HOW TO CONTACT "First review our website. Then send a query e-mail, and include a stock list or an active link to your website. If you don't hear from us in 3 weeks, send a reminder e-mail."

OXFORD SCIENTIFIC (OSF)

2nd Floor Waterside House, 9 Woodfield Rd., London W9 2BA, UK. (44)(0) 20 7432 8200. Fax: (44)(0) 20 7432 8201. E-mail: lwheatley@photolibrary.eu. Website: www.osf.co.uk. **Contact:** Creative director. Estab. 1968. Stock agency. Stills and footage libraries. Has 350,000 photos, over 2,000 feet of HD, film and video originated footage. Clients include: advertising agencies, design companies, audiovisual firms, book/encyclopedia publishers, magazine publishers, newspapers, merchandising companies, multimedia publishers, film production companies.

NEEDS Photos and footage of natural history: animals, plants, behavior, close-ups, life-histories, histology, embryology, electron microscopy, scenics, geology, weather, conservation, country practices, ecological techniques, pollution, special-effects, high-speed, time-lapse, landscapes, environmental, travel, sports, pets, domestic animals, wildlife, disasters, gardening, rural, agriculture, industry, medicine, science, technology/computers. Interested in seasonal.

SPECS Send via CD, e-mail at 72 dpi for initial review; 300 dpi (RGB TIFF files) for final submission. Review guidelines for details.

PAYMENT & TERMS Pays 40% commission. Negotiates fees below stated minimums on bulk deals. Average price per image (to clients): $100-2,000 for b&w and color photos; $300-4,000 for film or videotape. Offers volume discounts to regular customers; inquire about specific terms. Discount sale terms not negotiable. Works with photographers on contract basis only; needs image exclusivity. Offers image-exclusive contract, limited regional exclusivity, guaranteed subject exclusivity. Contracts renew automatically every 5 years. There is a charge for handling footage. Offers one-time, electronic media and agency promotion rights. Informs photographers and allows them to negotiate when client requests all rights. Model/property release required. Photo captions required; include common name, Latin name, behavior, location and country, magnification where appropriate, if captive, if digitally manipulated. Contact OSF for footage terms.

HOW TO CONTACT Submission guidelines available on website. Expects minimum initial submission of 100 images with quarterly submissions of at least 100 images. Interested in receiving high-quality, creative, inspiring work from both amateur and professional photographers. Responds in 1 month.

TIPS "Contact via e-mail, phone or fax, or visit our website to obtain submission guidelines." Prefers to see "good focus, composition, exposure, rare or unusual natural history subjects and behavioral and action shots, inspiring photography, strong images as well as creative shots. Read photographer's pack from website or e-mail/write to request a pack, giving brief outline of areas covered and specialties and size."

PACIFIC STOCK/PRINTSCAPES.COM

7192 Kalanianaole Hwy., Suite G-240, Honolulu HI 96825. (808)394-5100. Fax: (808)394-5200. E-mail: pics@pacificstock.com. Website: www.pacificstock.com. **Contact:** Barbara Brundage, owner/president. Member of Picture Archive Council of America (PACA). Has 100,000 photos in files; 25,000 digital images online. "Pacific Stock specializes exclusively in imagery from throughout the Pacific, Asia and Hawaii." Clients include: advertising agencies, public relations firms, book/encyclopedia publishers, magazine publishers, postcard companies, calendar companies, greeting card companies. "Printscapes caters to the professional interior design market at our new fine art website, www.printscapes.com."

NEEDS Photos and fine art of Hawaii, Pacific Islands, and Asia. Subjects for both companies include: people (women, babies/children/teens, couples, multicultural, families, parents, senior citizens), culture, marine science, environmental, landscapes, wildlife, adventure, food/drink, health/fitness, sports, travel, agriculture, business concepts." We also have an extensive vintage Hawaii file as well as fine art throughout the Pacific Rim."

SPECS We accept images from specialized professional photographers in digital format only. Send via hard drive or DVD as 16-bit TIFF files (guidelines on website at www.pacificstock.com/photographer_guidelines.asp).

PAYMENT & TERMS Pays 40% commission for color, b&w photos, or fine art imagery. Average price per image (to clients): $650. Works with photographers and artists on contract basis only. Statements and payments issued monthly. Contributors allowed to review account records to verify sales figures. Offers one-time or first rights; additional rights with contributor's permission. Informs contributors and allows them to negotiate when client requests all rights. Model/property release required for all people and certain properties, e.g., homes and boats. Accurate and detailed photo captions required; include: "who, what, where." See submission guidelines for more details.

HOW TO CONTACT "E-mail or call us after reviewing our website and our photo guidelines. Want lists distributed regularly to represented photographers; free via e-mail to interested photographers."

TIPS "Photographers must be able to supply a minimum of 500 image files (must be model-released) for initial entry and must make quarterly submissions of fresh material from Hawaii, Pacific and Asia area destinations. Image files must be captioned in File Info (i.e., IPTC headers) according to our submission guidelines. Please contact us to discuss the types of imagery that sell well for us: www.pacificstock.com/contactus.asp. We are also looking for fine artists whose work is representative of Hawaii and the Pacific Rim. We are interested in working with contributors who work with us and enjoy supplying imagery requested by our valued clients."

PAINET INC.

P.O. Box 171, 29 Skating Pond Rd., Montezuma NM 87731. (701)484-1251. E-mail: painet@stellarnet.com. Website: www.painetworks.com. Estab. 1985. Picture library. Has 650,000 digital photos in files. Painet is a stock photo agency that works mainly with advertising agencies, book publishers, photo researchers and graphic designers.

NEEDS "Anything and everything."

SPECS "Refer to www.painetworks.com/helppages/submit.htm for information on how to scan and submit images to Painet. The standard contract is also available from this page." We take a standard 40% agency commission and pay our photographers 60%, daily. You may view the individual contract and the agency contract by clicking the links online. Print out, complete and mail, or e-mail to painet@stellarnet.com, a copy of the contract when sending your first submission. *Note: upload highest quality JPEGs only!* Images should open to 24MB, or more, in a graphics application, such as Photoshop. As of February 22, 2010, due to bandwidth limitations, we no longer can support uploading of RAW or TIFF files. We have also changed our activation time period for new submissions to quarterly in lieu of weekly.

PAYMENT & TERMS Pays 60% commission (see contract). Works with photographers with or without a contract. Offers nonexclusive contract. Payment made immediately after a sale. Informs photographers and allows them to negotiate when client requests all rights. Provides buyer contact information to photographer by sending photographer copies of the original invoices on all orders of photographer's images.

HOW TO CONTACT "Occasionally receives a list of current photo requests."

TIPS "We have added an online search engine with 700,000 images. We welcome submissions from new photographers, since we add approximately 30,000 images quarterly. Painet markets color and b&w images electronically or by contact with the photographer. Because images and image descriptions are entered into a database from which searches are made, we encourage our photographers to include lengthy descriptions that improve the chances of finding their images during a database search. We prefer descriptions be included in the IPTC (File Info area of Photoshop). Photographers who provide us their e-mail address will receive a biweekly list of current photo requests from buyers. Photographers can then send matching images via e-mail or FTP, and we forward them to the buyer. Painet also hosts photographer's and photo agency websites. See details at www.painetworks.com/helppages/setupPT.htm."

PANORAMIC IMAGES

2302 Main St., Evanston IL 60202. (847)324-7000 or (800)543-5250. Fax: (847)324-7004. E-mail: images@panoramicimages.com. Website: www.panoramicimages.com. Estab. 1987. Stock photo agency. Member of ASPP, NANPA and IAPP. Clients include: advertising agencies, magazine publishers, newspapers, design firms, graphic designers, corporate art consultants, postcard companies, calendar companies.

NEEDS Photos of lifestyles, environmental, landscapes/scenics, wildlife, architecture, cities/urban, gardening, interiors/decorating, rural, adventure, automobiles, health/fitness, sports, travel, business concepts, industry, medicine, military, science, technology/computers. Interested in alternative process, avant garde, documentary, fine art, historical/vintage, seasonal. Works only with *panoramic formats* (2:1 aspect ratio or greater). Subjects include: cityscapes/skylines, international travel, nature, tabletop, backgrounds, conceptual.

SPECS "Transparencies preferred for initial submission. Call for digital submission guidelines or see website."

PAYMENT & TERMS Pays 40% commission for photos. Average price per image (to clients): $600. No charge for scanning, metadata or inclusion on website. Statements issued quarterly. Payments made quarterly. Offers one-time, electronic rights and limited exclusive usage. Model release preferred "and property release, if necessary." Photo captions required. Call or see website for submission guidelines before submitting.

HOW TO CONTACT Send e-mail with stock list or low-res scans/lightbox. Specific want lists created for contributing photographers. Photographer's work is represented on full e-commerce website and distributed worldwide through image distribution partnerships with Getty Images, National Geographic Society Image Collection, Amana, Digital Vision, etc.

TIPS Wants to see "well-exposed chromes or very high-res stitched pans. Panoramic views of well-known locations nationwide and worldwide. Also, generic beauty panoramics."

PAPILIO

155 Station Rd., Herne Bay, Kent CT6 5QA, United Kingdom. (44)(122)736-0996. E-mail: library@papiliophotos.com. Website: www.papiliophotos.com. **Contact:** Justine Pickett. Estab. 1984. Has 120,000 photos in files. Clients include: advertising agencies, book publishers, magazine publishers, newspapers, calendar companies, greeting card companies, postcard publishers.

NEEDS Photos of wildlife.

SPECS Prefers digital submissions. Uses digital shot in-camera as RAW and converted to TIFF for submission, minimum file size 17MB. See webpage for further details or contact for a full information sheet about shooting and supplying digital photos.

PAYMENT & TERMS Works with photographers on contract basis only. Offers nonexclusive contract. Statements issued quarterly. Payment made quarterly. Offers one-time rights, electronic media rights. Photo captions required; include Latin names and behavioral information and keywords.

HOW TO CONTACT Send query letter with résumé. Does not keep samples on file. Expects minimum initial submission of 150 images. Responds in 1 month to samples. Returns all unsuitable material with letter. Photo guidelines sheet free with SASE.

TIPS "Contact first for information about digital. Send digital submissions on either CD or DVD. Supply full caption listing for all images. Wildlife photography is very competitive. Photographers are advised to send only top-quality images."

PHOTO AGORA

3711 Hidden Meadow Ln., Keezletown VA 22832. (540)269-8283. Fax: (540)269-8283. E-mail: photoagora@aol.com. Website: www.photoagora.com. **Contact:** Robert Maust. Estab. 1972. Stock photo agency. Has over 65,000 photos in files. Clients include: businesses, book/encyclopedia and textbook publishers, magazine publishers, calendar companies.

NEEDS Photos of families, children, students, Virginia, Africa and other Third World areas, work situations, etc. Also needs babies/children/teens, couples, multicultural, parents, senior citizens, disasters, environmental, landscapes/scenics, wildlife, cities/urban, education, gardening, pets, religious, rural, health/fitness, travel, agriculture, industry, medicine, science, technology/computers.

SPECS Send high-res digital images. Ask for password to download agreement and submission guidelines from website.

PAYMENT & TERMS Pays 50% commission for b&w and color photos. Average price per image (to clients): $40 minimum for b&w photos; $100 minimum for color photos. Negotiates fees below standard minimum prices. Offers volume discounts to customers; inquire about specific terms. Photographers can choose not to sell images on discount terms. Works with photographers with or without a contract. Offers nonexclusive contract. Payment made quarterly. Photographers allowed to review account records. Offers one-time rights. Informs photographers and allows them to negotiate when client requests all rights. Model/property release preferred. Embedded photo captions required; include location, important dates, scientific names, etc.

HOW TO CONTACT Call, write or e-mail. No minimum number of images required in initial submission. Responds in 3 weeks. Photo guidelines free with SASE or download from website.

PHOTOEDIT INC.

3505 Cadillac Ave., Suite P-101, Costa Mesa CA 92626. (800)860-2098. Fax: (800)804-3707. E-mail: info@photoeditinc.com. Website: www.photoeditinc.com. Estab. 1987. Stock photo agency. Member of Picture Archive Council of America (PACA). Has 600,000 photos. Clients include: textbook/encyclopedia publishers, magazine publishers, advertising agencies, government agencies. "PhotoEdit Inc. is a leading multi-ethnic and multicultural stock agency specializing in diverse, culturally relevant imagery. Whether our images are used commercially, or as positive education tools, we keep in mind all of our clients' unique needs when selecting images for our 100% digital rights-managed collection. Our images capture real life as it happens all over the globe. We're in search of photographers who have access to models of every ethnicity who will shoot actively and on spec."

SPECS Uses digital images only.

PAYMENT & TERMS Pays 40% commission for color images. Works on contract basis only. Offers nonexclusive contract. Payments and statements issued monthly. Model release preferred.

HOW TO CONTACT Submit digital portfolio for review. Photo guidelines available on website.

THE PHOTOLIBRARY GROUP

Level 11, 54 Miller St., North Sydney, N.S.W. 2090, Australia. (61)(2)9929-8511. Fax: (61)(2)9923-2319. E-mail: creative@photolibrary.com. Website: www. photolibrary.com. **Contact:** Lucette Kenay. Estab. 1967. Stock agency. Has more than 7,000,000 high-res images online. Clients include: advertising agencies, graphic designers, corporate, newspapers, postcard publishers, public relations firms, book publishers, calendar companies, magazine publishers, greeting card companies, web designers.

> This agency also has an office in the UK at 83-84 Long Acre, London WC2E 9NG. Phone: (44)(207)836-5591. Fax: (44)(207)379-4650; other offices in New Zealand, Singapore, Malaysia, Thailand, Philippines, India, Dubai, USA, Indonesia, Hong Kong, France. Brands in The Photolibrary Group include OSF specializing in the natural world, Garden Picture Library, fresh food images, monsoon Images, Peter Arnold images, ticket and index stock images.

NEEDS "Contemporary imagery covering all subjects, especially model-released people in business and real life."

SPECS Images must be in digital format.

PAYMENT & TERMS Pays 40% commission. Offers volume discounts to customers. Discount sales terms not negotiable. Offers guaranteed subject exclusivity.

Statements issued quarterly. Photographers allowed to review account records. Offers one-time rights, electronic media rights, agency promotion rights. Model/property release required. Photo captions required; include date of skylines.

HOW TO CONTACT See website for information on how to make initial submissions under Contributor tab.

THE PHOTOLIBRARY GROUP

23 W. 18th St., 3rd Floor, New York NY 10011. (212)929-4644 or (800)690-6979. Fax: (212)633-1914. E-mail: ussales@photolibrary.us.com. Website: www.photolibrary.com. "The Photolibrary Group represents the world's leading stock brands and the finest photographers around the world, to bring memorable, workable content to the creative communities in America, Europe, Asia, and the Pacific. We provide customers with access to over 5 million images and thousands of hours of footage and full composition music. Photolibrary Group was founded in 1967 and, 40 years on has a global presence with offices in the United Kingdom (London), the USA (New York), Australia (Sydney and Melbourne), Singapore, India, Malaysia, the Philippines, Thailand, New Zealand and the United Arab Emirates. Photolibrary is always on the lookout for new and innovative photographers and footage producers. Due to the highly competitive market for stock imagery we are very selective about the types of work that we choose to take on. We specialize in high quality, creative imagery primarily orientated to advertising, business-to-business and the editorial and publishing markets. Interested contributors should go to the website and click on the Artists tab for submission information. For additional information regarding our house brands, follow the 'About Us' link."

PHOTOLIFE CORPORATION LTD.

2/F Eton Tower, 8 Hysan Ave., Causeway Bay, Hong Kong. (852)2808 0012. Fax: (852)2808 0072. E-mail: photo@photolife.com.hk. Website: www.photolife.com.hk. Estab. 1994. Stock photo library. Has over 1.6 million photos in files. Clients include: advertising agencies, newspapers, book publishers, calendar companies, magazine publishers, greeting card companies, corporations, production houses, graphic design firms.

NEEDS Contemporary images of architecture, interiors, garden, infrastructure, concepts, business, finance, sports, lifestyle, nature, travel, animal, marine life, foods, medical.

SPECS Accepts images in digital format only. "Use only professional digital cameras (capable of producing 24MB+ images) with high-quality interchangeable lenses; or images from high-end scanners producing a file up to 50 MB."

PAYMENT & TERMS Pays 50% commission for b&w and color photos. Average price per image (to clients): $105-1,550 for b&w photos; $105-10,000 for color photos. Offers volume discounts to customers; terms specified in photographers' contracts. Works with photographers on contract basis only. Contract can be initiated with minimum 300 selected images. Quarterly submissions needed. Informs photographers and allows them to negotiate when client requests all rights. Model release required; property release preferred. Photo captions required; include destination and country.

HOW TO CONTACT E-mail 50 low-res images (1,000 pixels or less), or send CD with 50 images.

TIPS "Visit our website. Edit your work tightly. Send images that can keep up with current trends in advertising and print photography."

PHOTO NETWORK

P.O. Box 317, Lititz PA 17543. (717)626-0296 or (800)622-2046. Fax: (717)626-0971. E-mail: info@heilmanphoto.com. Website: www.heilmanphoto.com. **Contact:** Sonia Wasco, president. Stock photo agency/library. Member of Picture Archive Council of America (PACA). Has more than 1 million photos in files. Clients include: agribusiness companies, ad agencies, textbook companies, graphic artists, public relations firms, newspapers, corporations, magazines, calendar companies, greeting card companies. Member ASPP, NANPA, AAEA.

    ⭘ Photo Network is now owned by Grant Heilman Photography.; Photo Network is now owned by Grant Heilman Photography.

NEEDS Photos of agriculture, families, couples, ethnics (all ages), animals, travel and lifestyles, babies/children/teens, parents, senior citizens, disasters, environmental, wildlife, architecture, cities/urban, education, gardening, interiors/decorating, pets, religious, rural, adventure, automobiles, food/drink, health/fitness/beauty, hobbies, humor, sports, business concepts, industry, medicine, military, political, science, technology/computers. Special subject needs include people over age 55 enjoying life; medical shots (patients and professionals); children and domestic animals.

SPECS Uses transparencies and digital format. Send via CD as JPEG files.

PAYMENT & TERMS Information available upon request.

HOW TO CONTACT Send query letter with stock list. Send a sample of 200 images for review; include SASE for return of material. Responds in 1 month.

TIPS Wants to see a portfolio "neat and well-organized and including a sampling of photographer's favorite photos." Looks for "clear, sharp focus, strong colors and good composition. We'd rather have many very good photos rather than one great piece of art. Would like to see photographers with a specialty or specialties and have it/them covered thoroughly. You need to supply new photos on a regular basis and be responsive to current trends in photo needs. Contract photographers are supplied with quarterly 'want' lists and information about current trends."

PHOTO RESEARCHERS, INC.

307 5th Ave., New York NY 10016. (212)758-3420 or (800)833-9033. E-mail: info@photoresearchers.com. Website: www.photoresearchers.com. Stock agency. Has over 1 million photos and illustrations in files, with 250,000 images in a searchable online database. Clients include: advertising agencies; graphic designers; publishers of textbooks, encyclopedias, trade books, magazines, newspapers, calendars, greeting cards; foreign markets.

NEEDS Images of all aspects of science, astronomy, medicine, people (especially contemporary shots of teens, couples and seniors). Particularly needs model-released people, European wildlife, up-to-date travel and scientific subjects. Lifestyle images must be no older than 2 years; travel images must be no older than 5 years.

SPECS Prefers images in digital format.

PAYMENT & TERMS Rarely buys outright; pays 50% commission on stock sales. General price range (to clients): $150-7,500. Works with photographers on contract basis only. Offers limited regional exclusivity. Contracts renew automatically with additional submissions for 5 years (initial term; 1 year thereafter). Charges $15 for web placement of transparencies. Photographers allowed to review account records upon reasonable notice during normal business hours. Statements issued monthly, bi-monthly or quarterly, depending on volume. Informs photographers and allows them to negotiate when a client requests to buy all rights, but does not allow direct negotiation with customer. Model/property release required for advertising; preferred for editorial. Photo captions required; include who, what, where, when. Indicate model release.

HOW TO CONTACT See submission guidelines on website.

TIPS "We seek the photographer who is highly imaginative or into a specialty (particularly in the scientific or medical fields). We are looking for serious contributors who have many hundreds of images to offer for a first submission and who are able to contribute often."

PHOTO RESOURCE HAWAII

111 Hekili St., #41, Kailua HI 96734. (808)599-7773. E-mail: prh@photoresourcehawaii.com. Website: www.PhotoResourceHawaii.com. **Contact:** Tami Kauakea Winston, owner. Estab. 1983. Stock photo agency. Has e-commerce website with electronic delivery of over 14,000 images. Clients include: ad agencies, audiovisual firms, businesses, book/encyclopedia publishers, magazine publishers, calendar companies, greeting card companies, postcard publishers.

NEEDS Photos of Hawaii and the South Pacific.

SPECS Accepts images online only via website submission in digital format only; 48MB or larger; JPEG files from RAW files preferred.

PAYMENT & TERMS Pays 50% commission. Enforces minimum prices. Offers volume discounts to customers. Discount sales terms not negotiable. Works with photographers on contract basis only. Offers nonexclusive contract. Contracts renew automatically with additional submissions. Statements issued monthly. Payment made monthly. Offers royalty-free and rights-managed images. Model/property release preferred. Photo captions and keywording online required.

HOW TO CONTACT Send query e-mail with samples. Expects minimum initial submission of 100 images with periodic submissions at least 5 times/year. Responds in 2 weeks. Offers photographer retreats in Hawaii to learn how to become a contributor and enjoy a healthy Hawaiian vacation!

PHOTOSOURCE INTERNATIONAL

Pine Lake Farm, 1910 35th Rd., Osceola WI 54020-5602. (715)248-3800. E-mail: info@photosource.com. Website: www.photosource.com. Estab. 1998. "We are the meeting place for photographers who want to sell their stock photos, and for editors and art directors who want to buy them. For more than 25 years we've been helping photographers and photo buyers from our world-wide connected electronic cottage on our farm in western Wisconsin."

SYLVIA PITCHER PHOTO LIBRARY

75 Bristol Rd., Forest Gate, London E7 8HG, United Kingdom. E-mail: SPphotolibrary@aol.com. Website: www.sylviapitcherphotos.com. Estab. 1965. Picture library. Has 70,000 photos in files. Clients include: book publishers, magazine publishers, design consultants, record and TV companies.

NEEDS Photos of musicians—blues, country, bluegrass, old time and jazz with views of America that could be used as background to this music. Also, other relevant subject matter such as recording studios, musicians' birth places, clubs, etc. Please see website for a good indication of the library's contents.

SPECS Accepts images in digital format.

PAYMENT & TERMS Pays 50% commission for b&w and color photos. Average fee per image (to clients): $100-1,000. Negotiates fees below stated minimum for budget CDs or multiple sale. Offers volume discounts to customers; terms specified in photographers' contracts. Photographers can choose not to sell images on discount terms, if specified at time of depositing work in library. Works with photographers with or without contract; negotiable. Offers nonexclusive contract. Contracts renew automatically with additional submissions for 3 years. Statements issued quarterly. Payment made on client's settlement of transaction. Offers one-time rights. Model/property release preferred. Photo captions required; include artist, place/venue, date taken.

HOW TO CONTACT Send query letter with CD of approximately 10 low-res sample images and stock list. Provide self-promotion piece to be kept on file. Expects minimum initial submission of 30 high-res images on CD with further submissions when available.

PIX INTERNATIONAL

3600 N. Lake Shore Dr., 612 Floor, Chicago IL 60613. (773)975-0158. E-mail: lmatlow@yahoo.com. Website: www.pixintl.com. **Contact:** Linda Matlow, president. Estab. 1978. Stock agency, news/feature syndicate. Has 200,000 photos in files. Clients include: advertising agencies, public relations firms, businesses, book publishers, magazine publishers, newspapers.

NEEDS Photos of celebrities, entertainment, performing arts.

SPECS Accepts images in digital format only. E-mail link to website. "Do not e-mail any images. Do not send any unsolicited digital files. Make contact first to see if we're interested."

PAYMENT & TERMS Pays 50% commission for b&w or color photos, film. Average price per image (to clients): $35 minimum for b&w or color photos; $75-3,000 for film. Enforces minimum prices. Offers volume discounts to customers; terms specified in photographers' contracts. Discount sales terms not negotiable. Works with photographers with or without a contract; negotiable. Statements issued monthly. Payments made monthly. Photographers allowed to review account records in cases of discrepancies only. Offers one-time rights. Informs photographers and allows them to negotiate when client requests all rights. Model release not required for general editorial. Photo captions required; include who, what, when, where, why.

HOW TO CONTACT "E-mail us your URL with thumbnail examples of your work that can be clicked for a larger viewable image." Responds in 2 weeks to samples, only if interested.

TIPS "We are looking for razor-sharp images that stand up on their own without needing a long caption. Let us know by e-mail what types of photos you have, your experience, and cameras used. We do not take images from the lower-end consumer cameras—digital or film. They just don't look very good in publications. For photographers we do accept, we would only consider high-res 300-dpi at 6×9 or higher scans submitted on CD. Please direct us to samples on your website."

☻ PLANS, LTD. (PHOTO LIBRARIES AND NEWS SERVICES)

5-17-2 Inamura, Kamakura 248-0024, Japan. 81-467-31-0330. Fax: 81-467-31-0330. E-mail: yoshida@plans. jp. Website: www.plans.jp. **Contact:** Takashi Yoshida, president. Estab. 1982. Was a stock agency. Now representing JaincoTech as JaincoTech Japan as a joint project such as scanning, key wording, dust busting, or color correction for photographers in the stock photo market. Has 100,000 photos in files. Clients include: photo agencies, newspapers, book publishers, magazine publishers, advertising agencies.

NEEDS "We do consulting for photo agencies for the Japanese market."

HOW TO CONTACT Send query e-mail. Responds only if interested.

☺ PONKAWONKA INC.

(416)638-2475. E-mail: contact@ponkawonka.com. Website: www.ponkawonka.com. Estab. 2002. Stock agency. Has 60,000+ photos in files. Clients include: advertising agencies, businesses, newspapers, public relations firms, book publishers, calendar companies, magazine publishers.

NEEDS Photos of religious events and holy places. Interested in avant garde, documentary, historical/vintage. "Interested in images of a religious or spiritual nature. Looking for photos of ritual, places of worship, families, religious leaders, ritual objects, historical, archaeological, anything religious, especially in North America."

SPECS Accepts images in digital format. Send via CD or DVD as TIFF or JPEG files.

PAYMENT & TERMS Pays 50% commission for any images. Offers volume discounts to customers. Works with photographers on contract basis only. Charges only apply if negatives or transparencies have to be scanned. Statements issued quarterly. Payments made quarterly. Offers one-time rights. Informs photographers and allows them to negotiate when client requests all rights. Model/property release preferred. Photo captions required; include complete description and cutline for editorial images.

HOW TO CONTACT Send query e-mail. Does not keep samples on file; cannot return material. Expects minimum initial submission of 200 images with annual submissions of at least 100 images. Responds only if interested; send 30-40 low-res samples by e-mail. Photo guidelines available on website.

TIPS "We are always looking for good, quality images of religions of the world. We are also looking for photos of people, scenics and holy places of all religions. Send us sample images. First send us an e-mail introducing yourself, and tell us about your work. Let us know how many images you have that fit our niche and what cameras you are using. If it looks promising, we will ask you to e-mail us 30-40 low-res images (72 dpi, no larger than 6 inches on the long side). We will review them and decide if a contract will be offered. Make sure the images are technically and esthetically salable. Images must be well-exposed and a large file size. We are an all-digital agency and expect scans to be high-quality files. Tell us if you are shooting digitally with a professional DSLR or if scanning from negatives with a professional slide scanner."

POSITIVE IMAGES

61 Wingate St., Haverhill MA 01832. (978)556-9366. Fax: (978)556-9448. E-mail: pat@positiveimages photo.com. Website: www.agpix.com/positiveimages. **Contact:** Patricia Bruno, owner. Stock photo agency and fine art gallery. Member of ASPP, GWAA. Clients include: advertising agencies, public relations firms, book/encyclopedia publishers, magazine publishers, greeting card and calendar companies, sales/promotion firms, design firms.

NEEDS Horticultural images showing technique and lifestyle, photo essays on property-released homes and gardens, travel images from around the globe, classy and funky pet photography, health and nutrition, sensitive and thought-provoking images suitable for high-end greeting cards, calendar-quality landscapes, castles, lighthouses, country churches. Model/property releases preferred.

PAYMENT & TERMS Pays 50% commission for stock photos; 60% commission for fine art. Average price per image (to clients): $250. Works with photographers on contract basis only. Offers limited regional exclusivity. Payments made quarterly. Offers one-time and electronic media rights. "We never sell all rights."

HOW TO CONTACT "Positive Images Stock is accepting limited new collections; however, if your images are unique and well organized digitally, we will be happy to review online after making e-mail contact. Our Gallery 61 will review fine art photography portfolios online as well and will consider exhibiting nonmembers' work."

TIPS "Positive Images has taken on more of a boutique approach, limiting our number of photographers so that we can better service them and offer a more in-depth and unique collection to our clients. Gallery 61 is a storefront in a small historic arts district. Our plan is to evolve this into an online gallery as well. We are always in search of new talent, so we welcome anyone with a fresh approach to contact us!"

PURESTOCK

7660 Centurion Pkwy., Jacksonville FL 32256. (904)565-0066 or (800)828-4545. Fax: (904)641-4480. E-mail: yourfriends@superstock.com; info@purestock.com. Website: wwwsuperstock.com/pure stock; www.purestock.com. "The Purestock royalty-free brand is designed to provide the professional creative community with high-quality images at high resolution and very competitive pricing. Purestock offers CDs and single-image downloads in a wide range of categories including lifestyle, business, education and sports to distributors in over 100 countries. Bold and fresh beyond the usual stock images."

NEEDS "A variety of categories including lifestyle, business, education, medical, industry, etc."

SPECS "Digital files which are capable of being output at 80MB with minimal interpolation. File must be 300 dpi, RGB, TIFF at 8-bit color."

PAYMENT & TERMS Statements issued monthly to contracted image providers. Model release required. Photo captions required.

HOW TO CONTACT Submit a portfolio including a subject-focused collection of 300+ images. Photo guidelines available on website at www.superstock. com/submissions.asp.

TIPS "Please review our website to see the style and quality of our imagery before submitting."

RAILPHOTOLIBRARY.COM

Newton Harcourt, Leicester, Leicestershire LE8 9FH, United Kingdom. (44)(116)259-2068. Website: www.railphotolibrary.com. Estab. 1969. Has 400,000 photos in files relating to railways worldwide. Clients include: advertising agencies, businesses, newspapers, postcard publishers, public relations firms, book publishers, calendar companies, audiovisual firms, magazine publishers, greeting card companies.

NEEDS Photos of railways.

SPECS Uses digital images; glossy b&w prints; 35mm, 2¼×2¼ transparencies.

PAYMENT & TERMS Buys photos, film or videotape outright depending on subject; negotiable. Pays 50% commission for b&w and color photos. Average price per image (to clients): $125 maximum for b&w and color photos. Works with photographers with or without a contract; negotiable. Statements issued quarterly. Photographers allowed to review account records in cases of discrepancies only. Photo captions preferred.

HOW TO CONTACT Send query letter with slides, prints. Portfolio may be dropped off Monday-Saturday. Does not keep samples on file; include SAE/IRC for return of material. Unlimited initial submission.

TIPS "Submit well-composed pictures of all aspects of railways worldwide: past, present and future; captioned digital files, prints or slides. We are the world's leading railway picture library, and photographers to the railway industry."

REX USA

1133 Broadway, Suite 1626, New York NY 10010. (212)586-4432. E-mail: requests@rexusa.com. Website: www.rexusa.com. Estab. 1935. Stock photo agency, news/feature syndicate. Affiliated with Rex Features in London. Member of Picture Archive Council of America (PACA). Has 1.5 million photos. Clients include: advertising agencies, public relations firms, audiovisual firms, businesses, book/encyclopedia publishers, magazine publishers, newspapers, postcard companies, calendar companies, greeting card companies, TV, film and record companies.

NEEDS Primarily editorial material: celebrities, personalities (studio portraits, candid, paparazzi), human interest, news features, movie stills, glamour, historical, geographic, general stock, sports and scientific.

SPECS Digital only.

PAYMENT & TERMS Pays 50-65% commission; payment varies depending on quality of subject matter and exclusivity. "We obtain highest possible prices, starting at $100-100,000 for one-time sale." Pays 50% commission for b&w and color photos. Works with or without contract. Offers nonexclusive contract. Statements issued monthly. Payments made monthly. Photographers allowed to review account records. Offers one-time, first and all rights. Informs photographers and allows them to negotiate when client requests all rights. Model release required. Photo captions required.

HOW TO CONTACT E-mail query letter with samples and list of stock photo subjects. Or fill out online submission form to offer material and discuss terms for representation.

ROBERTSTOCK/CLASSICSTOCK

4203 Locust St., Philadelphia PA 19104. E-mail: info@robertstock.com. Website: www.robertstock.com, www.classicstock.com. **Contact:** Bob Roberts, president. Estab. 1920. Stock photo agency. Member of the Picture Archive Council of America (PACA). Has 2 different websites: Robertstock offers contemporary rights-managed and royalty-free images; ClassicStock offers retro and vintage images. Clients include: advertising agencies, public relations firms, audiovisual firms, businesses, book/encyclopedia publishers, magazine publishers, newspapers, postcard publishers, calendar companies, greeting card companies.

NEEDS Uses images on all subjects in depth.

SPECS Accepts images in digital format. Send via CD, ZIP at 300 dpi, 50MB or higher.

PAYMENT & TERMS Pays 45-50% commission. Works with photographers with or without a contract; negotiable. Offers various contracts. Statements issued monthly. Payment made monthly. Payment sent with statement. Photographers allowed to review account records to verify sales figures "upon advance notice." Offers one-time rights. Informs photographers when client requests all rights. Model release required. Photo captions required.

HOW TO CONTACT Send query letter. Does not keep samples on file. Expects minimum initial submission of 250 images with quarterly submissions of 250 images. Responds in 1 month. Photo guidelines available.

SCIENCE PHOTO LIBRARY, LTD.

327-329 Harrow Rd., London W9 3RB, United Kingdom. +44(0)20 7432 1100. Fax: +44(0)20 7286 8668. E-mail: info@sciencephoto.com. Website: www.sciencephoto.com. Stock photo agency. Clients include: book publishers, magazines, newspapers, medical journals, advertising, design, TV and online in the U.K. and abroad. "We currently work with agents in over 30 countries, including America, Japan, and in Europe."

NEEDS Specializes in all aspects of science, medicine and technology.

SPECS Digital only via CD/DVD. File sizes at least 38 MB with no interpolation. Captions, model, and property releases required.

PAYMENT & TERMS Pays 50% commission. Works on contract basis only. Agreement made for 5 years; general continuation is assured unless otherwise advised. Offers exclusivity. Statements issued quarterly. Payments made quarterly. Photographers allowed to review account records to verify sales figures; fully computerized accounts/commission handling system. Model and property release required. Photo captions required. "Detailed captions can also increase sales so please provide us with as much information as possible."

HOW TO CONTACT "Please complete the inquiry form on our website so that we are better able to advise you on the saleability of your work for our market. You may e-mail us low-res examples of your work. Once you have provided us with information, the editing team will be in contact within 2-3 business weeks. Full photo guidelines available on website."

SILVER IMAGE® PHOTO AGENCY AND WEDDINGS

4104 NW 70th Terrace, Gainesville FL 32606. (352)373-5771. E-mail: carla@silverimagephotoagency.com. Website: www.silverimagephotoagency.com; www.facebook.com/silverimagefloridalink. **Contact:** Carla Hotvedt, president/owner. Estab. 1987. Stock photo agency and rep for award-winning wedding photojournalists. Assignments in Florida/southern Georgia. Photographers are based in Florida, but available for worldwide travel. Has 150,000 photos in files. Clients include: public relations firms, book/encyclopedia publishers, brides and grooms, magazine publishers, newspapers.

NEEDS Stock photos from Florida only: nature, travel, tourism, news, people.

SPECS Accepts images in digital format only. Send via CD, FTP, e-mail as JPEG files *upon request only*. No longer accepting new photographers.

PAYMENT & TERMS Pays 50% commission for image licensing fees. Average price per image (to clients): $150-600. Works with photographers on contract basis only. Offers non-exclusive contract. Payment made monthly. Statements provided when payment is made. Photographers allowed to review account records. Offers one-time rights. Informs photographer and allows them to be involved when client requests all rights. Model release preferred. Photo captions required; include name, year shot, city, state, etc.

HOW TO CONTACT Send query letter via e-mail only. Do not submit material unless first requested.

TIPS "I will review a photographer's work to see if it rounds out our current inventory. Photographers should review our website to get a feel for our needs. Photographers interested in our agency and in receiving photo requests should follow our Facebook page."

SKYSCAN PHOTOLIBRARY

Oak House, Toddington, Cheltenham, Gloucestershire GL54 5BY, United Kingdom. (44)(124)262-1357. Fax: (44)(124)262-1343. E-mail: info@skyscan.co.uk. Website: www.skyscan.co.uk. **Contact:** Brenda Marks, library manager. Estab. 1984. Picture library. Member of the British Association of Picture Libraries and Agencies (BAPLA) and the National Association of Aerial Photographic Libraries (NAPLIB). Has more than 450,000 photos in files. Clients include: advertising agencies, public relations firms, businesses, book publishers, magazine publishers, newspapers, calendar companies, postcard publishers.

NEEDS "Anything aerial! Air-to-ground; aviation; aerial sports. As well as holding images ourselves, we also wish to make contact with holders of other aerial collections worldwide to exchange information."

SPECS Uses color and b&w prints; any format transparencies. Accepts images in digital format. Send via CD, e-mail.

PAYMENT & TERMS Pays 50% commission for b&w and color photos. Average price per image (to clients): $100 minimum. Enforces strict minimum prices. Offers volume discounts to customers. Photographers can choose not to sell images on discount terms. Works with photographers with or without a contract; negotiable. Offers guaranteed subject exclusivity (within files); negotiable to suit both parties. Statements issued quarterly. Payment made quarterly. Photographers allowed to review account records in cases of discrepancies only. Offers one-time, electronic media and agency promotion rights. Informs photographers and allows them to negotiate when a client requests all rights. Will inform photographers and act with photographer's agreement. Model/property release preferred for "air-to-ground of famous buildings (some now insist they have copyright to their building)." Photo captions required; include subject matter, date of photography, location, interesting features/notes.

HOW TO CONTACT Send query letter or e-mail. Provide résumé, business card, self-promotion piece or tearsheets to be kept on file. Agency will contact photographer for portfolio review if interested. No minimum submissions. Photo guidelines sheet and catalog both free with SASE. Market tips sheet free quarterly to contributors only.

TIPS "We have invested heavily in suitable technology and training for in-house scanning, color management, and keywording, which are essential skills in today's market. Contact first by letter or e-mail with résumé of material held and subjects covered."

SOVFOTO/EASTFOTO, INC.

263 W. 20th St. #3, New York NY 10011. (212)727-8170. Fax: (212)727-8228. E-mail: info@sovfoto.com. Website: sovfoto.com. Estab. 1935. Stock photo agency. Has 500,000+ photos in files. Clients include: advertising firms, audiovisual firms, book/encyclopedia publishers, magazine publishers, newspapers.

NEEDS All subjects acceptable as long as they pertain to Russia, Eastern European countries, Central Asian countries or China.

SPECS Uses b&w historical; color prints; 35mm transparencies. Accepts images in digital format. Send via CD or DVD as TIFF files.

PAYMENT & TERMS Pays 50% commission. Average price per image (to clients): $150-500 for b&w or color photos for editorial use. Statements issued quarterly. Payment made quarterly. Photographers allowed to review account records to verify sales figures or account for various deductions. Offers one-time print, electronic media, and nonexclusive rights. Model/property release preferred. Photo captions required.

HOW TO CONTACT Arrange personal interview to show portfolio. Send query letter with samples, stock list. Keeps samples on file. Expects minimum initial submission of 50-100 images.

TIPS Looks for "news and general interest photos (color) with human element."

TOM STACK & ASSOCIATES, INC.

154 Tequesta St., Tavernier FL 33070. (305)852-5520. Fax: (305)852-5570. E-mail: tomstack@earthlink. net. Website: tomstackassociates.photoshelter.com. **Contact:** Therisa Stack. Has 500,000 photos in files. Clients include: advertising agencies, public relations firms, businesses, audiovisual firms, book publishers, magazine publishers, encyclopedia publishers, postcard companies, calendar companies, greeting card companies.

NEEDS Photos of wildlife, endangered species, marine life, landscapes; foreign geography; photomicrography; scientific research; whales; solar heating; mammals such as weasels, moles, shrews, fisher, marten, etc.; extremely rare endangered wildlife; wildlife behavior photos; lightning and tornadoes; hurricane damage; dramatic and unusual angles and approaches to composition, creative and original photography with impact. Especially needs photos on life science, flora and fauna and photomicrography. No run-of-the-mill travel or vacation shots. Special needs include photos of energy-related topics-solar and wind generators, recycling, nuclear power and coal burning plants, waste disposal and landfills, oil and gas drilling, supertankers, electric cars, geo-thermal energy.

SPECS Only accepts images in digital format. Send sample JPEGs or link to website where your images can be viewed.

PAYMENT & TERMS Pays 50% commission. Average price per image (to clients): $150-200 for color photos; as high as $7,000. Works with photographers on contract basis only. Contracts renew automatically with additional submissions for 3 years. Statements issued quarterly. Payments made quarterly. Offers one-time and electronic media rights. Informs photographers and allows them to negotiate when client requests all rights. Model release preferred. Photo captions preferred.

HOW TO CONTACT E-mail tomstack@earthlink. net.

TIPS "Strive to be original, creative and take an unusual approach to the commonplace; do it in a different and fresh way. We take on only the best so we can continue to give more effective service."

STILL MEDIA

714 Mission Park Dr., Santa Barbara CA 93105. (805)682-2868. Fax: (805)682-2659. E-mail: images@stillmedia.com; info@stillmedia.com. Website: www.stillmedia.com. Photojournalism and stock photography agency. Has 500,000 photos in files. Clients include: advertising agencies, public relations firms, businesses, book/encyclopedia publishers, magazine publishers, newspapers, calendar companies.

NEEDS Reportage, world events, travel, cultures, business, the environment, sports, people, industry.

SPECS Accepts images in digital format only. Contact via e-mail.

PAYMENT & TERMS Pays 50% commission for color photos. Works with photographers on contract basis only. Offers nonexclusive and guaranteed subject exclusivity contracts. Statements issued quarterly. Payment made quarterly. Photographers allowed to review account records. Offers one-time and electronic media rights. Model/property release preferred. Photo captions required.

STOCK CONNECTION

112 Frederick Ave., Suite H, Rockville MD 20850. (301)251-0720. Fax: (301)309-0941. E-mail: photos@scphotos.com. Website: www.scphotos.com. **Contact:** Cheryl Pickerell DiFrank, president and photographer relations. Stock photo agency. Member of the Picture Archive Council of America (PACA). Has over 200,000 photos in files. Clients: advertising agencies, graphic design firms, magazine and textbook publishers, greeting card companies.

NEEDS "We handle many subject categories including lifestyles, business, concepts, sports and recreation, travel, landscapes and wildlife. We will help photographers place their images into our extensive network of over 35 distributors throughout the world. We specialize in placing images where photo buyers can find them."

SPECS Accepts images in digital format (TIFF or high-res JPEG), minimum 50MB uncompressed, 300 dpi, Adobe RGB.

PAYMENT & TERMS Pays 65% commission. Average price per image (to client): $450-500. Works with photographers on contract basis only. Offers nonexclusive contract. Contracts renew automatically with additional submissions. Photographers may cancel contract with 60 days written notice. Charges for keywording average $3 per image, depending on volume. If photographer provides acceptable scans and keywords, no upload charges apply. Statements issued monthly. Photographers allowed to review account records. Offers rights-managed and royalty-free. Informs photographers when a client requests exclusive rights. Model/property release required. Photo captions required.

HOW TO CONTACT Please e-mail for submission guidelines. Prefer a minimum of 100 images as an initial submission.

TIPS "The key to success in today's market is wide distribution of your images. We offer an extensive network reaching a large variety of buyers all over the world. Increase your sales by increasing your exposure."

STOCKFOOD

Tumblingerstr. 32, Munich 80337, Germany. (49)(89)74720222. Fax: (49)(89)7211020. E-mail: petra.thierry@stockfood.com. Website: www.stockfood.com. **Contact:** Petra Thierry, manager photographers and art department. Estab. 1979. Stock agency, picture library. Member of the Picture Archive Council of America (PACA). Has over 250,000 photos in files. Clients include: advertising agencies, businesses, newspapers, postcard publishers, public relations firms, book publishers, calendar companies, magazine publishers, greeting card companies.

NEEDS Photos and video clips of food/drink, health/fitness/food, wellness/spa, people eating and drinking, interiors, nice flowers and garden images, eating and drinking outside, table settings.

SPECS Uses 2¼×2¼; 4×5, 8×10 transparencies. Accepts only digital format. Send via CD/DVD as TIFF files at 300 dpi, 34MB minimum. Submission guidelines on our website.

PAYMENT & TERMS Pays 40% commission for rights managed images. Enforces minimum prices. Works with photographers on contract basis only. Offers limited regional exclusivity, guaranteed subject exclusivity (within files). Contracts renew automatically. Statements issued quarterly. Photographers allowed to review account records. Offers one-time rights. Model release required; photo captions required.

HOW TO CONTACT Send e-mail with new examples of your work as JPEG files.

STOCK FOUNDRY IMAGES

Artzooks Multimedia Inc., P.O. Box 78089, Ottawa ON K2E1B1, Canada. (613)258-1551; (866)644-1644. Fax: (613)258-1551. E-mail: info@stockfoundry.com. Website: www.stockfoundry.com. Estab. 2006. Stock agency. Clients include: advertising agencies, businesses, newspapers, public relations firms, book publishers, audiovisual firms, magazine publishers.

NEEDS Photos of babies/children/teens, celebrities, couples, multicultural, families, parents, senior citizens, architecture, cities/urban, education, gardening, interiors/decorating, pets, religious, rural, agriculture, business concepts, industry, medicine, military, political, product shots/still life, science, technology/computers, disasters, environmental, landscapes/scenics, wildlife, adventure, automobiles, entertainment, events, food/drink, health/fitness/beauty, hobbies, humor, performing arts, sports, travel. Interested in alternative process, avant garde, documentary, erotic, fashion/glamour, fine art, historical/vintage, lifestyle, seasonal.

SPECS Accepts images in digital format. Send via CD. Save as EPS, JPEG files at 300 dpi. For film and video: .MOV.

PAYMENT & TERMS Buys photos/film/video outright. Pays $25 minimum for all photos, film and videotape. Pays $250 maximum for all photos, film and videotape. Pays 50% commission. Average price per image (to clients): $60 minimum for all photos, film and videotape. Negotiates fees below stated minimums. Offers volume discounts to customers. Terms specified in photographer's contracts. Works with photographers on contract basis only. Offers guaranteed subject exclusivity (within files). Contracts renew automatically with additional submissions. "Term lengths are set on each submission from the time new image submissions are received and accepted. There is no formal obligation for photographers to pay for inclusion into catalogs, advertising, etc.; however, we do plan to make this an optional item." Statements issued monthly or in real time online. Payment made monthly. Photographers allowed to review account records in cases of discrepancies only. Informs photographers and allows them to negotiate when a client requests all rights. Negotiates fees below stated minimums. "Volume discounts sometimes apply for preferred customers." Model/property release required. Captions preferred: include actions, location, event, and date (if relevant to the images, such as in the case of vintage collections).

HOW TO CONTACT E-mail query letter with link to photographer's website. Send query letter with tearsheets, stock list. Portfolio may be dropped off Monday–Friday. Expects initial submission of 100 images with monthly submission of at least 25 images. Responds only if interested; send nonreturnable samples. Provide resume to be kept on file. Photo guidelines sheet available online. Market tips sheet is free annually via e-mail to all contributors.

TIPS "Submit to us contemporary work that is at once compelling and suitable for advertising. We prefer sets of images that are linked stylistically and by subject matter (better for campaigns). It is acceptable to shoot variations of the same scene (orientation, different angles, with copy space and without, etc.); in fact, we encourage it. Please try to provide us with accurate descriptions, especially as they pertain to specific locations, places, dates, etc. Our wish list for the submission process would be to receive a PDF tearsheet containing small thumbnails of all the high-res images. This would save us time, and speed up the evaluation process."

STOCKMEDIA.NET

Stock Media Corporation, 10 E. 23rd St., Suite 500, New York NY 10010, United States. (212)463-8300. Fax: (212) 929-6965. E-mail: info@stockmedia.net. Website: www.stockmedia.net. Estab. 1998. Stock photo syndicate. Clients include: photographers, photo agencies, major publishers.

NEEDS "For photographers and stock photo agencies, we provide software and websites for e-commerce, image licensing, global rights control and fulfillment. We also serve as a conduit, passing top-grade, model-released production stock to foreign agencies."

SPECS Uses digital files only.

PAYMENT & TERMS Pays 40-60% commission. Works on contract basis only. Offers image exclusive contract only if distribution desired. Contracts renew automatically on annual basis. Statements are automated and displayed online. Payments made monthly. Photographers allowed to review account records to verify sales figures online at website or "upon reasonable notice, during normal business hours." Offers one-time rights. Requests agency promotion rights. Informs photographer and allows them to negotiate when client requests all rights. Model/property release required. Photo captions preferred; include "who, what, where, when, why and how."

HOW TO CONTACT Send query letter with résumé of credits. Responds "only when photographer is of interest." Photo guidelines sheet available. Tips sheet not distributed.

TIPS Has strong preference for experienced photographers. "For distribution, we deal only with top shooters seeking long-term success. If you have not been with a stock photo agency for several years, we would not be the right distribution channel for you."

STOCK OPTIONS

P.O. Box 1048, Fort Davis TX 79734. (432)426-2777. Fax: (432)426-2779. E-mail: stockoptions@sbc global.net. **Contact:** Karen Hughes, owner. Estab. 1985. Stock photo agency. Member of Picture Archive Council of America (PACA). Has 150,000 photos in files. Clients include: advertising agencies, public relations firms, audiovisual firms, corporations, book/

encyclopedia and magazine publishers, newspapers, postcard companies, calendar companies, greeting card companies.

NEEDS Emphasizes the southern U.S. Files include Gulf Coast scenics, wildlife, fishing, festivals, food, industry, business, people, etc. Also western folklore and the Southwest.

SPECS Uses 35mm, 2¼×2¼, 4×5 transparencies.

PAYMENT & TERMS Pays 50% commission for color photos. Average price per image (to client): $300-3,000. Works with photographers on contract basis only. Offers nonexclusive contract. Contracts renew automatically with each submission for 5 years from expiration date. When contract ends photographer must renew within 60 days. Charges catalog insertion fee of $300/image and marketing fee of $10/hour. Statements issued upon receipt of payment from client. Payment made immediately. Photographers allowed to review account records to verify sales figures. Offers one-time and electronic media rights. "We will inform photographers for their consent only when a client requests all rights, but we will handle all negotiations." Model/property release preferred for people, some properties, all models. Photo captions required; include subject and location.

HOW TO CONTACT Interested in receiving work from full-time commercial photographers. Arrange a personal interview to show portfolio. Send query letter with stock list. Contact by phone and submit 200 sample photos. Tips sheet distributed annually to all photographers.

TIPS Wants to see "clean, in-focus, relevant and current materials." Current stock requests include industry, environmental subjects, people in up-beat situations, minorities, food, cityscapes and rural scenics.

STOCKYARD PHOTOS

1410 Hutchins St., Houston TX 77003. (713)520-0898. Fax: (713)820-6966. E-mail: jim@stockyard.com. Website: www.stockyard.com. Estab. 1992. Stock agency. Niche agency specializing in images of Houston and China. Has thousands of photos in files. Clients include: advertising agencies, businesses, newspapers, postcard publishers, public relations firms, book publishers, calendar companies, audiovisual firms, magazine publishers, greeting card companies, real estate firms, interior designers, retail catalogs.

NEEDS Photos relating to Houston and the Gulf Coast.

SPECS Accepts images in digital format only. To be considered, e-mail link to photographer's website, showing a sample of 20 images for review.

PAYMENT & TERMS Average price per image (to clients): $250-1,500 for color photos. Offers volume discounts to customers. Photographers can choose not to sell images on discount terms.

STSIMAGES

225, Neha Industrial Estate, Off Dattapada Rd., Borivali (East), Mumbai 400 066, India. (91)(222)870-1586. Fax: (91)(222)870-1609. E-mail: info@STSimages.com. Website: www.stsimages.com. **Contact:** Mr. Pawan Tikku. Estab. 1993. Has over 200,000 photos on website. Clients include: advertising agencies, businesses, postcard publishers, public relations firms, book publishers, calendar companies, freelance web designers, audiovisual firms, magazine publishers, greeting card companies.

NEEDS Royalty-free and rights-managed images of babies/children/teens, celebrities, couples, multicultural, families, parents, senior citizens, disasters, environmental, landscapes/scenics, wildlife, architecture, cities/urban, education, gardening, interiors/decorating, pets, religious, rural, adventure, automobiles, entertainment, events, food/drink, health/fitness, hobbies, humor, performing arts, sports, travel, agriculture, business concepts, industry, medicine, military, political, product shots/still life, science, technology/computers. Interested in alternative process, avant garde, documentary, fashion/glamour, fine art, historical/vintage, seasonal. Also needs vector images.

SPECS Accepts images in digital format only. Send via DVD or direct upload to website, JPEG files at 300 dpi. Minimum file size 25MB, preferred 50MB or more. Image submissions should be made separately for royalty-free and rights-managed images

PAYMENT & TERMS Pays 50% commission. Average price per image (to clients): $20 minimum for b&w or color photos. Enforces minimum prices. Offers to customers. Works with photographers on contract basis only. Offers nonexclusive contract, limited regional exclusivity. Contracts renew automatically with additional submissions for 3 years. Statements issued quarterly. Payment made monthly. Photographers allowed to review account records. Offers royalty-free images as well as one-time rights. Model release required; property release preferred. Photo captions and keyword are mandatory in the file info area of the image. Include names, description, location.

HOW TO CONTACT Send e-mail with image thumbnails. Expects minimum initial submission of 200 images with regular submissions of at least some images every month. Responds in 1 month to queries. Ask for photo guidelines by e-mail. Market tips available to regular contributors only.

TIPS 1) Strict self-editing of images for technical faults. 2) Proper keywording is essential. 3) All images should have the photographer's name in the IPTC(XMP) area. 4) All digital images must contain necessary keywords and caption information within the "file info" section of the image file. 5) Send images in both vertical and horizontal formats.

SUGAR DADDY PHOTOS

Hanklooks Publications, 732 1/2 Alpine St., Los Angeles CA 90012. (626)627-5127. Website: www. sugardaddyphotos.com; www.facebook.com/Sugar daddyphotos; www.twitter.com/Sugardaddyphoto. **Contact:** Henry Salazar, editor-in-chief. Estab. 2000. Art collector and stock agency. Clients: advertising agencies, businesses, newspapers, postcard publishers, public relations firms, book publishers, calendar companies, audiovisual firms, magazine publishers, greeting card companies.

NEEDS Photos of babies/children/teens, celebrities, couples, multicultural, families, parents, senior citizens, architecture, cities/urban, education, gardening, interiors/decorating, pets, religious, rural, agriculture, business concepts, industry, medicine, military, political, product shots/still life, science, technology/computers, disasters, environmental, landscapes/scenics, wildlife, adventure, automobiles, entertainment, events, food/drink, health/fitness/beauty, hobbies, humor, performing arts, sports, travel, exotic locations. Interested in alternative process, avant garde, documentary, erotic, fashion/glamour, fine art, historical/vintage, lifestyle, seasonal.

SPECS Accepts images in digital format. Send RAW, TIFF or JPEG files at minimum 300 dpi. Pay 15% commission level. Average price per image (to clients): $100-1,000 for photos and streaming video. Enforces strict minimum prices. "We have set prices; however, they are subject to change without notice." Photographers can choose not to sell images on discount terms. Works with photographers with or without a contract; negotiable. Offers

nonexclusive contract. Statements issued quarterly. Payments made monthly. Offers one-time rights. Informs photographers and allows them to negotiate when a client requests all rights. Model/property release required. Photo captions required; include location, city, state, country, full description, related keywords, date image was taken.

HOW TO CONTACT "We are encouraging all new prospects to submit any work from any agencies or person who share a passion towards photography."

TIPS "Please e-mail through our form online before sending samples and make sure you include an online link to show your work. Arrange your work in categories to view. Clients expect the very best in professional-quality material."

SUPERSTOCK INC.

7660 Centurion Pkwy., Jacksonville FL 32256. (904)565-0066 or (800)828-4545. Fax: (904)641-4480. E-mail: yourfriends@superstock.com. Website: www. superstock.com. International stock photo agency represented in 192 countries. Offices in Jacksonville, New York and London. Extensive rights-managed and royalty-free content within 3 unique collections–contemporary, vintage and fine art. Clients include: advertising agencies, businesses, book and magazine publishers, newspapers, greeting card and calendar companies.

NEEDS "SuperStock is looking for dynamic lifestyle, travel, sports and business imagery, as well as fine art content and vintage images with releases."

SPECS Accepts images in digital format only. Digital files must be a minimum of 50MB (up-sized), 300 dpi, 8-bit color, RGB, JPEG format.

PAYMENT & TERMS Statements issued monthly to contracted contributors. "Rights offered vary, depending on image quality, type of content, and experience." Informs photographers when client requests all rights. Model release required. Photo captions required.

TIPS "Please review our website to see the style and quality of our imagery before submitting."

● TROPIX PHOTO LIBRARY

44 Woodbines Ave., Kingston-Upon-Thames, Surrey KT1 2AY, United Kingdom. (44)(020)8546-0823. E-mail: photographers@tropix.co.uk. Website: www. tropix.co.uk. **Contact:** Veronica Birley, proprietor. Picture library specialist. Has 100,000 photos in files. Clients include: book publishers, magazine publishers,

newspapers, government departments, design groups, travel companies, new media.

NEEDS *"Sorry, Tropix is currently closed to new contributing photographers. But any temporary exceptions to this will be posted on our website."*

SPECS Uses large digital files only, minimum 50MB when sent as TIFF files.

PAYMENT & TERMS Pays 40% commission for color photos. Average price per image (to clients): $118 for b&w and color photos. Offers guaranteed subject exclusivity. Charges cost of returning photographs by insured post, if required. Statements made quarterly with payment. Photographers allowed to have qualified auditor review account records to verify sales figures in the event of a dispute but not as routine procedure. Offers one-time, electronic media and agency promotion rights. Informs photographers when a client requests all rights, but agency handles negotiation. Model release always required. Photo captions required; accurate, detailed data to be supplied in IPTC, electronically, and on paper. "It is essential to follow captioning guidelines available from agency."

HOW TO CONTACT "E-mail preferred. Send no unsolicited photos or JPEGs, please."

ULLSTEIN BILD

Axel-Springer-Str. 65, Berlin 10888, Germany. +49(0)30 2591 72547. Fax: +49(0)30 2591 73896. E-mail: ramershoven@ullsteinbild.de. Website: www.ullsteinbild.de. Estab. 1900. Stock agency, picture library and news/feature syndicate. Has approximately 12 million photos in files. Clients include: advertising agencies, public relations firms, audiovisual firms, businesses, book publishers, magazine publishers, newspapers, calendar companies, greeting card companies, postcard publishers, TV companies.

NEEDS Photos of celebrities, couples, multicultural, families, parents, senior citizens, wildlife, disasters, environmental, landscapes/scenics, architecture, cities/urban, education, pets, religious, rural, adventure, automobiles, entertainment, events, health/fitness, hobbies, humor, performing arts, sports, travel, agriculture, buildings, computers, industry, medicine, military, political, portraits, science, technology/computers. Interested in digital, documentary, fashion/glamour, historical/vintage, regional, seasonal. Other specific photo needs: German history.

SPECS Accepts images in digital format only. Send via FTP, CD, e-mail as TIFF, JPEG files at minimum 25MB decompressed.

PAYMENT & TERMS Pays on commission basis. Works with photographers on contract basis only. Offers nonexclusive contract for 5 years minimum. Statements issued monthly, quarterly, annually. Payments made monthly, quarterly, annually. Photographers allowed to review account records in cases of discrepancies only. Offers one-time rights. Photo captions required; include date, names, events, place.

HOW TO CONTACT "Please contact Mr. Ulrich Ramershoven (ramershoven@ullsteinbild.de) before sending pictures."

VIEWFINDERS STOCK PHOTOGRAPHY

3245 SE Ankeny St., Portland OR 97214. (503)222-5222. Fax: (503)274-7995. E-mail: studio@viewfindersnw.com. Website: www.viewfindersnw.com. **Contact:** Bruce Forster, owner. Estab. 1996. Stock agency. Member of the Picture Archive Council of America (PACA). Has 70,000 photos in files. Clients include: advertising agencies, public relations firms, businesses, book publishers, magazine publishers, design agencies.

NEEDS "We are a stock photography agency providing images of the Pacific Northwest. Founded by Bruce Forster in 1996, our image collection has content from over 10 locally known photographers. whether you're looking for landscapes and landmarks, aerials, cityscapes, urban living, industry, recreation, agriculture or green energy images, our photography collection covers it all. Contact us for your image needs."

VIREO (VISUAL RESOURCES FOR ORNITHOLOGY)

1900 Ben Franklin Pkwy., Philadelphia PA 19103. (215)299-1069. Fax: (215)299-1182. E-mail: vireo@ansp.org. Website: vireo.ansp.org. **Contact:** Doug Wechsler, director. Estab. 1979. Picture library. "We specialize in birds only." Has 160,000 photos in files. Clients include: advertising agencies, businesses, book publishers, magazine publishers, newspapers, calendar companies, CD publishers.

NEEDS High-quality photographs of birds from around the world with special emphasis on behavior. All photos must be related to birds or ornithology.

SPECS Uses digital format primarily. See website for specs.

STOCK PHOTO AGENCIES

PAYMENT & TERMS Pays 50% commission for b&w and color photos. Average price per image (to clients): $125. Negotiates fees below stated minimums; "we deal with many small nonprofits as well as commercial clients." Offers volume discounts to customers. Discount sales terms negotiable. Works with photographers on contract basis only. Offers nonexclusive contract. Statements issued semiannually. Payments made semiannually. Offers one-time rights. Model release preferred. Photo captions preferred; include date, location.

HOW TO CONTACT Read guidelines on website. To show portfolio, photographer should send 10 JPEGs or a link to web pages with the images. Follow up with a call. Responds in 1 month to queries.

TIPS "Study our website and show us some bird photos we don't have or better than those we have. Write to us describing the types of bird photographs you have, the type of equipment you use, and where you do most of your bird photography. You may also send us a web link to a portfolio of your work. Edit work carefully."

WILDLIGHT

P.O. Box 1606, Double Bay, NSW Sydney 1360, Australia. +61 2 9043 3255. E-mail: wild@wildlight.net. Website: www.wildlight.net. Estab. 1985. Picture library specializing in Australian images only. Has 50,000 photos in files. Clients include: advertising agencies, public relations firms, audiovisual firms, businesses, book/encyclopedia publishers, magazine publishers, newspapers, postcard publishers, calendar companies, greeting card companies.

NEEDS Australian photos of babies/children/teens, couples, multicultural, families, parents, senior citizens, disasters, environmental, landscapes/scenics, wildlife, architecture, cities/urban, education, gardening, interiors/decorating, pets, religious, rural, adventure, entertainment, events, food/drink, health/fitness, hobbies, humor, performing arts, sports, travel, agriculture, business concepts, industry, medicine, military, political, product shots/still life, science, technology/computers. Interested in documentary, seasonal.

SPECS Accepts images in digital format only.

PAYMENT & TERMS Pays 40% commission for color photos. Works with photographers on contract basis only. Offers image exclusive contract within Australia. Statements issued quarterly. Payments made quarterly. Offers one-time rights. Model/property release required. Photo captions required.

HOW TO CONTACT Send CD to show portfolio. Expects minimum initial submission of 100 images with periodic submissions of at least 50 images per quarter. Photo guidelines available by e-mail.

ADVERTISING, DESIGN & RELATED MARKETS

Advertising photography is always "commercial" in the sense that it is used to sell a product or service. Assignments from ad agencies and graphic design firms can be some of the most creative, exciting, and lucrative that you'll ever receive.

Prospective clients want to see your most creative work—not necessarily your advertising work. Mary Virginia Swanson, an expert in the field of licensing and marketing fine art photography, says that the portfolio you take to the Museum of Modern Art is also the portfolio that Nike would like to see. Your clients in advertising and design will certainly expect your work to show, at the least, your technical proficiency. They may also expect you to be able to develop a concept or to execute one of their concepts to their satisfaction. Of course, it depends on the client and their needs: Read the tips given in many of the listings on the following pages to learn what a particular client expects.

When you're beginning your career in advertising photography, it is usually best to start close to home. That way, you can make appointments to show your portfolio to art directors. Meeting the photo buyers in person can show them that you are not only a great photographer but that you'll be easy to work with as well. This section is organized by region to make it easy to find agencies close to home.

When you're just starting out, you should also look closely at the agency descriptions at the beginning of each listing. Agencies with smaller annual billings and fewer employees are more likely to work with newcomers. On the flip side, if you have a sizable list of ad and design credits, larger firms may be more receptive to your work and be able to pay what you're worth.

Trade magazines such as *HOW*, *Print*, *Communication Arts*, and *Graphis* are good places to start when learning about design firms. These magazines not only provide information about how designers operate, but they also explain how creatives use photography. For ad agencies, try *Adweek* and *Advertising Age*. These magazines are more business oriented, but they reveal facts about the top agencies and about specific successful campaigns. (See Publications in the Resources section for ordering information.) The website of American Photographic Artists (APA) contains information on business practices and standards for advertising photographers (www.apanational.org).

⊘⊙ AMBIT MARKETING COMMUNICATIONS

Ambit Advertising and Public Relations, 2601 E. Oakland Park Blvd, Suite 301, Fort Lauderdale FL 33306. (954)568-2100. Fax: (954)568-2888. Website: www.ambitmarketing.com. Estab. 1977. Member of American Association of Advertising Agencies, American Advertising Federation, Public Relations Society of America. Ad agency. Firm specializes in ad campaigns, print collateral, direct mail.

◎ ○ ❀ THE AMERICAN YOUTH PHILHARMONIC ORCHESTRAS

4026 Hummer Rd., Annandale VA 22003. (703)642-8051, ext. 25. Fax: (703)642-8054. Website: www.aypo.org. **Contact:** Tomoko Azuma, executive director. Estab. 1964. Nonprofit organization that promotes and sponsors 4 youth orchestras. Photos used in newsletters, posters, audiovisual and other forms of promotion.

NEEDS Photographers usually donate their talents. Offers 8 assignments/year. Photos taken of orchestras, conductors and soloists. Photo captions preferred.

AUDIOVISUAL NEEDS Uses slides and videotape.

SPECS Uses 5×7 glossy color and b&w prints.

MAKING CONTACT & TERMS Arrange a personal interview to show portfolio. Works with local freelancers on assignment only. Keeps samples on file. Payment negotiable. "We're a résumé-builder, a nonprofit that can cover expenses but not service fees." **Pays on acceptance**. Credit line given. Rights negotiable.

AMPM, INC.

P.O. Box 1887, Midland MI 48641-1887. (989)837-8800. E-mail: solutions@ampminc.com. Website: www.ampminc.com/. **Contact:** Robert A. Saks, president. Estab. 1962. Member of Art Directors Club, Illustrators Club, National Association of Advertising Agencies and Type Directors Club. Ad agency. Approximate annual billing: $125 million. Number of employees: 265. Firm specializes in display design, direct mail, magazine ads, packaging. Types of clients: food, industrial, retail, pharmaceutical, health and beauty and entertainment. Examples of recent clients: Cadillac (ads for TV); Oxford (ads for magazines).

NEEDS Works with 6 photographers/month. Uses photos for consumer and trade magazines, direct mail, P-O-P displays, catalogs, posters, newspapers and audiovisual. Subjects include: landscapes/scenics, wildlife, commercials, celebrities, couples, architecture, gardening, interiors/decorating, pets, adventure, automobiles, entertainment, events, food/drink, health/fitness, humor, performing arts, agriculture, business concepts, industry, medicine, product shots/still life. Interested in avant garde, erotic, fashion/glamour, historical/vintage, seasonal. Reviews stock photos of food and beauty products. Model release required. Photo caption preferred.

AUDIOVISUAL NEEDS "We use multimedia slide shows and multimedia video shows."

SPECS Uses 8×10 color and/or b&w prints; 35mm, 2¼×2¼, 4×5, 8×10 transparencies; 8×10 film; broadcast videotape. Accepts images in digital format. Send via e-mail.

MAKING CONTACT & TERMS Arrange personal interview to show portfolio. Send unsolicited photos by mail for consideration. Provide résumé, business card, brochure, flier or tearsheets to be kept on file. Keeps samples on file. Responds in 2 weeks. Pays $50-250/hour; $500-2,000/day; $2,000-5,000/job; $50-300 for b&w photos; $50-300 for color photos; $50-300 for film; $250-1,000 for videotape. Pays on receipt of invoice. Credit line sometimes given, depending upon client and use. Buys one-time, exclusive product, electronic and all rights; negotiable.

TIPS Wants to see originality in portfolio or samples. Sees trend toward more use of special lighting. Photographers should "show their work with the time it took and the fee."

⊘⊙ ● AUGUSTUS BARNETT ADVERTISING/DESIGN

P.O. Box 197, Fox Island WA 98333. (253)549-2396. E-mail: charlieb@augustusbarnett.com. Website: www.augustusbarnett.com. Charlie Barnett, president/creative director. **Contact:** Augustus Barnett, president. Estab. 1981. Ad agency, design firm. Firm specializes in print, collateral, direct mail, business to business, package design and branding and identity systems. Types of clients: small business, industrial, financial, retail, small business, food & beverage, agriculture.

NEEDS Works with assignment photographers as needed. Uses photos for consumer and trade requirements. Subjects include: industrial, food-related product photography. Model release required; property release preferred for fine art, vintage cars, boats and documents. Photo captions preferred.

SPECS Accepts images in digital format. Send via CD, Jaz, Zip, e-mail, FTP as TIFF, EPS, GIF files at 300 dpi minimum.

MAKING CONTACT & TERMS Call for interview. Keeps samples on file. Responds in 2 weeks. Fees and payments are negotiable. Credit line sometimes given "if the photography is partially donated for a nonprofit organization." Buys one-time and exclusive product rights; negotiable.

BERSON, DEAN, STEVENS

P.O. Box 3997, Westlake Village CA 91359. (818)713-0134. E-mail: contact@bersondeanstevens.com; info@bersondeanstevens.com. Website: www.bersondeanstevens.com. **Contact:** Lori Berson, owner. Estab. 1981. Design firm. Number of employees: 3. Firm specializes in annual reports, display design, collateral, packaging, direct mail and video production. Types of clients: industrial, financial, food and retail. Examples of recent clients: Dole Food Company; Charles Schwab & Co., Inc.

NEEDS Works with 4 photographers/month. Uses photos for billboards, trade magazines, direct mail, P-O-P displays, catalogs, posters, packaging, signage and Web. Subjects include: product shots and food. Reviews stock photos. Model/property release required.

SPECS Accepts images in digital format only. Send via CD, DVD as TIFF, EPS, JPEG files at 300 dpi.

MAKING CONTACT & TERMS Provide résumé, business card, brochure, flier or tearsheets to be kept on file. Works on assignment only. Responds in 1-2 weeks. Payment negotiable. Pays within 30 days after receipt of invoice. Credit line not given. Rights negotiable.

⊗⊗ 🌓 BOB BOEBERITZ DESIGN

247 Charlotte St., Asheville NC 28801. (828)258-0316. E-mail: bob@bobboeberitzdesign.com. Website: www.bobboeberitzdesign.com. **Contact:** Bob Boeberitz, owner. Estab. 1984. Member of American Advertising Federation—Asheville Chapter, Asheville Freelance Network and Asheville Creative Services Group. Graphic design studio. Approximate annual billing: $100,000. Number of employees: 1. Firm specializes in annual reports, collateral, direct mail, magazine ads, packaging, publication design, signage, websites. Types of clients: management consultants,

retail, recording artists, mail-order firms, industrial, nonprofit, restaurants, hotels, book publishers.

NEEDS Works with 1 freelance photographer "every 6 months or so." Uses photos for consumer and trade magazines, direct mail, brochures, catalogs, posters. Subjects include: babies/children/teens, couples, multicultural, families, parents, senior citizens, environmental, landscapes/scenics, wildlife, architecture, cities/urban, education, pets, rural, adventure, entertainment, events, food/drink, health/fitness/beauty, hobbies, performing arts, sports, travel, business concepts, industry, medicine, product shots/still life, science, technology/computers; some location, some stock photos. Interested in fashion/glamour, seasonal. Model/property release required.

SPECS Accepts images in digital format. Send via CD, e-mail as TIFF, BMP, JPEG, GIF files at 300 dpi. E-mail samples at 72 dpi. No EPS attachments.

MAKING CONTACT & TERMS Provide résumé, business card, brochure, flier or postcard to be kept on file. Cannot return unsolicited material. Responds "when there is a need." Pays $75-200 for b&w photos; $100-500 for color photos; $75-150/hour; $500-1,500/day. Pays on per-job basis. Buys all rights; negotiable.

TIPS "Send promotional piece to keep on file. Do not send anything that has to be returned. I usually look for a specific specialty; no photographer is good at everything. I also consider studio space and equipment. Show me something different, unusual, something that sets you apart from any average local photographer. If I'm going out of town for something, it has to be for something I can't get done locally. I keep and file direct mail pieces (especially postcards). I do not keep anything sent by e-mail. If you want me to remember your website, send a postcard."

🌓 ◎ BRAGAW PUBLIC RELATIONS SERVICES

800 E. Northwest Hwy., Suite 700, Palatine IL 60074. (847)997-3876. Fax: (847)705-3812. E-mail: info@bragawpr.com, rbragaw@bragawpr.com. Website: bragawpr.com. **Contact:** Richard Bragaw, president. Estab. 1981. Member of Publicity Club of Chicago. PR firm. Number of employees: 3. Types of clients: professional service firms, high-tech entrepreneurs.

NEEDS Uses photos for trade magazines, direct mail, brochures, newspapers, newsletters/news releases.

Subjects include: "products and people." Model release preferred. Photo captions preferred.

SPECS Uses 3×5, 5×7, 8×10 glossy prints.

MAKING CONTACT & TERMS Provide résumé, business card, brochure, flier or tearsheets to be kept on file. Works with freelance photographers on assignment basis only. Payment is negotiated at the time of the assignment. Pays on receipt of invoice. Credit line "possible." Buys all rights; negotiable.

TIPS "Execute an assignment well, at reasonable costs, with speedy delivery."

◎ ◐ BRAINWORKS DESIGN GROUP

2460 Garden Road, Suite G, Monterey CA 93940. (831)657-0650. Fax: (831)657-0750. E-mail: info@brainwks.com. Website: www.brainwks.com. **Contact:** Alfred Kahn, president. Estab. 1986. Design firm. Approximate annual billing: $2 million. Number of employees: 8. Firm specializes in publication design and collateral. Types of clients: higher education, technology, medical, and pharmaceutical. Specializing in innovative and visually powerful communications, Brainworks pioneered Emotional Response Communications. This process, which includes photographic and conceptual images, is designed to induce an emotional reaction and connection on the part of the target market. It combines marketing, psychology, and design. Over the years, Brainworks has earned numerous awards.

NEEDS Works with 4 photographers/month. Uses photographs for direct mail, catalogs and posters. Subjects include: couples, environmental, education, entertainment, performing arts, sports, business concepts, science, technology/computers. Interested in avant garde, documentary. Wants conceptual images. Model release required.

SPECS Uses 35mm, 4×5 transparencies. Accepts images in digital format. Send via CD.

MAKING CONTACT & TERMS Arrange a personal interview to show portfolio. Send unsolicited photos by e-mail for consideration. Submit online. Works with freelancers on assignment only. Keeps samples on file. Cannot return material. Responds in 1 month. Pay negotiable. Pays on receipt of invoice. Credit line sometimes given, depending on client. Buys first, one-time and all rights; negotiable.

◎ ⊛ BRAMSON + ASSOCIATES

7400 Beverly Blvd., Los Angeles CA 90036. (323)938-3595. Fax: (323)938-0852. E-mail: gbramson@aol.com. **Contact:** Gene Bramson, principal. Estab. 1970. Ad agency. Approximate annual billing: $2 million. Number of employees: 7. Types of clients: industrial, financial, food, retail, health care. Examples of recent clients: Sumitomo Metal and Mining: Biotech, Japan; Lawry's Restaurants, Inc.; AF Growlabs, Division of Hairraising Personal Care Products, Inc.

NEEDS Works with 1-2 photographers/month. Uses photos for trade magazines, direct mail, posters, newspapers, signage, websites, corporate brochures, and collateral. Subject matter varies; includes babies/children/teens, couples, multicultural, families, architecture, cities/urban, gardening, interiors/decorating, pets, automobiles, food/drink, health/fitness/beauty, business concepts, medicine, science. Interested in avant garde, documentary, erotic, fashion/glamour, historical/vintage. Reviews stock photos. Model/property release required. Photo captions preferred.

AUDIOVISUAL NEEDS Works with 1 videographer/month. Uses videotape for industrial, product.

SPECS Mostly DVD and digital format.

MAKING CONTACT & TERMS Submit portfolio for review. Send unsolicited photos by mail for consideration; include SASE for return of material. Works with local freelancers on assignment only. Provide résumé, business card, brochure, flier or tearsheet to be kept on file. Responds in 3 weeks. Payment negotiable, depending on budget for each project. Pays on receipt of invoice. Credit line not given. Buys one-time and all rights.

TIPS "Innovative, crisp, dynamic, unique style—otherwise we'll stick with our photographers. If it's not great work, don't bother."

◎ ⊛ BRIGHT LIGHT VISUAL COMMUNICATIONS

602 Main St., Suite 810, Cincinnati OH 45202. (513)721-2574. Fax: (513)721-3329. E-mail: info@brightlightusa.com. Website: www.brightlightusa.com. **Contact:** Linda Spalazzi, CEO. Visual communication company. Types of clients: national, regional and local companies in the governmental, educational, industrial and commercial categories. Examples of recent clients: Procter & Gamble; U.S. Grains Council; Convergys.

ADVERTISING

NEEDS Model/property release required. Photo captions preferred.

AUDIOVISUAL NEEDS "Hires crews around the world using a variety of formats."

MAKING CONTACT & TERMS Provide résumé, flyer and brochure to be kept on file. Call to arrange appointment or send query letter with résumé of credits. Works on assignment only. Pays $100 minimum/day for grip; payment negotiable based on photographer's previous experience/reputation and day rate (10 hours). Pays within 30 days of completion of job. Buys all rights.

TIPS Sample assignments include camera assistant, gaffer or grip. Wants to see sample reels or samples of still work. Looking for sensitivity to subject matter and lighting. "Show a willingness to work hard. Every client wants us to work smarter and provide quality at a good value."

⊛ ⊖ ◑ BYNUMS MARKETING AND COMMUNICATIONS, INC.

1501 Reedsdale St., Suite 5003, Pittsburgh PA 15233. (412)471-4332. Fax: (412)471-1383. E-mail: rbynum 2124@earthlink.net; russell@bynums.com. Website: www.bynums.com. Estab. 1985. Ad agency. Number of employees: 8-10. Firm specializes in annual reports, collateral, direct mail, magazine ads, packaging, publication design, signage. Types of clients: financial, health care, consumer goods, nonprofit.

NEEDS Works with 1 photographer/month. Uses photos for billboards, brochures, direct mail, newspapers, posters. Subjects include: babies/children/teens, couples, multicultural, families, parents, senior citizens, environmental, wildlife, cities/urban, education, religious, adventure, automobiles, events, food/drink, health/fitness, performing arts, sports, medicine, product shots/still life, science, technology/computers. Interested in fine art, seasonal. Model/property release required. Photo captions preferred.

AUDIOVISUAL NEEDS Works with 1 videographer and 1 filmmaker/year. Uses slides, film, videotape.

SPECS Uses 8×10 glossy or matte color and b&w prints; 35mm, 4×5 transparencies. Accepts images in digital format. Send via ZIP, e-mail as TIFF files.

MAKING CONTACT & TERMS Send query letter with résumé, prints, tearsheets, stock list. Provide business card, self-promotion piece to be kept on file. Responds only if interested, send nonreturnable

samples. Pays $150-300 for b&w and color photos. "Payment may depend on quote and assignment requirements." Buys electronic rights.

⊛ ⊖ ⊖ ⊛ CARMICHAEL LYNCH

110 N. 5th St., Minneapolis MN 55403. (612)334-6000. Fax: (612)334-6090. E-mail: portfolio@clynch.com. Website: www.clynch.com. Bonnie Brown, Jill Kahn, Jenny Barnes, Andrea Mariash, art producers. **Contact:** Sandy Boss Febbo, executive art producer. Member of American Association of Advertising Agencies. Ad agency. Number of employees: 250. Firm specializes in collateral, direct mail, magazine ads, packaging. Types of clients: finance, health care, sports and recreation, beverage, outdoor recreational. Examples of recent clients: Harley-Davidson, Porsche, Northwest Airlines, American Standard.

NEEDS Uses many photographers/month. Uses photos for billboards, consumer and trade magazines, direct mail, P-O-P displays, brochures, posters, newspapers and other media as needs arise. Subjects include: environmental, landscapes/scenics, architecture, interiors/decorating, rural, adventure, automobiles, travel, product shots/still life. Model/property release required for all visually recognizable subjects.

SPECS Uses all print formats. Accepts images in digital format. Send TIFF, GIF, JPEG files at 72 dpi or higher.

MAKING CONTACT & TERMS Submit portfolio for review. To show portfolio, call Andrea Mariash. Provide résumé, business card, brochure, flyer or tearsheets to be kept on file. Payment negotiable. Pay depends on contract. Buys all, one-time or exclusive product rights, "depending on agreement."

TIPS "No 'babes on bikes'! In a portfolio, we prefer to see the photographer's most creative work—not necessarily ads. Show only your most technically, artistically satisfying work."

⊛ ⊖ ◑ DESIGN2MARKET

1973 O'Toole Way, San Jose CA 95131. (408)232-0440. Fax: (408)232-0443. E-mail: info@design2marketinc.com. Website: www.design2marketinc.com. **Contact:** Lior Taylor, senior designer. Design firm. Number of employees: 5. Firm specializes in publication design, display design, magazine ads, collateral, packaging, direct mail and advertising. Types of clients: industrial, retail, nonprofit and technology. Examples of recent clients: NEC (Tradeshow, promotions), Metropolis Retail (web), California Insurance Careers Program (web, promotions), Silicon Valley Charity Ball (invitation and posters); IDEC Corporation (advertising); City College of San Francisco (advertising); Polycom (packaging).

NEEDS Works with 6 photographers/month. Uses photos for trade magazines, direct mail, P-O-P displays, catalogs, posters, packaging and advertising. Subjects include: people, computers, equipment. Reviews stock photos. Model/property release required.

SPECS Accepts images in digital format. Send via CD as TIFF, EPS, PICT, JPEG files at 300 dpi minimum.

MAKING CONTACT & TERMS Send unsolicited photos by mail for consideration. Include SASE for return of material. Provide résumé, business card, brochure, flyer or tearsheets to be kept on file. Works on assignment and buys stock photos. Payment negotiable. Credit line sometimes given. Buys all rights.

☺ ⊛ DYKEMAN ASSOCIATES, INC.

4115 Rawlins St., Dallas TX 75219. (214)528-2991. E-mail: adykeman@airmail.net. Website: www.dyke manassociates.com. Estab. 1974. Member of Public Relations Society of America. PR, marketing, video production firm. Firm specializes in website creation and promotion, crisis communication plans, media training, collateral, direct marketing. Types of clients: industrial, financial, sports, technology.

NEEDS Works with 4-5 photographers and videographers. Uses photos for publicity, consumer and trade magazines, direct mail, catalogs, posters, newspapers, signage, websites.

AUDIOVISUAL NEEDS "We produce and direct video. Just need crew with good equipment and people and ability to do their part."

MAKING CONTACT & TERMS Arrange a personal interview to show portfolio. Pays $800-1,200/day; $250-400/1-2 days. "Currently we work only with photographers who are willing to be part of our trade dollar network. Call if you don't understand this term." Pays up to 30 days after receipt of invoice.

TIPS Reviews portfolios with current needs in mind. "If video, we would want to see examples. If for news story, we would need to see photojournalism capabilities."

☻☻ ◎ ◑ ⊛ FARNAM COMPANIES, INC.

301 W. Osborn, Phoenix AZ 85013-3997. (800)234-2269. E-mail: clsinfo@central.com. Website: www. farnam.com. **Contact:** Leslie Burger, creative director. Firm specializes in display design, magazine ads, packaging. Types of clients: retail.

◗ This company has an in-house ad agency called Charles Duff Advertising.

NEEDS Works with 2 photographers/month. Uses photos for direct mail, catalogs, consumer magazines, P-O-P displays, posters, AV presentations, trade magazines and brochures. Subject matter includes horses, dogs, cats, birds, farm scenes, ranch scenes, cowboys, cattle, horse shows, landscapes/scenics, gardening. Model release required.

AUDIOVISUAL NEEDS Uses film and videotape. Occasionally works with freelance filmmakers to produce educational horse health films and demonstrations of product use.

SPECS Uses 35mm, 2¼×2¼, 4×5 transparencies; 16mm and 35mm film and videotape. Accepts images in digital format. Send via CD, ZIP.

MAKING CONTACT & TERMS Send query letter with samples; include SASE for return of material. Provide résumé, business card, brochure, flyer or tearsheets to be kept on file. Works with freelance photographers on assignment basis only. Pays $50-350 for color photos. Pays on publication. Credit line given whenever possible. Buys one-time rights.

TIPS "Send me a number of good, reasonably priced for one-time use photos of dogs, horses or farm scenes. Better yet, send me good-quality dupes I can keep on file for *rush* use. When the dupes are in the file and I see them regularly, the ones I like stick in my mind and I find myself planning ways to use them. We are looking for original, dramatic work. We especially like to see horses, dogs, cats and cattle captured in artistic scenes or poses. All shots should show off quality animals with good conformation. We rarely use shots if people are shown and prefer animals in natural settings or in barns/stalls."

☻ ◑ ⊛ FLINT COMMUNICATIONS

101 N. 10th St., Suite 300, Fargo ND 58107. (701)237-4850. Fax: (701)234-9680. E-mail: gerriL@flintcom. com, dawnk@flintcom.com. Website: www.flintcom. com. **Contact:** Gerri Lien, creative director; Dawn Koranda, art director. Estab. 1946. Ad agency. Ap-

proximate annual billing: $9 million. Number of employees: 30. Firm specializes in display design, direct mail, magazine ads, publication design, signage, annual reports. Types of clients: industrial, financial, agriculture, health care and tourism.

NEEDS Works with 2-3 photographers/month. Uses photos for direct mail, P-O-P displays, posters and audiovisual. Subjects include: babies/children/teens, couples, parents, senior citizens, architecture, rural, adventure, automobiles, events, food/drink, health/fitness, sports, travel, agriculture, industry, medicine, political, product shots/still life, science, technology, manufacturing, finance, health care, business. Interested in documentary, historical/vintage, seasonal. Reviews stock photos. Model release preferred.

AUDIOVISUAL NEEDS Works with 1-2 filmmakers and 1-2 videographers/month. Uses slides and film.

SPECS Uses 35mm, 2¼×2¼, 4×5 transparencies. Accepts images in digital format. Send via CD, Zip as TIFF, EPS, JPEG files.

MAKING CONTACT & TERMS Send query letter with stock list. Submit portfolio for review. Provide résumé, business card, brochure, flier or tearsheets to be kept on file. Responds in 1-2 weeks. Pays $50-150 for b&w photos; $50-1,500 for color photos; $50-130/hour; $400-1,200/day; $100-2,000/job. Pays on receipt of invoice. Buys one-time rights.

$ ◐ 🎞 FRIEDENTAG PHOTOGRAPHICS

314 S. Niagara St., Denver CO 80224-1324. (303)333-0570. E-mail: harveyfriedentag@msn.com. Estab. 1957. AV firm. Approximate annual billing: $500,000. Number of employees: 3. Firm specializes in direct mail, annual reports, publication design, magazine ads. Types of clients: business, industry, financial, publishing, government, trade and union organizations. Produces slide sets, motion pictures and videotape. Examples of recent clients: Perry Realtors annual report (advertising, mailing); Lighting Unlimited catalog (illustrations).

NEEDS Works with 5-10 photographers/month on assignment only. Buys 1,000 photos and 25 films/year. Reviews stock photos of business, training, public relations, and industrial plants showing people and equipment or products in use. Other subjects include agriculture, business concepts, industry, medicine, military, political, science, technology/computers. Interested in avant garde, documentary, erotic, fashion/glamour. Model release required.

AUDIOVISUAL NEEDS Uses freelance photos in color slide sets and motion pictures. "No posed looks." Also produces mostly 16mm Ektachrome and some 16mm × ¾ inch and VHS videotape. Length requirement: 3-30 minutes. Interested in stock footage on business, industry, education and unusual information. "No scenics, please!"

SPECS Uses 8×10 glossy b&w and color prints; 35mm, 2¼×2¼, 4×5 color transparencies. Accepts images in digital format. Send via CD as JPEG files.

MAKING CONTACT & TERMS Send material by mail for consideration. Provide flier, business card, brochure and nonreturnable samples to show clients. Responds in 3 weeks. Pays $500/day for still; $700/day for motion picture plus expenses; $100 maximum for b&w photos; $200 maximum for color photos; $700 maximum for film; $700 maximum for videotape. **Pays on acceptance.** Buys rights as required by clients.

TIPS "More imagination needed—be different; *no scenics, pets or portraits*, and above all, technical quality is a must. There are more opportunities now than ever, especially for new people. We are looking to strengthen our file of talent across the nation."

$ ◎ 🎞 GIBSON ADVERTISING

928 Broadwater Ave., Suite 244, Billings MT 59101. (406)248-3555. Fax: (406)839-9006. E-mail: mike@gibsonad.com. Website: www.gibsonad.com. **Contact:** Mike Curtis, president. Estab. 1984. Ad agency. Number of employees: 2. Types of clients: industrial, financial, retail, food, medical.

NEEDS Works with 1-3 freelance photographers and 1-2 videographers/month. Uses photos for direct mail, P-O-P displays, catalogs, posters, newspapers, signage, audiovisual. Subjects vary with job. Reviews stock photos. "We would like to see more Western photos." Model release required. Property release preferred.

AUDIOVISUAL NEEDS Uses slides and videotape.

SPECS Uses color and b&w prints; 35mm, 2¼×2¼, 4×5, 8×10 transparencies; 16mm, VHS, Betacam videotape; and digital formats.

MAKING CONTACT & TERMS Send query letter with résumé of credits or samples. Provide résumé, business card, brochure, flier or tearsheets to be kept on file. Works with local freelancers on assignment only. Keeps samples on file. Cannot return material. Responds in 2 weeks. Pays $75-150/job; $150-250 for color photo; $75-150 for b&w photo; $100-150/hour for video. Pays on receipt of invoice, net 30 days. Credit line sometimes given. Buys one-time and electronic rights. Rights negotiable.

⊛ GOLD & ASSOCIATES, INC.

6000-C Sawgrass Village Cir., Ponte Vedra Beach FL 32082. (904)285-5669. Fax: (904)285-1579. E-mail: gold@strikegold.com. Website: www.strikegold.com. **Contact:** Keith Gold, creative director/CEO. Estab. 1988. Marketing/design/advertising firm. Approximate annual billing: $50 million in capitalized billings. Multiple offices throughout Eastern U.S. Firm specializes in health care, publishing, tourism, entertainment industries. Examples of clients: State of Florida; Harcourt; Time-Warner; GEICO; the PGA Tour. **NEEDS** Works with 1-4 photographers/month. Uses photos for print advertising, posters, brochures, direct mail, television spots, packaging. Subjects vary. Reviews stock photos and reels. Tries to buy out images.
AUDIOVISUAL NEEDS Works with 1-2 filmmakers/month. Uses 35mm film; no video.
SPECS Uses digital images.
MAKING CONTACT & TERMS Contact through rep. Provide samples to be kept on file. Works with freelancers from across the U.S. Cannot return material. Only responds to "photographers being used." Pays 50% on receipt of invoice, 50% on completion. Credit line given only for original work where the photograph is the primary design element; never for spot or stock photos. Buys all rights worldwide.

⊛ HALLOWES PRODUCTIONS & ADVERTISING

11260 Regent St., Los Angeles CA 90066-3414. (310)390-4767. Fax: (310)745-1107. E-mail: adjim@aol.com. Website: www.jimhallowes.com; www.hallowesproductions.com. **Contact:** Jim Hallowes, creative director/producer-director. Estab. 1984. Creates and produces TV commercials, corporate films and videos, and print and electronic advertising.
NEEDS Buys 8-10 photos/year. Uses photos for magazines, posters, newspapers and brochures. Reviews stock photos; subjects vary.
AUDIOVISUAL NEEDS Uses film and video for TV commercials and corporate films.

SPECS Uses 35mm, 4×5 transparencies; 35mm/16mm film; Beta SP videotape; all digital formats.
MAKING CONTACT & TERMS Send query letter with résumé of credits. "Do not fax unless requested." Keeps samples on file. Responds if interested. Payment negotiable. Pays on usage. Credit line sometimes given, depending upon usage, usually not. Buys first and all rights; rights vary depending on client.

⊛⊛ ◑ HENRY SCHMIDT DESIGN

P.O. Box 67204, Portland OR 97268. (503)652-1114. E-mail: hank@hankink.com. Website: www.hankink.com. **Contact:** Hank Schmidt, president. Estab. 1976. Design firm. Number of employees: 2. Approximate annual billing: $160,000. Firm specializes in branding, packaging, P-O-P displays, catalog/sales literature.
NEEDS Works with 1-2 photographers/month. Uses photos for catalogs and packaging. Subjects include product shots/still life. Interested in fashion/glamour. Model/property release required.
MAKING CONTACT & TERMS Contact via e-mail with samples attached and link to website. Buys all rights.

BERNARD HODES GROUP

Website: www.hodes.com. **Contact:** Gregg Petermann, creative director. Estab. 1970. Member of Western Art Directors Club, San Francisco Ad Club. Ad agency, design firm. Has over 90 offices and affiliates worldwide; approximately 700 employees. Firm specializes in annual reports, collateral, direct mail, magazine ads, packaging, publication design. Types of clients: industrial, retail, nonprofit.
NEEDS Works with 1 or more photographers/month. Uses photos for brochures, catalogs, consumer and trade magazines, direct mail. Model release preferred.
AUDIOVISUAL NEEDS Uses slides.
SPECS Uses 35mm, 2¼×2¼, 4×5 transparencies. Accepts images in digital format. Send via CD, SyQuest, ZIP, e-mail as TIFF, EPS, JPEG files.
MAKING CONTACT & TERMS Send query letter with résumé. Works with local freelancers only. Provide résumé, business card, self-promotion piece to be kept on file. Pays net 30 days. Buys all rights.

⊛ ◑ HOWARD, MERRELL AND PARTNERS, INC.

8521 Six Forks Rd., 4th Floor, Raleigh NC 27615. (919)848-2400. Fax: (919)845-9845. Website: www.

merrellgroup.com. **Contact:** Ann Neely, art buyer. Estab. 1945. Member of AAAA. Number of employees: 45.

NEEDS Works with 1-2 photographers/month. Uses photos for consumer and trade magazines, newspapers, collateral, outdoor boards and websites. Purchases stock images. Model/property release required.

SPECS Uses b&w prints; 2¼×2¼, 4×5 transparencies. Accepts images in digital format.

MAKING CONTACT & TERMS Query on the website form. Provide samples to be kept on file. Work on assignment and buys stock photos. Pays on receipt of invoice. Buys one-time and all rights.

⊗⊗⊗ ◐ HUTCHINSON ASSOCIATES, INC.

822 Linden Ave., Suite 200, Oak Park IL 60302. (312)455-9191. Fax: (312)455-9190. E-mail: hutch@hutchinson.com, or contact via website. Website: www.hutchinson.com. **Contact:** Jerry Hutchinson, president. Estab. 1988. Member of American Institute of Graphic Arts. Design firm. Number of employees: 3. Firm specializes in identity development, website development, annual reports, collateral, magazine ads, publication design, marketing brochures. Types of clients: industrial, financial, real estate, retail, publishing, nonprofit and medical. Recent client: Cardinal Growth.

NEEDS Works with 1 photographer/month. Uses photographs for annual reports, brochures, consumer and trade magazines, direct mail, catalogs, websites and posters. Subjects include: still life, real estate. Reviews stock photos.

SPECS Accepts images in digital format.

MAKING CONTACT & TERMS Send query letter with samples. Keeps samples on file. Responds "when the right project comes along." Payment rates depend on the client. Pays within 30-45 days. Credit line sometimes given. Buys one-time, exclusive product and all rights; negotiable.

TIPS In samples, "print quality and composition count."

⊗ ◉ ⊗ IDEA BANK MARKETING

P.O. Box 2117, Hastings NE 68902. (402)463-0588. Fax: (402)463-2187. Website: www.ideabankmarketing.com. **Contact:** Sherma Jones, vice president/creative director. Estab. 1982. Member of Lincoln Ad Federation. Ad agency. Approximate annual billing: $1.5 million. Number of employees: 13. Types of clients: industrial, financial, tourism and retail.

NEEDS Works with 1-2 photographers/quarter. Uses photos for direct mail, catalogs, posters and newspapers. Subjects include people and products. Reviews stock photos. Model release required; property release preferred.

AUDIOVISUAL NEEDS Works with 1 videographer/quarter. Uses slides and videotape for presentations.

SPECS Uses digital images.

MAKING CONTACT & TERMS Provide résumé, business card, brochure, flyer or tearsheets to be kept on file. Works with freelancers on assignment only. Responds in 2 weeks. Pays $75-125/hour; $650-1,000/day. Pays on acceptance with receipt of invoice. Credit line sometimes given depending on client and project. Buys all rights; negotiable.

⊗ IMAGE INTEGRATION

2619 Benvenue Ave., #A, Berkeley CA 94704. (510)841-8524. E-mail: vincesail@aol.com. **Contact:** Vince Casalaina, owner. Estab. 1971. Firm specializes in material for TV productions and Internet sites. Approximate annual billing: $100,000. Examples of recent clients: "Internet coverage of Melges 32 World Championship, 505 World Championship, Snipe World Championship, Snipe Women's World Championship. 30-Minute Documentary on the Snipe Class as it turns 80 in 2011.

NEEDS Works with 1 photographer/month. Reviews stock photos of sailing only. Property release preferred. Photo captions required; include regatta name, regatta location, date.

AUDIOVISUAL NEEDS Works with 1 videographer/month. Uses videotape. Subjects include: sailing only.

SPECS Uses 4×5 or larger matte color and b&w prints; 35mm transparencies; 16mm film and Betacam videotape. Prefers images in digital format. Send via e-mail, ZIP, CD (preferred).

MAKING CONTACT & TERMS Send unsolicited photos of sailing by mail with SASE for consideration. Keeps samples on file. Responds in 2 weeks. Payment depends on distribution. Pays on publication. Credit line sometimes given, depending upon whether any credits included. Buys nonexclusive rights; negotiable.

JUDE STUDIOS

8000 Research Forest, Suite 115-266, The Woodlands TX 77382. (281)364-9366. Fax: (281)364-9529. E-mail: jdollar@judestudios.com. **Contact:** Judith Dollar, art director. Estab. 1994. Number of employees: 2. Firm specializes in collateral, direct mail, packaging. Types of clients: nonprofits, builder, retail, destination marketing, event marketing, service. Examples of recent clients: home builder; festivals and events; corporate collateral; various logos; banking.

NEEDS Works with 1 photographer/month. Uses photos for newsletters, brochures, catalogs, direct mail, trade and trade show graphics. Needs photos of families, active adults, senior citizens, education, pets, business concepts, industry, product shots/still life, technology/computers. Model release required; property release preferred. Photo captions preferred.

SPECS Accepts images in digital format. Do not e-mail attachments.

MAKING CONTACT & TERMS Send e-mail with link to website, blog, or portfolio. Provide business card, self-promotion piece to be kept on file. Responds only if interested; send nonreturnable samples. Pays by the project. Pays on receipt of invoice.

KINETIC: THE TECHNOLOGY AGENCY

200 Distillery Commons, Suite 200, Louisville KY 40206-1990. (502)719-9500. Fax: (502)719-9509. E-mail: info@thetechnologyagency.com. Website: www.thetechnologyagency.com. Estab. 1968. Types of clients: industrial, financial, fashion, retail and food.

NEEDS Works with freelance photographers and/or videographers as needed. Uses photos for audiovisual and print. Model and/or property release required.

SPECS Prefers images in digital format. Send via CD, Jaz, ZIP as TIFF files.

MAKING CONTACT & TERMS Provide résumé, business card, brochure, flier or tearsheets to be kept on file. Works with local freelancers only. Responds only when interested. Payment negotiable. Pays within 30 days. Buys all rights.

KOCHAN & COMPANY

800 Geyer Ave., St. Louis MO 63104. (314)621-4455. Fax: (314)621-1777. Website: www.kochanandcompany.com. Estab. 1987. Member of AAAA. AAF/St. Louis. Ad agency. Number of employees: 10. Firm specializes in brand identity, print and magazine ads,

outdoor, direct mail, signage. Recent clients: Argosy Casino (billboards/duratrans); Pasta House Co. (menu inserts); Mystique Casino/billboards/print ads.

NEEDS Uses photos for billboards, brochures, catalogs, direct mail, newspapers, posters, signage. Reviews stock photos. Model/property release required. Photo captions required.

MAKING CONTACT & TERMS Send query letter with samples, brochure, stock list, tearsheets. To show portfolio, photographer should follow up with call and letter after initial query. Portfolio should include b&w, color, prints, tearsheets, slides, transparencies. Works with freelancers on assignment only. Keeps samples on file. Responds only if interested; send nonreturnable samples. Pays on receipt of invoice. Credit line given. Buys all rights.

LIGGETT STASHOWER

1422 Euclid Ave., Suite 400, Cleveland OH 44115. (216)348-8500. E-mail: info@liggett.com. Website: www.liggett.com. **Contact:** Tom Federico. Estab. 1932. (Formerly Ligget Stashower Advertising, Inc.) Ad and PR agency. Examples of recent clients: Forest City Management; Ritz-Carlton; Crane Performance Siding; Henkel Consumer Adhesives; TimberTech.

NEEDS Works with 10 photographers, filmmakers and videographers/month. Uses photos for billboards, websites, consumer and trade magazines, direct mail, P-O-P displays, catalogs, posters, newspapers, signage and audiovisual. Interested in reviewing stock photos/film or video footage. Model/property release required.

AUDIOVISUAL NEEDS Uses film and videotape for commercials.

SPECS Uses b&w and color prints (size and finish varies); 2¼×2¼, 4×5, 8×10 transparencies; 16mm film; ¼-¾-inch videotape. Accepts images in digital format.

MAKING CONTACT & TERMS Send query letter with samples. Provide résumé, business card, brochure, flyer or tearsheets to be kept on file. Responds only if interested. Pays according to project. Buys one-time, exclusive product, all rights; negotiable.

LINEAR CYCLE PRODUCTIONS

P.O. Box 2608, North Hills CA 91393-2608. (818)347-9880. Fax: (818)347-9880. E-mail: Lcp@Wgn.net.

Website: www.Linearcycleproductions.com. **Contact:** Mason Pandanceski, associate director. Estab. 1980. Number of employees 30. Approximate annual billing $500,000. AV firm. Specializes in display design, magazine ads, design and packaging signage. Current clients include: Katz, Inc.; Doland, Kilpatrich & Spear; Sterling Estates and United Twade, LLP. Serves industrial, publishing and retail clients.

NEEDS Uses freelance photos for billboards, consumer magazines, newspapers and signage. Needs recreational photographs of automobiles, entertainment, events, hobbies, humor, performing arts, sports and travel. Needs style art in lifestyle, historical/vintage, seasonal, erotic and documentary. Model releases and property releases are preferred. Photo captions are preferred. Reviews 35mm, film and video. Reviews digital images via CD or Zipped JPEG files at 400-600 dpi.

AUDIOVISUAL NEEDS Works with 8-12 filmmakers and 8-12 videographers/month. Uses slides and film or video for television/motion pictures. Subjects include: archival-humor material.

SPECS Uses 8×10 color and b&w prints; 35mm, 8×10 transparencies; 16mm-35mm film; ½-inch, ¾-inch, 1-inch videotape. Accepts images in digital format. Send via CD, floppy disk, Jaz as TIFF, GIF, JPEG files.

MAKING CONTACT & TERMS Submit portfolio for review. Send a query letter with résumé, business card, artist's statement, biography, photographs/slides/SASE/transparencies. Samples kept on file with résumé. Samples not returned. Responds within 90 days. Portfolio should include color, original art, photographs, slides, transparencies and tearsheets. Paid by the project, on acceptance. Buys all rights.

TIPS "Make sure all photos and multimedia elements are presented in original formats that show supreme quality of work. If originals are desired, no photocopies can be accepted. The same goes for video and related elements."

$$ LOHRE & ASSOCIATES INC.

126A W. 14th St., 2nd Floor, Cincinnati OH 45202-7535. (513)961-1174. Website: www.lohre.com. **Contact:** Chuck Lohre, president. Ad agency. Types of clients: industrial.

NEEDS Uses photos for trade magazines, direct mail, catalogs and prints. Subjects include: machine-industrial themes and various eye-catchers.

SPECS Uses high-res digital images.

MAKING CONTACT & TERMS Send query letter with résumé of credits. Provide business card, brochure, flier or tearsheets to be kept on file.

$ [O] MCGUIRE ASSOCIATES

1234 Sherman Ave., Evanston IL 60202. (847)328-4433. Fax: (847)328-4425. E-mail: jmcguire@ameritech.net. **Contact:** James McGuire, owner. Estab. 1979. Design firm. Specializes in annual reports, publication design, direct mail, corporate materials. Types of clients: industrial, retail, nonprofit.

NEEDS Uses photos for annual reports, consumer and trade magazines, direct mail, catalogs, brochures. Reviews stock photos. Model release required.

SPECS Prefers high-res digital images. Uses color and b&w prints, transparencies.

MAKING CONTACT & TERMS Provide résumé, business card, brochure, flyer or tearsheets to be kept on file. Cannot return material. Photo fee based on project budget. Pays on receipt of invoice. Credit line sometimes given depending upon client or project. Buys all rights; negotiable.

$$$ ⊘ THE MILLER GROUP

1516 Bundy Dr., Suite 200, Los Angeles CA 90025. (310)442-0101. Fax: (310)442-0107. E-mail: gary@millergroup.net. Website: www.millergroup.net. **Contact:** Gary Bettman. Estab. 1990. Member of WSAAA. Approximate annual billing: $12 million. Number of employees: 10. Firm specializes in print advertising. Types of clients: consumer.

NEEDS Uses photos for billboards, brochures, consumer magazines, direct mail, newspapers. Model release required.

MAKING CONTACT & TERMS Contact through rep or send query letter with photocopies. Provide self-promotion piece to be kept on file. Buys all rights; negotiable.

TIPS "Please, no calls!"

◐ MONDERER DESIGN, INC.

2067 Massachusetts Ave., 3rd Floor, Cambridge MA 02140. (617)661-6125. Fax: (617)661-6126. E-mail: info@monderer.com. Website: www.monderer.com. **Contact:** Stewart Monderer, president. Estab. 1981. Specializes in corporate identity, branding, print collateral, website, event and interactive solutions. Clients: corporations (technology, education, consulting and life science). Current clients include Solidworks, Thermo Scientific, MIT Sloan, Northeastern University, Progress Software, Kronos, Greenlight Fund, Canaccord Genuity.

NEEDS Works with 2 photographers/month. Uses photos for advertising, annual reports, catalogs, posters and brochures. Subjects include: environmental, architecture, cities/urban, education, adventure, automobiles, entertainment, events, performing arts, sports, travel, business concepts, industry, medicine, product shots/still life, science, technology/computers, conceptual, site specific, people on location. Interested in alternative process, avant garde, documentary, historical/vintage, seasonal. Model release preferred; property release sometimes required.

SPECS Accepts images in digital format. Send via CD as TIFF, EPS files at 300 dpi.

MAKING CONTACT & TERMS Send unsolicited photos by mail for consideration. Keeps samples on file. Follow up from photographers recommended. Payment negotiable. Pays on receipt of invoice. Credit line sometimes given depending upon client. Rights always negotiated depending on use.

⊛⊛ ◐ ⊛ MULLIN/ASHLEY ASSOCIATE

306 Cannon St., P.O. Box 118, Chesteron MD 21620. (410)778-2184. Fax: (410)778-6640. E-mail: mar@mullinashley.com; info@mullinashley.com. Website: www.mullinashley.com. **Contact:** Marlayn King, creative director. Estab. 1978. Approximate annual billing: $2 million. Number of employees: 6. Firm specializes in collateral and interactive media. Types of clients: industrial, business to business, health care. Examples of recent clients: W.L. Gore & Associates, Nevamar of International Paper, Community Hospitals.

NEEDS Works with 1 photographer/month. Uses photos for brochures and online. Subjects include: business concepts, industry, product shots/still life, technology. Also needs industrial, business to business, healthcare on location. Model release required; property release preferred. Photo captions preferred.

AUDIOVISUAL NEEDS Works with 1 videographer/year. Uses for corporate capabilities, brochure, training, videos.

SPECS Prefers images in digital format; also uses 2¼×2¼, 4×5 transparencies; high-8 video.

MAKING CONTACT & TERMS Send query letter or e-mail with résumé and digital files. Responds only if interested; send nonreturnable samples. Pays $500-5,000 for b&w or color photos; depends on the project or assignment. Pays on 30 days receipt of invoice. Credit line sometimes given depending upon assignment.

◎ ◐ MYRIAD PRODUCTIONS

415 Barlow Ct., Johns Creek GA 30022. (678)417-0041. E-mail: myriad@mindspring.com. **Contact:** Ed Harris, president. Estab. 1965. Primarily involved with sports productions and events. Types of clients: publishing, nonprofit.

NEEDS Works with photographers on assignment-only basis. Uses photos for portraits, live-action and studio shots, special effects, advertising, illustrations, brochures, TV and film graphics, theatrical and production stills. Subjects include: celebrities, entertainment, sports. Model/property release required. Photo captions preferred; include names, location, date, description.

SPECS Uses 8×10 b&w and color prints; 2¼×2¼ transparencies. Accepts images in digital format. Send "Mac-compatible CD or DVD. No floppy disks or ZIPs!"

MAKING CONTACT & TERMS Provide brochure, résumé or samples to be kept on file. Send material by mail for consideration. "No telephone or fax inquiries, please!" Cannot return material. Response time "depends on urgency of job or production." Payment negotiable. Credit line sometimes given. Buys all rights.

TIPS "We look for an imaginative photographer—one who captures all the subtle nuances. Working with us depends almost entirely on the photographer's skill and creative sensitivity with the subject. All materials submitted will be placed on file and not returned, pending future assignments. Photographers should not send us their only prints, transparencies, etc., for this reason."

⊛ NATIONAL BLACK CHILD DEVELOPMENT INSTITUTE

1313 L St., NW, Suite 110, Washington D.C. 20005. (202)833-2220. Fax: (202)833-8222. E-mail: moreinfo@nbcdi.org; vdavis@nbcdi.org. Website: www.nbcdi.org. Carol Brunson Day, president. **Contact:** Vicki L. Davis, vice president. Estab. 1970.

NEEDS Uses photos in brochures, newsletters, annual reports and annual calendar. Candid action photos of black children and youth. Reviews stock photos. Model release required.

SPECS Uses 5×7, 8×10 color and glossy b&w prints; color slides; b&w contact sheets. Accepts images in digital format. Send via CD.

MAKING CONTACT & TERMS Send query letter with samples; include SASE for return of material. Pays $70 for cover; $20 for inside. Credit line given. Buys one-time rights.

TIPS "Candid action photographs of one black child or youth or a small group of children or youths. Color photos selected are used in annual calendar and are placed beside an appropriate poem selected by organization. Therefore, photograph should communicate a message in an indirect way. B&w photographs are used in quarterly newsletter and reports. Obtain sample of publications published by organization to see the type of photographs selected."

⊗ ⊗ ◎ ◐ ⊛ NOVUS COMMUNICATIONS

121 E. 24th St., 12th Floor, New York NY 10010. (212)473-1377. Fax: (212)505-3300. E-mail: novuscom@aol.com. Website: www.novuscommunications.com. **Contact:** Robert Antonik, managing director. Estab. 1988. Integrated creative marketing and communications firm. Number of employees: 5. Firm specializes in multi-channel online and offline advertising, annual reports, publication design, display design, multimedia, packaging, direct mail, signage and website, Internet and DVD development. Types of clients: start ups and developers, industrial, financial, retail, health care, entertainment, nonprofit.

NEEDS Works with 1 photographer/month. Uses photos for cross-marketing campaigns, business-to-business direct mail, digital displays, online and print catalogs, posters, packaging and signage. Subjects include: babies/children/teens, couples, multicultural, families, parents, senior citizens, environmental, landscapes/scenics, wildlife, architecture, cities/urban, education, gardening, interiors/decorating, pets, religious, rural, adventure, automobiles, entertainment, events, food/drink, health/fitness, hobbies, humor, performing arts, sports, travel, agriculture, business concepts, industry, medicine, military, political, product shots/still life, science, technology/computers. Interested in alternative process, avant garde, documentary, fashion/glamour, fine art, historical/vintage,

seasonal. Reviews stock photos. Model/property release required. Photo captions preferred.

AUDIOVISUAL NEEDS Uses film, videotape, DVD.

SPECS Accepts images in digital format. Send via ZIP, CD as TIFF, JPEG files.

MAKING CONTACT & TERMS Arrange a personal interview to show portfolio. Works on assignment only. Keeps samples on file. Cannot return material. Responds in 1-2 weeks. Pays $85-175 for b&w photos; $175-800 for color photos; $300-1,000 for digital film; $175-800 for videotape. Pays upon client's payment. Credit line given. Rights negotiable.

TIPS "The marriage of photos and illustrations continues to be trendy. More illustrators and photographers are adding stock usage as part of their business. E-mail with link to website. Send a sample postcard; follow up with phone call. Use low-tech marketing."

⊛ ◎ OMNI PRODUCTIONS

P.O. Box 302, Carmel IN 46082-0302. (317)846-2345, ext.111. E-mail: winston@omniproductions.com; omni@omniproductions.com. Website: www.omniproductions.com. **Contact:** Winston Long, president. AV firm. Types of clients: industrial, corporate, educational, government, medical.

NEEDS Works with 6-12 photographers/month. Uses photos for AV presentations. Subject matter varies. Also works with freelance filmmakers to produce training films and commercials. Model release required.

SPECS Uses b&w and color prints; 35mm transparencies; 16mm and 35mm film and videotape. Accepts images in digital format.

MAKING CONTACT & TERMS Provide complete contact info, rates, business card, brochure, flyer, digital samples or tearsheets to be kept on file. Works with freelance photographers on assignment basis only. Cannot return unsolicited material. Payment negotiable. **Pays on acceptance.** Credit line given "sometimes, as specified in production agreement with client." Buys all rights on most work; will purchase one-time use on some projects.

◎ POINTBLANK AGENCY

(818)539-2282. Fax: (818)551-9681. E-mail: valn@pointblankagency.com. Website: www.pointblankagency.com. **Contact:** Valod Nazarian. Ad and design agency. Serves travel, high-technology and consumer-technology clients.

NEEDS Uses photos for trade show graphics, websites, consumer and trade magazines, direct mail, P-O-P displays, newspapers. Subject matter of photography purchased includes: conceptual shots of people and table top (tight shots of electronics products). Model release required. Photo captions preferred.

SPECS Uses 8×10 matte b&w and color prints; 35mm, 2¼×2¼, 4×5, 8×10 transparencies. Accepts images in digital format. Send via CD.

MAKING CONTACT & TERMS Arrange a personal interview to show portfolio. Provide résumé, business card, brochure, flyer or tearsheets to be kept on file. Works on assignment basis only. Does not return unsolicited material. Responds in 3 weeks. Pay is negotiable. Pays on receipt of invoice. Buys one-time, exclusive product, electronic, buy-outs, and all rights (work-for-hire); negotiable.

TIPS Prefers to see "originality, creativity, uniqueness, technical expertise" in work submitted. There is more use of "photo composites, dramatic lighting and more attention to detail" in photography.

❸ ⬤ POSEY SCHOOL

P.O. Box 254, Northport NY 11768. (631)757-2700. E-mail: EPosey@optonline.net. Website: www.poseyschool.com. **Contact:** Elsa Posey, president. Estab. 1953. Sponsors a school of dance, art, music, drama; regional dance company and acting company. Uses photos for brochures, news releases, newspapers.

NEEDS Buys 12-15 photos/year; offers 4 assignments/year. Special subject needs include children dancing, ballet, modern dance, jazz/tap (theater dance) and "photos showing class situations in any subjects we offer. Photos must include girls and boys, women and men. " Interested in documentary, fine art, historical/vintage. Reviews stock photos. Model release required.

SPECS Uses 8×10 glossy b&w prints. Accepts images in digital format. Send via CD, e-mail.

MAKING CONTACT & TERMS "Call us." Responds in 1 week. Pays $35-50 for most photos, b&w or color. Credit line given if requested. Buys one-time rights; negotiable.

TIPS "We are small but interested in quality (professional) work. Capture the joy of dance in a photo of children or adults. Show artists, actors or musicians at work. We prefer informal action photos, not posed pictures. We need photos of *real* dancers dancing. Call first. Be prepared to send photos on request."

◎ ⬤ QUALLY & COMPANY, INC.

1187 Wilmette Ave., Suite 160, Wilmette IL 60091-2719. (312)280-1898. E-mail: quallycompany@hotmail.com. Website: www.quallycompany.com. **Contact:** Mike Iva, creative director. Estab. 1979. Ad agency. Types of clients: new product development and launches.

NEEDS Uses photos for every media. "Subject matter varies, but it must always be a 'quality image' regardless of what it portrays." Model/property release required. Photo captions preferred.

SPECS Uses b&w and color prints; 35mm, 4×5, 8×10 transparencies. Accepts images in digital format.

MAKING CONTACT & TERMS Send query letter with photocopies, tearsheets. Provide résumé, business card, brochure, flyer or tearsheets to be kept on file. Responds only if interested; send nonreturnable samples. Payment negotiable. Pays net 30 days from receipt of invoice. Credit line sometimes given, depending on client's cooperation. Rights purchased depend on circumstances.

⬤ QUON DESIGN

543 River Rd., Fair Haven NJ 07704-3227. (732)212-9200. Fax: (732)212-9217. E-mail: studio@quondesign.com. Website: www.quondesign.com. **Contact:** Mike Quon, president/creative director. Design firm. Firm specializes in corporate identity/ logos, collateral, event promotion, advertising, illustration. Types of clients: industrial, financial, retail, publishers, nonprofit.

NEEDS Works with 1-3 photographers/year. Uses photos for direct mail, P-O-P displays, packaging, signage. Model/property release preferred. Photo captions required; include company name.

SPECS Uses color and b&w digital images.

MAKING CONTACT & TERMS Submit portfolio for review by mail only. No drop-offs. "Please, do not call office. Contact through mail only." Keeps samples on file. Responds only if interested; send nonreturnable samples. Pays net 30 days. Credit line given when possible. Buys first rights, one-time rights; negotiable.

TIPS "Currently using more stock photography and less assignment work."

❸❸ ⬤ TED ROGGEN ADVERTISING AND PUBLIC RELATIONS

101 Westcott St., Unit 306, Houston TX 77007. (713)426-2314. Fax: (713)869-3563. E-mail: sroggen@aol.com.

Contact: Ted Roggen. Estab. 1945. Ad agency and PR firm. Number of employees: 3. Firm specializes in magazine ads, direct mail. Types of clients: construction, entertainment, food, finance, publishing, travel.

NEEDS Buys 25-50 photos/year; offers 50-75 assignments/year. Uses photos for billboards, direct mail, radio, TV, P-O-P displays, brochures, annual reports, PR releases, sales literature and trade magazines. Subjects include adventure, health/fitness, sports, travel. Interested in fashion/glamour. Model release required. Photo captions required.

SPECS Uses 5×7 glossy or matte b&w and color prints; 4×5 transparencies. "Contact sheet OK."

MAKING CONTACT & TERMS Provide résumé to be kept on file. Pays $75-250 for b&w photos; $125-300 for color photos; $150/hour. **Pays on acceptance.** Rights negotiable.

ARNOLD SAKS ASSOCIATES

118 E. 28th St., Suite 401, New York NY 10016. (212)861-4300. Fax: (212)861-4347. E-mail: afiorillo @saksdesign.com. Website: www.saksdesign.com. **Contact:** Anita Fiorillo, vice president. Estab. 1967. Graphic design firm. Number of employees: 6. Approximate annual billing: $2 million. Types of clients: industrial, financial, legal, pharmaceutical, hospitals. Examples of recent clients: Alcoa; McKinsey; UBS; Wyeth; Xerox; Hospital for Special Surgery.

NEEDS Works with approximately 10 photographers during busy season. Uses photos for annual reports and corporate brochures. Subjects include corporate situations and portraits. Wants photos of babies/children/teens, couples, multicultural, families, parents, senior citizens, automobiles, health/fitness/beauty, performing arts, sports, business concepts, industry, medicine, product shots/still life, science, technology/computers. Reviews stock photos; subjects vary according to the nature of the annual report. Model release required. Photo captions preferred.

SPECS Accepts images in digital format. Send via e-mail as TIFF, EPS, JPEG files.

MAKING CONTACT & TERMS "Appointments are set up during the spring for summer review on a first-come only basis. We have a limit of approximately 30 portfolios each season." Call to arrange an appointment. Responds as needed. Payment negotiable, "based on project budgets. Generally we pay $1,500-2,500/day." Pays on receipt of invoice and payment

by client; advances provided. Credit line sometimes given depending upon client specifications. Buys one-time and all rights; negotiable.

TIPS Specializes in annual reports and corporate communications. Clients: Fortune 500 corporations. Current clients include Alcoa, Wyeth, and Hospital for Special Surgery. Client list available upon request.

❸❸❸ ✦ SIDES & ASSOCIATES

222 Jefferson St., Suite B, Lafayette LA 70501. (337)233-6473. E-mail: donny@sides.com; info@ sides.com. Website: www.sides.com. **Contact:** Larry Sides, agency president. Estab. 1976. Member of AAAA, PRSA, Association for Strategic Planning, Chamber of Commerce, Better Business Bureau. Ad agency. Number of employees: 13. Firm specializes in publication design, display design, signage, video and radio production. Types of clients: governmental, healthcare, financial, retail, nonprofit. Examples of recent clients: U.S. Dept of Homeland Security, ESF #14 (web, brochure, and special event planning); Lafayette Regional Airport (signs, brochures), Our Lady of Lourdes Regional Medical Center (TV, outdoor, print ads, brochures).

NEEDS Works with 2 photographers/month. Uses photos for billboards, brochures, newspapers, P-O-P displays, posters, signage. Subjects include: setup shots of people. Reviews stock photos of everything. Model/property release required.

AUDIOVISUAL NEEDS Works with 2 filmmakers and 2 videographers/month. Uses slides and/or film or video for broadcast, TV, newspaper.

SPECS Uses 35mm, 2¼×2¼, 4×5 transparencies.

MAKING CONTACT & TERMS Provide résumé, business card, self-promotion piece or tearsheets to be kept on file. Works with local freelancers only. Responds only if interested; send nonreturnable samples. Payment determined by client and usage. Pays "when paid by our client." Rights negotiable.

❸ ◯ ✦ SOUNDLIGHT

5438 Tennessee Ave., New Port Richey FL 34652. (727)842-6788. E-mail: keth@soundlight.org. Website: www.soundlight.org. **Contact:** Keith Luke. Estab. 1972. Approximate annual billing: $150,000. Number of employees: 2. Firm specializes in websites, direct mail, magazine ads, model portfolios, publication design. Types of clients: businesses, astrological and spiritual workshops, books, calendars, fashion, magazines, models, special events, products, nonprofit, webpages. Examples of recent clients: Sensual Women of Hawaii (calendars, post cards).

NEEDS Works with 1 freelance photographer every 7 months. Subjects include: women, celebrities, couples, Goddess, people in activities, landscapes/scenics, animals, religious, adventure, health/fitness/beauty, humor, alternative medicine, spiritual, travel sites and activities, exotic dance and models (art, glamour, lingerie, nude). Interested in alternative process, avant garde, erotic, fine art. Reviews stock photos, slides, computer images. Model release preferred for models and advertising people. Photo captions preferred; include who, what, where.

AUDIOVISUAL NEEDS Uses freelance photographers for slide sets, multimedia productions, videotapes, websites.

SPECS Uses 4×6 to 8×10 glossy color prints; 35mm color slides. Accepts images in digital format. Send via CD, floppy disk, e-mail as TIFF, GIF, JPEG files at 70-100 dpi.

MAKING CONTACT & TERMS Send query letter with résumé, stock list. Provide prints, slides, business card, computer disk, CD, contact sheets, self-promotion piece or tearsheets to be kept on file. Works on assignment; sometimes buys stock nude model photos. May not return unsolicited material. Responds in 3 weeks. Pays $100 maximum for b&w and color photos; $10-1,800 for videotape; $10-100/hour; $50-750/day; $2,000 maximum/job; sometimes also pays in "trades." Pays on publication. Credit line sometimes given. Buys one-time, all rights; various negotiable rights depending on use.

TIPS "In portfolios or demos, we look for unique lighting, style, emotional involvement; beautiful, artistic, sensual, erotic viewpoints. We see a trend toward manipulated computer images. Send query about what you have to show, to see what we can use at that time."

◎ 🎞 SOUTH CAROLINA FILM COMMISSION

1205 Pendleton St., Room 225, Columbia SC 29201. (803)737-0490. Fax: (803)737-3104. E-mail: tclark@scprt.com; danrogers@scprt.com. Website: www.filmsc.com. **Contact:** Tom Clark or Dan Rogers. Types of clients: motion picture and television producers.

🍁 $ ◎ 🎞 SUN.ERGOS

130 Sunset Way, Priddis AB T0L 1W0, Canada. (403)931-1527. Fax: (403)931-1534. E-mail: waltermoke@sunergos.com. Website: www.sunergos.com. **Contact:** Robert Greenwood, artistic and managing director. Estab. 1977. "A unique, professional, two-man company of theater and dance, touring nationally and internationally as cultural ambassadors to urban and rural communities."

NEEDS Buys 10-30 photos/year; offers 3-5 assignments/year. Uses photos for brochures, newsletters, posters, newspapers, annual reports, magazines, press releases, audiovisual uses, catalogs. Reviews theater and dance stock photos. Property release required for performance photos for media use. Photo captions required; include subject, date, city, performance title.

AUDIOVISUAL NEEDS Uses digital images, slides, film and videotape for media usage, showcases and international conferences. Subjects include performance pieces/showcase materials.

SPECS Uses 8×10, 8½×11 color and b&w prints; 35mm, 2¼×2¼ transparencies; 16mm film; NTSC/PAL/SECAM videotape.

MAKING CONTACT & TERMS Arrange a personal interview to show portfolio. Send query letter with résumé of credits. Provide résumé, business card, self-promotion piece or tearsheets to be kept on file. Works on assignment only. Response time depends on project. Pays $100-150/day; $150-300/job; $2.50-10 for color or b&w photos. Pays on usage. Credit line given. Buys all rights.

TIPS "You must have experience shooting dance and *live* theater performances."

$$$ 🎞 MARTIN THOMAS, INTERNATIONAL

42 Riverside Dr., Barrington RI 02806. (401)245-8500. Fax: (866)899-2710. E-mail: contact@martinthomas.com. Website: www.martinthomas.com. Estab. 1987. Ad agency, PR firm. Approximate annual billing: $7 million. Number of employees: 5. Firm specializes in collateral. Types of clients: industrial and business-to-business. Examples of recent clients: NADCA Show Booth, Newspaper 4PM Corp. (color newspaper); Pennzoil-Quaker State "Rescue," PVC Container Corp. (magazine article); "Bausch & Lomb," GLS Corporation (magazine cover); "Soft Bottles," McKechnie (booth graphics); "Perfectly Clear," ICI Acrylics (brochure).

NEEDS Works with 3-5 photographers/year. Uses photos for trade magazines. Subjects include: location shots of equipment in plants and some studio. Model release required.

AUDIOVISUAL NEEDS Uses videotape for 5- to 7-minute capabilities or instructional videos.

SPECS Uses 8×10 color and b&w prints; 35mm, 4×5 transparencies. Accepts images in digital format (call first). Send via CD, e-mail, floppy disk as GIF, JPEG files.

MAKING CONTACT & TERMS Send stock list. Provide résumé, business card, brochure, flier or tearsheets to be kept on file. Send materials on pricing, experience. "No unsolicited portfolios will be accepted or reviewed." Cannot return material. Pays $1,000-1,500/day; $300-900 for b&w photos; $400-1,000 for color photos. Pays 30 days following receipt of invoice. Buys exclusive product rights; negotiable.

TIPS To break in, demonstrate you can be aggressive, innovative, realistic, and can work within our clients' parameters and budgets. Be responsive; be flexible.

VIDEO I-D, TELEPRODUCTIONS

105 Muller Rd., Washington IL 61571. (309)444-4323. E-mail: videoid@videoid.com. Website: www.videoid. com. **Contact:** Sam B. Wagner, president. Estab. 1977. Number of employees: 10. Types of clients: health, education, industry, service, cable and broadcast.

NEEDS Works with 2 photographers/month to shoot digital stills, multimedia backgrounds and materials, films and videotapes. Subjects "vary from commercial to industrial—always high quality." Somewhat interested in stock photos/footage. Model release required.

AUDIOVISUAL NEEDS Uses digital stills, videotape, DVD, CD.

SPECS Uses digital still extension, Beta SP, HDV and HD. Accepts images in digital format. Send via DVD, CD, e-mail, FTP.

MAKING CONTACT & TERMS Provide résumé, business card, self-promotion piece or tearsheets to be kept on file. Also send video sample reel. Include SASE for return of material. Works with freelancers on assignment only. Responds in 3 weeks. Pays $10-65/hour; $160-650/day. Usually pays by the job; negotiable. **Pays on acceptance.** Credit line sometimes given. Buys all rights; negotiable.

TIPS "Sample reel—indicate goal for specific pieces. Show good lighting and visualization skills. Show me you can communicate what I need to see, and have a willingness to put out effort to get top quality."

WARNE MARKETING COMMUNICATIONS

65 Overlea Blvd., Suite 113, Toronto ON M4H 1P1, Canada. (416)927-0881; (888)279-7846. Fax: (416)927-1676. E-mail: john@warne.com; info@warne.com. Website: www.warne.com. John Coljee, studio manager. **Contact:** Scott Warne, president. Estab. 1979. Ad agency. Types of clients: business-to-business.

NEEDS Works with 4 photographers/month. Uses photos for trade magazines, direct mail, Internet, P-O-P displays, catalogs and posters. Subjects include: business concepts, science, technology/computers, in-plant photography and studio set-ups. Special subject needs include in-plant shots. Model release required.

AUDIOVISUAL NEEDS Uses PowerPoint and videotape.

SPECS Uses digital images or transparencies.

MAKING CONTACT & TERMS Send letter citing related experience plus 2 or 3 samples. Works on assignment only. Cannot return material. Responds in 2 weeks. Pays $1,000-1,500/day. Pays within 30 days. Buys all rights.

TIPS In portfolio/samples, prefers to see industrial subjects and creative styles. "We look for lighting knowledge, composition and imagination."

DANA WHITE PRODUCTIONS

2623 29th St., Santa Monica CA 90405. (310)450-9101. E-mail: dwprods@aol.com. **Contact:** Dr. Dana White, president. Estab. 1977. Full-service book development and design, video/film production studio. Types of clients: schools and community-based nonprofit institutions, corporate, government, publishing, marketing/advertising, art galleries. Examples of recent clients: Copper Cauldron Publishing, Toyota Hybrid Synergy: Mobile Experience Tour (video production); Los Angeles County (annual report); Back Forty Feature Films; Southern California Gas Company/South Coast AQMD (clean air environmental film trailers in 300 LA-based motion picture theaters); Glencoe/McGraw-Hill (textbook photography and illustrations, slide shows); Pepperdine University (awards banquet presentations, fundraising, biographical tribute programs); U.S. Forest Service (training programs); Venice Family Clinic (newsletter photography); Johnson & Higgins (brochure photography). "Stock photography is available through PhotoEdit: www.photoeditinc.com; locate Dana White in list of photographers."

NEEDS Works with 2-3 photographers/month. Uses photos for catalogs, audiovisual, books. Subjects include: people, products, still life, event documentation, architecture. Interested in reviewing 35mm stock photos by appointment. Model release required for people and companies. "If your portfolio is on flickr. com, please send a link to your images."

AUDIOVISUAL NEEDS Uses all AV formats including scanned and digital images for computer-based multimedia; 35mm slides for multi-image presentations; and medium-format as needed.

SPECS Uses color and b&w prints; 35mm, 2¼×2¼ transparencies; digital images (minimum 6mp files).

MAKING CONTACT & TERMS Arrange a personal interview to show portfolio and samples. "Please do not send originals." Works with freelancers on assignment only. Will assign certain work on spec. Do not submit unsolicited material. Cannot return material. Pays when images are shot to White's satisfaction—never delays until acceptance by client. Pays according to job: $25-100/hour, up to $750/day; $20-50/shot; or fixed fee based upon job complexity and priority of exposure. Hires according to work-for-hire and will share photo credit when possible.

TIPS In freelancer's portfolio or demo, wants to see "quality of composition, lighting, saturation, degree of difficulty, and importance of assignment. The trend seems to be toward more video, less AV. Clients are paying less and expecting more. To break in, freelancers should diversify, negotiate, be personable and flexible, go the distance to get and keep the job. Freelancers need to see themselves as hunters who are dependent upon their hunting skills for their livelihood. Don't get stuck in one-dimensional thinking. Think and perform as a team—service that benefits all sectors of the community and process."

○ WORCESTER POLYTECHNIC INSTITUTE

100 Institute Rd., Worcester MA 01609-2280. (508)831-6715. Fax: (508)831-5820. E-mail: charna@wpi.edu. Website: www.wpi.edu. **Contact:** Charna Westervelt, director of publications. Estab. 1865. Publishes periodicals; promotional, recruiting and fund-raising printed materials. Photos used in brochures, news-

letters, posters, audiovisual presentations, annual reports, catalogs, magazines, press releases, online.

NEEDS On-campus, comprehensive and specific views of all elements of the WPI experience.

SPECS Prefers images in digital format, but will use 5×7 (minimum) glossy b&w and color prints.

MAKING CONTACT & TERMS Arrange a personal interview to show portfolio or query with website link. Provide résumé, business card, brochure, flyer or tearsheets to be kept on file. "No phone calls." Responds in 6 weeks. Payment negotiable. Credit line given in some publications. Buys one-time or all rights; negotiable.

GALLERIES

The popularity of photography as a collectible art form has improved the market for fine art photographs over the last decade. Collectors now recognize the investment value of prints by Ansel Adams, Irving Penn, and Henri Cartier-Bresson, and therefore frequently turn to galleries for photographs to place in their private collections.

The gallery/fine art market can make money for many photographers. However, unlike commercial and editorial markets, galleries seldom generate quick income for artists. Galleries should be considered venues for important, thought-provoking imagery, rather than markets through which you can make a substantial living.

More than any other market, this area is filled with photographers who are interested in delivering a message. Many photography exhibits focus on one theme by a single artist. Group exhibits feature the work of several artists, and they often explore a theme from many perspectives, though not always. These group exhibits may be juried (i.e., the photographs in the exhibit are selected by a committee of judges who are knowledgeable about photography). Some group exhibits also may include other mediums such as painting, drawing, or sculpture. In any case, galleries want artists who can excite viewers and make them think about important subjects. They, of course, also hope that viewers will buy the photographs shown in their galleries.

As with picture buyers and art directors, gallery directors love to see strong, well-organized portfolios. Limit your portfolio to twenty top-notch images. When putting together your portfolio, focus on one overriding theme. A director wants to be certain you have enough quality work to carry an entire show. After the portfolio review, if the director likes your style, then you might discuss future projects or past work that you've done. Directors who see promise in your work, but don't think you're ready for a solo exhibition, may place your photographs in a group exhibition.

HOW GALLERIES OPERATE

In exchange for brokering images, a gallery often receives a commission of 40–50 percent. They usually exhibit work for a month, sometimes longer, and hold openings to kick off new shows. They also frequently provide pre-exhibition publicity. Some smaller galleries require exhibiting photographers to help with opening night reception expenses. Galleries also may require photographers to appear during the show or opening. Be certain that such policies are put in writing before you allow them to show your work.

Gallery directors who foresee a bright future for you might want exclusive rights to represent your work. This type of arrangement forces buyers to get your images directly from the gallery that represents you. Such contracts are quite common, usually limiting the exclusive rights to specified distances. For example, a gallery in Tulsa, Oklahoma, may have exclusive rights to distribute your work within a 200-mile radius of the gallery. This would allow you to sign similar contracts with galleries outside the 200-mile range.

FIND THE RIGHT FIT

As you search for the perfect gallery, it's important to understand the different types of exhibition spaces and how they operate. The route you choose depends on your needs, the type of work you do, your long-term goals, and the audience you're trying to reach.

- **Retail or commercial galleries.** The goal of the retail gallery is to sell and promote artists while turning a profit. Retail galleries take a commission of 40–50 percent of all sales.
- **Co-op galleries.** Co-ops exist to sell and promote artists' work, but they are run by artists. Members exhibit their own work in exchange for a fee, which covers the gallery's overhead. Some co-ops also take a commission of 20–30 percent to cover expenses. Members share the responsibilities of gallery-sitting, sales, housekeeping, and maintenance.
- **Rental galleries.** The rental gallery makes its profit primarily through renting space to artists and consequently may not take a commission on sales (or will take only a very small commission). Some rental spaces provide publicity for artists, while others do not. Showing in this type of gallery is risky. Rental galleries are sometimes thought of as "vanity galleries," and, consequently, they do not have the credibility other galleries enjoy.
- **Nonprofit galleries.** Nonprofit spaces will provide you with an opportunity to sell work and gain publicity, but will not market your work aggressively, because their goals are not necessarily sales-oriented. Nonprofits normally take a commission of 20–30 percent.

- **Museums.** Don't approach museums unless you have already exhibited in galleries. The work in museums is by established artists and is usually donated by collectors or purchased through art dealers.
- **Art consultancies.** Generally, art consultants act as liaisons between fine artists and buyers. Most take a commission on sales (as would a gallery). Some maintain small gallery spaces and show work to clients by appointment.

If you've never exhibited your work in a traditional gallery space before, you may want to start with a less traditional kind of show. Alternative spaces are becoming a viable way to help the public see your work. Try bookstores (even large chains), restaurants, coffee shops, upscale home furnishings stores, and boutiques. The art will help give their business a more pleasant, interesting environment at no cost to them, and you may generate a few fans or even a few sales.

Think carefully about what you take pictures of and what kinds of businesses might benefit from displaying them. If you shoot flowers and other plant life, perhaps you could approach a nursery about hanging your work in their sales office. If you shoot landscapes of exotic locations, maybe a travel agent would like to take you on. Think creatively and don't be afraid to approach a business person with a proposal. Just make sure the final agreement is spelled out in writing so there will be no misunderstandings, especially about who gets what money from sales.

COMPOSING AN ARTIST'S STATEMENT

When you approach a gallery about a solo exhibition, they will usually expect your body of work to be organized around a theme. To present your work and its theme to the public, the gallery will expect you to write an artist's statement, a brief essay about how and why you make photographic images. There are several things to keep in mind when writing your statement: Be brief. Most statements should be 100–300 words long. You shouldn't try to tell your life's story leading up to this moment. Write as you speak. There is no reason to make up complicated motivations for your work if there aren't any. Just be honest about why you shoot the way you do. Stay focused. Limit your thoughts to those that deal directly with the specific exhibit for which you're preparing.

Before you start writing your statement, consider your answers to the following questions: Why do you make photographs (as opposed to using some other medium)? What are your photographs about? What are the subjects in your photographs? What are you trying to communicate through your work?

ADDISON/RIPLEY FINE ART

1670 Wisconsin Ave., NW, Washington D.C. 20007. (202)338-5180. Fax: (202)338-2341. E-mail: addison rip@aol.com. Website: www.addisonripleyfineart. com. **Contact:** Christopher Addison, owner. Estab. 1981. Art consultancy, for-profit gallery. Approached by 100 artists/year; represents or exhibits 25 artists. Average display time 6 weeks. Gallery open Tuesday–Saturday, 11-6. Closed end of summer. Located in Georgetown in a large, open, light-filled gallery space. Overall price range $500-80,000. Most work sold at $2,500-10,000.

EXHIBITS Works of all media.

MAKING CONTACT & TERMS Gallery provides insurance, promotion, contract. Accepted work should be framed, mounted, matted.

SUBMISSIONS Mail portfolio for review. Send query letter with artist's statement, bio, photocopies, résumé, SASE. Responds in 1 month.

TIPS "Submit organized, professional-looking materials."

ADIRONDACK LAKES CENTER FOR THE ARTS

Route 28, P.O. Box 205, Blue Mountain Lake NY 12812. (518)352-7715. Fax: (518)352-7333. E-mail: info@ adirondackarts.org. Website: www.adirondackarts. org. **Contact:** Stephen Svodoba, executive director. Estab. 1967. "ALCA is a 501c, nonprofit organization showing national and international work of emerging to established artists. A tourist and second-home market, demographics profile our client as highly educated, moderately affluent, environmentally oriented and well-travelled. In addition to its public programs, the Arts Center also administers the New York State Decentralization Regrant Program for Hamilton County. This program provides grants to local nonprofit organizations to sponsor art and cultural events, including concerts, workshops, and lectures in their own communities. The area served by the Arts Center includes Hamilton County, and parts of Essex, Franklin, Warren, and Herkimer counties. Our intent, with this diversity, is to enrich and unite the entire Adirondacks via the arts. The busy season is June through September."

EXHIBITS Solo, group, call for entry exhibits of color and b&w work. Sponsors 15-20 exhibits/year. Average display time 1 month. Overall price range $100-2,000. Most work sold at $250.

MAKING CONTACT & TERMS Consignment gallery, fee structure on request. Payment for sales follows within 30 days of close of exhibit. White mat and black frame required, except under prior agreement. ALCA pays return shipping only or cover work in transit.

SUBMISSIONS Apply by CD or slides, résumé and bio. Must include SASE for return of materials. Upon acceptance notification, price sheet and artist statement required.

TIPS "ALCA offers a residency program, maintains a fully-equipped darkroom with 24 hour access."

⊘ AKRON ART MUSEUM

One S. High St., Akron OH 44308. (330)376-9185. Fax: (330)376-1180. E-mail: mail@akronartmuseum.org, btannenbaum@akronartmuseum.org. Website: www. akronartmuseum.org. **Contact:** Barbara Tannenbaum, director of curatorial affairs. Located on the corner of East Market and South High Streets in the heart of downtown Akron. Open Wednesday–Sunday, 11-5; Thursday 11-9. Closed holidays.

○ Annually awards the Knight Purchase Award to a living artist working with photographic media.

EXHIBITS To exhibit, photographers must possess "a notable record of exhibitions, inclusion in publications, and/or a role in the historical development of photography. We also feature area photographers (northeast Ohio)." Interested in innovative works by contemporary photographers; any subject matter. Interested in alternative process, documentary, fine art, historical/vintage.

MAKING CONTACT & TERMS Payment negotiable. Buys photography outright.

SUBMISSIONS Will review websites and CDs. Send material via e-mail or by mail with SASE if you want materials returned. Responds in 2 months, "depending on our workload."

TIPS "Send professional-looking materials with high-quality images, a résumé and an artist's statement. Never send original prints."

ALASKA STATE MUSEUM

395 Whittier St., Juneau AK 99801-1718. (907)465-2901. Fax: (907)465-2976. E-mail: paul.gardinier@ alaska.gov. Website: www.museums.state.ak.us. **Contact:** Paul Gardinier, curator of exhibits. Estab. 1900. Museum. Approached by 40 artists/year. Sponsors 1

photography exhibit every 2 years. Average display time 10 weeks. Downtown location with 3 galleries.

EXHIBITS Interested in historical and fine art.

SUBMISSIONS Finds artists through portfolio reviews.

THE ALBUQUERQUE MUSEUM OF ART & HISTORY

2000 Mountain Rd., NW, Albuquerque NM 87104. (505)243-7255. E-mail: aconnors@cabq.gov. Website: www.cabq.gov/museum. Glenn Fye, photo archivist. **Contact:** Andrew Connors, curator of art. Estab. 1967.

SUBMISSIONS Submit portfolio of slides, photos, or disk for review. Responds in 2 months.

AMERICAN PRINT ALLIANCE

302 Larkspur Turn, Peachtree City GA 30269-2210. E-mail: director@printalliance.org. Website: www.printalliance.org. **Contact:** Carol Pulin, director. Estab. 1992.

EXHIBITS "We only exhibit original prints, artists' books and paperworks." Usually sponsors 2 travelling exhibits/year—all prints, paperworks and artists' books; photography within printmaking processes but not as a separate medium. Most exhibits travel for 2 years. Hours depend on the host gallery/museum/arts center. "We travel exhibits throughout the U.S. and occasionally to Canada." Overall price range for Print Bin: $150-3,200; most work sold at $300-500. "We accept all styles, genres and subjects; the decisions are made on quality of work." Individual subscription: $32-39. Print Bin is free with subscription."

MAKING CONTACT & TERMS Subscribe to journal, *Contemporary Impressions* (www.printalliance.org/alliance/al_subform.html), send one slide and signed permission form (www.printalliance.org/gallery/printbin_info.html). Returns slide if requested with SASE. Usually does not respond to queries from non-subscribers. Files slides and permission forms. Finds artists through submissions to the gallery or Print Bin, and especially portfolio reviews at printmakers conferences.

AMERICAN SOCIETY OF ARTISTS

P.O. Box 1326, Palatine IL 60078. (847)991-4748 or (312)751-2500. E-mail: asoaartists@aol.com. Website: www.americansocietyofartists.org. **Contact:** Helen Del Valle, membership chairman.

EXHIBITS Members and nonmembers may exhibit. "Our members range from internationally known artists to unknown artists—quality of work is the important factor. We have about 25 shows throughout the year that accept photographic art.

MAKING CONTACT & TERMS Accepted work should be framed, mounted or matted.

SUBMISSIONS Send SASE and 4 slides/photos representative of your work, and request membership information and application. See our website for online jury. To jury via e-mail: submit only to: Asoaartists@aol.com. Accepted work should be framed, mounted or matted. Responds in 2 weeks. Accepted members may participate in lecture and demonstration service. Member publication: *ASA Artisan*.

ARC GALLERY

832 W. Superior St., #204, Chicago IL 60662. (312)733-2787. E-mail: info@arcgallery.com. Website: www.arcgallery.org. **Contact:** Iris Goldstein, president. Estab. 1973. Sponsors 5-8 exhibits/year. Average display time 1 month. Overall price range $100-1,200.

"ARC Gallery and Educational Foundation is a not-for-profit gallery and foundation whose mission is to bring innovative, experimental visual art to a wide range of viewers, and to provide an atmosphere for the continued development of artistic potential, experimentation and dialogue. ARC serves to educate the public on various community-based issues by presenting exhibits, workshops, discussion groups and programs for, and by, underserved populations."

EXHIBITS All styles considered. Contemporary fine art photography, documentary and journalism.

MAKING CONTACT & TERMS Charges no commission, but there is a space rental fee.

SUBMISSIONS Must send slides, résumé and statement to gallery for review; include SASE. Reviews JPEGs. Responds in 1 month.

TIPS Photographers "should have a consistent body of work. Show emerging and experimental work."

ARIZONA STATE UNIVERSITY ART MUSEUM

P.O. Box 872911, 10th St. and Mill Ave., Tempe AZ 85287-2911. (480)965-2787. Fax: (480)965-5254. Website: asuartmuseum.asu.edu. **Contact:** Gordon Knox, director. Estab. 1950. Has 2 facilities and approximately 8 galleries of 2,500 square feet each; mounts approximately 15 exhibitions/year. Average display time 3-4 months.

EXHIBITS Only a small number of solo shows are presented, but all proposals are reviewed by curatorial staff.

MAKING CONTACT & TERMS Accepted work should be framed, mounted, matted.

SUBMISSIONS Send query letter with résumé, reviews, images of current work and SASE. "Allow several months for a response since we receive many proposals and review monthly."

ARNOLD ART

210 Thames St., Newport RI 02840. (401)847-2273; (800)352-2234. E-mail: info@arnoldart.com. Website: www.arnoldart.com. **Contact:** William Rommel, owner. Estab. 1870. For-profit gallery. Represents or exhibits 40 artists. Average display time 1 month. Gallery open Monday–Saturday, 9:30-5:30; Sunday, 12-5. Closed Christmas, Thanksgiving, Easter. Art gallery is 17 ft × 50 ft., open gallery space (3rd floor). Overall price range $100-35,000. Most work sold at $300.

EXHIBITS Marine (sailing), classic yachts, America's Cup, wooden boats, sailing/racing. Artwork is accepted on consignment, and there is a 45% commission. Gallery provides promotion. Accepted work should be framed.

MAKING CONTACT & TERMS E-mail to arrange personal interview to show portfolio.

THE ARSENAL GALLERY

The Arsenal Bldg., Room 20, Central Park, 830 Fifth Ave., New York NY 10065. (212)360-8163. Fax: (212)360-1329. E-mail: artandantiquities@parks.nyc. gov; patricia.hamilton@parks.nyc.gov. Website: www. nycgovparks.org/art. Arsenal Gallery Curator; Jennifer Lantzas, public art coordinator. **Contact:** Patricia Hamilton. Estab. 1971. Nonprofit gallery. Approached by 100 artists/year; 8-10 exhibits/year. Sponsors 2-3 photography exhibits/year. Average display time 4-6 weeks. Gallery open Monday through Friday from 9 to 5. Closed weekends and holidays. Has 100 linear feet of wall space on the 3rd floor of the Administrative Headquarters of the Parks Department located in Central Park. Overall price range $100-5,000.

EXHIBITS Exhibits photos of environmental, landscapes/scenics, wildlife, architecture, cities/urban, adventure, NYC parks. Interested in alternative process, avant garde, documentary, fine art, historical/vintage. Artwork is accepted on consignment, and there is a

15% commission. Gallery provides promotion. "Contact us for submission deadlines."

MAKING CONTACT & TERMS Mail portfolio for review. Send query letter with artist's statement, bio, brochure, business card, photocopies, résumé, reviews, SASE. Responds within 6 months, only if interested. Artist should call. Finds artists through word of mouth, portfolio reviews, art exhibits, referrals by other artists.

TIPS "Appear organized and professional."

ART@NET INTERNATIONAL GALLERY

E-mail: artnetg@yahoo.com. Website: www.designbg. com. **Contact:** Yavor Shopov, photography director. Estab. 1998. Artwork is accepted on consignment; there is a 10% commission and a rental fee for space of $1/image per month or $5/image per year. First 6 images are displayed free of rental fee. Gallery provides promotion. Accepted work should be matted. Main usage of all works exhibited in our gallery is for limited edition (photos) or original (paintings) wall decoration of offices and homes, so photos must have quality of paintings.

EXHIBITS Photos of creative photography including: travel, landscapes/scenics, fashion/glamour, erotic, figure landscapes, beauty, abstracts, avant garde, fine art, silhouettes, architecture, buildings, cities/urban, science, astronomy, education, seasonal, wildlife, sports, adventure, caves, crystals, minerals and luminescence.

MAKING CONTACT & TERMS "We accept computer scans only; no slides, please. E-mail attached scans, 900×1200 px (300 dpi for prints or 900 dpi for 36mm slides), as JPEG files for IBM computers." E-mail query letter with artist's statement, bio, résumé. Responds in 6 weeks. Finds artists through submissions, portfolio reviews, art exhibits, art fairs, referrals by other artists." E-mail a tightly edited selection of less than 20 scans of your best work. All work must force any person to look over it again and again.

TIPS "We like to see strong artistic sense of mood, composition, light, color and strong graphic impact or expression of emotions. For us, only quality of work is important, so newer, lesser-known artists are welcome."

ARTEFACT/ROBERT PARDO GALLERY

805 Lake Ave., Lake Worth FL 33460. (561)585-2881. E-mail: robertpardogallery@yahoo.com. Website:

www.robertpardogallery.com (coming soon); sculplakeworth.com (coming soon). **Contact:** Dr. Giovanna Federico. Estab. 1986. Approached by 500 artists/year; represents or exhibits 18 artists. Sponsors 3 photography exhibits/year. Average display time 4-5 weeks. Gallery open 7 days a week until 6.

EXHIBITS Interested in avant garde, fashion/glamour, fine art.

SUBMISSIONS Arrange personal interview to show portfolio of slides, transparencies. Responds in 1 month.

ARTISTS' COOPERATIVE GALLERY

405 S. 11th St., Omaha NE 68102. (402)342-9617. E-mail: bronzesculptor@yahoo.com; ACGomahaneb@yahoo.com. Website: www.artistsco-opgallery.com. Estab. 1974. Gallery sponsors all-member exhibits and outreach exhibits; individual artists sponsor their own small group exhibits throughout the year. Overall price range $100-500. "Artist must be willing to work 13 days per year at the gallery. Sponsors 11 exhibits/year. Average display time 1 month. Fine art photography only. We are a member-owned-and-operated cooperative. Artist must also serve on one committee. Write for membership application. Membership committee screens applicants August 1-15 each year. Responds by September 1. New membership year begins October 1. Members must pay annual fee of $325. Our community outreach exhibits include local high school photographers and art from local elementary schools." Open Tuesday–Thursday, 11-5; Friday and Saturday, 11-10; Sunday, 12-6.

EXHIBITS Interested in all types, styles and subject matter. Charges no commission. Reviews transparencies. Accepted work should be framed work only.

SUBMISSIONS Send query letter with résumé, SASE. Responds in 2 months.

THE ARTS COMPANY

215 Fifth Ave., Nashville TN 37219. (615)254-2040; (877)694-2040. Fax: (615)254-9289. E-mail: art@theartscompany.com. Website: www.theartscompany.com. **Contact:** Anne Brown, owner. Estab. 1996. Art consultancy, for-profit gallery. Sponsors 6-10 photography exhibits/year. Average display time 1 month. Open Tuesday-Saturday, 11-5. Located in downtown Nashville, the gallery has 6,000 sq. ft. of contemporary space in a historic building. Overall price range $10-35,000. Most work sold at $300-3,000.

EXHIBITS Photos of celebrities, architecture, cities/urban, rural, environmental, landscapes/scenics, entertainment, performing arts. Interested in documentary, fine art, historical/vintage.

MAKING CONTACT & TERMS "We prefer an initial info packet via e-mail." Send query letter with artist's statement, bio, brochure, business card, photocopies, résumé, reviews, SASE, CD. Returns material with SASE.

SUBMISSIONS "Provide professional images on a CD along with a professional bio, résumé." Artwork is accepted on consignment. Gallery provides insurance, contract. Accepted work should be framed.

TIPS Finds artists through word of mouth, art fairs, art exhibits, submissions, referrals by other artists.

ARTS IOWA CITY

114 S. Dubuque St., Iowa City IA 52240. (319)337-7447. E-mail: gallery@artsiowacity.org. Website: www.artsiowacity.org. **Contact:** Richard Sjolund, president; Elise Kendrot, gallery director. Estab. 1975. Nonprofit gallery. Approached by more than 65 artists/year; represents or exhibits more than 45 artists. Average display time 1-2 months. Ped Mall gallery open limited hours. Several locations open during business hours; satellite galleries at Starbucks Downtown, US Bank, Melrose Meadows, and Englert Theatre. Overall price range: $200-6,000. Most work sold at $500.

EXHIBITS Photos of landscapes/scenics, architecture, cities/urban, rural. Interested in fine art.

MAKING CONTACT & TERMS Artwork is accepted on consignment, and there is a 20% commission. Gallery provides insurance (in gallery, not during transit to/from gallery), promotion and contract. Accepted work should be framed, mounted and matted. "We represent artists who are members of Arts Iowa City; to be a member, one must pay a membership fee. Most members are from Iowa City and the surrounding area."

SUBMISSIONS Call, write or e-mail to arrange personal interview to show portfolio of photographs, transparencies. No slides; JPEG advisable. Send query letter with artist's statement, bio, brochure, business card, photographs, résumé, reviews, CD and JPEGs. Responds to queries in 1 month. Finds artists through referrals by other artists, submissions and word of mouth.

TIPS "We are a nonprofit gallery with limited staff. Most work is done by volunteers. Artists interested in submitting work should visit our website to gain a better understanding of the services we provide and to obtain membership and show proposal information. Please submit applications according to our guidelines online."

ARTS ON DOUGLAS

123 Douglas St., New Smyrna Beach FL 32168. (386)428-1133. Fax: (386)428-5008. E-mail: mail@ artsondouglas.net; mmartin@artsondouglas.net. Website: www.artsondouglas.net. **Contact:** Mehgan Martin, gallery director. Estab. 1996. For-profit gallery. Represents 60 Florida artists in ongoing group exhibits and features 8 artists/year in solo exhibitions. Average display time 1 month. Gallery open Tuesday-Friday, 10-5; Saturday, 11-3; by appointment. Location has 5,000 sq. ft. of exhibition space. Overall price range varies.

EXHIBITS Photos of environmental. Interested in alternative process, documentary, fine art.

MAKING CONTACT & TERMS Artwork is accepted on consignment, and there is a 50% commission. Gallery provides insurance, promotion. Accepted work should be framed. Requires exclusive representation locally. *Accepts only professional artists from Florida.*

SUBMISSIONS Call in advance to inquire about submissions/reviews. Send query letter with artist's statement, bio, brochure, résumé, reviews, slides, SASE. Finds artists through referrals by other artists.

ART SOURCE L.A., INC.

2801 Ocean Park Blvd., #7, Santa Monica CA 90405. (310)452-4411. Fax: (310)452-0300. E-mail: info@ artsourcela.com; bonniek@artsourcela.com. Website: www.artsourcela.com. **Contact:** Francine Ellman, president; Dina Dalby, artist liason. Estab. 1980. Overall price range $300-15,000. Most work sold at $600.

EXHIBITS Photos of multicultural, environmental, landscapes/scenics, wildlife, architecture, cities/urban, gardening, interiors/decorating, rural, automobiles, food/drink, travel, technology/computers. Interested in alternative process, avant garde, fine art, historical/vintage, seasonal. "We do projects worldwide, putting together fine art for corporations, health care, hospitality, government and public space. We use a lot of photography."

MAKING CONTACT & TERMS Interested in receiving work from emerging and established photographers. Charges 50% commission.

SUBMISSIONS Prefers digital submissions via e-mail. Send a minimum of 20 JPEGs, photographs or inkjet prints (laser copies not acceptable), clearly labeled with name, title and date of work; plus catalogs, brochures, résumé, price list, SASE. Responds in 2 months maximum.

TIPS "Show a consistent body of work, well marked and presented so it may be viewed to see its merits."

ART WITHOUT WALLS, INC.

P.O. Box 341, Sayville NY 11782. (631)567-9418. Fax: (631)567-9418. E-mail: artwithoutwalls3@webtv.net. Website: www.artwithoutwalls.net. **Contact:** Sharon Lippman, executive director. Estab. 1985. Nonprofit gallery. Approached by 300 artists/year; represents or exhibits 100 artists. Sponsors 3 photography exhibits/year. Average display time 1 month. Open daily, 9-5. Closed December 22–January 5 and Easter week. Traveling exhibits in various public spaces. Overall price range $1,000-25,000. Most work sold at $3,000-5,000. "Price varies—especially if student work."

EXHIBITS Photos of multicultural, families, parents, senior citizens, disasters, environmental, landscapes/scenics, wildlife, architecture, cities/urban, education, rural, adventure, events, food/drink, health, performing arts, sports, travel, agriculture, medicine, political, product shots/still life, science, technology/computers. Interested in alternative process, avant garde, documentary, fashion, fine art, historical/vintage, seasonal.

MAKING CONTACT & TERMS Artwork is accepted on consignment, and there is a 20% commission. Gallery provides promotion, contract. Accepted work should be framed, mounted, matted.

SUBMISSIONS Mail portfolio for review. Send query letter with artist's statement, brochure, photographs, résumé, reviews, SASE, slides. Responds in 1 month. Finds artists through submissions, portfolio reviews, art exhibits.

TIPS "Work should be properly framed with name, year, medium, title, size."

ASIAN AMERICAN ARTS CENTRE

111 Norfolk St., New York NY 10002. (212)233-2154. Fax: (360)283-2154. E-mail: aaacinfo@artspiral.org. Website: www.artspiral.org. Estab. 1974. "Our mission is to promote the preservation and creative vitality of Asian American cultural growth through the arts, and its historical and aesthetic linkage to other communities." Exhibits should be Asian American or

significantly influenced by Asian culture and should be entered into the archive-a historical record of the presence of Asia in the U.S. Interested in "creative art pieces." Average display time 6 weeks. Open Monday–Friday, 12:30-6:30 (by appointment).

ATLANTIC GALLERY

135 W. 29th, Suite 601, New York NY 10001. (212)219-3183. E-mail: contact@atlanticgallery.org. Website: www.atlanticgallery.org. **Contact:** Pamela Talese, president. Estab. 1974. Cooperative gallery. Approached by 50 artists/year; represents or exhibits 40 artists. Average display time 3 weeks. Gallery open Tuesday-Saturday, 12-6. Closed August. Located in Soho. Overall price range $100-13,000. Most work sold at $1,500-5,000.There is a co-op membership fee plus a donation of time. Accepts mostly artists from New York, Connecticut, Massachusetts, New Jersey. Finds artists through word of mouth, submissions, art exhibits, referrals by other artists.

EXHIBITS Photos of multicultural, families, environmental, landscapes/scenics, wildlife, architecture, cities/urban, rural, performing arts, travel, product shots/still life, technology/computers. Interested in fine art.

MAKING CONTACT & TERMS Call or write to arrange a personal interview to show portfolio of slides.

SUBMISSIONS "Submit an organized folder with slides, bio, and 3 pieces of actual work. If we respond with interest, we then review again." Responds in 1 month. Views slides monthly.

AXIS GALLERY

50-52 Dobbin St., Brooklyn NY 11222. (212)741-2582. E-mail: info@axisgallery.com. Website: www.axisgallery. com. **Contact:** Lisa Brittan, director. Estab. 1997. For-profit gallery. Approached by 40 African artists/year; representative of 30 artists. Located in Williamsburg, 900 sq. ft. Hours during exhibitions: check gallery hours online; other times by appointment. Closed during summer. Overall price range $500-50,000.

EXHIBITS Interested in alternative process, avant garde, documentary, erotic, fine art, historical/vintage. Also interested in photojournalism, resistance.

MAKING CONTACT & TERMS Artwork is accepted on consignment, and there is a 50% commission. Gallery provides insurance, promotion, contract. *Only accepts artists from Africa.*

SUBMISSIONS Send query letter with résumé, reviews, SASE, slides, photographs or CD. Responds in 3 months. Finds artists through research, recommendations, submissions, portfolio reviews, art exhibits, referrals by other artists.

TIPS "Send letter with SASE and materials listed above. Photographers should research galleries first to check if their work fits the gallery program. Avoid bulk mailings."

BALZEKAS MUSEUM OF LITHUANIAN CULTURE ART GALLERY

6500 S. Pulaski Rd., Chicago IL 60629. (773)582-6500. Fax: (773)582-5133. E-mail: info@balzekasmuseum. org. Website: www.balzekasmuseum.org. **Contact:** Stanley Balzekas, Jr., president. Estab. 1996. Museum, museum retail shop, nonprofit gallery, rental gallery. Approached by 20 artists/year. Sponsors 2 photography exhibits/year. Average display time 6 weeks. Open daily, 10-4. Closed Christmas, Easter and New Year's Day. Overall price range $150-6,000. Most work sold at $545.

EXHIBITS Photos of babies/children/teens, celebrities, couples, multicultural, families, parents, senior citizens, disasters, environmental, landscapes/scenics, wildlife, architecture, cities/urban, education, gardening, interiors/decorating, pets, religious, rural, adventure, automobiles, entertainment, events, food/drink, health/fitness, hobbies, humor, performing arts, sports, travel, agriculture, buildings, business concepts, industry, medicine, military, political, product shots/still life, science, technology/computers. Interested in alternative process, avant garde, documentary, erotic, fashion/glamour, fine art, historical/vintage, seasonal.

MAKING CONTACT & TERMS Artwork is accepted on consignment, and there is a 33⅓% commission. Gallery provides promotion. Accepted work should be framed.

SUBMISSIONS Write to arrange personal interview to show portfolio. Responds in 2 months. Finds artists through word of mouth, art exhibits, referrals by other artists.

BARRON ARTS CENTER

1 Main St., Woodbridge NJ 07095. (732)634-0413. Website: www.twp.woodbridge.nj.us/Departments/BarronArtsCenter/tabid/251/Default.aspx. **Contact:** Cynthia Knight, director. Estab. 1977. The Barron Arts Center serves as a center for the arts for resi-

dents of Woodbridge Township and Central New Jersey. Overall price range $150-400. Most work sold at $150. Charges 20% commission.

🗨 "In terms of the market, we tend to hear that there are not enough galleries that will exhibit photography."

SUBMISSIONS Reviews transparencies but prefers portfolio. Submit portfolio for review; include SASE for return. Responds "depending upon date of review, but generally within a month of receiving materials." CDs of photos acceptable for review. "Make a professional presentation of work with all pieces matted or treated in a like manner."

⊕ BELIAN ART CENTER

5980 Rochester Rd., Troy MI 48085. (248)828-1001. E-mail: BelianArtCenter@aol.com. Estab. 1985. Sponsors 1-2 exhibits/year. Average display time 3 weeks. Sponsors openings. Average price range $200-2,000.

EXHIBITS Looks for originality, capturing the intended mood, perfect copy, mostly original editions. Subjects include landscapes, cities, rural, events, agriculture, buildings, still life.

MAKING CONTACT & TERMS Charges 40-50% commission. Buys photos outright. Reviews transparencies. Requires exclusive representation locally. Arrange a personal interview to show portfolio. Send query letter with résumé and SASE.

BELL STUDIO

3428 N. Southport Ave., Chicago IL 60657. (773)281-2172. Fax: (773)281-2415. E-mail: bellstudioinc@gmail.com; paul@bellstudio.net. Website: www.bellstudio.net. **Contact:** Paul Therieau, director. Estab. 2001. For-profit gallery. Approached by 60 artists/year; represents or exhibits 10 artists. Interested in alternative process, avant garde, fine art. Artwork is accepted on consignment, and there is a 50% commission. Gallery provides insurance, promotion, contract. Accepted work should be framed. Requires exclusive representation locally. Finds artists through referrals by other artists, submissions, word of mouth. Requires local representation.

EXHIBITS Sponsors 3 photography exhibits/year. Average display time 6 weeks. Open all year; Monday-Friday, 12-7; weekends 12-5. Located in brick storefront; 750 sq. ft. of exhibition space; high traffic. Overall price range: $150-3,500. Most work sold at $600.

MAKING CONTACT & TERMS Write to arrange personal interview to show portfolio; include bio and résumé. Responds to queries within 3 months, only if interested.

SUBMISSIONS Send SASE; type submission letter; include show history, résumé.

BENNETT GALLERIES AND COMPANY

5308 Kingston Pike, Knoxville TN 37919. (865)584-6791. Fax: (865)588-6130. E-mail: info@bennettgalleries.com. Website: www.bennettgalleries.com. Estab. 1985. For-profit gallery. Represents or exhibits 40 artists/year. Sponsors 1-2 photography exhibits/year. Average display time 1 month. Gallery open Monday–Thursday, 10-6; Friday–Saturday, 10-5:30. Conveniently located a few miles from downtown Knoxville in the Bearden area. The formal art gallery has over 2,000 sq. ft. and 20,000 sq. ft. of additional space. Overall price range $100-12,000. Most work sold at $400-600.

EXHIBITS Photos of landscapes/scenics, architecture, cities/urban, humor, sports, travel. Interested in alternative process, fine art, historical/vintage.

MAKING CONTACT & TERMS Artwork is accepted on consignment, and there is a 50% commission. Gallery provides insurance, promotion, contract. Accepted work should be framed. Requires exclusive representation locally.

SUBMISSIONS Mail portfolio for review. Send query letter with artist's statement, bio, photographs, SASE, CD. Responds within 1 month, only if interested. Finds artists through word of mouth, submissions, art exhibits, referrals by other artists.

TIPS When submitting material to a gallery for review, the package should include information about the artist (neatly written or typed), photographic material, and SASE if you want your materials back.

BONNI BENRUBI GALLERY

41 E. 57th St., 13th Floor, New York NY 10022-1908. (212)888-6007. Fax: (212)751-0819. E-mail: Benrubi@BonniBenrubi.com. Website: www.bonnibenrubi.com. Estab. 1987. Sponsors 7-8 exhibits/year. Average display time 6 weeks. Overall price range $500-50,000.

EXHIBITS Interested in 19th- and 20th-century photography, mainly contemporary.

MAKING CONTACT & TERMS Charges commission. Buys photos outright. Accepted work should be matted. Requires exclusive representation locally. No manipulated work.

SUBMISSIONS Submit portfolio for review; include SASE. Responds in 2 weeks. Portfolio review is the first Thursday of every month. Out-of-towners can send slides with SASE, and work will be returned.

BERKSHIRE ARTISANS GALLERY

Lichtenstein Center for the Arts, 28 Renne Ave., Pittsfield MA 01201. (413)499-9348. Fax: (413)442-8043. Website: www.pittsfield.com/artsculture.asap. **Contact:** Megan Whilden, artistic director. Estab. 1975. Sponsors 10 exhibits/year. Open Wednesday–Saturday, 12-5. Overall price range $50-1,500.

MAKING CONTACT & TERMS Charges 20% commission. Will review transparencies of photographic work. Accepted work should be framed, mounted, matted.

SUBMISSIONS "Photographer should send SASE with 20 slides or prints, résumé and statement by mail only to gallery."

TIPS "To break in, send portfolio, slides and SASE. We accept all art photography. Work must be professionally presented and framed. Send in by July 1 each year. Expect exhibition 2-3 years from submission date. We have a professional juror look at slide entries once a year (usually July-September). Expect that work to be tied up for 2-3 months in jury."

MONA BERMAN FINE ARTS

78 Lyon St., New Haven CT 06511. (203)562-4720. E-mail: info@monabermanfinearts.com. Website: www. monabermanfinearts.com. **Contact:** Mona Berman, director. Estab. 1979. Sponsors 0-1 exhibit/year. Average display time 1 month. Overall price range $500-5,000.

○ "We are art consultants serving corporations, architects and designers. We also have private clients. We hold very few exhibits; we mainly show work to our clients for consideration and sell a lot of photographs. Initial contact should be by e-mail, with link to website, etc. Always include a retail price list."

EXHIBITS "Photographers must have been represented by us for over 2 years. Interested in all except figurative, although we do use some portrait work."

MAKING CONTACT & TERMS Charges 50% commission. "Payment to artist 30 days after receipt of payment from client." Interested in seeing unframed, unmounted, unmatted work only.

SUBMISSIONS "E-mail digital images or web links. Inquire by e-mail; no calls, please. Always include retail prices." Materials returned with SASE only. Responds in 1 month.

TIPS "Looking for new perspectives, new images, new ideas, excellent print quality, ability to print in *very* large sizes, consistency of vision. Digital prints must be archival. Not interested in giclée prints."

B.J. SPOKE GALLERY

299 Main St., Huntington NY 11743. (631)549-5106. E-mail: managerbjs@verizon.net. Website: www. bjspokegallery.com. **Contact:** Marilyn Lavi, gallery manager. Estab. 1978.

MAKING CONTACT & TERMS Arrange a personal interview to show portfolio. Send query letter with SASE.

SUBMISSIONS Charges 30% commission. Photographer sets price.

BLOUNT BRIDGERS HOUSE/HOBSON PITTMAN MEMORIAL GALLERY

130 Bridgers St., Tarboro NC 27886. (252)823-4159. E-mail: edgecombearts@embarqmail.com. Website: www.edgecombearts.org. Estab. 1982. Museum. Gallery open Monday-Friday, 10-4; weekends 2-4. Closed major holidays, Christmas-New Year. Located in historic house in residential area of small town. Gallery is approximately 48×20 ft. Overall price range $250-5,000. Most work sold at $500.

○ Interested in fine art, historical/vintage.

EXHIBITS Photos of landscapes/scenics, wildlife. Approached by 1-2 artists/year; represents or exhibits 6 artists. Sponsors 1 exhibit/year. Average display time 6 weeks.

MAKING CONTACT & TERMS Artwork is accepted on consignment, and there is a 30% commission. Gallery provides insurance, limited promotion. Accepted work should be framed. Accepts artists from the Southeast and Pennsylvania. Finds artists through word of mouth, submissions, art exhibits, referrals by other artists.

SUBMISSIONS Mail portfolio review. Send query letter with artist's statement, bio, SASE, slides. Responds in 3 months.

BOOK BEAT GALLERY

26010 Greenfield, Oak Park MI 48237. (248)968-1190. Fax: (248)968-3102. E-mail: bookbeat@aol.com. Website: www.thebookbeat.com. **Contact:** Cary Loren, director. Estab. 1982. Sponsors 6 exhibits/year. Average display time 6-8 weeks. Overall price range $300-5,000. Most work sold at $600.

EXHIBITS "Book Beat is a bookstore specializing in fine art and photography. We have a backroom gallery devoted to photography and folk art. Our inventory includes vintage work from 19th- to 20th-century, rare books, issues of *Camerawork*, and artist books. Book Beat Gallery is looking for courageous and astonishing image makers, high quality digital work is acceptable. Artists are welcome to submit a handwritten or typed proposal for an exhibition, include artist bio, statement, and website, book or CD with sample images. We are especially interested in photographers who have published book works or work with originals in the book format, also those who work in 'dead media' and extinct processes."

SUBMISSIONS Responds in 6 weeks.

RENA BRANSTEN GALLERY

77 Geary St., San Francisco CA 94108. (415)982-3292. Fax: (415)982-1807. E-mail: info@renabranstengallery.com; calvert@renabranstengallery.com; rena@renabranstengallery.com. Website: www.renabranstengallery.com. **Contact:** Rena Bransten, owner. Estab. 1974. For-profit gallery. Approached by 200 artists/year; represents or exhibits 12-15 artists. Average display time 4-5 weeks. Open Tuesday–Friday, 10:30-5:30; Saturday, 11-5.

SUBMISSIONS E-mail JPEG samples at 72 dpi. Finds artists through word of mouth, art exhibits, submissions, art fairs, portfolio reviews, referrals by other artists.

J.J. BROOKINGS GALLERY

330 Commercial St., San Jose CA 95112. (408)287-3311. Fax: (408)287-6705. E-mail: info@jjbrookings.com. Website: www.jjbrookings.com. Sponsors rotating group exhibits. Sponsors openings. Overall price range $500-30,000.

EXHIBITS Interested in photography created with a "painterly eye."

MAKING CONTACT & TERMS Charges 50% commission.

SUBMISSIONS Send material by mail for consideration. Responds in 3-5 weeks if interested; immediately if not acceptable.

TIPS Wants to see "professional presentation, realistic pricing, numerous quality images. We're interested in whatever the artist thinks will impress us the most.

'Painterly' work is best. No documentary or politically oriented work."

BUSINESS OF ART CENTER

513 Manitou Ave., Manitou Springs CO 80829. (719)685-1861. Fax: (719)685-5276. E-mail: liz@thebac.org. Website: www.thebac.org. **Contact:** Liz Szabo, gallery curator and director. Estab. 1988. Nonprofit gallery situated in 2 renovated landmark buildings in the Manitou Springs National Historic District—Studio 513 and Venue 515. Sponsors 6 photography exhibits/year. Average display time 1 month. Gallery open Tuesday–Saturday, 11-6. Overall price range $50-3,000. Most work sold at $300.

EXHIBITS Photos of environmental, landscapes/scenics, wildlife, gardening, rural, adventure, health/fitness, performing arts, travel. Interested in alternative process, avant garde, documentary, fashion/glamour, fine art.

MAKING CONTACT & TERMS Artwork is accepted on consignment, and there is a 40% commission. Gallery provides insurance, promotion, contract. Accepted work should be framed.

SUBMISSIONS Write to arrange a personal interview to show portfolio. Send query letter with artist's statement, bio, slides. Finds artists through word of mouth, submissions, portfolio reviews, art exhibits, referrals by other artists.

WILLIAM CAMPBELL CONTEMPORARY ART

4935 Byers Ave., Ft. Worth TX 76107. (817)737-9566. Fax: (817)737-5466. E-mail: wcca@flash.net. Website: www.williamcampbellcontemporaryart.com. **Contact:** William Campbell, owner/director. Estab. 1974. Sponsors 8-10 exhibits/year. Average display time 5 weeks. Sponsors openings; provides announcements, press releases, installation of work, insurance, cost of exhibition. Overall price range $300-8,000.

EXHIBITS "Primarily interested in photography that has been altered or manipulated in some form."

MAKING CONTACT & TERMS Charges 50% commission. Reviews transparencies. Accepted work should be mounted. Requires exclusive representation within metropolitan area.

SUBMISSIONS Send CD (preferred) or slides and résumé by mail with SASE. Responds in 1 month.

CAPITOL COMPLEX EXHIBITIONS

500 S. Bronough St., R.A. Gray Bldg., 3rd Floor, Department of State, The Capitol, Tallahassee FL 32399-0250. (850)245-6470. Fax: (850)245-6492. E-mail: sshaughnessy@dos.state.fl.us. Website: www.florida-arts.org. Average display time 3 months. Overall price range $200-1,000. Most work sold at $400.

EXHIBITS "The Capitol Complex Exhibitions Program is designed to showcase Florida artists and art organizations. Exhibitions are displayed in the Capitol Gallery (22nd floor) and the Cabinet Meeting Room in Florida's capitol. Exhibitions are selected based on quality, diversity of media, and regional representation."

MAKING CONTACT & TERMS Does not charge commission. Accepted work should be framed. *Interested only in Florida artists or arts organizations.*

SUBMISSIONS Download application from website, complete and send with image CD. Responds in 3 weeks.

SANDY CARSON GALLERY

760 Santa Fe Dr., Denver CO 80204. (303)573-8585. Fax: (303)573-8587. E-mail: info@vanstraatengallery.com. Website: www.vanstraatengallery.com. Estab. 1975. Average display time 7 weeks. Open by appointment only.

EXHIBITS "We include all mediums and represent artists who are professional and committed, with an extensive body of work and continually producing more."

SUBMISSIONS "We are not presently seeking new artists. Please contact us by e-mail or call the gallery."

CENTER FOR CREATIVE PHOTOGRAPHY

University of Arizona, P.O. Box 210103, 1030 North Olive Rd., Tucson AZ 85721-0103. (520)621-7968. Fax: (520)621-9444. E-mail: oncenter@ccp.library.arizona.edu. Website: www.creativephotography.org. Estab. 1975. Museum/archive, research center, print study, library, museum retail shop. Sponsors 6-8 photography exhibits/year. Average display time 3-4 months. Gallery open Monday–Friday, 9-5; weekends, 1-4. Closed most holidays. 5,500 sq. ft.

➕ ⊛ CENTER FOR EXPLORATORY AND PERCEPTUAL ART

617 Main St., Suite 201, Buffalo NY 14203. (716)856-2717. Fax: (716)270-0184. E-mail: info@cepagallery.com. Website: www.cepagallery.org. **Contact:** Sean J. Donaher, executive director. Estab. 1974. "CEPA is an artist-run space dedicated to presenting photographically based work that is under-represented in traditional cultural institutions." Sponsors 5-6 exhibits/year. Average display time 6 weeks. Call or see website for hours. Total gallery space is approximately 6,500 sq. ft. Overall price range $200-3,500.

⊘ CEPA conducts an annual Emerging Artist Exhibition for its members. You must join the gallery in order to participate.

EXHIBITS Interested in political, digital, video, culturally diverse, contemporary and conceptual works. Extremely interested in exhibiting work of newer, lesser-known photographers.

MAKING CONTACT & TERMS Sponsors openings; reception with lecture. Accepted work should be framed or unframed, mounted or unmounted, matted or unmatted.

SUBMISSIONS Send query letter with artist's statement, résumé. Accepts images in digital format. Send via CD, ZIP as TIFF, JPEG, PICT files. Include SASE for return of material. Responds in 3 months.

TIPS "We review CD portfolios and encourage digital imagery. We will be showcasing work on our website."

THE CENTER FOR FINE ART PHOTOGRAPHY

400 S. College Ave., Fort Collins CO 80524. (970)224-1010. E-mail: contact@c4fap.org. Website: www.c4fap.org. **Contact:** Hamidah Glasgow, executive director; Azarie Furlong, exhibitions manager. Estab. 2005. Nonprofit gallery. Approached by 4,500 artists/year; represents or exhibits about 500 artists. Average display time 4-5 weeks. Office open Monday–Friday, 10-5; Saturday, 10-3. Closed between exhibitions. Consisting of an 1,600-sq.-ft. gallery, adjoining coffee shop, and events space. Overall price range $180-3,000. Most work sold at $150-500. "The Center provides and markets to buyers its online gallery of artists' portfolios—Artists' ShowCase Online, available to all members of the Center." Workshops and forums are also offered.

EXHIBITS Photos of babies/children/teens, celebrities, couples, multicultural, families, parents, senior citizens, architecture, cities/urban, interiors/decorating, rural, political, environmental, landscapes/scenics, wildlife, performing arts; abstract, experimental work. Interested in alternative process, avant garde, documentary, erotic, fine art. "The Center features fine art photography that incorporates all processes, many styles and subjects."

MAKING CONTACT & TERMS Art is accepted through either juried calls for entry or from portfolio review. Gallery provides insurance. Accepts only fine art photographic work.

SUBMISSIONS Work accepted for exhibition via the center's juried calls for entry. Details online.

TIPS "Only signed archival-quality work is seriously considered by art collectors. This includes both traditional and digital prints."

CENTER FOR PHOTOGRAPHIC ART

Sunset Cultural Center, P.O. Box 1100, Carmel CA 93921. (831)625-5181. Fax: (831)625-5199. E-mail: info@photography.org. Website: www.photography. org. Estab. 1988. Nonprofit gallery. Sponsors 7-8 exhibits/year. Average display time 5-7 weeks. Hours: Tuesday-Sunday, 1-5.

EXHIBITS Interested in fine art photography.

SUBMISSIONS "Currently not accepting unsolicited submissions. Please e-mail the center and ask to be added to our submissions contact list if you are not a member." Photographers should see website for more information.

CENTER FOR PHOTOGRAPHY AT WOODSTOCK

59 Tinker St., Woodstock NY 12498. (845)679-9957. Fax: (845)679-6337. E-mail: ariel@cpw.org. Website: www.cpw.org. **Contact:** Ariel Shanberg, executive director; Akemi Hiatt, program associate. Estab. 1977. Alternative space, nonprofit arts and education center. Approached by more than 500 artists/year. Hosts 10 photography exhibits/year. Average display time 7 weeks. Gallery open all year; Wednesday–Sunday, 12-5.

EXHIBITS Interested in presenting all aspects of contemporary creative photography including digital media, film, video, and installation by emerging and under-recognized artists. "We host 5 group exhibitions and 5 solo exhibitions annually. Group exhibitions are curated by guest jurors, curators, and CPW staff. Solo exhibition artists are selected by CPW staff. Visit the exhibition archives on our website to learn more."

MAKING CONTACT & TERMS CPW hosts exhibition and opening reception; provides insurance, promotion, a percentage of shipping costs, installation and de-installation, and honorarium for solo exhibition artists who give gallery talks. CPW takes 25% commission on exhibition-related sales. Accepted work should be framed and ready for hanging.

SUBMISSIONS Send introductory letter with samples, résumé, artist's statement, SASE. Responds in 4 months. Finds artists through word of mouth, art exhibits, open calls, portfolio reviews, referrals by other artists.

TIPS "Please send 10-20 digital work samples by mail (include an image script with your name, telephone number, image title, image media, size). Include a current résumé, statement, SASE for return. We are not responsible for unlabeled slides. We *do not* welcome solicitations to visit websites. We *do* advise artists to visit our website and become familiar with our offerings."

○ THE CHAIT GALLERIES DOWNTOWN

218 E. Washington St., Iowa City IA 52240. (319)338-4442. Fax: (319)338-3380. E-mail: info@thegalleries downtown.com; terri@thegalleriesdowntown. com; bpchait@aol.com. Website: www.thegalleries downtown.com. **Contact:** Benjamin Chait, director. Estab. 2003. For-profit gallery. Approached by 100 artists/year; represents or exhibits 150 artists. Open Monday–Friday, 10-6; Saturday, 11-5; Sunday by appointment or by chance. Located in a downtown building renovated to its original look of 1882 with 14-ft.-high molded ceiling and original 9-ft. front door. Professional museum lighting and Scamozzi-capped columns complete the elegant gallery. Overall price range: $50-10,000.

EXHIBITS Landscapes, oil and acrylic paintings, sculpture, fused glass wall pieces, jewelry, all types of prints.

MAKING CONTACT & TERMS Artwork is accepted on consignment, and there is a 50% commission. Gallery provides insurance, promotion and contract. Accepted work should be framed. Requires exclusive representation locally.

SUBMISSIONS Call; mail portfolio for review. Responds to queries in 2 weeks. Finds artists through art fairs, art exhibits, portfolio reviews and referrals by other artists.

CHAPMAN FRIEDMAN GALLERY

624 W. Main St., Louisville KY 40202. E-mail: friedman@imagesol.com; cheryl_chapman@bell

south.net. Website: www.chapmanfriedmangallery. com; www.imagesol.com. **Contact:** Julius Friedman, owner. Estab. 1992. For-profit gallery. Approached by 100 or more artists/year; represents or exhibits 25 artists. Sponsors 1 photography exhibit/year. Average display time 1 month. Open by appointment only. Located downtown; approximately 3,500 sq. ft. with 15-foot ceilings and white walls. Overall price range: $75-10,000. Most work sold at more than $1,000.

EXHIBITS Photos of landscapes/scenics, architecture. Interested in alternative process, avant garde, erotic, fine art.

MAKING CONTACT & TERMS Artwork is accepted on consignment, and there is a 50% commission. Gallery provides insurance, promotion and contract. Accepted work should be framed. Requires exclusive representation locally.

SUBMISSIONS Send query letter with artist's statement, bio, brochure, photographs, résumé, slides and SASE. Responds to queries within 1 month, only if interested. Finds artists through portfolio reviews and referrals by other artists.

CLAMPART

521-531 W. 25th St., Ground Floor, New York NY 10001. (646)230-0020. E-mail: portfolioreview@ clampart.com; info@clampart.com. Website: www. clampart.com. **Contact:** Brian Paul Clamp, director. Estab. 2000. For-profit gallery. Specializes in modern and contemporary paintings and photographs. Approached by 1,200 artists/year; represents 15 emerging, mid-career and established artists. Exhibited artists include Jill Greenberg (photography), Lori Nix (photography) and Mark Beard (painting). See portfolio review guidelines at www.clampart.com/ portfolio.html.

EXHIBITS Photos of couples, disasters, environmental, landscapes/scenics, architecture, cities/urban, humor, performing arts, travel, science, technology/ computers. Interested in alternative process, avant garde, documentary, erotic, fashion/glamour, fine art, historical/vintage.

MAKING CONTACT & TERMS Artwork is accepted on consignment, and there is a 50% commission. Gallery provides insurance, promotion and contract. Accepted work should be framed, mounted and matted.

SUBMISSIONS E-mail query letter with artist's statement, bio and JPEGs. Responds to queries in 2 weeks.

Finds artists through portfolio reviews, submissions and referrals by other artists.

TIPS "Include a bio and well-written artist's statement. Do not submit work to a gallery that does not handle the general kind of work you produce."

CATHARINE CLARK GALLERY

150 Minna St., Ground Floor, San Francisco CA 94105. (415)399-1439. Fax: (415)543-1338. E-mail: info@ cclarkgallery.com. Website: www.cclarkgallery.com. **Contact:** Catherine Clark, owner/director. Estab. 1991. For-profit gallery. Approached by 1,000 artists/ year; represents or exhibits 28 artists. Sponsors 1-3 photography exhibits/year. Average display time 4-6 weeks. Overall price range $200-150,000. Most work sold at $5,000. Charges 50% commission. Gallery provides insurance, promotion.

SUBMISSIONS Accepted work should be ready to hang. Requires exclusive representation locally. "Do not call." No unsolicited submissions. Finds artists through word of mouth, art exhibits, art fairs, referrals by other artists and colleagues.

TIPS Interested in alternative process, avant garde. "The work shown tends to be vanguard with respect to medium, concept and process."

JOHN CLEARY GALLERY

2635 Colquitt, Houston TX 77098. (713)524-5070. E-mail: info@johnclearygallery.com. Website: www. johnclearygallery.com. Estab. 1996. Fine art photography. Average display time 5 weeks. Open Tuesday–Saturday, 10-5 and by appointment. Located in upper Kirby District of Houston, Texas. Overall price range $500-40,000. Most work sold at $1,000-2,500.

EXHIBITS Photos of babies/children/teens, celebrities, couples, multicultural, families, parents, senior citizens, landscapes/scenics, wildlife, architecture, cities/urban, education, pets, religious, rural, adventure, automobiles, entertainment, events, humor, performing arts, travel, agriculture, industry, military, political, portraits, product shots/still life, science, technology/computers. Interested in alternative process, documentary, fashion/glamour, fine art, historical/vintage.

MAKING CONTACT & TERMS Artwork is bought outright or accepted on consignment with a 50% commission. Gallery provides insurance, promotion, contract.

SUBMISSIONS Call to show portfolio of photographs. Finds artists through submissions, art exhibits.

STEPHEN COHEN GALLERY

7358 Beverly Blvd., Los Angeles CA 90036. (323)937-5525. Fax: (323)937-5523. E-mail: info@stephencohen gallery.com; rick@stephencohengallery.com. Website: www.stephencohengallery.com. Estab. 1992. Photography and photo-based art gallery. Exhibits vintage and contemporary photography and photo-based art from the U.S., Europe and South America. The gallery is also able to locate work by photographers not represented in the gallery. Represents 40 artists. Sponsors 6 exhibits/year. Average display time 2 months. Open Tuesday–Saturday, 11-6. "We are a large, spacious gallery and are flexible in terms of types of shows we can mount." Overall price range $500-20,000. Most work sold at $2,000.

EXHIBITS All styles of photography and photo-based art. "The Gallery has exhibited vintage and contemporary photography and photo-based art from the United States, Europe and South America. The gallery is also able to locate work by photographers not represented by the gallery. As host gallery for Photo LA, Photo San Francisco, Photo NY and Art LA, the gallery has helped to expand the awareness of photography as an art form to be appreciated by the serious collector."

MAKING CONTACT & TERMS Charges 50% commission. Gallery provides insurance, promotion, contract. Requires exclusive representation locally.

SUBMISSIONS Mail portfolio for review. Send query letter with artist's statement, bio, brochure, business card, photographs, résumé, reviews, SASE. Responds within 3 months, only if interested. Finds artists through word of mouth, published work.

TIPS "Photography is still the best bargain in 20th-century art. There are more people collecting photography now, increasingly sophisticated and knowledgeable people aware of the beauty and variety of the medium."

CONTEMPORARY ARTS CENTER

900 Camp, New Orleans LA 70130. (504)528-3805. Fax: (504)528-3828. E-mail: amackie@cacno.org; info@cacno.org. Website: www.cacno.org. **Contact:** Amy Mackie, director of visual arts. Estab. 1976.

EXHIBITS Interested in alternative process, avant garde, fine art. Cutting-edge contemporary preferred.

MAKING CONTACT & TERMS Send query letter with bio, SASE, slides or CD. Responds in 4 months.

Finds artists through word of mouth, submissions, art exhibits, art fairs, referrals by other artists, professional contacts, art periodicals.

TIPS Submit only 1 slide sheet with proper labels (title, date, media, dimensions) or CD-ROM with the same information.

THE CONTEMPORARY ARTS CENTER

44 E. 6th St., Cincinnati OH 45202. (513)345-8400. Fax: (513)721-7418. E-mail: jmagoto@contemporary artscenter.org; pr@contemporaryartscenter.org. Website: www.contemporaryartscenter.org. Nonprofit arts center. Without a permanent collection, all exhibitions on view are temporary and ever-changing. Sponsors 9 exhibits/year. Average display time 6-12 weeks. Sponsors openings; provides printed invitations, music, refreshments, cash bar. Open Monday, 10-9; Wednesday–Friday, 10-6; Saturday and Sunday, 11-6. Closed Thanksgiving, Christmas and New Year's Day.

EXHIBITS Photographer must be selected by the curator and approved by the board. Exhibits photos of multicultural, disasters, environmental, landscapes/scenics, gardening, technology/computers. Interested in avant garde, innovative photography, fine art.

MAKING CONTACT & TERMS Photography sometimes sold in gallery. Charges 15% commission.

SUBMISSIONS Send query with résumé, slides, SASE. Responds in 2 months.

CONTEMPORARY ARTS COLLECTIVE

101 E. Charleston Blvd., Suite 120, Las Vegas NV 89104. (702)382-3886. Fax: (702)598-3886. E-mail: info@lasvegascac.org. Website: www.lasvegascac.org. Estab. 1989. "The CAC is a non-profit 501(c)3 art organization dedicated to presenting new, high quality, visual, and performing art, while striving to build, educate, and sustain audiences for contemporary art." Sponsors more than 9 exhibits/year. Average display time 1 month. Gallery open Tuesday–Saturday, 12-5, and by appointment; 1st Friday, 6-10. Closed Thanksgiving, Christmas, New Year's Day. 1,200 sq. ft. Overall price range $200-4,000. Most work sold at $400.

"The CAC is accepting submissions of work for East Side Projects, a series of monthly two-week projects in the gallery's front window space facing Charleston Blvd. This ongoing call is open to all contemporary artists working in any media. Artists must be current CAC members (defined as dues-paying members starting at the $25 level) in order to be eligible for consideration. To become a member go to cac.wildapricot.org/join. Site-specific work for the space is encouraged. We encourage artists to visit the gallery to see the space. Please note that the window receives a generous dose of Las Vegas sunshine."

EXHIBITS Interested in alternative process, avant garde, documentary, fine art.

MAKING CONTACT & TERMS Artwork is accepted through annual call for proposals of self-curated group shows, and there is a 30% requested donation. Gallery provides insurance, promotion, contract.

SUBMISSIONS Finds artists through annual call for proposals, membership, word of mouth, submissions, portfolio reviews, art exhibits, art fairs, referrals by other artists and walk-ins. Check website for dates and submission guidelines. Submissions must include a proposal, current CV/résumé, artist bio/statement, disc with JPEG images of original artwork (300 dpi at 2MB or less) and image reference sheet (including artist, title, media, dimensions, and filename). Send SASE for return.

TIPS Submitted slides should be "well labeled and properly exposed with correct color balance."

⊕ CORCORAN FINE ARTS LIMITED, INC.

12610 Larchmere Blvd., Cleveland OH 44120. (216)767-0770. Fax: (216)767-0774. E-mail: corcoranfinearts@gmail.com; gallery@corcoranfinearts.com. Website: www.corcoranfinearts.com. **Contact:** James Corcoran, director/owner. Estab. 1986. Represents 28 artists. Open Monday, Tuesday, Thursday, Friday 12-6; Saturday, 10-2 and by appointment.

EXHIBITS Interested in fine art. Specializes in representing high-quality 19th- and 20th-century work.

MAKING CONTACT & TERMS Gallery receives 50% commission. Requires exclusive representation locally.

SUBMISSIONS For first contact, send a query letter, résumé, bio, slides, photographs, SASE. Responds within 1 month. After initial contact, drop off or mail in appropriate materials for review. Portfolio should include slides, photographs. Finds artists through solicitation.

CORPORATE ART SOURCE/CAS GALLERY

2960-F Zelda Rd., Montgomery AL 36106. (334)271-3772. Fax: (334)271-3772. E-mail: casjb@mindspring.

com. Website: www.casgallery.com. Estab. 1990. Approached by 100 artists/year; represents or exhibits 50 artists. Sponsors 1 photography exhibit/year. Average display time 6 weeks. Gallery open Monday-Friday, 10-5:30; Overall price range $200-20,000. Most work sold at $1,000.

EXHIBITS Photos of landscapes/scenics, architecture, rural. Interested in alternative process, avant garde, fine art, historical/vintage.

MAKING CONTACT & TERMS Artwork is accepted on consignment, and there is a 50% commission. Gallery provides contract.

SUBMISSIONS E-mail from the website, or mail portfolio for review. Send query letter. Responds within 6 weeks, only if interested. Finds artists through submissions, portfolio reviews, art exhibits, art fairs, referrals by other artists.

TIPS "Have good photos of work, as well as websites with enough work to get a feel for the overall depth and quality."

CO/SO: COPLEY SOCIETY OF ART

158 Newbury St., Boston MA 02116. (617)536-5049. Fax: (617)267-9396. E-mail: info@copleysociety.org. Website: www.copleysociety.org. **Contact:** Caroline Vokey, gallery manager. Estab. 1879. Co/So is the oldest non-profit art association in the U.S. Sponsors 20-30 exhibits/year, including solo exhibitions, thematic group shows, juried competitions and fundraising events. Average display time 3-4 weeks. Open Tuesday–Saturday, 11-6; Sunday and Monday, 12-5. Overall price range $100-10,000. Most work sold at $700. Also offers workshops.

EXHIBITS Interested in all styles.

MAKING CONTACT & TERMS Must apply and be accepted as an artist member. "Once accepted, artists are eligible to compete in juried competitions. Artists can also display or show smaller works in the lower gallery throughout the year." Guaranteed showing in annual Small Works Show. There is a possibility of group or individual show, on an invitational basis, if merit exists. Charges 40% commission. Reviews digital images only with application. Preliminary application available via website. "If invited to apply to membership committee, a date would be agreed upon."

TIPS Wants to see "professional, concise and informative completion of application. The weight of the judgment for admission is based on quality of work.

Only the strongest work is accepted. We are in the process of strengthening our membership, especially photographers. We look for quality work in any genre, medium or discipline."

COURTHOUSE GALLERY, LAKE GEORGE ARTS PROJECT

1 Amherst St., Lake George NY 12845. (518)668-2616. E-mail: mail@lakegeorgearts.org. Website: www.lake georgearts.org. **Contact:** Laura Von Rosk, gallery director. Estab. 1986. Nonprofit gallery. Approached by more than 200 artists/year; represents or exhibits 10-15 artists. Sponsors 1-2 photography exhibits/year. Average display time 5-6 weeks. Gallery open Tuesday-Friday, 12-5; weekends, 12-4. Closed mid-December to mid-January. Overall price range $100-5,000. Most work sold at $500.

MAKING CONTACT & TERMS Artwork is accepted on consignment and there is a 25% commission. Gallery provides insurance, promotion, contract. Accepted work should be framed, mounted, matted.

SUBMISSIONS Mail portfolio for review. Deadline: January 31. Send query letter with artist's statement, bio, resume, slides, SASE. Responds in 4 months. Finds artists through word of mouth, submissions, portfolio reviews, art exhibits, art fairs, referrals by other artists.

O CREALDÈ SCHOOL OF ART

600 St. Andrews Blvd., Winter Park FL 32792. (407)671-1886. Fax: (407)671-0311. E-mail: rickpho@aol.com. Website: www.crealde.org. **Contact:** Rick Lang, director of photography. Estab. 1975. "The school's gallery holds 6-7 exhibitions/year, representing artists from regional/national stature." Open Monday–Thursday, 9-4; Friday–Saturday 9-1.

EXHIBITS All media.

MAKING CONTACT & TERMS Send 20 slides or digital images, resume, statement and return postage.

CROSSMAN GALLERY

950 W. Main St., Whitewater WI 53190. (262)472-5708 (office); (262)472-1207 (gallery). E-mail: flanagam@uww.edu. Website: blogs.uss.edu/crossman. **Contact:** Michael Flanagan, director. Estab. 1971. Photography is frequently featured in thematic exhibits at the gallery. Average display time 1 month. Overall price range $250-3,000. Located on the 1st floor of the Center of the Arts on the campus of the University of Wisconsin-Whitewater. Open Monday–Friday, 10-5; Monday–Thursday evening, 6-8; Saturday, 1-4. Special hours may apply when school is not in session. Please call before visiting to insure access.

EXHIBITS "We primarily exhibit artists from the Midwest but do include some from national and international venues. Works by Latino artists are also featured in a regular series at ongoing exhibits." Interested in all types of innovative approaches to photography. Sponsors openings; provides food, beverage, show announcement, mailing, shipping (partial) and possible visiting artist lecture/demo.

SUBMISSIONS Submit 10-20 slides or CD, artist's statement, résumé, SASE.

TIPS "The Crossman Gallery operates within a university environment. The focus is on exhibits that have the potential to educate viewers about processes and techniques and have interesting thematic content."

CSPS

1103 3rd St., SE, Cedar Rapids IA 52401-2305. (319)364-1580. Fax: (319)362-9156. E-mail: info@legionarts.org. Website: www.legionarts.org. **Contact:** Mel Andringa, producing director. Estab. 1991. Alternative space. Approached by 50 artists/year; represents or exhibits 15 artists. Sponsors 4 photography exhibits/year. Average display time 2 months. Open Wednesday–Sunday, 11-6. Closed July and August. Overall price range $50-500. Most work sold at $200.

EXHIBITS Interested in alternative process, avant garde, documentary, fine art.

MAKING CONTACT & TERMS Artwork is accepted on consignment and there is a 30% commission. Gallery provides insurance, promotion. Accepted work should be framed.

SUBMISSIONS Send query letter with artist's statement, bio, slides, SASE. Responds in 6 months. Finds artists through word of mouth, art exhibits, referrals by other artists, art trade magazine.

THE DALLAS CENTER FOR CONTEMPORARY ART

191 Glass St., Dallas TX 75204. (214)821-2522. Fax: (214)821-9103. E-mail: info@dallascontemporary.org. Website: www.dallascontemporary.org. **Contact:** Peter Doroshenko, director. Estab. 1981. Nonprofit gallery. Sponsors 1-2 photography exhibits/year. Other exhibits may include photography as well as other mediums. Average display time 6-8 weeks. Gallery open Tuesday-Saturday, 10-5.

EXHIBITS Variety of subject matter and styles.

MAKING CONTACT & TERMS Charges no commission. "Because we are nonprofit, we do not sell artwork. If someone is interested in buying art in the gallery, they get in touch with the artist. The transaction is between the artist and the buyer."

SUBMISSIONS Reviews slides/CDs. Send material by mail for consideration; include SASE. Responds October 1 annually.

TIPS "Memberships available starting at $50. See our website for info and membership levels."

➕ DARK ROOM GALLERY

12 Main St., Essex Jct. VT 05452. (802)777-3686. E-mail: ken@vermontphotospace.com. Website: www. vermontphotospace.com. **Contact:** Ken Signorello. Estab. 2010. (Formerly Vermont Photo Space Gallery.) For-profit and rental gallery. Approached by 1000 artists a year; represents or exhibits 500 emerging, mid-career and established artists. Exhibited artists include: Jeffrey A. Wolk, photography and Kathy Cline, photography. Sponsors 13 photography exhibits/year. Average display time 26 days. Open Sunday-Saturday, 11-4; closed on major holidays. The gallery is a freshly renovated 1300-sq.-ft. first floor store-front air conditioned space with hardwood floors and an 11 ft. ceiling. Our lighting system uses 3000K LED flood lights. Nearly every image has a dedicated light and hangs from a fully adjustable hanging system. We are located within 10 miles of the University of Vermont, three other colleges, downtown Burlington and Burlington International Airport. Clients include local community, students and tourists. Overall price range $100-2000. Most work sold for less than $200.

EXHIBITS Florals, landscapes, portraits and wildlife; considers all genres.

MAKING CONTACT & TERMS Model and property release are preferred. There is a rental fee for space; fee covers 1 month. Retail price of the art set by the artist. Gallery provides insurance, promotion and contract.

SUBMISSIONS Exhibits are juried with a small jury fee; selected entries are on consignment with 34-66% commission. Accepted work should be framed, mounted and matted. Call, e-mail query letter (with link to your website and JPEG samples at 72dpi), mail porfolio for review, send query letter or make submissions on the website. Responds in 1 week. Submitted materials filed include electronic files and unmounted prints only. Finds artists through submissions and Internet.

THE DAYTON ART INSTITUTE

456 Belmonte Park N., Dayton OH 45405-4700. (937)223-5277. Fax: (937)223-3140. E-mail: info@daytonart.org. Website: www.daytonartinstitute.org. Estab. 1919. Museum. Galleries open Wednesday–Saturday, 10-5; Sunday, 12-5; Thursday, 10-8; closed Monday and Tuesday.

EXHIBITS Interested in fine art.

DELAWARE CENTER FOR THE CONTEMPORARY ARTS

200 S. Madison St., Wilmington DE 19801. (302)656-6466. E-mail: info@thedcca.org. Website: www. thedcca.org. Alternative space, museum retail shop, nonprofit gallery. Approached by more than 800 artists/year; exhibits 50 artists. Sponsors 30 total exhibits/year. Average display time 6 weeks. Gallery open Tuesday, Thursday, Friday, and Saturday, 10-5; Wednesday and Sunday, 12-5. Closed on Monday and major holidays. Seven galleries located along rejuvenated Wilmington riverfront.

EXHIBITS Interested in alternative process, avant garde.

MAKING CONTACT & TERMS Gallery provides PR and contract. Accepted work should be framed, mounted, matted. Prefers only contemporary art.

SUBMISSIONS Send query letter with artist's statement, bio, SASE, 10 digital images. Returns material with SASE. Responds within 6 months. Finds artists through calls for entry, word of mouth, submissions, portfolio reviews, art exhibits, referrals by other artists.

DEMUTH MUSEUM

120 E. King St., Lancaster PA 17602. (717)299-9940. Fax: (717)299-9749. E-mail: information@demuth. org. Website: www.demuth.org. **Contact:** Gallery director. Estab. 1981. Museum. Average display time 2 months. Open Tuesday–Saturday, 10-4; Sunday, 1-4. Located in the home and studio of Modernist artist Charles Demuth (1883-1935). Exhibitions feature the museum's permanent collection of Demuth's works with changing, temporary exhibitions.

DETROIT FOCUS

P.O. Box 843, Royal Oak MI 48068-0843. (248)541-2210. Fax: (248)541-3403. E-mail: michael@sarnacki.

com. Website: www.detroitfocus.org. Estab. 1978. Artist alliance. Approached by 100 artists/year; represents or exhibits 100 artists. Sponsors 1 or more photography exhibit/year.

EXHIBITS Interested in photojournalism, avant garde, documentary, erotic, fashion/glamour, fine art.

MAKING CONTACT & TERMS No charge or commission.

SUBMISSIONS Call or e-mail. Responds in 1 week. Finds artists through word of mouth, submissions, art exhibits, referrals by other artists.

SAMUEL DORSKY MUSEUM OF ART

1 Hawk Dr., New Paltz NY 12561. (845)257-3844. Fax: (845)257-3854. E-mail: wallaceb@newpaltz.edu. Website: www.newpaltz.edu/museum. **Contact:** Brian Wallace, curator. Estab. 1964. Sponsors ongoing photography exhibits throughout the year. Average display time 2 months. Museum open Wednesday–Sunday, 11-5. Closed legal and school holidays and during intersession; check website to confirm your visit.

EXHIBITS Interested in alternative process, avant garde, documentary, fine art, historical/vintage.

SUBMISSIONS Send query letter with bio and SASE. Responds within 3 months, only if interested. Finds artists through art exhibits.

O DOT FIFTYONE GALLERY

51 NW 36 St., Wynwood Arts District, Miami FL 33127. (305)573-9994, ext. 450. Fax: (305)573-9994. E-mail: Dot@Dotfiftyone.com. Website: www.dotfiftyone.com. Estab. 2003. Sponsors 6 photography exhibits per year. Average display time: 30 days. Clients include the local community, tourists, and upscale corporate collectors. Art sold for $1,000-20,000 (avg. $5,000) with a 50% commission. Prices are set by the gallery and the artist. Gallery provides insurance, promotion and contract. Work should be framed, mounted and matted. Will respond within 1 month if interested.

MAKING CONTACT & TERMS Send letter with CD of digital art files in JPEG samples at 72 dpi.

GEORGE EASTMAN HOUSE

900 East Ave., Rochester NY 14607. (585)271-3361. Website: www.eastmanhouse.org. Estab. 1947. Museum. "As the world's preeminent museum of photography, Eastman House cares for and interprets hundreds of thousands of photographs encompassing the full history of this medium. We are also one of the oldest film archives in the U.S. and now considered to be among the top cinematic collections worldwide." Approached by more than 400 artists/year. Sponsors more than 12 photography exhibits/year. Average display time 3 months. Gallery open Tuesday, Wednesday, Friday, Saturday, 10-5; Thursday, 10-8; Sunday, 1-5. Closed Thanksgiving and Christmas. Museum has 7 galleries that host exhibitions, ranging from 50- to 300-print displays.

EXHIBITS GEH is a museum that exhibits the vast subjects, themes and processes of historical and contemporary photography.

SUBMISSIONS See website for detailed information: http://eastmanhouse.org/inc/collections/submissions.php. Mail portfolio for review. Send query letter with artist's statement, résumé, SASE, slides, digital prints. Responds in 3 months. Finds artists through word of mouth, art exhibits, referrals by other artists, books, catalogs, conferences, etc.

TIPS "Consider as if you are applying for a job. You must have succinct, well-written documents; a well-selected number of visual treats that speak well with written document provided; an easel for reviewer to use."

CATHERINE EDELMAN GALLERY

300 W. Superior St., Lower Level, Chicago IL 60654. (312)266-2350. Fax: (312)266-1967. Website: www.edelmangallery.com. **Contact:** Catherine Edelman, director. Estab. 1987. Sponsors 7 exhibits/year. Average display time 8-10 weeks. Open Tuesday–Saturday, 10-5:30. Overall price range $1,500-25,000.

EXHIBITS "We exhibit works ranging from traditional photography to mixed media photo-based work."

MAKING CONTACT & TERMS Charges 50% commission. Requires exclusive representation in the Midwest.

SUBMISSIONS Submissions policy on the website.

TIPS Looks for "consistency, dedication and honesty. Try to not be overly eager and realize that the process of arranging an exhibition takes a long time. The relationship between gallery and photographer is a partnership."

PAUL EDELSTEIN STUDIO AND GALLERY

540 Hawthorne St., Memphis TN 38112-5029. (901)496-8122. Fax: (901)276-1493. E-mail: henrygrove@yahoo.com. Website: www.askart.com. **Contact:** Paul R. Edelstein, director/owner. Estab. 1985. "Shows are

presented continually throughout the year." Overall price range: $300-10,000. Most work sold at $1,000.

EXHIBITS Photos of celebrities, children, multicultural, families. Interested in avant garde, historical/vintage, C-print, dye transfer, ever color, fine art and 20th-century photography that intrigues the viewer—figurative still life, landscape, abstract—by upcoming and established photographers.

MAKING CONTACT & TERMS Charges 50% commission. Buys photos outright. Reviews transparencies. Accepted work should be framed or unframed, mounted or unmounted, matted or unmatted work. There are no size limitations. Submit portfolio for review. Send query letter with samples. Cannot return material. Responds in 3 months.

TIPS "Looking for figurative and abstract figurative work."

THOMAS ERBEN GALLERY

526 W. 26th St., Floor 4, New York NY 10001. (212)645-8701. Fax: (212)645-9630. E-mail: info@thomaserben.com. Website: www.thomaserben.com. Estab. 1996. For-profit gallery. Approached by 100 artists/year; represents or exhibits 15 artists. Average display time 5-6 weeks. Gallery open Tuesday–Saturday, 10-6 (Monday–Friday in July). Closed Christmas/New Year's Day and August.

SUBMISSIONS Mail portfolio for review. Responds in 1 month.

ERNESTO MAYANS GALLERY

601 Canyon Rd., Santa Fe NM 87501. (505)983-8068. E-mail: arte2@aol.com. **Contact:** Ernesto Mayans, director. Estab. 1977. "We exhibit Photogravures by Unai San Martin; Pigment prints by Pablo Mayans, Silver Gelatin prints by Richard Faller (Vintage Southwest Works) and Johanna Saretzki and Sean McGann (Nudes)."

MAKING CONTACT & TERMS "Please call before submitting." Size limited to 16×20 maximum. Arrange a personal interview to show portfolio. Send query by mail with SASE for consideration. Responds in 4 weeks. Charges 50% commission. Consigns. Requires exclusive representation within area.

ETHERTON GALLERY

135 S. 6th Ave., Tucson AZ 85701. (520)624-7370. Fax: (520)792-4569. E-mail: info@ethertongallery.com. Website: www.ethertongallery.com. **Contact:** Terry Etherton. Estab. 1981. Retail gallery and art consul-

tancy. Specializes in vintage, modern and contemporary photography. Represents 50+ emerging, mid-career and established artists. Exhibited artists include Kate Breakey, Harry Callahan, Jack Dykinga, Elliott Erwitt, Mark Klett, Danny Lyon, Rodrigo Moya, Luis Gonzalez Palma, Lisa M. Robinson, Joel-Peter Witkin and Alex Webb. Sponsors 3-5 shows/year. Average display time 8 weeks. Open year round. Located in downtown Tucson; 3,000 sq. ft. gallery in historic building with wood floors and 16 ft. ceilings. Clientele: 50% private collectors, 25% corporate collectors, 25% museums. Overall price range $800-50,000; most work sold at $2,000-5,000. Media: Considers all types of photography, painting, works on paper. Etherton Gallery regularly purchases 19th-century, vintage, and classic photography; occasionally purchases contemporary photography and artwork. Interested in seeing work that is "well-crafted, cutting-edge, contemporary, issue-oriented."

MAKING CONTACT & TERMS Usually accepts work on consignment (50% commission). Retail price set by gallery and artist. Gallery provides insurance and promotion; shipping costs are shared; prefers framed artwork.

SUBMISSIONS Send CD or DVD, artist statement, résumé, reviews, bio; materials not returned. No unprepared, incomplete or unfocused work. Responds in 6 weeks only if interested.

TIPS "Become familiar with the style of our gallery and with contemporary art scene in general."

EVENTGALLERY 910ARTS

910 Santa Fe Dr., Denver CO 80204. (303)815-1779. E-mail: info@910arts.com. Website: www.910arts.com. **Contact:** Cheryl Spector, director. Estab. 2007. Community outreach gallery and event rental space whose mission is to create an open dialogue between artists and the community by raising awareness of social and environmental issues through creation of exceptional art. Average exhibition time is 2 months. Located in Denver's art district on Santa Fe with 1,500 sq. ft. of event space including full-service bar, gift shop featuring local artists, colorful open-air courtyard and catering kitchen. Open Tuesday–Saturday, 10-4; 1st Friday, 12-9; 3rd Friday, 12-8.

EXHIBITS Interested in fine art.

MAKING CONTACT & TERMS Artwork is accepted on a rental fee basis with 60% commission. Gallery provides insurance, promotion, contract. Artwork must be professionally displayed. See website for artist submission and event space rental guidelines. Responds to queries as soon as possible. Finds artists through word of mouth, art fairs, portfolio reviews, submissions, referrals by other artists.

EVERSON MUSEUM OF ART

401 Harrison St., Syracuse NY 13202. (315)474-6064. Fax: (315)474-6943. E-mail: everson@everson.org; smassett@everson.org. Website: www.everson.org. **Contact:** Steven Kern, executive director; Debora Ryan, senior curator; Sarah Massett; public relations director. Estab. 1897. Museum. "In fitting with the works it houses, the Everson Museum building is a sculptural work of art in its own right. Designed by renowned architect I.M. Pei, the building itself is internationally acclaimed for its uniqueness. Within its walls, Everson houses roughly 11,000 pieces of art; American paintings, sculpture, drawings, graphics and one of the largest holdings of American ceramics in the nation." Open all year; Tuesday-Friday, 12-5; Saturday, 10-5; Sunday, 12-5. Located in a distinctive I.M. Pie-designed building in downtown Syracuse, NY. The museum features four large galleries with 24 ft. ceilings, back lighting and oak hardwood, a sculpture court, Art Zone for children, a ceramic study center and five smaller gallery spaces.

FAHEY/KLEIN GALLERY

148 N. La Brea Ave., Los Angeles CA 90036. (323)934-2250. Fax: (323)934-4243. E-mail: fkg@earthlink.net. Website: www.faheykleingallery.com. **Contact:** David Fahey or Ken Devlin, co-owners. Estab. 1986. For-profit gallery. "Devoted to the enhancement of the public's appreciation of the medium of photography through the exhibition and sale of 20th century and contemporary fine art photography. The gallery, with over 8,000 photographs in stock, deals extensively in photographs as works of art in all genres including portraits, nudes, landscapes, still-life, reportage and contemporary photography. The website contains a broad range of over 10,000 images." Approached by 200 artists/year; represents or exhibits 60 artists. Sponsors 10 exhibits/year. Average display time 5-6 weeks. Open Tuesday–Saturday, 10-6. Closed on all major holidays. Sponsors openings; provides announcements and beverages served at reception. Overall price range $500-500,000. Most work sold at $2,500. Located in Hollywood; gallery features 2 exhibition spaces with extensive work in back presentation room.

EXHIBITS Interested in established work; photos of celebrities, landscapes/scenics, wildlife, architecture, entertainment, humor, performing arts, sports. Interested in alternative process, avant garde, documentary, erotic, fashion/glamour, fine art, historical/vintage. Specific photo needs include iconic photographs, Hollywood celebrities, photojournalism, music-related, reportage and still life.

MAKING CONTACT & TERMS Artwork is accepted on consignment, and the commission is negotiated. Gallery provides insurance, promotion, contract. Accepted work should be unframed, unmounted and unmatted. Requires exclusive representation within metropolitan area. Photographer must be established for a minimum of 5 years; preferably published.

SUBMISSIONS Prefers website URLs for initial contact, or send material (CD, reproductions, no originals) by mail with SASE for consideration. Responds in 2 months. Finds artists through art fairs, exhibits, portfolio reviews, submissions, word of mouth, referrals by other artists.

TIPS "Please be professional and organized. Have a comprehensive sample of innovative work. Interested in seeing mature work with resolved photographic ideas and viewing complete portfolios addressing one idea."

FALKIRK CULTURAL CENTER

1408 Mission Ave., San Rafael CA 94915-1560. (415)485-3328. Fax: (415)485-3404. E-mail: Beth.Goldberg@cityofsanrafael.org. Website: www.falkirkculturalcenter.org. **Contact:** Beth Goldberg, curator. Estab. 1974. Nonprofit gallery and national historic place (1888 Victorian) converted to multi-use cultural center. Approached by 500 artists /year; exhibits 300 artists. Sponsors 2 photography exhibits/year. Average display time 2 months. Open Tuesday–Friday, 1-5; Saturday, 10-1; by appointment.

MAKING CONTACT & TERMS Gallery provides insurance.

SUBMISSIONS Send query letter with artist's statement, bio, slides, résumé. Returns material with SASE. Please prepare a written proposal explaining the exhibition scope and content. Thematic exhibits are encouraged, and shows must include at least three artists. Include slides and/or photo samples of work to be included. Proposals should be delivered to Falkirk or mailed to Exhibition Committee, Falkirk Cultural Center. Finds artists through word of mouth, submissions, portfolio reviews, art exhibits, art fairs, referrals by other artists.

FAVA (FIRELANDS ASSOCIATION FOR THE VISUAL ARTS)

New Union Center for the Arts, 39 S. Main St., Oberlin OH 44074. (440)774-7158. Fax: (440)775-1107. E-mail: favagallery@oberlin.net. Website: www.fava gallery.org. Estab. 1979. Nonprofit gallery. Features changing exhibits of high-quality artwork in a variety of styles and media. Sponsors 1 photography exhibit/year. Average display time 1 month. Open Tuesday–Saturday, 11-5; Sunday, 1-5. Overall price range $75-3,000. Most work sold at $200.

EXHIBITS Open to all media, including photography. Exhibits a variety of subject matter and styles.

MAKING CONTACT & TERMS Charges 30% commission. Accepted work should be framed or matted. Sponsors 1 regional juried photo exhibit/year: Six-State Photography, open to residents of Ohio, Kentucky, West Virginia, Pennsylvania, Indiana, Michigan. Deadline for applications: March. Send annual application for 6 invitational shows by mid-December of each year; include 15-20 slides, slide list, résumé.

SUBMISSIONS Send SASE for exhibition opportunity flyer or 6-state photo show entry form.

TIPS "As a nonprofit gallery, we do not represent artists except during the juried show. Present the work in a professional format; the work, frame and/or mounting should be clean, undamaged, and (in cases of more complicated work) well organized."

FOCAL POINT GALLERY

321 City Island Ave., City Island NY 10464. (718)885-1403. Fax: (718)885-1451. E-mail: ronterner@gmail.com. **Contact:** Ron Terner, photographer/director. Estab. 1974. Overall price range $75-1,500. Most work sold at $175.

EXHIBITS Open to all subjects, styles and capabilities. "I'm looking for the artist to show me a way of seeing I haven't seen before." Nudes and landscapes sell best. Interested in alternative process, avant garde, documentary, erotic, fine art.

MAKING CONTACT & TERMS Charges 40% commission. Artist should call for information about exhibition policies.

TIPS Sees trend toward more use of alternative processes. "The gallery is geared toward exposure—let-

ting the public know what contemporary artists are doing—and is not concerned with whether it will sell. If the photographer is only interested in selling, this is not the gallery for him/her, but if the artist is concerned with people seeing the work and gaining feedback, this is the place. Most of the work shown at Focal Point Gallery is of lesser-known artists. Don't be discouraged if not accepted the first time. Continue to come back with new work when ready." Call for an appointment.

FREEPORT ART MUSEUM

121 N. Harlem Ave., Freeport IL 61032. (815)235-9755. Fax: (815)235-6015. E-mail: info@freeportart museum.org. Website: www.freeportartmuseum.org. **Contact:** Jennifer Kirker Priest, director. Formerly Freeport Arts Center. Sponsors 6 exhibits/year. Average display time: 8 weeks.

EXHIBITS All artists are eligible for solo or group shows. Exhibits photos of contemporary, abstract, avant garde, multicultural, families, landscapes/scenics, architecture, cities/urban, rural, performing arts, travel, agriculture. Interested in fine art.

MAKING CONTACT & TERMS Charges 30% commission. Accepted work should be framed.

SUBMISSIONS Send material by mail with SASE for consideration. Responds in 3 months.

FRESNO ART MUSEUM

2233 N. 1st St., Fresno CA 93703. (559)441-4221. Fax: (559)441-4227. E-mail: info@fresnoartmuseum.org; eva@fresnoartmuseum.org. Website: www.fresnoart museum.org. **Contact:** Eva Torres, associate director. Estab. 1948. "Approached by many California artists throughout the year." The museum highlights 6 areas of artwork: the work of women artists; support of professional mid-career local and California artists; modern masters; ethnographic art; emerging younger artists; and popular art. For more information on artist submissions, please call or e-mail us. Over 25 changing exhibitions/year including at least two photography exhibitions. Average display time 8 weeks. Gallery closed mid-August to early September.

EXHIBITS Focused on Modernist and Contemporary art.

MAKING CONTACT & TERMS Museum provides insurance. Send letter of inquiry through the mail with artist's statement, résumé, slides for curator to review (20 or more images). Studio visit arranged following review of material. "The museum shows the work of contemporary California artists; interested in sculpture, the work of mid-career and mature artists working in photography, sculpture, painting, mixed-media, installation work. The museum also draws exhibitions from its permanent collection."

⊘ THE G2 GALLERY

1503 Abbot Kinney Blvd., Venice CA 90291. (310)452-2842. Fax: (310)452-0915. E-mail: info@theg2 gallery.com. Website: www.theg2gallery.com. **Contact:** Jolene Hanson, gallery director. Estab. 2008. For-profit gallery exhibiting emerging, mid-career, and established artists. Approached by 100+ artists/year; represents or exhibits 45 artists. Exhibited photography by Robert Glenn Ketchum and Art Wolfe. Average display time 4-6 weeks. Open Tuesday–Saturday, 11-9; Sundays, 11-6. Closed Mondays. "The G2 Gallery is a green art space. The first floor features a gift shop and some additional exhibition space. In 2008, before the gallery opened, the building was renovated to be as eco-friendly as possible. The space is rich in natural light with high ceilings and there are large screen televisions and monitors for exhibition-related media. The G2 Gallery donates all proceeds to environmental causes and partners with conservation organizations related to exhibition themes. "Our motto is 'Supporting Art and the Environment.'" Clients include local community, tourists, upscale. Price range of work: $300-3,000. Most work sold at $500.

EXHIBITS Photography featuring environmental, landscapes/scenics, wildlife, alternative process, documentary, fine art, historical/vintage.

MAKING CONTACT & TERMS Art is accepted on consignment with a 40% commission. Retail price of the art is set by the artist. Gallery provides insurance, promotion, and contract. Accepted work should be framed, mounted, matted. Accepts photography only.

SUBMISSIONS All prospective artists are vetted through a juried application process. Please e-mail to request an application or download the application from website. Responds only if interested. "The G2 Gallery will contact artist with a confirmation that application materials have been received." Accepts only electronic materials. Physical portfolios are not accepted. Finds artists through word of mouth, submissions.

TIPS "Preferred applicants have a website with images of their work, inventory list, and pricing. Please do not contact the gallery once we have confirmed that your application has been received."

GALLERY 72

2709 Leavenworth St., Omaha NE 68105-2399. (402)345-3347. E-mail: gallery72@novia.net. **Contact:** Robert D. Rogers, director. Estab. 1972. Represents or exhibits 6 artists. Sponsors 2 photography exhibits/year. Average display time 3-4 weeks. Gallery open Monday–Saturday, 10-5; Sunday, 12-5. One large room, one small room.

EXHIBITS Photos of senior citizens, landscapes/scenics, cities/urban, interiors/decorating, rural, performing arts, travel.

MAKING CONTACT & TERMS Artwork is accepted on consignment, and there is a 50% commission. Gallery provides insurance, promotion. Requires exclusive representation locally. "No Western art."

SUBMISSIONS Call or write to arrange personal interview to show portfolio. Send query letter with artist's statement, brochure, photocopies, résumé. Accepts digital images. Finds artists through word of mouth, submissions, art exhibits.

GALLERY 110 COLLECTIVE

110 3rd Ave. S, Seattle WA 98104. (206)624-9336. E-mail: director@gallery110.com. Website: www.gallery 110.com. **Contact:** Sarah Dillon, director. Estab. 2002. "Gallery 110 presents contemporary art in a wide variety of media in Seattle's premiere gallery district, historic Pioneer Square. Our artists are emerging and established professionals, actively engaged in their artistic careers. We aspire to present fresh exhibitions of the highest professional caliber. The exhibitions change monthly and consist of solo, group and/or thematic shows in the main gallery and solo shows in our Small Space." Open Wednesday-Saturday, 12-5; hosts receptions every first Thursday of the month, 6-8 pm. Overall price range: $125-3,000; most work sold at $500-800.

MAKING CONTACT & TERMS Yearly active membership with dues, art on consignment, or available for rent.

TIPS "The artist should research the gallery to confirm it is a good fit for their work. The artist should be interested in being an active member, collaborating with other artists and participating in the success of the gallery. The work should challenge the viewer through concept, a high sense of craftsmanship, artistry, and expressed understanding of contemporary art culture and history. Artists should be emerging or established individuals with a serious focus on their work and participation in the field."

GALLERY 218

207 E. Buffalo St., Suite 218, Milwaukee WI 53202. (414)643-1732. E-mail: info@gallery218.com. Website: www.gallery218.com. **Contact:** Judith Hooks, president/director. Estab. 1990. Located in the Marshall Building of Milwaukee's historic Third Ward. Sponsors 12 exhibits/year. Average display time 1 month. Sponsors openings. "If a group show, we make arrangements and all artists contribute. If a solo show, artist provides everything." Overall price range $150-5,000. Most work sold at $350.

EXHIBITS Interested in alternative process, avant garde, abstract, fine art. Membership dues: $55/year plus $55/month rent. Artists help run the gallery. Group and solo shows. Photography is shown alongside fine arts painting, printmaking, sculpture, etc.

MAKING CONTACT & TERMS Charges 25% commission. There is an entry fee for each month. Fee covers the rent for 1 month. Accepted work must be framed.

SUBMISSIONS Send SASE for an application. "This is a cooperative space. A fee is required."

TIPS "Get involved in the process if the gallery will let you. We require artists to help promote their show so that they learn what and why certain things are required. Have inventory ready. Read and follow instructions on entry forms; be aware of deadlines. Attend openings for shows you are accepted into locally."

GALLERY 400

University of Illinois, 400 S. Peoria St., Chicago IL 60607. (312)996-6114. Fax: (312)355-3444. Website: gallery400.aa.uic.edu. **Contact:** Lorelei Stewart, director. Estab. 1983. Nonprofit gallery. Approached by 500 artists/year; exhibits 80 artists. Sponsors 1 photography exhibit/year. Average display time 4-6 weeks. Gallery open Tuesday–Friday, 10-6; Saturday, 12-6. Clients include local community, students, tourists, and upscale.

MAKING CONTACT & TERMS Gallery provides insurance and promotion.

SUBMISSIONS Check info section of website for guidelines. Responds in 5 months. Finds artists through word of mouth, art exhibits, referrals by other artists.

TIPS "Check our website for guidelines for proposing an exhibition and follow those proposal guidelines. Please do not e-mail, as we do not respond to e-mails."

GALLERY NORTH

90 N. Country Rd., Setauket NY 11733. (631)751-2676. Fax: (516)751-0180. E-mail: info@gallerynorth.org. Website: www.gallerynorth.org. **Contact:** Judith Levy, director.

SUBMISSIONS "Works to be exhibited are selected by our director, with input from our Artist Advisory Board. We encourage artist dialogue and participation in gallery events and community activities. Many artists associated with our gallery offer ArTrips and ArTalks, as well as teach in our educational programs. To present work in the gallery, send an e-mail with 2-5 medium-sized images; include a price list (indicating title, size, medium and date), artist's statement, biography and link to website. We encourage artists to visit the gallery and interact with our exhibitions."

GALLERY WEST

1213 King Str., Alexandria VA 22314. (703)549-6006. E-mail: gallerywest@verizon.net. Website: www.gallery-west.com. **Contact:** Judith Smith, president. Estab. 1979. Cooperative gallery. Owned and operated by Washington area artists of all media. Located in the historic district of Old Town Alexandria, Virginia, just across the Pomomac from Washington D.C. Approached by 30 artists/year; represents or exhibits 25 artists. Average display time 1 month. Open Wednesday–Sunday, 11-5 (January–March); the rest of the year, hours at 11-6. Overall price range $100-3,500. Most work sold at $500-700.

EXHIBITS Photos of babies/children/teens, multicultural, landscapes/scenics, wildlife, architecture, cities/urban, gardening, religious, rural, automobiles, food/drink, travel, product shots/still life. Interested in alternative process, avant garde, documentary, fine art, seasonal.

MAKING CONTACT & TERMS There is a co-op membership fee plus a donation of time. There is a 25% commission. Gallery provides promotion, contract. Accepted work should be framed.

SUBMISSIONS Call to show portfolio of slides. Send query letter with artist's statement, bio, SASE, slides. Responds in 1 month. Finds artists through word of mouth, portfolio reviews, art exhibits, referrals by other artists.

TIPS "Send high-quality slides."

⊘ GERING & LÓPEZ GALLERY

730 Fifth Ave., New York NY 10019. (646)336-7183. E-mail: info@geringlopez.com. Website: www.gering lopez.com. **Contact:** Director. Estab. 1991. For-profit gallery. Approached by 240 artists/year; represents or exhibits 12 artists. Sponsors 1 photography exhibit/year. Average display time 5 weeks. Gallery open Tuesday–Saturday, 10-6.

EXHIBITS Interested in alternative process, avant garde; digital, computer-based photography.

MAKING CONTACT & TERMS Artwork is accepted on consignment.

SUBMISSIONS E-mail with link to website or send postcard with image. Responds within 6 months, only if interested. Finds artists through word of mouth, art exhibits, art fairs, referrals by other artists. *Gering & López Gallery is currently NOT accepting unsolicited submissions.*

TIPS "Most important is to research the galleries and only submit to those that are appropriate. Visit websites if you don't have access to galleries."

GRAND RAPIDS ART MUSEUM

101 Monroe Center, Grand Rapids MI 49503. (616)831-1000. E-mail: pr@artmuseumgr.org. Website: www.gramonline.org. Estab. 1910. Museum. Sponsors 1 photography exhibit/year. Average display time 4 months. Gallery open Tuesday–Sunday, 11-6.

EXHIBITS Interested in fine art, historical/vintage.

CARRIE HADDAD GALLERY

622 Warren St., Hudson NY 12534. (518)828-1915. Fax: (518)828-3341. E-mail: carrie.haddad@carrie haddadgallery.com; cynthia.lathrop@carriehaddad gallery.com. Website: www.carriehaddadgallery.com. **Contact:** Carrie Haddad, owner. Estab. 1990. Art consultancy, for-profit gallery. "Hailed as the premier gallery of the Hudson Valley, the Carrie Haddad Gallery presents 8 large exhibits/year and includes all types of painting, both large and small sculpture, works on paper and a variety of techniques in photography." Approached by 50 artists/year; represents or exhibits 60 artists. Open daily, 11-5; closed Wednesday. Overall price range $350-6,000. Most work sold at $1,000.

EXHIBITS Photos of nudes, landscapes/scenics, architecture, pets, rural, product shots/still life.

MAKING CONTACT & TERMS Artwork is accepted on consignment, and there is a 50% commission. Gal-lery provides insurance, promotion. Requires exclusive representation locally.

SUBMISSIONS Send query letter with bio, photocopies, photographs, price list, SASE. Responds in 1 month. Finds artists through word of mouth, submissions, art exhibits, referrals by other artists.

THE HALSTED GALLERY, INC.

P.O. Box 7766, Bloomfield Hills MI 48302-7766. (248)894-0353. Fax: (248)332-0227. E-mail: thalsted@ halstedgallery.com. Website: www.halstedgallery. com. **Contact:** Wendy or Thomas Halsted. Sponsors 3 exhibits/year. Average display time 2 months. Sponsors openings. Overall price range $500-25,000.

EXHIBITS Interested in 19th and 20th century photographs.

SUBMISSIONS Call to arrange a personal interview to show portfolio only. Prefers to see scans. Send no slides or samples. Unframed work only.

TIPS This gallery has no limitations on subjects. Wants to see creativity, consistency, depth and emotional work.

LEE HANSLEY GALLERY

225 Glenwood Ave., Raleigh NC 27603. (919)828-7557. Fax: (919)828-7550. Website: www.leehansleygallery. com. **Contact:** Lee Hansley, gallery director. Estab. 1993. "Located in Raleigh's bustling Glenwood South, we are dedicated to showcasing quality fine art through a series of changing exhibitions, both group and solo shows, featuring works from professional artists from North Carolina, the Southeast and the nation. There are 35 artists in the gallery whose works are shown on a rotating basis. The gallery also hosts invitational exhibitions in which non-gallery artists show alongside stable artists. The gallery organizes at least 1 historical exhibition annually exploring the work of a single artist or group of stylistically-related artists." Sponsors 3 exhibits/year. Average display time 4-6 weeks. Overall price range $250-1600. Most work sold at $400. Open Tuesday–Friday, 11-6; 1st Friday, 11-10; Saturday, 11-6; or by appointment.

EXHIBITS Photos of environmental, landscapes/scenics, architecture, cities/urban, gardening, rural, performing arts. Interested in alternative process, avant garde, erotic, fine art. Interested in new images using the camera as a tool of manipulation; also wants minimalist works. Looks for top-quality work with an artistic vision.

MAKING CONTACT & TERMS Charges 50% commission. Payment within 1 month of sale.

SUBMISSIONS Send material by mail for consideration; include SASE. May be on CD. Does not accept e-mails. Responds in 2 months.

TIPS "Looks for originality and creativity—someone who sees with the camera and uses the parameters of the format to extract slices of life, architecture and nature."

JAMES HARRIS GALLERY

312 2nd Ave. S., Seattle WA 98104. (206)903-6220. Fax: (206)903-6226. E-mail: mail@jamesharrisgallery. com. Website: www.jamesharrisgallery.com. **Contact:** Jim Harris, director. Estab. 1999. Approached by 40 artists/year; represents or exhibits 26 artists. Average display time 6 weeks. Open Tuesday–Saturday, 11-5.

EXHIBITS Photos of landscapes and portraits. Interested in fine art.

SUBMISSIONS E-mail with JPEG samples at 72 dpi. Send query letter with artist's statement, bio, slides.

WILLIAM HAVU GALLERY

1040 Cherokee St., Denver CO 80204. (303)893-2360. Fax: (303)893-2813. E-mail: info@williamhavugallery. com. Website: www.williamhavugallery.com. **Contact:** Bill Havu, owner and director; Nick Ryan, gallery administrator. For-profit gallery. "Engaged in an ongoing dialogue through its 7 exhibitions a year with regionalism as it affects and is affected by both national and international trends in realism and abstraction. Strong emphasis on mid-career and established artists." Approached by 120 artists/year; represents or exhibits 50 artists. Sponsors 1 photography exhibit/year. Average display time 6-8 weeks. Open Tuesday–Friday, 10-6; Saturday, 11-5; 1st Friday of each month,10-9; Sundays and Mondays by appointment. Closed Christmas and New Year's Day. Overall price range $250-15,000. Most work sold at $1,000-4,000.

EXHIBITS Photos of multicultural, landscapes/scenics, religious, rural. Interested in alternative process, documentary, fine art.

MAKING CONTACT & TERMS Gallery provides insurance, promotion, contract. Accepted work should be framed. Requires exclusive representation locally. Accepts only artists from Rocky Mountain, Southwestern region.

SUBMISSIONS *Not accepting unsolicited submissions.* Mail portfolio for review. Send query letter with artist's statement, bio, brochure, résumé, SASE, slides.

Responds within 1 month, only if interested. Finds artists through word of mouth, submissions, referrals by other artists.

TIPS "Always mail a portfolio packet. We do not accept walk-ins or phone calls to review work. Explore website or visit gallery to make sure work would fit with the gallery's objective. We only frame work with archival quality materials and feel its inclusion in work can 'make' the sale."

HEARST ART GALLERY, SAINT MARY'S COLLEGE

P.O. Box 5110, Saint Mary's College of California, Moraga CA 94575-5110. (925)631-4379. Fax: (925)376-5128. E-mail: jarmiste@stmarys-ca.edu. Website: www.hearstartgallery.org. **Contact:** Julie Armistead, assistant curator. Estab. 1977. College gallery serving both Saint Mary's College community and the public. Sponsors 1 photography exhibit/year. Open Wednesday–Sunday, 11-4:30. Closed major holidays. 1,650 sq. ft. of exhibition space.

EXHIBITS Photos of multicultural, landscapes/scenics, religious, travel.

SUBMISSIONS Send query letter (Attn: Registrar) with artist's statement, bio, résumé, slides, SASE. Finds artists through submissions, art exhibits, art fairs, referrals by other artists.

⊘ HEMPHILL

1515 14th St., NW, Suite 300, Washington D.C. 20005. (202)234-5601. Fax: (202)234-5607. E-mail: gallery@ hemphillfinearts.com. Website: www.hemphill finearts.com. Estab. 1993. Art consultancy and for-profit gallery. Represents or exhibits 30 artists/year. Hemphill is a member of the Association of International Photography Art Dealers (AIPAD). Gallery open Tuesday–Saturday, 10-5 and by appointment. Overall price range $900-300,000.

EXHIBITS Photos of landscapes/scenics, architecture, cities/urban, rural. Interested in alternative process, fine art, historical/vintage.

SUBMISSIONS Gallery does not accept or review portfolio submissions.

HENRY STREET SETTLEMENT/ABRONS ART CENTER

466 Grand St., New York NY 10002. (212)766-9200; (212)598-0400. E-mail: info@henrystreet.org. Website: www.henrystreet.org/arts. **Contact:** Martin Dust, visual arts coordinator. Alternative space, nonprofit

gallery, community center. "The Abrons Art Center brings innovative artistic excellence to Manhattan's Lower East Side through diverse performances, exhibitions, residencies, classes and workshops for all ages and arts-in-education programming at public schools. Holds 9 solo photography exhibits/year. Open Tuesday–Friday, 10-10; Saturday, 9-10; Sunday, 11-6. Closed major holidays.

EXHIBITS Photos of multicultural, environmental, landscapes/scenics, architecture, cities/urban, rural. Interested in alternative process, avant garde, documentary, fine art, historical/vintage.

MAKING CONTACT & TERMS Artwork is accepted on consignment, and there is a 20% commission. Gallery provides insurance, space, contract.

SUBMISSIONS Send query letter with artist's statement, SASE. Finds artists through word of mouth, submissions, referrals by other artists.

HERA EDUCATIONAL FOUNDATION AND ART GALLERY

327 Main St., Wakefield RI 02879. (401)789-1488. E-mail: info@heragallery.org. Website: www.hera gallery.org. Estab. 1974. Cooperative gallery. "Hera Gallery/Hera Educational Foundation was a pioneer in the development of alternative exhibition spaces across the U.S. in the 70s and one of the earliest women's cooperative galleries. Although many of these galleries no longer exist, Hera is proud to have not only continued, but also expanded our programs, exhibitions and events." The number of photo exhibits varies each year. Average display time: 6 weeks. Open Wednesday, Thursday, Friday, 1-5; Saturday, 10-4; or by appointment. Closed during the month of January. Sponsors openings; provides refreshments and entertainment or lectures, demonstrations and symposia for some exhibits. Call for information on exhibitions. Overall price range: $100-10,000.

EXHIBITS Photos of disasters, environmental, landscapes/scenics. Interested in all types of innovative contemporary art that explores social and artistic issues. Interested in fine art.

MAKING CONTACT & TERMS Charges 25% commission. Works must fit inside a 6'6"×2'6" door. Photographer must show a portfolio before attaining membership.

SUBMISSIONS Inquire about membership and shows. Membership guidelines and application available on website or mailed on request.

TIPS "Hera exhibits a culturally diverse range of visual and emerging artists. Please follow the application procedure listed in the Membership Guidelines. Applications are welcome at any time of the year."

GERTRUDE HERBERT INSTITUTE OF ART

506 Telfair St., Augusta GA 30901-2310. (706)722-5495. Fax: (706)722-3670. E-mail: ghia@ghia.org. Website: www.ghia.org. **Contact:** Rebekah Henry, executive director. Estab. 1937. Nonprofit gallery. Has 5 solo or group shows annually; exhibits approximately 40 artists annually. Average display time 6-8 weeks. Open Tuesday–Friday, 10-5; weekends by appointment only. Closed 1st week in August, and December 17-31. Located in historic 1818 Ware's Folly mansion.

MAKING CONTACT & TERMS Artwork is accepted on consignment, and there is a 35% commission.

SUBMISSIONS Send query letter with artist's statement, bio, brochure, résumé, reviews, slides or CD of work, SASE. Responds to queries in 1-3 months. Finds artists through art exhibits, submissions, referrals by other artists.

HEUSER ART CENTER GALLERY & HARTMANN CENTER ART GALLERY

Bradley University, 1400 W. Bradley Ave., Peoria IL 61625. (309)677-2989. Website: art.bradley.edu/bug. **Contact:** Pamela Ayres, director of galleries, exhibitions and collections. Estab. 1984. Alternative space, nonprofit gallery, educational. "We have 2 formal exhibition spaces, one in the Heuser Art Center, where the art department is located, and one in the Hartmann Center, where the theatre department is housed." Approached by 260 artists/year; represents or exhibits 50 artists. Sponsors 1 photography exhibit/year. Average display time 4 to 6 weeks. Heuser Art Gallery open Monday–Friday, 9-7; Saturday, 12-4; and by appointment. Hartmann Center Gallery open Monday–Friday, 9-4; and by appointment. See website for more information.

EXHIBITS Photos of babies/children/teens, celebrities, couples, multicultural, families, parents, senior citizens, disasters, environmental, landscapes/scenics, wildlife, architecture, cities/urban, education, rural, entertainment, events, performing arts, travel, agriculture, business concepts, industry, medicine, military, political, product shots/still life, science, technology/computers. Interested in alternative process, avant garde, documentary, fashion/glamour, fine art, historical/vintage, large-format Polaroid.

MAKING CONTACT & TERMS Artwork is accepted on consignment, and there is a 35% commission. Gallery provides promotion and contract. Accepted work should be framed or glazed with Plexiglas. "We consider all professional artists."

SUBMISSIONS Mail portfolio of 20 slides for review. Send query letter with artist's statement, bio, brochure, business card, photocopies, photographs, résumé, reviews, SASE, slides and CD. Queries are reviewed in January and artists are notified in June. Finds artists through art exhibits, portfolio reviews, referrals by other artists and critics, submissions and national calls.

TIPS "No handwritten letters. Print or type slide labels. Send only 20 slides total."

EDWARD HOPPER HOUSE ART CENTER

82 N. Broadway, Nyack NY 10960. (845)358-0774. E-mail: info@hopperhouse.org. Website: hopperhouse.org. **Contact:** Kendra Yapyapan, assistant director; Carole Perry, director. Estab. 1971. Nonprofit gallery and historic house. Approached by 200 artists/year; exhibits 100 artists. Sponsors 1-2 photography exhibits/year. Average display time 1 month. Also offers an annual summer jazz concert series. Open Thursday–Sunday, 1-5; or by appointment. The house was built in 1858; there are 4 gallery rooms on the 1st floor. Overall price range: $100-12,000. Most work sold at $750.

EXHIBITS Photos of all subjects. Interested in alternative process, avant garde, documentary, fine art, historical/vintage, seasonal.

MAKING CONTACT & TERMS Artwork is accepted on consignment, and there is a 35% commission. Gallery provides insurance, promotion and contract. Accepted work should be framed, mounted and matted.

SUBMISSIONS Call. Mail portfolio for review. Send query letter with artist's statement, bio, brochure, business card, photocopies, photographs, résumé, reviews, slides and SASE. Responds to queries in 3 weeks. Finds artists through art fairs, art exhibits, portfolio reviews, referrals by other artists, submissions and word of mouth.

EDWYNN HOUK GALLERY

745 5th Ave., Suite 407, New York NY 10151. (212)750-7070. Fax: (212)688-4848. E-mail: info@houkgallery.com; julie@houkgallery.com. Website: www.houkgallery.com. **Contact:** Julie Castellano, director. For-profit gallery. The gallery is a member of the Art Dealers Association of America and Association of International Photography Art Dealers. The gallery represents the Estates of Ilse Bing, Bill Brandt, Brassaï and Dorothea Lange, and is the representative for such major contemporary photographers as Robert Polidorí, Joel Meyerowitz, Sally Mann, Herb Ritts, Bettina Rheims, Lalla Essaydi, Hannes Schmid, Sebastiaan Bremer, Danny Lyon and Elliott Erwitt. Open Tuesday–Saturday, 11-6.

EXHIBITS Specializes in masters of 20th-century photography with an emphasis on the 1920s and 1930s and contemporary photography.

HOWARD FINSTER VISION HOUSE

1346 N. Paulina St., Chicago IL 60622. (773)278-3058. E-mail: david@dlg-gallery.com. Website: www.dlg-gallery.com. **Contact:** David Leonardis, owner. Estab. 1992. For-profit gallery. Approached by 100 artists/year; represents or exhibits 12 artists. Average display time 30 days. Gallery open Tuesday–Saturday, 12-7; Sunday, 12-6. "One big room, four big walls." Overall price range $50-5,000. Most work sold at $500.

EXHIBITS Photos of celebrities. Interested in fine art.

MAKING CONTACT & TERMS Artwork is accepted on consignment, and there is a 50% commission. Gallery provides promotion. Accepted work should be framed.

SUBMISSIONS E-mail to arrange a personal interview to show portfolio. Mail portfolio for review. Send query letter via e-mail. Responds only if interested. Finds artists through word of mouth, art exhibits, referrals by other artists.

TIPS "Artists should be professional and easy to deal with."

HUNTSVILLE MUSEUM OF ART

300 Church St., SW, Huntsville AL 35801-4910. (256)535-4350. E-mail: info@hsvmuseum.org. Website: www.hsvmuseum.org. Estab. 1970. This nationally-accredited museum fills its 13 galleries with a variety of exhibitions throughout the year, including prestigious traveling exhibits and the work of nationally and regionally acclaimed artists. The museum's own 2,522-piece permanent collection also forms the basis for several exhibitions each year. Sponsors 1-2 exhibits/year. Average display time 2-3 months. Open Sunday, 1-4; Tuesday, Wednesday, Friday, Saturday, 11-4; Thursday, 11-8.

EXHIBITS No specific stylistic or thematic criteria. Interested in alternative process, avant garde, documentary, fine art, historical/vintage.

MAKING CONTACT & TERMS Buys photos outright. Accepted work may be framed or unframed, mounted or unmounted, matted or unmatted. Must have professional track record and résumé, slides, critical reviews in package (for curatorial review).

SUBMISSIONS Regional connection strongly preferred. Send material by mail with SASE for consideration.

ICEBOX QUALITY FRAMING & GALLERY

1500 Jackson St., NE, Suite #443, Minneapolis MN 55413. (612)788-1790. E-mail: icebox@bitstream.net. Website: www.iceboxminnesota.com. Estab. 1988. Exhibition, promotion and sales gallery. Represents photographers and fine artists in all media, predominantly photography. "A sole proprietorship gallery, Icebox sponsors installations and exhibits in the gallery's 1,700-sq.-ft. space in the Minneapolis Arts District." Overall price range $200-1,500. Most work sold at $200-800. Open Thursday and Friday, 10-6; Saturday, 12-5. Tuesday and Wednesday, by appointment only.

EXHIBITS Photos of multicultural, environmental, landscapes/scenics, rural, adventure, travel. Interested in alternative process, documentary, erotic, fine art, historical/vintage. Specifically wants "fine art photographs from artists with serious, thought-provoking work."

MAKING CONTACT & TERMS Charges 50% commission.

SUBMISSIONS "Send letter of interest telling why and what you would like to exhibit at Icebox. Include only materials that can be kept at the gallery and updated as needed. Check website for more details about entry and gallery history."

TIPS "We are experienced with the out-of-town artist's needs."

ILLINOIS STATE MUSEUM CHICAGO GALLERY

100 W. Randolph, Suite 2-100, Chicago IL 60601. (312)814-5322. E-mail: jstevens@museum.state.il.us. Website: www.museum.state.il.us/ismsites/chicago/exhibitions.html. **Contact:** Jane Stevens, assistant administrator. Estab. 1985. Sponsors 2-3 exhibits/year. Average display time 4 months. Sponsors openings; provides refreshments at reception and sends out announcement cards for exhibitions.

EXHIBITS *Must be an Illinois photographer.* Interested in contemporary and historical/vintage, alternative process, fine art.

SUBMISSIONS Send résumé, artist's statement, 10 slides, SASE. Responds in 6 months.

INDIANAPOLIS ART CENTER

Marilyn K. Glick School of Art, 820 E. 67th St., Indianapolis IN 46220. (317)255-2464. Fax: (317)254-0486. E-mail: ldehayes@indplsartcenter.org. Website: www.indplsartcenter.org. Estab. 1934. "Started in 1934 after the Great Depression to provide employment for artists, the IAC stays true to its mission by hiring professional artists as faculty, exhibiting the work of working artists and selling artist-made gifts and art. Sponsors 1-2 photography exhibits/year. Average display time 8 weeks. Overall price range $50-5,000. Most work sold at $500.

EXHIBITS Interested in alternative process, avant garde, documentary, fine art and "very contemporary work, preferably unusual processes." Prefers artists who live within 250 miles of Indianapolis.

MAKING CONTACT & TERMS Charges 35% commission. One-person show: $300 honorarium; 2-person show: $200 honorarium; 3-person show: $100 honorarium; plus $0.32/mile travel stipend (one way). Accepted work should be framed (or other finished-presentation formatted).

SUBMISSIONS Send minimum of 20 digital images with résumé, reviews, artist's statement and SASE between July 1 and December 31. No wildlife or landscape photography. Interesting color and mixed media work is appreciated.

TIPS "We like photography with a very contemporary look that incorporates unusual processes and/or photography with mixed media. Submit excellent images with a full résumé, a recent artist's statement, and reviews of past exhibitions or projects. Please, no glass-mounted slides. Always include a SASE for notification and return of materials, ensuring that correct return postage is on the envelope. Exhibition materials will not be returned. Currently booking 2012."

INDIVIDUAL ARTISTS OF OKLAHOMA

P.O. Box 60824, Oklahoma OK 73146. (405)232-6060. Fax: (405)232-6060. E-mail: stokes@iaogallery.org; info@iaogallery.org. Website: www.iaogallery.org. **Contact:** Clint Stone, executive director. Estab. 1979.

Alternative space. "IAO creates opportunities for Oklahoma artists by curating and developing socially relevant exhibitions in one of the finest gallery spaces in the region." Approached by 60 artists/year; represents or exhibits 30 artists. Sponsors 10 photography exhibits/year. Average display time 3-4 weeks. Open Tuesday–Saturday, 12-6. Gallery is located in downtown art district, 2,300 sq. ft. with 10 ft. ceilings and track lighting. Overall price range $100-2,000. Most work sold at $400.

EXHIBITS Interested in alternative process, avant garde, documentary, fine art, historical/vintage photography. Other specific subjects/processes: contemporary approach to variety of subjects.

MAKING CONTACT & TERMS Charges 20% commission. Gallery provides insurance, promotion, contract. Accepted work must be framed.

SUBMISSIONS Mail portfolio for review with artist's statement, bio, photocopies or slides, résumé, SASE. Reviews quarterly. Finds artists through word of mouth, art exhibits, referrals by other artists.

INTERNATIONAL CENTER OF PHOTOGRAPHY

1133 Avenue of the Americas, New York NY 10036. (212)857-0000. Fax: (212)768-4688. E-mail: info@icp.org. Website: www.icp.org. **Contact:** Department of Exhibitions & Collections. Estab. 1974.

SUBMISSIONS "Due to the volume of work submitted, we are only able to accept portfolios in the form of CDs or e-mail attachments. JPEG files are preferable; each image file should be a maximum of 1000 pixels at the longest dimension, at 72dpi. Slides must be labeled on the front with a name, address, and a mark indicating the top of the slide and should also be accompanied by a list of titles and dates. CDs must be labeled with a name and address. Submissions must be limited to 1 page of up to 20 slides or a CD of no more than 20 images. All files should be accompanied by a list of titles and dates. Portfolios of prints or of more than 20 images will not be accepted. Photographers may also wish to include the following information: cover letter, rèsumè or curriculum vitae, artist's statement and/or project description. ICP can only accept portfolio submissions via mail (or FedEx, etc.). Please include a SASE for the return of materials. ICP cannot return portfolios submitted without return postage."

INTERNATIONAL VISIONS GALLERY

2629 Connecticut Ave., NW, Washington D.C. 20008. (202)234-5112. Fax: (202)234-4206. E-mail: intvisions@aol.com. Website: www.inter-visions.com. **Contact:** Timothy Davis, owner/director. Estab. 1997. For-profit gallery. Approached by 60 artists/year; represents or exhibits 50 artists. Sponsors 1 photography exhibit/year. Average display time 4-6 weeks. Gallery open Wednesday–Saturday, 11-6. Located in the heart of Washington D.C.; features 1,000 sq. ft. of exhibition space. Overall price range $1,000-8,000. Most work sold at $2,500.

EXHIBITS Photos of babies/children/teens, multicultural.

MAKING CONTACT & TERMS Artwork is accepted on consignment, and there is a 50% commission. Gallery provides insurance, promotion, contract. Accepted work should be framed. Requires exclusive representation locally.

SUBMISSIONS Call. Send query letter with artist's statement, bio, photocopies, résumé, SASE. Responds in 2 months. Finds artists through word of mouth, art exhibits, referrals by other artists.

JACKSON FINE ART

3115 E. Shadowlawn Ave., Atlanta GA 30305. (404)233-3739. Fax: (404)233-1205. E-mail: info@jacksonfineart.com. Website: www.jacksonfineart.com. **Contact:** Malia Schramm, director. Estab. 1990. Specializes in 20th century and contemporary photography. Exhibitions are rotated every 6 weeks. Gallery open Tuesday–Saturday, 10-5. Overall price range $600-500,000. Most work sold at $5,000.

EXHIBITS Interested in innovative photography, avant garde, fine art.

MAKING CONTACT & TERMS Only buys vintage photos outright. Requires exclusive representation locally. Exhibits only nationally known artists and emerging artists who show long term potential. "Photographers must be established, preferably published in books or national art publications. They must also have a strong biography, preferably museum exhibitions, national grants."

SUBMISSIONS Send JPEG files via e-mail, or CD by mail with SASE for return. Responds in 3 months, only if interested. Unsolicited original work is not accepted.

ELAINE L. JACOB GALLERY AND COMMUNITY ARTS GALLERY

150 Community Arts Building, Detroit MI 48202. (313)577-2423. Fax: (313)577-8935. E-mail: s.dupret@ wayne.edu. Website: www.art.wayne.edu. **Contact:** Sandra Dupret, curator of exhibitions. Estab. 1995. Nonprofit university gallery. Approached by 30 artists/year; exhibits solo and group shows. Sponsors 1-2 photography exhibits/year. Average display time 1 month. Open Tuesday–Thursday, 10-6; Friday, 10-7. Closed Monday and Sunday, Thanksgiving weekend and Christmas. Community Arts Gallery: 3,000 sq. ft.; Elaine L. Jacob Gallery, level 1: 2,000 sq. ft., level 2: 1,600 sq. ft.

EXHIBITS Interested in fine art. "The Elaine L. Jacob Gallery and the Community Arts Gallery are university galleries, displaying art appropriate for an academic environment."

MAKING CONTACT & TERMS Gallery provides insurance, promotion. Accepted work should be framed.

SUBMISSIONS Send query letter with artist's statement, bio, résumé, SASE, slides, exhibition proposal, video, slide list. Responds in 3 months. Finds artists through word of mouth, portfolio reviews, art exhibits, referrals by other artists.

JADITE GALLERIES

413 W. 50th St., New York NY 10019. (212)315-2740. Fax: (212)315-2793. Website: www.jadite.com. **Contact:** Roland Sainz, director. Estab. 1985. "Exhibitions cover the spectrum of art form created by a myriad of talented artists from the U.S., Europe, Latin America and Asia. With 3 exhibition spaces, we have fostered a number of promising artists and attracted many serious collectors over the years." Sponsors 3-4 exhibits/year. Average display time 1 month. Open Monday–Saturday, 12-6. Overall price range $300-5,000. Most work sold at $1500.

EXHIBITS Photos of landscapes/scenics, architecture, cities/urban, travel. Interested in avant garde, documentary and b&w, color and mixed media.

MAKING CONTACT & TERMS Gallery receives 40% commission. There is a rental fee for space (50/50 split of expenses such as invitations, advertising, opening reception, etc.). Accepted work should be framed.

SUBMISSIONS Arrange a personal interview to show portfolio. Responds in 5 weeks.

ALICE AND WILLIAM JENKINS GALLERY

600 St. Andrews Blvd., Winter Park FL 32804. (407)671-1886. Fax: (407)671-0311. E-mail: Rberrie@ Crealde.org. Website: www.Crealde.org. **Contact:** Rick Lang, director of photo department. Estab. 1980. The Jenkins Gallery mission is to exhibit the work of noted and established Florida artists, as well as to introduce national and international artists to the Central Florida region. Each of the four to six annual exhibitions are professionally curated by a member of the Crealdé Gallery Committee or a guest curator.

JHB GALLERY

26 Grove St., Suite #4C, New York NY 10014. (212)255-9286. Fax: (212)229-8998. E-mail: info@jhbgallery. com. Website: www.jhbgallery.com. Estab. 1982. Private art dealer and consultant. Gallery open by appointment only. Overall price range $1,500-40,000. Most work sold at $2,500-15,000.

MAKING CONTACT & TERMS Artwork is accepted on consignment, and there is a 50% commission. Gallery provides promotion.

SUBMISSIONS Accepts online submissions. Send query letter with résumé, CD, slides, artist's statement, reviews, SASE. Finds artists through submissions, portfolio reviews, art exhibits, art fairs, referrals by other curators.

STELLA JONES GALLERY

201 St. Charles Ave., New Orleans LA 70170. (504)568-9050. Fax: (504)568-0840. Website: www.stellajones gallery.com. **Contact:** Stella Jones. Estab. 1996. For-profit gallery. "The gallery provides a venue for artists of the African diaspora to exhibit superior works of art. The gallery fulfills its educational goals through lectures, panel discussions, intimate gallery talks and exhibitions with artists in attendance." Approached by 40 artists/year; represents or exhibits 45 artists. Sponsors 1 photography exhibit/year. Average display time 6-8 weeks. Open Monday–Friday, 11-6; Saturday, 12-5; Sunday, by appointment only. Located on 1st floor of corporate 53-story office building downtown, 1 block from French Quarter. Overall price range $500-150,000. Most work sold at $5,000.

EXHIBITS Photos of babies/children/teens, multicultural, families, cities/urban, education, religious, rural.

MAKING CONTACT & TERMS Artwork is accepted on consignment, and there is a 50% commission.

Gallery provides insurance, promotion, contract. Accepted work should be framed. Requires exclusive representation locally.

SUBMISSIONS Call to show portfolio of photographs, slides, transparencies. Mail portfolio for review. Send query letter with artist's statement, bio, brochure, business card, photocopies, photographs, résumé, reviews, slides, SASE. Responds in 1 month. Finds artists through word of mouth, submissions, portfolio reviews, art exhibits, referrals by other artists.

TIPS "Photographers should be organized with good visuals."

KENT STATE UNIVERSITY SCHOOL OF ART GALLERIES

201 Art Building, Kent OH 44242. (330)672-7853. E-mail: haturner@kent.edu. Website: galleries.kent.edu/index.html. **Contact:** Anderson Turner, director of galleries. Located in the Art Building. Sponsors at least 6 photography exhibits/year. Average display time 4 weeks. Open Tuesday–Friday, 11-5.

EXHIBITS Interested in all types, styles and subject matter of photography. Photographer must present quality work.

MAKING CONTACT & TERMS Photography can be sold in gallery. Charges 40% commission. Buys photography outright.

SUBMISSIONS Will review transparencies. Write a proposal and send with slides/CD. Send material by mail for consideration; include SASE. Responds "usually in 4 months, but it depends on time submitted."

KIRCHMAN GALLERY

P.O. Box 115, 213 N. Nuget St., Johnson City TX 78636. (830)868-9290. E-mail: susan@kirchmangallery.com. Website: www.kirchmangallery.com. **Contact:** Susan Kirchman, owner/director. Estab. 2005. Art consultancy and for-profit gallery. Represents or exhibits 25 artists. Average display time 1 month. Sponsors 4 photography exhibits/year. Open Sunday, Monday and Thursday, 12-5; Friday and Saturday 11-6; anytime by appointment. Located across from Johnson City's historic Courthouse Square in the heart of Texas hill country. Overall price range $250-25,000. Most work sold at $500-1,000.

EXHIBITS Photos of landscapes/scenics. Interested in alternative process, avant garde, fine art.

MAKING CONTACT & TERMS Artwork is accepted on consignment, and there is a 50% commission.

SUBMISSIONS "Send 20 digital-format examples of your work, along with a résumé and artist's statement."

ROBERT KLEIN GALLERY

38 Newbury St., Boston MA 02116. (617)267-7997. Fax: (617)267-5567. E-mail: inquiry@robertklein gallery.com. Website: www.robertkleingallery.com. **Contact:** Robert L. Klein, owner; Eunice Hurd, director. Estab. 1980. Devoted exclusively to fine art photography, specifically 19th and 20th century and contemporary. Sponsors 10 exhibits/year. Average display time 5 weeks. Overall price range $1,000-200,000. Open Tuesday–Friday, 10-5:30; Saturday, 11-5 and by appointment.

EXHIBITS Interested in fashion, documentary, nudes, portraiture, and work that has been fabricated to be photographs.

MAKING CONTACT & TERMS Charges 50% commission. Buys photos outright. Accepted work should be unframed, unmatted, unmounted. Requires exclusive representation locally. Must be established a minimum of 5 years; preferably published.

SUBMISSIONS "The Robert Klein Gallery is not accepting any unsolicited submissions. Unsolicited submissions will not be reviewed or returned."

ROBERT KOCH GALLERY

49 Geary St., 5th Floor, San Francisco CA 94108. (415)421-0122. Fax: (415)421-6306. E-mail: info@kochgallery.com. Website: www.kochgallery.com. Estab. 1979. "Our gallery has exhibited and offered a wide range of museum quality photography that spans the history of the medium from the 19th century to the present. Our extensive inventory emphasizes Modernist and experimental work from the 1920s and 1930s, 19th century and contemporary photography." Sponsors 6-8 photography exhibits/year. Average display time 2 months. Located in the heart of San Francisco's downtown Union Square. Open Tuesday–Saturday, 10:30-5:30.

MAKING CONTACT & TERMS Artwork is accepted on consignment. Gallery provides insurance, promotion, contract. Requires West Coast or national representation.

SUBMISSIONS Finds artists through publications, art exhibits, art fairs, referrals by other artists and curators, collectors, critics.

LANDING GALLERY

8 Elm St., Rockland Maine 04841. (207)594-4544. E-mail: landinggallery@gmail.com. Website: www. landingart.com. **Contact:** Bruce Busko, president. Estab. 1985. For-profit gallery. Approached by 40 artists/year; represents or exhibits 50 artists. Sponsors 1 photography exhibit/year. Average display time 2-3 months. Two floors totalling 3,000 sq. ft., with 19-foot ceilings. Overall price range $100-12,000. Most work sold at $1,500. See website for exhibition schedule.

EXHIBITS Photos of landscapes/scenics, architecture, cities/urban, rural, adventure, automobiles, entertainment. Interested in alternative process, avant garde, erotic, fine art, historical/vintage. Seeking photos "with hand color or embellishment."

MAKING CONTACT & TERMS Artwork is accepted on consignment, and there is a 50% commission. Gallery provides insurance, promotion, contract. Accepted work should be framed. Requires exclusive representation locally.

SUBMISSIONS Call to show portfolio. Mail portfolio for review. Send query letter with artist's statement, bio, brochure, business card, photocopies, photographs, résumé, reviews, slides, SASE. Responds in 2 weeks. Finds artists through word of mouth, submissions, portfolio reviews, art exhibits, art fairs, referrals by other artists.

⊘ ELIZABETH LEACH GALLERY

417 NW 9th Ave., Portland OR 97209-3308. (503)224-0521. Fax: (503)224-0844. Website: www.elizabeth leach.com. Sponsors 3-4 exhibits/year. Average display time 1 month. "The gallery has extended hours every first Thursday of the month for our openings." Overall price range $300-5,000.

EXHIBITS Photographers must meet museum conservation standards. Interested in "high-quality concept and fine craftsmanship."

MAKING CONTACT & TERMS Charges 50% commission. Accepted work should be framed or unframed, matted. Requires exclusive representation locally.

SUBMISSIONS Not accepting submissions at this time.

LEEPA-RATTNER MUSEUM OF ART

St. Petersburg College, 600 Klosterman Rd., Tarpon Springs FL 34689. (727)712-5762. E-mail: lrma@sp college.edu. Website: www.spcollege.edu/museum.

Contact: R. Lynn Whitelaw, curator. The museum's 20th century collection is made up of art from Abraham Rattner's estate, donated by Allen and Isabelle Leepa, and a large donation made by the Tampa Museum of Art. The museum is filled with Rattner's retrospective works: lithographs, tapestries, sculptures, paintings and stained glass." Open Tuesday, Wednesday, Saturday, 10-5; Thursday, 10-8; Friday, 10-4, Sunday, 1-5. Closed Mondays and national holidays. Located on the Tarpon Springs campus of St. Petersburg College.

EXHIBITS Photos of babies/children/teens, celebrities, couples, multicultural, families, parents, senior citizens, architecture, cities/urban, education, gardening, interiors/decorating, pets, religious, rural, agriculture, business concepts, industry, medicine, military, political, product shots/still life, science, technology/computers, disasters, environmental, landscapes/scenics, wildlife, adventure, automobiles, entertainment, events, food/drink, health/fitness/beauty, hobbies, humor, performing arts, sports, travel. Interested in alternative process, avant garde, documentary, erotic, fashion/glamour, fine art, historical/vintage, seasonal.

LEHIGH UNIVERSITY ART GALLERIES

420 E. Packer Ave., Bethlehem PA 18015. (610)758-3619. Fax: (610)758-4580. E-mail: rv02@lehigh.edu. Website: www.luag.org. **Contact:** Ricardo Viera, director/curator. Sponsors 5-8 exhibits/year. Average display time 6-12 weeks. Sponsors openings.

EXHIBITS Fine art/multicultural, Latin American. Interested in all types of works. The photographer should "preferably be an established professional."

MAKING CONTACT & TERMS Reviews transparencies. Arrange a personal interview to show portfolio. Send query letter with SASE. Responds in 1 month.

TIPS "Don't send more than 10 slides or a CD."

LEOPOLD GALLERY

324 W. 63rd St., Kansas City MO 64113. (816)333-3111. Fax: (816)333-3616. E-mail: sharon@leopoldgallery. com. Website: www.leopoldgallery.com. **Contact:** Robin Elliott, assistant director. Estab. 1991. For-profit gallery. Approached by 100+ artists/year; represents or exhibits 50 artists/year. Sponsors 1 photography exhibit/year. Average display time 3 weeks. Open Monday–Friday, 1-6; Saturday, 10-5. "We are located in Brookside, a charming retail district built in 1920 with more than 70 shops, restaurants and of-

fices. The gallery has two levels of exhibition space, with the upper level dedicated to artist openings/exhibitions." Overall price range $50-25,000. Most work sold at $1,000.

EXHIBITS Photos of architecture, cities/urban, rural, environmental, landscapes/scenics, wildlife, entertainment, performing arts. Interested in alternative process, avant garde, documentary, fine art.

MAKING CONTACT & TERMS Artwork is accepted on consignment; there is a 50% commission. Gallery provides insurance, promotion, contract. Accepted work should be framed, mounted, matted. *Accepts artists from Kansas City area only.* Send query letter with artist's statement, bio, brochure, business card, résumé, reviews, SASE, disc with images. Responds in 2 weeks. Finds artists through word of mouth, art exhibitions, submissions, art fairs, portfolio reviews, referrals by other artists.

SUBMISSIONS E-mail 5-10 JPEG images of your body of work to email@leopoldgallery.com. Before sending, please scan your e-mail for viruses, as any viral e-mails will be deleted upon receipt. Images should be saved at 72 dpi, approximately 5×7 inches in measurement and compressed to level 3 JPEG. Please save for Windows. Or, send e-mail query letter with link to artist's website.

LIMITED EDITIONS & COLLECTIBLES

697 Haddon Ave., Collingswood NJ 08108. (856)869-5228. Fax: (856)869-5228. E-mail: jdl697ltd@juno.com. Website: www.ltdeditions.net. **Contact:** John Daniel Lynch, Sr., owner. Estab. 1997. For-profit online gallery. Approached by 24 artists/year; represents or exhibits 70 artists. Sponsors 20 photography exhibits/year. Overall price range $100-3,000. Most work sold at $450.

EXHIBITS Photos of landscapes/scenics, wildlife, adventure, automobiles, entertainment, events, food/drink, health/fitness/beauty, hobbies, humor, performing arts, sports, travel. Interested in alternative process, documentary, erotic, fashion/glamour, historical/vintage, seasonal.

MAKING CONTACT & TERMS Artwork is accepted on consignment, and there is a 30% commission. Gallery provides insurance, promotion, contract.

SUBMISSIONS Call or write to show portfolio. Send query letter with bio, business card, résumé. Responds in 1 month. Finds artists through word of mouth, portfolio reviews, art exhibits, referrals by other artists.

LIMNER GALLERY

123 Warren St., Hudson NY 12534. (518)828-2343. E-mail: thelimner@aol.com. Website: www.slowart.com. **Contact:** Tim Slowinski, director. Estab. 1987. Alternative space. Established in Manhattan's East Village. Approached by 200-250 artists/year; represents or exhibits 90-100 artists. Sponsors 2 photography exhibits/year. Average display time 4 weeks. Open Wednesday-Sunday, 11-5. Closed January, July-August (weekends only). Located in the art and antiques center of the Hudson Valley. Exhibition space is 1,000 sq. ft.

EXHIBITS Interested in alternative process, avant garde, documentary, erotic, fine art, historical/vintage.

SUBMISSIONS Artists should e-mail a link to their website; or download exhibition application at www.slowart.com/prospectus; or send query letter with artist's statement, bio, brochure or photographs/slides, SASE. Finds artists through submissions.

TIPS "Artist's website should be simple and easy to view. Complicated animations and scripted design should be avoided, as it is a distraction and prevents direct viewing of the work. Not all galleries and art buyers have cable modems. The website should either work on a telephone line connection or two versions of the site should be offered—one for telephone, one for cable/high-speed Internet access."

LIZARDI/HARP GALLERY

P.O. Box 91895, Pasadena CA 91109. (626)791-8123. Fax: (626)791-8887. E-mail: lizardiharp@earthlink.net. **Contact:** Grady Harp, director. Estab. 1981. Sponsors 3-4 exhibits/year. Average display time 4-6 weeks. Overall price range $250-1,500. Most work sold at $500.

EXHIBITS Primarily interested in the figure. Also exhibits photos of celebrities, couples, performing arts. Must have more than one portfolio of subject, unique slant and professional manner. Interested in avant garde, erotic, fine art, figurative, nudes, "maybe" manipulated work, documentary and mood landscapes, both b&w and color.

MAKING CONTACT & TERMS Charges 50% commission. Accepted work should be unframed, unmounted; matted or unmatted.

SUBMISSIONS Submit portfolio for review. Send query letter by e-mail résumé, samples. Responds in 1 month.

TIPS Include 20 labeled slides, résumé and artist's statement with submission. "Submit at least 20 images that represent bodies of work. I mix photography of figures, especially nudes, with shows on painting."

LOS ANGELES ART ASSOCIATION/ GALLERY 825

825 N. La Cienega Blvd., Los Angeles CA 90069. (310)652-8272. E-mail: peter@laaa.org. Website: www. laaa.org. **Contact:** Peter Mays, executive director. Estab. 1925. Holds approximately 1 exhibition/year. Average display time 4-5 weeks. Fine art only. Exhibits all media.

MAKING CONTACT & TERMS Gallery provides promotion, exhibition venues and resources.

SUBMISSIONS To become an LAAA Artist member, visit website for screening dates and submission requirements.

THE LOWE GALLERY

1555 Peachtree St., NE, Suite 100, Atlanta GA 30309. (404)352-8114. Fax: (404)352-0564. E-mail: info@ lowegallery.com; christina@lowegallery.com. Website: www.lowegallery.com. **Contact:** Christina Kwan. For-profit gallery. Approached by 300 artists/year; represents or exhibits approximately 67 artists. Average display time 4-6 weeks. Open Tuesday–Friday, 10-5:30; Saturday, 11-5:30; Sunday by appointment. Exhibition space is 6,000 sq. ft. with great architectural details, such as 22-ft.-high ceilings. Exhibition spaces range from monumental to intimate.

⊙ Additional gallery located in Santa Monica, California.

EXHIBITS Photos of babies/children/teens, multicultural. Interested in alternative process, mixed media.

MAKING CONTACT & TERMS Artwork is accepted on consignment, and there is a 50% commission. Requires exclusive representation locally.

SUBMISSIONS Send query letter with artists's statement, bio, photographs, résumé, reviews, SASE. Finds artists through word of mouth, art exhibits, submissions, art fairs, portfolio reviews, referrals by other artists. Submission guidelines available online.

TIPS "Look at the type of work that the gallery already represents, and make sure your work is an aesthetic

fit first! Send lots of great images with dimensions and pricing."

LUX CENTER FOR THE ARTS

2601 N. 48th St., Lincoln NE 68504. (402)466-8692. Fax: (402)466-3786. E-mail: info@luxcenter.org. Website: www.luxcenter.org. Estab. 1978. Non-profit gallery. Over 450 fine arts prints collected by the art center's benefactor are preserved in the Gladys M. Lux Historical Gallery. Exhibited artists include Guy Pene DuBois, Joseph Hirsch, Dois Emrick Lee, Fletcher Martin, Georges Schreiber, Margurite Zorach and many more. Represents or exhibits 60+ artists. Sponsors 3-4 photography exhibits/year. Average display time 1 month. Open Tuesday–Friday, 11-5; Saturday, 10-5; 1st Friday, 11-7.

EXHIBITS Photos of landscapes/scenics. Interested in alternative process, avant garde, fine art.

MAKING CONTACT & TERMS Artwork is accepted on consignment, and there is a 50% commission.

SUBMISSIONS Mail portfolio for review. Send query letter with artist's statement, bio, slides or digital images on CD, SASE. Finds artists through referrals by other artists and through research.

TIPS "To make your submission professional, you should have high-quality images (either slides or high-res digital images), cover letter, bio, résumé, artist's statement and SASE."

MACALESTER GALLERY

Janet Wallace Fine Arts Center, 1600 Grand Ave., St. Paul MN 55105. (651)696-6416. Fax: (651)696-6266. E-mail: fitz@macalester.edu; gallery@macalester.edu. Website: www.macalester.edu/gallery. **Contact:** Gregory Fitz, curator. Estab. 1964. Nonprofit gallery. Approached by 15 artists/year; represents or exhibits 3 artists. Sponsors 1 photography exhibit/year. Average display time 4-5 weeks. Gallery open Monday-Friday, 10-4; weekends, 12-4. Closed major holidays, summer and school holidays. Located in the core of the Janet Wallace Fine Arts Center on the campus of Macalester College. While emphasizing contemporary, the gallery also hosts exhibitions on a wide-range of historical and sociological topics. Gallery is approx. 1,100 sq. ft. and newly renovated. Overall price range: $200-1,000. Most work sold at $350.

EXHIBITS Photos of multicultural, environmental, landscapes/scenics, architecture, rural. Interested in avant garde, documentary, fine art, historical/vintage.

MAKING CONTACT & TERMS Gallery provides insurance. Accepted work should be framed, mounted, matted.

SUBMISSIONS Send query letter with artist's statement, bio, brochure, business card, photocopies, photographs, résumé, reviews, SASE, slides. Responds in 3 weeks. Finds artists through word of mouth, portfolio reviews, referrals by other artists.

TIPS "Photographers should present quality slides which are clearly labeled. Include a concise artist's statement. Always include a SASE. No form letters or mass mailings."

MACNIDER ART MUSEUM

303 2nd St. SE, Mason City IA 50401. (641)421-3666. Fax: (641)422-9612. E-mail: eblanchard@masoncity.net; macniderinformation@masoncity.net. Website: www.macniderart.org. Estab. 1966. Nonprofit gallery. Represents or exhibits 1-10 artists. Sponsors 2-5 photography exhibits/year (1 is competitive for the county). Average display time 2 months. Gallery open Tuesday and Thursday, 9-9; Wednesday, Friday, Saturday, 9-5; Sunday, 1-5. Closed Monday. Overall price range $50-2,500. Most work sold at $200.

MAKING CONTACT & TERMS Artwork is accepted on consignment, and there is a 40% commission. Gallery provides insurance, promotion, contract. Accepted work should be framed.

SUBMISSIONS Mail portfolio for review. Responds within 3 months, only if interested. Finds artists through word of mouth, submissions, portfolio reviews, art exhibits, art fairs, referrals by other artists. Exhibition opportunities: exhibition in galleries, presence in museum shop on consignment or booth at Festival Art Market in June.

MARKEIM ART CENTER

104 Walnut St., Haddonfield NJ 08033. (856)429-8585. E-mail: markeim@verizon.net. Website: www.markeimartcenter.org. **Contact:** Elizabeth H. Madden, executive director. Estab. 1956. Sponsors 10-11 exhibits/year. Average display time 4 weeks. The exhibiting artist is responsible for all details of the opening. Overall price range $75-1,000. Most work sold at $350.

EXHIBITS Interested in all types work. Exhibits photos of babies/children/teens, celebrities, couples, multicultural, families, parents, senior citizens, environmental, landscapes/scenics, wildlife, architecture, cities/urban, education, rural, adventure, automo-

biles, entertainment, performing arts, sports, travel, agriculture, product shots/still life. Interested in alternative process, avant garde, documentary, fine art, historical/vintage, seasonal.

MAKING CONTACT & TERMS Charges 30% commission. Accepted work should be framed and wired, ready to hang, mounted or unmounted, matted or unmatted. Artists from New Jersey and Delaware Valley region are preferred. Work must be professional and high quality.

SUBMISSIONS Send slides by mail or e-mail for consideration. Include SASE, résumé and letter of intent. Responds in 1 month.

TIPS "Be patient and flexible with scheduling. Look not only for one-time shows, but for opportunities to develop working relationships with a gallery. Establish yourself locally and market yourself outward."

MARLBORO GALLERY

Prince George's Community College, 301 Largo Rd., Largo MD 20772-2199. (301)322-0965. Fax: (301)808-0418. E-mail: tberault@pgcc.edu. Website: www.pgcc.edu. **Contact:** Tom Berault, curator-director. Estab. 1976. Average display time 6 weeks. Overall price range $50-2,000. Most work sells at $75-350.

EXHIBITS Fine art, photos of celebrities, portraiture, landscapes/scenics, wildlife/adventure, entertainment, events and travel. Also interested in alternative processes, experimental/manipulated, avant garde photographs. Not interested in commercial work.

MAKING CONTACT & TERMS "We do not take commission on artwork sold." Accepted work must be framed and suitable for hanging.

SUBMISSIONS "We are most interested in fine art photos and need 10-20 examples to make assessment. Reviews are done on an ongoing basis. We prefer to receive submissions February through April." Please send cover letter with résumé, CD with 15 to 20 JPEGs (300 ppi, 5×7), image list with titles, media and dimensions, artist statement, and SASE to return. Responds in 1 month.

TIPS "Send examples of what you wish to display, and explanations if photos do not meet normal standards (i.e., in focus, experimental subject matter)."

MASUR MUSEUM OF ART

1400 S. Grand St., Monroe LA 71202. (318)329-2237. Fax: (318)329-2847. E-mail: info@masurmuseum.org. Website: www.masurmuseum.org. **Contact:** Evelyn Stewart, director. Estab. 1963. Approached by 500 artists/year; represents or exhibits 150 artists. Sponsors 2 photography exhibits/year. Average display time 2 months. Museum open Tuesday–Friday, 9-5; Saturday, 12-5. Closed Mondays, between exhibitions and on major holidays. Located in historic home, 3,000 sq. ft. Overall price range $100-12,000. Most work sold at $300.

EXHIBITS Photos of babies/children/teens, celebrities, environmental, landscapes/scenics. Interested in alternative process, avant garde, documentary, fine art, historical/vintage.

MAKING CONTACT & TERMS Artwork is accepted on consignment, and there is a 20% commission. Gallery provides insurance, promotion. Accepted work should be framed.

SUBMISSIONS Send query letter with artist's statement, bio, résumé, reviews, slides, SASE. Responds in 6 months. Finds artists through word of mouth, submissions, art exhibits, referrals by other artists.

⊕ MAUI HANDS

P.O. Box 974, Makawao, HI 96768 (808)573-2021. Fax: (808)573-2021. E-mail: panna@mauihands.com. Website: www.mauihands.com. **Contact:** Panna Cappelli, owner. Estab. 1992. For-profit gallery. Approached by 50-60 artists/year. Continuously exhibits 300 emerging, mid-career and established artists. Exhibited artists include Linda Whittemore (abstract monotypes) and Steven Smeltzer (ceramic sculpture). Sponsors 15-20 exhibits/year; 2 photography exhibits/year. Average display time: 1 month. Open Monday-Sunday 10-7, weekends 10-6. Closed on Christmas and Thanksgiving. Three spaces: #1 on Main Highway, 1,200 sq. ft .gallery, 165 sq. ft. exhibition; #2 on Main Highway, 1,000 sq. ft. gallery, 80 sq.ft. exhibition; #3 in resort, 900 sq. ft. gallery, 50 sq. ft. exhibition. Clients include local community, tourists and upscale. 3% of sales are to corporate collectors. Overall price range: $10-7,000. Most work sold at $350.

EXHIBITS Considers all media. Most frequently exhibits oils, pastels, and mixed media. Considers engravings, etchings, linocuts, lithographs, and serigraphs. Styles considered are painterly abstraction, impressionism and primitivism realism. Most frequently exhibits impressionism and painterly abstraction. Genres include figurative work, florals, landscapes and portraits.

MAKING CONTACT & TERMS Artwork accepted on consignment with a 55% commission. Retail price of the art set by the gallery and artist. Gallery provides insurance and promotion. Artwork should be framed, mounted and matted, as applicable. Only accepts artists from Hawaii.

SUBMISSIONS Artists should call, write to arrange personal interview to show portfolio of original pieces, e-mail query letter with link to artist's website (JPEG samples at 72 dpi) or send query letter with artist's statement, bio, brochure, photographs, résumé, business cards and reviews. Responds in days. All materials filed. Finds artists through word of mouth, submissions, portfolio reviews, art exhibits, art fairs and referrals by other artists.

TIPS "Best to submit your work via our website."

MCDONOUGH MUSEUM OF ART

525 Wick Ave., One University Plaza, Youngstown OH 44555-1400. (330)941-1400. E-mail: labrothers@ ysu.edu. Website: www.fpa.ysu.edu. **Contact:** Leslie Brothers, director. Estab. 1991. A center for contemporary art, education and community, the museum offers exhibitions in all media, experimental installation, performance, and regional outreach programs to the public. The museum is also the public outreach facility for the Department of Art and supports student and faculty work through exhibitions, collaborations, courses and ongoing discussion.

SUBMISSIONS Send exhibition proposal.

MESA CONTEMPORARY ARTS AT MESA ARTS CENTER

1 E. Main St., P.O. Box 1466, Mesa AZ 85211. (480)644-6560. E-mail: patty.haberman@mesaartscenter.com. Website: www.mesaartscenter.com. **Contact:** Patty Haberman, curator. Estab. 1980. Not-for-profit art space. "Mesa Contemporary Arts is the dynamic visual art exhibition space at Mesa Arts Center. In 5 stunning galleries, Mesa Contemporary Arts showcases curated and juried exhibitions of contemporary art by emerging and internationally recognized artists. We also offer lectures by significant artists and arts professionals, art workshops and a volunteer docent program." Public admission: $3.50; free for children ages 7 and under; free on Thursdays (sponsored by Salt River Project); free on the first Sunday of each month, via the "3 for Free" program sponsored by Target (also includes free admission to the Arizona Museum for Youth and the Arizona Museum of Natural History).

EXHIBITS Photos of babies/children/teens, celebrities, couples, multicultural, families, parents, senior citizens, disasters, environmental, landscapes/scenics, wildlife, architecture, cities/urban, interiors/decorating, rural, adventure, automobiles, entertainment, events, performing arts, travel, industry, political, science, technology/computers. Interested in alternative process, avant garde, documentary, fine art, historical/vintage, seasonal, and contemporary photography.

MAKING CONTACT & TERMS Charges $25 entry fee, 25% commission.

TIPS "We do invitational or national juried exhibits. Submit professional-quality slides."

⊘ R. MICHELSON GALLERIES

132 Main St., Northampton MA 01060. (413)586-3964. Fax: (413)587-9811. E-mail: RM@RMichelson.com. Website: www.RMichelson.com. **Contact:** Richard Michelson, owner and president. Estab. 1976. Retail gallery. Sponsors 1 exhibit/year. Average display time 6 weeks. Open all year; Monday-Saturday, 10-6; Sunday, 12-5. Located downtown; Northampton gallery has 3,500 sq. ft.; Amherst gallery has 1,800 sq. ft. 50% of space for special exhibitions. Clientele 80% private collectors, 20% corporate collectors. Sponsors openings. Overall price range $1,200-15,000.

EXHIBITS Interested in contemporary, landscape and/or figure work.

MAKING CONTACT & TERMS Sometimes buys photos outright. Accepted work can be framed or unframed, mounted or unmounted, matted or unmatted. Requires exclusive representation locally. Not taking on new photographers at this time.

MILL BROOK GALLERY & SCULPTURE GARDEN

236 Hopkinton Rd., Concord NH 03301. (603)226-2046. E-mail: artsculpt@mindspring.com. Website: www.themillbrookgallery.com. Estab. 1996. Exhibits 70 artists. Sponsors 1 photography exhibit/year. Average display time 6 weeks. Gallery open Tuesday–Sunday, 11-5, April 1–December 24; open by appointment December 25–March 31. Outdoor juried sculpture exhibit. Three rooms inside for exhibitions, 1,800 sq. ft. Overall price range $8-30,000. Most work sold at $500-1,000.

MAKING CONTACT & TERMS Artwork is accepted on consignment, and there is a 50% commission.

Gallery provides insurance, promotion, contract. Accepted work should be framed, matted.

SUBMISSIONS Write to arrange a personal interview to show portfolio of photographs, slides. Send query letter with artist's statement, bio, photocopies, photographs, résumé, slides, SASE. Responds within 1 month, only if interested. Finds artists through word of mouth, submissions, art exhibits, referrals by other artists.

PETER MILLER GALLERY

118 N. Peoria St., Chicago IL 60607. (312)226-5291. Fax: (312)226-5441. E-mail: director@petermiller gallery.com. Website: www.petermillergallery.com. **Contact:** Peter Miller and Natalie R. Domchenko, directors. Estab. 1979. The Peter Miller Gallery exhibits contemporary art by emerging and mid-career artists. The gallery's current direction spans a broad range of contemporary art practice, including photo-based work, sound and video installations as well as painting and sculpture. The current location in Chicago's West Loop Gallery District occupies approximately 1800 square feet on the ground floor. The main exhibition gallery has its own project space and the office/reception area has two smaller project rooms. Overall price range $1,000-40,000. Most work sold at $5,000.

EXHIBITS Painting, sculpture, photography and new media.

MAKING CONTACT & TERMS Charges 50% commission. Accepted work can be framed or unframed, mounted or unmounted, matted or unmatted. Requires exclusive representation locally.

SUBMISSIONS Send CD with minimum of 20 images (no details) from the last 18 months with SASE, or e-mail a link to your website to director@peter millergallery.com.

TIPS "We look for work we haven't seen before; i.e., new images and new approaches to the medium."

MILLS POND HOUSE GALLERY

Smithtown Township Arts Council, 660 Route 25 A, St. James NY 11780. E-mail: exhibits@stacarts.org. Website: www.stacarts.org. **Contact:** Krista Biedenbach, program coordinator. Non-profit gallery. Sponsors 9 exhibits/year (1-2 photography). Average display time is 5 weeks. Hours: Monday–Friday 10-5; weekends, 12-4. Considers all types of prints, media and styles. Prices set by the artist. Gallery provides insurance and promotion. Work should be framed. Clients: local and national community.

MOBILE MUSEUM OF ART

4850 Museum Dr., Mobile AL 36608-1917. (251)208-5200. E-mail: eric.gallichant@cityofmobile.org. Website: www.mobilemuseumofart.com. **Contact:** Tommy McPherson, director. Sponsors 4 exhibits/year. Average display time 3 months. Sponsors openings; provides light hors d'oeuvres and cash bar.

EXHIBITS Open to all types and styles.

MAKING CONTACT & TERMS Photography sold in gallery. Charges 20% commission. Occasionally buys photos outright. Accepted work should be framed.

SUBMISSIONS Arrange a personal interview to show portfolio; send material by mail for consideration. Returns material when SASE is provided "unless photographer specifically points out that it's not required."

TIPS "We look for personal point of view beyond technical mastery."

MONTEREY MUSEUM OF ART

559 Pacific St., Monterey CA 93940. (831)372-5477. Fax: (831)372-5680. E-mail: info@montereyart.org. Website: www.montereyart.org. **Contact:** Mary De Groat, director of communications. Estab. 1969. Two locations, on Pacific Street and La Mirada (see website for a full description of each). Sponsors 3-4 exhibitions/year. Average display time approximately 10 weeks. Open Wednesday–Saturday, 11-5; Sunday, 1-4. Closed Thanksgiving, Christmas, New Year's and July 4.

EXHIBITS Interested in all subjects.

MAKING CONTACT & TERMS Accepted work should be framed.

SUBMISSIONS Send slides by mail for consideration; include SASE. Responds in 1 month.

TIPS "Send 20 slides and résumé at any time to the attention of the museum curator."

MULTIPLE EXPOSURES GALLERY

Torpedo Factory Art Center, 105 N. Union St., #312, Alexandria VA 22314. (703)683-2205. E-mail: multipleexposuresgallery@verizon.net. Website: www.multipleexposuresgallery.com. Estab. 1986. Cooperative gallery. Represents or exhibits 14 artists. Sponsors 12 photography exhibits/year. Average display time 1-2 months. Open daily, 11-5. Closed on 5 major holidays throughout the year. Located in Torpedo Factory Art Center; 10-ft. walls with about 40 ft. of running wall space; 1 bin for each artist's matted photos, up to 20×24 in size with space for 25 pieces.

EXHIBITS Photos of landscapes/scenics, architecture, beauty, cities/urban, religious, rural, adventure, automobiles, events, travel, buildings. Interested in alternative process, documentary, fine art. Other specific subjects/processes: "We have on display roughly 300 images that run the gamut from platinum and older alternative processes through digital capture and output."

MAKING CONTACT & TERMS There is a co-op membership fee, a time requirement, a rental fee and a 15% commission. Accepted work should be matted. *Accepts only artists from Washington, D.C., region.* Accepts only photography. "Membership is by jury of active current members. Membership is limited. Jurying for membership is only done when a space becomes available; on average, 1 member is brought in about every 2 years."

SUBMISSIONS Send query letter with SASE to arrange a personal interview to show portfolio of photographs, slides. Responds in 2 months. Finds artists through word of mouth, referrals by other artists, ads in local art/photography publications.

TIPS "Have a unified portfolio of images mounted and matted to archival standards."

MICHAEL MURPHY GALLERY M

2701 S. MacDill Ave., Tampa FL 33629. (813)902-1414. Fax: (813)835-5526. Website: www.michaelmurphygallery.com. **Contact:** Michael Murphy. Estab. 1988. (Formerly Michael Murphy Gallery Inc.) For-profit gallery. Approached by 100 artists/year; exhibits 35 artists. Sponsors 1 photography exhibit/year. Average display time 1 month. See website for current gallery hours. Overall price range $500-15,000. Most work sold at less than $1,000. "We provide elegant, timeless artwork for our clients' home and office environment as well as unique and classic framing design. We strongly believe in the preservation of art through the latest technology in archival framing."

EXHIBITS Photos of babies/children/teens, celebrities, couples, multicultural, families, parents, senior citizens, disasters, environmental, landscapes/scenics, wildlife, architecture, cities/urban, education, gardening, interiors/decorating, pets, religious, rural, agriculture, business concepts, industry, medicine, military, political, product shots/still life, science, technology/computers. Interested in alternative process, avant garde, documentary, erotic, fashion/glamour, fine art, historical/vintage, seasonal.

MAKING CONTACT & TERMS Artwork is accepted on consignment, and there is a 50% commission. Accepted work should be framed. Requires exclusive representation locally.

SUBMISSIONS Send query with artist's statement, bio, brochure, business card, photocopies, photographs, résumé, reviews, slides and SASE. Responds to queries in 1 month, only if interested.

MUSEO DE ARTE DE PONCE

P.O. Box 9027, Ponce, Puerto Rico 00732-9027. (787)848-0505, ext. 231. Fax: (787)841-7309. E-mail: map@museoarteponce.org, aserna@museoarteponce.org. Website: www.museoarteponce.org. **Contact:** curatorial department. Estab. 1959. Museum. Approached by 50 artists/year; mounts 3 exhibitions/year. Satellite gallery in Plaza las Americas, San Juan. Open Wednesday-Monday, 10-6. Closed New Year's Day, January 6, Good Friday, Thanksgiving and Christmas Day. Admission: $6 for adults, $3 for senior citizens, students with an ID card, and children.

EXHIBITS Interested in avant garde, fine art, European and Old Masters.

SUBMISSIONS Send query letter with artist's statement, résumé, images, reviews, publications. Responds in 3 months. Finds artists through research, art exhibits, studio and gallery visits, word of mouth, referrals by other artists.

MUSEO ITALOAMERICANO

Fort Mason Center, Bldg. C, San Francisco CA 94123. (415)673-2200. Fax: (415)673-2292. E-mail: sfmuseo@sbcglobal.net. Website: www.museoitaloamericano.org. Estab. 1978. Museum. "The first museum in the U.S. devoted exclusively to Italian and Italian-American art and culture." Approached by 80 artists/year; exhibits 15 artists. Sponsors 1 photography exhibit/year (depending on the year). Average display time 2-3 months. Open Tuesday–Sunday, 12-4; Monday by appointment. Closed major holidays. Gallery is located in the San Francisco Marina District, with a beautiful view of the Golden Gate Bridge, Sausalito, Tiburon and Alcatraz; 3,500 sq. ft. of exhibition space.

EXHIBITS Photos of babies/children/teens, celebrities, couples, multicultural, families, parents, senior citizens, environmental, landscapes/scenics, architecture, cities/urban, education, religious, rural, entertainment, events, food/drink, hobbies, humor, performing arts, sports, travel, product shots/still life.

Interested in alternative process, avant garde, documentary, fine art, historical/vintage.

MAKING CONTACT & TERMS "The museum rarely sells pieces. If it does, it takes 20% of the sale." Museum provides insurance, promotion. Accepted work should be framed, mounted, matted. *Accepts only Italian or Italian-American artists.*

SUBMISSIONS Call or write to arrange a personal interview to show portfolio of photographs, slides, catalogs. Send query letter with artist's statement, bio, brochure, photographs, résumé, reviews, slides, SASE. Responds in 2 months. Finds artists through word of mouth, submissions.

TIPS "Photographers should have good, quality reproduction of their work with slides, and clarity in writing their statements and résumés. Be concise."

MUSEUM OF CONTEMPORARY ART SAN DIEGO

700 Prospect St., La Jolla CA 92037-4291. (858)454-3541. E-mail: jsiman@mcasd.org; info@mcasd.org. Website: www.mcasd.org. **Contact:** Lucia Sanroman, associate curator. Estab. 1941. Museum. With 2 locations, MCASD is the region's foremost forum devoted to the exploration and presentation of the art of our time, presenting works across all media since 1950. Located in the heart of downtown San Diego and the coastal community of La Jolla. Open Thursday–Tuesday, 11-5; 11-7 on 3rd Thursday of the month (both locations). Closed Wednesday and during installation (both locations).

EXHIBITS Photos of families, architecture, education. Interested in avant garde, documentary, fine art.

SUBMISSIONS See artist proposal guidelines at www.mcasd.org/information/proposals.asp.

MUSEUM OF CONTEMPORARY PHOTOGRAPHY, COLUMBIA COLLEGE CHICAGO

600 S. Michigan Ave., Chicago IL 60605. (312)663-5554. Fax: (312)344-8067. E-mail: jarnett@colum.edu. Website: www.mocp.org. **Contact:** Jeffrey Arnett, manager of development and communication. Estab. 1984. "We offer our audience a wide range of provocative exhibitions in recognition of photography's roles within the expanded field of imagemaking." Sponsors 6 main exhibits and 4-6 smaller exhibits/year. Average display time 2 months. Open Monday–Friday, 10-5; Thursday, 10-8; Saturday, 10-5; Sunday 12-5.

EXHIBITS Exhibits and collects national and international works including portraits, environment, architecture, urban, rural, performance art, political issues, journalism, social documentary, mixed media, video. Primarily interested in experimental work of the past ten years.

SUBMISSIONS Reviews of portfolios for purchase and/or exhibition held monthly. Submission protocols on website. Responds in 2-3 months. No critical review guaranteed.

TIPS "Professional standards apply; only very high-quality work considered."

MUSEUM OF PHOTOGRAPHIC ARTS

1649 El Prado, San Diego CA 92101. (619)238-7559. Fax: (619)238-8777. E-mail: page@mopa.org. Website: www.mopa.org. **Contact:** Debra Klochko, executive director; Carole McCusker, curator of photography. Estab. 1983. MOPA is devoted to collecting, conserving and exhibiting the entire spectrum of the photographic medium. Sponsors 12 exhibits/year. Average display time 3 months.

EXHIBITS Interested in the history of photography, from the 19th century to the present.

MAKING CONTACT & TERMS "The criteria is simply that the photography be of advanced artistic caliber, relative to other fine art photography. MoPA is a museum and therefore does not sell works in exhibitions." Exhibition schedules planned 2-3 years in advance. Holds a private members' opening reception for each exhibition.

SUBMISSIONS "For space, time and curatorial reasons, there are few opportunities to present the work of newer, lesser-known photographers." Send a CD, website or JPEGs to curator. Curator will respond, and if interested, will request materials for future consideration. Files are kept on contemporary artists of note for future reference. Send return address and postage if you wish your materials returned. Responds in 2 months.

TIPS "Exhibitions presented by the museum represent the full range of artistic and journalistic photographic works. There are no specific requirements. The executive director and curator make all decisions on works that will be included in exhibitions. There is an enormous stylistic diversity in the photographic arts. The museum does not place an emphasis on one style or technique over another."

⊕ MUSEUM OF PRINTING HISTORY

1324 W. Clay, Houston TX 77019. (713)522-4652. E-mail: astevenson@printingmuseum.org. Website: www.printingmuseum.org. **Contact:** Ann Kasman, executive director; Amanda Stevenson, curator. Estab. 1982. "The mission of the museum is to promote, preserve and share the knowledge of printed communication and art as the greatest contributors to the development of the civilized world and the continuing advancement of freedom and literacy." Represents or exhibits 4-12 artists. Sponsors 1-12 photography exhibits/year. Average display time 6-16 weeks. Open Tuesday–Saturday, 10-5. Closed 4th of July, Thanksgiving, Christmas Eve, Christmas, New Year's Eve/Day. Three rotating exhibit galleries. Overall price range $10-1,500.

EXHIBITS Photos of multicultural, landscapes/scenics, architecture, cities/urban, rural. Interested in alternative process, documentary.

MAKING CONTACT & TERMS Artwork is accepted on consignment, and there is a 30% commission. Gallery provides insurance. Accepted work should be mounted, matted.

SUBMISSIONS Write to arrange a personal interview to show portfolio of photographs, slides. Mail portfolio for review. Send query letter with artist's statement, bio, brochure, business card, photocopies, photographs, résumé, reviews, slides, SASE. Responds within 2 months, only if interested. Finds artists through word of mouth, submissions, portfolio reviews, art exhibits, referrals by other artists.

MUSEUM OF THE PLAINS INDIAN

P.O. Box 410, Browning MT 59417. (406)338-2230. Fax: (406)338-7404. E-mail: mpi@3rivers.net. Website: www.iacb.doi.gov/museums/museum_plains2.html. Estab. 1941. Open daily, 9-4:45 (June-September); Monday–Friday, 10-4:30 (October-May). Admission is free of charge October–May. Contact for additional information.

NEVADA MUSEUM OF ART

160 W. Liberty St., Reno NV 89501. (775)329-3333. Fax: (775)329-1541. E-mail: wolfe@nevadaart.org. Website: www.nevadaart.org. **Contact:** Ann Wolfe, curator. Estab. 1931. Sponsors 12-15 exhibits/year in various media. Average display time 4-5 months.

SUBMISSIONS See website for detailed submission instructions. No phone calls, please."

TIPS "The Nevada Museum of Art is a private, non-profit institution dedicated to providing a forum for the presentation of creative ideas through its collections, educational programs, exhibitions and community outreach. We specialize in art addressing the environment and the altered landscape."

NEW GALLERY/THOM ANDRIOLA

2627 Colquitt, Houston TX 77098. (713)520-7053. Fax: (713)520-1145. E-mail: info@newgallery.net. Website: www.newgallery.net. **Contact:** Thom Andriola, director. For-profit gallery. Represents or exhibits 22 artists/year. Sponsors 1 photography exhibit/year. Average display time 1 month. Open Tuesday–Saturday, 11-5.

MAKING CONTACT & TERMS Artwork is accepted on consignment, and there is a 50% commission. Requires exclusive representation locally.

NEW MEXICO STATE UNIVERSITY ART GALLERY

P.O. Box 30001, Las Cruces NM 88003-8001. (575)646-2545. Fax: (575)646-8036. E-mail: artglry@nmsu.edu; pthayer@nmsu.edu. Website: www.nmsu.edu/~artgal. **Contact:** Preston Thayer, director. Estab. 1969. Museum. Average display time 2-3 months. Gallery open Tuesday–Saturday, 11-4. Closed Christmas through New Year's Day and university holidays. See website for summer hours. Located on university campus, 3,900 sq. ft. of exhibit space.

NEW ORLEANS MUSEUM OF ART

P.O. Box 19123, New Orleans LA 70179-0123. (504)658-4100. Fax: (504)658-4199. E-mail: staylor@noma.org. Website: www.noma.org. **Contact:** Susan Taylor, director. Estab. 1973. "The city's oldest fine arts institution, NOMA has a magnificent permanent collection of more than 40,000 objects. The collection, noted for its extraordinary strengths in French and American art, photography, glass, African and Japanese works, continues to grow." Sponsors exhibits continuously. Average display time 1-3 months. Open Tuesday–Sunday, 10-5.

EXHIBITS Interested in all types of photography.

MAKING CONTACT & TERMS Buys photography outright; payment negotiable. "Current budget for purchasing contemporary photography is very small." Sometimes accepts donations from established artists, collectors or dealers.

SUBMISSIONS Send query letter with color photocopies (preferred) or slides, résumé, SASE. Accepts images in digital format; submit via website. Responds in 3 months.

TIPS "Send thought-out images with originality and expertise. Do not send commercial-looking images."

NEXUS/FOUNDATION FOR TODAY'S ART

1400 N. American St., Philadelphia PA 19106. (215)684-1946. E-mail: info@nexusphiladelphia.org. Website: nexusphiladelphia.org. **Contact:** Nick Cassway, executive director. Estab. 1975. Alternative space; cooperative, nonprofit gallery. Approached by 40 artists/year; represents or exhibits 20 artists. Sponsors 2 photography exhibits/year. Average display time 1 month. Open Wednesday–Sunday, 12-6; closed July and August. Located in Fishtown, Philadelphia; 2 gallery spaces, approximately 750 sq. ft. each. Overall price range: $75-1,200. Most work sold at $200-400.

EXHIBITS Photos of multicultural, families, environmental, architecture, rural, entertainment, humor, performing arts, industry, political. Interested in alternative process, documentary, fine art.

SUBMISSIONS Send query letter with artist's statement, bio, photocopies, photographs, slides, SASE. Finds artists through portfolio reviews, referrals by other artists, submissions, and juried reviews 2 times/year. "Please visit our website for submission dates."

TIPS "Learn how to write a cohesive artist's statement."

NICOLAYSEN ART MUSEUM & DISCOVERY CENTER

400 E. Collins Dr., Casper WY 82601. (307)235-5247. E-mail: info@thenic.org. Website: www.thenic.org. **Contact:** Connie Gibbons, executive director; Lisa Hatchadoorian, curator of exhibitions. Estab. 1967. Sponsors 10 exhibits/year. Average display time 3-4 months. Sponsors openings.

NICOLET COLLEGE ART GALLERY

5364 College Dr., P.O. Box 518, Rhinelander WI 54501. (715)365-4556. E-mail: Kralph@Nicoletcollege.edu. Website: www.nicoletcollege.edu. **Contact:** Katherine Ralph, gallery director. Nicolet College is a public community college serving Northern Wisconsin from its campus situated along Lake Julia south of Rhinelander, and from outreach centers located within the Nicolet District. The College offers 1- and 2-year career diplomas and degrees, liberal arts university transfer studies, and a comprehensive continuing education program.

MAKING CONTACT & TERMS Call or e-mail for further information.

NKU GALLERY

Northern Kentucky University, Art Galleries, Nunn Dr., Highland Heights KY 41099. (859)572-5148. Fax: (859)572-6501. E-mail: knight@nku.edu. Website: www.nku.edu/~art/galleries/index.php. **Contact:** David Knight, director of collections and exhibitions. Estab. 1970. The NKU Art Department Galleries are located on the 3rd floor of the Fine Arts Center. There are 2 gallery spaces: The Main Gallery and the Third Floor Gallery. Approached by 30 artists/year; represents or exhibits 5-6 artists. Average display time 1 month. Open Monday–Friday, 9-9; closed weekends and major holidays. Main Gallery is 2,500 sq. ft.; Third Floor Gallery is 600 sq. ft. Overall price range $25-3,000. Most work sold at $500.

MAKING CONTACT & TERMS Gallery provides insurance, promotion, contract. Accepted work should be framed, mounted, matted.

SUBMISSIONS Finds artists through word of mouth, art exhibits, referrals by other faculty.

TIPS "Submission guidelines, current exhibitions and complete information available on our website."

NORTHWEST ART CENTER

Minot State University, 500 University Ave. W., Minot ND 58707. (701)858-3264. Fax: (701)858-3894. E-mail: nac@minotstateu.edu. Website: www.minotstateu.edu/nac. **Contact:** Avis R. Veikley, director. Estab. 1969. Nonprofit gallery. Represents emerging, mid-career and established artists. Represents 20 artists. Sponsors 20 total exhibits/year; 2 photography exhibits/year. Model and property release preferred. Average display time: 4 weeks. Open Monday-Friday, 9-4. Two galleries located on university campus, each gallery approximately 100 linear feet. Clients include local community and students. 50% of sales are to corporate collectors. Overall price range: $100-1,000; most work sold at $350.

EXHIBITS Special interest in printmaking, works on paper, contemporary art and drawings.

MAKING CONTACT & TERMS Accepted work should be framed and mounted. Artwork is accepted on consignment with a 30% commission. Retail price set by the artist. Gallery provides insurance, promotion and contract.

SUBMISSIONS Send query letter with artist's statement, photocopies bio, résumé and reviews. Returns material with SASE. Responds, if interested, within 3 months. Finds artists through art exhibits, submissions, referrals by other artists and entries in our juried competitions.

NORTHWESTERN UNIVERSITY DITTMAR MEMORIAL GALLERY

1999 S. Campus Dr., Evanston IL 60208. (847)491-2348. E-mail: dittmargallery@northwestern.edu. Website: www.norris.northwestern.edu/recreation/dittmar. **Contact:** gallery coordinator. Estab. 1972. Nonprofit, student-operated gallery. Approached by 30 artists/year; represents or exhibits more than 10 artists. Sponsors 1-2 photography exhibits/year. Average display time 6 weeks. Open daily 10-10. Closed December. The gallery is located within the Norris Student Center on the main floor behind the information desk.

EXHIBITS Photos of babies/children/teens, couples, multicultural, families, parents, disasters, environmental, landscapes/scenics, wildlife, architecture, cities/urban, education, gardening, adventure, automobiles, entertainment, events, food/drink, health/fitness, hobbies, humor, performing arts, sports, travel. Interested in avant garde, erotic, fashion/glamour, fine art, historical/vintage, seasonal.

MAKING CONTACT & TERMS Artwork is accepted on consignment, and there is a 20% commission. Gallery provides promotion, contract. Accepted work should be mounted.

SUBMISSIONS Mail portfolio for review. Send query letter with 10-15 slides, artist's statement, brochure, résumé, reviews. Responds in 3 months. Finds artists through word of mouth, submissions, referrals by other artists.

TIPS "Do not send photocopies. Send a typed letter, good photos or color photocopies. Send résumé of past exhibits, or if emerging, a typed statement."

THE NOYES MUSEUM OF ART

733 Lily Lake Rd., Oceanville NJ 08231. (609)652-8848. Fax: (609)652-6166. E-mail: info@noyesmuseum.org. Website: www.noyesmuseum.org. **Contact:** Michael Cagno, executive director; Dorrie Papademetriou, director of exhibitions. Estab. 1983. Sponsors 10-12 exhibits/year. Average display time 12 weeks. The Noyes Museum of Art of The Richard Stockton College of New Jersey presents exhibitions and events

that benefit students and enthusiasts of the arts, as well as the entire southern New Jersey community. In 2010, Stockton partnered with the Noyes Museum, bringing an expanded array of educational opportunities, events, exhibits and performances to the nearby off-campus facility. Stockton is also home to one of the area's top performing arts centers, and its own art gallery.

EXHIBITS Interested in alternative process, avant garde, fine art, historical/vintage.

MAKING CONTACT & TERMS Charges 30% commission. Accepted work must be ready for hanging, preferably framed. Infrequently buys photos for permanent collection.

SUBMISSIONS Any format OK for initial review; most desirable is a challenging, cohesive body of work. Send material by mail for consideration; include résumé, artist's statement, slide samples or CD. May include photography and mixed media.

TIPS "Send a challenging, cohesive body of work."

OAKLAND UNIVERSITY ART GALLERY

208 Wilson Hall, 2200 N. Squirrel Rd., Rochester MI 48309-4401. (248)370-3005. Website: www.oakland. edu/ouag. Estab. 1962. Nonprofit gallery. Represents 10-25 artists/year. Sponsors 6 exhibits/year. Average display time 4-6 weeks. Open September–May: Tuesday–Sunday, 12-5; evenings during special events and theater performances (Wednesday–Friday, 7 through 1st intermission, weekends, 5 through 1st intermission). Closed Monday, holidays and June–August. Located on the campus of Oakland University; exhibition space is approximately 2,350 sq. ft. of floor space, 301-ft. linear wall space, with 10-ft. 7-in. ceiling. The gallery is situated across the hall from the Meadow Brook Theatre. "We do not sell work, but do make available price lists for visitors with contact information noted for inquiries."

EXHIBITS Considers all styles and all types of prints and media.

MAKING CONTACT & TERMS Charges no commission. Gallery provides insurance, promotion and contract. Accepted work should be framed, mounted, matted. No restrictions on representation; however, prefers emerging Detroit artists.

SUBMISSIONS E-mail bio, education, artist's statement and JPEG images. Mail portfolio for review. Send query letter with artist's statement, bio, photocopies, curriculum vitae. Returns material with SASE. Responds to queries in 1-2 months. Finds artists through referrals by other artists, word of mouth, art community, advisory board and other arts organizations.

O.K. HARRIS WORKS OF ART

383 W. Broadway, New York NY 10012. (212)431-3600. Fax: (212)925-4797. E-mail: okharris@okharris.com. Website: www.okharris.com. **Contact:** Ivan C. Karp, director. Estab. 1969. Commercial exhibition gallery. Represents 40 emerging, mid-career and established artists. Sponsors 30 solo shows/year. Average display time 1 month. Open Tuesday–Saturday, 10-6; in July, Tuesday–Friday, 12-5; closed from mid-July through August and December 24–January 1. "Four separate galleries for four separate one-person exhibitions. The back room features selected gallery artists which also change each month." 90% of sales are open to private collectors, 10% corporate clients. Overall price range $50-250,000; most work sold at $12,500-100,000.

EXHIBITS Considers all media. Most frequently exhibits painting, sculpture and photography. Exhibits realism, photorealism, minimalism, abstraction, conceptualism, photography and collectibles. Genres include landscapes, Americana, but little figurative work. "The gallery's main concern is to show the most significant artwork of our time. In its choice of works to exhibit, it demonstrates no prejudice as to style or materials employed. Its criteria demands originality of concept and maturity of technique. It believes that its exhibitions have proven the soundness of its judgment in identifying important artists and its pertinent contribution to the visual arts theme." Accepts work on consignment (50% commission). Retail price set by gallery. Customer discounts and payment by installment are available. Exclusive area representation required. Gallery provides insurance and limited promotion. Prefers artwork ready to exhibit. Send query letter with 1 CD of recent work with labeled images size, medium, etc." and SASE. Responds in 1 week.

TIPS "We suggest the artist be familiar with the gallery's exhibitions and the kind of work we prefer to show. Visit us either in person or online at www. okharris.com. Always include SASE. Common mistakes artists make in presenting their work are submissions without return envelope and inappropriate work. We affiliate about 1 out of every 10,000 applicants."

⊕ ONLY ORIGINALS GALLERY OF FINE ART

P.O. Box 592, Benton AR 72015. (501)778-8830. E-mail: onlyoriginals@sbcglobal.net. Website: www.onlyoriginals.org. **Contact:** Carol Samsel, owner. Estab. 2010. Online gallery displaying the work of emerging and mid-career artists. Exhibits are rotated every 6 months. At this time, the gallery exhibits only 2D work. Sponsors 2 exhibits/year. Clients are upscale. Overall price range: $2,500.

EXHIBITS Considers acrylic, collage, drawing, fiber, glass, mixed media, oil, paper, pastel, pen & ink and watercolor. Types of prints include engravings, etchings, linocuts, lithographs, mezzotints, serigraphs and woodcuts.

MAKING CONTACT & TERMS "We seek artists through a national and international art competition. All 2D works of fine art are considered. Finalists are showcased on the website, with a link to their private galleries. There is no commission on artworks sold by finalists." Retail price set by the artist. Gallery provides promotion. Accepted work should be well photographed.

SUBMISSIONS Artists are currently reviewed twice a year through competitions. See the website for dates. Materials can not be returned. Responds in 1 week. Files MUST be in JPEG format; 1200 pixels (longest side) or larger. Remember, very small files are difficult to judge and very large files difficult to download. Also, scaled-down JPEGs are often used on websites. They can be copied and submitted by individuals other than the artist, making provenance difficult to establish.

TIPS "Submit clear JPEG photographs from which distracting backgrounds have been cropped."

OPALKA GALLERY

The Sage Colleges, 140 New Scotland Ave., Albany NY 12208. (518)292-7742. E-mail: opalka@sage.edu. Website: www.sage.edu/opalka. **Contact:** Jim Richard Wilson, director. Estab. 2002. Nonprofit gallery. "The Opalka Gallery replaced Rathbone Gallery, which served The Sage Colleges for 25 years." Approached by 90-120 artists/year; represents or exhibits approximately 24 artists. Average display time 5 weeks. Open Monday-Friday, 10-8; Sundays, 12-4; June-July 10-4 and by appointment. Open by appointment only between exhibitions and when classes are not in session. Closed July 4. Located on the Sage Albany campus,

The Opalka's primary concentration is on work by professional artists from outside the region. The gallery frequently features multidisciplinary projects and hosts poetry readings, recitals and symposia, often in conjunction with its exhibitions. The 7,400-sq.-ft. facility includes a vaulted gallery and a 75-seat lecture/presentation hall with Internet connectivity. Overall price range $50-260,000.

EXHIBITS Interested in fine art.

MAKING CONTACT & TERMS Artwork is accepted on consignment; there is no commission. "We primarily accept artists from outside our region and those who have ties to The Sage Colleges. We host the local Photography Regional every three years." Requires exclusive representation locally.

SUBMISSIONS E-mail query with pertinent information and images. Finds artists through word of mouth, art exhibits, submissions, portfolio reviews, referrals by other artists.

TIPS "Submit all correspondence in a professional manner. Include an artist's statement, bio, reviews, with visuals of your work (slides, CD, etc.)."

OPENING NIGHT GALLERY

2836 Lyndale Ave. S., Minneapolis MN 55408-2108. (612)872-2325. Fax: (612)872-2385. E-mail: deen@onframe-art.com; info@onframe-art.com. Website: www.onframe-art.com. **Contact:** Deen Braathen. Estab. 1975. Rental gallery. Approached by 40 artists/year; represents or exhibits 15 artists. Sponsors 1 photography exhibit/year. Average display time 6-10 weeks. Gallery open Monday–Friday, 8:30-5; Saturday, 10:30-4. Overall price range $300-12,000. Most work sold at $2,500.

EXHIBITS Photos of landscapes/scenics, architecture, cities/urban.

MAKING CONTACT & TERMS Artwork is accepted on consignment, and there is a 50% commission. Gallery provides insurance, promotion, contract. "Accepted work should be framed by our frame shop." Requires exclusive representation locally.

SUBMISSIONS Mail slides for review. Send query letter with artist's statement, bio, résumé, slides, SASE. Responds in 2 months. Finds artists through word of mouth, submissions, portfolio reviews.

PALO ALTO ART CENTER

1313 Newell Rd., Palo Alto CA 94303. (650)329-2366. Fax: (650)326-6165. E-mail: artcenter@cityofpalo alto.org. Website: www.cityofpaloalto.org/artcenter.

Contact: Exhibitions Department. Estab. 1971. Average display time 1-3 months. Museum hours: Tuesday–Saturday, 10-5; Sunday, 1-5, Tuesday–Thursday, 7-10. Gallery hours: Tuesday–Saturday, 10-5; Sunday, 1-5, Thursday, 7-9. Sponsors openings.

EXHIBITS "Exhibit needs vary according to curatorial context." Seeks "imagery unique to individual artist. No standard policy. Photography may be integrated in group exhibits." Interested in alternative process, avant garde, fine art; emphasis on art of the Bay Area.

SUBMISSIONS Send slides/CD, bio, artist's statement, SASE.

PARKLAND ART GALLERY

2400 W. Bradley Ave., Champaign IL 61821. (217)351-2485. Fax: (217)373-3899. E-mail: parklandart gallery@parkland.edu. Website: www.parkland.edu/gallery. **Contact:** Lisa Costello, director. Estab. 1980. Nonprofit gallery. Approached by 130 artists/year; 7 exhibitions per year. Average display time 4-6 weeks. Open Monday–Friday, 10-3; Monday–Thursday, 6-8; Saturday, 12-2 (fall and spring semesters). Summer: Monday–Thursday, 10-3; Monday–Thursday, 6-8. Parkland Art Gallery at Parkland College seeks exhibition proposals in all genres of contemporary approaches to art making by single artists, collaborative groups, or curators. Parkland Art Gallery is a professionally designed gallery devoted primarily to education through contemporary art. Parkland Art Gallery hosts 7 exhibitions per year including two student exhibitions, one art and design faculty show, and a Biennial Watercolor Invitational that alternates with a National Ceramics Invitational. Other shows vary depending on applications and the vision of the Art Gallery Advisory Board. Exhibits are scheduled on a 4- to 6-week rotation. Closed college and official holidays. Overall price range $100-5,000. Most work sold at $300.

EXHIBITS Interested in alternative process, avant garde, documentary, fine art, historical/vintage.

MAKING CONTACT & TERMS Gallery provides insurance, promotion. Accepted work should be framed.

SUBMISSIONS Send 20 slides or a CD containing 20 images; an identifying list with titles, sizes, dates, and media; a résumé; an artist statement; and a SASE (if necessary) to attention of the Director, Parkland Art Gallery, Parkland College. Only complete proposal packages including all information listed on the Proposal Guidelines will be reviewed. Responds in 4 months. No online proposals accepted. Finds artists through word of mouth, portfolio reviews, art exhibits, referrals by other artists. Call for entry.

LEONARD PEARLSTEIN GALLERY

Drexel University, 33rd and Market Streets, Philadelphia PA 19104. (215)895-1029. Fax: (215)895-4917. E-mail: gallery@drexel.edu. Website: www.drexel.edu/academics/comad/gallery. **Contact:** Filiz O'Brien. Estab. 1986. Nonprofit gallery. Located in Nesbitt Hall in the Antoinette Westphal College of Media Arts and Design at Drexel. Committed to exhibiting the work of local, national and international contemporary artists and designers. Sponsors 8 total exhibits/year; 1 or 2 photography exhibits/year. Average display time 1 month. Open Monday–Friday, 11-5. Closed during summer.

MAKING CONTACT & TERMS Artwork is bought outright. Gallery takes 20% commission. Gallery provides insurance, promotion. Accepted work should be framed, mounted, matted. "We will not pay transport fees."

SUBMISSIONS Write to arrange a personal interview to show portfolio. Send query letter with artist's statement, bio, résumé, SASE. Returns material with SASE. Responds by February, only if interested. Finds artists through referrals by other artists, academic instructors.

PETERS VALLEY CRAFT CENTER

19 Kuhn Rd., Layton NJ 07851. (973)948-5202. Fax: (973)948-0011. E-mail: store@petersvalley.org. Website: www.petersvalley.org. **Contact:** Brienne Rosner, gallery manager. Estab. 1970. Nonprofit gallery and store. Approached by about 100 artists/year; represents about 350 artists. Average display time 1 month in gallery; varies for store items. Open year round; call for hours. Located in northwestern New Jersey in Delaware Water Gap National Recreation Area; 2 floors, approximately 3,000 sq. ft. Overall price range $5-3,000. Most work sold at $100-300.

EXHIBITS Considers all media and all types of prints. Also exhibits non-referential, mixed media, collage and sculpture.

MAKING CONTACT & TERMS Artwork is accepted on consignment, and there is a 60% commission to artist. "Retail price set by the gallery in conjunction with artist." Gallery provides insurance and promotion. Accepted work should be framed, mounted and matted.

SUBMISSIONS Submissions reviewed in March. Send query letter with artist's statement, bio, résumé and images (slides or CD of JPEGs). Returns material with SASE. Responds in 2 months. Finds artists through submissions, art exhibits, art fairs, referrals by other artists.

TIPS "Submissions must be neat and well-organized throughout."

PHILLIPS GALLERY

444 E. 200 S., Salt Lake City UT 84111. (801)364-8284. Fax: (801)364-8293. Website: www.phillips-gallery. com. **Contact:** Meri DeCaria, director/curator. Estab. 1965. Commercial gallery. We represent artists working in a variety of media including painting, drawing, sculpture, photography, ceramics, printmaking, jewelry, and mixed media. Our artists, many of whom have been with us since 1965, are primarily from Utah or the surrounding area. Phillips Gallery also represents national and international artists who have an association with Utah. You will discover a full range of subject matter from traditional to contemporary. Average display time 4 weeks. Sponsors openings; provides refreshments, advertisement, and half of mailing costs. Overall price range $300-2,000. Most work sold at $600.

EXHIBITS Accepts all types and styles.

MAKING CONTACT & TERMS Charges 50% commission. Accepted work should be matted. Requires exclusive representation locally. *Photographers must have Utah connection.* Must be actively pursuing photography.

SUBMISSIONS Submit portfolio for review; include SASE. Responds in 2 weeks.

THE PHOENIX GALLERY

210 11th Ave. #902, New York NY 10001. (212)226-8711. E-mail: info@phoenix-gallery.com. Website: www.phoenix-gallery.com. **Contact:** Linda Handler, director. Estab. 1958. Sponsors 10-12 exhibits/year. Average display time 1 month. Overall price range $100-10,000. Most work sold at $3,000-8,000.

EXHIBITS "The gallery is an artist-run nonprofit organization; an artist has to be a member in order to exhibit in the gallery. There are 3 types of membership: active, inactive and associate." Interested in all media; alternative process, documentary, fine art.

MAKING CONTACT & TERMS Charges 25% commission.

SUBMISSIONS Artists wishing to be considered for membership must submit an application form, slides and résumé. Call, e-mail or download membership application from website.

PHOTO-EYE GALLERY

376 Garcia St., Santa Fe NM 87501. (505)988-5122, ext.202. Fax: (505)988-4482. E-mail: gallery@photo eye.com. Website: www.photoeye.com. **Contact:** Anne Kelly, associate gallery director. Estab. 1991. Approached by 40+ artists/year. Exhibits 30 established artists/year. Exhibited artists include Nick Brandt, Julie Blackmon, Tom Chambers (all fine-art photographers). Sponsors 3-4 photography exhibits/year. Average display time 3 months. Open Tuesday–Saturday, 10-5. Closed Sunday and Monday. The gallery is located approximately 1 mile from The Plaza; approximately 1,000 sq. ft. Clients include: local community, tourists, upscale and collectors. 30% of sales are to corporate collectors. Overall price range: $100-50,000. Most work sold at $2,500.

EXHIBITS Photography only. Fine-art photographs using only archival methods. Considers all styles. Most frequently exhibits contemporary photography projects and bodies of work.

MAKING CONTACT & TERMS Retail price of the art set by the artist. Gallery provides insurance, promotion and contract. Accepted work should be matted. "Prefers fine-art photography with exciting, fresh projects that are cohesive and growing."

SUBMISSIONS "Submit your work via 'The Photographer's Showcase' on our website." Material can not be returned. Responds in 2 weeks if dropped off at gallery, but prefers online submissions. Finds artists through word of mouth, art fairs, portfolio review and online through "The Photographer's Showcase".

TIPS "Be consistent, professional and only submit approximately 20 images. Call or e-mail gallery to find out the submission policy."

PHOTOGRAPHIC RESOURCE CENTER

832 Commonwealth Ave., Boston MA 02215. (617)975-0600. Fax: (617)975-0606. E-mail: info@prcboston. org. Website: www.prcboston.org. "The PRC is a nonprofit arts organization founded to facilitate the study and dissemination of information relating to photography." The PRC brings in nationally recognized artists to lecture to large audiences and host workshops

GALLERIES

on photography. Open Tuesday-Friday, 10-5, and Saturday and Sunday, 12-5. Please check our website for the current exhibition schedule.

PHOTOGRAPHY ART

107 Myers Ave., Beckley WV 25801. (304)252-4060 or (304)575-6491. Fax: (304)252-4060 (call before faxing). E-mail: bruceburgin@photographyart.com. Website: www.photographyart.com. **Contact:** Bruce Burgin, owner. Estab. 2003. Internet rental gallery. "Each artist deals directly with his/her customers. I do not charge commissions and do not keep records of sales."

EXHIBITS Photos of landscapes/scenics, wildlife. Interested in fine art.

MAKING CONTACT & TERMS There is a rental fee for space. The rental fee covers 1 year. The standard gallery is $240 to exhibit 40 images with biographical and contact info for 1 year. No commission charged for sales. Artist deals directly with customers and receives 100% of any sale. Gallery provides promotion.

SUBMISSIONS Internet sign-up. No portfolio required.

TIPS "An artist should have high-quality digital scans. The digital images should be cropped to remove any unnecessary background or frames, and sized according to the instructions provided with their Internet gallery. I recommend the artist add captions and anecdotes to the images in their gallery. This will give a visitor to your gallery a personal connection to you and your work."

THE PHOTOMEDIA CENTER

P.O. Box 8518, Erie PA 16505. (617)990-7867. E-mail: info@photomediacenter.org. Website: www.photomediacenter.org. Estab. 2004. Nonprofit gallery. Sponsors 12 "new" photography exhibits/year. "Previously featured exhibits are archived online. We offer many opportunities for artists, including sales, networking, creative collaboration and promotional resources; maintain an information board and slide registry for members; and hold an open annual juried show in the summer."

EXHIBITS Interested in alternative process, avant garde, documentary, fine art.

MAKING CONTACT & TERMS Artwork is accepted on consignment, and there is a 25% commission. Gallery provides promotion. Prefers only artists working in photographic, digital and new media.

SUBMISSIONS "We have a general portfolio review call in the fall for the following year's exhibition schedule. If after December 31, send query letter with artist's statement, bio, résumé, slides, SASE." Responds in 2-6 months. Finds artists through word of mouth, submissions, portfolio reviews, art exhibits, referrals by other artists.

TIPS "We are looking for artists who have excellent technical skills, a strong sense of voice and cohesive body of work. Pay careful attention to our guidelines for submissions on our website. Label everything. Must include a SASE for reply."

PIERRO GALLERY OF SOUTH ORANGE

Baird Center, 5 Mead St., South Orange NJ 07079. (973)378-7754. Fax: (973)378-7833. E-mail: pierrogallery@southorange.org;. Website: www.pierrogallery.org. **Contact:** Sandy Martiny, gallery director. Estab. 1994. Nonprofit gallery. Approached by 75-185 artists/year; represents or exhibits 25-50 artists. Average display time 7 weeks. Open Friday–Sunday, 1-4 and by appointment. Closed mid-December through mid-January and the month of August. Overall price range $100-10,000. Most work sold at $800.

EXHIBITS Interested in fine art, "which can be inclusive of any subject matter."

MAKING CONTACT & TERMS Artwork is accepted on consignment, and there is a 15% commission. Gallery provides insurance, promotion, contract. Accepted work should be framed.

SUBMISSIONS Mail portfolio for review. Send cover letter, biography and/or résumé, brief artist statement, up to 3 reviews/press clippings, representation of work in either CD or DVD format; no more than 10 labeled representative images. Responds in 2 months from review date. Finds artists through word of mouth, submissions, portfolio reviews, referrals by other artists.

POLK MUSEUM OF ART

800 E. Palmetto St., Lakeland FL 33801-5529. (863)688-7743, ext. 241. Fax: (863)688-2611. E-mail: kpope@polkmuseumofart.org. Website: www.polkmuseumofart.org. **Contact:** Adam Justice, curator of art. Estab. 1966. Approached by 75 artists/year; represents or exhibits 3 artists. Sponsors 1-3 photography exhibits/year. Galleries open Tuesday–Saturday, 10-5; Sunday, 1-5. Closed major holidays. Four different galleries of various sizes and configurations.

EXHIBITS Interested in alternative process, avant garde, documentary, fine art, historical/vintage.

MAKING CONTACT & TERMS Museum provides insurance, promotion, contract. Accepted work should be framed.

SUBMISSIONS Mail portfolio for review. Send query letter with artist's statement, bio, résumé, slides or CD, SASE.

✚ POUDRE RIVER GALLERY

406 N. College Ave., Fort Collins CO 80524. E-mail: gallery@poudrestudioartists.com. Website: www. poudrestudioartists.com. **Contact:** Tracey Kazimir-Cree, gallery manager. Estab. 2006. Nonprofit co-operative, rental gallery with alternative space. Approached by 100+ artists/year; exhibits 200+ emerging, mid-career and established artists/year. Exhibited artists include Barbara McCulloch (watermedia) and Carol Simmons (polymer clay). Exhibits rotate monthly. Open Thursday-Saturday, 11-3. Closed major holidays. Located just north of Old Town Fort Collins and participates in the city's monthly Gallery Walk. "Our gallery is 1,100 sq. ft, L-shaped with wood floors in a funky old building." Clients: local community, students, tourists and upscale. Overall price range: $50-10,000.

EXHIBITS Considers all media, prints, genres and styles. Most frequently exhibits acrylics, mosaic and watercolor and painterly abstraction.

MAKING CONTACT & TERMS Artwork accepted on consignment with a 25% commission. There is a co-op membership fee, plus a donation of time with a 25% commission. Contact museum for details on rental fee. Retail price of art set by the artist. Gallery provides promotion. Accepted work should be framed, mounted and matted.

SUBMISSIONS E-mail with link to artist's website and JPEG samples at 72 dpi or send query letter with artist's statement, bio, brochure and résumé. Material returned with SASE. Responds in 2-3 weeks. Brochures and printed materials filed. Finds artists through word of mouth, submissions and referrals by other artists.

TIPS "Read instructions carefully and follow them to the letter!"

PRAKAPAS GALLERY

One Northgate 6B, Bronxville NY 10708. (914)961-5091. Fax: (914)961-5192. E-mail: eugeneprakapas@ optonline.net. **Contact:** Eugene Prakapas, director. Estab. 1976. Overall price range $500-100,000.

MAKING CONTACT & TERMS Commission "depends on the particular situation."

TIPS "We are concentrating primarily on vintage work, especially from between the World Wars, but some as late as the 1970s. We are not currently doing exhibitions and so are not a likely home for contemporary work. People expect vintage, historical work from us."

THE PRINT CENTER

1614 Latimer St., Philadelphia PA 19103. (215)735-6090. Fax: (215)735-5511. E-mail: info@printcenter. org. Website: www.printcenter.org. **Contact:** Ashley Peel Pinkham, assistant director. Estab. 1915. Nonprofit gallery and Gallery Store. Represents over 75 artists from around the world in Gallery Store. Sponsors 5 photography exhibits/year. Average display time 2 months. Open all year Tuesday-Saturday, 11-5:30. Closed Christmas to New Year's. Three galleries. Overall price range $15-15,000. Most work sold at $200.

EXHIBITS Contemporary prints and photographs of all processes. Accepts original artwork only—no reproductions.

MAKING CONTACT & TERMS Accepts artwork on consignment (50% commission). Gallery provides insurance, promotion, contract. Artists must be printmakers or photographers.

SUBMISSIONS Must be member to submit work. Member's work is reviewed by curator and gallery store manager. See website for membership application. Finds artists through submissions, art exhibits and membership.

PUCKER GALLERY, INC.

171 Newbury St., Boston MA 02116. (617)267-9473. Fax: (617)424-9759. E-mail: contactus@pucker gallery.com. Justine Choi (justine@puckergallery. com). **Contact:** Bernard H. Pucker, director. Estab. 1967. For-profit gallery. Pucker Gallery is always willing to review artist's slides and submissions. Approached by 100 artists/year; represents or exhibits 50 artists. Sponsors 2 photography exhibits/year. Average display time 1 month. Open Monday–Saturday, 10-5:30; Sunday, 10:30-5. Five floors of exhibition space. Overall price range $500-75,000.

EXHIBITS Photos of multicultural, environmental, landscapes/scenics, architecture, cities/urban, religious, rural. Interested in fine art, abstracts, seasonal.

MAKING CONTACT & TERMS Gallery provides promotion.

SUBMISSIONS Send query letter with artist's statement, bio, slides/CD, SASE. "We do not accept e-mail submissions nor do we visit artists' websites." Finds artists through submissions, referrals by other artists.

PUMP HOUSE CENTER FOR THE ARTS

P.O. Box 1613, Chillicothe OH 45601. (740)772-5783. Fax: (740)772-5783. E-mail: info@pumphouseart gallery.com. Website: www.pumphouseartgallery. com. **Contact:** Priscilla V. Smith, director. Estab. 1991. Nonprofit gallery. Approached by 6 artists/year; represents or exhibits more than 50 artists. Average display time 6 weeks. Gallery hours: Closed Monday and Tuesday; Wednesday–Friday, 11-4 and Thursday evening 6-8; Saturday, 10-4; Sunday, 1-4. Overall price range $150-600. Most work sold at $300. Facility is also available for rent (business, meetings, reunions, weddings, receptions or rehearsals, etc.).

EXHIBITS Photos of landscapes/scenics, wildlife, architecture, gardening, travel, agriculture. Interested in fine art, historical/vintage.

MAKING CONTACT & TERMS Artwork is accepted on consignment, and there is a 30% commission. Gallery provides insurance, promotion. Accepted work should be framed, matted, wired for hanging. Call or stop in to show portfolio of photographs, slides. Send query letter with bio, photographs, slides, SASE. Responds in 1 month. Finds artists through word of mouth, submissions, portfolio reviews, art exhibits, art fairs, referrals by other artists.

TIPS "All artwork must be original designs, framed, ready to hang (wired—no sawtooth hangers)."

QUEENS COLLEGE ART CENTER

Benjamin S. Rosenthal Library, Flushing NY 11367. (718)997-3770. Fax: (718)997-3753. E-mail: suzanna. simor@qc.cuny.edu; artcenter@qc.cuny.edu. Website: qcpages.qc.cuny.edu/art_library/artcenter.html. Tara Tye Mathison, assistant curator. **Contact:** Suzanna Simor, director; Alexandra de Luise, curator. Estab. 1955. Queens College Art Center is a successor since 1987 of the Klapper Library Art Center that was based in the Queens College Art Library's gallery founded in 1960. Focuses on modern and contemporary art, presenting the works of both emerging and es-

tablished artists in diverse media, in programming expressive of the best of the art of our time. Open Monday–Thursday, 9-8; Friday 9-5. Average display time approximately 6-7 weeks. Overall price range $200-600.

EXHIBITS Open to all types, styles, subject matter; decisive factor is quality.

MAKING CONTACT & TERMS Charges 40% commission. Accepted work can be framed or unframed, mounted or unmounted, matted or unmatted. Sponsors openings. Photographer is responsible for providing/arranging refreshments and cleanup.

SUBMISSIONS Send query letter with résumé, samples and SASE. Responds after May annual review.

☺ MARCIA RAFELMAN FINE ARTS

10 Clarendon Ave., Toronto ON M4V 1H9, Canada. (416)920-4468. Fax: (416)968-6715. E-mail: info@ mrfinearts.com. Website: www.mrfinearts.com. **Contact:** Marcia Rafelman, president; Meghan Richardson, gallery director. Estab. 1984. Semi-private gallery. Average display time 1 month. Gallery is centrally located in Toronto; 2,000 sq. ft. on 2 floors. Overall price range $800-25,000. Most work sold at $1,500.

EXHIBITS Photos of environmental, landscapes. Interested in alternative process, documentary, fine art, historical/vintage.

MAKING CONTACT & TERMS Charges 50% commission. Gallery provides insurance, promotion, contract. Requires exclusive representation locally.

SUBMISSIONS Mail (must include SASE) or e-mail portfolio (preferred) for review; include bio, photographs, reviews. Responds only if interested. Finds artists through word of mouth, submissions, art fairs, referrals by other artists.

TIPS "We only accept work that is archival."

THE RALLS COLLECTION INC.

1516 31st St., NW, Washington D.C. 20007. (202)342-1754. Fax: (202)342-0141. E-mail: rallscollection@ gmail.com. Website: www.rallscollection.com. **Contact:** Marsha Ralls, owner. Estab. 1991. Approached by 125 artists/year; represents or exhibits 60 artists. Sponsors 7 photography exhibits/year. Average display time 1 month. Gallery open Tuesday-Saturday, 11-4 and by appointment. Closed Thanksgiving, Christmas. Overall price range $1,500-50,000. Most work sold at $2,500-15,000.

EXHIBITS Photos of babies/children/teens, celebrities, parents, landscapes/scenics, architecture, cities/urban, gardening, interiors/decorating, pets, rural, entertainment, health/fitness, hobbies, performing arts, sports, travel, product shots/still life. Interested in alternative process, avant garde, documentary, fashion/glamour, fine art, historical/vintage.

MAKING CONTACT & TERMS Artwork is accepted on consignment, and there is a 50% commission. Gallery provides insurance, promotion, contract. Accepted work should be framed, matted. Requires exclusive representation locally. Accepts only artists from America.

SUBMISSIONS Mail portfolio for review. Send query letter with artist's statement, bio, brochure, business card, photocopies, photographs, résumé, reviews, slides, SASE. Responds in 2 months. Finds artists through word of mouth, submissions, portfolio reviews, art exhibits, art fairs, referrals by other artists.

ROCHESTER CONTEMPORARY

137 East Ave., Rochester NY 14604. (585)461-2222. Fax: (585)461-2223. E-mail: info@rochestercontem porary.org. Website: www.rochestercontemporary.org. **Contact:** Elizabeth Switzer, programming director. Estab. 1977. Located in Rochester's downtown "East End" cultural district. The 4,500-sq.-ft. space is handicapped accessible. Sponsors 10-12 exhibits/year. Average display time 4-6 weeks. Gallery open Wednesday–Sunday, 1-5; Friday 1-10. Overall price range $100-500.

MAKING CONTACT & TERMS Charges 25% commission.

SUBMISSIONS Send slides/CD, letter of inquiry, résumé and statement. Responds in 3 months.

ROCKPORT CENTER FOR THE ARTS

902 Navigation Circle, Rockport TX 78382. (361)729-5519. E-mail: john@rockportartcenter.com. Website: www.rockportartcenter.com. Estab. 1969. Rockport Center for the Arts boasts a state-of-the-art main gallery as the result of building renovations and expansions in 1998 and 2000. The two parlor galleries are now dedicated entirely to the works of its member artists, while the main gallery allows the center to host local, regional, national, and internationally acclaimed artists in both solo and group exhibitions. In 2000, the Garden Gallery was added, allowing the center for the first time to simultaneously feature 3 distinct exhibitions, at times displaying over 100 original works of art. Today the building also houses 2 visual arts classrooms which are home to numerous workshops, classes, seminars, and open studio sessions. A well-furnished pottery studio is always active, and includes a kiln room which hosts daily firings. Visitors enjoy the art center gift shop where member artists display a wide range of art and craft. Open Tuesday–Saturday, 10-4; Sunday, 1-4; closed Monday.

MAKING CONTACT & TERMS Call, e-mail or visit website for more information.

THE ROTUNDA GALLERY

33 Clinton St., Brooklyn NY 11201. (718)875-4047. E-mail: jtaylor@bricartsmedia.org. Website: www.bric online.org/rotunda. Estab. 1981. Nonprofit gallery. Average display time 6 weeks. Open Tuesday–Saturday, 12-6.

EXHIBITS Interested in contemporary works.

MAKING CONTACT & TERMS Gallery provides photographer's contact information to prospective buyers. Shows are limited by walls that are 22 feet high.

SUBMISSIONS Send material by mail for consideration; include SASE. "View our website for guidelines and artist registry form."

SAN DIEGO ART INSTITUTE: MUSEUM OF THE LIVING ARTIST

1439 El Prado, San Diego CA 92101. (619)236-0011. Fax: (619)236-1974. E-mail: admin@sandiego-art.org. Website: www.sandiego-art.org. **Contact:** Kerstin Robers, executive administrator. Estab. 1941. Nonprofit gallery. SDAI's most visible activity focuses on showcasing the work of San Diego's emerging area visual artists through a program of over 30 juried shows a year. Different art professionals are selected as jurors for each show assuring exhibitions of high-quality and great variety. Jurors' Choice and Honorable Mention certificates are awarded at monthly public receptions. Represents or exhibits 500 member artists. Overall price range $50-3,000. Most work sold at $700. Open Tuesday–Saturday, 10-4; Sunday, 12-4.

EXHIBITS Photos of babies/children/teens, couples, multicultural, families, parents, senior citizens, disasters, environmental, landscapes/scenics, wildlife, architecture, cities/urban, education, gardening, pets, rural, adventure, entertainment, events, food/drink, health/fitness/beauty, hobbies, humor, performing arts, sports, travel, agriculture, political, product shots/still life, science, technology. Interested in alternative process, avant garde, documentary, erotic, fine art, historical/vintage, seasonal.

MAKING CONTACT & TERMS Artwork is accepted on consignment with a 40% commission. Membership fee: $125. Accepted work should be framed. Work must be carried in by hand for each monthly show except for annual international show, JPEG online submission.

SUBMISSIONS Membership not required for submission in monthly juried shows, but fee required. Artists interested in membership should request membership packet. Finds artists through referrals by other artists.

TIPS "All work submitted must go through jury process for each monthly exhibition. Work must be framed in professional manner. No glass—plexiglass or acrylic only."

⊘ THE JOSEPH SAXTON GALLERY OF PHOTOGRAPHY

520 Cleveland Ave., NW, Canton OH 44702. (330)438-0030. E-mail: gallery@josephsaxton.com. Website: www.josephsaxton.com. **Contact:** Stephen McNulty, curator and general manager. Estab. 2009. A premier photography gallery with nearly 7,000 sq. ft. of display space, more than 160 master photographers represented, and over 200 pieces on display. Upscale clients. 20% of sales are to corporate collectors. Overall price range of work sold is from $500-20,000. Most work sold at $1,500. Approached by 150 artists/year; represents or exhibits 4-6 artists. Exhibited artists include: Steve McCurry, photography; Art Wolfe, photography. Average display time 2-3 months. Open Wednesday–Saturday, 12-5.

EXHIBITS Color field, expressionism, surrealism, painterly abstraction, conceptualism, impressionism, postmodernism, minimalism, primitivism realism, geometric abstraction. Considers all genres. Exhibits people: celebrities, multicultural, families; home & garden: architecture, cities/urban, religious, rural; business & technology: agriculture, industry, military, political, product shots/still life; outdoors: disasters, environmental, landscapes/scenics, wildlife; recreation: adventure, automobiles, entertainment, events, performing arts, sports, travel; style: alternative process, avant garde, documentary, fashion/glamour, fine art, historical/vintage, lifestyle, seasonal.

MAKING CONTACT & TERMS Artwork is accepted on consignment and there is a 50% commission. Retail price of the art set by the artist. Gallery provides insurance, promotion, contract. Requires exclusive representation locally. Also offers a limited contract. Model release and property release are preferred.

SUBMISSIONS Accepted work should be framed. E-mail query letter with link to artists's website. Responds only if interested within 2 weeks. Returns material with SASE. Finds artists through word of mouth, portfolio reviews, referrals by other artists, our annual Canton Luminaries Photography Competition.

TIPS "We prefer to see work that was created as a cohesive body which exhibits a personal style or technique.

WILLIAM & FLORENCE SCHMIDT ART CENTER

Southwestern Illinois College, 2500 Carlyle Ave., Belleville IL 62221. (618) 641-5143. Website: schmidtart. swic.edu. Estab. 2002. Nonprofit gallery. Sponsors 1-2 photography exhibits/year.

EXHIBITS Interested in fine art and historical/vintage photography.

SUBMISSIONS Mail portfolio for review. Send query letter with artist's statement, bio and slides. Finds artists through art fairs and exhibits, portfolio reviews, referrals by other artists, submissions and word of mouth.

SCHMIDT/DEAN

1710 Samsom St., Philadelphia PA 19103. (215)569-9433. Fax: (215)569-9434. E-mail: schmidtdean@netzero.com. Website: www.schmidtdean.com. **Contact:** Christopher Schmidt, director. Estab. 1988. For-profit gallery. Houses eclectic art. Sponsors 4 photography exhibits/year. Average display time 6 weeks. Gallery open Tuesday–Saturday, 10:30-6. August hours are Tuesday–Friday, 10:30-6. Overall price range $1,000-70,000.

EXHIBITS Interested in alternative process, documentary, fine art.

MAKING CONTACT & TERMS Charges 50% commission. Gallery provides insurance, promotion. Accepted work should be framed, mounted, matted. Requires exclusive representation locally.

SUBMISSIONS Call/write to arrange a personal interview to show portfolio. Send query letter with SASE.

"Send digital images on CD and a résumé that gives a sense of your working history. Include a SASE."

SECOND STREET GALLERY

115 2nd St., SE, Charlottesville VA 22902. (434)977-7284. Fax: (434)979-9793. E-mail: ssg@secondstreetgallery.org. Website: www.secondstreetgallery.org. **Contact:** Rebecca Schoenthal, executive director. Estab. 1973. Sponsors approximately 2 photography exhibits/year. Average display time 1 month. Open Tuesday–Saturday, 11-6; 1st Friday of every month, 6-8 with artist talk at 6:30. Overall price range $300-2,000.

MAKING CONTACT & TERMS Charges 30% commission.

SUBMISSIONS Reviews slides/CDs in fall; $15 processing fee. Submit 10 slides or a CD for review; include artist statement, cover letter, bio/résumé, and most importantly, a SASE. Responds in 2 months.

TIPS Looks for work that is "cutting edge, innovative, unexpected."

➕ SIOUX CITY ART CENTER

225 Nebraska St., Sioux City IA 51101-1712. (712)279-6272. Fax: (712)255-2921. E-mail: siouxcityartcenter@sioux-city.org. Website: www.siouxcityartcenter.org. **Contact:** Todd Behrens, curator. Estab. 1938. Museum. Exhibits emerging, mid-career and established artists. Approached by 50 artists/year; represents or exhibits 2-3 artists. Sponsors 15 total exhibits/year. Average display time: 10-12 weeks. Gallery open Tuesday, Wednesday, Friday, Saturday 10-4; Thursday 10-9; Sunday 1-4. Closed on Mondays and municipal holidays. Located in downtown Sioux City; 2 galleries, each 40×80 ft. Clients include local community, students and tourists.

EXHIBITS Considers all media and types of prints. Most frequently exhibits paintings, sculpture and mixed media.

MAKING CONTACT & TERMS Artwork is accepted on consignment with a 30% commission. "However, the purpose of our exhibitions is not sales." Retail price of the art set by the artist. Gallery provides insurance, promotion and contract.

SUBMISSIONS Artwork should be framed. Only accepts artwork from upper-Midwestern states. E-mail query letter with link to artist's website; JPEG samples at 72 dpi. Or send query letter with artist's statement, résumé and digital images. Returns materials if SASE

is enclosed. Responds, only if interested, within 6 months. Files résumé, statement and images if artist is suitable. Finds artists through word of mouth, art exhibits, submissions, art fairs, portfolio reviews and referrals by other artists.

TIPS "Submit good photography with an honest and clear statement."

SOHO MYRIAD

1250 Menlo Dr., Atlanta GA 30318. (404)351-5656. Fax: (404)351-8284. E-mail: info@sohomyriad.com. Website: www.sohomyriad.com. Estab. 1977. Art consulting firm and for-profit gallery. Represents and/or exhibits over 2,000 artists. Sponsors 1 photography exhibit/year. Average display time: 2 months. Overall price range $500-20,000. Most work sold at $500-5,000.

  🔾 Additional offices in Los Angeles and London. See website for contact information.

EXHIBITS Photos of landscapes/scenics, architecture, floral/botanical and abstracts. Interested in alternative process, avant garde, fine art, historical/vintage.

MAKING CONTACT & TERMS Artwork is accepted on consignment, and there is a 50% commission. Gallery provides insurance.

SOUTH DAKOTA ART MUSEUM

South Dakota State University, Medary Ave. & Harvey Dunn St., P.O. Box 2250, Brookings SD 57007. (605)688-5423. Fax: (605)688-4445. E-mail: Dianne.Hawks@sdstate.edu. Website: www.southdakotaartmuseum.com. **Contact:** John Rychtarik, curator of exhibits. Estab. 1970. Museum. Sponsors 1-2 photography exhibits/year. Average display time 4 months. Gallery open Monday–Friday, 10-5; Saturday, 10-4; Sunday, 12-4. Closed state holidays and Sundays from January through March. Seven galleries offer 26,000 sq. ft. of exhibition space. Overall price range $200-6,000. Most work sold at $500.

EXHIBITS Interested in alternative process, documentary, fine art.

MAKING CONTACT & TERMS Artwork is accepted on consignment, and there is a 30% commission. Gallery provides insurance, promotion. Accepted work should be framed.

SUBMISSIONS Send query letter with artist's statement, bio, résumé, slides, SASE. Responds within 3 months, only if interested. Finds artists through word of mouth, portfolio reviews, art exhibits, referrals by other artists.

SOUTHSIDE GALLERY

150 Courthouse Square, Oxford MS 38655. (662)234-9090. E-mail: southside@southsideartgallery.com. Website: www.southsideartgallery.com. **Contact:** Will Cook, director. Estab. 1993. For-profit gallery. Average display time 4 weeks. Gallery open Tuesday–Saturday, 10-6; Sunday, 12-5. Overall price range $300-20,000. Most work sold at $425.

EXHIBITS Photos of landscapes/scenics, architecture, cities/urban, rural, entertainment, events, performing arts, sports, travel, agriculture, political. Interested in avant garde, fine art.

MAKING CONTACT & TERMS Artwork is accepted on consignment, and there is a 55% commission. Gallery provides promotion. Accepted work should be framed.

SUBMISSIONS Mail between 10 and 25 slides that reflect current work with SASE for review. CDs are also accepted with images in JPEG or TIFF format. Include artist statement, biography, and résumé. Responds within 4-6 months. Finds artists through submissions.

SRO PHOTO GALLERY AT LANDMARK ARTS

School of Art, Texas Tech University, Box 42081, Lubbock TX 79409-2081. (806)742-1947. Fax: (806)742-1971. E-mail: srophotogallery.art@ttu.edu. Website: www.landmarkarts.org. **Contact:** Joe R. Arredondo, director. Estab. 1984. Nonprofit gallery. Hosts an annual competition to fill 8 solo photography exhibition slots each year. Average display time 4 weeks. Open Monday–Friday, 8-5; Saturday, 10-5; Sunday, 12-4. Closed university holidays.

EXHIBITS Interested in art utilizing photographic processes.

MAKING CONTACT & TERMS "Exhibits are for scholarly purposes. Gallery will provide artist's contact information to potential buyers." Gallery provides insurance, promotion, contract. Accepted work should be matted.

SUBMISSIONS Exhibitions are determined by juried process. See website for details (under call for entries). Deadline for applications is end of March.

THE STATE MUSEUM OF PENNSYLVANIA

300 North St., Harrisburg PA 17120. (717)787-4980. Fax: (717)783-4558. E-mail: hpollman@state.pa.us. Website: www.statemuseumpa.org. **Contact:** N. Lee Stevens, senior curator of art collections. Offers visitors 4 floors representing Pennsylvania's story, from Earth's beginning to the present. Features archaeological artifacts, minerals, paintings, decorative arts, animal dioramas, industrial and technological innovations and military objects representing the Commonwealth's heritage. Number of exhibits varies. Average display time 2 months. Overall price range $50-3,000. Open Wednesday–Saturday, 9-5; Sunday 12-5.

EXHIBITS Fine art photography is a new area of endeavor for The State Museum, both collecting and exhibiting. Interested in works produced with experimental techniques.

MAKING CONTACT & TERMS Work is sold in gallery, but not actively. Connects artists with interested buyers. No commission. Accepted work should be framed.

STATE OF THE ART GALLERY

120 W. State St., Ithaca NY 14850. (607)277-1626. E-mail: gallery@soag.org. Website: www.soag.org. Estab. 1989. Cooperative gallery. Sponsors 1 photography exhibit/year. Average display time 1 month. Gallery open Wednesday–Friday, 12-6; weekends, 12-5. Located in downtown Ithaca, 2 rooms about 1,100 sq. ft. Overall price range $100-6,000. Most work sold at $200-500.

EXHIBITS Photos in all media and subjects. Interested in alternative process, avant garde, fine art, computer-assisted photographic processes.

MAKING CONTACT & TERMS There is a co-op membership fee plus a donation of time. There is a 10% commission for members, 30% for nonmembers. Gallery provides promotion, contract. Accepted work must be ready to hang. Write for membership application.

STATE STREET GALLERY

1804 State St., La Crosse WI 54601. (608)782-0101. E-mail: ssg1804@yahoo.com. Website: www.statestreetartgallery.com. **Contact:** Ellen Kallies, president. Estab. 2000. Wholesale, retail and trade gallery. Approached by 15 artists/year; exhibits 12-14 artists/quarter in gallery. Average display time 4-6 months. Open Tuesday, Thursday and Friday, 10-4, Wednesday, 11:15-5:15, Saturday, 10-2; other times by chance or appointment. Located across from the University of Wisconsin/La Crosse. Overall price range $50-12,000. Most work sold at $500-1,200 and above.

EXHIBITS Photos of environmental, landscapes/scenics, architecture, cities/urban, gardening, rural, travel, medicine.

MAKING CONTACT & TERMS Artwork is accepted on consignment, and there is a 40% commission. Gallery provides insurance, promotion, contract. Accepted work should be framed, matted.

SUBMISSIONS Call or mail portfolio for review. Send query letter with artist's statement, photographs, slides, SASE. Responds in 1 month. Finds artists through word of mouth, art exhibits, art fairs, referrals by other artists.

TIPS "Be organized, professional in presentation, flexible."

PHILIP J. STEELE GALLERY

Rocky Mt. College of Art + Design, 1600 Pierce St., Denver CO 80214. (303)753-6046. Fax: (303)759-4970. Website: www.rmcad.edu/gallery-exhibitions/philip-j-steele-gallery. **Contact:** Lisa Spivak, director. Estab. 1962. Nonprofit gallery. Located in the Mary Harris Auditorium building on the southeast corner of the quad. Approached by 25 artists/year; represents or exhibits 6-9 artists. Sponsors 1 photography exhibit/year. Average display time 1 month. Open Monday—Saturday, 11-4. Photographers should call or visit website for more information.

EXHIBITS No restrictions on subject matter.

MAKING CONTACT & TERMS No fee or percentage taken. Gallery provides insurance, promotion. Accepted work should be framed.

SUBMISSIONS Send query letter with artist's statement, bio, slides, résumé, reviews, SASE. Reviews in May, deadline April 15. Finds artists through word of mouth, submissions, referrals by other artists.

STEVENSON UNIVERSITY ART GALLERY

1525 Greenspring Valley Rd., Stevenson MD 21153. (443)334-2163. Fax: (410)486-3552. E-mail: exhibitions@stevenson.edu. Website: www.stevenson.edu/explore/gallery/index.asp. **Contact:** Diane DiSalvo, director of cultural programs. Estab. 1997. College/university gallery. Sponsors at least 2 photography exhibits/year. Average display time 6 weeks. Gallery open Monday, Tuesday, Thursday, Friday, 11-5; Wednesday, 11-8; Saturday, 1-4. "Two beautiful spaces." "Since its 1997 inaugural season, the Stevenson University Art Gallery has presented a dynamic series of substantive exhibitions in diverse media and has achieved the reputation as a significant venue for regional artists and collec-

tors. The museum quality space was designed to support the Baltimore arts community, provide greater opportunities for artists, and be integral to the educational experience of Stevenson students. Our exhibitions program offers a series of 7 shows per year in a variety of media including paintings, prints, sculpture and photography."

EXHIBITS Interested in alternative process, avant garde, documentary, fine art, historical/vintage. "We are looking for artwork of substance by artists from the mid-Atlantic region."

MAKING CONTACT & TERMS "We facilitate inquiries directly to the artist." Gallery provides insurance. *Accepts artists from mid-Atlantic states only; emphasis on Baltimore artists.*

SUBMISSIONS Write to show portfolio of slides. Send artist's statement, bio, résumé, reviews, slides, SASE. Responds in 3 months. Finds artists through word of mouth, submissions, portfolio reviews, referrals by other artists.

TIPS "Be clear, concise. Have good representation of your images."

⊕ STILL POINT ART GALLERY

193 Hillside Rd., Brunswick ME 04011. (207)837-5760. E-mail: info@stillpointartgallery.com. Website: www.stillpointartgallery.com. **Contact:** Christine Cote, owner/director. Estab. 2009. For-profit online gallery. Exhibits emerging, mid-career and established artists. Approached by 750 artists/year. Represents 500 artists. Sponsors 6 juried shows/year. Distinguished artists earn representation. Model and property release preferred. Average display time: 14 months. Overall price range: $200-5,000; most work sold at $800.

EXHIBITS Considers all media and styles. Most frequently exhibits oil and acrylic photography. Considers engravings, etchings, serigraphs, linocuts, woodcuts, lithographs and mezzotints. Considers all genres.

MAKING CONTACT & TERMS Artwork is accepted on consignment with a 20% commission. Retail price set by the artist. Gallery provides promotion. Responds to calls for artists posted on website.

SUBMISSIONS E-mail query letter with link to artist's website. Returns material with SASE.

TIPS "Follow the instructions posted on my website."

○ THE STORE AND SALLY D. FRANCISCO GALLERY AT PETERS VALLEY CRAFT CENTER

19 Kuhn Rd., Layton NJ 07851. (973)948-5202. Fax: (973)948-0011. E-mail: Store@Petersvalley.org. Website: www.petersvalley.org. **Contact:** Brienne Rosner, store and gallery manager. Estab. 1977. "National Delaware Water Gap Recreation Area in the Historic Village of Bevans, Peters Valley Craft Center hosts a large variety of workshops in the spring and summer. The Store and Gallery is located in an old general store; first floor retail space and second floor rotating exhibition gallery."

SYNCHRONICITY FINE ARTS

106 W. 13th St., New York NY 10011. (646)230-8199. Fax: (646)230-8198. E-mail: synchspa@bestweb.net. Website: www.synchronicityspace.com. **Contact:** John Amato, director. Estab. 1989. Nonprofit gallery. Approached by hundreds of artists/year; represents or exhibits over 60 artists. Sponsors 2-3 photography exhibits/year. Gallery open Tuesday–Saturday, 12-6. Closed 2 weeks in August. Overall price range $1,500-20,000. Most work sold at $3,000.

EXHIBITS Photos of multicultural, environmental, landscapes/scenics, architecture, cities/urban, education, rural, events, agriculture, industry, medicine, political. Interested in avant garde, documentary, fine art, historical/vintage.

MAKING CONTACT & TERMS Gallery provides insurance, promotion, contract. Accepted work should be framed, mounted, matted.

SUBMISSIONS Submissions may be made via electronic or e-mail as JPEG small files as well as the other means. Write to arrange a personal interview to show portfolio of photographs, transparencies, slides. Send query letter with photocopies, SASE, photographs, slides, résumé. Responds in 3 weeks. Finds artists through art exhibits, submissions, portfolio reviews, referrals by other artists.

LILLIAN & COLEMAN TAUBE MUSEUM OF ART

2 N. Main St., Minot ND 58703. (701)838-4445. E-mail: taube@srt.com. Website: www.taubemuseum.org. **Contact:** Nancy Walter, executive director. Estab. 1970. Established nonprofit organization. Sponsors 1-2 photography exhibits/year. Average display time 4-6 weeks. Museum is located in a renovated historic landmark building with room to show 2 exhibits simultaneously. Overall price range $15-225. Most work sold at $40-100.

EXHIBITS Photos of babies/children/teens, couples, multicultural, families, parents, senior citizens, disasters, landscapes/scenics, wildlife, beauty, rural, travel, agriculture, buildings, military, portraits. Interested in avant garde, fine art.

MAKING CONTACT & TERMS Charges 30% commission for members; 40% for nonmembers. Sponsors openings.

SUBMISSIONS Submit portfolio along with a minimum of 6 examples of work in digital format for review. Responds in 3 months.

TIPS "Wildlife, landscapes and floral pieces seem to be the trend in North Dakota. We get many portfolios to review for our photography exhibits each year. We also appreciate figurative, unusual and creative photography work."

NATALIE AND JAMES THOMPSON ART GALLERY

School of Art Design, San Jose State University, San Jose CA 95192-0089. (408)924-4723. Fax: (408)924-4326. E-mail: thompsongallery@cadre.sjsu.edu. Website: www.sjsu.edu. **Contact:** Jo Farb Hernandez, director. Nonprofit gallery. Approached by 100 artists/year. Sponsors 1-2 photography exhibits/year. Average display time 1 month. Gallery open Monday, Wednesday-Friday, 11-4; Tuesday, 11-4 and 6-7:30.

EXHIBITS All genres, aesthetics and techniques.

MAKING CONTACT & TERMS Works not generally for sale. Gallery provides insurance, promotion. Accepted work should be framed and/or ready to hang.

SUBMISSIONS Send query letter with artist's statement, bio, résumé, reviews, slides, SASE. Responds as soon as possible. Finds artists through word of mouth, submissions, portfolio reviews, art exhibits, art fairs, referrals by other artists.

THROCKMORTON FINE ART

145 E. 57th St., 3rd Floor, New York NY 10022. (212)223-1059. Fax: (212)223-1937. E-mail: info@throckmorton-nyc.com. Website: www.throckmorton-nyc.com. **Contact:** Kraige Block, director. Estab. 1993. For-profit gallery. A New-York based gallery specializing in vintage and contemporary photography of the Americas for over 25 years. Its primary focus is Latin American photographers. The gallery also specializes in Chinese jades and antiquities, as well as pre-Columbian art. Located in the Hammacher Schlem-

mer Building; 4,000 square feet; 1,000 square feet exhibition space. Clients include local community and upscale. Approached by 50 artists/year; represents or exhibits 20 artists. Sponsors 5 photography exhibits/year. Average display time 2 months. Overall price range $1,000-10,000. Most work sold at $2,500. Open Tuesday–Saturday, 11-5.

EXHIBITS Photos of babies/children/teens, landscapes/scenics, architecture, cities/urban, rural. Interested in erotic, fine art, historical/vintage, Latin American photography.

MAKING CONTACT & TERMS Charges 50% commission. Gallery provides insurance, promotion.

SUBMISSIONS Write to arrange a personal interview to show portfolio of photographs/slides/CD, or send query letter with artist's statement, bio, photocopies, slides, CD, SASE. Responds in 3 weeks. Finds artists through word of mouth, portfolio reviews.

TIPS "Present your work nice and clean."

TOUCHSTONE GALLERY

901 New York Ave., NW, Washington D.C. 20001-2217. (202)347-2787. E-mail: info@touchstone gallery.com. Website: www.touchstonegallery.com. Estab. 1976. Cooperative member gallery. Representing 50 artists in various media uses exhibiting a new show monthly. "Our newly renovated contemporary space is available for event rental. Located near the heart of the bustling Penn Quarter district in downtown Washington D.C., our large beautifully lit gallery can be found at street level and is easily accessible. Open Wednesday and Thursday, 11-6; Friday, 11-8; Saturday and Sunday, 12-5. Closed Christmas through New Year's Day. Overall price range: $400-7,000. As a functioning co-op gallery, there is a monthly membership fee, plus a donation of time. A 40% commission is taken from sold works. To become a member, visit the website for further information, or contact the gallery directly.

UCR/CALIFORNIA MUSEUM OF PHOTOGRAPHY

University of California, 3824 Main St., Riverside CA 92501. (951)784-3686. Fax: (951)827-4797. Website: www.cmp.ucr.edu. **Contact:** Director. Sponsors 10-15 exhibits/year. Average display time 8-14 weeks. Open Tuesday–Saturday, 12-5. Located in a renovated 23,000-sq.-ft. building. "It is the largest exhibition space devoted to photography in the West."

EXHIBITS Interested in technology/computers, alternative process, avant garde, documentary, fine art, historical/vintage.

MAKING CONTACT & TERMS Curatorial committee reviews CDs, slides and/or matted or unmatted work. Photographer must have highest-quality work.

SUBMISSIONS Send query letter with résumé, SASE. Accepts images in digital format; send via CD, ZIP.

TIPS "This museum attempts to balance exhibitions among historical, technological, contemporary, etc. We do not sell photos but provide photographers with exposure. The museum is always interested in newer, lesser-known photographers who are producing interesting work. We're especially interested in work relevant to underserved communities. We can show only a small percent of what we see in a year."

UNI GALLERY OF ART

University of Northern Iowa, 104 Kamerick Art Bldg, Cedar Falls IA 50614-0362. (319)273-6134. Fax: (319)273-7333. E-mail: galleryofart@uni.edu. Website: www.uni.edu/artdept/gallery. **Contact:** Darrell Taylor, director. Estab. 1976. Sponsors 9 exhibits/year. Average display time 1 month. Approximately 5,000 sq. ft. of space and 424 ft. of usable wall space.

EXHIBITS Interested in all styles of high-quality contemporary art works.

MAKING CONTACT & TERMS "We do not sell work."

SUBMISSIONS Please provide a cover letter and proposal as well as an artist's statement, CV, and samples. Send material by mail for consideration or submit portfolio for review; include SASE for return of material. Response time varies.

UNION STREET GALLERY

1527 Otto Blvd., Chicago Heights IL 60411. (708)754-2601. E-mail: unionstreetart@sbcglobal.net. Website: www.unionstreetgallery.org. **Contact:** Jessica Freudenberg, gallery administrator. Estab. 1995. Nonprofit gallery. Represents or exhibits more than 100 artists. "We offer group invitations and juried exhibits every year." Average display time 5 weeks. Hours: Wednesday and Thursday, 12-5; Friday, 12-6; Saturday, 11-4. Overall price range $30-3,000. Most work sold at $300-600.

SUBMISSIONS Finds artists through submissions, referrals by other artists and juried exhibits at the gallery. "To receive prospectus for all juried events, call, write or e-mail to be added to our mailing list. Prospectus also available on website. Artists interested in studio space or solo/group exhibitions should contact the gallery to request information packets."

UNIVERSITY ART GALLERY IN THE D.W. WILLIAMS ART CENTER

P.O. Box 30001, Las Cruces NM 88003. (575)646-2545 or (575)646-5423. Fax: (575)646-8036. E-mail: artglry@nmsu.edu. Website: www.nmsu.edu/~artgal. **Contact:** Preston Thayer, director. Estab. 1973. The largest visual arts facility in South Central New Mexico, the gallery presents 6-9 exhibitions annually. Overall price range $300-2,500. Features contemporary and historical art of regional, national and international importance. Focus includes the work of NMSU Art Department faculty, graduate students, undergraduates, traveling exhibitions and over 3,000 works from the university's permanent collection. The latter includes the country's largest collection of Mexican retablos (devotional paintings on tin) as well as photographs, paintings, prints and graphics, book art, and small scale sculpture and metals.

MAKING CONTACT & TERMS Buys photos outright.

SUBMISSIONS Arrange a personal interview to show portfolio. Submit portfolio for review. Send query letter with samples. Send material by mail with SASE by end of October for consideration. Responds in 3 months.

TIPS Looks for "quality fine art photography. The gallery does mostly curated, thematic exhibitions. Very few one-person exhibitions."

UNIVERSITY OF KENTUCKY ART MUSEUM

116 Singletary Center, Rose St. and Euclid Ave., Lexington KY 40506. (859)257-5716. Fax: (859)323-1994. E-mail: janie.welker@uky.edu. Website: www.uky.edu/artmuseum. **Contact:** Janie Welker, curator. Estab. 1979. Museum. The University of Kentucky Art Museum serves Central and Eastern Kentucky through art exhibitions, educational outreach, and other special events including lectures, sympsia and family festivals.

EXHIBITS Annual photography lecture series and exhibits.

SUBMISSIONS Prefers e-mail query with digital images. Responds in 6 months.

UNIVERSITY OF RICHMOND MUSEUMS

28 Westhampton Way, Richmond VA 23173. (804)289-8276. Fax: (804)287-1894. E-mail: rwaller@richmond.edu; museums@richmond.edu. Website: museums.richmond.edu. **Contact:** Richard Waller, director. Estab. 1968. University Museums comprises Joel and Lila Harnett Museum of Art, Joel and Lila Harnett Print Study Center, and Lora Robins Gallery of Design from Nature. The museums are home to diverse collections and exhibitions of art, artifacts and natural history specimens. Sponsors 18-20 exhibits/year. Average display time 8-10 weeks. See website for hours for each gallery.

EXHIBITS Interested in all subjects.

MAKING CONTACT & TERMS Charges 10% commission. Work must be framed for exhibition.

SUBMISSIONS Send query letter with résumé, samples. Send material by mail for consideration. Responds in 1 month.

TIPS "If possible, submit material that can be left on file and fits standard letter file. We are a nonprofit university museum interested in presenting contemporary art as well as historical exhibitions."

UNTITLED [ARTSPACE]

1 NE 3rd St., Oklahoma City OK 73104. (405)815-9995. Fax: (405)813-2070. E-mail: info@artspaceatuntitled.org. Website: www.1ne3.org. Estab. 2003. Alternative space, nonprofit gallery. Average display time 6-8 weeks. Open Tuesday–Friday, 10-5; Saturday, 10-4. Closed Sunday and Monday. "Located in a reclaimed industrial space abandoned by decades of urban flight. Damaged in the 1995 Murrah Federal Building bombing, Untitled [ArtSpace] has emerged as a force for creative thought. As part of the Deep Deuce historic district in downtown Oklahoma City, Untitled [ArtSpace] brings together visual arts, performance, music, film, design and architecture. Our mission is to stimulate creative thought and new ideas through contemporary art. We are committed to providing access to quality exhibitions, educational programs, performances, publications, and to engaging the community in collaborative outreach efforts." Most work sold at $750.

MAKING CONTACT & TERMS Artwork is accepted on consignment, and there is a 50% commission.

SUBMISSIONS Mail portfolio for review. Send query letter with artist's statement, bio, résumé, slides, or CD of images. Prefers 10-15 images on a CD. Include

SASE for return of materials or permission to file the portfolio. Reviews occur twice annually, in January and July. Finds artists through submissions, portfolio reviews. Responds to queries within 1 week, only if interested.

TIPS "Review our previous programming to evaluate if your work is along the lines of our mission. Take the time to type and proof all written submissions. Make sure your best work is represented in the images you choose to show. Nothing takes away from the review like poorly scanned or photographed work."

UPSTREAM GALLERY

26B Main St., Dobbs Ferry NY 10522. (914)674-8548. E-mail: upstreamgallery26@gmail.com. Website: www.upstreamgallery.com. Estab. 1990. Represents or exhibits 22 artists. Sponsors 1 invitational/juried photography exhibit/year. Average display time 1 month. Open Thursday–Sunday, 12:30-5:30. Closed July and August (but an appointment can be made by calling 914-375-1693). Gallery contains 2 store fronts, approximately 15×30 sq. ft. each. Overall price range: $300-2,000.

EXHIBITS Only fine art. Accepts all subject matters and genres for jurying.

MAKING CONTACT & TERMS There is a co-op membership fee plus a donation of time. There is a 20% commission. Gallery provides insurance. Accepted work should be framed, mounted and matted.

SUBMISSIONS Write to arrange a personal interview to show portfolio of photographs and slides. Send query letter with artist's statement, bio, brochure, business card, photographs, résumé, reviews, slides and SASE. Responds to queries within 2 months, only if interested. Finds artists through referrals by other artists and submissions.

UPSTREAM PEOPLE GALLERY

5607 Howard St., Omaha NE 68106-1257. (402)991-4741. E-mail: shows@upstreampeoplegallery.com. Website: www.upstreampeoplegallery.com. **Contact:** Laurence Bradshaw, curator. Estab. 1998. Exclusive online virtual gallery with over 40 international exhibitions in the archives section of the website. Represents mid-career and established artists. Approached by approximately 1,500 artists/year; represents or exhibits 20,000 artists. Sponsors 12 total exhibits/year and 7 photography exhibits/year. Average display time is 12 months to 4 years. Overall price range $100-60,000. Most work sold at $300. 15% of sales are to corporate collectors.

EXHIBITS Considers all media except video and film. Most frequently exhibits oil, acrylic and ceramics. Considers all prints, styles and genres. Most frequently exhibits Neo-Expressionism, Realism and Surrealism.

MAKING CONTACT & TERMS Artwork is accepted on consignment; there is no commission if the artists sells, but a 20% commission if the gallery sells. Retail price set by the artist. Gallery provides promotion and contract.

SUBMISSIONS Accepted work should be photographed. Call or write to arrange personal interview to show portfolio, e-mail query letter with link to website and JPEG samples at 72 dpi or send query letter with artist's statement and CD/DVD. Returns material with SASE. Responds to queries within 1 week. Files résumés. Finds artists through art exhibits, referrals and online and magazine advertising.

TIPS "Make sure all photographs of works are in focus."

URBAN INSTITUTE FOR CONTEMPORARY ARTS

2 W. Fulton St., Grand Rapids MI 49503. (616)454-7000. Fax: (616)459-9395. E-mail: jteunis@uica.org. Website: www.uica.org. **Contact:** Janet Teunis, managing director. Estab. 1977. Alternative space and non-profit gallery. Approached by 250 artists/year; represents or exhibits 20 artists. Sponsors 3-4 photography exhibits/year. Average display time 6 weeks. Gallery open Tuesday-Saturday, 12-10; Sunday, 12-7.

EXHIBITS Most frequently exhibits mixed media, avant garde, and nontraditional work. Style of exhibits are conceptual and postmodern.

SUBMISSIONS Please check our website for gallery descriptions and how to apply. Artists should visit the website, go to Exhibitions, then Apply for a Show and follow the instructions. UICA exhibits artists through submissions.

VIENNA ARTS SOCIETY ART CENTER

115 Pleasant St., Vienna VA 22180. (703)319-3971. E-mail: teresa@tlcillustration.com. **Contact:** Teresa Ahmad, director. Estab. 1969. Nonprofit gallery and work center. Art center acquired in 2005. Approached by 200-250 artists/year; represents or exhibits 50-100 artists. Average display time 3-4 weeks. Open Tuesday–Saturday, 10-4. Closed on federal holi-

days, county cancellations, or delays. Historic building with spacious room with modernized hanging system. Overall price range $100-1,500. Most work sold at $250-$500.

EXHIBITS Photos of all subject matter: celebrities, architecture, gardening, pets, environmental, landscapes/scenics, wildlife, entertainment, performing arts, travel. Exhibits fine arts of all subject matter and mediums throughout the year as well; oil, watercolor, acrylic, mixed media, collage, mosaic, sculpture, jewelry, pottery, and stained glass. Hosts 2 judged shows per year and one juries show. Annual judged show in July, focuses on photography only, all other shows welcomes each medium.

MAKING CONTACT & TERMS Artwork is accepted on consignment, and there is a 25% commission. The rental fee covers one month. "Rental fee is based on what we consider a 'featured artist' exhibit. For one month, VAS handles publicity with the artist."

SUBMISSIONS Call. Responds in 2 weeks. Finds artists through art exhibits, art fairs, referrals by other artists, membership.

VIRIDIAN ARTISTS, INC.

530 W. 25th St., #407, New York NY 10001. (212)414-4040. Fax: (212)414-4040. Website: www.viridian artists.com. **Contact:** Vernita Nemec, director. Estab. 1968. Artist-owned gallery. Approached by 200 artists/year. Exhibits 25-30 emerging, mid-career and established artists/year. Sponsors 15 total exhibits/year; 2-4 photography exhibits/year. Average display time 3 weeks. Open Tuesday–Saturday, 12-6. Closed in August. "Classic gallery space with 3 columns, hard-wood floor, white walls and track lights, approximately 1100 sq. ft. The gallery is located in Chelsea, the prime area of contemporary art galleries in New York City." Clients include: local community, students, tourists, upscale and artists. 15% of sales are to corporate collectors. Overall price range: $100-8,000. Most work sold at $1,500.

EXHIBITS Considers all media except craft, traditional glass and ceramic, unless it is sculpture. Most frequently exhibits paintings, photography and sculpture. Considers engravings, etchings, linocuts, lithographs, mezzotints, serigraphs, woodcuts and monoprints/limited edition digital prints. Considers all styles (mostly contemporary). Most frequently exhibits painterly abstraction, imagism and neo-expressionism. "We are not interested in particular styles, but in professionally conceived and professionally executed contemporary art. Eclecticism is our policy. The only unifying factor is quality. Work must be of the highest technical and aesthetic standards."

MAKING CONTACT & TERMS Artwork accepted on consignment with a 30% commission. There is a co-op membership fee plus a donation of time with a 30% commission. Retail price of the art is set by the gallery and artist. Gallery provides promotion and contract. "Viridian is an artist-owned gallery with a director and gallery assistant. Artists pay gallery expenses through monthly dues, but the staff takes care of running the gallery and selling the art. The director writes the press releases, helps install exhibits and advises artists on all aspects of their career. We try to take care of everything but making the art and framing it." Prefers artists who are familiar with the NYC art world and are working professionally in a contemporary mode which can range from realistic to abstract to conceptual and anything in between.

SUBMISSIONS Submitting art for consideration is a 2-step process: first through website or JPEGs, then if accepted at that level, by seeing 4-6 samples of the actual art. Artists should call, e-mail query letter with link to artist's website or JPEG samples at 72 dpi (include image list) or send query letter with artist's statement, bio, reviews, CD with images and SASE. Materials returned with SASE. Responds in 2-4 weeks. Files materials of artists who become members. Finds artists through word of mouth, submissions, art exhibits, portfolio reviews or referrals by other artists.

TIPS "Present current art completed within the last 2 years. Our submission procedure is in 2 stages: first we look at websites, JPEGs that have been e-mailed, or CDs that have been mailed to the gallery. When e-mailing JPEGs, include an image list with title, date of execution, size, media. Also, include a bio and artist's statement. Reviews about your work are helpful if you have them, but not necessary. If you make it through the first level, then you will be asked to submit 4-6 actual art works. These should be framed or matted, and similar to the work you want to show. Realize it is important to present a consistency in your vision. If you do more than one kind of art, select what you feel best represents you, for the art you show will be a reflection of who you are."

VISUAL ARTS CENTER OF NORTHWEST FLORIDA

19 E. 4th St., Panama City FL 32401. (850)769-4451. E-mail: vacoffice@knology.net. Website: www.vac.org.cn. **Contact:** Exhibition manager. Estab. 1988. Approached by 20 artists/year; represents local and national artists. Sponsors 1-2 photography exhibits/year. Average display time 6 weeks. Open Tuesday and Thursday, 10-8; Wednesday, Friday and Saturday, 10-6; closed Sunday and Monday. The Center features a large gallery (200 running ft.) upstairs and a smaller gallery (80 running ft.) downstairs. Overall price range $50-1,500.

EXHIBITS Photos of all subject matter, including babies/children/teens, couples, families, parents, senior citizens, environmental, landscapes/scenics, wildlife, architecture, product shots/still life. Interested in alternative process, avant garde, documentary, fashion/glamour, fine art, historical/vintage, seasonal, digital, underwater.

MAKING CONTACT & TERMS Artwork is accepted on consignment, and there is a 30% commission. Gallery provides promotion, contract, insurance. Accepted work must be framed, mounted, matted.

SUBMISSIONS Send query letter with artist's statement, bio, résumé, SASE, 10-12 slides or images on CD. Responds within 4 months. Finds artists through word of mouth, submissions, art exhibits.

VISUAL ARTS GALLERY

University of Alabama Department of Art & Art History, 1530 3rd Ave., S., Birmingham AL 35294-1260. (205)934-0815. Fax: (205)975-2836. E-mail: blevine@uab.edu. Website: www.uab.edu/art/gallery/vag.html. **Contact:** Brett Levine, director. Nonprofit university gallery. Sponsors 1-3 photography exhibits/year. Average display time 3-4 weeks. Gallery open Monday–Thursday, 11-6; Friday, 11-5; Saturday, 1-5. Closed major holidays and last 2 weeks of December. Located on 1st floor of Humanities Building: 2 rooms with a total of 2,000 sq. ft. and 222 running ft.

EXHIBITS Photos of multicultural. Interested in alternative process, avant garde, fine art, historical/vintage.

MAKING CONTACT & TERMS Gallery provides insurance, promotion. Accepted work should be framed.

SUBMISSIONS Does not accept unsolicited exhibition proposals. Write to arrange a personal interview to show portfolio of slides. Send query letter with artist's statement, bio, brochure, photographs, résumé, reviews, slides, SASE.

THE WAILOA CENTER GALLERY

P.O. Box 936, Hilo HI 96721. (808)933-0416. Fax: (808)933-0417. E-mail: wailoa@yahoo.com. **Contact:** Ms. Codie King, director. Estab. 1967. A division of State Parks, Department of Land and Natural Resources. Free and open to the public. Sponsors 24 exhibits/year. Average display time 1 month. Open Monday, Tuesday, Thursday, Friday, 8:30-4:30; Wednesday, 12-4:30. Closed designated furlough Fridays, Saturday, Sunday and state holidays.

EXHIBITS Photos must be submitted to director for approval. "All entries accepted must meet professional standards outlined in our pre-entry forms."

MAKING CONTACT & TERMS Gallery receives 10% "donation" on works sold. No fee for exhibiting. Accepted work should be framed. "Photos must also be fully fitted for hanging. Expenses involved in shipping, insurance, invitations and reception, etc., are the responsibility of the exhibitor."

SUBMISSIONS Submit portfolio for review. Send query letter with résumé of credits, samples, SASE. Responds in 3 weeks.

TIPS "The Wailoa Center Gallery is operated by the State of Hawaii, Department of Land and Natural Resources. We are unique in that there are no costs to the artist to exhibit here as far as rental or commissions are concerned. We welcome artists from anywhere in the world who would like to show their works in Hawaii. Wailoa Center is booked 2-3 years in advance. The gallery is also a visitor information center with thousands of people from all over the world visiting."

WASHINGTON COUNTY MUSEUM OF FINE ARTS

P.O. Box 423, 401 Museum Dr., Hagerstown MD 21741. (301)739-5727. Fax: (301)745-3741. E-mail: info@wcmfa.org. Website: www.wcmfa.org. **Contact:** Curator. Estab. 1929. The museum has a long tradition of cultural leadership in the Cumberland Valley region, providing residents and visitors with access to a permanent collection and an active schedule of exhibitions, musical concerts, lectures, film, art classes and special events for children and adults. Approached by 30 artists/year. Sponsors 1 juried photography exhibit/year. Average display time 6-8 weeks. Open Tuesday–Friday, 9-5; Saturday, 9-4; Sunday, 1-5. Closed legal holidays. Overall price range $50-7,000.

EXHIBITS Photos of babies/children/teens, celebrities, couples, multicultural, families, parents, senior citizens, disasters, environmental, landscapes/scenics, wildlife, architecture, cities/urban, education, gardening, interiors/decorating, pets, religious, rural, adventure, automobiles, entertainment, events, food/drink, health/fitness/beauty, hobbies, humor, performing arts, sports, travel, agriculture, business concepts, industry, medicine, military, political, product shots/still life, science, technology/computers. Interested in alternative process, avant garde, documentary, fashion/glamour, fine art, historical/vintage, seasonal.

MAKING CONTACT & TERMS Museum handles sale of works, if applicable, with 40% commission. Accepted work shall not be framed.

SUBMISSIONS Write to show portfolio of photographs, slides. Mail portfolio for review. Responds in 1 month. Finds artists through word of mouth, portfolio reviews, art exhibits, referrals by other artists.

TIPS "We sponsor an annual juried competition in photography. Entry forms are available in the fall of each year. Send name and address to be placed on list."

⊘ WEINSTEIN GALLERY

908 W. 46th St., Minneapolis MN 55419. (612)822-1722. Fax: (612)822-1745. E-mail: weingall@aol.com. Website: www.weinstein-gallery.com. **Contact:** Leslie Hammons, director. Estab. 1996. For-profit gallery. Approached by hundreds of artists/year; represents or exhibits 12 artists. Average display time 6 weeks. Open Tuesday–Saturday, 12-5, or by appointment. Overall price range $4,000-250,000.

EXHIBITS Interested in fine art. Most frequently exhibits contemporary photography.

SUBMISSIONS "We do not accept unsolicited submissions."

WISCONSIN UNION GALLERIES

WUD Art Committee, 5210 Memorial Union, 800 Langdon St., Madison WI 53706-1495. (608)262-7592. Fax: (608)262-8862. E-mail: art@union.wisc.edu. Website: www.union.wisc.edu/wud/art-events.htm. **Contact:** Robin Schmoldt, art collection manager. Estab. 1928. Nonprofit gallery. Estab. 1928. Approached by 100 artists/year; exhibits 30 shows/year. Average display time 4-6 weeks. Open Monday–Sun-

day, 10-8. Closed during winter break and when gallery exhibitions turn over. Visit the website for the gallery's features.

EXHIBITS Interested in fine art. "Photography exhibitions vary based on the artist proposals submitted."

MAKING CONTACT & TERMS All sales through gallery during exhibition only.

SUBMISSIONS Current submission guidelines available at www.union.wisc.edu/wud/art-submissions.htm. Finds artists through art fairs, art exhibits, referrals by other artists, submissions, word of mouth.

WOMEN & THEIR WORK ART SPACE

1710 Lavaca St., Austin TX 78701. (512)477-1064. Fax: (512)477-1090. E-mail: info@womenandtheirwork.org. Website: www.womenandtheirwork.org. **Contact:** Rachel Koper, director. Estab. 1978. Alternative space, nonprofit gallery. Approached by more than 400 artists/year; represents or exhibits 6 solo and 1 juried show/year. Sponsors 1-2 photography exhibits/year. Average display time 5 weeks. Gallery open Monday–Friday, 9-6; Saturday, 12-5. Closed December 24–January 2, and other major holidays. Exhibition space is 2,000 sq. ft. Overall price range $500-5,000. Most work sold at $800-1,000.

EXHIBITS Interested in contemporary, alternative process, avant garde, fine art.

MAKING CONTACT & TERMS "We select artists through a juried process and pay them to exhibit. We take 25% commission if something is sold." Gallery provides insurance, promotion, contract. Accepted work should be framed, mounted, matted. Texas women in solo shows only. "All other artists, male or female, in curated show. Online Artist Slide Registry on website."

SUBMISSIONS Finds artists through nomination by art professional.

TIPS "Provide quality images, typed résumé and a clear statement of artistic intent."

WORLD FINE ART GALLERY

179 E. 3rd St., Suite 16, New York NY 10009-7705. (646)336-1677. Fax: (646)478-9361. E-mail: info@worldfineart.com; wfagallery@gmail.com. Website: www.worldfineart.com. **Contact:** O'Delle Abney, director. Estab. 1992. Online gallery since 2010. Services include online websites (www.worldfineart.com/join.html) and personal marketing (www.worldfineart.com/Navigating_the_New_York_Art_Scene.html). Group exhibitions around the New York City Area.

SUBMISSIONS Responds to queries in 1 week. Non-exclusive agent to 12 current portfolio artists. Finds artists online.

TIPS "Have website available or send JPEG images for review."

YESHIVA UNIVERSITY MUSEUM

15 W. 16th St., New York NY 10011. (212)294-8330. Fax: (212)294-8335. E-mail: info@yum.cjh.org. Website: www.yumuseum.org. Estab. 1973. The museum's changing exhibits celebrate the culturally diverse intellectual and artistic achievements of 3,000 years of Jewish experience. Sponsors 6-8 exhibits/year; at least 1 photography exhibit/year. Average display time 4-6 months. The museum occupies 4 galleries and several exhibition arcades. All galleries are handicapped accessible. Open Sunday, Tuesday and Thursday, 11-5. Monday, 3:30-8, Wednesday, 11-8, Friday, 11-2:30.

EXHIBITS Seeks "individual or group exhibits focusing on Jewish themes and interests; exhibition-ready work essential."

MAKING CONTACT & TERMS Accepts images in digital format. Send CD and accompanying text with SASE for return. Send color slide portfolio of 10-12 slides or photos, exhibition proposal, résumé with SASE for consideration. Reviews take place 3 times/year.

TIPS "We exhibit contemporary art and photography based on Jewish themes. We look for excellent quality, individuality, and work that reveals a connection to Jewish identity and/or spirituality."

MIKHAIL ZAKIN GALLERY

561 Piermont Rd., Demarest NJ 07627. (201)767-7160. Fax: (201)767-0497. E-mail: gallery@tasoc.org. Website: www.tasoc.org. **Contact:** John J. McGurk, gallery director. Estab. 1974. Nonprofit gallery associated with the Art School at Old Church. "10-exhibition season includes contemporary, emerging, and established regional artists, NJ Annual Small Works show, student and faculty group exhibitions, among others." Gallery hours: Monday–Friday, 9:30-5:00. Call for weekend and evening hours. Exhibitions are mainly curated by invitation. However, unsolicited materials are reviewed and will be returned with the inclusion of a SASE. The gallery does not review artist websites, e-mail attachments or portfolios in the presence of the artist. Please follow the submission guidelines on our website.

EXHIBITS All styles and genres are considered.

MAKING CONTACT & TERMS Charges 35% commission fee on all gallery sales. Gallery provides promotion and contract. Accepted work should be framed, mounted.

SUBMISSIONS Guidelines are available on gallery's website. Small Works prospectus is available online. Mainly finds artists through referrals by other artists and artist registries.

TIPS "Follow guidelines available online."

ZENITH GALLERY

P.O. Box 55295, Washington D.C. 20040. (202)783-2963. Fax: (202)783-0050. E-mail: margery@zenithgallery.com. E-mail: art@zenithgallery.com. Website: www.zenithgallery.com. **Contact:** Margery E. Goldberg, founder/owner/director. Estab. 1978. For-profit gallery. Open by appointment. Curates shows throughout Chevy Chase Pavilion at 5533 Wisconsin Avenue in Chevy Chase, D.C. Open Monday–Saturday, 10-8; Sunday, 11-6. Level 2 Gallery open Saturdays, 10-6 and by appointment. Curates The Gallery at 1111 Pennsylvania Ave., NW, Washington D.C., open Monday–Friday, 8-7; Saturday and Sunday, by appointment. Overall price range: $500-15,000.

EXHIBITS Photos of landscapes/scenics and other. Interested in avant garde, fine art.

SUBMISSIONS Mail portfolio for review. Send query letter with artist's statement, bio, brochure, business card, résumé, reviews, photocopies, photographs, slides, CD, SASE. Responds to queries within 1 year, only if interested. Finds artists through art fairs and exhibits, portfolio reviews, referrals by other artists, submissions and word of mouth.

ART FAIRS

//

How would you like to sell your art from New York to California, showcasing it to thousands of eager art collectors? Art fairs (also called art festivals or art shows) are not only a good source of income for artists but an opportunity to see how people react to their work. If you like to travel, enjoy meeting people, and can do your own matting and framing, this could be a great market for you.

Many outdoor fairs occur during the spring, summer, and fall months to take advantage of warmer temperatures. However, depending on the region, temperatures could be hot and humid, and not all that pleasant! And, of course, there is always the chance of rain. Indoor art fairs held in November and December are popular because they capitalize on the holiday shopping season.

To start selling at art fairs, you will need an inventory of work—some framed, some unframed. Even if customers do not buy the framed paintings or prints, having some framed work displayed in your booth will give buyers an idea of how your work looks framed, which could spur sales of your unframed prints. The most successful art fair exhibitors try to show a range of sizes and prices for customers to choose from.

When looking at the art fairs listed in this section, first consider local shows and shows in your neighboring cities and states. Once you find a show you'd like to enter, visit its website or contact the appropriate person for a more detailed prospectus. A prospectus is an application that will offer additional information not provided in the art fair's listing.

Ideally, most of your prints should be matted and stored in protective wraps or bags so that customers can look through your inventory without damaging prints and mats. You will also need a canopy or tent to protect yourself and your wares from the elements as well as some bins in which to store the prints. A display wall will allow you to show off your best framed prints. Generally, artists will have 100 square feet of space in which to set up their tents and canopies. Most listings will specify the dimensions of the exhibition space for each artist.

If you see the ☻ icon before a listing in this section, it means that the art fair is a juried event. In other words, there is a selection process artists must go through to be admitted into the fair. Many art fairs have quotas for the categories of exhibitors. For example, one art fair may accept the mediums of photography, sculpture, painting, metal work, and jewelry. Once each category fills with qualified exhibitors, no more will be admitted to the show that year. The jurying process also ensures that the artists who sell their work at the fair meet the sponsor's criteria for quality. So, overall, a juried art fair is good for artists because it means they will be exhibiting their work along with other artists of equal caliber.

Be aware there are fees associated with entering art fairs. Most fairs have an application fee or a space fee, or sometimes both. The space fee is essentially a rental fee for the space your booth will occupy for the art fair's duration. These fees can vary greatly from show to show, so be sure to check this information in each listing before you apply to any art fair.

Most art fair sponsors want to exhibit only work that is handmade by the artist, no matter what medium. Unfortunately, some people try to sell work that they purchased elsewhere as their own original artwork. In the art fair trade, this is known as "buy/sell." It is an undesirable situation because it tends to bring down the quality of the whole show. Some listings will make a point to say "no buy/sell" or "no manufactured work."

For more information on art fairs, pick up a copy of *Sunshine Artist* (www.sunshine artist.com) or *Art Calendar* (www.artcalendar.com), and consult online sources such as www.artfairsource.com.

4 BRIDGES ARTS FESTIVAL

30 Frazier Ave., Chattanooga TN 37405. (423)265-4282. Fax: (423)265-5233. E-mail: jdmcfadden@avarts.org. Website: www.4bridgesartsfestival.org. **Contact:** Jerry Dale McFadden, director. Estab. 2001. Fine arts & crafts show held annually in mid-April. Held in a covered, open-air pavilion. Accepts photography and 24 different mediums. Juried by 3 different art professionals each year. Awards: $10,000 in artist merit awards; the on-site jurying for merit awards will take place Saturday morning. Number of exhibitors: 150. Public attendance: 20,000. Public admission: $7/day or a 2-day pass for $10; children are free. Artists should apply at www.zapplication.org. Deadline for entry: early November (see website for details). Application fee: $40. Space fee: $425 for 10×12 ft. Exhibit space: 10×12 ft.; double: 20×12 ft. Average gross sales/exhibitor: $3,091. For more information, e-mail, visit website or call.

TIPS "Have a compelling, different body of work that stands out among so many other photographers and artists."

AFFAIRE IN THE GARDENS ART SHOW

Greystone Park, 501 Doheny Rd., Beverly Hills CA 90210-2921. (310)285-6836. E-mail: kmclean@beverlyhills.org. Website: www.beverlyhills.org/attractions/affaire. Estab. 1973. Fine arts & crafts show held bi-annually 3rd weekend in May and 3rd weekend in October. Outdoors. Accepts photography, painting, sculpture, ceramics, jewelry, digital media. Juried. Awards/prizes: 1st Place in category, cash awards, Best in Show cash award; Mayor's Purchase Award in October show. Number of exhibitors: 225. Public attendance: 30,000-40,000. Free to public. Deadline for entry: mid-February for the May show; mid-July for the October show. For more information, artists should e-mail, visit website, call or send SASE.

TIPS "Art fairs tend to be commercially oriented. It usually pays off to think in somewhat commercial terms—what does the public usually buy? Personally, I like risky and unusual art, but the artists who produce esoteric art sometimes go hungry! Be nice and have a clean presentation."

AKRON ARTS EXPO

Hardesty Park, 1615 W. Market, Akron OH 44313. (330)375-2836. Fax: (330)375-2883. E-mail: PBomba@akronohio.gov. Website: www.akronartsexpo.org. **Contact:** Penny Bomba, event planner. Estab. 1979. Held in late July (4th weekend). "The Akron Arts Expo is a nationally recognized juried fine arts & crafts show held outside with over 160 artists, ribbon and cash awards, great food, an interactive children's area, and entertainment for the entire family. Participants in this festival present quality fine arts and crafts that are offered for sale at reasonable prices. For more information, see the website."

ALDEN B. DOW MUSEUM SUMMER ART FAIR

1801 W. St. Andrews Rd., Midland MI 48640. Fax: (989)631-7890. E-mail: mills@mcfta.org. Website: www.mcfta.org. **Contact:** Emmy Mills, business manager/art fair coordinator. Estab. 1966. Fine art & crafts show held annually in early June. Outdoors. Accepts photography, ceramics, fibers, jewelry, mixed media 3D, painting, wood, drawing, glass, leather, sculpture, basket, furniture. Juried by a panel. Awards: $500 for 1st place, $300 for 2nd place, $100 for 3rd place. Average number of exhibitors: 150. Public attendance: 5,000-8,000. Free to public. Artists should apply at www.mcfta.org/specialevents.html. Deadline for entry: early March; see website for details. Application fee: jury $25, second medium $5/each. Space fee: $180/single booth, $350/double booth. Exhibition space: approximately 12×12 ft. Average gross sales/exhibitor: $1,500. Artists should e-mail or visit website for more information.

ALLEN PARK ARTS & CRAFTS STREET FAIR

16850 Southfield Rd., Allen Park MI 48101-2599. (313)928-1370. Fax: (313)382-7946. Website: www.cityofallenpark.org/visitors-street-fair.php. **Contact:** Allen Park Festivities Commission. Estab. 1981. Arts & crafts show held annually the 1st Friday and Saturday in August. Outdoors. Accepts photography, sculpture, ceramics, jewelry, glass, wood, prints, drawings, paintings. All work must be of fine quality and original work of entrant. Such items as imports, velvet paintings, manufactured or kit jewelry and any commercially produced merchandise are not eligible for exhibit or sale. Juried by 3 photos of work. Number of exhibitors: 400. Free to the public. Deadline: Applications must be postmarked by late February (see website for specifics). Application fee: $5. Space fee:

$100. Exhibition space: 10×10 ft. Artists should call or see website for more information.

ALLENTOWN ART FESTIVAL

P.O. Box 1566, Buffalo NY 14205. (716)881-4269. Fax: (716)881-4269. E-mail: allentownartfestival@verizon. net. Website: www.allentownartfestival.com. **Contact:** Mary Myszkiewicz, president. Estab. 1958. Fine arts & crafts show held annually 2nd full weekend in June. Outdoors. Accepts photography, painting, watercolor, drawing, graphics, sculpture, mixed media, clay, glass, acrylic, jewelry, creative craft (hard/soft). Slides juried by hired professionals that change yearly. Awards/prizes: 41 cash prizes totaling nearly $20,000; includes Best of Show awarding $1,000. Number of exhibitors: 450. Public attendance: 300,000. Free to public. Artists should apply by downloading application from website. Deadline for entry: late January. Exhibition space: 10×13 ft. For more information, artists should e-mail, visit website, call or send SASE.
TIPS "Artists must have attractive booth and interact with the public."

AMERICAN ARTISAN FESTIVAL

P.O. Box 41743, Nashville TN 37204. (615)429-7708. Fax: (423)265-5233. E-mail: americanartisanfestival@gmail. com. Website: www.american-artisan.com. **Contact:** Jerry Dale McFadden, co-director. Estab. 1971. Fine arts & crafts show held annually mid-June, Father's Day weekend. Outdoors. Accepts photography and 21 different medium categories. Juried by 3 different art professionals each year. 3 cash awards presented. Number of exhibitors: 165. Public attendance: 30,000. No admission fee for the public. Artists should apply online at www.zapplication.org. Deadline for entry: early March (see website for details). Application fee: $40. Space fee: $450 for 10×10 ft.; $675 for 15×15 ft.; $900 for 10×20 ft. Average gross sales/exhibitor: $3,000. For more information, e-mail or visit the website.

AMISH ACRES ARTS & CRAFTS FESTIVAL

1600 W. Market St., Nappanee IN 46550. (574)773-4188 or (800)800-4942. E-mail: amishacres@ amishacres.com; jenniwysong@amishacres.com; beckymaust@amishacres.com. Website: www. amishacres.com. **Contact:** Jenni Pletcher Wysong and Becky Maust Cappert, contact coordinators. Estab. 1962. Arts & crafts show held annually first week-end in August. Outdoors. Accepts photography, crafts, floral, folk, jewelry, oil, acrylic, sculpture, textiles, watercolors, wearable, wood. Juried by 5 images, either 35mm slides or e-mailed digital images. Awards/prizes: Cash including Best of Show and $1,500 Purchase Prizes. Number of exhibitors: 350. Public attendance: 60,000. Children under 12 free. Artists should apply by sending SASE or printing application from website. Deadline for entry: April 1. Exhibition space: 10×12, 15×12, 20×12 or 30×12 ft.; optional stable fee, with tent, also available. Average gross sales/exhibitor: $7,000. For more information, artists should e-mail, visit website, call or send SASE.
TIPS "Create a vibrant, open display that beckons to passing customers. Interact with potential buyers. Sell the romance of the purchase."

ANACORTES ARTS FESTIVAL

505 O Ave., Anacortes WA 98221. (360)293-6211. Fax: 360-299-0722. E-mail: staff@anacortesarts festival.com. Website: www.anacortesartsfestival. com. Fine arts & crafts show held annually 1st full weekend in August. Accepts photography, painting, drawings, prints, ceramics, fiber art, paper art, glass, jewelry, sculpture, yard art, woodworking. Juried by projecting 3 images on a large screen. Works are evaluated on originality, quality and marketability. Each applicant must provide 3 high-quality digital images or slides—2 of the product and 1 of the booth display. Awards/prizes: last year, the arts festival matched funds with 3 sponsors to award $3,600 in cash prizes. Number of exhibitors: 250. We only accept online applications. Application fee: $25. Deadline for entry: early March. Space fee: $300. Exhibition space: 10×10 ft. For more information, artists should see website.

ANN ARBOR'S SOUTH UNIVERSITY ART FAIR

118 N. 4th Ave., Ann Arbor MI 48104. (734)662-3382. Fax: (734)662-0339. E-mail: info@theguild.org. Website: www.theguild.org/art_fair_summer.html. Estab. 1960. Fine arts & crafts show held annually 3rd Wednesday through Saturday in July. Outdoors. Accepts photography, clay, drawing, digital, fiber, jewelry, metal, painting, sculpture, wood. Juried. Awards/prizes: $3,000. Number of exhibitors: 190. Public attendance: 750,000. Free to public. Deadline for entry: January. Exhibition space: 10×10 to 20×10 ft. Average gross sales/exhibitor: $7,000. For more information artists should e-mail, visit website or call.

ANN ARBOR STREET ART FAIR

721 E. Huron, Suite 200, Ann Arbor MI 48104. (734)994-5260. Fax: (734)994-0504. E-mail: production@artfair.org. Website: www.artfair.org. Estab. 1958. Fine arts & crafts show held annually 3rd Saturday in July. Outdoors. Accepts photography, fiber, glass, digital art, jewelry, metals, 2D and 3D mixed media, sculpture, clay, painting, drawing, printmaking, pastels, wood. Juried based on originality, creativity, technique, craftsmanship and production. Awards/prizes: cash prizes for outstanding work in any media. Number of exhibitors: 175. Public attendance: 500,000. Free to the public. Artists should apply through www.zapplication.org. Deadline for entry: January. Application fee: $40. Space fee: $650. Exhibition space: 10×12 ft. Average gross sales/exhibitor: $7,000. For more information, artists should e-mail, visit website, call.

APPLE ANNIE CRAFTS & ARTS SHOW

4905 Roswell Rd., Marietta GA 30062. (770)552-6400, ext. 6110. Fax: (770)552-6420. E-mail: appleannie@st-ann.org. Website: www.st-ann.org/apple_annie.php. Estab. 1981. Arts & crafts show held annually the 1st weekend in December. Indoors. Accepts photography, woodworking, ceramics, pottery, painting, fabrics, glass. Juried. Number of exhibitors: 135. Public attendance: 5,000. Artists should apply by visiting website to print an application form, or call to have one sent to them. Deadline: late April (see website for details). Application fee: $10, nonrefundable, along with photos (1 of overall display and up to 5 of your work). Exhibition space: 72 sq. ft. For more information, artists should e-mail, call or visit website.

TIPS "Have an open, welcoming booth and be accessible and friendly to customers."

ART FAIR ON THE COURTHOUSE LAWN

P.O. Box 795, Rhinelander WI 54501. (715)365-7464. E-mail: info@rhinelanderchamber.com. Website: www.rhinelanderchamber.com. **Contact:** Events coordinator. Estab. 1985. Arts & crafts show held annually in June. Outdoors. Accepts woodworking (includes furniture), jewelry, glass items, metal, paintings and photography. Number of exhibitors: 150. Public attendance: 3,000. Free to the public. Space fee: $75-125. Exhibit space: 10×10 to 10×30 ft. For more information, artists should e-mail, call or visit website.

TIPS "We accept only items handmade by the exhibitor."

ART FESTIVAL BETH-EL

400 S. Pasadena Ave., St. Petersburg FL 33707. (727)347-6136. Fax: (727)343-8982. E-mail: administrator@templebeth-el.com. Website: www.templebeth-el.com. Estab. 1972. Fine arts & crafts show held annually the last weekend in January. Indoors. Accepts photography, painting, jewelry, sculpture, woodworking, glass. Juried by special committee on-site or through slides. Awards/prizes: over $7,000 prize money. Number of exhibitors: 150-175. Public attendance: 8,000-10,000. Free to the public. Artists should apply by application with photos or slides; show is invitational. Deadline for entry: September. For more information, artists should call or visit website.

TIPS "Don't crowd display panels with artwork. Make sure your prices are on your pictures. Speak to customers about your work."

ART IN THE PARK FALL FOLIAGE FESTIVAL

16 S. Main St., Rutland VT 05701. (802)775-0356. Fax: (802)773-4401. E-mail: info@chaffeeartcenter.org. Website: www.chaffeeartcenter.org. **Contact:** Sherri Birkheimer Rooker, event coordinator. Estab. 1961. Fine arts & crafts show held annually in early October. Accepts fine art, photography, clay, fiber, floral, glass, art, specialty foods, wood, jewelry, handmade soaps, lampshades, baskets, etc. Juried by a panel of 10-15 judges who perform a blind review of slide submissions. Number of exhibitors: 130. Public attendance: 8,000. Public admission: voluntary donation. Artists should apply online and submit a CD of three photos of work and one of booth (photos upon pre-approval). Deadline for entry: ongoing but to receive discount for doing both shows, must apply by late May; $25 late fee after that date. Space fee: $200-350. Exhibit space: 10×12 or 20×12 ft. For more information, artists should e-mail, visit website, or call.

TIPS "Have a good presentation and variety, if possible (in pricing also), to appeal to a large group of people."

ART IN THE PARK (GA)

P.O. Box 1540, Thomasville GA 31799. (229)227-7020. Fax: (229)227-3320. E-mail: roseshowfest@rose.net; felicia@thomasville.org. Website: www.downtown

thomasville.com. **Contact:** Felicia Brannen, festival coordinator. Estab. 1998-1999. Arts in the park (an event of Thomasville's Rose Show and Festival) is a one-day arts & crafts show held annually in April. Outdoors. Accepts photography, handcrafted items, oils, acrylics, woodworking, stained glass, other varieties. Juried by a selection committee. Number of exhibitors: 60. Public attendance: 2,500. Free to public. Artists should apply by submitting official application. Deadline for entry: early February. Space fee: $75, varies by year. Exhibition space: 20×20 ft. For more information, artists should e-mail, call or visit website.

TIPS "Most important, be friendly to the public and have an attractive booth display."

ART IN THE PARK (HOLLAND MI)

c/o Holland Friends of Art, P.O. Box 1052, Holland MI 49422. (616)395-3278. E-mail: info@hollandfriends ofart.com. Website: www.hollandfriendsofart.com. **Contact:** Bonnie Lowe, art fair chairperson. This annual fine arts and crafts fair is held on the first Saturday of August in Holland. The event draws one of the largest influx of visitors to the city on a single day, second only to Tulip Time. More than 300 fine artists and artisans from 8 states will be on hand to display and sell their work. Juried. All items for sale must be original. Public attendance: 15,000+. Entry fee: $80 (HFA members $70); includes a $20 application fee. Deadline: late March. Space fee: $150 for a double-wide space; $140 for a double-deep space. Exhibition space: 12×12 ft. Details of the jury and entry process are explained on the application. Application available online. Call, e-mail or visit website for more information.

TIPS "Create an inviting and neat booth. Offer well-made quality artwork and crafts at a variety of prices."

ART IN THE PARK (SIERRA VISTA)

P.O. Box 247, Sierra Vista AZ 85636-0247. (520)803-1511. E-mail: dragnfly@theriver.com. Website: www.artintheparksierravista.com. Estab. 1972. Oldest longest running Arts & Crafts fair in Southern AZ. Fine arts & crafts show held annually 1st full weekend in October. Outdoors. Accepts photography, all fine arts and crafts created by vendor. No resale retail strictly applied. Juried by Huachaca Art Association Board. Artists submit 3-5 photos. Returnable with SASE. Number of exhibitors: 240. Public attendance:

15,000. Free to public. Artists should apply by downloading the application www.artintheparksierra vista.com. Deadline for entry: postmarked by late June. Last minute/late entries always considered. No application fee. Space fee: $175, includes jury fee. Exhibition space: 15×30 ft. Some electrical. Some RV space available at $15/night. For more information, artists should see website, e-mail, call or send SASE.

ART IN THE PARK (VA)

1 Gypsy Hill Park, Staunton VA 24401. (540)885-2028. E-mail: info@saartcenter.org. Website: www.saartcenter.org. **Contact:** Beth Hodges, exec. director; Leah Dubinski, office manager. Estab. 1966. Fine arts & crafts show held annually 3rd Saturday in May. Outdoors. Accepts photography, oil, watercolor, pastel, acrylic, clay, porcelain, pottery, glass, wood, metal, almost anything as long as it is handmade fine art/craft. Juried by submitting 4 photos or slides that are representative of the work to be sold. Award/prizes: Grand Winner. Number of exhibitors: 100. Public attendance: 3,000-4,000. Free to public. Artists should apply by sending in application. Application fee: $15. Space fee: $100, $90 for SAAC members. Exhibition space: 10×10 ft. For more information, artists should e-mail, call or visit website.

ART IN THE PARK (WARREN MI)

8707 Forest Ct., Halmich Park, Warren MI 48093. (586)795-5471. E-mail: wildart@wowway.com. Website: www.warrenfinearts.org. **Contact:** Paula Wild, chairperson. Estab. 1990. Fine arts & crafts show held annually 2nd weekend in July. Indoors and outdoors. Accepts photography, sculpture, basketry, pottery, stained glass. Juried. Awards/prizes; monetary awards. Number of exhibitors: 70. Public attendance: 7,500. Free to public. Deadline for entry: mid-May. Jury fee: $20. Space fee: $125/outdoor; $135/indoor. Exhibition space: 12×12 ft./tent; 12×10 ft./atrium. For more information, artists should e-mail, visit website or send SASE.

ART IN THE PARK SUMMER FESTIVAL

16 S. Main St., Rutland VT 05701. (802)775-8836. Fax: (802)773-0672. E-mail: info@chaffeeartcenter.org. Website: www.chaffeeartcenter.org/art_park.html. **Contact:** Sherri Birkheimer Rooker, event coordinator. Estab. 1961. Fine arts & crafts show held outdoors annually in mid-August. Accepts fine art, pho-

tography, clay, fiber, floral, glass, art, specialty foods, wood, jewelry, handmade soaps, lampshades, baskets, etc. Juried by a panel of 10-15 judges who perform a blind review of slide submissions. Number of exhibitors: 130. Public attendance: 8,000. Public admission: voluntary donation. Artists should apply online and submit a CD with 3 photos of work and 1 of booth (photos upon pre-approval). Deadline for entry: ongoing but to receive discount for doing both shows, must apply by late March; $25 late fee after that date. Space fee: $200-350. Exhibit space: 10×12 or 20×12 ft. For more information, artists should e-mail, visit website, or call.

TIPS "Have a good presentation, variety if possible (in price ranges, too) to appeal to a large group of people."

⊕ ARTISPHERE

16 Augusta St., Greenville SC 29601. (864)271-9355. Fax: (864)467-3133. E-mail: liz@greenvillearts.com. Website: www.artisphere.us. Kerry Murphy, executive director. **Contact:** Liz Rundorff, program director. Fine arts & crafts show held annually in early May (see website for details). Showcases local artists and top regional galleries in a gallery row at various venues along Main Street. Free to public. E-mail, call or visit website for more information and to display your work.

⊕ 🎧 ART ON THE LAWN

Village Artisans, 100 Corry St., Yellow Springs OH 45387. (937)767-1209. E-mail: artonthelawn@aol.com. Website: www.shopvillageartisans.com. **Contact:** Village Artisans. Estab. 1983. Fine arts & crafts show held annually the 2nd Saturday in August. Outdoors. Accepts photography, all hand-made media and original artwork. Juried, as received, from photos accompanying the application. Awards: "Best of Show" receives a free booth space at next year's event. Number of exhibitors: 90-100. Free to public. Request an application by calling or e-mailing, or download an application from the website. Deadline for entry: early August; however, the sooner received, the better the chances of acceptance. Jury fee: $15. Space fee: $65 before May; $75 until late July; $95 thereafter. Exhibition space: 10×10 ft. Average gross sales vary. For more information, artists should visit website, e-mail, call, send SASE or stop by Village Artisans at above address.

🎧 AN ARTS & CRAFTS ADVENTURE

P.O. Box 1326, Palatine IL 60078. (312)751-2500. Fax: (847)221-5853. E-mail: asoa@webtv.net or asoaartists@aol.com. Website: www.americansociety ofartists.org. **Contact:** Office personnel. Estab. 1991. Fine arts & crafts show held annually in early May and mid-September. Outdoors. Event held in Park Ridge, Illinois. Accepts photography, pottery, paintings, sculpture, glass, wood, woodcarving, and more. Juried by 4 slides or photos of work and 1 slide or photo of display; #10 SASE; a résumé or show listing is helpful. See our website for on-line jury. To jury via e-mail: Asoaartists@aol.com. Number of exhibitors: 75. Free to the public. Artists should apply by submitting jury materials. If juried in, you will receive a jury/approval number. Deadline for entry: 2 months prior to show or earlier if spaces fill. Space fee: $80. Exhibition space: approximately 100 sq. ft. for single space; other sizes available. For more information, artists should send SASE, submit jury material.

TIPS "Remember that when you are at work in your studio, you are an artist. But when you are at a show, you are a business person selling your work."

🎧 AN ARTS & CRAFTS AFFAIR, AUTUMN & SPRING TOURS

P.O. Box 184, Boys Town NE 68010. (402)331-2889. Fax: (402)445-9177. E-mail: hpifestivals@cox.net. Website: www.hpifestivals.com. **Contact:** Huffman Productions. Estab. 1983. An arts & crafts show that tours different cities and states. The Autumn Festival tours annually October-November; Spring Festival tours annually in April. Artists should visit website to see list of states and schedule. Indoors. Accepts photography, pottery, stained glass, jewelry, clothing, wood, baskets. All artwork must be handcrafted by the actual artist exhibiting at the show. Juried by sending in 2 photos of work and 1 of display. Awards/prizes: 4 $30 show gift certificates; $50, $100 and $150 certificates off future booth fees. Number of exhibitors: 300-500 depending on location. Public attendance: 15,000-35,000. Public admission: $7-8/adults; $6-7/seniors; 10 & under, free. Artists should apply by calling to request an application. Deadline for entry: varies for date and location. Space fee: $400-650. Exhibition space: 8×11 ft. up to 8×22 ft. For more information, artists should e-mail, call, or visit website.

TIPS "Have a nice display, make sure business name is visible, dress professionally, have different price points, and be willing to talk to your customers."

◎ ARTS & CRAFTS EXPRESSIONS

P.O. Box 1326, Palatine IL 60078. (312)751-2500. Fax: (847)221-5853. E-mail: asoa@webtv.net or asoaartists@aol.com. Website: www.american societyofartists.org. **Contact:** Office personnel. Estab. 1979. Fine arts & crafts show held annually indoors in Walton, Illinois, in spring and fall, usually March and September. Accepts quilting, fabric crafts, artwear, photography, sculpture, jewelry, glass works, wood-working and more. Juried by 4 slides or photos of your work and 1 slide or photo of your display; #10 SASE; a résumé or show listing is helpful. "See our website for online jury information." Number of exhibitors: 50. Free to the public. Artists should apply by submit-ting jury materials. If you want to jury via internet see our website and follow directions given there. To jury via e-mail submit to: Asoartists@aol.com. If juried in, you will receive a jury/approval number. Deadline for entry: 2 months prior to show or earlier if spaces fill. Space fee: $125. Exhibition space: approximately 100 sq. ft. for single space; other sizes available. For more information, artists should send SASE, submit jury material.

TIPS "Remember that when you are at work in your studio, you are an artist. But when you are at a show, you are a business person selling your work."

◎ ARTS & CRAFTS FESTIVAL

Simsbury Woman's Club, P.O. Box 903, Simsbury CT 06070. (860)651-0788. E-mail: simsburywom-ansclub@hotmail.com. **Contact:** Janice Johnson, co-chairman. Estab. 1978. Juried arts & crafts show held annually 2nd weekend after Labor Day. Outdoors rain or shine. Accepts photography, clothing, accessories, jewelry, toys, wood objects, floral arrangements. Ju-ried. Applicants should submit photos or JPEG files. Number of exhibitors: 120. Public attendance: 5,000-7,000. Free to public. Artists should apply by submit-ting completed application, 4 photos including 1 of display booth. Deadline for entry: June 30. Space fee: $150-175. Exhibition space: 11×14 ft. or 15×14 ft. frontage. For more information, artists should e-mail or call.

TIPS "Display artwork in an attractive setting."

◎ ARTS ADVENTURE

P.O. Box 1326, Palatine IL 60078. (312)571-2500. Fax: (847)221-5853. E-mail: asoa@webtv.net or asoaartists@aol.com. Website: www.american societyofartists.org. Estab. 2001. American Society of Artists. Fine arts & crafts show held annually the end of July. Event held in Chicago, Illinois. Outdoors. Ac-cepts photography, paintings, pottery, sculpture, jew-elry and more. Juried. Send 4 slides or photos of your work and 1 slide or photo of your display; #10 SASE; a résumé or show listing is helpful. See our website for online jury. To jury via e-mail: Asoaartists@aol.com. Number of exhibitors: 50. Free to the public. Artists should apply by submitting jury materials. If juried in, you will receive a jury/approval number. Deadline for entry: 2 months prior to show or earlier if spaces fill. Entry fee: $135. Exhibition space: approximately 100 sq. ft. for single space; other sizes available. For more information, artists should send SASE, submit jury material.

TIPS "Remember that when you are at work in your studio, you are an artist. But when you are at a show, you are a business person selling your work."

◎ ART'S ALIVE

Ocean City City Hall, 301 Baltimore Ave., Ocean City MD 21842. (410)250-0125. Fax: (410)250-5409. Website: oceancitymd.gov/Recreation_and_Parks/ specialevents.html. **Contact:** Brenda Moore, event co-ordinator. Estab. 2000. Fine art show held annually in mid-June. Outdoors. Accepts photography, ceramics, drawing, fiber, furniture, glass, printmaking, jewelry, mixed media, painting, sculpture, fine wood. Juried. Awards/prizes: $5,250 in cash prizes. Number of ex-hibitors: 110. Public attendance: 10,000. Free to pub-lic. Artists should apply by downloading application from website or call. Deadline for entry: February 28. Space fee: $200. Jury Fee: $25. Exhibition space: 10 x 10 ft. For more information, artists should visit web-site, call or send SASE.

TIPS Apply early.

◎ ARTS EXPERIENCE

P.O. Box 1326, Palatine IL 60078. (312)751-2500 or (847)991-4748. Fax: (847)221-5853. E-mail: asoa@ webtv.net or asoaartists@aol.com. Website: www. americansocietyofartists.org. Estab. 1979. Fine arts & crafts show held in summer in Chicago. Outdoors. Accepts photography, paintings, graphics, sculpture, quilting, woodworking, fiber art, hand-crafted candles, glass works, jewelry and more. Juried by 4 slides/photo representative of work being exhibited; 1 photo of display set-up, #10 SASE, résumé with show listings helpful. Number of exhibitors: 50. Free to public. Artists should apply by submitting jury material and indicate you are interested in this particular show. If you wish to jury online please see our website and follow directions given there. To jury via e-mail: submit only at Asoaartists@aol.com. When you pass the jury, you will receive jury approval number and application you requested. Deadline for entry: 2 months prior to show or earlier if space is filled. Space fee: to be announced. Exhibition space: 100 sq. ft. for single space; other sizes are available. For more information, artists should send SASE to submit jury material.

TIPS "Remember that at work in your studio, you are an artist. When you are at a show, you are a business person selling your work."

ARTS IN THE PARK

302 2nd Ave. East, Kalispell MT 59901. (406)755-5268. E-mail: information@hockadaymuseum.org. Website: www.hockadaymuseum.org. Estab. 1968. Fine arts & crafts show held annually 4th weekend in July (see website for details). Outdoors. Accepts photography, jewelry, clothing, paintings, pottery, glass, wood, furniture, baskets. Juried by a panel of 5 members. Artwork is evaluated for quality, creativity and originality. Jurors attempt to achieve a balance of mediums in the show. Number of exhibitors: 100. Public attendance: 10,000. Artists should apply by completing the online application form and sending 5 images in JPEG format; 4 images of work and 1 of booth. Application fee: $25. Exhibition space: 10×10 or 10×20 ft. For more information, artists should e-mail, call or visit website.

ARTS ON FOOT

1250 H St., NW, Suite 1000, Washington D.C. 20005. (202)638-3232. E-mail: artsonfoot@downtowndc.org. Website: www.artsonfoot.org. Fine arts & crafts show held annually in September. Outdoors. Accepts photography, painting, sculpture, fiber art, furniture, glass, jewelry, leather. Juried by 5 color images of the artwork. Send images as 35mm slides, TIFF or JPEG files on CD or DVD. Also include artist's résumé and SASE for return of materials. Free to the public. Deadline for entry: July. Exhibition space: 10×10

ft. For more information, artists should call, e-mail, visit website.

ARTS ON THE GREEN

Arts Association of Oldham County, 104 E. Main St., LaGrange KY 40031. (502)222-3822. Fax: (502)222-3823. E-mail: maryklausing@bellsouth.net. Website: www.aaooc.org. **Contact:** Mary Klausing, director. Estab. 2001. Fine arts & crafts show held annually 1st weekend in June. Outdoors. Accepts photography, painting, clay, sculpture, metal, wood, fabric, glass, jewelry. Juried by a panel. Awards/prizes: cash prizes for Best of Show and category awards. Number of exhibitors: 100. Public attendance: 7,500. Free to the public. Artists should apply online or call. Deadline for entry: March 15. Jury fee: $15. Space fee: $150. Electricity fee: $15. Exhibition space: 10×10 or 10 ×12 ft. For more information, artists should e-mail, visit website, call.

TIPS "Make potential customers feel welcome in your space. Don't overcrowd your work. Smile!"

ARTSPLOSURE

313 S. Blount St., #200B, Raleigh NC 27601. (919)832-8699. Fax: (919)832-0890. E-mail: Info@Artsplosure.org. Website: www.artsplosure.org. **Contact:** Dylan Morris, operations manager. Estab. 1979. Annual outdoor art/craft fair held the 3rd weekend of May. Accepts ceramics, glass, fiber art, jewelry, metal, painting, photography, wood, 2D and 3D artwork. Juried event. Awards: 6 totaling $3,500 cash. Number of exhibitors: 170. Public attendance: 75,000. Free admission to the public. Applications available in October, deadline is mid-January. Application fee: $30. Space fee: $225 for 12×12 ft. Average sales: $2,500. For more information visit website or e-mail.

TIPS "Professional quality photos of work submitted for jurying are preferred, as well as a well executed professional booth photo. Keep artist statements concise and relevant."

BLACK SWAMP ARTS FESTIVAL

P.O. Box 532, Bowling Green OH 43402. (419)354-2723. E-mail: info@blackswamparts.org. Website: www.blackswamparts.org. The Black Swamp Arts Festival (BSAF), held early September, connects art and the community by presenting an annual arts festival and by promoting the arts in the Bowling Green community. Apply online at www.zapplication.org. Call, e-mail or visit website for more information.

TIPS Offer a range of prices, from $5 to $500.

🎧 BRICK STREET MARKET

E-mail: info@zionsvillechamber.org. Website: www.zionsvilleart.org. Estab. 1985. Fine art, antique & craft show held annually the Saturday after Mother's Day. Outdoors. In collaboration with area merchants, this annual event is held on the Main Street Gallery District in the Historic Village of Zionsville, Indiana. Please submit up to 3 JPEG images. All mediums are welcome. Artists are encouraged to perform demonstrations of their work and talk with visitors during the event. No tents are required although artists must supply display equipment. Selection committee chooses from the following criteria: antiques, art, food, green/organic products, photography, plants/flowers, and handmade/hand crafted textiles. Committee discourages catalog or mass-produced products. Number of exhibitors: 150-160. Public attendance: 3,000-4,000. Free to public. Artists should apply by requesting application by mail or on website. Space fee: $165. Exhibition space: 10×8 ft. For more information, artists should e-mail.

TIPS "Display is very important. Be creative by making booth space interesting and appealing."

🎧 CAIN PARK ARTS FESTIVAL

40 Severance Circle, Cleveland Heights OH 44118-9988. (216)291-3669. Fax: (216)291-3705. E-mail: jhoffman@clvhts.com; ksenia@clvhts.com. Website: www.cainpark.com. Estab. 1976. Fine arts & crafts show held annually 2nd full week in July. Outdoors. Accepts photography, painting, clay, sculpture, wood, jewelry, leather, glass, ceramics, clothes and other fiber, paper, block printing. Juried by a panel of professional artists; submit 5 slides. Awards/prizes: cash prizes of $750, $500 and $250; also Judges' Selection, Director's Choice and Artists' Award. Number of exhibitors: 155. Public attendance: 60,000. Free to the public. Artists should apply by requesting an application by mail, visiting website to download application or by calling. Deadline for entry: early March. Application fee: $25. Space fee: $350. Exhibition space: 10×10 ft. Average gross sales/exhibitor: $4,000. For more information, artists should e-mail, call or visit website.

TIPS "Have an attractive booth to display your work. Have a variety of prices. Be available to answer questions about your work."

🎧 CALABASAS FINE ARTS FESTIVAL

100 Civic Center Way, Calabasas CA 91302. (818)224-1657. E-mail: artcouncil@cityofcalabasas.com. Website: www.calabasasartscouncil.com/Thefineartsfestival artistinfo. Estab. 1997. Fine arts & crafts show held annually in late April/early May. Outdoors. Accepts photography, painting, sculpture, jewelry, mixed media. Juried. Number of exhibitors: 250. Public attendance: 10,000+. Free to public. Application fee: $25. Artists should apply online through www.zapplication.org; must include 3 photos of work and 1 photo of booth display. For more information, artists should call, e-mail or visit website.

➕ 🎧 CAREFREE FINE ART & WINE FESTIVAL

101 Easy St., Carefree AZ 85377. (480)837-5637. Fax: (480)837-2355. E-mail: info@thunderbirdartists.com. Website: www.thunderbirdartists.com. **Contact:** Denise Dodson, president. Estab. 1993. Fine arts & crafts show held annually in mid-January, the first weekend in March, and the first weekend in November (see website for specifics). Outdoors. Accepts photography and paintings, bronzes, baskets, jewelry, stone and pottery. Juried; CEO blind juries by medium. Number of exhibitors: 165. Public attendance: 45,000. Public admission: $3. Applications available at www.zapplication.com. Deadlines for entry: mid-August (for January festival); late November (for March festival); early June (for November festival). See website for specifics. Application fee: $30. Space fee: $410-1,230. Exhibition space: 10×10 to 10×30 ft. For more information, artists should e-mail, call or visit website.

TIPS "A clean gallery-type presentation is very important."

🎧 CEDARHURST CRAFT FAIR

P.O. Box 923, Richview Rd., Mt. Vernon IL 62864. (618)242-1236, ext. 234. Fax: (618)242-9530. E-mail: linda@cedarhurst.org. Website: www.cedarhurst.org. **Contact:** Linda Wheeler, staff coordinator. Estab. 1977. Arts & crafts show held annually in early September (see website for details). Outdoors. Accepts photography, paper, glass, metal, clay, wood, leather, jewelry, fiber, baskets, 2D art. Juried. Awards/prizes: Best of each category. Number of exhibitors: 125. Public attendance: 12,000. Public admission: $5. Artists should apply by filling out online application form. Deadline for entry: March. Application fee: $25. Space fee: $280. Exhibition space: 10×15 ft. For more information, artists should e-mail, call or visit website.

CENTERVILLE/WASHINGTON TOWNSHIP AMERICANA FESTIVAL

P.O. Box 41794, Centerville OH 45441-0794. (937)433-5898. Fax: (937)433-5898. E-mail: americanafestival@sbcglobal.net. Website: www.americanafestival.org. Estab. 1972. Arts & crafts show held annually on the Fourth of July, except when the 4th falls on a Sunday and then festival is held on Monday the 5th. Festival includes entertainment, parade, food, car show and other activities. Accepts photography and all mediums. "No factory-made items accepted." Awards/prizes: 1st Place; 2nd Place; 3rd Place; certificates and ribbons for most attractive displays. Number of exhibitors: 275-300. Public attendance: 70,000. Free to the public. Artists should send SASE for application form, or apply online. Deadline for entry: early June (see website for details). Space fee: $50. Exhibition space: 12×10 ft. For more information, artists should e-mail, call or visit website.

TIPS "Artists should have moderately priced items, bring business cards and have an eye-catching display."

CHARDON SQUARE ARTS FESTIVAL

Historic Chardon Square, 107 Center St., Chardon OH 44024. (440)285-8686. Website: www.tourgeauga.com/default.aspx. **Contact:** Jan Gipson, chairman. Estab. 1980. Fine arts & crafts show held annually in early August (see website for details). Outdoors. Accepts photography, pottery, weaving, wood, paintings, jewelry. Juried. Number of exhibitors: 105. Public attendance: 3,000. Free to public. Artists should apply by calling for application. Exhibition space: 10×10 ft. For more information, artists should call or visit website.

TIPS "Make your booth attractive; be friendly and offer quality work."

CHATSWORTH CRANBERRY FESTIVAL

P.O. Box 286, Chatsworth NJ 08019. (609)726-9237. Fax: (609)726-1459. E-mail: lgiamalis@aol.com. Website: www.cranfest.org. Estab. 1983. Arts & crafts show held annually in mid-October (see website for details). Outdoors. The festival is a celebration of New Jersey's cranberry harvest, the 3rd largest in the country, and offers a tribute to the Pine Barrens and local culture. Accepts photography. Juried. Number of exhibitors:

200. Public attendance: 75,000-100,000. Free to public. Artists should apply by sending SASE to above address (application form online). Deadline: September 1. Space fee: $200. Exhibition space: 15×15 ft. For more information, artists should visit website.

CHRISTMAS CRAFT SHOW

Cumus Radio, 5989 Susquehanna Plaza Dr., York PA 17406-8910. (717)764-1155, ext. 1367. Fax: (717)252-4708. E-mail: jolene.kirsch@cumulus.com. Website: www.warm103.com. Estab. 1985. Arts & crafts show held annually in early December. Indoors. Accepts photography and all hand crafts. Number of exhibitors: 250. Public attendance: 3,000. Public admission: $3. Artists should apply by visiting website, calling or mailing for an entry form. Space fee: $95. Exhibition space: 10×10 ft. Average gross sales/exhibitor: $1,000-$2,000. For more information, artists should e-mail, visit website or call.

CHUN CAPITOL HILL PEOPLE'S FAIR

1290 Williams St., Suite 102, Denver CO 80218. (303)830-1651. Fax: (303)830-1782. E-mail: andrea furness@chundenver.org; nicoleanderson@chun denver.org. Website: www.peoplesfair.com; www.chundenver.org. **Contact:** Andrea Furness, assistant director. Estab. 1971. Arts & crafts show held annually 1st weekend in June. Outdoors. Accepts photography, ceramics, jewelry, paintings, wearable art, glass, sculpture, wood, paper, fiber, children's items, and more. Juried by professional artisans representing a variety of mediums and selected members of fair management. The jury process is based on originality, quality and expression. Awards/prizes: Best of Show. Number of exhibitors: 300. Public attendance: 250,000. Free to public. Artists should apply by downloading application from website. Deadline for entry: March. Application fee: $35. Space fee: $300. Exhibition space: 10×10 ft. For more information, artists should e-mail, visit website or call.

CHURCH STREET ART & CRAFT SHOW

Downtown Waynesville Association, P.O. Box 1409, Waynesville NC 28786. (828)456-3517. E-mail: down townwaynesville@charter.net. Website: www.down townwaynesville.com. Estab. 1983. Fine arts & crafts show held annually 2nd Saturday in October. Outdoors. Accepts photography, paintings, fiber, pottery, wood, jewelry. Juried by committee: submit 4 slides or photos of work and 1 of booth display. Number of exhibitors: 100. Public attendance: 15,000-18,000. Free to public. Space fee: $100 ($195 for two booths). Exhibition space: 10×12 ft. (option of two booths for 12×20 space). For more information and application, see website. Deadline: mid-August.

TIPS Recommends "quality in work and display."

CITY OF FAIRFAX FALL FESTIVAL

4401 Sideburn Rd., Fairfax VA 22030. (703)385-7949. Fax: (703)246-6321. E-mail: lherman@fairfaxva.gov; ParksRec@fairfaxva.gov. Website: www.fairfaxva.gov. **Contact:** Leslie Herman, special events manager. Estab. 1975. Arts & crafts show held annually the 2nd Saturday in October. Outdoors. Accepts photography, jewelry, glass, pottery, clay, wood, mixed media. Juried by a panel of 5 independent jurors. Number of exhibitors: 500. Public attendance: 25,000. Free to the public. Deadline for entry: early March (see website for details). Application fee: $10. Space fee: $150. Exhibition space: 10×10 ft. For more information, artists should e-mail.

TIPS "Be on site during the event. Smile. Price according to what the market will bear."

CITY OF FAIRFAX HOLIDAY CRAFT SHOW

10455 Armstrong St., Fairfax VA 22030. (703)385-7949. Fax: (703)246-6321. E-mail: ParksRec@fairfaxva.gov; leslie.herman@fairfaxva.gov. Website: www.fairfaxva.gov. **Contact:** Leslie Herman, special events coordinator. Estab. 1985. Arts & crafts show held annually 3rd weekend in November. Indoors. Accepts photography, jewelry, glass, pottery, clay, wood, mixed media. Juried by a panel of 5 independent jurors. Number of exhibitors: 247. Public attendance: 7,000. Public admission: $5 for age 18 an older. $8 for two day pass. Artists should apply by contacting Leslie Herman for an application. Deadline for entry: early March (see website for details). Application fee: $10. Space fee: 10×6 ft.: $185; 11×9 ft.: $235; 10×10 ft.: $260. For more information, artists should e-mail.

TIPS "Be on-site during the event. Smile. Price according to what the market will bear."

CODORUS SUMMER BLAST

Codorus State Park, 2600 Smith Station Rd., Hanover PA 17331. (717)434-4042. E-mail: freedomloghouse@comcast.net. Website: codorusblast.com. **Contact:** Vicki Senft. Estab. 2000. Arts & crafts show held as part of a 3-day family-friendly festival. Held annually in late June (see website for details). Outdoors. Accepts photography and all crafts. Number of exhibitors: 50. Public attendance: 15,000. Free to the public. Artists should apply on website or through the mail. Space fee: $100-300. Exhibition space: 10 x 12, 20 x 12 or 30 x 12 ft. For more information, artists should e-mail, visit website or call.

York Craft Shows also sponsors Christmas Craft Show in mid-December. See listing for this event in this section.

COLORSCAPE CHENANGO ARTS FESTIVAL

P.O. Box 624, Norwich NY 13815. (607)336-3378. E-mail: info@colorscape.org. Website: www.colorscape.org. Estab. 1995. A juried exhibition of art & fine crafts held annually the weekend after Labor Day. Outdoors. Accepts photography and all types of media. Juried. Awards/prizes: $5,000. Number of exhibitors: 90-95. Public attendance: 12,000-14,000. Free to public. Deadline for entry: see website for details. Application fee: $15 jury fee. Space fee: $175. Exhibition space: 12×12 ft. For more information, artists should e-mail, visit website, call or send SASE.

TIPS "Interact with your audience. Talk to them about your work and how it is created. People like to be involved in the art they buy and are more likely to buy if you involve them."

CONYERS CHERRY BLOSSOM FESTIVAL

1184 Scott St., Conyers GA 30012. (770)929-4270. E-mail: harriet.gattis@conyersga.com. Website: www.conyerscherryblossomfest.com. Estab. 1981. Arts & crafts show held annually in late March (see website for details). Outdoors. The festival is held at the Georgia International Horse Park at the Grand Prix Plaza overlooking the Grand Prix Stadium used during the 1996 Centennial Olympic Games. Accepts photography, paintings and any other handmade or original art. Juried. Number of exhibitors: 300. Public attendance: 40,000. Free to public. Space fee: $75. Exhibition space: 10×10 ft. Application fee: $10; apply online. For more information, artists should e-mail, call or visit website.

CRAFT FAIR AT THE BAY

38 Charles St., Rochester NH 03867. (603)332-2616. Fax: (603) 332-8413. E-mail: info@castleberryfairs.com. Website: www.castleberryfairs.com. Estab. 1988.

Arts & crafts show held annually in July in Alton Bay, New Hampshire. Outdoors. Accepts photography and all other mediums. Juried by photo, slide or sample. Number of exhibitors: 85. Public attendance: 7,500. Free to the public. Artists should apply by downloading application from website. Deadline for entry: until full. Exhibition space: 100 sq. ft. For more information, artists should visit call, e-mail or visit website.

TIPS "Do not bring a book; do not bring a chair. Smile and make eye contact with everyone who enters your booth. Have them sign your guest book; get their e-mail address so you can let them know when you are in the area again. And, finally, make the sale—they are at the fair to shop, after all."

CRAFTS AT RHINEBECK

6550 Springbrook Ave., Rhinebeck NY 12572. (845)876-4001. Fax: (845)876-4003. E-mail: vimperati@dutchessfair.com. Website: www.craftsatrhinebeck.com. Estab. 1981. Fine arts & crafts show held biannually in late June and early October. Indoors and outdoors. Accepts photography, fine art, ceramics, wood, mixed media, leather, glass, metal, fiber, jewelry. Juried by 3 slides of work and 1 of booth display. Number of exhibitors: 350. Public attendance: 25,000. Public admission: $7. Artists should apply by calling for application or downloading application from website. Deadline for entry: early February. Application fee: $20. Space fee: $300-730. Exhibition space: inside: 10×10 and 10×20 ft.; outside: 15×15 ft. For more information, artists should e-mail, visit website or call.

TIPS "Presentation of work within your booth is very important. Be approachable and inviting."

CRAFTWESTPORT

P.O. Box 28, Woodstock NY 12498. (845)331-7484. Fax: (845)331-7484. E-mail: crafts@artrider.com. Website: www.craftwestport.com. Estab. 1975. Fine arts & craft show held annually in mid-November. Indoors. Accepts photography, wearable and nonwearable fiber, metal and nonmetal jewelry, clay, leather, wood, glass, painting, drawing, prints, mixed media. Juried by 5 images of work and 1 of booth, viewed sequentially. Number of exhibitors: 160. Public attendance: 5,000. Public admission: $9. Artists should apply by downloading application from www.artrider.com or can apply online at www.zapplication.org. Deadline for entry: early July. Application fee: $45.

Space fee: $545. Exhibition space: 10×10 ft. For more information, artists should e-mail, visit website, call.

CUNEO GARDENS ART FESTIVAL

3417 R.F.D., Long Grove IL 60047. E-mail: dwevents@comcast.net. Website: www.dwevents.org. **Contact:** D&W Events, Inc. Estab. 2005. Fine arts & crafts show held outdoors in late May (see website for details). Accepts photography, fiber, oil, acrylic, watercolor, mixed media, jewelry, sculpture, metal, paper, painting. Juried by 3 jurors. Awards/prizes: Best of Show; First Place and awards of excellence. Number of exhibitors: 75. Public attendance: 10,000. Entrance to festival is free, however there is a $5/car parking fee. Artists should apply by downloading application from website, e-mail or call. Exhibition space: 100 sq. ft. For more information, artists should e-mail, visit website, call.

TIPS "Artists should display professionally and attractively, and interact positively with everyone."

CUSTER'S LAST STAND FESTIVAL OF THE ARTS

P.O. Box 6013, Evanston IL 60202. (847)328-2204. Fax: (847)823-2295. E-mail: office@custerfair.com. Website: www.custerfair.com. Estab. 1972. Outdoor fine art craft show held in June. Accepts photography and all mediums. Number of exhibitors: 400. Public attendance: 70,000. Free to the public. Application fee: $10. Deadline for entry: early May. Space fee varies, email, call or visit website for more details.

TIPS "Be prepared to speak with patrons; invite them to look at your work and discuss."

A DAY IN TOWNE

Boalsburg Memorial Day Committee, 117 E. Boal Ave., Boalsburg PA 16827. (814)466-6311 or (814)466-9266. E-mail: office@boalmuseum.com. Website: www.boalmuseum.com/memorialday.village.htm. Arts & crafts show held annually the last Monday in May/Memorial Day weekend. Outdoors. Accepts photography, country fabric & wood, wool knit, soap, jewelry, dried flowers, children, pottery, blown glass. Vendor must make own work. Number of exhibitors: 125-135. Public attendance: 20,000. Artists should apply by writing an inquiry letter and sending 2-3 photos; 1 of booth and 2 of the craft. Deadline for entry: January 1–February 1. Space fee: $75. Exhibition space: 10×15 ft.

TIPS "Please do not send fees until you receive an official contract. Have a neat booth and nice smile. Have fair prices—if too high, product will not sell here."

☺ DEERFIELD FINE ARTS FESTIVAL

3417 R.F.D., Long Grove IL 60047. (847)438-4517. E-mail: dwevents@comcast.net. Website: www.dwevents.org. **Contact:** D&W Events, Inc. Estab. 2000. Fine arts & crafts show held annually during the first weekend of June; hours are 10-5. Outdoors. Accepts photography, fiber, oil, acrylic, watercolor, mixed media, jewelry, sculpture, metal, paper, ceramics, painting. Juried by 3 jurors. Awards/prizes: Best of Show; First Place, awards of excellence. Number of exhibitors: 150. Public attendance: 35,000. Free to public. Artists should apply by downloading application from website, e-mail or call. Exhibition space: 100 sq. ft. For more information artists should e-mail, visit website, call.

TIPS "Artists should display professionally and attractively, and interact positively with everyone."

☺ DELAWARE ARTS FESTIVAL

P.O. Box 589, Delaware OH 43015. (740)363-2695. E-mail: info@delawareartsfestival.org. Website: www.delawareartsfestival.org. Estab. 1973. Fine arts & crafts show held annually the Saturday and Sunday after Mother's Day. Outdoors. Accepts photography; all mediums, but no buy/sell. Juried by committee members who are also artists. Awards/prizes: Ribbons, cash awards, free booth for the following year. Number of exhibitors: 160. Public attendance: 25,000. Free to the public. Submit 3 slides or photographs that best represent your work. Your work will be juried in accordance with our guidelines. Photos will be returned only if you provide a SASE. Artists should apply by visiting website for application. Application fee: $10, payable to the Delaware Arts Festival. Deadline: April 15. Space fee: $125. Exhibition space: 120 sq. ft. For more information, artists should e-mail or visit website.

TIPS "Have high-quality, original stuff. Engage the public. Applications will be screened according to originality, technique, craftsmanship and design. The Delaware Arts Festival, Inc., will exercise the right to reject items during the show that are not the quality of the media submitted with the applications. No commercial buy and resell merchandise permitted. Set up a good booth."

☺ DOWNTOWN FESTIVAL & ART SHOW

P.O. Box 490, Gainesville FL 32602. (352)393-8536. Fax: (352)334-2249. E-mail: Piperlr@Cityofgainesville.org. Website: www.gvlculturalaffairs.org. **Contact:** Linda Piper, events coordinator. Estab. 1981. Fine arts & crafts show held annually in November (see website for more details). Outdoors. Accepts photography, wood, ceramic, fiber, glass, and all mediums. Juried by 3 digital images of artwork and 1 digital image of booth. Awards/prizes: $14,000 in cash awards; $5,000 in purchase awards. Number of exhibitors: 250. Public attendance: 100,000. Free to the public. Artists should apply by mailing 4 slides. Deadline for entry: May. Space fee: $215, competitive, $195 non-competitive. Exhibition space: 12×12 ft. Average gross sales/exhibitor: $6,000. For more information, artists should e-mail, visit website, call.

TIPS "Submit the highest-quality slides possible. A proper booth slide is so important."

☺ DURANGO AUTUMN ARTS FESTIVAL

802 E. 2nd Ave., Durango CO 81301. (970)259-2606. Fax: (970)259-6571. E-mail: info@durangoarts.org. Website: www.durangoarts.org. Estab. 1993. Fine arts & crafts show. Mid-September. Outdoors. Accepts photography and all mediums. Juried. Number of exhibitors: 100. Public attendance: 8,000. Free to public. Exhibition space: 10×10 ft. For more information, artists should e-mail, visit website or send SASE.

☺ EDENS ART FAIR

P.O. Box 1326, Palatine IL 60078. (312)2500. Fax: (847)5853. E-mail: asoa@webtv.net or asoaartists@aol.com. Website: www.americansocietyofartists.com. **Contact:** Office personnel. Estab. 1995. American Society of Artists. Estab. 1995 (after renovation of location; held many years prior to renovation). Fine arts & fine selected crafts show held annually in mid-July. Outdoors. Event held in Wilmette, Illinois. Accepts photography, paintings, sculpture, glass works, jewelry and more. Juried. Send 4 slides or photos of your work and 1 slide or photo of your display; #10 SASE; a résumé or show listing is helpful. Number of exhibitors: 50. Free to the public. Artists should apply by submitting jury materials. If you wish to jury online please see our website and follow directions given. To jury via e-mail: Asoaartists@aol.com. If juried in, you will receive a jury/approval number. Deadline for entry: 2 months prior to show or earlier if spaces fill. Entry fee: $145. Exhibition space: approximately 100 sq. ft. for single space; other sizes available. For more information, artists should send SASE, submit jury material.

TIPS "Remember that when you are at work in your studio, you are an artist. But when you are at a show, you are a business person selling your work."

☺ EDWARDS FINE ART & SCULPTURE FESTIVAL

27 Main St., Edwards CO 81632. (480)837-5637. Fax: (480)837-2355. E-mail: info@thunderbirdartists. com. Website: www.thunderbirdartists.com. **Contact:** Denise Dodson, vice president. Estab. 1999. Fine art & craft show. Held annually in mid-July (see website for specifics). Outdoors. Accepts photography, painting, bronzes, baskets, jewelry, stone, pottery. Juried; blind jury by CEO. Number of exhibitors: 75. Public attendance: 10,000. Free to public. Apply online at www.zapplication.com. Deadline for entry: see website for details. Application fee: $30. Space fee: $410-1,230. Exhibition space: 10×10 to 10 x 30 ft. For more information, artists should e-mail, call or visit website.

TIPS "A clean, gallery-type presentation is very important."

☺ ELMWOOD AVENUE FESTIVAL OF THE ARTS, INC.

P.O. Box 786, Buffalo NY 14213-0786. (716)830-2484. E-mail: directoreafa@aol.com. Website: www.elm woodartfest.org. Estab. 2000. Arts & crafts show held annually in late August, the weekend before Labor Day weekend. Outdoors. Accepts photography, metal, fiber, ceramics, glass, wood, jewelry, basketry, 2D media. Juried. Awards/prizes: to be determined. Number of exhibitors: 170. Public attendance: 80,000-120,000. Free to the public. Artists should apply by e-mailing their contact information or by downloading application from website. Deadline for entry: April. Space fee: $250. Exhibition space: 10×15 ft. Average gross sales/exhibitor: $3,000. For more information, artists should e-mail, call or visit website.

TIPS "Make sure your display is well designed, with clean lines that highlight your work. Have a variety of price points—even wealthy people don't always want to spend $500 at a booth where they may like the work."

☺ EVERGREEN ARTS FESTIVAL

Evergreen Artists Association, P.O. Box 3931, Evergreen CO 80437-3931. (303)679-1609. E-mail: info@ evergreenartists.org. Website: www.evergreenartists. org/Shows_Festivals.htm; www.fairsandfestivals. net/events/details/evergreen-fine-arts-festival-2011. **Contact:** EAA Fine Arts Festival Coordinator. Estab. 1966. Fine arts show held annually the last weekend in August. Outdoors in Historic Grove Venue, next to Hiwan Homestead. Accepts both 2D and 3D media, including photography, fiber, oil, acrylic, pottery, jewelry, mixed media, ceramics, wood, watercolor. Juried event with jurors that change yearly. Artists should submit a CD with 4 views of work and 1 of booth display by digital photograph high-res. Awards/prizes: Best of Show; 1st, 2nd, 3rd places in each category. Number of exhibitors: approximately 96. Public attendance: 3,000-6,000. Free to public. Deadline for entry: April 15. Application fee: $25. Space fee: $350, and space is limited. Exhibition space: 10×10 ft. Submissions on www.zapplication.org begin in February and jurying completed in early May. For more information, artists should call or send SASE.

TIPS "Have a variety of work. It is difficult to sell only high-ticket items."

FAIRE ON THE SQUARE

Prescott Courthouse Plaza, 120 S. Cortez St., Prescott AZ 86303, United States. (928)445-2000, ext. 112. E-mail: chamber@prescott.org; scott@prescott.org. Website: www.visit-prescott.com/details/222-faire-on-the-square.html. Estab. 1985. Arts & crafts show held annually Labor Day weekend. Outdoors. Accepts photography, ceramics, painting, sculpture, clothing, woodworking, metal art, glass, floral, home décor. No resale. Juried. Photos of work and artist creating work are required. Number of exhibitors: 170. Public attendance: 10,000-12,000. Free to public. Application can be printed from website or obtained by phone request. Deadline: spaces are sold until show is full. Space fee: $425. Exhibition space: 10×15 ft. For more information, artist should e-mail, visit website or call.

☺ A FAIR IN THE PARK

906 Yew St., Pittsburgh PA 15224. (412)370-0695. E-mail: info@craftsmensguild.org. Website: www. craftsmensguild.org. **Contact:** Katie Horowitz, director. Estab. 1969. Contemporary fine arts & crafts show held annually the weekend after Labor Day

outdoors. Accepts photography, clay, fiber, jewelry, metal, mixed media, wood, glass, 2D visual arts. Juried. Awards/prizes: 1 Best of Show and 4 Craftsmen's Guild Awards. Number of exhibitors: 115. Public attendance: 25,000+. Free to public. Artists should apply by sending application with jury fee, booth fee and 5 digital images. Deadline for entry: early May. Exhibition space: 11×12 ft. Average gross sales/exhibitor: $1,000 and up. For more information artists should e-mail, visit website or call.

TIPS "It is very important for artists to present their work to the public, to concentrate on the business aspect of their artist career. They will find that they can build a strong customer/collector base by exhibiting their work and by educating the public about their artistic process and passion for creativity."

FALL FEST IN THE PARK

117 W. Goodwin St., Prescott AZ 86303. (928)445-2000 or (800)266-7534. E-mail: chamber@prescott.org. Website: www.prescott.org. Estab. 1981. Arts & crafts show held annually in mid-October. Outdoors. Accepts photography, ceramics, painting, sculpture, clothing, woodworking, metal art, glass, floral, home décor. No resale. Juried. Photos of work and artist creating work are required. Number of exhibitors: 150. Public attendance: 6,000-7,000. Free to public. Application can be printed from website or obtained by phone request. Deadline: Spaces are sold until show is full. Exhibition space; 10×15 ft. For more information, artists should e-mail, visit website or call.

⊕ FALL FESTIVAL OF ART AT QUEENY PARK

P.O. Box 31265, St. Louis MO 63131. (314)889-0433. E-mail: info@gslaa.org. Website: www.gslaa.org. Estab. 1976. Fine arts & crafts show held annually Labor Day weekend at Queeny Park. Indoors. Accepts photography, all fine art and fine craft categories. Juried by 5 jurors; 5 slides shown simultaneously. Awards/prizes: 3 levels, ribbons, $4,000+ total prizes. Number of exhibitors: 130. Public attendance: 2,000-4,000. Admission: $5. Artists should apply online. Deadline for entry: late May, see website for specific date. Exhibition space: 80 sq. ft. For more information, artists should e-mail or visit website.

TIPS "Excellent, professional slides; neat, interesting booth. But most important—exciting, vibrant, eye-catching art work."

⊕ ⊙ FALL FINE ART & CRAFTS AT BROOKDALE PARK

473 Latchung Ave., Bloomfield NJ 07003. (908)874-5247. Fax: (908)874-7098. E-mail: info@rosesquared.com. Website: www.rosesquared.com. **Contact:** Howard Rose, vice president. Estab. 1998. Fine arts & crafts show held annually in mid-October. Outdoors. Accepts photography and all other mediums. Juried. Number of exhibitors: 160. Public attendance: 12,000. Free to public. Artists should apply on the website. Deadline for entry: mid-September. Application fee: $25. Space fee varies by booth size; see application form on website for details. For more information, artists should visit the website.

TIPS "Have a range of products and prices."

⊕ ⊙ FALL FINE ART & CRAFTS AT THE WESTFIELD ARMORY

500 Rahway Ave., Westfield NJ 07090. (908)874-5247. Fax: (908)874-7098. E-mail: info@rosesquared.com. Website: www.rosesquared.com. **Contact:** Howard Rose, vice president. Estab. 2010. Fine arts & crafts show held annually in mid-November. Indoors. Accepts photography and all other mediums. Juried. Number of exhibitors: 130. Public attendance: 4,000. Admission fee: $6. Artists should apply on the website. Deadline for entry: early November. Application fee: $25. Space fee varies by booth size; see application form on website for details. For more information, artists should visit the website.

TIPS "Create a unique booth."

⊙ FARGO'S DOWNTOWN STREET FAIR

Downtown Community Partnership, 203 4th Ave. North, Fargo ND 58102. (701)241-1570; (701)451-9062. Fax: (701)241-8275. E-mail: steph@fmdowntown.com. Website: www.fmdowntown.com. Estab. 1975. Fine arts & crafts show held annually in July (see website for dates). Outdoors. Accepts photography, ceramics, glass, fiber, textile, jewelry, metal, paint, print/drawing, sculpture, 3D mixed media, wood. Juried by a team of artists from the Fargo-Moorehead area. Awards/prizes: Best of Show and best in each medium. Number of exhibitors: 300. Public attendance: 130,000-150,000. Free to pubic. Artists should apply online or by mail. Deadline for entry: mid-February. Space fee: $275/booth; $50/corner. Exhibition space: 10×10 ft. For more information, artists should e-mail, visit website or call.

FAUST FINE ARTS & FOLK FESTIVAL

Greensfelder Recreation Complex, 15185 Olive St., St. Louis MO 63017. (314)615-8482. E-mail: toconnell@stlouisco.com. Website: www.stlouisco.com/parks. **Contact:** Tonya O'Connell, recreation supervisor. Fine arts & crafts show held bi-annually in May and September. Outdoors. Accepts photography, oil, acrylic, clay, fiber, sculpture, watercolor, jewelry, wood, floral, baskets, prints, drawing, mixed media, folk art. Juried by a committee. Awards/prizes: $100. Number of exhibitors: 90-100. Public attendance: 5,000. Public admission: $2 for May show and $5 for September show—includes free hayrides and carousel rides. Deadline for entry: March for spring show and July for fall show. Application fee: $15. Space fee: $85. Exhibition space: 10×10 ft. For more information, artists should call.

FERNDALE ART SHOW

Integrity Shows, 2102 Roosevelt, Ypsilanti MI 48197. E-mail: markloeb@aol.com. Website: www.michiganartshow.com. **Contact:** Mark Loeb, president. Estab. 2004. Fine arts & crafts show held annually in September. Outdoors. Accepts photography and all fine art and craft mediums; emphasis on fun, funky work. Juried by 3 independent jurors. Awards/prizes: purchase and merit awards. Number of exhibitors: 120. Public attendance: 30,000. Free to the public. Application is available in March. Deadline for entry: July. For more information, artists should e-mail.

TIPS "Show enthusiasm. Keep a mailing list. Develop collectors."

FESTIVAL IN THE PARK

1409 East Blvd., Charlotte NC 28203. (704)338-1060. E-mail: festival@festivalinthepark.org. Website: www.festivalinthepark.org. Estab. 1964. Fine arts & crafts show held annually the 3rd Friday after Labor Day. Outdoors. Accepts photography, decorative and wearable crafts, drawing and graphics, fiber and leather, jewelry, mixed media, painting, metal, sculpture, wood. Juried by slides or photographs. Awards/prizes: $4,000 in cash awards. Number of exhibitors: 150. Public attendance: 100,000. Free to the public. Artists should apply by visiting website for application. Application fee: $35. Space fee: $350. Exhibition space: 10×10 ft. For more information, artists should e-mail, visit website, call.

FILLMORE JAZZ FESTIVAL

Steven Restivo Event Services, LLC, P.O. Box 151017, San Rafael CA 94915. (800)310-6563. Fax: (415)456-6436. Website: www.fillmorejazzfestival.com. Estab. 1984. Fine arts & crafts show and jazz festival held annually 1st weekend of July in San Francisco, between Jackson & Eddy Streets. Outdoors. Accepts photography, ceramics, glass, jewelry, paintings, sculpture, metal clay, wood, clothing. Juried by prescreened panel. Number of exhibitors: 250. Public attendance: 90,000. Free to public. Deadline for entry: ongoing; apply online. Exhibition space: 8×10 ft. or 10×10 ft. Average gross sales/exhibitor: $800-11,000. For more information, artists should visit website or call.

FINE ART & CRAFTS AT ANDERSON PARK

274 Bellevue Ave., Upper Montclair NJ 07043. (908)874-5247. Fax: (908)874-7098. E-mail: info@rosesquared.com. Website: www.rosesquared.com. Estab. 1984. Fine art & craft show held annually in mid-September. Outdoors. Accepts photography and all other mediums. Juried. Number of exhibitors: 160. Public attendance: 12,000. Free to the public. Artists should apply on the website. Deadline for entry: mid-August. Application fee: $25. Space fee varies by booth size; see application form on website for details. For more information, artists should visit the website.

TIPS "Create a range of sizes and prices."

FINE ART & CRAFTS AT VERONA PARK

542 Bloomfield Ave., Verona NJ 07044. (908)874-5247. Fax: (908)874-7098. E-mail: info@rosesquared.com. Website: www.rosesquared.com. **Contact:** Howard Rose, vice president. Estab. 1986. Fine arts & crafts show held annually in mid-May. Outdoors. Accepts photography and all other mediums. Juried. Number of exhibitors: 140. Public attendance: 10,000. Free to public. Artists should apply on the website. Deadline for entry: mid-April. Application fee: $25. Space fee varies by booth size; see application form on website for details. For more information, artists should visit the website.

TIPS "Have a range of sizes and price ranges."

FOOTHILLS CRAFTS FAIR

2753 Lynn Rd., #A, Tryon NC 28782-7870. (828)859-7427. E-mail: info@blueridgebbqfestival.com. Website: www.blueridgebbqfestival.com. **Contact:** Julie

McIntyre. Estab. 1994. Fine arts & crafts show and Blue Ridge BBQ Festival/Championship held annually the 2nd Friday and Saturday in June. Outdoors. Accepts photography, arts and handcrafts by artist only; nothing manufactured or imported. Juried. Number of exhibitors: 50. Public attendance: 25,000+. Public admission: $8; 12 and under free. Artists should apply by downloading application from website or sending personal information to e-mail or mailing address. See website for deadline for entry. Jury fee: $25, nonrefundable. Space fee: $160. Exhibition space: 12×12 ft. For more information, artists should e-mail or visit website.

TIPS "Have an attractive booth, unique items, and reasonable prices."

🎭 FORD CITY HERITAGE DAYS

P.O. Box 205, Ford City PA 16226-0205. (724)763-1617. E-mail: fcheritagedays@gmail.com. Estab. 1980. Arts & crafts show held annually over the Fourth of July weekend. Outdoors. Accepts photography, any handmade craft. Juried. Public attendance: 35,000-50,000. Free to public. Artists should apply by requesting an application by e-mail or telephone. Deadline for entry: mid-April. Application fee: $200. Space fee included with application fee. Exhibition space: 12×17 ft. For more information, artists should e-mail, call or send SASE.

TIPS "Show runs for five days. Have quality product, be able to stay for length of show, and have enough product."

🎭 FOREST HILLS FESTIVAL OF THE ARTS

P.O. Box 477, Smithtown NY 11787. (631)724-5966. Fax: (631)724-5967. E-mail: Showtiques@aol.com. Website: www.showtiques.com. Estab. 2001. Fine arts & crafts show held annually in May/June. Outdoors. Accepts photography, all arts & crafts made by the exhibitor. Juried. Number of exhibitors: 300. Public attendance: 175,000. Free to public. Deadline for entry: until full. Exhibition space: 10×10 ft. For more information, artists should visit website or call.

➕ 🎭 FOUNTAIN HILLS FINE ART & WINE AFFAIRE

16810 E. Avenue of the Fountains, Fountain Hills AZ 85268. (480)837-5637. Fax: (480)837-2355. E-mail: info@thunderbirdartists.com. Website: www.thunderbirdartists.com. **Contact:** Denise Dodson, president. Estab. 2005. Fine arts & crafts show held annually in

mid-March (see website for specifics). Outdoors. Accepts photography, paintings, bronzes, baskets, jewelry, stone, pottery. Juried; CEO blind juries by medium. Number of exhibitors: 125. Public attendance: 25,000. Public admission: $3. Apply online at www.zapplication.com. Deadline for entry: November (see website for specifics). Application fee: $30. Space fee: $410-1,230. Exhibition space: 10×10 - 10×30 ft. For more information, artists should e-mail, call or see website.

TIPS "A clean, gallery-type presentation is very important."

🎭 FOURTH AVENUE SPRING STREET FAIR

434 E. 9th St., Tucson AZ 85705. (520)624-5004 or (800)933-2477. Fax: (520)624-5933. E-mail: kurt@fourthavenue.org. Website: www.fourthavenue.org. Estab. 1970. Arts & crafts fair held annually in late March/early April (see website for details). Outdoors. Accepts photography, drawing, painting, sculpture, arts & crafts. Juried by 5 jurors. Awards/prizes: Best of Show. Number of exhibitors: 400. Public attendance: 300,000. Free to the public. Artists should apply by completing the online application at www.zapplication.org. Exhibition space: 10×10 ft. Average gross sales/exhibitor: $3,000. For more information, artists should e-mail, visit website, call, send SASE.

🎭 FOURTH AVENUE WINTER STREET FAIR

434 E. 9th St., Tucson AZ 85705. (520)624-5004 or (800)933-2477. Fax: (520)624-5933. E-mail: kurt@fourthavenue.org. Website: www.fourthavenue.org. Estab. 1970. Arts & crafts fair held annually in December. Outdoors. Accepts photography, drawing, painting, sculpture, arts & crafts. Juried by 5 jurors. Awards/prizes: Best of Show. Number of exhibitors: 400. Public attendance: 300,000. Free to the public. Artists should apply by completing the online application at www.zapplication.org. Deadline for entry: September. Exhibition space: 10×10 ft. Average gross sales/exhibitor: $3,000. For more information, artists should e-mail, visit website, call, send SASE.

🎭 FOURTH OF JULY STREET FAIR

501 Poli St., #226, Ventura CA 93002. (805)654-7749. Fax: (805)648-1030. E-mail: mgodoy@ci.ventura.ca.us. Website: www.venturastreetfair.com. **Contact:** Michelle Godoy. Estab. 1976. Fine arts & crafts show

held annually in July. Outdoors. Accepts photography. Juried by a panel of 3 artists who specialize in various mediums; photos of work required. Number of exhibitors: 75-300. Public attendance: 30,000-50,000. Free to public. Artists should apply by downloading application from website or call to request application. Space fee: $175-225. Exhibition space: 10×10 ft. For more information, artists should e-mail, visit website or call.

TIPS "Be friendly, outgoing; know the area for pricing."

ⓘ FOURTH STREET FESTIVAL FOR THE ARTS & CRAFTS

P.O. Box 1257, Bloomington IN 47402. (812)335-3814. E-mail: info@4thstreet.rg. Website: www.4thstreet. org. Estab. 1976. Fine arts & crafts show held annually Labor Day weekend. Outdoors. Accepts photography, clay, glass, fiber, jewelry, painting, graphic, mixed media, wood. Juried by a 4-member panel. Awards/prizes: Best of Show ($750), 1st, 2nd, 3rd in 2D and 3D. Number of exhibitors: 105. Public attendance: 25,000. Free to public. Artists should apply by sending requests by mail, e-mail or download application from website at www.zapplication.org. Exhibition space: 10×10 ft. Average gross sales/exhibitor: $2,700. For more information, artists should e-mail, visit website, call or send for information with SASE.

TIPS Be professional.

ⓘ FRANKFORT ART FAIR

P.O. Box 566, Frankfort MI 49635. (231)352-7251. Fax: (231)352-6750. E-mail: fcofc@frankfort-elberta. com. Website: www.frankfort-elberta.com. **Contact:** Joanne Bartley, executive director. Fine art fair held annually in August. Outdoors. Accepts photography, clay, glass, jewelry, textiles, wood, drawing/graphic arts, painting, sculpture, baskets, mixed media. Juried by 3 photos of work, 1 photo of booth display and 1 photo of work in progress. Prior exhibitors are not automatically accepted. No buy/sell allowed. Artists should apply by downloading application from website, e-mailing or calling. Deadline for entry: early May. Jury fee: $15. Space fee: $105 for Friday and Saturday. Exhibition space: 12×12 ft. For more information, artists should e-mail or visit website.

FREDERICK FESTIVAL OF THE ARTS

15 W. Patrick St., Frederick MD 21701. (301)662-4190. Fax: (301)663-3084. E-mail: info@frederickarts

council.org. Website: www.frederickarts.org. Juried 2-day fine arts festival held annually the 1st weekend of June along Carroll Creek Linear Park in downtown Frederick. Features approximately 115 artists from across the country, two stages of musical performances, children's crafts and activities, artist demonstrations, as well as interactive classical theater performances. Apply online at www.zapplication.org. Application fee: $25. Space fee: starts at $395, depending on size and needs. For more information, call, e-mail or visit website.

TIPS "Pricing is key. People like to feel like they are getting a deal."

ⓘ GARRISON ART CENTER FINE ART & CRAFT FAIR

23 Garrison's Landing, P.O. Box 4, Garrison NY 10524. (845)424-3960. E-mail: info@garrisonart center.org. Website: www.garrisonartcenter.org. Fine arts & crafts show held annually 3rd weekend in August. Outdoors. Accepts all mediums. Juried by a committee of artists and community members. Number of exhibitors: 100. Public attendance: 10,000. Artists should call for application form or download from website. Deadline for entry: April. Exhibition space: 10×10 ft. For more information, artists should e-mail, visit website, call, send SASE.

TIPS "Have an inviting booth and be pleasant and accessible. Don't hide behind your product-engage the audience."

ⓘ GENEVA ARTS FAIR

8 S. 3rd St., Geneva IL 60134. (630)232-6060. Fax: (630)232-6083. E-mail: chamberinfo@geneva chamber.com. Website: www.genevachamber.com/festivals. Fine arts & crafts show held annually in late-July (see website for details). Outdoors. Juried. "Victorian homes-turned-businesses in the downtown historic district serve as a backdrop for the fine arts show." Showcases over 150 artists from across the country. Accepts photography, pottery, fiber, printmaking, glass, mixed media, watercolor, oil/acrylic, wood, sculpture and jewelry. Application fee: $20. Application deadline: early February. Space fee: $280. Exhibit space: 1 "wall" approximately 6×8 ft. long. *A limited number of photography spaces are available.* Call, e-mail or visit website for more information, and to apply.

GERMANTOWN FESTIVAL

P.O. Box 381741, Germantown TN 38183. (901)757-9212. E-mail: gtownfestival@aol.com. Website: www.germantownfest.com. **Contact:** Melba Fristick, coordinator. Estab. 1971. Arts & crafts show held annually the weekend after Labor Day. Outdoors. Accepts photography, all arts & crafts mediums. Number of exhibitors: 400+. Public attendance: 65,000. Free to public. Artists should apply by sending applications by mail. Deadline for entry: until filled. Application/space fee: $190-240. Exhibition space: 10×10 ft. For more information, artists should e-mail, call or send SASE.

TIPS "Display and promote to the public. Price attractively."

GLOUCESTER WATERFRONT FESTIVAL

38 Charles St., Rochester NH 03867. (603)332-2616. E-mail: terrym@worldpath.net. Website: www.castleberryfairs.com. **Contact:** Terry Mullen, events coordinator. Estab. 1971. Arts & crafts show held the 3rd weekend in August in Gloucester, Massachusetts. Outdoors in Stage Fort Park. Accepts photography and all other mediums. Juried by photo, slide or sample. Number of exhibitors: 225. Public attendance: 50,000. Free to the public. Artists should apply by downloading application from website. Deadline for entry: until full. Space fee: $375. Exhibition space: 10×10 ft. Average gross sales/exhibitor: "Generally, this is considered an 'excellent' show, so I would guess most exhibitors sell ten times their booth fee, or in this case, at least $3,500 in sales." For more information, artists should visit website.

TIPS "Do not bring a book; do not bring a chair. Smile and make eye contact with everyone who enters your booth. Have them sign your guest book; get their e-mail address so you can let them know when you are in the area again. And, finally, make the sale—they are at the fair to shop, after all."

GOLD RUSH DAYS

P.O. Box 774, Dahlonega GA 30533. (706)864-7247. E-mail: festival@dahlonegajaycees.com. Website: www.dahlonegajaycees.com. Arts & crafts show held annually the 3rd full week in October. Accepts photography, paintings and homemade, handcrafted items. No digitally originated art work. Outdoors. Number of exhibitors: 300. Public attendance: 200,000. Free to the public. Artists should apply online under "Gold Rush," or send SASE to request application. Deadline:

March. Exhibition space: 10×10 ft. Artists should e-mail, visit website for more information.

TIPS "Talk to other artists who have done other shows and festivals. Get tips and advice from those in the same line of work."

GOOD OLD SUMMERTIME ART FAIR

P.O. Box 1753, Kenosha WI 53141. (262)654-0065. E-mail: KenoshaArtAssoc@yahoo.com. Website: www.kenoartassoc.tripod.com/events.html. Estab. 1975. Fine arts show held annually the 1st Sunday in June. Outdoors. Accepts photography, paintings, drawings, mosaics, ceramics, pottery, sculpture, wood, stained glass. Juried by a panel. Photos or slides required with application. Number of exhibitors: 100. Public attendance: 3,000. Free to public. Artists should apply by completing application form, and including fees and SASE. Deadline for entry: early April. Exhibition space: 12×12 ft. For more information, artists should e-mail, visit website or send SASE.

TIPS "Have a professional display, and be friendly."

GRADD ARTS & CRAFTS FESTIVAL

3860 US Hwy 60 W., Owensboro KY 42301. (270)926-4433. Fax: (270)684-0714. E-mail: bethgoetz@gradd.com. Website: www.gradd.com. **Contact:** Beth Goetz, festival coordinator. Estab. 1972. Arts & crafts show held annually 1st full weekend in October. Outdoors. Accepts photography taken by crafter only. Number of exhibitors: 180-200. Public attendance: 15,000+. Artists should apply by calling to be put on mailing list. Exhibition space: 15×15 ft. For more information, artists should e-mail, visit website or call.

TIPS "Be sure that only hand-crafted items are sold. No buy/sell items will be allowed."

GRAND FESTIVAL OF THE ARTS & CRAFTS

P.O. Box 429, Grand Lake CO 80447-0429. (970)627-3372. Fax: (970)627-8007. E-mail: glinfo@grandlakechamber.com. Website: www.grandlakechamber.com. Fine arts & crafts show held annually in June and September. Outdoors. Accepts photography, jewelry, leather, mixed media, painting, paper, sculpture, wearable art. Juried by chamber committee. Awards/prizes: Best in Show and People's Choice. Number of exhibitors: 60-75. Public attendance: 1,000+. Free to public. Artists should apply by submitting slides or photos. Deadline for entry: early June and early September. Application fee: $175; includes space fee and business license. Exhibition space: 10×10 ft. For more information, artists should e-mail or call.

GREAT LAKES ART FAIR

46100 Grand River Ave., Novi MI 48374. (248)348-5600. Fax: (248)347-7720. E-mail: info@great lakesartfair.com. Website: www.greatlakesartfair. com. **Contact:** Kristina Jones, event manager. Estab. 2009. Held twice a year. Accepts paintings, sculptures, metal and fiber work, jewelry, 2D and 3D art, ceramics and glass. Cash prizes are given. Number of exhibitors: 150-200. Public attendance: 12,000-15,000. Application fee: $30. Space fee: $400. Exhibition space: 10×12 ft.

TIPS E-mail, call or visit website for more information.

GREAT NECK STREET FAIR

Showtiques Crafts, Inc., P.O. Box 477, Smithtown NY 11787. (631)724-5966. Fax: (631)724-5967. E-mail: Showtiques@aol.com. Website: www.showtiques. com. Estab. 1978. Fine arts & crafts show held annually in early May (see website for details) in the Village of Great Neck. "Welcomes professional artists, craftspeople and vendors of upscale giftware." Outdoors. Accepts photography, all arts & crafts made by the exhibitor. Juried. Number of exhibitors: 250. Public attendance: 50,000. Free to public. Deadline for entry: until full. Space fee: $150; corner space for $175. Exhibition space: 10×10 ft. For more information, artists should e-mail, visit website or call.

GREENWICH VILLAGE ART FAIR

711 N. Main St., Rockford IL 61103. (815)968-2787. Fax: (815)316-2179. E-mail: ldennis@rockfordart museum.org. Website: www.rockfordartmuseum.org. Estab. 1948. Fine arts & crafts show held annually in September. Outdoors. Our application will open late October and close early January. Download prospectus to apply. Accepts photography and all mediums. Juried by a panel of artists and committee. Awards/prizes: Best of Show and Best of Categories. Number of exhibitors: 120. Public attendance: 7,000. Artists should apply by mail or locating prospectus on the website. Deadline for entry: April 30. Exhibition space: 10×10 ft. For more information, artists should e-mail, visit website or call.

GUILFORD CRAFT EXPO

P.O. Box 28, Woodstock NY 12498. (845)331-7900. E-mail: crafts@artrider.com. Website: guilfordart center.org; artrider.com. Estab. 1957. Fine craft & art show held annually in mid-July. Outdoors. Accepts photography, wearable and nonwearable fiber, metal and nonmetal jewelry, clay, leather, wood, glass, painting, drawing, prints, mixed media. Juried by 5 images of work and 1 of booth, viewed sequentially. Number of exhibitors: 180. Public attendance: 14,000. Public admission: $7. Artists should apply by downloading application from www.artrider.com or can apply online at www.zapplication.org. Deadline for entry: early January. Application fee: $45. Space fee: $630-655. Exhibition space: 10×10 ft. For more information, artists should e-mail, visit website, call.

GUNSTOCK SUMMER FESTIVAL

38 Charles St., Rochester NH 03867. (603)332-2616. Fax: (603)332-8413. E-mail: info@castleberryfairs. com. Website: www.castleberryfairs.com. Estab. 1971. Arts & crafts show held annually in early July in Gilford, New Hampshire (see website for details). Indoors and outdoors. Accepts photography and all other mediums. Juried by photo, slide or sample. Number of exhibitors: 100. Public attendance: 10,000. Free to the public. Artists should apply by downloading application from website. Deadline for entry: until full. Space fee: $275. Exhibition space: 10×8 (indoor) or 10×10 (outdoor). For more information, artists should visit website.

TIPS "Do not bring a book; do not bring a chair. Smile and make eye contact with everyone who enters your booth. Have them sign your guest book; get their e-mail address so you can let them know when you are in the area again. And, finally, make the sale-they are at the fair to shop, after all."

HIGHLAND MAPLE FESTIVAL

P.O. Box 223, Monterey VA 24465. (540)468-2550. Fax: (540)468-2551. E-mail: info@highlandcounty. org. Website: www.highlandcounty.org. Estab. 1958. Fine arts & crafts show held annually the 2nd and 3rd weekends in March. Indoors and outdoors. Accepts photography, pottery, weaving, jewelry, painting, wood crafts, furniture. Juried by 3 photos or slides. Number of exhibitors: 150. Public attendance: 35,000-50,000. "Vendors accepted until show is full." Exhibition space: 10×10 ft. For more information, artists should e-mail, visit website, call.

TIPS "Have quality work and good salesmanship."

⊕ HIGHLANDS ART LEAGUE'S ANNUAL FINE ARTS & CRAFTS FESTIVAL

1989 Lakeview Dr., Sebring FL 33870. (863)385-6682. Fax: (863)385-6611. E-mail: director@highlands artleague.org. Website: www.highlandsartleague.org. **Contact:** Martile Blackman, festival director. Estab. 1966. Fine arts & crafts show held annually 2nd weekend in November. Outdoors. Accepts photography, pottery, painting, jewelry, fabric. Juried based on quality of work. Awards/prizes: monetary awards up to $3,100 and purchase awards. Number of exhibitors: 100+. Public attendance: more than 15,000. Free to the public. Artists should apply by calling or visiting website for application form. Deadline for entry: October. Exhibition space: 10×14 and 10×28 ft. Artists should e-mail for more information.

⊕ HINSDALE FINE ARTS FESTIVAL

22 E. First St., Hinsdale IL 60521. (630)323-3952. Fax: (630)323-3953. E-mail: info@hinsdalechamber.com. Website: www.hinsdalechamber.com. Fine arts show held annually in mid-June. Outdoors. Accepts photography, ceramics, painting, sculpture, fiber arts, mixed media, jewelry. Juried by 3 slides. Awards/prizes: Best in Show, President's Award and 1st, 2nd and 3rd place in 2D and 3D categories. Number of exhibitors: 140. Public attendance: 2,000-3,000. Free to public. Artists should apply online at www.zapplication.org. Deadline for entry: First week in March. Application fee: $30. Space fee: $225. Exhibition space: 10×10 ft. For more information, artists should e-mail or visit website.

TIPS "Original artwork sold by artist."

⊕ HOLIDAY ARTS & CRAFTS SHOW

60 Ida Lee Dr., Leesburg VA 20176. (703)777-1368. Fax: (703)737-7165. E-mail: lfountain@leesburgva. gov. Website: www.idalee.org. Estab. 1990. Arts & crafts show held annually the 1st weekend in December. Indoors. Accepts photography, jewelry, pottery, baskets, clothing, accessories. Juried. Number of exhibitors: 95. Public attendance: 2,500. Free to public. Artists should apply by downloading application from website. Deadline for entry: August 31. Space fee: $110-150. Exhibition space: 10×7 ft. and 10×10 ft. For more information, artists should e-mail or visit website.

⊕ HOLIDAY CRAFTMORRISTOWN

P.O. Box 28, Woodstock NY 12498. (845)331-7900. Fax: (845)331-7484. E-mail: crafts@artrider.com. Website: www.craftsatmorristown.com. Estab. 1990. Fine arts & crafts show held annually in early December. Indoors. Accepts photography, wearable and nonwearable fiber, metal and nonmetal jewelry, clay, leather, wood, glass, painting, drawing, prints, mixed media. Juried by 5 images of work and 1 of booth, viewed sequentially. Number of exhibitors: 150. Public attendance: 5,000. Public admission: $7. Artists should apply by downloading application from www.artrider.com or can apply online at www.zapplication.org. Deadline for entry: early July. Application fee: $45. Space fee: $495. Exhibition space: 10×10 ft. For more information, artists should e-mail, visit website, call.

⊕ HOLLY ARTS & CRAFTS FESTIVAL

P.O. Box 2122, Pinehurst NC 28370. (910)295-7462. E-mail: sbharrison@earthlink.net. Website: www. pinehurstbusinessguild.com. **Contact:** Susan Harrison. Estab. 1978. Annual arts & crafts show held 3rd Saturday in October. Outdoors. Accepts quality photography, arts and crafts. Juried based on uniqueness, quality of product and overall display. Awards/prizes: plaque given to Best in Show. Number of exhibitors: 200. Public attendance: 7,000. Free to the public. Artists should apply online. Deadline for entry: late March. Space fee: $75. Exhibition space: 10×10 ft. For more information, artists should call or visit website.

HOME, CONDO AND GARDEN ART & CRAFT FAIR

P.O. Box 486, Ocean City MD 21843. (410)213-8090. Fax: (410)213-8092. E-mail: oceanpromotions@ beachin.net. Website: www.oceanpromotions.info. Estab. 1984. Fine arts & crafts show held annually in March. Indoors. Accepts photography, carvings, pottery, ceramics, glass work, floral, watercolor, sculpture, prints, oils, pen and ink. Number of exhibitors: 125. Public attendance: 12,000. Public admission: $7/adults; $6/seniors & students; 13 and under free. Artists should apply by e-mailing request for info and application (can also be completed online). Deadline for entry: until full. Space fee: $250. Exhibition space: 8×12 ft. For more information, artists should e-mail, visit website or call.

HOME DECORATING & REMODELING SHOW

P.O. Box 230699, Las Vegas NV 89105-0699. (702)450-7984; (800)343-8344. Fax: (702)451-7305. E-mail: spvandy@cox.net. Website: www.nashvillehomeshow.com. Estab. 1983. Home show held annually in early September (see website for details). Indoors. Accepts photography, sculpture, watercolor, oils, mixed media, pottery. Awards/prizes: Outstanding Booth Award. Number of exhibitors: 300-350. Public attendance: 25,000. Public admission: $8. Artists should apply by calling. Marketing is directed to middle and above income brackets. Deadline for entry: open until filled. Space fee: $900+. Exhibition space: 9×10 ft. For more information, artists should call or visit website.

HOT SPRINGS ARTS & CRAFTS FAIR

308 Pullman, Hot Springs AR 71901. (501)623-9592. E-mail: sephpipkin@aol.com. Website: www.hotspringsartsandcraftsfair.com. Contact: Peggy Barnett. Estab. 1968. Fine arts & crafts show held annually the 1st full weekend in October at the Garland County Fairgrounds. Indoors and outdoors. Accepts photography and varied mediums ranging from heritage, crafts, jewelry, furniture. Juried by a committee of 12 volunteers. Number of exhibitors: 350+. Public attendance: 50,000+. Free to public. Deadline for entry: August. Space fee: $100-200. Exhibition space: 10×10 or 10×20 ft. For more information, and to apply, artists should e-mail, call or visit website.

HYDE PARK ARTS & CRAFTS ADVENTURE

P.O. Box 1326, Palatine IL 60078. (312)751-2500, (847)991-4748. Fax: (847)21-5853. E-mail: asoa@webtv.net or asoaartists@aol.com. Website: www.americansocietyofartists.org. Estab. 2006. Arts & crafts show held once a year in late September. Event held in Chicago, Illinois. Outdoors. Accepts photography, painting, glass, wood, fiber arts, hand-crafted candles, quilts, sculpture and more. Juried by 4 slides or photos of work and 1 slide or photo of display; #10 SASE; a résumé or show listing is helpful. Number of exhibitors: 50. Free to the public. Artists should apply by submitting jury materials. To jury via e-mail: Asoaartists@aol.com. If juried in, you will receive a jury/approval number. See website for jurying online. Deadline for entry: 2 months prior to show or earlier if spaces fill. Entry fee: $155. Exhibition space: approximately 100 sq. ft. for single space; other sizes are available. For more information, artists should send SASE, submit jury material.

TIPS "Remember that when you are at work in your studio, you are an artist. But when you are at a show, you are a business person selling your work."

STAN HYWET HALL & GARDENS WONDERFUL WORLD OF OHIO MART

714 N. Portage Path, Akron OH 44303. (330)836-5533 or (888)836-5533. E-mail: info@StanHywet.org. Website: www.stanhywet.org. Estab. 1966. Arts & crafts show held annually 1st full weekend in October. Outdoors. Accepts photography and all mediums. Juried 2 Saturdays in January and via mail application. Awards/prizes: Best Booth Display. Number of exhibitors: 115. Public attendance: 15,000-20,000. Deadline: June 1. Application fee: $25, nonrefundable. Application available online. Space fee: $525-750. Exhibition space: 10×10 or 10×15 ft. For more information, artists should visit website or call.

INDIANA ART FAIR

650 W. Washington St., Indianapolis IN 46204. (317)232-8293. Fax: (317)233-8268. E-mail: jhahn@dnr.in.gov. Website: www.indianamuseum.org. Estab. 2004. Annual art/craft show held the third weekend of February. Indoors. Juried event; 5-6 judges award points in 3 categories. 80 exhibitors; 3,000 attendees. $7 admission for the public. Application fee $25. Space fee 4165; 80 square feet. Accepts ceramics, glass, fiber, jewelry, painting, sculpture, mixed media, drawing/pastels, garden, leather, surface decoration, wood, metal, printmaking, and photography.

TIPS "Make sure that your booth space complements your product and presents well. Good photography can be key for juried shows."

INDIAN WELLS ARTS FESTIVAL

78-200 Miles Ave., Indian Wells CA 92210. (760)346-0042. Fax: (760)346-0042. E-mail: info@indianwellsartsfestival.com. Website: www.indianwellsartsfestival.com. Contact: Dianne Funk, producer. "A premier fine arts festival attracting thousands annually. The Indian Wells Arts Festival brings a splash of color to the beautiful grass concourse of the Indian Wells Tennis Garden. This spectacular venue transforms into an artisan village featuring 200 judged and juried artists and hundreds of pieces of one-of-a-kind artwork available for sale. Watch glass blowing, monumental rock sculpting, wood carving, pottery wheel demonstrations, weaving and mural painting. Wine tasting, gourmet market, children's activities, entertainment and refreshments add to the festival atmosphere." See Website for information and an application.

TIPS "Have a professional display of work. Be approachable and engage in conversation. Don't give up—people sometimes need to see you a couple of times before they buy."

🎧 INTERNATIONAL FOLK FESTIVAL

201 Hay St., Fayetteville NC 28302. (910)323-1776. Fax: (910)323-1727. E-mail: ashleyh@theartscouncil. com. Website: www.theartscouncil.com. **Contact:** Ashley Hunt, special events coordinator; Kelvin Culbreth, director of special events. Estab. 1978. Fine arts & crafts show held annually the last weekend in September. Outdoors. Accepts photography, painting of all mediums, pottery, woodworking, sculptures. Work must be original. Juried. Awards: $1,000 in cash prizes. Number of exhibitors: 120+. Public attendance: 85,000-100,000 over two days. Free to public. Artists should apply on the website. Deadline for entry: early September. Application fee: $75; includes space fee. Exhibition space: 10×10 ft. For more information, artists should e-mail or visit website.

TIPS "Have reasonable prices."

🎧 ISLE OF EIGHT FLAGS SHRIMP FESTIVAL

18 N. 2nd St., Fernandina Beach FL 32034. (904)271-7020. Fax: (904)261-1074. E-mail: mailbox@islandart. org. Website: www.islandart.org. Estab. 1963. Fine arts & crafts show and community celebration held annually the 1st weekend in May. Outdoors. Accepts all mediums. Juried. Awards: $9,700 in cash prizes. Number of exhibitors: 300. Public attendance: 150,000. Free to public. Artists should apply by downloading application from website. Deadline for entry: late January. Application fee: $30. Space fee: $200. Exhibition space: 10×12 ft. Average gross sales/exhibitor: $1,500+. For more information, artists should visit website.

TIPS "Quality product and attractive display."

🎧 JOHNS HOPKINS UNIVERSITY SPRING FAIR

3400 N. Charles St., Mattin Suite 210, Baltimore MD 21218. (410)513-7692. Fax: (410)516-6185. E-mail: springfair@gmail.com. Website: www.jhuspringfair. com. Estab. 1972. Fine arts & crafts, campus-wide festival held annually in April. Outdoors. Accepts photography and all mediums. Juried. Number of exhibitors: 80. Public attendance: 20,000+. Free to public. Artists should apply via website. Deadline for entry: early March. Application fee: $200. Space fee: $200. Exhibition space: 10×10 ft. For more information, artists should e-mail, visit website or call.

TIPS "Artists should have fun displays, good prices, good variety and quality pieces."

JUBILEE FESTIVAL

Eastern Shore Chamber of Commerce, P.O. Drawer 310, Daphne AL 36526. (251)621-8222 or (251)928-6387. Fax: (251)621-8001. E-mail: specialevents@ eschamber.com. Website: www.eschamber.com. Estab. 1952. Fine arts & crafts show held in late September in Olde Towne of Daphne, Alabama. Outdoors. Accepts photography and fine arts and crafts. Juried. Awards/prizes: ribbons and cash prizes totaling $4,300 with Best of Show awarding $750. Number of exhibitors: 258. Free to the public. Space fee: $100. Exhibition space: 10×10 ft. For more information, and application form, artists should e-mail, call, see website.

KENTUCK FESTIVAL OF THE ARTS

503 Main Ave., Northport AL 35476. (205)758-1257. Fax: (205)758-1258. E-mail: kentuck@kentuck.org. Website: www.kentuck.org. Call or e-mail for more information. General information about the festival available on the Website. "Celebrates a variety of artistic styles ranging from folk to contemporary arts as well as traditional crafts. Each of the 250+ artists participating in the festival is either invited as a guest artist or is juried based on the quality and originality of their work. The guest artists are nationally recognized folk and visionary artists whose powerful visual images continue to capture national and international acclaim."

🎧 KETNER'S MILL COUNTY ARTS FAIR

P.O. Box 322, Lookout Mountain TN 37350. (423)267-5702. E-mail: contact@ketnersmill.org. Website: www.ketnersmill.org. **Contact:** Dee Nash, event coordinator. Estab. 1977. Arts & crafts show held annually the 3rd weekend in October held on the grounds of the historic Ketner's Mills, in Whitwell, Tennessee, and the banks of the Sequatchie River. Outdoors. Accepts photography, painting, prints, dolls, fiber arts, baskets, folk art, wood crafts, jewelry, musical instruments, sculpture, pottery, glass. Juried. Number of exhibitors: 170. Number of attendees: 10,000/day, depending on weather. Artists should apply online. Space fee: $125. Exhibition space: 15×15 ft. Average gross sales/exhibitor: $1,500.

TIPS "Display your best and most expensive work, framed. But also have smaller unframed items to sell. Never underestimate a show: Someone may come forward and buy a large item."

☺ KIA ART FAIR

Kalamazoo Institute of Arts, 314 S. Park St., Kalamazoo MI 49007. (269)349-7775. Fax: (269)349-9313. E-mail: museum@kiarts.org. Website: www.kiarts.org/artfair. Estab. 1951. Fine arts & crafts show held annually the 1st Friday and Saturday in June. Outdoors. "The KIA's annual art fair has been going strong for 60 years. Still staged in shady, historic Bronson Park, the fair boasts more hours, more artists and more activities. It now spans 2 full days. The art fair provides patrons with more time to visit and artists with an insurance day in case of rain. Some 210 artists will be invited to set up colorful booths. Numerous festivities are planned, including picnics in the park, public art activities, street performers and an artist dinner. For more information, visit www.kiarts.org/artfair."

✚ ☺ KINGS MOUNTAIN ART FAIR

13106 Skyline Blvd., Woodside CA 94062. (650)851-2710. E-mail: kmafsecty@aol.com. Website: www.kingsmountainartfair.org. **Contact:** Carrie German, administrative assistant. Estab. 1963. Fine arts & crafts show held annually Labor Day weekend. Fundraiser for volunteer fire dept. Accepts photography, ceramics, clothing, 2D, painting, glass, jewelry, leather, sculpture, textile/fiber, wood. Juried. Number of exhibitors: 138. Public attendance: 10,000. Free to public. Deadline for entry: late January. Application fee: $10 (online). Exhibition space: 10×10 ft. Average gross sales/exhibitor: $3,500. For more information, artists should e-mail, visit website, call or send SASE.

TIPS "Read and follow the instructions. Keep an open mind and be flexible."

☺ KRASL ART FAIR ON THE BLUFF

707 Lake Blvd., St. Joseph MI 49085. (269)983-0271. Fax: (269)983-0275. E-mail: info1@krasl.org. Website: www.krasl.org. Estab. 1962. Fine arts & crafts show held annually in early July (see website for details).

Outdoors. Accepts photography, painting, digital art, drawing, pastels, wearable and nonwearable fiber art, glass, jewelry, sculpture, printmaking, metals and woods. Number of exhibitors: 216. Number of attendees: more than 70,000. Free to public. Application fee: $30. Applications are available online through www.zapplication.com. Deadline for entry: approximately mid-January. There is on-site jurying the same day of the fair and approximately 50% are invited back without having to pay the $30 application fee. Space fee: $250. Exhibition space: 15×15 ft. or $275 for 20×20 ft. (limited). Average gross sales/exhibitor: $3,000. For more information, artists should e-mail or visit website.

TIPS "Be willing to talk to people in your booth. You are your own best asset!"

☺ LAKE CITY ARTS & CRAFTS FESTIVAL

P.O. Box 1147, Lake City CO 81235. E-mail: info@lakecityarts.org. Website: www.lakecityarts.org. Estab. 1975. Fine arts/arts & craft show held annually 3rd Tuesday in July. One-day event. Outdoors. Accepts photography, jewelry, metal work, woodworking, painting, handmade items. Juried by 3-5 undisclosed jurors. Prize: Winners are entered in a drawing for a free booth space in the following year's show. Number of Exhibitors: 85. Public Attendance: 500. Free to the public. Space fee: $75. Exhibition space: 12×12 ft. Average gross sales/exhibitor: $500-$1,000. For more information, and application form, artists should visit website.

TIPS "Repeat vendors draw repeat customers. People like to see their favorite vendors each year or every other year. If you come every year, have new things as well as your best-selling products."

☺ LEEPER PARK ART FAIR

22180 Sundancer Ct., Villa 504, Estero FL 33928. (239)495-1783. E-mail: Studio266@aol.com. Website: www.leeperparkartfair.org. **Contact:** Judy Ladd, director. Estab. 1967. Fine arts & crafts show held annually in June. Indoors. Accepts photography and all areas of fine art. Juried by slides. Awards/prizes: $3,500. Number of exhibitors: 120. Public attendance: 10,000. Free to public. Artists should apply by going to the website and clicking on "To Apply." Deadline for entry: early March. Exhibition space: 12×12 ft. Average gross sales/exhibitor: $5,000. For more information, artists should e-mail or send SASE.

TIPS "Make sure your booth display is well presented and, when applying, slides are top notch!"

🎧 LES CHENEAUX FESTIVAL OF ARTS

Les Cheneaux Islands Chamber of Commerce, P.O. Box 301, Cedarville MI 49719. (906)484-3935; (888)364-7526. Fax: (906)484-6107. Website: www.les cheneaux.net/?annualevents. Estab. 1976. Fine arts & crafts show held annually 2nd Saturday in August. Outdoors. Accepts photography and all other media; original work and design only; no kits or commercially manufactured goods. Juried by a committee of 10. Submit 4 slides (3 of the artwork; 1 of booth display). Awards: monetary prizes for excellent and original work. Number of exhibitors: 70. Public attendance: 8,000. Public admission: $7. Artists should fill out application form to apply. Deadline for entry: April 1. Application fee: $65. Exhibition space: 10×10 ft. Average gross sales/exhibitor: $5-500. For more information, artists should call, send SASE, or visit website.

⭕ 🎧 LIBERTY ARTS SQUARED

P.O. Box 302, Liberty MO 64069. E-mail: staff@libertyartssquared.org. Website: www.liberty artssquared.org. Estab. 2010. Outdoor fine art/craft show held annually. Accepts all mediums. Awards: prizes totaling $4,000; Literary Arts for Awards–$500; Visual Arts for Awards–$1,500; Folk Art for Awards–$1,500; Overall Best of Show Award–$500. Free admission to the public; free parking. Application fee: $25. Space fee: $75. Exhibition space: 10×10 ft. For more information, e-mail or visit website.

🎧 LILAC FESTIVAL ARTS & CRAFTS SHOW

E-mail: lilacfestival@gmail.com. Website: www.lilac festival.com. Estab. 1985. Arts & crafts show held annually in mid-May (see website for details). Outdoors. Accepts photography, painting, ceramics, woodworking, metal sculpture, fiber. Juried by a panel. Number of exhibitors: 150. Public attendance: 25,000. Free to public. Exhibition space: 10×10 ft. Space fee: $200. For more information, and to apply, artists should e-mail or visit website.

🎧 LOMPOC FLOWER FESTIVAL

Sponsored by Cyprus Gallery, ATTN: Flower Festival, c/o LVAA, 119 E. Cypress Ave., Lompoc CA 93436. (805)737-1129. E-mail: jazzybec@verizon.net. Website: www.lompocvalleyartassociation.com. **Contact:** Becky Jazo. Estab. 1942. Show held annually last week in June. Festival event includes a parade, food booths, entertainment, beer garden and commercial center, which is not located near arts & crafts area. Outdoors. Accepts photography, fine art, woodworking, pottery, stained glass, fine jewelry. Juried by 5 members of the Lompoc Valley Art Association. Vendor must submit 5 photos of their craft and a description on how to make the craft. Free to public. Artists should apply by calling for application or download application from website. Deadline for entry: early May. Application fee: $200, plus insurance. Exhibition space: 12×16 ft. For more information, artists should visit website, call the gallery or send SASE.

TIPS "Artists should have prices that are under $100 to succeed."

MADISON CHAUTAUQUA FESTIVAL OF ART

601 W. First St., Madison IN 47250. (812)265-6100. Fax: (812)273-3694. E-mail: georgie@madison chautauqua.com. Website: www.madisonchautauqua.com. **Contact:** Georgie Kelly, coordinator. Estab. 1971. "Enjoy this juried fine arts & crafts show, featuring painting, sculpture, stained glass, textiles, pottery and more amid the tree-lined streets of Madison's Historic district. Stop by the Riverfront Food-Fest for delicious treats. Relax and listen to the Live Performances on the Lanier Mansion lawn on the riverfront, and enjoy strolling performers." Takes place in late September. "Painting (2D artists may sell prints but must include originals as well), drawing, photography, sculpture, weaving, wearables, jewelry, fiber, wood, baskets, clay/pottery, glass, paper and leather. Other media will be considered, individually. No buy-sell, imports or kits. The number of artists in each category is limited to protect the integrity of the show. "

TIPS "Be honest with products. Communicate with organizers. Fair market price for area."

🎧 MASON ARTS FESTIVAL

Mason-Deerfield Arts Alliance, P.O. Box 381, Mason OH 45040. (513)309-8585. E-mail: masonarts@gmail.com. Website: www.masonarts.org. Fine arts & crafts show held annually in mid-September (see website for details). Indoors and outdoors. Accepts photography, graphics, printmaking, mixed media; painting and drawing; ceramics, metal sculpture; fiber, glass, jewelry, wood, leather. Juried. Awards/prizes: $3,000+.

Number of exhibitors: 75-100. Public attendance: 3,000-5,000. Free to the public. Artists should apply by visiting website for application, e-mailing or calling. Deadline for entry: April 1. Jury fee: $25. Space fee: $75. Exhibition space: 12×12 ft.; artist must provide 10×10 ft. pop-up tent.

○ City Gallery show is held indoors; these artists are not permitted to participate outdoors and vice versa. City Gallery is a juried show featuring approximately 30-50 artists who may show up to 2 pieces.

○ MEMORIAL WEEKEND ARTS & CRAFTS FESTIVAL

38 Charles St., Rochester NH 03867. (603)332-2616. Fax: (603) 332-8413. E-mail: info@castleberryfairs. com. Website: www.castleberryfairs.com. Estab. 1989. Arts & crafts show held annually on Memorial Day weekend in Meredith, New Hampshire. Outdoors. Accepts photography and all other mediums. Juried by photo, slide or sample. Number of exhibitors: 85. Public attendance: 7,500. Free to the public. Artists should apply by downloading application from website. Deadline for entry: until full. Space fee: $325. Exhibition space: 10×10 ft. For more information, artists should visit website.

TIPS "Do not bring a book; do not bring a chair. Smile and make eye contact with everyone who enters your booth. Have them sign your guest book; get their e-mail address so you can let them know when you are in the area again. And, finally, make the sale-they are at the fair to shop, after all."

○ MICHIGAN STATE UNIVERSITY HOLIDAY ARTS & CRAFTS SHOW

319 MSU Union, East Lansing MI 48824. (517)355-3354. E-mail: uab@hfs.msu.edu. Website: www.uabevents.com. Estab. 1963. Arts & crafts show held annually 1st weekend in December. Indoors. Accepts photography, basketry, candles, ceramics, clothing, sculpture, soaps, drawings, floral, fibers, glass, jewelry, metals, painting, graphics, pottery, wood. Juried by a panel of judges using the photographs submitted by each vendor to eliminate commercial products. They will evaluate on quality, creativity and crowd appeal. Number of exhibitors: 220. Public attendance: 15,000. Free to public. Artists should apply online. Exhibition space: 8×5 ft. For more information, artists should visit website or call.

○ MICHIGAN STATE UNIVERSITY SPRING ARTS & CRAFTS SHOW

University Activities Board, Spring Arts & Crafts Show, ATTN: Stephanie Bierlein, 319 MSU Union, East Lansing MI 48824. (517)355-3354. Fax: (517)432-2448. E-mail: artsandcrafts@uabevents.com. Website: www.uabevents.com. Estab. 1963. Arts & crafts show held annually the weekend before Memorial Day Weekend in mid-May in conjunction with the East Lansing Art Festival. Both shows are free for the public to attend. Outdoors. Accepts photography, basketry, candles, ceramics, clothing, sculpture, soaps, drawings, floral, fibers, glass, jewelry, metals, painting, graphics, pottery, wood. Juried by a panel of judges using the photographs submitted by each vendor to eliminate commercial products. They will evaluate on quality, creativity and crowd appeal. Number of exhibitors: 329. Public attendance: 60,000. Free to public. Artists can apply online beginning in February. Online applications will be accepted until show is filled. Application fee: $260 ($240 if apply online). Exhibition space: 10×10 ft. (double booth available, $500 or $480 online). For more information, artists should visit website or call.

○ MID-MISSOURI ARTISTS CHRISTMAS ARTS & CRAFTS SALE

P.O. Box 116, Warrensburg MO 64093. (660)747-6092. E-mail: rlimback@iland.net. Estab. 1970. Holiday arts & crafts show held annually in November. Indoors. Accepts photography and all original arts and crafts. Juried by 3 good-quality color photos (2 of the artwork, 1 of the display). Number of exhibitors: 50. Public attendance: 1,200. Free to the public. Artists should apply by e-mailing or calling for an application form. Deadline for entry: early November. Space fee: $50. Exhibition space: 10×10 ft. For more information, artists should e-mail or call.

TIPS "Items under $100 are most popular."

MONTAUK POINT LIONS CLUB

PO Box 683, Montauk NY 11954. (631)668-2428. E-mail: info@onmontauk.com. Website: www.onmontauk.com/index.shtml. Estab. 1970. Arts & crafts show held annually Labor Day weekend. Outdoors. Accepts photography, arts & crafts. Number of exhibitors: 100. Public attendance: 1,000. Free to public. Exhibition space: 100 sq. ft. For more information, artists should call or visit website.

MOUNTAIN STATE FOREST FESTIVAL

P.O. Box 388, 101 Lough St., Elkins WV 26241. (304)636-1824. Fax: (304)636-4020. E-mail: msff@forestfestival.com; djudy@forestfestival.com. Website: www.forestfestival.com. **Contact:** Renee Heckel, executive director. Estab. 1930. Arts, crafts & photography show held annually in early October. Accepts photography and homemade crafts. Awards/prizes: cash awards for photography only. Number of exhibitors: 50. Public attendance: 50,000. Free to the public. Artists should apply by requesting an application form. For more information, artists should visit website, call, or visit Facebook page (Search "Mountain State Forest Festival").

MOUNT GRETNA OUTDOOR ART SHOW

P.O. Box 637, Mount Gretna PA 17064. (717)964-3270. Fax: (717)964-3054. E-mail: mtgretnaart@comcast.net. Website: www.mtgretnaarts.com. Estab. 1974. Fine arts & crafts show held annually 3rd full weekend in August. Outdoors. Accepts photography, oils, acrylics, watercolors, mixed media, jewelry, wood, paper, graphics, sculpture, leather, clay/porcelain. Juried by 4 professional artists who assign each applicant a numeric score. The highest scores in each medium are accepted. Awards/prizes: Judges' Choice Awards: 30 artists are invited to return the following year, jury exempt; the top 10 are given a monetary award of $250. Number of exhibitors: 250. Public attendance: 15,000-19,000. Public admission: $8; children under 12 free. Artists should apply via www.zapplication.org. Deadline for entry: early April. Application fee: $25. Space fee: $350 per 10×12 ft. space; $700 per 10×24 ft. double space. For more information, artists should e-mail, visit website, call.

NAPA RIVER WINE & CRAFTS FAIR

After the Gold Rush, P.O. Box 5171, Walnut Creek CA 94596. (707)257-0322. E-mail: julie@napadowntown.com. Website: www.napadowntown.com; www.afterthegoldrushfestivals.com. Wine and crafts show held annually in early September (see website for details). Outdoors. Accepts photography, jewelry, clothing, woodworking, glass, dolls, candles and soaps, garden art. Juried based on quality, uniqueness, and overall craft mix of applicants. Number of exhibitors: over 200. Public attendance: 20,000-30,000. Artists should apply online. Space fee: $200. Exhibition space: 10×10

ft. For more information, artists should e-mail, visit website or call.

TIPS "Electricity is available, but limited. There is a $40 processing fee for cancellations."

NEW ENGLAND ARTS & CRAFTS FESTIVAL

38 Charles St., Rochester NE 03867. (603)322-2616. Fax: (603)332-8413. E-mail: info@castleberryfairs.com. Website: www.castleberryfairs.com. Estab. 1988. Arts & crafts show held annually on Labor Day weekend in Topsfield, Massachusetts. Indoors and outdoors. Accepts photography and all other mediums. Juried by photo, slide or sample. Number of exhibitors: 250. Public attendance: 25,000. Artists should apply by downloading application from website. Deadline for entry: until full. Exhibition space: 100 sq. ft. Average gross sales/exhibitor: "Generally, this is considered an 'excellent' show, so I would guess most exhibitors sell ten times their booth fee, or in this case, at least $3,500 in sales." For more information, artists should visit website.

TIPS "Do not bring a book; do not bring a chair. Smile and make eye contact with everyone who enters your booth. Have them sign your guest book; get their e-mail address so you can let them know when you are in the area again. And, finally, make the sale—they are at the fair to shop, after all."

NEW ENGLAND CRAFT & SPECIALTY FOOD FAIR

38 Charles St., Rochester NH 03867. (603)332-2616. Fax: (603) 332-8413. E-mail: info@castleberryfairs.com. Website: www.castleberryfairs.com. Estab. 1995. Arts & crafts show held annually on Veteran's Day weekend in Salem, New Hampshire. Indoors. Accepts photography and all other mediums. Juried by photo, slide or sample. Number of exhibitors: 200. Public attendance: 15,000. Artists should apply by downloading application from website. Deadline for entry: until full. Space fee: $350-450. Exhibition space: 10×6 or 10×10 ft. Average gross sales/exhibitor: "Generally, this is considered an 'excellent' show, so I would guess most exhibitors sell ten times their booth fee, or in this case, at least $3,000 in sales." For more information, artists should visit website.

TIPS "Do not bring a book; do not bring a chair. Smile and make eye contact with everyone who enters your booth. Have them sign your guest book; get their e-mail address so you can let them know when you are in the area again. And, finally, make the sale—they are at the fair to shop, after all."

NEW MEXICO ARTS AND CRAFTS FAIR

2501 San Pedro St., NE, Suite 110, Albuquerque NM 87110. (505)884-9043. Fax: (505)884-9084. E-mail: info@nmartsandcraftsfair.org. Website: www.nmarts andcraftsfair.org. Estab. 1962. Fine arts & craft show held annually in June. Indoors. Accepts decorative and functional ceramics, digital art, drawing, precious and nonprecious jewelry, photography, paintings, printmaking, mixed media, metal, sculpture and wood. *Only New Mexico residents 18 years and older are eligible.* See website for more details.

NEW ORLEANS JAZZ & HERITAGE FESTIVAL

336 Camp St., Suite 250, New Orleans LA 70130. (504)410-4100. Fax: (504)410-4122. Website: www. nojazzfest.com. Estab. 1970. This festival showcases music, cuisine, arts and crafts from the region and around the world. The Louisiana Heritage Fair is held at the Fair Grounds Race Course over the course of 2 weekends (late April/early May; see website for details). Contact the Crafts Dept (at the above address) for an application. Deadline: late December (see website for details). Call or visit website for more information.

NEW SMYRNA BEACH ART FIESTA

New Smyrna Beach Visitors Bureau, 2238 State Road 44, New Smyrna Beach FL 32168. (386)424-2175; (800)541-9621. Fax: (386)424-2177. E-mail: kshelton@ cityofnsb.com. Website: www.cityofnsb.com; nsbfla. com/index.cfm. Estab. 1952. Arts & crafts show held annually the last full weekend in February. Outdoors. Accepts photography, oil, acrylics, pastel, drawings, graphics, sculpture, crafts, watercolor. Awards/prizes: $15,000 prize money; $1,600/category; Best of Show. Number of exhibitors: 250. Public attendance: 14,000. Free to public. Artists should apply by calling to get on mailing list. Applications are always mailed out the day before Thanksgiving. Deadline for entry: until full. Application/space fee: $150 plus tax. Exhibition space: 10×10 ft. For more information, artists should call.

NEW WORLD FESTIVAL OF THE ARTS

P.O. Box 994, Manteo NC 27954. (252)473-2838. Fax: (252)473-6044. E-mail: edward@outerbanks

christmas.com. Website: www.townofmanteo.com. **Contact:** Edward Greene. Estab. 1963. Fine arts & crafts show held annually in mid-August (see website for details). Outdoors. Juried. Location is the Waterfront in downtown Manteo. Features 80 selected artists from Vermont to Florida exhibiting and selling their works.

NORTH CONGREGATIONAL PEACH & CRAFT FAIR

17 Church St., New Hartford CT 06057. (860)379-2466. Estab. 1966. Arts & crafts show held annually in mid-August. Outdoors on the Green at Pine Meadow. Accepts photography, most arts and crafts. Number of exhibitors: 50. Public attendance: 500-2,000. Free to public. Artists should call for application form. Deadline for entry: August. Application fee: $60. Exhibition space: 11×11 ft.

TIPS "Be prepared for all kinds of weather."

OAK PARK AVENUE-LAKE ARTS & CRAFTS SHOW

P.O. Box 1326, Palatine IL 60078. (312)751-2500, (847)991-4748. Fax: (847)221-5853. E-mail: asoa@ webtv.net or asoaartists@aol.com. Website: www. americansocietyofartists.org. Estab. 1974. Fine arts & crafts show held annually in mid-August. Event held in Oak Park, Illinois. Outdoors. Accepts photography, painting, graphics, sculpture, glass, wood, paper, fiber arts, mosaics and more. Juried by 4 slides or photos of work and 1 slide or photo of display; #10 SASE; a résumé or show listing is helpful. Number of exhibitors: 150. Free to the public. Artists should apply by submitting jury materials. If you want to jury online please see our website and follow directions given there. To jury via e-mail: Asoaartists@aol.com. If juried in, you will receive a jury/approval number. Deadline for entry: 2 months prior to show or earlier if spaces fill. Entry fee: $170. Exhibition space: approximately 100 sq. ft. for single space; other sizes available. For more information, artists should send SASE, submit jury material.

TIPS "Remember that when you are at work in your studio, you are an artist. But when you are at a show, you are a business person selling your work."

OFFICIAL TEXAS STATE ARTS & CRAFTS FAIR

4000 Riverside Dr., Kerrville TX 78028. (830)896-5711; (888)835-1455. Fax: (830)896-5569. E-mail:

fair@tacef.org. Website: www.theartoftexas.com. Fine arts & crafts show held annually Memorial Day weekend on the grounds of the River Star Arts & Event Park. One of the top ranked arts & crafts events in the nation. Outdoors. Public admission: $10 (adult 3-day), $7 (adult Monday-only), $2 (children 12 & under). Application fee: $20. Space fee: $300-650. Exhibition space: 10×10 or 10×20 ft. (outdoor tent or indoor exhibit hall available). Application form online. Deadline: early December. For more information, artists should call, e-mail or visit website.

TIPS "Market and advertise."

OLD TOWN ART FAIR

1763 N. North Park Ave., Chicago IL 60614. (312)337-1938. E-mail: info@oldtowntriangle.com. Website: www.oldtownartfair.com. Fine art festival held annually in early June (see website for details). Located in the city's historic Old Town Triangle District. Artists featured are chosen by an independent jury of professional artists, gallery owners and museum curators. Features a wide-range of art mediums, including 2D- and 3D-mixed media, drawing, painting, photography, printmaking, ceramics, fiber, glass, jewelry and works in metal, stone and wood. Apply online at www.zapplication.org. For more information, call, e-mail or visit website.

🎧 ORCHARD LAKE FINE ART SHOW

P.O. Box 79, Milford MI 48381-0079. (248)684-2613. Fax: (248)684-0195. E-mail: patty@hotworks.org. Website: www.hotworks.org. **Contact:** Patty Narozny, show director. Estab. 2003. Fine arts & crafts show held annually late July (see website for details). Outdoors. Accepts photography, clay, glass, fiber, wood, jewelry, painting, prints, drawing, sculpture, metal, multimedia. Artist applications available via Zapplication, Juried Art Services, or via "manual" application. Awards $2,500 in prizes: $1,000 Best of Show; two $500 Purchase Awards; and five $100 Awards of Excellence. Admission $5; 12 & under free; free parking. Deadline: early March (see website for details). Space fee: $200. Exhibition space: 10×10, 10×15 or 10×20 ft. For more information, call, e-mail or visit website.

TIPS "Be attentive to your customers. Do not ignore anyone."

🎧 PANOPLY ARTS FESTIVAL, PRESENTED BY THE ARTS COUNCIL, INC.

700 Monroe St. SW, Suite. 2, Huntsville AL 35801. (256)519-2787. E-mail: tac@artshuntsville.org; vhinton@artshuntsville.org. Website: www.panoply.org. Estab. 1982. Fine arts show held annually the last weekend in April. Also features music and dance. Outdoors. Accepts photography, painting, sculpture, drawing, printmaking, mixed media, glass, fiber. Juried by a panel of judges chosen for their in-depth knowledge and experience in multiple mediums, and who jury from slides or disks in January. During the festival 1 judge awards various prizes. Number of exhibitors: 60-80. Public attendance: 140,000+. Public admission: $5/day or $10/weekend (children 12 and under free). Artists should e-mail, call, or go online for an application form. Deadline for entry: January. Space fee: $185. Exhibition space: 10×10 ft. (tent available, space fee $390). Average gross sales/exhibitor: $2,500. For more information, artists should e-mail or visit website.

🎧 PARADISE CITY ARTS FESTIVALS

30 Industrial Dr. E., Northampton MA 01060. (800)511-9725. Fax: (413)587-0966. E-mail: artist@paradisecityarts.com. Website: www.paradisecityarts.com. Estab. 1995. Five fine arts & crafts shows held annually in March, April, May, October and November. Indoors. Accepts photography, all original art and fine craft media. Juried by 5 slides or digital images of work and an independent board of jury advisors. Number of exhibitors: 150-275. Public attendance: 5,000-20,000. Public admission: $12. Artists should apply by submitting name and address to be added to mailing list or print application from website. Deadline for entry: September 9. Application fee: $30-45. Space fee: $650-1,500. Exhibition space: 8×10 and 10×20 ft. For more information, artists should e-mail, visit website or call.

🎧 PATTERSON APRICOT FIESTA

P.O. Box 442, Patterson CA 95363. (209)892-3118. Fax: (209)892-3388. E-mail: patterson_apricot_fiesta@hotmail.com. Website: www.apricotfiesta.com. **Contact:** Sandra Stobb, chairperson. Estab. 1984. Arts & crafts show held annually in May/June. Outdoors. Accepts photography, oils, leather, various handcrafts. Juried by type of product. Number of exhibitors: 140-150. Public attendance: 30,000. Free to the public.

Deadline for entry: mid-April. Application fee/space fee: $225/craft; $325/commercial. Exhibition space: 12×12 ft. For more information, artists should call, send SASE.

TIPS "Please get your applications in early!"

◯ PEND OREILLE ARTS COUNCIL ANNUAL ARTS & CRAFTS FAIR

P.O. Box 1694, Sandpoint ID 83864. (208)263-6139. E-mail: art@sandpoint.net. Website: www.artin sandpoint.org. Estab. 1978. Arts & crafts show held annually, second week in August. Outdoors. Accepts photography and all handmade, noncommercial works. Juried by 8-member jury. Number of exhibitors: 120. Public attendance: 5,000. Free to public. Artists should apply by sending in application, available in February, along with 4 images (3 of your work, 1 of your booth space). Deadline for entry: May 1. Application fee: $15. Space fee: $185-250, no commission taken. Exhibition space: 10×10 ft. or 10×15 ft (shared booths available). For more information, artists should e-mail, call or visit website.

◯ PETERS VALLEY ANNUAL CRAFT FAIR

19 Kuhn Rd., Layton NJ 07851. (973)948-5200. Fax: (973)948-0011. E-mail: craftfair@petersvalley.org, or via online contact form. Website: www.petersvalley. org. Estab. 1970. Arts & crafts show held annually in late September at the Sussex County Fairgrounds in Augusta. Indoors. Accepts photography, ceramics, fiber, glass, basketry, metal, jewelry, sculpture, printmaking, paper book art, drawing, painting. Juried. Awards/prizes: cash awards. Number of exhibitors: 185. Public attendance: 7,000-8,000. Public admission: $8. Artists should apply at www.zapplication.org. Deadline for entry: June 1. Application fee: $35. Space fee: $395. Exhibition space: 10 x 10 ft. Average gross sales/exhibitor: $2,000-5,000. For more information artists should e-mail, visit website or call.

◯ PRAIRIE ARTS FESTIVAL

201 Schaumburg Ct., Schaumburg IL 60193. (847)923-3605. Fax: (847)923-2458. E-mail: rbenvenuti@ ci.schaumburg.il.us. Website: www.prairiecenter.org. **Contact:** Roxane Benvenuti, special events coordinator. Event held in late May. "With thousands of patrons in attendance, an ad in the Prairie Arts Festival program is a great way to get your business noticed. Rates are reasonable, and an ad in the program gives you access to a select regional market. Sponsorship opportunities are also available. For more information, see the website."

TIPS "Submit your best work for the jury since these images are selling your work."

PUNGO STRAWBERRY FESTIVAL

P.O. Box 6158, Virginia Beach VA 23456. (757)721-6001. Fax: (757)721-9335. E-mail: pungofestival@aol. com. Website: www.pungostrawberryfestival.info. Estab. 1983. Arts & crafts show held annually on Memorial Day Weekend. Outdoors. Accepts photography and all media. Number of exhibitors: 60. Public attendance: 120,000. Free to Public; $5 parking fee. Artists should apply by calling for application or downloading a copy from the website and mail in. Deadline for entry: early March; applications accepted from that point until all spaces are full. Notice of acceptance or denial by early April. Application fee: $50 refundable deposit. Space fee: $200 (off road location); $450 (on road location). Exhibition space: 10×10 ft. For more information, artists should e-mail, visit website or call.

⊕ ◯ PYRAMID HILL ANNUAL ART FAIR

1763 Hamilton Cleves Rd., Hamilton OH 45013. (513)868-8336. Fax: (513)868-3585. E-mail: pyramid@ pyramidhill.org. Website: www.pyramidhill.org. Art fair held the last Saturday and Sunday of September. Call, e-mail or visit website for more information.

TIPS "Make items affordable! Quality work at affordable prices will produce profit."

◯ QUAKER ARTS FESTIVAL

P.O. Box 202, Orchard Park NJ 14127. (716)667-2787. E-mail: opjaycees@aol.com. Website: www.opjaycees. com. Estab. 1961. Fine arts & crafts show held annually in mid-September (see website for details). Outdoors. Accepts photography, painting, graphics, sculpture, crafts. Juried by 4 panelists during event. Awards/prizes: over $10,000 total cash prizes. Number of exhibitors: 330. Public attendance: 75,000. Free to the public. Artists should apply online, or by sending SASE. Deadline for entry: late August (see website for details). Space fee: $175 ($250 for double space). Exhibition space: 10×12 ft. (outdoor), 10×6 ft. (indoor). For more information, artists should call or visit website.

TIPS "Have an inviting booth and be pleasant and accessible. Don't hide behind your product—engage the audience."

RATTLESNAKE ROUNDUP

Evans County Wildlife Club, P.O. Box 292, Claxton GA 30417. (912)739-3820. Fax: (912)739-3827. E-mail: thall@claxtonevanschamber.com. Website: www.claxtonevanschamber.com. Estab. 1968. Arts & crafts show held annually 2nd weekend in March. Outdoors. Accepts photography and various mediums. Number of exhibitors: 150-200. Public attendance: 15,000-20,000. Artists should apply by filling out an application. Click on the "Registration Tab" located on the Rattlesnake Roundup home page. Deadline for entry: late February/early March (see website for details). Space fee: $85. Exhibition space: 10 ×16 ft. For more information, artists should e-mail, visit website or call.

TIPS "Your display is a major factor in whether people will stop to browse when passing by. Offer a variety."

🎧 RILEY FESTIVAL

312 E. Main St., Suite C, Greenfield IN 46140. (317)462-2141. Fax: (317)467-1449. E-mail: info@rileyfestival.com. Website: www.rileyfestival.com. **Contact:** Sarah Kesterson, public relations. Estab. 1970. Fine arts & crafts festival held in October. Outdoors. Accepts photography, fine arts, home arts, quilts. Juried. Awards/prizes: small monetary awards and ribbons. Number of exhibitors: 450. Public attendance: 75,000. Free to public. Artists should apply by downloading application on website. Deadline for entry: mid-September. Space fee: $185. Exhibition space: 10×10 ft. For more information, artists should visit website.

TIPS "Keep arts priced for middle-class viewers."

🎧 RIVERBANK CHEESE & WINE EXPOSITION

6618 3rd St., Riverbank CA 95367-2317. (209)863-9600. Fax: (209)863-9601. E-mail: events@riverbankcheese andwine.org. Website: www.riverbankcheeseand wine.org. **Contact:** Chris Elswick, event coordinator. Estab. 1977. Arts & crafts show and food show held annually 2nd weekend in October. Outdoors. Accepts photography, other mediums depends on the product. Juried by pictures and information about the artists. Number of exhibitors: 250. Public attendance: 60,000. Free to public. Artists should apply by calling and requesting an application. Applications also available on website. Deadline for entry: early September. Space fee: $345/arts & crafts; $465/commercial. Exhibition

space: 12×12 ft. For more information, artists should e-mail, visit website, call or send SASE.

TIPS Make sure your display is pleasing to the eye.

RIVERFRONT MARKET

The Riverfront Market Authority, P.O. Box 565, Selma AL 36702-0565. (334)874-6683. E-mail: info@ selmaalabama.com. Website: www.selmaalabama.com. Estab. 1972. Arts & crafts show held annually the 2nd Saturday in October. Outdoors. Accepts photography, painting, sculpture. Number of exhibitors: 200. Public attendance: 8,000. Public admission: $2. Artists should apply by calling or mailing to request application. Deadline for entry: September 1. Space fee: $40; limited covered space available at $60. Exhibition space: 10×10 ft. For more information, artists should call or visit website.

ROYAL OAK OUTDOOR ART FAIR

Recreation Dept., P.O. Box 64, Royal Oak MI 48068-0064. (248)246-3180. E-mail: artfair@ci.royal-oak.mi.us. Website: www.ci.royal-oak.mi.us. **Contact:** Recreation Office Staff. Estab. 1970. Fine arts & crafts show held annually in July. Outdoors. Accepts photography, collage, jewelry, clay, drawing, painting, glass, wood, metal, leather, soft sculpture. Juried. Number of exhibitors: 110. Public attendance: 25,000. Free to pubic. Artists should apply with online application form and 3 slides of current work. Space fee: $250 (plus a $20 non-refundable processing fee per medium). Exhibition space: 15×15 ft. For more information, artists should e-mail, call or visit website.

TIPS "Be sure to label your slides on the front with name, size of work and 'top'."

🎧 SACO SIDEWALK ART FESTIVAL

P.O. Box 336, 12½ Pepperell Square, Suite 2A, Saco ME 04072. (207)286-3546. E-mail: sacospirit@ hotmail.com. Website: www.sacospirit.com. Estab. 1970. Event held in late June. The Saco Sidewalk Arts Festival is an annual event organized and managed by Saco Spirit Inc., a non-profitorganization committed to making Saco a better place to live and work by enhancing the vitality of our downtown. The Saco Sidewalk Arts Festival is dedicated to promoting art and culture in our community. Space fee: $75. Exhibition space: 10×10. See website for more details.

TIPS "Offer a variety of pieces priced at various levels."

ART FAIRS

SANDY SPRINGS FESTIVAL

P.O. Box 422571, Atlanta GA 30342. (404)851-9111. Fax: (404)851-9807. E-mail: info@sandysprings festival.org; Patrick@affps.com; Randall@affps.com. Website: www.sandyspringsfestival.com. Estab. 1985. Fine arts & crafts show held annually in mid-September (see website for details). Outdoors. Accepts photography, painting, sculpture, jewelry, furniture, clothing. Juried by area professionals and nonprofessionals who are passionate about art. Awards/prizes: change annually; usually cash with additional prizes. Number of exhibitors: 100+. Public attendance: 20,000. Public admission: $5. Artists should apply via application on website. Application fee: $10 ($35 for late registration). Space fee: $200-350. Exhibition space: 10×10 or 10×20 ft. Average gross sales/exhibitor: $1,000. For more information, artists should e-mail or visit website.

TIPS "Most of the purchases made at Sandy Springs Festival are priced under $100. The look of the booth and its general attractiveness are very important, especially to those who might not know art."

SANTA CALI GON DAYS FESTIVAL

210 W. Truman Rd., Independence MO 64050. (816)252-4745. E-mail: tsingleton@independence chamber.org; tfreeland@independencechamber.org. Website: www.santacaligon.com. **Contact:** Terri Singleton or Teresa Freeland. Estab. 1973. Market vendors show held annually Labor Day weekend. Outdoors. Accepts photography, all other mediums. Juried by committee. Number of exhibitors: 240. Public attendance: 225,000. Free to public. Artists should apply by requesting application. Application requirements include completed application, application fee, 4 photos of product/art and 1 photo of display. Exhibition space: 8×8 ft. and 10×10 ft. For more information, artists should e-mail, visit website or call.

SANTA FE COLLEGE SPRING ARTS FESTIVAL

3000 NW 83rd St., Gainesville FL 32606. (352)395-5355. Fax: (352)336-2715. E-mail: Kathryn.lehman@ sfcollege.edu. Website: springartsfestival.com. **Contact:** Kathryn Lehman, coordinator-cultural programs. Fine arts festival held in early April (see website for details). "The festival is one of the 3 largest annual events in Gainesville and is known for its high quality, unique artwork." Held in the downtown his-

toric district. Public attendance: 130,000+. Call, e-mail or visit website for more information.

SAUSALITO ART FESTIVAL

P.O. Box 10, Sausalito CA 94966. (415)332-3555. Fax: (415)331-1340. E-mail: apply@sausalitoartfestival. org. Website: www.sausalitoartfestival.org. Estab. 1952. Fine arts & crafts show held annually Labor Day weekend. Outdoors. Accepts painting, photography, 2D and 3D mixed media, ceramics, drawing, fiber, functional art, glass, jewelry, printmaking, sculpture, watercolor, woodwork. Juried. Jurors are elected by their peers from the previous year's show (1 from each category). They meet for a weekend at the end of March and give scores of 1, 2, 4 or 5 to each applicant (5 being the highest). Number of exhibitors: 280. Public attendance: 40,000. Artists should apply by visiting website for instructions and application. Applications are through Juried Art Services. Deadline for entry: March. Exhibition space: 100 or 200 sq. ft. Average gross sales/exhibitor: $7,700. For more information, artists should visit website.

SCOTTSDALE ARTS FESTIVAL

7380 E. 2nd St., Scottsdale AZ 85251. (480)874-2787. Fax: 480-874-4699. Website: www.scottsdalearts festival.org. Estab. 1970. Fine arts & crafts show held annually in March. Outdoors. Accepts photography, jewelry, ceramics, sculpture, metal, glass, drawings, fiber, paintings, printmaking, mixed media, wood. Juried. Awards/prizes: 1st, 2nd, 3rd Places in each category and Best of Show. Number of exhibitors: 200. Public attendance: 40,000. Public admission: $7. Artists should apply through www.zapplication. org. Deadline for entry: October. Exhibition space: 100 sq. ft. For more information, artists should visit website.

SIDEWALK ART MART

Downtown Helena, Inc., Mount Helena Music Festival, 225 Cruse Ave., Suite B, Helena MT 59601. (406)447-1535. Fax: (406)447-1533. E-mail: hlnabid@ mt.net. Website: www.downtownhelena.com. Estab. 1974. Arts, crafts and music festival held annually in June in conjunction with the Mount Helena Music Festival. Outdoors. Accepts photography. No restrictions except to display appropriate work for all ages. Number of exhibitors: 50+. Public attendance: 5,000. Free to public. Artists should apply by visiting website to download application. Space fee: $100 ($125 if received after deadline). Exhibition space: 10 ×10 ft. For more information, artists should e-mail, visit website or call.

TIPS "Greet people walking by and have an eye-catching product in front of booth. We have found that high-end artists or expensively priced art booths that had business cards with e-mail or website information received many contacts after the festival."

◑ SIERRA MADRE WISTARIA FESTIVAL

37 Auburn Ave., Suite 1, Sierra Madre CA 91024. (626)355-5111. Fax: (626)306-1150. E-mail: info@ sierramadrechamber.com. Website: www.SierraMadre chamber.com. Fine arts, crafts and garden show held annually in March. Outdoors. Accepts photography, anything handcrafted. Juried. Craft vendors send in application and photos to be juried. Most appropriate are selected. Awards/prizes: Number of exhibitors: 175. Public attendance: 12,000. Free to public. Artists should apply by sending completed and signed application, 3-5 photographs of their work, application fee, license application, space fee and 2 SASEs. Deadline for entry: late December. Application fee: $25. Public Safety Fee (non-refundable) $25. Space fee: $175 and a city license fee of $31. Exhibition space: 10×10 ft. For more information, artists should e-mail, visit website or call. Applications can be found on chamber website.

TIPS "Have a clear and simple application. Be nice."

SKOKIE ART GUILD'S ART FAIR

5211 W. Oakton, Skokie IL 60076. (847)677-8163. E-mail: skokieart@aol.com. Website: www.skokieart guild.org. **Contact:** B. Willerman, chairperson. Outdoor fine art/craft show open to all artists (18+). Held on second weekend of July. Space fee: $150 for 10×10 ft. space. Awards: Guild awards, a Mayor's award and community business gift certificates are rallied. Deadline for application: mid-May.

TIPS Display your work in a professional manner: matted, framed, etc.

◑ SMITHVILLE FIDDLERS' JAMBOREE AND CRAFT FESTIVAL

P.O. Box 83, Smithville TN 37166. (615)597-8500. Website: www.smithvillejamboree.com. Estab. 1971. Arts & crafts show held annually the weekend nearest the Fourth of July holiday. Indoors. Juried by photos and personally talking with crafters. Awards/prizes: ribbons and free booth for following year for Best of Show, Best of Appalachian Craft, Best Display, Best New Comer. Number of exhibitors: 235. Public attendance: 130,000. Free to public. Artists should apply online. Deadline: June 1. Space fee: $125. Exhibition space: 12×12 ft. Average gross sales/exhibitors: $1,200+. For more information, artists should call or visit website.

◑ SOLANO AVENUE STROLL

1563 Solano Ave., #PMB 101, Berkeley CA 94707. (510)527-5358. E-mail: SAA@solanoavenueassn.org. Website: www.solanoave.org. Estab. 1974. Fine arts & crafts show held annually 2nd Sunday in September. Outdoors. "Since 1974, the merchants, restaurants, and professionals, as well as the twin cities of Albany and Berkeley have hosted the Solano Avenue Stroll, the east bay's largest street festival." Accepts photography and all other mediums. Juried by board of directors. Number of exhibitors: 140 spaces for crafts; 600 spaces total. Public attendance: 300,000. Free to the public. Artists should apply online in April, or send SASE. Space fee: $150. Exhibition space: 10×10 ft. For more information, artists should e-mail, visit website, send SASE.

TIPS "Artists should have a clean presentation; small-ticket items as well as large-ticket items; great customer service; enjoy themselves."

THE SOUTHWEST ARTS FESTIVAL

Indio Chamber of Commerce, 82921 Indio Blvd., Indio CA , 92201. (760)347-0676. Fax: (763)3476069. E-mail: swaf@indiochamber.org. Website: www.south westartsfest.com. Estab. 1986. Featuring over 275 acclaimed artists showing traditional, contemporary and abstract fine works of art and quality crafts, the festival is a major, internationally recognized cultural event attended by nearly 10,000 people. The event features a wide selection of clay, crafts, drawings, glass work, jewelry, metal works, paintings, photographs, printmaking, sculpture and textiles. Application fee: $50 before August 31; $65 after. Easy check-in and check-out procedures with safe and secure access to festival grounds for setup and breakdown. Allow advance set-up for artists with special requirements (very large art requiring the use of cranes, forklifts, etc., or artists with special needs.) Artist parking is free. Disabled artist parking is available. Apply online. For more information, artists should call, e-mail or visit website.

⊕ SPRING CRAFTMORRISTOWN

P.O. Box 28, Woodstock NY 12498. (845)331-7900. Fax: (845)331-7484. E-mail: crafts@artrider.com. Website: artrider.com. Estab. 1990. Fine arts & crafts show held annually in March or April. Indoors. Accepts photography, wearable and nonwearable fiber, metal and nonmetal jewelry, clay, leather, wood, glass, painting, drawing, prints, mixed media. Juried by 5 images of work and 1 of booth, viewed sequentially. Number of exhibitors: 150. Public attendance: 5,000. Public admission: $7. Artists should apply by downloading application from www.artrider.com or apply online at www.zapplication.org. Deadline for entry: January 1. Application fee: $45. Space fee: $475. Exhibition space: 10×10 ft. For more information, artists should e-mail, visit website, call.

⊕ SPRING CRAFTS AT LYNDHURST

P.O. Box 28, Woodstock NY 12498. (845)331-7900. Fax: (845)331-7484. E-mail: crafts@artrider.com. Website: artrider.com. Estab. 1984. Fine arts & crafts show held annually in early May. Outdoors. Accepts photography, wearable and nonwearable fiber, metal and nonmetal jewelry, clay, leather, wood, glass, painting, drawing, prints, mixed media. Juried by 5 images of work and 1 of booth, viewed sequentially. Number of exhibitors: 250. Public attendance: 14,000. Public admission: $10. Artists should apply by downloading application from www.artrider.com or can apply online at www.zapplication.org. Deadline for entry: January 1. Application fee: $45. Space fee: $745-845. Exhibition space: 10×10 ft. For more information, artists should e-mail, visit website, call.

SPRINGFEST

Southern Pines Business Association, P.O. Box 831, Southern Pines NC 28388. (910)315-6508. E-mail: spbainfo@southernpines.biz. Website: www.southernpines.biz. Estab. 1979. Arts & crafts show held annually last Saturday in April. Outdoors. Accepts photography and crafts. We host over 160 vendors from all around North Carolina and the country. Enjoy beautiful artwork and crafts including paintings, jewelry, metal art, photography, woodwork, designs from nature and other amazing creations. Event is held in conjunction with Tour de Moore, an annual bicycle race in Moore County, and is co-sponsored by the town of Southern Pines. Public attendance: 8,000. Free to the public. Deadline: March (see website for more details).

Space fee: $75. Exhibition space: 10×12 ft. For more information, artists should e-mail, visit website, call, send SASE. Apply online.

➕ ⊕ SPRING FINE ART & CRAFTS AT BROOKDALE PARK (BLOOMFIELD, NJ)

473 Latchung Ave., Bloomfield NJ 07003. (908)874-5247. Fax: (908)874-7098. E-mail: info@rosesquared.com. Website: www.rosesquared.com. **Contact:** Howard Rose, vice president. Estab. 1988. Fine arts & crafts show held annually in mid-June. Outdoors. Accepts photography and all other mediums. Juried. Number of exhibitors: 160. Public attendance: 12,000. Free to public. Artists should apply on the website. Deadline for entry: mid-May. Application fee: $25. Space fee varies by booth size; see application form on website for details. For more information, artists should visit the website.

TIPS "Have a range of priced items."

⊕ SPRING FINE ART & CRAFTS AT BROOKDALE PARK (MONTCLAIR, NJ)

12 Galaxy Court, Montclair NJ (908)874-5247. Fax: (908)874-7098. E-mail: info@rosesquared.com. Website: www.rosesquared.com. Estab. 1988. Fine arts & craft show held annually in mid-June Father's Day weekend. Outdoors. Accepts photography and all other mediums. Juried. Number of exhibitors: 180. Public attendance: 16,000. Free to the public. Artists should apply by downloading application from website or call for application. Deadline: 1 month before show date. Application fee: $25. Space fee: $340. Exhibition space: 120 sq. ft. For more information, artists should e-mail, visit website, call.

TIPS "Create a professional booth that is comfortable for the customer to enter. Be informative, friendly and outgoing. People come to meet the artist."

➕ ⊕ SPRING FINE ART & CRAFTS AT THE WESTFIELD ARMORY

500 Rahway Ave., Westfield NJ 07090. (908)874-5247. Fax: (908)874-7098. E-mail: info@rosesquared.com. Website: www.rosesquared.com. **Contact:** Howard Rose, vice president. Estab. 2010. Fine arts & crafts show held annually in early April. Indoors. Accepts photography and all other mediums. Juried by 4 images of your work. Number of exhibitors: 130. Public attendance: 4,000. Admission fee: $6. Artists should apply on the website. Deadline for entry: early March. Application fee: $25. Space fee varies by booth size;

see application form on website for details. For more information, artists should visit the website.

TIPS "Create a unique booth."

ST. CHARLES FINE ART SHOW

213 Walnut St., St. Charles IL 60174. (630)513-5386. E-mail: jennifer@dtown.org; adorsch@dtown.org; info@dtown.org. Website: www.dtown.org. Fine art fair held annually in late May. Outdoors. Accepts photography, painting, sculpture, glass, ceramics, jewelry, nonwearable fiber art. Juried by committee: submit 4 slides of art and 1 slide of booth/display. Awards/prizes: Cash awards of $3,500 awarded in several categories. $14,000 of art has been purchased through this program since its inception in 2005. Number of exhibitors: 100. Free to the public. Artists should apply by downloading application from website or call for application. Deadline for entry: February. Jury fee: $25. Space fee: $200. Exhibition space: 12×12 ft. For more information, artists should e-mail, or visit website.

STEPPIN' OUT

Downtown Blacksburg, Inc., P.O. Box 233, Blacksburg VA 24063. (540)951-0454. E-mail: dbi@downtown blacksburg.com. Website: www.downtownblacks burg.com. Estab. 1981. Arts & crafts show held annually 1st Friday and Saturday in August. Outdoors. Accepts photography, pottery, painting, drawing, fiber arts, jewelry, general crafts. All arts and crafts must be handmade. Number of exhibitors: 170. Public attendance: 45,000. Free to public. Space fee: $150. Exhibition space: 10×16 ft. Artists should apply by e-mailing, calling or downloading an application on website. Deadline: early May.

TIPS "Visit shows and consider the booth aesthetic—what appeals to you. Put the time, thought, energy and money into your booth to draw people in to see your work."

ST. GEORGE ART FESTIVAL

86 S. Main St., George UT 84770. (435)627-4500. E-mail: leisure@sgcity.org. Website: www.sgcity.org/artfestival. Estab. 1979. Fine arts & crafts show held annually Easter weekend in either March or April. Outdoors. Accepts photography, painting, wood, jewelry, ceramics, sculpture, drawing, 3D mixed media, glass. Juried from digital submissions, CDs and slides. Awards/prizes: $5,000 Purchase Awards. Art pieces selected will be placed in the city's permanent collec-

tions. Number of exhibitors: 110. Public attendance: 20,000/day. Free to public. Artists should apply by completing application form, nonrefundable application fee, slides or digital format of 4 current works in each category and 1 of booth, and SASE. Deadline for entry: January. Exhibition space: 10×11 ft. For more information, artists should e-mail.

TIPS "Artists should have more than 50% originals. Have quality booths and set-up to display art in best possible manner. Be outgoing and friendly with buyers."

STILLWATER ARTS FESTIVAL

P.O. Box 1449, Stillwater OK 74074. (405)533-8539. Fax: (405)533-3097. E-mail: jnovak@stillwater.org. Estab. 1977. Fine arts & crafts show held annually in April. Outdoors. Accepts photography, oil, acrylic, watercolor and multimedia paintings, pottery, pastel work, fiber arts, jewelry, sculpture, glass art. Juried. Awards are based on entry acceptance on quality, distribution and various media entries. Awards/prizes: Best of Show, $500; 1st Place, $200; 2nd Place, $150 and 3rd Place, $100. Number of exhibitors: 80. Public attendance: 7,500-10,000. Free to public. Artists should apply online at http://stillwater.org/content/arts-festival.php. Deadline for entry: early spring (visit website for details). Application fee: $150. Exhibition space: 10×10 ft. Average gross sales/exhibitor: $700. For more information, artists should e-mail.

ST. JAMES COURT ART SHOW

P.O. Box 3804, Louisville KY 40201. (502)635-1842. Fax: (502)635-1296. E-mail: mesrock@stjamescourt artshow.com. Website: www.stjamesartshow.com. Estab. 1957. Annual fine arts & crafts show held the first full weekend in October. Accepts photography; has 16 medium categories. Juried in April; there is also a street jury held during the art show. Awards/prizes: Best of Show-3 places; $3,000 total prize money. Number of exhibitors: 300. Public attendance: 200,000. Free to the public. Artists should apply by visiting website and printing out an application or via www.zapplication.org. Deadline for entry: late March (see website for details). Application fee: $30. Space fee: $500. Exhibition space: 10×12 ft. For more information, artists should e-mail or visit website.

TIPS "Have a variety of price points. Don't sit in the back of the booth and expect sales."

☉ STOCKLEY GARDENS FALL ARTS FESTIVAL

801 Boush St., Suite 302, Norfolk VA 23510. (757)625-6161. Fax: (757)625-7775. E-mail: AKnox@hope-house.org. Website: www.hope-house.org. **Contact:** Anne Knox, development coordinator. Estab. 1984. Fine arts & crafts show held bi-annually in the 3rd weekend in May and October. Outdoors. Accepts photography and all major fine art mediums. Juried. Number of exhibitors: 150. Public attendance: 25,000. Free to the public. Artists should apply by submitting application, jury and booth fees, 5 slides. Deadline for entry: February and July. Exhibition space: 10×10 ft. For more information, artists should visit the website.

☉ STONE ARCH FESTIVAL OF THE ARTS

(763)438-9978. E-mail: mplsriverfront@msn.com. Website: www.stonearchfestival.com. **Contact:** Sara Collins, manager. Estab. 1994. Fine arts & crafts show and culinary arts show held annually Father's Day weekend in the Riverfront District of Minneapolis. Outdoors. Accepts drawing/pastels, printmaking, ceramics, jewelry (metals/stone), mixed media, painting, photography, sculpture metal works, bead work (jewelry or sculpture), glass, fine craft, special consideration. Juried by committee. Awards/prizes: free booth the following year; $100 cash prize. Number of exhibitors: 230. Public attendance: 80,000. Free to public. Artists should apply by application found on website or through www.zapplication.org. Application fee: $25. Deadline for entry: mid-March. Space fee: depends on booth location (see website for details). Exhibition space: 10×10 ft. For more information, artists should call, e-mail or visit website.

TIPS "Have an attractive display and variety of prices."

ST. PATRICK'S DAY CRAFT SALE & FALL CRAFT SALE

P.O. Box 267, Maple Lake MN 55358-2331. Website: www.maplelakechamber.com. **Contact:** Irene Hudek. Estab. 1988. Arts & crafts show held bi-annually in March and early November. Indoors. Number of exhibitors: 40-50. Public attendance: 300-600. Free to public. Artists should apply by requesting an application. Deadline for entry: 1 month-2 weeks before the event. Exhibition space: 10×10 ft. For more information, artists should visit website.

TIPS "Don't charge an arm and a leg for the items. Don't over crowd your items. Be helpful, but not pushy."

☉ STRAWBERRY FESTIVAL

2815 2nd Ave. N., Billings MT 59101. (406)294-5060. Fax: (406)294-5061. E-mail: info@strawberryfun.com; mikaly@downtownbillings.com. Website: www.strawberryfun.com. Estab. 1991. Fine arts & crafts show held annually 2nd Saturday in June. Outdoors. Accepts photography and only finely crafted work. Hand crafted works by the selling artist will be given priority. Juried. Public attendance: 15,000. Free to public. Artists should apply online. Deadline for entry: April. Space fee: $150. Exhibition space: 10×10 ft. For more information, artists should e-mail or visit website.

☉ SUMMER ARTS & CRAFTS FESTIVAL

38 Charles St., Rochester NH 03867. (603)332-2616. Fax: (603)332-8413. E-mail: info@castleberryfairs.com. Website: www.castleberryfairs.com. Estab. 1992. Arts & crafts show held annually 2nd weekend in August in Lincoln, New Hampshire. Outdoors. Accepts photography and all other mediums. Juried by photo, slide or sample. Number of exhibitors: 100. Public attendance: 7,500. Free to the public. Artists should apply by downloading application from website. Space fee: $225. Exhibition space: 10×10 ft. For more information, artists should visit website.

TIPS "Do not bring a book; do not bring a chair. Smile and make eye contact with everyone who enters your booth. Have them sign your guest book; get their e-mail address so you can let them know when you are in the area again. And, finally, make the sale—they are at the fair to shop, after all."

☉ SUMMERFAIR

7850 Five Mile Rd., Cincinnati OH 45230. (513)531-0050. Fax: (513)531-0377. E-mail: exhibitors@summerfair.org. Website: www.summerfair.org. Estab. 1968. Fine arts & crafts show held annually the weekend after Memorial Day. Outdoors. Accepts photography, ceramics, drawing, printmaking, fiber, leather, glass, jewelry, painting, sculpture, metal, wood and mixed media. Juried by a panel of judges selected by Summerfair, including artists and art educators with expertise in the categories offered at Summerfair. Submit application with 5 digital images (no booth image) through www.zapplication.com. Awards/prizes:

$10,000 in cash awards. Number of exhibitors: 300. Public attendance: 20,000. Public admission: $10. Deadline: February. Application fee: $30. Space fee: $375, single; $750, double space; $75 canopy fee (optional—exhibitors can rent a canopy for all days of the fair.). Exhibition space: 10×10 ft. for single space; 10×20 ft. for double space. For more information, artists should e-mail, visit website, call.

SUN FEST, INC.

P.O. Box 2404, Bartlesville OK 74005. (918)331-0456. Fax: (918)331-3217. E-mail: wcfd90@sbcglobal.net. Website: www.bartlesvillesunfest.org. Estab. 1982. Fine arts & crafts show held annually in early June. Outdoors. Accepts photography, painting and other arts and crafts. Juried. Awards: $2,000 in cash awards along with a ribbon/award to be displayed. Number of exhibitors: 95-100. Number of attendees: 25,000-30,000. Free to the public. Artists should apply by e-mailing or calling for an entry form, or completing online, along with 3-5 photos showing your work and booth display. Deadline: early May. Space fee: $125. Exhibition space: 10×10 ft. For more information, artists should e-mail, call or visit website.

SYRACUSE ARTS & CRAFTS FESTIVAL

572 South Salina St., Syracuse NY 13202. (315)422-8284. Fax: (315)471-4503. E-mail: mail@downtown syracuse.com. Website: www.syracuseartsandcrafts festival.com. **Contact:** Laurie Reed, director. Estab. 1970. Fine arts & crafts show held annually in late July. Outdoors. Accepts photography, ceramics, fabric/fiber, glass, jewelry, leather, metal, wood, computer art, drawing, printmaking, painting. Juried by 4 independent jurors. Jurors review 4 slides of work and 1 slide of booth display. Number of exhibitors: 170. Public attendance: 50,000. Free to public. Artists should apply by calling for application or downloading from website. Application fee: $25. Space fee: $260. Exhibition space: 10×10 ft. For more information, artists should e-mail, visit website or call.

TARPON SPRINGS FINE ARTS FESTIVAL

11 E. Orange St., Tarpon Springs FL 34689. (727)937-6109. Fax: (727)937-2879. E-mail: scottie@tarpon springschamber.org. Website: www.tarponsprings chamber.com. Estab. 1974. Fine arts & crafts show held annually in early April. Outdoors. Accepts photography, acrylic, oil, ceramics, fiber, glass, graph-ics, drawings, pastels, jewelry, leather, metal, mixed media, sculpture, watercolor, wood. Juried by CD. Awards/prizes: cash and ribbons. Number of exhibitors: 250. Public attendance: 20,000. Public admission: $2; free age 12 and under. Artists should apply by submitting signed application, CD, slides, fees and SASE. Deadline for entry: early December. Jury fee: $25. Space fee: $225. Exhibition space: 10×12 ft. For more information, artists should e-mail, call or send SASE.

TIPS "Produce good CDs for jurors."

THREE RIVERS ARTS FESTIVAL

803 Liberty Ave., Pittsburgh PA 15222. (412)471-3191. Fax: (412)471-6917. Website: www.artsfestival.net. **Contact:** Sonja Sweterlitsch, director. Estab. 1960. "Three Rivers Arts Festival has presented, during its vast and varied history, more than 10,000 visual and performing artists and entertained millions of residents and visitors. Three Rivers Arts Festival faces a new turning point in its history as a division of The Pittsburgh Cultural Trust, further advancing the shared mission of each organization to foster economic development through the arts and to enhance the quality of life in the region." See website for more information.

TUBAC FESTIVAL OF THE ARTS

P.O. Box 1866, Tubac AZ 85646. (52)398-2704. Fax: (520)398-1704. E-mail: assistance@tubacaz.com. Website: www.tubacaz.com. Estab. 1959. Fine arts & crafts show held annually in early February (see website for details). Outdoors. Accepts photography and considers all fine arts and crafts. Juried. A 7-member panel reviews digital images and artist statement. Names are withheld from the jurists. Number of exhibitors: 170. Public attendance: 65,000. Free to the public; parking: $6. Deadline for entry: late October (see website for details). Application fee: $30. Artists should apply online and provide images on a labeled CD (see website for requirements). Space fee: $575. Exhibition space: 10×10 ft. (a limited number of double booths are available). For more information, artists should e-mail, call or visit website.

TULIP FESTIVAL STREET FAIR

P.O. Box 1801, Mt. Vernon WA 98273. (360)336-3801. E-mail: edmvdt@gmail.com. Website: www.mount vernondowntown.org. Estab. 1984. Arts & crafts show held annually 3rd weekend in April. Outdoors. Accepts photography and original artists' work only. No manufactured work. Juried by a board. Jury fee: $10 with application and prospectus. Number of exhibitors: 220. Public attendance: 30,000-35,000. Free to public. Artists should apply by calling or e-mailing. Deadline for entry: late January. Application fee: $10. Space fee: $300. Exhibition space: 10×10 ft. Average gross sales/exhibitor: $2,500-4,000. For more information, artists should e-mail, visit website, call or send SASE.

TIPS "Keep records of your street fair attendance and sales for your résumé. Network with other artists about which street fairs are better to return to or apply for."

TULSA INTERNATIONAL MAYFEST

P.O. Box 521146, Tulsa OK 74152. (918)582-6435. Fax: (918)517-3518. E-mail: comments@tulsamayfest.org. Website: www.tulsamayfest.org. Estab. 1972. Fine arts & crafts show annually held in May. Outdoors. Accepts photography, clay, leather/fiber, mixed media, drawing, pastels, graphics, printmaking, jewelry, glass, metal, wood, painting. Juried by a blind jurying process. Artists should apply online at www.zapplication.org and submit 4 images of work and one photo of booth set-up. Awards/prizes: Best in Category and Best in Show. Number of exhibitors: 125. Public attendance: 350,000. Free to public. Artists should apply by downloading application in the fall. See website for deadline entry. Application fee: $35. Space fee: $300. Exhibition space: 10×10 ft. For more information, artists should e-mail or visit website.

UPTOWN ART FAIR

1406 W. Lake St., Lower Level C, Minneapolis MN 55408. (612)823-4581. Fax: (612)823-3158. E-mail: maude@uptownminneapolis.com; info@uptown minneapolis.com. Website: www.uptownminneapolis. com. Estab. 1963. Fine arts & crafts show held annually 1st full weekend in August. Outdoors. Accepts photography, painting, printmaking, drawing, 2D and 3D mixed media, ceramics, fiber, sculpture, jewelry, wood. Juried by 4 images of artwork and 1 of booth display. Awards/prizes: Best in Show in each category; Best Artist. Number of exhibitors: 350. Public attendance: 375,000. Free to the public. The Uptown Art Fair uses www.zapplication.com. Each artist must submit 5 images of his or her work. All artwork must be in a high-quality digital format. Five highly

qualified artists, instructors, and critics handpick Uptown Art Fair exhibitors after previewing projections of the images on 8-foot screens. The identities of the artists remain anonymous during the entire review process—all submitted images must be free of signatures, headshots or other identifying marks. Three rounds of scoring determine the final selection and waitlist for the show. Artists will be notified shortly after of their acceptance. For additional information, see the links on website. Deadline for entry: March. Application fee: $30. Space fee: $450 for 10×10 space; $900 for 10×20 space. For more information, artists should call or visit website.

A VICTORIAN CHAUTAUQUA

P.O. Box 606, Jeffersonville IN 47131-0606. (812)283-3728 or (888)472-0606. Fax: (812)283-6049. E-mail: hsmsteam@aol.com. Website: www.steamboat museum.org. Estab. 1993. Fine arts & crafts show held annually 3rd weekend in May. Outdoors. Accepts photography, all mediums. Juried by a committee of 5. Number of exhibitors: 80. Public attendance: 3,000. Exhibition space: 12×12 ft. For more information, artists should e-mail, call or visit website.

VILLAGE SQUARE ARTS & CRAFTS FAIR

P.O. Box 1105, Saugatuck MI 49453. (269)857-2677. Fax: (269)857-7717. E-mail: artclub@saugatuck douglasartclub.org. Website: www.saugatuckdouglas artclub.org. **Contact:** Bonnie Lowe, art fair co-chairperson. Estab. 2004. The art club offers two fairs each summer. See website for upcoming dates. This fair has some fine artists as well as crafters. Both fairs take place on the two busiest weekends in the resort town of Saugatuck's summer season. Both are extremely well attended. Generally the vendors do very well.

TIPS "Create an inviting booth. Offer well-made artwork and crafts for a variety of prices."

VIRGINIA CHRISTMAS MARKET

The Farm Bureau Center at Meadow Event Park, 13111 Dawn Blvd., Doswell VA 23047. Website: www. vashowsinc.com. Indoors. Virginia Christmas Market is held the 2nd weekend in November at Farm Bureau Center at Meadow Event Park. Virginia Christmas Market will showcase over 300 quality artisans, crafters, boutiques and specialty food shops. Features porcelain, pottery, quilts, folk art, fine art, reproduction furniture, flags, ironwork, carvings, leather, toys, tinware, candles, dollcraft, wovenwares, book authors, musicians, jewelry, basketry, gourmet foods—all set amid festive Christmas displays. Accepts photography and other arts and crafts. Juried by 3 photos of artwork and 1 of display. Attendance: 17,000. Public admission: $7. Artists should apply by calling, e-mailing or downloading application from website. Space fee: $335. Exhibit spaces: 10×10 ft. For more information, artists should call, e-mail or contact through website.

○ VIRGINIA CHRISTMAS SHOW

P.O. Box 305, Chase City VA 23924. (804)253-6284. Fax: (800)253-6285. E-mail: vashowsinc@comcast. net. Website: www.vashowsinc.com. Estab. 1986. Arts and crafts show held annually in November in Richmond, Virginia. Accepts photography and other arts and crafts. Juried by 3 slides of artwork and 1 of display. Attendance: 30,000. Public admission: $7. Artists should apply by calling or e-mailing for application or downloading online application. Space fee: $435. Exhibition space: 10×10 ft. Included in this fee are booth curtains, 24-hour security in the show exhibit area, signage, a complimentary listing in the show directory and an extensive multi-media advertising campaign—radio, television, billboards, direct mail, magazines and newspapers—we do it all! Set-up is always easy, organized and convenient. The building is climate-controlled and many RVs may park on the premises for a nominal fee.

TIPS "If possible, attend the shows before you apply."

○ VIRGINIA SPRING SHOW

11050 Branch Rd., Glen Allen VA 23059. (804)253-6284. Fax: (804)253-6285. E-mail: vashowsinc@ comcast.net. Website: www.vashowsinc.com. Estab. 1988. Holiday arts & crafts show held annually 2nd weekend in March in Richmond, Virginia. Indoors at the Showplace Exhibition Center. Accepts photography and other arts and crafts. Juried by 3 slides of artwork and 1 of display. Awards/prizes: Best Display. Number of exhibitors: 300. Public attendance: 20,000. Public admission: $7. Exhibitor application is online at website. Artists can also apply by writing or e-mailing for an application. Space fee: $335. Exhibition space: 10×10 ft. For more information, artists should e-mail or visit website.

TIPS "If possible, attend the show before you apply."

○ WASHINGTON SQUARE OUTDOOR ART EXHIBIT

P.O. Box 1045, New York NY 10276. (212)982-6255. Fax: (212)982-6256. E-mail: jrm.wsoae@gmail.com. Website: www.wsoae.org. Estab. 1931. Fine arts & crafts show held semiannually Memorial Day weekend and the following weekend in May/early June and Labor Day weekend and following weekend in September. Outdoors. Accepts photography, oil, watercolor, graphics, mixed media, sculpture, crafts. Juried by submitting 5 slides of work and 1 of booth. Awards/prizes: certificates, ribbons and cash prizes. Number of exhibitors: 150. Public attendance: 100,000. Free to public. Artists should apply by sending a SASE or downloading application from website. Deadline for entry: March, Spring Show; July, Fall Show. Exhibition space: 5×10 ft. up to 10×10 ft., double spaces available. For more information, artists should call or send SASE.

TIPS "Price work sensibly."

⊕ WATERFRONT FINE ART & WINE FESTIVAL

7135 E. Camelback Rd., Scottsdale AZ 85251. (480)837-5637. Fax: (480)837-2355. **Contact:** Denise Dodson, vice president. Estab. 2011. Fine art/craft show held annually over Valentine's Day weekend. Outdoors. Accepts photography, paintings, bronzes, baskets, jewelry, stone, pottery. Juried; blind jury by CEO. Number of exhibitors: 150. Public attendance: 40,000. Public admission: $3. Apply online at www. zapplication.com. Deadline for entry: late August (see website for specifics). Application fee: $30. Space fee: $410-1,230. Exhibition space: 10×10 to 10×30 ft. For more information, artists should e-mail, call or visit website.

TIPS "A clean, gallery-type presentation is very important."

WATERFRONT FINE ART FAIR

P.O. Box 1105, Saugatuck MI 49453. (269)857-2677. Fax: (269)857-7717. E-mail: artclub@saugatuck douglasartclub.org. Website: www.saugatuckdouglas sartclub.org. **Contact:** Bonnie Lowe and Jim Hanson, art fair co-chairs. For information, e-mail, call or visit the website.

TIPS "Create a pleasing, inviting booth. Offer well-made, top-quality fine art."

WESTMORELAND ART NATIONALS

252 Twin Lakes Rd., Latrobe PA 15650-3554. (724)834-7474. E-mail: info@artsandheritage.com. Website: www.artsandheritage.com. **Contact:** Diana Morreo, executive director. Estab. 1975. Fine arts & crafts show held annually in early July (see website for details). Photography displays are indoors. Accepts photography, all handmade mediums. Juried by 2 jurors. Awards/prizes: $7,000 in prizes. Number of exhibitors: 100. Public attendance: 155,000. Free to public. Artists should apply by downloading application from website. Application fee: $25/craft show vendors; $35/art nationals exhibitors. Deadline: early March. Space fee: $375-750. Exhibition space: 10×10 or 10×20 ft. For more information, artists should visit e-mail, call or visit website.

WHITEFISH ARTS FESTIVAL

P.O. Box 131, Whitefish MT 59937. (406)862-5875. Website: www.whitefishartsfestival.org. Estab. 1979. Fine arts & crafts show held annually 1st full weekend in July. Outdoors. Accepts photography, pottery, jewelry, sculpture, paintings, woodworking. Juried. Art must be original and handcrafted. Work is evaluated for creativity, quality and originality. Awards/prizes: Best of Show awarded half-price booth fee for following year with no application fee. Number of exhibitors: 100. Public attendance: 3,000. Free to public. Entry fee: $29. Deadline: see website for details. Space fee: $215. Exhibition space: 10×10 ft. For more information, and to apply, artists should visit website.

TIPS Recommends "variety of price range, professional display, early application for special requests."

WHITE OAK CRAFTS FAIR

P.O. Box 111, Woodbury TN 37190. (615) 563-2787 or (800)235-9073. E-mail: mary@artscenterofcc.com. Website: www.artscenterofcc.com. Estab. 1985. Arts & crafts show held annually in early September (see website for details) featuring the traditional and contemporary craft arts of Cannon County and Middle Tennessee. Outdoors. Accepts photography; all handmade crafts, traditional and contemporary. Must be handcrafted displaying excellence in concept and technique. Juried by committee. Send 3 slides or photos. Awards/prizes: more than $1,000 cash in merit awards. Number of exhibitors: 80. Public attendance: 6,000. Free to public. Applications can be downloaded from website. Deadline: early July. Space fee: $100

($70 for Artisan member) for a 10×10 ft. under tent; $80 ($50 for Artisan member) for a 12×12 ft. outside. For more information, artists should e-mail, call or visit website.

WILD WIND FOLK ART & CRAFT FESTIVAL

P.O. Box 719, Long Lake NY 12847. (814)723-0707 or (518)624-6404. E-mail: wildwindcraftshow@yahoo.com. Website: www.wildwindfestival.com. **Contact:** Liz Allen and Carol Jilk, directors. Estab. 1979. Traditional crafts show held annually the weekend after Labor Day at the Warren County Fairgrounds in Pittsfield, Pennsylvania. Barn locations and outdoors. Accepts traditional country crafts, photography, paintings, pottery, jewelry, traditional crafts, prints, stained glass. Juried by promoters. Three photos or slides of work plus one of booth, if available. Number of exhibitors: 160. Public attendance: 9,000. Artists should apply by visiting website and filling out application request, calling or sending a written request.

WILMETTE FESTIVAL OF FINE ARTS

P.O. Box 902, Wilmette IL 60091. (847)256-2080. E-mail: wilmetteartsguild@gmail.com. Website: www.wilmetteartsguild.org. Estab. 1992. Fine arts & crafts show held annually in September (see website for details). Outdoors. Accepts photography, paintings, prints, jewelry, sculpture, ceramics, and any other appropriate media; no wearable. Juried by a committee of 6-8 artists and art teachers. Number of exhibitors: 100. Public attendance: 4,000. Free to the public. Deadline for entry: April. Exhibition space: 12×12 ft. For more information, artists should e-mail, visit website, call, send SASE.

TIPS "Maintain a well-planned, professional appearance in booth and person. Greet viewers when they visit the booth. Offer printed bio with photos of your work. Invite family, friends and acquaintances."

WINNEBAGOLAND ART FAIR

South Park Avenue, Oshkosh WI 54902. E-mail: oshkoshfaa@gmail.com. Estab. 1957. Fine arts show held annually the second Sunday in June. Outdoors. Accepts photography, watercolor, oils & acrylics, 3D, drawing, pastels, mixed media. Artwork must be the original work of the artist in concept and execution. Juried. Applicants send in photographs to be reviewed. Awards/prizes: monetary awards, purchase, merit and Best of Show awards. Number of exhibitors: 125-160. Public attendance: 5,000-8,000. Free to public. Deadline for entry: Previous exhibitors due mid-March. New Exhibitors due late March. $25 late entry fee after March. Exhibition space: 20×20 ft. For more information, artists should e-mail or see website. The updated entry form will be added to the website in early January.

TIPS "Artists should send clear, uncluttered photos of their current work which they intend to show in their booth as well as a photo of their booth setup."

✪ WYANDOTTE STREET ART FAIR

3131 Biddle Ave., Wyandotte MI 48192. (734)324-4502. Fax: (734)324-7296. E-mail: info@wyan.org. Website: www.wyandottestreetartfair.org. **Contact:** Heather Thiede, special events coordinator. Estab. 1961. Fine arts & crafts show held annually 2nd week in July. Outdoors. Accepts photography, 2D mixed media, 3D mixed media, painting, pottery, basketry, sculpture, fiber, leather, digital cartoons, clothing, stitchery, metal, glass, wood, toys, prints, drawing. Juried. Awards/prizes: Best New Artist: $500; Best Booth Design Award: $500; Best of Show: $1,200. Number of exhibitors: 300. Public attendance: 200,000. Free to the public. Artists may apply online or request application. Deadline for entry: early February. Application fee: $20 jury fee. Space fee: $225/single space; $450/double space. Exhibition space: 10×10 ft. Average gross sales/exhibitor: $2,000-$4,000. For more information, and to apply, artists should e-mail, visit website, call, send SASE.

CONTESTS

//

Whether you're a seasoned veteran or a newcomer still cutting your teeth, you should consider entering contests to see how your work compares to that of other photographers. The contests in this section range in scope from tiny juried county fairs to massive international competitions. When possible, we've included entry fees and other pertinent information in our limited space. Contact sponsors for entry forms and more details.

Once you receive rules and entry forms, pay particular attention to the sections describing rights. Some sponsors retain all rights to winning entries or even *submitted* images. Be wary of these. While you can benefit from the publicity and awards connected with winning prestigious competitions, you shouldn't unknowingly forfeit copyright. Granting limited rights for publicity is reasonable, but you should never assign rights of any kind without adequate financial compensation or a written agreement. If such terms are not stated in contest rules, ask sponsors for clarification.

If you're satisfied with the contest's copyright rules, check with contest officials to see what types of images won in previous years. By scrutinizing former winners, you might notice a trend in judging that could help when choosing your entries. If you can't view the images, ask what styles and subject matters have been popular.

AESTHETICA CREATIVE WORKS COMPETITION

P.O. Box 371, York YO23 1WL, UK. E-mail: pauline@ aestheticamagazine.com. E-mail: submissions@ aestheticamagazine.com. Website: www.aesthetica magazine.com. The Aesthetica Creative Works Competition represents the scope of creative activity today, and provides an opportunity for both new and established artists to nurture their reputations on an international scale. There are three categories: Artwork & Photography, Fiction and Poetry. See guidelines online.

AFI FEST

2021 N. Western Ave., Los Angeles CA 90027. (323)856-7707. Website: www.afifest.com. **Contact:** Director of festivals. Cost: $40 shorts; $50 features. "LA's most prominent annual film festival." Various cash and product prizes are awarded. Open to filmmakers of all skill levels. Deadline: July (see website for details). Photographers should write, call or e-mail for more information.

ALEXIA COMPETITION

Professional Division, S.I. Newhouse School of Communications, 215 University Place, Syracuse NY 13244-2100. (315)443-7388. E-mail: trkenned@ syr.edu. Website: www.alexiafoundation.org. **Contact:** Tom Kennedy. Annual contest. Provides financial ability for students to study photojournalism in England, and for professionals to produce a photo project promoting world peace and cultural understanding. Students win cash grants plus scholarships to study photojournalism at Syracuse University in London. A professional wins $15,000 cash grant. Photographers should e-mail or see website for more information.

ARC AWARDS

500 Executive Blvd., Ossining-on-Hudson NY 10562. (914)923-9400. Fax: (914)923-9484. E-mail: info@ mercommawards.com. Website: www.mercomm awards.com. Cost: $185-290. Annual contest. The International ARC Awards, celebrating its 24th year, is the "Academy Awards of Annual Reports," according to the financial media. It is now the largest international competition honoring excellence in annual reports. The competition is open to corporations, small companies, government agencies, non-profit organizations, and associations, as well as agencies and individuals involved in producing annual reports. The purpose of the contest is to honor outstanding achievement in annual reports. Major category for annual report photography—covers and interiors. "Best of Show" receives a personalized trophy. Grand Award winners receive personalized award plaques. Gold, silver, bronze and finalists receive a personalized award certificate. Every entrant receives complete judge score sheets and comments. Photographers should see website, write, call or e-mail for more information.

ARTIST FELLOWSHIP GRANTS

Oregon Arts Commission, 775 Summer St. NE, Salem OR 97301-1280. (503)986-0082. Fax: (503)986-0260. E-mail: oregon.artscomm@state.or.us. Website: www. oregonartscommission.org. A highly competitive juried grant process offering $3,000 in cash awards to Oregon visual artists, in odd-numbered years. Deadline: October. See website for more information.

ARTIST FELLOWSHIPS/VIRGINIA COMMISSION FOR THE ARTS

223 Governor St., Richmond VA 23219-2010. (804)225-3132. Fax: (804)225-4327. E-mail: arts@arts.virginia. gov. Website: www.arts.virginia.gov. Applications accepted in alternating years. The purpose of the Artist Fellowship program is to encourage significant development in the work of individual artists, to support the realization of specific artistic ideas, and to recognize the central contribution professional artists make to the creative environment of Virginia. Grant amounts: $5,000. Emerging and established artists are eligible. Open only to photographers who are legal residents of Virginia and at least 18 years of age. Applications are available in July. See Guidelines for Funding and application forms on the website or write for more information.

ARTISTS ALPINE HOLIDAY

Ouray County Arts Association, P.O. Box 167, Ouray CO 81427. (970)626-3212. E-mail: ouraybelle@ yahoo.com. Website: ourayarts.org/aah.html. **Contact:** Deann McDaniel, president. Cost: $25, includes up to 2 entries. Annual fine arts show. Juried. Cash awards for 1st, 2nd and 3rd prizes in all categories total $4,850. Best of Show: $500; People's Choice Award: $50. Open to all skill levels. Photographers and artists should call or see website for more information.

ASTRID AWARDS

500 Executive Blvd., Ossining-on-Hudson NY 10562. (914)923-9400. Fax: (914)923-9484. E-mail: info@mercommawards.com; contacts@mercommawards.com. Website: www.mercommawards.com. Annual contest. Cost: $295/classification; there is a multiple entry discount. The purpose of the contest is to honor outstanding achievement in design communications. Major category for photography, including books, brochures and publications. "Best of Show" receives a personalized trophy. Grand Award winners receive personalized award plaques. Gold, silver, bronze and finalists receive a personalized award certificate. Every entrant receives complete judge score sheets and comments. Deadline: late February (see website for details). Photographers should see website, write, call or e-mail for more information.

ATLANTA PHOTOJOURNALISM SEMINAR CONTEST

PMB 301, 541 Tenth St. NW, Atlanta GA 30318-5713. E-mail: contest@photojournalism.org. Website: www.photojournalism.org. Annual contest. This is an all-digital contest with several different categories (all related to news and photojournalism). Photographs may have been originally shot on film or with a digital camera, but the entries must be submitted in digital form. Photographs do not have to be published to qualify. No slide or print entries are accepted. Video frame grabs are not eligible. Rules are very specific. See website for official rules. More than $5,000 in prizes, including $1,000 and Nikon camera gear for Best Portfolio. Open to all skill levels. Deadline: November (see website for more details).

☼ BANFF MOUNTAIN PHOTOGRAPHY COMPETITION

P.O. Box 1020, 107 Tunnel Mountain Dr., Banff AB T1L 1H5, Canada. (403)762-6347. Fax: (403)762-6277. E-mail: BanffMountainPhotos@banffcentre.ca. Website: www.BanffMountainFestivals.ca. **Contact:** Competition Coordinator. Annual contest. Maximum of 7 images (digital) in photo essay format. The theme is mountain exploration and adventure. Entry fee: $10/essay. Entry form and regulations available on website. Approximately $5,000 in cash and prizes to be awarded. Open to all skill levels. Photographers should write, e-mail or fax for more information.

THE CENTER FOR FINE ART PHOTOGRAPHY

400 S. College Ave., Fort Collins CO 80524. (907)224-1010. E-mail: contact@c4fap.org. Website: www.c4fap.org. Cost: typically $35 for first 3 entries; $10 for each additional entry. Competitions held 10 times/year. "The Center's competitions are designed to attract and exhibit quality fine art photography created by emerging and established artists working in traditional, digital and mixed-media photography. The themes for each exhibition vary greatly. The themes, rules, details and entry forms for each call for entry are posted on the Center's website." All accepted work is exhibited in the Center gallery. Additionally, the Center offers monetary awards, scholarships, solo exhibitions and other awards. Awards are stated with each call for entry. Open to all skill levels and to all domestic and international photographers working with digital or traditional photography or combinations of both. Photographers should see website for deadlines and more information.

COLLEGE PHOTOGRAPHER OF THE YEAR

101B Lee Hills Hall, University of Missouri, Columbia MO 65211-1370. (573)884-2188. E-mail: info@cpoy.org. Website: www.cpoy.org. **Contact:** Rita Reed, director. Annual contest to recognize excellent photography by currently enrolled college students. Portfolio winner receives a plaque, cash and camera products. Other category winners receive cash and camera products. Open to beginning and intermediate photographers. Photographers should see website for more information.

COLLEGE PHOTOGRAPHY CONTEST

Serbin Communications, 813 Reddick St., Santa Barbara CA 93103. (805)963-0439 or (800)876-6425. Fax: (805)965-0296. E-mail: admin@serbin.com. Website: www.pfmagazine.com. **Contact:** Julie Simpson, managing editor. Annual student contest; runs September through mid-November. Sponsored by *Photographer's Forum Magazine* and Nikon. Winners and finalists have their photos published in the hardcover book *The Best of College Photography*. See website for entry form.

COMMUNICATION ARTS ANNUAL PHOTOGRAPHY COMPETITION

110 Constitution Dr., Menlo Park CA 94025-1107. (650)326-6040. E-mail: shows@commarts.com. Web-

site: www.commarts.com/competitions. Entries must be accompanied by a completed entry form. "Entries may originate from any country. Explanation of the function in English is very important to the judges. The work will be chosen on the basis of its creative excellence by a nationally representative jury of designers, art directors and photographers." Cost: $35 single entry/$70 series. Categories include advertising, books, editorial, for sale, institutional, cinemaphotography, self-promotion, and unpublished. Deadline: late March (see website for details). See website for more information.

⊕ CREATIVE QUARTERLY CALL FOR ENTRIES

244 5th Ave., Suite F269, New York NY 10001-7604. (212)591-2566. Fax: (212)537-6201. E-mail: shows@CQjournal.com. Website: www.cqjournal.com. Entry fee: $10/entry. Quarterly contest. "Our publication is all about inspiration." Open to all art directors, graphic designers, photographers, illustrators and fine artists in all countries. Separate categories for professionals and students. We accept both commissioned and uncommissioned entries. Work is judged on the uniqueness of the image and how it best solves a marketing problem. Winners will be requested to submit an image of a person, place or thing that inspires their work. We will reprint these in the issue and select one for our cover image. *Creative Quarterly* has the rights to promote the work through our publications and website. Complete rights and copyright belong to the individual artist, designer or photographer who enters their work. Enter online or by sending a disc. Winners will be featured in the next issue of *Creative Quarterly* corresponding with the call for entries and will be displayed in our online gallery. Runners-up will be displayed online only. Winners and runners-up both receive a complimentary copy of the publication. Open to all skill levels. Deadline: Last Friday of January, April, July and October. See website for more information.

CURATOR'S CHOICE AWARDS

Center, P.O. Box 2483, Santa Fe NM 87504. (505)984-8353. E-mail: programs@visitcenter.org. Website: www.visitcenter.org. **Contact:** Laura Pressley, executive director. Cost: $25/members $35/non-members. Annual contest. Center's Choice Awards are in three different categories with different jurors and prizes. "You can submit to one, two or all categories.

Our jurors are some of the most important and influential people in the business. Photographers are invited to submit their most compelling images. Open to all skill levels." Prizes include exhibition and more. Photographers should see submissions guidelines at: centeryourcareer.org/programs.cfm?p=Competition Guidelines.

⭘ Center, the organization that sponsors this competition, was formerly known as The Santa Fe Center for Photography. "Get a second opinion on your edit and your artist statement. Be very clear in your concepts and execution. Look at the work of your contemporaries and work that preceded yours. If it resembles others it will be too 'familiar' and not as potent to the national and international community. So keep going, keep working, until it is ripe, until it is mainly your voice, your vision that others see.

✵ DANCE ON CAMERA FESTIVAL

48 W. 21st St., #907, New York NY 10010. (212)727-0764. E-mail: info@dancefilms.org. Website: www.dancefilms.org. Sponsored by Dance Films Association, Inc. The oldest annual dance festival competition in the world for films and videotapes on all aspects of dance. Co-presented by the Film Society of Lincoln Center in New York City; also tours internationally. Entry forms and deadline dates available on website.

⊕ THE DEALER'S CHOICE AWARDS

P.O. Box 2483, Santa Fe NM 87504. (505)984-8353. E-mail: programs@visitcenter.org. Website: www.visitcenter.org. Recognizes outstanding photographers through the dealer's perspective. Cost: $25/members $35/non-members. Annual contest. Photographers are invited to submit their most compelling images. Open to all skill levels. Prizes include exhibition and more. Deadline: January (see website for details). Photographers should see website for more information.

⭘ Center, the organization that sponsors this competition, was formerly known as The Santa Fe Center for Photography.

DIRECT ART MAGAZINE PUBLICATION COMPETITION

123 Warren St., Hudson NY 12534. (845)688-7129. E-mail: slowart@aol.com. Website: www.slowart.com. **Contact:** Tim Slowinski, director. Cost: $35. Annual contest. National magazine publication of new and

emerging art in all medias. Cover and feature article awards. Open to all skill levels. Send SASE or see website for more information. SlowArt Productions presents the annual group thematic exhibition. Open to all artists, national and international, working in all media. All forms of art are eligible. *Entrants must be 18 years of age or older to apply.* 96" maximum for wall hung work, 72" for free-standing sculpture.

THE EDITOR'S CHOICE AWARDS

Center, P.O. Box 2483, Santa Fe NM 87504. (505)984-8353. E-mail: programs@visitcenter.org. Website: www.visitcenter.org. Annual contest. This award recognizes outstanding photographers working in all processes and subject matter. Open to all skill levels. Awards/prizes: 1st, 2nd, 3rd Prize and Honorable Mention awarded; 1st Prize includes exhibition at Center space, $125 gift certificate for Singer Editions printing, publication in *Fraction* magazine and online exhibition at VisitCenter.org; see website for listing of prizes. Photographers should see website for more information.

> ○ Center, the organization that sponsors this competition, was formerly known as The Santa Fe Center for Photography.

FIFTYCROWS INTERNATIONAL FUND FOR DOCUMENTARY PHOTOGRAPHY

49 Geary St., Suite 225, San Francisco CA 94108. (415)647-1100. E-mail: info@fiftycrows.org. Website: www.fiftycrows.org. Grants, career and distribution assistance to emerging and mid-career documentary photographers to help complete a long-term documentary project of social, political, ethical, environmental or economic importance. FiftyCrows maintains a by-appointment gallery and reference library, and creates short films about documentary photographers. E-mail us to receive a call-for-entry notification and updates.

FIRELANDS ASSOCIATION FOR THE VISUAL ARTS

39 S. Main St., Oberlin OH 44074. (440)774-7158. E-mail: favagallery@oberlin.net. Website: www.favagallery.org. Cost: $15/photographer; $12 for FAVA members. Biennial juried photography contest (odd-numbered years) for residents of Ohio, Kentucky, Indiana, Michigan, Pennsylvania and West Virginia. Both traditional and experimental techniques welcome. Photographers may submit up to 3 works

completed in the last 3 years. Annual entry deadline: March-April (date varies, see website for details). Photographers should call, e-mail or see website for entry form and more details.

● HUMANITY PHOTO AWARD (HPA)

E-mail: hpa@china-fpa.org. Website: www.worldfpa.org. **Contact:** Organizing Committee HPA. Cost: free. Biennial contest. Open to all skill levels. See website for more information and entry forms.

INFOCUS

Palm Beach Photographic Centre, 415 Clematis St., West Palm Beach FL 33401. (561)253-2600. E-mail: cs@workshop.org. Website: www.workshop.org. **Contact:** Fatima NeJame, CEO. Cost: $20/image, up to 5 images. Annual contest. Awards: Best of Show: $950. Merit awards of free tuition for a PBPC photography workshop of choice. Open to members of the Palm Beach Photographic Center. Interested parties can obtain an individual membership for $95. Photographers should write, call or see website for more information.

LAKE CHAMPLAIN MARITIME MUSEUM'S ANNUAL JURIED PHOTOGRAPHY EXHIBIT

4472 Basin Harbor Rd., Vergennes VT 05491. (802)475-2022. E-mail: eloiseb@lcmm.org. Website: www.lcmm.org. **Contact:** Eloise Beil. Annual exhibition, Lake Champlain Through the Lens, images of Lake Champlain. "Amateur and professional photographers are invited to submit framed prints in color or black & white. Professional photographers will judge and comment on the work." Additional prints of work accepted for exhibition can be placed on consignment at museum store. Call for entries begins in June, photograph delivery in August, on view September and October. Photographers should call, e-mail, or visit website for registration form.

LAKE SUPERIOR MAGAZINE AMATEUR PHOTO CONTEST

P.O. Box 16417, Duluth MN 55816-0417. (888)244-5253. Fax: (218)722-4096. E-mail: edit@lakesuperior.com. Website: www.lakesuperior.com. **Contact:** Konnie LeMay, editor. Annual contest. Photos must be taken in the Lake Superior region and should be labeled for categories: lake/landscapes, nature, people/humor. Accepts up to 10 b&w and color images—prints no larger than 8×10, and transparencies. Digital images can be submitted as prints with accompanying CD. Grand Prize: $200 prize package, plus a 1-year subscription to *Lake Superior Magazine* and a Lake Superior wall calendar. Other prizes include subscriptions and calendars; all prize winners, including honorable mentions and finalists, receive a Certificate of Honor. Although there is no cost to enter, entries will not be returned without a SASE. No e-mailed submissions accepted. Photographers should write, e-mail or see website for more information.

LARSON GALLERY JURIED BIENNUAL PHOTOGRAPHY EXHIBITION

Yakima Valley Community College, P.O. Box 22520, Yakima WA 98907. (509)574-4875. Fax: (509)574-6826. E-mail: gallery@yvcc.edu. Website: www.larson gallery.org. **Contact:** Denise Olsen, assistant gallery director. Cost: $12/entry (limit 4 entries). National juried competition. Awards: Approximately $3,500 in prize money. Held odd years in April. First jurying held in February. Photographers should write, fax, e-mail or visit the website for prospectus.

LOS ANGELES CENTER FOR DIGITAL JURIED COMPETITION

107 W. 5th St., Los Angeles CA 90013. (323)646-9427. E-mail: rexbruce@lacda.com. Website: www.lacda. com. LACDA is dedicated to the propagation of all forms of digital art, supporting local, international, emerging and established artists in our gallery. Entry fee: $30. Its juried competition is open to digital artists around the world. It also sponsors other competitions throughout the year. Visit website, e-mail, call for more information, including deadline dates.

MERCURY AWARDS

500 Executive Blvd., Ossining-on-Hudson NY 10562. (914)923-9400. Fax: (914)923-9484. E-mail: rwitt@ mercommawards.com. Website: www.mercomm awards.com. **Contact:** Ms. Reni L. Witt, president. Cost: $190-250/entry (depending on category). Annual contest. The purpose of the contest is to honor outstanding achievement in public relations and corporate communications. Major category for photography, including ads, brochures, magazines, etc. "Best of Show" receives a personalized trophy. Grand Award winners receive award plaques (personalized). Gold, silver, bronze and finalists receive a personalized award certificate. All nominators receive complete judge score sheets and evaluation comments. Dead-

line: November. Photographers should write, call or e-mail for more information.

THE MOBIUS AWARDS FOR ADVERTISING

713 S. Pacific Coast Hwy., Suite A, Redondo Beach CA 90277-4233. (310)540-0959. Fax: (310)316-8905. E-mail: kristengluckman@mobiusawards.com. Website: www.mobiusawards.com. **Contact:** Kristen Gluckman, exec. director. Annual international awards competition founded in 1971 for TV, cinema/in-flight and radio commercials, print, outdoor, new media, direct, online, mixed media campaigns and package design. Student and spec work welcome. Deadline: October 1. Late entries accepted. "Entries are judged by an international jury on their effectiveness and creativity. Mobius Awards reflects the most current trends in the advertising industry by updating the competition regularly, such as adding new media types and categories. We are dedicated to consistently providing a fair competition with integrity."

MYRON THE CAMERA BUG

c/o Educational Dept., 2106 Hoffnagle St., Philadelphia PA 19152-2409. E-mail: cambug8480@aol.com. Website: www.shutterbugstv.com. **Contact:** Len Friedman, director. Open to all photography students and educators. Photographers should e-mail for details and/or questions.

NEW YORK STATE FAIR PHOTOGRAPHY COMPETITION AND SHOW

581 State Fair Blvd., Syracuse NY 13209. (315)487-7711, ext. 1336 or 1337. Website: www.nysfair.org/competitions. You may enter by downloading and mailing in the entry form, or directly online (any competition marked "N/A" is not available for online entry). All works must be received in person at the entry department office at the State Fairgrounds by 4:30pm or online by 12:00 midnight on the specified competition deadline date. See website for complete details, and to enter.

ONLY ORIGINALS INTERNATIONAL ART COMPETITION

P.O. Box 592, Benton AR 72018-0592. (501)778-8830. E-mail: onlyoriginals@sbcglobal.net. Website: www. onlyoriginals.org. **Contact:** Carol Fullerton-Sansel, gallery owner. $20. Annual contest to find emerging artists to showcase on the website and to help interested clients link to their sites. The gallery charges no commission, but instead encourages clients to contact artists directly. Open to artists 18 years of age or older, residing in 1 of 44 selected countries and all skill levels. All 2D work will be considered, including painting, drawing, printmaking, photography, digital imagery, mosaics, artistic quilts, etc. Up to 20 finalists will have 6 works showcased on the website. There is a single cash award, which varies in amount. $5 from each entry goes toward the cash prize, with minimum and maximum prizes defined in the prospectus. If the winner lives outside the U.S., the prize money is deposited into a PayPal account. **Next deadline: March 1, 2012.** Artists should e-mail or see website for more information.

⊕ ONLY ORIGINALS NATIONAL INVITATIONAL

P.O. Box 592, Benton AR 72018-0592. (501)778-8830. E-mail: onlyoriginals@sbcglobal.net. Website: www.onlyoriginals.org. **Contact:** Carol Fullerton-Samsel, gallery owner. Cost: $20. Annual contest to find emerging U.S. artists to showcase on the website and to help interested clients link to their sites. The gallery charges no commission, but instead encourages clients to contact artists directly. Open to all artists 18 years of age or older of all skill levels. All 2D work will be considered, including painting, drawing, printmaking, photography, digital imagery, mosaics, artistic quilts, and more. Up to 20 artists will have 6 works showcased on the website. There is a single cash award, which varies in amount. $5 from each entry goes toward the cash prize, with minimum and maximum prizes defined in the prospectus. **Next deadline: September 1, 2012.** Artists should e-mail or see website for more information.

THE GORDON PARKS PHOTOGRAPHY COMPETITION

Fort Scott Community College, 2108 S. Horton, Fort Scott KS 66701-3140. (620)223-2700. Fax: (620)223-6530. E-mail: photocontest@fortscott.edu. Website: www.fortscott.edu. **Contact:** Jill Warford. The annual Gordon Parks Photography Competition is in tribute to Fort Scott, Kansas, native Gordon Parks. This competition is open to anyone. Photographs submitted should have been taken within the last five years. "Freedom" was the theme of all of his work, Parks said. Not allowing anyone to set boundaries, cutting loose the imagination and then making the new horizons.

Each photographer may submit up to 4 photographs which will be judged as an individual entry. Each photo entry is $15. Awards: $500 first place, $350 second place, $200 third place will be awarded and up to 3 Honorable Mentions will receive $50 each. See complete details and access entry forms online.

PERKINS CENTER FOR THE ARTS JURIED PHOTOGRAPHY EXHIBITION

395 Kings Hwy., Moorestown NJ 08057. (856)235-6488 or (800)387-5226. Fax: (856)235-6624. E-mail: create@perkinscenter.org. Website: www.perkinscenter.org. Cost: $8/entry; up to 3 entries. Regional juried photography exhibition. Works from the exhibition are considered for inclusion in the permanent collection of the Philadelphia Museum of Art and the Woodmere Art Museum. Past jurors include Merry Foresta, former curator of photography at the Smithsonian American Art Museum; Katherine Ware, curator of photographs at the Philadelphia Museum of Art; and photographers Emmett Gowin, Ruth Thorne-Thomsen, Matthew Pillsbury, and Vik Muniz. All work must be framed with wiring in back and hand-delivered to Perkins Center. Prospectus must be downloaded from the Perkins site. Photographers should call, e-mail or see website for more information.

PHOTOGRAPHY NOW

Center for Photography at Woodstock, 59 Tinker St., Woodstock NY 12498. (845)679-9957. Fax: (845)679-6337. E-mail: info@cpw.org. Website: www.cpw.org. **Contact:** Akemi Hiatt, CPW, program associate. Two annual contests: 1 for exhibitions, 1 for publication. Juried annually by renowned photographers, critics, museum and gallery curators. Deadlines vary. General submission is ongoing. Photographers must call or write for guidelines.

THE PHOTO REVIEW ANNUAL PHOTOGRAPHY COMPETITION

140 E. Richardson Ave., Suite 301, Langhorne PA 19047. (215)891-0214. E-mail: info@photoreview.org. Website: www.photoreview.org. **Contact:** Stephen Perloff, editor. Cost: $30 for up to 3 images; $5 each for up to 3 additional images. National annual contest. All types of photographs are eligible—b&w, color, nonsilver, computer-manipulated, etc. Submit prints (unmatted, unframed, 16×20 or smaller), or images on CD. All entries must be labeled. Awards include

SilverFast HDR Studio digital camera RAW conversion software from LaserSoft Imaging ($499), a $270 gift certificate from Lensbabies for a Composer lens or other items on the Lensbaby.com webstore, a $250 gift certificate from Calumet Photographic, a 24"×50" role of Museo Silver Rag ($240), a 20"×24" silver gelatin fiber print from Digital Silver Imaging ($215), camera bags from Lowepro, and $250 in cash prizes. All winners reproduced in summer issue of *Photo Review* magazine and prizewinners exhibited at photography gallery of the University of Arts/Philadelphia. Open to all skill levels. Deadline: May 15. Photographers should send SASE or see website for more information.

PHOTOSPIVA

222 W. 3rd St., Joplin MO 64801. (417)623-0183. Fax: (417)623-3805. E-mail: spiva@spivaarts.org. Website: www.spivaarts.org; www.photospiva.org. **Contact:** Jo Mueller, director. Annual national fine art photography competition. Awards: over $2,000 cash. Open to all photographers in the U.S. and its territories; any photographic process welcome. Enter online. See website for updates on deadlines and exhibition dates.

PICTURES OF THE YEAR INTERNATIONAL

315 Reynolds Journalism Institute, Columbia MO 65211. (573)884-7351. E-mail: info@poyi.org. Website: www.poyi.org. **Contact:** Rick Shaw. Cost: $50/entrant. Annual contest to reward and recognize excellence in photojournalism, sponsored by the Missouri School of Journalism and the Donald W. Reynolds Journalism Institute. Over $20,000 in cash and product awards. Open to all skill levels. January deadline. Photographers should write, call, e-mail or see website for more information.

○ The Missouri School of Journalism also sponsors College Photographer of the Year. See website for details.

⊕ ○ PROFESSIONAL WOMEN PHOTOGRAPHERS INTERNATIONAL WOMEN'S CALL FOR ENTRY

(212)410-3865. Fax: (212)289-7979. E-mail: open.calls@pwponline.org. Website: www.pwponline.org. **Contact:** Terry Berenson, development director. Cost: $35 for first three images; $10 for each additional image. Contest held annually. "Professional Women Photographers (PWP) helps fulfill its mission of advancing women in photography by hosting international Calls for Entry open to all women photographers around the world." Awards: "First Prize: One photographer will receive $600 and her selected image will appear in the Spring/Summer issue of *Imprints* magazine. Her image will be exhibited in the Soho Photo Gallery show and the online exhibition. Second Prize: One photographer will receive $500 and her image will appear in *Imprints* Spring/Summer issue. Her image will be exhibited in the Soho-Photo Gallery show and the online exhibition. Third Prize: One photographer will receive $400 and her image will appear in the Spring/Summer issue of *Imprints*. Her image will be exhibited in the SohoPhoto Gallery show and the online exhibition." Deadlines vary; see website for details.

THE PROJECT COMPETITION

Center, P.O. Box 2483, Santa Fe NM 87504. (505)984-8353. Website: www.visitcenter.org. Annual contest. The Project Competition honors committed photographers working on documentary projects and fine-art series. Three jurors reach a consensus on the First Prize and 10-25 Honorable Mentions. Each individual juror also selects a project to receive 1 of the 3 Juror's Choice Awards. Prizes include $5,000, a 2-person exhibition and reception during Review Santa Fe, a year-long Photographer's Showcase at Photoeve.com, publication in *Fraction* magazine, workshop tuition vouchers, $250 gift certificate to Blurb books and an online exhibition at VisitCenter.org. Photographers should see website for more information.

RHODE ISLAND STATE COUNCIL ON THE ARTS FELLOWSHIPS

One Capitol Hill, 3rd Floor, Providence RI 02908. (401)222-3880. Fax: (401)222-3018. Website: www.arts.ri.gov. Rhode Island residents only. Cost: free. Annual contest "to encourage the creative development of Rhode Island artists by enabling them to set aside time to pursue their work and achieve specific career goals." Awards $5,000 fellowship; $1,000 merit award. Open to advanced photographers. Deadline: April 1. Photographers should go to www.arts.ri.gov/grants/guidelines/fellow.php for more information.

☺ SAN DIEGO COUNTY FAIR ANNUAL EXHIBITION OF PHOTOGRAPHY

2260 Jimmy Durante Blvd., Del Mar CA 92014. (858)792-4207. E-mail: entry@sdfair.com. Website: www.sdfair.com. **Contact:** Entry office. Sponsor: San

Diego County Fair (22nd District Agricultural Association). Annual event for still photos/prints. This is a juried competition open to individual photographers. Entry information is posted on the website as it becomes available in February and March. Pre-registration deadline: April/May. Access the dates and specifications for entry on website. Entry form can be submitted online.

○ SPRING PHOTOGRAPHY CONTEST

Serbin Communications, 813 Reddick St., Santa Barbara CA 93103. (805)963-0439 or (800)876-6425. Fax: (805)965-0496. E-mail: admin@serbin.com. Website: www.pfmagazine.com. Annual amateur contest, runs January thru mid-May. Sponsored by *Photographer's Forum Magazine*. Winners and finalists have their photos published in the hardcover book, *Best of Photography*. See website for entry form.

TAYLOR COUNTY PHOTOGRAPHY CLUB MEMORIAL DAY CONTEST

P.O. Box 613, Grafton WV 26354-0613. (304)265-5405. E-mail: hsw123@comcast.net. **Contact:** Harry S. White, Jr., club secretary. Cost: $3/print (maximum of 10). Annual juried contest (nationally judged) held in July/August during the May observance of Memorial Day in Grafton. Color and b&w, all subject matter. All prints must be mounted or matted, with a minimum overall size of 8×10 and maximum overall size of 16×20. No framed prints or slides. No signed prints or mats. All prints must be identified on the back as follows: name, address, phone number, title, and entry number of print (e.g., 1 of 6). All entries must be delivered in a reusable container. Entrant's name, address and number of prints must appear on the outside of the container. Open to amateur photographers only. Six award categories.

TEXAS PHOTOGRAPHIC SOCIETY, NATIONAL COMPETITION

6338 N. New Braunfels #174, San Antonio TX 78209. (210)824-4123. E-mail: clarke@texasphoto.org. Website: www.texasphoto.org. Cost: $35 for 5 images, plus $5 for each image over 5, and membership fee if joining Texas Photographic Society. You do not have to be a member to enter. See website or call for information on membership fees. TPS has a membership of 1,300 from 49 states and 12 countries. Contest held annually. Cash awards: 1st Place: $750; 2nd Place: $350; 3rd Place: $200; 5 honorable mentions at $100 each.

The exhibition will open in Austin, TX and be exhibited at galleries in Odessa, Abilene, and San Antonio. Open to all skill levels. See website or call for more information.

TEXAS PHOTOGRAPHIC SOCIETY ANNUAL MEMBERS' ONLY SHOW

Website: www.texasphoto.org. Photographers should see website for more information. Cost: $35 for 5 images, plus $5 for each image over 5, and membership fee if joining Texas Photographic Society. You must be a member to enter. TPS has a membership of 1,300 from 48 states and 12 countries. Contest held annually. Cash awards: 1st place: $500; 2nd place: $300; 3rd place $200; 5 honorable mentions at $100 each. The Members' Only show opens in different cities with a juror from that city and has opened in Austin, Beaumont, Longview, Lubbock, El Paso, Dallas, Galveston, San Marcos, San Antonio, and San Francisco, CA. Open to all skill levels. See website or call Clarke for more information.

◐ ◯ UNLIMITED EDITIONS INTERNATIONAL JURIED PHOTOGRAPHY COMPETITIONS

Competition Chairman, 319. E. Shay Circle, Hendersonville NC 28791. (828)489-9609. E-mail: Ultd EditionsIntl@aol.com. **Contact:** Gregory Hugh Leng, president/owner. Sponsors juried photography competitions several times yearly offering cash, award certificates and prizes. Photography accepted from amateurs and professionals. Open to all skill levels and ages. Prizes awarded in different categories or divisions such as commercial, portraiture, journalism, landscape, digital imaging, and retouching. We accept formats in print film, transparencies and digital images. B&w, color, and digital imaging CDs or DVDs may be submitted for consideration. Prints and large transparencies may be in mats, no frames. All entries must be delivered in a reusable container with prepaid postage to insure photography is returned. Unlimited Editions International also offers the unique opportunity to purchase photography from those photographers who wish to sell their work. All images submitted in competition remain the property of the photographer/entrants unless an offer to purchase their work is accepted by the photographer. All photographers must send SASE for entry forms, contest dates, and detailed information on how to participate in our International juried photography competitions.

YOUR BEST SHOT

E-mail: YourBestShot@bonniercorp.com. Website: www.popphoto.com. Monthly contest; submit up to 5 entries/month. Submit digital photographs: 50-75KB recommended, 1000KB maximum, JPEG format only; if accepted for publication, an image file size of at least 9MB (uncompressed) will be required. Each file should be named with your full name. Multiple entries should be named with your full name followed by consecutive numbers. "If your photo is selected for first place you will receive $300; $200 for second place; $100 for third place; and $50 for honorable mention. And your photo will be published in *Popular Photography* magazine and may be showcased in a gallery on the Pop Photo website. Include your name, address, phone number, and e-mail address. Also, any technical information you can supply about the photo—camera, lens, settings, film, software, and printer. Submitting a composite? Tell us! If you win and we need more material, we will contact you."

PHOTO REPRESENTATIVES

Many photographers are good at promoting themselves and seeking out new clients, and they actually enjoy that part of the business. Other photographers are not comfortable promoting themselves and would rather dedicate their time and energy solely to producing their photographs. Regardless of which camp you're in, you may need a photo rep.

Finding the rep who is right for you is vitally important. Think of your relationship with a rep as a partnership. Your goals should mesh. Treat your search for a rep much as you would your search for a client. Try to understand the rep's business, who they already represent, etc., before you approach them. Show you've done your homework.

When you sign with a photo rep, you basically hire someone to get your portfolio in front of art directors, make cold calls in search of new clients, and develop promotional ideas to market your talents. The main goal is to find assignment work for you with corporations, advertising firms, or design studios. And, unlike stock agencies or galleries, a photo rep is interested in marketing your talents rather than your images.

Most reps charge a 20- to 30-percent commission. They handle more than one photographer at a time, usually making certain that each shooter specializes in a different area. For example, a rep may have contracts to promote three different photographers—one who handles product shots, another who shoots interiors, and a third who photographs food.

DO YOU NEED A REP?

Before you decide to seek out a photo representative, consider these questions:

- Do you already have enough work, but want to expand your client base?
- Are you motivated to maximize your profits? Remember that a rep is interested in working with photographers who can do what is necessary to expand their businesses.

- Do you have a tightly edited portfolio with pieces showing the kind of work you want to do?
- Are you willing to do what it takes to help the rep promote you, including having a budget to help pay for self-promotional materials?
- Do you have a clear idea of where you want your career to go, but need assistance in getting there?
- Do you have a specialty or a unique style that makes you stand out?

If you answered yes to most of these questions, perhaps you would profit from the expertise of a rep. If you feel you are not ready for a rep or that you don't need one, but you still want some help, you might consider a consultation with an expert in marketing and/or self-promotion.

As you search for a rep, there are numerous points to consider. First, how established is the rep you plan to approach? Established reps have an edge over newcomers in that they know the territory. They've built up contacts in ad agencies, magazines, and elsewhere. This is essential since most art directors and picture editors do not stay in their positions for long periods of time. Therefore, established reps will have an easier time helping you penetrate new markets.

If you decide to go with a new rep, consider paying an advance against commission in order to help the rep financially during an equitable trial period. Usually it takes a year to see returns on portfolio reviews and other marketing efforts, and a rep who is relying on income from sales might go hungry if he doesn't have a base income from which to live.

Whatever you agree upon, always have a written contract. Handshake deals won't cut it. You must know the tasks that each of you is required to complete, and having your roles discussed in a contract will guarantee there are no misunderstandings. For example, spell out in your contract what happens with clients that you had before hiring the rep. Most photographers refuse to pay commissions for these "house" accounts, unless the rep handles them completely and continues to bring in new clients.

Also, it's likely that some costs, such as promotional fees, will be shared. For example, photographers often pay 75 percent of any advertising fees (such as sourcebook ads and direct mail pieces).

If you want to know more about a specific rep, or how reps operate, contact the Society of Photographers and Artists Representatives, 60 E. 42nd St., Suite 1166, New York NY 10165, (212)779-7464, www.spar.org. SPAR sponsors educational programs and maintains a code of ethics to which all members must adhere.

ACHARD & ASSOCIATES

611 Broadway, Suite 803, New York NY 10012. (212)614-0962. Fax: (212)254-9751. E-mail: philippe@p-achard.com. Website: www.p-achard.com; www.achardimages.com. **Contact:** Philippe Achard, Malado Baldwin or Suzie Mellring, art directors. Estab. 1990. Commercial photography representative. Represents 12 photographers. Agency specializes in fashion, portraiture, interiors and still life. Markets include advertising agencies, editorial/magazines, direct mail firms, corporate/client direct, design firms, publishing/books.

HANDLES Photography only.

TERMS Rep receives 25% commission. Exclusive area representation required. For promotional purposes, talent must provide images and money. Advertises in *Le Book*.

HOW TO CONTACT Send portfolio. Responds only if interested within 1 week. Portfolios may be dropped off every day. To show portfolio, photographer should follow up with a call.

TIPS Finds new talent through recommendations from other artists, magazines. "Be original."

ROBERT BACALL REPRESENTATIVES INC.

4 Springwood Dr., Princeton Junction NJ 08550. (212)695-1729. Fax: (212)695-1739. E-mail: rob@bacall.com. Website: www.bacall.com. **Contact:** Robert Bacall. Estab. 1988. "We represent commercial photographers, CGI and motion content providers for both print and video animation needs. Agency specializes in digital imaging, healthcare, food, still life, fashion, beauty, kids, corporate, environmental, portrait, lifestyle, location, landscape. Markets include advertising agencies, corporations/clients direct, design firms, editorial/magazines, publishing/books, sales/promotion firms.

TERMS Rep receives 30-35% commission. Exclusive area representation required. For promotional purposes, talent must provide portfolios, cases, tearsheets, prints, etc. Advertises in *Found Folios*, *Workbook*, *Le Book*, *Alternative Pick*, *PDN-Photoserve*, *At-Edge* and all of their respective websites. Bacall reps can also be found on Facebook, Twitter and LinkedIn.

HOW TO CONTACT Send query letter/e-mail, direct mail flier/brochure. Responds only if interested. After initial contact, drop off or mail materials for review.

TIPS "Seek representation when you feel your portfolio is unique and can bring in new business." Also offering consulting services to photographers that are not represented but are looking to improve their business potential.

MARIANNE CAMPBELL ASSOCIATES

354 Panoramic Hwy., Mill Valley CA 94941. (415)433-0353. E-mail: marianne@mariannecampbell.com; quinci@mariannecampbell.com. Website: www.MarianneCampbell.com. **Contact:** Marianne Campbell or Quinci Payne. Estab. 1989. Commercial photography representative. Member of APA, SPAR, Western Art Directors Club. Represents 6 photographers. Markets include advertising agencies, corporations/clients direct, design firms, editorial/magazines.

HANDLES Photography.

TERMS Negotiated individually with each photographer.

HOW TO CONTACT Send printed samples of work. Responds in 2 weeks, only if interested.

TIPS Obtains new talent through recommendations from art directors and designers and outstanding promotional materials.

MARGE CASEY & ASSOCIATES

20 W. 22nd St., #1605, New York NY 10010. (212)929-3757. E-mail: info@margecasey.com. Website: www.margecasey.com. Represents photographers. Agency specializes in representing commercial photographers. Markets include advertising agencies, corporate/client direct, design firms, editorial/magazines, direct mail firms.

HANDLES Photography.

HOW TO CONTACT Send brochure, promo cards. Responds only if interested. Portfolios may be dropped off Monday through Friday. To show portfolio, photographer should follow up with call. Rep will contact photographer for portfolio review if interested.

TIPS Finds new talent through submission, recommendations from other artists.

RANDY COLE REPRESENTS, LLC

115 W. 30th St., Suite 404, New York NY 10001. (212)760-1212. Fax: (212)760-1199. E-mail: randy@randycole.com. Website: www.randycole.com. Estab. 1989. Commercial photography representative. Member of SPAR. Represents 10 photographers. Staff in-

cludes an assistant. Markets include advertising agencies, editorial companies and magazines, corporate clients, design firms, publishers and entertainment and music companies.

HANDLES Photography.

TERMS Rep receives commission on the creative fees; dependent upon specific negotiation. Advertises in *At Edge*, *Archive* and *Le Book* as well as online creative directories, e.g., *Workbook* and Photoserve.

HOW TO CONTACT Send e-mail or promo piece and follow up with call. Portfolios may be dropped off; set up appointment.

TIPS Finds new talent through submissions and referrals.

FRANCOISE DUBOIS/DUBOIS REPRESENTS

305 Newbury Lane, Newbury Park CA 91320. (805)376-9738. Fax: (805)376-9738. E-mail: fd@francoisedubois.com. Website: www.francoisedubois.com. **Contact:** Françoise Dubois, owner. Commercial photography representative and creative and marketing consultant. Represents 3 photographers. Staff includes Michel Dubois (still life/people) and Michael Baciu (photo impressionism). Agency specializes in commercial photography for advertising, editorial, creative, marketing consulting. Markets include advertising agencies, corporations/clients direct, design firms, editorial/magazines, publishing/books, sales/promotion firms.

HANDLES Photography.

TERMS Rep receives 25% commission. Charges FedEx expenses (if not paid by advertising agency or other potential client). Exclusive area representation required. Advertising costs are paid by talent. For promotional purposes, talent must provide "3 portfolios, advertising in national sourcebook, and 3 or 4 direct mail pieces per year. All must carry my name and number."

HOW TO CONTACT Not looking at portfolios at this time. Send e-mail with link to site.

TIPS "Do not look for a rep if your target market is too small a niche. Do not look for a rep if you're not somewhat established. Hire a consultant to help you design a consistent and unique portfolio and marketing strategy, and to make sure your strengths are made evident and you remain focused."

MICHAEL GINSBURG & ASSOCIATES, INC.

345 E. 94th St., #10F, New York NY 10128. (212)369-3594. Fax: (212)679-3495. E-mail: mg@michaelginsburg.com. Website: www.michaelginsburg.com. **Contact:** Michael Ginsburg. Estab. 1978. Commercial photography representative. Represents 9 photographers. Agency specializes in advertising and editorial photographers. Markets include advertising agencies, corporations/clients direct, design firms, editorial/magazines, sales/promotion firms.

HANDLES Photography.

TERMS Rep receives 30% commission. Charges for messenger costs, FedEx expenses. Exclusive area representation required. Advertising costs are paid 100% by talent. For promotional purposes, talent must provide a minimum of 5 portfolios—direct mail pieces 2 times per year—and at least 1 sourcebook per year. Advertises in *Workbook*, source books and online source books.

HOW TO CONTACT Send query letter, direct mail flier/brochure, or e-mail. Responds only if interested within 2 weeks. After initial contact, call for appointment to show portfolio of tearsheets, slides, photographs.

TIPS Obtains new talent through personal referrals and solicitation.

CAROL GUENZI AGENTS, INC.

865 Delaware St., Denver CO 80204. (303)820-2599. E-mail: carol@artagent.com. Website: www.artagent.com. **Contact:** Carol Guenzi, president. Estab. 1984. Commercial illustration, photography, new media, film/animation representative. Member of Art Directors Club of Denver, AIGA and ASMP. Represents 30 illustrators, 8 photographers, 6 computer multimedia designers, 3 copywriters, 2 film/video production companies. Agency specializes in a "worldwide selection of talent in all areas of visual communications." Markets include advertising agencies, corporations/clients direct, design firms, editorial/magazine, paper products/greeting cards, sales/promotions firms.

HANDLES Illustration, photography, new media, film and animation. Looking for unique styles and applications and digital imaging.

TERMS Rep receives 25-30% commission. Exclusive area representation required. Advertising costs are split: 70-75% paid by talent; 25-30% paid by representative. For promotional purposes, talent must provide "promotional material after 6 months, some restrictions on portfolios." Advertises in *Directory of Illustration* and *Workbook*.

HOW TO CONTACT E-mail JPEGs or send direct mail piece, tearsheets. Responds in 2-3 weeks, only if interested. After initial contact, call or e-mail for appointment or to drop off or ship materials for review. Portfolio should include tearsheets, prints, samples and a list of current clients.

TIPS Obtains new talent through solicitation, art directors' referrals and active pursuit by individual. "Show your strongest style and have at least 12 samples of that style before introducing all your capabilities. Be prepared to add additional work to your portfolio to help round out your style. We do a large percentage of computer manipulation and accessing on network. All our portfolios are both electronic and prints."

PAT HACKETT/ARTIST REP

Website: www.pathackett.com. Estab. 1979. Commercial illustration and photography representative. Member of Graphic Artists Guild. Represents 12 illustrators and 1 photographer. Markets include advertising agencies, corporations/client direct, design firms, editorial/magazines.

HANDLES Illustration, photography.

TERMS Rep receives 25-33% commission. Exclusive area representation required. No geographic restrictions. Advertising costs are split: 75% paid by talent; 25% paid by representative. For promotional purposes, talent must provide "standardized portfolio, i.e., all pieces within the book are the same format." Advertises in *Showcase* and *Workbook* (www.portfolios.com and www.theispot.com).

HOW TO CONTACT Send direct mail flier/brochure or e-mail. Responds within 3 weeks if interested.

TIPS Looks for "experience in the *commercial* art world, professional presentation in both portfolio and person, cooperative attitude and enthusiasm."

JG + A

(323)464-2492. Fax: (323)465-7013. E-mail: info@jgaonline.com. Website: www.jgaonline.com. Estab. 1985. Commercial photography representative. Member of APA. Represents 12 photographers. Staff: Sherwin Taghdiri, sales rep. Agency specializes in photography. Markets include advertising agencies, design firms.

HANDLES Photography.

TERMS Rep receives 25% commission. Charges shipping expenses. Exclusive representation required. No geographic restrictions. Advertising costs are paid by talent. For promotional purposes,

talent must provide promos, advertising and a quality portfolio. Advertises in various source books.

HOW TO CONTACT Send direct mail flier/brochure.

TRICIA JOYCE INC.

79 Chambers St., New York NY 10007. (212)962-0728. E-mail: info@triciajoyce.com. Website: www.triciajoyce.com. **Contact:** Tricia Joyce; Amy Fraher. Estab. 1988. Commercial photography representative. Represents photographers and stylists. Agency specializes in fashion, advertising, lifestyle, still life, travel, cosmetics/beauty, interiors, portraiture. Markets include advertising agencies, corporations/clients direct, design firms, editorial/magazines and sales/promotion firms.

HANDLES Photography, stylists, hair and makeup artists, and fine art.

TERMS Agent receives 25% commission for photography; 20% for stylists, 50% for stock.

HOW TO CONTACT Send query letter, résumé, direct mail flier/brochure and photocopies. Responds only if interested. After initial contact, "wait to hear, please don't call."

CRISTOPHER LAPP PHOTOGRAPHY

1211 Sunset Plaza Dr., Suite 413, Los Angeles CA 90069. (310)612-0040. Fax: (310)943-3793. E-mail: Cristopherlapp@yahoo.com. Website: www.cristopherlapp.com. Estab. 1994. Specializes in fine art prints, hand-pulled originals, limited edition, monoprints, monotypes, offset reproduction, unlimited edition, posters.

HANDLES Decorative art, fashionable art, commercial and designer marketing. Clients include: Posner Fine Art, Gilanyi Inc., Jordan Designs.

TERMS Keeps samples on file.

HOW TO CONTACT Send an e-mail inquiry.

LEE + LOU PRODUCTIONS INC.

211 N. Dianthus St., Manhattan Beach CA 90266. (310)374-1918. Fax: (310)287-1814. E-mail: leelou@earthlink.net. Website: www.leelou.com. **Contact:** Lee Pisarski. Estab. 1981. Commercial illustration and photography representative, digital and traditional photo retouching. Represents 2 retouchers, 5 photographers, 5 film directors, 2 visual effects companies, 1 CGI company. Specializes in automotive. Markets include advertising agencies.

HANDLES Photography, commercial film, CGI, visual effects.

TERMS Rep receives 25% commission. Charges for shipping, entertainment. Exclusive area representation required. Advertising costs are paid by talent. For promotional purposes, talent must provide direct mail advertising material. Advertises in *Creative Black Book*, *Workbook* and *Single Image, Shoot, Boards*.

HOW TO CONTACT Send direct mail flyer/brochure, tearsheets. Responds in 1 week. After initial contact, call for appointment to show portfolio of photographs.

TIPS Obtains new talent through recommendations from others, some solicitation.

THE BRUCE LEVIN GROUP

601 W. 26th St, Suite 1223, New York NY 10001. (212)627-2281. E-mail: brucelevin@mac.com. Website: www.brucelevingroup.com. **Contact:** Bruce Levin, president. Estab. 1983. Commercial photography representative. Estab. 1983. Member of SPAR and ASMP. Represents 10 photographers. Agency specializes in advertising, editorial and catalog; heavy emphasis on fashion, lifestyle and computer graphics.

HANDLES Photography.

TERMS Rep receives 25% commission. Exclusive area representation required. Advertising costs are paid by talent. Advertises in *Workbook* and other sourcebooks.

HOW TO CONTACT Send brochure, photos; call. Portfolios may be dropped off every Monday–Friday.

TIPS Obtains new talent through recommendations, research, word of mouth, solicitation.

NORMAN MASLOV AGENT INTERNATIONALE

879 Florida St., San Francisco CA 94110. (415)641-4376. Fax: (415)695-0921. E-mail: maslov@maslov.com. Website: maslov.com. Estab. 1986. Member of APA. Represents 12 photographers. Markets include advertising agencies, corporations/clients direct, design firms, editorial/magazines, paper products/greeting cards, publishing/books, private collections.

HANDLES Photography. Looking for "original work not derivative of other artists. Artist must have developed style."

TERMS Rep receives 30% commission. Exclusive US national representation required. Advertising costs split varies. For promotional purposes, talent must provide 3-4 direct mail pieces/year. Advertises in *Archive*, *Workbook* and *At Edge*.

HOW TO CONTACT Send query letter, direct mail flier/brochure, tearsheets. Do not send original work. Responds in 2-3 weeks, only if interested. After initial contact, call to schedule an appointment, or drop off or mail materials for review. Individual and group consulting available in person or via phone or website.

TIPS Obtains new talent through suggestions from art buyers and recommendations from designers, art directors, other agents, sourcebooks and industry magazines and social networks. "We prefer to follow our own leads rather than receive unsolicited promotions and inquiries. It's best to have represented yourself for several years to know your strengths and be realistic about your marketplace. The same is true of having experience with direct mail pieces, developing client lists, and having a system of follow up. We want our talent to have experience with all this so they can properly value our contribution to their growth and success—otherwise that 30% becomes a burden and point of resentment. Enter your best work into competitions such as *Communication Arts* and *Graphis* photo annuals. Create a distinctive promotion mailer if your concepts and executions are strong."

JUDITH MCGRATH

P.O. Box 133, 32W040 Army Trail Rd., Wayne IL 60184. (312)945-8450. Fax: (312)465-1638. E-mail: judy@judymcgrath.net. Website: www.judymcgrath.net. Estab. 1980. Commercial photography representative. Represents photographers. Markets include advertising agencies, corporate/client direct, design firms, editorial/magazines, paper products/greeting cards, publishing/books, direct mail firms.

HANDLES Photography.

TERMS Rep receives 25% commission. Exclusive area representation required. Advertising costs paid by talent. Advertises in *Workbook*.

HOW TO CONTACT Send query letter, bio, tearsheets, photocopies. Rep will contact photographer for portfolio review if interested.

MUNRO CAMPAGNA ARTISTS REPRESENTATIVES

630 N. State St., #2109, Chicago IL 60654. (312)335-8925. E-mail: steve@munrocampagna.com. Website: www.munrocampagna.com. **Contact:** Steve Munro, president. Estab. 1987. Commercial photography and

illustration representative. Member of SPAR, CAR (Chicago Artist Representatives). Represents 1 photographer, 30 illustrators. Markets include advertising agencies, corporations/clients direct, design firms, publishing/books.

HANDLES Illustration, photography.

TERMS Rep receives 30% commission. Exclusive national representation required. Advertising costs are paid by talent. For promotional purposes, talent must provide 2 portfolios, leave-behinds, several promos. Advertises in *Workbook*, other sourcebooks.

HOW TO CONTACT Send query letter, bio, tearsheets, SASE. Responds within 2 weeks, only if interested. After initial contact, write to schedule an appointment.

TIPS Obtains new talent through recommendations, periodicals. "Do a little homework and target appropriate rep. Try to get a referral from an art buyer or art director."

PHOTOKUNST

725 Argyle Ave., Friday Harbor WA 98250. (360)378-1028. Fax: (360)370-5061. Website: www.photokunst.com. **Contact:** Barbara Cox, principal. Estab. 1998. Consulting and marketing of photography archives and fine art photography, nationally and internationally. "Accepting select number of photographers on our website. Works with artists on licensing, curating and traveling gallery and museum exhibitions; agent for photo books."

HANDLES Emphasis on cause-oriented photography, photojournalism, documentary and ethnographic photography. Vintage and contemporary photography.

TERMS Charges for consultation, per project rate or annual for full representation; for representation, website fee and percentage of sales and licensing.

HOW TO CONTACT Send website information. Responds in 2 months.

TIPS Finds new talent through submissions, recommendations from other artists, publications, art fairs, portfolio reviews. "In order to be placed in major galleries, a book or catalog must be either in place or in serious planning stage."

PHOTOTHERAPY

11977 Kiowa Ave., Los Angeles CA 90049-6119. E-mail: rhoni@phototherapists.com. Website: www.phototherapists.com. **Contact:** Rhoni Epstein, acquisitions. Estab. 1983. Commercial and fine art photography consultant. "Consulting with a knowledgeable and well-respected industry insider is a valuable way to get focused and advance your career in a creative and cost-efficient manner. You will see how to differentiate yourself from other photographers and get to where you want to be. Inexpensive ways to customize your portfolio, marketing program, branding materials and websites will show the market who you are and why they need you. You will be guided to embrace your point of view and learn how to focus your images on making money!" Rhoni Epstein is an Assistant Professor at Art Center College of Design, a panel moderator, portfolio reviewer, lecturer and contest judge.

HOW TO CONTACT Via e-mail.

TIPS "Work smart, remain persistent and enthusiastic; there is always a market for creative and talented people."

MARIA PISCOPO

2973 Harbor Blvd., #341, Costa Mesa CA 92626-3912. (714)356-4260. Fax: (888)713-0705. E-mail: maria@mpiscopo.com. Website: www.mpiscopo.com. **Contact:** Maria Piscopo. Estab. 1978. Commercial photography representative. Member of SPAR, Women in Photography, Society of Illustrative Photographers. Markets include advertising agencies, design firms, corporations.

HANDLES Photography. Looking for "unique, unusual styles; established photographers only."

TERMS Rep receives 25% commission. Exclusive area representation required. No geographic restrictions. Advertising costs are split: 50% paid by talent; 50% paid by representative. For promotional purposes, talent must have a website and provide 3 traveling portfolios, leave-behinds and at least 6 new promo pieces per year. Plans web, advertising and direct mail campaigns.

HOW TO CONTACT Send query letter and samples via PDF to maria@mpiscopo.com. Do not call. Responds within 2 weeks, only if interested.

TIPS Obtains new talent through personal referral and photo magazine articles. "Do lots of research. Be very businesslike, organized, professional and follow the above instructions!"

ALYSSA PIZER

13121 Garden Land Rd., Los Angeles CA 90049. (310)440-3930. Fax: (310)440-3830. E-mail:

alyssapizer@earthlink.net. Website: www.alyssapizer.com. Estab. 1990. Member of APCA. Represents 12 photographers. Agency specializes in fashion, beauty and lifestyle (catalog, image campaign, department store, beauty and lifestyle awards). Markets include advertising agencies, corporations/clients direct, design firms, editorial/magazines.

HANDLES Photography. Established photographers only.

TERMS Rep receives 25% commission. Photographer pays for FedEx and messenger charges. Talent pays 100% of advertising costs. For promotional purposes, talent must provide 10 portfolios, leave-behinds and quarterly promotional pieces.

HOW TO CONTACT Send query letter or direct mail flier/brochure or e-mail website address. Responds in a couple of days. After initial contact, call to schedule an appointment or drop off or mail materials for review.

WALTER SCHUPFER MANAGEMENT CORPORATION

413 W. 14th St., 4th Floor, New York NY 10014. (212)366-4675. Fax: (212)255-9726. E-mail: mail@wschupfer.com. Website: www.wschupfer.com. **Contact:** Walter Schupfer, president. Estab. 1996. Commercial photography representative. Represents photographers, stylists, designers. Staff includes producers, art department, syndication. Agency specializes in photography. Markets include advertising agencies, corporate/client direct, design firms, editorial/magazines, record labels, galleries.

HANDLES Photography, design, stylists, make-up artists, specializing in complete creative management.

TERMS Charges for messenger service. Exclusive area representation required. For promotional purposes, talent must provide several commercial and editorial portfolios. Advertises in *Le Book* .

HOW TO CONTACT Send promo cards, "then give us a call." To show portfolio, photographer should follow up with call.

TIPS Finds new talent through submissions, recommendations from other artists. "Do research to see if your work fits our agency."

TM ENTERPRISES

P.O. Box 18644, Beverly Hills CA 90210. E-mail: tmarques1@hotmail.com. **Contact:** Tony Marques. Estab. 1985. Commercial photography representa-

tive and photography broker. Member of Beverly Hills Chamber of Commerce. Represents 50 photographers. Agency specializes in photography of women only: high fashion, swimsuit, lingerie, glamour and fine (good taste) *Playboy*-style pictures, erotic. Markets include advertising agencies, corporations/clients direct, editorial/magazines, paper products/greeting cards, publishing/books, sales/promotion firms, medical magazines.

HANDLES Photography.

TERMS Rep receives 50% commission. Advertising costs are paid by representative. "We promote the standard material the photographer has available, unless our clients request something else." Advertises in Europe, South and Central America, and magazines not known in the U.S.

HOW TO CONTACT Send everything available. Responds in 2 days. After initial contact, drop off or mail appropriate materials for review. Portfolio should include slides, photographs, transparencies, printed work.

TIPS Obtains new talent through worldwide famous fashion shows in Paris, Rome, London and Tokyo; by participating in well-known international beauty contests; recommendations from others. "Send your material clean and organized. Do not borrow other photographers' work in order to get representation. Always protect yourself by copyrighting your material. Get releases from everybody who is in the picture (or who owns something in the picture)."

DOUG TRUPPE

121 E. 31st St., New York NY 10016. (212)685-1223. E-mail: doug@dougtruppe.com. Website: www.dougtruppe.com. **Contact:** Doug Truppe, artist representative. Estab. 1998. Commercial photography representative. Member of SPAR, Art Directors Club. Represents 10 photographers. Agency specializes in lifestyle, food, still life, portrait and children's photography. Markets include advertising agencies, corporate, design firms, editorial/magazines, publishing/books, direct mail firms.

HANDLES Photography. "Always looking for great commercial work." Established, working photographers only.

TERMS Rep receives 25% commission. Exclusive area representation required. Advertising costs are paid by talent. For promotional purposes, talent must provide directory ad (at least 1 directory per year), direct mail promo cards every 3 months, e-mail promos every month, website. Advertises in *Workbook*.

HOW TO CONTACT Send e-mail with website address. Responds within 1 month, only if interested. To show portfolio, photographer should follow up with call.

TIPS Finds artists through recommendations from other artists, source books, art buyers. "Please be willing to show some new work every 6 months. Have 3-4 portfolios available for representative. Have website and be willing to do direct mail every 3 months. Be professional and organized."

VICKI SANDER/FOLIO FORUMS

48 Gramercy Park N., New York NY 10010. (212)420-1333. E-mail: vicki@vickisander.com. Website: www.vickisander.com; www.folioforums.com. **Contact:** Vicki Sander. Estab. 1985. Commercial photography representative. Member of SPAR, The One Club for Art and Copy, The New York Art Directors Club. Represents photographers. Markets include advertising agencies, corporate/client direct, design firms, editorial/magazines, paper products/greeting cards. "Folio Forums is a company that promotes photographers by presenting portfolios at agency conference rooms in catered breakfast reviews. Accepting submissions for consideration on a monthly basis."

HANDLES Photography, fine art. Looking for lifestyle, fashion, food.

TERMS Rep receives 30% commission. Exclusive representation required. Advertising costs are paid by talent. For promotional purposes, talent must provide direct mail and sourcebook advertising. Advertises in *Workbook*.

HOW TO CONTACT Send tearsheets. Responds in 1 month. To show portfolio, photographer should follow up with a call and/or letter after initial query.

TIPS Finds new talent through recommendation from other artists, referrals. Have a portfolio put together and have promo cards to leave behind, as well as mailing out to rep prior to appointment.

THE WILEY GROUP

1535 Green St, Suite 301, San Francisco CA 94123. (415)441-3055. Fax: (415)520-0999. E-mail: info@thewileygroup.com. Website: www.thewileygroup.com. **Contact:** David Wiley, owner. Estab. 1984. Representing commercial illustration. Established as an artist agency that promotes and sells the work of illustrators for commercial use worldwide. "David Wiley has over 27 years of experience in the industry, and an extensive knowledge about the usage, pricing, and marketing of commercial art. Represents 13 illustrators. All digital work. The artist agency services accounts in advertising, design, and publishing as well as corporate accounts. Clients include Disney, Coca Cola, Smithsonian, Microsoft, Nike, Oracle, Google, Random House, Eli Lilly Pharmaceuticals, *National Geographic,* Kraft Foods, FedEx, Nestle Corp., and Apple Computers."

TERMS Rep receives 25% commission with a bonus structure. No geographical restriction. Artist pays 75% of ADBASE subscription, www.theispot.com, www.workbook.com and postcard mailings. Each year, the artists are promoted using online agencies, monthly postcard mailings, and biweekly eMailers from adbase.com.

HOW TO CONTACT For first contact, e-mail URL and one visual image representing your style. If interested, agent will e-mail or call back to discuss representation.

TIPS "The bottom line is that a good agent will get you more work at better rates of pay while freeing you to focus on right brain."

WORKSHOPS & PHOTO TOURS

Taking a photography workshop or photo tour is one of the best ways to improve your photographic skills. There is no substitute for the hands-on experience and one-on-one instruction you can receive at a workshop. Besides, where else can you go and spend several days with people who share your passion for photography?

Photography is headed in a new direction. Digital imaging is here to stay and is becoming part of every photographer's life. Even if you haven't invested a lot of money into digital cameras, computers or software, you should understand what you're up against if you plan to succeed as a professional photographer. Taking a digital imaging workshop can help you on your way.

Outdoor and nature photography are perennial workshop favorites. Creativity is another popular workshop topic. You'll also find highly specialized workshops, such as underwater photography. Many photo tours specialize in a specific location and the great photo opportunities that location affords.

As you peruse these pages, take a good look at the quality of workshops and the skill level of photographers the sponsors want to attract. It is important to know if a workshop is for beginners, advanced amateurs, or professionals. Information from a workshop organizer can help you make that determination.

These workshop listings contain only the basic information needed to make contact with sponsors, and a brief description of the styles or media covered in the programs. We also include information on costs when possible. Write, call, or e-mail the workshop/photo tour sponsors for complete information. Most have websites with extensive information about their programs, when they're offered, and how much they cost.

A workshop or photo tour can be whatever the photographer wishes—a holiday from the normal working routine, or an exciting introduction to new skills and perspectives on the craft. Whatever you desire, you're sure to find in these pages a workshop or tour that fulfills your expectations.

○ ◑ EDDIE ADAMS WORKSHOP

540 E. 11th St., New York NY 10009. (646)263-8596. E-mail: info@eddieadamsworkshop.com. Website: www.eddieadams.com. **Contact:** Mirjam Evers, workshop producer. Annual, tuition-free photojournalism workshop. The Eddie Adams Workshop brings together 100 promising young photographers with over 150 of the most influential picture journalists, picture editors, managing editors and writers from prestigious organizations such as the Associated Press, CNN, The White House, *Life*, *National Geographic*, *Newsweek*, *Time*, *Parade*, *Entertainment Weekly*, *Sports Illustrated*, *The New York Times*, *The Los Angeles Times* and *The Washington Post*. Pulitzer-prize winning photographer Eddie Adams created this program to allow young photographers to learn from experienced professionals about the storytelling power and social importance of photography. Participants are divided into 10 teams, each headed by a photographer, editor, producer, or multimedia person. Daily editing and critiquing help each student to hone skills and learn about the visual, technical, and emotional components of creating strong journalistic images. Open to photography students and professional photographers with 3 years or less of experience. Photographers should e-mail for more information.

◑ ● AERIAL AND CREATIVE PHOTOGRAPHY WORKSHOPS

Hangar 23, Box 470455, San Francisco CA 94147. (415)771-2555. Website: www.aerialarchives.com. Aerial and creative photography workshops in unique locations from helicopters, light planes and balloons.

◑ ● ALASKA'S SEAWOLF ADVENTURES

P.O. Box 312, Gustavus AK 99826. (907)957-1438. E-mail: kimber@seawolfadventures.net. Website: www.seawolfadventures.net. "Photograph glaciers, whales, bears, wolves, incredible scenics, etc., while using the Seawolf, a 97-foot, 12-passenger expedition ship, as your base camp in the Glacier Bay area."

○ ◑ ● ANCHELL PHOTOGRAPHY WORKSHOPS

1127 Broadway NE, Salem OR 97301. (503)375-2163. Fax: (503)588-4003. E-mail: steve@steveanchell.com; sanchell@ctelco.net. Website: www.anchellworkshops.com. **Contact:** Steve Anchell. Film or digital, group or private workshops held throughout the year, including large-format, 35mm, studio lighting, figure, darkroom, both color and b&w. Open to all skill levels. Upcoming workshop: March 16-23, 2012 in Cuba. Since 2001, Steve has been leading successful humanitarian missions for photographers to Cuba. On each visit, the photographers deliver medicine to a community clinic in Havana and then have time to explore Havana and the Vinales tobacco region. This is a legal visit with each member possessing a U.S. Treasury license allowing them to travel for humanitarian reasons. Though we will be in Cuba for humanitarian reasons, there will be discussion and informal instruction on street photography. See website for more information.

◑ ● ANDERSON RANCH ARTS CENTER

P.O. Box 5598, Snowmass Village CO 81615. (970)923-3181. Fax: (970)923-3871. E-mail: info@anderson ranch.org. Website: www.andersonranch.org. Digital media and photography workshops featuring distinguished artists and educators from around the world. Classes range from traditional silver and alternative photographic processes to digital formats and use of the computer as a tool for time-based and interactive works of art. Program is diversifying into video, animation, sound and installations.

○ ◑ ● ANDY LONG'S FIRST LIGHT PHOTOGRAPHY WORKSHOP TOURS

P.O. Box 2123, Castle Rock CO 80101. (303)601-2828. E-mail: andy@firstlighttours.com. Website: www.first lighttours.com. **Contact:** Andy Long, owner. Tours cover a variety of locations and topics, including: Penguins of Falkland Islands, Alaskan northern lights, Florida, south Texas birds, Glacier National Park, Iceland, Maine coast, eagles of southwest Alaska, Alaskan northern lights, Florida, Mt. Rainier National Park, Colorado wildflowers, Alaska bears, and more. See website for more information on locations, dates and prices. Open to all skill levels. Upcoming workshops: October 7-10 in Great Sand Dunes, Colorado ($1,495); October 8-13 in Monument Valley and Canyon de Chelly ($2,195); December 2-5 in Bosque del Apache, Albuquerque ($1,495). See website for more details, detailed pricing information and registration.

○ ◑ ● ANIMALS OF MONTANA, INC.

170 Nixon Peak Rd., Bozeman MT 59715. (406)686-4224. Fax: (406)686-4224. E-mail: animals@animals

ofmontana.com. Website: www.animalsofmontana. com. See website for pricing information. Held annually. Workshops held year round. "Whether you're a professional photographer or amateur or just looking for a Montana Wildlife experience, grab your camera and leave the rest to us! Please visit our tour page for a complete listing of our tours." Open to all skill levels. Photographers should call, e-mail, see website for more information.

○ ◐ ● SEAN ARBABI

508 Old Farm Rd., Danville CA 94526-4134. (925)855-8060. Fax: (925)855-8060. E-mail: workshops@ seanarbabi.com. Website: www.seanarbabi.com/ workshops.html. **Contact:** Sean Arbabi, photographer/instructor. Online and seasonal workshops held in spring, summer, fall, winter. Taught around the world (online) and in locations including Digital Photo Academy (PPSOP.com), Point Reyes Field Seminars, Santa Fe Photographic Workshops, as well as locations around the U.S. Sean Arbabi teaches through computer presentations, software demonstrations, slide shows, field shoots and hands-on instruction. All levels of workshops are offered from beginner to advanced. Subjects include exposure, digital photography, composition, HDR, panorama, technical aspects of photography, lighting, fine-tuning your personal vision, utilizing equipment, a philosophical approach to the art, as well as how to run a photography business.

○ ◐ ● ARIZONA HIGHWAYS PHOTO WORKSHOPS

2039 W. Lewis Ave., Phoenix AZ 85009. (888)790-7042. Fax: (602)256-2873. E-mail: friends@friends ofazhighways.com. Website: www.friendsofazhigh ways.com. **Contact:** Roberta Lites, customer service manager. Offers photo adventures to the American West's most spectacular locations with top professional photographers whose work routinely appears in *Arizona Highways* magazine.

○ ◐ ARROWMONT SCHOOL OF ARTS AND CRAFTS

556 Parkway, Gatlinburg TN 37738. (865)436-5860. Fax: (865)430-4101. E-mail: info@arrowmont.org. Website: www.arrowmont.org. Offers weekend, 1- and 2-week workshops in photography, drawing, painting, clay, metals/enamels, kiln glass, fibers, surface design, wood turning and furniture. Residencies, studio as-

sistantships, work-study, and scholarships are available. See individual course descriptions for pricing.

○ ◐ ● ART NEW ENGLAND SUMMER WORKSHOPS @ BENNINGTON VT

621 Huntington Ave., Boston MA 02115. (617)879-7200. Fax: (617)879-7171. E-mail: ce@massart.edu. Website: www.massartplus.org. **Contact:** Nancy McCarthy. Week-long workshops in August, run by Massachusetts College of Art. Areas of concentration include b&w, alternative processes, digital printing and many more. See website for more information and upcoming workshops.

○ ◐ ● ART OF NATURE PHOTOGRAPHY WORKSHOPS

211 Kirkland Ave., Suite 503, Kirkland WA 98033-6408. (425)968-2884. E-mail: charles@charlesneedlephoto. com. Website: www.charlesneedlephoto.com. **Contact:** Charles Needle, founder/instructor. U.S. and international locations such as Monet's Garden (France); Keukenhof Gardens (Holland), and Gardens of England; includes personalized one-on-one field and classroom instruction and supportive image evaluations. Emphasis on creative camera techniques in the field and digital darkroom, allowing students to express "the art of nature" with unique personal vision. Topics include creative macro, flower/garden photography, multiple-exposure impressionism, intimate landscapes and scenics, dynamic composition and lighting, etc. Open to all skill levels. Upcoming workshop: Indian Harbor and Peggy's Cove, Nova Scotia. See website for more information and all upcoming workshops.

ART WORKSHOPS IN GUATEMALA

4758 Lyndale Ave. S, Minneapolis MN 55419-5304. (612)825-0747. E-mail: info@artguat.org. Website: www.artguat.org. **Contact:** Liza Fourre, director. Estab. 1995. Annual workshops held in Antigua, Guatemala. See website for a list of upcoming workshops.

○ ◐ ● BACHMANN TOUR OVERDRIVE

P.O. Box 950833, Lake Mary FL 32746. (407)333-9988. E-mail: Bill@Billbachmann.com. Website: www.bill bachmann.com. **Contact:** Bill Bachmann, owner. "Bill Bachmann shares his knowledge and adventures with small groups several times a year. Past trips have been to China, Tibet, South Africa, Antarctica, India,

Nepal, Australia, New Zealand, New Guinea, Greece, Vietnam, Laos, Cambodia, Malaysia, Singapore, Guatemala, Honduras, Greece and Cuba. Future trips will be back to Cuba, Antarctica, Eastern Canada, Italy, Eastern Europe, Peru, Argentina, Brazil and many other destinations. Programs are designed for adventure travelers who love photography and want to learn stock photography from a top stock photographer." Open to all skill levels.

○ ◑ ● NOELLA BALLENGER & ASSOCIATES PHOTO WORKSHOPS

P.O. Box 457, La Canada CA 91012. (818)954-0933. Fax: (818)954-0910. E-mail: Noella1B@aol.com. Website: www.noellaballenger.com. **Contact:** Noella Ballenger. Travel and nature workshops/tours, West Coast locations. Individual instruction in small groups emphasizes visual awareness, composition, and problem-solving in the field. All formats and levels of expertise welcome. Also offers online photo classes and articles at www.apogeephoto.com.

◑ ● FRANK BALTHIS PHOTOGRAPHY WORKSHOPS

P.O. Box 255, Davenport CA 95017. (831)426-8205. E-mail: frankbalthis@yahoo.com. Website: pa.photoshelter.com/c/frankbalthis. **Contact:** Frank S. Balthis, photographer/owner. "Workshops emphasize natural history, wildlife and travel photography, often providing opportunities to photograph marine mammals." Worldwide locations range from Baja California to Alaska. Frank Balthis runs a stock photo business and is the publisher of the Nature's Design line of cards and other publications.

○ ◑ ● BETTERPHOTO.COM ONLINE PHOTOGRAPHY COURSES

16544 NE 79th St., Redmond WA 98052. (888)927-9992. Fax: (425)881-0309. E-mail: course.sales@betterphoto.com. Website: www.betterphoto.com. **Contact:** Karen Orr, executive director. BetterPhoto is the worldwide leader in online photography education, offering an approachable resource for photographers who want to improve their skills, share their photos, and learn more about the art and technique of photography. BetterPhoto offers over 100 photography courses that are taught by top professional photographers. Courses begin the 1st Wednesday of every month. Courses range in skill level from beginner to advanced and consist of inspiring weekly lessons

and personal feedback on students' photos from the instructors. "We provide websites for photographers, photo sharing solutions, free online newsletters, lively Q&A and photo discussions, a monthly contest, helpful articles and online photography courses." Open to all skill levels.

◑ BIRDS AS ART/INSTRUCTIONAL PHOTO-TOURS

P.O. Box 7245, 4041 Granada Dr., Indian Lake Estates FL 33855. (863)692-0906. E-mail: birdsasart@verizon. net. Website: www.birdsasart.com. **Contact:** Arthur Morris, instructor. The tours, which visit the top bird photography hot spots in North America, feature evening in-classroom lectures, breakfast and lunch, in-the-field instruction, 6 or more hours of photography, and most importantly, easily approachable yet free and wild subjects.

○ ◑ ● BLUE PLANET PHOTOGRAPHY WORKSHOPS AND TOURS

201 N. Kings Rd., Suite 107, Nampa ID 83687. (208)466-9340. Website: www.blueplanetphoto.com. Award-winning professional photographer and former wildlife biologist Mike Shipman conducts small group workshops/tours emphasizing individual expression and "vision-finding" by Breaking the Barriers to Creative Vision™. Workshops held in beautiful locations away from crowds and the more-often-photographed sites. Some workshops are semi-adventure-travel style, using alternative transportation such as hot air balloons, horseback, llama, and camping in remote areas. Group feedback sessions, digital presentations and film processing whenever possible. Workshops and tours held in western U.S., Alaska, Canada and overseas. On-site transportation and lodging during workshop usually included; meals included on some trips. Specific fees, optional activities and gear list outlined in tour materials. Digital photographers welcome. Workshops and tours range from 2 to 12 days, sometimes longer; average is 9 days. Custom tours and workshops available upon request. Open to all skill levels. Photographers should write, call, e-mail or see website for more information.

BLUE RIDGE WORKSHOPS

4831 Keswick Court, Montclair VA 22025. (703)967-2531. E-mail: blueridgews@mac.com. Website: www.blueridgeworkshops.com. **Contact:** Elliot Stern, owner/photographer. These workshops sell out, so book early. See website for more information and a list of all upcoming workshops.

○ ◐ ● NANCY BROWN HANDS-ON WORKSHOPS

381 Mohawk Lane, Boca Raton FL 33487. (561)988-8992. Fax: (561)988-1791. E-mail: nbrown50@bell south.net. Website: www.nancybrown.com. **Contact:** Nancy Brown. Offers one-on-one intensive workshops all year long in studio and on location in Florida. You work with Nancy, the models and the crew to create your images. Photographers should call, fax, e-mail or see website for more information.

☾ ○ ◐ ● BURREN COLLEGE OF ART WORKSHOPS

(353)65-7077200. Fax: (353)65-7077201. E-mail: anna@burrencollege.ie. Website: www.burrencollege. ie. **Contact:** Anne McKeown, resident artist. "These workshops present unique opportunities to capture the qualities of Ireland's western landscape. The flora, prehistoric tombs, ancient abbeys and castles that abound in the Burren provide an unending wealth of subjects in an ever-changing light. Workshop #1—Creatively Using Your Digital Camera, with Martina Cleary: Participants will explore the technical as well as creative range of possibilities offered on the average digital SLR camera. Suitable for beginners as well as intermediate students, the courses involve a mixture of both fieldwork and instruction in the digital darkroom. Maximum of 10 participants. Workshop #2—Digital Photography II, with Martina Cleary: This course is for students who already know the basic principles of using the digital camera, but would like to concentrate more on the creative potential of photography. Over the five days of the course, we will explore differences between a variety of photographic genre, including the portrait, the documentary shot, the snapshot, the photo-story, the deadpan image and the tableaux vivant. The intention of the course is to introduce students to the language of photography as an expressive medium. During the course, we will explore a selection of important photographic pioneers and through practical guided assignments, discover new ways to describe our experience through the lens. Fieldwork will involve short excursions into the immediate local environment of the burren. Photographers should e-mail for more information or go to website."

● CALIFORNIA PHOTOGRAPHIC WORKSHOPS

2500 N. Texas St., Fairfield CA 94533. (888)422-6606. E-mail: cpwschool@sbcglobal.net. Website: www. cpwschool.com. **Contact:** James Inks. 3 and 5-day workshops in professional photography.

☾ ● CAMARGO FOUNDATION VISUAL ARTS FELLOWSHIP

1, Avenue Jermini, Cassis 13260, France. E-mail: apply@ camargofoundation.org. Website: www.camargo foundation.org. **Contact:** Emily Roberts, applications coordinator. Residencies awarded to visual artists, creative writers, composers, and academics. Artists may work on a specific project, develop a body of work, etc. Fellows must live on-site at foundation headquarters for the duration of the fellowship. Self-catering accommodation provided, stipend of $1,500 available. Open to advanced photographers. See website for deadline. Photographers should visit website to apply. **Note:** The fellowship is suspended for the 2011-12 academic year and is not currently accepting applications. If you are interested in applying for future fellowships, please revisit the website in October 2011.

○ ◐ ● JOHN C. CAMPBELL FOLK SCHOOL

One Folk School Rd., Brasstown NC 28902. (828)837-2775 or (800)365-5724. Fax: (828)837-8637. Website: www.folkschool.org. The Folk School offers year-round weekend and weeklong courses in photography. Please call for free catalog or see website for more information and upcoming workshops.

○ ◐ ● THE CENTER FOR FINE ART PHOTOGRAPHY

400 N. College Ave., Fort Collins CO 80524. (907)224-1010. E-mail: contact@c4fap.org. Website: www. c4fap.org/workshops_intro.asp. **Contact:** Hamidah Glasgow, executive director. The Center for Fine Art Photography offers a range of workshops for the novice photographer to the advanced professional. Each workshop is presented by a photographer who has extensive knowledge and skills in the subject he or she presents. All classes are limited to a certain number of attendees to maximize your learning experience. New courses are added frequently. See website for more information and upcoming workshops.

CHICAGO PHOTO SAFARIS

9171 Raven Crest Lane, Byron IL 61010. (815)222-2824. E-mail: Info@Chicagophotosafaris.com. Website: www.ChicagoPhotoSafaris.com. **Contact:** Gary Gullett, owner/operations manager. Held daily. "Local travel photography workshops are held daily in convenient locations in Chicago. These are 'hands-on' workshops with participants learning the creative camera controls and concepts of photography in easy-to-understand language. There are also regional, national and worldwide safaris for the more adventurous. Extreme photography opportunities include adventures such as mountain climbing and/or scuba diving, all in great photographic venus. Check the website for details." Open to photographers of all skill levels and types of cameras (film or digital).

KATHLEEN T. CARR PHOTOGRAPHY

P.O. Box 335, Honaunau HI 96726. (808)328-2162. E-mail: workshops@kathleencarr.com. Website: www.kathleencarr.com.workshops. **Contact:** Kathleen T. Carr. Photographing special places, digital infrared, model shoots, Photoshop, Polaroid/Fuji transfers, handcoloring and more. November 5-12. Location is Tropical Hideaway, South Kona, Big Island of Hawaii. Limited to 6 individuals. See website for more information and registration.

CATHY CHURCH PERSONAL UNDERWATER PHOTOGRAPHY COURSES

P.O. Box 479, GT, Grand Cayman KY1 1106, Cayman Islands. (345)949-7415 or (607)330-3504 (U.S. callers). Fax: (345)949-9770 or (607)330-3509 (U.S.). E-mail: cathy@cathychurch.com. Website: www.cathychurch.com. **Contact:** Cathy Church. Hotel/dive package available at Sunset House Hotel. Private and group lessons available for all levels throughout the year; classroom and shore diving can be arranged. Lessons available for professional photographers expanding to underwater work. Photographers should e-mail for more information.

THE CENTER FOR PHOTOGRAPHY AT WOODSTOCK

59 Tinker St., Woodstock NY 12498. (845)679-9957. E-mail: info@cpw.org. Website: www.cpw.org. **Contact:** Lindsay Stern. "Held at CPW in Woodstock, NY, our hands-on workshops allow you to expand your craft, skills and vision under the mentorship of a leading image-maker." Workshops are kept intimate by limited enrollment and taught by highly qualified support staff. Photographers should call, e-mail or see website for more information and a list of upcoming workshops.

CLICKERS & FLICKERS PHOTOGRAPHY NETWORK—LECTURES & WORKSHOPS

P.O. Box 60508, Pasadena CA 91116-6508. (310)457-6130. E-mail: dawnhope@clickersandflickers.com; photographer@clickersandflickers.com. Website: www.clickersandflickers.com. **Contact:** Dawn Hope Stevens, organizer. Estab. 1985. Monthly networking dinners with outstanding guest speakers (many award winners, including the Pulitzer Prize), events and free activities for members. "Clickers & Flickers Photography Network, Inc., was created to provide people with an interest and passion for photography (cinematography, filmmaking, image making) the opportunity to meet others with similar interests for networking and camaraderie. It creates an environment in which photography issues, styles, techniques, enjoyment and appreciation can be discussed and viewed as well as experienced with people from many fields and levels of expertise (beginners, students, amateur, hobbyist, or professionals, gallery owners and museum curators). We publish a bimonthly color magazine listing thousands of activities for photographers and lovers of images." Most of its content is not on our website for a reason. Membership and magazine subscriptions help support this organization. Clickers & Flickers Photography Network, Inc., is a 21-year-old professional photography network association that promotes information and offers promotional marketing opportunities for photographers, cinematographers, individuals, organizations, businesses, and events. "C&F also provides referrals for photographers. Our membership includes photographers, videographers, and cinematographers who are skilled in the following types of photography: outdoor and nature, wedding, headshots, fine art, sports, events, products, news, glamour, fashion, macro, commercial, landscape, advertising, architectural, wildlife, candid, photojournalism, marquis gothic—fetish, aerial and underwater; using the following types of equipment: motion picture cameras (Imax, 70mm,

65mm, 35mm, 16mm, 8mm), steadicam systems, video, high-definition, digital, still photography—large format, medium format and 35mm." Open to all skill levels. Photographers should call or e-mail for more information.

◐ ● COMMUNITY DARKROOM

713 Monroe Ave., Rochester NY 14607. (585)244-1730. E-mail: gcae@geneseearts.org. Website: www.geneseearts.org. The Genesee Center for the Arts & Education offers programs in all of our visual arts areas: Community Darkroom, Genesee Pottery, and the Printing and Book Arts Center. We offer youth programs, classes and workshops, rent studio space to individuals and exhibit work in our galleries. Anyone may take classes, though you must be a member to use some of the facilities. See website for more information and upcoming workshops.

○ ◐ ● CONE EDITIONS WORKSHOPS

P.O. Box 51, East Topsham VT 05076. (802)439-5751, ext. 101. E-mail: cathy@cone-editions.com. Website: www.cone-editions.com. See website for details on workshop dates and prices. Cone Editions digital printmaking workshops are hands-on and cover a wide range of techniques, equipment and materials. The workshops take place in the studios of Cone Editions Press and offer attendees the unique opportunity to learn workflow and procedures from the masters. These workshops are an excellent opportunity to learn proven workflow in a fully equipped digital printmaking studio immersed in the latest technologies. Open to all skill levels. See website for more information and upcoming workshops.

◐ ● THE CORTONA CENTER OF PHOTOGRAPHY, ITALY

665 Cooledge Ave., N.E., Atlanta GA 30306. (404)876-6341. E-mail: allen@cortonacenter.com. Website: www.cortonacenter.com. Robin Davis and Allen Matthews lead a personal, small-group photography workshop in the ancient city of Cortona, Italy, centrally located in Tuscany, once the heart of the Renaissance. Dramatic landscapes; Etruscan relics; Roman, Medieval and Renaissance architecture; and the wonderful and photogenic people of Tuscany await. Photographers should write, e-mail or see website for more information.

○ ◐ ● CORY PHOTOGRAPHY WORKSHOPS

P.O. Box 42, Signal Mountain TN 37377. (423)886-1004. E-mail: tompatcory@aol.com. Website: www.tomandpatcory.com. **Contact:** Tom or Pat Cory. Small workshops/field trips (8-12 maximum participants) with some formal instruction, but mostly one-on-one instruction in the field. "Since we tailor this instruction to each individual's interests, our workshops are suitable for all experience levels. Participants are welcome to use film or digital cameras or even video. Our emphasis is on nature and travel photography. We spend the majority of our time in the field, exploring our location. Cost and length vary by workshop. Many of our workshop fees include single-occupancy lodging. We offer special prices for 2 people sharing the same room. Workshop locations vary from year to year but include the Eastern Sierra of California, Colorado and Arches National Park, Olympic National Park, Acadia National Park, the Upper Peninsula of Michigan, Death Valley National Park, Smoky Mountain National Park, and Glacier National Park. We offer international workshops in Ireland, Scotland, Provence, Brittany, Tuscany, New Zealand, Newfoundland, Wales, Iceland, Morocco, Costa Rica and Panama. We also offer a number of short workshops throughout the year in and around Chattanooga, Tennessee. We offer individual instruction and custom-designed workshops for groups." Photographers should write, call, e-mail or see our website for more information.

○ ◐ CREALDÉ SCHOOL OF ART

600 St. Andrews Blvd., Winter Park FL 32792. (407)671-1886. E-mail: pschreyer@crealde.org; rickpho@aol.com. Website: www.crealde.org. Rick Lang, director of photography. **Contact:** Peter Schreyer, executive director. Crealdé School of Art is a community based non-profit arts organization established in 1975. It features a year-round curriculum of over 90 visual arts classes for students of all ages, taught by a faculty of over 40 working artists; a renowned summer art camp for children and teens; a visiting artist workshop series, 3 galleries, the contemporary sculpture garden, and award-winning outreach programs. Offers classes covering traditional and digital photography; b&w darkroom techniques; landscape, portrait, documentary, travel, wildlife and abstract

photography; and educational tours. See website for more information and upcoming workshops.

○ ◑ ● **CREATIVE ARTS WORKSHOP**

80 Audubon St., New Haven CT 06511. (203)562-4927. E-mail: hshapiro8@aol.com. Website: www.creativeartsworkshop.org. **Contact:** Harold Shapiro, photography department head. Creative Arts Workshop is a nonprofit regional center for education in the visual arts that has served the Greater New Haven area since 1961. Located in the heart of the award-winning Audubon Arts District, CAW offers a wide-range of classes in the visual arts in its own three-story building with fully equipped studios and an active exhibition schedule in its well known Hilles Gallery. Offers exciting classes and advanced workshops. Digital and traditional b&w darkroom. See website for more information and upcoming workshops.

○ ◑ ● **BRUCE DALE PHOTOGRAPHIC WORKSHOPS**

1546 N. Ivanhoe St., Arlington VA 22205. (703)241-8297. E-mail: bruce@brucedale.com. Website: www.brucedale.com. Bruce teaches throughout the world. Send an e-mail or visit his website for current information on his workshops and lectures.

○ ✳ ◑ ● **DAWSON COLLEGE CENTRE FOR TRAINING AND DEVLOPMENT**

4001 de Maisonneuve Blvd. W., Suite 2G.1, Montreal QC H3Z 3G4, Canada. (514)933-0047. Fax: (514)937-3832. E-mail: ctd@dawsoncollege.qc.ca. Website: www.dawsoncollege.qc.ca/ciait. Workshop subjects include imaging arts and technologies, computer animation, photography, digital imaging, desktop publishing, multimedia, and web publishing and design. See website for course and workshop information.

○ ◑ ● **THE JULIA DEAN PHOTO WORKSHOPS**

755 Seward St., Los Angeles CA 90038. (323)464-0909. Fax: (323)464-0906. E-mail: workshops@juliadean.com. Website: www.juliadean.com. **Contact:** Brandon Gannon, director. The Julia Dean Photo Workshops (JDPW) is a practical education school of photography devoted to advancing the skills and increasing the personal enrichment of photographers of all experience levels and ages. Photography workshops of all kinds held throughout the year, including al-ternative and fine art, photography & digital camera fundamentals, lighting & portraiture, specialized photography, Photoshop and printing, photo safaris, and travel workshops. Open to all skill levels. Photographers should call, e-mail or see website for more information.

◑ ● **CYNTHIA DELANEY PHOTO WORKSHOPS**

168 Maple St., Elko NV 89801. (775)753-5833. Fax: (775)753-5833. E-mail: cynthia@cynthiadelaney.com. Website: www.cynthiadelaney.com. **Contact:** Cynthia Delaney. "In addition to her photography classes, Cynthia offers outdoor photography workshops held in many outstanding locations. It is our hope to bring photographers to new and unusual places where inspiration comes naturally." See website for more information and upcoming workshops.

○ ◑ **DIGITAL WILDLIFE PHOTOGRAPHY FIELD SCHOOL**

P.O. Box 236, S. Wellfleet MA 02663. (508)349-2615. E-mail: wellfleet@massaudubon.org. Website: www.massaudubon.org/wellfleetbay. **Contact:** Melissa Lowe, education coordinator. Enjoy learning in the beautiful coastal setting of Cape Cod. Mass Audubon's Wellfleet Bay Wildlife Sanctuary offers a wide variety of field courses for adults which focus on the unique coastal environment and wildlife of Cape Cod. Sponsored by Massachusetts Audubon Society. Classes held on a regular basis. For a more detailed course descriptions and itineraries, call, e-mail or see website.

○ ◑ **DRAMATIC LIGHT NATURE PHOTOGRAPHY WORKSHOPS**

2292 Shiprock Rd., Grand Junction CO 81503. (800)20-PHOTO (74686). E-mail: josephklange@aol.com; joe.lange@dramaticlightphoto.com. Website: www.dramaticlightphoto.com. Cost: $1,295-1,695 for North American (6-day) workshops; includes motel, transportation, continental breakfast and instruction in the field and classroom. Maximum workshop size: 10 participants. Specializing in the American West. Upcoming workshop: January 7-21, 2012 in Falkland Islands; $6,495 all inclusive; 4 participants max. See website for more information.

○ ◐ ELOQUENT LIGHT PHOTOGRAPHY WORKSHOPS

903 W. Alameda St., #115, Santa Fe NM 87501. (505)983-2934. E-mail: cindylane@eloquentlight.com. Website: www.eloquentlight.com. **Contact:** Cindy Lane, managing director. "Eloquent Light Photography Workshops was founded in 1986 to provide exceptional educational photographic workshop experiences based on the history, character and beauty of the American Southwest. We pride ourselves on offering real photographic education that helps participants become better photographers. We keep our group sizes small in order to address participants needs. Open to all skill levels. In our traditional workshops, you are encouraged to bring your own images with you for informal comment by the instructor and fellow participants. Photographs made during the week of your workshop will also be reviewed. The instructor and assistant are available to look at digital captures on participants' laptops during our adventure workshops when requested." Upcoming workshop: The Antelope Slot Canyon Workshop, $1,995 (includes tuition, round-trip ground transportation during the workshop, air-conditioned double occupancy lodging and all entrance, tour & permit fees. Single rooms available for additional fee); 8-10 participants; all skill levels. This is a shooting-intensive workshop providing hands-on, one-on-one guidance in the field as needed. Images you will see in your viewfinder include the various spectacular red rock formations in and around the Slot Canyons, shafts of light coming through the rocks, the desert landscape and gorgeous sunsets. See website for more information and registration.

● JOE ENGLANDER PHOTOGRAPHY WORKSHOPS & TOURS

P.O. Box 1261, Manchaca TX 78652. (512)922-8686. E-mail: info@englander-workshops.com. Website: www.englander-workshops.com. **Contact:** Joe Englander. Instruction in beautiful locations throughout the world, all formats and media, color/b&w/digital, photoshop instruction. Locations include Europe, Asia with special emphasis on Bhutan and the Himalayas and the U.S. See website for more information.

○ ◐ ● EUROPA PHOTOGENICA PHOTO TOURS TO EUROPE

3920 W. 231st Pl., Torrance CA 90505. (310)378-2821. Fax: (310)378-2821. E-mail: fraphoto@aol.com. Website: www.europaphotogenica.com. **Contact:** Barbara Van Zanten-Stolarski, owner. (Formerly France Photogenique/Europa Photogenica Photo Tours to Europe). Tuition provided for beginners/intermediate and advanced level. Workshops held in spring (1-2) and fall (1-2). Five- to 11-day photo tours of the most beautiful regions of Europe. Shoot landscapes, villages, churches, cathedrals, vineyards, outdoor markets, cafes and people in France, Paris, Provence, England, Italy, Greece, etc. Tours change every year. Open to all skill levels. Photographers should call or e-mail for more information.

○ ◐ ● EXPOSURE36 PHOTOGRAPHY

805 SE 176th Pl., Portland OR 97233. (866)368-6736. E-mail: workshop@exposure36.com. Website: www.exposure36.com. Open to all skill levels. Workshops offered at prime locations in the U.S. and Canada, including Yosemite, Smoky Mountains, Bryce Canyon, the Oregon coast. Also offers classes on the basics of photography in Portland, Oregon (through the Experimental College or Mt. Hood Community College) and Seattle, Washington (through the Experimental College of the University of Washington). Photographers should write, call, e-mail, see website for more information and upcoming workshops.

● FINDING & KEEPING CLIENTS

2973 Harbor Blvd., Suite 341, Costa Mesa CA 92626-3912. (714) 356-4260. E-mail: maria@mpiscopo.com. Website: www.mpiscopo.com. **Contact:** Maria Piscopo, instructor. "How to find new photo assignment clients and get paid what you're worth!" Maria Piscopo is the author of *The Photographer's Guide to Marketing & Self Promotion*, 4th edition (Allworth Press). See website for more information and upcoming workshops.

FINE ARTS WORK CENTER

24 Pearl St., Provincetown MA 02657. (508)487-9960. Fax: (508)487-8873. E-mail: workshops@fawc.org. Website: www.fawc.org. **Contact:** Dorothy Antczak, summer program director. Estab. 1968. Faculty includes Constantine Manos, David Graham, Amy Arbus, Marian Roth, Gabe Greenburg, Joanne Dugan,

David Hilliard, and Connie Imboden. Write, call or e-mail for more information.

PETER FINGER PHOTOGRAPHER
1143 Blakeway St., Daniel Island SC 29492. (843)377-8652. E-mail: images@peterfinger.com. Website: www.peterfinger.com. **Contact:** Peter Finger, president. Offers over 20 weekend and week-long photo workshops, held in various locations. Workshops planned include Charleston, Savannah, Carolina Coast, Outer Banks, and the Islands of Georgia. "Group instruction from dawn till dusk." Write or visit website for more information.

◯ ◑ ● FIRST LIGHT PHOTOGRAPHIC WORKSHOPS AND SAFARIS
10 Roslyn, Islip Terrace NY 11752. (631)581-0400. Website: www.firstlightphotography.com. **Contact:** Bill Rudock, president. Photo workshops and photo safaris for all skill levels, specializing in national parks, domestic and international; also presents workshops for portrait and wedding photographers. "We will personally teach you through our workshops and safaris, the techniques necessary to go from *taking pictures* to *creating* those unique, magical images while experiencing some of life's greatest adventures." Upcoming workshops: "Great Smoky Mountains", October 17-21 in Gatlinburg, Tennessee; "Winter in Yellowstone", February 13-17, 2012 in Wyoming and Montana. See website for more information, pricing and registration.

◯ ◑ ● FOCUS ADVENTURES
P.O. Box 771640, Steamboat Springs CO 80477. (970)879-2244. E-mail: karen@focusadventures.com. Website: www.focusadventures.com. **Contact:** Karen Gordon Schulman, owner. Photo workshops and tours emphasize photography and the creative spirit and self-discovery through photography. Summer photo workshops in Steamboat Springs, Colorado and at Focus Ranch, a private guest ranch in NW Colorado. Customized private and small-group lessons available year-round. International photo tours run with Strabo Photo Tour Collection to various destinations including Ecuador, Bali, Morocco, Barcelona, and Western Ireland. Upcoming workshop: "Magical Morocco, A Photographic and Cultural Adventure, September 21-October 5, 2012. Cost: $3,745; includes transportation, accommodations, meals, photo instruction. "We will enjoy the sights in vibrant Mar-rakech and ancient Fes, rug shopping, palace visits, and an unforgettable journey into the Sahara on camelback for sunrise, and much more." See website for more details and registration.

◯ ◑ ● FOTOFUSION
415 Clematis St., West Palm Beach FL 33401. (561)276-9797. Fax: (561)276-9132. E-mail: cs@workshop.org. Website: www.fotofusion.org. America's foremost festival of photography and digital imaging is held each January. Learn from more than 90 master photographers, picture editors, picture agencies, gallery directors, and technical experts, over 5 days of field trips, seminars, lectures and Photoshop workshops. Open to all skill levels interested in nature, landscape, documentary, portraiture, photojournalism, digital, fine art, commercial, etc. 2012 FOTOfusion is January 24-28; details coming soon online.

☼ ◯ ◑ ● FREEMAN PATTERSON PHOTO WORKSHOPS
Shamper's Cove Limited, 3487 Route 845, Long Reach NB E5S 1X4, Canada. (506)763-2189. Fax: (506)763-2035. E-mail: freepatt@nbnet.nb.ca. Website: www.freemanpatterson.com. Freeman made several visits to Africa between 1967 and 1983, three of them at the request of the Photographic Society of Southern Africa. As a result of these contacts and others, he co-founded (with Colla Swart) the Namaqualand Photographic Workshops in 1984, and travels to the desert village of Kamieskroon once or twice a year to teach three or four week-long workshops. This project has expanded so rapidly that Freeman now works with several other instructors and no longer participates in every program. Freeman has also given numerous, week-long workshops in the United States, New Zealand, and Israel and has completed lecture tours in the United Kingdom, South Africa and Australia. See website for more information and a list of upcoming workshops.

◑ ● GALÁPAGOS TRAVEL
783 Rio Del Mar Blvd., Suite 49, Aptos CA 95003. (831)689-9192 or (800)969-9014. E-mail: info@galapagostravel.com. Website: www.galapagostravel.com. **Contact:** Mark Grantham. Landscape and wildlife photography tour of the islands with an emphasis on natural history. Spend either 11 or 15 days aboard the yacht in Galápagos, plus three nights in a first-class hotel in Quito, Ecuador. Upcoming tours:

October 27-November 9, November 10-23, November 24-December 7, December 8-21, December 22-January 4. See website for additional information and registration.

○ ◐ ● GERLACH NATURE PHOTOGRAPHY WORKSHOPS & TOURS

P.O. Box 642, Ashton ID 83420. (208)652-4444. E-mail: michele@gerlachnaturephoto.com. Website: www.gerlachnaturephotocom. **Contact:** Michele Smith, office manager. Professional nature photographers John and Barbara Gerlach conduct intensive field workshops in the beautiful Upper Peninsula of Michigan in August and during October's fall color period. They lead a photo safari to the best game parks in Kenya in January. They also lead winter photo tours of Yellowstone National Park and conduct high-speed flash hummingbird photo workshops in British Columbia in late May and early June. Barbara and John work for an outfitter a couple weeks a year leading photo tours into The Yellowstone Back Country and Lee Metcalf Wilderness with the use of horses. This is a wonderful way to experience Yellowstone. They conduct an inspirational one-day seminar on how to shoot beautiful nature images in major cities each year. Their two highly rated books, *Digital Nature Photography-The Art and the Science*, and *Digital Landscape Photography* have helped thousands master the art of nature photography. Photographers should visit their website for more information.

○ ◐ ● GLOBAL PRESERVATION PROJECTS

P.O. Box 30866, Santa Barbara CA 93130. (805)682-3398 or (805)455-2790. E-mail: timorse@aol.com. Website: www.globalpreservationprojects.com. **Contact:** Thomas I. Morse, director. Offers photographic workshops and expeditions promoting the preservation of environmental and historic treasures. Produces international photographic exhibitions and publications. GPP uses a 24-ft. motor home with state-of-the art digital imaging and printer systems for participants use. Upcoming workshops: October 2-5 "White Sands, City of Rock," October 8-10 "Very Large Array," November 16-20 "Death Valley, Alabama Hills." See website for more details, pricing and registration.

● ⊘ GOLDEN GATE SCHOOL OF PROFESSIONAL PHOTOGRAPHY

P.O. Box F, San Mateo CA 94402-0018. (650)548-0889. E-mail: goldengateschool@yahoo.com. Website: www.goldengateschool.org. **Contact:** Martha Bruce, director. Offers 1-3 day workshops in traditional and digital photography for professional and aspiring photographers in the San Francisco Bay Area.

○ ◐ ● ROB GOLDMAN CREATIVE PHOTOGRAPHY WORKSHOPS

Huntington NY (631)424-1650. Fax: (631)424-1650. E-mail: rob@rgoldman.com. Website: www.rgoldman.com. **Contact:** Rob Goldman, photographer. Custom-design your photographic education through Rob Goldman's proven 8-level learning system. Enter at your own level and advance quickly toward photographic mastery. Rob's hands-on classes are stimulating and fun, balancing technical training with creative inspiration. Rob has developed a variety of personal and professional growth programs for people who are ready to express their passion, their creativity and their extraordinariness in both their lives and their work. His creativity workshops and seminars have been offered internationally and have been designed specifically for the art, self-development, education and business communities. Open to all skill levels. See website for more information and a list of all upcoming workshops.

○ ◐ GREAT SMOKY MOUNTAINS INSTITUTE AT TREMONT

9275 Tremont Rd., Townsend TN 37882. (865)448-6709. Fax: (865) 448-9250. E-mail: mail@gsmit.org. Website: www.gsmit.org. **Contact:** Registrar. Workshop instructors: Bill Lea, Will Clay and others. Next workshop: October 21-24, 2011. Emphasizes the use of natural light in creating quality scenic, wildflower and wildlife images.

◐ ● HALLMARK INSTITUTE OF PHOTOGRAPHY

P.O. Box 308, Turners Falls MA 01376. (413)863-2478. E-mail: info@hallmark.edu. Website: www.hallmark.edu. Lindsay O'Neil, director of admissions. **Contact:** George J. Rosa III, president. Offers an intensive 10-month resident program teaching the technical, artistic and business aspects of traditional and digital professional photography for the career-minded individual.

JOHN HART PORTRAIT SEMINARS

344 W. 72nd St., New York NY 10023. (212)877-0516. E-mail: johnhartstudio1@mac.com. Website: www. johnhartpics.com. One-on-one advanced portraiture seminars covering lighting and other techniques. John Hart is a New York University faculty member and author of 50 Portrait Lighting Techniques, Professional Headshots, Lighting For Action and Art of the Storyboard. Seminars will contain a new emphasis on *digital portrait photography*—the subject of which will be a new book by the author.

○ ◐ ● HEART OF NATURE PHOTOGRAPHY WORKSHOPS

P.O. Box 1033, Volcano HI 96785. (808)345-7179. E-mail: info@heartofnature.net. Website: www.heartof nature.net. **Contact:** Robert Frutos. "Photograph nature in the magnificent wonder of Hawaii, capture compelling and dynamic images that convey the beauty and spirit of the islands." Upcoming workshop: Bali Photo Tour, October 29-November 3 ($2,450); more details coming soon. Photographers can e-mail or see website for more information.

○ ◐ ● HORIZONS: ARTISTIC TRAVEL

P.O. Box 634, Leverett MA 01054. (413)367-9200. Fax: (413)367-9522. E-mail: horizons@horizons-art. com. Website: www.horizons-art.com. **Contact:** Jane Sinauer, director. One-of-a-kind small-group travel adventures: 1 and 2-week programs in the American Southwest, Mexico, Ecuador, Peru, Burma, Laos, Vietnam, Cambodia, Southern Africa, Morocco, Northern India. Upcoming workshops: October 9-15 "Off-Beat Southwest: Canyon Country," January 13-22 "Southeast Asia Explorer," March 7-13 "Ecuador: Treasures of the Andean Highlands." See website for more information, including pricing and registration.

○ ◐ ● HUI HO'OLANA

P.O. Box 280, Kualapuu, Molokai HI 96757. (808)567-6430. E-mail: hui@aloha.net. Website: www.huiho. org. **Contact:** Rik Cooke. "Hui Ho'olana is a non-profit organization on the island of Molokai, Hawaii. We are dedicated to the fine art of teaching. Through workshops and volunteer residencies, our mission is to create a self-sustaining facility that supports educational programs and native Hawaiian reforestation projects. Our goal is to provide an environment for inspiration, a safe haven for the growth and nurturing of the creative spirit." Upcoming workshops 2011:

November 5-12 "Photoshop for the Soul," November 19-26 To Be Announced, December 4-10 "Ukulele." Photographers should e-mail, call or visit website for more information.

○ ◐ ● INFINITY WORKSHOPS

P.O. Box 27555, Seattle WA 98165. (206)367-6864. Fax: (206)367-8102. E-mail: mark@infinitywork shops.com. Website: www.infinityworkshops.com. **Contact:** Mark Griffith, director. Location workshops on the Oregon coast and Southern Utah. Open to all digital and film users, color or black and white. Call, e-mail, or see website for information.

◐ IN FOCUS WITH MICHELE BURGESS

20741 Catamaran Lane, Huntington Beach CA 92646. (714)536-6104. E-mail: maburg5820@aol.com. Website: www.infocustravel.com. **Contact:** Michele Burgess, president. Offers overseas tours to photogenic areas with expert photography consultation at a leisurely pace and in small groups (maximum group size: 20).

○ ◐ ● INTERNATIONAL EXPEDITIONS

One Environs Park, Helena AL 35080. (800)633-4734. Fax: (205)428-1714. E-mail: nature@ietravel.com. Website: www.ietravel.com. **Contact:** Charlie Weaver, photo tour coordinator. Includes scheduled ground transportation; extensive pre-travel information; services of experienced English-speaking local guides; daily educational briefings; all excursions, entrance fees and permits; all accommodations; meals as specified in the respective itineraries; transfer and luggage handling when taking group flights. Guided nature expeditions all over the world: Amazon, Costa Rica, Machu Picchu, Galapagos, Laos & Vietnam, Borneo, Kenya, Patagonia and many more. Open to all skill levels. Photographers should write, call, e-mail, see website for more information.

○ ◐ ● JIVIDEN'S NATURALLY WILD PHOTO ADVENTURES

P.O. Box 333, Chillicothe OH 45601. (800)866-8655 or (740)774-6243. Fax: (740)774-2272 (call first). E-mail: mail@imagesunique.com. Website: www.naturally-wild.net. **Contact:** Jerry or Barbara Jividen. "Offering a limited number of photo workshop as we undertake several photo and writing projects and speaking engagements." See website for more information and a list of upcoming workshops.

◑ ● JORDAHL PHOTO WORKSHOPS

P.O. Box 3998, Hayward CA 94540. (510)785-7707. E-mail: kate@jordahlphoto.com. Website: www.jordahl photo.com. **Contact:** Kate or Geir Jordahl, directors. Intensive 1- to 5-day workshops dedicated to inspiring creativity and community among artists through critique, field sessions and exhibitions.

○ ◑ ● ART KETCHUM HANDS-ON PHOTOGRAPHIC MODEL WORKSHOPS

3540 Seagate Way, Oceanside CA 92056. (773)551-8751. E-mail: artketchum@sbcglobal.net. Website: www.artketchum.com. **Contact:** Art Ketchum, owner. Art Ketchum's extensive lighting and posing workshops allow the participant to learn and build a super portfolio of images in the workshop. Call, e-mail or see website for more information and a list of upcoming workshops.

BOB KORN IMAGING

46 Main St., P.O. Box 1687, Orleans MA 02653. (508)255-5202. E-mail: bob@bobkornimaging.com. Website: www.bobkornimaging.com. **Contact:** Bob Korn, director. Photography workshops for the digital photographer. All skill levels. Workshops run year-round. Photographers should call, e-mail or see website for more information.

✳ ○ ◑ ● THE LIGHT FACTORY

Spirit Square, Suite 211, 345 N. College St., Charlotte NC 28202. (704)333-9755. E-mail: dkiel@@light factory.org; julietteMontauk-Smith@lightfactory.org; info@lightfactory.org. Website: www.lightfactory.org. **Contact:** Dennis Kiel, chief curator. Estab. 1972. The Light Factory is a nonprofit arts center dedicated to exhibition and education programs promoting the power of photography and film. From classes in basic point-and-shoot to portraiture, Photoshop, and more, TLF offers 3-8 week-long courses that meet once a week in our uptown Charlotte location. Classes are taught by professional instructors and cater to different expertise levels: introductory, intermediate and advanced in both photography and filmmaking. See website for a listing of classes and registration.

LIGHT PHOTOGRAPHIC WORKSHOPS

Lepp Institute of Digital Imaging, 1062 Los Osos Valley Rd., Los Osos CA 93402. (805)528-7385. Fax: (888)254-6211. E-mail: info@lightworkshops.com. Website: www.lightworkshops.com. Offers small groups workshops, private tutoring, Alaska and worldwide photography instruction cruises and tours, printing and canvas gallery wrap services, Canon gear rental, studio and classroom rental. "New focus on digital tools to optimize photography, make the most of your images and improve your photography skills at the premier digital imaging school on the West Coast."

◒ ○ ◐ LLEWELLYN PHOTOGRAPHY WORKSHOPS & PHOTO TOURS, PETER

645 Rollo Rd., Gabriola BC VOR 1X3, Canada. (250)247-9109. E-mail: peter@peterllewellyn.com. Website: www.peterllewellyn.com. **Contact:** Peter Llewellyn. "All workshops and photo tours feature small groups, maximum 6 for workshops and 10 for photo tours to allow maximum personal attention. Workshops include basic Photoshop skills, digital photography and digital workflow. Photo Tours are designed to provide maximum photographic opportunities to participants with the assistance of a professional photographer. Trips include Brazil, Africa, Canada and U.S. New destinations coming soon." Open to all skill levels. For further information, e-mail or see website.

○ ◑ ● C.C. LOCKWOOD WILDLIFE PHOTOGRAPHY WORKSHOP

P.O. Box 14876, Baton Rouge LA 70898. (225)769-4766. Fax: (225)767-3726. E-mail: cactusclyd@aol.com. Website: www.cclockwood.com. **Contact:** C.C. Lockwood, photographer. Lockwood periodically teaches hands-on photography workshops in the Grand Canyon, Yellowstone National Park, and The Atchafalaya Basin Swamp. Informative slide show lectures precede field trips into these great photo habitats. Call, write, e-mail or see website for a list of upcoming workshops.

○ LONG ISLAND PHOTO WORKSHOP

(516)221-4058. E-mail: jerry@jsmallphoto.com; info@jsmallphoto.com. Website: www.liphotoworkshop.com. **Contact:** Jerry Small, director. Annual 4-day workshop covering professional wedding, portrait, and digital photography and photographic skills.

Open to all skill levels. See website for upcoming dates. Every year there are two full scholarships given to deserving members of PPGNY. See website for more info.

◐ THE MACDOWELL COLONY

100 High St., Peterborough NH 03458. (603)924-3886. Fax: (603)924-9142. E-mail: admissions@macdowell colony.org. Website: www.macdowellcolony.org. Estab. 1907. Provides creative artists with uninterrupted time and seclusion to work and enjoy the experience of living in a community of gifted artists. Residencies of up to 8 weeks for writers, playwrights, composers, film/video makers, visual artists, architects and interdisciplinary artists. Artists in residence receive room, board and exclusive use of a studio. Average length of residency is 5 weeks. Ability to pay for residency is not a factor; there are no residency fees. Limited funds available for travel reimbursement and artist grants based on need. Application deadlines: January 15: summer (June-September); April 15: fall/winter (October-January); September 15: winter/spring (February-May). Photographers should see website for application and guidelines. Questions should be directed to the admissions director.

○ ◐ ● MAINE MEDIA WORKSHOPS

70 Camden St., P.O. Box 200, Rockport ME 04856. (207)236-8581 or (877)577-7700. Fax: (207)236-2558. E-mail: info@theworkshops.com. Website: www.mainemedia.edu. "Maine Media Workshops is a nonprofit educational organization offering year-round workshops for photographers, filmmakers and media artists. Students from across the country and around the world attend courses at all levels, from absolute beginner and serious amateur to working professional; also high school and college students. Professional certificate and low-residency MFA degree programs are available through Maine Media College." See website for the fall calendar.

○ ◐ ● WILLIAM MANNING PHOTOGRAPHY

6396 Birchdale Ct., Cincinnati OH 45230. (513)624-8148. E-mail: williammanning@fuse.net. Website: www.williammanning.com. Digital photography workshops worldwide with emphasis on travel, nature, and architecture. Offers small group tours. Upcoming workshops: October 19-23 "Art-tecture" in Cincinnati. This workshop will offer creative challenges and possibilities that will open you to a whole new way of thinking when shooting the ordinary and creating something new and fresh. Participants will learn how to photograph with an open mind and shoot with post-production in mind and all of its possibilities. Participants should have a basic knowledge of Adobe Photoshop and own 1 or more plug-ins such as Topaz Adjust, Nik software and/or Auto FX (Mystical Lighting and Ambiance) software. See website for more information and registration.

○ ◐ ● JOE & MARY ANN MCDONALD WILDLIFE PHOTOGRAPHY WORKSHOPS AND TOURS

73 Loht Rd., McClure PA 17841-9340. (717)543-6423. Fax: (717)543-6423. E-mail: info@hoothollow.com. Website: www.hoothollow.com. **Contact:** Joe McDonald, owner. "We are wildlife photographers who not only maintain a huge inventory of stock images for editorial and advertising use, but who have dedicated ourselves to the sharing of photographic and natural history information through our various courses, tours, workshops, and safaris." Offers small group, quality instruction with emphasis on nature and wildlife photography. See website for more information and a list of upcoming workshops.

○ ◐ ● MENTOR SERIES WORLDWIDE PHOTO TREKS

Bonnier Technology Group, 2 Park Ave, 9th Floor, New York NY 10016. (888)676-6468 or (212)779-5473. Fax: (212)376-7057. E-mail: michelle.cast@bonniercorp.com; erica.johnson@bonniercorp.com. Website: www.mentorseries.com. **Contact:** Michelle Cast, director of special events. Workshops that build not only your skill as a photographer but your sense of the world around you. Enjoy many days of photo activities led by world-renowned professional shooters, all experienced and charismatic photographers who will offer in-the-field advice, lectures, slide shows and reviews. "The chance of getting good photos is high because we have invested in getting great teachers and permits for private access to some cool places. Some of our upcoming destinations include Santa Fe, Savannah, Colorado, Dominican Republic, London, Arizona, Montana and Switzerland." Open to all skill levels. Photographers should call, e-mail or see website for more information.

○ ◑ ● **MID-ATLANTIC REGIONAL SCHOOL OF PHOTOGRAPHY**

666 Franklin Ave., Nutley NJ 07110. (888)267-MARS. E-mail: adele@marsschool.com. Website: www.photoschools.com. Covers many aspects of professional photography from digital to portrait to wedding. Open to photographers of all skill levels. Check website for information on the 2012 workshop.

○ ◑ ● **MIDWEST PHOTOGRAPHIC WORKSHOPS**

28830 W. Eight Mile Rd., Farmington Hills MI 48336. (248)471-7299. E-mail: officemanager@mpw.com. Website: www.mpw.com. **Contact:** Bryce Denison, owner. "One-day weekend and week-long photo workshops, small group sizes and hands-on shooting seminars by professional photographers/instructors on topics such as portraiture, landscapes, nudes, digital, nature, weddings, product advertising and photojournalism. Workshops held regularly. See website for more information and registration.

MISSOURI PHOTOJOURNALISM WORKSHOP

109 Lee Hills Hall, Columbia MO 65211. (573)882-4882. Fax: (573)884-4999. E-mail: reesd@missouri.edu. Website: www.mophotoworkshop.org. **Contact:** Photojournalism department. Workshop for photojournalists. Participants learn the fundamentals of documentary photo research, shooting, and editing. Held in a different Missouri town each year.

● ⊘ **MOUNTAIN WORKSHOPS**

Western Kentucky University, 1906 College Heights, MMTH 131, Bowling Green KY 42101-1070. (502)745-6292. E-mail: mountainworkshops@wku.edu; kurt.fattic@wku.edu. Website: www.mountainworkshops.org. **Contact:** Jim Bye, workshop coordinator. Annual documentary photojournalism workshop held in October. Open to intermediate and advanced shooters. See website for upcoming dates.

○ **TOM MURPHY PHOTOGRAPHY**

402 S. Fifth, Livingston MT 59047. (406)222-2302. E-mail: tom@tmurphywild.com. Website: tmurphywild.com. **Contact:** Tom Murphy, president. Offers programs in wildlife and landscape photography in Yellowstone National Park and special destinations.

◑ **NATURAL HABITAT ADVENTURES**

833 W. South Boulder Rd., Louisville CO 80027. (303)449-3711 or (800)543-8917. Fax: (303)449-3712. E-mail: info@nathab.com. Website: www.nathab.com. Guided photo tours for wildlife photographers. Tours last 5-27 days. Destinations include North America, Latin America, Canada, the Arctic, Galápagos Islands, Africa, the Pacific and Antarctica. See website for more information.

○ ◑ ● **NATURAL TAPESTRIES**

1208 St. Rt. 18, Aliquippa PA 15001. (724)495-7493. Fax: (724)495-7370. E-mail: nancyrotenberg@aol.com. Website: www.naturaltapestries.com. **Contact:** Nancy Rotenberg, photographer/writer/educator. We will be traveling to Mexico, Guatemala, Oregon Coast, Callaway Gardens, Ireland, Zion, New Hampshire, and Alaska. Open to all skill levels. Photographers should e-mail or check website for more information.

○ ◑ ● **NEVERSINK PHOTO WORKSHOP**

P.O. Box 641, Woodbourne NY 12788. (212)929-0009. E-mail: lou@loujawitz@mac.com; louisjawitz@mac.com. Website: www.neversinkphotoworkshop.com. **Contact:** Louis Jawitz, owner. Spend a weekend in the Catskills developing your photographic techniques while expanding your visual horizons! These workshops concentrate on scenic and nature photography with supervised field trip shooting, as well as portfolio review and critique, discussions related to composition and perspective, technical skills, visual design, using color for impact, exposure control, basic digital workflow and developing a personal style. Group workshops held every weekend in August, with the possibility of an additional "Fall Foliage" weekend in October (see website for specifics). Photographers should call, e-mail or see website for more information.

◑ ● **NEW ENGLAND SCHOOL OF PHOTOGRAPHY**

537 Commonwealth Ave., Boston MA 02215. (617)437-1868 or (800)676-3767. E-mail: info@nesop.com. Website: www.nesop.com. Instruction in professional and creative photography in the form of workshops or a professional photography program.

○ ◐ ● NEW JERSEY HERITAGE PHOTOGRAPHY WORKSHOPS

124 Diamond Hill Rd., Berkeley Heights NJ 07922. (908)790-8820. E-mail: nancyori@comcast.net. Website: www.nancyoriphotography.com. **Contact:** Nancy Ori, director. Estab. 1990. Workshops held every spring. Nancy Ori, well-known instructor, freelance photographer and fine art exhibitor of landscape and architecture photography, teaches how to use available light and proper metering techniques to document the man-made and natural environments of Cape May. A variety of film and digital workshops taught by guest instructors are available each year and are open to all skill levels, especially beginners. Topics include hand coloring of photographs, creative camera techniques with Polaroid materials, intermediate and advanced digital, landscape and architecture with alternative cameras, environmental portraits with lighting techniques, street photography; as well as pastel, watercolor and oil painting workshops. All workshops include an historic walking tour of town, location shooting or painting, demonstrations and critiques.

○ ◐ ● NEW JERSEY MEDIA CENTER LLC WORKSHOPS AND PRIVATE TUTORING

124 Diamond Hill Rd., Berkeley Heights NJ 07922. (908)790-8820. E-mail: nancyori@comcast.net. Website: www.nancyoriworkshops.com. **Contact:** Nancy Ori. **1. Italy Photography Workshop: Delicious Photography in Italy** with Nancy Ori. Explore the Italian countryside, cities and small villages, with emphasis on architecture, documentary, portrait and landscape photography. The group will venture in non-tourist areas to explore the culture with cooking lessons and visits to small shops and industrial locations to see how the real people live and eat. Significant others welcome and will have plenty to see and do while you photograph, sketch or paint. Cost: call for this year's price; includes tuition, accommodations at a 15th Century fully-renovated hilltop retreat with all the modern amenities, breakfasts and some dinners. Open to all skill levels. **2. Private Photography Tutoring** with Nancy Ori in Berkeley Heights, New Jersey. This unique and personalized approach to learning photography is designed for the beginning or intermediate student who wants to expand his/her understanding of the craft and work more creatively with the camera, develop a portfolio and create an exhibit. The goal is to refine individual style while exploring the skills necessary to make expressive photographs. The content will be tailored to individual needs and interests. Cost: $350 for a total of 8 hours. **3. Capturing the Light of the Southwest**, a painting, sketching and photography workshop with Nancy Ori, held every other year in October, will focus on the natural landscape and man-made structures of the area around Santa Fe and Taos. Participants can be at any level in their media. All will be encouraged to produce a substantial body of work worthy of portfolio or gallery presentation. Features special evening guest lecturers from the photography community in the Santa Fe area. Artists should e-mail for more information. **4. Cape May Photography Workshops** are held annually in April and May. Also, a variety of subjects such as photojournalism, environmental portraiture, landscape, alternative cameras, Polaroid techniques, creative digital techniques, on-location wedding photography, large-format, and how to photograph birds in the landscape are offered by several well-known East-Coast instructors. Open to all skill levels. Includes critiques, demonstrations, location shooting of Victorian architecture, gardens, seascapes, and, in some cases, models in either film or digital. E-mail for dates, fees and more information. Workshops are either 3 or 4 days. **5. Capture the Light and Color of New England** will emphasize time for careful study of the relationship between the natural environment, light, color and simple country architecture, which may effectively lead to paintings or photographs with insight and emotional value.

○ ◐ ● NIKON SCHOOL DIGITAL SLR PHOTOGRAPHY

1300 Walt Whitman Rd., Melville NY 11747. (631)547-8666. Fax: (631)547-0309. E-mail: nikonschool@nikon.net. Website: www.nikonschool.com. **Contact:** Ellen Coburn, operations manager. Weekend seminars traveling to 30 major U.S. cities 9:30-4:30; lunch is included; no camera equipment is required. Intro to Digital SLR Photography—Cost: $129; those new to digital SLR photography or those coming back after many years away. Expect a good understanding of the basics of photography, terminology, techniques and solutions for specific challenges allowing you to unleash your creative potential. Next steps—Cost: $159; for experienced digital SLR photographers and those comfortable with the basics of digital photography and key camera controls. Take your digital photography to a higher level creatively and technically.

NORTHERN EXPOSURES

4917 Evergreen Way #383, Everett WA 98203. (425)341-4981 or (425)347-7650. Fax: (425)347-7650. E-mail: abenteuerbc@yahoo.com. **Contact:** Linda Moore, director. Offers 3- to 8-day intermediate to advanced nature photography workshops in several locations in Pacific Northwest and western Canada; spectacular settings including coast, alpine, badlands, desert and rain forest. Also, 1- to 2-week Canadian Wildlife and Wildlands Photo Adventures and nature photo tours to extraordinary remote wildlands of British Columbia, Alberta, Saskatchewan and Yukon.

NYU TISCH SCHOOL OF THE ARTS

Department of Photography & Imaging, 721 Broadway, 8th Floor, New York NY 10003. (212)998-1930. E-mail: photo.tsoa@nyu.edu. Website: www.photo.tisch.nyu.edu. **Contact:** Department of Photography and Imaging. Summer classes offered for credit and noncredit covering digital imaging, career development, basic to advanced photography, darkroom techniques, photojournalism, and human rights & photography. Open to all skill levels.

OREGON COLLEGE OF ART AND CRAFT

8245 SW Barnes Rd., Portland OR 97225. (503)297-5544 or (800)390-0632. Fax: (503)297-9651. E-mail: admissions@ocac.edu. Website: www.ocac.edu. Offers workshops and classes in photography throughout the year: b&w, color, alternative processes, studio lighting, digital imaging. Also offers MFA in photography. For schedule information, call or visit website.

OTTER CREEK PHOTOGRAPHY

(304)478-3586. E-mail: ottercreekphotography@yahoo.com. **Contact:** John Warner. Intensive weeklong, hands-on workshops held throughout the year in the most visually rich regions of Mexico. Photograph snow-capped volcanoes, thundering waterfalls, pre-Columbian ruins, botanical gardens, fascinating people, markets and colonial churches in jungle, mountain, desert and alpine environments. Photographers should call or e-mail for more information.

PACIFIC NORTHWEST ART SCHOOL/PHOTOGRAPHY

15 NW Birch St., Coupeville WA 98239. (360)678-3396. Fax: (877)678-3396. E-mail: info@pacific northwestartschool.org. Website: www.pacificnorth westartschool.org. **Contact:** Registrar. "Join us for workshops taught by a well known faculty offering on site (beautiful Whidbey Island) and on location classes." Workshops held frequently throughout the year. See website for more details and registration.

PALM BEACH PHOTOGRAPHIC CENTRE

415 Clematis St., West Palm Beach FL 33401. (561)253-2600. Fax: (561)253-2604. E-mail: cs@workshop.org. Website: www.workshop.org. The center is an innovative learning facility offering 1- to 5-day seminars in photography and digital imaging year round. Also offered are travel workshops to cultural destinations such as South Africa, Bhutan, Myanmar, Peru, and India. Emphasis is on photographing the indigenous cultures of each country. Also hosts the annual Fotofusion event (see separate listing in this section). Photographers should call for details.

RALPH PAONESSA PHOTOGRAPHY WORKSHOPS

509 W. Ward Ave., Suite B-108, Ridgecrest CA 93555-2542. (800)527-3455. E-mail: ralph@rpphoto.com. Website: www.rpphoto.com. **Contact:** Ralph Paonessa, director. Various workshops repeated annually. Nature, bird and landscape trips to the Eastern Sierra, Death Valley, Falkland Islands, Alaska, Costa Rica, Ecuador, and many other locations. Open to all skill levels. Upcoming workshop: "Ecuador Hummingbirds," October 16-29 in Quito. See website for more information.

PETERS VALLEY CRAFT CENTER

19 Kuhn Rd., Layton NJ 07851. (973)948-5200. Fax: (973)948-0011. E-mail: info@petersvalley.org. Website: www.petersvalley.org. Offers workshops May, June, July, August and September; 3-6 days long. Offers instruction by talented photographers in a wide range of photographic disciplines—from daguerreotypes to digital and everything in between. Also offers classes in blacksmithing/metals, ceramics, fibers, fine metals, weaving and woodworking. Located in northwest New Jersey in the Delaware Water Gap National

Recreation Area, 70 miles west of New York City. Artists and photographers should call for catalog or visit website or more information.

◐ ◐ ● PHOTO EXPLORER TOURS

2506 Country Village, Ann Arbor MI 48103-6500. (800)315-4462 or (734)996-1440. E-mail: decox photo@aol.com. Website: www.photoexplorertours. com. **Contact:** Dennis Cox, director. Photographic explorations of China, southern Africa, India, Turkey, Indonesia, Morocco, Burma, Iceland, Croatia, Bhutan, and Vietnam. "Founded in 1981 as China Photo Workshop Tours by award-winning travel photographer and China specialist Dennis Cox, Photo Explorer Tours has expanded its tours program since 1996. Working directly with carefully selected tour companies at each destination who understand the special needs of photographers, we keep our groups small, usually from 5 to 16 photographers, to ensure maximum flexibility for both planned and spontaneous photo opportunities." On most tours, individual instruction is available from professional photographer leading tour. Open to all skill levels. Photographers should write, call or e-mail for more information.

◐ ◐ ● PHOTOGRAPHERS' FORMULARY

P.O. Box 950, 7079 Hwy 83 N, Condon MT 59826-0950. (800)922-5255. Fax: (406)754-2896. E-mail: lynnw@blackfoot.net; formulary@blackfoot.net. Website: www.photoformulary.com; www.work-shopsinmt.com. **Contact:** Lynn Wilson, workshop program director. Photographers' Formulary workshops include a wide variety of alternative processes, and many focus on the traditional darkroom. Located in Montana's Swan Valley, some of the best wilderness lands in the Rocky Mountains. See website for details on costs and lodging. Open to all skill levels. Workshops held frequently throughout the year. See website for listing of dates and registration.

◐ ◐ PHOTOGRAPHIC ARTS WORKSHOPS

P.O. Box 1791, Granite Falls WA 98252. (360)691-4105. Fax: (360)691-4105. E-mail: PhotoArtsWrkshps@aol. com. Website: www.barnbaum.com. **Contact:** Bruce Barnbaum. Offers a wide range of workshops across the U.S., Latin America and Europe. Instructors include masters of both traditional and digital imagery.

Workshops feature instruction in the understanding and use of light, composition, exposure, development, printing, photographic goals and philosophy. All workshops include reviews of student portfolios. Sessions are intense but highly enjoyable, held in field, darkroom and classroom with outstanding photographer/instructors. Ratio of students to instructors is always 8:1 or fewer, with detailed attention to problems students want solved. All camera formats, color and b&w. The deposit for each workshop is $150, except the Escalante backpack, which is $200. Final payment is requested 5 weeks prior to the start of the workshop. The deposit is non-refundable. If a workshop is cancelled for any reason, your deposit will be returned in full. Upcoming workshops: October 16-21 "Autumn Complete Photographic Process Workshop" (Granite Falls, Washington), Cost: $1,125 (includes complete lab fees); November 13-19 "The High Sierra to Death Valley: the Highs and Lows of the American West," Cost: $1,125. See website for more information and registration.

PHOTOGRAPHIC CENTER NORTHWEST

900 12th Ave., Seattle WA 98122. (206)720-7222. E-mail: pcnw@pcnw.org; jbrandicke@pcnw.org. Website: www.pcnw.org. **Contact:** Annie Van Avery, executive director. Frequent day and evening classes and workshops in fine art photography (b&w, color, digital) for photographers of all skill levels; accredited certificate program. See website for more information and a listing of upcoming workshops.

◐ ● PHOTOGRAPHY AT THE SUMMIT: JACKSON HOLE

Rich Clarkson & Associates, LLC, 1099 18th St., Suite 2840, Denver CO 80202. (303)295-7770 or (800)745-3211. Fax: (303)295-7771. E-mail: bwilhelm@rich clarkson.com. Website: www.photographyatthe summit.com. **Contact:** Brett Wilhelm, administrator. Annual workshops held in spring (May) and fall (October). Weeklong workshops with top journalistic, nature and illustrative photographers and editors. See website for more information.

↪ ◐ ◐ ● PHOTOGRAPHY IN PROVENCE

La Chambre Claire, Rue du Buis, Ansouis 84240, France. E-mail: andrew.squires@photography-provence.com. Website: www.photography-provence. com. **Contact:** Andrew Squires, M.A. Workshops May to October. Theme: What to Photograph and Why? Designed for people who are looking for a subject and an approach they can call their own. Explore photography of the real world, the universe of human imagination, or simply let yourself discover what touches you. Explore Provence and photograph on location. Possibility to extend your stay and explore Provence if arranged in advance. Open to all skill levels. Photographers should send SASE, call or e-mail for more information.

○ PHOTO WALKING TOURS WITH RALPH VELASCO

422½ Carnation Ave., Corona del Mar CA 92625. (888)9PHOTO9 (974-6869). Fax: (888)974-6869. E-mail: ralph@RalphVelasco.com. Website: www.photo walkingtours.com. **Contact:** Ralph Velasco, founder/lead instructor. Designed to provide a unique opportunity for hands-on experience with a professional photography instructor. Learn to see like a photographer, develop skills that will allow you to readily notice and take advantage of more and better photo opportunities and begin to think outside the camera!" Includes: local (Southern California), domestic (San Francisco, Chicago) and international photo tours with award-winning photography instructor, international tour guide and author Ralph Velasco. Tours concentrate on various locations throughout Southern California including Orange County (Newport Beach, Corona del Mar, Crystal Cove, Long Beach, Laguna Beach, the Mission San Juan Capistrano), San Diego County (Balboa Park, Old Town San Diego, Point Loma, La Jolla Cove, downtown, San Diego by Train and Los Angeles/Pasadena (Santa Monica Pier), Walt Disney Concert Hall, Downtown L.A. Theatre District, The Huntington, San Gabriel Mission. Other parts of California include Temecula, The Flower Fields of Carlsbad, Catalina Island, Joshua Tree National Park, Death Valley, Santa Barbara, Central California Coast. International destinations include Cuba, Eastern Europe, Egypt, Spain, Russia, the Rhine River, Nantucket and much more. Other destinations are being added all the time. Many more will follow. Costs: varies depending on tour, some by appointment or special arrangement. Open to all levels of photographers with any equipment. Photographers should call, e-mail or visit the website for more information.

○ ◑ PRAGUE SUMMER SEMINARS

Division of International Education, 2000 Lakeshore Dr., ED 120, University of New Orleans, New Orleans LA 70148. (504)280-6388. E-mail: prague@uno.edu. Website: inst.uno.edu/Prague. **Contact:** Mary I. Hicks, program director. Challenging courses which involve studio visits, culture series, excursions within Prague and field trips to Vienna, Austria, and Cesky Krumlov, Bohemia. Open to beginners and intermediate photographers. Photographers should call, e-mail or see website for more information.

● ⊘ PROFESSIONAL PHOTOGRAPHER'S SOCIETY OF NEW YORK STATE PHOTO WORKSHOPS

2175 Stuyvesant St., Niskayuna NY 12309. (518)377-5935. E-mail: tmack1@nycap.rr.com; linda@ppsnys workshop.com. Website: www.ppsnysworkshop.com. **Contact:** Tom Mack, director. Weeklong, specialized, hands-on workshops for professional photographers in mid-July. See website for more information.

↺ ○ ◑ ● PYRENEES EXPOSURES

10 rue Edgar Quinet, 66190 Collioure, 66820, France. E-mail: explorerimages@yahoo.com. Website: www.explorerimages.com. **Contact:** Martin N. Johansen, director. Workshops held year-round. Offers 1- to 5-day workshops and photo expeditions in the French- and Spanish Pyrenees, including the Andorra, with emphasis on landscapes, wildlife and culture. Workshops and tours are limited to small groups. Open to all skill levels. Photographers should e-mail or see website for more information.

◑ ● JEFFREY RICH WILDLIFE PHOTOGRAPHY TOURS

P.O. Box 66, Millville CA 96062. (530)410-8428. E-mail: jrich@jeffrichphoto.com. Website: www.jeff richphoto.com. **Contact:** Jeffrey Rich. Estab. 1990. Leading wildlife photo tours in Alaska and western U.S.—bald eagles, whales, birds, Montana babies and predators, Brazil's Pantanal, Borneo, and Japan's winter wildlife. Photographers should call or e-mail for brochure.

○ ◑ ● ROCKY MOUNTAIN FIELD SEMINARS

1895 Fall River Rd., Estes Park CO 80517. (970)586-3262. E-mail: fieldseminars@rmna.org. Website: www.rmna.org. Rachel Balduzzi, field seminar director and NGF manager. **Contact:** Seminar Coordinator. "We have seminars starting at $10 for kids and families; up to $500 for a John Fielder seminar. We also have a seminar (around $3,000), which is a special trip to the Tatra National Park in Poland." Day and weekend seminars covering photographic techniques for wildlife and scenics in Rocky Mountain National Park. Professional instructors include David Halpern, W. Perry Conway, Don Mammoser, Glenn Randall, Allan Northcutt and Lee Kline. Call or e-mail for a free seminar catalog listing over 50 seminars.

○ ◑ ● ROCKY MOUNTAIN SCHOOL OF PHOTOGRAPHY

216 N. Higgins, Missoula MT 59802. (406)543-0171 or (800)394-7677. Fax: (406)721-9133. E-mail: work shops@rmsp.com. Website: www.rmsp.com. "RMSP offers three types of photography programs: Career Training, Workshops and Weekend events. There are varied learning opportunities for students according to their individual goals and educational needs. In a non-competitive learning environment we strive to instill confidence, foster creativity and build technical skills."

⊕ SAN FRANCISCO PHOTO SAFARIS

(415)891-7092. Website: www.sanfranphotosafaris. com. **Contact:** Gary Gullett, owner/operations manager. "Local travel photography workshops are held daily in convenient locations in San Francisco. These are hands-on workshops with participants learning the creative camera controls and concepts of photography in an easy-to-understand language. There are also regional, national and worldwide safaris for the more adventurous. Extreme photography opportunities include adventures such as mountain climbing and/or scuba diving, all in great photographic venues." See the website for more details. Open to all skill levels and types of cameras (film or digital).

○ ◑ ● SANTA FE PHOTOGRAPHIC WORKSHOPS

P.O. Box 9916, Santa Fe NM 87504-5916. (505)983-1400. Fax: (505)989-8604. E-mail: info@santafework shops.com. Website: www.santafeworkshops.com. Over 120 week-long workshops encompassing all levels of photography and more than 35 digital lab workshops and 12 week-long workshops in Mexico—all led by top professional photographers. The workshops campus is located near the historic center of Santa Fe.

Call or e-mail to request a free catalog. Upcoming workshops: October 18-November 2 "Bhutan: Land of the Thunder Dragon;" October 19-23 "A Natural Eye: Ghost Ranch, New Mexico;" October 19-23 "Autumn on the Coast of Maine." See website for more details and registration.

○ ◑ ● SELLING YOUR PHOTOGRAPHY

2973 Harbor Blvd., #341, Costa Mesa CA 92626-3912. (714) 356-4260. E-mail: maria@mpiscopo.com. Website: www.mpiscopo.com. **Contact:** Maria Piscopo. One-day workshops cover techniques for marketing and selling photography services. Open to photographers of all skill levels. See website for dates and locations. Maria Piscopo is the author of *Photographer's Guide to Marketing & Self-Promotion*, 4th edition (Allworth Press).

◑ ● SELLPHOTOS.COM

Pine Lake Farm, 1910 35th Rd., Osceola WI 54020. (715)248-3800, ext. 21. Fax: (715)248-3800. E-mail: psi2@photosource.com; info@photosource.com. Website: www.sellphotos.com, www.photosource. com. **Contact:** Rohn Engh. Offers half-day workshops in major cities. Marketing critique of attendees' slides follows seminar.

◑ ● JOHN SEXTON PHOTOGRAPHY WORKSHOPS

P.O. Box 30, Carmel Valley CA 93924. (831)659-3130. Fax: (831)659-5509. E-mail: info@johnsexton.com. Website: www.johnsexton.com. Director: John Sexton. **Contact:** Laura Bayless, administrative assistant. Offers a selection of intensive workshops with master photographers in scenic locations throughout the U.S. All workshops offer a combination of instruction in the aesthetic and technical considerations involved in making expressive b&w prints. Instructors include John Sexton, Charles Cramer, Ray McSavaney, Anne Larsen and others.

○ ◑ ● SHENANDOAH PHOTO-GRAPHIC WORKSHOPS

P.O. Box 54, Sperryville VA 22740. (540)937-5555. **Contact:** Frederick Figall, director. Three-day to 1-week photo workshops in the Virginia Blue Ridge foothills, held in summer and fall. Weekend workshops held year round in Washington, D.C. area. Prefers contact by phone.

○ ◑ THE SHOWCASE SCHOOL OF PHOTOGRAPHY

1135 Sheridan Road, Atlanta GA 30324. (404)965-2205. E-mail: staff@theshowcaseschool.com. Website: www.theshowcaseschool.com. Offers photography classes to the general public, including beginning digital camera, people photography, nature photography and Photoshop. Open to beginner and intermediate amateur photographers. Classes offered frequently throughout the year; see website for upcoming dates.

☺ ○ ◑ ● SINGING SANDS WORKSHOPS

(519)800-2099. E-mail: donmartelca@yahoo.ca. Website: www.singingsandsworkshops.com. Film shooters welcome. Semiannual workshops held in June and October. Creative photo techniques in the rugged coastline of Georgian Bay and the flats of Lake Huron, taught by Don Martel and James Sidney. Open to all skill levels. Photographers should send SASE, call, e-mail or see website for more information.

◔ SKELLIG PHOTO TOURS

(00353)66 9479022. E-mail: michaelherrmann@email.de. Website: www.skelligphototours.com. **Contact:** Michael Herrmann. Several held June-September and on demand. Learn, or improve, your photography skills through landscape photography, exposure, composition, low-light photography. HDR photo editing in Photoshop and Lightroom. Open to all skill levels. Photographers should call, e-mail or see website for more information.

○ ◑ ● SMOKY MOUNTAIN LEARNING CENTER

414 Whittier School Rd., Whittier NC 28789. (828)736-8450. E-mail: info@mountainlearning.com. Website: www.mountainlearning.com. Offers workshops on portraiture and wedding photography, Photoshop and Painter. Open to all skill levels. Upcoming workshop: "The Wonders of Macro Photography," October 15-18. Cost: $799. See website for more details and registration.

○ ◑ ● SOUTH SHORE ART CENTER

119 Ripley Rd., Cohasset MA 02025. (781)383-2787. Fax: (781)383-2964. E-mail: info@ssac.org. Website: www.ssac.org. South Shore Art Center is a non-profit organization based in the coastal area south of Boston. The facility features appealing galleries and teaching studios. Offers exhibitions and gallery programs, sales of fine art and studio crafts, courses and workshops, school outreach and special events. See website for more information and a list of upcoming workshops and events.

◑ ● SPORTS PHOTOGRAPHY WORKSHOP: COLORADO SPRINGS, CO

Rich Clarkson & Associates, 1099 18th St., Suite 2840, Denver CO 80202. (303)295-7770 or (800)745-3211. Fax: (303)295-7771. E-mail: info@richclarkson.com. Website: www.sportsphotographyworkshop.com. **Contact:** Brett Wilhelm, administrator. Annual workshop held in June. Weeklong workshop in sports photography at the U.S. Olympic Training Center with *Sports Illustrated* and Associated Press photographers and editors. See website for more information.

○ ◑ ● SUMMIT PHOTOGRAPHIC WORKSHOPS

P.O. Box 67459, Scotts Valley CA 95067. (831)440-0124. E-mail: b-and-k@pacbell.net. Website: www.summitphotographic.com. **Contact:** Barbara Brundege, owner. Offers several workshops per year, including nature and landscape photography; wildlife photography classes; photo tours from 5 days to 3 weeks. Open to all skill levels. Photographers should see website for more information and a listing of upcoming workshops.

◑ ● SUPERIOR/GUNFLINT PHOTOGRAPHY WORKSHOPS

P.O. Box 19286, Minneapolis MN 55419. (612)824-2999. E-mail: lk@laynekennedy.com. Website: www.laynekennedy.com. **Contact:** Layne Kennedy, director. Lodging and meals for North Shore session are paid for by participants. Offers wilderness adventure photo workshops 3 times/year. Winter session includes driving your own dogsled team in northeastern Minnesota. Summer sessions include kayaking/camping trip in the Apostle Islands with first and last nights in lodges, and a new session along Minnesota's North Shore, at the famed North House Folk School, covering Lake Superior's north shore. All trips professionally guided. Workshops stress how to shoot effective and marketable magazine photos in a story-telling format. Photographers should call, e-mail or see website for more information and a list of upcoming workshops.

○ ◐ ● SYNERGISTIC VISIONS WORKSHOPS

2435 E. Piazza Ct., Grand Junction CO 81506. (970)245-6700. Fax: (970)245-6700. E-mail: steve@synvis.com. Website: www.synvis.com. **Contact:** Steve Traudt, director. Offers a variety of digital photography and Photoshop classes at various venues in Grand Junction, Moab, Ouray, and others. "Steve is also available to present day-long photo seminars to your group." See website for more information and upcoming workshops.

○ ◐ ● TEXAS SCHOOL OF PROFESSIONAL PHOTOGRAPHY

P.O. Box 1120, Caldwell TX 77836. (979)272-5200. Fax: (979)272-5201. E-mail: don@texasschool.org. Website: texasschool.org/index.html. **Contact:** Don Dickson, director. Twenty-five different classes offered, including portrait, wedding, marketing, background painting and video. See website for more information and a list of upcoming workshops.

○ ◐ ● TRAVEL IMAGES

P.O. Box 2434, Eagle ID 83616. (800)325-8320. E-mail: phototours@travelimages.com. Website: www.travelimages.com. **Contact:** John Baker, owner/guide. Small-group photo tours. Locations include U.S., Canada, Wales, Scotland, Ireland, England, New Zealand, Tasmania, Galapagos Islands, Machu Picchu, Patagonia, Provence, Tuscany, Cinque Terre, Venice, Austria, Switzerland, Germany, and Greece.

○ ◐ ● JOSEPH VAN OS PHOTO SAFARIS, INC.

P.O. Box 655, Vashon Island WA 98070. Fax: (206)463-5484. E-mail: info@photosafaris.com. Website: www.photosafaris.com. **Contact:** Joseph Van Os, director. Offers over 50 different photo tours and workshops worldwide. At least 1 tour offered each month; several 2012 tours already planned. Fall/winter destinations include Antartica (November 5-December 2), Cambodia & Myanmar (November 8-22), Chilkat River, Alaska (November 13-19) and Sri Lanka (December 2-17). See website for more details and a list of all upcoming tours.

○ ◐ ● VIRGINIA CENTER FOR THE CREATIVE ARTS

154 San Angelo Dr., Amherst VA 24521. (434)946-7236. Fax: (434)946-7239. E-mail: vcca@vcca.com. Website: www.vcca.com. **Contact:** Sheila Gulley Pleasants, director of artists' services. The Virginia Center for the Creative Arts (VCCA) is an international working retreat for writers, visual artists and composers. Located on 450 acres in the foothills of the Blue Ridge Mountains in central Virginia, VCCA provides residential fellowships ranging from 2 weeks to 2 months. VCCA can accommodate 25 fellows at a time and provides separate working and living quarters and all meals. There is one fully equipped b&w darkroom at VCCA. Artists provide their own materials. Cost: "There is no fee to attend, but a daily contribution of $45-90 is suggested." VCCA application and work samples required. Photographers should call or see website for more information. Application deadlines are January 15, May 15, and September 15 each year.

○ ◐ ● VISION QUEST PHOTO WORKSHOPS CENTER

2370 Hendon Ave., St. Paul MN 55108-1453. (651)644-1400. Fax: (651)644-2122. E-mail: info@douglasbeasley.com. Website: www.beasleyphotography.com. **Contact:** Doug Beasley, director. Annual workshops held February through November. Hands-on photo workshops that emphasize content, vision and creativity over technique or gimmicks. Workshops held in a variety of locations. Open to all skill levels. Upcoming workshops: October 21-23: Renewing your Creative Spirit, Granstburg, Wisconsin; October 27-November 5: The Art Workshops in Guatemala; December 2-4: Zen and the Art of Photography, New York Open Center. Photographers should call, e-mail or see website for more information, a list of all upcoming workshops and registration.

◐ ● VISUAL ARTISTRY & FIELD MENTORSHIP PHOTOGRAPHY WORKSHOP SERIES

P.O.Box 963, Eldersburg MD 21784. (410)552-4664. Fax: (410)552-3332. E-mail: tony@tonysweet.com. Website: tonysweet.com. **Contact:** Tony Sweet or Susan Milestone, susan@tonysweet.com. Five-day workshops, limit 8-10 participants. Formats: Digital preferred; 35mm film; xpan. Extensive personal attention and instructional slide shows. Post-workshop support and image critiques for 6 months after the workshop (for an additional fee). Frequent attendees discounts and inclement weather discounts on subsequent workshops. Dealer discounts available from major vendors. "The emphasis is to create in the participant a greater awareness of composition, subject selection, and artistic rendering of the natural world using the raw materials of nature: color, form and line." Open to intermediate and advanced photographers. See website for more information.

○ ◑ ● WILDLIFE PHOTOGRAPHY WORKSHOPS AND LECTURES

Len Rue Enterprises, LLC, 138 Millbrook Rd., Blairstown NJ 07825. (908)362-6616. E-mail: rue@rue.com. Website: www.rue.com; www.rueimages.com. **Contact:** Len Rue, Jr. Taught by Len Rue, Jr., who has over 35 years experience in outdoor photography by shooting photographic stock for the publishing industry. Also leads tours and teaches photography.

○ ◑ ● WILD WINGS PHOTO ADVENTURES

2035 Buchanan Rd., Manning SC 29102. (803)473-3414. E-mail: doug@totallyoutdoorsimaging.com. Website: www.totallyoutdoorsimaging.com/work shops.html. **Contact:** Doug Gardner, photographer. Annual workshops held various times throughout the year in North and South Carolina: waterfowl (ducks, snow geese, tundra swan), osprey & swamp critters. "The purpose of Wild Wings Photo Adventures is to offer one on one instruction and great opportunities to photograph 'wild' animals up close. Students will learn valuable techniques in the field with internationally recognized wildlife photographer Doug Gardner." See website for more information and registration.

◑ ● ROBERT WINSLOW PHOTO, INC.

P.O. Box 334, Durango CO 81302-0334. (970)259-4143. E-mail: rwinslow@mydurango.net. Website: www.robertwinslowphoto.com. **Contact:** Robert Winslow, president. "We arrange and lead custom wildlife and natural history photo tours to East Africa and other destinations around the world." See website for more information.

○ ◑ ● WORKING WITH ARTISTS

(303)837-1341. E-mail: info@workingwithartists.org. Website: www.workingwithartists.org. Offers monthly workshops on Photoshop, digital, alternative process, portraiture, landscape, creativity, studio lighting and more. Open to all skill levels. They also have a gallery with changing juried photo exhibits. Pho-

tographers should call, e-mail, see website for more information and a list of upcoming workshops.

THE HELENE WURLITZER FOUNDATION

P.O. Box 1891, Taos NM 87571. (505)758-2413. Fax: (575)758-2559. E-mail: hwf@taosnet.com. Website: www.wurlitzerfoundation.org. **Contact:** Michael A. Knight, executive director. Estab. 1953. The foundation offers residencies to artists in the creative fields-visual, literary and music composition. There are three thirteen week sessions from mid-January through November annually. Application deadline: January 18 for following year. For application, request by e-mail or visit website to download.

◑ ● YADDO

The Corporation of Yaddo Residencies, Box 395, 312 Union Ave., Saratoga Springs NY 12866-0395. (518)584-0746. Fax: (518)584-1312. E-mail: chwait@yaddo.org; Lleduc@yaddo.org. Website: www.yaddo.org. **Contact:** Candace Wait, program director. Estab. 1900. Two seasons: large season is mid-May-August; small season is October-May (stays from 2 weeks to 2 months; average stay is 5 weeks). Accepts 230 artists/year. Average attendance: Accommodates approximately 35 artists in large season. Those qualified for invitations to Yaddo are highly qualified writers, visual artists (including photographers), composers, choreographers, performance artists and film and video artists who are working at the professional level in their fields. Artists who wish to work collaboratively are encouraged to apply. An abiding principle at Yaddo is that applications for residencies are judged on the quality of the artists' work and professional promise. Site includes four small lakes, a rose garden, woodland, swimming pool, tennis courts. Yaddo's non-refundable application fee is $30, to which is added a fee for media uploads ranging from $5-10 depending on the discipline. Application fees must be paid by credit card. Two letters of recommendation are requested. Applications are considered by the Admissions Committee and invitations are issued by March 15 (deadline: January 1) and October 1 (deadline: August 1). Information available on website.

○ ◑ ● YELLOWSTONE ASSOCIATION INSTITUTE

P.O. Box 117, Yellowstone National Park WY 82190. (406)848-2400. Fax: (406)848-2847. E-mail: Registrar@yellowstoneassociation.org. Website:

www.yellowstoneassociation.org. Offers workshops in nature and wildlife photography during the summer, fall and winter. Custom courses can be arranged. Photographers should see website for more information.

○ ◑ ● YOSEMITE OUTDOOR ADVENTURES

P.O. Box 230, El Portal CA 95318. (209)379-2646. Fax: (209)379-2486. E-mail: info@yosemiteconservancy. org. Website: www.yosemite.org. Offers small (8-15 people) workshops in Yosemite National Park in outdoor field photography and natural history year round. Photographers should see website for more information and a list of upcoming workshops.

◐ ○ ◑ ● ZORBA PHOTO WORKSHOPS

15 Thermopilon Str., Analipsi Thessaloniki 54248, Greece. +30 6944 257125. E-mail: Angelou Photography@gmail.com. Website: www.zorbaphoto workshops.com. **Contact:** John Angelou, owner/instructor. Workshop held annually. Workshops focus on landscape photography, the introduction of the human form into the landscape, creation of fashionable and conceptual images, and post-production. Open to all skill levels. E-mail or see website for more information.

STOCK PHOTOGRAPHY PORTALS

These sites market and distribute images from multiple agencies and photographers.

AGPix www.agpix.com
Alamy www.alamy.com
Digital Railroad www.digitalrailroad.net
Find a Photographer www.asmp.org/find-a-photographer
Independent Photography Network (IPNStock) www.ipnstock.com
PhotoServe www.pdnonline.com/pdn/photoserve/index.jsp
PhotoSource International www.photosource.com
Shutterpoint Photography www.shutterpoint.com
Veer www.veer.com
Workbook Stock www.workbook.com

PORTFOLIO REVIEW EVENTS

//

Portfolio review events provide photographers the opportunity to show their work to a variety of photo buyers, including photo editors, publishers, art directors, gallery representatives, curators, and collectors.

Art Director's Club, International Annual Awards Exhibition, New York City, www.adc-global.org

Atlanta Celebrates Photography, held annually in October, Atlanta GA, www.acpinfo.org

Center for Photography at Woodstock, New York City, www.cpw.org

Festival of Light International Directory of Photography Festivals, an international collaboration of more than twenty photography festivals, www.festivaloflight.net

Fotofest, March, Houston TX, www.fotofest.org. Biennial—held in even-numbered years.

Fotofusion, January, Delray Beach FL, www.fotofusion.org

North American Nature Photographers Association, annual summit held in January. Location varies. www.nanpa.org

Photo LA, January, Los Angeles CA, www.photola.com

Photo Miami, held annually in December, Miami FL, http://fotomarketart.com

Photo San Francisco, July, San Francisco CA, www.photosanfrancisco.net

Photolucida, March, Portland OR, www.photolucida.org. Biennial—held in odd-numbered years.

The Print Center, events held throughout the year, Philadelphia PA, www.printcenter.org

Review Santa Fe, July, Santa Fe NM, http://visitcenter.org. The only juried portfolio review event.

Rhubarb-Rhubarb, July, Birmingham UK, www.rhubarb-rhubarb.net
Society for Photographic Education National Conference, March, different location each
year, www.spenational.org0

GRANTS

State, Provincial & Regional

///

Arts councils in the United States and Canada provide assistance to artists (including photographers) in the form of fellowships or grants. These grants can be substantial and confer prestige upon recipients; however, only state or province residents are eligible. Because deadlines and available support vary annually, query first (with a SASE) or check websites for guidelines.

UNITED STATES ARTS AGENCIES

Alabama State Council on the Arts, 201 Monroe St., Montgomery, AL 36130-1800. (334) 242-4076. E-mail: staff@arts.alabama.gov. Website: www.arts.state.al.us.

Alaska State Council on the Arts, 161 S. Klevin St., Suite 102, Anchorage, AK 99508-1506. (907) 269-6610 or (888) 278-7424. E-mail: aksca.info@alaska.gov. Website: www.eed.state.ak.us/aksca.

Arizona Commission on the Arts, 417 W. Roosevelt St., Phoenix, AZ 85003-1326. (602) 771-6501. E-mail: info@azarts.gov. Website: www.azarts.gov.

Arkansas Arts Council, 1500 Tower Bldg., 323 Center St., Little Rock, AR 72201-2606. (501) 324-9766. E-mail: info@arkansasarts.com. Website: www.arkansasarts.org.

California Arts Council, 1300 I St., Suite 930, Sacramento, CA 95814. (916) 322-6555 or (800) 201-6201. E-mail: info@caartscouncil.com. Website: www.cac.ca.gov.

Colorado Creative Industries, 1625 Broadway, Suite 2700, Denver, CO 80202. (303) 892-3802. E-mail: online form. Website: www.coloarts.state.co.us.

Connecticut Commission on Culture & Tourism, One Constitution Plaza, 2nd floor, Hartford, CT 06103. (860) 256-2800. Website: www.cultureandtourism.org.

Delaware Division of the Arts, Carvel State Office Bldg., 4th Floor, 820 N. French St., Wilmington, DE 19801. (302) 577-8278 (New Castle County) or (302) 739-5304 (Kent or Sussex Counties). E-mail: delarts@state.de.us. Website: www.artsdel.org.

District of Columbia Commission on the Arts & Humanities, 1371 Harvard St. NW, Washington, DC 20009. (202) 724-5613. E-mail: cah@dc.gov. Website: www.dcarts. dc.gov.

Florida Division of Cultural Affairs, R.A. Gray Building, 3rd Floor, 500 S. Bronough St., Tallahassee, FL 32399-0250. (850) 245-6470. E-mail: info@florida-arts.org. Website: www.florida-arts.org.

Georgia Council for the Arts, 260 14th St. NW, Atlanta, GA 30318-5360. (404) 685-2787. E-mail: gaarts@gaarts.org. Website: www.gaarts.org.

Guam Council on the Arts & Humanities, P.O. Box 2950, Hagatna, GU 96932. (671) 475-2781/2782/3661. E-mail: info@caha.guam.gov. Website: www.guamcaha.org.

Hawai'i State Foundation on Culture & the Arts, 250 S. Hotel St., 2nd Floor, Honolulu, HI 96813. (808) 586-0300. E-mail: vivien.lee@hawaii.gov. Website: www.state. hi.us/sfca.

Idaho Commission on the Arts, P.O. Box 83720, Boise, ID 83720-0008. (208) 334-2119 or (800) 278-3863. E-mail: info@arts.idaho.gov. Website: www.arts.idaho.gov.

Illinois Arts Council, James R. Thompson Center, 100 W. Randolph, Suite 10-500, Chicago, IL 60601-3230. (312) 814-6750 or (800) 237-6994. E-mail: iac.info@illinois.gov. Website: www.arts.illinois.gov.

Indiana Arts Commission, 100 N. Senate Ave., Room N505, Indianapolis, IN 46204. (317) 232-1268. E-mail: IndianaArtsCommission@iac.in.gov. Website: www.in.gov/ arts.

Iowa Arts Council, 600 E. Locust, Des Moines, IA 50319-0290. (515) 242-6194. Website: www.iowaartscouncil.org.

Kansas Arts Commission, 700 SW Jackson, Suite 1004, Topeka, KS 66603-3774. (785) 296-3335 or (866) 433-0688. E-mail: kac@arts.ks.gov. Website: http://arts.ks.gov.

Kentucky Arts Council, Capital Plaza Tower, 21st Floor, 500 Mero St., Frankfort, KY 40601-1987. (502) 564-3757 or (888) 833-2787. E-mail: kyarts@ky.gov. Website: www. artscouncil.ky.gov.

Louisiana Division of the Arts, P.O. Box 44247, Baton Rouge, LA 70804-4247. (225) 342-8180. E-mail: arts@crt.state.la.us. Website: www.crt.state.la.us/arts.

Maine Arts Commission, 193 State St., 25 State House Station, Augusta, ME 04333-0025. (207) 287-2724. E-mail: MaineArts.info@maine.gov. Website: http://mainearts. maine.gov.

Maryland State Arts Council, 175 W. Ostend St., Suite E, Baltimore, MD 21230. (410) 767-6555. E-mail: msac@msac.org. Website: www.msac.org.

Massachusetts Cultural Council, 10 St. James Ave., 3rd Floor, Boston, MA 02116-3803. (617) 727-3668. E-mail: mcc@art.state.ma.us. Website: www.massculturalcouncil.org.

Michigan Council for Arts & Cultural Affairs, 300 N. Washington Square, Lansing, MI 48913. (517) 241-4011. E-mail: artsinfo@michigan.org. Website: www.themedc. org/Arts.

Minnesota State Arts Board, Park Square Court, Suite 200, 400 Sibley St., St. Paul, MN 55101-1928. (651) 215-1600 or (800) 866-2787. E-mail: msab@arts.state.mn.us. Website: www.arts.state.mn.us.

Mississippi Arts Commission, 501 N. West St., Suite 1101A, Woolfolk Bldg., Jackson, MS 39201. (601) 359-6030 or (800) 582-2233. Website: www.arts.state.ms.us.

Missouri Arts Council, 815 Olive St., Suite 16, St. Louis, MO 63101-1503. (314)340-6845 or (866)407-4752. E-mail: moarts@ded.mo.gov. Website: www.missouriartscouncil.org.

Montana Arts Council, P.O. Box 202201, Helena, MT 59620-2201. (406) 444-6430. E-mail: mac@mt.gov. Website: http://art.mt.gov.

National Assembly of State Arts Agencies, 1029 Vermont Ave. NW, 2nd Floor, Washington, DC 20005. (202) 347-6352. E-mail: nasaa@nasaa-arts.org. Website: www.nasaa-arts.org.

Nebraska Arts Council, 1004 Farnam St., Burlington Bldg., Plaza Level, Omaha, NE 68102. (402) 595-2122 or (800) 341-4067. Website: www.nebraskaartscouncil.org.

Nevada Arts Council, 716 N. Carson St., Suite A, Carson City, NV 89701. (775) 687-6680. E-mail: online form. Website: http://nac.nevadaculture.org.

New Hampshire State Council on the Arts, 21/2 Beacon St., Suite 225, Concord, NH 03301-4447. (603) 271-3584 or (800) 735-2964. Website: www.nh.gov/nharts.

New Jersey State Council on the Arts, 225 W. State St., 4th floor, P.O. Box 306, Trenton, NJ 08625. (609) 292-6130. E-mail: online form. Website: www.njartscouncil.org.

New Mexico Arts, Dept. of Cultural Affairs, P.O. Box 1450, Santa Fe, NM 87504-1450. (505) 827-6490 or (800) 879-4278. Website: www.nmarts.org.

New York State Council on the Arts, 175 Varick St., New York, NY 10014. (212) 627-4455 or (800) 895-9838. Website: www.nysca.org.

North Carolina Arts Council, 109 East Jones St., Cultural Resources Building, Raleigh, NC 27601. (919) 807-6500. E-mail: ncarts@ncdcr.gov. Website: www.ncarts.org.

North Dakota Council on the Arts, 1600 E. Century Ave., Suite 6, Bismarck, ND 58503-0649. (701)328-7590. E-mail: comserv@nd.gov. Website: www.state.nd.us/arts.

Ohio Arts Council, 727 E. Main St., Columbus, OH 43205-1796. (614) 466-2613. Website: www.oac.state.oh.us.

Oklahoma Arts Council, Jim Thorpe Building, 2101 N. Lincoln Blvd., Suite 640, Oklahoma City, OK 73152-2001. (405) 521-2931. E-mail: okarts@arts.ok.gov. Website: www.arts.state.ok.us.

Oregon Arts Commission, 775 Summer St. NE, Suite 200, Salem, OR 97301-1280. (503) 986-0082. E-mail: oregon.artscomm@state.or.us. Website: www.oregonartscommission.org.

Pennsylvania Council on the Arts, 216 Finance Bldg., Harrisburg, PA 17120. (717) 787-6883. Website: www.pacouncilonthearts.org.

Institute of Puerto Rican Culture, P.O. Box 9024184, San Juan, PR 00902-4184. (787) 724-0700. E-mail: webicp@icp.gobierno.pr. Website: www.icp.gobierno.pr.

Rhode Island State Council on the Arts, One Capitol Hill, Third Floor, Providence, RI 02908. (401) 222-3880. E-mail: info@arts.ri.gov. Website: www.arts.ri.gov.

American Samoa Council on Culture, P.O. Box 1995, Pago Pago, AS 96799. (684) 633-4347. E-mail: amssc@prel.org. Website: www.prel.org/programs/pcahe/ptg/terr-asamoa1.html.

South Carolina Arts Commission, 1800 Gervais St., Columbia, SC 29201. (803) 734-8696. E-mail: info@arts.state.sc.us. Website: www.southcarolinaarts.com.

South Dakota Arts Council, 711 E. Wells Ave., Pierre, SD 57501-3369. (605) 773-3301. E-mail: sdac@state.sd.us. Website: www.artscouncil.sd.gov.

Tennessee Arts Commission, 401 Charlotte Ave., Nashville, TN 37243-0780. (615) 741-1701. Website: www.arts.state.tn.us.

Texas Commission on the Arts, E.O. Thompson Office Building, 920 Colorado, Suite 501, Austin, TX 78701. (512) 463-5535. E-mail: front.desk@arts.state.tx.us. Website: www.arts.state.tx.us.

Utah Arts Council, 617 E. South Temple, Salt Lake City, UT 84102-1177. (801) 236-7555. Website: http://arts.utah.gov.

Vermont Arts Council, 136 State St., Montpelier, VT 05633-6001. (802) 828-3291. E-mail: online form. Website: www.vermontartscouncil.org.

Virgin Islands Council on the Arts, 5070 Norre Gade, St. Thomas, VI 00802-6876. (340)774-5984. Website: http://vicouncilonarts.org.

Virginia Commission for the Arts, Lewis House, 223 Governor St., 2nd Floor, Richmond, VA 23219. (804) 225-3132. E-mail: arts@arts.virginia.gov. Website: www.arts.state.va.us.

Washington State Arts Commission, 711 Capitol Way S., Suite 600, P.O. Box 42675, Olympia, WA 98504-2675. (360) 753-3860. E-mail: info@arts.wa.gov. Website: www.arts.wa.gov.

West Virginia Commission on the Arts, The Cultural Center, Capitol Complex, 1900 Kanawha Blvd. E., Charleston, WV 25305-0300. (304) 558-0220. Website: www. wvculture.org/arts.

Wisconsin Arts Board, 101 E. Wilson St., 1st Floor, Madison, WI 53702. (608) 266-0190. E-mail: artsboard@wisconsin.gov. Website: http://artsboard.wisconsin.gov.

Wyoming Arts Council, 2320 Capitol Ave., Cheyenne, WY 82002. (307) 777-7742. E-mail: online form. Website: http://wyoarts.state.wy.us.

CANADIAN PROVINCES ARTS AGENCIES

Alberta Foundation for the Arts, 10708 - 105 Ave., Edmonton, AB T5H 0A1. (780) 427-9968. Website: www.affta.ab.ca.

British Columbia Arts Council, P.O. Box 9819, Stn. Prov. Govt., Victoria, BC V8W 9W3. (250) 356-1718. E-mail: BCArtsCouncil@gov.bc.ca. Website: www.bcartscouncil. ca.

The Canada Council for the Arts, 350 Albert St., P.O. Box 1047, Ottawa, ON K1P 5V8. (613) 566-4414 or (800) 263-5588 (within Canada). E-mail: online form. Website: www.canadacouncil.ca.

Manitoba Arts Council, 525-93 Lombard Ave., Winnipeg, MB R3B 3B1. (204) 945-2237 or (866) 994-2787 (within Manitoba). E-mail: info@artscouncil.mb.ca. Website: www.artscouncil.mb.ca.

New Brunswick Arts Board (NBAB), 61 Carleton St., Fredericton, NB E3B 3T2. (506) 444-4444 or (866) 460-2787. E-mail: online form. Website: www.artsnb.ca.

Newfoundland & Labrador Arts Council, P.O. Box 98, St. John's, NL A1C 5H5. (709) 726-2212 or (866) 726-2212 (within Newfoundland). E-mail: nlacmail@nfld.net. Website: www.nlac.nf.ca.

Nova Scotia Department of Tourism, Culture, and Heritage, Culture Division, World Trade Center, 6th floor, 1800 Argyle St., P.O. Box 456, Halifax, NS B3J 2R5. (902) 424-4510. E-mail: culture@gov.ns.ca. Website: www.gov.ns.ca/tch.

Ontario Arts Council, 151 Bloor St. W., 5th Floor, Toronto, ON M5S 1T6. (416) 961-1660 or (800) 387-0058 (within Ontario). E-mail: info@arts.on.ca. Website: www.arts. on.ca.

Prince Edward Island Council of the Arts, 115 Richmond St., Charlottetown, PE C1A 1H7. (902) 368-4410 or (888) 734-2784. E-mail: info@peica.ca. Website: www. peiartscouncil.com.

Québec Council for Arts & Literature, 79 boul. René-Lévesque Est, 3e étage, Québec, QC G1R 5N5. (418) 643-1707 or (800) 897-1707. E-mail: info@calq.gouv.qc.ca. Website: www.calq.gouv.qc.ca.

The Saskatchewan Arts Board, 1355 Broad St., Regina, SK S4P 7V1. (306) 787-4056 or (800) 667-7526 (within Saskatchewan). E-mail: info@artsboard.sk.ca. Website: www. artsboard.sk.ca.

Yukon Arts Section, Cultural Services Branch, Dept. of Tourism & Culture, Government of Yukon, Box 2703, Whitehorse, YT Y1A 2C6. (867) 667-8589 or (800) 661-0408 (within Yukon). E-mail: arts@gov.yk.ca. Website: www.tc.gov.yk.ca/138.html.

REGIONAL GRANTS & AWARDS

The following opportunities are arranged by state since most of them grant money to artists in a particular geographic region. Because deadlines vary annually, check websites or call for the most up-to-date information.

California

Flintridge Foundation Awards for Visual Artists, 1040 Lincoln Ave., Suite 100, Pasadena, CA 91103. (626) 449-0839 or (800) 303-2139. Fax: (626) 585-0011. Website: www. flintridge.org. For artists in California, Oregon, and Washington only.

James D. Phelan Art Awards, Kala Art Institute, Don Porcella, 1060 Heinz Ave., Berkeley, CA 94710. (510)549-2977. Website: www.kala.org. For artists born in California only.

Connecticut

Martha Boschen Porter Fund, Inc., 145 White Hallow Rd., Sharon, CT 06064. For artists in northwestern Connecticut, western Massachusetts, and adjacent areas of New York (except New York City).

Idaho

Betty Bowen Memorial Award, c/o Seattle Art Museum, 100 University St., Seattle, WA 98101. (206)654-3131. E-mail: bettybowen@seattleartmuseum.org. Website: www. seattleartmuseum.org/bettybowen/. For artists in Washington, Oregon and Idaho only.

Illinois

Illinois Arts Council, Individual Artists Support Initiative, James R. Thompson Center, 100 W. Randolph, Suite 10-500, Chicago, IL 60601. (312)814-6750. Website: www. arts.illinois.gov/grants-programs/funding-programs/individual-artist-support. For Illinois artists only.

Kentucky

Kentucky Foundation for Women Grants Program, 1215 Heyburn Bldg., 332 W. Broadway, Louisville, KY 40202. (502) 562-0045 or (866) 654-7564. E-mail: info@kfw.org. Website: www.kfw.org/grants.html. For female artists living in Kentucky only.

Massachusetts

See **Martha Boschen Porter Fund, Inc.,** under Connecticut.

Minnesota

McKnight Artist Fellowships for Photogographers, University of Minnesota Dept. of Art, Regis Center for Art, E-201, 405 21st Ave. S., Minneapolis, MN 55455. (612) 626-9640. E-mail: info@mnartists.org. Website: www.mcknightphoto.umn.edu. For Minnesota artists only.

New York

A.I.R. Gallery Fellowship Program, 111 Front St., #228, Brooklyn, NY 11201. (212) 255-6651. E-mail: info@airgallery.org. Website: www.airgallery.org. For female artists from New York City metro area only.

Arts & Cultural Council for Greater Rochester, 277 N. Goodman St., Rochester, NY 14607. (585) 473-4000. Website: www.artsrochester.org.

Constance Saltonstall Foundation for the Arts Grants and Fellowships, 435 Ellis Hollow Creek Rd., Ithaca, NY 14850 (include SASE). (607) 539-3146. E-mail: artscolony@saltonstall.org. Website: www.saltonstall.org. For artists in the central and western counties of New York.

New York Foundation for the Arts: Artists' Fellowships, 20 Jay St., 7th floor, Brooklyn, NY 11201. (212) 366-6900. E-mail: fellowships@nyfa.org. Website: www.nyfa.org. For New York artists only.

Oregon

See **Flintridge Foundation Awards for Visual Artists,** under California.

Pennsylvania

Leeway Foundation—Philadelphia, Pennsylvania Region, The Philadelphia Building, 1315 Walnut St., Suite 832, Philadelphia, PA 19107. (215) 545-4078. E-mail: online form. Website: www.leeway.org. For female artists in Philadelphia only.

Texas

Individual Artist Grant Program—Houston, Texas, Houston Arts Alliance, 3201 Allen Pkwy., Suite 250, Houston, TX 77019-1800. (713) 527-9330. E-mail: online form. Website: www.houstonartsalliance.com. For Houston artists only.

Washington

See **Flintridge Foundation Awards for Visual Artists,** under California.

PROFESSIONAL ORGANIZATIONS

//

American Photographic Artists, National, P.O. Box 725146, Atlanta, GA 31139. (800) 272-6264, ext. 12. E-mail: membership@apanational.com. Website: www.apanational.com

American Photographic Artists, Atlanta, 2221-D Peachtree Rd. NE, Suite #553, Atlanta, GA 30309. (888) 889-7190, ext. 50. E-mail: director@apaatlanta.com. Website: www.apaatlanta.com

American Photographic Artists, Los Angeles, 9190 W. Olympic Blvd., #212, Beverly Hills, CA, 90212. (323) 933-1631. E-mail: director@apa-la.org. Website: http://midwest.apanational.com

American Photographic Artists, Midwest, 28 E. Jackson, Bldg. #10-A855, Chicago, IL 60604. (877) 890-7375. E-mail: apamidwest@gmail.com. Website: www.apamidwest.org

American Photographic Artists, New York, 27 W. 20th St., Suite 601, New York, NY 10011. (212) 807-0399. Fax: (212) 727-8120. E-mail: jocelyn@apany.com. Website: www.apany.com

American Photographic Artists, San Diego, P.O. Box 84321, San Diego, CA 92138. (619) 417-2150. E-mail: webmaster@apasd.org. Website: http://sandiego.apanational.com

American Photographic Artists, San Francisco, 560 Fourth St., San Francisco, CA 94107. (415) 882-9780. Fax: (415) 882-9781. E-mail: info@apasf.com. Website: http://sanfrancisco.apanational.com

American Society of Media Photographers (ASMP), 150 N. Second St., Philadelphia, PA 19106. (215) 451-2767. Fax: (215) 451-0880. Website: www.asmp.org

American Society of Picture Professionals (ASPP), 117 S. St. Asaph St., Alexandria, VA 22314. (703) 299-0219. Fax: (703) 299-9910. Website: www.aspp.com

The Association of Photographers, 81 Leonard St., London EC2A 4QS, United Kingdom. (44) (020) 7739-6669. Fax: (44) (020) 7739-8707. E-mail: general@aophoto.co.uk. Website: www.the-aop.org

British Association of Picture Libraries and Agencies, 59 Tranquil Vale, Blackheath, London SE3 OBS, United Kingdom. (44) (020) 7713-1780. Fax: (44) (020) 8852-7211. E-mail: online form. Website: www.bapla.org.uk

British Institute of Professional Photography (BIPP), 1 Prebendal Ct., Oxford Rd., Aylesbury, Bucks HP19 8EY, United Kingdom. (44) (012) 9671-8530. Fax: (44) (012) 9633-6367. E-mail: membership@bipp.com. Website: www.bipp.com

Canadian Association of Journalists, 1106 Wellington St, Box 36030, Ottawa, ON K1Y 4V3 Canada. (613) 526-8061. Fax: (613) 521-3904. E-mail: online form. Website: www.caj.ca

Canadian Association of Photographers & Illustrators in Communications, 720 Spadina Ave., Suite 202, Toronto, ON M5S 2T9, Canada. (416) 462-3677 or (888) 252-2742. Fax: (416) 929-5256. E-mail: administration@capic.org. Website: www.capic.org

Canadian Association for Photographic Art, Box 357, Logan Lake, BC V0K 1W0, Canada. (604) 855-4848. Fax: (604) 855-4824. E-mail: capa@capacanada.ca. Website: www.capacanada.ca

The Center for Photography at Woodstock (CPW), 59 Tinker St., Woodstock, NY 12498. (845) 679-9957. Fax: (845) 679-6337. E-mail: info@cpw.org. Website: www.cpw.org

Evidence Photographers International Council, Inc. (EPIC), 229 Peachtree St. NE, Suite 2200, Atlanta, GA 30303. (866) 868-3742. Fax: (404) 614-6406. E-mail: csc@evidencephotographers.com. Website: www.epic-photo.org

International Association of Panoramic Photographers, 9207 Warriors Creek, San Antonio, TX 78230. (210) 748-0800. E-mail: bryan@snowprophoto.com. Website: www.panoramicassociation.org

International Center of Photography (ICP), 1133 Avenue of the Americas at 43rd St., New York, NY 10036. (212) 857-0000. E-mail: membership@icp.org. Website: www.icp.org

The Light Factory (TLF), 345 N. College St., Charlotte, NC 28202. (704) 333-9755. E-mail: info@lightfactory.org. Website: www.lightfactory.org

National Association of Photoshop Professionals (NAPP), 333 Douglas Rd. E., Oldsmar, FL 34677. (813) 433-5005 or (800) 738-8513. Fax: (813) 433-5015. Website: www.photoshopuser.com

National Press Photographers Association (NPPA), 3200 Croasdaile Dr., Suite 306, Durham, NC 27705. (919) 383-7246. Fax: (919) 383-7261. E-mail: members@nppa.org. Website: www.nppa.org

North American Nature Photography Association (NANPA), 10200 W. 44th Ave., Suite 304, Wheat Ridge, CO 80033-2840. (303) 422-8527. Fax: (303) 422-8894. E-mail: info@nanpa.org. Website: www.nanpa.org

Photo Marketing Association International, 3000 Picture Place, Jackson, MI 49201. (517) 788-8100. Fax: (517) 788-8371. E-mail: PMA_Information_Central@pmai.org. Website: www.pmai.org

Photographic Society of America (PSA), 3000 United Founders Blvd., Suite 103, Oklahoma City, OK 73112-3940. (405) 843-1437. Fax: (405) 843-1438. E-mail: hq@psa-photo.org. Website: www.psa-photo.org

Picture Archive Council of America (PACA), 23046 Avenida de la Carlota, Suite 600, Leguna Hills, CA 92653-1537. (714) 815-8427. Fax: (949) 282-5066. E-mail: pacnews@pacaoffice.org. Website: www.pacaoffice.org

Professional Photographers of America (PPA), 229 Peachtree St. NE, Suite 2200, Atlanta, GA 30303. (404) 522-8600 or (800) 786-6277. Fax: (404) 614-6400. E-mail: csc@ppa.com. Website: www.ppa.com

Professional Photographers of Canada (PPOC), 209 Light St., Woodstock, ON N4S 6H6 Canada. (519) 537-2555 or (888) 643-7762. Fax: (888) 831-4036. Website: www.ppoc.ca

The Royal Photographic Society, Fenton House, 122 Wells Rd., Bath BA2 3AH United Kingdom. (44) (012) 2532-5733. E-mail: reception@rps.org. Website: www.rps.org

Society for Photographic Education, 2530 Superior Ave., #403, Cleveland, OH 44114. (216) 622-2733. Fax: (216) 622-2712. E-mail: membership@spenational.org. Website: www.spenational.org

Society of Photographers and Artists Representatives (SPAR), 60 E. 42nd St., Suite 1166, New York, NY 10165. E-mail: info@spar.org. Website: www.spar.org

Volunteer Lawyers for the Arts, 1 E. 53rd St., 6th Floor, New York, NY 10022. (212) 319-2787, ext. 1. Fax: (212) 752-6575. Website: www.vlany.org

Wedding & Portrait Photographers International (WPPI), 6059 Bristol Pkwy., Suite 100, Culver City, CA 90230. (310) 846-4770. Fax: (310) 846-5995. Website: www.wppi-online.com

White House News Photographers' Association (WHNPA), 7119 Ben Franklin Station, Washington, DC 20044-7119. E-mail: online form. Website: www.whnpa.org

PUBLICATIONS

PERIODICALS

Advertising Age: www.adage.com
> Weekly magazine covering marketing, media and advertising.

Adweek: www.adweek.com
> Weekly magazine covering advertising agencies.

American Photo: www.popphoto.com
> Monthly magazine emphasizing the craft and philosophy of photography.

Art Calendar: www.artcalendar.com
> Monthly magazine listing galleries reviewing portfolios, juried shows, percent-for-art programs, scholarships, and art colonies.

ASMP Bulletin: www.asmp.org
> Newsletter of the American Society of Media Photographers published five times/year. Subscription with membership.

Communication Arts: www.commarts.com
> Trade journal for visual communications.

Editor & Publisher: www.editorandpublisher.com
> Monthly magazine covering latest developments in journalism and newspaper production. Publishes an annual directory issue listing syndicates and another directory listing newspapers.

Folio: www.foliomag.com
> Monthly magazine featuring trends in magazine circulation, production, and editorial.

Graphis: www.graphis.com

Magazine for the visual arts.

HOW: www.howdesign.com

Bimonthly magazine for the design industry.

News Photographer: www.nppa.org

Monthly news tabloid published by the National Press Photographers Association. Subscription with membership.

Outdoor Photographer: www.outdoorphotographer.com

Monthly magazine emphasizing equipment and techniques for shooting in outdoor conditions.

Photo District News: www.pdnonline.com

Monthly magazine for the professional photographer.

Photosource International: www.photosource.com

This company publishes several helpful newsletters, including PhotoLetter, Photo-Daily, and PhotoStockNotes.

Popular Photography & Imaging: www.popphoto.com

Monthly magazine specializing in technical information for photography.

Print: www.printmag.com

Bimonthly magazine focusing on creative trends and technological advances in illustration, design, photography, and printing.

Professional Photographer: www.ppmag.com

Professional Photographers of America's monthly magazine emphasizing technique and equipment for working photographers.

Publishers Weekly: www.publishersweekly.com

Weekly magazine covering industry trends and news in book publishing; includes book reviews and interviews.

Rangefinder: www.rangefindermag.com

Monthly magazine covering photography technique, products, and business practices.

Selling Stock: www.selling-stock.com

Newsletter for stock photographers; includes coverage of trends in business practices such as pricing and contract terms.

Shutterbug: www.shutterbug.net

Monthly magazine of photography news and equipment reviews.

BOOKS & DIRECTORIES

Adweek Agency Directory, VNU Business Publications. Annual directory of advertising agencies in the U.S.

Adweek Brand Directory, VNU Business Publications. Directory listing top 2,000 brands, ranked by media spending.

ASMP Copyright Guide for Photographers, American Society of Media Photographers.

ASMP Professional Business Practices in Photography, 7th Edition, American Society of Media Photographers. Handbook covering all aspects of running a photography business.

Bacon's Media Directories, Cision. Contains information on all daily and community newspapers in the U.S. and Canada, and 24,000 trade and consumer magazines, newsletters, and journals.

The Big Picture: The Professional Photographer's Guide to Rights, Rates & Negotiation, by Lou Jacobs, Writer's Digest Books, F+W Media, Inc. Essential information on understanding contracts, copyrights, pricing, licensing and negotiation.

Business and Legal Forms for Photographers, 4th Edition, by Tad Crawford, Allworth Press. Negotiation book with thirty-four forms for photographers.

The Business of Photography: Principles and Practices, by Mary Virginia Swanson, available through her Website (www.mvswanson.com) or by emailing Lisa@mvswanson.com.

The Business of Studio Photography, Third Edition, by Edward R. Lilley, Allworth Press. A complete guide to starting and running a successful photography studio.

Children's Writers & Illustrator's Market, Writer's Digest Books, F+W Media, Inc. Annual directory including photo needs of book publishers, magazines and multimedia producers in the children's publishing industry.

Color Confidence: The Digital Photographer's Guide to Color Management, by Tim Grey, Sybex.

Color Management for Photographers: Hands-On Techniques for Photoshop Users, by Andrew Rodney, Focal Press.

Creative Careers in Photography: Making a Living With or Without a Camera, by Michal Heron, Allworth Press.

Digital Stock Photography: How to Shoot and Sell, by Michal Heron, Allworth Press.

How to Succeed in Commercial Photography: Insights from a Leading Consultant, by Selina Maitreya, Allworth Press.

How to Grow as a Photographer: Reinventing Your Career, by Tony Luna, Allworth Press.

LA 411, 411 Publishing. Music industry guide, including record labels.

Legal Guide for the Visual Artist, 4th Edition, by Tad Crawford, Allworth Press. The author, an attorney, offers legal advice for artists and includes forms dealing with copyright, sales, taxes, etc.

Licensing Photography, by Richard Weisgrau and Victor Perlman, Allworth Press.

Literary Market Place, Information Today. Directory that lists book publishers and other book publishing industry contacts.

O'Dwyer's Directory of Public Relations Firms, J.R. O'Dwyer Company, available through website (www.odwyerpr.com). Annual directory listing public relations firms, indexed by specialties.

Photo Portfolio Success, by John Kaplan, Writer's Digest Books, F+W Media, Inc.

The Photographer's Guide to Marketing & Self-Promotion, 4th Edition, by Maria Piscopo, Allworth Press. Marketing guide for photographers.

Photographer's Market Guide to Building Your Photography Business, Second Edition, by Vic Orenstein, Writer's Digest Books, F+W Media, Inc. Practical advice for running a profitable photography business.

Pricing Photography: The Complete Guide to Assignment & Stock Prices, by Michal Heron and David MacTavish, Allworth Press.

The Professional Photographer's Legal Handbook, by Nancy Wolff, Allworth Press.

Real World Color Management: Industrial-Strength Production Techniques, Second Edition, by Bruce Fraser, Chris Murphy, and Fred Bunting, Peachpit Press.

Sell & Resell Your Photos, 5th Edition, by Rohn Engh, Writer's Digest Books, F+W Media, Inc. Revised edition of the classic volume on marketing your own stock.

Selling Your Photography: How to Make Money in New and Traditional Markets, by Richard Weisgrau, Allworth Press.

Shooting & Selling Your Photos, by Jim Zuckerman, Writer's Digest Books, F+W Media, Inc.

Songwriter's Market, Writer's Digest Books, F+W Media, Inc. Annual directory listing record labels.

Standard Rate and Data Service (SRDS), Kantar Media. Directory listing magazines and their advertising rates.

Starting Your Career as a Freelance Photographer, by Tad Crawford, Allworth Press.

Workbook, Scott & Daughter Publishing. Numerous resources for the graphic arts industry.

Writer's Market, Writer's Digest Books, F+W Media, Inc. Annual directory listing markets for freelance writers. Many listings include photo needs and payment rates.

WEBSITES

PHOTOGRAPHY BUSINESS

The Alternative Pick www.altpick.com
Black Book www.blackbook.com
Copyright Website www.benedict.com
EP: Editorial Photographers www.editorialphoto.com
MacTribe www.mactribe.com
ShootSmarter.com www.shootsmarter.com
Small Business Administration www.sba.gov

MAGAZINE AND BOOK PUBLISHING

American Journalism Review's News Links www.ajr.org
Bookwire www.bookwire.com

STOCK PHOTOGRAPHY

Global Photographers Search www.photographers.com
PhotoSource International www.photosource.com
Stock Photo Price Calculator www.photographersindex.com/stockprice.htm
Selling Stock www.selling-stock.com
Stock Artists Alliance www.stockartistsalliance.org
The STOCKPHOTO Network www.stockphoto.net

ADVERTISING PHOTOGRAPHY

Advertising Age www.adage.com
Adweek, Mediaweek and Brandweek www.adweek.com
Communication Arts Magazine www.commarts.com

FINE ART PHOTOGRAPHY

The Art List www.theartlist.com
Art Support www.art-support.com
Art DEADLINES List www.artdeadlineslist.com
Photography in New York International www.photography-guide.com
Mary Virginia Swanson www.mvswanson.com

PHOTOJOURNALISM

The Digital Journalist www.digitaljournalist.org
Foto8 www.foto8.com
National Press Photographers Association www.nppa.org

MAGAZINES

Afterimage www.vsw.org
Aperture www.aperture.org
Art Calendar www.artcalendar.com
Black and White Photography www.bandwmag.com
Blind Spot www.blindspot.com
British Journal of Photography www.bjphoto.co.uk
Lens Work www.lenswork.com
Photo District News www.pdnonline.com
Photograph Magazine www.photography-guide.com
The Photo Review, The Photography Collector, and The Photographic Art Market Magazines www.photoreview.org
Shots Magazine www.shotsmag.com
View Camera www.viewcamera.com

E-ZINES

The following publications exist online only. Some offer opportunities for photographers to post their personal work.
Apogee Photo www.apogeephoto.com

American Photo Magazine www.popphoto.com
American Photography Museum www.photographymuseum.com
Art in Context www.artincontext.org
Art Business News www.artbusinessnews.com
Art Support www.art-support.com
Artist Register http://artistsregister.com
Digital Journalist www.digitaljournalist.org
En Foco www.enfoco.org
Fotophile www.fotophile.com
Handheld Magazine www.handheldmagazine.com/index.html
Musarium www.musarium.com
Fabfotos www.fabfotos.com
Foto8 www.foto8.com
One World Journeys www.oneworldjourneys.com
PhotoArts www.photoarts.com
Pixel Press www.pixelpress.org
Photo Imaging Information Council www.takegreatpictures.com
Photo Links www.photolinks.com
Online Photo Workshops www.photoworkshop.com
Picture Projects www.pictureprojects.com
Sight Photo www.sightphoto.com
Zone Zero www.zonezero.com

TECHNICAL

About.com www.photography.about.com
BetterPhoto.com® http://betterphoto.com
Photo.net www.photo.net
PhotoflexLightingSchool® www.photoflexlightingschool.com
The Pixel Foundry www.thepixelfoundry.com
Shoot Smarter www.shootsmarter.com
Wilhelm Imaging Research www.wilhelm-research.com
Web Photo School www.webphotoschool.com

HOW TO

Adobe Tutorials www.adobe.com.designcenter
Digital Photographers www.digitalphotographers.net
Digital Photography Review www.dpreview.com
Fred Miranda www.fredmiranda.com/forum/index.php

Imaging Resource www.imaging-resource.com
Lone Star Digital www.lonestardigital.com
The National Association of Photoshop Professionals www.photoshopuser.com
Photography Review www.photographyreview.com
Steve's Digicams www.steves-digicams.com

GLOSSARY

Absolute-released images. Any images for which signed model or property releases are on file and immediately available. For working with stock photo agencies that deal with advertising agencies, corporations and other commercial clients, such images are absolutely necessary to sell usage of images. Also see Model release, Property release.

Acceptance (payment on). The buyer pays for certain rights to publish a picture at the time it is accepted, prior to its publication.

Agency promotion rights. Stock agencies request these rights in order to reproduce a photographer's images in promotional materials such as catalogs, brochures and advertising.

Agent. A person who calls on potential buyers to present and sell existing work or obtain assignments for a client. A commission is usually charged. Such a person may also be called a photographer's rep.

All rights. A form of rights often confused with work for hire. Identical to a buyout, this typically applies when the client buys all rights or claim to ownership of copyright, usually for a lump sum payment. This entitles the client to unlimited, exclusive usage and usually with no further compensation to the creator. Unlike work for hire, the transfer of copyright is not permanent. A time limit can be negotiated, or the copyright ownership can run to the maximum of 35 years.

Alternative Processes. Printing processes that do not depend on the sensitivity of silver to form an image. These processes include cyanotype and platinum printing.

Archival. The storage and display of photographic negatives and prints in materials that are harmless to them and prevent fading and deterioration.

Artist's statement. A short essay, no more than a paragraph or two, describing a photographer's mission and creative process. Most galleries require photographers to provide an artist's statement.

Assign (designated recipient). A third-party person or business to which a client assigns or designates ownership of copyrights that the client purchased originally from a creator such as a photographer. This term commonly appears on model and property releases.

Assignment. A definite OK to take photos for a specific client with mutual understanding as to the provisions and terms involved.

Assignment of copyright, rights. The photographer transfers claim to ownership of copyright over to another party in a written contract signed by both parties.

Audiovisual (AV). Materials such as filmstrips, motion pictures and overhead transparencies which use audio backup for visual material.

Automatic renewal clause. In contracts with stock photo agencies, this clause works on the concept that every time the photographer delivers an image, the contract is automatically renewed for a specified number of years. The drawback is that a photographer can be bound by the contract terms beyond the contract's termination and be blocked from marketing the same images to other clients for an extended period of time.

Avant garde. Photography that is innovative in form, style or subject matter.

Biannual. Occurring twice a year. Also see Semiannual.

Biennial. Occurring once every two years.

Bimonthly. Occurring once every two months.

Bio. A sentence or brief paragraph about a photographer's life and work, sometimes published along with photos.

Biweekly. Occurring once every two weeks.

Blurb. Written material appearing on a magazine's cover describing its contents.

Buyout. A form of work for hire where the client buys all rights or claim to ownership of copyright, usually for a lump sum payment. Also see All rights, Work for hire.

Caption. The words printed with a photo (usually directly beneath it), describing the scene or action.

CCD. Charged Coupled Device. A type of light detection device, made up of pixels, that generates an electrical signal in direct relation to how much light strikes the sensor.

CD-ROM. Compact disc read-only memory; non-erasable electronic medium used for digitized image and document storage and retrieval on computers.

Chrome. A color transparency, usually called a slide.

Cibachrome. A photo printing process that produces fade-resistant color prints directly from color slides.

Clips. See Tearsheet.

CMYK. Cyan, magenta, yellow and black—refers to four-color process printing.

Color Correction. Adjusting an image to compensate for digital input and output characteristics.

Commission. The fee (usually a percentage of the total price received for a picture) charged by a photo agency, agent or gallery for finding a buyer and attending to the details of billing, collecting, etc.

Composition. The visual arrangement of all elements in a photograph.

Compression. The process of reducing the size of a digital file, usually through software. This speeds processing, transmission times and reduces storage requirements.

Consumer publications. Magazines sold on newsstands and by subscription that cover information of general interest to the public, as opposed to trade magazines, which cover information specific to a particular trade or profession. See Trade magazine.

Contact Sheet. A sheet of negative-size images made by placing negatives in direct contact with the printing paper during exposure. They are used to view an entire roll of film on one piece of paper.

Contributor's copies. Copies of the issue of a magazine sent to photographers in which their work appears.

Copyright. The exclusive legal right to reproduce, publish and sell the matter and form of an artistic work.

Cover letter. A brief business letter introducing a photographer to a potential buyer. A cover letter may be used to sell stock images or solicit a portfolio review. Do not confuse cover letter with query letter.

C-print. Any enlargement printed from a negative.

Credit line. The byline of a photographer or organization that appears below or beside a published photo.

Cutline. See Caption.

Day rate. A minimum fee that many photographers charge for a day's work, whether a full day is spent on a shoot or not. Some photographers offer a half-day rate for projects involving up to a half-day of work.

Demo(s). A sample reel of film or sample videocassette that includes excerpts of a filmmaker's or videographer's production work for clients.

Density. The blackness of an image area on a negative or print. On a negative, the denser the black, the less light that can pass through.

Digital Camera. A filmless camera system that converts an image into a digital signal or file.

DPI. Dots per inch. The unit of measure used to describe the resolution of image files, scanners and output devices. How many pixels a device can produce in one inch.

Electronic Submission. A submission made by modem or on computer disk, CD-ROM or other removable media.

Emulsion. The light-sensitive layer of film or photographic paper.

Enlargement. An image that is larger than its negative, made by projecting the image of the negative onto sensitized paper.

Exclusive property rights. A type of exclusive rights in which the client owns the physical image, such as a print, slide, film reel or videotape. A good example is when a portrait is shot for a person to keep, while the photographer retains the copyright.

Exclusive rights. A type of rights in which the client purchases exclusive usage of the image for a negotiated time period, such as one, three or five years. May also be permanent. Also see All rights, Work for hire.

Fee-plus basis. An arrangement whereby a photographer is given a certain fee for an assignment—plus reimbursement for travel costs, model fees, props and other related expenses incurred in completing the assignment.

File Format. The particular way digital information is recorded. Common formats are TIFF and JPEG.

First rights. The photographer gives the purchaser the right to reproduce the work for the first time. The photographer agrees not to permit any publication of the work for a specified amount of time.

Format. The size or shape of a negative or print.

Four-color printing, four-color process. A printing process in which four primary printing inks are run in four separate passes on the press to create the visual effect of a full-color photo, as in magazines, posters and various other print media. Four separate negatives of the color photo—shot through filters—are placed identically (stripped) and exposed onto printing plates, and the images are printed from the plates in four ink colors.

GIF. Graphics Interchange Format. A graphics file format common to the Internet.

Glossy. Printing paper with a great deal of surface sheen. The opposite of matte.

Hard Copy. Any kind of printed output, as opposed to display on a monitor.

Honorarium. Token payment—small amount of money and/or a credit line and copies of the publication.

Image Resolution. An indication of the amount of detail an image holds. Usually expressed as the dimension of the image in pixels and the color depth each pixel has. Example: a 640×480, 24-bit image has higher resolution than a 640×480, 16-bit image.

IRC. International Reply Coupon. IRCs are used with self-addressed envelopes instead of stamps when submitting material to buyers located outside a photographer's home country.

JPEG. Joint Photographic Experts Group. One of the more common digital compression methods that reduces file size without a great loss of detail.

Licensing/Leasing. A term used in reference to the repeated selling of one-time rights to a photo.

Manuscript. A typewritten document to be published in a magazine or book.

Matte. Printing paper with a dull, nonreflective surface. The opposite of glossy.

Model release. Written permission to use a person's photo in publications or for commercial use.

Multi-image. A type of slide show that uses more than one projector to create greater visual impact with the subject. In more sophisticated multi-image shows, the projectors can be programmed to run by computer for split-second timing and animated effects.

Multimedia. A generic term used by advertising, public relations and audiovisual firms to describe productions using more than one medium together—such as slides and full-motion, color video—to create a variety of visual effects.

News release. See Press release.

No right of reversion. A term in business contracts that specifies once a photographer sells the copyright to an image, a claim of ownership is surrendered. This may be unenforceable, though, in light of the 1989 Supreme Court decision on copyright law. Also see All rights, Work for hire.

On spec. Abbreviation for "on speculation." Also see Speculation.

One-time rights. The photographer sells the right to use a photo one time only in any medium. The rights transfer back to the photographer on request after the photo's use.

Page rate. An arrangement in which a photographer is paid at a standard rate per page in a publication.

Photo CD. A trademarked, Eastman Kodak-designed digital storage system for photographic images on a CD.

PICT. The saving format for bit-mapped and object-oriented images.

Picture Library. See Stock photo agency.

Pixels. The individual light-sensitive elements that make up a CCD array. Pixels respond in a linear fashion. Doubling the light intensity doubles the electrical output of the pixel.

Point-of-purchase, point-of-sale (P-O-P, P-O-S). A term used in the advertising industry to describe in-store marketing displays that promote a product. Typically, these highly-illustrated displays are placed near checkout lanes or counters, and offer tear-off discount coupons or trial samples of the product.

Portfolio. A group of photographs assembled to demonstrate a photographer's talent and abilities, often presented to buyers.

PPI. Pixels per inch. Often used interchangeably with DPI, PPI refers to the number of pixels per inch in an image. See DPI.

Press release. A form of publicity announcement that public relations agencies and corporate communications staff people send out to newspapers and TV stations to generate news coverage. Usually this is sent with accompanying photos or videotape materials.

Property release. Written permission to use a photo of private property or public or government facilities in publications or for commercial use.

Public domain. A photograph whose copyright term has expired is considered to be "in the public domain" and can be used for any purpose without payment.

Publication (payment on). The buyer does not pay for rights to publish a photo until it is actually published, as opposed to payment on acceptance.

Query. A letter of inquiry to a potential buyer soliciting interest in a possible photo assignment.

Rep. Trade jargon for sales representative. Also see Agent.

Resolution. The particular pixel density of an image, or the number of dots per inch a device is capable of recognizing or reproducing.

Resume. A short written account of one's career, qualifications and accomplishments.

Royalty. A percentage payment made to a photographer/filmmaker for each copy of work sold.

R-print. Any enlargement made from a transparency.

SAE. Self-addressed envelope.

SASE. Self-addressed, stamped envelope. (Most buyers require a SASE if a photographer wishes unused photos returned to him, especially unsolicited materials.)

Self-assignment. Any project photographers shoot to show their abilities to prospective clients. This can be used by beginning photographers who want to build a portfolio or by photographers wanting to make a transition into a new market.

Self-promotion piece. A printed piece photographers use for advertising and promoting their businesses. These pieces generally use one or more examples of the photographer's best work, and are professionally designed and printed to make the best impression.

Semiannual. Occurring twice a year. Also see Biannual.

Semigloss. A paper surface with a texture between glossy and matte, but closer to glossy.

Semimonthly. Occurring twice a month.

Serial rights. The photographer sells the right to use a photo in a periodical. Rights usually transfer back to the photographer on request after the photo's use.

Simultaneous submissions. Submission of the same photo or group of photos to more than one potential buyer at the same time.

Speculation. The photographer takes photos with no assurance that the buyer will either purchase them or reimburse expenses in any way, as opposed to taking photos on assignment.

Stock photo agency. A business that maintains a large collection of photos it makes available to a variety of clients such as advertising agencies, calendar firms and periodicals. Agencies usually retain 40-60 percent of the sales price they collect, and remit the balance to the photographers whose photo rights they've sold.

Stock photography. Primarily the selling of reprint rights to existing photographs rather than shooting on assignment for a client. Some stock photos are sold outright, but most are rented for a limited time period. Individuals can market and sell stock images to individual clients from their personal inventory, or stock photo agencies can market photographers' work for them. Many stock agencies hire photographers to shoot new work on assignment, which then becomes the inventory of the stock agency.

Subsidiary agent. In stock photography, this is a stock photo agency that handles marketing of stock images for a primary stock agency in certain US or foreign markets. These are usually affiliated with the primary agency by a contractual agreement rather than by direct ownership, as in the case of an agency that has its own branch offices.

SVHS. Abbreviation for Super VHS. Videotape that is a step above regular VHS tape. The number of lines of resolution in a SVHS picture is greater, thereby producing a sharper picture.

Tabloid. A newspaper about half the page size of an ordinary newspaper that contains many photos and news in condensed form.

Tearsheet. An actual sample of a published work from a publication.

TIFF. Tagged Image File Format. A common bitmap image format developed by Aldus.

Trade magazine. A publication devoted strictly to the interests of readers involved in a specific trade or profession, such as beekeepers, pilots or manicurists, and generally available only by subscription.

Transparency. Color film with a positive image, also referred to as a slide.

Unlimited use. A type of rights in which the client has total control over both how and how many times an image will be used. Also see All rights, Exclusive rights, Work for hire.

Unsolicited submission. A photograph or photographs sent through the mail that a buyer did not specifically ask to see.

Work for hire. Any work that is assigned by an employer who becomes the owner of the copyright. Stock images cannot be purchased under work-for-hire terms.

World rights. A type of rights in which the client buys usage of an image in the international marketplace. Also see All rights.

Worldwide exclusive rights. A form of world rights in which the client buys exclusive usage of an image in the international marketplace. Also see All rights.

GEOGRAPHIC INDEX

Colorado

INTERNATIONAL INDEX

SUBJECT INDEX

Agriculture

Architecture

Celebrities

Cities/Urban

SUBJECT INDEX

Erotic

Events

Families

Fashion/Glamour

Gardening

Health/Fitness/Beauty

Interiors/Decorating

Landscapes/Scenics

Lifestyle

Military

Nudes/Figure

Parents

Portraits

Product Shots/Still Life

Religious

Rural

Seasonal

Senior Citizens

Technology/Computers

GENERAL INDEX

Ideas. Instruction. Inspiration.

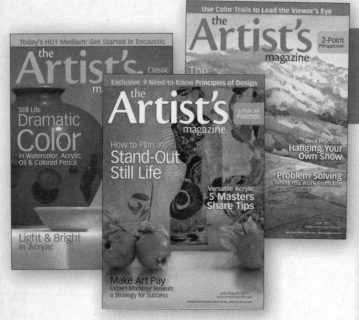
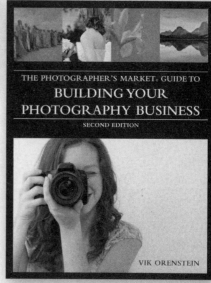
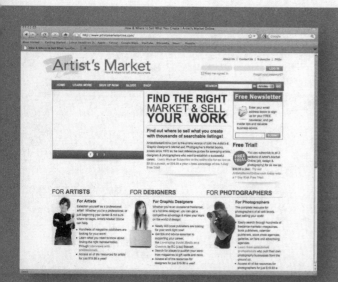